For H.M.R., the most supportive of wives

The author of this work, as of the official histories
of the Second World War, has been given
free access to official documents. He alone
is responsible for the statements made and
the views expressed; also for the accuracy
of any information *not* obtained from
official British documents.

Secret Flotillas

*The clandestine sea lines to France
and French North Africa 1940–1944*

The artist, Mr Sebastien Briec Junior, was serving in the *Veach-Vad* as a 14 year old cabin-boy under his father's command when she carried Robert Alaterre and Jean Le Roux of the JOHNNY network, Jean Lavalou and a son of Dr Vourch to an offshore rendezvous with the British submarine *Sea Lion*. The artist is said to have been arrested five times and was lucky to escape being shot a week before the OVERLORD landings.

A newspaper article about Mr Sebastien Briec Senior is reproduced on the endpapers at the back of the book.

Secret Flotillas

The clandestine sea lines to France and French North Africa 1940–1944

BROOKS RICHARDS

London : HMSO

Published by HMSO and available from:

HMSO Publications Centre
(Mail, fax and telephone orders only)
PO Box 276, London SW8 5DT
Telephone orders 0171 873 9090
General enquiries 0171 873 0011
(Queuing system in operation for both numbers)
Fax orders 0171 873 8200

HMSO Bookshops
49 High Holborn, London WC1V 6HB 0171 873 0011   Fax 0171 831 1326
(Counter service only)
68–69 Bull Street, Birmingham B4 6AD 0121 236 9696   Fax 0121 236 9699
33 Wine Street, Bristol BS1 2BQ 0117 9264306   Fax 0117 9294515
9–21 Princess Street, Manchester M60 8AS 0161 834 7201 Fax 0161 833 0634
16 Arthur Street, Belfast BT1 4GD 01232 238451   Fax 01232 235401
71 Lothian Road, Edinburgh EH3 9AZ 0131 228 4181   Fax 0131 229 2734
The HMSO Oriel Bookshop
The Friary, Cardiff CF1 4AA 01222 395548   Fax 01222 384347

HMSO's accredited Agents
(see Yellow Pages)

and through good booksellers

Printed in the United Kingdom for HMSO
Dd298171 12/95 C12 G559 10170

CONTENTS

Introduction   xi
Acknowledgements   xvi

Part One   Operations from the United Kingdom to the
            North and West Coasts of France   1

I   May–June 1940: The Lost Battle for France   3
II   The British Clandestine Services in the New
            Strategic Context   15
III   Slocum's Section and the First Operations to
            Northern France   24
IV   First Contacts with the West Coast of France   31
V   August–October 1940   46
VI   November 1940–March 1941   73
VII   Did the Abwehr Allow *L'Émigrant* to Escape?   83
VIII   SOE's Aspirations and Operations: August
            1940–June 1941   87
IX   SOE's Endeavours to Set up Independent Sea
            Transport to Brittany, 1941   99
X   April – November 1941   105
XI   October 1941–February 1942   114
XII   November 1941–June 1942   126
XIII   January 1942–March 1943   145
XIV   West Coast: November 1942–October 1943   164
XV   North Coast: Winter 1943–44   174
XVI   The Aber-Benoît Saga:
            November–December 1943   184
XVII   North Coast and the 'Var' Line:
            August 1943–April 1944   218
XVIII   The 'Shelburne' Escape Line:
            January–March and July–August 1944   240
XIX   July–August 1944   269
XX   Operations for SIS: January–August 1944   273
XXI   Escapes by Sea from Brittany: 1940–44   289

Footnotes   294
Appendix A Clandestine Sea Transport Operations to
            North and West Coasts of France, 1940–44   304

Appendix B   Clandestine Escapes and Contacts at Sea by
             Vessels from Breton Ports, 1940–44   322
Appendix C   Recommendations by Captain Slocum for
             awards to members of the 15th MGB Flotilla
             and Inshore Patrol Flotilla   330
Appendix D   Comments on MARIE-LOUISE Rendez-Vous   343

Part Two   Operations from Gibraltar and other bases in
             the Western Mediterranean   345
XXII   The Polish Predicament   347
XXIII   Mass Evacuation from the Marseilles Area and
             the FIDELITY Tragedy   361
XXIV   Operations from Gibraltar to Morocco:
             July–October 1941   370
XXV   Krajewski's Operations to Western Algeria:
             October 1941–January 1942   409
XXVI   Krajewski's Further Plans for Operations to
             North Africa and Southern France:
             December 1941–March 1942   445
XXVII   Operations from Gibraltar to Southern France:
             April–June 1942   453
XXVIII   The Coast Watching Flotilla and the Polish
             Special Operations Group   495
XXIX   Problems and Methods of Operating from
             Gibraltar to the South of France   500
XXX   Operations by *Seawolf*, *Seadog* and *Tarana*:
             July–September 1942   504
XXXI   Last of the Polish Evacuation Missions   545
XXXII   The Changing Strategic Context in the
             Western Mediterranean   552
XXXIII   Renewed Priority for Operations to French
             North Africa   556
XXXIV   SOE and OSS Prepare for TORCH   561
XXXV   The Last Phase of the CWF's Operations:
             October–November 1942   569
XXXVI   Final Preparations for TORCH   573
XXXVII   Unsuccessful Attempts to Revive Felucca
             Operations   577
XXXVIII   Operations by Sea for SIS and SOE in Tunisia   581
XXXIX   Clandestine Sea Transport Operations in the
             Western Mediterranean after TORCH   594
XL   Missions to Sardinia and Corsica:
             January–March 1942   616
XLI   Last Missions to Corsica before the Italian
             Armistice and its Liberation   629

XLII   Operations from Bastia   644
            Epilogue   656

Footnotes   661
Appendix E Clandestine Sea Operations from Gibraltar to
            French North Africa and the South Coasts of
            France and Spain   669

Bibliography   690
Index   694

Introduction

The Fall of France in June 1940, coming hard on the heels of Hitler's seizure of Denmark, Norway and the Low Countries, left the whole coastline of western Europe from the North Cape to the Spanish frontier in hostile hands. It was as great a strategic threat to the British Isles as any since the Spanish Armada. Even the Channel Islands, whose seamen had so often over the previous two and a half centuries kept watch for any concentration of enemy shipping in neighbouring French ports and far down into the Bay of Biscay, had been abandoned as indefensible in the face of air power.

The British clandestine services, hastily reorganised to meet the emergency, came under great pressure: there were urgent requirements for intelligence, of which timely warning of any attempt to mount a cross-Channel invasion was the most pressing. Agents needed to be landed and picked up. Commander F.A. Slocum, the officer charged with the task of establishing physical communications with enemy-occupied territory for the Secret Intelligence Service, could find no relevant official records to help him.

What he was probably hoping to find was some form of report by Lt Augustus Agar, VC, DSO, RN who had between June and August 1919 used two of the then new 40-ft Thornycroft coastal motor boats (CMBs) to make nine trips from the small Finnish port of Terrioki into Bolshevik-held Petrograd, successfully landing or picking up couriers on six of these occasions. In doing so, he had re-established contact with Sir Paul Dukes, SIS's agent ST25, who had been sent into the field 18 months previously to obtain political intelligence. Dukes had been living in Petrograd disguised as a workman, a soldier or a member of the Cheka. His reports had originally been sent out by couriers across the Finnish border. But Bolshevik counter-espionage had captured many of those working for him and nothing had been heard from him for some time before Agar's arrival.

London's plan had been that Agar should transport agents across the Gulf of Finland and land them on the coast of Estonia. Once he had taken stock of the situation, Agar decided on a much more daring course of action – to run agents directly into Petrograd through the chain of forts guarding the approaches. The forts mounted batteries of searchlights and guns, while between them ran a boom in the form of a chain, whose maximum immersion of 3 ft could be crossed even by a shallow-draught CMB with only a few inches to spare. There was also an ever-present danger from floating mines, but Agar succeeded in the hazardous enterprise he had set himself. On his last expedition, CMB 7 came under fire and crashed into the boom, losing both rudder and propeller shaft. He got back to base only after 12 hours at sea, with an improvised mast and sail and a cable streamed astern to steer the boat.

As though these risks were not enough, Agar from an early stage involved himself in offensive action when opportunity offered. It was for sinking the 6,000-ton cruiser Oleg on his second mission that he was awarded the Victoria Cross.

In August 1919 he was joined by a small flotilla of seven 55-ft CMBs. In a combined operation, they destroyed the whole of the Bolshevik battle fleet lying in the Kronstadt naval basin – an action for which Commander C.C. Dobson, RN, senior officer of the flotilla, and Lt G.C. Steele, his second in command, were each awarded the VC, while Agar received the DSO.

It is hardly surprising that soon after this Agar's operations for SIS came to an end. In the Second World War motor gunboats (MGBs) carrying out operations for the clandestine services were strictly discouraged from indulging in heroics.

If anyone in 1940 had had leisure to look for even earlier precedents in the age when sail and oar were master, they would have found that when war broke out with Revolutionary France in 1793 Jersey became a main base for collecting intelligence about the situation on the mainland. Its importance was enhanced when Royalist revolts occurred in the Vendée, Brittany and Normandy. The central personage in what became known as 'the Channel Islands correspondence' was a Jersey-born Royal Navy post-captain named Phillippe d'Auvergne, Prince de Bouillon, who had French *émigré* connections. From a hut below the ramparts of Gorey Castle d'Auvergne commanded a small flotilla of fast-sailing local craft, some manned by Royalist Frenchmen. These vessels carried secret agents to and from the French coast. Intelligence collection was their primary task and they were allowed to engage in offensive action and join in the defence of the Islands only when this responsibility had been discharged. D'Auvergne had a dispatch vessel standing by to carry his reports to England. He addressed them directly to William Wyndham, Secretary at War, rather than to any naval authority. In addition to the intelligence that his own flotilla brought him, a procession of Royalist small craft arrived from French ports with information and collected arms and ammunition from stocks held by him.

By the time counter-revolutionary resistance had collapsed in 1797, fear of a French invasion of the Channel Islands, Ireland or England lent fresh importance to Jersey as a base for intelligence collection. D'Auvergne, a key figure as spymaster and local naval commander, was promoted Commodore in 1801 and Rear Admiral in 1805. He retired from the Navy only in 1812.

For nearly 20 years d'Auvergne provided a centralised control, which had been lacking earlier in what has been well called the Second Hundred Years' War with France. At that period a swarm of small privateers, mostly based on Guernsey, preyed on French coastal shipping, ranging deep down into the Bay of Biscay and, posing as local craft, ventured far enough into French harbours to look for strategically threatening concentrations of vessels. Though this combination of free enterprise and self-defence had previously been effective in detecting any build-up of French forces in the neighbouring harbours of Granville, Saint-Malo, Tréguier or Morlaix, it failed spectacularly to prevent a French invasion of Jersey in the winter of 1781. The Governor was surprised in his bed and forced to order all British forces in the island to surrender. The situation was redressed only by the action of one regular officer of the garrison, Major Pierson, who refused to obey the Governor's order and attacked the French. In a short, sharp action both Pierson and de Rullecourt, the French commander, were killed, but the French were defeated and the island was saved. This episode may have had something to do with the institution of more systematic intelligence arrangements in Jersey under d'Auvergne when France and Great Britain were next at war.

Notwithstanding the advent of the internal combustion engine, aircraft and radar, fishing vessels and craft which could pass as such played an important part in clandestine sea transport in the Second World War.

One big difference from previous occasions when a line of war separated England and France was that parachuting from aircraft and the clandestine landing of aircraft by moonlight now provided alternatives to infiltration and exfiltration by sea. Air landing and pick-up of agents had been pioneered by the French intelligence services in the First World War, but the RAF was not ready for a first such operation to France until October 1940. Only five took place in 1941. The build-up of the RAF's Special Duties squadrons was swift thereafter, but, as weather not infrequently bedevilled flying, clandestine operations to France by sea retained their importance until the Liberation.

When the French edition of Hugh Verity's *We Landed by Moonlight* was published in 1982, Jacques Maillet, one of General de Gaulle's Compagnons de la Libération, wrote in a preface that it was surprising and regrettable that the subject of clandestine air landings in France during the Occupation had before then been treated only incidentally in accounts of the clandestine struggle. Group Captain Verity's record of these operations was an extraordinary adventure story, but the author had also striven to achieve meticulous historical accuracy. He had drawn on official RAF records and a great deal of evidence from British and French participants: his book was therefore a valid contribution to historiography. Moreover, these operations had exercised a profound influence on the course of French history. The flights were few in number: no more than a few dozen pilots had been involved and passengers amounted to a few hundred at the most. But their historical importance was immense.

They were significant firstly for military reasons. It was essential that those responsible for radio communications and for intelligence and those designated to take charge of the secret army should be able to report back to London. In the fighting that led to the Liberation, the excellent cooperation between the French Forces of the Interior and the armies that had landed owed much to the contacts thus established.

But, above all, M Maillet pointed out, one must not forget that these were the links that made it possible to unite French internal Resistance and General de Gaulle's Free France in a single combat. Without them the Jean Moulins, the Brossolettes, the Morandats could not have built the structures by which the French Resistance movement organised itself under General de Gaulle's command. If France was able, notwithstanding the armistice of 1940 and the Vichy regime, to reclaim her status as a great power, it was because de Gaulle was, and had in the end to be recognised as, the man who spoke for all of France. That was possible only because men who had come out of France had been able to unite around him.

Without clandestine air operations, the Free French would have remained a group – unquestionably a heroic and admirable group – of combatants, but one isolated from evolving attitudes in France. The air operations, however, enabled men and ideas to be exchanged between London and Algiers on the one hand and the French Resistance on the other. He might well have added that France was thereby spared the fragmentation and confrontation of internal and external resistance that embittered the Liberation of, for example, Greece and Yugoslavia.

It was, M Maillet concluded, no exaggeration to say that clandestine air operations had modified the course of French history. Those associated with the Special Duties squadrons were equally deserving of Sir Winston Chruchill's tribute to the airmen of the Battle of Britain: 'Never in the field of human conflict was so much owed by so many to so few.'

As head of SOE's North African French country section in 1943 and 1944, I was a customer of the RAF's Special Duties squadrons and my admiration of them is as great as that of M Maillet. But from two years' earlier service in SOE's Naval Section, I know that their seagoing counterparts, the Secret Flotillas, made a far from insignificant contribution to the historic process he describes. It is high time that their story be recorded, not as a series of incidental episodes, but as a subject in its own right.

Brooks Richards

21 March 1995

Folly Barn
Norton Lane
Durweston
Blandford Forum
Dorset DT11 0QP

Acknowledgements

This book grew out of a chance encounter with Professor Guy Vourc'h in Paris in 1979. It was a name that awoke echoes: we had met soon after the Liberation. I knew that he and his three younger brothers had escaped in turn from Brittany to England during the Occupation and that he had been one of the first Frenchmen to fight their way ashore on D-Day. I told him that I had been involved in contacts with Brittany in 1941 and 1942: he knew more of the Breton side of my first operation than I did. And he sent me Roger Huguen's *Par les Nuits les Plus Longues*.

The book was a professionally researched account of wartime escapes from Brittany, which I found fascinating. It covered a number of British-organised evacuations by sea and he had had help from various British sources. But most naval and paranaval operations to Brittany did not concern evacuation of escapers and evaders and fell outside the scope of M. Huguen's researches. I knew too that Brittany was not the only part of France to which sea lines had operated. I found myself regretting the lack of a comprehensive record of clandestine sea transport into and out of French territory during the war years. This lacuna seemed anomalous since Hugh Verity, who commanded the Lysander and Hudson Flight of 161 Special Duties Squadron in 1943 when it was at the peak of its activity, had long since published a history of the corresponding air operations. This had been translated and published also in France, where it evoked much interest. Unless a maritime counterpart were produced promptly, it would be too late to draw on the testimony of surviving participants to amplify any surviving official records. Since no-one seemed better placed to tackle the job, I decided to set about it myself.

My especial thanks are due to Gervase Cowell, SOE Adviser to the Foreign and Commonwealth Office, for his help in enabling me to gain access to the essential records on the terms applied to Official Historians. He later helped me to surmount pitfalls on the way to publication. I am grateful to Professor M.R.D. Foot and John Debenham Taylor for helpful advice and briefing.

The records provided an indispensable armature of fact and chronology, but they contained important gaps and were too lacking in detail to yield a satisfactory narrative on their own. I have had help from many quarters in redressing these deficiencies.

Operations to the west coast of Brittany had to be carried out by fishing boats or a combination of submarines and fishing boats as the distances involved were beyond the reach of high-speed vessels such as motor gunboats. In dealing with the sea lines to this area I have received invaluable help from Daniel Lomenech, Steven Mackenzie, Patrick Whinney, Richard Townsend, Jean Le Roux, Roger Huguen, René Pichavant and Capitaine de Vaisseau Jean Pillet. Daniel Lomenech's assistance extended beyond his own remarkable involvement to that of Hubert Moreau, his precursor, the first man to return to France on an intelligence mission. He found copies of an incomplete series of articles by Moreau published in the 1950s. Lt Col Moreau, Hubert's son, who was approached on my behalf by Claude Huan, produced a most interesting unpublished article in which his father carries forward his account of the three missions he undertook in July, August and September 1940.

I am most grateful to Steven Mackenzie for allowing me to reprint his scintillating account of the MARIE-LOUISE operations, which appeared in *Blackwood's Magazine* not long after the end of the war.

Operations on the north coast of Brittany by motor gunboats from Dartmouth or Falmouth enjoyed spectacular success from October 1943 onwards. In this field, papers that were in the possession of the late David Birkin, longest-serving of the specialist navigating officers attached to the 15th MGB Flotilla, are by far the most important supplementary source. Not only did he keep copies of 33 official reports of operations in which he was involved, but he and his widow, Judy, allowed me to make use of two unpublished articles by David, track charts, diagrams and photographs from his collection. I am much indebted to them for their help.

I am also most grateful to Peter Williams, Charles Martin, Lloyd Bott, Tom Long, Michel Guillot and Derek Carter for help with this section of the book.

When I arrived in Gibraltar at the end of October 1942, a brilliantly successful run of operations by Polish-manned feluccas was just coming to an end. Little has appeared in print about them but, on the advice of Professor M.R.D. Foot, I approached Dr Josef Garliński, who remembered seeing records of the Polish Naval Mission at Gibraltar in the Sikorski Institute. I am most grateful for that tip; the Institute possessed an almost complete set of operational reports and related correspondence in Polish, which I was able to sample thanks to the kindness of Dr Andrjez Suchcitz, who is in charge of the collection and who most helpfully summarised their contents. Full translations of all the key documents were needed, so I enlisted the help of Dr Keith Sword of the School of Slavonic and Eastern European Languages. I am most grateful for his translations, researches and background advice. I hope that we have between us rescued a small-scale epic from oblivion. Captain Marian Kadulski added valuable personal details to the narrative represented by the reports and correspondence that he wrote, under very great pressure, at the time. I am most grateful to the Sikorski Institute for permission to publish material of which they hold the copyright.

In relation to operations to and from Corsica, I am much indebted to Pat Whinney and Andrew Croft and Michael Lumby.

Throughout my researches, I received much help and advice from Capitaine de Vasseau Claude Huan, the well-known French naval historian. His knowledge of the French naval archives and his energy and skill in extracting information from them and other documentary and human sources only accessible in Paris helped my project forward very greatly. I am particularly grateful to him for compiling a list of the special operations undertaken by French submarines from Algiers in 1943 and 1944 for the French clandestine services and for obtaining from Capitaine Paul Paillole the names of more than 100 of the 150 passengers who travelled to or from France by this route.

The subject of operations by British submarines for SOE and SIS also required basic research. I am grateful to David Brown, Head of the Naval Historical Branch at the Ministry of Defence; to Commodore Bob Garson; to Commander Compton-Hall and Commander Jeff Tall, successively Directors of the RN Submarine Museum; to Gus Britten; and to Charles Beatty for their help in this connection. It was the last-named who kindly lent me Jean L'Herminier's book.

I am much indebted to Roger Huguen for generous advice and help and allowing me to make use of maps prepared for his book; to Daniel Lomenech, Richard Townsend, Derek Carter, Pat Whinney, Judy Birkin, Andrew Croft, Charles Martin, Lloyd Bott, Mary Holdsworth, Hilary Rust, the Musée de la Marine and the Etablissement Cinématographique et Photographique des Armées (ECPA) in Paris for help over photographs. My thanks are due to Mrs E.A.G. Davis for permission to use a painting of MGB 318 on the dust jacket; and to my brother Robin for resolving various problems of chart-work and nomenclature. It is to him and to Mrs. Honer that I owe the drawing of Seawolf by the late Eric Honer. My brother and his wife, Kate, kindly photographed and transcribed the panels in the museum on the Ile-de-Sein recording escapes by Breton vessels during the Occupation.

While the project was still trying to make its way, the Imperial War Museum gave it unconditional backing, whether publication ensued or not. On the strength of this the Leverhulme Foundation gave it an invaluable two-year grant. Without their generous help it could never have come to maturity.

At a critical stage, the interest of Admiral Sir Julian Oswald, the First Sea Lord, and of Kenneth Carlisle, MP, Parliamentary Under-Secretary at the Ministry of Defence, were a great encouragement, as was that of Amiral Emile Chaline, historian of the Free French naval forces.

I owe an immense debt to Patricia Andrews, Head of the Historical and Records Section of the Cabinet Office; without her support the book would never have been published. I am most grateful to Margaret Russell, who undertook the task of putting the text on to word processor and seeing it through many revisions of detail.

I am much obliged to Ingrid Cranfield for her careful editing of the text; to Steven Carruthers at HMSO for further editing and proof-reading; to Arthur Spencer for compiling the index and to my wife for critical advice and much practical help.

HMSO wishes to acknowledge with grateful thanks the following for their kind permission to reproduce photographs: Beken of Cowes, marine photographers for the photograph of S502; Mrs. Mary Collins, for the photographs of RAF 360 and *Sunbeam II*; Conway Maritime Press for the photograph of *Minna*, taken from *Model Shipwright* (Vol II, No. 3, Spring 1974); M le Capitaine de Vaisseau Jannot, director of the Service d'Information et de Relations Publiques des Armées/Établissement Cinématographique et Photographique des Armées (SIRPA/ECPA) of the French Ministry of Defence for the photographs of Capitaine de Frégate Jean L'Herminier one taken in the boardroom of *Casabianca* and the other of Capitaine de Frégate Jean L'Herminier and Admiral Darlan; the Musée de la Marine in Paris for the photograph of Capitaine de Frégate Jean L'Herminier standing by *Casabianca*'s periscope and the photograph of *Casabianca* at Algiers; Universal Pictorial Press & Agency Ltd. for the photograph of Commander F.A. Slocum at his CMG investiture in 1953; M. Sebastien Briec for his painting used on the frontispiece. Extracts from *Michelin Green Guide to Brittany*, 1991 edition, are reproduced by permission of Michelin, authorisation no. 95–027.

The author and publisher have attempted to trace Gordon Ellis, the artist whose painting *Mayflower* has been used on the dust jacket for this publication, and T.H. Maxted whose photograph of the Felucca *Seawolf* has been reproduced in this publication. They wish to thank both artists for their work. If the legal copyright holders of these (or other material not acknowledged above) wish to contact HMSO, we shall ensure that the correct acknowledgement appears in any future edition of this book.

PART ONE

*Operations from the
United Kingdom to the
North and West coasts of France*

CHAPTER I

May–June 1940: The Lost Battle for France

Hitler's long-awaited attack in the west began at dawn on 10 May 1940, barely a month after his swift occupation of Denmark and pre-emptive descent on Norway.[1] He had assembled 136 divisions for the new Blitzkrieg campaign – a force that gave him a two-to-one numerical ascendancy. The first thrusts were into neutral Holland and Belgium. He knew from intercepted signals of the French High Command that this would draw three French armies and most of the British Expeditionary Force forward in support of the Belgians. Then seven German Panzer divisions advanced through the Ardennes forest, outflanking the northern end of the Maginot Line defensive system, and crossed the Meuse into French territory near Sedan, the third such invasion in 70 years.

The French General Staff had discounted the risk of a major German attack in this sector: Pétain, the victor of Verdun, had in 1938 described the Ardennes as 'impenetrable'. To a questioner, who had expressed concern about the fact that the Maginot Line stopped short of the Ardennes, he had said that, if the Germans were imprudent enough to get entangled in that forest, the French forces would seize them as they emerged.[2] But General Heinz Guderian's[3] Panzers stood Pétain's prediction on its head: they smashed the small French force that guarded the pivotal point between the Maginot defences and the Allied Northern Armies. By 13 May they had established a substantial bridgehead across the Meuse on French soil.

Within 24 hours this German lodgement had expanded considerably and, with the Allied field armies heavily engaged in Belgium, there was little to prevent Generals Guderian and Kleist, who could count on overwhelming Luftwaffe support, from breaking out on a narrow front in whatever direction best suited overall German strategy. The French High Command called for RAF support, which was promptly given, but the German bridges across the Meuse were so heavily defended that by nightfall on 14 May more than half the 70 bomber aircraft engaged had been destroyed.

By seven o'clock next morning, 15 May, a hastily improvised French counter-attack had also failed. Paul Reynaud, the French Prime Minister, telephoned to Winston Churchill – called to office only five days previously as a result of the disastrous Allied campaign in Norway – to say that the road to Paris lay open to the Germans and that the battle was lost.

Paris was not in fact the immediate objective of Guderian's and Kleist's Panzers: they struck westwards towards the mouth of the Somme with a view to cutting the Allied armies in two.

Colonel Charles de Gaulle was at Le-Vésinet forming the French Fourth Armoured Division, which he had been appointed to command. Still unknown outside professional military circles, he was notorious within them as a heterodox military intellectual. His pre-war campaign to persuade France to adopt a strategy of attack and movement using massed armoured fighting vehicles, such as she now faced at German hands, had been a public challenge by a serving officer to the French General Staff and its preoccupation with defence. It was an outlook born out of the carnage of the First World War battlefields and embodied in the Maginot Line fortifications. Though he had managed to assemble only a third of his division's planned armoured strength, he was ordered forward to Laon on 15 May to delay the Panzers' advance. He was under no illusion as to the gravity of the situation and advised his wife to seek a place of safety for herself and their children as 'anything may be expected'.

The full ignominy of the disaster struck him on the following day. As his division probed forward of Laon, he ran into routed French troops whom the Blitzkrieg thrust had put to disorderly flight. Overtaken by the enemy's motorised formations, they had been ordered to throw away their rifles and hurry away southwards so as not to block roads needed by the German advance: the enemy's vanguard simply could not spare the time to take them prisoner. Writing about these painful memories 15 years later, de Gaulle identified that traumatic day as the turning-point, when he realised the war in Europe had begun so unspeakably badly that the only hope was to continue the struggle elsewhere. If he lived, he would fight on wherever it was necessary and as long as was necessary, until the enemy was beaten and the nation's stain was washed away.[4]

His division was in action next day (17 May) and again, after a march of 200 km. (125 miles), on 28 May, when they struck at a bridgehead which the Panzers had established across the Somme near Abbeville. It was a last, though vain, attempt to prevent the complete encirclement of the Allies' Northern Armies. In these two engagements he had the sour satisfaction of demonstrating that counter-attack by massed tanks, if given appropriate air support, was the only way to defeat a Panzer onslaught and prevail in the new form of warfare, whose prophet and passionate advocate he had been. His efforts, though doomed then to failure for lack of back-up and air cover, earned him promotion to the rank of two-star general and, on 6 June, a summons to join the Government of his friend Paul Reynaud as Under-Secretary of State for War. This translation from soldier to politician was, in the view of his biographer Jean Lacouture, fundamental to all that followed.

The Battle of France was already lost and the new minister's main concern was to enable the Government and a maximum of French troops to withdraw by sea to Algeria, as the only alternative to abject capitulation. He immediately asked Reynaud to give him responsibility for arranging the necessary shipping, and flew to London to enlist British help to that end. Churchill received him on 9 June. The Prime Minister left no record of that first meeting but General Sir Edward Spears, Churchill's personal representative to Reynaud in his role as Minister of War, who was present, recorded that de Gaulle listened to Churchill's reasons for rejecting his plea for more RAF support in France and then said, 'I think you are right' – a remark that no doubt made an impact. Admiral Odend'hal, head of the French Naval Mission in London, who was also present, confirmed that de Gaulle greatly impressed Churchill.[5] De Gaulle said that the situation in France was very serious and the French Cabinet was divided: some, such as Reynaud, Mandel and Campinchi, were determined to continue the fight, others, above all Pétain and Weygand, insisted on negotiating at any price. De Gaulle's pen-portrait of Churchill at this point in his war memoirs reveals that the British Prime Minister made an immediate and profound impression on him also.[6] The two men met again at Briare a couple of days later. Churchill, who had begun to fear that a collapse of France might lead to a reversal of alliances, with the French fleet at Hitler's beck and call, was convinced by de Gaulle and saw his as the only French hand outstretched towards him.

Churchill had flown out to Briare with Eden, then Secretary of State for War, to try to stiffen the resolve of the French Government, which had left Paris during the previous night. Churchill arranged to have de Gaulle seated next to him when dinner was served at the conference table and listened with rapt attention and warm approval as de Gaulle expounded his idea of carrying on guerilla warfare after France had been overrun. De Gaulle's relentless determination to carry on the fight was in striking contrast to the defeatism of Pétain, Weygand, Baudouin and a growing number of other members of the French Government, who were already pressing for an armistice. When reporting to the War Cabinet next day, the Prime Minister mentioned de Gaulle as a young and energetic minister who had made a very favourable impression on him.

By the time Churchill and Eden flew back to England on the morning of 12 June, the German vanguard was poised to outflank the refugee French administration by crossing the Loire to the north-west of them, ministers therefore took to the roads again and headed west across the mainstream of the civilian exodus into Touraine, where historic châteaux afforded them temporary lodging.

Pressure was mounting on Reynaud from those in favour of an armistice, among them his mistress, the Comtesse Hélène de Portes. Churchill had to fly out once more on 13 June, this time to Tours, accompanied by Lord Halifax, the Foreign Secretary. Reynaud asked them what would be the attitude of the British Government if an armistice were obtained. Churchill's reply, delivered in his idiosyncratic Franglais, was wilfully misconstrued by Baudouin to advance the defeatists' cause. Late that night de Gaulle wrote a letter of resignation; but Georges Mandel, Minister of the Interior, warned by a member of the General's staff, persuaded him that he still had great duties to fulfil and that he had the advantage of being an untarnished man.[7]

The situation was deteriorating so fast that further retreat became imperative on the morning of 14 June. Reynaud decided they should head for Bordeaux rather than Quimper in Brittany as de Gaulle had wished.

According to Lacouture, de Gaulle was, like Churchill, until the middle of June an ardent supporter of the idea that Brittany might be held as a redoubt open to the Atlantic. He had gone up to Rennes on 12 June to discuss the idea with General Altmeyer, the regional military commander, and his own family had taken refuge at Carentec, a fishing village on the north coast near Morlaix. De Gaulle made no mention of this expedition in his memoirs, however, as though he wished to forget it.[8] He must have known by 13 June that Weygand, who was already demanding an armistice, would never have provided the resources to mount a successful defence of the peninsula. His advocacy of Quimper, as he went out of his way to explain in his memoirs, was based on a conviction that, if the Government took refuge there, it would within a matter of days be obliged to put to sea and head for North Africa, if only to avoid capture.

De Gaulle, unable to find a plane at Bordeaux, went to Brittany again by road on 14 June on his way to London for a second attempt to seek shipping for this planned evacuation. At Brest he paused to arrange for the embarkation of as many troops as possible. He stopped briefly at Paimpont to see his mother, who died not long afterwards; and he made a detour to Carentec to see his wife and family. He arranged for passports to be issued for them and for his mother before boarding the French destroyer *Milan*, which was evacuating a team of French nuclear scientists and their stock of heavy water to Plymouth.[9]

With Churchill's support, the General's request for British shipping was rapidly granted. This business concluded, he was on the point of leaving London when he found himself drawn into a desperate last bid to prevent the French Government from suing for peace. A scheme for a Franco-British Union had originated at a meeting between Jean Monnet, René Pleven and Vansittart a couple of days earlier. In more normal circumstances, such a project would probably not have been espoused by de Gaulle, who was a highly sensitive nationalist and whose Action Française background was scarcely Anglophile, but he played a leading part in selling the idea to his new friend Churchill; Churchill sold it to the War Cabinet that afternoon, 16 June; and de Gaulle flew off to Bordeaux very shortly thereafter in an RAF aircraft which Churchill placed at his disposal. Their hope was that the proposed Union would tip the balance within the French Cabinet in favour of continuing the war from North Africa.

De Gaulle had telephoned the text of the draft agreement through to Reynaud before leaving London. Reynaud's initial reaction had been enthusiastic, but when he laid the proposal before a hastily-summoned meeting of the Council of Ministers half an hour later he found himself outmanoeuvred by those who wanted an armistice: Madame de Portes, who haunted his outer office, had forewarned her ally Baudouin of what she had seen being typed. He in turn told Pétain and Weygand, so that Reynaud, instead of achieving the dramatic and positive impact for which he had hoped, fell into an ambush. Full of confidence, he read the text of Churchill's offer to his colleagues, only to be engulfed in a derisive uproar. When President Lebrun, who was in the chair, managed to quell the tumult, Reynaud reread the proposal slowly in the hope that its historic import would rally support, adding that he would be meeting Churchill off Concarneau to carry the matter forward. Someone shouted that there was no need for him to go: they didn't wish to become a British dominion. When Mandel, his friend, interjected that it would be better to be a British dominion than a Nazi province, Ybarnégaray shouted back, 'Yes, it would be better to be a Nazi province. We at least know what that means.'

Reynaud found himself deserted by both his Vice-Presidents and not even Mandel and Campinci were prepared to speak in favour of the idea. No vote was taken but Reynaud drew a line down a sheet of paper, listing, on one side, the names of those who favoured asking for the forms of an armistice and, on the other, those who wished to continue the war from Algeria. There were 14 of the former and only 10 of the latter. He adjourned the meeting and placed his resignation in the hands of the President of the

Republic, fully expecting to be called upon to form a new administration.

Such was the situation when de Gaulle landed at Mérignac. It was to Reynaud and to him alone that the General owed his 11-day political career; and Reynaud still remained his only hope of preventing an armistice. He went straight to see his friend and patron in the office he was using on the Rue Vital-Carlès. When he arrived, he was told that President Lebrun had asked Pétain to form a government. Pétain had there and then produced from his pocket a list of his intended ministerial appointments and had handed it to the President.

Pétain had been de Gaulle's first commanding officer and thereafter his chief, patron and protector, though they in fact represented antithetical schools of military thought. Relations between them had cooled well before the war, as de Gaulle had increasingly asserted his independence as a thinker and writer on military matters. Now, however, an unbridgeable gulf opened up between the two men over the burning issue of whether to fight on from North Africa or seek an armistice. De Gaulle apparently decided to leave France as soon as he knew that Pétain had formed a government intent on abandoning the struggle.[10] He found Reynaud exhausted, but clinging to the hope that the German terms for an armistice would prove so unacceptable that he would be recalled to office; and unwilling for this reason to leave Bordeaux, though it was clear that the city must fall to the Germans within a matter of days. De Gaulle seems not at that stage to have told even Reynaud of the decision he had just taken to return to England.

Sir Edward Spears had arrived in Bordeaux with Sir Ronald Campbell, the British Ambassador, only half an hour after Reynaud on 14 June. Spears wrote a scintillating account of the events that took place in the hours following Reynaud's resignation and of de Gaulle's escape to London the next morning. Some French historians have treated this record with suspicion, for Spears, though an ardent and effective supporter of de Gaulle at the time, fell out with him a year later over policy in Syria. His account may indeed be coloured by a desire to emphasise how much de Gaulle owed to him at that decisive juncture; certainly de Gaulle was in very real danger of arrest at the hands of Weygand that night. Weygand had never been his friend: he had strenuously opposed de Gaulle's proposals for reform of the army and was reliably reported to have said, only a few days previously, that he would like to shoot the recently promoted, very junior general who had suddenly become his ministerial superior. On arrival in Bordeaux, Weygand, convinced that he was about to be relieved of office, had made plans to use the French Air Force cadets under training at Mérignac to arrest and depose Reynaud by force if necessary. The plot had come to light by the merest chance and the cadets had been disarmed at Mandel's behest.[11] There is therefore no doubt that Weygand, with Pétain's backing, would have done whatever was necessary to prevent the departure for England of the man who had been a leading proponent of continuing the war from Algeria.

De Gaulle, no doubt warned by his staff, had therefore every reason to keep his departure a secret. He had, however, the assistance of his personal staff headed by Jean Laurent, who had been Director General of the Banque d'Indo-Chine and was not quite the cowering foundling that Spears perhaps implied.[12] However, de Gaulle urgently needed the help of the senior British representative in Bordeaux, whoever that might be, to make sure that the aircraft that had brought him from London would be available to fly him out next morning, and he cannot have known where to find such an authority in a town packed with refugees; indeed, it would have been dangerous for him to be seen, or known, to be looking for such help. But luck – or destiny – smiled upon him as he was making his way down the unlit hall that led from Reynaud's office into the street. Two figures entered it on their way to see the ex-Prime Minister: they proved to be Campbell and Spears. A hurried consultation in the hall, where he had waited for them to re-emerge from Reynaud's office, was later continued at the Hôtel St Mandé, where Campbell was staying. De Gaulle made his way there on foot, since it would have been highly imprudent for him to have been seen in the Ambassador's car.

Spears had a lively eye for detail, which de Gaulle, with his mind on loftier matters, did not. Spears's version of those epic events records that in the ensuing conversation de Gaulle said it was essential he should return to England without delay. The fate of the French Empire was at stake: there was no-one in France who would, or could, rally it now that Pétain and a team of defeatists had taken over. The call to continued resistance must be made at once, before any statement accepting defeat was sent out from Bordeaux. He would give that call himself; let anyone join him who would.

The circumstances were so altered by Reynaud's resignation and the fact that de Gaulle was no longer a member of the French Government that Campbell and Spears telephoned Churchill to persuade him to allow de Gaulle to use the aircraft to leave France and return to England; and to agree that Spears should accompany him. Churchill, roused from sleep, understood the danger de Gaulle faced and the advantage of getting him out of the country, though he was somewhat reluctant to accept that, with Reynaud's resignation, Spears's mission was at an end and that he could do nothing useful by staying on in Bordeaux. This conversation must have taken place on an open telephone line but things were in such turmoil that neither the new French Government nor the Germans could have been in a position to benefit thereby.

The plan was that de Gaulle and his ADC, a young English-speaking diplomat named Geoffroy Chaudron de Courcel, should accompany Spears to the airport next morning, ostensibly to see him off. Spears left the meeting to attempt to persuade Georges Mandel, who had been Clemenceau's *éminence grise* in the darkest days of the First World War, to fly to England too. Mandel felt it was impossible for him, as a Jew, to leave French territory in the hour of catastrophe; and that he must carry on the fight from French soil in North Africa. It was a courageous decision that was to cost him his life.[13]

Someone, probably Jean Laurent, had found the General a room at the Hôtel de Normandie. It was only when he had made his escape plan that de Gaulle sent Laurent with a message to inform Reynaud of his intention. From the secret funds he had in his office, Reynaud sent him the equivalent of £500: this was all the General had with him on arrival in England.

De Gaulle and de Courcel were half an hour late arriving at the Hôtel St Mandé next morning, which caused Spears to fear the General might indeed have been arrested. They had brought rather more luggage with them than the 'two small suitcases' of popular legend and Spears thought a trunk had been sent on to Mérignac in advance. De Gaulle took the precaution of calling at his office and, without leaving the car, made various appointments for later in the day to give the impression that he planned to remain in Bordeaux.

The aerodrome was filled with more aircraft than Spears had seen before or since: they were parked wing to wing and stretched away into the distance. Every machine capable of flying had been assembled in readiness to leave for Morocco, but none was taking off. They soon found the RAF aircraft but the congestion was such that it proved difficult to get Spears's car close to it in order to conceal the transfer of the luggage.

The pilot, who had slept in the aircraft, went on foot to reconnoitre for space to take off, so closely were the planes parked. Then a new problem arose: the pilot insisted that de Gaulle's luggage, some of which was heavy, should be lashed down. De Courcel was sent off at the double to find a ball of string: he was gone for some ten minutes and the wait was very trying to both Spears and de Gaulle. The boxes contained important documents and Spears gathered that there could be no question of leaving them behind to be investigated by Weygand's people. De Courcel eventually returned with the indispensable string and quite soon the engines sputtered into life. The story goes that the plane had actually started to move before Spears, with hooked hands, hoisted de Gaulle's very considerable bulk aboard; Lacouture discounts this version as another case in which Spears projected himself as rescuer. It is hard, however, to see how anyone wearing the uniform of a French two-star general could have boarded the plane earlier or with more dignity without giving the whole game away. De Courcel, future French Ambassador to the Court of St James, had proved more nimble: he was up in a trice and no doubt helped haul his master on to the aircraft.

The plane taxied out and found space to take off. Within a few minutes they were flying north over the sea between the Ile-d'Oléron and La-Pallice. Spears had spent a pleasant sailing holiday on that coast two years before and was busy identifying remembered coves and landmarks when he beheld a terrible sight: a great ship was lying on her side sinking and hundreds of tiny figures could be seen in the water. It was the liner *Champlain* which had 2,000 British troops aboard.

As they cut across the Breton peninsula, flying low, the whole countryside seemed to be on fire, for there was smoke everywhere. Spears supposed the Germans had set fire to villages but he was told later that the fires came from the destruction of British Army supply dumps: there must, he commented, have been very many of them in the abandoned Breton redoubt. De Gaulle reflected on his dying mother at Paimpont and the family he had left at Carentec.[14]

The plane touched down to refuel in Jersey, where Spears asked de Gaulle if he wanted anything to drink, neither of them having breakfasted. De Gaulle said he would like a cup of coffee. Spears handed him one in the canteen. De Gaulle took a sip, and in a voice which indicated that, without implying criticism, he must nevertheless proclaim the truth, said this was tea. It was, Spears wrote, the General's introduction to the tepid liquid that in England passed for one or the other.

As he watched de Gaulle with a sense of contrition deepening into self-reproach, Spears felt more vividly than before that there was nothing but this man's courage to kindle into flame the tiny spark of hope he had brought with him – all that was left of the spirit of France. It was a deserved tribute, but events were to prove that the same spirit and hope were still alive in the hearts of a number of other French men and women, mostly of even more modest status than that of the most junior general of the French army.

They landed at Heston in beautiful weather in time for a late lunch at the Royal Automobile Club. Then Spears took de Gaulle to call on Churchill. The Prime Minister had only just completed his own move from Admiralty House to No. 10 Downing Street. He was sitting in the garden enjoying the fine weather. He had already decided to help the General to rally such Frenchmen as might be willing to continue the fight, and he placed the BBC at de Gaulle's disposal.

The two men must also have discussed the urgent problem of ensuring that Mme de Gaulle and their three children did not become hostages in German hands. The first idea seems to have been to send a British destroyer to evacuate them from Brest, but Carentec, where they had taken refuge, is over 50 km. (30 miles) distant and communications had become almost impossible. Instead, Major Norman Hope, head of the Belgian Section of Section D of the Secret Intelligence Service, was sent to Plymouth that evening to attempt to bring the family out of France by air.[15]

Carentec is a fishing village lying on Morlaix Bay where there are large expanses of beach at low tide and it was presumably for this reason that an amphibious aircraft was thought best for the job. In addition to Hope and the aircrew, it had to be able to carry five passengers: Anne, the de Gaulles' handicapped daughter, Marguerite Potel, a maid who looked after her, the two other children and Mme de Gaulle herself. At RAF Mount Batten on Plymouth Sound there was a Supermarine Walrus amphibian L2312 with the required characteristics, which had been borrowed from time to time by the Plymouth-based No. 10 Squadron, Royal Australian Air Force, for communications flights. Flight Lieutenant J.N. Bell, who had flown this aircraft to Brest two days previously, volunteered for the job. A signal from Commander-in-Chief, Western Approaches, at 2100 hrs on the evening of 17 June, ordered 'one Walrus' to proceed with 'an Admiralty passenger' to the north coast of Brittany 'at earliest 18/6'. The passenger would give details of destination on arrival 'about 2358/17'. The aircraft was to be 'fully armed, especially when waterborne' and was to return to base on completion.[16]

Hope, who had worked for Shell in peacetime, was briefed to make a visual reconnaissance of the Shell fuel storage facilities at Brest as a subsidiary task. He landed at Plymouth's Roborough Airport on schedule. He had been described as 'attached to the Naval Intelligence Directorate'. Hope and Bell were to be accompanied by Flight Sergeant C.W. Harris and a wireless electrical mechanic from the RAF's ground staff, who had had to be given a rapid course of instruction in the operation of the relevant wireless equipment that evening before take-off.

The Walrus left Mount Batten at 0200 hrs on 18 June, though a secondary source reported 0255 as the actual time of take-off. The aircraft was never heard from again. It was not until many months later that London learned through the International Red Cross that the site of the graves of Hope, Bell, Harris and the wireless mechanic had been located. The aircraft had crashed in fog two miles from Ploudaniel, a village rather nearer Brest than Carentec, and those on board had been buried in the churchyard there.

De Gaulle spent much of that day, 18 June, the anniversary of Waterloo, working on his broadcast with the help of a typist borrowed from the French Blockade Mission. Churchill was incommunicado that morning, writing his 'This was their finest hour' speech for an impending debate in the House of Commons and, in his absence, the War Cabinet, chaired by Neville Chamberlain, took fright at the diplomatic implications of what was afoot and decided to ban de Gaulle's planned broadcast. Churchill had to send one of his staff round Whitehall that afternoon to approach individually the ministers concerned and persuade them to change their minds. This they did and the General went on the air that evening with the first of his two now famous appeals. He did so 24 hours after Pétain had asked, through the Spanish Government, for the Germans' terms for an armistice. It was therefore a public act of dissidence: de Gaulle had crossed his Rubicon.

In Brittany, the motorised infantry of General von Kluge's 4th Army reached Rennes that day and swept on westwards towards Brest, whose quays were still crowded with troops, including a British division landed only a few days earlier, and French and Polish troops evacuated from Narvik. Among those who had come from Narvik and were waiting to embark were a Captain Koenig of the 13th Demi-Brigade of the French Foreign Legion and a Staff Captain named André Dewavrin. Both were to join de Gaulle and to play key parts under his orders.[17]

There was still no news of Madame de Gaulle and her children, nor of the missing Walrus L2312 and her crew. On 19 June – the day the Germans occupied Brest – a Belgian RNVR officer named Van Riel, who had been serving as deputy to the missing Major Hope in Section D of the Secret Intelligence Service (SIS or MI6), was sent to Plymouth to make a further attempt to find de Gaulle's family and discover what had happened to the Walrus. He had in peacetime been the secretary of a Belgian yacht club, assuming the name Vann for cover purposes. He sailed from Plymouth that evening, 19 June, in a motor torpedo boat named MTB 29 and landed at Carentec at 0600 the next day. He found that the first German troops had appeared in the village nearly 24 hours before, and that the de Gaulle family had left.[18]

Vann had thought of taking the MTB up to Morlaix to seek news of Hope and the missing Walrus but they had already been spotted by hostile aircraft and it would have been folly to pursue the search further in broad daylight into what had evidently become enemyheld territory, so they returned to Plymouth.

Mme de Gaulle had in fact taken her children and the maid into Brest on 17 June, before the arrival of the German vanguard. She borrowed money from an aunt who lived there and sought news of her husband at the British Vice-Consulate, which was closing down. Staff advised her to embark on one of the last two ships sailing for England, one Polish, one British. The de Gaulles took passage in the latter and reached Falmouth safely on 19 June: they were therefore in England before MTB 29 sailed to find them. The Polish ship was sunk on the way over.[19]

The abortive mission to rescue General de Gaulle's family has been claimed as the RAF's first attempt to carry out a clandestine pick-up operation in German-occupied territory in the Second World War. Although until the end of 1940 only one such RAF operation to France succeeded, 6 did so in 1941, 38 in 1942 and altogether more than 220 by the time France was liberated.[20] These operations were almost all carried out by Lysander and Hudson aircraft of 161 Special Duties Squadron, the records of which are kept in the Public Record Office. A well-researched account of these flights has been published and their importance at a critical period of French history is widely recognised. The available RAF records of parachute drops of men and supplies to occupied Europe, which were many more in number than the pick-up operations, have formed the basis of an even more wide-ranging study.

Clandestine contacts by sea, though numerous, were initially under less centralised control and until now the most important British record in this field has been inaccessible. In the case of Norway, sea traffic was far more important than air supply during the German occupation, and was carried on largely by Norwegians; British records are thus incomplete and of marginal importance. Clandestine sea transport to and from France, on the other hand, was until 1943 predominantly in British and Polish hands and no systematic account of it is possible without recourse to their respective archives. This book draws on both these sources, on relevant French records, published accounts and the memories of participants, to provide a framework of firm, historical fact before the subject sinks into oblivion or drifts beyond reach into the realm of legend.

CHAPTER II

The British Clandestine Services in the New Strategic Context

T he news that German forces were flooding into Holland and Belgium on the morning of 10 May 1940, coming on top of the bloodless occupation of Denmark and the pre-emption of Allied strategy in Norway, led Neville Chamberlain reluctantly to accept the necessity of forming a National Coalition Government. As the Labour Party proved unwilling to serve under his leadership, he summoned Lord Halifax and Winston Churchill to Downing Street. Halifax, whom Chamberlain would have preferred, said it would be difficult for him, as a peer, to control the parliamentary situation in a war such as this. So the choice fell on Churchill.

When the new Prime Minister got to grips with shaping the Government to deal with the perilous situation that arose from the collapse of the Allied front in France, it became apparent that the clandestine services needed to be strengthened for the forthcoming tasks. The stock of the SIS stood low in Whitehall. Indeed, Mr Chamberlain had been so beset by complaints about the Service's ineffectiveness that he had, in December 1939, asked Lord Hankey, Chancellor of the Duchy of Lancaster, to look into the matter in detail. Hankey was also to consider bids for additional funding by Colonel Stewart Menzies, who had become Chief of the SIS only a month earlier on the death of Admiral Sinclair; the budget was seriously overspent.

Hankey, the architect of so much of Britain's 20th-century machinery of government, had an unusual qualification for this task, which incidentally was still not completed when the Chamberlain Government fell. A report he had written as a young Captain in the Royal Marines, for a subcommittee of the Committee of Imperial Defence, had led in 1909 to the creation of a Secret Service Bureau, whose home and foreign departments had evolved into MI5, the Security Service, and MI6, its overseas counterpart. It was only at that late date that the growth of tension between Edwardian England and the Kaiser's Germany, both stimulating and stimulated by a popular literature of invasion scares and spy thrillers, had led to a high-level review of the nation's need for professional espionage and counter-espionage. Victorian Britain had neglected these traditional skills as largely irrelevant to the protection of the country's far-flung interests, except in India and

Ireland. The long, if piecemeal, tradition of British intelligence systems in continental Europe, stretching back through the spy-masters and code-breakers of the Napoleonic and French Revolutionary wars to those who served Marlborough, Thurloe and Walsingham, had received little attention for 70 years. The Boer War had found British intelligence resources so run-down that it was followed by a mood of popular alarm in which every German waiter and barber came under suspicion as a spy preparing the way for an invasion.

MI1c, the future SIS, had little time to get going before the outbreak of the First World War. Its achievements were limited, not least because the Admiralty, its first tutelary department, set it to discover non-existent German plans to invade the United Kingdom.[1] During the war, it was transferred to the supervision of the War Office and thence to that of the Foreign Office. After a somewhat hesitant start, it developed into a useful component of the ramified intelligence structure created for wartime needs. In support of the Allied armies on the Western Front, it came to run, via Holland, the largest and most successful of the train-watching networks operating behind the lines in German-occupied France and Belgium.[2]

At that time the Admiralty's Naval Intelligence Division was by far the most comprehensive of Britain's intelligence resources and its pre-eminence was enhanced when, before the end of 1914, it began to read German naval codes, though senior officers were slow to take advantage of this achievement. The Admiralty's Room 40 went on to break German diplomatic ciphers and it was their decryption of what has become known as the 'Zimmerman telegram' at the beginning of 1917 that precipitated the entry into the war of the United States.[3]

At the end of the war and of Allied intervention in Russia, it was the Admiralty's code-breakers who successfully attacked the cipher used by the Soviet trade delegation in London and produced a flow of evidence of Moscow's plans to promote revolution in the United Kingdom and subversion in Ireland and India.[4] The Director of Naval Intelligence, under whose aegis Room 40 operated, the Service chiefs and Lord Curzon, then Foreign Secretary, were so provoked by the Komintern intercepts that in 1920[5] and again in 1923[6] they thought it right to publicise and to base diplomatic action on them – that is to say, they were prepared to kill the goose that laid the golden eggs, although, curiously enough, not all access to Soviet telegrams was lost as a consequence, even in 1923.

It was clearly an anomaly that the Admiralty should in peacetime pay for the production of intelligence to be used primarily by the Foreign Office and the Home Office. Admiral 'Quex' Sinclair was given the task of creating a civilian cryptanalytical facility, drawing upon staff who had worked in Room 40 and its War Office equivalent. This new organisation took the name Government Code and Cipher School (GC&CS)[7] and was made responsible to the Foreign Office. It was not long before the Directors of Service Intelligence objected that civilian control would lead to neglect of their longer-term interests. The solution adopted in 1923 was to appoint Sinclair to succeed Sir Mansfield Cumming, who had been head of what had become MI6 or the Secret Intelligence Service from its inception, and to make him at the same time Director of GC&CS.[8]

SIS's position had been strengthened in 1921 with the dismissal of Sir Basil Thomson, head of the Special Branch during the war and then Director of Intelligence at the Home Office with wide-ranging powers to collect intelligence about subversion from overseas sources without reference to Cumming. SIS thereby acquired a monopoly of espionage and counter-espionage outside the United Kingdom and the British Empire.[9]

However, the inter-war years were a lean time both for SIS and GC&CS. SIS's relations with the Foreign Office were prickly: funds were so scarce that many of the Service's small stations in European capitals had to be closed. Recruitment was suspended and the Service, lacking new blood, remained too long preoccupied with the old post-Russian Revolution intelligence targets and was slow to recognise the new danger represented by the advent of the Nazis and German rearmament.

GC&CS continued to read Soviet ciphers until 1927. Austen Chamberlain, the Foreign Secretary, and his officials had by then recognised that there was a wide gap between Komintern rhetoric and Komintern achievements. Still a group of Tory die-hards, led by Joynson-Hicks, the Home Secretary, Churchill and Birkenhead, the Secretary of State for India, persuaded the Baldwin Cabinet that a breach of diplomatic relations was the best way to halt Soviet interference in British domestic affairs, Komintern use of London as a base for subversion in the British Empire, and Moscow's attempts to supplant British by Soviet influence in Afghanistan and incite the British armed forces to mutiny. Police raids were mounted on premises occupied by the All-Russia Cooperative Society (Arcos) and the Soviet trade delegation in the hope of finding evidence that could be used to justify the planned breach without compromising GC&CS's intercepts, but the results were disappointing. Baldwin, Joynson-Hicks and Austen Chamberlain all in turn quoted intercepted Soviet telegrams in the ensuing House of Commons debate and after this appalling series of indiscretions GC&CS inevitably lost access to this most valuable traffic.[10]

In the prevailing atmosphere of financial stringency, the visa fees

collected by the Passport Control Offices, which provided cover for
SIS's overseas deployment, were an important resource. By 1935,
however, Nazi persecution of the Jews flooded those offices with
long queues of applicants for Palestine visas. The workload became
crippling and the temptations fatal to security. Desperate German
Jews were ready to pay large sums to jump visa queues or circum-
vent visa requirements. The temptations proved irresistible not only
to poorly-paid visa clerks at Warsaw and the Hague but also to SIS's
Head of Station in the Netherlands, a Major Dalton, who pocketed
several thousand pounds, was blackmailed by one of his clerks and
committed suicide in 1936.[11] Following an enquiry by an officer
from SIS headquarters the blackmailer was sacked. He was
promptly taken on by Abwehr IIIf to whom he betrayed SIS's
best source of intelligence about German naval construction. The
hard-pressed Passport Control Office, under Dalton's successor, a
decent ex-Indian Army Officer who spoke fluent Dutch, then
excelled themselves by re-employing the blackmailer-turned-Ger-
man spy. The Germans went on to infiltrate a second mole into the
PCO, the door of which they kept under surveillance from a barge
moored in a nearby canal.[12] As the Hague was a main base for
SIS's operations against intelligence targets in Germany, the consequences were far-reaching.

SIS suffered two further serious setbacks, when German entry
into Austria in the spring of 1938 led to the arrest of the head of its
Vienna station and, a year later, when Hitler's seizure of Prague
brought about the collapse of its organisation in Czechoslovakia.[13]

As war approached, there was a series of false alarms both from
SIS sources and from the private informants of Sir Robert Vansittart, who played the role of Cassandra as Chief Diplomatic Adviser
to the Government, even after Chamberlain had eased him out of
his post as Permanent Under-Secretary at the Foreign Office. False
intelligence planted by Admiral Canaris, head of the Abwehr and a
secret opponent of Hitler, in the hope of galvanising British resistance to the Fuehrer's adventurism along with information from
tainted sources in the Netherlands, fed to SIS for purposes of
strategic deception, vied for attention in Whitehall with soundly
based reports. The result was confusion. At Easter 1939, the
Foreign Office gave credence to a number of intelligence plans
and false alarms, but none to accurate indications of the impending German occupation of Prague and the Italian invasion of
Albania. Consequently, interdepartmental machinery in Whitehall
was belatedly established for the assessment of raw intelligence –
something the Foreign Office had long resisted. It was a step in the
right direction but the new arrangements were still not functioning
effectively when war broke out.[14]

It would be unjust to impute to SIS prime responsibility for the confusion that prevailed in Whitehall in 1939. It has been well observed that Great Britain suffered from built-in disadvantages in her intelligence battles with her three main rivals in Europe – Germany, Italy and the Soviet Union: secrets are easier to protect in authoritarian than in open societies.[15] Treasury parsimony, coupled with Foreign Office Pharisaism and the sometimes comic amateurism of Foreign Office security at home and abroad, exacerbated that handicap. The Foreign Office was chiefly responsible for the inadequate resources devoted to intelligence collection in the inter-war years; for inattention to the quality of SIS's recruitment;[16] and for the delay in establishing a Joint Intelligence Committee to analyse and assess raw intelligence, as well as to coordinate and manage the national intelligence effort to best effect.[17]

Whitehall collectively misjudged the danger of a Soviet–German pact in August 1939 and all but the Treasury underestimated the ability of the German economy to sustain a long war. SIS failed to report German preparations for the invasion of Poland; its chief, 'Quex' Sinclair, understood that the creation of the Ministerial Council for the Defence of the Reich, under Goering's chairmanship, was the coping-stone on Germany's preparations for war, but Cadogan and other senior officials in the Foreign Office clung to the hope that it betokened the ascendancy of 'moderate' elements in the German leadership.[18]

SIS shared the not wholly unfounded belief of the Foreign Office that there was a powerful conservative opposition to Hitler's adventurist policies; they were deluded in believing that contact could be made with that opposition through Dr Franz Fischer, who posed as a Catholic refugee in the Netherlands but was in fact an informer of the Sicherheitsdienst. Fischer arranged a first meeting in the Hague with an emissary from Germany, who purported to represent a powerful group within the German armed forces, which was planning to overthrow Hitler should he order an offensive in the West. On 7 November 1939, despite a warning from Schofield, the Naval Attaché, that the meeting might be a trap, Stevens, head of the SIS Station at the Hague, and a British resident named Payne Best, who had been running an independent SIS network in Holland, were lured to a rendezvous at Venlo on the Dutch–German border. They were accompanied by an observer from Dutch military intelligence. The trap was sprung and the three were dragged across the border into Germany. The Dutch observer offered resistance and was mortally wounded.

Whitehall had no idea what had happened. Menzies, who succeeded Sinclair as Chief of SIS on the latter's death (which occurred just as the affair was reaching its climax), continued even in 1947 to believe that the conspiracy had been genuine, even if the contact with the plotters had gone wrong.[19] Heydrich

(Himmler's chief lieutenant in the SS) decided to exploit the affair as a propaganda victory, thereby compounding SIS's humiliation.[20]

Menzies survived the débâcle, but, Halifax, the Foreign Secretary, when informing him of his appointment, spoke of the possible need for a review of SIS's organisation. Shortly afterwards Chamberlain asked Hankey to conduct this scrutiny.

In March 1940 Hankey put in an interim report on SIS's affairs, which did not foresee any need for structural change; but by the end of May the disastrous tide of events on the Continental battlefield obliged the British Chiefs of Staff to reappraise their whole strategy, including some major reshaping of the clandestine services. On 25 May the Chiefs submitted to the War Cabinet that, even if France fell, 'Germany might still be defeated by economic pressure; by a combination of air attacks on economic objectives inside Germany and on German morale; and the creation of widespread revolt in the conquered territories.' To stimulate this revolt was, they considered, 'of the very highest importance. A special organisation [would] be required, and plans . . . should be prepared, and all the necessary preparations and training should be proceeded with, as a matter of urgency.'[21]

Apart from Section D of SIS, whose disavowable activities had so far secured almost no tangible results except the removal from Amsterdam of a large stock of industrial diamonds immediately before the city fell into German hands, there were two other bodies in Whitehall that had been set up before the outbreak of hostilities with terms of reference relevant to this new strategy. Since 1938 the War Office had had a small staff (MI(R)) studying, *inter alia*, the technical aspects of guerilla warfare and its relevance to Allied strategy, given that Allied guarantees to Poland and Czechoslovakia could manifestly not be honoured by the use of British and French conventional forces. Also in 1938, the Foreign Office had set up a small organisation in Electra House (EH) to look into the use of propaganda as a means of influencing enemy public opinion.

Another matter requiring urgent attention was the use of amphibious raiding forces. Brigadier Colin Gubbins, one of the officers engaged in MI(R)'s study of guerilla warfare, had been sent to Norway in command of what were termed the Independent Companies. In an otherwise disastrous campaign, he had demonstrated the effectiveness of small raiding parties landed by local fishing vessels behind the enemy lines to disrupt communications. There was, however, no existing organisation that could prepare for and direct operations of this type. Beaumont-Nesbitt, the Director of Military Intelligence, whose small staff in MI(R) had made striking contributions to Whitehall's thinking in all these fields, including strategic deception and escape techniques for prisoners of war, made a bid to set up a directorate of irregular warfare within the War Office, but the subject had too many interdepartmental implications to be pursued from within a single ministry.

With Churchill's warm backing, Hankey rapidly solved the problem of responsibility for organising amphibious raids by uniformed troops: a Directorate of Combined Operations was created under Admiralty auspices. Hankey and the heads of MI(R) and Section D concluded at a meeting on 13 June that the fall of France would require that raiding and subversion should be placed under the control of a single Minister. However, Churchill's decision on 10 June to set up a new Security Executive increased his political hold on the Security Service (MI5): this development was most unwelcome to the Labour component of the National Government, who had long regarded both the Security Service and the SIS with suspicion as nests of reactionaries. Attlee, Lord Privy Seal and Leader of the Labour Party and Dalton, the Minister of Economic Warfare, inisted that any new agency created to deal with sabotage and subversion must be responsible to a Labour minister. Dalton was present at a meeting on 1 July called by Lord Halifax about this subject, at which the general feeling, voiced by Lord Lloyd, the Colonial Secretary, who had experience of guerilla warfare under T.E. Lawrence, was that the multiplicity of bodies dealing with these matters required a controller armed with 'almost dictatorial powers'.[22]

Dalton wrote next day to Halifax calling for a 'new organisation to coordinate, inspire, control and assist the nationals of the oppressed countries, who must be direct participants.' 'We have got,' he argued, 'to organise movements in enemy-occupied territory comparable to the Sinn Fein movement in Ireland, to the Chinese guerillas operating against Japan, to the Spanish irregulars who played a notable part in Wellington's campaign or – one might as well admit it – to the organisations the Nazis themselves have developed so remarkably in almost every country in the world. This "democratic international" must use many different methods, including industrial and military sabotage, labour agitation and strikes, continuous propaganda, terrorist acts against traitors and German leaders, boycotts and riots.' It was a radical call that fitted the perceived needs and mood of the hour: Churchill and the Chiefs of Staff, bereft of a major ally to mount a credible challenge to the Wehrmacht's 250 triumphant divisions on the European field of battle, had compelling reasons to espouse a strategy that might weaken the enemy from within: traumatic memories of the battlefield losses of the First World War loomed large in the minds of Britain's strategists as in the minds of the French General Staff.

Dalton, with Attlee's backing, pressed hard to be given charge of the new organisation for which he had called. Though both the Foreign Office and the War Office also made bids for control, Churchill invited Dalton to take the job on and the Special Operations Executive came formally into existence on 1 August 1940. It had two components; SO1 for propaganda and SO2 for operations.

To Col Menzies, who had been present at Lord Halifax's meeting on 1 July, the amputation of Section D and the creation of SOE as a separate agency were most unwelcome: SIS's business was to collect secret intelligence secretly. It cut across the professional instincts and interests of the SIS to have their in-house capability for small-scale sabotage and deniable subversion become part of a new and independent service under an activist minister of left-wing views and with a mandate from Churchill to 'set Europe ablaze'. The new arrangement was bound to cause friction; moreover the lack of common ministerial responsibility for the two sister services at any level below that of the very busy Prime Minister meant that no arbiter was readily available when trouble arose. Yet it is difficult to believe that the SIS of 1940 was capable of summoning up the 'certain fanatic enthusiasm' for which Dalton called in putting the new strategic concept into effect.

SOE thus got off to a sticky start as far as its relations with SIS were concerned. Notwithstanding SIS's own recent disasters and the fact that SOE had taken over a number of their own officers, SIS affected to regard the new organisation as a bunch of ignorant and potentially dangerous amateurs. They did what they could to contain any threat the SOE cuckoo's egg might pose to their interests: they were able, for the time being, to control SOE's ciphers and signals. They also got the Chiefs of Staff to award priority to their own needs for clandestine transport by both sea and air.

Menzies had an asset of enormous potential significance in his dealings with Churchill and the Chiefs of Staff; and after what had happened in 1926, he was shrewd enough to keep it very much under his personal control. The Government Code and Cipher School had begun the war in no very confident mood: Denniston, its operational head from the outset, had believed that ENIGMA, the machine cipher system adopted by the Germans for their highest-grade security traffic, was unbreakable. During the 1930s the Poles had made most progress towards doing so, with the help of a long-forgotten patent application for the system and of key material bought by the French from a venal German diplomatic courier. It was only under the imminent threat of German invasion that the Polish cryptanalysts had revealed to their French and British counterparts the extent of their achievement, delivering into their safekeeping two copies of a prototype ENIGMA machine built in great secrecy. The copy destined for Bletchley Park, to which GC&CS had been evacuated at the outbreak of war, had been brought from Paris to England in a heavily escorted diplomatic bag and met at Victoria Station by Menzies, then deputy to Admiral Sinclair, dressed in a dinner jacket, with the rosette of the Légion d'Honneur in his buttonhole.[23]

At Bletchley, some of Cambridge's finest mathematical intellects concentrated on discovering how to break ENIGMA signals traffic regularly and promptly, despite last-minute protective measures introduced by the Germans at the outbreak of war. On 22 May 1940, 12 days after Churchill formed his National Government and as the British Expeditionary Force pulled back towards Dunkirk, GC&CS broke the ENIGMA key most commonly used by the Luftwaffe and they were able to maintain their coverage from day to day. Although there were still enormous difficulties to overcome, the breakthrough afforded possibilities of a kind that had never before been available to any belligerent: the Germans were obliged to use radio links and continued to rely on variants of the ENIGMA system to protect their most sensitive secrets. At that time SIS's fortunes lay at a low ebb and Whitehall mandarins such as Cadogan had little confidence in reports from agents even when Menzies thought these worth bringing to them in person. The ENIGMA advance therefore came none too soon. But in July 1940 it did not make the need for intelligence from human sources in enemy-occupied territory or for physical lines of communication any less pressing.

CHAPTER III

Slocum's Section and the First Operations to Northern France

I n the weeks following the fall of France, SIS came under
particular pressure from the Directors of Naval, Military and
Air Intelligence to provide at least 72 hours' warning of any
impending German invasion of the United Kingdom. A second
urgent requirement was for intelligence that would enable the
Navy and the Royal Air Force to mount effective attacks on
commerce-raiders, blockade-runners and U-boats operating from
ports on the French Atlantic coast. This pressure on SIS was all the
greater in that none of the other possible sources of coverage of
these intelligence targets could be relied on to supply, or even make
a regular contribution to, the required information. The Admiralty's own direction-finding organisation was new and at first
produced little, if anything, of value; and the same was then true
of GC&CS's cryptanalysts and the RAF's photographic reconnaissance units. Indeed, cooperation between the Admiralty and the Air
Ministry over air reconnaissance had reached what Godfrey, the
Director of Naval Intelligence, called its 'nadir'.[1]

SIS had no immediately available assets in France, where it had
had a gentlemen's agreement with its French counterpart, the
Service de Renseignements, not to conduct espionage; and whatever coverage it had had in the Low Countries had been severely
disrupted by the Germans. It had therefore to start from scratch by
recruiting, training and briefing agents; devising means of transport
to get them into, and out of, German-occupied territory; and
developing clandestine radio (W/T) communications for agents'
use and training operators to use them.[2] They sought help wherever they could in France, not only from de Gaulle's Deuxième
Bureau (later BCRA) but also from intelligence professionals who
had remained in France and were now working for the Vichy
Government; and from the intelligence service of the exiled Polish
Government.

Menzies established two new staff sections to produce intelligence on French targets: one under Commander W.H. Dunderdale,
who had been head of SIS's Paris station until the fall of France, the
other under Commander Kenneth Cohen, RN. Dunderdale's brief
was to operate independently of the Free French, as far as possible,
though he found it necessary, particularly in the early days, to

borrow personnel from them: Cohen's role, on the other hand, was to cooperate fully with, and provide facilities for, the Free French embryo intelligence service under Captain André Dewavrin, who had adopted the *nom de guerre* 'Passy' for security reasons.

At the same time an Operations Section was created to reopen physical communications with occupied Europe. It was headed by Commander F.A. Slocum, a regular naval officer who had served in the Grand Fleet in the First World War, become a navigation specialist and retired from the Navy in 1936 as a Lieutenant-Commander. He had returned to uniform at the outbreak of war as a Commander RN.

Slocum's Section was at this stage responsible for arranging both sea and air transport operations, but the RAF was not immediately ready to begin such operations for the clandestine services. Experiments had to be conducted on how to adapt the available types of bomber aircraft for the parachute dropping of agents and how to land Lysander aircraft, originally intended for Army needs, on short improvised runways by moonlight.[3] All the earliest attempts to infiltrate agents into France and the Low Countries and to bring them back to report – for initially no radio facilities were available – had to be made by sea.

The motorised vanguard of the German army had broken through surprisingly quickly in the Battle of France, the mechanised 'teeth' troops running far ahead of the administrative 'tail', which, still largely dependent on horse-drawn transport, followed as best it could. This feature of their logistic arrangements was to persist until the end of the war, for the inventors of Blitzkrieg remained chronically short of oil. It meant that, from June through to September 1940, the whole coast that was accessible from the United Kingdom on overnight operations by high-speed craft, from Brest to the Hook of Holland, lay wide open.

Until radio sets suitable for agents' use became available towards the end of 1940 – even then in very limited numbers – and until agents had been found and trained to use them, more traditional methods of *de visu* reconnaissance and reporting back in person, or by pigeon or mail, had to be employed. Between June and October, agents were landed in Holland, Belgium and on the north coast of France from whatever fast surface craft were available. MTBs from Dover – and even a small RAF seaplane-tender – put a number ashore between Oostende and La Panne; MTBs and an old submarine from Portsmouth operated to the Normandy beaches, the Cherbourg peninsula and the Channel Islands. The only common factor in these operations was the provision by Slocum of a specialist navigating and conducting officer in each case: Lt H.W. Goulding, DSO, RNR, who knew the Channel coast intimately, and Lt Cdr J.W.F. Milner-Gibson, DSC, RNVR, between them carried the responsibility for navigating and conducting clandestine cross-Channel operations by high-speed craft for SIS, SOE and the Commandos until September 1941.

The first operation to France recorded by Slocum, carried out by a French MTB with a French crew, successfully landed an agent near Brest on the night of 20 June – the night following Vann's landing at Carentec in search of Mme de Gaulle and her family and only 24 hours after Brest and its strategic dockyard had been occupied by German troops. The code name allocated to this operation, AFB/SLO1, indicates that it was the first sea-landing operation carried out for an ephemeral organisation entitled the Anglo-French Bureau. The object was presumably to collect intelligence about the state in which the naval dockyard and its fuel stocks had fallen into German hands. The unfortunate Major Hope had had the same brief when he set out to rescue the de Gaulle family 48 hours earlier. This anonymous agent had better luck than Hope for he was picked up by the same means 11 nights after he had been landed.

On the following night, 1 July, a second French MTB with a French crew was sent to land two further agents for the Anglo-French Bureau near Cherbourg, on what may have been a similar reconnaissance, but the operation failed owing to a faulty compass and no further attempts were made.

At the beginning of July 1940 there were six MTBs being built for the French Navy at the British Power Boat Company yard in Hythe on Southampton Water. These were the Scott-Paine-designed vessels subsequently used as motor anti-submarine boats (MA/SBs) by Coastal Forces.[4]

By 1 July these boats were virtually ready and were completing their trials from Hythe with French crews who were already living on board. An agreement had been reached between the Admiralty, the French Admiral Muselier and Slocum's Section that they should be commissioned in the Free French Navy and put at Slocum's disposal for use in cross-Channel operations.

Pat Whinney and Steven Mackenzie, who had been serving on the British Naval Mission at Admiral Darlan's headquarters at the Château de Maintenon and made their way back from Saint-Jean-de-Luz on a Canadian destroyer, HMCS *Fraser*, which was run down and cut in two by the anti-aircraft cruiser *Calcutta* during the night, were sent by Ian Fleming to join Slocum's staff. On 2 July, they arrived in Hythe to liaise with the flotilla commander about operations planned for the very near future. On 3 July, however, a Captain Talbot brought Admiralty orders from London that the boats should be impounded and the crews taken ashore. This was on the eve of the action against the French squadron at Mers el-

Kebir; all French naval vessels lying in British ports were treated similarly.

Once vacated by their French crews, Coastal Forces decided to take the boats over for their own needs. Mackenzie remained at Hythe for about ten days until it was clear that their loss was final: he then took the French crews to Portsmouth for other duties.

On 22 July Mackenzie accompanied Milner-Gibson and Goulding, who were working as specialist navigators for Slocum, on an operation from Dover to the Dutch coast, but brilliant moonlight prevented a landing. On 24 July Whinney and Mackenzie were sent by Slocum to HMS *Vernon* in Portsmouth to take over a motor dispatch vessel named MDV 1, which was lying under the care of an engineer commander called Stallybrass. This boat was one of a series built in France for the Spanish Republican Government but never delivered, since the Civil War ended before they were ready for sea. They had been bought and brought to England by a Monsieur Westblatt, and Slocum, desperate for any craft, took two of them. They were fitted with four engines and electromagnetic clutches, which evinced a fine disregard for orders regarding going ahead or astern. On one occasion their contrariness had most of the crew flat on deck. They could cruise at about 18 knots on half-throttle but anything above that caused the clutches to slip and break down.[5]

At the end of July Slocum was finding it difficult, indeed impossible, to cope with the demands placed upon him. Section D of SIS, just about to become part of the new SOE, wanted three agents landed in Brittany. Then the Director of Combined Operations also wanted him to land a Sergeant, who was a native of the Channel Islands, on Guernsey to attempt to round up and rescue a small group of Commandos left behind on one of their first two operations, which Churchill described as a 'silly fiasco'. Slocum did so, and sent a Portsmouth-based MTB back to collect Sergeant Ferbrache, their would-be rescuer, but the men had surrendered to the Germans before Ferbrache got there.

At much the same time Passy's Deuxième Bureau wanted an agent landed on the north coast of Brittany – their first such demand, but one that failed since the agent proved unwilling to disembark at the pinpoint. Slocum dated this event 30 July. The Prime Minister, too, wanted an agent sent to Normandy to report on any signs of an impending cross-Channel invasion.

When de Gaulle's headquarters were asked to find a volunteer to go to the Ouistreham area to carry out the reconnaissance Churchill had requested, Passy thought of going in person, but the idea was vetoed as he was Chief of Staff to the General as well as organiser of the Deuxième Bureau and up to his eyes in work. It then emerged that Captain Maurice Duclos, another member of Passy's small staff, knew the stretch of coast intimately, as his parents had a holiday villa at Lagrune. Duclos, who had adopted the *nom de guerre* 'Saint-Jacques', volunteered for the job and suggested he might go on to Paris thereafter to contact friends who were known patriots and, with their assistance, try to set up an intelligence network covering the whole coast of Normandy and Picardy. This proposal was welcomed by all concerned but, since the Prime Minister wanted an immediate report on any invasion preparations, it was agreed that a second officer should accompany him but return by high-speed craft three days later. The choice fell on yet another survivor of the Norwegian disaster, a man named Beresnikov, who, like Passy and Saint-Jacques, had adopted the name of a Paris Métro station, 'Corvisart', for cover purposes.

No-one in London knew at that stage what identity papers might be required by the Germans and anyone of military age without suitable exemption ran the risk of being rounded up for failing to constitute himself a prisoner of war. There was some discussion in de Gaulle's headquarters as to how Saint-Jacques could justify his presence on the Normandy coast if questioned at a German check-point. Saint-Jacques caused some hilarity when he said he would tell the Germans he had been sent by his mother to see if his sister's piano was safe.[6]

On 3/4 August, after ten days spent doing trials in the Solent, MDV 1 carried out her one and only operation with Whinney as Commanding Officer, Mackenzie as No.2 and Milner-Gibson and Goulding navigating. Saint-Jacques and Corvisart were successfully landed with some carrier pigeons at Bella-Riva near the mouth of the River Orne at Ouistreham. Her magnetic clutches failed and the vessel managed only with difficulty to stem an adverse tide in the Solent when she got back to the English coast on the following afternoon.[7]

The beach used for this operation was close to that on which a French Commando would be put ashore on D-Day nearly four years later, as the first French component of the OVERLORD invasion force to land on their native soil.

As neither of Slocum's MDVs was in a usable state, a borrowed 63-foot motor anti-submarine boat was sent to re-embark Corvisart on the agreed night of 7 August. Unfortunately no-one was seen at what Slocum's navigator and conducting officer considered the proper pinpoint. Saint-Jacques returned in due course via Vichy, Oran, Casablanca and Lisbon, by which time he had laid the foundations of the intelligence network he had proposed. Corvisart came back through Spain.

MDV 1 was bombed during a daylight raid on Portsmouth on 12 August and one seaman was killed. Mackenzie stayed on in Portsmouth to take over MDV 2 and spent about two months in protracted efforts to solve her mechanical problems. Just when they were finally solved towards the end of September, this vessel was also destroyed during a night raid on the dockyard.

For the next 18 months the Admiralty, though ready to lend Slocum Coastal Forces high-speed vessels for the needs of the clandestine services, was unwilling to allocate them permanently for such duties. This meant that overnight sea-transport operations in the Narrow Seas between Brest and the Hook of Holland would be conducted under a grave handicap. Indeed, it was not until late in 1943, after prolonged and frustrating battles on Slocum's part, that reliable and suitable motor gun boats (MGBs) were permanently allocated by the Admiralty in adequate numbers for such purposes.

Between 20 June and 12 October 1940, when their operations by high-speed craft were closed down for the winter, Slocum's section had been able to arrange 16 attempted missions to the north coast of France, as well as five to the Channel Islands, six to Belgium and five to Holland, but the success rate to France was low. Setting aside the abortive attempt to rescue Mme de Gaulle, which had been arranged through other channels, there had been only the two successful missions by a French-manned MTB, on 20 June (the day before the armistice) and 1 July; and the landing of Saint-Jacques and Corvisart on 4 August by MDV 1. Not one of the ten operations arranged by Slocum's Section for SOE had led to a successful landing: on the final occasion on 12 October, the three agents had come under German machine-gun fire when trying to get ashore at the Anse-de-Bréhec, south of Paimpol.

Dunderdale's Section of SIS were at the time running successful operations to Brittany using Breton fishing vessels and the Free French were doing the same. Slocum also arranged for the RAF to parachute a first agent into France and had him picked up by Lysander.[8] But SOE, under political pressure from Dalton to get something started in France, had at the end of 1940 failed to infiltrate a single agent.

CHAPTER IV

First Contacts with the West Coast of France

N one of the high-speed craft available in 1940 or, indeed, for a long time afterwards, had sufficient range and speed to operate from bases in the United Kingdom to pinpoints further south than Brest. Clandestine sea-transport operations into the Bay of Biscay, which contained intelligence targets of the highest strategic importance, could therefore be carried out only by submarines or by craft that could pass as fishing vessels; or by a combination of the two.

Slocum arranged for an early, but unidentified, Free French agent to be landed with two SIS agents near Bordeaux from the British submarine *Talisman* on 2 August 1940.[1] By then, ten Italian submarines were already operating from that port and it was not long before that number grew to 20; some were of substantial tonnage. These vessels were of considerable importance to the Axis powers as blockade-runners.[2]

Slocum's Section was initially not concerned with such contacts as were arranged with the west coast using fishing boats with French fishermen as crews. These required minimal use of scarce Admiralty resources, and sea lines of this type were established by Dunderdale's Section of SIS, and by the Free French working independently.

The fishing industry on the west coast of Brittany was substantial, with large numbers of small and medium-size vessels operating from an array of little harbours between Ushant and the Loire. In 1940 many of these boats were still working under sail, though mechanisation had begun during the 1930s. As von Kluge's 4th Army broke into Brittany almost unopposed, vessels of all sorts and sizes, including many fishing boats, put to sea carrying refugees, both civilian and military. This improvised evacuation took place in utter confusion, with some remaining military authorities actively opposing it. General de Gaulle wrote glowingly of the 'flotilla of fishing boats' that arrived in Cornwall in the last days of June bringing to him 'all the able-bodied men' from the Ile-de-Sein. This was an overstatement[3] but, motivated perhaps as much by fear as courage, there were, indeed many Breton fishermen who sought refuge in Cornish harbours and who on 14 July, paraded at Olympia to be reviewed by the Free French leader. The contingent from the Ile-de-Sein was impressive enough to provoke the General's remark that they were 'a quarter of France', an early manifestation of his black humour.

Among those who arrived in Cornwall at that time was a young cavalry cadet named Hubert Moreau, son of a French Vice-Admiral, who had escaped when being moved from a barracks at Lorient on the first stage of transfer to Germany as a prisoner of war.[4] Along with a distant cousin, and with the encouragement of the parish priest of Concarneau, he had appropriated a small sailing boat at Beg-Meil and set off for England. They arrived at Polperro a week later, on 1 July. When asked for his passport by the local police constable, Moreau had to reply that he had left it in Paris; his cousin Gérard, lying in the bottom of the boat, was, after seven days of sea-sickness and almost complete lack of nourishment, incapable of answering any questions.

They were taken to Plymouth, housed briefly in a lunatic asylum, taken on a pub-crawl and finally to a sumptuous dinner in a smart hotel, where the intelligence officer who had interrogated them introduced them to his wife, who was not only French by birth but from a family known to Moreau. In the course of dinner their host said that he would be very interested to know exactly what was happening in France at the time of their departure. 'We are completely without information about the present situation,' he continued, 'and I know that up-to-date intelligence would be very much appreciated in London. It would be really useful to be able to follow from day to day what the Germans are doing in occupied France.' He went on to ask what Moreau's own plans were. By the end of the evening Moreau had accepted, in principle, the idea of a clandestine return to France.

Next day they arrived in London, where Moreau left his cousin to stay with relations and recover from his nautical adventures. Moreau was lunching alone at the Rubens Hotel, which was very close to SIS's headquarters in Broadway Buildings, to which he had been directed by the officer who had received them at Plymouth. At the end of the meal, when he was appraising the hole it was going to make in his slender financial resources, two French officers in uniform came into the dining room. One of them, tall and a general, was unknown to Moreau but the other, clearly his aide-de-camp, seemed vaguely familiar, though he could not immediately put a name to him. Moreau, notwithstanding his ragamuffin appearance, which had evoked the silent disapproval of the head waiter, went over and introduced himself: it was his first contact with General de Gaulle and Lt de Courcel. From them he learned of the creation in London of the Free French movement and of the presence in London of Admiral Muselier and Commandant d'Argenlieu, of whom he had often heard talk in naval circles.

Moreau told the General of the degree to which he had that very morning committed himself to the British services. De Gaulle raised no objection, but stipulated that Moreau must get British approval to come and report to him in person what he had seen and learned each time he returned from France. Some who reached England from France later in 1940 and were caught in the crossfire that had by then developed between Dunderdale and Passy have regarded this anecdote with suspicion, but Moreau published his account in 1955, evidently fearing no contradiction from de Gaulle.

Moreau decided that he would return to France by the same means as he had left it, by fishing boat. Needing a crew and a suitable vessel, he went to Olympia, which was being used as a barracks, and, in the corner where the Breton fishermen were congregated, found a solid and obstinate boy he liked at first sight. Raymond Le Corre had the further merit of being 19 years old – younger than Moreau, a fact the latter thought important for his authority.

On 10 July they went to Falmouth and chose a cutter-rigged crabber from the Ile-de-Sein, the *Rouanez-ar-Peoc'h* (Queen of Peace), whose crew of five immediately volunteered for the job. Moreau was about to make a last visit to London when he learned by chance that the five good islanders had left 26 children behind them: he decided he could not in such circumstances honestly accept their help on such a dangerous venture into the unknown.

He and Le Corre then decided to refit for the job a Douarnenez sardine pinnace that had been requisitioned by the French navy and had ended up in Falmouth Harbour. She was 16 metres overall and about to sink because of a small leak, which however proved easy to repair. Her excellent engine had been under water, but a mechanic promised to have it back in running order within 24 hours. Moreau, leaving the work to be carried out by a small boat-yard under the supervision of Le Corre and of the RN's Base Engineer Officer, went back to London in search of additional crew. Armed with a letter of authority, he went down to Portsmouth where he interviewed a procession of fishermen serving on the old battleship *Courbet*; this vessel had been the pride of the French Navy in 1915 but was now lying without steam or electricity, serving in effect as a floating anti-aircraft battery, the dockyard being under frequent attack by the Luftwaffe. He picked three men from Le-Guilvinec, who already knew Le Corre, as they had all arrived in Cornwall on the sardine pinnace *Korrigan* on 27 June, having escaped from their home port shortly after the Germans had occupied it.

When Moreau returned to Falmouth with his three new recruits, work on the boat had almost finished and 'Uncle Tom' Greene, Dunderdale's assistant, was there to lend a hand and see them on their way. It was a nickname that his age and unfailing kindness had earned the burly 6'6" Anglo-Irishman, son of a one-time mayor of Drogheda and owner of a family whiskey distillery as

well as a large flat in Paris. Moreau and his crew found in him 'a
father, rather than an uncle'.

It remained to take on board 2,000 litres of petrol and to victual
the ship, which the crew decided to call Le-Petit-Marcel. The
British naval rations that were sent on board for the purpose
proved alien to French tastes. Seeing the faces that the crew pulled
as they took the rations on board, Moreau and Uncle Tom set off
on a foraging expedition. They returned with a small barrel of
Algerian red wine Uncle Tom had found on board the temporarily
abandoned French hydrographic vessel *Président-Théodore-Tissier* and
had managed single-handed to pass up through a hatchway out on
to the deck: Moreau thought this an incredible feat of strength.
Endless tins of French bully beef and French biscuits were also
found and stowed away in the pinnace's lockers and fish-hold.

They ran trials and found that, thus laden, they could maintain
a cruising speed of about 6 knots. On 26 July they were ready: they
decided to leave in the afternoon to take advantage of the good
weather and make maximum use of the short hours of darkness, so
that they would be close to the French coast at daybreak. Such
information as was available suggested that French fishing boats
were obliged to sail within four miles of the coast; that they were
required to fly a white flag over their national colours; and that they
had to return to port before sunset.

Uncle Tom and Mills, the Port Engineer Officer, came to have
a farewell lunch with them on the otherwise deserted *Président-
Théodore-Tissier*. The ship's red wine failed, on the whole, to deliver
good cheer and everyone felt rather emotional when, at 3.30, the
time came for them to return to their own vessel. Uncle Tom, in
particular, seemed suddenly to have developed a bad cold, which
obliged him to blow his nose frequently. At 4 o'clock they sailed
and, from the harbour mouth, Moreau could still see Tom on the
deck of the *Tissier* frenetically waving what may have been an
outsize handkerchief. They were halted by a vessel of the Contraband Control Service stationed at the entrance to the harbour, who
had received no instructions about the pinnace. Moreau therefore
had to produce the only really compromising document he carried,
a letter from the local Naval Officer-in-Charge, a retired Admiral,
calling on all British naval authorities to give them 'aid and
protection'.

The crossing was uneventful and at first light next day they were
some miles west of Ushant, having decided not to attempt the
Chenal-du-Four passage inside that island, which is studded with
rocks and scoured by one of the most vicious tidal streams on the
whole French coast. At about 8 o'clock, when they were heading for
the Raz-de-Sein in calm conditions, a Dornier, which they had not
heard until it was very close, flew over them almost at masthead

height. It provoked great agitation on board for it was their first contact with the occupation authorities and much depended on what would happen next. They reduced speed and headed towards the nearest land, for they were far outside any four-mile limit that might be in force, meanwhile busying themselves with ropes on the deck aft, hoping that these would, at the Dornier's altitude and speed, be taken for nets. They had not omitted to hoist an enormous French flag and a towel to serve as the white one they understood to be required. After a first pass at an altitude of some 50 metres, the plane turned and came back towards them at greater speed: for some seconds, Moreau fully expected to see bullets spattering the sea or the deck. Fortunately nothing of the kind happened, except that on its third passage the aircraft fired a red, yellow and green rocket. They had no idea what that meant, but supposed it was a signal that would have been known to genuine fishermen, indicating that they were outside the permitted limits. So they headed for land at full speed, not without keeping an eye on their aerial sheep-dog, which in fact soon flew off towards base. It remained only to be seen whether the aircraft had reported them and some surface vessel would follow wanting to know what they were doing in that position.

As soon as the aircraft was out of sight, they headed south at top speed – 7–8 knots – with the idea of disappearing in the fine drizzle that had begun to fall.

The time had come to decide where to land: Uncle Tom had given Moreau latitude to go where they could and to bring back, when they could, such intelligence as they could collect. For security reasons, Moreau had thought it better not even to discuss their destination before they sailed.

The north coast, being nearest to England, was no doubt under particular watch, so it seemed better to land somewhere between the Raz-de-Sein and Lorient. He had himself sailed from that area a month previously and there had at that time been minimal surveillance of the coast.

During the night, Moreau had discussed the matter with Le Corre, who had mentioned several possible beaches and, in particular, some near Le-Guilvinec, which he knew well as it was his home port. Moreau, who knew the immediate area only from the charts they had borrowed from the *Tissier*, thought it right to consult the other three members of the crew. They all agreed that a small beach lying a kilometre or two west of Le-Guilvinec was the most suitable: it was the private foreshore of a château belonging to a 'Parisian' (which for a Breton meant someone from outside his own village) and, as the owner was rarely there, it seemed unlikely they would be disturbed. This seemed a sensible choice, as it would enable them to make rapid contact with Le Corre's parents or those of some other member of the crew.

They passed through the Raz-de-Sein that afternoon quite close to the Pointe-du-Raz, carried by a swingeing tide and in rain so dense that any German lookout post would have been unable to see them. At 10 o'clock that evening they were getting near Le-Guilvinec. The rain had given way to light drizzle, there was no moon, the wind had dropped and the sea was calm enough to offer the prospect of an easy landing. Moreau thought it better not to hazard the pinnace by too close an approach, so he told Baltas, Guénolé and Le Goff, the three other members of the crew, to heave to and remain about 300 metres from the shore, with the engine running dead slow, ready to put to sea at the smallest sign of trouble. Le Corre and he would land from the dinghy and leave it on the beach until they were ready to return.

Thus at 11.30, in complete darkness, they set off for the beach, having told the crew not to wait for them after 4.30 next morning, as their presence outside the port at daybreak would be inexplicable. They landed successfully and, as the tide was falling, forbore to pull the dinghy further up the beach, which would have made a considerable noise on the shingle. They then set off along the beach in the direction of the village. They had not covered more than ten metres when they heard voices raised in excitement quite close to them, together with the sound of heavy boots on the shingle.

They took refuge behind a rock and waited, in some trepidation. Soon electric torches were being flashed in all directions and there were cries that were definitely in German, which made it clear that something or someone was being pursued by members of the occupation forces. This was not reassuring, but it seemed improbable that they could have been reported in the course of the day and even more improbable that their landing point could have become known so rapidly. They had, however, fallen into a hornet's nest and Moreau even contemplated swimming back to the pinnace, since there was no way in which they could retrieve the dinghy, even supposing it had not already been discovered.

On reflection, however, he thought it would be better to get to the house of Le Corre's parents and find out what on earth was happening. Since it would be tempting providence to try to walk, or even crawl, among these excited people who might at any moment pick them up in the beams of their electric torches, he decided it would be better to wade through the water with little more than their heads showing, particularly since any noise they might make would be muffled by the sound of waves breaking on the beach. They therefore crawled on their stomachs to the edge of the water and paused to regain breath only when they were suitably immersed. They made their way gently towards the eastern end of the beach, which was delimited by a small wall, hoping that, once beyond it, they would be safe from further unpleasant surprises.

Suddenly Le Corre caught Moreau by the arm and whispered, 'There is one of them there.' Opening his eyes wide in the darkness, Moreau could at first make out nothing at all, but then he heard the sound of rapid breathing. Soon he perceived a man, only a few metres from where they stood; he too was half in and half out of the water, trying to hide behind a rock. Since he was hiding, it must be him, and not themselves, whom the Germans were for some reason hunting: Moreau already felt a degree of reassurance. He came within a whisker of approaching the unknown victim and offering to rescue him: it would have been so easy to take him back to England! But the prime object of their mission was not to help evaders and escapers and their boat was not a doss-house. Moreover, there was no way of telling whether he could provide the intelligence they had come to collect. Having weighed all these considerations carefully, Moreau decided to leave him where he was, though he had undoubtedly seen and heard them. No doubt he was just as afraid as they were. They continued on their way to the village where they arrived an hour later.

Leading Moreau with one hand and carrying his sabots in the other, Le Corre went to his parents' house. Once they were compelled to flatten themselves into a corner to let pass a German, whose heavy footfalls had warned them of his approach. They had to scratch away at the ground-floor shutters for some time before they got a cautious response: a pair of shutters on the first floor opened slightly and a tremulous voice asked what they wanted. When Raymond had been recognised, the door was opened, with a warning to make no noise: the Kommandantur was very close by and they were at the mercy of any belated German stroller. Once inside, with doors shut and curtains drawn, they explained to an astonished to M and Mme Le Corre how they came to be there.

Moreau's first concern was to discover what had been going on where they landed. It quickly emerged that the 'château' belonging to the 'Parisian' was no more than a villa. This had been requisitioned by the Germans, who had installed a headquarters in it: they could not have chosen a worse place for their landing. As for the man-hunt they had witnessed, it was no doubt the sequel to a quarrel at some drunken party organised by the occupants. Moreau and Le Corre realised, with small shudders, that the individual hiding behind the rock must have been a German, who would no doubt rapidly have composed his differences with his pursuers if presented with Moreau's offer of 'escape'.

They were at the Le Corre house for two well-spent hours. Moreau was able to elicit a mass of information on identity documents and permits, travel restrictions and the state of morale in Le-Guilvinec and the surrounding villages, and to gather a complete collection of the local newspapers since the beginning of the Occupation, which included, among other things, all the notices put out by the local Kommandantur. Having changed clothes, Moreau was decked out in a pair of red canvas trousers and a blue fisherman's blouse, amd his shoes had been replaced by a pair of heavy sabots.

The question was whether it was prudent to go back and collect their dinghy from where they had left it. Le Corre's parents begged them not to but after much discussion Moreau convinced them that in his new disguise there would be no great danger in his going for a walk along the foreshore. Once he had located the dinghy, he should be able to see, by the first light of dawn, whether it had yet attracted the attention of the authorities, which it inevitably would when daylight came, revealing the metal plaque – Moreau had just remembered its existence with anguish – fixed to the dinghy's transom bearing the name of its English builder's Cornish yard. A full-scale investigation with house-searches would be launched immediately throughout the village: the consequences for the inhabitants would be unthinkable. In any case, there was nothing irrevocable in Moreau's sallying forth with a basket on his arm to take a stroll along the beach. There was, however, no good reason for Le Corre to go too: he would instead accompany Moreau to the edge of the property and wait there for five minutes. If he did not see Moreau returning and heard nothing suspicious, he would go back home and then rejoin Moreau at 10 o'clock that evening in Beg-Meil, at the house of Moreau's friends, whence he had escaped to England a month previously.

It was still not daylight, but M Le Corre had told Moreau that the Germans made no difficulty about fishermen moving about the harbour area at any time after 4.30 a.m. Footsteps in the street outside indicated that they would not be the only people abroad at that hour. The beach, when they reached it, was calm and Moreau quite quickly found the dinghy. It lay further from the water than when they had landed, the tide having ebbed considerably, but it did not seem to have been disturbed. Moreau could, however, make out through the morning mist the figure of a sentry at the top of the beach: he seemed to be marching to and fro at the entrance to the garden. Making no attempt at concealment, Moreau dragged the boat noisily across the pebbles down to the water's edge. Five minutes later, heartily relieved, he was back on board. He had returned in the nick of time, for day was beginning to break and the crew were getting seriously concerned: they had decided that if nobody returned within quarter of an hour they must head back to England.

They stood out to sea at slow speed, so as to avoid making more noise than was strictly necessary, and wondered how best to kill time until the evening rendezvous with Le Corre. Moreau turned in and snatched a couple of hours' sleep before the crew called him up on deck, saying that they could see a large number of boats leaving the ports along the coast. Moreau reckoned that they could safely go alongside one or other of these vessels, for he felt confident they would not be given away by such splendid people, who, after all, were the friends and relatives of his crew. The crew of the first boat they spoke to guessed immediately why they were on the coast and assured Moreau of their discretion. They exchanged a few litres of petrol for some fish and spoke for a moment. The locals pointed out how dangerous it was to be seen in a motor pinnace that was not even rigged to sail: it was some time since petrol had last been issued to the fishing fleet and the boats at sea were all working under sail. Moreau took good note of this for his next trip. Another feature that marked them out from the other boats was that, in addition to the 300 litres of petrol in the pinnace's tank, they carried several hundred more on deck in 40-gallon barrels, stowed along both sides of the deck; these upended drums stood higher than the bulwarks, and were thus visible from a considerable distance.

The morning mist had lifted and it was such a fine day that Moreau felt emboldened to take the pinnace over to Beg-Meil, which lies half-way to Concarneau, to warn his friend Gauchard of the rendezvous he had arranged with Le Corre for that evening at his house. They set course for the bay and picked up the mooring buoy that Moreau had dropped overboard on 24 June when, in his flight from France as an escaped prisoner of war, he had 'borrowed' the 4.5-metre *Albatros* to take him to England.

There were Germans all over the beach: some were bathing, some playing football and some tinkering with the motor of a small motor launch tied up alongside a jetty in the middle of the beach. A single Frenchman was mending his nets on a boat close to where they were moored. Moreau thought it a good idea to have a word with him before going ashore. 'I hear a boat was stolen from here a month ago,' he said. 'Oh yes,' the fisherman replied in a broad Breton accent, 'it belonged to Caradec the baker.' 'Do they know who did it?' 'It must have been young people who wanted to get away to England on it, but of course they never can have got there; it was much too small a boat.' 'Any idea who they were and how many they were?' The fisherman assumed a knowing air. 'Some people hereabouts seem to know. They found his shoes on the beach. Some say he was the son of an admiral.'

Moreau was thunderstruck that the village Sherlock Holmeses had been able to discover so much of his identity from his shoes – a heavy pair of hob-nailed boots. Nevertheless, since everybody thought him dead, there was little risk of trouble on that score. He had spent no more than a few hours at Beg-Meil in June.

It was time to go ashore. Taking the dinghy, from which they had removed the offending plaque, Moreau rowed himself ashore and landed on the slipway. No-one paid any attention to him. Pausing briefly, his oars on his shoulder, to watch the Germans dismantling the motor of their launch, he noted that they lacked tools for the job. They asked him in very bad French and with the help of gestures whether he had by any chance an adjustable spanner. It seemed an easy way to make friends, so he rowed back on board and fetched what they needed. Then he made his way slowly – the sabots hurt his feet atrociously – towards the villa of his friend, which lay at some little distance.

His friend's 12-year old son opened the door and, seeing who it was, had difficulty in suppressing a cry of surprise. Mme Gauchard told him that her husband had gone off to Paris a few days earlier, in the car that Moreau had appropriated at Brest during his escape and had left at Beg-Meil when he put to sea. Unfortunately, she told Moreau, it would be impossible for Le Corre to get to Beg-Meil that evening unless he hitched a lift from the Germans, who were almost the only people with cars. The ferry across the Odet River, which crossed the direct route from Le-Guilvinec to Beg-Meil, was no longer running and he would be forced to make his way round through Quimper.

That complicated matters. Le Corre, when he discovered the problem, might either decide to stay at home or try willy-nilly to get to Beg-Meil, hoping that Moreau would wait for him there. Unfortunately, Moreau did not feel able to prolong his stay on the coast, since they would soon be the subject of gossip in the bistros among the fishermen they had encountered that morning, or of the curiosity of some German bather who might try to come on board the pinnace. Moreau told Mme Gauchard that he must return to Le-Guilvinec that same day. If Raymond turned up on her doorstep, she should tell him to make his way back home and stay there so that Moreau could pick him up on his next voyage, probably in a fortnight's time.

Moreau reclaimed his spanner, receiving thanks for the loan, and put to sea. At about 7 p.m. when the sun was getting low, they entered Le-Guilvinec harbour at the same time as all the other boats returning to port before nightfall as required. They secured the pinnace alongside a sailing vessel lying near the entrance to the harbour, so as to be able to leave with a minimum of manœuvring. After a light meal, Moreau went ashore at about 8 p.m. with Baltas and Guénolé, leaving Le Goff on board with strict orders not to leave the boat, not to fall asleep and, if they were not back aboard by sunrise, to get back to Falmouth as best he could.

They had an hour left before curfew and they used it to visit two or three bistros – fearing they would find Le Corre there recounting his adventures to an admiring audience. He was nowhere to be seen, so they went round finally to his parents' house. They had not seen him since the morning and, as there was no news of an arrest in the village, it looked as though he must be trying to make his way round to Beg-Meil.

In the course of their wandering through the village they fell in with a mechanic who was a specialist in marine engines. M. Frélhaud made no secret of his Communist convictions but, wanting to help, placed himself at their complete disposal. Moreau asked him to give a message to Raymond Le Corre and prepared to return to the ship.

It was now well beyond the time of the curfew. Once more, Moreau made his way through the village, slipping along walls as inconspicuously as possible, followed by his two acolytes and by Frélhaud, who was determined to check over the pinnace's engine to make sure they would have no trouble with it on their return passage. They boarded the dinghy and headed across the port towards the place where they had left Le Goff. Taking care not to attract the attention of the sentry on the jetty, they reached the harbour mouth. When they got there Moreau experienced a moment of sheer panic: the pinnace had disappeared and, as far as they could make out in the darkness, there was nothing that remotely resembled its familiar silhouette.

Le Goff could hardly have set off single-handed in defiance of his orders since, in the calm of the evening, the sound of the engine would have stirred up the whole village. As there was no wind and very little tidal current, he could not have drifted out to sea. Nor was there any sign that the pinnace had sunk. Moreau simply could not understand what had happened but he decided, before giving up and going ashore, to examine the boats one by one to see if, by chance, it had changed its berth and, while he was about it, to look into the possibility of stealing another to replace it. After searching for half an hour, groping about in the dark, Moreau suddenly thought he saw, outlined against the sky near the breakwater at the entrance to the port, the silhouette of *Le-Petit-Marcel*, though curiously deformed. The mast and the exhaust pipe, which took the form of a funnel, seemed foreshortened, and the boat itself astonishingly tall. Moreau and his colleagues went towards the dinghy and, when they were ten metres away, she ran hard aground, making what seemed to them a considerable noise. They saw then, with consternation, that the pinnace was out of the water, as high and dry as could possibly be and that one could walk right round her without getting one's feet wet.

After complicated gymnastics, Moreau found himself on the

deck, inclined at more than 45°, and on all fours he crawled into the after-cabin. There was frightful disorder caused by the ship's listing, but no sign of damage. Armed with an electric torch they next inspected the engine-room in which there was quite a lot of water, proving at least that there was no hole in the hull. A 50-litre tin of oil had fallen over and made a splendid mess, but that was a minor misadventure.

It was almost impossible to get into the fish-hold: all the provisions garnered from the *Président-Tissier* were swimming in a sea of red wine, the inadequately stoppered barrel having emptied itself over the noodles, tea and so on. Still no sign of Le Goff. In the crew's quarters right forward, similar disorder prevailed. Moreau was just about to climb back out of the fo'c's'le, cursing the missing man on watch, when he discovered him in a bunk covered with a mass of objects that had fallen on top of him – out for the count. A paraffin lamp had even tipped its contents into his bunk without waking him. Since Le Goff was stretched out in his bunk, he had clearly intended to take a rest, in spite of Moreau's orders to the contrary. Moreau suspected that his deep sleep was due not only to fatigue but to a visit to the wine barrel, which he felt sure had been perfectly well stoppered when they had gone ashore.

It was not, in any case, the right time to ask for explanations. Instead, they held a council of war in the after-cabin to decide what to do. High water had been just before 11 p.m.; the boat, having gone ashore somewhere near the top of the tide, would not float before 10 o'clock the following morning. Given that it would be light from 5 o'clock onwards, how were they to pass off their predicament until the tide was high enough to enable them to leave? For good measure, Frélhaud threw in that the fishermen did not go to sea on Saturday because of some professional agreement; consequently there would be no lack of bystanders and attention would be guaranteed. There was only one thing they could do in the circumstances; to gamble on the discretion, or at least the patriotism, of the inhabitants and, at the same time, on the ignorance of the Germans. After all, they were only soldiers and probably not particularly well informed about seafaring matters.

In the hold they had a number of long-handled scrubbing brushes and Frélhaud suggested to Moreau that they should 'repair' their propeller, thus giving the impression that they had dried the ship out deliberately to scrub the ship's bottom and carry out repairs. This ruse might convince soldiers, but sailors would know that none of their number would choose such a rocky and uneven spot to dry out a boat, when there was a satisfactory and unobstructed hard only a short distance away.

What taxed Moreau most severely was how the boat, which had to the best of his knowledge been properly moored, had come thus to drift across the harbour. He was no nearer the answer 15 years later. Had the boat been badly secured? Had it been victim of the malevolence of another fisherman? He rued his failure to have checked the mooring lines more carefully .

At first light, the sentry on the breakwater saw them busying themselves around the hull with pails and brushes while one of them struck blows with a blunt chisel in the vicinity of the propeller. Moreau wondered how long this charade could be kept up, for the boat was in perfect condition, having been scrubbed only three days before in England. However that might be, the sentry, delighted by the distraction, climbed down onto the rocks and came to watch them at work without manifesting any surprise. He even walked round the stern and tried to see if he was strong enough to turn the propeller, not noticing that the pinnace's transom above his head lacked the name and number that all fishing vessels were obliged to carry. Satisfied, smiling and offering some apparently friendly German words, he left, to their great relief, and resumed his normal position on the jetty. Neither the drums of petrol nor the lack of fishing gear struck him as suspect. If there is a divinity who takes care of drunks, Le Goff, who had let them in for all this, had made serious calls on his services.

At about 7 a.m. Moreau's fear was realised. Fishermen, who had gathered in groups on the quay, began to approach; hitherto those who had seen them had been remarkably discreet, but among the newcomers many seemed very surprised to see the pinnace in her predicament. No-one tried to engage them in conversation, however, though there were friendly gestures to Moreau's crew from relatives and acquaintances watching from the top of the quay. But how long could the reprieve last? Moreau wondered. The tide was rising – too slowly for their liking – but the water was still far from lapping against the hull. Moreau foresaw that, because the boat had grounded at the very top of high water, she would float for only a short time, if at all.

At about 8 o'clock a man in uniform appeared, pushing a bicycle, and joined the group of fishermen. He seemed to examine the crew with particular attention. In due course he recognised Guénolé, who was, of course, a native of Le-Guilvinec, and asked him to come up and have a word on the quay. Moreau felt he must at any price prevent that from happening; the fellow seemed to be some kind of an official and therefore potentially very dangerous to them. Moreau was responsible and if they were going to be arrested it was better that he should from the outset assert his authority. He therefore told Guénolé to stay where he was, climbed up on to the quay so as to avoid having to shout and approached the man, whom he recognised as a maritime gendarme. Moreau asked him what he wanted, guessing what would be his rejoinder:

'What on earth are you doing with that boat?'

'As you can see, we are scrubbing the hull and repairing our stuffing gland, which is leaking.'

'Where have you come from?'

'Just from Douarnenez. Why?'

'Why are the name and numbers not shown on the hull? Have you any papers?'

Moreau knew that there was now no way of avoiding the issue, but the first thing was to gain time. He asked the man for whom he was working, the Germans or the French maritime administration?

'For the Administrator, of course.'

'In that case, let's go and see him. He will explain everything to you.'

Moreau did not pluck that reply out of the air: one of the crew had spoken in very warm terms of the Administrator, whose name was Québriac. He had for some time been mobilised as a reserve officer at Quiberon, organising maritime convoys, and had therefore served under Moreau's father. Moreau thought that he might, through that, find a way to settle the matter. Anyway, it was their only chance.

The crowd had fallen silent around them and the gendarme, who looked anything but well-disposed, seized his bicycle with one hand and Moreau's arm with the other and led him to the maritime administration building on the other side of the harbour.

They were soon there and, still holding Moreau's arm very firmly, the gendarme swept with him into the entrance hall. He was so puffed up with his own importance that he did not even bother to answer the questions coming from a head that appeared round the office door; instead, they went straight upstairs to M. Québriac's office. On the way Moreau reflected that things would probably go more smoothly without the presence of this Cerberus. He decided to bluff matters out and opened the door of the office without knocking, saying to the gendarme, 'Wait for me in the passage, I have something to say to the Administrator.' With which, he shut the door in the gendarme's face.

M. Québriac, seated at his desk, muttered something and, thinking no doubt it was some member of his own staff who had come into the office, did not immediately look up from his work. When the silence caused him to do so, he asked, with some bewilderment, what Moreau wanted.

'Nothing at all: it is your gendarme who has brought me here.'

'But why ? What have you done ?'

'Nothing in particular, but I don't have papers for the boat that you can see from the window, dried out over there.'

'But is it your boat ? Where have you come from and what is all this about?'

Moreau could see that his interlocutor was getting impatient at being made to waste time on some petty contravention.

'Oh, it is quite simple; we have come from England and we shall be returning there shortly. We haven't time to equip ourselves with papers and permits at the Kommandantur.'

At these words the Administrator sprang to his feet in astonishment. He made Moreau repeat his statement and his face lit up. 'At last!' he exclaimed. Then he explained that he had been convinced he would one day be able to make contact with 'the other side' and that he was happy the opportunity had arisen.

Moreau scarcely dared to believe his luck, of which he needed to take advantage straight away. First he asked M. Québriac to do something about his gendarme, who was waiting outside and might eventually realise that Moreau had made a fool of him. Opening the door very slightly, the Administrator told the gendarme to let the matter drop as he would be dealing with it himself. Then, seating himself at his table, he offered Moreau a cigarette and put himself at the latter's disposal with respect to giving intelligence. Moreau began by explaining who he was, although he told a lie in pretending to be a naval officer – justified he thought, because it might induce the Administrator to consider him a colleague. To enable M. Québriac to enter the story, Moreau talked about his father, whom the Administrator had met on a number of occasions. Having created a climate of confidence, Moreau told him of their adventures and of his concern that half the population of the village already knew what they were doing there and that a word was all that was needed to put the Germans in the picture too. However, a glance through the window reassured Moreau: his men were still busying themselves, undisturbed, around the ship's side, which the sea would shortly reach.

Moreau spent more than two hours with M. Québriac, who gave him an assessment of the attitude of the population in his area and valuable information about the troops who garrisoned it. The Germans often used him as a means of promulgating administrative decisions of the Kommandantur and, in a more general sense, as liaison officer. Moreau could thus not have found a better source of intelligence.

Moreover, Québriac's official functions often took him to Quimper, Rennes and Lorient, so he was able to inform Moreau in great detail about the occupiers' regulations concerning navigation and the possibilities of landing in different ports. Finally, to avoid any future misadventure such as they had experienced that morning, he gave Moreau a stock of crew lists and customs clearance forms already stamped and signed, which they could fill up as and when required. With these papers a number of other boats were able to come and go in the course of the following months. At about 9.45,

Moreau thought that he ought to get back on board: the ship was beginning to right herself and it was important not to miss the few minutes during which she might be afloat. It would be fatal if they were to miss this tide.

Before leaving Québriac, Moreau asked for his help in trying to find the missing Le Corre. Québriac promised to do whatever he could, including, if necessary, making him stay at home to stop him from talking, until Moreau came to collect him on a later trip.

Moreau was greeted with a sigh of relief by his three men, who were wondering what had happened to him. They started the engine so as to be able, with the aid of the bilge pump, to get rid of the water, red wine and noodles in the ship's bottom. At 10.30 a.m., as foreseen, the boat thus lightened at last came afloat, and without more ado they put to sea, to the accompaniment of friendly waves from many bystanders and particularly from Québriac standing at his office window. The sentry registered no surprise at their departure, pleased, on their behalf, that the repairs had been so successful.

That evening, while they were off Ushant, Moreau was wakened by sudden silence owing to a breakdown of the engine. This caused concern for a short time, until it was realised that the petrol pipes needed to be dismantled and cleaned, which took an hour. They were off again, and by next morning were within sight of the English coast. One last excitement awaited them on arrival: when they failed to reply to a challenge from the signal station on Pendennis Castle at the entrance to Falmouth Harbour, a small-calibre shot was fired across their bows to convey the order to heave to, according to the best privateering traditions. They were soon boarded, recognised and allowed to proceed, while Mills, the Base Engineer Officer, was warned by telephone of their impending arrival. From far off, they saw his little silhouette moving rapidly about on the quay and soon, unable to wait any longer, he jumped into a boat and came off to meet them. He was as moved and relieved as they were.

CHAPTER V

August–October 1940

After a telephone call to London, in the course of which both parties found it difficult to make themselves understood, so excited was 'Uncle Tom' at the other end of the line, Moreau warned Mills that it would be madness to return to France in that 'floating petrol barrel': it was far too conspicuous, since there was now no fuel for French fishermen.

They had over the last few days had to deal only with land-lubbers from the Wehrmacht, but Moreau foresaw that the coast would soon be guarded by the Kriegsmarine, who knew all about maritime matters. Mills pointed out that the Ile-de-Sein boat, the *Rouanez-ar-Peoc'h*, which Moreau had very nearly employed the week before, was still lying in the harbour and could no doubt be chartered for a modest sum. That would enable them to proceed under sail when in sight of the coast, but they could also from time to time use her quite powerful auxiliary engine. Mills promised to make enquiries and telephone Moreau in London within a few days.

Before going to bed that evening, Moreau had one important thing to do, – to take a bath. He disappeared into a bath-tub at half past nine and was astonished to wake up in it at four o'clock next morning. The night watchman, concerned to see the bathroom occupied so long, had made a noise to rouse him. After spending the rest of the night in a dry bed, Moreau caught the first train to London at about seven o'clock. He was met by Dunderdale and Uncle Tom, who was ready to have a celebration. The intelligence brought back was not of strategic importance, but it did give an idea of the conditions of life and, more particularly, of travel, in Brittany. Moreover, the documents Québriac had given to Moreau were of real value in that they opened up the possibility of future missions. While the newspapers were being dissected and each article studied in detail, Moreau was put to work writing a full report on the operation.

Before he settled down to this on the day after he arrived in London, Moreau was received by General de Gaulle, who expressed lively interest in what could be told in a few minutes. He received the same welcome from Muselier, who clasped him to his breast and formally forbade him to undertake a second voyage – a prohibition which Moreau did not take too seriously. Muselier's Chief of Staff, Commandant Moullec, who was known in London by the name of Moret, tried to persuade Moreau to go to see a certain 'Capitaine Passy', who had just been appointed head of General de Gaulle's Deuxième Bureau. Moreau had already had enough time to perceive that the offices in the Carlton Gardens building that were in the process of being organised were still in a state of chaos. The atmosphere was pleasant enough, for a spirit of close comradeship seemed to prevail (unfortunately it did not last long). An instinct for self-preservation, however, made him loth to go and tell his tale once more to people he did not know at all and who might, by talking too much, compromise him in France.

However, on the second or third day, before Moreau had finished dictating his report, Moret telephoned and again urged him to go to see Passy, who was expecting him. Dunderdale was consulted and saw no insuperable objection to the visit, though he did tell Moreau to ask Passy not to make notes of what he heard. He would in due course be informed of all that might interest him in the report, which still needed to be translated.

At Carlton Gardens, Moreau was shown up to the fourth floor and into a small office with a glazed door and partitions, where a Captain was awaiting him. Having carefully arranged a screen across the door to avoid Moreau's being seen from the corridor, he asked Moreau to tell him about his mission. Passy abstained from taking notes but asked some searching questions and gave evidence of a certain interest. As Moreau rose to take his however, leave, the Captain said to him:

'This is all very well, young man, but you have no proof of what you contend. Trust my long experience: in this kind of work one must have proof.'

'It seems to me,' replied Moreau, rather taken aback, 'quite useless, to send to France people in whom one does not have confidence, and I can pledge my word that everything happened just as I have told you.'

Passy admitted in his memoirs that at that time he knew nothing about the technical side of secret intelligence work – which he was to learn later from Sir Claude Dansey of SIS. Nonetheless he put his two thumbs under his uniform belt – a familiar gesture of de Gaulle's – and said, unabashed:

'Of course, if you had burgled a Kommandantur or brought back prisoners, that would have been different. You should have made a point of doing something of that kind.'

Moreau thought at first that Passy was joking, but his superior and very solemn air indicated otherwise. Anger rising in him, Moreau replied 'that one judged matters from entirely different points of view when one was behind a desk in Carlton Gardens or when one was alone in the wilds of France, without contacts and with very limited means.' Passy's shrug of shoulders indicated that he took his visitor for an obvious amateur (which he was, and proud of it). Moreau then left, still surprised at the attitude of this man who was responsible for de Gaulle's intelligence service – a service surely destined to acquire considerable importance.

Once his report was finished and corrected, Moreau had nothing more to detain him in London, so a second operational voyage was arranged. After a telephone call from Mills to say that the new boat, the *Rouanez-ar-Peoc'h*, was ready, Moreau left for Falmouth with the faithful Uncle Tom. He said goodbye to Admiral Muselier, who voiced objections, which Moreau again disregarded, since he knew they stemmed from his solicitude. A passenger, to whom Moreau had been introduced by Dunderdale, was to join them just before they sailed.

This time, Moreau was given complete freedom of movement in France. It was agreed that, after landing him and the passenger, the boat would return to England, then make a fresh voyage to France about 17 August to pick them up, if possible with Le Corre. During the 12 days they would thus have, Moreau's passenger was to go to Paris and he himself proposed to make contact with as many people as possible and more particularly – for the British attached great importance to it – to find out what the Germans might be preparing by way of an invasion. To this end, he planned to see Théry, an engineer at Lorient, whom he had met at the time of his first departure. If the latter was still at liberty, he would no doubt be able to give Moreau useful leads.

During the two days he spent at Falmouth settling final details, Moreau was invited aboard the *Commandant-Dominé*, which was being fitted out and commissioned with a new French crew under the command of Jacquelin de la Porte des Vaux, whom Moreau had met in London some weeks before. On the day Moreau took lunch on board, a very moving ceremony took place: Jacquelin, who was formally assuming command, made a short and well-turned speech to the crew in which one could sense the overtones of his burning wish to make his new ship an efficient fighting unit. In response, and breaking with all French naval tradition, the senior Warrant Officer made a speech to the Captain, the extraordinarily moving text of which Moreau was very sorry not to have been able to preserve. She was to be one of the most distinguished Free French ships, notable too for the high morale that always prevailed on board. After lunch, Jacquelin took Moreau aside and said to him, 'If you go to Brest, don't fail to see my wife and children and give them my news and some money.' On the latter score, he no doubt thought that what the French term the *'cavalerie de Saint-Georges'* – British secret service funds – would come to the rescue, for he would have been hard put to it to give Moreau any money at all.

Next day everything was ready, and in the early afternoon they headed towards the mouth of the harbour, passing the *Commandant-Dominé* as they did so. She saluted them, very indiscreetly, with a fanfare of bugles, and the ship's company lined the rails. The farewell was cheering but, for Moreau and his companions, mixed with a little envy: they were sailing unarmed against an enemy who would, should the occasion arise, pay them no greater honour than a bullet in the back of the neck, while the crew of the *Commandant-Dominé* had the prospect of fighting openly.

The new boat was far from comfortable. In their previous vessel, Moreau had had a large after-cabin in which he could almost stand up, while the crew were housed in a fo'c's'le with four bunks. The *Rouanez-ar-Peoc'h* was much smaller. Down aft, there was a cabin with two bunks – too short for Moreau in any case – and it was encumbered with a folding table, which was usually dismantled, since it covered the engine. The latter, which, it must be said, never gave the slightest trouble, was neither boxed in nor ventilated, which no doubt had the advantage of heating the cabin but the more serious drawback of dispensing a smell of hot oil, exhaust fumes and petrol, to say nothing of the steam when clothes were spread out to dry on the silencer. Finally, there was scarcely more than 1.3 metres headroom, which made it necessary to move around practically on all fours. Forward, there was a large fish-hold and a fish-well, open to the sea through a series of holes in the hull, which in this area resembled a sieve. In this fish-well, designed to preserve a catch of crabs or crayfish, they hid, in watertight tins, anything that might prove compromising, including their reserve of petrol; their provisions were piled up alongside. They usually cooked down there in the hold on a petrol stove, which was the source of endless trouble, like all its tribe. . . Finally, right in the bows, there were the crew's quarters – a 'rat hole' which contained, in theory, two bunks, but these were used only when in port, since Moreau's crew preferred to 'shake down' in the fish-hold beside the fish-well. The rig was quite simple, consisting of jib, foresail and mainsail, which gave the boat a good turn of speed. She was an excellent seaboat.

At sunset the English coast was still in sight on the horizon, but the breeze seemed steady and, with further help from the engine, which was turning over at half-throttle, Moreau hoped to be near Ushant in the morning. That evening he told his passenger that, in the light of their previous experience, they were not going to risk a secret landing at night; instead, he planned to enter the port of Douarnenez at the end of the afternoon. It would, of course, be mad to return to Le-Guilvinec, and a boat would be much more likely to attract attention putting into a creek or even a small isolated port than into a large and important port such as Douarnenez, just when all the fishing fleet was returning to harbour. The passenger was not very enthusiastic, but had the good sense not to argue: and the crew, whom he told of his decision, were cheered up by the thought of the Pernod they promised themselves on arrival. Douarnenez had, moreover, the advantage of being right next door to Tréboul, where Moreau knew that Madame Cariou of the Ty-Mad pension would afford them discreet hospitality.

The patent log, whose log-line and propeller they had streamed on leaving Falmouth harbour, was showing nearly 100 sea miles when, at about 3 a.m., they stopped the engine. They reckoned that they must be getting near the Chenal-du-Four, the passage between Ushant and the mainland, which they planned to take. If the Germans had finally got around to patrolling the coastal areas, it would be well to be as quiet as possible; moreover, it would be wise, in the mist that precedes sunrise, to refrain from piling themselves up on one of the many rocks with which that area is peppered. They therefore took a certain satisfaction, when daylight came, in sighting the coast to port (or east), less than two miles away, while to the west they could just make out the Isle of Ushant. Moreau claimed no credit for the precision of the landfall, which even radar assistance could not have bettered, but providence and the tide had stood them in good stead. Their nerves had been tried between the hours of 5 and 8, for most of which time there was not a single vessel to be seen on the horizon. However, at about half past seven some sails appeared, coming from Le-Conquet, and they made haste to join them. Following the orders of their Kommandantur, these boats all flew white flags at their mastheads, as did *Rouanez*, and the latter's presence seemed to arouse no curiosity.

They had plenty of time from then until the evening to get to Douarnenez, so, disposing themselves comfortably in the sunshine, they streamed fishing lines. To an observer on the coast, their movement would have been imperceptible as they drifted south to join the group of fishermen who had emerged from the Iroise and, further on, those working at the entrance to Douarnenez Bay. Their fishing was not productive but they took a relaxed view of that, having already in their hold fish brought from England as part of their cover. On the other hand, they all caught the sun during this holiday-like day before they entered Douarnenez Bay and headed for the port.

The burning, unanswered question was: what sort of inspection did the Occupation authorities exercise on boats returning to port? Was there a regular on-board check? And how far could the Germans be led to believe that the moon was made of green cheese? They stood on for some distance – some hundreds of metres – beyond the Rosmeur breakwater so as to have a better view of the inside of the port; this course could legitimately be explained, having regard to the direction of the wind, as an over-long tack.

Meanwhile, Moreau attentively watched through his binoculars what happened to the boats entering ahead of them. There were, indeed, some grey-green uniforms at the seaward end of the breakwater and, after a while, he saw four of them get into a boat that put out and went alongside a sailing tunnyman that had just entered the harbour. The preceding boat, however, did not seem to have been inspected. They must try therefore to take advantage of a moment when the patrol was on board another boat to get to the far end of the port and as far as possible from the breakwater. Moreau reckoned that those soldiers – from the uniforms, it was not the Kriegsmarine they had to deal with – would not be keen, at the end of the day, to make a long excursion, sculling their boat right across the harbour to catch up with them. In any case, once the boat was tied up, if they were quick to put things in order and nip off ashore, there was a good chance they would have made themselves scarce before the Germans arrived. There would still be time after that to watch developments from the bistro across the quay.

They had hung about long enough and, if they were not to draw attention to themselves by over-complicated manœuvres designed only to waste time, they must go in straight away. Almost side by side with a big tunnyman, they passed the critical position. The patrol paid neither of them a visit. It took them no time at all to moor the boat, stow the sails and lock the cabin hatch carefully. With three strokes of the dinghy's oars – the same dinghy they had used at Le-Guilvinec, but now without its tell-tale builder's plaque and with carefully chipped paint the same colour as *Rouanez* – they were at the foot of a ladder in the quay wall.

At the end of the breakwater, the guard seemed to be changing and the soldiers were deep in conversation together. All the while, other boats were entering without any form of hindrance. Moreau, fearing the cumulative effect of the numerous rounds of drinks his men intended to absorb, tried to persuade them not to linger, but he was told 'it will be much better than that disgusting tea the English drink.'

They were to leave next morning about seven o'clock at the same time as the fishing fleet put to sea. Moreau proposed to come down when they sailed in case there was any hitch.

After the long detour necessary to get to Tréboul by the bridge, Moreau and his companion reached the Ty-Mad pension where Moreau and his cousin had been kindly received by Mme Cariou, the proprietor, during their escape at the end of June. A glance through the window of the dining-room revealed a number of Germans having dinner but, as there were also French families being served, the place was clearly not requisitioned and they could enter. They went in through the kitchen, where Moreau's reappearance caused a sensation, but Mme Cariou, understanding the need for discretion, immediately told her cook, who knew Moreau from his earlier visit, to be quiet. She passed them off as a pair of old friends who had come to pay her a visit on their way elsewhere. After an excellent dinner at a table next to the Germans, who were having a party, Moreau, left his companion behind and went for a little stroll. A hundred metres from the *pension* where Christopher Wood, the English painter, had stayed before the war and of which he had painted a picture, Moreau found a tobacconist's shop and on impulse went in to buy a packet of Gauloises. Inside the shop was a German who had bought a considerable supply of tobacco, probably with the idea of sending it back home to Germany. He was collecting his parcels on one side of the counter when Moreau brought out money to pay for his purchase. Moreau experienced a moment of panic when he saw that he had spread out on the counter, under the wide eyes of the tobacconist, a fistful of English small change: what danger lay in failing to go through one's pockets in such circumstances! The German fortunately saw nothing and, with some embarrassment, Moreau expressed astonishment at finding these coins in an 'old suit'. That evening, to avoid further trouble, he entrusted this small change to his hostess.

Next morning when he arrived on the quay at seven o'clock, the *Rouanez*, with all sail set, was already out of the port on her way back to England. Seeing her leaving with so little difficulty among the flock of blue-netted sardine boats, Moreau remembered the poor, much-travelled fish in the fish-hold. Later in the morning Moreau and his passenger took the train to Quimper where they went their separate ways: the latter to Paris, while Moreau was to tour the Breton coast. They had arranged to meet at Ty-Mad on the evening of 17 August. The boat, was due back that evening but would in any case leave on the 18th.

While in London he had run into one of his old friends from Brest who had given him letters for his family and had recommended him to call on his uncle, a Canon who was the director of charitable works in the Quimper diocese. He decided to do this straight away and, having found his address, was received by a secretary who, for some reason Moreau could not understand, seemed stupefied by the sight of him. Before going to announce his visit she asked his name. Faced with her obvious alarm, Moreau presented himself as M Etienne, an inspiration of the moment. At the same time out of the corner of his eye he took good note of the way out of the building. After a few minutes, he was ushered in to the office of the Canon, a rather tall man with a purposeful air, who seemed very surprised to find that he spoke French, his secretary having just warned him that an Englishman wanted to talk to him. 'Indeed,' said the Canon, 'your grey suit and your build could very well enable you to pass for a British citizen.' There was nothing British about his clothing, except for the pressing it had had from an English flat-iron after it had lain for a week in a soaking suitcase when he first arrived in England. Moreau had no great difficulty in convincing the Canon of his real nationality, but the incident was a salutary warning that he would need to modify his appearance if he did not want to attract attention. It also alerted him to the fact that people in France were extremely nervous and more fearful than ever of spies. For all that, the Canon was friendly, providing Moreau not only with bed and board during his stay in Quimper but also a room he could use whenever he passed that way.

Over lunch they talked at length of the situation in France as well as in England; they discussed above all how French opinion had reacted to General de Gaulle's stand. The Canon said, and Moreau had confirmation of it subsequently, that the great majority of people in France were loyal to Pétain as the only leader capable of standing up to the Germans, or at least of inspiring them with a certain respect. The General's stand was unanimously approved. The Bretons, who had so many of their kin in England, were legitimately proud that many of their compatriots were continuing to fight. Up to that point the BBC's attacks on the Marshal had not been too virulent and in the Canon's view, which he shared, 90 per cent of Bretons were convinced that the two leaders were really in agreement.

Next day, Moreau went to Le-Guilvinec by taxi – *the* Quimper taxi – and, leaving it at the edge of the village, went and rang Québriac's doorbell. Québriac had been called away to Lorient, but his wife told Moreau of the intelligence he had been able to collect since his last visit. She told him, too, that Le Corre had been found and was shut up at home in his own room to prevent him from telling tales in the bistros, since all Le-Guilvinec knew that he had gone to England at the end of June. Moreau left messages for Québriac and asked him to send Le Corre to Mme Cariou at Ty-Mad.

Moreau published articles covering his first two missions up to that point in a Gaullist periodical in 1955, but the series was then broken off without explanation. Its appearance must have caused little pleasure to Passy, who had claimed in his memoirs that the title of 'first special envoy to occupied France' belonged to Jacques Mansion, who, he said, had set foot in France on 19 July, eight days before 'another French officer named Hubert Moreau', who had been recruited by the SIS. British records make it clear, however, that Mansion cannot have returned to France until perhaps a fortnight later than Passy claimed. Passy admitted in 1992 that he knew why Moreau's series of articles had been interrupted, but refused to say more.

Passy's own account of this first mission under Free French auspices is, apart from the matter of chronology, a good deal more credible than some of Mansion's own claims. According to Passy, Mansion was 26 or 28 years old at the time and both keen and brave.[1] He had been severely wounded in the 'Phoney War' and had been invalided out of the French Army. His papers were therefore in order and he would be able to circulate in German-occupied France without the risk of being arrested and held as a prisoner of war. This was a rare case among the volunteers, most of whom de Gaulle's nascent Deuxième Bureau would be able to send into the field only after they had obtained the indispensable personal documents to copy. Mansion, moreover, knew Brittany, having worked there before the war and married a girl from Camaret; and the coastal area was of course of particular interest to Churchill and the British Chiefs of Staff at that time. Captain Maurice Duclos ('Saint-Jacques'), who was working for Passy before undertaking his mission to Normandy and Paris, had found Mansion at Olympia, which was being used as a barracks for French volunteers, spotted his unusual qualifications and had him transferred to the Gaullist Deuxième Bureau. He was stuffed with questionnaires and embarked on a fast launch on 17 July, but that attempt to land him failed and he was put ashore some days later by two Bénodet fishermen somewhere near Cap-de-la-Chèvre, which lies on the north side of Douarnenez Bay and conveniently close to his wife's home town of Camaret. It had not been possible to give him a radio transmitter because these were still not available. He would therefore have to find his own way back to England to report and deliver the urgently needed personal documents.

The only person able to produce a 'fast launch' for a cross-Channel landing of this kind was Commander Slocum of SIS, whose records show his first attempt to carry out a sea landing operation for the Free French was on 30 July 1940, not 17 July as Passy claimed. The agent, according to Slocum's record, was taken by MTB to Saint-Pabu, which lies on the Aber-Benoît estuary due north of Brest, but refused to land and later landed and returned by fishing boat. Since this conforms with Passy's account, there is little room for doubt about the identity of the agent, but it shows quite clearly that Moreau's return to France was the earlier of the two.

Mansion claimed many years later that the pinpoint of the MTB operation was Plougasnou, near Morlaix, rather than Saint-Pabu, this is credible, as Saint-Pabu would have been an extremely difficult nocturnal venue for an MTB with the navigational equipment available in 1940, as later operations to the Aber-Benoît estuary demonstrated.[2] Where exactly Mansion was landed by fishing boat is another minor mystery: when questioned by Lomenech and Le Roux in 1982 he named Pointe-Saint-Mathieu, which is on the other side of the Iroise from Cap-de-la-Chèvre.[3]

Mansion's courage and the importance of his first mission are not in question: when General de Gaulle in due course created the Ordre de la Libération, Mansion became one of its first Compagnons. Nevertheless, he seems to have embellished the record. He told Pichavant (chronicler of some of these missions to Brittany in 1940–42; see Footnotes), for example, that he returned to France single-handed for his first mission on the small (4.75 m) Bénodet fishing boat *Jiji* with a 10 h.p. engine and that he scuttled the boat on arrival. Not only is this at variance with Passy's statement that he was put ashore by two fishermen (from Bénodet, indeed), but it also defies belief that, with no previous seafaring experience, he would have been sent off in sole charge of a boat he had not seen before for a voyage of well over 100 miles into enemy waters.

Mansion's credibility has been even more seriously questioned in connection with a photograph of him in SS uniform exhibited in the museum of the Ordre de la Libération; the label states that he used this disguise to penetrate the German headquarters in the Hotel Majestic in Paris in search of intelligence. To judge from Moreau's account of his interview with Passy, this is how the latter would have liked his agents to behave but, since Mansion spoke no German, this looks more like hagiography than history, and the picture was probably taken for some reason in England before his first mission.[4]

Such claims have led some wartime colleagues and fellow agents to suggest that Mansion was already in England for medical treatment before the exodus and that he returned to France for his first mission on a hospital ship via Spain. There is, however, independent corroboration of his statement to Pichavant that he escaped from France in June 1940 by persuading a local Camaret fisherman to ferry him over to Ushant, whence he took passage to England on a large trawler named *Frêne*. And his return by fishing boat cannot seriously be doubted.

Moreau's unpublished account of the latter part of his second mission to France was found in 1992 among his papers. It shows that, in the course of a visit to Brest, he ran into Mansion a few days after the latter's arrival.[5]

After a second night at Quimper as guest of the hospitable Canon, Moreau took a train to Brest. He avoided spending the night at a hotel since he had no false identity documents and it was highly probable that hotel registers were inspected from time to time. Instead, he went to his parents' flat in the Boulevard Gambetta, to which he had a key, though he did not know whether or not they were still living there. On his way he greeted various neighbours and acquaintances, who did not seem particularly surprised to see him. He opened the door, to find the flat stripped of its contents and uninhabited.

Carefully relocking the door, he went back into the town with the idea of finding friends who might be willing to give him a bed. At the flat of Engineer-General Fayolle, the maid told him that her master, who was under police surveillance, was away and would not be back until the following morning, but she willingly made up a bed for Moreau in the sitting-room. Loth to ask her to make dinner for him, he went out to a restaurant.

As he emerged into the street, he remembered that Jacquelin de la Porte des Vaux had asked him to see to his wife's financial needs and, since he was in the right quarter, he decided to call on her. There was no reply when he rang the doorbell: the owners told him that she and her children had gone back to Paris that very morning. Since she had heard of her husband's death, she had been in a pitiable situation. She planned to live with her mother, whose address they gave Moreau. He thought it better not to ask why Jacquelin, whom he had seen at Falmouth only a few days previously very full of life, was thought to have been dead for several weeks, so he gave some vague explanation of his call and left.

Out on the pavement again, he bumped into three people, two women and a man, who were passing the door. Apologising, he was transfixed with astonishment: less than a week before he had met the man in London. Equally taken aback, the man escorted the two sailor's molls who were with him to the corner of the street and returned to Moreau. To avoid a discussion on the pavement, they agreed to meet for lunch on the following day at a bistro on the Rue de Siam.

When the two had met in London under Dunderdale's auspices, they had been told that they were both being sent to France, but not to which parts of the country. Moreau, having already returned from his first mission, had given the other man tips he thought might be of interest, but they parted without even learning each other's names. Moreau's movements were governed by no pre-established plan, so it was an extraordinary coincidence that they should have run into each other.

After dinner, Moreau went back to M Fayolle's flat. The staircase of the block was, he noted, in constant use by Germans in every sort of uniform.

Next morning, a Monday, he was awakened by a grumbling sound. At the foot of the bed stood M Fayolle, suitcase in hand. Not having been warned by the maid, he was rather surprised to find Moreau installed in the flat. His surprise gave way to incredulity when Moreau tried to explain how he came to be there, and then went on to give him news of his son, whom M Fayolle believed to be in Algeria training as a fighter pilot. Young Fayolle had indeed been there but, after the armistice, he and some of his friends had helped themselves to aircraft from their base near Oran and had reached the United Kingdom via Gibraltar. Moreau had seen him at Olympia towards the end of July. He was serving in the first Free French fighter squadron and was to die two years later, leading an RAF Squadron during the Dieppe raid.

Though glad to have news of his son, M Fayolle was none too pleased at Moreau's presence in his flat: he had to report each day at the Kommandantur and all the other apartments in the block had been requisitioned by the Germans. Moreau therefore shaved, washed, dressed and left as soon as possible by the back stairs.

He spent the morning gathering information from friends about what was going on in the dockyard, telling them that he had been away in Paris for some time. Large-scale building works were being carried out for the Germans, but he concluded that they could not be connected with a planned invasion of the United Kingdom, which would have to take place before the end of September, if at all. It seemed clear that Brest was to become a base for U-boats and perhaps also for capital ships, but M Fayolle, who was well placed to know, had said that to his certain knowledge there were no German vessels in the dockyard at that time.

At 12.30, he met Mansion as planned and only then learned his name. Mansion had arrived some days previously by unspecified means to carry out an intelligence mission on rather similar lines to Moreau's own, but directly for the Free French and with the dockyard as his main target: hence his interest in the girls he was escorting when they met in the street. He hoped to garner from them intelligence gleaned from their patrons among the Kriegs-marine.

At the end of the meal, at which a good deal was drunk, Mansion, who had given Moreau an outline of his plans, produced from his pockets an array of weapons, including an enormous pistol and one of the elegant little daggers worn by Luftwaffe officers, which he had filched from a hotel cloakroom. Mansion was so proud of his pistol, the use of which he insisted on demonstrating under the tablecloth, that Moreau had difficulty in persuading him to put it away. They then went their separate ways and did not meet again until a year later in London.

Moreau arranged for two of his former schoolmates to make a reconnaissance on bicycles along the north coast of Brittany looking for any signs of preparations for a German invasion of England, while he pursued a similar investigation further east at Saint-Brieuc, Saint-Malo and possibly in the Cotentin. Before leaving Brest, however, he met in the street a couple whom he had known for many years. The husband belonged to an auxiliary service of the Navy, where Moreau felt sure he made a highly successful career both under Vichy and subsequently. He predicted that the war would end with a victorious invasion of England before the end of the summer. Then it would be possible, with German help, to instil order in France and to apply the Hitlerian discipline that the country sorely needed. He went on to extol the benefits that would flow from this new order.

This officer's loss of patriotism in the space of two months under the influence of German propaganda, did not, in Moreau's view, say much for his intelligence, although he was considered to be brilliant and had already reached a rank equivalent to Lieutenant Commander. When Moreau innocently asked why he was so confident that a German invasion of the British Isles would succeed, he was unable to adduce any concrete facts or reasons, let alone name the ports where the invasion force was being assembled, which was what Moreau most wanted to know.

On the following evening, Moreau took the train to Rennes, which he found sadly changed since he had been there in June. He had some hours to wait before the train left for Saint-Brieuc and the waiting room was thronged with demobilised conscripts, who were celebrating with red wine the release from military service that they owed to their numerous progeny or to their age. There, too, he had to listen to a surprising number of predictions of an early end to hostilities. No-one seemed to give a thought to what sort of peace would follow.

There were no signs of any suspicious concentration of shipping at Saint-Brieuc. After another night on the railway station at Rennes, he arrived at Saint-Malo where he had been given the address of a radio shop whose owner might be worth contacting. The man, a former naval telegraphist, had just got home after being demobilised at Toulon. When Moreau, with much circumlocution, asked whether he might be prepared to use a small W/T transmitter, the man's response was positive, though he stipulated that he would need to be supplied with a suitable set as he could not build one himself. Moreau felt quite cock-a-hoop about this prospective recruit and was on the point of leaving when the man brought him up short by asking about payment. Not only was Moreau unqualified to deal with such an approach but he felt instinctively that anyone who undertook such a job for money could not be trusted. Nothing came, therefore, of the interview.

Moreau was able to collect some information from shopkeepers and from the owner of the bistro where he was the only customer. A certain amount of maritime activity was observable and on several occasions there had been a temporary concentration of barges in the port, but this was on so small a scale that it could not have been more than an exercise. At Saint-Malo he encountered for the first time a story that there had been a raid on the English coast – a sort of Dieppe in reverse – causing serious German losses. All the hospitals of Brittany and Normandy were said to be full of soldiers suffering from serious burns. He later on heard versions of this apocryphal story in other parts of Brittany.

When he stepped off the train at Brest next day, French and German gendarmes were checking the identity documents of passengers as they left the platform. His own papers were genuine, but his date of birth showed that he was of an age to have been called up for military service and thus become a prisoner of war at the armistice. Rather than face questions on this score, he put his local knowledge to good effect and slipped up a small staircase leading to the station restaurant where he had often been a customer. As he had no luggage, his arrival there attracted no attention. When in due course he finished his drink and went down into the station concourse by the main stairs, the gendarmes had disappeared.

Next day, 14 August, he debriefed his two school-friends who had bicycled to Aber-Wrac'h and Morlaix without seeing anything significant. He then took the train to Quimper, where he was due to meet his friend M Québriac in front of the cathedral next day. Borrowing a bicycle from the helpful Canon, he went over to Beg-Meil in search of Gauchard, but found that he was still in Paris. Mme Gauchard told him that Le Corre had in fact managed to reach Beg-Meil at the appointed time, having thumbed a lift in a German truck, only to find that they had already taken LE-PETIT-MARCEL round to Le-Guilvinec. After waiting two days in the Gauchard garage in case they came back to pick him up, he had made his way home, where Québriac had taken charge of him.

The latter turned up punctually next morning in front of the cathedral, where the aged Bishop of Quimper had just created a sensation by preaching a patriotic sermon to a large congregation at High Mass. Resorting to the Breton language to obviate interruptions, he had belaboured both the Germans and the Breton separatists. The separatists of the newly formed Conseil National Breton, who enjoyed active German support, had made a practice of trying to distribute their weekly broadsheet, *L'Heure Bretonne*, to congregations as they left church. There was a furious disturbance on the steps of the cathedral and the next day the Bishop was put under house arrest in his episcopal palace.

While they were lunching at a nearby *crêperie*, Québriac brought Moreau up to date on events at Le-Guilvinec. The Germans had picked up echoes of *Le-Petit-Marcel*'s visit at the end of July, though they had no precise details; it would not be possible to take such liberties there in future. The two breakwaters now had machine-guns mounted on them and boats were searched more methodically than at Douarnenez. As regards a possible invasion of Great

Britain, Québriac had nothing specific to report but thought it unlikely in the short term.

Before they parted, it was agreed that Le Corre would be driven over to Tréboul on 17 August by Frélhaud and put in Mme Cariou's care.

There remained one further potential, and important, source of intelligence: Théry, the Chief Engineer at Lorient. Moreau caught a train there that same evening and spent part of the next day walking round the port and a secondary airbase near the town. That evening, he used a small garden gate, with which he was already familiar, to slip discreetly into Théry's garden. Théry promised to deliver to him on the following day (17 August) a detailed plan of the naval base, showing the new installations built by the Germans, together with full details of the ships, launches and U-boats lying there.

Moreau spent the afternoon of 17 August on a jetty in the fishing port, from which he could watch the entrance to the naval dockyard and whence he was able (very discreetly, for a German sentry was posted not 15 metres away) to photograph two German launches as they proceeded to sea. That evening, Théry handed over a plan and a report of the highest importance on the state of the dockyard. He had done everything possible to ensure that German workmen and sailors were segregated from the French dockyard personnel. These precautions were intensified following their talk, for Moreau warned him that the RAF were likely to strike as a consequence of this intelligence.

On the afternoon of 18 August, Moreau was back at Tréboul, where his still unidentified fellow passenger had already arrived from Paris and Le Corre was waiting, relieved to be released from his preventive detention. The *Rouanez-ar-Peoc'h*, if she had sailed from Falmouth on the 17th as agreed, was due in before nightfall, and Moreau kept watch at the window with a view of the bay, only tearing himself away to make a quick trip to the beach.

After dinner, having still seen nothing, he could not resist making a reconnaissance of the port in Douarnenez. As he reached the quay, he saw his three men landing. They had only just arrived and were on their way to fill themselves up with assorted liquors.

They arranged to meet at 7 next morning and Moreau, much relieved, went back to Ty-Mad, where his two companions and Mme Cariou were awaiting his return with an anxiety that bordered on panic, for it was long past the beginning of the curfew. Mme Cariou scolded him so severely for what she called his recklessness that he was left feeling that, if they stayed 24 hours longer in France, 'nanny' would stop his sweets.

By the time Moreau returned from this second mission to France, Dunderdale's fishing boats were using Mylor Creek, a discreet and sheltered anchorage further up Falmouth Harbour, as their operational base and an SIS officer named Oxley had been given the job of looking after their needs. He did this on a visiting basis from SIS's London headquarters. The crews of these vessels were technically Free French naval volunteers on secondment to SIS. The Free French themselves set up a second and parallel liaison structure under a Free French naval officer, Georges Lequien, who based himself at Falmouth to maintain contact with the refugee French fishermen working out of Newlyn. These men – again preponderantly Bretons – were civilians actively engaged in fishing and Lequien arranged operations with them on an *ad hoc* basis when need arose. Slocum often heard what these two separate structures were up to in an operational sense only after the event. He regarded them both with suspicion as amateur ventures that might well compromise the work of his own Section.[6]

Dunderdale, for all his naval rank of Commander RNVR, had really never been a seafarer. His father was a Constantinople-based shipowner and Black Sea merchant who represented a variety of British and American shipbuilding and armament manufacturers in Imperial Russia during the First World War. Young Wilfred Dunderdale, whom some people called Bill and others Biffy, had been educated at a Russian gymnasium at Nikolayev on the Black Sea and had gone on to study naval architecture in St Petersburg when the Russian Revolution broke out in 1917. He was not yet 17 when, on his father order's, he went out to Vladivostok, took delivery of an American-built submarine and successfully arranged for its transport, still in five sections, by rail right across Siberia, then in the throes of Revolution, to the Black Sea.

He spoke fluent Russian, German and French and made himself so useful to naval intelligence as an undercover agent during operations in the Black Sea and the Sea of Marmora that, by the age of 21, he held the honorary rank of Lieutenant RNVR, and had been mentioned in despatches twice and awarded the MBE. He joined SIS in 1921 and served in their Constantinople station while that city was under Allied occupation and during the crisis that led to the exile of Sultan Mohammed V and the downfall of Lloyd George. An obituary published when he died in New York at the age of 91 described his part in these events as 'domestic rather than epic': he was made responsible for the repatriation of members of the Sultan's harem who were not Turkish nationals, including one houri from Leamington Spa, who was packed off home on the Orient Express.

Dunderdale had been sent to Paris by SIS in 1926 and remained there until June 1940. As head of the SIS station, he built up a good working relationship with the French Service de Renseignements under Colonel Rivet, with the French counter-intelligence service under Captain Paillole and with Colonel Gustave Bertrand, the chief French cryptanalyst. His duties had also brought him into close contact with the Polish cipher-breakers. He had been one of the last members of the British Embassy staff to leave Paris before it fell into German hands. He made his way south through the chaos of the exodus, keeping such contact as was possible with his French colleagues as they retreated from one château to another. With the armistice looming, he took his leave of Rivet and was flown out from Bordeaux by an RAF Anson, which SIS had sent to ensure he could get home.[7]

*   *   *

Moreau was landed at Douarnenez for his third mission by the *Rouanez-ar-Peoc'h*. Though his personal file in the French naval archives records this mission as covering 5-22 September, another document shows that he must have been back in England before 19 September.[8]

Moreau and his crew were at this time using the Buvette du Rosmeur as their safe house and point of contact at Douarnenez. It was conveniently close to the port and little frequented by Germans. The three Kerivel sisters who ran it knew exactly what was going on and were ready to provide lodgings for the crew on their overnight visits to the port, though their readiness to do so caused some unkind gossip.[9]

The *Rouanez-ar-Peoc'h* sailed the morning after landing Moreau, to return towards the end of the month to pick him up. However, Moreau returned to the Buvette du Rosmeur from a week-long intelligence-collecting foray, during which he had obtained important German plans from Lorient, to find that in his absence a fishing boat named *Ma-Gondole*, which had sailed to England during the exodus, had returned to Douarnenez. He thought her crew had recognised him as someone who had been in England and decided to leave as soon as possible, without waiting for his own boat to pick him up as previously agreed. The sisters put him in touch with the skipper of a sailing-tunnyman from Etel lying anchored outside the harbour. The skipper agreed to get him back to England, no doubt for a suitable price. Moreau called on the Abbé Deniel, whose house was to serve as a collecting-point for intelligence from his subagents, and left a message for his crew before sailing that night under cover of darkness. He and a man named Burgaud, whom he met by chance, were taken safely to English waters and transferred at sea to a Newlyn-based vessel before the tunnyman returned to fish on the Grand Sole Bank.[10]

As Moreau had now to be considered compromised as a result of *Ma-Gondole*'s return to France, his usefulness to Dunderdale was at an end. He went on a course at the Royal Naval College at Dartmouth, from which the erstwhile cavalry cadet emerged as Enseigne de Vaisseau de Deuxième Classe and then joined the Free French destroyer *Léopard*.[11]

Slocum had not been involved in any of Moreau's three missions, but on 30 August he sent Patrick Whinney, one of his staff officers, to Cornwall bearing a letter from Admiral Muselier's Chief of Staff to Georges Lequien, the link between Carlton Gardens and the Breton fishermen at Newlyn.[12] The letter said that Command's intention was to have three agents landed as near Lorient as possible. The first would stay a month, but the two others would come back after a short visit of about four days to occupied territory. Whinney was authorised to study with Lequien how this mission could best be carried out. He would return to London on Sunday evening bearing up-to-date information that would allow Moret, the Chief of Staff, to issue final instructions.[13]

The letter ended by laying down the scale of remuneration that Carlton Gardens had decided to grant: a bonus of 1,500 Francs for each volunteer crew member for the voyage over and back; an additional bonus of 500 Francs per passenger per voyage in either direction; and 1,000 Francs for each German prisoner.

Whinney was met off the train at Penzance by an interesting anachronism – a very senior member of the Russian imperial family, the Grand Duke Dimitri, in the uniform of a Lieutenant RNVR. He was representing the interests of the Director of Naval Intelligence in the area and proved most helpful.[14]

The boat chosen by Lequien and Whinney was Prosper Couillandre's 17-ton, cutter-rigged *Rouanez-ar-Mor*, one of the Ile-de-Sein fishing boats that had sailed to England shortly after the armistice with, in her case, 37 islanders on board. Lequien set out his proposals in three notes, which Whinney carried back to London. Orders were then issued to Lequien to sail Couillandre's boat at the hour of his choice after the evening of the following Wednesday, 4 September. The three agents were to be landed and the boat was then to return to Newlyn, Penzance or Falmouth. She was to remain ready to collect the two due to return on 11 September. Gloaguen and Labasque, two members of the crew, were authorised to bring back their wives and there would be additional bonuses for any volunteers for the Free French Forces landed in England.

One of the agents involved in this expedition was Jan Doornik,[15] a Dutch businessman born in Paris, where his brother ran a number of commercial concerns. He had left the Hague when the Germans arrived, made his way down to Bordeaux and managed to get on to a ship which landed him in Falmouth. He joined the Netherlands forces in England but subsequently transferred to the Free French and on their behalf was returning to France.

The other two agents were young French-speaking Englishmen whom Slocum was sending to France to collect samples of current identity and travel documents, urgently needed to enable SIS and its Free French counterpart to send agents into the field. This mission was very similar to that from which Mansion had not yet returned. One of the emissaries was Robert Barclay, a stepson of Sir Robert Vansittart: the other, who spoke even better French, was an RAF Flight Sergeant named René Arthur.[16] Couillandre, Lequien and Whinney decided that these three agents should be landed on the Ile-de-Sein.

The *Rouanez-ar-Mor* put to sea at 0600 hrs on 5 September, made part of the crossing under sail and arrived at Sein at 0800 hrs next day. The Germans did not at that time keep a permanent garrison on the island. Six soldiers who had been stationed there had left in a hurry two days earlier, explaining 'Nous partir, mauvais pour nous' and cutting the telephone and electric supply cables from the mainland.[17]

The Couillandre family gave Doornik clothes so that he could assume the identity of a sailor from Boulogne. That afternoon he was taken over to the mainland by Couillandre's father-in-law in his crabber and landed at Porz-Loubous-en-Plogoff, a concrete jetty built among the tumbled rocks south of the Pointe-du-Raz, an area known as the Enfer-de-Plogoff. He received help and hospitality from the Normant family, fisherfolk who lived in the first house on the road up from the landing-place. Next morning he caught a bus into Quimper and a train to Paris, where his brother proved a source of interesting information.

Barclay and Arthur were taken for Belgians by Prosper Couillandre and his family. People with firsthand experience of the conditions that prevailed on the mainland decided their identity documents would not pass muster, but, as no-one on the island could provide them with anything better, they were obliged to renounce their plan. After eating a delicious *homard à l'armoricaine* with the Couillandre family and collecting such documents as were available, they re-embarked on the *Rouanez-ar-Mor*, which sailed at 0700 hrs on 7 September. She made her way north under power and was overflown by German aircraft at low altitude from soon after sailing until 1230 hrs. They reached Newlyn at 1500 hrs next day. Couillandre, when reporting to Lequien such information as he had gleaned, said he had brought forward the time of his departure from the Ile-de-Sein because of the arrival in the island of two gendarmes from Brest.

Jacques Mansion had by this time also returned to England on a Camaret crabber named *Marie-Louise*, bringing with him Roger

Lefèvre, a pre-war acquaintance from Brest, who was a trained W/T (wireless-telegraphy) operator.

An unsigned record has survived of Lefèvre's debriefing in London. He said he had found Mansion very excitable and over-nervous. His questioner asked parenthetically whether the relevant Free French services knew about Mansion's accident at the beginning of the war, when he had been buried in an underground sap-work and had received head injuries, since when he had been subject to frequent crises. The French Police Special Branch, for whom he had been an unpaid and sometimes clumsily over-zealous informer, had made a report on the subject.[18] In Lefèvre's view, Mansion was rather self-satisfied and had made himself too conspicuous during his stay in Brest, so that several people knew he was an agent of the Deuxième Bureau. Mansion had also acted very indiscreetly in arranging his return to England: he had revealed his identity and the objects of his mission to a fisherman he did not know at all, who turned down Mansion's offer, and pointed out the *Marie-Louise*, which was about to set off for Morocco. Mansion had told the skipper and crew of that vessel, whom he also did not know, that he was an agent of the British services. Thus from Thursday 29 August all the crew knew that Mansion and Lefèvre were to sail to England on the following Monday. Lefèvre was much concerned about possible indiscretions by the families of these fishermen, among whom was a boy only 15 years old. On his return to the Free French barracks at Olympia, Mansion had again made himself far too conspicuous and been publicly congratulated in the hall.

For all these reasons, Lefèvre refused to work with Mansion, whose return to Brest would, he thought, probably compromise all the Free French agents with whom he might come into contact. This adverse report does not seem to have eroded Passy's confidence in Mansion. Mansion was sent back to France for two further missions and in 1944 visited the United States with Passy, who had been eventually invited there by General Donovan, head of the Office of Strategic Services (OSS).[19]

Lefèvre, who had been W/T operator on a lifeboat, needed no more than a fortnight's training in the use of ciphers and was then ready to be put back into the field. He sailed from Falmouth on 26 September on Dunderdale's *Rouanez-ar-Peoc'h*, which had mail to collect from Moreau's small network (Moreau himself being back in England).

After an uneventful crossing, the *Rouanez-ar-Peoc'h* made a brief call at the Ile-de-Sein at midday on 27 September. During this visit, someone from the boat, probably Lefèvre, called on the Abbé Guillerm, the island's priest. Although he had some initial difficulty in persuading Guillerm of his *bona fides* he eventually delivered to him a sum of money to be used for the benefit of the families of islanders who were in the United Kingdom, and also a letter destined for the Abbé Deniel, Moreau's contact at Tréboul.[20]

Prosper Couillandre, skipper of the *Rouanez-ar-Mor*, had decided to take advantage of the *Rouanez-ar-Peoc'h*'s call at Sein to spend another night with his wife, so he took passage on Dunderdale's ship and was dropped off. He was met on the quay by his brother-in-law, who warned him that he was 'blown'. The island was occupied by 12 German soldiers who had arrived on 8 September just after his departure. Revolver in hand, they had interrogated Couillandre's wife, the mayor, the parish priest and various other people. They warned the mayor that he must inform them if any suspicious vessel arrived in the island. Couillandre spent the night at home, in hiding, while *Rouanez-ar-Peoc'h* continued her voyage to Douarnenez to land Roger Lefèvre, in time for him to catch an evening train. The ship's movements had not been interfered with, although she had not been flying the coloured pennant required by the Germans.

Couillandre was taken out from the Ile-de-Sein next morning by his brother and brother-in-law in their boat, the *Corbeau-des-Mers*, to an agreed rendezvous with *Rouanez-ar-Peoc'h* at 0900, north of Tévennec islet, between the Pierres-Noires and Ar-Men light-house. Pierre Couillandre and Jos Guilcher, who with their boat had taken refuge in England at the end of June, had come back to Sein three weeks earlier, homesick, disappointed with the fishing conditions imposed in Cornish waters and with no desire to return. They had trouble attracting the attention of the *Rouanez-ar-Peoc'h*'s crew, who seemed oblivious of the arrangement they had made and intent on sailing back to Falmouth without a thought for Prosper Couillandre.

Lefèvre was the first W/T operator sent back to occupied territory by the Free French. Though landed at Douarnenez with codes and a W/T set, he seems never to have established radio contact with London; if he had done so, it would have been, by three months or so, their first such link. Lefèvre reportedly carried a letter from Passy to his wife. He seems to have spent his first three months between the Bar du Zinc at Brest and the Buvette du Rosmeur at Douarnenez. He took to borrowing large sums of money for imaginary Resistance activities and kept company that made him highly suspect thereafter. By 1942, he had moved to Oran. Pichavant records that London had by then so far lost confidence in him that orders had been issued to Brittany that he should be shot on sight. He escaped that fate but underwent imprisonment both in Morocco and at Fresnes. The BCRA, as the Gaullist secret service was by then styled, noted in his favour that he had prevented the Americans from parachuting him back into France.

If it was, as Le Roux believes, Free French naval intelligence that had sent Lefèvre back to France, it was not their only attempt to collect intelligence during September 1940, for they also sent Joseph Gloaguen's *Dom-Michel-de-Nobletz* on a voyage of reconnaissance into the Bay of Biscay to see what she could glean from fishing vessels encountered at sea.[21] She sailed from Newlyn at noon on 24 September. On 25 September she fell in with a Concarneau tunnyman whose crew told them that fishing vessels were operating entirely under sail, there being no diesel oil. Food supplies were becoming scarce even for fishermen. They were forbidden to enter any port at night, but could anchor outside in the bay. A German permit was required for fishing. That evening, 90 miles west of Ushant, they were overflown by six large German aircraft heading west at low altitude.

On 26 September they fell in with, and spoke to, a fishing vessel from the Ile-de-Groix, whose crew said there had been 800 German troops in the island, but only about ten customs men and gendarmes remained. There was no diesel fuel or petrol. The coal-fired Lorient trawlers were fishing, probably on the Grand Sole Bank. There were no German patrols at sea. British bombing had caused damage at Lorient and other places. The population was hostile to the Germans.

On 28 September in the evening, when about 50 miles from the Longships, the *Dom-Michel* was overflown by two German aircraft heading out into the Atlantic, and on the following morning, when she was off St Mary's in the Scillies, she was overflown by a single German aircraft, flying south. With that meagre harvest of information, she reached Newlyn at midday.

The Free French decided to make operational use of the *Marie-Louise*, which had brought Mansion and Lefèvre to England. She set off from Newlyn at 1000 on 9 October in the hope of collecting Doornik from Porz-Loubous. Lequien was on board to look into the possibility of using the Normant house at Penneac'h-en-Plogoff, where Doornik had received help and shelter, as a reception-point for future operations. François Follic, the *Marie-Louise's* new skipper, took with him Arsène Celton, who had brought the boat over to England.[22]

They sighted a single German aircraft on an easterly course at 1730 hrs that afternoon and two tunnymen, about 50 miles west of Ushant, on the morning of 10 October. They were under sail from 0700 that morning. At 1730 on 10 October they anchored off Porz-Loubous, having approached the coast from the south. The boat was within sight of the signal station on the Pointe-du-Raz at 1200 and was under observation from it until they weighed anchor. Lequien went ashore on the slip with three members of the crew on the pretext of going to buy bread. After breaking down initial reticence, he picked up the trace of Doornik's passage. Lequien's report states clearly that Doornik was not at Penneac'h on either 9 or 10 October. Lequien wrote him a letter at his Paris address, telling him to come back to his landing-place. He also gave the Normant family a note for Doornik telling him to present himself to a M Lomenech at Pont-Aven, using the latter's son Daniel's name as an introduction. It might be possible to find a boat there that would carry him over to England. Lequien re-embarked at 1930 hrs, being obliged to leave as the Germans did not allow vessels to remain overnight in the open roadstead. The return passage was without incident. They sighted nothing and reached Newlyn at 1030 on 12 October.

Lequien's statement that Doornik was not at Penneac'h on either 9 or 10 October was contradicted by Mme Normant and her daughter, who told Pichavant that he arrived at their house on the 9th and left in the early afternoon of the following day, saying he could wait no longer.

According to François Follic, skipper of the *Marie-Louise*, the ship's departure from England was delayed by at least two days owing to bad weather: he remembered this because it was his first operation. They had, of course, no means of warning Doornik, who would seem to have missed them by a narrow margin. As he had left an address, Lequien was able to write to him.

Doornik resumed his mission, visiting Vichy, Nice, Toulon and Perpignan, whence he tried without success to cross the Spanish frontier. He next tried the Swiss frontier, which was less well guarded, crossed it and delivered an abundant harvest of intelligence to a kindly British Vice-Consul in Geneva. Doornik then returned to Lyon and set to work collecting a further crop of information.

Moreau had demonstrated vividly that German control of fishing ports and of the comings and goings of French fishing vessels on the west coast of Brittany was still ineffective. This fact was of considerable importance at a time when SIS was still trying hard to produce the prototype of the suitcase W/T set for use by agents. Before June 1940, the Poles had maintained W/T links between the government-in-exile in France and their diplomatic missions in Budapest and Bucharest, which relayed traffic on to the Home Army command in occupied Poland.[23] M.Z. Rygor-Slowikowski claimed credit for persuading one of their diplomatic wireless engineers he met at Toulouse to build a transmitter–receiver: using this, a clandestine radio contact was established with Sikorski's headquarters in London on 16 September 1940.[24] The Free French made a major attempt to set up clandestine radio communications under Comte Honoré d'Estiennes d'Orves in December 1940 but this was a disaster and the W/T set was in

German hands before the latter's arrest on 22 January 1941. A link between SIS and the Polish 'Interallié' intelligence network was working by the end of 1940, but Dunderdale's 'Johnny' came on the air from Quimper only on 27 March 1941 and Rémy's highly efficient 'Confrérie Notre Dame' did not have radio communications between the occupied zone and London until the end of May 1941.

During the autumn of 1940 fishing boats continued to arrive in England carrying French volunteers for General de Gaulle's forces. This was a more purposeful migration than the chaotic exodus of June, which comprised many who were intent on escaping from the Germans rather than continuing to fight them. The owners of the boats that served to transport the volunteers, however, had no intention of remaining in England and were in a great hurry to get back to fishing before their absence was noticed. The tunnyman *Lusitania*, for example, left Concarneau on 16 September with four volunteers who had had to pay each of the eight crew members 2,000 Francs. The skipper and crew were trustworthy but timid and they became increasingly nervous as they approached the coast of England. About 20 miles off Penzance they encountered a British trawler and, putting their passengers into the dinghy, they turned on their heels in such haste that they did not even wait to recover the boat.[25]

The organiser of the *Lusitania* escape was a 19-year-old Breton named Daniel Lomenech, whose parents owned a fish and vegetable cannery at Pont-Aven, between Concarneau and Lorient. It was his third attempt to escape to England. The German customs control of boats leaving port for the fishing grounds was at that time summary and consisted mainly in scrutiny of the ship's papers, crew list and the individual documents showing that each member of the crew was an *inscrit maritime*. No search was made below decks, so it was not difficult to stow away, which Lomenech and his friends twice did on tunnymen from Concarneau, hoping to meet some British ship or convoy out on the tunny fishing grounds at the edge of the Continental Shelf. Having twice failed, they concluded that they would have to pay a skipper and crew to deviate from their normal fishing routine and take them where they wanted to go, with all the concomitant risks.

One of Lomenech's three companions was a determined 35-year-old commercial traveller named Maurice Barlier, who was married and had four children, came from the Vosges and had worked for Breton canning firms. He had been demobilised in November 1939, presumably on account of his family responsibilities, but had returned to the army in May 1940. He had been taken prisoner but escaped very promptly and came down to the coast seeking means to get across to England. He later returned to France as an agent.

On arrival in London Lomenech and his companions went through the normal interrogation and screening process. They said that 98 per cent of the French population – at all social levels – hoped for the victory of Great Britain and the Free French forces. In the cafés people listened quite openly to the BBC News. They did not accept the Germans and mocked them about the difficulties of landing in England. Despite the Germans' efforts, there was no social contact with them and no-one attended their open-air concerts. All stocks of tinned food were blocked by the Germans. Industrialists were producing as little as possible. Food production was proceeding on a very reduced scale. At Nantes, 2,000 workers were losing their jobs each week. Married women were prostituting themselves on the streets to feed their children.

Lomenech was interviewed by a man called Jacolot, a former member of the French naval mission in London, who had joined Dunderdale's staff after the fall of France. Dunderdale employed him as a talent-spotter when new arrivals from France were undergoing security screening at the Royal Patriotic School on Wandsworth Common. Jacolot recommended Lomenech to his chief as someone with an exceptional knowledge of the south-western coast of Brittany and Dunderdale took him on as a replacement for Moreau, an arrangement at least tacitly accepted by Passy and his staff.

Lomenech was fortunate in having parents who shared his outlook and seconded his efforts. By contrast, Moreau's father, who was a friend of Admiral Darlan, Pétain's deputy, adopted a more equivocal attitude.

Rear-Admiral Jacques Moreau had sailed from Brest on 17 June in command of a convoy bound for Casablanca. On Sunday 23 June, the day before his son set out from Beg-Meil to England in a stolen boat, he wrote in his diary:

> A rumour is spreading that a certain General de Gaulle, who has been stripped of his rank by Weygand, has broadcast from London raising the standard of dissidence. He seems to have announced the formation of a French Committee in England, to have distanced himself from the Bordeaux Government, to be ready to continue the war and to have called on the French Empire to follow him. . .
>
> This is a serious matter. If de Gaulle were not unknown, there would be every reason to follow him. If he were a Lyautey, everyone would march, but to follow a General of whom one knows so very little. . ?[26]

Admiral Moreau had been reckoned a close friend by the last two British Naval Attachés in Paris. When the fall of France was imminent, he had told Holland that he hoped to see the day when their two countries would again be fighting side by side. In October 1942 he was appointed Préfét Maritime at Algiers and in that capacity received Darlan when he arrived there shortly before the TORCH landings. The elements of the French navy under his command actively opposed these landings. Even after the war he never accepted his son's right to wear the decorations he had won as a Free French naval officer and there were frequent arguments between father and son about the wartime years.

Lomenech's parents and sister threw themselves into the struggle as he did and were arrested when the 'Johnny' group was destroyed. M and Mme Lomenech did not return from deportation to Germany; his sister came back, but died not long afterwards.

Although many Breton skippers and crews were nervous about crossing the Channel to carry volunteers for de Gaulle's forces, there were two brave exceptions.

The first, Jacques Guéguen from Pont-de-la-Corde on the Penzé River, not far above Carentec (whence Madame de Gaulle and her children escaped to England), was 70 years old in 1940 when France fell. He was a veteran of Charcot's 1908–10 Antarctic Expedition and he had named his small, sloop-rigged fishing boat *Pourquoi-Pas?* after Charcot's ship. How many boatloads of stragglers from the British Expeditionary Force and volunteers for de Gaulle's Forces he took out in the summer of 1940 is uncertain. A list in the little museum on the Ile-de-Sein credits him with four double crossings in July. Another account says he had carried 32 passengers out of France before the engine of his boat broke down at the end of June and that his friend and neighbour Ernest Sibiril, owner of a local boat-yard, repaired it, which allowed him to continue. Both men later had distinguished careers in the Resistance. In January 1941, as the result of an indiscretion, the Germans caught up with Guéguen when he was preparing to ship out the mail from a Polish intelligence network, but he was freed within a month for lack of evidence and not in the least deterred.[27]

The second brave skipper was Raymond Morvan of Camaret. On 8 October 1940 he sailed his small crabber *L'Étourdi* from that port in broad daylight with volunteers on board. One account says they were four in number; the Sein Museum credits him with eleven.

L'Étourdi had no auxiliary engine and there would have been no fuel for it even had one been fitted. However, she had the fine lines and sailing qualities for which the cutter- and yawl-rigged crabbers of Camaret were justly famous. The Germans tended to underestimate the capabilities of Breton seamen and their ships, no doubt reckoning it impossible for so small a boat to reach England under sail alone. In fact, the small and medium-size Camaret boats had fished regularly off the Longships and Wolf Rock, while their larger, ketch-rigged counterparts sought catches on the coasts of Morocco, Mauretania, Brazil and the Caribbean.

In spite of a gale that struck *L'Étourdi* in mid-Channel, she arrived at Newlyn 48 hours later and landed her passengers. Morvan went up to London and met d'Estiennes d'Orves, then in charge of de Gaulle's Deuxième Bureau and planning his own subsequent mission to Brittany. He then sailed his boat back to Camaret, pausing only to pick up the lobster-pots he had laid on his outward passage as a precaution, so as to have some catch to show for his fortnight's absence.[28]

CHAPTER VI

November 1940–March 1941

E arly in November 1940, the dashing young Daniel Lomenech began what was to prove a long and brilliant involvement in intelligence-gathering and clandestine sea operations to wartime Brittany. He landed on a beach at Rospico between Raguenès and Port-Manech from an elderly and rather nondescript Lorient trawler named *Le-Grec*, which had been added to Dunderdale's Mylor flotilla. She was considerably larger and more comfortable than *Rouanez-ar-Peoc'h*, but she adopted the latter's name and registration number because it was felt that Germans would find it more difficult to remember a Breton name accurately. He was accompanied by another agent working for Dunderdale, Jean Milon. They were to be picked up a month later.[1]

Milon's case history is of interest for the light it throws on contemporary attitudes in France.[2] Son of an academic who became Dean of the Faculty of Sciences at Rennes University and Mayor of the city after the Liberation, he had been serving in the French navy and had been present at Mers-el-Kebir when Admiral Somerville found himself obliged, by Churchill's very specific and precise orders for Operation CATAPULT, to open fire on the French warships concentrated there, killing 1,295 French sailors in a bombardment that lasted only five minutes. Milon arrived home at Rennes in August with the strongly Anglophobe sentiments of his naval background, but contact with his family produced a complete change in his attitude: it was now the German occupation that seemed to him intolerable and he decided to resume the fight. Finding no immediately available means of escape by sea, he crossed into the non-occupied zone, made his way across the Spanish frontier and approached the British Embassy in Madrid. The Embassy got him out to Gibraltar and arranged a passage for him to the United Kingdom, where he arrived in October. His odyssey evoked enough interest in Broadway Buildings for him to be recruited by Dunderdale and entrusted with an intelligence mission back to France.

The ship sent at the beginning of December to collect Lomenech and Milon from the area where they had landed was again *Le-Grec*. But as her Bolinders two-cylinder engine was giving trouble, the crew decided to make an unprogrammed call at Quiberon in the hope of effecting repairs. Henri Le Goff, who had fished sardines in the area before the war, knew the local representative of the manufacturers at Port-Maria and they put into nearby Port-Haliguen, thinking that three or four hours would be enough to put the engine to rights. Unfortunately the defect turned out to be more serious than they had suspected: that, anyway, is what they subsequently told Lomenech.

The crew went ashore to seek consolation and, while they were gone, the wind got up and the boat, obviously inadequately secured, was blown adrift. She was nowhere to be seen when the crew returned, having patronised most of the local bars.

It was an awkward situation: four sailors without a boat, cut off from their home base and without resources: two spies stranded with their intelligence becoming stale. The crew telephoned the Inscription Maritime at La-Trinité to report that a disabled and unmanned ship was adrift and a potential danger to shipping. The Inscription Maritime sent a launch, which found the drifting vessel, managed to get a grapnel aboard and towed her into La-Trinité. She was found to have tell-tale stocks of British provisions on board. The French administration tried to conceal both the provisions and the facts from the German military customs service, the GAST, but failed. The matter was reported to the Abwehr regional office at Angers, who reported it to Berlin as the first known case of a fishing boat's being used to convey persons back from England.[3]

Lomenech rounded up most of his aberrant crew, though the engine mechanic deserted and preferred to remain at home in Douarnenez. He took them to Camaret, where a long-laid-up local crabber named, appropriately enough, *L'Émigrant*, was being repaired and prepared for an escape to England. The ship had been bought by, and registered in the name of, Jacques Andrieux, son of a local doctor, who had a distinguished subsequent career in the Free French air force. Lomenech paid the shipyard bill and the crew of the *Grec* and a sailor from Camaret manned her when she sailed for Cornwall on 16 December with no fewer than 12 clandestine passengers, including two British and two Polish evaders, hidden behind false bulkheads and in empty water tanks. Her skipper had planned to arrive off the west coast of Ushant at nightfall so as to cross under cover of darkness the northern limit of the zone in which the Germans allowed fishing. But they ran into deteriorating weather, and when the hull began to work and take in significant quantities of water, he took the short cut through the Fromveur Channel between Ushant and the mainland, in spite of the danger posed to sailing craft in winter conditions by the narrowness of the channel and the violent tidal streams. The gamble paid off: they sighted the English coast next day and made port at Newlyn. The ship was also added to Dunderdale's little flotilla at Mylor, in Falmouth Harbour, after having had an auxiliary engine installed.

The Abwehr noted her disappearance on the day she sailed and rightly surmised she must be lying at Falmouth. On the same day, 16 December, they learned that the *Marie-Louise* had been missing from her home port, also Camaret, since the beginning of September.[4]

The *Marie-Louise* had in fact made a second clandestine voyage to Porz-Loubous at the beginning of December. François Follic, who was in command, carried with him for the Free French Deuxième Bureau Jacques Mansion, who was this time to report on German troop dispositions on the Channel coast, and Maurice Barlier, who had volunteered to go back to prepare for the arrival of Frigate Captain Henri Honoré, Comte d'Estiennes d'Orves and a radio operator. The passage from Newlyn was rougher than in October and, on arrival, there was too much sea running for the ship to make a landing at Porz-Loubous. Follic opted therefore for Brézel-lec in Douarnenez Bay, behind the shelter of the Pointe-du-Van, where the two agents were safely disembarked. The ship somehow or other ended up at Weymouth on her return voyage to England, where she was of course not expected, with the result that Follic and his crew were initially detained as suspects.[5]

Barlier went to see his contacts in Nantes and on 9 December travelled to Paris, where he made contact with Jan Doornik's brother Yves. He had tracked down Jan at Vichy and was back in Finistère by 15 December, where he established himself at the Ville d'Ys inn on the Baie-des-Trépassés and settled to await the arrival of d'Estiennes d'Orves.[6]

D'Estiennes d'Orves (*nom de guerre* 'Châteauvieux') had taken over as head of de Gaulle's Deuxième Bureau in autumn 1940, leaving Passy to concentrate on his duties as the General's Chief of Staff, which had become very much a full-time job as a result of the expedition to Dakar in October. However, Passy thought him quite unsuitable for the job – too candid, too kind, too conformist and too little on guard when dealing with the British.[7] He had, more-over, strongly opposed Châteauvieux's wish to go into the field in person, not only because he thought him too trusting to make a good secret agent, but because he considered it still far too soon for the chief of de Gaulle's secret service to undertake a mission in occupied France – a perfectly valid point, although Passy had himself volunteered to go into Normandy in August. Muselier took the same view and they both begged de Gaulle not to allow d'Estienne d'Orves to go. However the General finally gave way to the latter's repeated entreaties.[8]

The plan was that he and his W/T operator should set up an organisation ('Nemrud') to coordinate the efforts of the agents previously sent into the field and establish for them the vital radio communications with the United Kingdom base that had so far been lacking.

Gaessler, whom d'Estiennes d'Orves had selected to accompany him as his W/T operator, was a fully qualified Petty Officer Telegraphist from the Free French submarine *Le-Triomphant*. An Alsatian, he was, at 21, the older and more experienced of the only two candidates for the job, but it was to prove a disastrous choice.[9]

François Follic had only just returned to Newlyn from fishing when Lequien contacted him and introduced 'M. Châteauvieux'. They sailed early on 21 December and landed their two passengers the following evening at Porz-Loubous. Gaessler came on the air two days later with the news that d'Estiennes d'Orves was going to Paris. What happened next is, even now, a matter of conjecture: neither d'Estiennes d'Orves's children, in a book that they wrote about their father,[10] nor historians of the Resistance in Brittany have espoused the theory that Gaessler was a German agent on a mission to England. More likely it was his enthusiasm for riotous living in the bars and bordellos of Nantes that made d'Estiennes d'Orves threaten to send him home in disgrace. Unable to resist temptation and faced with this unpalatable prospect, he seems to have offered his services to the enemy. His Alsatian background may have been a factor in his defection, for his father sought, and acquired, German citizenship in 1943. Any careful process of selection ought to have shown him to be quite unsuitable for the lonely and nerve-racking job of a clandestine radio operator, but in 1940 security vetting procedures were still in their infancy. One French historian has noted that at least four equally disastrous choices of W/T operators were made by the Free French at this period.[11]

After d'Estiennes d'Orves's arrest on 22 January – exactly a month after his landing – Colonel Dernbach of the Abwehr installed Gaessler at Nantes and ordered him to continue to maintain radio contact with the United Kingdom base. It was the first case of *Funkspiel* of the Occupation (the capture and offensive use of the enemy's radio link) and through it the Abwehr learned of the plan to send out, at d'Estiennes d'Orves's request, a second radio operator, J.-J. Le Prince, who was due to be landed on 5 February at Porz-Loubous. When the Abwehr, guided by Gaessler, went to the Normant house at Plogoff to await the arrival of the *Marie-Louise*, they found and arrested Jan Doornik, who had hoped to return to the United Kingdom by the same boat.[12]

The *Marie-Louise* did not turn up: she had to return to base because of compass trouble. Dernbach, through Gaessler's W/T channel, informed London of this failure and urged them to try again. London agreed, asking only to be told the colour of the pennant that fishing boats on the Brittany coast were required to fly. The colour had just been changed; Dernbach told them to use the colour that had ceased to be valid.[13]

The *Marie-Louise*, under command of Follic, set off again on the morning of 14 February with Le Prince, the W/T operator, and his equipment on board. They sailed into a trap and were captured by enemy trawlers some 43 km. (27 miles) west of the Pointe-du-Raz and towed into Brest.[14] Barlier, Doornik, d'Estiennes d'Orves and all those captured in the *Marie-Louise* were condemned to death, but Hitler commuted the sentences of all but the first three to 15 years' hard labour.[15]

The halcyon days, epitomised by a humorous notice 'Service Régulier Tréboul–Penzance' on a wall in the Royal Patriotic School security screening centre on Wandsworth Common, were coming to an end. The French are not taciturn by nature and in that period of national humiliation they found it doubly difficult to keep silent if they could see that some spark of hope was still alive; the results were often disastrous.[16]

At the beginning of January 1941, an over-ambitious attempt by a precocious Nantes Resistance group to smuggle 23 people out of Douarnenez on the Camaret motor crabber *Monique* backfired badly. The boat was seized; Bocq and Adam, the two main organisers, were arrested. The town was invested by troops and placed under a state of siege, while a large-scale, if only partly successful, manhunt was mounted for the would-be passengers, mostly volunteers for the Free French forces but including also Maître André Weil-Curiel, a well-known Socialist member of the Paris Bar, and two colleagues. Weil-Curiel, who had been evacuated from Dunkirk, had been one of the first people to join de Gaulle.[17] He had undertaken a political reconnaissance mission for the General under the cover of voluntary repatriation to France via Spain and was now on his way back to London to report. He slipped through the German net at Douarnenez, though they knew of, or actually captured, 16 of the 23 would-be passengers. Unfortunately the Musée de l'Homme group in Paris, with which he had been in contact, contained a double agent, who was one of the men who accompanied him to Douarnenez. Weil-Curiel was arrested on the demarcation line near Toulouse a few days later. He was released after an intervention by Abetz, the German Ambassador, but only after agreeing to work for the enemy.[18] On arriving in England Weil-Curiel punctiliously reported this, was tried and exonerated by a *jury d'honneur*, but was never forgiven by de Gaulle, who at the end of the war denied him the Médaille de la Résistance.[19]

Just before Christmas there had been another bungled escape, this time on the north coast of Brittany: 16 would-be volunteers for the Free French forces appropriated a fishing boat named *La-Jeanine* from the harbour of Dorduff near Morlaix, but they quickly got into trouble with the boat and were carried east towards Guernsey, where they were intercepted and arrested.[20] The Occupation authorities were sufficiently exasperated by these attempted escapes, and by the *Monique* case in particular, to ban all forms of fishing and navigation on the coasts of the three Breton departments from 14 January, even within 3 km. of the shore. This draconian measure had, for economic reasons, to be rescinded only 11 days later when coastal fishing for mackerel, sardines, fish caught by line, oysters, shellfish, lobsters and crayfish in undecked vessels was conditionally authorised. Other forms of fishery remained prohibited. But the implicit threat of reimposition of the ban caused many people in Breton ports to turn hostile towards activities that might disrupt their livelihoods.[21] The combination of stricter German controls and enhanced risks of denunciation were enough greatly to limit escapes from west coast ports: there were indeed only three in the ensuing 28 months.[22] Escapes from the north coast in small boats and vessels continued with varying success. A sand-barge named *Gustave*, which left Paimpol on 9 February 1941 with 30 persons on board, reached England safely but a boat, well named *Misère*, which sailed from Kerity with 9 passengers only days later, was lost with all hands.

Fishing by larger, fully-decked vessels was resumed in due course on the west coast, but only south of a line running south-west from Ushant. The implications of the new restrictions on the north coast seem not to have been known or understood in London, since attempts were made in March and in April to carry out operations using fishing vessels of a type and size no longer allowed by the Germans to fish, or indeed navigate, in these waters.

Surprisingly enough, two operations undertaken in March by boats of Dunderdale's Mylor flotilla on the north coast were successful. On 18 March, a mission code-named ALLAH, but by Dunderdale most frequently called 'Johnny's Group', embarked at Mylor on *L'Émigrant*, now bearing the name *Marcel-Elénore*. The party was led by Robert Alaterre, a former archivist of the French Embassy in London. Its second-in-command and W/T operator was Jean Le Roux, who had escaped from Camaret on this same boat in December with Daniel Lomenech and Jean Milon, the other two members of the ALLAH mission.[23]

They were due to be landed on the west coast, but the Breton crew got drunk on rum, lost their way and made a landfall on the north coast near Ile-Vierge. The mission was put ashore near Lampaul-Ploudalmézeau. They concealed their luggage and equipment in the sand dunes. Daniel Lomenech contacted his father at Pont-Aven and they came back together in the latter's car to collect the baggage, including Le Roux's transmitters.

The mission's task was to set up an intelligence-collecting network for Dunderdale covering the ports of north-western France and, in particular, Brest, which acquired much enhanced importance as an intelligence target owing to the arrival there for repairs of the German battle-cruisers *Scharnhorst* and *Gneisenau* on 21 March – the day after the landing of ALLAH. The ships were being frequently bombed by the RAF and there was an urgent need to find a source in the dockyard to monitor the damage caused and ascertain the time required to repair and ready them for sea. For nearly a year many of Le Roux's telegrams concerned these ships.

Slocum had resumed his MTB operations on 19 March with an attempt to land an SOE agent in the Ile-Vierge area, but the operation was frustrated by a mechanical breakdown. A further, this time successful, attempt to disembark this unidentified man was made on 28 March by Dunderdale's Mylor team, using the Le-Guilvinec pinnace *Korrigan*.[24] The seaman who rowed the agent ashore was none other than Henri Le Goff, the member of Moreau's crew, who had allowed the original *Petit-Marcel* to go adrift and dry out in Le-Guilvinec harbour when he was supposed to be on watch. Le Goff seems to have been accident-prone: his dinghy was caught in a tidal current on his way back to *Korrigan* and he failed to find her. When he did not return within the agreed time-limit, *Le-Korrigan* got underway without him. Le Goff got back to the shore only after sculling the boat for four hours: he then sank it, threw himself into the sea and swam to the beach. He made his way into Brest looking conspicuous in his wet clothes and wooden-soled seaboots, caught a train to Le-Guilvinec, went back to his home in the nearby village of Saint-Guénolé and told his friend Yves Frélaud that he had, of necessity, suddenly become available again. Though he was soon back in touch with Daniel Lomenech and the new 'Johnny' organisation, he was victim of a denunciation, was arrested in October 1941 and deported to Buchenwald, from which he did not return.[25]

L'Émigrant, bearing the name *Le-Petit-Marcel* for this operation, was sent to pick up Jean Milon from a beach at Bréhec-en-Lanloup between Paimpol and Plouha on 19 April 1941. Two German patrol boats intercepted her when she was still 10 km. (6 miles) offshore and towed her into Cherbourg. Raymond Le Corre, Marcel Guénolé and Jules Kerloc'h, the Breton members of the crew, were imprisoned at Caen, Angers and Romainville before being deported to Buchenwald. Three crew members from Fécamp who had been taken off the Grand Banks barquentine *Georges-Duhamel* by a British man-of-war, were more fortunate: they were released after a few months in prison.[26]

The loss of the renamed *L'Émigrant* was a severe setback for Dunderdale, as the arrest of d'Estiennes d'Orves and the loss of the

Marie-Louise had been to the Free French. Moreover Dunderdale's agent Jean Milon was lost at sea while trying to get back to England by his own means, after the promised passage in *L'Émigrant* had failed to materialise. He had appropriated a heavy, undecked 6-metre-long sailing boat from a small harbour between Trébeurden and Trégastel for the crossing. Jacques Mansion, de Gaulle's first emissary, who should have been picked up by *L'Émigrant* at the same time as Milon, had gone off on his own and a man named Chemine, who had been *L'Émigrant*'s third prospective passenger, drew back because he thought the risks involved in Milon's improvised attempt to cross the Channel too great. So Milon put to sea single-handed. He was sighted at dawn by the keeper on the offshore Triagoz lighthouse: the boat, under jib and mainsail, seemed to be heading towards Morlaix, but neither she nor Milon was ever seen again.[27]

By the end of 1940 Dunderdale was anyway in difficulties over his relations with the Free French. His was not an easy hand to play: he had had to look to them initially for agents and boats' crews, but his section was supposed to operate in France independently of de Gaulle's Deuxième Bureau. He had to attempt to re-establish contact with his old professional counterparts, now working for the Vichy administration, which in August had tried de Gaulle *in absentia* and condemned him to death. Moreover, Dunderdale's French friends in London, including the former French Consul-General, who subsequently returned to Vichy, tended to be strong anti-Gaullists and Passy became convinced that Biffy shared his French friends' anti-Gaullist views; in this, he was not very wide of the mark. Dunderdale, conversely, felt that Passy's nascent organisation had begun to interfere with his own networks of agents in France. A further dimension was added to this imbroglio by the fact that, in the period following the abortive Dakar expedition of October 1940, the Gaullists' security had come under grave suspicion.

Matters came to a head over Christmas and the New Year of 1940–41 when Churchill high-handedly and, as it turned out, ill-advisedly, had Admiral Muselier, de Gaulle's deputy, arrested and thrown into Brixton gaol on the strength of letters passed to the British Security Service by a man called Meffre, appointed by Passy to tighten up Free French security. The letters were found to have been forged at Meffre's behest. De Gaulle's wrath was not appeased by Churchill's attempts to make amends: his worst suspicions about the British Government's perfidy had been confirmed. He believed that Muselier's arrest had been deliberately engineered by British intelligence to discredit the Free French movement and that Meffre had been planted in Passy's organisation for this express purpose. His belief was ill-founded: it was in fact Spears, still at that stage de

Gaulle's ardent admirer and supporter, who had recommended Meffre to Passy.[28]

What this state of strained relations meant in practical terms is well illustrated by the case of Jean Le Roux, second in command and radio operator of the ALLAH mission. When he arrived in England in December 1940, Le Roux impressed his British interrogators with his knowledge as a radio electrician and they suggested he return to France as a W/T operator in one of Dunderdale's intelligence circuits. Le Roux agreed to do so provided he was given the status of a member of the Free French forces. This stipulation was accepted, but he discovered that Dunderdale much preferred to employ individual Frenchmen without any prior arrangement with de Gaulle's headquarters, if he could get away with it. On the eve of his departure for France with the ALLAH mission, having still been given no opportunity to join the Free French forces, he categorically refused to leave unless he was allowed to do so, at which he was taken round to 4 Carlton Gardens and allowed to sign a voluntary engagement *in extremis*. He went to France next night, assuming that copies of his signals would be passed automatically to de Gaulle's people. Not until he returned to London from this mission did he find, to his displeasure, that nothing of the kind had ever been intended.[29]

In these circumstances there was inevitably friction within SIS itself between Dunderdale's section and Cohen's, whose job was to maintain a good working liaison with Passy and the Free French Deuxième Bureau. Cohen could in such matters count on firm support from Claude Dansey, Assistant Chief of SIS, whose deputy he had been in the pre-war period. Dunderdale, on the other hand appealed to Menzies himself for support, so that SIS was uncomfortably divided against itself on French issues.

Slocum emerged from this mêleé with his position, and that of his Section, strengthened. He was still working with no more than tacit approval of the Admiralty, but the organisation under Lequien, through which the Free French had been able to arrange operations using the French boats and crews at Newlyn, had ceased to function with the loss of the *Marie-Louise*; and that which Dunderdale, Jacolot and Oxley had created at Mylor was closed down after the loss of *L'Émigrant*; this left Slocum as SIS's sole purveyor of clandestine sea and air transport to France.

His resources for the job were slender. As his struggle to get reliable high-speed craft allocated for his needs in the Channel had still borne no fruit, operations between Brest and the Hook of Holland could be mounted on a hand-to-mouth basis only. No operations to France had been attempted during the preceding five winter months and none of the ten undertaken during the spring and summer of 1941 was successful. In April 1941, he made a first attempt to use a small French cargo ship for operations in the western Mediterranean. It remained to be seen whether the British submarines patrolling off Brest and lying in wait for the *Scharnhorst* and the *Gneisenau* could be of assistance, for air operations were still on a very small scale.

There remained also the problem of what to do about SOE and its tiresome, if still rather hypothetical, mandate 'to set Europe ablaze'. If SOE wanted to run fishing boats in and out of Norway, the coastline was so long, ramified and remote that no great harm could ensue. The Greek archipelago, which had fallen into German hands by the end of May 1941, might be a similar case, but that was a problem for Cairo rather than Whitehall. Brittany, however, was an area where SOE's maritime ambitions must be held firmly in check and subordinated to those of SIS.

It would be wrong not to pay tribute here to the spirit and independence of the Breton fisherfolk who, in the dark days of 1940, were pioneers of the Resistance. There was a negative side to their idiosyncratic ways in that they were very reluctant to accept discipline. Those who manned the boats of Dunderdale's Mylor flotilla were young and, in some cases, as irresponsible as they were courageous. The stranding of Moreau's boat at Guilvinec and the loss of *Le-Grec* at Quiberon were directly attributable to poor discipline. *Le-Grec*'s engineman deserted. Dunderdale's men were in theory Free French naval ratings, but they were certainly not under anything like normal naval discipline: the Mylor flotilla had been in danger of running out of control.[30] The Breton fishermen at Newlyn, on whom Lequien relied, were not even theoretically subject to naval discipline. Pierre Couillandre and his crew of the *Corbeau-des-Mers* returned permanently to the Ile-de-Sein, as did *Ma-Gondole* to Douarnenez, while Prosper Couillandre chose to go home to the Ile-de-Sein for shore leave, an act that at that time (mid-September 1940) proved dangerous to both himself and his family.

CHAPTER VII

Did the Abwehr Allow *L'Émigrant* to Escape?

L ike all those who left Camaret on 16 December 1940 on
L'Émigrant, Jean Le Roux believed he had made a genuine
escape. Indeed, the citation drafted by Alaterre after the war
when Le Roux was awarded the Légion d'Honneur began with
the words 'Evadé de France dans des conditions périlleuses en
décembre 1940, le Chargé de Mission de Première Classe Le
Roux Jean. . . .'[1] But one day, after the war, Le Roux was invited
by a police inspector of the DST, the French counter-intelligence
service, to hear what one of their prisoners, Alois Gross, had to say.
Throughout the Occupation Gross had worked for successive heads
of the Abwehr for western France.

Le Roux had never heard of Gross, but Gross knew a lot about
Le Roux and his disclosures took the second in command of the
ALLAH mission aback. Gross told him that their network had been
broken up as a result of betrayal by one of their W/T operators who
had been arrested at Carhaix on 9 September 1941. Gross also
made some allegations about the circumstances in which
L'Émigrant had set sail for England: so surprising were these that
Le Roux asked him to put them in writing. Two days later Gross
handed him a statement, which he had written in his cell, in
pencil and in German. Le Roux spoke no German, so he took
Gross's document straight away to the office that Dunderdale's
Section of SIS had set up at Uncle Tom Greene's Paris address,
69 Avenue Victor Hugo.

Gross declared that in December 1940 he was sent to Camaret
to contact a man named Drévillion, whose mother worked as a cook
for the local GAST, the German military customs service, which
was in charge of all movements of fishing vessels. Corvette Captain
Pfeiffer, alias Dr André, who entrusted Gross with this mission, told
him that Drévillion had informed the GAST in Camaret some 10–
12 days previously that a cutter-rigged fishing vessel would shortly
sail for England with British Intelligence Service agents on board.
Gross's job was to report to the GAST at Camaret, to whom
Drévillion would introduce him; to receive further information;
and to take note of a declaration made to the GAST at an earlier
date.

When he arrived in Camaret, Drévillion was introduced to
Gross in the presence of an inspector and reported that Jacques
Andrieux, the son of a doctor from Carhaix, had acquired the

cutter *Émigrant* from a M Morvan in order to get agents to England. As cover, Andrieux had stated that he wished to sail the cutter to Lorient to have a diesel engine installed and later to arrange transport of vegetables between Roscoff and Lorient.

The GAST confirmed this information. At the same time they informed Drévillion that there was something suspicious about Andrieux's statement, as enquiry had shown that some of the details given on his identity card were wrong. The street in Lorient market where he claimed to live did not exist and, indeed, he was not known in Lorient. This information had been sent to Brest and the GAST received orders that preparations for the sailing of the cutter should not be interfered with in any way. Gross was ordered to stay with the GAST and to report to Brest any possible news from Drévillion. The deed of sale between Morvan and Andrieux was deposited by Andrieux at the GAST and photographed there.

On the first day Drévillion had already started dropping hints to Gross about money, intimating that for more pay he could produce more information. Gross explained to Drévillion that he had no authority to bargain with him about this and that he must deal with the GAST. The following day Drévillion brought Gross the names of the crew of the *Marie-Louise*, which, he said, had escaped from Camaret and was making trips from England. Gross claimed that he did not forward to Brest the list Drévillion gave him without witnesses, but kept it for several weeks in case Drévillion should make a further report. He could then pretend to have forgotten it.

Drévillion again demanded money and Gross again referred him to the GAST. Within the next day or two, Drévillion also betrayed the *Monique* to the GAST. He said he hoped that, with the sum he would receive, he could become a master and would no longer need to work for others.

Meanwhile, the preparation of *L'Émigrant* was completed and Andrieux came to get his clearance, which was given immediately. Pfeiffer again gave strict orders that under no circumstances was anything abnormal to happen during the inspection by the GAST, which took place at 0930 next morning. Gross saw the customs officers go on board in a small boat. Shortly afterwards *L'Émigrant* weighed anchor and set sail. Notification was sent immediately to Pfeiffer, who ordered a torpedo boat to be sent to shadow the cutter. An hour later the GAST received a report of a 'cutter steering north island Ushant direction England'. Gross added that there had been a lot of people on the quay when the cutter sailed, who commented on its departure and could easily have guessed what was going on.

Gross concluded his statement with the report of the staff that carried out the inspection. They came aboard and were received by the captain in an extremely friendly way. He immediately offered them cognac, which they refused, saying they might have some when they had finished their work. The skipper tried to divert their attention with a small black cat. The inspection over, the officials then went on deck and had a drink with the skipper, who was bursting with pleasure over the favourable outcome of the inspection. The inspector said subsequently that he was sure that, if he had found anything amiss, he would not have left the boat alive. The GAST had taken precautionary measures, including having machine-guns in readiness.

Gross left Drévillion the same day without paying him. Later Drévillion made reports to the GAST in which he again accused Morvan, who was arrested but released for lack of evidence.

On Gross's return to Brest, Pfeiffer asked for a report. He was extremely pleased about the smooth resolution of the matter. He told Gross that *L'Émigrant* had had wind Force 7 and Gross said he found it hard to believe that anyone would venture out on the high seas in such an old sieve. One must hand it to the Bretons: they were the best seamen in the world.

Later a rumour went round the Abwehr's local headquarters that two agents had been got to England successfully. Gross did not know where and how, but thought it must certainly be by means of *L'Émigrant*. Anyhow, Pfeiffer was extremely interested in the sailing of the cutter and reminded Gross of his duty to preserve complete secrecy, warning him also of the consequences should he break his silence.

In April 1955, Le Roux wrote to Gross to propose that Gross should come to Brittany at his expense, or that he should himself travel up to Vitry-sur-Orne in the Moselle, an address he had obtained from the Direction de Surveillance du Territoire (DST). Gross's wife replied, saying that her husband did not know Le Roux, and indeed that his sufferings during and after the war, compounded by illness two years previously, had caused him substantial loss of memory.

Le Roux gave his Gross papers to Pichavant, who, he felt, paid too little attention to his testimony on the matter. Pichavant had concluded a chapter on the *Émigrant* affair in his book *Clandestins de l'Iroise* with the words:

> The enigma, if one still holds to it, rests at last on a single declaration by a prisoner who was struck almost immediately thereafter by a strange amnesia.

As Le Roux has pointed out, this charge of instant amnesia is not fair, since in fact ten years had elapsed between the events and the protagonists' attempts to recall them.

Le Roux's concluding questions were:

1. How could a German agent describe so precisely the departure of *L'Émigrant* unless he had been directly involved in it?

2. What interest could he have had in inventing such a story (even if he were able to do so), when he had already given a mass of information to the DST on all the cases in which he had been involved over the last four years? Gross had, together with Charlotte Pillon, Dernbach's secretary, been the most important source available to the DST at Rennes.

3. In Le Roux's judgement, the departure of *L'Émigrant* unquestionably took place with German complicity. Again, Gross could not have invented all the accurate details of this aspect of the matter.

4. Why, finally, did the Germans want *L'Émigrant* to sail? Was it to allow the two Poles,[2] who joined the escape venture at a late stage, to get over to the United Kingdom? Obviously Le Roux had no proof but he was profoundly convinced that there could be no other explanation. He thought it probable that when these two Poles arrived in England they explained the circumstances in which they had left France: Dunderdale was, probably aware of the situation. When his staff handed the translation of Gross's statement over to Le Roux at their Paris office, they made no comment if any kind on it.

Hinsley's *British Intelligence in the Second World War* (Vol. IV)[3] makes it clear that, at the end of 1940, the Germans were having very real difficulty in infiltrating agents illegally into the United Kingdom and in these circumstances the Abwehr may well have thought it a price worth paying to allow the Frenchmen and a crew to escape to England if at the same time they could get two agents established there as refugees or escapers – a technigue they used in a score of cases during 1942. That these two Poles never attempted to work for the Abwehr in Great Britain seems certain: they are not mentioned in the official history, which records that from July 1942 MI5 was virtually cetain that all Abwehr agents operating in the United Kingdom were under control.[4]

Daniel Lomenech, on the other hand, disbelieved Gross's story, claiming it may have been invented *ex post facto* by the local Abwehr to explain away to their superiors their failure to stop *L'Émigrant* from sailing. He remained in touch with one of the two Poles, who became a doctor in the United Kingdom after the war. Lomenech also pointed out that the Mlles Barbarin of Pont-Aven gave shelter to the two Polish evaders for many weeks before they left for England via Camaret and that they were never subsequently arrested or troubled by the Germans for having done so. However, their immunity perhaps confirms, rather than disproves, that the Germans wanted the Poles to get away.

Hubert Moreau, the first intelligence agent to return to German-occupied French territory.

Daniel Lomenech in British naval uniform.

Raymond Le Corre, Michel Baltas, Marcel Guénolé and Henri Le Goff of Le Guilvinec on the *Rouanez-ar-Peoc'h* in the Iroise off Brest heading back to Falmouth. Photograph by Hubert Moreau when returning from his second mission in August 1940.

Mutin ashore below Budock Vean, Port Navas on the Helford River for a scrub and coat of anti-fouling paint. Drawing by the author.

The diminutive RAF 360 in the Helford River. The house on the right was
'Ridifarne' used by Gerry Holdsworth as his headquarters.

Gerry Holdsworth
ocean racing at the
end of the war.

MGB 325 (Lt Peter Williams, DSC, RNVR) on trials off Brixham, where she was built in 1941. She was used for operations to Britain and Holland shortly after this picture was taken. MGBs 314 (Lt Dunstan Curtis, DSO, RNVR) and 318 (Lt Charles Martin DSC, RNVR) and Lt Cdr J T McQuoid Mason, S.A.N.F. (v) were identical sister ships.

CHAPTER VIII

SOE's Aspirations and Operations: August 1940–June 1941

L eslie Humphreys had returned from his assignment as Section D's representative in Paris after parting on good terms with Brochu, head of the French Cinquième Bureau and Rivet, head of the Service de Renseignements, who had been moving from one château to another as the French Government made its way through chaotic traffic to Bordeaux. He had been evacuated to England by a series of warships and on arrival in London he had, like Dunderdale of SIS, been told to organise a section to work back to France; in Humphreys's case this was of course, for Section D, soon to be merged into SOE. Brochu actually sent a liaison officer to join him in London and within a month he had, with the help of this man and a variety of other sources, collected over two dozen agents and sent them to Brickendonbury Hall in Hertfordshire for training.[1]

Humphreys held that good communications are the essential basis of all clandestine activities and his work as head of SOE's French Section was, in this respect, a continuation of his earlier efforts to organise clandestine routes into Germany and sabotage behind the enemy lines as the invasion of France began. He gradually developed a blueprint for a system that would serve SOE throughout western Europe for secret travel and supply. This took time and he was concerned to send three of the men he had recruited back to France to conduct a reconnaissance as a first step in this longer-term programme. He wanted these agents, Tilly, Clech and Bernard, landed by sea and, since no W/T link was available, his plan was for them to be picked up three weeks after their arrival in the field and brought back to report. It was a simple and very traditional concept but it depended on getting hold of a vessel to land them as soon as possible and to re-embark them at the agreed date.[2]

Section D was still formally part of SIS in July 1940 when this requirement arose and Humphreys had a number of meetings with Slocum to thrash out the details of a plan. It was agreed that the Pointe-de-Primel on the east side of Morlaix Bay would be a suitable pinpoint but, owing to some unrecorded mishap, the mission was not ready to leave at the agreed date. It thereby lost its place in the queue waiting to use the only MTB available to

Slocum. As his section was at the time beset by bids that SIS regarded as of higher priorty, it looked as though substantial delay might ensue; nor was there any means of ensuring that the same situation would not arise over the mission's return passage.

In the circumstances, Humphreys did exactly what Dunderdale and the Free French were doing in the hectic closing days of July 1940, namely to seek alternative means of transport that would be under their exclusive control. Just as Dunderdale sent Oxley and Passy sent Lequien into the West Country to improvise sea lines of communication for their needs, so D sent an Army officer, Captain John Dolphin, to find some suitable small vessel. After a rapid tour of the ports, his choice fell on a refugee Belgian motor yacht lying at Newlyn. This was requisitioned and fitted out as well as was possible with local resources and within the time available. She was renamed No. 77 and a gallant French merchant navy officer called Hélie, described as the best type of *loup de mer*, was chosen as skipper. After training and many rehearsals of the light signals that were to announce their presence to the boat picking them up for the return passage, the agents were put on a train from Paddington to Penzance with an escorting officer. They were joined on the train by Captain Holdsworth of the Intelligence Corps who had worked for Section D as an agent in Scandinavia and had been chosen to take charge of the Newlyn expedition because he was one of the few members of D who knew anything about boats and the sea.

Holdsworth was not best pleased by what he found on arrival at Newlyn. No. 77 had major defects and shortcomings, chief among which was that she was slow and noisy. He decided nevertheless to make the attempt and on the afternoon of 1 August – only 24 hours after Hubert Moreau had returned from the first of all clandestine missions by fishing boat to Brittany – Tilly, Clech and Bernard were discreetly embarked at Penzance on a naval launch, which proceeded as if on a routine trip until it met NO. 77 at an agreed rendezvous some 6 km. (4 miles) out to sea. The three agents were transferred to the larger vessel, which set out for the open sea in the gathering twilight, punctiliously dipping her ensign to the naval launch as it headed back to Penzance: Holdsworth was a stickler for such marks of deference to the senior service. The Hon. Tony Samuel, the escorting officer who had brought the agents down from London, caught the train from Penzance to Paddington next morning, but at Truro he was handed a telegram asking him to return at once to Penzance. He did so and was met on arrival by Holdsworth: the expedition had been abandoned after coming under fire from German vessels, which were thought to have been in the area by chance on convoy duties. With luck and good seamanship on Hélie's part, No. 77 had been brought safely back to Penzance.

The three agents, comparatively unshaken, were sent back to London to await another opportunity. All concerned felt that NO. 77 had shown herself unsuitable for clandestine operations of this type. Holdsworth's report emphasised that far more preparations were necessary for such work, including arrangements for cooperation with RAF Coastal Command. But Slocum's ensuing ten failures to deliver these three agents by MTB strengthened SOE's feeling that it must try to develop more satisfactory independent facilities of the kind Holdsworth recommended.

SOE regarded sea transport to France as essential to its plans because, in the autumn of 1940, it had no idea when, and on what scale, air transport would be available to it, even when the RAF's experiments with live parachute drops from Whitleys and with landing Lysanders by moonlight on improvised runways had been satisfactorily completed. Flight 419 had been established in August with two Whitleys for parachuting agents into the field, two Lysanders for landing and picking them up and two DC3s for communication flights, but it had been formed specifically to cater for SIS's needs; even thus endowed, it was not until October that the first SIS agent was parachuted into France. Pilot Officer Philip Schneidau was dropped near Fontainebleau to investigate for Slocum the possibility of setting up a network in the Paris area. He was brought back on the night of 20/21 October by the first of all operational pick-ups from enemy territory by Lysander aircraft, and it was a hair-raising event. A single rifle bullet hit the aircraft as it took off from France with Schneidau on board and demolished the compass – the aircraft's only navigational aid – between the knees of the pilot, Flight Lieutenant W.R. Farley. He climbed to a height of 16,000 feet and flew blind all the way to Oban on the west coast of Scotland, where he made a crash landing with the fuel tank empty. These were the only flights carried out successfully to France before the end of 1940, even for SIS, though an attempt to parachute a Gaullist agent into France failed only because he refused to jump.[3]

SOE had some commitments that could not be tackled at all unless aircraft were available to it. This was the case with regard to Poland and Czechoslovakia, for which it had taken over responsibility from the War Office. The Poles had agents standing by to be dropped in to the Secret Army well before the end of 1940 and this operation was SOE's highest priority requirement for air transport. It could, however, be carried out in ideal conditions only, since the flight across Jutland and along the Baltic to western Poland was at the extreme limit of a Whitley's range. In those early days sea transport was felt to be all that could be hoped for in planning operations to France. A paper put up to SOE's chief executive at the very beginning of August 1940 argued that one of SOE's main tasks would be to recruit a carefully selected body of saboteurs who would operate exclusively against objectives on, or near, the coasts, at widely spaced points and at short notice; and in March 1941, though SOE's first two parachute operations had by then included one to Brittany as well as one to Poland, Brigadier Gubbins, SOE's Director of Training and Operations, was still expressing the view that 'all the parties of men we are now training . . . may well have to be landed by sea as no other means exist.'[4]

SAVANNAH, SOE's first air operation into France, was of particular interest to the RAF since its object was to strike at the aircrews of Kampfgeschwader 100, the Luftwaffe's pathfinder force, then operating from Meuçon airfield near Vannes to guide the German night bombers to targets such as Coventry. It was only with great difficulty that Spears persuaded de Gaulle to make five trained parachutists, all veterans of the campaign in Norway, available to SOE for it, since relations between Carlton Gardens and Downing Street had not yet recovered from the Muselier affair. Then the RAF, despite their interest in the target of the operation, made an aircraft available only very reluctantly, after a protracted argument between SOE and Portal, the Chief of Air Staff, about the ethics of employing agents in civilian attire to attack uniformed Luftwaffe personnel. By the time this argument had been won by SOE and the team belatedly dropped into the Morbihan Department near Elven during the March 1941 moon period, the operation was no longer feasible since the aircrews were no longer travelling to and from the airfield by bus, the target they had been briefed to expect.[5]

The original intention had been to pick up the SAVANNAH team 15 days later from the Golfe-de-Morbihan, using a chartered refugee mackerel drifter from Audierne named *La-Brise*, one of those fishing out of Newlyn and available to de Gaulle's Deuxième Bureau through Lequien.[6] One of the team, Sergeant Joel Le Tac, had some familiarity with small boats from childhood holidays spent at Saint-Pabu on the Aber-Benoît estuary, where his parents had a villa, and he was sent down to Newlyn with Geoffrey Appleyard of SOE to discuss details. However, a row developed between SOE and Passy and it was decided that Appleyard and two other-ranks personnel trained for amphibious operations should be sent in the British submarine *Tigris* to evacuate them from a beach to the south of Saint-Gilles-Croix-de-Vie, near Les-Sables-d'Olonne. Only three of the five-man SAVANNAH team, including Le Tac and Lieutenant Bergé, its commander, got to the beach on the first night on which the submarine was expected. Having flashed the agreed light signal in vain, they had to make themselves inconspicuous for a further four days in Les-Sables-d'Olonne before the second attempt to embark them was due. The same trio returned to the beach on the night of 4/5 April 1941 and repeated the light signal until the end of the agreed period. When they were about to leave the beach for the second and last time, in low spirits, a shadow appeared on their left and showed a shaded blue light: it was Appleyard in a Folboat canoe. He explained that, on the night of 30/31 March, the three canoes that were to pick them up had been carried by a current on to a rocky point and two of them had been so damaged that they had to be abandoned. Appleyard had had to use his own undamaged Folboat to rescue their two crewmen and get them back to the *Tigris*. He could therefore now embark only two passengers in this surviving canoe. Bergé and Forman, the other member of the SAVANNAH team, clambered aboard, while Le Tac kept the canoe's head to sea. He pushed them off through the breakers. There was a vague promise to come back for him. With no great illusions, he stayed on the beach flashing the signal until day began to break. He then made his way to Paris where he had friends in the Free French 'Copernic' intelligence network. He did not have long to wait before an opportunity arose to join, and indeed play a decisive part in, another SOE-sponsored Free French *coup de main* operation named JOSEPHINE B, which destroyed the transformers supplying current to the submarine base at Bordeaux.

The trouble, from SIS's point of view, was that SOE, not content to wait for resistance to develop spontaneously, saw itself as a striking force whose blows would help convince opinion in occupied Europe that Great Britain was fighting on and was neither beaten nor cowed. This was why they planned small-scale raids on targets accessible from the sea as well as landing agents and cargoes of arms and explosives for subsequent use. The conflict of interest between the two services, both mandated at the highest level to pursue incompatible objectives, surfaced at a meeting on 16 December 1940 to coordinate the activities of SIS, SOE and Combined Operations. The SIS representative said there and then that his service was 'against raiding parties as they might interfere with their organisation for getting agents into occupied territory.' The implication, as the official historian of SOE in France pointed out, was clear: commando raids and SOE attacks on coastal targets might imperil work of a different, and perhaps greater, strategic importance.[7]

Holdsworth's recommendation to set up a 'transport outfit' to run clandestine sea lines to Brittany because, as he put it, 'other people kept letting them down', was, on the face of it, no more preposterous an ambition than that of Slocum, of Dunderdale or of the Free French to do the same thing. Indeed SOE was proceeding to organise sea lines to Norway from the Shetlands on just this basis, using refugee Norwegian fishing boats and crews. Though the distances were considerable and the weather in winter – the only season when cover of darkness was available in those high latitudes

– atrocious, the Norwegian fishing fleet was so large and the indented coastline so difficult to defend that the venture was eminently successful. In fact, the scale of SOE's operations from Lunna Voe rapidly outstripped that of the separate series of missions conducted by Slocum's representative for SIS. By 1944 it was SIS who had to hitch lifts from SOE in the American submarine-chasers that had by then, thanks to the Office of Strategic Services (OSS), replaced the fishing boats. Nor was this the only area where SOE catered for its own sea-transport needs: it ran dhows in the Red Sea and a flotilla of caiques and schooners in the Aegean. But Brittany was different and SOE found SIS prepared to go to great lengths to make sure that they acquired no such autonomy.

SOE became involved in an unusual paranaval operation to French waters, which was not in fact of its own devising. This was an enterprise code-named SHAMROCK, which took place at the end of November 1940. The moving spirit behind it was Merlin Minshall, an RNVR officer who belonged to the Admiralty's Naval Intelligence Division (NID) rather than SOE, though to carry it out he borrowed six French agents who were being trained for Leslie Humphreys's Section.[8] Minshall had taken part in the unsuccessful attempt to block the Danube at the Iron Gates, his participation being crowned by his drawing a pistol on the local Romanian chief of police in a night-club at Braila.

The immediate background to SHAMROCK appears to have been an argument within the NID about whether German U-boats had begun to operate from French Atlantic ports and, if so, how they might best be attacked when proceeding on, or returning from, patrol.

Minshall volunteered to lead a team of six who would be carried into the Bay of Biscay by a British submarine to capture a French fishing boat and use it to conduct the required reconnaissance. The team he picked for the job from Brickendonbury Hall included Marcel Clech, already the veteran of 11 unsuccessful attempts to land him in Brittany, and Jean Pillet, who subsequently joined the French navy and rose to the rank of Captain. They embarked on 16 November on HM S/m *Talisman* at Greenock.

Some days later, *Talisman* unsuccessfully attacked a German tanker off Lorient; one of the torpedoes hit the sea-bed before exploding. They were then subjected to a depth-charge counter-attack, which the submarine survived. At last they sighted a sailing-tunnyman some miles to the west of the Ile-de-Groix: because of wartime shortage of fuel she had been fitted out as a trawler and was on her way out to the fishing grounds. Minshall and the submarine's captain decided she would be a suitable prize. They surfaced, ordered the skipper and half the crew to row over and board the submarine, impressed the other half and put their SOE team on board the fishing boat as a prize crew. She was named *Le-Clipper* and had no auxiliary engine.

Minshall subsequently claimed that they observed the procedures used by U-boats entering and leaving the Gironde and his version found its way into the official history of SOE in France; but that river enters the Bay of Biscay 240 km. (150 miles) south of where the interception seems to have taken place and Pillet has recorded that, after interrogating the skipper, they started their passage northwards under sail, passing close to Groix, being escorted during that first night by *Talisman*. On 1 December, when they were 160 km. (100 miles) west of the Scillies, they were twice inspected by a Dornier seaplane, but fortunately they were on both occasions becalmed and appeared to be heading back to France. They made port at Falmouth safely on 5 December.

The interrogation of *Le-Clipper*'s crew no doubt resolved some of NID's queries, for Lorient had been brought into service as a U-boat base very promptly in July 1940 and, by August, Brest and La-Pallice were being similarly used. However, had Minshall really reconnoitred the Gironde estuary before heading for home, he would have found no German U-boats but instead ten Italian submarines, some of them large and of value to the German war effort as blockade-runners. Their number was doubled soon afterwards.

Minshall, who was in contact with Ian Fleming in NID, wrote a book in which he did not even mention the existence of the six SOE French members of the prize crew, giving the impression that he, a prototype of 007, sailed *Le-Clipper* back single-handed.

At Port-Tudy, *Le-Clipper*'s home port, her disappearance was attributed to her having sunk with all hands and no trace: the death of the seven members of her crew was officially declared by the administrator of the Inscription Maritime and their families went into mourning. But a German aircraft had happened to overfly *Le-Clipper* at a time when the crew were engaged in changing the ship's name and the Occupation authorities were suspicious about the disappearance of LGX 3501. The crew's wives were called to the Kommandatur several times and questioned, but they all asserted, and indeed believed, that their husbands had been lost at sea. They were duly dumbfounded when the missing men arrived back in Groix in July 1945.

Professor M.R.D. Foot expressed surprise in the official history that SOE should have been involved in an operation so clearly mounted to acquire intelligence, but presumably it was the fact that they had agents trained and qualified to take part in a piratical *coup de main* that made them a suitable, though subordinate, participant in a project devised by NID. SOE were however themselves the prime movers in setting up a small-scale amphibious raiding party entitled *Maid Honor* Force – and this was exactly the type of enterprise that SIS saw as a threat to their interests.

Brigadier Colin Gubbins, SOE's director of training and operations, was much involved in this project. He had a pre-war army background as a training specialist and had written a handbook on guerilla warfare for MI(R), the War Office think-tank on unconventional warfare. During the Norwegian campaign, he had commanded the Independent Companies, precursors of the Commandos. While there he had demonstrated the value of small raids from local fishing vessels as a means of disrupting communications behind the enemy's lines. No doubt he would have gone on to occupy an important position in the new Combined Operations set-up had fate not placed him next to Dr Dalton, the Minister of Economic Warfare, at dinner one evening soon after his return from Norway. Dalton had just won his battle to take charge of the new SOE and Gubbins impressed him in much the same way as de Gaulle had earlier impressed Churchill. Gubbins's drive, enthusiasm for unconventional warfare and experience as a specialist in training were exactly what were needed to launch SOE into action. Dalton arranged for him to join the new organisation at the end of 1940.[9]

He brought with him into SOE from Combined Operations a dashing, romantic and high-handed Gunner Captain named Gustavus March-Phillipps who, early in 1941, put forward a scheme for small-scale raids against enemy territory. His intention was to help develop resistance movements in France and elsewhere by demonstrating Great Britain's vitality and determination to strike at Hitler's New Order, by establishing personal contact with local patriots and bringing back information. An ardent and impecunious Catholic, cast in the mould of the warrior saints or the recusant martyrs, he had before the war been a professional kennel huntsman, so that he could indulge his taste for fox-hunting, and a professional racing driver, so as to pursue another favourite sport beyond the limits of his financial means. He was also a keen yachtsman and, after joining SOE, proceeded to requisition a 65-ton Brixham trawler yacht, the *Maid Honor*. He had no authority to do this, but told Baker Street that he was anxious to try out a sailing vessel for the type of operation he had in mind.[10]

Maid Honor was sailed up from Brixham to Poole and moved to Russell Quay on the Arne peninsula, a secluded part of that vast harbour, where March-Phillipps was joined by a nucleus of like-minded enthusiasts. After a number of experiments, the ship was refitted and armed. A crew was selected and trained: suitable boats for beach landings were acquired, all of which took longer than expected.

The Admiralty had refused permission for *Maid Honor* to

operate outside coastal waters until a specific project had been put up and approved. In June 1941, a plan worked out with the Dutch Section of SOE was submitted but turned down, which is not surprising given that March-Phillipps's intention had been to sail over to the vicinity of a major port, wait until a German vessel arrived to investigate his presence and, once she had been tempted into easy range, sink her with a concealed weapon variously known as the spigot-mortar or Blackler bombard. In addition to criticising the plan in detail, the Admiralty made it clear that they objected to giving information of a secret character to Army officers who might get captured; and that it was contrary to policy to place any restrictions on RAF attacks on shipping generally, even for the purpose of special operations of this kind.

It was evident that, for the time being at least, *Maid Honor* would not be allowed to operate in home waters at all and the scheme for small-scale raiding had to be temporarily abandoned. In July, SOE decided to transfer the ship and her crew, together with the rest of the unit 'Gus' had assembled and accommodated on two house-boats in his secluded anchorage, to their West African organisation, where March-Phillipps's burning desire to strike at the Germans was less likely to conflict with Admiralty policy and SIS's interests. She was seen off from Poole Harbour by Gubbins in person on 9 August with March-Phillipps in command and a crew of seven in all, three of whom were Danes. However, one of the Danes was chronically seasick and another did not measure up to expectations as a navigator, so March-Phillipps put into Dartmouth and landed them, continuing the voyage with a total crew of five. She reached Freetown via Funchal in six weeks, entirely under sail, where they were joined by the rest of the Force, who had travelled out by more conventional means.

SOE West Africa had already, in August 1941, put up a plan for the seizure of a German tug, the *Likomba*, and the immobilisation of an Italian cargo-liner, the *Duchessa d'Aosta*, lying in the harbour of Santa Isabel in the Spanish island of Fernando Po. March-Phillipps took over this scheme and, at midnight on 14 January 1942, his *Maid Honor* Force, augmented by civilian volunteers from Nigeria, carried out Operation POSTMASTER, a highly successful para-naval cutting-out expedition in which the *Duchessa d'Aosta*, the *Likomba* and a smaller German tug, the *Bibundi*, were towed to sea, while most of their crews were ashore at a party organised by a local SOE agent. The three ships, after various vicissitudes, reached Lagos as prizes.

In recognition of his part in this operation, which was a considerable stimulus to morale within SOE itself, March-Phillipps was awarded a DSO. A Danish private named Anders Lassen, who had been the only professional sailor in the *Maid Honor's* crew on the voyage out to Freetown, distinguished himself by being the first man to board the *Duchessa d'Aosta* and by his conspicuous efficiency in making the towing arrangements, while military members of the boarding party severed her moorings with explosive charges and mastered the skeleton crew, left behind while their colleagues went ashore. He was commissioned in the field and awarded an immediate MC: it was to prove the beginning of a remarkable military career.

Maid Honor, severely affected by teredo worm in her unsheathed bottom planking, was left to finish her days in Africa, but March-Phillipps and his unit, now styled the Small-Scale Raiding Force or 62 Commando, returned to Dorset and by the middle of 1942 were ready to begin attacks on targets in the Channel Islands and on the adjacent French coasts. These were now to be under the operational control of Combined Operations rather than SOE, which removed one potential source of friction between the two clandestine services; others, however, remained.

The anonymous SOE agent whom Slocum arranged for one of Dunderdale's boats to land near the Ile-Vierge on 28 March 1941 – the last successful operation by the Mylor flotilla – disappeared without trace. SOE's French Section preferred to remember their next agent, a W/T operator named Georges Begué, who was parachuted into France on 6 May 1941 near Valençay in the Indre. It is therefore at Valençay rather than at the Ile-Vierge that a memorial was unveiled 50 years later to commemorate 104 officers of SOE's Independent French Section who lost their lives on active service.

Slocum made a further five attempts in May and June 1941 to land three more agents for SOE's F Section to join the Vomécourt brothers' pioneer AUTOGYRO circuit, but none of these operations, mounted with another borrowed MTB, was successful. Two of these failures were recorded as due to bad weather, three to the agents' refusal to disembark. One of the three, Marcel Clech, had already been involved in all 16 of Slocum's unsuccessful MTB sorties for SOE, as well as in the abortive original attempt by No. 77 on 1 August 1940, and in Operation SHAMROCK, so it was certainly not a lack of courage and pertinacity on his part that prevented him from getting ashore at the Anse-de-Bréhec in the course of this series. This brave man was subsequently trained as a W/T operator and landed by felucca from Gibraltar on the south coast of France during the summer of 1942. He survived that first mission but was arrested in the course of a second. His is one of the names commemorated at Valençay.

Three of these five unsuccessful MTB operations at the Anse-de-Bréhec in May and June were combined with attempts to pick up Daniel Lomenech, who was on the run as a result of his activities in Dunderdale's 'Johnny' organisation.[11] A fourth and separate attempt to pick him up from the same pinpoint also failed. Thanks to W/T contact via Jean Le Roux, the radio operator and second in command of the ALLAH mission, Lomenech was in the end evacuated on 2 July 1941 by the British submarine *Sea Lion.* Her rendezvous with the Saint-Guénolé fishing vessel *Vincent-Michelle* took place 20 miles south-west of the Pointe-de-Penmarc'h. Lomenech had been brought out from his native Pont-Aven on a much smaller boat and transferred to the *Saint-Guénolé* ship, which was authorised to remain at sea overnight, at a pre-arranged meeting off the Glénan Islands. The other people evacuated on this occasion included Passy's agent Jacques Mansion, who had hoped to leave with Milon in April from Plouha on the north coast by *L'Émigrant* – the voyage on which she was captured; Henri Péron, part owner of the *Vincent-Michelle,* a chemist by profession, who was in imminent danger of arrest, having rejected a German proposal to use her to carry out a clandestine mission to Cork on their behalf; and the Comte Michel de Kerdrel, whose parents owned the Château de Kérembleis on the Odet between Bénodet and Quimper. His father had represented the French state railways in London before the war and his mother was English. He used her maiden name of Halsey when he joined the RAF and was killed in action. The *Vincent-Michelle* took back to Saint-Guénolé mail, W/T sets and money from Dunderdale for the 'Johnny' organisation.

This operation was a considerable technical achievement in that it involved coordinated action by the two fishing boats and then a rendezvous with the submarine at sea far out of sight of land. The Admiralty had questioned whether a fishing boat's navigation would be accurate enough to make this possible. The successful outcome opened up the possibility of subsequent operations, in which submarines patrolling off the Goulet-de-Brest in the hope of intercepting the *Scharnhorst, Gneisenau* and *Prinz Eugen,* could be used to collect mail from 'Johnny'.

Daniel Lomenech, like Moreau before him, had been compromised as an agent and could not return to France, but he went back to the Bay of Biscay twice in July on submarines to collect reports from the *Vincent-Michelle.* Both these attempts failed owing to difficulties experienced by the 'Johnny' agents concerned, but the operation, code-named VALISE, was eventually carried out on 16 September at a rendezvous with the Loctudy boat *Voltaire* (Pierre Dréau and Jean Bonoure) 65 km. (40 miles) south-west of Penmarc'h. Lomenech was aboard HM S/m *P37* to identify the agents concerned. There was a further successful rendezvous at sea on 27 November when Alaterre, three other men and a consignment of mail were embarked from the *Veac'h-Vad* (Sébastien Briec). But the submarines used in these VALISE operations had all been deployed

on offensive patrols in the approaches to Brest because of the
presence in the dockyard of the three big German ships and SIS
knew that they could not reckon on their being available as often,
and as long, as the mail-run from 'Johnny' required. One further
attempt was made in January 1942 by HM S/m *Tuna* to pick up an
agent and the mail, but the operation was cancelled by the agent at
the last moment when the submarine had already reached the
rendezvous area. The most she could achieve was to interrogate
other trawlers working in the vicinity.

The submarines were withdrawn once the German ships had
escaped up the Channel on 12 February 1942, but Daniel
Lomenech and Steven Mackenzie, Slocum's staff officer in charge
of operations from bases in the United Kingdom, had been working
for some time on an alternative scheme for maintaining sea lines to
the west coast by fishing vessels. Indeed one such operation had
been attempted already at Christmas 1941. It failed, but in circumstances that suggested that access to the area south of Penmarc'h
was still perfectly possible with the right ship and the right crew.

CHAPTER IX

SOE's Endeavours to Set up Independent Sea Transport to Brittany, 1941

G erry Holdsworth, whom Section D had sent to Newlyn on 1 August 1940 to take charge of the attempt to land their first three agents from the lumbering and unsuitable Belgian yacht, had been a cadet on a rubber plantation in Borneo, but the Depression that afflicted the world economy in 1929 brought him back to England, where he found work making films for an advertising agency.[1] He became part-owner of a Bristol Channel pilot-cutter yacht named *Mischief* and, when Section D was set up in 1938, he was one of a very select group of members of the Royal Cruising Club who were recruited to survey, and familiarise themselves with, parts of the continental coastline that might be of strategic significance in wartime. They were a distinguished company of amateur sailors including Frank Carr, Assistant Librarian of the House of Lords, who sailed another Bristol Channel pilot cutter; Roger Pinckney, architect of Melbourne Cathedral, who, with his mother, owned and sailed the Laurent Giles-designed *Dyarchy*; as well as Augustine Courtauld, the Arctic explorer, who sailed a handsome Fife yawl named *Duet*. Holdsworth's allotted task covered part of the Norwegian coast but, in the autumn of 1939, when war had begun, he was given a short course in demolition techniques by a sapper major in the St Ermin's Hotel, and sent to Norway under commercial cover to see how and where the flow of Swedish iron ore from Narvik to the Ruhr might best be disrupted; and how explosives for the purpose might be infiltrated by fishing vessels either via the Shetlands or direct from Aberdeen. This was viewed in Whitehall and in Paris as an operation of high strategic importance and when Menzies, the new Chief of the Secret Service, first called on Churchill, then First Lord of the Admiralty, on 11 December 1939 it was to discuss this very subject.

The idea stemmed from Churchill's friend, the Canadian industrialist 'Little Bill' Stephenson in New York. It was eventually decided that the best point of attack was not in Norway, from which the ore traffic was vulnerable to Allied naval patrols, but in Sweden at Oxelösund, the country's northernmost ice-free port, where ore was loaded on to ships after rail transport from the mines. Section D's agents, led by a man named Rickman, set about building up a stock of explosives but they were badly informed and had no idea how to attack the German-built ore-loading machinery; nor did they realise that the advent of new big ice-breakers meant that ports further north on the Gulf of Bothnia could be kept open, so that Oxelösund's importance was no longer what had been supposed. By the end of the winter of 1939–40 no attack had been mounted. In April, while German and Allied forces grappled with each other in Norway, the Swedish police arrested Rickman and his accomplices on suspicion of conducting propaganda and they discovered the stock of explosive. Holdsworth, who had only recently arrived in Stockholm, was also arrested, but he was carrying a diplomatic courier's passport and was released within the hour. He was able to make his way out via Finland and take passage home as a deckhand on an iron-ore carrier from Petsamo to Barrow-in-Furness. He was lucky to have emerged from what a friend in the British Legation has castigated as a disastrously stupid and appallingly badly handled affair. Rickman was less fortunate: he spent the war years in a Swedish prison.

Back in England, Holdsworth was put to work by Section D organising stay-behind resistance under Home Guard cover in East Anglia, at a time when the lost battle of France made German invasion seem very likely. From here, being one of the few people in Section D who had experience of small boats, he was summoned to Newlyn. In the autumn of 1940, he was asked; no doubt for the same reason, to create better-organised facilities to enable SOE to conduct its own sea-transport operations to Brittany, as he had recommended. In October 1940 he was authorised to obtain the necessary ships, recruit personnel and find a suitable base. He was given the sum of £1,000 to cover the cost of fitting-out.

Holdsworth's plan as regards the west coast was to use French fishing boats, with picked British naval crews and an admixture of Breton pilots and fishermen, to contact the fishing fleets working on the banks off that coast, with a view to obtaining information, and eventually to land supplies and arms to the Resistance.

Holdsworth arranged for two refugee French craft to be requisitioned. His first choice fell upon a robust 60-ton yawl named *Mutin*. She was not in fact a fishing boat, having been built for, and used by, the French navy as a training ship for the petty officer coastal pilots carried by all French naval vessels of more than a certain size. She had however been built at Les-Sables-d'Olonne on similar lines to those of the local sailing-tunnymen, several hundred of which were still working in the Bay of Biscay at that time, making a magnificent spectacle with their many-coloured sails. Not the least of *Mutin*'s attractions was that she already had a spacious mess-deck where the fish-hold would have been in a working fishing boat. She had an auxiliary motor, but it was unreliable and not very powerful. A suitable replacement was found: it was one of two German Deutz diesels that had arrived in England, still in their packing-cases, in a large, unfinished yacht, which had been building at Deauville for Ettore Bugatti, designer and builder of the famous racing cars, and which had been towed over to England during the exodus of June 1940. Holdsworth took *Mutin* to Dartmouth where she was refitted and re-engined at the Philips shipyard by the upper chain-ferry. The bill swallowed most of the money allocated for fitting out two boats.

Shortage of funds may have had much to do with his choice of his second vessel, which was a small motor long-liner from Honfleur in Normandy, named *Denise-Louise*. She was in good condition and required little conversion or repair. The idea was that she would be sent to Newlyn to try to earn her keep, as the boats employed by the Free French Deuxième Bureau were doing. Holdsworth clearly did not regard the fact that she was not a local Breton vessel as a significant drawback. No doubt he assumed that in wartime conditions fishing craft from ports further up the Channel, denied access to their normal fishing grounds, would be found working on the west coast. Considering the mixture of Belgian and Breton boats based on Newlyn at the time it was not an unreasonable assumption, but it proved controversial, since photographs brought back by RAF Coastal Command from their anti-submarine patrols in the Bay of Biscay showed nothing that looked like *Denise-Louise*.

The Admiralty agreed to let Holdsworth select 12 volunteer naval ratings from the Royal Naval Patrol Service depot at Lowestoft. These were peacetime fishermen and yacht-hands whom the Navy used to crew requisitioned steam trawlers, drifters and other minor war vessels. It was agreed that they would continue to draw naval pay and victuals but that Holdsworth would be free to employ them in civilian clothes at his discretion.

Holdsworth's first recruit, John Louis Newton, was in fact sent to him by Ian Fleming of NID: he was a physically diminutive but otherwise larger-than-life Guernsey fisherman and small-time smuggler. Newton was well known in his native island, where he was envied, admired and distrusted for an energy and resourcefulness that were no longer as common there as when the islanders lived by privateering, smuggling and the Nova Scotia cod-fishery. He had worked in summer as boatman for the Saumarez family, heirs to a distinguished 18th-century family naval tradition, and had been a favourite with lady guests at Saumarez Manor house parties. In June 1940, as France was falling, an emergency committee of Guernsey notables had sent the Admiralty a telegram asking for Newton to be released from naval service and sent home urgently: he was the only man who might be able and ready to smuggle food into the island during the impending German occupation. There was some delay in tracing Newton and, by the time he had been found, serving as a leading seaman in a minesweeping trawler at

Scapa Flow, and brought south, the Channel Islands had long since fallen into enemy hands. He was interviewed by Fleming, then special assistant to Rear Admiral John Godfrey, the Director of Naval Intelligence. Fleming concluded that Newton had potentially useful knowledge as a pilot in his home waters and that his buccaneering spirit of enterprise deserved greater scope. Knowing of Holdsworth's plans and need for crew, he sent Newton to see him and Holdsworth took him on immediately.

On 5 November 1940 Holdsworth called on the retired Admiral serving as Naval Officer-in-Charge at Falmouth and obtained his permission to establish a small base on the Helford River, whose long estuary, famed for its oysters, runs east and west across the landward side of the Lizard peninsula and opens into Falmouth Bay. The tide-water, overhung by scrubby oaks, flows deep into the countryside. The river forms a well-sheltered anchorage for small vessels, except when it blows hard from the east: in these conditions there is only one really sheltered berth – what would be called a 'hurricane hole' in the Caribbean – just inside the entrance to Port Navas Creek. Some God-fearing Cornish skipper of an earlier age endowed it with the evocative name 'Abraham's Bosom'. Daphne du Maurier's Frenchman's Creek lies a little higher up, on the opposite bank of the river. It was a beautiful and conveniently secluded place. At that stage the only other naval presence on the estuary was a Resident Naval Officer called Herbert Warington Smyth, mining engineer, barrister, artist and author, who had retired to 'Calamansack', a picturesque bungalow hidden among the oaks above Port Navas Creek. He went about his naval duties in a smart little St Ives motor fishing boat, the *Nazarène*, which was his own property.

Holdsworth first took over a house at Helston to serve as shore base, but it proved inconveniently far upstream and only accessible at high water, so he moved to another on the north bank just above Helford Passage, overlooking a pool where the ships could lie afloat at all states of the tide. 'Ridifarne' was the summer retreat of a family which manufactured the Bickford fuse, originally developed for Cornish mining and quarrying needs, but destined to become widely known in enemy-occupied territories as an essential ingredient in SOE's demolition charges.

For direct landings, the north coast of Brittany offered obvious advantages since the sea passage involved was much shorter, but, after the loss of Dunderdale's *Emigrant*, it was clear that high-speed craft, such as the MTBs Slocum had been borrowing from Coastal Forces, were required. The acquisition of a vessel fast enough to cross the Channel in reasonable safety, disembark or pick up agents and return to base under cover of the darkness of a single night, proved a matter of immense difficulty: the Admiralty, which was still denying Slocum exclusive use of any craft of this type, apart from a small 63-foot motor anti-submarine boat (MA/SB 36), was even more unwilling to meet Holdsworth's needs. The best he could achieve was a diminutive 41'6" RAF seaplane-tender, RAF 360, which the RAF had made available in the hope it might be a means of rescuing shot-down aircrew. Holdsworth found it difficult to acknowledge help from Slocum, whom he regarded as hostile to SOE's needs, but the records show that RAF 360, had been used by Slocum for a trip to Belgium on 23 June 1940, long before she was passed on to Holdsworth. It is therefore probable that it was Slocum, finding her too small for his requirements, who made her available to SOE.

RAF 360 belonged to a class developed for the RAF by Hubert Scott-Paine's British Power Boat Company at Hythe on South-ampton Water. T.E. Lawrence (Lawrence of Arabia), in the guise of 'Aircraftman Shaw', worked with this firm on developing marine craft for the RAF's needs when he was stationed at Calshot, and may well have been involved in the trials of 360's prototype. She was really too slow, too small and too vulnerable for the work Holdsworth hoped to carry out for SOE. While handy for man-oeuvring in rock-strewn waters such as abound on the Brittany coast, her small size was a handicap in that it allowed no room on deck for any form of rigid boat and the wheelhouse forward lacked space for satisfactory navigational facilities. Her top speed in smooth water was a bare 20 knots and, when laden down with additional fuel, stores and personnel for an operation, her cruising speed, even under the most favourable conditions, was no better than 15. This meant that, like the much bigger 'C'-class motor gunboats, she could not operate safely across the Channel during the short summer nights. What is more, her smallness and her large cockpit, at the forward end of which her two 100 h.p. Perkins diesels were installed, made her very vulnerable to bad weather. It was therefore both difficult and hazardous to operate her in winter across the widest and most exposed part of the English Channel to a coast notorious for its strong tides, which quickly raise a steep sea when wind and tide are in conflict. Her fuel-tank capacity gave her a range of just 160 km. (100 miles) – enough to get her across from Helford to the north-western tip of Brittany, but her tanks had to be replenished for the return passage from 40-gallon drums of diesel oil carried in the cockpit, using a semi-rotary hand pump, a slow and slippery job if any sort of a sea was running. Her only armament was a pair of Vickers gas-operated .303 machine-guns mounted on a steel stanchion in the middle of the cockpit. If used against a surface target, the field of fire was restricted by the coach-roof and any boat carried on top of it. There was absolutely no form of armoured protection for anything or anybody, which would have made her a remarkably soft target for a prowling E-boat, convoy escort or enemy aircraft. But it was Hobson's choice. Small and vulnerable she undoubtedly was, but to Slocum, who had not had a successful operation on the north coast for a year, she represented a potential he was now ready to use for SIS's needs. Holdsworth too could derive advantage from her capacity to operate to the north coast of Brittany independently for SOE, until something larger and more suitable became available.

As far as relations with SIS were concerned, it was a grave complication that SOE continued to take the view that it could legitimately use clandestine sea transport to France to land raiding parties and cargoes of arms and explosives as well as agents. SOE's basic objectives in France, as elsewhere, were offensive, and Leslie Humphreys, miscast as an executant of Churchill's mandate to set Europe ablaze, had been moved over at the beginning of December 1940 to concentrate on clandestine communications, a task well suited to his temperament and abilities. He was replaced as head of SOE's Independent French Section first by H.R. Marriott and in due course by Maurice Buckmaster.

CHAPTER X

April–November 1941

T owards the end of April 1941 – the month in which Dunderdale's *L'Émigrant*, alias *Le-Petit-Marcel*, had been lost – Holdsworth's *Denise-Louise*, which had been trying to build up cover as a
commercial fishing boat working out of Newlyn, was sent on a
reconnaissance of the fishing grounds west of Ushant. The thinking
behind this was that ships met at sea might be used to infiltrate
arms. The sortie had to be cut short because of engine trouble and
was therefore inconclusive. An attempt to conduct a night reconnaissance of the same area using ML 107, in conjunction with
aircraft flown from St Eval, was equally unproductive. The air
search was carried out in a Hudson aircraft of 54 Squadron by
Slocum's liaison officer with RAF Coastal Command, a retired
naval officer named W.B. Luard.

Luard had been invalided out of the Navy soon after the First
World War with a tubercular hip, which had followed injury in a
submarine accident.[1] He had become interested in the Breton
fishing industry while having a yacht built at Carentec in 1929
for the then new sport of ocean racing. He augmented his small
naval disability pension by writing novels and articles for *Blackwood's
Magazine* and he had made voyages, both on a Concarneau sailing-
tunnyman and in a Hull trawler to Bear Island, in search of
material. Having raced across the Atlantic in 1931 and taken part
in several gruelling Fastnet Races, he was chagrined that his 100 per
cent disability pension prevented him from being recalled for active
service on the outbreak of war. He lived at Falmouth and, with his
Breton background, did not take long to conclude that Dunderdale's boats at Mylor were crossing to and from Brittany in the
autumn of 1940. Here, he felt, was a field in which his knowledge
might be put to good use.

The author knew Luard well from before the war, when they
worked together in the building of several yachts in Cornish yards
to the author's designs. When he was sent to Falmouth in October
1940 in command of *Sevra*, a 400-ton whale-catcher that had been
brought back from South Georgia and converted into a magnetic
minesweeper, they were quickly in touch. Luard begged the author
to take him to sea so that he could write an article about this new
form of minesweeping, if censorship allowed. Luard was thus on
board *Sevra* when she was sunk on the morning of Guy Fawkes Day
1940 by an acoustic mine – then a new hazard – while completing

the daily search for aircraft-laid magnetic mines in the approach channel to Falmouth Harbour. By curious coincidence, just at that moment Holdsworth was calling on the Naval Officer-in-Charge at Falmouth to ask permission to set up his small base on the Helford River, and he witnessed the event from the windows of the Admiral's office at the Bay View Hotel. Luard, of course, should not have been on board *Sevra*, but fortunately, though bruised and shaken, he sustained no serious injury. The author had a broken leg and when Luard hobbled round to see him next day in the little Seamen's Hospital at Falmouth they set to wondering how to get themselves involved in whatever was going on with Brittany. They decided that the best gambit would be to write a joint paper on the use of refugee fishing boats as a means of making contact with German-occupied France; this, they hoped, would draw attention to Luard's genuine knowledge of the Breton fisheries and to the author's readiness to volunteer for work of this kind. The paper, forwarded through the local naval headquarters, must have passed through Slocum's in-tray, since he offered Luard the St Eval liaison job quite early in 1941. The timing is itself of interest, as Slocum's operations section had thus far had only a limited involvement in the Bay of Biscay, which is where Coastal Command's submarine-hunting patrols were of potential relevance. Luard was given an honorarium of only £100 per annum from the Secret Vote, to add to his disability pension, and a petrol allowance to enable him to drive to and from St Eval, but he was allowed to return to uniform as a rather over-age Lieutenant RN, which meant a lot to him. His main contact at St Eval was Squadron Leader Edward Shackleton, son of the Antarctic explorer and future member of the House of Lords, who, as the station Intelligence Officer, arranged for the regular anti-submarine patrol Hudsons of 54 Squadron to observe and photograph the French and Spanish fishing boats they encountered. The joint reconnaissance in May by ML 107 and Luard in a Hudson was, however, no more rewarding than *Denise-Louise*'s foray the month before: the tunny fishermen were mainly to be found, so early in the season, on the edge of the Continental Shelf much deeper down in the Bay, though mackerel-drifters from Audierne and Douarnenez were sometimes to be found in that latitude.

ML 107 was yet another in the long series of Slocum's borrowings from Coastal Forces. She was an 'A'-Class Fairmile boat, 33.5 metres (110 feet) long and therefore considerably bigger than the Coastal Forces craft previously available to him, but the Class, which had hard-chined hulls and were designed for higher speeds than their immediate and numerous successors, the round-bottomed 'B'-Class Fairmiles, was not reckoned a success and production was rapidly halted. This presumably explained why Slocum had her at his disposal for at least four months in the summer of

1941, though he got little operational work out of her and she seems not to have been used for the four abortive sorties to the Anse-de-Bréhec in May and June that failed to evacuate Lomenech. She was, however, sent on 11 September to escort the lightly armed RAF 360 on Holdsworth's first operation with that diminutive vessel.

The author had at that point been summoned from a mine-sweeping job at Hartlepool and interviewed at the Admiralty about the paper he had written with Luard. Confirming that he was indeed a volunteer for special duties, he was appointed as Holdsworth's second in command at Helford in place of Vann, the Belgian RNVR officer who had been sent in June 1940 to look for de Gaulle's family but who was now being transferred to SO1 to work on political warfare. The author arrived at Helford just in time for an operation in RAF 360, whose code name was POLISH: it was not for SOE but for Dunderdale's Section of SIS.

Dunderdale's Polish Deuxième Bureau friends had at that stage an extensive intelligence network built up by a Polish Air Force officer, Roman Garby-Czerniawski. Though based on Paris, it had coverage of a number of major ports and has passed into history as 'Interallié', though its offshoots in Brittany were known to those working in them as F1 and F2. A consignment of clandestine mail from this organisation was to be picked up at a nocturnal rendez-vous with a small boat off a rock named Le-Trépied, which was crowned with a latticed steel sea-mark and lay at the eastern entrance to the Channel between the Ile-de-Batz and the mainland at the north-western extremity of Morlaix Bay.

Since trials with ML 107 had proved disappointing, it was decided to use RAF 360 for the job, but to send ML 107 to escort her at a discreet distance. During the final approach, which on this occasion had to be made after moonrise, the ML was to stay well offshore, as she was both noisy and far more conspicuous than 360. The timing was critical, as the local boat had to drop down the Penzé River on the last of the ebb tide under the noses of the Germans patrolling the low cliffs and woods to the west of the estuary, meet 360 at slack water and return home on the first of the flood tide – all by moonlight and without attracting attention – no mean task, it seems in retrospect.

RAF 360 had an RAF grid compass which her naval quarter-masters found confusing at first: her sole other navigational aids were a sophisticated Chernikeef log and an echo sounder. As navigator, the author had worked out in advance the tidal sets to be expected hour by hour during the crossing. No navigational lights would be working on the enemy coast unless one of their convoys was in the vicinity. It would be necessary therefore to make an identifiable landfall by moonlight, a practice subsequently abandoned as too dangerous for inshore approaches, so that clandestine contacts by sea normally took place in the no-moon period, while RAF Lysander pick-ups were planned for moonlight conditions.

Unless a landfall was immediately recognisable, first visual contact with the coast required difficult decisions: a wrong choice of course at that juncture could mean losing so much time that the night's work would be wasted. On this occasion, one of the salient landmarks on the north coast of Brittany, the lighthouse on the Ile-de-Batz, offered itself as an ideal target, though it lay to the west of the rendezvous: if they could pick up the tall, but now normally unlit, tower in the moonlight from a safe distance offshore, all would be well, for they would know exactly where they were; they would still have to stem the last hour of a spring ebb tide for their final approach to Le-Trépied at reduced speed, using 360's improvised underwater exhaust-silencers. That was unavoidable for there was no landmark further to the east capable of being identified at a distance of 8–10 km. (5 or 6 miles).

In view of the importance of exact timing, they made an early start from the Helford River so as to make the crossing with a reserve of speed in hand. Their limit of 15 knots meant that they would be half-way to France by nightfall, and they could only hope that the Luftwaffe would not fly a reconnaissance at last light across the all too visible wake of the two ships.

They were in luck: the sea was smooth; there was no German mid-Channel air patrol and the echo-sounder gave them good positions as they crossed the Hurd Deep. The moon had risen, unclouded and bright, as they closed in to the still-invisible coast. Pierre Guillet had volunteered to join the cross-Channel sortie: he had come to Helford to advise on how to fit *Mutin* out as a tunny fisherman after he had been taken off his own tunnyman by a British warship and brought in to Plymouth for interrogation. He sat on deck up forward, with his back against the shuttered wheelhouse windows, his eyes glued to a pair of night binoculars, scanning the horizon. At last his back straightened: yes, he had picked up the moonlit lighthouse tower, which is immensely tall. The author could see it too, almost dead ahead at the hoped-for distance of 8–10 km. Alter course to the eastward; down silencers; reduce speed. They began their crab-like approach across the tide in to Le-Trépied. The moon was embarrassingly bright: one could have read a newspaper by it without difficulty. The contrast was acute when one dived into the darkened wheelhouse to plot a running fix: only the glow of the compass and the shaded light on the chart table. Progress against the ebb tide was frustratingly slow, but they were still on schedule. It was Pierre again who eventually sighted the Trépied: he clearly knew every inch of that coast, though his home port was Noirmoutier, way down in the Bay of

Biscay. He had in fact been in the coasting trade at one stage of his life, but only a year later did it emerge that he held a master mariners' ticket in both sail and steam and as a young man had been round Cape Horn in a sailing ship.

They edged in towards the Trépied: surely they must be visible to any lookout on the coast or on the Ile-de-Batz. Then they saw the boat. A small single-masted sailing vessel, no bowsprit, no sail set. An old man with a beard stood aft sculling her with a long sweep. There was a much younger figure further forward. RAF 360 closed in with what seemed exaggerated caution, keeping the boat – 7 or 8 metres long at the most – covered with Thompson sub-machine guns. A packet was handed across. Holdsworth disappeared below to make sure it did not contain a bomb: he was better versed than the author in the ways of the clandestine *demi-monde*. Then the two boats drifted apart, with waved farewells as they went their respective ways: the Bretons to catch the flood tide back; RAF 360 to join ML 107, which had waited offshore and fell in astern as they set course back to Helford for breakfast and bed. It was the first successful operation to France by high-speed craft for 13 months.

There was a comic interlude as they landed on the beach below the house that served as SOE's shore base: they were intercepted by an elderly customs officer who had been redeployed from Dover or some other port because the suspension of normal cross-Channel sailings had left nothing for the water-guard to do. He demanded to see the contents of the precious bag of clandestine mail that Holdsworth was carrying. Holdsworth refused point-blank, but, when next in London, he did have to call on the head of the customs service and get from him a licence granting him immunity from inspection for the duration of the war.

By September 1941, the Belgian coast and the coast of north-eastern France had been highly fortified and it had become necessary to land agents either east of the Scheldt or west of Cherbourg. This made Dover and Portsmouth less suitable as departure points than Felixstowe and Dartmouth, which became then and remained for the rest of the war the main bases used by Slocum for operations by high-speed craft to Holland, on the one hand, and the north coast of Brittany, on the other. Great Yarmouth and Falmouth were also used when pinpoints lay near the Hook or Brest.

During the winter of 1941–42 a long series of operations was carried out to the Dutch coast, in spite of the difficulties experienced by agents in penetrating enemy defences on shore and by ships in finding exact pinpoints on the featureless coast. On 23 November MGB 320, after eight false starts, landed a Netherlands navy signalman in the lee of the pier at Scheveningen, a major coastal resort. Eight successful operations to this pinpoint followed. It was known that the nearby Palace Hotel had been taken over by the Germans as an officers' mess and that the area was frequented by late-night revellers, so one agent was landed there wearing full evening dress with a specially designed rubber oversuit to keep his clothes dry while wading ashore. If challenged by a sentry, he was to pretend to be a drunken guest from the mess taking some fresh air; to sustain him in this role he carried an empty champagne bottle. On another occasion, a Dutch officer who accompanied an operation to embark some of his friends on the 'Scheveningen ferry', walked into town to telephone them as they had not appeared on the beach. Wearing British naval uniform, he was seen and illuminated on the front by a Dutch policeman who said 'Good evening' and passed on! Unfortunately this successful run ended when the Germans arrested the reception committee; if they had stayed longer, they might have captured the landing party and, with Kriegsmarine help, MGB 320 as well. This was only the beginning of a two-year series of disasters that struck both SIS and SOE networks in Holland. The extent of the penetration, to which the Germans gave the code name NORDPOL, was not revealed until the end of 1943. After the war it was the subject of a Dutch parliamentary commission of enquiry, to which three SIS officers gave evidence.

At the other end of the Channel, Slocum made arrangements to set up a permanent base at Dartmouth. His representative, Lt E.A.G. Davis, RNR, was appointed for cover purposes to the staff of the local Naval Officer-in-Charge, but he was in fact directly responsible to Slocum in London. He was joined by Lt Angus Letty, RNR, who had taken part in all the Dutch operations as navigating and conducting officer.

Operations to Brittany during the winter of 1941–42 were mainly carried out by 'C'-Class Fairmile motor gunboats, with occasional use of MA/SB 36 (motor anti-submarine boat), which was smaller and faster, but mainly used as a 'dispatch boat' for SIS communications needs in home waters. MGBs 325 and 319 were used until December and between them made five unsuccessful attempts to repeat RAF 360's Operation POLISH; while 360 had gone on in mid-October to carry out a second successful operation from Helford, this time to Aber-Benoît.

Davis had been navigating officer on the Cunard liner *Queen Mary* on a pre-war round-the-world cruise and had joined Slocum's Section in September 1941 as commanding officer of a converted trawler named *Breeze*.

His record of Operation CELERY, using MA/SB 36, the largest high-speed vessel permanently allocated to Slocum's Section at that stage, is of more than passing interest for the light it throws on the unsuitability of the craft and the lack of training of her crew. The object was to enable an agent to paddle himself ashore in Morlaix

Bay in a Folboat canoe. This unidentified agent probably belonged to the Free French service as his departure was arranged by Commander Cohen's section of SIS with which Passy had close liaison.

MA/SB 36 sailed at 1617 hrs on 20 November. When she passed through the gate in the protective boom at the mouth of the Dart five minutes later, she encountered a fresh south-westerly wind, with a moderate sea and swell, which made heavy going for a chine-bottomed craft of her type. At 1640 the crew began to assemble the canoe – something that would have been far better done in harbour before sailing. Only then was it discovered that some of the ribs belonging to the canoe's framework were broken and that warping of the constituent parts made assembly difficult. The screws and wing-nuts provided could consequently not be fitted and wire lashings had to be used instead. While this was being done, the ship had to be kept running before the sea and by the time the job was completed 20 minutes later they had made a considerable detour and fetched up off Berry Head close to Brixham.

Davis then set course to bring Start Point abeam at a distance of 4 km. (2½ miles) and took his departure from this point. She was making 18.4 knots with the engines opened up to 1,400 r.p.m., but this was reduced to 1,200 r.p.m. at 2301 hrs and to 1,000 at 2339 hrs. At 2341 hrs the centre engine was stopped. The boat itself had frequently to be stopped to allow the horizon to be swept with the night binoculars. The continual spray made this impossible when underway. MA/SB 36's mean course was about S13°W.

At 0031 hrs rocks were sighted on the starboard beam and the ship was stopped. There was a loom of land on the starboard bow. Davis concluded they must be to the east of the Pointe-de-Primel. Course was altered to north-west at 0034 and to west at 0049. At 0056 Davis had speed reduced to 800 r.p.m. and course brought round to S80°W. At 0111 the engines were throttled right back and at 0136 the starboard engine was stopped. Land was visible ahead to 60° on the starboard bow. At 0140 course was altered to S25°W: rocks were visible to starboard and two white lights were observed bearing south. Three minutes later Davis had the ship stopped again to allow the position to be checked. The agent verified the land to starboard as the Ile-de-Batz before they proceeded further to southward. At 0146 the boat was stopped and the canoe was lowered into the water. The agent clambered down, took his seat on the bottom boards of the canoe and was away at 0153. A minute later Davis had the boat's head brought round to N11°W to get a clearer view of the land. The night was very dark and the weather was freshening.

At 0211 course was again altered to N16°E, but not until 0245 did Davis order the starboard engine to be started. The tip of the land then bore almost astern. At 0250 the centre engine was restarted and speed gradually increased. At 0416 an aircraft dropped a green flare astern and speed was increased to clear the illuminated area, but nothing was heard. The wind was SSW force 6, the sea rough, swell moderate to heavy, sky 10/10 with showers.

At approximately 0755 they were back off Start Point and at 0832 they entered the gate in the boom at Dartmouth.

Davis reported to Slocum that the boat had throughout been lively in the extreme. On the southward passage bumping was bad but speed had to be maintained owing to the time factor and poor visibility. The view from the bridge was very poor, the two Lewis gun 'dustbins', searchlight, mast and rigging, signal halyards and compasses wooding most of the horizon to about 75° on each bow. Spray was continual and the boat had to be stopped to allow a clear view. Communications from the bridge to the coxswain were poor. Facilities for chart work were negligible.

Officers and men stood up to the buffeting very well indeed and remained cheerful throughout. Little provision had been made for hot drinks and food. Organisation in the boat appeared to be slap-happy: the crew moved about constantly; men left gun positions without permission, apparently causing no comment whatsoever; and one or two of them fell asleep on watch, which did not elicit an 'imperial raspberry' but only a reminder to stay awake. The coxswain stood out favourably from the rest of the crew. The officers suffered from a sad lack of experience.

The men RAF 360 had met at sea on Operation POLISH were 71-year-old Jacques Guéguen and his son François.[2] Guéguen was arrested by the Germans on 31 January 1941 as the result of an indiscretion concerning his earlier evacuation operations in his little sand-barge *Pourquoi-Pas?* At the time of his arrest, he had been preparing to ship out a consignment of mail for Garby-Czerniawski's Polish 'Interallié' intelligence network and he had imprudently left this compromising material in a drawer in his house. Anne Le Duc, the young and attractive wife of a Morlaix doctor, who had himself been arrested at the same time as Guéguen, had the presence of mind to find and destroy this *courrier*, as it was termed. She then sent a man to stand outside Morlaix Prison, where Guéguen and Dr Le Duc were being held, and shout in Breton, which the Germans could not understand, that their captors would find nothing incriminating when they searched Guéguen's house. Thus the prisoners could and did safely deny any charges brought against them, and were accordingly released a month later for lack of evidence, which enabled them to resume their Resistance activities. The exception was a 16-year-old-boy, who had been found with a plan of a German airbase in his possession; he was executed.

At the beginning of 1942, Guéguen found himself in prison again condemned to two months' detention, under suspicion of anti-German activities. He was temporarily released because of his age and chronic rheumatism. When summoned to present himself at Rennes Prison on 14 February 1942 to serve the rest of his sentence, he asked his friend Ernest Sibiril, the boat-builder from Carentec who had helped him by repairing the engine of *Pourquoi-Pas?* at the end of June 1940, to help him and his son to escape to England. Sibiril consented and, on 10 February, the Guéguens sailed in a 7-metre-long fishing boat, the *André*, taking with them a Belgian intelligence officer named Van Hacker and Mme Bruley de Vourane, a senior French nursing sister.

They arrived at Fowey; and when the author read the Security Service interrogation report on their escape, he took 360 to Fowey where he had business to transact at the Polruan shipyard, and found Guéguen's boat lying at moorings half-full of water. Nobody seemed to want her so she was towed back to Helford, where she was repaired, had her rusty old auxiliary engine removed and was endowed with a new mainsail. Tom Long, one of Holdsworth's Leading Seamen, and his friend Pierre Guillet used her for fishing at the end of the day's work. Whatever the boat's original name, *Pourquoi-Pas?* was the name Guéguen used when he was interrogated at the Royal Patriotic School and what she was always called at Helford.

This was the first of a remarkable series of escapes, involving 173[3] people in all, that Ernest Sibiril and his father organised from their boatyard between February 1942 and February 1944 and which is now part of Breton folklore.

CHAPTER XI

October 1941–February 1942

Joël Le Tac, the member of the SAVANNAH team whom Geoffrey Appleyard had had to leave on the beach at St Gilles-Croix-de-Vie in April 1941, had got back to England via Spain in August after playing a key role in Operation JOSEPHINE B, an SOE-organised attack by a Gaullist team parachuted in to destroy the electrical transformers supplying the German and Italian submarine base at Bordeaux. The team, which had replaced a group of Polish parachutists who were originally briefed for the attack but were killed in a crash-landing of their aircraft, were initially daunted by the perimeter defences of the installation at Pessac, but when Le Tac joined them from Paris he quickly found a way round the difficulty. It was SOE's first success in the field of industrial sabotage in France. It had now been decided that Le Tac should return by sea from Helford to build up an organisation through which further infiltrations and exfiltrations could be conducted by sea, primarily for the Free French 'Service Action' which de Gaulle's Secret Service had set up as a counterpart to SOE and which, at this point, became part of a structure styled the Bureau Central de Renseignements et d'Action, or BCRA, under Passy.[1]

Joël's parents, both teachers, had a villa at Saint-Pabu, on the west side of the Aber-Benoît estuary at the north-western tip of the Breton peninsula. The family had spent their holidays there and knew the area extremely well. Though the long Aber-Benoît approach channel is studded with rocks and very exposed to westerly and north-westerly winds, it possessed natural advantages for clandestine comings and goings by sea in the shape of three rocky islets – Guennoc,[2] Tariec and Rosservor – none of which was permanently occupied by the Germans. Tariec and Rosservor were even accessible from the mainland on foot at low tide. All three were used for landing and pick-up operations at various times during the German Occupation, though boatwork was often difficult because of the exposed conditions and strong tidal streams. One hazard, of which SOE were not aware at the time, was that the Le Tac family were from the outset conspicuous for their anti-German sentiments. In August 1940 Madame Le Tac and her future daughter-in-law Andrée had already been in trouble with the Occupation authorities for the warm welcome they accorded to a British pilot who had come down in the sea and been picked up and brought ashore by the Germans. Andrée's youth allowed her to get away with nothing worse than a kick in the backside, but Mme Le Tac spent 48 hours in gaol.

A reception organisation in north-western Brittany was what Holdsworth and his Helford team most needed. Joël was sent down to train with them in boatwork and plan the details of his own return to France and of the future operations which it was hoped would follow.

Joël was to be accompanied into the field by a W/T operator, Comte Alain de Kergorlay, member of a well-known family, who was taking with him a B-type suitcase transmitter-receiver. They would be got ashore by means of a pair of Folboat canoes, which could be dismantled and used in subsequent operations. Joël was used to small boats and quickly proved able to handle a Folboat, but de Kergorlay, even with training, showed no such aptitude and seemed likely, left to his own devices, to capsize the frail canoe and lose his precious radio set. The two canoes were therefore to be joined together, catamaran-fashion, by lashing stout spars athwartships at the forward and after ends of their cockpits. This not only enhanced stability but meant that the Comte could paddle away under direction of Joël, who could concentrate more on getting them to the right place.

At last, on 14 October, just over a month after 360's first successful cross-Channel operation, all was ready. The linked canoes were lifted aboard and loaded to the top of 360's coach-roof and the expedition headed south, this time without any escort. Heavily laden with canoes, crew, passengers, stores, weapons and extra fuel for the return journey, 360 could make no more than 15 knots, so it was a six-hour run before they picked up the Ile-Vierge lighthouse just to the east of the Aber-Wrac'h estuary, which enabled them, with Pierre Guillet's unerring pilotage, to alter course for the Petite-Fourche buoy, marking the seaward end of the Aber-Benoît channel.

Conditions were far from ideal: though wind and swell had been with them on the outward leg, there was a nasty short sea running in the tideway on the French coast. Holdsworth brought 360 round head to sea at the chosen spot inside the fairway buoy, and slipped the engines into neutral as the canoes were manhandled over the side. Le Tac and de Kergorlay were helped down into them and baggage, radio set and paddles were passed over. This manoeuvre had been rehearsed several times at night, but it was not easy in the prevailing choppy sea. Then they were off into the darkness, paddling with the flood tide under them.

RAF 360 needed to refill her fuel tanks from the 40-gallon drums before setting off homewards. Fred Walsh, the violin-playing engine-man, a yacht-hand from Lymington in less troubled times, looked deathly-pale green and thoroughly seasick but he worked at the semi-rotary pump as though his life depended on it, while water broke over 360 now that she was head to sea. It was a rough passage back and Holdsworth's report on the operation, which SOE called OVERCLOUD and Slocum listed, with scant regard for security, as LATAK, described RAF 360 as having been at the 'reasonable limit of her endurance'. She was, in the author's view as well, far too small and vulnerable, with her large open cockpit, for cross-Channel work in winter conditions.

Holdsworth had been trying for some time, without success, to obtain two RAF 64-foot air/sea rescue high-speed launches, which would not only be faster and more seaworthy than 360 but able to carry a larger quantity of stores and also a rigid boat for landing work. He probably hoped his report would strengthen the case he had made for the larger craft, but in this he was disappointed. Slocum, ruled, quite rightly, that 360 was too small and unseaworthy for work to the north coast of Brittany except during the summer months – when, however, in practice her lack of speed and the short hours of darkness precluded her use. This ruling was not accompanied by any offer of the larger RAF craft requested by Holdsworth: it was instead agreed that whatever gunboats were available to Slocum should also be used for SOE transport work.

Slocum, who had just been accorded the title NID(C) and attached to Admiral Godfrey's Naval Intelligence Division, in fact put paid to SOE's hopes of running a 'private navy' even on the most modest scale to the north coast of Brittany. This is not entirely surprising: high-speed craft were scarce resources. The Admiralty had not at this stage allocated any gunboats permanently to Slocum, whose operations rated higher priority than those of SOE, and he had found that the Coastal Forces craft lent to him for limited periods were liable to be called back for offensive requirements at times when he most needed them. However, the Admiralty were beginning to address the problem, and in December 1941 it was for the first time agreed that the 'C'-Class MGB 314 would be permanently assigned to Slocum, but not until the spring of 1942. Until that time, she would be on loan to NID(C) from Combined Operations and subject to recall. She was, as 'C'-Class MGBs went, a good boat and her captain, Lt Dunstan Curtis, RNVR, an able and well-regarded officer.

Thus, when Joël Le Tac came on the air at Christmas with a request to pick up four persons, including his brother Yves and himself, from Aber-Benoît, and the BCRA decided to take the opportunity to send him a second radio operator named Moureau for his new OVERCLOUD organisation, it fell to MGB 314 to carry out the operation from Falmouth. Ted Davis, Slocum's representative from Dartmouth, was in charge of the expedition. Holdsworth was responsible only for any boatwork, and for acting as conducting officer on behalf of SOE. This change of status was by no means congenial to a man of a highly independent disposition who had previously commanded his own ship on operations. Still there was no gainsaying the fact that a 'C'-Class Fairmile was a much better boat for the job than the minuscule RAF 360 or the lumbering ML 107; although, by 1944, when larger and faster craft were forthcoming, the 'C'-Class MGBs in their turn were regarded as too slow, too small and too unseaworthy to be ideal for cross-Channel operations in winter.

The rendezvous was expected to be on Ile-Guennoc and on 30 December Holdsworth and the author embarked with two small yacht's dinghies and a team of their own ratings from Helford to launch and recover them, taking Moureau with them. There was no sign of the agreed light signal from Guennoc that night, so they returned empty-handed. On the following night they made a second and similar attempt.

At 2300 hrs they were in sight of land and beginning the final approach using one silenced engine when, quite suddenly, all hell broke loose ashore on the southern skyline: rockets and flares were fired and anti-aircraft guns blazed tracer ammunition into the sky from several positions on the coast ahead. Further away to the south and inland, a similar display of pyrotechnics marked where Brest and its anti-aircraft defences lay. Davis stopped engines entirely and allowed MGB 314 to drift with the tide. Everyone assumed that a major air-raid must be taking place: the scale and nature of the display were quite disproportionate to the approach of one small vessel. Then everything fell silent as suddenly as it had begun. After perhaps ten minutes, in which 314 continued to drift, Davis told Curtis to have one engine restarted and they resumed their silent approach. They passed the Petite-Fourche buoy and entered the Aber-Benoît channel. There was still 1.6 km. (1 mile) to go to the position where the gunboat was due to anchor off Guennoc, using a grass warp which would run out almost noiselessly while a seaman stood ready to cut it with an axe if rapid withdrawal became necessary. Still no signals from the direction where Guennoc lay: then they saw a shaded torch beam from somewhere right down at sea-level not very far away. It emanated from a Folboat canoe, which came alongside. Two figures climbed aboard using the scrambling-net the gunboat had already lowered to facilitate their own boatwork. It was Joël Le Tac's brother Yves, whom they had not previously met; he introduced his passenger, Fred Scamaroni. Yves laughed when they asked him about the firework display. No, it was not an alert: the Germans had been celebrating the New Year, which by Central European Time had been ushered in an hour ahead of British reckoning. They were all drunk by now: the expedition could do anything it liked on the coast tonight while the enemy made wassail.

The author and Yves needed to talk and went into the shelter of the wheelhouse. Yves said his brother Joël had come out to the rendezvous in the Folboat with Scamaroni on the previous night. There had been a considerable sea running and they could see only the shadows of the rocks when they were on the crests of the waves. At the point where they had hoped to meet the gunboat they had suddenly been blinded by a bright light, which shone on them for perhaps three seconds from no great distance. They stopped paddling and crouched in the bottom of the canoe, wondering if it was not a German patrol boat. In the interval the flood tide had carried them to the east of the channel and they decided to make their way back to the Le Tac villa: it was almost the only one not requisitioned by the Germans, who had a radar station nearby. They carried the canoe up the steps cut in the cliff and hid it in the garden. Joël had had to go to Rennes as he was expecting a first parachute supply operation: he would not be ready to be picked up for another week, when he would like to be collected with other passengers from Ile-Guennoc. Meanwhile, would they please take Scamaroni, an air force officer who had come from Dakar and was on his way to report to General de Gaulle. A repeat operation was agreed for the same day and time a week later. Yves took charge of Moureau, the new radio operator for OVERCLOUD. They climbed down into the canoe, were handed Moureau's radio and went off into the night.

The author thought at the time that Scamaroni was just another volunteer for the Free French forces, but his story was far more complicated than that.[3] He had been a Sous-Préfet serving in the Préfecture at Caen at the outbreak of war, but fretted at being in a reserved civilian occupation and obtained a transfer to the French air force, where he qualified as an observer. At the armistice, after hearing de Gaulle's historic appeal, he made his way to Saint-Jean-de-Luz and boarded the Polish liner *Sobieski*, which brought him to England. He offered his services to the Free French forces and was appointed to de Gaulle's staff. In October de Gaulle sent him to Dakar as a member of a four-man mission headed by Hettier de Boislambert: their job was to try to ensure that Dakar, which had remained loyal to Vichy, would change sides and allow de Gaulle to occupy it peacefully.

The Anglo-Free French expedition of October 1940 was a fiasco. Scamaroni and his colleagues were arrested by the Vichy authorities and thrown into prison. When they refused to give their parole not to escape, they were chained, manacled and relegated to vermin-infested cells. Scamaroni heard that they were to be transferred to Bamako by rail and that, from the French Sudan, they would be sent to Algeria. He decided to escape and, with a friend, jumped off the train when it was 40 km. (25 miles) from the frontier of British Gambia. Just when they were congratulating themselves on a successful get-away, they were captured by two armed native tribesmen, who handed them back to the Vichy authorities. They were sick and exhausted enough to welcome a spell of enforced rest in gaol. Finally, he and his three Gaullist colleagues were sent by plane to Algiers and thence by boat to the unoccupied zone of France, where they were escorted to Clermont-Ferrand and incarcerated in a military prison. Fully expecting to be court-martialled and sentenced to death, they were surprised to be told that Pétain had granted clemency. They were demobilised and set free. Scamaroni was given a minor post in the Ministry of Food, with the prospect of a higher appointment when he had demonstrated his loyalty to Vichy.

Friends sent news of his whereabouts to the BCRA in London. He was ordered to return to London but was allowed, at his request, to remain in France for the time being. He made contact with various Resistance groups and, with the help of Spanish republican refugees, organised an escape route over the Pyrenees. His dream, however, was to get back to his native Corsica and to organise resistance there. Having obtained a few days' leave, he took one of the rare boats plying between Corsica and the mainland. Local resistance existed but was fragmented and badly in need of coordination. Returning to Paris, Scamaroni found that the 'Copernic' intelligence network, with which both he and the Le Tacs had been involved, had been penetrated. He wondered whether to make a dash back to Corsica, but the BCRA now insisted he go to London. This was how he became a passenger in MGB 314 on New Year's Day 1942. Exactly a year later he returned to Corsica by submarine on a mission that ended in his death.

Joël Le Tac and Scamaroni had in fact sighted MGB314 on the previous night: the light that had alarmed them and deterred them from making their presence known to us had come from behind one of the chart-house windows, revealed briefly when a blackout screen fell out of position.

MGB 314 was back at the agreed rendezvous on the night of 6/7 January. As they were expecting to pick up eight passengers from Ile-Guennoc, including both the Le Tac brothers, Holdsworth planned to use two small dinghies from Helford, rather than rely on the Le Tacs' Folboat canoes.

The passengers had arrived one after the other at the Le Tac villa: Forman, a member of both the SAVANNAH and JOSEPHINE B missions, returning now from a third operational sortie; Labit, already twice parachuted into France for the Service Action side of the BCRA (later that year he took his own life rather than fall into the hands of the Germans); Chenal, a lieutenant of the French air force: Peulevé, an intelligence agent of Austrian Jewish origin, who had been working as a radio operator at Rennes in a BCRA intelligence network known as 'Georges France 31'; and Paul Simon, head of the Paris-based 'Valmy' intelligence circuit. The eighth passenger never materialised but they filled the house. If all went well, they would be on their way within 24 hours. The weather was cold but clear. From the bottom of the garden, which was surrounded by tall, thick bushes, the transit passengers were able furtively to watch the dogfights that were taking place between the RAF and the Luftwaffe fighters in the limpid sky over Brest.

On the evening of 6 January the agreed message *'Aide-toi et le Ciel t'aidera'* was broadcast on the BBC French Service, signalling that the gunboat was on its way. After nightfall, Joël and Yves, accompanied by their mother, led the party to a small sandy beach between Corn-ar-Gazel Point and another rocky headland to the west of it that was more or less separated from the coast at high water. The canoe was already waiting there, Joël having paddled it round to the embarkation point shortly beforehand.

Two by two, the passengers were paddled the 4 km. (2½ miles) from Corn-ar-Gazel to the Ile-Guennoc, in the Folboat, crewed in turns by Yves and Joël, who left together on the last trip. The little group found shelter at the top of the island, which is covered with grass and heather and is ringed with enormous rocks; it also contains the well-preserved remains of a prehistoric settlement. At the appointed hour, Yves climbed to the highest point and flashed the agreed signal. The gunboat slipped round the point and moored 500 metres from the island.

Holdsworth and the author each manned one of the small yacht's dinghies they had brought from Helford and pulled over to the island, where they each picked up two passengers and ferried them off to the MGB, before returning to the island for a second load. They had a much shorter distance to cover than the Le Tacs had done in their canoe, but the dinghies were far from ideal for the job and the whole operation took far longer than they would have wished. It was after 2 o'clock before they had got all seven down in the gunboat's wardroom, where they were met with hot tea, whisky and sandwiches before they turned in for a rest. When they were awakened from their bunks, day was breaking and the flashing light dead ahead was that of the buoy marking the entrance to the Helford River.

Three weeks later, on the night of 1/2 February, they went back to Ile-Guennoc, again using MGB 314. This time there were only three passengers, the Le Tac brothers and Peulevé. It was a bright, moonlit night. They embarked Yves and Peulevé in one Folboat, Joël went with the luggage and Peulevé's new suitcase set in the other. The operation proceeded without a hitch, though the tide was out and there was more than a kilometre (0.6 miles) of beach between their landing point and the Le Tac villa, across which they had to lug the two canoes and their baggage. Fortunately it was very cold indeed and no sleepless German was loitering on the balcony of any of the requisitioned villas.

But disaster was awaiting: de Kergorlay had been arrested during their absence in England.[4] Peulevé was also arrested on arrival at Rennes; three days later Joël fell into a trap that had been set for him in the flat of a Resistance colleague in the same city, which was his chosen operational headquarters. Yves, whose propaganda mission took him to Paris, was arrested there two days after his brother and wounded into the bargain. The Le Tac parents and Andrée, their daughter-in-law, shared the same fate. They were all deported but, miraculously, returned from concentration camps three and a half years later. De Kergorlay, a nephew of Vladimir d'Ormesson of the Académie Française, continued to operate his wireless set under enemy control until 1943, but he omitted his security check and SOE's RF Section recognised the traffic as a *Funkspiel* and handled it accordingly. De Kergorlay was condemned for collaboration with the enemy after the war, but Yeo-Thomas of RF Section was able to clear him of the charges relating to OVER-CLOUD and his life sentence was reduced.

The extent to which OVERCLOUD was in contact with a whole series of other organisations whose security was under systematic attack had proved fatal: 'Georges France 31' had been penetrated by a Frenchman working for the Germans and its destruction was completed by a certain Roger Martin, working with a man called Robert or Bob, purportedly a Canadian. These two gained the confidence of a member of a group of student Resistance activists in Rennes who called themselves 'Les Ibériques' and who were in touch with the Le Tacs.

The rot continued long after OVERCLOUD's destruction: in spite of London's instructions to 'Georges France 31' to cease all activity, the group refused to obey, saying that since the beginning of hostilities they had pledged their lives to this cause and were even prepared to sacrifice them. This disregard of all the basic security rules of clandestine activity led to the deportation of 25 people, 14 of whom died in concentration camps. It was magnificent, but it was not the kind of war to wage against Hitler's security machine.

MGB 314 carried out three operations for SOE directly from Dartmouth during January and February 1942. The first of these, which involved the landing of a female Soviet agent in Lannion Bay, took place only four nights after the return of the Le Tacs and Peulevé to Aber-Benoît. Though SOE had served as the channel through which PICKAXE was arranged, the woman is thought to have been an intelligence agent on the way to join the well-known Rote Kappelle organisation.[5]

The other two operations – WATERWORKS and ROWAN – both involved attempts to embark Pierre de Vomécourt, the organiser of SOE's first independent F Section circuit, 'Autogyro', and a woman named Mathilde Carré, alias 'La Chatte'.[6] La Chatte had been assistant to Garby-Czerniawski, the Polish animator of the 'Interallié' intelligence network working for Dunderdale of SIS. Interallié, which was run from Paris, had been betrayed to the Germans by a French subagent in Cherbourg. Mme Carré was arrested while her chief was on a visit to England, but released after agreeing to work for her captors. She became, moreover, the mistress of an Abwehr sergeant named Bleicher who was working on the case and they used the telegram traffic passing through her hands to arrest many of her former colleagues. De Vomécourt, who was out of radio contact with London, was introduced to La Chatte, known in London by the name 'Victoire', as someone who might be able to pass a message for him to his Baker Street SOE headquarters. It was only after several exchanges through this channel that de Vomécourt, who was known in SOE as 'Lucas', realised that Victoire, his only link with London, was a double agent. Instead of breaking contact, as by all the normal rules he should have done, Lucas had the temerity to attempt to re-enlist this woman of remarkable character and cool nerves for the cause of the Resistance; and he succeeded. Through her and Bleicher, Lucas got the Abwehr to agree to a complicated and improbable bargain, as part of which both he and Victoire would be picked up on the north coast of Brittany by the Royal Navy, while the Germans watched.

There was, at the outset, a suggestion that the author should have the job of landing two agents destined to join Autogyro and of picking up Lucas, Victoire – by then a treble agent – and Ben Cowburn, another F Section agent returning from sabotaging an oil refinery he had helped to build before the war. For some reason, however, it was instead Ian Black, Dunstan Curtis's Australian First Lieutenant, who took charge of the two boats that rowed ashore from MGB 314 on the night of 11/12 February 1942 at Moulin-de-la-Rive, near Loquirec. He got ashore with Abbot and Redding, the two outward-bound agents, but at that point the sea suddenly began to get rough and a heavy swell began to develop with the rising tide. The dinghy that had landed the two F Section agents overturned when Victoire tried to embark. Lucas dragged her ashore, where she stood 'furious and dripping in a fur coat, lamenting her lost suitcase which had gone overboard with herself and the new agents' luggage.'[6]

Two sailors eventually righted the dinghy, but they could not get close enough inshore to embark those waiting on the beach, and the second boat could do no better. Cowburn's report, written after he had come out via Spain, described the dinghies as 'absurd little things . . . about as seaworthy as an inverted umbrella.' Black, who was in uniform, soon gave himself up to the Germans, who were watching from behind the dunes. He was treated as a prisoner of war. Abbot and Redding were handed over to the Germans by a farmer in whose barn they had taken refuge. De Vomécourt, who was eventually arrested and tried after his return to France, persuaded the Germans to treat them too as officer prisoners of war and they were sent to Colditz. Cowburn, being a very professional operator, slipped his German 'tail' and got away over the Pyrenees.

That night the *Scharnhorst, Gneisenau, Prinz Eugen* and their destroyer escort passed by unseen on their way up the Channel. MGB 314 was inshore of them, but she saw nothing; nor did the Hudson aircraft flying a chevron-shaped patrol across the approaches to the Goulet-de-Brest, which stayed on the job for two hours after its radar had packed up. According to Foot, signals passed by the Germans through the 'Interallié' radio link played a part in enabling the squadron to escape through the Chenal-du-Four. Though there were many red faces about the incident, the fact remains that, for over a year before that escape, accurate intelligence from within Brest dockyard and RAF bombing attacks each time they were nearly ready for sea had made it impossible for the Kriegsmarine to use Brest as a satisfactory base for their Atlantic squadron, and they never again attempted to do so.

Further attempts on 13 and 14 February to complete the WATERWORKS pick-up failed again owing to surf. Finally a separate operation – ROWAN – was mounted on 20 February to a pinpoint at the Pointe-de-Bihit, once again using MGB 314. They found no agents at the rendezvous, then or two nights later; it was 27 February before Lucas and Victoire were collected, in almost perfect conditions and by an almost full moon. It was MGB 314's swan-song in the role of clandestine transporter: before being permanently assigned to Slocum, she was withdrawn by Coastal Forces to do 'just one more job', namely to act as headquarters ship for the raid on the St-Nazaire dry-dock gates. The 'C'-Class MGBs were chosen because their silhouettes resembled E-boats. They were fitted with extra deck tanks to extend their range. When MGB 314's deck tanks were empty, Curtis had them filled up with sea water; but the other two or three MGBs were left with tanks unfilled. When the flotilla came under heavy fire the empty deck tanks exploded, but 314's did not.[7]

HMS Campbelltown, one of the fifty lend-lease United States vintage destroyers, successfully rammed and blew up the dry-dock gates, the essential target of the raid, for which Sam Beatty, her captain, got the VC. MGB 314 was so badly damaged that she had to be sunk by British forces on the way home, when bad weather was encountered. Her fore-gunner was awarded a posthumous vc.[8]

After that, there were no further attempts to work to the north coast of Brittany until the following winter. The low speed of the 'C'-Class Fairmile MGBs precluded operations during the summer months, although that was when better sea and landing conditions might have been hoped for.

Though the loss of MGB 314 was a setback, Slocum's prospects of obtaining permanently allocated high-speed craft for clandestine sea-transport operations in the English Channel now seemed to have taken a turn for the better. On 12 December 1941, two members of his staff, Ted Davis and Steven Mackenzie, went down to Southampton to inspect the first of a series of motor gunboats ordered by the Turkish Government before the outbreak of war from the firm of Camper and Nicholson but much delayed by the onset of hostilities.[9] Though the prototype of this class, subsequently designated MGB 501, was to be fitted with Packard petrol engines of 3,600 h.p., her slightly larger sisters were, as part of the original contract, to be equipped with a new type of Paxman diesel. These engines were still under development and Coastal Forces, all of whose craft were petrol-engined, were not interested in taking over diesel-powered vessels, so that the whole of this series of ex-Turkish MGBs, which would seem at this stage to have consisted of the prototype and at least six other boats, were provisionally allocated to Slocum's NID(C). Moreover, Curtis's MGB 314 was replaced within a matter of weeks by a sister ship, MGB 318, whose captain, Charles Martin, had been well known before the war in motor-racing circles, when he drove for Bugatti. MGB 318 was permanently allocated to Slocum's Section and by June she had been joined at Dartmouth by 501, first of the ex-Turkish gunboats, under command of Dunstan Curtis. However, at some point during the summer of 1942, four of the ex-Turkish hulls, that Slocum had been promised, were reallocated to the Ministry of Economic Warfare to be completed as civilian-manned blockade-runners for fetching Swedish ball-bearings from Göteborg to Hull – at the time this task was deemed to merit even higher priority than landing and embarking agents in France and the Low Countries. Then, on 27 July 1942, 501 set out, in company with 318 and MA/SB 36, the other boats permanently allocated to Slocum, on passage to the Scillies with Slocum, Davis and Mackenzie on board, along with a ship's company of 25 ratings and three officers. When nearing the Longships lighthouse, 501 blew up and sank after a Primus stove exploding in the galley started a fire. Fortunately no-one was injured, though Slocum was narrowly missed by the falling mast. MGB 318 picked them up.

It was not until November 1943 that the next ship in the

Camper and Nicholson series, the diesel-engined 502, was available to Slocum for her first operation. During the intervening 16 months, he had to rely for operational purposes on 318, with the occasional assistance of other 'C'-Class Fairmiles made temporarily available by Coastal Forces.

The accident that had led to the loss of Black at Moulin-de-la-Rive showed that the yacht dinghies used there and by Holdsworth at Aber-Benoît were quite unsuitable for the job. What type of surf-boats should be carried in MGBs thus became the subject of much research and experiment, after which two standard 14-foot boats were produced and used with much success in the following winters. A third variant, a dory built in Cornwall to the author's design, was later used to good effect for submarine operations in the Mediterranean.

CHAPTER XII

November 1941–June 1942

B etween July 1941 and January 1942 submarines patrolling in the Bay of Biscay to watch for the emergence of the *Scharnhorst* and *Gneisenau* from Brest had been used six times in attempts to collect agents, passengers and mail from small Le-Guilvinec and Pont-Aven fishing boats working for Dunderdale's 'Johnny' group of agents in the Lorient area. The first of these contacts, only three of which had been successful, brought Daniel Lomenech back to England in HM S/m *Sealion*.

Lomenech, compromised as an agent and unable to be sent back to France, had been used as conducting officer on four of the ensuing submarine operations during the next four months. His job was to identify fishing boats owned and operated by his friends in Le-Guilvinec. His considerable knowledge of the fishing grounds and the types of craft working from western French ports made him an ideal choice. Slocum saw a lot of him and obtained a commission for him as a Sub Lieutenant RNVR. Discussions between Lomenech and Steven Mackenzie gave rise to the idea of using converted fishing vessels to maintain this link. Mackenzie, a founder member of Slocum's Section – now known in Whitehall as NID(C) – and Slocum's staff officer dealing with operations from bases in the United Kingdom, had served previously on the British naval mission attached to Admiral Darlan's headquarters.[1]

Submarines were in most respects the best of all craft for clandestine operations by sea, but in most cases use had to be made of a submarine carrying out a pre-arranged patrol in the area. Agents who had recruited a fishing boat in occupied territory therefore had to conform with the operating plan of the submarine as regards date, time and place of any meeting. This coordination was difficult for agents, working as they did under strict enemy control, with shortage of fuel and having only scrappy communications with their friendly base.

Lomenech and Mackenzie pointed out that the chances of success would be improved if a diesel trawler, fitted out in England, were to take the place of the submarines for these meetings at sea with fishing boats under agents' control. A craft operated by NID(C) with no reference to any other controlling authority would be able to fit in with the requirements of the agents rather than vice versa. Such a vessel could approach closer inshore than a submarine could normally be hazarded; could lie off the French west coast in the permitted fishing zone for days if necessary, waiting for an agent or mail to be brought out; and could make contact in daylight, which no submarine could do.

Slocum was much attracted by these arguments. The idea of using tunny vessels to reach the French coast had often been considered and rejected as too uncertain, since these craft depended on sail and consequently on favourable conditions. Moreover, the areas where the tunny shoals were normally encountered lay well offshore, near the edge of the Continental Shelf, and tunnymen had no legitimate reason to hang about closer inshore. Lomenech and Mackenzie had gone to considerable trouble to identify a more suitable type of vessel for the purpose they had in mind. Apart from Lomenech's up-to-date personal knowledge of the area and the industry, photographic coverage of craft encountered by RAF Coastal Command patrols seeking U-boats in the Bay of Biscay was obtained through Luard, Slocum's liaison officer at St Eval, and carefully examined. Their proposal was to use a 60-foot diesel-engined trawler of a type found in fair numbers in Concarneau, Lorient and other west coast Breton ports. These vessels fished grounds 30–50 km. (20–30 miles) off the coast and were allowed by the Germans to remain at sea for two or three nights at a time. They did not depend on favourable winds.

In November 1941 Slocum decided to acquire and fit out a vessel of this type. Lomenech had found two such refugee Concarneau motor-trawlers on the Sussex coast, Le-Dinan and Fée-des-Eaux. They were typical examples of a class of boat known in the Breton-speaking parts of the west coast of Brittany as malamoks, which had begun to be built there during the 1930s. Their pointed 'Norwegian' sterns were a notable departure from the wide, flat overhangs that had previously prevailed and had represented an effort to build the largest possible boat for the available money, misguided since the price depended on the length of keel rather than on overall dimensions. These old-style sterns were widely thought to have caused the loss of many ships of the tunny fleet in a great gale of August 1931, when vessels running in for shelter from the offshore fishing grounds 'pitch-poled', or capsized heels over head, owing to an unbalanced distribution of buoyancy between their slab-sided, sharp bows and over-broad sterns.

Le-Dinan, 65 feet long, was chosen as being the quicker of the two malamoks to reconvert to her original appearance. She had been serving at Newhaven as a patrol boat under the local registration N51 and had been converted below decks to accommodate a crew of eight men and two officers. This accommodation was suitable for Slocum's purpose, but the gun mounted forward had to be removed and her original masts, which had been discarded as an impediment to the gun's field of fire, were found and restepped, wireless was installed and the engine overhauled. Daniel Lomenech had unhappy memories of disciplinary problems with Dunderdale's French crews at Mylor and it was decided, for better security, to man her with a volunteer British crew from the Royal Naval Patrol Service.

In December 1941 an urgent project was put forward through Dunderdale's section of SIS to land food and stores on the Glénan Islands off Concarneau for the use of RAF evaders and escapers. *Le-Dinan*, still usually known by her old patrol number N51, was still far from having completed her refit at Shoreham so *La-Brise*, the Audierne mackerel drifter fishing out of Newlyn, which had been considered earlier in the year for use in picking up the SAVANNAH team, was chartered for the job on a 'bare boat' basis. The French crew were put ashore and N51's British crew took over *La-Brise* and sailed from the Scillies on Christmas Day 1941. This first venture of this type by Slocum ended in disaster: the RNR skipper, who had commanded a Bear Island trawler in peacetime, ran the ship on to the rocks at Ushant and, in extracting her from this danger, struck further rocks. He got extremely drunk on whisky and announced his intention of surrendering to the Germans. He was prevented from doing so by the explosion of a Mills hand-grenade, which killed him. Lomenech, who was on board to act as pilot for entering the Glénan Islands channel, took charge and brought the boat back to Falmouth with the skipper's body in the forepeak. A court of inquiry found the death to be accidental and Lomenech's service with Slocum went forward from strength to strength. *La-Brise* had, moreover, reached Penmarc'h before he turned her head north, which proved that it was still possible for a ship of this type to cross the western approaches to the English Channel by night and that she could safely close in to the French coast south of Ushant by day.

N51's refit was completed in February 1942 and she was sailed to Dartmouth. The RNR Lieutenant who was put in command of her was ordered to make a trial voyage to the Scillies, before attempting to carry out the operation to the Glénan Islands. Once again there was trouble in the shape of two serious engine breakdowns which were not repaired until mid-March. The ship's speed proved, moreover, to be little more than 6 knots at best.

The unreliability of the full-diesel engines fitted to French and Danish fishing boats and of the semi-diesels normal in Norwegian fishing vessels proved a very widespread problem when these ships were used for clandestine sea-transport operations. Normal fishing boats are fitted with slow-turning engines designed for trawling at slow speeds. To run such engines at their maximum revolutions for long periods to obtain speed rather than power is an abuse of the original purpose of the design and breakdowns are bound to ensue. The lack of normal stocks of spare parts for engines of Continental manufacture during the war was a further very real difficulty: when needed urgently they often had to be made on a one-off basis. Slocum found it better to re-engine French boats with British diesels of higher horsepower than those originally fitted in order to obtain reliability and a slight increase in speed, but in 1942 and 1943 there was often much difficulty and delay in obtaining the engines required.

The commanding officer of N51 had to be changed once more owing to serious breaches of security. Steven Mackenzie was then put in charge with Lomenech as First Lieutenant until the latter was sufficiently familiar with naval procedure to take over the ship himself.

While this work on the engine was going forward, Dunderdale's 'Johnny' group of agents in the Quimper area was disbanded and it became questionable whether the ship would be needed. At this time, however, Rémy (Colonel Gilbert Renault), creator and head of the 'Confrérie de Notre Dame' (CND), which was to become the largest and most productive of all the Free French intelligence networks in France, was in London. He had returned from the field by Lysander at the very end of February 1942 and representatives of Slocum's Section, including Mackenzie and Lomenech, were invited to meet him. Mackenzie gave an account of this first contact:[2]

> We met first in a mews flat; one of those flats which hide themselves so discreetly all over London off the fashionable squares and down unexpected alleyways. You open the door and find a narrow staircase directly in front of you, the neat carpet and pale distempered walls contrasting oddly with the cobbles on which you stand. But over the stables, now used for garages and stores, you may find rooms more spacious than you expect, more filled with character and the decorator's art than any of your box-like luxury flats can show. In such a room, then, we met him.
>
> I do not retain any strong impression of him at that first meeting. The room was clouded with blue smoke, the slightly acrid smoke of French cigarettes; a colonel and maybe a captain or two sat round the fire. By the polished oak table stood the object of our visit, a man of middle height, apparently of middle age, with a tendency to stoutness, a tendency to baldness, with the softest and yet the brightest brown eyes you could imagine.
>
> 'This is M. Roulier,' our escort introduced us. We bowed and shook hands.
>
> 'Enchanté, m'sieur!'
>
> 'Enchanté, messieurs!'
>
> This was our first meeting with a man whom later we came

to know as an outstanding personality in the Resistance; a man with the courage of a lion, the determination of a bulldog, and the charm of a royal ambassador . . . But in that smoke-filled mews flat on a foggy . . . afternoon he was just another Frenchman, another customer.

We unrolled our charts upon the table, asked the stock questions, recieved precise replies. He was returning to France in a few days, required assistance in his future journeys back to England.

'I may have to evacuate my wife and family from France. Already it is dangerous for them in France. They may be taken as hostages, you see.'

Even in 1941 we knew what that meant. We saw and agreed. In what area would he work? For the Navy to help him he must reach the coast. Brittany? Excellent! North or west coast? West? Hm! Not so easy. Rapidly we explained the naval aspects of the case. The north coast could be reached by night: an MTB could pick him up under given conditions. The west coast was too far from Britain for such an undertaking; it would mean a submarine – a more delicate undertaking altogether.

'But surely the Royal Navy can arrange a submarine for such a purpose? M Rémy is our most important man in northern France!' It was the colonel who spoke, the colonel who was sitting by the fire and had not appeared to be introduced.

We agreed somewhat nervously, knowing that submarines were like gold to the Admiralty. M Rémy would have to abide by many added regulations with which he might not be able to comply. This we explained, showing the reasons on our chart, doubting if he would understand the real necessity for accurate navigation, timing and a detailed plan. But Rémy was an exception; he understood our reasons, presented his own plan, and after some discussion settled the navigational difficulties into the bargain.

'I have the possibility of a fishing boat,' he jabbed at the chart with his finger. 'On board, I will have the most trustworthy crew. If you insist I will provide a pilot – how do you say, a navigator? – from a *Transatlantique*. If you say "be twenty miles from the coast" we will be twenty miles, not more, not less. I can meet you where you like with this man!'

In the end we arranged three meeting places and gave them code names; *Juliette* was far out to sea, too far out we thought for accuracy in a fishing boat: *Marie-Louise* was closer inshore, where bearings could be taken, while a third was fixed on the coast itself in case the fishing smack did not materialise at all. I knew what Flag Officer (Submarines) would say to the second and third; the waters inside the 100-fathom line were hotly patrolled by aircraft and on the surface between Brest and Lorient. No submarine would be allowed to risk herself there without some formidable guarantee that the game was worth the candle.

But although we made more than one rash promise about the availability of a submarine, there was at the back of my mind a second plan which might redeem our promises if put to the test. For some weeks previously we had been discussing it, and although she would never be ready in time for M Roulier's purpose unless considerable pressure were applied, there was already a ship earmarked and fitted out which might take the place of the hypothetical submarine. We did not mention this possibility to M Rémy: we were not anxious that details of it should be known to anyone who was visiting France. But in promising that on receipt of a given signal his fishing boat would be met by the Royal Navy, we felt justified in making the mental reservation, 'Even if the Royal Navy is represented by another fishing boat of similar design and appearance'.

Mackenzie's recollection of this first meeting with Rémy was at fault in one particular: he thought it took place in November, when work on N51 had only just started, but it must have taken place some four months later, in March 1942, since Rémy returned by Lysander from his first mission to France only on the night of 27/28 February and went back into the field on 26/27 March by the same means.[3] N51 was therefore more nearly ready for sea than he remembered, though very probably the engineers were still trying to deal with her second serious engine breakdown and he had still not been called to take over command of her in person.

The crew Mackenzie chose were for the most part North Sea fishermen who spoke seldom but who knew the sea from childhood. They could not have been better. Few RN active service ratings would have cared for the cramped quarters or the eternal smell of fish and diesel oil that N51's bilges exuded no matter what steps were taken to clean them. These men had lived for fishing before the war; they asked for nothing better than to resume their normal lives under naval auspices. In time a few misfits were weeded out but from the start they were a first-class crew. The coxswain, 'Jasper' Lawn, was a short stocky man with grizzled hair and bright blue eyes. He was, Mackenzie supposed, about 35 and had fished from Grimsby and Hull since boyhood. He was a man of few words but these few were all gold: expletives for the most part and wonderfully phrased derogatory remarks about the crews' ability.

Then there was Cookie Nash, red-cheeked and bespectacled, always cheerful, always anxious to take a watch on deck; and Jock, the ancient engineman (Mackenzie reckoned he must have been about 45 but looked over 60), whose stories of his past life were no less amusing when it was discovered they were lifted bodily from the Wild West fiction that he read so avidly. Jock was almost a real-life version of J.M. Barrie's Smee; he related vividly the story of his escape from Dartmoor, his life as a cowboy, as a dope pedlar in Chinatown, as almost everything disreputable, but all the time Mackenzie knew that he had a wife and two bairns in Edinburgh to whom he was devoted. On his leaves he never missed going up north to them, even when it meant four days of corridor travelling in order to spend two days at home.

Altogether the crew totalled eight, with two officers additional. The wardroom was built in the fish-hold amidships and though cramped was well fitted. In good weather it was splendid, but when the skylight was battened down and covered by the fish-hatch the fug below grew intolerable. This, combined with the heavy smell of fish and oil, was too much for Mackenzies' stomach. In bad weather he preferred to face the elements on deck.

Operation MARIE-LOUISE was eventually arranged for April, by which time N51 was in as good shape mechanically as she was ever likely to be. After so many false starts, Mackenzie and Lomenech had no great expectation of doing the job when they sailed from Dartmouth for the Scillies to put on their war-paint. In the secluded New Grimsby Sound anchorage between Tresco and Bryher the painting was done – blue hull, brown upperworks and a French name and number. Daniel, as First Lieutenant, chose the colour scheme and they had a fine old time getting the coloured paint out of the naval stores officer!

> The day for sailing dawned bright and clear, with a light sou'westerly breeze; the weather report was good and the crew, who had awaited this moment eagerly for four months, were in high spirits. But the blow fell at the eleventh hour; a signal was received from France asking for a further delay. The permit for the French craft to sail had not been received from the German authorities. Rather than return once more to Dartmouth, we asked permission to make a reconnaissance voyage to the Brittany coast to get experience and confirm that our vessel was the right type and capable of doing the job. To our surprise and joy permission was granted and we sailed within the hour.
>
> That first voyage was a confirmation of our highest hopes. Daniel had assured us that we would see a dozen ships of our own type on the fishing grounds west of Lorient. We saw them all and a hundred more besides. We left Scillies in the afternoon and had an air escort until dusk; by midnight we were off Ushant and when dawn broke we made a landfall off the Pointe-du-Raz, picking up the Saints Buoy after a 150-mile

run. From there to the Iles-de-Glénan we sighted crabbers from Audierne, motor trawlers from Le-Guilvinec and finally the bigger diesel craft from Concarneau and Lorient.

It was too early in the season for tunnymen to be out, but of these we sighted a number on later voyages, majestic shadowy ghosts by comparison with chugging trawlers, beautiful shapely craft spreading blue, orange and white sails to the breeze as they came out from the islands heading for the broad Atlantic.

At night we hove to and rocked in the long Atlantic swell until dawn, when we closed the coast to make a landing near Concarneau. The landing itself was to show what could be done with impunity on the German back doorstep. We went ashore on a small islet half a mile from the mainland coast and photographed the shoreline from Concarneau itself to the Port-Manech entrance, sailing in and out in the ship's dinghy while the N51 herself patrolled up and down a couple of miles offshore.

It is hard to describe the atmosphere of peaceful activity which filled the great bay formed by the Pointe-de-Penmarc'h and the Pointe-de-Rousbicout. Every size and description of fishing boat, large and small, appeared to be at sea. From time to time convoys passed along the route from Brest to Lorient. Minesweepers and patrol boats formed their escort, driving relentlessly through the busy fleets and paying no attention to the craft around them. In the blue sky over Penmarc'h itself white puffs of smoke showed where an anti-aircraft battery held a practice shoot, and through glasses one could see the target plane towing a drogue. As far as we were concerned we might have been in Lyme Bay for all the attention anyone paid us.

On the following day we made our way back along the coast, photographing the convoys as they passed and noting the types of fishing boat at sea. Without incident we reached the Scillies once more and there reverted to our grey paintwork and white ensign. Naturally the voyage had done much to give us confidence in what had until then been no more than a well-documented theory. The theory had been proved, and we knew it could be done again and again, until the secret leaked out and the German restrictions were tightened. On our side we could take precautions to keep things quiet; what we feared was talk in the Brittany cafés when, if ever, we succeeded in meeting M Rémy's craft.

In May the procedure was repeated. This time there was no cancellation and we left the Scillies a month later to the day. A beam wind helped us across the Channel and down the French coast with all sails set. Although the weather was worse than before, there were plenty of boats out; we lay off the coast the night before our rendezvous was due, with half a dozen trawlers around us.

About midnight the sky cleared, and above the creaking of the ship as she rolled we heard the hum of bombers. Searchlights on the coast lit up, probing the sky and fixing in great clusters on the tiny silver specks at their apex. Orange and red shell bursts twinkled above the land whilst, down below, the increasing glow of fire showed where Lorient was getting a pasting. This was a satisfactory feeling indeed, watching the RAF delivering the goods from a front-row seat.

But all next day we searched in vain for the ship we were to have met, and the day after as well. Green hull, white sail, name *Les-Deux-Anges*; that was the description, but none fitted it. During the third night we received a signal. *Les-Deux-Anges* had been in Lorient for repairs when the RAF raid closed the port with mines. We had sat and watched the fun, little knowing that it was defeating the very purpose for which we had come. Deeply disappointed we returned to the Scillies.

One small but quite interesting detail that Mackenzie was too tactful to put into print was that on the evening of 20 May, the date on which they arrived off the Glénans, a small boat did come out from the islands. When she failed to respond to their recognition signals, Lomenech, whose reflexes were rapid and bold in the extreme, suggested they should capture the boat and force the crew to return with them to England to make sure they did not report the presence of a suspicious-looking craft to the authorities. Mackenzie vetoed this proposal.

Third time lucky? We were growing a little sceptical of success. The delays on the French side were not, I know, of Rémy's choosing. Indeed his position was growing desperate, for his wife and children were being sought by the Gestapo, and it is not easy to conceal an entire family. But to our crew, who knew nothing of the reasons behind our project, the operation now seemed doomed to failure. True, they enjoyed the sensation of fooling the Hun, but we seemed to be getting little dividend out of it other than enjoyment. In June, nevertheless, all was arranged once more, and once more we set sail for the Scillies.

This was to be our last attempt. If it failed there was little point in keeping men uselessly employed when they were badly needed elsewhere. But if it succeeded, we would have formed the first link of confidence with the fishermen from Brittany. If it succeeded, we would establish a regular service to France, through which men and arms could be passed to the hard-pressed Resistance, and by which escapers, helpers and information could return to Britain.

Once again we picked up the moorings in New Grimsby Harbour and piped all hands to paint. The old ship's hull was getting its fifth coat in three months and it took but a forenoon to apply. Hull, bulwarks, deckhouse and masts hid their naval grey under shades of green and brown. We chose a slightly different colour scheme each time; after mingling with the French fleet, we knew there were plenty to choose from. Douarnenez boats were all painted black, with a white line round the bulwarks; Audierne crabbers are mostly green-hulled, with tanned sails and ochre decks; but from Penmarc'h southward, the French fisherman fairly lets himself go on the question of paint. Concarneau trawlers vary between green, blue, brown and orange in different combinations, and we had even sighted one vessel freshly painted throughout in a delicate shade of mauve.

As soon as the hull was dry, registration numbers and a Breton name were painted on in white and covered over with canvas. French flags painted close to the waterline at either bow were required by German regulations, and these were also covered over. It was not possible to disguise from the few Scillonians on the two islands that we were up to something strange, but we did not intend them to guess exactly what, nor to see the numbers and name we had chosen. The appearance of our bows with canvas patches tacked over the painted flags gave rise to a rumour on shore that these concealed torpedo tubes, and we did nothing to counteract the idea that we were engaged on anti-submarine patrols of a 'Q-ship' nature.

Was ever such perfect weather! For a week before sailing we basked in the hot sunshine, and fished over the side in that amazingly clear water which looks so tempting to the bather and is in reality so icy cold on the hottest days of summer. We carried out exercises on shore, held revolver and small-arms shoots, perfecting our drill in case of need. In our disguise as an innocent fishing boat there was no room or opportunity to mount a proper gun, so we relied on the surprise element, together with Sten guns, grenades and pistols in case we should be hailed for examination by a German fishery patrol boat. We had practised such a surprise attack off Dartmouth with an M.L.,[4] of which only the captain knew of our intentions. The result had given us confidence and much assistance in the question of where best to conceal guns and grenades.

At length the date for sailing came. The weather remained unbroken; too fine to suit us well since the visibility was extreme while the short hours of darkness gave little time to pass the German air cordon west of Ushant. At seven knots one makes agonizingly slow progress through waters patrolled from the air, and if sighted by a reconnaissance plane one has scarcely moved at all in the time it takes an aircraft to report to base and bring out a strike of fighter-bombers. For this reason we had an escort of Beaufighters to protect us half-way across the Channel, three planes circling widely round the ship, relieved in relays from St Eval. Even so we had three hours of unescorted daylight sailing to put us twenty miles from Ushant by the time darkness fell.

No signal of cancellation came; indeed this time we had a message relayed from France that all was in order the other side, and we sailed accordingly on June 16th. South of the Bishop our escort picked us up. The lightest of southerly breezes rippled the water. Not even a child could feel sick in that weather, an encouraging thought since we expected to embark Rémy's children, and had taken a special supply of rice and tinned milk for their diet on the homeward journey!

At 10 p.m. our air escort left us, rearing overhead and waggling wings in farewell. This was the most dangerous part of the voyage, crossing the No Man's Land forbidden to fishing craft, where a sighting by German air patrols would give the game away completely. With doubled lookouts we chugged on, while the cloudless sky turned slowly from blue to gold in the west, and from gold to a deepening violet. The sheer beauty of the sunset was a joy to watch apart from the welcome darkness it foreshadowed. By dawn we were slightly south of Brest, not too far north to pass a longline vessel from Douarnenez. From here southward our appearance was natural enough to pass without comment; on this voyage it was to be tested thoroughly. The sea, I remember, was like a mirror reflecting the deepening blue of the early morning sky. No breath of wind rippled the still surface, and in that curious calm our exhaust echoed as though in an empty room, infinitely loud and clanging. To the south-ward the topsails of the day's first crabbers appeared over the horizon. There, it was evident, a breeze was making up to end the uncanny calm and silence of the dawn. The Ile-de-Sein raised its tall wireless masts to port; and the Pointe-du-Raz loomed on the horizon, hard and menacing.

By ten in the morning we were among the crabbing fleet and encountered our first incident. Passing between two crab-bers and trying to keep as far from both as possible we ran into a line of trammel nets. By the time the line of bobbing corks was seen it was too late to avoid them; we drove on, putting the engine out of gear and praying that the nets would not catch on our rudder or propeller. In the clear water we could see the rope as the ship passed over it skidding safely along the keel until it reached the prop. There for five interminable seconds it caught, stretching like a bowstring; then the strain pulled it clear and with a satisfying plop the line of corks bobbed up astern. That saved a cold and tricky dip for someone as well as unwanted delay.

As we sailed down the Baie-d'Audierne we could see the golden sands and the white villas at their edge shimmering in the sun. The great lighthouse of Penmarc'h, reputedly the tallest in the world, raised itself on the skyline, beckoning us on; beyond it lay the Glénan Isles where our business called us. On this occasion we had fixed our meeting time for 5 p.m. and intended to reach the position by that time the day after leaving the Scillies. By keeping our appointment so late we would save a day on the whole operation, but it meant we could afford no delays on the outward journey. The sense of urgency to be on time made our seven knots seem even slower; the lighthouse was a chimera, a mirage on the horizon that never drew nearer.

It was a busy day in the air. Heinkels and Arados crossed and recrossed overhead whilst two or three convoys passed us going north. They were well escorted with sweepers and armed trawlers but none paid attention to us. At length the light was reached and passed and we set course for our meeting place. Fishing boats abounded, diesel boats like our own, tunny boats and a few big steam trawlers on the outer banks. The Glénan Isles appeared, low and rocky, five miles to the eastward.

1630. We reached the position with half an hour in hand and proceeded to steam up and down as though we were trawling. All eyes turned to the islands round which *Les-Deux-Anges* should appear; we saw precisely nothing. Five o'clock, six o'clock passed while our hopes gradually faded away. Another failure, another voyage for nothing. A little after six, black smoke appeared on the southern horizon, quickly followed by the appearance of five German corvettes steaming up the convoy route towards us. We held our course watching them anxiously, for they would pass all too close. Or would they pass, was this a trap? Had Rémy been caught and our plans uncovered?

As the corvettes came on Jasper, the coxswain, nudged my arm and pointed towards the islands. A tiny white sail had appeared there, too far off to identify but clearly making out to sea. The excitement grew intense, the corvettes lent the final touch of colour to the situation. We reached the end of our run and turned, letting them overtake us to starboard, between us and the islands. They passed us belching black smoke, the nearest less than a cable distant. We could see the captain examining us through glasses from the bridge, watched by German sailors idling on deck, holding our thumbs and turning our backs on them. Then they were past, the casual inspection over.

We watched the white sail tacking to and fro till the corvettes had disappeared. At last it steadied on a seaward course making directly for us. We let it approach until we could identify it; everything fitted with the description we held. 30 feet long, single mast, green hull and finally, to dispel the last doubts, the name painted in clear white letters on the quarter: *Les-Deux-Anges—C'neau*. We made our signal, identified ourselves and went alongside.[5]

One thing puzzled me; on the deck of *Les-Deux-Anges* stood only three persons, all obviously fishermen. Yet we expected to see three passengers at least besides the children. It was not until the two ships were fast alongside, heaving up and down unevenly in the light swell, that they appeared. It seemed amazing that so many people could be hidden in that little cockleshell of a boat. They certainly had been hidden and had survived a German inspection when the vessel left harbour. Now they emerged in lengthy succession, a woman; Mme Rémy; three children ranging between 11 and 5 years old, a man with several suitcases, and finally Rémy himself, with a bagful of papers in one hand and, in the other, a six-month-old baby.

Rapidly they were helped on board, choosing the moments when the deck of *Les-Deux-Anges* heaved up to our gunwale. The stores we had brought for the fishermen were handed over, petrol, oil, and some food and tobacco. In five minutes it was all over, the warps were cast off and *Les-Deux-Anges* turned away in a wide circle. As she passed us again to wave goodbye, the French skipper pointed to the sky and we looked up. A patrolling Heinkel was approaching from the north'ard, still too far distant to have seen us together. We made suitable gestures of contempt, and headed out to sea.

M. Roulier was by my side and together we went to join the party below, where Cookie Nash was serving hot coffee and rum to welcome them on board. I ordered a tot to all hands to celebrate this long-awaited moment, and took my own up in the wheelhouse. I felt deeply moved by the sight we had seen; four young children and their mother helped to safety, their smile of thanks, their obvious confidence of security in our hands. Jasper was at the wheel staring straight ahead. His voice was gruffer, his language more picturesque than usual. After a few moments I left him and went out on deck. Cookie Nash, still grasping his coffee pot, was gazing at the retreating coast, and there were tears in his eyes. This is no exaggeration; there was not a man amongst the crew who did not feel the sentimental strength of that dramatic meeting.

There were still a few hours of daylight left, but it was pointless for us to start for home at once. Had we done so we should have passed Ushant at noon the following day and so entered the prohibited area for fishing boats in broad daylight. Accordingly we made an offing from the coast and hove-to for the night. As dusk fell, the engine coughed into silence for the first time since we had left the Scillies; in the unwonted silence the wash of the waves and the creaking of the rigging sounded strangely loud. From where we lay, we could see the flashing of Penmarc'h light, the red beacon on the Ile-aux-Moutons, and the loom of the light on the Ile-de-Groix, getting a comforting 'fix' each hour as the tide drifted us southwards.

At dawn the engine was started again and we began a slow cruise up the coast, planning to reach the latitude of Ushant by midnight and the Scillies by noon the following day. There was more wind today and an increase in the swell, but nothing to worry about and the sunshine was as brilliant as before. The long hours dragged by interminably; for the first time since we had started the whole plan of the operation I felt acutely nervous. Now that we had on board the cargo for which we had searched so long, each aircraft that approached seemed especially inquisitive, each convoy escort that passed threatened to stop and examine us.

At one moment in the afternoon, off the Ile-de-Sein, an armed trawler came up from astern to pass us close on the port side. As luck would have it we were on top of a line of unattended trammel nets; while she passed we stopped to haul them in, and were busy picking the spider crabs from them when the officer of the watch swept us with his glasses from the bridge. A double triumph this, for Cookie had the crabs boiled within half an hour and we ate them on deck, wondering at the lack of public demand which makes British fishermen throw them back and curse them for tangling the nets.

The last and nastiest shock came at about ten in the evening. We were passing Brest well to seaward when we sighted three destroyers steaming parallel to the coast some five miles to starboard. In a craft purporting to be an innocent French fisherman we felt a little conspicuous at this particular moment making our maximum speed northwards with dusk coming on. As though to confirm our worst fears one of the destroyers broke away from the flotilla and headed out to sea towards us. For five minutes, or was it five years, she held her course, gathering speed. We waited hopelessly for a challenge

to blink imperiously from her lamp. Then she turned away
and stopped. Exercise? We did not wait to see. The sky ahead
was turning grey and grew darker every minute. Thankfully
we watched the darkness surround us, and set about getting up
the Lewis guns. From dawn onwards we should be in British
waters, no longer in disguise, and allowed to hit back if
necessary.

The sea that night was alive with fish. Mackerel in great
shoals, glinting in the phosphorescent water, lit up huge
patches of the sea. At one moment two dolphins swam with
us, rubbing their backs against the ship's side and playing
round the bows. In the darkness, their outlines were clearly
picked out by the phosphorescence, beautiful streamlined
shapes darting easily through the water with a trailing wake
of fire.

At six the following morning, our air escort found us, a
fine tribute to the accuracy of 'Coastal', for a 65-foot boat is a
small target to find in the Western Approaches even when you
know approximately where to look. Rémy was much impressed
by the escort, and so were the children who were now allowed
on deck for the first time. For nearly 36 hours they and their
mother had been shut up in the tiny wardroom cabin, with the
engine clattering behind the thin wooden bulkhead. They had
not once complained; the baby had not even cried, or certainly we never heard it. But alas, Cookie's carefully prepared
milk puddings had hardly been touched; the entire family felt
unwell and ate almost nothing until they reached England.

We did not make New Grimsby until three in the afternoon. A contrary tide and a sad accident to one of our
Beaufighters delayed us on the last lap. From the moment
when the escort had arrived, by reaction I had felt irritable
and tired. Now, as we turned the last headland and the blue
placid waters of the anchorage unfolded before us, this irrit-
ability vanished in an instant. The entrance is narrow, passing
between two craggy points whose wild beauty was now
painted a golden brown by the summer sun. White water
boiled and tumbled on the treacherous rocks outside, whilst
within, the water shimmered transparent and motionless.
Cromwell's Castle, solid and ancient, guarded our mooring-
buoys. All was friendly, welcoming, unchanged.

The final scene of our small drama was yet to come, an
unforgettable moment, born of coincidence perhaps, but one
of those moments whose dramatic effect exceeds by far the
sum of the factors which build it up. We had already signalled
to the Admiralty the happy result of the expedition, and had
expected to find a gunboat waiting at the Scillies to take our

N 51 photographed by RAF Coastal Command.

Gol Gilbert Renault
('Rémy'), Daniel
Lomenech, Mme Renault,
her children and members
of the crew of N 51
approaching the Scillies
at the end of Operation
MARIE-LOUISE, June
1942.

BELOW Rémy's children
Jean-Claude and Catherine
on N 51 when approaching
the Scillies at the end of
Operation MARIE-LOUISE.

Attaching a watertight
SOE container by chain
to the La Sumart Buoy
off the Glénan Islands on
N 51s first operation in
1942.

N 51 (*Le-Dinan*) at New Grunsby Sound, Scilly Isles, prior to an operation.

The crew of N 51. The group includes Daniel Lomenech, Richard Townsend, Jasper Lawn, Joe Houghton, Peter Fryer (Chief of N 51), Ted (Cookie) Nash.

Steven Mackenzie when in command of N 51 (*Le-Dinan*).

Jasper Lawn, Coxswain of N 51, with Cromwell's Castle, Tresco, in the background.

Louis Yéquel, with his first crew Gildas Bihan and Paul Bihan (not relations) bring *Les-Deux-Anges* alongside N 51 off the Glénan Islands.

chard Townsend DSC, RNVR, first lieutenant to
el Lomenech on N 51 and P 11, later CO of
2028 (*Président-Herriot*).

Daniel Lomenech in the Scillies.

Les-Deux-Anges: Three adults and four children were successfully hidden from
German inspection of this small, undecked vessel – an essential link in the fishing
vessel operations for 'Rémy'. (Photograph of a model built for the Imperial War
Museum).

ABOVE A Helford dory, as used in the Western Mediterranean, in surf-boat trials at Prah Beach, Cornwall.

LEFT The Warington Smythe SN 1 14 foot surf-boat on the beach, Helford River. The sailor's face has been obliterated for wartime security reasons.

BELOW Four SN 1 surf-boats could be carried on the deck of an MGB. The 25 foot SN 2 was designed for HMS *Minna*. A very similar SN 6 was used to rescue 28 people from Ile Tariec.

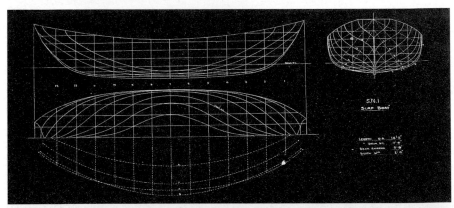

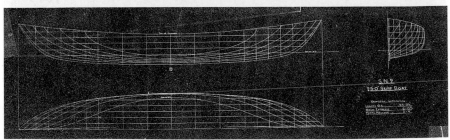

ABOVE AND BELOW P 11 (*Ar-Morscoul*) in New Grunsby Sound, Scilly Isles, before Operation GUILLOTINE.

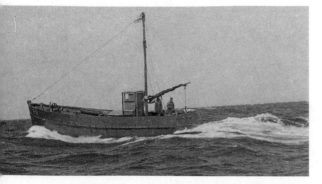

ABOVE MFV 2023 (*L'Angèle-Rouge*), the high speed despatch boat built by Groves & Gutteridge at Cowes to a Laurent Giles design for the mail run to Rémy's Confrérie Notre Dame.

RIGHT P 11 (*Ar-Morscoul*).

BELOW HM Yacht *Sunbeam II* served as depot ship for the 'Inshore Fisheries Patrol', moored in the Helford River from June 1943 onwards.

passengers to the mainland. But as luck would have it the chosen MGB had encountered a minor breakdown, and was late in arriving; later than we were ourselves. But within half an hour of our making fast we heard the drone of her engines beyond the point, and waited idly for her coming.

The sun shone hot into our protected anchorage, its rays reflected from the rocky hills which surrounded us; a few gulls floated lazily around us. Otherwise the place was deserted; except for those droning engines there was no sound, no sign of life. Then round the headland appeared the expected MGB,[6] pennants fluttering green and white, bow wave creaming in the deep blue water, and from her loudhailer came the martial crash of a Souza march. On she came without slackening speed, the music resounding from the hills, contrasting strangely with their wildness, challenging their unmoving solitude.

Then she drew nearer, engines and music stopped and we could see the cheery faces on her bridge. Swinging in a wide circle she came alongside. This was the end of a venture, a fittingly dramatic end to a voyage full of excitement. The passengers were quickly transferred to the gunboat to start the first stage of their journey; and N51 was left to herself at the anchorage to resume the drab grey of an auxiliary naval trawler. How many times she changed colours in the succeeding months and years I would not like to guess. Suffice it to say that the link had been forged; it endured for more than two years!

The future of what Slocum decided to call the 'Inshore Patrol Flotilla' had indeed been assured and it was to maintain the sea line to Rémy's network until October 1943. Thereafter the 'Confrérie' (CND) was in trouble and the link with Brittany by sea was taken over by MGBs working to the north coast and to other organisations.

By the time of the operation that brought out Rémy and his family, a second and smaller trawler had been brought into service. Lomenech and Mackenzie found this boat, the *Ar-Morscoul*, lying half-submerged in Newlyn harbour, but her hull was sound and Slocum obtained Admiralty approval to salvage her. She was of the inshore type known as a *pinasse*, which was used both for the sardine fishery and as a small trawler or longliner. She was taken to Falmouth to be patched up and re-engined. After being fitted with a new and larger diesel engine, this vessel, which was given the name P11, proved capable of 9 knots, a welcome bonus when compared with N51's 6 or 7. P11 was too small for a crew to live aboard in harbour and she was therefore manned by N51's crew

for operations. She carried out a first operation in August and a
second in September under Lomenech's command. The August
operation took P11 further south to a meeting at sea with a
cutter-rigged crabber from Léchiagat, a small fishing port next
door to Le-Guilvinec.[7] This boat was named *L'Audacieux* and the
expedition to the vicinity of the Ile-d'Yeu involved P11 in a five-day
voyage. She carried a small consignment of SOE stores on this
occasion, which was successfully transferred, though the expected
two agents from Rémy's CND organisation did not appear. She was
back on 16 September for another rendezvous with *Les-Deux-Anges*
off the Glénans Islands. Her two passengers on this occasion were
Rémy himself and another member of his CND organisation,
Michel Pichard.

The rendezvous worked perfectly and the mail was collected,
but the skipper of *Les-Deux-Anges* said that the German controls in
force at Concarneau, from which she had sailed and to which she
must return, were so stringent that it would be impossible for him to
land Rémy and Pichard, who had therefore to return to England.
The author, who was on board P11 for this operation to see how
Lomenech worked, found his confidence, courage and local knowledge extremely impressive.

By September 1942 Rémy's 'Confrérie de Notre Dame' was on
a vast scale. It had for more than a year extended along the Atlantic
coast and up into Brittany, with particularly good coverage of
Bordeaux and Brest: now it covered the whole of France. In 1941
and 1942 Dunderdale's networks had suffered such a run of
disasters that SIS had become critically dependent on the CND's
output. Rémy had, moreover, stepped into the breach caused by the
destruction of Dunderdale's 'Johnny' organisation in the Lorient
area and had taken over its capacity to handle fishing boat operations on the south-west coast of Brittany. This sea link became of
such overriding importance to SIS that Slocum ruled that NID(C)'s
fishing vessels must be reserved exclusively for this purpose and
must not undertake operations for other organisations in the Bay of
Biscay for fear of compromising the system.

Unless disaster befell the 'Confrérie' it was clear that a regular
monthly voyage would be needed during the coming winter to take
supplies to, and collect mail from, this network, particularly since
the declaration of the whole north coast of France as a forbidden
zone in the summer of 1942 made the future of cross-Channel
operations by high-speed craft from Dartmouth or Falmouth look
uncertain. It was hoped that these monthly contacts by fishing boat
on the west coast, which would take place in the 'dark' phase of the
moon, could be supplemented by RAF Lysander or Hudson pick-up
operations during the periods of moonlight.

Since P11 was too small and vulnerable to be employed in

winter conditions, NID(C) fitted out and commissioned a second 60-foot *malamok*-type trawler, the *Président-Herriot* (renamed AO4 and subsequently MFV 2022), again with a British crew, but including one Breton rating in case she was hailed on the French coast. She was placed under the command of Sub Lt Richard Townsend, RNVR, with Sub Lt John Garnett as first lieutenant.

Lomenech made two more voyages with the N51 in October and November, but her engine was in a bad state and needed reboring. It was thought better to re-engine her completely and a long battle began to obtain and fit a suitable British diesel, which was to last until June 1943, with the result that she was out of action for more than six months.

There seems to have been no sortie in December, but the AO4, under the command of Richard Townsend, who had taken part in six operations as first lieutenant of N51 and P11 with Daniel Lomenech, picked up to the 'Confrérie' mail in January and did so again in February. The first of these contacts was achieved only at a second attempt, owing to bad weather, while the February operation was delayed because Rémy's boat had been bombed. In spite of these delays, the sea communications line had been kept running and its importance enhanced by the repeated cancellation of air pick-up operations as a result of winter gales: only one of these had so far been carried out successfully for Rémy's CND since Rémy himself returned by this means in March 1942.

One fact alone conveys the qualitative importance of the intelligence carried back from France during these expeditions: a parcel brought to England by N51 when she evacuated Rémy's family in June 1942 proved to be a blueprint of the coastal defences that the Todt organisation was just beginning to build on the coast of Normandy.[8]

Rémy himself did not at the time realise the importance of that parcel. Twenty years later he wrote:

'Quite recently I heard someone say that Hitler told his advisers that the Allies would try to make their landing on the beaches of Lower Normandy. The generals of the Army High Command disagreed with this view for logistic reasons, whose recapitulation reminded me of a scene which I had entirely forgotten.

It took place in my flat in the Square Henri Paté, where Loiseau had come to call. The map spread out on the carpet was more than three metres long and 75 centimetres in width. It covered the whole of the Normandy coastline from Cherbourg to Honfleur. Marked on it were a great number of concrete blockhouses, machine-gun nests, barbed-wire entanglements and minefields. The calibre of the guns to be mounted was indicated.

'What an extraordinary document! it shows every sign of being genuine', said Loiseau. 'You have there nothing less than a precise description of what will be a large stretch of the famous Atlantic Wall, about which enemy propaganda is always boasting. How did it come into your hands?'

'In a parcel tied up with string, which was brought to me.'

'But it is a special printing, of the utmost secrecy. It must therefore have been spirited out of some German office?'

'You ask too many questions.'

'You don't seem very enthusiastic?'

'My dear friend, I would be if that plan covered the coast between Le Havre and Dunkirk. But what can be the use of this one? I shall send it to London, but I don't think it will be of any greater value than to show how the enemy conceive their Wall. I agree that is better than nothing.'

I, like the German generals, was wrong.

CHAPTER XIII

January 1942–March 1943

E arly in 1942 when Slocum became NID(C) and was attached to Rear Admiral John Godfrey's Naval Intelligence Division, his position *vis-à-vis* Naval Commands and establishments was thereby enhanced. In March 1942 he relinquished responsibility for SIS's air operations, which were on an increasing scale, to a new Air Ministry Liaison Section. Thenceforward he dealt with sea operations only.

At the same time, a post designated NID(Q) was created and filled by a retired Rear Admiral named Holbrook, head of SOE's Naval Section. However any suggestion that NID(C) and NID(Q) enjoyed similar status as far as operations to France were concerned was dispelled from the outset: Slocum had always been in a position to approve or veto any proposals put forward by SOE. As NID(C), he was still faced with a good deal of scepticism within the Admiralty and at Naval Commands towards all matters clandestine. But SIS was important to NID in a way SOE was not and Slocum's star was in the ascendant. In January 1942, not long after Slocum's ruling that RAF 360 was too small and unseaworthy for operations to the north coast of Brittany, an Admiralty directive was issued placing SOE vessels at Helford under the operational control of NID(C). This step was apparently considered necessary to avoid possible overlapping and clashing of operational interests, and was doubtless wise in principle. In practice, however, certain controversial issues at once arose which engendered friction between NID(C) and SOE.

SOE operating personnel, who had carried out successful operations with 360, were fully aware of her limitations, but they resented the ruling depriving them of any craft of their own that could be used on the north coast and relegating them to the role of passengers in NID(C) vessels. It produced, moreover, an awkward system of divided control – the commanding officer of the gunboat had overriding conduct of the expedition, while the SOE officer's responsibility was confined to the command of the landing party when going ashore. Since Slocum still had no permanently allocated MGB, SOE personnel were at the time the only people who had been able to train systematically for this part of the work; moreover, after the collapse of Le Tac's OVERCLOUD operation, they continued to develop and improve their skills and techniques for landing agents and material with keenness and enthusiasm. Nevertheless, there was no gainsaying the fact that SOE's purely naval role had been largely nullified with respect to operations to France.

This sense of frustration was compounded during the summer of 1942 when NID(C) ruled that Holdsworth's fishing vessels were not to be used on west coast operations as they were of unsuitable type. There was something to be said for this view as far as *Denise-Louise* and *Sérénini*, Holdsworth's second and third choices, were concerned: they were both north coast vessels and, although they had been structurally altered and camouflaged to make them as suitable as possible for work in the Bay of Biscay, NID(C) maintained, perhaps rightly, that they would not pass muster when seen by Breton west coast fishermen at close range. But, as Lt Cdr Bevil Warington Smyth, RNVR, Holdsworth's successor at the SOE Helford River base, wrote in 1946, certain SOE officers thought that the NID(C) case was spoilt when *Mutin*, which he described (not wholly accurately) as a genuine west coast tunnyman, was also condemned as unsuitable for operations, although she had been passed as correct in every detail by a Breton tunny-fishing skipper. Moreover, NID(C) themselves employed a specially built, high-speed motor vessel on west coast operations, which was meant to look like a *pinasse* but which, owing to her excessively wide stern, could not be expected to deceive a Breton fisherman for an instant, except at a considerable distance.[1]

In the summer of 1942 Captain H. A. Simpson, RN, son of a Scottish family of Jacobite exiles who had lived in St Petersburg until the Russian Revolution of 1917, took over control of the SOE Naval Section in London from Holbrook. To overcome these difficulties, he arranged for the acquisition of four new west coast vessels approved by NID(C) representatives as being suitable for operations. The layout below decks was converted to allow for the storage of four tons of stores in special lockers.

The first of these ships was ready for sea in the autumn of 1942, when Brigadier Gubbins and Captain Simpson visited the Helford base and discussed future plans with Holdsworth, who was by now a Lieutenant Commander, RNVR. From this visit and subsequent discussions with SOE's Independent French Section came a plan for an operation to be carried out in the new ship to the Quiberon Bay area. At the last moment, however, when all details had been worked out, a ban was placed by Slocum on all SOE operations to the west coast of France for fear of compromising the SIS fishing-vessel mail service: NID(C) claimed that this had become increasingly important as a result of the Germans' entry into what had been unoccupied France and the consequent tightening–up of control on the French Mediterranean seaboard. The ban, which was not lifted until several months after the OVERLORD landings in Normandy, came as a severe disappointment to SOE personnel at Helford. At the beginning of December, Holdsworth, denied any active operational role by NID(C)'s ruling, handed over command of the base to Lt Cdr Bevil Warington Smyth and sailed for North Africa with most of the base's operational personnel in two of the fishing vessels, *Mutin* and *Sérénini*, to set up a new SOE sea-transport service in the western Mediterranean, where it was hoped that conflict with NID(C) could be avoided.

Gus March-Phillipps and his *Maid Honor* Force, that other SOE thorn in NID(C)'s side, had come home from West Africa early in 1942. March-Phillipps, with a DSO, had established a shore base for his unit – now styled the 'Small Scale Raiding Force' (SSRF) – at Anderson Manor, a beautiful but long-neglected early 17th-century Dorset manor-house not far from Poole Harbour. During that summer the SSRF mounted cross-Channel forays against targets on the coast of the Cotentin and in the Channel Islands, the most spectacular of which was the capture of the entire eight-man German crew from the Casquets lighthouse, eight miles north-west of Alderney.[2] John Newton from Helford was the pilot and guide. Numbering nine at the time the *Maid Honor* Force was formed, the SSRF grew to 55 officers and men. Though numerically small, it was very high in quality. At that stage in the war it fulfilled the need to make gestures of vitality and prove thereby that there was still some kick in Great Britain. The SSRF was, in fact, the beginning of the maritime and amphibious side of the SAS tradition, the Special Boat Squadron.

Hitler paid close attention to the SSRF's raids during the summer of 1942 and they made him very angry. But there was such a high proportion of officer material in the Force that casualties were disproportionately expensive. Of the 11 men who landed with March-Phillipps at Port-en-Bessin on 12 September, not one returned to base. March-Phillipps was killed and the only man who got away to Spain was extradited into German hands and executed to assuage the Führer's wrath at these impertinent and unconventional gestures of defiance of his proclaimed 'Thousand Year Reich'.

Soon afterwards, a raid was led on Sark by Appleyard, March-Phillipps' second in command, and Anders Lassen, who was consumed by a passionate determination to erase the shame of Denmark's tame submission to the Germans in April 1940. The morning after the raid, German prisoners were found dead with their hands tied. Eleven days later Hitler, hardly a stickler for the Geneva Convention, issued a secret order – marked 'In no circumstances to fall into enemy hands' – which accused the Commandos of 'brutal underhand behaviour'; of 'recruiting animals'; and of being instructed 'not only to tie up prisoners, but also to kill unarmed captives'. He further authorised the extermination of captured raiders.

Although this order remained secret, the Germans made an immediate outcry about the Sark raid, which they linked with the tying up of seven German soldiers and five civilians during the Combined Operations raid on Dieppe six weeks earlier, in August 1942. By way of reprisal, 1,376 British and Canadian prisoners of war taken at Dieppe were shackled: the Canadians retaliated by shackling a similar number of Germans and there were months of international tit-for-tat. SSRF was in trouble: it was wound up and its surviving personnel, including Appleyard and Lassen, were transferred to No.1 SAS in the Middle East. Both were killed during the Italian campaign: Lassen's posthumous Victoria Cross – he already had three Military Crosses – was the only one awarded to a member of the Regiment.

Ironically enough, at the very moment when NID(C) had thus acquired sole operational use of the north coast of Brittany, SIS's demands for the services of the Dartmouth motor gunboats fell away to nothing. This was because, by the summer of 1942, the whole north coast of France had been declared a Prohibited Zone; this extended 25 km. (c. 15 miles) inland. SIS concluded that access to and from landing beaches on the Channel coast of Brittany was thereby made too difficult for agents to use this route. Subsequent events were to prove this an over-reaction on SIS's part. Still, during the winter of 1942/43, the sea line of communications for intelligence from France was maintained exclusively by the fishing-boat operations to the west coast. Slocum's problem therefore was what use to make of MGB 318. SOE, however, came forward with a scheme to land arms on the north coast of Brittany. As no reception parties were available, the consignments, which included explosives as well as weapons, packed into watertight aluminium boxes fitted with shoulder straps, were to be landed by SOE boats' crews from Helford on the chosen beach, carried as backpacks to some point well above high-water mark and buried for later collection. The place of concealment needed simultaneously to be safe from accidental discovery and identifiable by those who were eventually to take delivery. All traces of the operation had then to be effaced before the landing party withdrew. These were remarkably difficult desiderata in the circumstances: moonless nights, enemy-held territory and the expenditure of toil, sweat, tears and, in one case, blood. These operations, were given the name LARDERING by Holdsworth, their originator.

In October 1942 four attempts were made to land half a ton of stores from Dartmouth on the Breton coast near the Ile-de-Batz. The operation went under the name CARPENTER. The landing party, under the command of Dick Laming, a Dutch officer belonging to

SOE's Naval Section who had been earlier involved in the Scheveningen Ferry, came up from Helford in *Mutin* with the cargo and the necessary boats. Also among the team, and on their first operation, were the author's brother, who had recently joined the Helford unit straight from finishing an Engineering degree at Cambridge, and a young Ordinary Seaman named Gordon Baker, a Poole fisherman who had been the paid hand on *Astrape*, a yacht built at Lymington to the author's design in 1939 for his father.

The first attempt, on 9 October, ran into wind and sea conditions in the Channel off Start Point that were too bad for operating: MGB318 shipped a sea up to the wheel-house, leaving both anchors adrift from their lashings and moving several dog-clips off the pom-pom ammunition lockers. Speed was reduced to slow to allow the damage to be made good. The course was held for a short while to see if conditions were better to seaward, but they were not; then 318 and her escort, 323, returned to Dartmouth. The two Beaufighters from St Eval that were to have escorted them on the first part of the crossing left them as they neared the river entrance.[3]

The second attempt, on 11 October, again using MGB 318 with MGB 323 to escort her, made a landfall on the French coast 3 km. (2 miles) further west than expected. A running fix was obtained on the Ile-de-Batz lighthouse and course was altered to pick up the submerged offshore rocks at Méan-Névez. The night was very dark and speed was kept down to slow on the wing engines, giving 8 knots. At 0007 hrs engines were stopped as rocks were observed on both bows, distant about 50 metres. When an attempt was made to go astern, rocks were reported on each quarter, or, more accurately, white water. It seemed that whatever course they turned on to, rocks appeared. It was almost an hour before they could clear this collection of rocks. A second attempt was made after another running fix on the Ile-de-Batz at 0226 put their position between Méan-Névez and Brouillerézon: this was recorded by Davis as 'partly due to slight panic from the chart-room from soundings and insufficient allowance for tide'. The coastline gave no lead whatever, being a level black smudge on the horizon. Méan-Névez rock was just visible from 50 metres. At 0229 the operation was abandoned. Davis concluded his report by saying that, despite the natural hazards that surround the pinpoint, he felt sure it could be reached. The flatness of the coastline and absence of outstanding features did not help but, with a very careful fix on the Ile-de-Batz and careful computation of the height of the tide, small errors in the strength of the tidal streams could be overcome. The whole of the period in the area had been quite exciting and had left Martin, the commanding officer of MGB 318, shaken. This was his first experience of operating conditions on the blacked-out Breton coast and Davis 'gave, as usual, the extra smoothing-down work'.

The third attempt was abandoned at an early stage owing to re-routing made necessary by local naval operations in the Plymouth area. When the operation was replotted, it was clear that an extra 37 km. (23 miles) had been added to their distance and that MGB 318 could not arrive in the target area before 0100 hrs on 14 October on the most optimistic assumptions, which was too late to be any good.

The fourth attempt, on 15 October, was made with what seemed a favourable weather forecast that the wind would back to south-west and the swell moderate. Unfortunately this did not happen and the passage from Start Point was most uncomfortable. Running at the maximum speed possible in these conditions made steering very difficult, the boat continually running up to the westward of her intended course in leaps of about 30 degrees. No allowance could be made for this, as it was almost impossible to check between the two compasses owing to the movement of the boat and the continuous showers of spray. Engines were silenced at 2235 on the 15th and the uncomfortable feeling was spreading among the crew that the swell would prove too much for a landing. A white light was sighted ahead at 0005 on the 16th: five minutes later, breakers were seen and land was just visible. The exact spot could not be recognised but the general appearance and the breakers indicated it to be the Pointe-du-Ponsuval and accordingly course was altered to the eastwards. It was soon realised that boatwork would be impossible, as the swell was quite heavy on the banks and a white line of surf was visible along the base of the land. Davis did not begin the return passage immediately as he wanted to observe the effect of the swell in the vicinity of the pinpoint. They were off it outside the rocks between 0125 and 0140 and, although the land could not be distinguished easily with the naked eye, the breakers were easily discernible.

At 0141 they turned back. Nothing untoward happened, except that the boat seemed continually to be 'using her chines as keels', which made things most uncomfortable. As the boat approached the English coast, the steering gear packed up and the auxiliary gear was brought into use, but it lasted only 3 minutes, so they were forced to use the hand tiller. The engine room staff worked on the steering gear and had it in action again at 0805.

It was noticed throughout that the extra deck cargo made the ship's movement more uncomfortable – the boat hanging on to the end of each roll, as if deciding to steam along on her beam ends. It was, Davis recorded, frightening at first, but everybody soon became used to it.

When weapons were being cleaned after one of these four abortive sorties, Ordinary Seaman Gordon Baker, who had been so keen to join the author when he was called up for National

Service, was accidentally killed by another member of the Helford landing party who was fooling about with a gun he didn't realise was loaded. It was a very personal tragedy for the author and his brother, who had known him and his family since they were children.

When *Mutin* returned to Helford at the end of the no-moon period, SOE's Baker Street headquarters wanted to know why Pierre Guillet, SOE's local pilotage expert, had on this occasion failed to find the chosen pinpoint. It then emerged that he had not been on board MGB 318 at the material times. Pierre, the name by which he chose to be known out of concern for the safety of his family at Noirmoutier, had gone to Helford 14 months before to advise on fitting *Mutin* out as a tunny fisherman, and had volunteered to stay on as a member of Holdsworth's unit. He had never missed an opportunity to go on an operation or a major exercise and his skills as a coastal pilot were much valued by the naval side of SOE. He had originally been commissioned as a Skipper, RNR, the appropriate rank for the captain of a fishing boat, but it eventually transpired not only that he had been round Cape Horn on a square-rigged ship but also that he held master mariner's tickets for sail and steam: these entitled him to promotion to Lieutenant, RNR, which was duly granted. In July 1942 he was awarded the DSC. He had therefore gone up to Dartmouth with Laming, everyone on the SOE side having assumed that he would go with them on CARPENTER. However, nobody had explained his presence to Davis and when the Helford landing party trans-shipped from *Mutin* to MGB 318, Davis, as Slocum's senior representative at Dartmouth and the man in charge of the operation, was on the bridge of the gunboat. History does not relate how Pierre was attired, but he was no doubt wrapped up in an anonymous duffel coat or something similar. As the gunboat was about to cast off, Davis's eye lit on the bearded, fiftyish figure of Pierre, a generation older than the members of the landing party. He turned to Laming, the man in charge of the Helford contingent, and, pointing at Pierre, asked, 'What is that?' Laming explained that Pierre was a French fishing skipper with a remarkable knowledge of that part of the coast of Brittany. According to Leading Seaman Tom Long, a member of the landing party and a particular friend of Pierre's, Davis looked at Pierre 'as though he was something the cat had brought on board' and said loudly, 'I was navigating officer of the *Queen Mary* when she did a world cruise and I don't need a stupid fisherman to tell me where I am.' Pierre stayed behind in Dartmouth and was not involved in any of the first four attempts to carry out CARPENTER.[4]

SOE's headquarters in Baker Street must have taken the matter up with NID(C) and, when the team went back to Dartmouth for a further crack at CARPENTER, Pierre went with them, Davis having been instructed to take him on the operation. The fifth attempt took place early in the November dark period. Pierre went straight up to Davis on MGB 318's bridge and said, 'Me go this time.' Davis assented, but he must have had quite a shock when Pierre added, 'If me go this time, then you f... off ashore. If you go, me f... off ashore.' It was, of course, Davis who went to sea once more that night and once again bad weather put paid to the success of the operation.

Morale in the Helford landing party was sagging and Tom Long recalls that requests were being made to return to general service.[5] Then someone in London had a brainwave: Davis was called to London for an urgent meeting and Letty, his second in command, took his place on MGB 318's bridge. Laming knew him well from the time they were both working on Dutch operations and Pierre went to sea with them on 10 November. He found the beach straight away and the operation was successful.

A very similar operation, CARPENTER II, was mounted in the January no-moon period: the beach chosen on this occasion was 11 km. (8 miles) south-west of the Ile-de-Batz, very much in the same vicinity as before. The weather reports from RAF Coastal Command, St Eval and Admiralty seemed promising on 4 January, so arrangements were made to make an attempt that night. For some five hours before MGB 318 left Dartmouth it had been snowing quite heavily, which promised much fun at the Ile-de-Batz if it continued. Davis, by now a Lieutenant Commander, RNR, was again in charge but this time the landing party had been provided by NID(C) Dartmouth.

Troubles started quite soon after their departure: the seascape promised what Davis described as 'one of those nights'. Once clear of the race off Start Point, the weather was much worse than forecast, which made 318's movements violent. Spray was continuous and 'the farms astern of them were eyed with envy'.

The Ile-de-Batz was sighted at 2220 fine on the starboard bow. At 2225 engines were silenced and speed reduced. Frequent rain squalls obscured the light but soundings remained at 30 fathoms. At 2340 the commanding officer MGB 318 remarked, 'There's a big so-and-so rock now passing along the port side'; at the same time Davis noticed 'much rock embroidery from right ahead to Green 45 on the starboard now' and everything was stopped. Soundings gave 10 fathoms. MGB 318 was turned slowly to north-west on one engine and the run to Méan-Névez began with the definite fix they had obtained on the unlit Ile-de-Batz lighthouse – 211°, 1.2 miles. Squalls were very frequent and no land was visible.

At 0102 they assumed they were in position – Méan-Névez south-east ¼ mile – and a careful run to the southward was begun, as the rocks now had about a metre of water on them. Dinghies were lowered and towed astern. At 0116 hrs, 318 was anchored and the transfer of stores began. During the anchoring, Davis and Lt Uhr-Henry, RANVR, the officer in charge of the landing party, discussed the approach for the boats – a landmark, a course and a prominent star were given to Uhr-Henry for him to steer by. Unfortunately the binoculars supplied to him were not fitted with spray shields and became useless during the squalls. Davis had therefore to share the only serviceable pair of glasses with Uhr-Henry when explaining the coastline to him and pointing out his landmarks. It later emerged that they had been looking at different, but almost identical, landmarks.

The boats left at 0124 and were given until 0330, with a 15-minute allowance after that. The boat's compass proved inefficient and the star given was almost immediately obscured by a squall.

The weather at the anchorage was wind WSW Force 4; slight sea and swell; cloudy and frequent rain squalls. While the boats were away only glimpses of the land were obtained, although it was less than half a mile away. Davis started to worry. MGB 318 had to weigh and re-anchor owing to dragging, the current being about 3 knots.

The boats returned at 0230 with the shore party: they had proceeded to the wrong bay. A conference was held immediately; the bay they had been to was pinpointed and the reason for the mistake discovered and cleared: it was due to the original misunderstanding about the landmarks. The stores were taken on board and the dinghies hoisted. Anchor was weighed at 0346 and 318 proceeded. The wind had veered and on the return passage was NW. The ship's motion was just as violent as on the way out. Of all those on board only two were not seasick, while two others were completely incapacitated on the southward passage.

A further attempt two nights later, again in MGB 318, started with very favourable weather reports and everyone was confident that the operation would be completed this time. But 318 was already making heavy work of a moderate south-westerly swell soon after clearing the race at Start Point. As the direction of the swell promised a weather shore on the Breton side of the Channel, Davis decided to plug into it at reduced speed, as they had left sufficiently early to allow for a slow crossing. Wind and swell slowly increased; however, Davis recorded that, although there was not enough wind 'to worry a top hat', it was just enough to push over the tops of the swell and make it dangerous. Steering was 15 to 20 degrees either side of the course. Frequent heavy showers made a nice change from spray soakings. MGB 318 was labouring but 'not liable to break up'. At 2020 speed had to be further reduced as she was now really starting to 'scoop it up' forward, and, with propellers out of the water, engine-racing was becoming worse. At 2035 'the Atlantic in solid form arrived on the forecastle, quickly followed by the Pacific': speed was reduced to 12 knots. To make life even more amusing, the masthead steaming light started to flash intermittently. At 2045, after bouncing in the same hole for ten minutes, the operation was abandoned. On the return passage, the exhaust pipe of the centre engine was found to be fractured and the engine-room had to be cleared of all personnel, except for occasional visits.

Because of the navigational hazards revealed by these first two LARDERING operations, MGB 318[6] was sent on 24/25 January to lay two submerged position-finding sonar buoys, one near the Triagoz plateau, the other off Ile-Losquet, in the Ile-Grande area, as an adjunct to future operations.

Weather reports promised wind increasing to Force 5–6 about midnight, but as it was south by west, this was considered favourable as it offered the prospect of a good weather shore for working at the time they planned to arrive. They took their departure from Start Point at 1735: weather was not favourable to a fast passage as there was a slight to moderate sea with a confused swell. Though not big, it threw the boat about, causing personal discomfort but no danger. By 1900 it was obvious that the weather was determined not to be neutral; wind and sea were increasing rapidly and spray becoming continuous. By 1936 they were forced to reduce speed further as 318 was now shipping solid water forward. Davis expected to pick up Hurd Deep at 2040: he was particularly anxious to check speed on the Deep and decided that if it did not show up on the echo-sounder by 2130 the operation would have to be abandoned. The Deep was picked up at 2128, which indicated that they were losing 3.2 knots on estimated speed, rather than the 1-knot reduction Davis had allowed for on account of weather, but he decided to carry on as to return would be 'a shocking waste of engine hours' and the operation – code-named, ironically enough, TENDERLY – required no boatwork.

Wind was now Force 6 direction south and engines were silenced at 2330; the sea moderate to rough. Land was sighted at 2336 on the port bow but not identified. At 2340 a flashing light was sighted on the starboard bow. It was suspected to be the Ile-de-Batz light, but, knowing how misleading a landfall can be along that collection of rocks, Davis altered course for the light as they appeared to be on dipping-range and it was necessary to make certain of its characteristics. At 0004 Triagoz rocks and lighthouse were sighted bearing SSE, Ile-de-Batz light was verified and course altered to the buoy position. As they approached the Triagoz plateau, it was obvious there was not going to be any work done near the rocks, as the swell was tumbling and breaking a good distance out and the current would carry them down on to what Davis called 'the stone embroidery'. The movement of the boat made bearings difficult and several fixes were necessary before they could be certain of the exact position. The buoy was slipped at 0044 in 28 fathoms of water – Triagoz lighthouse bearing 044°, 1.7 miles. Lt Whalley used the Asdic set to ascertain whether the buoy was working properly and expressed satisfaction. The trek to Ile-Losquet now began.

The mainland was plainly visible, the moon being brilliant and the sky almost cloudless. They arrived off Ile-Losquet at 0129, one hour before low water. Their position was most uncertain, as Davis reported to Slocum two days later:

> 'of all the festering collections of rocks on this rotten coast, the Ile-Losquet area wins the Hamburger. Not one of the islands on the chart could be distinguished. The swell here was most uncomfortable and its action on the outlying reefs was most impressive. It would start as a white break with a rumble and develop as a white express train with about the same volume of sound. As this entertainment was going on outside of us (Le Crapaud and adjacent banks) as well as inside of us, and I could not fix our position with any certainty, I desperately looked for other means. The Commanon Bank was our only hope. At 0152 we commenced a run to the westward to try to pick up the Commanon Bank, praying rapidly all the time that it wouldn't be so ungracious as to break when we arrived on top of it. At 0200 it was found – 5 fathoms recorded, allowing for the height of tide. We continued on this course for a while as it was necessary to recross and check bearings of outstanding objects at the same time. At 0212 we recrossed the bank and ran in until time and sounding and a bearing of Triagoz gave our position. The buoy (No. 6) was slipped at 0218 in 22 fathoms in position Triagoz bearing 352° distance 4.6 miles . . . Lt Whalley again expressed his satisfaction with the working of the buoy.'

Course was set for the western end of the Triagoz plateau. Weather was wind south Force 6 gusting to 7, moderate sea, moderate westerly swell, clear sky and visibility very good. At 0259 course was altered for the return to base.

At 0304, five or six enemy trawlers were sighted about 15° on the port bow, course ENE, speed about 9 knots. These challenged 318 a few seconds later with O for Orange. The MGB, unsilenced, rang for full speed and turned to south-east. The enemy took about a minute and a half before opening fire, at a range of about 2,000 metres. The German vessels must have seen them some time before, as they were directly in their moon-path. Their fire at first was quite accurate, passing down both sides of the boat, with small stuff (2-pounder) bursting overhead. MGB 318's smoke-screen was beginning to take effect and the enemy fire was aimed at both ends of the screen and at two or three points along it. At about 0308 smoke was stopped so that the enemy's position could be guessed. Shortly after this they started using 3- or 4-inch ammunition: some of these shells burst ahead and about six metres above the water. MGB 318 restarted their smoke and turned to south to gain cover of the land and rocks. The enemy appeared to be confused by this second smoke-screen and their shooting became haphazard. At 0314 they engaged each other and through the screen 318 watched with delight their tracers flying backwards and forwards to each other. The Germans ceased fire about 0302 and 318 altered course to south-west.

Throughout this time the gunboat's engines were misfiring and large quantities of water were breaking over her. Over the next half-hour, speed had gradually to be reduced as course was progressively brought round to north. By 0430, when Plymouth was called for the second time on the W/T and an enemy report broadcast twice, the wind was south Force 7 and the sea very rough, with a heavy swell. The boat had to be watched continuously as she took the hit and rode a swell at exceptionally high speed; on several occasions engines had to be stopped to allow the swell to pass underneath.

At 0917 they asked Plymouth to give them a fix but this was not obtainable. It was assumed they were somewhere west of Bolt Tail. The weather was wind south Force 8 gusting to 9, high sea and swell, overcast and rain. The sea length was about 40–50 metres and seemed to be about 10 metres high, although Davis supposed it to be 6–7 metres in fact. A destroyer that passed about 3,000 metres away could be seen only when on the top of a sea. These conditions worried Martin and scared Davis 'almost stiff. We were all thinking about the steering gear,' he wrote, 'but nobody dared mention it. Actually the steering did not break down until the following day.' At 1000 they were in sight of land and the Mewstone was recognised bearing N 30° W. This presented a pretty problem on a lee shore, as it was impossible to run across the sea to make Plymouth entrance. It was decided to turn the boat to SW and try to make westing, so as to run up with the sea to the entrance. They waited for some sort of a smooth, then turned the boat with one engine going slow ahead. It seemed to take about an hour and everybody looked fairly grim. They managed to get the sea about two points on the port bow and had the wing engines on slow ahead; centre engine was then cut. She rode this fairly well and was surprisingly dry, but the many vertical positions she insisted on assuming were hair-raising. At 1055 they had made between about 3 and 3½ miles and decided to turn for Plymouth. This turn to the northward, the climax of a night of horrors, seemed endless and finally, in absolute desperation, they were forced to use half-speed on one engine.

The turn was eventually completed and they endeavoured to

keep the ship's head about N 10° W. They could not run with the sea as they would not then make the entrance: they actually went about two points off it. They were in a very nasty spot: every sea had to be watched and on one occasion a sea broke across the boat abaft the bridge carrying away both surf-boat lashings and filling the engine-room vents, which got rid of their overflow direct into the engine-room. Rolling was of the 50-degree order now: she was making a good course, though unfortunately land was only visible on the top of the seas, otherwise they could have made better steering.

Davis recalled that no-one appeared to dare breathe for about an hour during the run to the entrance. At 1225 they entered the gate and beautiful still, or almost still, water was their reward. At 1310, after being within 5 miles of Plymouth for four hours, they secured to HMS *Defiance*. They could now eat and drink for the first time since leaving Dartmouth. Davis reported that this was the first operation during which not one officer had had any sleep whatsoever. Of the 20 hours that the operation lasted, the coxswain, P.O. Boyle, was on the bridge for 15, and Davis considered that they owed their partly successful return to harbour to his skill and unfailing cheerfulness. The behaviour of the motor mechanic, P.O. Barker, had also been splendid: his efforts to keep the engines running at high speed while in contact with the enemy, despite the obvious difficulties audible to those on deck, and his constant care of the engines on the return passage, when they were endeavouring to race themselves to pieces, enabled the gunboat to return safely.

Davis reported to the Commander-in-Chief's staff shortly after arriving and was disappointed to find that neither of 318's enemy reports had been received. He was instructed to return next day to report to the Chief of Staff and to the Commander-in-Chief, who offered his personal congratulations to 318 for a successful operation and safe return.

Damage to 318 was negligible: the port guard rails were all bent owing to sea damage; both rubbing strakes were sprung from the hull and there were various small items damaged. Nearly all the crockery on board had been cracked or broken.

CARPENTER II was never completed, though it was not finally cancelled until April. A sortie by MGB 324 to Clogourouan on 9 March for SOE failed to contact two RAF evaders, but was able to confirm that the stores landed on CARPENTER I were still intact: one case had a corner exposed and was again covered.

CARPENTER III to Ile Stagadon, which lies to the east of the Malouine subsidiary entrance channel to Aber-Wrac'h was attempted by MGB 326 on 27 February, but failed because there was no sand of sufficient depth to bury containers. A further operation, code-named DRAPER, was mounted on 10 March with MGB 318 to contact the solitary inhabitant of Stagadon and to enlist his help in establishing an arms dump on the island. The landing party encountered a horse and three noisy dogs, whose barking had to be stilled with lumps of meat. Whether for this or for some other reason, they failed to check the house for inhabitants, though they established an arms dump in a cranny in the rocks. It would seem from Davis's report on the subsequent Operation COOK that this visit to Stagadon drew the attention of the Germans to SOE's LARDERING activities and brought the whole Aber-Wrac'h area to a constant state of alertness.

COOK, the last operation in the 1942/43 winter LARDER-ING series, was first attempted in MGB 318 from Falmouth on 28/29 March 1943. The object was to land 15 cases, each weighing 80 lb., on Ile Guennoc, which lies to the east of the main channel into Aber-Benoît and which had been used 14 months earlier when the Le Tac brothers and their passengers were picked up by Holdsworth and the author, working from MGB 314. This first attempt foundered when they failed to pick up the Petite-Fourche buoy at the seaward end of the channel. It was obviously a frustrating night and when Davis came to write his report he had some hard things to say about SOE. He pointed out that the operation orders mentioned 1,000 lb. of stores, though the actual weight of consignment was 1,200 lb. On his last visit to London he thought he had made it quite clear to Lt Cdr Esplen[7] (of SOE's Naval Section) and his assistant that it would be impossible for the landing party to deal with this quantity of stores in the time available. On this last attempt they had the full load of stores, two boats and an increased landing party consisting of three officers and six men. If the SOE representatives in London were not prepared to listen to suggestions concerning 'their operations which I have a hand in, then I suggest one of the SOE London staff be sent on one of these joy rides to ensure [sic] them that I am not talking merely from the end of a pen. As there have been suggestions that Letty and I are "not trying" to complete LARDER operations, which I admit are suggestions I have been unable to track down, but if I do, I intend taking up officially, perhaps it would be better if Letty and I were confined to our own operations and that SOE supplied their own navigators for LARDER operations.'

'It is becoming increasingly obvious to Letty and I [sic],' he continued, 'that we are not considered capable of anything except thumping away in an MGB and the fact that we might have an interest in or ideas about the particular work we are engaged upon is discounted.'

Fortunately the weather reports on 3 April 1943 for the second attempt at Operation COOK were most promising, though the southern horizon from Falmouth looked banked with fog. MGB

318 left *Forte IV* at 1732 to rendezvous with 360 off Helford River. Praam dinghies of a type that had been specially developed at Helford that winter for landing in surf were transferred with the stores and shore party and 318 proceeded towards the Lizard via the Manacles.

After they had passed the Manacles buoy the echo-sounder packed up, but the motor mechanic managed somehow to repair it to a state in which it at least gave an indication whether the sea bed was rushing to meet them or whether it was wise to proceed.

Air escort, consisting of two Beaufighters, joined them at 1946 hrs and recognition signals were exchanged. Speed was increased to 1500 r.p.m. at 1849 and departure was taken from D3 buoy at 1908.

Weather was light airs and smooth sea, slight WNW swell, sky 1/10 hazy. The conditions were, for once, really delightful and speed could have been increased to maximum cruising, but, as it was almost cloudless and they had been requested to leave the D3 buoy at 1900, it was decided that they would be much too far to the southward by dusk, so speed was reduced to 1400 r.p.m. At 2038 speed was increased to 1,500 r.p.m. The air escort made their departure signal at 2051, just as night was beginning to darken, although it was not really dark until 2130. At 2103 a flash was seen bearing Red 40, but it could not be defined as flak, bomb or gun-flash. Speed was reduced and engines silenced.

'Pocket battleships, cruisers, destroyers and E-boats' were sighted, or thought to have been sighted on the horizon quite frequently: this was a combination of haze and swell, 'amusing to some but rather wearing', as Davis recorded.

At 2253 speed was reduced to 1,000 r.p.m. for the land approach. Land was sighted, indistinctly at 2328. Speed was reduced to 800 r.p.m. At 2335 engines were stopped as Ile-Vierge lighthouse was sighted and they were 'looking up' at it, about 1.3 miles distant. As they stopped engines, a white flare or Very light was fired from the top of the lighthouse towards the mainland; had they been seen? A position was quickly fixed and a run to the south-westward begun until 2342, when rocks were sighted right ahead: these were the north-western corner of the Libenter plateau. While they were in this position, a searchlight of quite some power came on in the Stagadon-Malouine area to the eastward and illuminated the Aber-Wrac'h Grand-Chenal for some time before sweeping to the southward, illuminating the rocks and islands and finally, Davis was almost certain, Stagadon Island. MGB 318 proceeded again as the searchlight beam was sweeping towards the sea. They did their best to imitate a rock, which proved unnecessary as the searchlight seemed unable to shine seawards, and its arc to be bounded by Ile-Vierge through south to Le-Trépieds. The searchlight was constantly switched on and off with the beam on a different bearing each time.

At 2359 they altered course to S 20° W expecting to make the Petite-Fourche buoy. From this time on, a most unreliable echo-sounder provided many scares until at 0014 it indicated no water at all. They were mixed up in foam, but remedied this by means of a short period at half-astern. Their position was fixed again by guess and good luck and course set to the NE. At 0020 the buoy was sighted. Trying to avoid a collision with it afforded a few lively moments.

The run down the Aber-Benoît Channel started at 0023 and dinghies were launched and towed astern. Course was set to allow for a flood tide and before long they found themselves mixed up with the shoals on the west side. They then commenced loading the dinghies, while towing them, and rounded the end of Ile-Guennoc to the chosen anchorage. The anchor was let go at 0042, and the praams left at 0045, when the boat was brought up to 20 fathoms. The commanding officer of the SOE shore party[8] was instructed to return by 0215. Engines were cut at 0047.

The dinghies returned at 0217 and reported that, once again, the landing party, which included an officer from SOE's Independent French Section, found too little sand or soil to allow containers to be dug in, but 12 of the 15 cases had been hidden among the rocks and prehistoric structures. Unfortunately no stowage place could be found for the other three. They commenced heaving in the grass anchor warp, started engines and got the dinghies aboard.

At 0230 they proceeded slow ahead and at 0234 increased to 800 r.p.m. They took departure from the Petite-Fourche buoy at 0240, set course and increased speed. Owing to a restriction imposed by Commander-in-Chief Plymouth, they could not be north of the line 40 km. (25 miles) south of the Lizard before first light, so speed was reduced to 1200 r.p.m at 0521. As the dawn broke at 0600, speed was increased to 1,400 r.p.m. and six minutes later to 1,500 r.p.m.

Air escort, consisting of two Beaufighters, joined at 0627, and D3 buoy was passed at 0730. At 0809 they stopped at the rendez-vous off the Helford River to await RAF 360's arrival. Between 0825 and 0830, men, boats and stores were trans-shipped. They moored alongside *Forte IV* at 0855.

The weather had remained constant throughout and the whole operation had been 'a most pleasant joy ride'. The echo-sounder alone had misbehaved. The air escort had been very good indeed and most reassuring. However, Davis reported, the last visit to Stagadon had brought that area to a constant state of alertness.

This was the end of the winter's LARDERING operations and

they were never resumed. It was, however, the beginning of a long association between MGB 318 and Aber-Benoît.

The net result of all this effort was three caches of arms and explosives: one was found by a fisherman, who informed the Germans; one disappeared almost certainly into German hands; one reached the local Resistance by chance rather than as a result of arrangements made by SOE. It was, on the face of it, a disappointing outcome to a winter's work. Slocum took the more positive view that these LARDERING operations provided experience that later proved invaluable: the training of ships' crews, boats' crews and navigators was standardised and, when the 15th MGB Flotilla was formed officially at Dartmouth, 'a really strong team spirit centred round the crews which had worked together during the previous winter.' In fact this rather curious scheme – devised originally by a hard-pressed, but always inventive, Holdsworth to provide training and operational experience for his Helford crews after the Admiralty vetoed his plans to endow SOE with an independent capacity for secret sea lines to Brittany – proved a godsend to Slocum by providing employment and training for the first MGB to be permanently allocated to him. MGB 318 and her sisters were too slow to operate across the Channel in the short summer nights when the weather was most likely to be favourable, but if they had failed to find work during the stormy winter of 1942/43, when SIS was unwilling to route agents or mail in and out of France via the north coast of Brittany, it would have been difficult for Slocum to sustain his case for larger and faster craft to be made available to him at Dartmouth.

At this point SOE's two French Country Sections ceased to regard sea transport as relevant to their needs and concentrated on trying to get more help from the RAF. The availability of RAF Special Duties missions for SOE in western Europe was gradually improving. During the first six months of 1941 there had been only 18 successful sorties for SIS and SOE, but there were 38 between July 1941 and February 1942, when a second Special Duties squadron (161) was formed. From a total of 22 completed operations to France for SOE in 1941 (37 agents and 1.5 tons of material), the figure rose to 93 in 1942 (195 agents and 25 tons of stores). There had been a seven-month window of opportunity to carry agents into and out of the unoccupied south coast of France by felucca, and 51 SOE-sponsored passengers did travel by this rather roundabout route between April and November 1942; but this sea line ceased to work after the Allies landed in French North Africa and the Germans moved into the Vichy-administered rump of metropolitan France. In the first three months of 1943, the RAF delivered 20 tons to France for SOE – almost as much as in the whole of 1942.

As has been recounted, Slocum's Operations Section had at the outset worked with the tacit consent of the Admiralty; not until 1942 was he given a measure of recognition and status outside SIS, accorded the title of NID(C) and attached to the Naval Intelligence Division. But there was a clear need for central control where significant demands for naval resources were involved and conflicts of interest arose between the maritime ambitions of the clandestine services. The solution adopted in June 1943 was to appoint Slocum to a newly created post of Deputy Director Operations Division (Irregular), or DDOD(I). This gave him authority to call upon naval commands and bases for support for clandestine sea transport needs and was a conveniently tidy arrangement from the Admiralty's point of view, but it caused understandable resentment in SOE, since Slocum retained his previous responsibility for SIS's own sea operations and continued to do so until the end of the war. This dual role placed Slocum in a difficult position and in his final report as DDOD(I), written in 1946, he admitted that he never entirely succeeded in convincing SOE that he was not prejudiced in favour of SIS.

Against this background it caused much annoyance in Baker Street when Leslie Humphreys's DF Section bypassed SOE's own Naval Section and arranged directly with DDOD(I) for an agent and for one of DF Section's own officers, Captain Peter Harratt, to be trained at Dartmouth with a view to setting up a DF sea line to the north coast of Brittany. Harratt, who had been a regular soldier in the 1920s and had farmed in south-western France before fighting briefly on the Republican side in Spain, was Humphreys's staff officer in charge of operations by sea. He had been closely in touch with SOE's own paranaval outfit at Helford and had accompanied Uhr-Henry ashore on Operation MIRFIELD, the reconnaissance of the beach at Clogourouan on 9/10 March 1943 when the CARPENTER I cache had been inspected and the corner of an exposed container covered up. He and Humphreys had evidently decided that, after Holdsworth's departure to North Africa and Slocum's emergence as DDOD(I) with a permanently allocated MGB and other high speed-craft in prospect, it was better to do business with the organ-grinder than with his monkey. Harratt went down to Dartmouth with DF's chosen agent, Erwin Deman, a cosmopolitan Jew born in Vienna in 1904, who had been in business at Lisbon before the war and spoke fluent German, French and English. His hatred of Nazism – a sentiment he shared with Harratt – had led him to join the French army as a corporal. He was taken prisoner in 1940, but escaped from Germany and joined the Foreign Legion in North Africa. He reached England after deserting from the Legion and was recruited by SOE. After the normal training given to agents, Harratt took him on as his team-mate. They lived for two months on a small boat in the Dart, becoming, in cooperation with DDOD(I)'s local representatives, experts in map-reading and mapmaking, navigation, beach reconnaissance, clandestine beach landing from the surf-boats used by the MGBs and the use of the S-Phone, a secure form of 'walkie-talkie' developed by SOE.[9]

A first attempt to land Deman was made in MGB 326 on 29 April 1943 using the Clogourouan beach, but was defeated by bad weather (Operation MANGO). Though Letty's report spoke of awaiting the first opportunity, no new attempt was made, probably because the nights were getting too short. Letty foresaw that to maintain a consistent speed of 28 knots, which was evidently expected of this particular boat, 'practically ideal weather conditions would be needed.'

In the end Deman was landed by an RAF Hudson aircraft of 161 Special Duties Squadron on 19/20 August 1943 and set about organising what became SOE's 'Var' land line, responsible for evacuating agents in trouble and conveying W/T sets, crystals and codes for other SOE circuits.

CHAPTER XIV

West Coast: November 1942–October 1943

T he disasters suffered by Dunderdale's Section in 1941 and 1942 were a reflection of greatly improved German counter-measures in the Occupied Zone. Rémy's Gaullist CND was also badly affected by these in 1942, but showed remarkable powers of regeneration and, during the winter of 1942/43, its output was important enough to SIS for its communications both by W/T and by fishing-boat operations to the west coast of Brittany to command very high priority: this was further enhanced when the Germans occupied southern France following the Allied landings in North Africa in November 1942 and brought a series of Polish-manned felucca operations from Gibraltar to a halt.

In a number of other respects too, the North African landings altered the context in which SIS and SOE had to work as far as France was concerned. Roosevelt's preponderant stake in the North African venture and his entrenched mistrust of de Gaulle meant that, for much of 1943, there were two separate French clandestine services working into occupied France. General Giraud, on becoming High Commissioner for the North African Territories after Admiral Darlan's assassination, took over Colonel Rivet's Service de Renseignements, and Captain Paul Paillole's counter-espionage service, the Direction de Surveillance du Territoire (DST), both of which had managed to go on working against the Germans under Vichy auspices. SIS and SOE continued to cooperate with de Gaulle's BCRA in London but they were also in liaison with Giraud's Special Services in Algiers and with missions he set up in London. But the main part of the BCRA under Passy moved to Algiers when de Gaulle became Co-President of the French Committee of National Liberation in the summer of 1943, leaving a rear-link in London under Commandant André Manuel, Passy's second in command. By the winter of that year de Gaulle had emerged as master of this complex political battlefield and Giraud rapidly faded from the picture, as did Rivet and General Ronin, who had been in overall charge of intelligence at the Palais d'Eté under Giraud's aegis.

From the TORCH landings onwards, the American Office of Strategic Services (OSS) also aspired to operate independently of British tutelage in France. SIS did all they could to prevent this development: they had grounds to mistrust OSS's inexperience. SOE, under Dodds-Parker, its senior officer in the Western Mediterranean, took a more accommodating line. Henceforward Britain no longer had a monopoly of clandestine communications with occupied Europe, as French submarines also operated as a covert link between Algiers and occupied France from December 1942 onwards.

The effect of these changes was, of course, confined to the Western Mediterranean: links between the United Kingdom base and France remained in British hands and they became increasingly sophisticated.

By the end of November 1942 both 138 and 161 Special Duties squadrons had been re-equipped completely with Halifaxes, which were a great improvement on the Whitleys originally used. 'Rebecca' radio beacons were increasingly widely deployed, which meant that agents and supplies could be dropped even in the no-moon periods. Three double Lysander operations were flown during November – the first of their kind – one of these for Rémy. Two Havocs, which had been carrying out trials for 161 Squadron with an ultra-shortwave radio-telephone system developed by SIS, were detached to St Eval for operational trials with NID(C)'s Breton fishing vessels and with an agent in Brittany. Contact was established with N51 (*Le-Dinan*) on 13 November to pick up reports on enemy shipping in the Brest-Lorient area in the course of Operation GRENVILLE III. Two Albemarles sent by 161 to St Eval for an evaluation of their suitability for maintaining this secure radio telephone link were further evidence of the importance attached by SIS to communications with Rémy's CND, but these ASCENSION operations were eventually suspended and the Albemarles withdrawn.

On the first three voyages undertaken by N51 in the summer of 1942, Lomenech and Mackenzie had been struck by the very large number of small 40–50-foot trawlers working the inshore fishing grounds off the Pointe-de-Penmarc'h. These were of a type similar to the P11, square-sterned *pinasses* which fished by day only. P11's performance when re-engined for NID(C)'s use gave Lomenech the idea that a satisfactory copy of such a craft could be built, with a flat bottom and powerful engines to give it a much higher speed. These features would increase the safety of the line, by reducing the amount of daylight steaming in crossing from the Scillies to Ushant, and also the safety of the crews, by giving them, as a last resort, the legs of any German patrol craft that might chase them. The Director of Naval Construction was approached through the Naval Intelligence Directorate and, to everyone's surprise, Admiralty approval was obtained for the project – a clear indication of Slocum's increasing influence and of the importance attached to the sea line with Rémy's CND organisation. Laurent Giles, well known in peacetime as a Lymington yacht designer, was working for the Admiralty in DNC's office at Bath and produced plans for a 55-foot craft, which resembled the P11 above water but whose two 500 h.p. Hall-Scott engines and underwater lines were designed to give her a speed of 18–20 knots. The first vessel built to these plans was unfortunately destroyed during an air raid before she had left her builders' yard at East Cowes, belonging to the firm of Groves and Gutteridge, which in peacetime specialised in producing lifeboats for the Royal National Lifeboat Institution. A second and identical vessel was laid down immediately. It was thought prudent to launch her without her fisherman-style bulwarks, deckhouse and mast, so as to disguise her ultimate purpose, and in that state, under Mackenzie's eye, she completed her acceptance trials in the Solent satisfactorily. She was then finished off in another yard and commissioned in time to take over from the slow trawlers in May 1943. Immediately before this, there had been a series of arrests in France, which caused SIS and the BCRA much concern: contact with Rémy's organisation was temporarily disrupted and DDOD(I)'s monthly fishing-boat operations to collect the mail could not take place in March and April. By May these difficulties had been overcome and the new high-speed vessel re-established the sea line.

The new vessel was known officially as MFV 2023 (Motor Fishing Vessel), part of a more general renaming of DDOD(I)'s growing collection of French fishing vessels, but Slocum called her *L'Angèle-Rouge* – a compliment to his auburn-haired secretary, Miss Sykes-Wright, who had recently married Steven Mackenzie.[1]

MFV 2023, which had, among other weight-saving features, a mast made of balsa wood, proved suitable for operations in the summer months only, but she undertook five missions between the beginning of May and the end of September 1943, three of which were successful, her high speed enabling her to make the crossing even in the shortest nights and in spite of heavily increased enemy air patrols north and west of Ushant.

MFV 2023 (*L'Angèle-Rouge*) was commanded on her first three operations by Daniel Lomenech. His log abstract, his report on the general conduct of the operation, his notes on the vessel's behaviour at sea and his report on the fishing fleets encountered during EFFINGHAM, her maiden voyage, have happily survived.[2] The operation required another rendezvous with Rémy's *Les-Deux-Anges* 5 miles off the La-Jument buoy that marks the seaward entrance to the channel into the Glénans archipelago.

Repainted in fisherman colours, 2023 slipped her mooring in New Grimsby sound off Tresco in the Scillies at 1645 hrs on 5 May. Her crew consisted of seven hands – Lomenech, Sub Lt Harding, Petty Officer Lawn, Seaman Rive, Telegraphist Mankelow, Motor Mechanic Robinson and Stoker Petty Officer Blackby. Her Beaufighter escort joined soon after she passed Cromwell's Castle and set course for the Bishop Rock, from which she took her departure at 1755, setting course S 6° E to pass 32 km. (20 miles) SSW of the Basse-Froide buoy in order to take her through the area where the mackerel-fishing fleet was likely to be found.

The wind was northerly, with a moderate sea and swell. With the following sea, the vessel was difficult to steer at 1,200 r.p.m. on the two 500 h.p. Hall-Scott engines, as she was inclined to broach to. Relieving Beaufighters took over at 2100. Steering improved when speed was increased to 1,600 r.p.m. on both engines at 2155 but the ship tended to pound and light water was shipped forward on several occasions. At 2230 hrs the Beaufighters returned to base and 2023 was on her own, but under cover of darkness.

Steering had to be watched carefully as there was a tendency for the ship to pay off to starboard when proceeding on both engines. Periods of more than half an hour at the wheel were found inadvisable because of the strain on the quartermaster. Watch on and watch off were kept by all hands, with an officer, a deckhand and an engineer on duty at all times.

At 0320 lights of the mackerel fleet were observed and action was taken to avoid passing close: they were, as anticipated, roughly 20 miles SSW of the Basse-Froide buoy. At 0325 course was altered to S 65° E for the position south of Penmarc'h lighthouse, where they expected to contact trawlers of the P11 type. At 0400 speed was reduced to slow ahead on the starboard engine (800 r.p.m.) and petrol was transferred from the deck tanks to replenish the main tankage. Considerable difficulty was experienced owing to the violent movements of the ship, and some 50 gallons of fuel were lost. At 0500, the three pumps were removed on completion of the operation and the deck tanks were cut open and thrown overboard, together with the crates that had protected them, so that the deck was clear before daylight.

On arrival off Penmarc'h, course was set for the La-Jument buoy, various alterations of course being necessary to avoid passing close to local fishermen of the P11 type from Le-Guilvinec, Pen-marc'h and Saint-Guénolé. This entailed an hour's delay. At 1130, *Les-Deux-Anges*, which they were due to meet, was sighted to star-board in a position 3 miles south of La-Jument. The recognition procedure was carried out and precautions were taken in case of treachery, but all was well and at 1230 *Les-Deux-Anges* was alongside and stores were transferred, though the adverse weather conditions caused considerable difficulty. One bag of mail, one passenger and five empty 10-gallon petrol drums were taken on board MFV 2023. The stores transferred to *Les-Deux-Anges* consisted of four 10-gallon drums of petrol, a coil of 2″ manila rope, three balls of cod-line, 6lb. of cocoa, seven tins of coffee, a bottle of whisky, 10 tots of rum, 15 packets of cigarettes and 6 bars of soap. The crew of the rendezvous craft were in the best of spirits but refused to take 'any sails whatsoever [sic]' and some trawl-doors and a trawl, these being far too heavy for their craft. However, they suggested that a smaller trawl should be provided when opportunity offered. By 1240 the transfer was completed and a course was set for La-Jument buoy, which was abeam at 1250. The old-fashioned Patent log was streamed and set as the more up-to-date Chernikeef log, worked by a small impeller projecting through the ship's bottom, had packed up on the outward passage.

Lomenech, who preferred to sail as close inshore as possible during these expeditions, decided that, in view of the obviously impending bad weather, it would be right to begin the homeward passage immediately, as speeds of over 8 knots were out of the question. Course was set to make a position 7 miles south of Penmarc'h, where they arrived at 1430. Course was then set for the Basse-Froide buoy. This coastal route was deemed appropriate because of the prevailing violent conditions, which made interception by hostile craft very improbable. At 1455 the P11-type trawlers, of which they had seen about 30 in that vicinity, were returning to port because of the deteriorating weather conditions. Larger sailing fishing vessels continued about their business: a Concarneau tunnyman was proceeding west and they encountered four *Émigrant*-type cutters during the afternoon, as well as three large German whale-catchers minesweeping. By 1850 Ar-Men lighthouse was abeam at a distance of 4.8 nautical miles and at 1920 they were off the Basse-Froide buoy; here speed was reduced owing to the confused sea and strong north-easterly wind. Course was now set for the Scillies, but very little progress was made before midnight, when it became possible to increase speed to 1,000 r.p.m. After they left the Basse-Froide buoy, the compass was completely useless, swinging at times through 360°. At dusk, the Pole Star was observed and kept ahead.

At 0420 the sea had moderated sufficiently for speed to be increased to 1,200 r.p.m. and by 0500 it was increased to 1,600 on both engines. At 0730 Land's End was sighted on the starboard bow. At 0800 the Wolf Rock was observed to starboard and course was set for the Scillies. By 1000 Round Island was abeam and by 1020 the operation had been successfully completed and MFV 2023 was moored alongside MGB 318, which left New Grimsby Sound with the mail and passenger at 1130.

The homeward passage had been a hard one. MFV 2023 pounded badly and heavy water was shipped forward even at 8 knots. Steering was difficult and the vessel's movements made life aboard 'unbearable'. But Lomenech reported that the vessel's appearance compared favourably with its prototypes on the French coast and the crew of *Les-Deux-Anges* were unable to tell her actual character. The favourable outcome of EFFINGHAM was, he considered, full proof that the ship overall was an outstanding success. On the other hand, bad accommodation, lack of food for 42 hours and unfavourable weather put a mental strain on the crew that was more noticeable than on previous occasions. The behaviour of the ship's company as a whole under these conditions was, however, exemplary. Lomenech recommended that the ship should undergo a major overhaul before undertaking another operation: he enclosed a defect list and was critical of the standard of engineering maintenance at the Helford base over the three weeks before the expedition, as a result of which the vessel had been found to have major engine-room defects during the operation. A competent authority on high-speed engines was needed to supervise any major repairs that might in future be required. As things were, the engine-room personnel felt they could not be held responsible for any major defect that might occur.

On 2023's second operation (JERVIS) on 6 June, she was attacked by enemy aircraft when c. 50 km. (30 miles) south of the Scillies and obliged to return after one of her two escorting RAF Mustangs had been shot down. The operation was then postponed by the agents from Rémy's CND organisation whom she was to have met at the usual rendezvous with *Les-Deux-Anges* off the Glénans to pick up three passengers and mail.

Lomenech's final operation, ANSON, the object of which was to land one agent and embark two others together with the usual mail, was completed only on 18 August after 24 changes of date. For much, if not all, of the ten preceding weeks, 2023 lay at NID(C)'s specially laid mooring in New Grimsby Sound, and contact with Slocum's office in Palace Street, Westminster, was maintained by a field-telephone line, connected to the island's exchange. The handset was hidden among the rocks and bracken above the rough-hewn steps below Cromwell's Castle that were their usual landing place on Tresco. It was not an unpleasant life: the crew became regular patrons of the one and only pub at New Grimsby and anything less than 20 pints of the weak beer was considered a subnormal evening's performance. Daniel, a strikingly handsome young man, found female company among the Land Girls; they were trying to practise wartime agriculture in small fields where the normal crop was daffodils, which proved impossible to eradicate by ploughing. The fisherman from neighbouring Bryher used to row off and come alongside 2023 to ask how many lobsters Daniel had removed from his pots laid in the Sound on that particular morning. However, Daniel had already in April applied for a transfer to submarines. Enough was enough: he was by temperament a man of action and longed to strike at the enemy. After almost exactly three years' involvement in clandestine operations in and to Brittany – a period during which his parents and sister had been victims of the break-up of the 'Johnny' organisation – he relinquished command of 2023.[3] He took the necessary training course and embarked on a completely new career in Royal Navy submarines. He had done a number of operations with them in 1941 and had much liked what he had seen.

Slocum paid tribute to him at the end of the war in the following terms:

'(1) I have been associated with Lieut Lomenech since 1940, firstly as a civilian and later as a Naval Officer.

(2) Prior to receiving his commission in the Royal Navy in October 1941, this officer rendered distinguished service to the Allied cause in Occupied France under conditions of considerable danger.

(3) Subsequently, he embarked in HM Submarines as liaison officer on expeditions into enemy-controlled waters of France.

(4) Later a flotilla of French fishing vessels was formed and trained by DDOD(I) for operations to the Biscay coast of France and Lieut Lomenech was the original executive officer and later commanding officer of the first of these ships.

(5) By August 1942 he had taken part in eleven expeditions to the north and west coast of France, on the last three occasions in command. He displayed outstanding qualities of leadership, courage and seamanship and surmounted all the difficulties of adverse weather, mechanical breakdown and the risk of detection and capture by the enemy, which last hazard, in his case, would have resulted in certain summary execution, since his identity and previous activities were known to the enemy.

(6) For the above services he was, in October 1942, awarded the Distinguished Service Cross.

(7) Subsequent to this award Lieut Lomenech continued to display undiminished courage and initiative and commanded no fewer than eight additional expeditions to the coasts of France, all of which were successful.

(8) In carrying out these operations he enabled a vital line of intelligence between Great Britain and France to be kept open, with results of the highest value to the Allied cause.

(9) Finally, at his own request and after two years of brilliant service as a commissioned officer with DDOD(I), he transferred to duty in submarines and his chapter of distinguished service

with DDOD(I) was closed with the award of a bar to the Distinguished Service Cross in November 1943.

F. A. Slocum'

Lomenech was succeeded as commanding officer of MFV 2023 by Lt J.J. Allen who also used the name Tremayne, a French officer who had joined the Royal Navy in 1940 and served in HMS *Fidelity*.

On Allen's first operation – REMEDY, which was successfully carried out between 7 and 9 September – *L'Angèle Rouge* ran into an awkward situation.[4] She was returning from the usual rendezvous off the Glénans with two agents and the mail on board, steaming at 8 knots, on her auxiliary engine, up the coast of the Ile-de-Sein. A fleet of crabbers was fishing nearby and a German convoy zigzagging southwards to seaward of the ship. As 2023 was passing the crabbers, keeping as far to seaward of them as possible, the convoy altered course towards her. Allen could not move in among the crabbers, nor avoid the convoy by making out to sea without revealing his exceptional speed. He stopped and allowed the convoy to pass either side of him. One of the escort vessels passed him close enough for his crew to hear a gramophone playing on the German ship, while the German captain scrutinised 2023 through glasses at a range of no more than 100 metres. It was a tense moment, as *L'Angèle Rouge*'s stern was wider than that of a genuine fishing boat. However, the convoy, which included a crippled U-boat, passed by and MFV 2023 resumed her passage to England. The author was in the Mediterranean when this happened but he heard on the grapevine that Allen had tried for over an hour to make W/T contact with his SIS base station, which was supposed to be keeping constant watch on the relevant frequency, as he felt he should report the alluring target of opportunity represented by the damaged submarine. Considering how close they were to Brest, it was a brave thing to do. Fortunately the Germans were keeping no better radio watch than their counterparts at Helford.

Since June 1943 Helford had been reorganised on an ambitious scale. The SIS fishing-boat flotilla, which now included N51, P11, AO4, MFV 2023 and the engineless tunnyboat *Le-Clipper* from Operation SHAMROCK, which had been used as a store ship, was moved there from Falmouth. It was to be enlarged to meet an anticipated large-scale SOE programme and was consequently put on a more official footing. It now became officially known as the Inshore Patrol Flotilla (IPF) and the vessels renumbered as MFVs, becoming, respectively, MFVs 2020 (N51) *Le-Dinan*; 2021 (P11) *Ar-Morscoul*; 2022 (AO4) *Président-Herriot*; and 2023 (*L'Angèle-Rouge*). The additional vessels were MFV 2025 (*Fée-des-Eaux*); 2026 (*Sirène*), a converted 55-foot French crabber; 2027 (*Korrigan*), a 50-foot French trawler; 2028 (*L'Oeuvre*), a 65-foot French fishing vessel.

Two considerably larger trawlers, the 105-foot *Breeze* and 106-foot *Jacques-Morgand*, were added and the flotilla was given as base ship HM Yacht *Sunbeam II*, a three-masted, square-topsail schooner that had belonged to Lord Runciman and was herself a near-replica of the original *Sunbeam*, in which Lord Brassey has sailed round the world.

'As though to crush so presumptuous a move,' wrote Slocum in his final report, 'fate stepped in as soon as the IPF was well established.' A fifth operation by MFV 2023 in September failed because of bad weather, in which 2023 displayed fine sea-keeping qualities but reached the meeting-place to find herself the only fishing boat at sea. Two further attempts by MFV 2022 (AO4) in October were frustrated by gales and on the second occasion the ship returned with damage to her propeller. At the end of that month MFV 2022 (*Président-Herriot*) made what proved to be a final attempt to make contact, but the weather was such that she could not maintain sufficient speed and the operation was abandoned. At this point a fresh series of arrests broke out in France and Rémy's sea line closed down for good. Many further operations for other organisations were projected, but none got beyond the discussion stage.

The Senior Officer Inshore Patrol Flotilla (SOIP) appointed by DDOD(I) was Lt Cdr Nigel Warington Smyth, RNVR, brother of Lt Cdr Bevil Warington Smyth, RNVR, who was in command of the SOE naval base. Since their father was Resident Naval Officer in the Helford River, the arrangement had a distinctly dynastic character. Bevil, who had lost a foot in a Fleet Air Arm flying accident, considered that the move of DDOD(I)'s fishing vessel flotilla from Falmouth to Helford opened up a new era in the relations between SOE personnel at Helford and men of the IPF. It enabled everyone to get to know everyone else and it came as a source of great surprise to more than one officer (and to some of the more intelligent ratings) to discover that – contrary to what they had been led to believe – the principal enemy was Hitler and not that member's opposite number in the sister organisation. In his view nothing but good came of this amalgamation at the same base, and the personnel of the two organisations at Helford worked thereafter in the closest cooperation with 'the discomforture of the Hun' as their sole objective. Ironically enough, this improved state of relations was achieved just when the centre of all operational activity had moved back to Dartmouth, where it remained for the next 12 months, leaving Helford as little more than a training base.

One field where cooperation between the Warington Smyths yielded valuable results, during the winter of 1943 and the spring of 1944, was small-boat training and surf practice. Under their able direction, exercises were carried out tirelessly in all types of rubber boats, canoes and dinghies. The recurring problem of landing through surf had been the subject of tests at Prah Beach, which were filmed so that the results could be studied at leisure and conclusions drawn. The surf-boats that Nigel designed won the confidence of the boat officers working with DDOD(I)'s 15th Motor Gunboat Flotilla. Guy Hamilton, the film director, who was one of them, was always amazed at the amount of stores and bodies that could be piled aboard the 14-foot SN1 model and at the same time ride smoothly with just two stout matelots at the oars. After a little practice in the surf at Prah Sands, the boats were even more impressive.

Clinker-built by yacht builders Camper and Nicholson, the surf-boats were double-ended, with a diminutive transom at both ends designed to take a steering oar. All that was needed when leaving a beach was that the two oarsmen should swivel round on their thwarts and move oars and rowlocks to the available alternative position; then, when the coxswain boarded the boat over what had been the bow when landing, he would be in the right place to use the steering oar for the return journey to the waiting gunboat. It was a very sophisticated arrangement.

The 24′9″ SN2 version had been designed to fit the same boat chocks as the standard Montagu whaler carried by frigates and destroyers as their sea-boat. In tests, the Warington Smyth boat proved far easier to pull than the Montagu whaler. The Navy's Chief Hydrographer ordered six for his own use, but he was the only user from outside Slocum's private navy. Perhaps his interest in this outstanding surf-boat had something to do with the fact that the Warington Smyths' grandfather had previously been Chief Hydrographer. The SN2 was used from Helford on Christmas Day 1943 to rescue 28 people from the Aber-Benoît estuary.

CHAPTER XV

North Coast: Winter 1943–44

'The Breton coast is extraordinarily indented. . . The jag-
gedness of this coastline with its islands, islets and reefs,
which is due only in part to the action of the sea, is one of the
characteristics of Brittany. . .

Sombre cliffs, rugged capes . . . , islands, rocks and reefs
give the coastline a grimness which is reflected in local names
with a sinister ring; the Channel of Great Fear (Fromveur), the
Bay of the Dead (Baie des Trépassés), the Hell of Plogoff (Enfer
de Plogoff). . . On the north coast, the tide sweeps in, in
exceptional cases to a height of 13.50 m – 43 ft in the Bay of
St-Malo. . . When the wind blows, the battering-ram effect of
the sea is tremendous. Sometimes the shocks given to the rocks
of Penmarc'h are felt as far off as Quimper, 30 km. – 18 miles
away. . .'

From the Michelin Guide to Brittany, 1991 edition

There can be few less hospitable coastlines than that of north
Brittany, but for David Birkin, and no doubt for others who had
to find their way to pinpoints on moonless nights during autumn
and winter, without the aid of lighthouses, lightbuoys, land-based
navigation aids or radar, it came to exercise a peculiar fascination.[1]

In 1942, while at the Naval Signal School, Birkin was suddenly
and surprisingly summoned to an interview with Slocum and,
having been vetted and security-screened, he was offered a job on
his staff. After two years as a rating-telegraphist, a period spent
largely in hospital, thanks to a string of sinus and eye operations,
with dwindling hopes of ever seeing the war at first hand, he leapt at
the opportunity, signed the Official Secrets Act and was promoted
to Sub-Lieutenant overnight as one of Slocum's assistants.

At this stage Slocum still had responsibility for air operations for
SIS as well as for sea transport, but Birkin was chiefly concerned
with the latter and he was occasionally sent down to Dartmouth
with orders, both real and dummy, the latter to be carried on
operations in case of capture. This first-hand contact with the
flotilla made him increasingly dissatisfied with his staff appointment: from the start he found the Scarlet Pimpernel character of
the work fascinating and quite unlike normal naval routine.
Although for cover purposes MGB 318 and MA/SB 36 formed
part of Coastal Forces, they were in fact responsible to Commander

Operations to Guennoc 1943 – Chart 2649

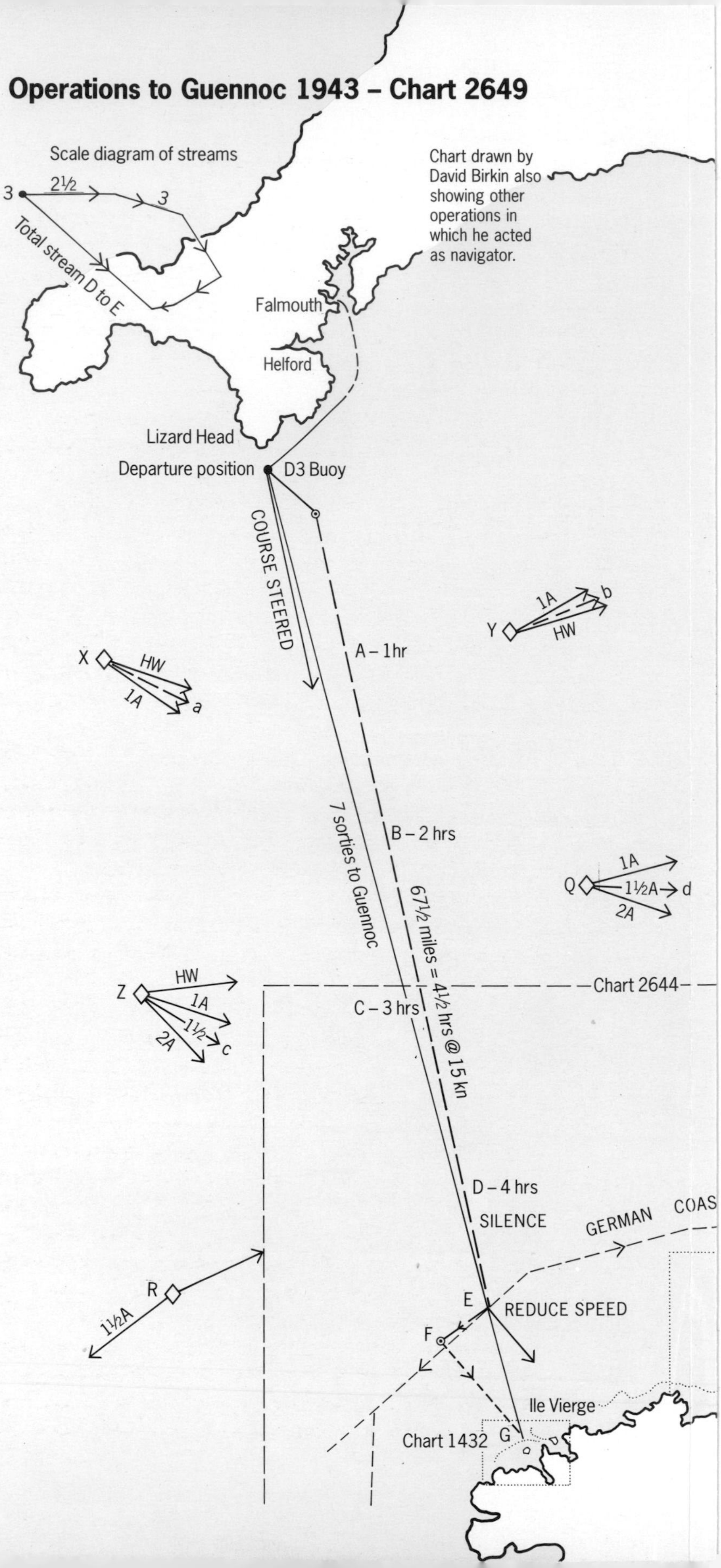

Scale diagram of streams

Chart drawn by David Birkin also showing other operations in which he acted as navigator.

3

2½

3

Total stream D to E

Falmouth

Helford

Lizard Head

Departure position • D3 Buoy

COURSE STEERED

A – 1 hr

Y

1A

HW

b

X

HW

1A

a

7 sorties to Guennoc

B – 2 hrs

67½ miles = 4½ hrs @ 15 kn

Q

1A

1½A → d

2A

Chart 2644

Z

HW

1A

1½

2A

c

C – 3 hrs

D – 4 hrs

SILENCE

GERMAN COAST

R

1½A

E

REDUCE SPEED

F

Ile Vierge

Chart 1432

G

Davis and controlled by NID(C). Birkin's described how passengers would arrive at Kingswear by the last through train from London, carrying outsize suitcases and strange bulky parcels, board the liberty boat that would take them to *Westward Ho!*, the paddle-steamer that served as base-ship to NID(C)'s gunboats, and then, a few hours later, scramble ashore from rowing boats on the enemy-occupied coast of Brittany. Looked at in the cold light of day, this picture is hardly typical of most of 1942 and 1943. MGB 314, the predecessor of 318, had done a flurry of such operations from Falmouth and Dartmouth in the first two months of 1942 but it was not until October 1943 that agents were again landed on the north coast. Anyway, Birkin was 'hooked', and he approached Captain Slocum, who was sympathetic enough to turn a blind eye to his poor health record (a medical board had pronounced David unfit for any form of military service), and sent him on a crash course in navigation with Captain O.M. Watts at Bursledon, after which he joined the Dartmouth set-up on probation.

'O', as Slocum was known in SIS, also overlooked the fact that Birkin had not done the usual officer-training course and had no seagoing experience: indeed, the first time on board 318 he distinguished himself by treading on the commanding officer's fingers as he was coming up the companion way and David was eagerly hurrying down. He feared his career at sea would end before it had begun, but he was let off with a volley of four-lettered abuse and joined in most of the operations that winter, which were almost all concerned with the SOE LARDERING scheme.

The first operation he went on was somewhat untypical. MGB 318 was used at the end of August 1942 in an attempt to contact the French tunny fleet at sea and persuade them to leave their fishing grounds and head for England, since the campaign against U-boats leaving and entering the French Atlantic ports was to be stepped up. Attacks would be made at night on any target that showed up on the radar screens of the patrolling aircraft, which included a number of additional squadrons diverted from Bomber Command to Coastal Command for the purpose. The Battle of the Atlantic was then at its height, but Luard at St Eval pointed out that, as few sailing tunnymen carried radio receivers, broadcast warnings would be unlikely to reach them and many were likely to be sunk in night attacks by our aircraft. As a consequence of his intervention, large numbers of leaflets were dropped on vessels at sea, but the attempt to contact and speak to tunnymen using two MGBs and, subsequently, two destroyers and trawlers, had minimal effect – only two were persuaded to sail to British ports. Lomenech, who had not been consulted but was put on board one of these two tunnymen, thought the whole scheme misconceived and a vast waste of time and effort. The tunny-fishing season would come to an end in

August in the ordinary course of events. Operation NEPTUNE, as it was called, involved 318s being continuously at sea for 36 hours – a record for 'C'-Class MGBs. Birkin had been dropped in at the deep end.

Under the eye of Ted Davis – Slocum's senior officer at Dartmouth – David rapidly began to learn the practical difficulties of wartime navigation on the wild, romantic, rock-infested north coast of Brittany and to appreciate the challenge. Most of the French charts were out of date and the gunboat was not allowed to use radar for fear of being spotted by the enemy. At that time compass, log and echo-sounder were the only navigational aids and the sounder was by no means always in good working order after a crossing of 90 to 100 miles, involving a steaming time of six to seven hours or more. So they had to rely mainly on dead reckoning to find an exact pinpoint, on time, on a pitch-black winter's night, when a two-degree compass error might take them 8 km. (5 miles) off course, or a slight miscalculation of tide levels put the gunboat literally on the rocks. In theory this was not easy and in practice it sometimes looked impossible. Time was always a scarce and crucially important factor and could not be wasted looking for a meeting-place when passengers might be waiting to be embarked uncomfortably close to German lookout posts.

The mid-Channel tidal streams were fickle enough but those within 10 or 15 miles of the French coast were not only very strong at the high spring tides but ran at right angles to their approach course. Even in the finest weather, a long, low Atlantic ground swell pounds relentlessly against cliffs and beaches. When autumn comes, the south-westerly winds blowing in from the Atlantic reach gale force in a surprisingly short time: then great waves smash shorewards like express trains, breaking far out to sea and gathering pace as they rush in, transforming the whole jagged coastline into a cauldron of boiling surf and filling the air with salt-laden spray that penetrates miles inland.

The 'C'-Class gunboats were, moreover, top-heavy and, particularly when carrying stores and boats for one of the SOE LARDERING operations, rolled alarmingly, as well as being exceedingly wet. Because of their speed, they could carry out cross-Channel operations only during the long nights of autumn and winter. Conditions were never ideal: even the rare dead-calm night brought the problem of phosphorescence: anything that touched the water, especially the gunboat's wake and bow-wave, but also the surf-boat's oars, glowed with what seemed, to those involved, extraordinary brightness. There were occasions when St Elmo's fire danced along the rigging, making them feel they were on an illuminated float at Blackpool. Moreover, a calm sea exposed them to detection by enemy radar.

As luck would have it, Birkin's first operation in sole charge of navigation was TENDERLY, one of the most trying of those carried out by Dartmouth gunboats during the whole war. Since the FH830 submarine buoys they were to lay as an adjunct to future operations were navigational aids, it fell to Birkin to fit them with the self-destruction charges: he was sent far from human habitation with a pensioner rating recalled to active service, the two long cylinders, 4lb. of TNT, detonators, a do-it-yourself assembly diagram and a rusty penknife.

Having survived that preliminary ordeal and been up for several nights on end planning the courses, Birkin found himself cooped up in a wooden box measuring about 2.1 x 1.8 m., with under 1.8 m. of headroom. As he was well over average height, this represented a permanent threat to his cranium. This so-called chart-room was separated from the gunboat's bridge by a ladder and a finger-slicing bullet-proof door. David was later to discover that, while the bridge was surrounded by armour plate, the space in which he had to spend the next 23 hours and undergo his baptism of enemy fire was constructed of nothing more solid than plywood. Two paces back from the chart-table, which was designed to be collapsible and in rough weather invariably did just that, was an open, man-size hole from which a ten-rung ladder led down to the mess deck: he described it as 'a vicious mantrap sprung for action'. Up through the same hole, the smell of stale cabbage and engine oil hung about at all hours of the day and night, ready to turn the stoutest stomach. David's stomach was in any case not robust: like Nelson and Captain O.M. Watts, his first navigation instructor, he never overcame seasickness and he had to work with a bucket and towel at hand.

Over the chart-table a feeble electric lamp – the bulb painted red for black-out reasons – just illuminated half a chart of standard size. Other fixed objects included an echo-sounder, a magnetic compass, a radar set – the use of which was forbidden – a maze of switches and wires, and a voice-pipe over the chart-table, connecting with the bridge, down which, as he was soon to discover, a Bovril-like mixture of salt water and rust would drip or pour, depending on the weather, on to carefully prepared charts and notebooks, reducing them to a pulpy mess unless immediate countermeasures were taken, such as plugging the pipe with any soft material to hand.

Birkin was so busy arranging his charts and diagrams that he did not even realise that 318 had left harbour until Davis shouted down the voice-pipe, 'Got the time of slipping, did you, Birkin?' The weather forecast had been Force 5–6 south-westerly wind, but this turned out to be the underestimate of the year. 'What time's high water ?' came down the voice-pipe, and David was just thumbing his way through *Reed's Nautical Almanac*, finding everything else from moonset to the declination of Jupiter, when the ship first nosed into the swell and he was up to his ankles in rusty water; then crash!, the collapsible chart-table duly collapsed; the lamp went out as it joined everything else on the deck; and David was violently sick in the darkness. Somehow he righted the chart-table and got a new bulb into the lamp and was scrabbling about trying to rescue the sodden charts and log-book, when the ship lurched, shook even more convulsively and seemed almost to explode. A mine, perhaps, to put the neophyte navigator out of his misery? But the voice merely noted, 'Testing guns,' adding, 'Log that, Birkin'.

The movable features of the chart room were more numerous. To start with there was the highly mobile Birkin himself. All items of the navigator's equipment – chair, dividers, parallel rulers, pencils, notebooks and the like – were free to move in any direction and usually did. Evidently devices to make life easier, such as clips to clamp down the charts, containers for the basic tools of the trade and handholds were beyond the designer's imagination. In rough weather other heavy objects invariably worked loose, such as boxes of distress signals which the crew were naturally never allowed to use; spare batteries of enormous size and weight, only too willing to spill their contents on the unwary; and a lot of other formidable appliances, each capable of dealing out a nasty cut, if not an actual death-blow.

Until he tried, Birkin would never have believed that the motion of an MGB's chart-room could have been so horrible: it was like being shut in a hen-coop attached to a universal joint, placed in a high-speed lift operated by a madman, whose object was to make it bump at the bottom. Added to that was an occasional douching of freezing sea water. He also had problems peculiar to himself: double vision, lungs which invariably bled, a constant frontal sinus head-ache; and, of course, the propensity to be seasick in the most moderate of seas.

His remarkable success in navigating was attributable to the infinitely painstaking calculations he made before setting out on an operation, and to the second sense he developed for knowing the position of the MGB when approaching the pinpoint area. Both of these, he found, were liable to nasty shocks in the course of a sortie. The most valuable sea-marks were the charted rocks off the Breton coast and he always worked out the height above, or depth below, the water-level of every rock on their approach course for every half hour the MGB might be in the vicinity. These he drew to scale diagrammatically, so that he had a ready reckoner at his fingertips and could tell the commanding officer what to look for, and in what direction, at any time during the night. In theory, too, he knew which rocks would be submerged far enough to allow the MGB to

Rock diagram as used by David Birkin to show amount of exposure or immersion hour by hour on a given night.

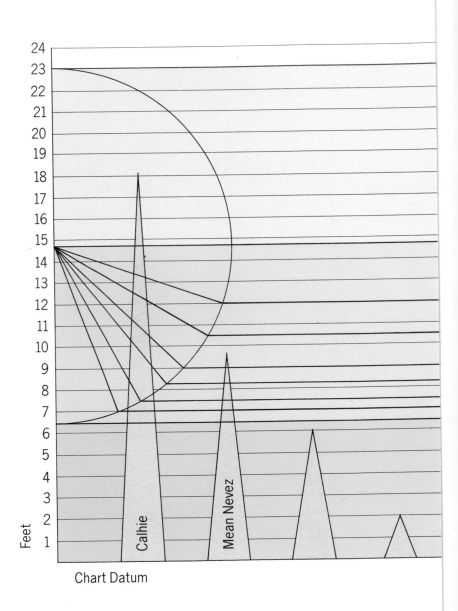

pass over them safely, which would be awash and which were so exposed as to provide usable sea-marks.

As time went by, their names became familiar and, to Birkin, romantic. Indeed, he always calculated courses to one or other of the rocks that would be showing well above the surface near their rendezvous – Méan-Névez, Brouillezou and Calhic off the Ile-de-Batz pinpoint; Les-Boeufs and Le-Mouton-Noir a mile from Beg-an-Fry; Le-Crapaud for Ile-Losquet; Le-Taureau off the Plouha beach; and La-Petite-Fourche, Le-Trépieds and Le-Relec in the Aber-Benoît estuary. They very seldom let him down. To the end of his life he remembered most vividly how, as the MGB; crept silently towards the Brittany coast in absolute darkness, he would wonder, with apprehension and excitement, whether his outward show of confidence in his calculations would be justified or rudely shattered.

David Birkin learned his skills as a cross-Channel navigator in the winter of 1942/43 when 318 was the only gunboat available to Slocum and the SOE LARDERING operations were the only work on offer; but, as 1943 drew to a close, conditions in France improved from the agents' point of view. German controls in the Prohibited Zone along the north coast of Brittany grew easier to avoid and a number of agents were trained specially for SOE and SIS by DDOD(I) to work with the Dartmouth-based motor gun-boats. Thus, just as the sea line to Rémy's 'Confrérie de Notre Dame', which had been maintained for 18 months by the fishing boats from Falmouth and Helford, broke down, three new lines were opened up from Dartmouth and Falmouth to the north coast. One of these was for SOE, one for SIS and the third for MI9, the organisation established to rescue evaders and escapers.

The countdown to a clandestine sea-transport operation for one of these customer services was quite complex, but by the time the 15th MGB Flotilla was officially formed in the autumn of 1943 it had assumed the following more or less standard form:

Stage I: The DDOD(I) head office in Palace Street, Westminster, in conjunction with whichever of the clandestine services was involved and via their radio link with the *réseau* in Brittany, would decide that seatransport was needed to infiltrate or collect agents or mail or pick up escapers. There might also be a requirement to land warlike stores, radio sets or money. The proposed operation would at this point be given a code name.

Stage II: A rendezvous (pinpoint) on the coast would be arranged in general terms for an approximate date some way ahead, in a no-moon period. From then on every scrap of information about the pinpoint would be collected and filed – German coastal defences, troop movements, shipping, etc – together with its appearance at various states of the tide from RAF Photographic Reconnaissance Unit coverage.

Stage III: As the night of the operation approached, operation orders were prepared by DDOD(I)'s office and ship-to-shore recognition signals and their reply agreed with the customer service and, through them, signalled to the field. From the shore these were usually by a dimmed flashlight of agreed colours but various forms of secure walkie-talkie radio-telephone link were used increasingly as the equipment became available to both parties. Dummy operation orders were also prepared to be carried on the MGB so that, in case of capture, there would be a cover story to explain her presence and safeguard the network. Real and dummy orders would be taken (sealed) by a staff officer from London and delivered to Davis a day before the sailing date, or Birkin might travel to London to collect them.

On one fearful occasion a junior staff officer was entrusted with this most secret delivery assignment. He found his reserved seat on the waiting train at Paddington, placed his locked briefcase on it and reckoned he had just enough time to grab a sandwich and a cup of coffee at the station waiting-room. Alas, there was a queue, the guard's whistle blew and, before he could reach it, the train was puffing on its way to Kingswear. The Special Branch intercepted the train at Exeter and the briefcase was duly delivered to Davis the same evening. Needless to say, the officer concerned was found alternative employment – not in intelligence.

Stage IV: An MGB, a landing party, a conducting officer and a navigating officer would be allocated and work began in earnest. The MGB was got ready for the sortie. All compasses were corrected for deviation errors, engines and communications systems were tested and retested, guns, echo-sounder and radio were checked. Although chance played a big part in the success or otherwise of a sortie, as little as possible was left to it.

The officer in charge of the landing party would make quite sure that his surf-boats and their equipment were in perfect condition and that his boats' crews were ready for all eventualities, including shipwreck.

The navigating officer started sweating over charts and navigational data such as sunrise and sunset, moonrise and moonset, tidal information, etc, for all of which he relied on Captain O.M. Watts's *Reed's Almanac.* Long- and short-range weather forecasts were studied and RAF Photographic Reconnaissance coverage of the pin-point area given close attention.

Stage V - Operation Day: Birkin always had a disturbed and almost sleepless night before the fateful day. For days before, he had pored over Channel and local charts so intensely that every island, bay or rock in the vicinity of the pinpoint was imprinted on his over-sensitive brain. When sleep did come, it took the form of night-mares involving navigational errors of every description and enor-mous rocks with sinister shapes.

David spent the morning in the office checking and rechecking his calculations; providing, that is, that there were no last-minute hitches – which he always prayed there would be – such as a sudden change of weather, warnings from the field of trouble at the pinpoint, or even sabotage at Dartmouth.[2] At lunchtime, nervous indigestion, usually coupled with a thumping headache from his ever-changing double vision, eliminated any desire for food. This was probably just as well, as he was invariably seasick.

An hour and a half before departure, which in autumn and winter was usually between 1600 and 1800 GMT + 2, to ensure that the gunboat would not be more than half-way to France before darkness fell, Davis and Birkin would be ferried across the harbour to *Westward Ho!*. All the officers taking part would attend a final briefing by Davis in the base-ship, at which the latest intelligence reports relating to the operation area would be discussed in detail, photographic reconnaissance coverage and likely enemy shipping movements would be studied and ill-timed jokes from those not actually going on the operation would fail to raise smiles from those who were.

Ten minutes before sailing any agents due to be landed went discreetly on board the MGB with their conducting officer and containers of stores would be stowed on deck. Meanwhile, the navigating officer, who had come aboard with his charts and an attaché case full of sharpened pencils and notebooks, and wishing the sea outside the harbour mouth didn't look so rough, would have a brief talk with the ratings on the mess deck, indicating in fairly general terms the area of the operation in case of disaster and their being left ashore in enemy-held territory. Birkin always carried in his jacket pockets his pipe, enough tobacco for two days, his box of survival rations, a bottle of cascara pills, a razor in case he too were marooned ashore, plus a bottle of morphine tablets and a Luger pistol.

Stage VI: At exactly the appointed time, mooring lines would be cast off, the engines would bark into action and slowly the ship – usually alone, but sometimes in company with a second gunboat from the flotilla or borrowed from Coastal Forces – would move off down-stream into the gathering darkness of a winter evening, the crew standing to attention along the ship's rail. Until silence became a necessity, their progress would be accompanied by the strains of the ship's radio – usually the voice of Vera Lynn. On the way out to

their departure position off Start Point or, if they had sailed from
Falmouth, the Lizard, guns would be tested, alarming the seabirds,
which rose in clouds into the sky.

Stage VII: An accurate compass fix of the departure position was
vital and by no means easy when the weather was poor and visibility
bad. In winter, mist and salt-laden spray often obscured Start Point
or the Lizard and on those occasions they got as close to the
headland as possible and prayed for a break in the low scudding
clouds. Usually the dim gaunt shape of the lighthouse was visible for
long enough to get a quick bearing and to judge its distance. Then,
on to the pre-calculated course.

The ideal weather conditions were a slightly choppy sea and
overcast sky, but they seldom prevailed – perhaps three or four
times in Birkin's 33 sorties as navigating officer. Usually it was
either too smooth and starlit or too rough for personal comfort
and for boatwork, and there was the occasional unexpected south-
westerly gale for good measure.

After a six-hour passage during which the QH position-finding
system might or might not be working, an approximate position
check could also be derived from the echo-sounder when crossing
the Hurd Deep, a depression 138 km. (86 miles) long stretching
from off Alderney to a point 51km. (32 miles north) of the Ile-de-
Batz. At their usual point of crossing from Dartmouth, it was about
$2\frac{1}{2}$ miles wide and gave a dramatic increase of soundings on entering
and an equally sudden decrease on leaving. One could also make an
inspired guess at one's position from the time it took to cross.

Lighthouses on the Breton coast were usually extinguished, but
occasionally might be working at about half or quarter strength.
This provided a useful compass bearing, but it meant that a German coastal convoy was moving along the convoy route c. 15 km.
(10 miles) offshore and parallel to it. So at about 24 km. (15 miles)
off the coast, engines were silenced and all eyes strained for signs of
ships moving across their approach course.

At 10 miles from the coast they would alter course to counter
the fierce tidal stream; which at spring tide reaches over 5 knots,
and all available binoculars would be trained on the darkness ahead
for the first indication of the denser darkness that represented the
Breton coast, or for surf breaking on outlying rocks. All the while
the echo-sounder would be at work to indicate any dramatic
changes of depth. Of Birkin's 33 missions as navigator, 24 succeeded in reaching the agreed pinpoint: most of the failures were
due to bad weather or poor visibility and none to navigational
error. Quite good for a beginner!

Anchorage positions might be anything between 140 and 800
m. (half a mile) from the pinpoint. Then the long wait began;

sometimes it was as little as an hour and a half; the absolute maximum was four hours. Walkie-talkie contact was maintained between ship and surf-boat at infrequent intervals, as the danger of the transmissions being picked up by the Germans was always present (on one occasion they picked up the Brighton Police). Minutes seemed like hours and hours like days. David remembered well how, lying at anchor, he had the strange, creepy sensation of being unprotected and exposed and knowing that within a few hundred metres, certainly within earshot, the enemy were on the look-out from their gun emplacements, searchlight and radar positions. The pinpoint and anchorage were almost always in the field of fire of German artillery or machine-guns. It was difficult to believe that a 110-foot ship so close to a hostile shore could not be seen, especially on a starry, still night when every splash or ripple glowed with phosphorescence. They could occasionally see the enemy lighting cigarettes on the clifftop and their vehicles with dimmed headlights crawling along the coast roads.

Total quietness was ordained on board the anchored MGB and the slightest noise, a cough or a rubber-soled footstep, jarred heavily on the nerves. Occasionally there were horrid shocks, such as the short-circuits that switched on the MGB's navigation lights or set the gun-buzzer blaring.

When the surf-boats returned, an engine had to be started up: though silenced, it seemed to their over-sensitive ears like a lion's roar. It was considered wise to be at least 30 miles offshore on the way back to England before dawn. Occasionally they were seen by the Germans and fired on; several times they were spotted by French lighthouse keepers, but on the whole they were remarkably lucky. Their luck owed a good deal, however, to the fact that by the beginning of the 1943/44 winter season, the 15th MGB Flotilla had become highly professional.

was expecting at the beginning of November to evacuate 15 evaders who could leave immediately.

As mentioned before, Slocum had been hoping for nearly two years to receive gunboats from a series being built at Southampton by Camper and Nicholson for the Turkish Government. The hulls of these boats, built and finished to a high specification, had been launched and laid up in mud-berths in the Itchen pending a decision as to their future. When the Admiralty took over the contract at the end of 1941 or beginning of 1942, Slocum had been led to expect that all seven boats of this class would be made available to him as and when they were completed: indeed, the petrol-engined prototype, MGB 501, had been delivered to NID(C) by the early summer of 1942, though she sank as a result of an accidental explosion before she had carried out any operations.[3]

The loss of 501 was a major set-back to NID(C) since she was superior to the 'C'-Class MGB 318 in every way. She was longer, broader, drier and drew less water. Having a round-bilged hull, she was a better sea-boat than the hard-chined 'C'-Class Fairmiles. Her three Packard engines gave her speeds up to 30 knots, greatly in excess of the maximum available to 318, and her range and armament were also greatly superior. She had, moreover, been fitted with a tilting ramp to enable her to launch and recover a specially designed 14-foot surf-boat over her stern.

A further blow to NID(C) followed when four of the other hulls in the series were reallocated to the Ministry of Economic Warfare to be completed as civilian-manned blockade-runners for ferrying desperately needed cargoes of Swedish ball-bearings out through the German-controlled Kattegat and Skagerrak.

The remaining two[4] ex-Turkish gunboat hulls, relegated thus to lower priority, became available to Slocum only after major delays. Charles Martin, erstwhile captain of 318, had been appointed to 'stand by' 503 in her builder's yard in November 1942 but, even when she had been engined and put through her trials, her teething troubles were unusually protracted. Martin's recollection was that 503's Paxman-Ricardo main engines caused fewer difficulties than her auxiliary hydraulic and electrical systems. Although she was the earlier of the two sister ships to arrive at Dartmouth, she was still not ready for operations in November 1943 when Martin, after a whole year of frustrations, was transferred to a steam-gunboat and replaced by Lt R. M. (Mike) Marshall, RNVR, a former Rugby international who had already distinguished himself in Coastal Forces. It was not until 23 January 1944 that 503 did her first operation.

Peter Williams, who had undertaken three operations for Slocum to Brittany and three to Holland when he had been in command of MGB 325, had been recruited by Slocum and 'standing by' 502 at Southampton since April 1943. She followed 503 to Dartmouth before the end of the summer, but carried out her first cross-Channel operation only in late November.

Not only did 502 and 503, when eventually ready for sea, possess the superior armament and sea-keeping qualities of the ill-fated 501, but their three diesels gave them speeds up to 31 knots, and their range of 3,200 km. (2,000 miles) was four times that of the 'C'-Class Fairmile boats. Their diesel fuel, too, was far less likely to be ignited by an incendiary or tracer bullet than 318's 2,600 gallons of high-octane petrol or 501's even larger inflammable fuel load. However, the operation for Maho, code name ENVIOUS, was due to be carried out on 3/4 November, at which time 318 was still the only vessel of the newly formed 15th MGB Flotilla ready and available. Her new commanding officer was Lt Jan McQuoid Mason, South African Naval Force (Volunteer). Birkin was navigating and Davis was in charge of the expedition, which was mounted from Falmouth.

The rendezvous that DDOD(I) gave 318 on this occasion was Rosservor, the most westerly of the three islets that flank the Aber-Benoît estuary, scene of earlier operations with the Le Tac brothers in the winter of 1941/42 and of Operation COOK in March 1943. Like Ile-Tariec to the east of the approach channel, Rosservor is joined to the mainland at low tide, while Guennoc is a true island and can be approached only by boat.

The crossing from Falmouth began with favourable weather reports and hopes ran high, though there was a bigger swell than Davis had expected, once clear of the land, and speed had to be reduced to save 318 from a thrashing.

The new QH set, a naval adaptation of the RAF's GEE position-finding system, was not giving satisfactory reception of signals, but Birkin made good with what little was available. Less than an hour after they had taken their departure from the D3 buoy at the seaward end of the mine-swept approach channel to Falmouth, the centre engine began to suffer from fuel starvation: it would have to be supplied with fuel by hand pump throughout the night.

By 2000 hrs the sudden appearance of very low cloud and drizzle with variable visibility stopped light-hearted chatter on 318's bridge. By 2200 it was definitely misty, but this was not at that stage considered a risk as the QH was giving them positions.

At 2225 engines were silenced and speed maintained. At 2243 a flashing white light was sighted bearing Green 40–45 degrees on the starboard bow. This was obviously the Ushant lighthouse. Only a few glimpses could be had of it in the mist, but Davis thought from peacetime experience that it was working at almost full power – a clear indication that enemy vessels were in the vicinity.

They reduced speed as they approached the land. Unfortunately, the QH aid to navigation, by which they intended to 'home' on the prominent Le-Relec rock, ceased functioning at 2335. Then the echo-sounder, which they hoped to use instead, also resigned and, as Davis subsequently reported to Slocum, 'terror reigned supreme'. They continued on the course given by the QH to make Le-Relec and at 2355 sighted white water fine on the port bow, about 200 metres distant. They closed it slowly and at 2359 stopped engines and 'attacked the echo-sounder in a body', eliciting intermittent soundings They continued the approach at 0007. Land was not visible and Porsal lighthouse was not available, but the Ile-Vierge light was on at this point, which helped considerably.

Land was sighted at 0010 and five minutes later they anchored and lowered boats. Davis was doubtful of his position and no signal was visible from the shore, but he sent Sub Lt Uhr-Henry away in the boats to reconnoitre the land to which they were nearest.

At 0105 a white navigational light group flashing twice every seven seconds came on at the headland of the Presqu'île-Sainte-Marguerite, inside Guennoc and Tariec. At 0115 the Aber-Wrac'h leading lights were lit and a definite position was obtained, but Davis decided against approaching the islands closer as the starboard silencer had been found defective on the run in and barely dulled the exhaust noise at all. In any case, starting engines always grated on nerves that were already somewhat on edge.

At 0125 Uhr-Henry returned with verification of the position and reported he could see no sign of life on either Rosservor or the nearby Ile-du-Bec. Davis decided to send both boats in with the stores they were carrying for Maho, but with strict orders to be back by 0300, as it was clear from the lights already on that there was an enemy shipping movement from the westward. At 0245 the boats returned and again reported no sign of life, but scouting had taken up the time they would have needed to unload the stores – a consignment of inflatable rubber dinghies requested from the field. Uhr-Henry said that in any case a working party would have been necessary to handle and conceal the stores, as it was rough going.

The moderate westerly swell running at the time made boat-work difficult and, although the surf on reefs and beaches could be heard, poor visibility meant that it could be seen only occasionally. At 0300 they started up one engine and reluctantly weighed anchor.

At 0315 they dropped a submarine sonar buoy, in a position noted, as a navigational aid for the future. At 0319 they proceeded slow ahead on all three engines and four minutes later sighted two enemy Flak trawlers bound east at a range of about 2,000 metres. They stopped engines and gave them the honour of crossing 318's bows. The second trawler was well astern and a beautiful target but they passed up the opportunity, as it would have looked peculiar for a hostile vessel to come sauntering out of the rocks close inshore to attack. Besides, they were still very close to their own operational rendezvous. They went gently ahead and altered course round the second trawler's stern. The return to Falmouth was uneventful: the swell was lower and speed was maintained throughout.

It subsequently transpired that the 15 evaders, along with two young men from Ploudalmézeau who were on the run from the German police, had waited for them on Ile-Guennoc and that Hentic's signal informing Dunderdale's Section, his London controllers, of the change of pick-up point had not been received in time to save 318 a fruitless sortie. The shore party had seen 318 in the distance and flashed the recognition signal in her direction to no avail.

This particular group of evaders seems to have included some troublesome and badly behaved characters.[5] Madame Broc'h, secretary at the Mairie at Guisseny, whose help Maho had invoked, asked one of the Lannilis gendarmerie, Jean-François Derrien, to find a vehicle to take them from Landerneau to Landéda at short notice on 3 November. Jean Galliou, a grain merchant, agreed to act as driver without realising he was being asked to carry Allied airmen. They set off for Landéda accompanied by Maho, his radio operator and Mme Broc'h's husband, who thought one would have needed to be blind not to realise who the passengers were: had they been stopped, they could not conceivably have passed muster, since all their identity cards described them as deaf and dumb. Clearly oblivious to the risks they were running, they began to shout and sing at the tops of their voices, completely disregarding their escorts' attempts to quieten them. One American went so far as to tell to M Broc'h that the French, having lost the war, had only one right and duty – to stay silent.

At Lannilis they picked up the two young Frenchmen who were candidates for embarkation. Then they were led by local guides along the beach at low tide in small groups, pretending to be gathering shellfish, and crossed dry-shod on to Ile Tariec under the noses of German look-outs, who scanned the foreshore through their binoculars. From Tariec they were ferried across to Ile-Guennoc – a distance of some 600 metres – by Job Mouden, a local fisherman. Once they were safely across, Maho and Sarol went back to their forward base in the attic of a café run by one of their helpers. Their radio operator and his set were installed at this point and Maho sent a signal to confirm that everything was ready for the pick-up, while Sarol and the café proprietor kept discreet watch from across the square. Maho arranged for the 7.15 p.m. BBC French news to be monitored. An agreed personal message, twice repeated, confirmed that the operation would take place that night.

It came therefore as a great shock next day at noon when Job Mouden rushed into the café and announced that the operation could not have gone ahead during the night because he had seen a man on Ile-Guennoc. A message was sent to Maho, who had returned to Brest, and someone was sent after Jeannot, the radio operator, who had left on a bicycle to catch the train at Landerneau: he was intercepted and returned to Lannilis, where he attempted in vain to make contact with the base station in the home counties with a view to arranging an alternative date for the pick-up. Maho hoped the gunboat would come back that night. Although Sarol went off to Landerneau to try to collect blankets, by nightfall no help had been got to the stranded party, who passed a miserable night, wet to the skin, frozen to the marrow and ravenously hungry, having eaten nothing for 36 hours. On 5 November, the local Resistance did contrive to land some food on Guennoc.

On 6 November, Jeannot had still not managed to make contact with his base station. Two volunteers ferried more food over to the island where the 17 would-be passengers were in a state of distress and utter demoralisation. Mouden, whose boat was again used, had great difficulty in preventing them from climbing aboard and was pursued by their curses when he left. Maho, thoroughly exasperated by the breakdown of communications, decided that, if the gunboat failed to appear that night, he would have to bring the whole party ashore. He even thought of sending them to England in a fishing boat. The Germans were at this point carrying out an exercise and were moving about the beach continuously: Maho and his friends were afraid that some untimely manifestation by the Guennoc party would attract the attention of the enemy look-outs, but fortunately rain at midday compelled the Germans to take shelter, though it added to the misery of the evaders. The morning of 7 November dawned without any major catastrophe. Maho asked Job Mouden and his brother to ferry the party back to the mainland, which was done rapidly at low water. They were escorted by three of the local Resistance to the Le-Guen farm at Prat-ar-Lann. Mme Le Guen, terrified by their unexpected arrival so early in the morning, leapt from bed and disappeared through the window. It required much persuasion on the part of Amédée Rolland, owner of the café where Maho had installed himself, to reassure her and bring her back into her house. That evening the castaways, starving, bearded and looking like hunted animals after their four days of exposure and isolation, were escorted by unfrequented by-ways to the Château de Kérouartz, with Derrien and two other gendarmes from Lannilis providing security for their passage. At Kerouartz, Rose Visot,

Maho's original local contact, Mme de la Marnière, wife of a Brest doctor who was a leading figure in the local Resistance, and her daughter did what was possible to relieve the airmen's distress and make them comfortable. Next morning seven of them were fetched by Louis Bodiger of Lannilis and his son-in-law and taken to a safe house in Brest: the remaining members of the group followed later in the day in another vehicle. M Bodiger's passengers, having celebrated their rescue by drinking more than was sensible, made a considerable, and worryingly uncomforatble, commotion during the journey.

Bodiger dropped Maho and Sarol at Landerneau: Maho surprised the local transport contractor by telling him that he had decided to go to London by a forthcoming Lysander operation he had organised. He and five others connected with the 'Jade-Fitzroy' network were, indeed, collected from a landing strip east of Reims in the course of a double Lysander operation (SALVIA), carried out by Sqn Ldr Hugh Verity and Flt Lt Stephen Hankey of 161 Special Duties Squadron on the night of 11/12 November. He was therefore able to discuss with Dunderdale, Slocum and their respective staffs the reasons for the failure of ENVIOUS, among which the lack of adequate radio contact quickly emerged as the most important. He renewed his plea for inflatable rubber dinghies to transport evaders out to Guennoc, a demand that had already been accepted in principle. Bad weather prevented his return to the field by parachute with this bulky material, however, and it was agreed that instead he would be landed back by gunboat on an operation that would also embark as many airmen as possible. Once again there was no reply from Brittany to his signals but he decided to return nevertheless.

The operation (ENVIOUS II(a)) was again entrusted to MGB 318, with Birkin as navigator, Uhr-Henry in charge of boatwork and Davis in command of the expedition, which took place from Falmouth on 26/27 November. Maho came out from Helford on board RAF 360 and was transferred to the gunboat at 1637.

The swell was larger than expected or reported and was not to Maho's liking, though he remained remarkably cheerful. The QH system was working but by the time they were 40 miles from the Cornish coast signals were, as usual, much reduced.

At 2127 engines were silenced as they crossed the German convoy route. Twenty minutes later searchlights and many other lights were seen ahead in the Aber-Wrac'h area: Ted Davis described the glare on the cloud base as 'similar to the peacetime glow of a town'. They had a glimpse of the Ile-Vierge lighthouse and took a rough bearing. While on the final run in at about 10 knots they found themselves in among the Grande-Fourche rocks, with a number of them on the port quarter. During their retreat, they located these rocks and the buoy shortly thereafter. The run down the Aber-Benoît channel was at slow speed with the dinghies towing astern. They rounded the Ile-Guennoc, anchored and cut the engines. The dinghies were loaded and left at midnight. The weather 'now remembered it was November', as Davis put it: the sky was heavily overcast with low cloud, and intermittent drizzle restricted the visibility. The dinghies returned at 0115, reporting that nobody was present on Ile-Guennoc. One minute later a signal light similar to a white Very pistol cartridge was fired from the vicinity of Brouennou, away to the south-east at the base of the Presqu'île Sainte-Marguerite, opposite Saint-Pabu. This illuminated the houses and a mile or more of foreshore and appeared to come from behind the houses but to be falling in front of them on the seaward side. By 0126 the dinghies were inboard and 318, losing no time in moving from so conspicuous a spot, had weighed anchor, was rounding the island and creeping up the channel back to the Petite-Fourche buoy. All went well except for the weather; the rain had become continuous, reducing visibility to about 600 metres. At the buoy, they altered course to port for the Relec rock, the turning-point for the Rosservor anchorage. The approach to it was a new experience: the swell breaking on the Relec was heard in the chart-room before they saw or heard it abeam at 50 metres. Then it appeared dramatically like an iceberg out of the mist. They altered course to the south-west and the dinghy was lowered and towed astern. At 0157 they anchored again: no land was visible, but the swell was breaking like a collection of white express trains ahead of them and began, indeed, to break unpleasantly close. Davis decided to up anchor and search for the land.

At 0222 they were anchored off Rosservor and the dinghy left to disembark a seasick but otherwise cheerful Maho on the mainland. At 0305 the dinghy returned and reported that he had been put ashore on the Ile-du-Bec, which, like Rosservor, was joined to the mainland at low tide. This position was far more uncomfortable than the Guennoc anchorage and 318 left it without regret. She cleared the rocks without seeing any of them, as visibility was minimal, and for this reason speed was kept low until they were north of the convoy route. At 0630 the usual engine troubles began: the port engine timing had slipped and the centre was suffering from water in the carburettor. But they crawled back to Falmouth and tied up there after 20 hours at sea. Davis noted that without QH the operation would not have succeeded; Birkin's navigation had again been superb and Uhr-Henry's boatwork in uncomfortable breakers commendable.

A further attempt to evacuate the airmen and the accumulated mail from 'Jade-Fitzroy' (ENVIOUS II(b)) was due to take place five nights later, with the pick-up point on Ile-Guennoc. However, Job

Mouden, who had been involved in ENVIOUS I, persuaded Maho that it would be better on this occasion to concentrate them on Ile-Tariec, which could be reached on foot at low water. Since Maho knew that the gunboat would be expecting them on Guennoc, 600 metres offshore, he got Mouden to land and hide a Folboat collapsible canoe on Tariec. Uhr-Henry had landed this when Maho returned from England via Ile-du-Bec on 27 November. Maho planned to paddle himself off to Guennoc and warn the gunboat of the changed rendezvous.

On 1 December the airmen were collected from their hiding-places in Brest, taken by truck to Landéda and thence by footpaths down to the long beach leading to Tariec. As this took place in daylight, some had been equipped with forks, others with baskets, to disguise them as seaweed-gatherers, and collectors of shellfish respectively. They made their way along the shore in small groups without attracting attention from the German look-outs. In the course of the afternoon Maho had Jeannot transmit two messages from the attic of Amédée Rolland's café at Lannilis, which was much frequented by the Germans: 'Le radiateur tient bien' and 'Le Loing est une rivière rapide'. London acknowledged reception on the BBC French-language news bulletin at 1945; so the MGB was on its way. Maho and Sarol took time off for a drink at the bar of the café before making their way across country to Tariec.

In fact two gunboats, not one, were engaged in ENVIOUS II(b): DDOD(I) had decided that, in view of number of evaders awaiting evacuation, 318 should be joined on this occasion by a sister ship, MGB 329, which he had borrowed from Coastal Forces for this one job.

The weather reports were promising and the receipt of Maho's signal confirming that the men were on the island set hopes running high. The two ships slipped from the Coast Lines wharf at Falmouth at 1600 and made a rendezvous with RAF 360 outside the Helford River, where stores were transferred on board. They took their departure from the D3 buoy at 1730 and the long passage began: QH fixes checked their position throughout. On the French coast the usual searchlights were seen, both high- and low-angle.

Wind had increased to Force 5 by the time they were half-way to France, but its direction was south-west and, since this offered a prospect of working in the shelter of a weather shore, no change of plan was deemed necessary. The usual procedure for silencing engines and reducing speed was followed and MGB 329 was ordered to do likewise by the secure SOE S-phone radio–telephone link.

The night turned out to be very dark. The search for the Petite-Fourche buoy began at 2330 hrs, when breaking water was seen close on the starboard bow. A QH fix was taken and course set to the north-east to the buoy. It was not seen until they were 30 metres off it and violent avoiding action had to be taken, especially with 329 close on their tail.

MGB 318 set course down the Aber-Benoît channel, lowering their dinghies and trailing them astern. They suddenly spotted 329 heading in to the Grande-Fourche rocks: this was stopped by S-phone and, as their sister ship had completely lost them, she had to be guided down the channel: 329 was plainly visible to 318, but not vice versa. The two gunboats proceeded thus in company to the anchorage. There was then some delay as 318 found she was dragging her anchor and 329 had to be told to move to prevent the two boats from running foul of each other. The dinghies finally left at 0025: Uhr-Henry was in the first with two ratings, Sub Lt Pollard, first lieutenant of 318, in the second with two; and the coxswain of 329 in the third, also with two oarsmen. They proceeded in line ahead, carrying stores and one S-phone.

Maho had planned to meet them on Guennoc and direct them on to Tariec, where the passengers were waiting, but he set out late in his canoe, and, having had no previous experience of its use, was completely lost for an hour, when he saw the red torch signal being flashed from Tariec and made his way back there.

At 0045 Uhr-Henry reported to 318 that he had found nobody on Guennoc: he was instructed to 'turn over every stone' on the island, using the boats' crews. At 0130 he reported a negative outcome but said he could see a red light flashing, apparently on Ile-Tariec. He was told to investigate and at 0155 he reported success: there were 20 to be embarked and he was having the stores unloaded.

At 0200 a violent squall came down, together with heavy rain, and the barometer was falling fast. As they had received a W/T signal to the effect that the weather would deteriorate to SSW Force 5 to 6, Davis ignored this development, but the squall continued at far greater strength than predicted and 318 was forced to start up the centre engine to take some of the strain off the coir-grass anchor line. During this time at anchor, 329 made several nerve-racking moves trying to find a better holding-ground: the climax came when they fouled 318's anchor line with their propellers.

At 0220 Uhr-Henry reported that the boats were leaving with all the passengers, and closed down: this was passed to 329 by the secure radio–telephone link and instructions were given to anchor closer to 318.

The sea was getting worse by the minute. Still no news over the surf-boat's S-phone walkie-talkie. At 0335 the already tense nerves of those on 318 were jangled by the gun-buzzers blaring out in unison, having short-circuited from the inundations of sea and pelting rain. Wrenching the wires away from the buzzers was the only way to cut off the noise.

In view of the weather, Davis decided at 0428 that they had waited long enough and that the boats were probably sheltering at Guennoc, having found wind and sea too much for them. At this juncture one dinghy was sighted astern of 318: heavy seas were breaking over her and she was making practically no progress at all. MGB 318 cut their anchor line with the axe that was always kept ready for such an eventuality when anchored in enemy waters. She slipped down on the dinghy and towards the reef round which the dinghy had negotiated. Davis reported that the next few minutes were 'beyond description', with a series of frights that 'should satisfy anyone's craving for a thrill'. A heaving line was thrown, but the wind hurled it back. Scrambling nets were lowered as dinghy and gunboat bumped into each other. All available hands dragged the men out and finally hoisted the sinking praam dinghy on board while every second the reef got closer. They got under way at 0440 and instructed 329 to follow.

Uhr-Henry reported to Davis that he had seven escapers with him. The second boat had been with him at the reef but he had seen nothing of the third dinghy. It appeared that the second boat had gone off in a different direction after rounding the reef.

At 0445 course was set for the Petite-Fourche buoy. Visibility was now down to nothing but a red light could be seen flashing to the stern, either from Guennoc or Tariec, so someone else had evidently survived the ordeal. When, at 0510, they estimated that they must be clear of the invisible buoy, speed was increased on all three engines to about 10 knots and a nightmarish return passage began.

At 0530 they were clear of the banks and fully subject to the weather. The sky was starting to lighten and Birkin wrote in his log book: 'Wind west-south-west Force 7, sea very rough; heavy and confused swell; sea covered with streaks of foam.' The movements of a small, flat-bottomed, over-top-hampered ship in such conditions almost defy description. The motion was so violent that course was altered at 0550 to the east, parallel to the French coast, to avoid their being rolled over by a beam sea.

By 0930 and in full daylight they were still only 30 miles from the Breton coast and making good a mere 8 or 9 knots. Crisis was in the air, for neither MGB had enough fuel to be able to continue for long on a course that brought them no nearer home. The rolling of the ships was estimated at the time to be in the region of 50 degrees: lashings parted and heavy objects started rocketing across the deck. The small, box-like chart-room under the forward end of the ship's bridge, where David Birkin was ensconced, was chaotic and he had to wedge himself against the chart-table to remain on two feet. The working surface of the table had accumulated the usual repulsive mixture of rusty water cascading down the voice-pipe from the bridge, plus, on this occasion, vomit and blood from the bashings his head had received against every kind of projection; pulpy charts were slithering in every direction, parallel rulers careering madly across the table and on to the deck, and pencils and notes flying through the air.

At 1000, with the wind gradually veering, Davis decided to turn into it and bash their way back northwards. Four fighters passed ahead about 3 km. (2 miles) away on a course from west to east, which was frightening given that the mist and spray prevented them from being recognised: the crew went to action stations, but the aircraft did not reappear.

At 1032 the centre engine was cut to conserve fuel as they were making no more than 6 knots' headway. They plodded on, more like a semi-submerged submarine than a normal surface craft. Personnel on the bridge hung on to the side rails with their legs clear of the deck. From now on, starboard and port engines competed with each other to be first to pack up. It was even possible that the ship would have to be towed back.

At 1430 the wonderful sight of land appeared: never had it looked so good. At 1450 their Hurricane fighter escort joined them. It was not until 1720 – 25 hours after sailing, with no break of any sort for anyone on board – that 318 and 329 were secured alongside the Coast Lines jetty in Falmouth Harbour.

It was a great disappointment, Davis reported to Slocum, not to have completed the operation. The decision to leave without recovering the other two dinghies was hard but, he thought, justified, as at 0800 they were no more than 20 miles off the enemy coast making about 7½ knots. That Uhr-Henry had done a magnificent job with a sinking boat was beyond doubt. This dinghy had had its bung knocked out on a rock and fingers did not fit the hole. He had completely ruined his uniform cap by using it for bailing and in an attempt to block the bung-hole. The disappearance of the other dinghies was a mystery. The sterling efforts of the engine-room crew under motor mechanic Sealey had certainly spared 318 the ignominy of being towed the last 90 or 100 km. (60–70 miles). Davis regretted that he had not been able to set minds at rest back at base by reporting sooner, but the uncertain engines had deterred him from making a W/T signal earlier on a wavelength that the enemy could have picked up by direction-finder. He concluded his report by paying tribute to his companion officers.

It emerged later that Maho had arrived back on Tariec, soaked to the skin and completely exhausted from his efforts in the canoe, at almost the same time as the three surf-boats from the MGBs with their cargoes of food and equipment. His failure to reach Guennoc was not altogether surprising in view of the extreme conditions and his almost total lack of experience in handling such a craft. It proved extremely difficult to get the 20 escapers on board the surf-boats, which were rolling and pitching on the reef-fringed island in the surf. Moreover, the passage from Tariec off to Guennoc is dangerous even for local fishermen familiar with the submerged rocks that lie all around the Presqu'île Sainte-Marguerite and the fierce currents that run between them; and therefore particularly hazardous on a dark and stormy night. For the crews of the three surf-boats, who had no such local knowledge, the crossing was a nightmare. Only one reached 318, as recounted above. The boat manned by the coxswain and two crew members from 329 lagged behind. But Pollard's surf-boat was in company with Uhr-Henry's praam dinghy until they reached the reef on the south-western side of Guennoc. Owing to the force of the wind and the sea that was then running, Pollard found it impossible to make further headway. Communication between the two boats became impossible and in a heavy squall, when visibility dropped to nil, they parted company. The third boat had by this time been lost to sight to leeward.

During this squall Pollard's boat shipped quite a lot of water, being close to the reef all the time. Owing to this extra weight and the exhausted condition of the boat's crew, even with the help of the airmen, both on the oars and bailing with shoes and caps, Pollard decided that the best thing to do was to land on Guennoc and to try to tell 318 of their predicament. When the boat had been emptied of water and the oarsmen a little rested, he hoped to make a further attempt to reach the MGB if time permitted.

They landed on the lee side of the island at 0455 hrs. Pollard crossed over to the hill overlooking the anchorage and tried to make visual signal contact. However, the MGBs could not be seen and Pollard assumed they had left – the time then being 0510.

Returning to the dinghy, Pollard talked the situation over with Pierrot, Maho's W/T operator, who had taken passage with him. They decided the best course would be to get in touch with the escape organisation on the mainland and arrange for the crew to be looked after until the MGBs could return.

With this in view Pollard left the seven airmen on Guennoc and started off with Pierrot for Tariec, reckoning that the boat would be easier to handle with only four on board and that, should they fail to make contact with Maho, the airmen would be safer on Guennoc, which was seldom visited by the Germans, than on Tariec, where they went every day.

The wind had now freshened to Force 6, gusting 7, with rain. Visibility was very poor and nil in squalls, which were frequent. The wind had gone round to the south-west – a fact that Pollard had not noticed. As he could see no marks and set a course to Tariec largely by the feel of the wind, the boat was carried by the north-going tide right into the middle of the first reef between the two islands. Pollard altered course and tried to get to the south of this obstacle but the adverse wind and tide were too strong, so he went north of it, hoping to be able to work south on the leeward side. However, they found themselves in a ring of surf and when they broke through this there were further rocks ahead. Pollard thought this must be the mainland but what they saw were off-lying rock formations named Tielan and Kerquenn. They managed to get down the channel between them and went ashore on Kerquenn for a rest. The time was then 0700 hrs. Bartley and Clancey, the boat's crew, were greatly fatigued by this time, having been rowing hard for about 90 minutes since leaving Guennoc and having had little respite since leaving the MGB seven hours previously. Pierrot thought they would probably be able to walk ashore at low tide. It was beginning to get light and the wind showed no sign of abating, so they hauled the boat on to the reef, turned her over, covered her with rocks and seaweed as best they could and took shelter underneath.

To their relief the tide started to drop about 0900 hrs and by 1100 the sands and rocks were drying out. Local fishermen appeared on the beaches gathering clams and picking up seaweed which they loaded into carts. By noon the reef on which they had found refuge was only separated from the mainland by two small channels some 3 feet deep and 30 metres wide. A fisherman came quite close and Pierrot waded across to him and explained their predicament. The fisherman agreed to take them inland and went away, returning two hours later with a cart and a companion. By this time they had worked their way towards Tariec and, after concealing themselves behind a large rock, they destroyed everything that might give them away – badges, gold braid and uniform buttons. They then walked down to the cart. Bartley and Clancey got into it and were covered with seaweed, while Pierrot and Pollard walked on under the noses of the Germans, to the mainland. They met the fisherman and his cart again briefly at the foot of the sand cliffs and then, followed his companion about 3 km. to the west to Joseph Le Guen's farmhouse near Landéda. Here they were given food and sat down by a fire to dry out their clothes.

At this farm Pollard and Pierrot found the crew and passengers from the third boat. The coxswain from 329, who was in charge of this, had lost sight of the other two dinghies in a rain squall just before reaching Guennoc. Finding he could not get back to their MGB, he too had looked for somewhere to land and rest. Finally he found one of the small islands south of Tariec, where they hauled their surf-boat out of the water and waited. At low water a Frenchman in their party was able to contact a local fisherman who led them to the farm.

Pollard arranged with Pierrot for the local fisherman to dispose of their two dinghies. The boat from MGB 329 was quite sound, but Pollard's had a gash in her port bilge – sustained just before they pulled her out of the water. The boat from 329 was towed out to sea by the fishermen and sunk with weights in her. Unfortunately she was subsequently washed up on the beach.

They all remained at the farm that night (2/3 December), being joined during the day by the seven airmen Pollard had left on Guennoc.

Maho had left Tariec as soon as the three surf-boats had set off into the darkness because the tide was rising and he needed to get across to the mainland while he still could. Having reached a safe house in the rue Voltaire at Brest, he announced to those who were sheltering him that the operation had been a total success.

A French member of the group made his way from the Le Guen farm to Lannilis, where Sarol and Jean-François Derrien, the senior local gendarme, were waiting: they were unable to contact Maho straight away and it was easy to imagine how he must have felt when he learned next day that ENVIOUS II(b) had been very largely a failure and that he had new refugees to take care of.

Sarol and Rolland, another of the helpful Lannilis gendarmes, were unable to get through to the Le Guen farm at Prat-ar-Lann straight away as the Germans had found the two wrecked surf-boats and had thrown up road-blocks on all the roads leading into the Sainte-Marguerite peninsula. Derrien managed to reach the farm that evening alone but it was only next day, 3 December, that he was able to send Rolland and Coum through to collect the ship-wrecked party and escort them across fields and by little paths to a point where a van was waiting to drive them into Brest. The naval party of six were separately catered for: they had local lodgings and were taken next day into Landerneau in another van. Some days later, Maho took Sub Lt Pollard to Paris with him by train: he hoped to be able to repatriate him by Lysander.

The moonlit period of December 1943 was in fact a particularly bad month for the Lysander Flight of 161 Special Duties Squadron, and there was no pick-up operation for 'Jade-Fitzroy'. On 10/11 December two Lysanders were engaged in an operation for the BCRA to bring out Pierre Brossolette and Michel Pichard, who had now left Rémy's CND and been given charge of all air operations for the Service Action in northern France; one was shot down and the other forced back by bad weather. Bob Hodges with Squadron Leader Wagland as navigator, managed on 16/17 December, at a second attempt, to pick up Robin Hooper, one of the Flight's pilots, who had had to burn his own Lysander in November when it became immovably stuck in mud near Niort. The weather on the night of his rescue, however, was so foggy that all the airfields in southern England were closed down for operations and two other Lysanders trying to land at Tangmere only a few minutes after Hodges both crashed, killing their pilots. Maho was therefore back at Lannilis with Pollard on 20 December for another attempt to evacuate the accumulated backlog of passengers and mail from Ile-Tariec by sea. This operation, to which DDOD(I) allocated the code name FELICITATE, was scheduled to take place on 23/24 December and was once more entrusted to MGB 318, operating from Falmouth, this time alone and without Ted Davis, who was due to take part in another operation (JEALOUS III) from Dartmouth that night. However, Steven Mackenzie came down from DDOD(I)'s London office on 18 December to join the expedition. The weather he found at Falmouth was discouraging, as he subsequently recorded:

Cold, hard rain lashed the quayside, forming broad lakes of water along its uneven surface. If anything was needed to add to the desolation of the scene, those puddles did the trick. Piles of rusting paravanes, coils of wire, broken sweeps lay against the black gleaming sheds; empty crates exuding sodden paper, disintegrating straw, were heaped under the hand-crane. Standing out sharply on the white wood of the crates were the black stencilled addresses: 'S.A.S.O. Falmouth', 'B.E.O. Forte IV, Falmouth'. I picked my way miserably through the puddles, conscious that my shoes were leaking, that my Burberry was absorbing water like blotting paper.

Above the level of the quayside rose the masts of an ML flotilla, masts prickled like hedgehogs with every sort of aerial; 'B'-Class Fairmiles on air-sea rescue duty, with characteristic splashes of yellow paint, and a big sick-bay built up on deck in place of the after Oerlikon. Beyond them, in the outer berth, lay a 'C'-Class MGB, painted mauve. She was the one I was looking for; damply I climbed down the ladder in the dock wall, water seeping up my sleeves as I clung to the iron rungs, water oozing past my white starched collar as I twisted round to find the deck of the innermost craft.

With hatches tight closed and water drumming on the wooden decks, MGB 318 looked deserted as the grave. I climbed to her bridge, washed clean and slippery by the rain, entered the chart-house and peered down the ladder which led thence to the wardroom. A warm moist smell came up, and a buzz of conversation. The wardroom door was closed and my first efforts to push it inwards were unsuccessful. A shuffling of feet and chairs within resulted in a gap just wide enough to squeeze through. In the tiny wardroom, designed by the builders for two, six officers were crowded, fortifying the inner man against the rain outside.

'Hallo, Jan! Had a good trip round?'

'Hallo, Steven! Glad to see you. We got in before the worst of it yesterday'.

'How long d'you think this'll last?'

'God knows! There's a gale warning just come in!'

The weather! For a week that was to be our conversation. How long would it blow, how soon would the sea and swell outside moderate?

Two of the ML skippers laughed at us. They were all right; no flying was likely in that weather.

'Personally I hope it keeps up till after Christmas,' said the first. 'I'm putting in for a '48' if it blows any harder tomorrow. The sea won't go down for days after this lot. What are you worrying about?'

'Oh, they're keen types from Dartmouth!' said the second. 'Colonials, you know!'

This was a sure rise in 318, whose captain, Jan, was South African, whilst Number One, Tassy, as his name implied, was an Australian from Tasmania. Nevertheless we had reason to worry about the weather. I had the orders in my pocket and when the ML types had gone I pulled them out to go through them with Jan.

'Same place?' he asked.

'Yes, any day from the 20th onwards.'

'Impossible with this wind. It's a lee shore.'

'Well, we'll have to hope for the best. Today's the eighteenth. I don't see much chance before the 22nd, even if the gale blows over tomorrow.'

Jan pushed his fingers through his sandy hair. He had the traditional ruddy face and blue eyes of the sailor, but he looked older than his 30 years. Nights of straining through the darkness at the shadowy form of the French coast, nights of rock-dodging at low speed in a yawing 110-ft craft, had left their mark. . .

Jan finished reading and pushed the papers aside.

'No good trying till the wind's south of west. That's what ditched us last month. It was just possible for boatwork when we anchored, but the squall came up after Michael had left. We'd only be chucking another boat away in this weather.'

Tassy grinned broadly.

'Don't mind me!'

'You staying to dinner?' Jan asked.

'No thanks. I must get back. They're expecting me at the base. Philip will be here tomorrow to give us the latest from the other side. Meet you at the Duty Staff office at 10?'

'O.K.!'

I clambered back up to the rain-swept deck. Heavy grey clouds were scudding overhead; the wind was whistling in the masts now. A dismal outlook for fifteen or more hopeful men separated from us by 100 miles of storm-tossed Channel.

Next morning there was little change. Even in the Helford River there was a sea running which made it a wet business getting ashore from the depot-ship. At least the rain had cleared, and a watery sun shone fitfully through gaps in the cloud. I met Jan at the base office, where we read the weather report. 'Strong winds continuing, west or south-west.' Hopeless. We finished our business there and walked together to the hotel to meet Philip.[6]

Philip was our liaison with the Section in London where messages from the fugitives could be received. He was short, stocky and irrepressible, wore a DSO ribbon which bore witness to his own adventures in France. When it came to a question of conditions over there, he knew what he was talking about. We found him in the billiard room playing snooker with another airman, an RAAF officer on leave at the hotel.

'The bar's not open yet, you cads,' he greeted us, 'but I can fix the waiter. What'll you have?'

Philip could fix anything. He had a natural flair for achieving the impossible. I knew that, even if he had only arrived off the night train an hour before, he would by now have been given the best room and the biggest breakfast the hotel could offer and been noted down as the most favoured guest by the hawk-eyed knitters in the lounge. He rang the bell, and we drank beer. After a time the Australian airman drifted out; we stood in the glass-fronted 'sun-trap' watching the white horses foaming across the bay.

'Any hope for tomorrow night?' Philip asked.

Jan shook his head. 'The local forecast's lousy. Could you get us a long-range one from Air Ministry?'

'Sure; and I hope it's a good one. The boys are all ready on the far side. We had a message last night asking for the boat as soon as possible. The trouble is food, mostly. It's a big party for the farmers to support if you're held up here.'

'We're ready to go as soon as the weather clears. I'd like to get it over by Christmas.'

Philip went over to the base to telephone, and came back with the Air Ministry forecast. It gave a pretty detailed picture of the situation and we decided, if it worked out right, to sail on the 22nd. There was likely to be a two- or three-day lull in the gale, with worse weather to follow. Two days to wait, two days of wind and heavy seas. The looked-for break in the gale was slow in coming.

Personally I had welcomed the chance to come to Falmouth, since my wife was working in a naval base nearby, and was sharing a cottage in Helford with some old friends. Jan and Philip came over to dinner there, and we sat round the big log fire visualising Michael and his party in a similar cottage on the Brittany coast sitting round a similar fire, waiting and hoping.

On the 21st another member joined our party: Ray Guest, a United States Commander from London. Ray was the advance guard of the American PT craft which came over later to join in the Channel patrols. Officially he was an observer, and had been on a number of trips across to the French coast already. With him he brought the latest thing in R/T sets, a portable two-way machine with a direction-finding device; just the thing for boatwork, light, waterproof and easily handled. We carried out tests in the harbour and agreed to use it on the job, but conditions in daylight in a substantial launch are not the same thing as heaving up and down at midnight in a 14-foot surf-boat, so there was just a chance it would not work as faultlessly as Ray claimed.

On the 22nd the wind had eased considerably but there was still a big sea running off the Lizard. The weather report was dubious, so with regret we postponed matters for 24 hours. Philip in particular was worried.

'There was a message last night,' he told us when we met. 'Including Michael, one Petty Officer and four ratings, the party's grown to 24, and that's a hell of a number to hide over there.'

'Sorry,' said Jan. 'We couldn't make it with this sea, and even if we got there in time, I don't think boatwork would be possible. I'm afraid they'll have to hang on.'

By next morning things were better, and though Jan was still uneasy about the swell, he agreed to sail at 4 p.m. Taking things easily, that would allow about two hours for boatwork, and we should need all of it with so big a party to embark. Six passengers per boat would be the limit in bad weather, and the MGB could only carry two boats. Philip was delighted, and went to arrange the message which would warn the shore party to expect us.

Everything was ready; tanks full, engines tested, those last-minute defects corrected; surf-boats lashed down, equipment checked.

In Brittany that day Claude Tanguy had gone in his truck to pick up Maho, Sarol and the six naval castaways from MGBs 318 and 329, some airmen and Maho's two radio operators, Jeannot and Pierrot, from Landerneau; and had dropped them off at Bel-Air-en-Landéda, the point from which they were later to be led to Ile-Tariec by Guillaume Le Guen and his two nephews. The secret mail from 'Jade-Fitzroy' had accumulated since the beginning of the month on such a scale that it had to be loaded on to a horse-drawn cart. By the time it was ready to set out, the expedition consisted of 32 persons, who were divided into three groups for the next stage of their journey.

At 1600 precisely [as Steven Mackenzie recorded], MGB 318 cast off. The crew watched the Coast Lines quay slip away with regret, knowing they were in for a dirty night, whatever the outcome of the operation. From the windows of the Bay Hotel, 50 feet above sea-level, the swell had looked insignificant but as we passed the boom it was distinctly uncomfortable. Soon the flared bow was lifting to the swell and slamming down with a shudder into the troughs, ploughing into the next wave, only to be lifted up and slammed down again by hostile grey seas.

Jan didn't like it and I thought he was right. There was plenty of wind left in the darkening sky, enough still to whip the tops off the waves and throw showers of spray in a stinging icy stream across the open bridge. Too late to cancel the expedition now: those on the other side would be expecting us. I could visualise the expectation,the ragged men collected in some barn probably, waiting for their guides to lead them through the minefield and along the beach. Home for Christmas! Up the Navy! Michael Pollard, at least, must realise it was only a borderline chance tonight: perhaps he would curb their hopes a bit. We were still uncertain whether it was worth going on: we were down to 12 knots already.

South of the Lizard we changed course for France. This was the critical time really; if we could keep up speed on the new course, we should push on; otherwise it was a waste of time and engine-hours to go further. The westerly swell was on our beam now, lifting us bodily but with an easier roll. Jan leaned forward to the telegraphs and wound the indicator up to 1,200 revs – 15 knots. The exhaust roar rose in pitch and the bow lifted perceptibly. At least it was drier on this course, but the 'C'-Class boats, with their hard chine, hung on to the end of their roll in a sea like this, treating their chine as a keel, I reflected. With each wave we rolled heavily to port and hung there for an interminable second, waiting for the next grey sea to topple us over completely; but each time when it seemed irretrievably too late, 318 started to heave slowly back on to an even keel, only to be rolled on to her chine again as the sea checked her and

pushed her back. It was hard work for the coxswain trying to
steer an even course, while the bow sheered off the crest of each
wave; wet work for the look-outs, wedged damply into the 0.5
turrets beside the bridge; anxious work for Jan, weighing the
safety of the ship against the safety of 28 evaders and escapers
awaiting him, expecting him.

'Say, Lootenant, do you think w'll make it?' Lt Cdr Raymond Guest, USN, the man who evacuated General MacArthur
from Bataan and was a distant kinsman of Winston Churchill,
really did talk American: his transatlantic epithets on the
weather were bright and expressive beside the single adjective
used by the British seamen. But you could see he was enjoying
it; this was a holiday for him, an excuse to escape from a
London desk where he was called on to answer endless questions from Washington before his PT craft could be sent. What
facilities were available at which port? What about fuel supplies? What local labour could be used for repairs? In a sea of
paper he floundered, but here he knew better how to act.
Naturally tall, and broad in proportion, he looked gargantuan
in his kapok-lined 'zoot suit', dwarfing McQuoid Mason's
slighter figure and filling a good proportion of the small open
bridge.

Jan nodded to him, 'If it gets no worse we'll be there in time.
But I doubt if the boats will be able to do much. Might as well
try, though, now we've started.'

'Mind if I take a look at the chart?' Ray squeezed his
massive bulk through the narrow entrance to the wheel-house
where David Birkin, who was navigating, was wedged up
against the chart-table, surrounded by instruments and the
tools of his trade. The usual dim red light burned over the
chart, illuminating the log-recorder and various tables pinned
on to the bulkhead showing speed against revs, and the times of
high water at Brest. I reckoned the wheel-house floor at no
more than about four feet long by two feet across and Ray
Guest filled it comfortably. David was lighting his second pipe;
the air was already thick, with the fumes of shag tobacco
triumphing over the smell of wet oilskins. He worked apparently on the Sherlock Holmes principle, smoking continuously
all night, and it took a strong stomach to remain with him for
long on a rough passage.

'Bridge to Navigator!' A tinny voice spoke through the
voice-pipe from the bridge above his head. 'Increasing to
1,400 revs.'

David noted the time on his pad and plotted a position on
the chart. The engine whine rose and the movement of the ship
became, if anything, a trifle more alarming. After five minutes

the voice-pipe spoke again. The revs dropped back to 1,200. Ray climbed back to the bridge, welcoming the cold air after the fug of the wheel-house.

'Trying to make up time, Cap'n?' he asked.

'No, trying to gain it! I'd like to have half an hour to spare when we get there, but she won't take it. Safer to push on slowly.'

Slowly was right; at this rate it would take us seven hours to make the crossing: seven hours of violent movement with a tricky landfall at the end of it on a low-lying rock-strewn coast. A bad landfall, if not disastrous, could mean another hour's delay in reaching the beach, since off the French coast they would have to reduce speed and silence the open exhausts.

Maho followed Le Guen's advice as to the route to be followed for the first mile or so to the beach at Toul-an-Dour that evening. By keeping to cart tracks and crossing fields, the party kept clear of all but one house, whose barking dog was the only incident that befell them. The critical point was reached when they had to cross a newly laid minefield, which the Germans had established all along the foreshore above high-water mark. Le Guen, who was a coast-guard as well as a farmer, had watched them at work and knew that each mine was buried leaving three antennae standing 2–3 cm. (1 inch) or so clear of the surface: he volunteered to lead the column, bent double, passing his hand gently over the sand. The others followed him Indian-file in a long line, each holding on to the shoulder of the man in front, and in this fashion they passed in safety through the danger.

Once through on to the sand below high-water mark, they could follow the beach for 2½ kilometres (1½ miles) to Tariec. They managed to avoid attracting the attention of the three German observation posts guarding that stretch of the foreshore, though the look-outs manning them must have been particularly on the alert since the two dinghies had been found smashed on the beach after ENVIOUS II(b).

When all 32 had reached Ile-Tariec, dry-shod, as the tide was low, Jeannot transmitted the agreed message, 'Les troènes sont en fleur', which was repeated as one of the personal messages following the BBC French Service evening news bulletin to confirm that the gunboat was on its way.

The swell in the southern half of the Channel was greater than forecast and upset several members of the crew, including the coxswain. By 2045 hrs visibility had become bad owing to contin-uous drizzle, but the wind eased off by 2200, and the sea grew calmer as they approached the French coast. Speed crept up to 18 knots for the last hour's run.

At about 2345 mugs of steaming cocoa appeared miraculously from the galley and, as we were gulping them down, the look-out reported:

'Lights flashing Green 20, Sir.'

Jan took a quick bearing and passed it to the chart-house

'Ile-Vierge!' came back David's voice. 'That puts us about two miles east of our track.' He gave a corrected course and they ran on for ten minutes before the light started flashing again, this time on their port bow, just clear of the horizon. Jan reduced speed and rang down for the silencers to be engaged. He handed Ray a pair of night glasses and said:

'There must be a convoy about if they've put the light on. Will you keep an extra look-out to port?'

'OK by me, pal!'

Ray was pleased to be doing something useful: on the passage across there had been little he could do to help but now every pair of eyes was important; and at the anchorage he could help with the boatwork.

The light flashed intermittently for another ten minutes, then stopped. Against the dark sky one could just make out through night glasses the black shadow of the coast, very low and hardly to be distinguished from the sea.

At 0025 hrs breaking water was seen again to port and identified as the Libenter rocks from a QH fix after they had stopped. Another change of course and with it a change of movement. They were heading west now and looking for the Petite-Fourche buoy, which marked the channel into Aber-Benoît.

Jan was straining ahead into the darkness and calling through the voice-pipe to the wheel-house. David would have the large-scale chart out now, plotting with his stop-watch and checking each bearing Jan could give him. It was curious to think that the ship's safety depended entirely on one who never watched the approaching coast from the bridge, and only saw it when the ship lay anchored in the chosen spot. To him the rocks outside were simply marks on a chart, marks between which a fine pencil line could be drawn; while to Jan, following the courses he received through that impersonal voice-tube, they were patches of angry white foam, seething in the darkness, so close that one could almost reach out and touch them.

Later I showed Ray the instructions in the *Channel Pilot* for that part of the coast. The gist of them was that it should be approached cautiously in daylight, and then only with a local pilot on board. He understood why Jan's language had become so picturesque during the run in, and why his insistence on finding that buoy had been extreme.

'How much longer on this course?' said Jan to the voice-pipe.

'Another 45 seconds! Can't you see the buoy yet?'

'N-Yes!'

We were almost on top of it – a great narrow pillar buoy, difficult to make out in the darkness against the land and the dark sky. The time was 0040 on Christmas Eve.

'Port wheel. Course from the buoy, navigator?'

Round swung 318 and we were safely in the channel, proceeding down it at 8 knots. Here in the shallow water with an uneven bottom punctuated with spikes of rock reaching far towards the surface, the sea was unpleasantly bumpy. The swell poured up the channel as if in a funnel, making conditions worse than outside. There was increasing wind and breaking water on both sides. We might just get a lee from Ile-Guennoc, otherwise boat-work would be impossible. Another few minutes of slow rock-dodging and at 0050 Mason gave the order to anchor off Guennoc. He looked worried for there was little room for the ship to swing and conditions were far from ideal for boat-work. A strong ebb tide was running round the inshore end of the island and would sweep across the surf-boats' track both on their way into and back from the beach at Tariec.

Shortly after anchoring, a squall – NE Force 5 – reduced visibility to half a cable. Jan knew that Michael had had a walkie-talkie with him when he landed a month previously and that, if it was still working, he would probably try to call them up at each half hour from midnight onwards. He told Tassy to get the boats into the water and stand by while he attempted to make contact with the shore. He switched on the walkie-talkie and waited. Nothing disturbed the crackle of the set for some minutes; then at 0125 the crackling increased strongly. A throaty voice came through loud and clear:

'Hullo, gunboat! Hallo, gunboat! Can you hear me? Michael calling! Can you hear me?'

Broad smiles spread around the bridge: the shore party were waiting! Jan took the microphone and answered briefly, asking about the surf and whether a boat could make a landing. Pollard replied that the sea was calm inshore at Tariec and a landing could easily be made. There were, however 25 people waiting on the beach; could they take them all? They would try for as many as possible, Jan answered: they would call up again at half-hourly intervals.

By this time the ship appeared to be dragging and at 0135 the wing engines were started, the anchor was weighed and they moved closer to Guennoc before reanchoring. However the 'creep' of the ship with the engines running carried them over their grass anchor line, though it had a spring bent on to it, and it parted, with the loss of the anchor. A spare anchor was made up with a slightly used grass line, while they manoeuvred under power, and they reanchored ten minutes later.

Jan waited for the squall to pass before sending Tassy away in the boats, but by 0215 conditions seemed more propitious. The wind was NE Force 4, with lulls of Force 3, and the swell was slight to moderate NE.

The boats used on this occasion were two of the PD1 praam dinghies that had been designed for DDOD(I) by Lt Whalley, a member of his own staff, on the basis of a Dutch prototype that had turned up at Felixstowe. Whalley had found it necessary to modify the lines of the original boat to give them additional stability and carrying power. They rode light on the water, being designed to transport a heavy load with enough buoyancy to get through broken surf when landing. Tassy decided to concentrate his four oarsmen on one boat and to tow the other, reckoning that the four seamen waiting ashore would be available to pull the second PD back once they had been picked up. He distrusted the conditions and did not feel that two oarsmen would be enough to contend with the elements. It was a fortunate precaution.

With Tassy himself on the steering sweep, the boat bobbed up and down wildly, which made rowing difficult: the towed boat was a cockle-shell, subject to the lightest whims of wind and tide. From the bridge they watched the two boats drawing slowly away, keeping close in under the lee of Guennoc until they reached the point round which the tide swirled: then they were off into the darkness, struggling to make headway across the tidal stream.

No sooner were they out of sight than the second grass warp parted at the anchor and this anchor was also lost. Thereafter, the ship had to be kept in position by using the two wing engines.

They called the shore party at half-hourly intervals but, even at 0400, there was no sign of the boat where Pollard and the others were waiting. This was distinctly worrying as Jan knew that he would quite shortly have to leave Guennoc so that the MGB herself and all her crew could get clear of the enemy coast by dawn. Conditions at sea would be even more unfavourable for the return passage. Jan asked the shore party to wait until the last possible moment in case Tassy and his crew had landed further down the coast, but in sober fact they knew that conditions had beaten them at the last lap and, what was worse, they could not recall the boats, with whom they had had no walkie-talkie contact at all since they lost sight of them two hours earlier. Tassy was a sticker and they knew he would not give up until the crew were exhausted. Jan was cursing himself for having let the boats go at all, although it was not his fault that the attempt had failed but a combination of sea and tide. The PD surf-boat could have dealt with either separately and no-one could have predicted with any certainty that the two together would be too much. Had they returned to base without making the attempt, there would always have been a gnawing doubt about whether it might not have succeeded.

Then, at 0420 hrs, when the gunboat was already overdue to leave and more than two hours after the boats had set off, Uhr-Henry made contact on the walkie-talkie and reported that he was returning to the ship but could make no headway against wind, swell and tidal stream. He had been set well to the south-west of his course and his crew had been rowing for an hour without any progress to show for it. McQuoid Mason ordered him to slip, and if possible destroy, the second PD1. Tassy did so by removing the bung of the boat so that it would fill with water and break up against the rocks. Relieved of its tow, the other dinghy's prospects improved and soon it could just be seen to the westward of 318, in the middle of the Aber-Benoît channel, struggling hard to reach the MGB, with great waves breaking over it. The wind was freshening again as the tide turned.

Ray Guest had put on the R/T set they had tested before sailing from Falmouth and was trying to establish two-way communications with Tassy, but answers came there none. In harbour the portable unit had seemed so simple to operate – just a button to press and then a microphone to speak into. Circumstances were now very different: Steven could picture Tassy with both hands working at the steering sweep, one eye on the compass and the other on the rocks. The whip-aerial fitted at the side of the set strapped to his chest came up beside his head, and each time he lent forward to see the compass it would catch him in the face. When he brushed it aside with a toss of his head the fitting would become disconnected from the set. Poor Tassy would not even be able to get rid of it for he hadn't a free hand. A Presbyterian by upbringing, he would no doubt have caused his minister some pain with his present reactions.

On the bridge, Ray was not discouraged by his failure to evoke a reply and, assuming that Tassy would at least be listening even if too busy to transmit, set himself to encourage the rowers in the style of a Harvard boat-race coach:

'Come on, boys! Come on, Tassy! Keep going now! Give it punch, give 'em hell! Good lad, Tassy – you'll make it – pull!'

If the situation had not been so serious, it would have seemed as funny at the time as it did in retrospect. As it was, even without benefit of Ray's advice, the four ratings pulled, very literally, for their lives as wave after wave broke over the sinking boat; and by 0438 they had made it. With skill born of long practice, Jan manoeuvred 318 alongside the surf-boat, stopping for just long enough to enable the boat's crew to be hauled aboard up the scrambling-net, battered and exhausted. Then the waterlogged PD1 was taken inboard and 318 proceeded up channel just before the wind drifted her dangerously close to the rocks that edged it. It was a well-executed manoeuvre but a very close shave for all concerned.

They were underway at 0445. As they had thought, the tide had swept Tassy's boat down to the westward and he had had to steer seawards to get out of it. That, coupled with the big sea running up the entrance channel, had frustrated every attempt he made to get through to the beach and it was only his own determination that spurred on his crew to make a final effort to rejoin 318. With disappointment tempered with relief, they crept out to face the long passage home. It was worse than the outward leg, with a heavy north-easterly swell running in the southern half of the Channel and a moderate sea on top of it. Dawn at 0800 found them 30 miles off the enemy coast and making 12 knots: they had overstayed their safety limit by 20 minutes to recover Tassy and the boat's crew, but at least they were now in no hurry to complete the voyage. The entire ship's company, including Ray Guest, were extremely seasick. Davis recorded in the log-book that some passed out and others were injured by the ship's gyrations.

Two Spitfires appeared at 1100 and maintained air cover until they were close under the lee of the Lizard: everyone was heartened by their punctuality in finding the MGB and remaining on guard. MGB 318 secured alongside HMS *Forte IV*, the Falmouth Coastal Forces base, at 1315 on Christmas Eve. There would have been no hope of a second attempt that night, even if the weather had allowed it, keen though they had all been to finish the job before Christmas: after 22 hours of almost continuous running, 318 had several defects that required attention and it would be a hard job to get dockyard hands to work on Christmas Eve or Christmas Day.

Philip already knew of their failure: they had signalled to the Helford base that morning. He was full of sympathy for the wasted effort and their hard night, but brightened visibly when they told him of their R/T talk with Michael Pollard on the beach.

'That makes all the difference,' he remarked. 'It was worth while, if you spoke to them, because it'll keep the Frenchmen happy to know you came even in that appalling weather.'

McQuoid Mason reported to Slocum that, though the operation had produced no results, the fact that they had been so close to the party ashore filled them all with the resolution to succeed the next time. He ventured the opinion that the PD dinghies were not suitable for use in that area: the water outside the reef south of Ile-Guennoc was always subject to a swell of varying strength and it was here that Uhr-Henry had encountered his greatest difficulty, despite the fact that the water inside the reef was fairly calm. A surf-boat on the lines of the 25-foot SN6, specially built for Slocum's HMS *Minna* to use in operations from Gibraltar, or a motor surf-boat with an engine of at least 7 h.p., like those carried on the MGBs used by Combined Operations, would prove more suitable when operating in weather of up to Force 4 or 5.

Philip Philipson was right: the party waiting on Ile-Tariec at least knew, via the S-phone, more or less what had happened. At low tide, towards 0500, members of the expedition carrying the suitcases containing the secret mail were sent off to Guillaume Le Guen's house, passing very close to a German observation post. A second group was taken care of by Joseph Le Guen at Prat-ar-Lann. Maho went very early in the morning to the gendarmerie at Lannilis to tell Derrien of the new set-back and asked him to arrange for evaders to be moved from the Presqu'île Sainte-Marguerite to Lannilis and found shelter with friends for one or two days. The gendarme went to Claude Tanguy, the local garage owner, to borrow his delivery van. Robert Jestin, accompanied by Derrien, used this to pick up a group of the men at about 0800 that morning and bring them back to Lannilis. The mail, much of which came from central Europe, was dropped off at Derrien's house. Amédée Rolland, the Lannilis café proprietor, and a friend brought back a second group to take them to the château at Kerouartz.

Maho quickly overcame his discouragement at these successive and persistent misfortunes: he got Louis Bodiger to drive him over to Landerneau on Christmas morning and sent a signal to London asking for the return of 318 that same night.

As repairs were needed on 318 and the wind was still high, Steven and Jan decided that Boxing Day would be the earliest date on which to sail for the next attempt. Everyone who had been on board 318 was dispirited at the failure of FELICITATE and, even after a night's rest in harbour, still dog-tired. As was usual at Christmas, 'make and mend' and 'splicing the main brace' were the order of the day – a holiday, in short, for all the Coastal Forces craft at Falmouth.

Steven was due to meet Philip at midday for a drink, but the latter rang up earlier to ask if there was a chance of sailing that same evening.

'But, dash it, Philip, it's Christmas Day. Have a heart.'

'Have you seen the weather report?'

'No, and I don't want to!'

'Well, it's the best ever. They'll never forgive us on the other side if we miss a chance like this.'

'How d'you mean? Much better give the sea another 24 hours to calm down.'

'No, not that. Don't you see? On Christmas Day the Huns will be celebrating. They'll all be blind from noon today. It's the best night of the year for us. No patrols, no look-outs, nothing!'

Together they went to visit Jan, who refused to talk until they had gone round 318's mess deck and been suitably entertained by the crew. The party was going well already as officers and crew set about countering the general gloom, and Steven did not think that the ship could conceivably be got ready to sail that evening. But Jan, quite recovered from the recent outing, declared that most of the damage had been repaired and what was outstanding could be fixed in an hour or two. He had seen the weather report and was anxious to fall in with Philip's plan. It was too late to stop the party: a vast quantity of gin had been downed already in the wardroom mess. Then they had set about a Christmas lunch of turkey and plum pudding, finished off with liqueurs, before turning in for the afternoon to sleep off their over-indulgence.

At 3 o'clock a telephone call came through from London to confirm that the operation was indeed 'on' again that night. The weather reports were excellent but, as David Birkin put it, operating conditions within the stomachs of 318's ship's company were less than favourable. In the circumstances, even the toughest constitution would quail at the prospect of at least another 20 hours of tossing and rolling. But there it was, and many a head went under the cold tap in a desperate attempt to bring its owner back to a state of operational viability, if not high-grade mental alertness. McQuoid Mason had taken preliminary steps already to get essential work done and had arranged with the nearby SIS/SOE base in the Helford River to make available the large, 25-foot SN6 surf-boat and an SOE crew to man it. Since 318 was not yet fitted with a derrick capable of hoisting it, Jan declared he would tow it across, carrying two smaller boats on deck in case of accidents.

They had been practising with their new and larger boat some weeks before and knew its capabilities. It would carry more passengers, row faster and more easily than the smaller surf-boats and, provided the sea had gone down somewhat, would be no trouble to tow. Arrangements were made accordingly but, since an extra crew would have to be carried for the big SN6, Steven and Ray had to surrender their places to make room for the trained eight-man team.

David Birkin, with the greatest difficulty in getting eyes and brain to coordinate, had meanwhile been working out the night's courses.

Thus, at ten minutes to four in the fading light of Christmas afternoon, MGB 318 slipped unobtrusively from her berth alongside the Coast Lines wharf at Falmouth and, on the last of the ebb tide, nosed slowly and silently downstream towards the open sea. She was the only ship on the move that day and, as she cleared the boom that protected the harbour mouth between Pendennis Head and St Anthony's Point and turned westward into the wind towards her rendezvous with RAF 360, she must, to those on board the boom defence vessel and to the look-outs in the signal station on Pendennis Castle, have looked a lonely speck retreating on an empty sea.

The weather had unquestionably taken a turn for the better and there was a prevailing mood of optimism on board 318, in spite of the hangovers. Surely nothing could go wrong on Christmas Day! David Birkin had even strung Christmas decorations across the tiny chart-room where he wrestled with the navigation, and the ship's radio was on full blast until the moment they actually set course for France. Vera Lynn's voice rose from the mess deck with 'Yours' and 'We'll Meet Again', bringing a lump to David's throat, as they always did.

Half-way across Falmouth Bay, all guns were tested with a shattering roar, sending sea-birds high into the sky as usual. They stopped off the Helford River entrance to transfer from little 360 the boat's crew that had been provided by SOE: it consisted of six oarsmen, with Skipper Howard Rendle as coxswain and Sub Lt John Garnett of the Inshore Patrol Flotilla to take charge of the towing arrangements. They had brought with them the big SN2 to add to the SN1 and two PD1 praam dinghies carried on deck. Then 318 set off, towing the SN2, and 360 followed her towards the Lizard. The sea was blue and calm, with a long low swell from the south-west. For a time 360, with Steven and Ray Guest on board, kept level, watching the tow. The new boat, light in the water though it weighed 7 cwt. and could carry 3 tons, rode delicately on the gun-boat's foaming wake. At 1742, with a north-westerly Force 3 wind behind them, they took their departure from the D3 buoy at the outer end of the swept channel from the Lizard to Falmouth, increased speed to 15½ knots and headed S 5° E for Aber-Benoît, while the sun sank behind the land, casting purple shadows from the cliffs.

Ray, Philip and Steven had their Christmas dinner at Helford at the cottage where Steven's wife was living. The prevailing optimism was due not only to the Christmas spirit: there was also a feeling of calm after the storm and of confidence that this time the operation would succeed.

In Brittany the men awaiting evacuation and their Breton hosts had also wished to celebrate Christmas, in spite of the circumstances. A party had taken place the previous evening at the house of Mme Pallier, a widow living in the road leading to the railway station at Lannilis. Claude Tanguy brought along Harold Pickles and Roger Bartley, two of the stranded seamen from 318, who had lodged with him; Amédée Rolland came with the sailors and airmen he had sheltered. They drank a good deal and went so far as to sing the 'Marseillaise' and 'Tipperary', which was rash considering that the Germans were installed in a nearby shed. The sentry on duty was invited to drink a toast with the assembled company. Maho's two radio operators and Sarol, his assistant, spent the night of 24 December at the house of Mme Pallier's son-in-law.

On the evening of Christmas Day, Maho, Sarol, the two radio operators, Amédée Rolland and another local helper left the village with small groups of the sailors and airmen who had been hidden there. London had confirmed that the operation would be laid on again that night. The agreed meeting-place for the shore party was Bel-Air-en-Landéda and those in charge of each group established its identity by whistling 'La Madelon'. Doctor de la Marnière turned up in an ambulance, which he had chosen as the form of transport most likely to get through German road-blocks and vehicle checks: he had used it to collect some of the evaders who had been lodged further afield. The expedition consisted of 32 people, 28 of whom were due to be embarked. Apart from the six British naval personnel, they included Sarol, who was due to report to London, five other agents, two women and 16 aircrew. The party was divided into two groups and guided to Ile-Tariec by Guillaume Le Guen and two members of the Coum family from Landéda, without attracting the attention of the German sentinels. This time everything worked like clockwork.

The same held true on board 318: the weather was good and, by skilful navigation, Birkin put the ship on a course that led straight to the Petite-Fourche buoy, with which they had all become so familiar. Men on the gunboat's bridge had the feeling of being on top of everything as they watched the land take shape and realised that their navigator had managed so good a landfall. Birkin, too, was elated that his course had been so precisely on target. Fourteen minutes later they were anchored very close indeed to the southern tip of Guennoc.

Five minutes after anchoring, contact had been established with Michael Pollard ashore who passed the heart-warming news that the mail and 28 bodies were waiting to be taken off. At 2355 hrs the boats were away: Tassy with four oarsmen in a PD1 led the SN6 with Howard Rendle, John Garnett and six oarsmen, direct to Tariec in 20 minutes. At 0045 they reported on the S-phone that they were on the way back, and 15 minutes later they were along-side, transferring their passengers and mail. The inclusion in the party of a Frenchman and his wife, who wished to escape to England, made a second trip to the beach necessary: the SN2 left the ship again at 0110 and was back at 0152. The embarkation had been completed without a hitch.

The return passage to England in the small hours of Boxing Day gave everyone on 318 a tremendous feeling of achievement and euphoria – success at last after four failures. Their elation was such that nobody really cared when, at 0600, somewhere south of the Lizard, all three of the MGB's engines began spluttering and finally cut through lack of fuel pressure. Filters were cleaned and the voyage was completed on two.

Steven, who spent the night on *Sunbeam II*, the depot ship at Helford, had not expected a signal before 0800 but already at 0600 the telephone rang with the brief message, 'Successful, 28 passengers', and gave the time of return as 0930. He woke Philip and Ray, who had spent the night on board, and they made sure that everything was ready to receive the party on arrival. At 0900 360 came alongside and they left to meet 318, embark the passengers and bring them straight in to the reception camp while the MGB returned to the Coastal Forces base. It was a clear fresh morning, giving promise of another day of sunshine; the sea undulated in a gentle swell. For an hour they rocked gently outside the Helford River, waiting for the sound of engines, while the gulls screamed and wheeled above the cliffs and the Manacles buoy clanged mournfully a mile away. The sun grew hotter, the sea bluer, and still they seemed to have the Channel to themselves. Then a faint droning was heard, increasing slowly to a rumble in the south.

'There she is!' cried Philip. And there she was, limping slowly home on two engines, with a slight list to port, as though she was leaning over on one elbow. As she approached, 318 looked grim and warlike in that golden, peaceful setting on the Cornish coast. But as she drew nearer they could see the narrow deck crowded with raffish figures, like a holiday river-launch. From the mess deck below they swarmed up to see the English coast at last – men in the remnants of battledress and flying kit, in shapeless ancient coats and black French berets, men of all shapes and sizes but with one feature in common – a broad grin of welcome and relief.

The two vessels met at 0945 and proceeded together towards the Helford River entrance, where mail and passengers were transferred to 360 and the very buoyant reception party on board her. At 1012 hrs, 318 was on her way again and at 1050 she slid unobtrusively back into her berth at the Coast Lines wharf in

Falmouth Harbour, attracting as little attention as when she had put to sea 19 hours earlier.

That evening, 28 people took the night train to London in Philip Philipson's charge. They had been bathed and fed, examined and lectured. They included Englishmen, Australians, Americans and one Polish airman, six agents, including Sarol, and two women. The French couple, who had joined the party at the eleventh hour and thus avoided most of the tribulations that had befallen many of the others during the previous seven weeks, were quite overwhelmed by the whole proceedings.

McQuoid Mason's report to Slocum wound up by saying, 'This operation will long be remembered by those on board not because it took place on Christmas Day but because of the smooth way in which the internal organisation of the ship ran. All the Officers and Men, including those lent by SOE, fulfilled their duties in a highly efficient manner, sparing the Commanding Officer of the Expedition all unnecessary worries.' Congratulations were in the air: 318 even earned a good mark from General Eisenhower, for the mail they brought back for Dunderdale included detailed intelligence about the V1 and V2 rocket sites.

Slocum was displeased that Pollard had left Brittany and accompanied Maho to Paris. He took the view that, by doing so, 318's first lieutenant had unnecessarily risked capture and thus endangered DDOD(I)'s operations in Brittany. Pollard left the Flotilla not long afterwards.

For those involved in the French side of these five sorties, however, a disastrous period had begun. The gallant Maho and Guillaume Le Guen met on 27 December, the day following the successful embarkation, to plan another such operation for 19 January, the beginning of the next no-moon period. But before this could take place, Maho was arrested with one of his W/T operators in Paris. After being tortured by the notorious Masuy-Fallot gang in the Avenue Henri-Martin, he was deported to Dachau, although he did survive the war. His assistant Sarol returned to France in January and was in his turn arrested and deported. In consequence, London was obliged to consider not only the Ile-Tariec and Ile-Guennoc pinpoints but the whole area as compromised and thus to be avoided. It was clear from the searchlights observed in the adjacent Aber-Wrac'h estuary on each of the ENVIOUS and FELICITATE sorties that this area was already in a high state of alert. On the other hand, the complete success achieved in the early hours of Boxing Day encouraged MI9 and DDOD(I) in the view that large-scale evacuation of evaders and escapers by sea, such as had earlier been achieved by the Poles in Morocco and by the Poles and Pat O'Leary on the south coast of France, was possible in Brittany, if some more accessible and sheltered pinpoint could be found. David Birkin, after eight sorties to Aber-Benoît, rated it one of the most treacherous venues ever visited by the 15th MGB Flotilla.

Nevertheless, aircraft continued to be shot down in the Brest peninsula, Allied airmen continued to receive unstinting and heroic assistance from the local population and, in the spring of 1944, the local Resistance suffered severe retribution for the help they had given to these evaders. Dr de la Marnière, a main organiser in Brest itself, narrowly escaped arrest and had to go into hiding. Louis Bodiger, the garage proprietor at Lannilis, avoided arrest by seconds and also had to go underground. Joseph Mouden, the fisherman and farmer who had played such a key role in the ENVIOUS and FELICITATE operations, was less fortunate. Though he knew he was under surveillance, he refused to take to the maquis, as he knew this would leave his wife and children as potential hostages. In May 1944 the Germans found a cache of parachuted arms buried under one of his fields of corn: he must have been denounced by someone who knew him extremely well. He was subjected to savage torture by Shad, the Gestapo chief at Saint-Brieuc, and died in deportation.

CHAPTER XVII

North Coast and the 'Var' Line: August 1943 – April 1944

E rwin Deman, whose training at Dartmouth for operations with the 15th MGB Flotilla had so annoyed SOE's own Naval Section, was held up in England for nearly four months after the failure to land him at Clogourouan on 19 April 1943. This was because the 'C'-Class motor gunboats, which were all that were then available to Slocum, were deemed too slow for operations to Brittany in the short summer nights. He was landed by the future Air Chief Marshal Sir Lewis Hodges in a Hudson aircraft of 161 Special Duties Squadron 16 km. north-east of Angers on the night of 19/20 August. It was the second time Hodges had used that particular water-meadow and he had to contend with mist and the presence of cattle.[1] A potentially even more serious hazard, of which no-one was aware at the time, was that Gilbert Déricourt, air-landing operations officer for SOE's F Section, who had arranged the operation, was in touch with Bomelberg of the Abwehr in Paris.

Deman carried with him half a sheet of a letter written by a Mme Jestin, living at Rennes, to the sister of an SOE staff officer, whose childhood nanny she had been.[2] He made immediate contact with this lady, using this scrap of paper as introduction, and her two unmarried daughters, active women in their early forties, agreed to work for him as guides and couriers. Moreover, the elder sister, Aline, had a job in the Préfecture at Rennes which enabled her to produce as many blank permits for access to the prohibited coastal zone as might be needed. With their help, Deman established himself at Rennes, with cover as an insurance salesman.

Harratt had briefed Deman to investigate a possible landing beach in the Saint-Cast area west of Dinard: this lay below a villa owned by an Irish yachtswoman, Cecily Lefort, who was under training in England as an agent for SOE's 'Buckmaster' Independent French Section. He had been given an ancient Irish ring which would be immediately recognised as Mrs Lefort's by the maid who had been left in charge of the villa. Deman carried out a reconnaissance and concluded that the beach would be suitable from his point of view. It was called the Grêve-du-Mousselet and lay near the Pointe-du-Châtelet on the face of the Saint-Cast peninsula overlooking the Baie-de-la-Fresnaie. A further advantage was that it was close to the house of the parents of a promising local recruit, Aristide Sicot, which could be used to shelter inward- and outward-bound passengers.

After two months, Harratt flew over one night, as had been agreed before Deman's departure, and had a conversation with him on the secure S-phone link. Deman was able to report that the basic structure of what became known as the 'Var' line was in place and it was agreed he should pay a short visit to London to tie up outstanding points of detail with SOE and DODD(I). He told his local acquaintances that he would be taking a fortnight's holiday: he then used SOE's existing land line, the extremely efficient 'Vic', to cross the Pyrenees and reach Gibraltar, whence he flew to England, accomplishing the whole journey in a record time of seven days.

DDOD(I) accepted the Mousselet beach, though the whole Baie-de-la-Fresnaie area was uncomfortably close to the major German coast-watching radar station on Cap-Fréhel, whose 60-metre-high cliffs stand less than 5 km. (3 miles) to the west. A further drawback was that, in order to bring the beach within practicable rowing distance, the gunboat would have to anchor inside the mouth of the bay, which is less than 2.5 km. (4 miles) wide at that point. Navigational access was, on the other hand, excellent: the Roches-Douvres lighthouse provided a good offshore landfall even when unlit. The Les-Hanois light on Guernsey was frequently available as a further check and Cap-Fréhel and the mediaeval Fort-de-Latte at the western side of the entrance to the Baie-de-la-Fresnaie were distinctive and likely to be visible even on a moonless night; the approach was, moreover, free of submerged hazards. Deman and Raymond Langard, the excellent W/T operator who was to work with him, were to be the first passengers landed on the Mousselet beach. They needed to get over to France promptly in order to maintain the timetable that Deman had laid down in saying he would be away for only a fortnight.

MGB 318 was not available as she was 'standing by' to make her first attempt from Falmouth to pick up the 'Jade-Fitzroy' mail and passengers from the Aber-Benoît area. Neither MGB 502 nor 503 was yet ready to operate, so DDOD(I) had once again to borrow a gunboat from Coastal Forces for the operation to the Pointe-de-Saint-Cast, on which he bestowed the code name JEALOUS, though SOE called it MANGO 4 The boat chosen for the job was MGB 697, one of the 'D'-Class Fairmiles. Her first sortie, on 25 October, had to be abandoned owing to her late arrival in the pinpoint area; but a renewed attempt on 28 October was entirely successful.

SIS also had plans to use the Baie-de-la-Fresnaie to land two agents,[3] though the pinpoint they chose for this was at Saint-Géran on the opposite side of the bay, close to the Fort-de-Latte. MGB 697 attempted this operation (code-named INDIFFERENT) on the night of 3 November, but this failed, again because the gunboat arrived in the area too late. The waxing moon precluded a further attempt until the last week of that month, by which time SOE had asked Slocum to land four agents to Deman and pick up between three and six others. DDOD(I) decided to do the two operations (JEALOUS II and INDIFFERENT II) in conjunction, using two gunboats to tackle the two pinpoints on opposite sides of the Baie-de-la-Fresnaie.

MGB 502, by now fully operational, was detailed to carry out JEALOUS II as her first job. Lt Peter Williams, RNVR, her commanding officer, was the senior MGB captain of the Dartmouth flotilla. His considerable experience with Coastal Forces included two cross-Channel operations (POLISH III and IV) with Ted Davis and Angus Letty in the autumn of 1941, carried out at short notice from Portland in his MGB 325 when another boat, which they had hoped to use to collect mail from Garby-Czerniawski's 'Interallié' network, broke down. He had also worked for DDOD(I) from Felixstowe to Holland. As navigator, Williams took with him on JEALOUS II Lt R. ('Titch') Salmond, RNR. The records show another 'borrowed' gunboat, 673, as the ship tasked to carry out INDIFFERENT II.

Deman and Sicot, told to expect JEALOUS II, stood on the top of the cliff on the night of 26 November, and managed to make contact with MGB 502 using their secure S-phone link. The two gunboats had had to stop some miles short of their respective destinations in the Baie-de-la-Fresnaie because they had run into a long and straggling German convoy heading into Saint-Malo. It is said to have been two hours before they were able to get underway again. In the interval Deman had concluded that the operation would not take place that night and had stood down the reception committee at the Grêve-du-Mousselet. 502 and 673 had in fact made their way into the entrance to the Baie de la Fresnaie and had anchored at positions suitable for their respective pinpoints. They sent their boats inshore, but in both cases there was no reception committee: one of the two SIS agents decided to land in spite of this, but his colleague and the four SOE agents on 502 preferred to return to Dartmouth.

A second attempt to complete these two operations was mounted on 1 December, using the same two gunboats. On this occasion everything went well with the SOE landing at Mousselet, though Peter Harratt, who was in the first of the two surf-boats, very nearly opened fire on the unfortunate Aristide Sicot as he waded out to meet the boat: they agreed that in future, when acting as beach-master, he would hold his hands above his head to avoid any misunderstanding. One of the four men landed on this occasion was an OSS officer named Emile Minerault, who was intended to act as deputy to Deman, but the two men failed to establish a satisfactory working relationship and in practice Sicot acted as Deman's chief organiser of operations. The five passengers embarked that night included a French-Canadian SOE agent who was on the run and three members of the same 'Buckmaster' circuit, which had been broken up by the Germans. The fifth outward-bound passenger was the son of one of Deman's helpers who wanted to join the Fighting French Forces. The 'Var' line had begun to work, though Peter Williams recalls that one of those landed on this occasion was a Dutchman who was in an extremely apprehensive state, a condition exacerbated when he had to climb down into the surf-boat. Williams heard subsequently that this man had to be sent back to England as unsuitable, though it is difficult to understand how such a misfit can have survived the scrutiny that had by then become a feature of the programme for training potential agents.

The shore party from MGB 673 on the western side of the Baie-de-la-Fresnaie had no such luck. Once again they could find no reception committee, though their search lasted an hour and a half. Thus the second of the two SIS agents involved in INDIFFERENT II could again not be landed.

The next moonless period began just before the last Christmas of the Occupation and by this time Deman's 'Var' line was in full working order: there was a considerable build-up of candidates for evacuation at 'Les Feux Follets', the Sicot family villa behind Saint-Cast. London expected nine and had six SOE agents, including two women, to be landed.

Deman's orders from Leslie Humphreys, head of SOE's DF Section, which was supposed to cater exclusively for SOE's own needs, were that he was not to accept passengers who were not known to, and approved by, the Baker Street organisation. The conditions prevailing in Brittany, however, were such that it was difficult to apply this instruction in practice. Increasing numbers of RAF and USAAF planes were being shot down and their surviving aircrews needed shelter and evacuation. They gravitated into the hands of any organised branch of the Resistance in Brittany, whatever its original purpose. It was therefore a mixed party of agents and airmen who awaited collection at 'Les Feux Follets'. A French account describes them as about a dozen in number and says that Aristide had set them to work excavating an underground shelter beneath the dining-room floor of his parents' villa so that the transients could be hidden in the event that Germans conducted searches of properties close to the sea. Each day, Sicot himself distributed some of the accumulated soil round the garden, using a wheelbarrow.

The next operation was due to take place on the 23/24 December and at the last minute Félix Jouan, the miller from Bedée, whose van was being used by the 'Var' organisation to transport passengers through the Prohibited Zone that covered the coast, came to say that a General Allard, whose wife had already been arrested by the Gestapo, was urgently seeking evacuation to England. Deman felt he could not do other than accept this distinguished additional passenger, whom Jouan then delivered in his van. The party, now expanded to considerable size, left the villa that night in Indian file behind Aristide Sicot. They passed through La-Pisotte and made their way down to the Grêve-du-Mousselet, using a coastguard path cut into the face of the cliff.

Though there was no moon, the night had become calm and clear after earlier rain and the visibility by starlight was good enough to cause Peter Williams, on the bridge of MGB 502, considerable apprehension as he approached the Baie-de-la-Fresnaie, its entrance, 2.5 km. (1½ miles) wide, dominated by high cliffs on each side.

Sicot and Deman had hurried back from the beach to the top of the cliff at the Pointe-du-Châtelet to try to establish contact with the approaching gunboat as soon as possible; when they did, they warned Williams that the party awaiting embarkation was even larger than he had been told to expect. This severely complicated an already difficult task, as the surf-boats with their three-man crews would need to make two trips to the shore to pick up the whole group. There were therefore strong reasons to bring the gunboat as close inshore as possible so as to cut to a minimum the time required.

Williams came close enough to surprise those waiting ashore. Sicot recalled that the gunboat seemed to drift over to the Saint-Cast shore. She passed under the noses of the Germans, that is to say, within a hundred metres of their block-houses. Even though she was steaming at slow speed on one silenced engine, the Germans would have had to be deaf not to hear her. She came on in until she was off the Pointe-du-Châtelet and there anchored. Deman and Sicot watched from the top of their rocky headland, astonished by the audacity of the proceedings. Although there was no moon, the visibility to seaward was such that, even at a distance of over half a mile, the ship's silhouette seemed outlined by a sort of phosphorescent mist. Sicot said after the war that he asked Deman to advise the British to clear out as quickly as possible: the Germans had certainly been alerted.

It is difficult to know how literally to take this evidence: if the MGB had been only 100 metres from the German block-houses, it seems odd that she should have been ten times that distance off the Pointe-du-Châtelet when she dropped anchor. The recollection of events by those on board the gunboat differ from those of Sicot in other respects as well.

Signalman George College was on MGB 502's bridge as she entered the bay. Suddenly he saw a light ashore and at almost the same time Williams saw it too. A door had been opened and a man rushed out, briefly silhouetted against the lighted room behind him. As there was no immediate sequel, Williams concluded that they had not necessarily been spotted, and continued cautiously into the bay. When he had reached his chosen position, they anchored to a grass warp, as was standard practice, and the surf-boats were hoisted out and lowered into the water. Deman and Sicot heard the noise of a winch quite clearly at this point. Then a white flare burst overhead, turning night into day.

MGB 502's surf-boats were hoisted back on board, the grass warp was cut and her main engines were started up. But the ship was lying with her head facing into the bay. As the white flare sank exhausted, it was replaced by a red one and this was clearly a signal for all guns that could be brought to bear to open fire. The gunboat was so far into the bay that she was beyond the field of fire of the cannon mounted on both sides of the entrance, but machine-guns and small arms opened up immediately and tracer bullets fell all around her as she turned at full speed, heading over to the Fort-de-Latte shore as she did so. Williams knew that heavier-calibre fire was to be expected as he passed out of the bay. Those ashore said she laid a smoke screen. Those on board recalled frantic entreaties over the S-phone for the boats to be sent in; they found it difficult to understand how the reception committee could have been so unaware of what was happening.

MGB 502 adopted violent alterations of course as she headed towards the open sea. Her luck was in and the enemy artillery shells fell harmlessly astern of her. Incredible as it may seem, the only damage she sustained that night was to a signals halliard that was severed by a bullet, thus bringing the recognition signals crashing down behind the bridge. If the Germans had used a searchlight the outcome might have been different.

When the firing began, Sicot had dashed down to the beach to collect those waiting there: they rushed up the cliff path helter-skelter and all got back to 'Les Feux Follets' safely.

As a result of the tunnelling operation under the house, three or four cubic metres of soil were still in the garage. Sicot foresaw that, as an immediate consequence of the alert caused by their discovery of MGB 502 in the bay, the Germans were all too likely to under-take a house-to-house search of all the villas near the coast. If they discovered the garage full of soil, his parents would be in great danger, so he set to work immediately, with the assistance of some of the would-be evacuees, distributing the tell-tale earth round the garden. By breakfast-time the task was virtually complete and a council of war ensued. His father thought they had all better stay where they were in the hope that another operation might be arranged to the Mousselet beach. Deman, on the other hand, knew that the British would never again hazard a gunboat by sending her back to the Baie-de-la-Fresnaie area and that the passengers must be got away from the area as soon as possible.

The Germans' suspicions fell, in fact, on the opposite side of the bay and they concentrated their search operations there. No doubt they thought that the array of bunkers they had built on the Saint-Cast promontory made it an unlikely site for a landing. Aristide Sicot was therefore able, with the assistance of Jouan, the miller, and his wood-burning *gazogène* van, to evacuate all the 'Var' passengers to Bedée in the course of the following night. They ran tremendous risks in doing so, as Jouan's van was registered in the Ille-et-Vilaine Department and was not authorised to circulate in the prohibited coastal zone at all, let alone after the curfew. Perhaps the fact that it was Christmas Day meant that German guards and check-points were less vigilant than usual. Baker Street decided to transfer the passengers to their highly efficient 'Vic' line, which never lost any of the 'parcels' it handled, and in due course they all got back to the United Kingdom via Spain and Gibraltar.

As Deman had foreseen, there was no question of any further operations to the Baie-de-la-Fresnaie after the failure of JEALOUS III. Baker Street gave 'Var' two alternative pinpoints to investigate. One of these was at Paramé, close to Saint-Malo, where there was a shut-up hotel that offered potential shelter for transit passengers, but Aristide Sicot judged the site unsuitable because of convoy movements in and out of Saint-Malo; and entering and leaving the hotel itself would present further problems. He turned his attention therefore to London's second suggestion, a place named Beg-an-Fry near Guimaëc, north-east of Morlaix. As he had no local contacts there his presence aroused some curiosity among the inhabitants when he turned up there at the end of the first week of January 1944. He hoped to satisfy them by explaining that he was interested in the geography of the region, left his bicycle at the Hôtel du Prajou in Guimaëc and went off on foot to reconnoitre the coast. He thought that the beach proposed by London was too close to the headland feature of Beg-an-Fry, which was crowned with a German gun emplacement from which it could be overlooked; slightly further to the east, however, there were two long spurs of rock running out into the sea with a beach between them that was easily accessible from landward. This seemed to him a much better site, indeed, exactly what he was looking for.

When he got back from his excursion on foot and went to collect his bicycle, he was confronted by the gendarmes from Lanmeur, accompanied by a civilian. They ordered him to put his hands up and began to search him. His papers were genuine and, as he lived at Saint-Cast, which was in the coastal zone, it was perfectly in order for him to move around along the coast as he was doing. He could therefore not be charged with any offence, but the gendarmes decided to keep his papers and told him to come back and collect them next day. He discovered subsequently that he had been denounced by someone who demanded that he be handed over to the Occupation authorities. The danger was that, if the matter were referred to the German police, they would put two and two together and link his presence at Guimaëc with recent events at Saint-Cast. Above all he was determined not to leave his genuine identity papers in the hands of the gendarmerie for fear that he would thereby compromise his parents. He therefore asked to speak to the gendarmes privately. They met at the back of a café, where he told them in effect that he was as well known on the far side of the Channel as he was in Brittany and that, if any harm should come to him, retribution would certainly be visited upon anyone responsible for his capture. His papers were returned to him immediately. At this point Sicot decided to try to take further advantage of his questioners' change of attitude. If they wanted confirmation of his story, he said, he would arrange for an agreed message to be broadcast on the BBC's French Service at the time of the news bulletin. Since the gendarmes did not know what to suggest, Sicot proposed a play on words (since they came from Lanmeur): *'Quarante-quatre n'est pas l'an qui meurt.'* Afterwards Sicot returned to Rennes, where he told Deman that he had found a suitable beach and of the narrow escape he had just had at Guimaëc. Deman drafted a signal to DF Section of SOE accepting Beg-an-Fry as a pinpoint for the next operation by sea and asking for Sicot's message for the gendarmes to be broadcast by the BBC to confirm his *bona fides* as a British agent. This was done a few days later, though the message was transmitted in a form that spoiled Sicot's punning allusion to Lanmeur. More ominously, the signal from 'Var' must have failed to make clear that the beach at Beg-an-Fry that Sicot wished to use was not the one London had proposed but another 300 metres to the east of it. Sicot, who had not been trained in England and whose experience was thus far limited to a single successful landing, may have thought that the change was of little operational significance, as his light signal from the new position would be equally visible to the gunboat and would automatically bring the surf-boats in to where he was waiting. He was to be proved wrong on both counts.

Aristide had left some equipment, including an S-phone, at Paramé and it was agreed that Félix Jouan, the miller, would drive him there in his *gazogène* van to collect it. They set out on 13 January, barely a week after Sicot's expedition to Beg-an-Fry. After a stop at Bedée, where they picked up some additional suitcases, they set off to Rennes, where they arrived just at the hour of curfew and stopped in the square in front of the theatre. While Sicot was dealing with the suitcases, two German Feldgendarmen approached Jouan, who was still in the driving seat, and drew his attention to the fact that the van's number-plate was so mud-bespattered as to be illegible; this, of course, was exactly as Jouan wanted it, for he was not at all anxious to have the vehicle identified. Just as Jouan was paying the fine and moving off, one of the Germans flashed his torch into the back of the van and his eye lit on a series of identical, rather distinctive suitcases. He drew his pistol and was just taking aim at the moving vehicle when it broke down and spluttered to a halt only 20 metres down the street. By this time Sicot was sheltering in a doorway, but he was unarmed and had to watch helplesly as his friend was arrested.

Jouan told so plausible a story that he might well have got away with it had he not been denounced quite independently. The Germans had been told that his son had left France to join de Gaulle.

Sicot was able to warn Mme Jouan and the Jestin sisters, who moved to Paris. By mid-January the 'Var' organisation had pulled out of Rennes and was operating from Fougères and Redon, with Deman's headquarters at the latter.

Sicot took Deman with him when he went back to Lanmeur to look for a safe house where agents and airmen could be sheltered when in transit. His first call was on the gendarmerie. He went alone to see them while Deman waited near by. They agreed that, if he was not back within five minutes, Deman must take to his heels. But the gendarmes, having heard the BBC message, promised to cooperate by warning Sicot if the Germans seemed to be suspicious. They even provided names and addresses of reliable people who might help. Deman returned to Redon leaving Sicot to follow up the leads.

The first contact led nowhere, but the second – Yvonne Jacob, who ran a tobacconist's shop at Guimaëc – evoked so positive a response that Sicot feared he had perhaps fallen into the hands of a Gestapo informant. But the offer of help proved genuine: Yvonne discussed the matter with her sisters, took the precaution of consulting the gendarmerie and confirmed that they were all ready to join the 'Var' organisation.

The search for a safe house close to the sea was protracted but, by asking from farm to farm, Sicot eventually found a blacksmith at Plouigneau, which had a station on the main Paris–Brest railway line, though it was some way inland. The blacksmith was not only willing to provide shelter, but he had a trusted friend, a wine merchant, with a van that could be used to transport passengers from Plouigneau to the coast.

Deman wanted to make a visit to England to consult Harratt and Humphreys, taking with him Langard, his W/T operator, who had been experiencing a great deal of atmospheric interference

with his traffic. A first operation to Beg-an-Fry was therefore arranged for the night of 28/29 January, 1944.

MGB 502 was the vessel chosen for the job, with Birkin as navigator; Peter Harratt was also on board as conducting officer for SOE. They found the wind south-westerly Force 5 with a heavy swell running off Start Point, and both wind and swell increased for a brief period, but they were making better than the requisite speed of 15 knots and conditions improved as they neared the French coast. No difficulty was experienced in finding Les-Boeufs, the distinctive group of rocks to seaward of Beg-an-Fry. By 0015 the ship was anchored three cables N 60° E of them. Both surf-boats had been lowered into the water during the approach to this anchorage and at 0027 they were on their way to the shore. Beg-an-Fry was clearly distinguishable, its easterly slope rising sheer from the beach. Lt Uhr-Henry, the Australian officer who had been involved in so many of MGB 318's operations over the previous 15 months, was now 502's first lieutenant and boats officer: he took Harratt with him in the first boat, and an SOE agent (or agents) who were to be landed followed in the second. There was considerable surf on the beach but both boats touched down and were hauled up while Harratt carried out a search for the reception party. At 0150, he concluded that the rendezvous had not been kept and the boats were launched through the surf, returning to the ship at 0210. The boats were difficult to get inboard as they had both made a certain amount of water. However, both were on deck at 0225, and at 0238 the anchor was weighed and the ship proceeded on the return journey to Dartmouth.

Sicot, Deman, Langard and two other would-be evacuees had been guided to the beach by the Jacob sisters and were waiting on the beach chosen by Sicot 300 metres to the east. Here they were effectively screened from view by one of the two rocky spurs that separated it from the beach at the base of Beg-an-Fry on which the surf-boats had landed. The misunderstanding was sorted out on the W/T link the following day. The blame for this wasted night's work must be laid at the door of Sicot, who had changed the pinpoint without telling London, but it must be said in mitigation that he lacked training and had been under great pressure since the failure of JEALOUS III four weeks before.

The passengers who should have left on *Easement* on the night of 28/29 January were lodged in an empty house just opposite the Jacob sisters' shop at Guimaëc until the next operation could be mounted, which was not until 26/27 February. In the interval Deman and Langard had been back in Redon and had arranged a first parachute drop to deliver a new W/T transmitter/receiver for Langard. The single container should have been dropped to a reception committee they had organised at Saint-Jacques-en-Rieux, but the aircraft made a mistake and it came down at a small place called Allaire. The farmer on whose land it fell reported the matter to the local gendarmes and the Germans took possession of the container. As this incident was certain to lead to further searches and enquiries in the area, Deman decided to move Langard and his existing set to Quimper. He established himself in a house belonging to the Henriot family, owners of the well-known pottery business, but Mme Henriot seemed surprised to find the young people she had agreed to lodge there operating a radio transmitter. Deman decided to move without delay, though Langard would have liked to stay, as the site was on the top of a small hill and he was obtaining excellent results. Deman insisted, which was lucky because the girl who loaded the suitcase containing the set on to the luggage-rack of her bicycle passed a group of German soldiers on their way to the house she had just left. It was not clear whether they had been denounced or located by a German direction-finding operation.

Just before the next operation, EASEMENT II, was due to take place, the party awaiting evacuation was increased by the arrival of an RAF pilot, who had landed by parachute near Morlaix. He was a Southern Rhodesian named Wally Mollet. The Jacob sisters collected him from the local Morlaix Resistance group under Doctor Le Duc and escorted him to Guimaëc on bicycles. Deman subjected him to a strenuous cross-examination about the geography of London and decided that he was what he claimed to be. London agreed that he be included in the operation, which was to embark Deman, Langard and Sicot among others. Deman felt the need to reshape the whole 'Var' organisation, as well as to explain to SOE and DDOD(I) that Sicot's beach, which they called Le Studio, was far safer than the beach London still insisted on using, right under the Beg-an-Fry headland and code-named (by 'Var') L'Atelier.

The gunboat employed for EASEMENT II on the night of 25/26 February was again Peter Williams's 502. No detailed report of this operation has been preserved, which is a pity, as one of the two inward passengers at Beg-an-Fry that night was the young François Mitterrand, future President of the Republic, who had been flown out of France by Bob Hodges on 15/16 November the previous year from the same improvised landing strip north-east of Angers on which he had landed Deman three months previously. De Gaulle had refused to help Mitterrand return to France, perhaps because he had left it under SOE F Section auspices, but perhaps also because of the latter's known connections with the Vichy administration.

The group awaiting embarkation, hidden among the rocks at the foot of Beg-an-Fry, heard 502's engine stop when she dropped anchor once more off Les-Boeufs. Although fitted with silencers, the sound was audible at sea-level at surprising distances in calm conditions.

The drill followed by those on board the MGBs had by now been carefully standardised: no talking or smoking on deck; S-phone contact would be established with the beach where possible, failing which the reception party would be flashing the agreed light signal to seaward. The first surf-boat carried an armed look-out in its bows. The agents to be landed would be following in the second boat. They would be wearing gas-capes over their clothes to avoid tell-tale salt-water stains and would be carried the last metre or two on to the beach to ensure that they landed dry-shod. They were on no account to contact the people waiting to embark or indeed to talk at all. No-one involved was allowed to wear headgear in case it should fall, or be blown, off. Passengers 'should be briefed to behave as much like luggage as possible. While waiting they should always sit down, except on first disembarkation, when they should stand by the boats.' The gas-capes would be collected and taken back by the surf-boats. The actual time spent by the seamen on the beach was supposed to be only three or four minutes. Usually the MGB was at anchor for about an hour and a half; Harratt recorded 35 minutes as the shortest time. The longest, three and a half hours, occurred during EASEMENT II, when the shore party's return was delayed by a sudden fog. Landings were made on a rising tide to minimise footprint traces and someone from the shore party would visit the beach again at first light to ensure that there was nothing suspicious to be seen.

On this particular night Sicot, who had waded out to meet the first surf-boat, identified himself to Harratt as 'Jeanette', his field name, whereas he should have said 'Aristide'; this nearly produced another crisis. The two incoming passengers were taken in charge by the resident members of the reception committee, Le Corvaisier, who would be in charge during Deman's absence, and Raymonde and Alice Jacob. Deman, Langard, Sicot and perhaps as many as seven other passengers were embarked.

Harratt was using an S-phone of American manufacture for the first time and soon hit the problem that, while the gunboat could hear him, he could not hear them. Then, to their consternation, the fog enveloped them like a blanket, and they were quite unable to find the gunboat, although she could still receive them on the S-phone channel. After a long and tantalising search, they gave up looking for the anchored 502 and tried to attract her attention by shining their torches at sea-level. That stratagem worked and they suddenly saw a high ship's bow slicing through the white fog. For a brief moment, they wondered whether it might not be an enemy vessel, but they were soon reassured by the sight of the scrambling-net that had been lowered down the gunboat's side amidships to enable them to board her.

The return passage to Dartmouth was uneventful. Sicot's main memory of it was that of regaining a sense of security he had not known for months. They berthed next morning alongside the paddle-steamer *Westward Ho!*, depot-ship for the 15th MGB Flotilla, a mere 100 metres off the railway station and ferry terminal on the Kingswear side of the Dart. At almost the same time, their sister ship 503 berthed, having embarked 18 passengers at the Anse-Cochat during the night on Operation BONAPARTE II.

Westward Ho! provided a large wardroom and cabins for the use of the base staff of the 15th MGB Flotilla, as well as for agents in transit. Its closeness to the Kingswear railway terminus meant that passengers and their baggage could be ferried between her and the station without attracting much attention. On a morning such as this, the first train out of Kingswear might wait an extra minute or two after the guard's whistle while a bunch of weary civilians climbed on board and collapsed exhausted behind the drawn blinds of their reserved compartments. Little did the other passengers guess that in the early hours of that same morning these late arrivals had been crawling over Breton rocks 150 km. away under the noses of German coastal look-outs, and unpleasantly close to the Gestapo headquarters at Saint-Brieuc and Morlaix.

The two passengers left at Beg-an-Fry by 502 had been escorted to the house of a retired gendarme named Lucas at Kergoriou. The nameless companion of M Mitterrand must have been destined for an intelligence mission, for he bombarded Le Corvaisier and Raymonde Jacob with questions about the German submarine base at Lorient. The Jacob sisters, who found him good company, took the new arrivals on to Guimaëc, their home village, where Louis Mercier, a local fish merchant, came and picked them up to drive them to Doctor Le Duc's house at Morlaix, whence they were to take trains to their respective destinations. The future President left Mme Le Duc a ration card made out in the name of Morland.

MGB 502 went back to Beg-an-Fry only three nights later to land two further SOE agents. One was a spirited Corsican named Defendini, who was on his way to establish, and lead, a circuit named 'Priest', but who was captured soon after his arrival and was killed in captivity at Buchenwald in September 1944. The other was a Lt Schwatschko, who was destined for the 'Stationer' circuit but was transferred to the 'Shipwright' circuit following the capture of Maurice Southgate, organiser of 'Stationer' (and, unusually, recipient of the award of DSO while he was still in captivity). Schwatschko was killed in action near Eguzon (Indre) on 7 June 1944. This landing was code-named EASEMENT III.

During March there were three further successful operations to

Beg-an-Fry. MGB 503 (Lt R.M. Marshall, RNVR) went there on the night of 17/18 for Operation SEPTIMUS, in the course of which Deman and Langard must have been disembarked, for they certainly returned to France on that date and there was no appropiriate RAF Lysander or Hudson operation at the time. (Besides, Deman was allergic to the idea of a parachute jump.) The four other passengers were BCRA agents on an intelligence mission. Their leader, Gilbert Védy ('Médéric'), already had behind him a long and distinguished Resistance career. He had been appointed to represent the 'Ceux de la Libération' movement in the Algiers Consultative Assembly and, as Vice-President of the Assembly's Defence Committee, had been to Italy to visit the French Expeditionary Corps. He was, in fact, such a well-known figure that his return to France involved exceptional risks, but he accepted them without hesitation. Though he did not know it at the time, his elder brother, Maxime, had been executed by a German firing-squad at Mont-Valérian ten days previously. He told Mme Le Duc that it was his fourth mission and that, if arrested, he would certainly use the lethal cyanide tablet he carried. It was no idle boast designed to impress his attractive young hostess. From Morlaix he and his companions took the train to Paris. There, Védy moved into a hotel where he was given a room just vacated by a notorious black-marketeer whom the police were actively pursuing. They raided the hotel and took Védy with them to police headquarters for identification. David, head of the Anti-Terrorist Brigade and a zealous collaborator with the occupying power, quickly recognised him as a man he had long been seeking. Knowing he would be handed over to the Germans, Védy swallowed his cyanide tablet.

It is tempting to say that so well known a figure should never have been allowed to return to France. But if men of the calibre of Jean Moulin, Pierre Brossolette, Fred Scamaroni, Emmanuel d'Astier de la Vigerie and Gilbert Védy had not been willing to undertake such missions – and to commit suicide if things went wrong – de Gaulle would never have acquired the right to speak for the Resistance or to claim for a resurgent France the Great Power status Roosevelt felt she had forfeited in June 1940. Indeed, if a gulf had been allowed to develop between internal and external French Resistance, the country might, when Liberation came, have been racked by conflict such as arose in Greece and Yugoslavia.

SEPTIMUS took place in extremely favourable weather. Birkin was navigating and he had by this stage become adept at using the QH navigational aid as a check on his own dead-reckoning. After about an hour's run, QH fixes showed a position too far to the westward and it eventually became clear that 503's standard compass must be at fault. Course was altered accordingly. The ship had come back into commission only very recently after a refit: the compass must have developed this deviation while in dockyard hands and no opportunity for checking it had arisen since her return.

The Triagoz light was sighted at the expected time and it was working, which suggested that enemy vessels were somewhere in the vicinity. The sea was flat calm and the sky clear, but the horizon was at times difficult to distinguish, owing to a slight haze. There was also some intermittent phosphorescence, but this disappeared entirely as they closed in to the enemy coast. Long streaks of light seen in the distance on the smooth sea were disconcerting at first, until they were recognised as reflections of stars. No enemy vessels were encountered. Birkin homed in to the coast on QH and, on his information, the MGB was stopped at 0041 hrs to get the surf-boats out for towing. While this was being done and 503 was still moving through the water, the Les-Boeufs rocks were sighted fine on the starboard bow at about half a mile. They were approached with caution and the ship eventually anchored at 0055. Gear was stowed in the boats during anchoring and, as soon as the agents were embarked and the secure-speech walkie-talkies tested, the surf-boats left for the pinpoint, with Sub Lt Andrew Smith in charge.

The boats proceeded first to Les-Boeufs before setting course for the beach. However, there proved to be a stronger westerly set than anticipated and the boats were carried towards the Beg-an-Fry headland: when this was observed, Smith altered course to the eastward. The pinpoint was found without much difficulty and the boats were beached in practically no surf. The reception committee was waiting, business was quickly transacted and the boats as quickly launched for the return journey. They had been told to expect up to ten outward passengers, but only one was waiting – a Canadian airman named Gérald Racine, who had been collected by Dr Le Duc a fortnight previously and sheltered by a M Marzin.

Allowing for the stronger set of tide, Smith steered straight for the parent ship and came right up to it without using the homing facility available on the new MAB type of walkie-talkie. Boats were alongside at 0218 and haste was made to unload and haul them aboard. The return to Dartmouth, which was uneventful, was made at slow speed until 0515 as they had been ordered to keep clear of dispositions of British forces until that time.

Operation SEPTIMUS II was carried out by MGB 502 to the Beg-an-Fry pinpoint only four nights later, on 21/22 March. Six SOE agents were landed that night and one was embarked. The arrivals included Virginia Hall, an early and key 'Buckmaster' Section agent, now returning as a W/T operator; and Charles Rechenmann, who had previously worked with Ben Cowburn, the specialist in destroying the oil refineries that, before the war, he had helped to build. As Birkin was engaged on another operation by

MGB 503 that night for SIS, no detailed record of the naval side of SEPTIMUS II has survived, but on 26/27 March he navigated 503 back to Beg-an-Fry for SEPTIMUS III, the penultimate operation to this pinpoint, when four further agents were landed for SOE. One agent who went in on SEPTIMUS II or III was a woman called Mme Fontaine, on her way to join Mulsant's 'Minister' circuit in the Seine-et-Marne as courier. SEPTIMUS III's passengers had a comfortable passage in ideal weather: no wind, a flat calm sea and no swell, with visibility up to 3 km. (2 miles).

It was a fast crossing at 1,400 r.p.m., which speed was maintained, except for a short time while a minor defect was repaired, until they reached the point where they had to begin the silenced approach. Once again the Triagoz light was working, but no enemy shipping was encountered. Visibility was low as they crossed the German convoy route, but improved again as they closed in on the coast. Birkin used QH to home in on the final approach, with excellent results, as was proved by the appearance of the Les-Boeufs rocks fine on the starboard bow at 0051 at a distance of one mile. As they were cautiously approaching their anchoring position, star-shell, at first thought to be flares not far distant, was seen, bearing N 80° W: it was assumed this might indicate activity by other British forces.

The two boats got away at 0119 with Sub Lt Smith again in charge, carrying Captain Harratt, the four agents and a quantity of stores. The passage to the beach on a compass course with allowance for tide was uneventful: and a good landfall was made on a sandy beach with practically no surf. Smith attempted to make radio-telephone contact while the gear was being unloaded. The ship could hear faint signals, but two-way contact was impossible from that distance. The boats left within five minutes of landing and course was set for Les-Boeufs. Visibility had improved considerably and was up to 3–4 miles. They were no more than 100 metres away from the beach on the return journey when an unexplained yellow light was seen, for about 10 seconds, to the eastward on top of the cliff somewhere near the Pointe-du-Corbeau. Les-Boeufs were sighted at a range of about half a mile. The gunboat saw the boats returning at 0215 and a course was passed to them on the secure MAB link, but this was unnecessary, although it was not until the boats were quite close that the parent ship was sighted. The return passage to Dartmouth was uneventful.

By this time the 'Var' organisation was snowballing in a way that Leslie Humphreys's DF Section networks rarely did: the Jestin sisters in Paris had developed contacts in Brussels on the one hand and far down the Rhône valley on the other. Langard's friends in southern Brittany, from where he was now transmitting, could not understand why it was not possible to conduct sea operations from the relatively unguarded beaches in that area. Deman held a conference in Paris on Easter Day in an endeavour to sort out a programme of future action, but London decided that, with the onset of shorter nights and the need to suspend sea operations because of the imminence of D-Day, the time had come to recall Deman for consultations about restructuring the whole organisation. He left on the night of 15/16 April by the most ambitious, but also the last, of the 'Var' sea-line operations.

MGB 502 sailed from Dartmouth on Operation SCARF in company with a new 'D'-Class addition to the 15th MGB Flotilla – MGB 718 (Lt R. Seddon, RNVR) – a ship destined to carry out two outstanding operations for Slocum from Aberdeen to Norway later that year. On this, the first such mission she had undertaken, she carried, in addition to her normal complement of officers and men, Lt Jan McQuoid Mason, the commanding officer of MGB 318, as commanding officer of the expedition. Since Peter Williams of MGB 502 was the most senior of the Dartmouth gunboat captains and the record shows that 718 was under his orders on this occasion, Seddon must have been under instruction from Mason, who had brought with him one complete boat's crew from 318 as well. MGB 718 also carried Lt M.P. Salmond, RNR, as navigating officer. In addition to the commanding officer of 318, her first lieutenant, Sub Lt D.N. Miller, SANF, was on board 502 as boats officer and Lt Cdr A.H. Smith, RNR, and Sub Lt B.K. Fraser, RNR, as additional navigating and assistant navigating officers respectively.

MGB 502 carried six agents. Two of these – Captain Martin Rendier and Félix Duffour – had been entrusted by Col Maurice Buckmaster of SOE's Independent French Section with a mission to sabotage and delay any redeployment of the armoured forces which the Germans had concentrated around Guers (Ille-et-Vilaine) in a position from which, in the event of an Allied landing, they could move either to the Channel or the Atlantic coasts to oppose it. Rendier and Duffour were to prove brilliantly successful: on the night of 5/6 June, teams equipped and trained by them cut the four relevant railway lines out of Guers and destroyed fuel dumps and telecommunications to such good effect that the armoured unit had to proceed to the Normandy battlefront on its own tracks and took nine days to get into battle. A similar, and equally important, delaying action was taken by SOE against the 'Das Reich' 2nd SS Armoured Division on its redeployment from Moutauban to the Normandy battle.

The six outward-bound agents included two other officers of SOE's F Section, M.H. Rouneau, a Belgian who was being sent in something of a hurry to try to get a circuit going in Brittany to take the place of J.F.A. Antelme's 'Bricklayer'; and A.P.A. Watt, who had been W/T operator to Déricourt's 'Farrier' and had left France just before the Gestapo closed in on it after Déricourt's withdrawal to England. He was now on his way to join M.M.L. Dupont's 'Diplomat' circuit, in the Aube, which was preparing to isolate Troyes when ordered to do so.

The other two agents travelling over to Brittany on MGB 502 that night were on missions for de Gaulle's secret service, by then based in Algiers and styled the Direction Générale des Études et Recherches (DGER). Col P. Ely ('Algèbre') was on his way to take over as Délégué Militaire for the old occupied zone in the place of Col Rondelay ('Sapeur'), who had been captured and shot. Lazare Racheline ('Socrate'), the other emissary, was the sole member of CLE, a one-man, politico-military mission of considerable importance. Lazare and his brother had been closely involved in setting up SOE's 'Vic' land-line structure in 1942[4] and he had been withdrawn from France late in 1943 as he was well known to the Gestapo in Lyons. SOE's Security Section had ruled that he must not return to the field for this reason. As M.R.D. Foot remarked, how the Gaullists got round this ban is not recorded, but they did. Racheline's principal task was to persuade Alexandre Parodi, who had been chosen by the French provisional government in Algiers to become their delegate to the Conseil National de la Résistance (CNR) in place of Émile Bollaert; Bollaert had been arrested with Pierre Brossolette after being shipwrecked near Audierne on the west coast of Brittany while attempting to return to England on a small coastal cargo-carrier, the *Jouet-des-Flots*. Having persuaded Parodi to take the job, Racheline was to help him decentralise authority as far as possible and to make sure that he and his principal assistants all understood that it would be folly to precipitate a national insurrection once the OVERLORD landings began. Racheline, who had learnt his clandestine trade-craft at the hands of Vic Gerson, the star turn of Leslie Humphreys's DF Section, was thoroughly security-conscious and his advice must have been of great value to Parodi, although Racheline returned to England after only four weeks by his own old 'Vic' line.

MGB 718 carried nine suitcases and one motor tyre to be landed at Beg-an-Fry with this important party of agents. The outward passage was uneventful until midnight, when the Ile-de-Batz and Sept-Iles lights were sighted, both burning brightly. As this suggested enemy shipping near by, Williams reduced the speed of both gunboats from 20 to 18 knots. Almost immediately, an extremely bright light appeared ahead, resembling a brilliant diamond, flashing red, white and green almost simultaneously. An accurate bearing of this light, which lasted for three seconds or more, showed it to be somewhere on the Pointe-de-Locquirec and that it was probably an aircraft beacon. At 0041 the Triagoz light was sighted on the port beam, but no shipping was seen during the crossing of the outer and inner convoy routes.

At 0046 speed was reduced to 10 knots for the approach to the anchoring position. A steady dim light was then seen fine on the port bow, presumably the Locquirec aircraft beacon burning on low power.

At 0145 the Les-Boeufs rocks were just visible bearing N 22° W, about 1 km. ($\frac{3}{4}$ mile) away; the surf-boats were lowered over the side and 502 was anchored in $7\frac{1}{2}$ fathoms. Williams's orders for reductions of speed and the like were passed by the secure S-phone link to 718, which anchored about three cables to the eastward of 502. At 0153 the two surf-boats from 718 came alongside and the flotilla of four boats, led by Sub Lt Miller, set off for the pinpoint on a course of S 60° W.

They reached the beach without any difficulty in 20 minutes and the six SOE-sponsored agents were handed over to the 'Var' reception committee, together with their luggage. Then ten passengers, including three women and one small boy, were embarked on the boats and brought back to 502 and 718 respectively. The boats were on the beach this time for about ten minutes, twice as long as normal: Miller subsequently reported to Williams that a lot of time was taken up with unnecessary chatter and fond partings with those remaining behind. At 0242, the American MAB/DAV equipment on MGB 502 received a request for a homing signal, which the directional qualities built into the set were designed to interpret, and at 0248 the boats were sighted about 400 metres off. They were alongside at 0252 and by 0306 the anchor was aweigh in both ships and course set for the return passage.

At 0336, 502 sighted three ships on the port bow about 800 metres (half a mile distant). They were very low in the water and had a strong resemblance to a tank landing craft or armed coaster of a type known to be used by the Germans. An enemy sighting signal was passed by S-phone to 718, together with an order to increase speed to 15 knots; all engines in both ships were thus working. The range decreased rapidly until, when the enemy ships were abeam of 502, it was not more than 500 metres ($\frac{1}{3}$ mile). The enemy showed no signs of activity until they were just abaft the beam of 502, when they challenged, first 718 and then 502, with the letter 'V' by small white lamp. MGB 502 replied with 'KA'. There was another pause and then the enemy opened fire on both ships with one burst which lasted about 15 seconds. By this time they were well abaft the beam of 718, and, although the order to return fire was given on 502, it was cancelled before it could be carried out, as the enemy were fast losing bearing and appeared to be shooting high and missing. Instead, Williams ordered complete silence from 502 and 718, in the hope of misleading the enemy, which it apparently did. Fire ceased abruptly and was not renewed, nor did the enemy make any attempt to follow. At 0338 full speed was ordered, although at this juncture 718 was capable only of $19\frac{1}{2}$ knots owing to a defective starboard engine. This meant that the two ships lost contact for a few minutes until this was realised, when Williams reduced speed to 15 knots to allow 718 to catch up. No order to make smoke was given as the wind was south-westerly and a smoke-screen could not have been in any way effective.

At 0340 the rating manning 502's No.4 gun reported that a young 18-year-old Ordinary Seaman was wounded. Sub Lt Miller and one rating carried him into the chart-house, but he was found to be very badly wounded in the arms, chest and stomach and he died before they could even get him inside. Nobody else on board was hit nor was either of the ships damaged, apart from one hit on 718's port aft towing-plate, which in no way incapacitated her. The enemy's fire appeared to consist of Oerlikon tracer, although McQuoid Mason in 718 believed he saw some 40-mm cannon fire.

The remainder of the return passage was uneventful and Dartmouth was reached at 0848, with 502's white ensign at half-mast.

The encounter with the enemy had taken place about 8 km. (5 miles) off the coast and, although it would have been desirable to alter course to the eastward to avoid close contact, the danger of running on to a submerged hazard named Le-Crapaud, which had been sighted awash on at least one previous occasion, outweighed all other considerations. The 'KA' signal must have greatly confused the enemy: as Williams pointed out in his report, no British force would have allowed itself to be overtaken without reaching a decision as to whether it was by friend or foe. Presumably the silence from 502 and 718 made the enemy fear that they had, after all, fired on their own forces. Williams had been given a recognition signal-letter group, 'VAW', before sailing, for use in an emergency. He decided not to use this after the 'KA' signal – meaning 'Hold on, we're fetching the captain' – had been passed, as the enemy were drawing rapidly astern. Williams felt that giving the emergency 'VAW' signal on this occasion would have compromised its future use.

Williams ended his report on SCARF by expressing the hope that the 15th MGB Flotilla might have occasion to engage the enemy in circumstances compatible with the operation in hand, as it would increase the confidence of the crews in their ships and their armament.

The six agents landed that night were escorted from the beach with their luggage by Le Corvaisier and the two Jacob sisters up the narrow path that climbs the heavy clay of the cliff. It had been raining and they were soon floundering up to the ankles in the mud of the Breton countryside. They had gone no more than 500 metres when they heard the motors of the two gunboats leaving the anchorage. Rendier reported later that the Germans must also have heard their withdrawal as their searchlights were turned on and coastal batteries opened fire. As Williams recorded no such reaction from the shore, Rendier may well have misinterpreted the sound of the firing that was taking place 8 km. to seaward. Whatever the source, the sound greatly alarmed the party making their way inland and they cleared the coast as fast as they could. After an exhausting scramble through the mud, interspersed with clambering over banks and walls, they reached an abandoned house that was used by the 'Var' organisation as a shelter. They rested for a while, and then four members of the party caught the morning train to Paris. Rendier and Duffour stayed on in Guimaëc for a couple of days with the Jacob sisters before being driven to Morlaix by M Barron, the local vet.

Apart from Deman himself, the party of ten evacuated on this occasion included Suzanne Warenghem, who had worked in an escape line, and her friend Blanche Charlet. As the latter scrambled aboard 502, the gunboat's W/T operator, seeing an attractive young lady, thought the moment had come to use his schoolboy French. Having ventured, 'Ici, mademoiselle', he was momentarily disconcerted to receive in reply, 'It's OK, Jack. I've been aboard these boats before.' She had, indeed, arrived in the south of France on one of the Polish felucca operations.

SCARF was the last 'Var' operation as a sea line and its attempts to turn itself into a land line through Spain came to nothing. Humphreys told Deman in London to avoid expanding his organisation too fast and attempted to send him back into the field through Spain, but his nerves were by this time overstrained and, as the official historian concluded, it was just as well that, when his false papers were stolen by one of the guides who was supposed to take him across the Pyrenees, he turned back and was subsequently recalled to London. Langard was arrested while transmitting at the end of June, stayed silent under torture and died in Buchenwald some weeks later. Émile Minerault, the American OSS member of the organisation, fell into a German trap in Paris and died at Ellrich, one of the camps in the Buchenwald complex.

'Var' never achieved the smooth efficiency of Gerson's 'Vic' line[4] but the operations it organised by sea at Beg-an-Fry, after the false start at the unsuitable Saint-Cast pinpoint, were a valuable achievement. They provided SOE's F Section with a way into and out of France that was much needed at a time when the suspicions accumulated around Déricourt had led to his recall and thus deprived Buckmaster of his main organiser of Lysander and Hudson landings. Moreover, the line became available just when the pre-D-Day build-up of traffic was at its height. It demonstrated what could be achieved with goodwill on SIS's part and common sense on SOE's, and highlighted the needless waste of those 20 months, from February 1942 to October 1943, when not one SOE agent entered or left France via the north and west coasts.

CHAPTER XVIII

The 'Shelburne' Escape Line: January–March and July–August 1944

T he nine operations carried out between January and August 1944 to a beach near Plouha, for MI9's 'Shelburne' escape line, were, in Slocum's estimation, the most interesting work accomplished by his Dartmouth-based 15th MGB Flotilla. 'Shelburne', which collected shot-down airmen from all over northern France and conveyed them to this embarkation point with exemplary efficiency, has been the subject of books in both French and English.[1] Bonaparte Beach, from which the first five evacuations (code name BONAPARTE) were carried out, has become a tourist attraction and a tunnel has been built to enable it to be visited at all states of the tide without the need to slither down the huge rock-fall by which, in 1944, evaders were led down and heavy suitcases of arms were hauled up. Ironically, none of the detailed naval operation reports of this series appears in the Birkin collection.[2]

MI9, drawing on experience accumulated in the First World War, had been active since the outbreak of the Second in briefing members of the armed forces on how to evade capture and how to escape should they fall into enemy hands. But it was not until 1942 that, with Polish assistance, they organised a first mass evacuation by sea of evaders and escapers from the south coast of France. The possibility of doing so from Brittany had been contemplated even earlier, and Slocum, at MI9's behest, had sent the chartered refugee Audierne fishing boat *La-Brise* south at Christmas 1941 with the mission of establishing a food dump on the Glénan Islands off Concarneau so that evaders could be collected there and subsequently embarked.[3] Although the venture failed in tragic circumstances, it proved that access to the area was still possible using suitable fishing vessels operating from England.

MI9's mass evacuations by felucca and trawler from southern France are recounted in Part II of this book. Until the Germans took over what had been the non-occupied zone in November 1942, that area, from which it was possible to walk out across the Pyrenees into Spain, had offered the main escape route from France. By the end of 1942, however, MI9's pioneering escape line – created by Pat O'Leary – had been penetrated and was being broken up by enemy action. O'Leary's 'Pat' organisation had been attempting to extend its reach into Brittany, where

many airmen were hiding. These evaders were stranded there by its demise.

On 20 March 1943, to deal with this situation, MI9 parachuted into France an agent of Russian origin named Bouryschkine, who called himself Val Williams for cover purposes. He had been the trainer of the Monte Carlo basketball team and he had played an important part in two mass escapes of Allied internees from Fort-de-la-Révère, at La-Turbie in the Monégasque hinterland, before leaving France by O'Leary's last sea evacuation. He landed back in France with his French–Canadian W/T operator, Raymond Labrosse, near the Étangs-de-la-Hollande in the Forêt-de-Rambouillet, only after nine previous attempts. Even then it was not a smooth landing: Labrosse's W/T set was damaged, which meant that Williams began his 'Oaktree' mission under the grave handicap of having no means of communication with his London base. In an attempt to overcome this, but in breach of all the normal security safeguards, he had recourse to the W/T facilities of other organisations in both Paris and Brittany. Williams's personality seems to have been a security problem in its own right; those who worked with him found him indiscreet to the point of flamboyance.

Williams's lack of a direct W/T link with London did not prevent him from setting about creating a departure base for evacuation in the Baie-de-Saint-Brieuc area, a matter he must have discussed with DDOD(I)'s staff before he left London. Indeed, the Comtesse Geneviève de Poulpiquet, who had worked with Louis Nouveau of 'Pat', and subsequently with the ebullient Williams, considered that the latter's main achievement had been to flood the Saint-Quay-Portrieux neighbourhood with Allied evaders.

Williams had hoped to organise a first operation to embark these men in May, but Slocum refused, via the Free French BCRA's 'Mithridate' W/T link: the nights were by then too short for cross-Channel operations by the slow 'C'-Class Fairmile motor gunboats that were still all he had to work with, and, in any case the lack of direct W/T contact with 'Oaktree' made the prospects too uncertain to be worth risking a precious motor gunboat. Then Williams was arrested on 4 June 1943. Labrosse got away through Spain with the help of Georges Broussine and his 'Bourgogne' escape line. He reached England at the beginning of September and was able to report to MI9 in detail.

MI9's hopes of organising the evacuation of large numbers of Allied evaders by sea from Brittany, as O'Leary had done from the south coast of France during the summer of 1942, had suffered a severe setback, for which the lack of a direct W/T link between 'Oaktree' and the London base was primarily responsible. A second lesson that stood out was that Williams's use of other people's clandestine radio facilities had led directly to the destruction of the escape line he had been attempting to set up. The organisations with which he had entered into contact were all in deep trouble. Not only was O'Leary's 'Pat' by now so compromised as to be a death-trap, but the BCRA's 'Mithridate' intelligence network and the Belgian 'Comète' escape organisation were also doomed and 'Oaktree' had been sucked into the vortex. Nevertheless, the balance sheet that emerged from MI9's debriefing of Labrosse was by no means wholly negative. Williams had managed to send out through Spain some 100 Allied airmen, most of them picked up in Brittany in the early summer of 1943, when it had become clear that there was no early prospect of evacuating them by sea. And whereas Louis Nouveau, Pat O'Leary's emissary to Brittany, had noted how difficult it was at the beginning of 1943 to find goodwill, and recruit helpers, from the middle-class circles in which he moved before the war, both he and the 'Oaktree' mission after him received remarkable support from more modest levels of the population, particularly in Brittany. All the basic elements of an escape line as prescribed by MI9 had worked perfectly: the search for pilots, the means of sheltering them at centres such as Carhaix, Rostrenen and Paris, and the lines for convoying them to the coastal region where other safe houses had been established to receive them. Simple people had shown the most extraordinary courage, never hesitating spontaneously to help airmen overtaken by disaster, in spite of the risk of dire retribution. At the risk of being irremediably compromised in the eyes of the Occupation authorities, many were ready to shelter airmen under their own roofs. Moreover, as Huguen pointed out, the process evoked an upsurge of solidarity among large numbers of people, since the problems of feeding and clothing evaders and escapers could not be solved without a wide circle of complicity. This friendly attitude on the part of the population towards shot-down Allied air-crew, who had in many cases just bombed French cities or shot up French trains, disconcerted the Germans and surprised even MI9. It also provided a solid reason for making further efforts to arrange evacuations by sea from Brittany, where aircraft continued to be shot down in considerable numbers in the course of the heavy Allied bombing of German bases in the French Atlantic ports throughout the Occupation as part of the struggle to safeguard the Allied lifeline from North America.

A central feature of the disasters that befell 'Oaktree' in Brittany was that Williams had taken over parts of Louis Nouveau's Breton branch of the 'Pat' organisation, which had been infiltrated by a German agent named Roger Le Neveu, alias 'Roger Le Légionnaire'. This man's duplicity had been unmasked in March 1943, the month of Williams's arrival, but adequate countermeasures were not taken and Le Légionnaire continued his destructive activities like a worm within the 'Oaktree' bud. By the time Labrosse got back to report, 'Oaktree's' groups at Pontivy, Carhaix, Plourivo and Saint-Quay-Portrieux had practically been wiped out, although the Paris centre under Paul Campinchi, which was of great potential importance, was, in Labrosse's view, still untouched. Labrosse volunteered to return to Brittany via Paris and find out whether this was indeed the case. After all that had happened, Patrick Windham-Wright and Airey Neave, who had succeeded Jimmy Langley at MI9, were determined that the security of any new organisation should be really effective. As professionals, they were obliged to consider the possibility that, if Campinchi was at liberty, it might be because he had betrayed 'Oaktree' to the Germans. They did not, however, reject the idea that Labrosse might undertake a second mission to France.

When those evacuated by Pat O'Leary on his fourth and last felucca operation had reached London nearly a year earlier, Langley of MI9 had been much impressed by a French–Canadian Sergeant-Major named Lucien Dumais and had asked him if he would consider returning to France to organise an escape line. Dumais had been taken prisoner on the Dieppe raid in August 1942 but had escaped and made his way south into what was then still the non-occupied zone, where he had discovered that there was an American Consul at Marseilles. He was travelling at the time with two Frenchmen, who were on the run from the Gestapo and wanted to get to England and join General de Gaulle. All three went to the Consulate, only to be told by the Consul that he could do nothing to help. Dumais's French friends felt that it was their presence that had led to this negative response and insisted that Dumais return to see the Consul alone. This time the Consul sent him round to see a French doctor of Greek origin, who was a key figure in O'Leary's 'Pat' escape line and whose flat gave shelter to Allied evaders awaiting means to leave France. The doctor, a heroic and saintly man named Georges Rodocanachi,[4] put him in touch a few days later with O'Leary, who was in process of organising a large-scale evacuation by felucca from a beach near the Spanish frontier. Dumais, being French-speaking, became one of the organisers and accompanied O'Leary to the beach, armed with an iron bar to deal with intruders. This story brought him to Langley's attention.

Langley found him articulate and determined, though he was uncertain whether his forceful personality would not be a problem when it came to handling local French Resistance groups. Dumais was, however, not at that stage prepared to return to France as an agent and rejoined his regiment. Langley told him that, if he should ever change his mind, he would be glad to see him again.

Dumais was sent to Tunisia to observe the winter campaign of

1942/43 but, when he returned to his battalion of the Fusiliers de Mont Royal four months later, he found himself under a new platoon commander who had arrived straight from Canada. After enduring this man's airs and ignorance for a week or two, Dumais remembered his interview with the one-armed Major Langley in Intelligence and the invitation with which it had ended. He asked Canadian Intelligence to arrange a second meeting with him, which took place in St James's Park.

Langley had by this time left MI9 and been replaced by Airey Neave. Patrick Windham-Wright, his assistant, who, like Langley, had lost an arm, probably interviewed Dumais. The meeting was coolly professional; nothing was done specifically to encourage Dumais. It was only after a fortnight, during which Dumais was subjected to close surveillance and a variety of interviews and tests, that he was told he had been accepted. Windham-Wright then arranged for him to meet Labrosse, whose quiet, unflappable personality was in marked contrast to his own forceful ways. Dumais was impressed by the fact that Labrosse had brought out 27 evaders after Williams's arrest, when he could have made his escape into Spain far more easily without them. Dumais decided Labrosse was someone with whom he could work: Labrosse, conversely, was ready to accept him as his chief. They spent much time going over the lessons that were to be drawn from the destruction of 'Oaktree', and the training they undertook together included exercises in which Labrosse operated his W/T set from Scotland, as well as intensive security instruction. Their course finished up with sessions during which Steven Mackenzie and Sir Colville Barclay of DDOD(I)'s staff taught them how to select a beach for clandestine embarkation operations, how to identify the chosen pinpoint in signals to London, the use of personal messages on the BBC's French-language programme to convey last-minute operational information, use of light signals and various forms of secure radio-telephone equipment to establish contact between shore and ship, the handling of boats and of inward and outward passengers on the beach, and how to avoid leaving tell-tale evidence on the foreshore after an operation had taken place.

Dumais would have preferred to go into France by sea, but DDOD(I) rejected the idea of a blind landing with no reception committee, so he opted to return by Lysander. It was only after two abortive sorties that what was to be known as the 'Shelburne' mission was safely landed at Chauny in the Aisne Department.[5]

Since Windham-Wright feared that Campinchi, the main 'Oaktree' organiser in the Paris area, had been compromised in the collapse of that network, the 'Shelburne' team had been given as their initial contact Mme Georges, who ran a hairdressing salon in the Rue des Capucines. She and a nurse named Suzanne had lodged evaders in Paris and sent them on their way to Spain with varying success. They were splendid people, but with no sense of security and there had already been arrests in the small organisation to which they belonged. Suzanne escorted them to Rueil-Malmaison in the western suburbs of Paris where she lived.

Labrosse's initial attempts to make contact with London using his suitcase W/T set were unsuccessful and, after discussion, the two men agreed that he should try to do so from Normandy, where Dumais had been helped after the Dieppe raid: this would be very much nearer the base station in England. Before they could try this, however, they returned to the flat one day to find a note slipped under the door warning them that Mme Georges and Suzanne had been arrested.

Labrosse suggested they should go to see Campinchi. Dumais, mindful of Langley's warning, at first demurred, but then agreed when Labrosse declared that he could guarantee the patriotism of his friend and former colleague. Labrosse went, and came back 20 minutes later accompanied by Campinchi. He explained that they were a new mission from London. Campinchi told them how he had avoided arrest thanks to a timely telephone call to his office saying that two individuals were waiting to see him. Since Williams and a number of other members of 'Oaktree' had already been arrested, he had been sure his visitors were Gestapo and he had gone into hiding in another part of Paris for nearly six months. When Dumais asked if he was ready to resume the same work, Campinchi said that Williams had been guilty of unimaginable indiscretions and that his arrest had been only a matter of time: the only folly he had not committed was to advertise in the press for recruits for the Intelligence Service. Labrosse said security was a matter that his new chief took very seriously indeed and he explained some of Dumais's ideas on the subject. In the end Campinchi suggested they should come to stay with his hostess for a few days so that they could talk the matter over in detail. Relieved not to be forced to stay in a hotel, Dumais and Labrosse agreed.

The planned excursion to Normandy enabled Labrosse to establish W/T contact with London and Dumais and Campinchi decided to work together in building the new 'Shelburne' line. Dumais, who had of course seen O'Leary's sea-evacuation operations in the Mediterranean and had discussed the possibility of doing similar embarkations from Brittany before he left London, decided to try to use Anse-Cochat near Plouha on the western side of the Baie-de-Saint-Brieuc, but he lacked local contacts with which to build a new organisation to shelter would-be evacuees and convoy them to the beach. The resourceful Campinchi saw a way out of this difficulty: he knew that a doctor named Meynard, who had been practising at Plouézec, some 10 km. (6 miles) north of Anse-Cochat on the road to Paimpol, had left the village because he no longer felt safe there after the arrests of Williams's helpers at Saint-Quay-Portrieux and Plourivo. Among those who had helped 'Oaktree' in Paris was a young house surgeon at Saint-Denis named Le Balch and if he could be persuaded to take over the abandoned practice at Plouézec, which was in the forbidden coastal zone, the necessary first foothold would have been secured. Le Balch agreed and moved to Plouézec forthwith, taking over Méynard's house and a small ten-bed clinic that went with it. Within three weeks of their arrival in France the two Canadians, armed with identity papers and the necessary permit to enter the coastal zone, procured for them by Campinchi, were calling on the newly installed Dr Le Balch, who had been warned by Campinchi to expect them. Dumais explained his interest in Anse-Cochat. At the local Hôtel du Commerce, where he frequently took his meals, Le Balch had met a travelling inspector who represented the French Office des Céréales in the Côtes-du-Nord Department. Le Balch felt sure that this man, Henri Le Blais, was a patriot: moreover, he had an official car and the necessary papers giving him permission to use it by both day and night. The doctor went on foot to see Le Blais, who lived only a couple of kilometres away, and asked him point-blank whether he was willing to work for the 'good cause' by for example, putting up, foreign agents. He agreed straight away and Dumais told him of his need for a beach somewhere between Saint-Quay-Portrieux and Plougrescant, suitable for the evacuation of Allied evaders and for a team of volunteers to accommodate airmen awaiting embarkation and escort them to the chosen pinpoint. Le Blais did not know Plouha well, but he was a friend of the schoolteacher at Pludual, Adolphe Le Trocquer, who was, like himself, a member of the Front National and likely therefore to have good local contacts in Resistance circles – people whose activities had thus far been limited, but who could probably be persuaded to embrace the new tasks that 'Shelburne' required. Le Trocquer's first contact thought himself too old and corpulent to lead such a group, but he suggested a fellow member of the Front National, François Le Cornec, who had a *café-charcuterie* on the village square at Plouha. Le Cornec, on his guard as a result of the earlier wave of arrests at Saint-Quay-Portrieux, wanted to think the matter over, but agreement was reached within a matter of days.

At Dumais's request, the embryo group at Plouha set about looking for a suitable beach. They thought first of the Pointe-de-Plouha, but there was no beach there on which boats could conveniently embark passengers; there were many dangerous off-shore rocks and tidal streams were strong; there was also a German post near by. Then Pierre Huet, a French fleet air arm pilot, suggested a pinpoint to the north of Plouha and the valley road leading to the tiny quay at Anse-Cochat – a cleft in the cliffs with a nearby small beach known locally as 'Sous-Kéruzeau'. The problem here was one of access, for it lay at the foot of steep cliffs rising in places to a height of 60 metres, but Huet and Joseph Mainguy, a merchant navy captain, both of whom had grown up in the area and knew it intimately, reconnoitred it carefully. The beach consisted of shingle, with a wide expanse of sand at low tide, and the seaward approach was acceptable. Though Anse-Cochat, with its easy landward access – the pinpoint DDOD(I) had suggested – lay only 100 metres to the south of the end of Sous-Kéruzeau beach, the seaward approach to that pinpoint was encumbered with off-lying rocks which would be dangerous on a moonless night. Sous-Kéruzeau was cut off from Anse-Cochat at high tide: Huet and Mainguy thought, however, that a massive rock-fall would provide a practicable, if steep and uncomfortable, access route to the beach at all states of the tide. They made a detailed sketch plan of the site, based on a large-scale chart, and Dumais sent the relevant particulars to London,[6] though he felt doubtful about the proposed means of access: there was, however, no alternative and the airmen were young and must be prepared to slither down on their backs if necessary, clutching brambles to check their descent. DDOD(I) accepted the venue, which presented no significant problems from the navigational point of view; and Dumais appointed Le Cornec to act as beach-master, since operations might have to take place in his absence.

They discussed how 'parcels', as candidates for evacuation seem always to have been termed, arriving from Paris by train should be handled; it was agreed that they should leave the Paris–Brest overnight express at Saint-Brieuc, where they could be taken over by local guides. Le Cornec stipulated that they should not arrive at Plouha in full daylight, as the village was so small that people would quickly realise who was getting off the little departmental train. This meant that there was need for a reception centre at Saint-Brieuc, where they would arrive early in the morning. Henri Le Blais undertook to arrange this, using his Front National contacts to do so: this Communist-dominated Resistance organisation was strong in the departmental capital.

Dumais, whose memory has sometimes proved at fault, has stated that 'Shelburne' was ready to carry out the first BONA-PARTE operation on 15 December, but that bad weather caused nine successive 24-hour postponements, during which time he and Labrosse had to sleep in flea-infested beds; and that at the end of this period Labrosse and he returned to Paris to await the next moonless period, which began in mid-January, leaving the 15 'parcels' in Brittany, where they were far safer than they would have been in Paris. Huguen, the historian of escapes from wartime Brittany, who clearly interviewed many of the other people involved in Shelburne, has stated that it was not until the beginning of January 1944 that Dumais was able to report that preparations for BONAPARTE were complete. Since Dumais and Labrosse did not set foot in Brittany until 5 or 6 December, it is hard to believe that all the above preparations could have been made as early as 15 December. Since MGB 318 was tied up during December with operations to Aber-Benoît and MGB 502 with the abortive final operation to Saint-Cast, a third gunboat would have been required to stand by for nine successive nights if there had been any question of carrying out BONAPARTE by so early a date as the 15th. MGB 503, which succeeded in carrying out the operation (its first cross-Channel operation) on 28 January, may conceivably have been ready and available in the December no-moon period but, if so, and if 'Shelburne' had really been standing by for their first evacuation as early as Dumais claimed, why was no attempt made to carry it out on either 23 or 25 December, when the weather was good enough to permit other ships of her flotilla to operate? Indeed, the weather experienced by MGB 502 on the earlier of those two dates at Saint-Cast, not many miles to the east, was far from extreme. In January, on the other hand, the 15th MGB Flotilla attempted no operations before the night on which BONAPARTE was carried out, which does suggest earlier bad weather.

The first two airmen Campinchi sent by the overnight train from Paris to Saint-Brieuc were arrested on arrival for lack of documents showing them to be resident in the prohibited coastal zone. This mistake was not repeated and a second batch of 15 'parcels' were safely dropped off the small local train from Saint-Brieuc to Plouha in little groups at five successive stops, where they were met and escorted by members of the local group of helpers. The series of 24-hour postponements for bad weather – signalled by the message '*Yvonne pense souvent à l'heureuse occasion*', which Dumais had kept to himself, for his security precautions were systematic – was replaced on 28 January on the BBC programme 'Les Français Parlent aux Français' by '*Bonjour tout le monde à la Maison d'Alphonse*'; this was repeated on the evening bulletin at 2100 hrs. Dumais thus knew that the MGB was already on its way. Messengers were sent to alert the nine guides whose business it was to collect the airmen from their hiding-places and escort them across country on what proved to be a particularly dark night, taking care to avoid German patrols and isolated farms where the barking of dogs might betray their passage. Finally they were all assembled in an unoccupied house belonging to Jean Gicquel, which was not more than about 1½ km. (1 mile) from the beach: it was soon to be known as La Maison d'Alphonse. The house stood with its back to a road regularly patrolled by the Germans, but a path led from it to fields in the valley that was part of the route to Anse-Cochat and Sous-Kéruzeau.

When the 17 airmen – 13 USAAF, 4 RAF – had been assembled in the room at the end of the house, Dumais surprised them by addressing them in accentless English. He told them they now faced the last but most dangerous lap of their long journey. They were now about 1½ km. from the Channel and, if everything went well, they would be aboard a British warship in two hours and in England by 9 o'clock in the morning. There were excited, but subdued, reactions of pleasure. Dumais went on to say that, when the guides were ready to leave, they would form up in single file. The first man would hold on to the coat-tail of the third guide – the first and second guides being left free to lead the column and bring up the rear – and each other man was to hold on to the coat-tail of the man in front, so as not to lose sight of him in the darkness. If contact did break, the man behind was to stand still and make no noise: the guides would straighten things out. The third guide in question was an 18-year-old girl, Marie-Thérèse Le Calvez, who was to play a prominent part in all these operations.[7]

When they reached the coast, they would have to go down a steep cliff. They should lie on their backs and slide down. When they got to the bottom they would be told where to sit. There would be no smoking, talking or coughing, either on the way or on the beach. Small boats would come to pick them up. When ordered to, and not before, they were to wade out to the boats and get in.

If they were attacked, they were to remember that they were soldiers and they would all be expected to fight back. The guides had pistols and, if they had a knife, they were to use it. If not, they were to use their hands, feet and teeth, taking care that, if they laid hands on anyone, it was a German and that they knew what to do with him. They were to remember that many brave Frenchmen had risked their lives to get them thus far and that, if they talked, their protectors would be tortured or shot or both, and so would their families.

Dumais gave the senior officer a package containing a carefully wrapped bottle of cognac, which was to be handed to the first British security officer they met on arrival in England. If they were attacked on land, it was to be broken and thrown into the bushes, if at sea, thrown overboard, where it would sink. He gave the next senior officer a small folded piece of paper to be carried in his hand. If he was attacked, it was to be thoroughly chewed and then swallowed. Otherwise it must be delivered with the bottle of cognac.

The cognac was for Langley: it was wrapped in a 30-page report, in which all names and addresses had been replaced by numbers. The key to these numbers was on the folded piece of paper carried by the second man.

At midnight the column was formed up and, when eyes had grown accustomed to the dark, they moved off across country. Pierre Huet was in the lead, Le Cornec brought up the rear. Only once was the chain broken and then Le Cornec ran forward and put matters to rights.

At the cliff edge, Dumais was the last to slide down: it was so steep a descent that he marvelled they had all got down safely. Mainguy, who knew Morse, had stopped part-way down and was signalling the letter 'B' to seaward, using a torch masked by a cardboard tube, at intervals of one minute. Dumais had given a second torch, this one masked by a blue plastic screen, to Marie-Thérèse, who flashed it on and off continuously from a position at the foot of the cliff: this blue light would be visible only at comparatively close range. In case of danger, the blue plastic screen was to be replaced by a red one and the torch to be switched on and wedged between two rocks, pointing to seaward. Huet and Mainguy had chosen this pinpoint because it was out of sight of German look-outs and the nearest block-house, which was 1,200 metres to the north on the Pointe-de-la-Tour.

From a navigational point of view, this was a fairly straightforward pinpoint. The gunboat needed to make a first landfall on a group of rocks surmounted by a tower, Le-Grand-Léjon, which lies in the middle of the Baie-de-Saint-Brieuc. This involved steering a south-easterly course from the departure point off Dartmouth or, more probably, Start Point. At the Grand-Léjon, a change of course of at least 90° was necessary and the ship headed in towards the Pointe-de-Plouha on one of her three engines at the reduced speed of 800 r.p.m. At the appropriate point, the engine was stopped and three (on subsequent operations four) 14-foot surf-boats were hoisted out by hand, to port and to starboard – a job that required a dozen men. Once they were in the water, the silenced centre engine was restarted and course was resumed until the Le-Taureau rock, which was crowned with another tower, came in sight, fine on the starboard bow. As soon as the agreed light signal was picked up, Mike Marshall, captain of MGB 503, would give the order to anchor, using, as always, a grass warp. Then the boats would be manned – two oarsmen to each boat, each with a pair of muffled oars and a coxswain to steer the boat with a long sweep. A fourth man, MI9's conducting officer, would take position in the bows of the leading boat, armed no doubt with a sub-machine-gun. On this first BONAPARTE operation of 28/29 January no radio-telephone was used, simply because Dumais had not yet been equipped with the required sister set; subsequently this secure speech link was used.

The MGB's anchorage for the operations in this series was

somewhere between 1,500 and 1,800 metres from the German bunker on the Pointe-de-la-Tour, which was armed with a 76-mm. cannon, heavy machine-guns and searchlights. Sixteen km. to the north on the Pointe-de-Guilben was an enemy coast-watching radar station and a battery of medium artillery. Dumais, who knew about these defences, wondered whether the Royal Navy did not believe in the efficacy of the German radar or whether they had some method of jamming its transmissions. In fact, small wooden vessels were hard to detect and anchoring close to offshore rocks made the MGBs doubly inconspicuous.

The first operation involved a long wait. The ebb had finished and the tide was coming in when, just as they were beginning to despair, they saw three dark specks to seaward. As they watched, they became more substantial, moving steadily towards the shore in line abreast. Dumais waded out to the centre one, flanked by Le Cornec and Huet with pistols drawn. A figure jumped from the bows of the boat. Dumais called out the password 'Dinan'.

'Saint-Brieuc' came the reply: it was Patrick Windham-Wright, of MI9. What a relief! Pistols were put away and Dumais and MI9's emissary had a brief talk while stores packed in carefully marked suitcases were unloaded. Then the waiting passengers – 17 airmen and two young Frenchmen who were on the run from the Germans – were brought forward and loaded into the surf-boats. In 12 minutes the transfer was complete and the three boats were on their way back to the anchored gunboat. Once they were alongside and passengers and boat crews had scaled the waiting scrambling-nets and reached the MGB's deck, the anchor was weighed and the homeward passage began on a silenced centre engine, towing the surf-boats. When Marshall judged they were sufficiently far offshore, the engine was stopped and the boats were hauled back on board, stowed and secured, scrambling-nets picked up and course resumed for the Grand-Léjon. Only when they had closed into it and turned north-west for Dartmouth did they attain full speed, 1,800 r.p.m. on all three main engines.

The 'Shelburne' beach party, soaked to the shoulders in the chilling January sea, clambered back up the rock-fall, lugging the six suitcases with them. When they reached the Maison d'Alphonse, Dumais could not resist the temptation of examining the contents: there were .45 Colt pistols and ammunition for the Plouha protection group, a more powerful W/T transmitter/receiver for Raymond Labrosse, Gauloise cigarettes of British manufacture, gin and whisky as presents for helpers and a suitcase containing four million Francs. In retrospect, it was a mistake to have shown such a large sum of money to helpers who daily risked their lives for 'Shelburne' even if they were being paid (on scales suggested by Le Cornec): they imagined that Dumais was about to distribute handfuls of these notes among them; instead of which he closed the case, remarking that the money was for the rest of the escape line. Cold and wet though they were, they waited for the end of the curfew at 0600 hrs before making their respective ways home. Mainguy thought subsequently that it would have been better not to wait and to go home in the dark.

The suitcases were collected by Le Blais that afternoon in his official car and taken to Saint-Brieuc. He had disconnected the car's milometer and adapted the engine to run on alcohol – obtainable from local farmers – in the main tank, while for starting it would switch to a small additional tank under the bonnet, which contained petrol. He booked places on the night train to Paris for Dumais and Labrosse.

Although Dumais was punctilious about security and had by this time begun to construct a separate security section in Paris to keep a watch on 'Shelburne' in this field, he had a very narrow escape when he arrived back in Paris carrying the suitcase full of the money. As he emerged from the Lamarck-Caulincourt Métro station he ran into a police check. They were looking for black-marketeers. He picked on the youngest and most amenable-looking of the policemen, told him that the suitcase was destined for the Resistance, that his number had been noted and that, if he wanted to keep out of harm's way, it would be better not to interfere. The bluff worked and he was allowed to pass.

Next the Gestapo attempted to plant an agent in Campinchi's network. The man, a Dane who claimed to be a Norwegian airman and to have two brothers serving in England, came under immediate suspicion because he knew little about aircraft and a signal to London brought a quick reply that neither brother could be traced. At this point, the Dane took fright and disappeared.

Then Le Blais was reported to have got drunk in a Saint-Brieuc café and to have been boasting that he belonged to the British Intelligence Service. When the same story reached Dumais via London, he caught the next train to Saint-Brieuc. In the course of the ten-hour journey his anger subsided sufficiently for him to consult Le Cornec before confronting Le Blais. The upshot was that Dumais told Le Blais that London had decided the operations from Plouha should be discontinued, as they were too dangerous, and on this ground he was paid off on generous terms. Dumais rather liked the look of a girl Le Blais had brought to their meeting. Afterwards he followed her and asked her to come and work for 'Shelburne' in Paris, where she became his liaison agent. Louisette Lorre proved brave to the point of recklessness.

Suddenly Bouryschkine, alias Williams, who in Dumais's view had destroyed the 'Oaktree' organisation with his vanity and garrulity, reappeared in Paris with a broken leg and in company

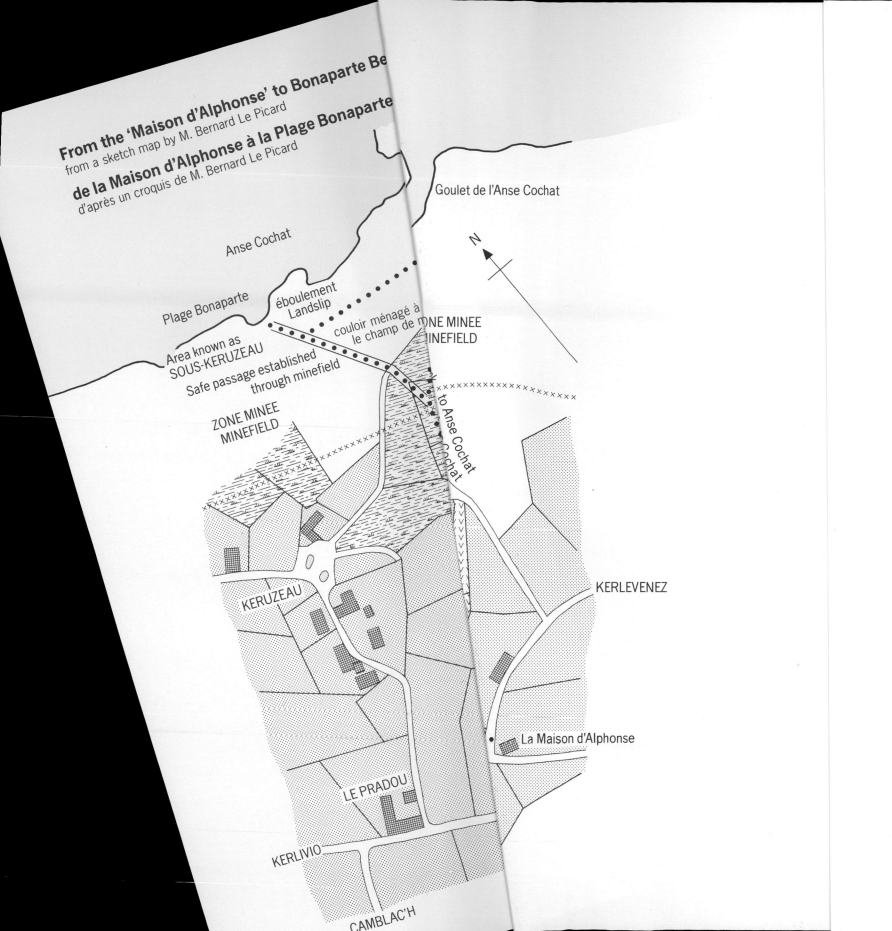

From the 'Maison d'Alphonse' to Bonaparte Be[ach]
from a sketch map by M. Bernard Le Picard

de la Maison d'Alphonse à la Plage Bonaparte
d'après un croquis de M. Bernard Le Picard

Goulet de l'Anse Cochat

N

Anse Cochat

Plage Bonaparte

éboulement
Landslip

couloir ménagé à
le champ de [mi]ne ZONE MINEE
[M]INEFIELD

Area known as
SOUS-KERUZEAU

Safe passage established
through minefield

to Anse Cochat
Cochat

ZONE MINEE
MINEFIELD

KERLEVENEZ

KERUZEAU

La Maison d'Alphonse

LE PRADOU

KERLIVIO

CAMBLAC'H

of a Russian, who had been his prison warder at Rennes and who had helped him to escape. Campinchi not only helped his former chief but gave a party to celebrate his new-found liberty, to which he invited a number of those who had worked for him in the Paris area and had avoided arrest. He then put him on a train to Saint-Brieuc so that he could be evacuated on the next BONAPARTE operation. Dumais was furious with Campinchi for forcing his hand and for the needless risk he had run in resuming contact with friends from the shipwrecked 'Oaktree'. He was angry with Labrosse too, for his part in the affair. He had the two Russians, whom he had found speaking English on the train, rounded up and placed under guard on one of the farms. In the end Bouryschkine was carried to the beach on an improvised stetcher and evacuated by MGB 503 on the night of 26 February. On that date a total of 18 were embarked, including two young volunteers for the Fighting French forces. Four surf-boats were used and eight suitcases of equipment were landed. There had been disciplinary problems with the airmen and one was evacuated on BONAPARTE II with his hands tied. A fighter pilot who was picked up on this operation had been shot down near Boulogne only five days previously and brought to Plouha in a postal van. Campinchi at one point had 75 airmen hidden at various points in Paris. Dumais fixed up a land line across the Pyrenees and shipped out 24 evaders from the Beauvais area on it.

Dumais asked for three BONAPARTE operations in the March no-moon period but no sooner was 'Shelburne' committed to this programme than they ran into problems. The local railway from Saint-Brieuc to Plouha stopped running for passengers, as it was taken over by the 'Todt' organisation for its own needs, strengthening coastal defences, so that 'parcels' arriving from Paris had to be collected from Guingamp or Châtelaudren. The latter turned out to be unsuitable, as it was too small a place for strangers to pass unnoticed and controls were particularly rigorous there as it was in the prohibited coastal zone. Then, before the first of the three March operations, the loss of a substantial sum of money from one of the suitcases landed on BONAPARTE II somewhere between Plouha and Paris led to a temporary cooling of relations between Dumais and Le Cornec. Dumais had a row, too, with Le Trocquer over a sub-machine-gun, which the latter had retained, contrary to his instructions. As Windham-Wright had foreseen, Dumais, who was a regular Sergeant Major and used to being obeyed, found it difficult to work with the Communist-controlled Front National.

When they arrived at Guingamp for the first of the March operations, scheduled for the night of the 16th, Dumais and Labrosse noted that there were no fewer than four German radio-direction-finding vans in the town. They were not unduly worried by this, as Labrosse had never transmitted from there. But Le Cornec met them with the news that there seemed to be a state of alert on the coast too; and that the local fishing boats were not allowed to leave port. Dumais did not see how this could be a result of the operation they had carried out nearly three weeks previously but he was worried enough to contemplate cancelling the operation due for that night. However, a puncture prevented them from reaching Plouha in time for Labrosse to send a signal and, at the end of the day, the agreed BBC messages confirmed that, as far as London was concerned, the operation was going ahead. So, notwithstanding the alert, they once more gathered at La Maison d'Alphonse and proceeded to the beach. Dumais by now had a R/T walkie-talkie set and was able to speak to Windham-Wright as the gunboat closed in from the Grand-Léjon towards Le-Taureau, and warn him to be especially careful. Then there was the sound of a distant explosion, though it was difficult to locate it because it echoed round the amphitheatre of cliffs. A second explosion followed. Windham-Wright announced that the MGB – it was Peter Williams's 502 this time – was being fired on. They proposed to withdraw and return later.

There were three or four further shots, then silence and a long wait, with Dumais monitoring the situation closely with his walkie-talkie. Eventually he was rewarded with confirmation that the MGB had returned.

Lloyd Bott, who was working with Andrew Smith that night, says that there were four surf-boats in the first wave, each of which embarked seven airmen; then he and Smith came back with two of the boats to pick up the others. Dumais claimed to have shipped out 30 evaders on that occasion; Slocum gave the number as 25. When the embarkation took place, the tide was very low and the departing airmen had to cross 200–300 metres of shingle and then sand to get to the boats. Here they were absolutely without cover. If the enemy sentries manning the strongpoint on the Pointe-de-la-Tour had turned a searchlight beam in that direction while the operation was in progress, nearly 50 people – evaders, escorts and boats' crews – would have been revealed in the fields of fire of two of the three heavy machine-guns and the 76-mm. field gun mounted there. As these machine-guns had a range in excess of 1,100–1,200 metres, the whole expedition could hardly have avoided being wiped out. The gunboat, too, lay within easy range of the 76-mm. cannon. Considering the number of lives at stake, these were probably the riskiest 20 minutes in the whole cycle of wartime sea contacts with Brittany. Dumais, who was a good soldier, must have been aware of the enormous risk, particularly after the gunfire that had delayed the arrival of the MGB. According to Le Cornec,

Dumais told him and Baudet during that night that there would be no more BONAPARTE operations, and that he had already sent Labrosse to Paris to cancel the others that had been planned.

By the time the surf-boats returned to their mother ship, dawn was about to break. Le Cornec, listening for 502's engine, heard it start up quite distinctly. They were in a hurry to get clear of the coast, but Dumais told the ship that they were audible and they slowed down. Dawn overtook 502 before she was out of sight of the coast, though by then she was well out. Fortunately the enemy were off their guard, as they had been when the surf-boats were inshore.

Dumais may indeed have hoped to cancel BONAPARTE III, but the vagaries of clandestine W/T communications made that impossible. In sending Labrosse back to Paris he felt sure that his signal would reach London in time to cancel BONAPARTE IV, which was scheduled to take place four nights later. So convinced was he that he left Plouha immediately after the operation of 16/17 March. But Labrosse had not been able to pass the message and BONAPARTE IV took place on 19/20 March without Dumais and without a hitch of any kind. At high tide, the Sous-Kéruzeau beach was an altogether better operational proposition, since the surf-boats came right in to the pebble beach at the foot of the cliff, where they were screened from sight and from fire. Dumais has stated that on this occasion two agents destined for an intelligence mission in central France were landed, together with stores. Slocum did not mention this but recorded that 19 airmen were brought out. Windham-Wright was surprised not to find Dumais on the beach: he wanted to confer with him.

Dumais was back at Plouha for BONAPARTE V on 23 March, when MGB 503 picked up 30 airmen, according to Slocum's record, and landed stores. There were at least two Frenchmen among those embarked: an agent named Le Bourhis from another organisation and a young and active member of the Plouha group, Jean Tréhiou, who wanted to join the Fighting French forces.

Even the participants in this remarkable series of operations seem to have found it difficult to keep track of dates and numbers, but Slocum's record, based no doubt on reports of each sortie by the commanding officers of the MGBs concerned, must be correct in outline, if not necessarily in detail. By his reckoning, at least 111 people were embarked from a heavily defended enemy coastline in the ten-day dark periods of January, February and March 1944, 74 of them within the span of seven days. But at this point the Plouha operations came to a halt. Dumais wrote in his book, 'In April we put on another operation from Plouha,' but his recollection is contradicted by the record of the MGBs' employment: it was not until three months later that a sixth group of airmen was shipped out by 'Shelburne' from Sous-Keruzeau. No doubt Dumais's organisation had been put under great strain by the three March operations in such rapid succession and needed time to recover. Windham-Wright had told Le Cornec when they met on the beach on 19 March that it would be necessary to suspend the series because the nights were getting shorter, but this was not the real reason. As in the case of the 'Var' line's operations at Beg-an-Fry, clandestine sea-transport work by DDOD(I) on the north coast of Brittany was halted in April 1944 because of the risk of increasing German vigilance and defence measures in the weeks before the invasion of Normandy. The same embargo applied to MI9's operations, which were even larger in scale and therefore more likely to stir up the defence system. For security reasons 'Shelburne' was not given the real reason. Dumais was curiously reticent about this subject when he came to write his book long after the war, as he was about his difficult relations with Le Cornec and other members of the Plouha group in the spring of 1944. Those who had been working with him at Plouha seem not to have understood the reasons for his sudden disappearance and, after what had been achieved in March, must have felt let down.

Dumais went off at this point to see whether he could find some means of evacuating airmen from the west coast of Brittany, since the safe houses that had been emptied by the run of operations in March soon filled up again, as the existence and efficacy of 'Shelburne' had become widely known in Resistance circles.

Dumais enlisted the help of Captain Dréau of Lesconil, who had been involved in a rendezvous between a fishing boat and a British submarine in autumn 1941.[8] They examined the possibility of converting a Concarneau trawler to enable it to conceal clandestine passengers on board when undergoing German inspection on leaving port, but the inspections were extremely thorough and no crew could be found willing to run the risks involved. They also made an extensive search to try to find a beach on the west coast that could be used for direct embarkation operations on the BONAPARTE model. Dumais seems not to have known that DDOD(I) was not then in a position to send any form of ship so far south. The big MGBs 502 and 503 had indeed sufficient range for the job, but the hours of darkness would not have been enough to cover so long a double passage by a vessel of this type. What is more, fishing-boat operations had come to a halt at the end of the previous October, among other reasons because fuel shortages had so restricted French fishing that the vessels of DDOD(I)'s so-called Inshore Patrol Flotilla would have been far too conspicuous.

Dumais went to look at the Aber-Wrac'h/Aber-Benoît area to see if it might be possible to arrange for Allied evaders to be taken to sea in open boats and picked up from them by the Royal Navy, but he was discouraged by the desolate and exposed nature of the coast and by garbled accounts of the difficulties experienced in the operations carried out there by the 15th MGB Flotilla at the end of 1943. When he published his book in the 1970s he still believed that sailors had been drowned in the course of these attempts, which was not true, though the troubles encountered had made DDOD(I) decide there would be no further operations there.

Even though the work of the 15th MGB Flotilla for SOE and MI9 had been halted because of the prior claims of OVERLORD, operations to the north coast of Brittany continued for SIS on a small scale, although only one of four such attempted contacts succeeded in the period between mid-April and D-Day.

Dumais and Labrosse were in Paris when the Allied assault on the Normandy coast began on 6 June. They had demurred when told by MI9 to return to the United Kingdom and, on 7 June, MI9 ordered them back to Brittany instead. The rail service was no longer running and they set off on the 450-km. journey on bicycles, accompanied by Louisette Lorre, Dumais's courier. The journey was very difficult: Dumais had his bicycle confiscated by a German sergeant when he was leaving Rennes, but he insisted on a written receipt and used this to thumb a lift on a series of German military vehicles as far as Saint-Brieuc. It took him almost three weeks to get that far and he was suffering from a boil on his bottom. The little local train to Plouha was running a partial service again and, on boarding it, Dumais ran into Job Mainguy, who was returning from an intelligence mission for the 'Cohors Asturies' network. Dumais seemed surprised to see him and said he thought they had all been arrested. Mainguy told him briefly what had happened in the three months since he and Labrosse had left immediately after BONAPARTE V. Dumais's reaction to this account was positive: in that case, he said, they would be able to resume operations.

Though the Plouha group was intact, access to the Sous-Kéruzeau beach had become more difficult, the Germans having laid minefields all along the coast following an inspection of coastal defences by Rommel in February. Mainguy, Huet and Marie-Thérèse Le Calvez had taken it in turns to watch the minelaying in the vicinity of the route they had used between the Maison d'Alphonse and the top of the rock-fall down which they got to the beach. From their hiding-place behind some gorse bushes they had obtained a very good idea of the emplacement and spacing of the Teller mines. Dumais estimated the width of the minefield at 50 metres and, having been a regular soldier, he was probably right though some French accounts suggested far greater widths. It was marked on its landward side by barbed wire.

Mainguy and Huet had also been able to get down to the Anse-Cochat gully in daylight and examine the positions of the five Teller mines laid across its entrance, together with two old French naval 203-mm. shells buried in the roadway, their detonating mechanisms rather clumsily concealed by clods of turf, like molehills.

Very soon after D-Day, MI9 and Slocum resumed operations to Saint-Brieuc Bay by sending MGB 718, the 'D'-Class Fairmile boat that had joined the Dartmouth flotilla in mid-March, to land Jean Tréhiou, who had left Plouha on BONAPARTE V to join the Fighting French forces, and was now being sent back by MI9 with two agents named Parent and Hamon to carry out missions further to the west. Tréhiou had belonged to 'Shelburne' and of course knew the Sous-Kéruzeau pinpoint. One account has stated that he and his companions were landed at the Pointe-de-Plouézec some miles to the north, but this seems to have been a misapprehension on the part of the writer (Hampshire).

MGB 718, which had arrived at Dartmouth straight from her builder's yard on the Clyde, was more powerful than the other boats of the 15th Flotilla. She was 120 feet long, with a displacement of 120 tons and her four 1,500-h.p. Packard engines, fuelled by 100-octane petrol, gave her a top speed of 42 knots, which matched that of the most powerful German E-boats. Her cruising speed on two engines was 14 knots. She was armed with two automatic 6-pounder guns mounted in power-operated turrets fore and aft; twin 20-mm. Oerlikons were carried forward in two other power-operated turrets and there were .5-inch Vickers machine-guns on both sides of the bridge. Because she was destined for work with DDOD(I), her four torpedo tubes had been removed to provide more deck space for carrying and handling surfboats.

MGB 718's first cross-Channel operation had been SCARF, when she accompanied MGB 502 to Beg-an-Fry on 15 April and had come under fire on the way out. Shortly after this, Lt Ronald Seddon, RNVR, her commanding officer, had been ordered to take her north via the Caledonian Canal to Lerwick in the Shetlands to carry out operation CYGNUS, which involved rescuing the SIS agents manning one of a chain of clandestine naval reporting stations on the coast of Norway – a task successfully accomplished at the end of May. It had been the first operation by one of DDOD(I)'s high-speed craft to Norway and it was carried out in conditions of almost continuous daylight. Eleven people were picked up from small boats off Batalden Island, 130 km. (c. 80 miles) north of Bergen, without a hitch. She had returned to Dartmouth only ten days before being sent to carry out REFLEXION, her first solo cross-Channel mission.

They arrived late at their chosen anchorage, which, as Guy Hamilton, her first lieutenant, observed, was par for the course.

The surf-boat was lowered and the conducting officer poured into it his three 'joeys'.[9]

As the surf-boat approached the coast, the loom of Pointe-de-la-Tour could be made out to the north and also Le-Pommier away to the south. They came in to rocks and steep cliff-side. Since there was to be no reception committee, a decision forced on MI9 by lack of radio communication with 'Shelburne' at the material time, by doubt whether the Plouha group had escaped destruction and since Tréhiou and his companions were to carry several suitcases and rucksacks, it was imperative to find the Anse-Cochat gully leading inland, so as to spare them the steep climb up the Sous-Kéruzeau rock-fall.

An instinct that the surf-boat had drifted too far south made Hamilton turn north: they rowed for about 150 metres until, much to his relief, there it was – Le Goulet-de-l'Anse-Cochat. '*Bonne chance*' was whispered a few times and the heavily laden trio vanished. Hamilton had a feeling that they knew the area, which was certainly true of Tréhiou. Although they had landed in ignorance of the new minefield, which now stretched continuously along the coast, somehow or other they must have walked safely carrying their equipment, straight through the array of mines laid across the landward end of the Goulet. No-one in the area knew of their arrival until Tréhiou, having no doubt assured himself that they were not walking into a trap, knocked at the door of Pierre Huet at the Le Dernier Sou hamlet.

Raoul Parent and Jean Hamon had been briefed to collect military intelligence and hidden airmen from the Josselin/Forêt-de-Quénécan area. They were to send the airmen north to the coast, where Tréhiou was to set up a new group to arrange evacuation by sea from some suitable point between Aber-Wrac'h in the west and the Ile-de-Sieck/Santec area, just short of the Ile-de-Batz, in the east, should the area remain in enemy hands for long enough to enable this to be done.

The surf-boat's return to 718 was a good deal less successful. It was a dark night with an overcast sky, for the weather had deteriorated after D-Day and the English Channel had seen some of the highest winds and stormiest seas experienced in June for many years. At the Anse-Cochat pinpoint, conditions had not been unfavourable, for the wind was off the shore.

As 718 had turned south-west at the Grand-Léjon they could see from the gun-flashes and bomb-bursts that an Allied air raid was in progress on Saint-Malo, 40 km. (25 miles) away to the south-east. They reached the chosen area at about 0200 hrs and anchored about a kilometre ($\frac{3}{4}$ mile) offshore. When the surf-boat set off for the beach, the walkie-talkie R/T link was not working well and it was difficult to pass course instructions to Hamilton. Incidentally,

Hamilton was then a Sub Lieutenant in the RNVR, but subsequently rose to fame as director of many successful films for Alexander Korda and other producers. His boat's crew that night consisted of Leading Seaman Albert 'Lofty' Dellow and Able Seaman 'Rocky' Rockwood, an 18-year-old Newfoundlander.

By the time the surf-boat was lost to view against the land, Seddon found that 718's anchor was dragging. More grass warp was paid out, but still the anchor did not hold, so he had the anchor brought aboard and decided to maintain his position using silenced engines.

They did so for some considerable time. Hamilton should by then have been on the way back but attempts to make contact with him on the walkie-talkie were vain. The echo-sounder was switched on in the hope that it would enable the surf-boat to home in on it, using a small hydrophone that it carried for this purpose – a device invented by Peter Williams of MGB 502 – but still the surf-boat did not reappear. Then Seddon decided to take the gunboat closer inshore in the hope of finding it. They flashed signals to seaward and even showed a shaded light towards the land: it was a risky thing to do, but two hours had elapsed since the surf-boat's departure and time was running out. Dawn would soon be upon them and they needed to be as far as possible offshore before daylight, even though the Luftwaffe was now no more than a shadow of its former self. They still could see no sign of the surf-boat and Seddon, unable to wait any longer, decided with extreme reluctance that he must begin the return passage to Dartmouth. The only crumb of comfort was that, with the prevailing offshore wind, they would probably have heard had any shots been fired on the beach.

After landing the three agents, the surf-boat had rowed off to where Hamilton had expected to find the gunboat anchored, but his efforts to coax the walkie-talkie into life were fruitless. After half an hour of rowing, Dellow and Rockwood rested on their oars and they all listened intently. Then, just as dawn was beginning to break, they heard the unmistakable sound of 718's silenced engines inshore of them, but gradually retreating. There was really nothing to be done: one cannot catch a 120-ton gunboat by rowing after it, so they rowed back towards the shore. Poor Dellow and Rockwood were by now exhausted. They beached on some rocks, which Hamilton estimated must have been some 500 metres south-east of the Sous-Kéruzeau beach and in the vicinity of Porz-Moguer. They hid their arms and Rockwood piled boulders into the surf-boat and sank her. Their preoccupation to remove all trace of the boat before daylight was such that Hamilton broke one of his fingers hacking holes in the boat's clinker-planked bottom with a jack-knife. The walkie-talkie had already been consigned to the deep with curses on its manufacturer.

Then they climbed the cliff and hid in the gorse near to the cliff-top. They were greatly relieved to watch the tide go down without revealing any trace of the surf-boat. Hamilton was much concerned to avoid capture, particularly where their presence might compromise the BONAPARTE beach and prevent its further use for operations, but they could not move far by daylight. He had told the two seamen that if they fell into German hands they were to claim to be survivors from the Canadian destroyer *Athabascan*, which had been sunk in the Channel, but, as that had occurred six weeks previously, one wonders whether the story would have passed muster. But there was no sign of activity anywhere and Hamilton had plenty of time to take in his bearings, with what he took to be Pointe-de-la-Tour on their left and Gouine-Ségal and Le-Pommier on their right. Only later, when Hamilton climbed a fence to get a better view, while the other two remained in hiding, did he see a notice that read *Achtung – Minen* and realise that they had walked through a minefield.

They lay hidden until the following night before setting off to get away from the BONAPARTE beach and its immediate vicinity. They covered some miles during the night, in the general direction of Plouha, as Hamilton intended to try to contact the local Resistance in due course. They managed to avoid falling foul of German patrols.

By that time they were very hungry and thirsty, and surprisingly cold considering that it was mid-summer. Finally Hamilton, who had grown up in France and spoke French well, threw caution to the winds and explained their plight to an old man who was working in a field. He went off to a nearby house without uttering a word, while Hamilton waited, fearing the worst; but he returned with a bottle of cider and some Breton pancakes and was offended when Hamilton offered him money – an attitude typical of the other Bretons they were to meet.

They moved on and, although they covered a considerable distance, could find no-one who would admit to being in contact with the Resistance. At last, when they were about to cross a main road, a man who was working near by warned them that it was much used by the Germans: he led them to a pit in the middle of a field, where he hid them. He must have been the channel through which news of their presence reached Joseph Mainguy, because this was the spot where Marie-Thérèse Le Calvez eventually found them.

Three days after Tréhiou's return, Mainguy was accosted in the village square at Plouha by a man named Pen, who told him that three individuals were hiding on rough ground near the farm of M Harscoët and asking to be put in touch with the Plouha Resistance. Mainguy went immediately to consult Le Cornec: they agreed that this was almost certainly a Gestapo trap. The impression that they had been under close German surveillance was reinforced by the frequent loitering in the village of black, front-wheel-drive Citroën cars with Saint-Brieuc registration plates. They were not therefore disposed to respond; but messages from the three evaders became increasingly desperate in tone and Marie-Thérèse Le Calvez volunteered to go and investigate, since she was felt to be less at risk than her male colleagues. She returned with the news that they were the crew of the surf-boat that had landed Tréhiou and his companions and that they had been unable to join their mother ship after carrying out the disembarkation.

At the outset Marie-Thérèse and the three evaders mistrusted each other but, when the girl went back after nightfall, Hamilton decided to follow her. Dellow and Rockwood remained sceptical and thought their officer was after 'a bit of skirt'. They therefore fell in behind Hamilton with some reluctance. But as they followed Marie-Thérèse along a lane they heard the ominous 'clump-clump' of an approaching enemy patrol. The three men dived for cover, Hamilton falling into a 14-foot-deep anti-tank ditch, which the Germans had recently compelled the local population to dig for many miles parallel to the coast. In doing so, he added a broken nose to the finger he had broken in disposing of the surfboat. Marie-Thérèse stood her ground as the Germans passed, though it was long after the curfew. After that she could do no wrong in the eyes of the evaders.

After 22 June, when Hamilton was lodged with the Ropers family, his excellent French made it possible for him to accompany Huet and Mainguy on various expeditions, particularly to the bowling alleys of the Café Le Meur, where he rubbed shoulders with the Germans, who also frequented it.

Dumais and Labrosse arrived back in Plouha after their long and trying post-D-Day bicycle ride from Paris shortly after Hamilton, Dellows and Rockwood had been found and given shelter by the local Resistance. They were able to tell London, via Labrosse's W/T link, that the missing surf-boat's crew from MGB 718 were well and safe, news that occasioned much relief and rejoicing at Dartmouth.

Dumais also got Mainguy and Huet to find and mark the Teller mines that had been laid on the old path to the rock-fall above the Sous-Kéruzeau beach. They located 17 and, to make sure they could find them in the dark, they prepared to tie strips of white cloth to the sticks with which they had marked the mines' positions. By the end of June Dumais had a new headquarters and a new safe house for Labrosse to transmit from: after a three-month interval, 'Shelburne' was ready to resume operations.

The scope of Dumais's mission had by now been broadened to

include paramilitary action: he arranged a parachute drop on 27 June to a new Maquis group at Bois-de-la-Salle, south of Pléguen and this included two mine-detectors as well as arms and munitions. There was a second parachute drop to the same Maquis on the night of 5/6 July.

The Plouha group resumed contact with the group at Guingamp and on the night of 2/3 July Mainguy collected 15 airmen who had been driven over from Guingamp in a van. With the three naval evaders already at Plouha, there were therefore 18 candidates for evacuation, but from 1 July and for the next ten days a strong north-easterly gale made landing impossible.

The German troops stationed near the coast were at this stage thoroughly on edge: they included Vlasov Russians,[10] among whom the Georgians were particularly aggressive and ill-disciplined. Like other units of this kind on the coast since late 1943, they were a sore affliction, with their exactions, thefts and attempted rapes, and the area north of Plouha, where Gicquel's Maison d'Alphonse stood, suffered particularly from their habit of calling at houses and demanding drink at all hours of the day and night. The Resistance thought it prudent to evacuate some of the arms stocked in the farms there since the BONAPARTE landings. In spite of this state of tension, Gicquel and Mainguy used the newly arrived mine-detectors to check the road down to Anse-Cochat. This they did in broad daylight, one keeping watch while the other worked. Once this operation was completed, 'Shelburne' had, at low tide, a second and far easier route to the Sous-Kéruzeau beach.

The gale was at its height on 5 July and it had still not sufficiently abated to make an embarkation possible when the Gestapo told the gendarmerie two days later that they knew an organisation was active in the area. The gendarmerie passed on the warning to 'Shelburne' and the 15 candidates for evacuation were moved from the Gicquel and Ropers houses. By now they had been in the hands of the Plouha group for nearly a month. Then, on 11/12 July, the agreed message was broadcast by the BBC and, when it was repeated on the evening programme, they knew that the gun-boat must be on its way.

After nightfall, Mainguy ventured into the minefield and tied strips of white cloth on to the sticks marking the mines. The evacuees were briefed as usual by Dumais and made their way to the beach with every precaution. MGB 503 had been sent to carry out this operation, which was code-named CROZIER, and the landing and embarkation of the passengers went without a hitch. The 'Shelburne' beach party made their way back through the minefield, picking up the white cloth markers as they went.

Labrosse had, as usual, not been a member of the beach party but was standing by at Pludual, where his radio set was installed at the time. When he heard an aircraft circling round and apparently looking in vain for its appointed dropping zone, he rushed out and flashed 'OK' to the plane with his torch, so 'Shelburne' received a third and unexpected parachute drop of arms while CROZIER was in progress on the Sous-Kéruzeau beach. But the advent of this aircraft was itself a sign that the moonless period was over and that there would have to be a pause before another sea evacuation would be possible.

The land battle was drawing nearer and paramilitary activity was now in full swing inland and further south. On 20 July, the Maquis at Bois-de-la-Salle became a permanent group of 160 men under training to use the arms supplied via 'Shelburne'.

No. 4 SAS, a French unit under the indomitable one-armed Commandant Bourgoin, had parachuted an advance party into Brittany soon after midnight on D-Day-minus-one. They landed north-east of Vannes on the Landes-de-Lanvaux, accompanied by an SOE French Section team under Hunter-Hue. Their allocated task was to sever, as far as possible, all communications between Brittany and the rest of France. Within a few days a crowd of some 2,000 Maquisards had congregated round Bourgoin's Dingson base to collect small arms, uniforms, boots and food; and a very similar situation had developed at Bourgoin's second concentration area, Samwest, near Guingamp. Inevitably these over-large gatherings attracted German attention. Samwest was attacked on 12 June and scattered; Dingson's turn came on 18 June, but Bourgoin received air support and beat the Germans to a standstill before ordering his force to disperse during the night, thereby avoiding a disaster such as was to befall the unwise defenders of the Vercors a month later.

A small team was dropped into the Morbihan on 21/22 June to find out what had happened to the Dingson base and to bring Bourgoin orders to protect port installations at Morlaix, Saint-Malo and Vannes. This was because General Eisenhower's Supreme Headquarters Allied Expeditionary Force (SHAEF) at that time entertained the idea that a landing in Brittany, probably on the west coast at Port-Navalo and the Vilaine estuary in the Morbihan, might be a means of circumventing the tenacious German resistance to enlargement of the Normandy beach-head. This mission, which rejoiced in the code name LOST, was led by Major Oswald Cary-Elwes; Lieutenant Fleuriot of the French 2e Régiment de Chasseurs Parachutistes was second in command; there was a batman named Mills and a French Sergeant named Marty, with three W/T Operators from the 2e RCP under his orders.

By 17/18 July the prospects of a break-out from the Normandy beach-head were bright enough for SHAEF to lay aside all thought of a second landing in Brittany. When Bourgoin was told of this, *Lost* was ordered to return to the United Kingdom via 'Shelburne'. As

Cary-Elwes and Mills made their way north towards Plouha with the help of local Maquisards, they heard that Marty had been killed, together with Captain Marienne, Bourgoin's second in command. A further Maquis group at Coat-Mallouen, which had been linked with Bourgoin's Samwest base near Guingamp, gave them civilian identity cards and clothes: thus equipped, the party reached Plouha, where Dumais and Le Cornec escorted them to the Maison d'Alphonse. They were at this stage five in number: Cary-Elwes and another SAS Major named Smith, Mills, Cary-Elwes's batman, Flight Sergeant Philip Farger, an RAF fighter pilot shot down near Saint-Gildas, and Major William A. Jones, USAAF. Ten minutes after Dumais and Le Cornec had left them, they were all seated at the table in the kitchen of the farmhouse when Mme Gicquel thought she heard a noise outside. They stopped talking: there could be no doubt that someone was walking round the house. Gicquel, thinking that perhaps Dumais and Le Cornec had returned, opened the door and found himself face to face with two soldiers in German uniform. He shut the door in their faces and rushed to tell his Allied guests to hide in the loft as quickly as possible. It was at that moment that the first shots were fired somewhere outside. Gicquel was on his way back to the front door when he was confronted in the passage by two soldiers, who were in time to see his five guests disappearing through the trapdoor in the kitchen ceiling. The soldiers – Vlasov Russians – called on the fugitives to surrender. Bursts of fire must have been directed towards the ceiling, as Mills recalled bullets reaching the loft after passing through its floor, while others made holes in the roof. Then everything fell silent: the Russians stopped short of attempting to climb into the loft, which was just as well for them as Mills had a grenade ready to throw. Instead, they ordered Gicquel out into the yard where one of their patrol lay wounded: he had been hit in the backside by ill-directed fire from one of his compatriots positioned on a bank that overlooked the house and was in agony. They ordered Gicquel to go and fetch a horse and cart from a nearby farm. When he returned with it, they lifted their wounded comrade into it and left without posting a sentry.

The five Allied evaders in the Gicquel loft, caught in a trap in civilian clothes with arms in their possession, felt that the outlook was very bleak indeed. When they heard the cart approaching, they imagined that reinforcements had arrived, but after cries and lamentations from the wounded man, they were surprised to hear the cart leave the yard and their host call out 'Bonne nuit'. Gicquel appeared shortly afterwards on the ladder leading to the loft and announced that all the Russians had thanked him for his help, taken the cart and left. He predicted that they would attribute their comrade's injury to the terrorists seen disappearing into the roof and would soon return in strength. The house must therefore be evacuated immediately.

Mme Gicquel, who was mother of a six-week-old baby, was ready to leave and made off straight away with the child for her mother-in-law's house, which was no more than 400 metres distant. Gicquel stayed behind. When his five guests came down from their attic, they saw with dismay that in their hasty retreat they had left a number of compromising articles, including a British Army cap, on the kitchen table. They snatched up their possessions and were just about to leave when Major Jones remembered that he, too, had lost his cap. Cary-Elwes remarked that he now understood why a Frenchman never took his headgear off, which provoked a laugh. The cap was retrieved and Gicquel led them off to a field of corn, where they hid, damp and cold, in a ditch to await daylight.

When day began to break, Mills set off along the bank to see whether anyone was around. After going some 300 metres, he saw two silhouettes but was unable to identify them, so he crawled back to warn his fellow evaders: they prepared to do battle, but it turned out to be Dumais and Le Cornec, who had been told by Gicquel what had happened and had come to find them. Dumais first armed each of them with a Colt automatic and some grenades and then led them off across country at a spanking pace, walking in circles so as to confuse any tracker dogs the Germans might use. Though none of them had slept for 48 hours, they all felt fit and alert. After they had covered some kilometres Dumais found them a refuge where there was plenty of natural cover. A church clock could be heard striking eight when he left them, promising to return after nightfall. They had a long wait before them.

As foreseen, the Germans and their Russian satellites returned in strength to the Maison d'Alphonse and, after a vain search for the fugitives, sacked it, blew it up and set the ruins on fire. The enemy failed to find a stock of arms hidden in the stable since the CROZIER landing earlier that month, and it blew up when the fire reached it.

Thus was the Maison d'Alphonse, so important a link in six 'Shelburne' operations, reduced to a collection of charred walls and rubble, never to be rebuilt.

At the end of that eventful day, 24 July, Dumais announced that the operation to evacuate Cary-Elwes and his companions would take place that night. The countryside between the Pointe-de-la-Tour and the Pointe-de-Plouha was in a high state of alert and criss-crossed by trigger-happy enemy patrols. Dumais got Le Cornec to provide half a platoon of Maquisards armed with Sten sub-machine-guns and a light machine-gun to escort and cover the column on its 3-km. progress from Kerlerot, just north of Plouha, to the beach. He also arranged to have a horse and cart waiting, concealed, at Kerlerot to carry away any arms that might be landed. Then at last they set off, with Huet and Mainguy as scouts and guides, keeping well away from roads where patrols might be encountered. As they struck across the fields, dogs in the farms they skirted fell to barking, but they were already so unsettled by the bursts of indiscriminate firing and the intensified patrol action that it made little difference to them, nor did the sound attract the attention of the enemy. The tide would be low, so they made their way across country to the gulley leading down to the Anse-Cochat, where Huet and Mainguy had noted and marked the mines. The column halted where they had to cross a track much frequented by enemy patrols. On their left, where the ruins of the Maison-d'Alphonse lay smouldering, there was firing which seemed to be getting nearer. It was no place to linger, so they crossed quickly into the area where the coastal minefield lay, beyond the last habitation. The Germans, reckoning that no-one would be stupid enough to venture into such a danger zone, particularly on a dark night, did not bother to patrol it.

When their long single-file column reached the barbed wire that marked the landward side of the mined zone, and was about to enter the narrow gully leading to the beach, the light machine-gun and its crew were posted on a rise from which they could dominate the track. With this three-man rearguard to protect them, the procession made its way down to Anse-Cochat, past the marked mine positions and on to the beach.

It was nearly low tide and a wide expanse of sand lay uncovered as they turned left and made their way along the shingle at the foot of the cliff to the usual position at the rock-fall. Mainguy climbed part-way up it and the business of signalling began. It was strangely quiet.

At 0130 on 25 July Mainguy heard the sound of oars, and three surf-boats from MGB 502 materialised out of the night. In the bows of the first boat was Major John Verney of the Special Boat Squadron of the SAS, future author of *On Going to the Wars*, who had been taken prisoner in Sardinia and escaped down the Apennines after the Italian armistice. Dumais conferred with him while 15 suitcases of arms were brought ashore and the departing passengers embarked: they were six in number, as it had been decided that Jean Gicquel must also leave for safety's sake. Then the surf-boats were off into the night as quietly as they had come: they were the double-ended SN1 variety and did not even need to be turned round.

The large size of the shore party was a great help in handling the heavy suitcases. As they left the beach, they were overflown by a number of RAF fighter aircraft, which crossed and recrossed the area at low altitude without provoking any reaction from the

German defences. Dumais assumed they had come to cover the gunboat's withdrawal. As their column left the mined zone, they picked up their three-man rearguard, who had seen nothing, though they had heard much shooting from the patrol routes. Somehow or other, they carried their heavy cargo of arms the further 2 km. (1.2 miles), cutting across fields of wheat to get to the point where the horse and cart had been hidden. The cart set off soon after daybreak with the arms hidden under a load of hay and next night they were delivered to the Maquis at Bois-de-la-Salle. The operation was timely, coinciding with the American 3rd Army's break-out from the Cherbourg peninsula and the beginning of General Patton's armoured sweep into Brittany. The German units thus cut off were few in number and not of high quality: as they fell back westwards, the Maquis ambushed and harassed their withdrawal. Liberation came to Plouha on 6 August in the form of four (or perhaps five) light Sherman tanks followed by trucks carrying petrol and rations, very much as the German Panzers had thrust through Brittany towards Brest in June 1940.

'Shelburne' had had its last clandestine sea operation. When MGB 718 came back on the night of 8/9 August to collect one SIS and two French agents and any Allied evaders still in the hands of the Plouha group, the enemy forces who had manned the block-house on the Pointe-de-la-Tour had already surrendered several days previously, so the operation took place in daylight; and, when the party escorting the three outward-bound passengers, armed to the teeth – for there were still isolated German and Russian stragglers in the area – emerged from the gully at Anse-Cochat on to the beach, they could for the first time see the gunboat riding at anchor.

Dumais had already gone about other business. After helping a confused and non-French-speaking American town mayor deal with the post-Liberation power vacuum at Saint-Brieuc, he made his way east with Louisette Lorre to contact Major Airey Neave, MI9's new head, and find out what had happened to the redoubtable Campinchi, the Paris linchpin in turn of the 'Pat' organisation, of 'Oaktree' and of 'Shelburne', who had collected another 70 aircrew but had been prevented by the battle from sending them on to Brittany.

Dumais's firm discipline and punctilious security arrangements had stopped the rot that destroyed MI9's two previous French networks and allowed the 'Shelburne' organisation to flourish and achieve its outstanding results. Altogether, the 'Shelburne' Plouha group shipped out between 138 and 145 people by the Dartmouth gunboats – an achievement exceeded only by the 'Pat' line and the Poles working with their Gibraltar-based feluccas. Remarkably not a single member of the 'Shelburne' organisation was lost. La Maison d'Alphonse was the only victim.

ABOVE MGB 318 'Took avoiding action . . . at full speed' (Operation TENDERLY).
BELOW MGB 318 (Lt Jan McQuoid Mason).

Lt D L Birkin, RNVR

MGB 502 (Lt Cdr Peter Williams RNVR) undergoing trials in the Solent.

MGB 503 (Lt Cdr R. M. Marshall) coming alongside the Depot Ship *Westward Ho!* at Dartmouth.

MGB 503's bow-wave photographed at speed from the stern of MGB 502 by Lloyd Bott, her Australian First Lieutenant.

Ile Guennoc showing the MGBs' trackline (solid) to the anchorage at its landward southern end and the route (dotted) followed by the surf-boat to Ile Tariec, dried out at low tide.

Left to right, seated: Jan McQuoid Mason, Mike Marshall and Peter Williams, commanding officers of MGBs 318, 503 and 502, with a group of their officers.

From left to right. Able Seamen Harold Pickles and Roger Bartley flanked by Mme Tanguy (centre) and two employees of her husband's road transport company. Right, Mr Claude Tanguy and Edonard Tanguy. Back row, Lt Guy Hamilton, Cdr Ted Davis and Lt Cdr David Birkin at Lannilis near Aber-Benoît, in August 1944.

Captain F. H. Slocum outside Buckingham Palace, after
an Investiture at which he received the CMG.

Captain F. H. Slocum, S/Lt Jean Trehiou, Cdr E. A. G. Davis and F. Le Cornec at Plouha.

Monument erected above
BONAPARTE beach (Anse Cochat)

David Birkin and his
daughter Jane Birkin,
the actress, at a post-
war reunion at Plage
BONAPARTE.

CHAPTER XIX

July–August 1944

Jean Tréhiou, Raoul Parent and Jean Hamon, the three MI9 agents landed at Anse-Cochat on 16/17 June 1944 to set up a new organisation for the evacuation of aircrew, were to have only two months before the Germans fell back on Brest before the United States 3rd Army. A point on the coast was sought between Aber-Wrac'h and the Ile-de-Sieck/Ile-de-Batz area, and the beach Tréhiou chose was Grach-Dzu, near Clogourouan, scene of CARPENTER I and of Peter Harratt's unsuccessful first attempt in April 1943 to land Erwin Deman to set up SOE's 'Var' line. A successful first contact with Tréhiou was established there by MGB 502 a month after he arrived back in France, and four suitcases of stores were landed to him, but there were no airmen waiting to be picked up.

This operation – ROBESPIERRE – was carried out on 14/15 July 1944. MGB 502 sailed from Dartmouth at 2001 hrs with David Birkin as navigating officer and Ron Seddon, commanding officer of MGB 718, and Lt M. Carroll, USNR, as observers. A Captain Ford was conducting officer for MI9.[1]

The weather – wind W and SW Force 3, sea slight with a slight SW swell, and good visibility – was fairly constant throughout the night and the outward passage, with an air escort of two Spitfires until nightfall, was without incident except that the QH position-finder broke down and took three quarters of an hour to repair.

The Ile-de-Batz light was showing at full strength with its usual characteristics, but was only on for every alternate ten minutes. Lights were observed in the Morlaix River and off the Pointe-de-Bloscon to the east of it, but no enemy shipping was encountered. The approach to the pinpoint, which had proved so troublesome on earlier operations in less favourable circumstances, presented no great difficulties this time and the beach could easily be seen from the anchoring position. Porz-Névez could also be distinguished. Time was spent fixing the ship's position accurately before anchoring as no contact with the reception committee could be obtained by walkie-talkie. At 0201, however, a white light was seen flashing the letter 'R' from the pinpoint and the 20-foot SN6 surf-boat was hoisted out and lowered into the water, using the specially designed davit that had been fitted to enable this large boat to be handled. Ten suitcases of arms were loaded and the SN6 left the ship's side at 0215 under command of Sub Lt D. N. Miller, SANF(V). For once, S-phone contact between surf-boat and mother ship worked perfectly. A hydrophone was carried in the SN6 in case of homing difficulties, as there was haze over the land, but it was not in fact used, as Miller could see 502 when he was half-way back from the beach.

The surf-boat grounded at 0231 and there was immediate contact with the reception committee. There were no passengers to be embarked, but four of the suitcases were handed over (they could not manage more). Captain Ford had a few minutes' consultation in French, after which the surf-boat returned to the ship, coming alongside at 0245.

Owing to a moderate swell which arose at the most inopportune moment, there was some difficulty in getting the SN6 inboard, but the anchor was weighed at 0300 and the ship proceeded to sea. The return passage to Dartmouth was entirely uneventful except that at 0422 the ship was suddenly illuminated by a blue searchlight mounted on an aircraft, which flew across the stern. The two-star recognition signal was fired and the aircraft, which looked like a Wellington, proceeded on its patrol. MGB 502 entered the gate of the Dartmouth protective boom at 0819.

ROBESPIERRE II was entrusted to MGB 318, which sailed at 1825 on 12 August, with Jan McQuoid Mason in command, David Birkin as navigator, Captain Ford of MI9 as conducting officer, Sub Lt Guy Hamilton as boats officer and Sub Lt R. G. King, RNR, as observer.

The weather was wind WNW Force 2, slight WSW swell, slight sea, cloud 9/10, visibility 16 km. (10 miles). For about an hour the wind freshened to Force 3 and the crests were beginning to break: then it quietened down and the rest of the operation enjoyed fine weather. As they now knew to be customary at the Grach-Dzu anchorage even in fine weather, there was a good swell running, though the surf on the beach was slight. When they made the run-in visibility was only about 1.5 km. (1 mile), which made distances appear greater. After they had anchored, visibility improved and the coastline could be seen clearly.

At 2312 speed was reduced to 15 knots, as they were ahead of schedule, and engines were silenced. The Triagoz light was sighted (lit) at 2351 and Ile-de-Batz (unlit) at 0010. They anchored in 9 fathoms at 0057. Owing to the poor visibility, Mason had difficulty in identifying the Grach-Dzu beach and made the error of pointing out and even giving the compass course to the two false beaches that had caused confusion on the earliest expeditions to this pinpoint in the winter of 1942–43. The reception committee was called up on the American handy-talkie, but no reply was received so at 0134 the two surf-boats were sent away with Guy Hamilton in charge and Sub Lt Bell, first lieutenant of 318, in the second boat. Their orders were to lie off the beach until a light flashed the letter 'R' or R/T contact was established. At 0149 Hamilton reported that he had closed the beach but sighted nothing and that he was still without R/T contact. The surf-boats were ordered to return to the ship and came alongside at 0204. Hamilton reported that he thought he had gone to the correct beach, but a remark from Captain Ford suggested to Mason that he had in fact been to one of the two false beaches instead. From seaward, to the west of the true beach, these beaches look just like the correct pinpoint, particularly in bad visibility.

The gunboat continued to call the shore party on the R/T, in particular at the times specified in the operation orders, and at 0242 Mason sent Hamilton away again to investigate the correct beach. He went inside the rock at the entrance and had a good look at the beach but saw no-one on it. He also called them on the R/T set. He returned to the ship at 0255, quite satisfied that the beach he had inspected was the correct pinpoint and that there was no reception party waiting. The boats were hoisted inboard and they weighed anchor and proceeded clear of the area at 0316.

At 0347 the centre engine developed a cracked manifold – a defect all too familiar to them. It was not serious and they were able to continue at 19 knots, sighting land at 0700 and entering Dartmouth at 0911. No enemy shipping had been seen and the only item of interest was what looked like the bombing and shelling of the beleaguered city of Brest.

Except for these German enclaves round the main Atlantic ports, some of which continued to hold out until the final VE-Day surrender, Brittany was by now liberated and when ROBESPIERRE III was undertaken on 25 August it was a daylight promenade. MGB 318 left Dartmouth at 0530 with Birkin navigating once more and sundry observers on board. The weather was excellent throughout and the outward passage uneventful. The Ile-de-Batz light was sighted at 1023 and they were able to identify the Grach-Dzu beach when still a good distance offshore. They ran straight in and anchored at 1138 in 12 fathoms, fixing their position by bearings of the Ile-de-Batz lighthouse, Cléder Church and Saint-Pol-de-Léon Church.

Numerous fishing boats were busy in the area, but the sight that gave the ship's company the greatest pleasure, after two years of clandestine nocturnal visits to the Breton coast, was that of people rushing from all over the countryside to meet the landing party as the news of their arrival spread. Of the passengers they had come to collect – three agents of MI9, Jean Tréhiou of Plouha and his two team-mates Parent and Hamon – only Parent was present. He was accompanied by Dr and Mme Le Duc and by Captain Rendier's ADOLPHE-AMÉDÉ mission and an intelligence mission known as LA GIRAFE, who wished to be evacuated. At 1150 two SN1 surf-boats and a small motorboat they were carrying left for the shore.

The welcome they received was enthusiastic and it did not take long for the boats' crews to be invited to the peasants' houses for lunch. Gifts were offered of bread and of onions, which were particularly welcome, and cigarettes given in return. At 1250 the boats shoved off, with the shore party giving Churchill's 'V' sign. At 1316 hrs 318 weighed and proceeded to sea, arriving back at Dartmouth at 1940.

Mason reported a considerable amount of shipping off the Brittany coast: the Morlaix estuary had some American 'PC' craft lying in it and they sighted a small convoy of two merchant ships and numerous landing-craft making for Morlaix harbour. There were many escort groups and destroyers patrolling off the coast: indeed they sighted far more shipping on the French coast than on the British.

Brest was undergoing a 'softening process' and the sound of gunfire was almost continuous. There was a large pall of smoke rising high above the fortress city. On the return passage they sighted several waves of American heavy bombers going over to help the bombardment.

By daylight, Mason noted, the beach and coast looked much lower and smaller than by night, and landmarks less pronounced. Most surprising of all was the number of houses in the area: it looked almost like a seaside resort. In conclusion, he reported, a most enjoyable 'picnic' was had by all.

CHAPTER XX

Operations for SIS: January–August 1944

T he 15th MGB Flotilla carried out two discrete series of operations to the north coast of Brittany on behalf of Cohen's Section of SIS between January and August 1944. But Cohen's Section worked both in conjunction with de Gaulle's BCRA and independently: one of these Breton groups worked through SIS for the BCRA, while the other operated directly for SIS.

The BCRA series began with the landing by MGB 318 on 28/29 January of three of their agents on the west side of the estuary leading to the ancient port of Tréguier. The team's leader was Yvon Jézéquel, who had escaped from his native Lézardrieux in November 1943 on the lighthouse-tender *La-Horaine*.[1] He had been a conspicuously able student at the Lycée Anatole-Le-Braz at Saint-Brieuc and, after completing his baccalaureate in 1942, he had gone to Paris with the intention of preparing for the École Navale entrance examination. When the naval intake was suspended, he began to plan an escape to England, so as to be able to pursue his vocation as a sailor, though it took him most of 1943 to find the means to do so.

Jézéquel was accompanied by two W/T operators named Weybel or Neybel and July: they waited for low tide and then walked over to the mainland where they knocked at the door of a fisherman living at Plougrescant at 4 o'clock in the morning and asked for help. This three-man mission, code-named BLAVET, was to form part of a network named 'Turquoise', which in turn formed part of an organisation known as 'Phidias' in Paris. 'Phidias' was (dangerously) linked with a number of other subordinate intelligence groups. Jézéquel built up a group extending from Brittany to Paris, with July transmitting first from Saint-Brieuc and then from Guingamp.[2]

The operation that landed Jézéquel was code-named FLANNELFOOT and, after he had collected a quantity of secret mail, a repeat operation (FLANNELFOOT II) was arranged to collect it from the Toul-Tan side of the Île-d'Er and to land at least three further agents. MGB 318's first attempt to carry this out on 23/24 March was a failure: radio-telephone contact was established with the reception party, but, owing to the low tide, the surf-boats could not reach them and the operation had to be abandoned. A second attempt two nights later was successful; the outward-bound passengers were landed and the mail was picked up from the west of the island. In mid-March, however, the central organisation of 'Phidias' was seized by the Germans who found documents that enabled the whole structure to be dismantled. Very few of those involved avoided arrest. Jézéquel was picked up at the Gare-de-Montparnasse in Paris on 24 April. He and his young sister died as deportees in Germany.

At the time of his arrest, Jézéquel must have been on his way to Brittany for Operation SPLINT, which MGB 502 undertook on the following night, 25/26 April. The pinpoint chosen was on the east bank of the Tréguier River and Williams considered it the most difficult rendezvous 502 ever had to make, for it lay inside the estuary. The approach to this is strewn with rocks and a strong tide runs across the entrance. During the war years, the channel was unlit and marked with stakes. The MGB had therefore to find her way from stake to stake at slow speed while stemming this strong, cross-tidal current. David Birkin has been credited with the feat of pilotage that brought them to their chosen anchorage, but his own papers make it clear that SPLINT was not one of the 33 operations in which he took part. The navigator was in fact probably his colleague Sub Lt Brian Fraser, RNR. The gunboat waited at anchor for more than an hour but there was neither the expected light signal from the shore nor R/T contact, so Peter Williams regretfully gave orders to weigh anchor and began the homeward passage to Dartmouth. But as they emerged from the screen of rocky islets that fringe that part of the coast, the sky ahead of them was suddenly lit by star-shell and they found themselves confronted at short range by a full-scale naval battle.

During 1943 there had been increasingly frequent offensive sweeps by Coastal Force vessels from the Plymouth and Portsmouth commands against enemy shipping moving along the French coast and, as time went on, these patrols had often been reinforced by the addition of a destroyer. Gunboats from the 15th Flotilla proceeding on their clandestine descents on that same coast had normally been routed by the operations staff of the Commander-in-Chief, Western Approaches, at Mount Batten so as to keep clear of these sweeps, though they quite often saw star-shell and heard distant gunfire. Tonight the action was to take place right across their northward course.[3]

The Lézardrieux River, which lies between the Tréguier estuary and the Ile-de-Bréhat, a few miles to the east, offers a well-sheltered, deep-water anchorage and the Germans had mounted anti-aircraft guns and an array of barrage balloons on the cliffs overlooking the river, which was frequently used by their naval vessels staging between nocturnal forays. Williams had been warned before sailing from Dartmouth that three German fleet torpedo-boats lying there were expected to sail westwards and that the cruiser *Black Prince* with four destroyers, three of which were Canadian, would be operating in the area.

By the light of the star-shell, the three German torpedo-boats were revealed not more than 1 km. ($\frac{3}{4}$ mile) ahead of 502, heading west at full speed, with the Allied force in hot pursuit. Very soon, the nearest of the enemy vessels was seen to be on fire, as the destroyers closed in, raking her decks with heavy machine-gun fire. MGB 502 had stopped her engines and could see German sailors mown down like ninepins as they manned their guns or were swallowed up in the flames rapidly engulfing their ship.

MGB 502 was in an unenviable situation, clearly visible to both sides as star-shell burst overhead, a sitting duck as regards position and a silhouetted target for the German coastal batteries. Williams therefore restarted engines and took her clear of the battle at top speed, heading east into the night.

One of the Canadian destroyers, the *Athabascan*, not only saw her but assumed she must be a German E-boat and opened fire, without even bothering to challenge. MGB 502 switched on her navigation, masthead and recognition lights and fired two-star recognition signals from the Very pistol. These produced no immediate respite, but fortunately all the shells fell astern of her.

In the midst of the battle, an unexpected danger loomed briefly. An officer from DDOD(I)'s office, on board as an observer, had decided to carry on him a loaded .45 Colt automatic pistol. When the shooting began he rushed up on to the gunboat's bridge, no doubt bent on personal defence, at which his pistol was accidentally fired. The bullet ricocheted off the armoured plating of the bridge, narrowly missing Williams and Signalman College.

The second series of operations for SIS carried out by the Dartmouth gunboats during the months before the Liberation consisted of nine missions to collect mail, first from Ile-à-Canton and then from Ile-Grande, which lie a few miles west of the Tréguier River, on the east side of Lannion Bay. Slocum cited these GLOVER operations, alongside the BONAPARTE/CROZIER series, as examples of the success that a determined and well-briefed agent could achieve.

French sources identify the principal agent involved in this series as Georges Charaudeau and the group that formed the reception committee as members of a subsection of his 'Alibi' network known as 'Alibi-Maurice'.[4] Charaudeau claimed to have created the little-known 'Alibi' organisation, at the behest of the British, in July 1940, working from Spain. Its field of activity spread rapidly to both occupied and non-occupied zones as a result of a 40-day visit he made to France. His contacts were in extreme right-wing nationalist circles, such as the 'Cagoule' and the 'Croix de Feu': they included

Loustaunau-Lacau, founder of the 'Alliance' network, which in 1943 had 2,000 subagents and 20 active W/T links, also working directly for SIS. Whether SIS regarded 'Alibi' as a genuinely independent network or as a subsection of 'Alliance' is not clear, but Charaudeau claimed to have been autonomous throughout and, in 1944, when 'Alliance' had lost its original leadership and two of those who had taken their place were in fact working for the Germans, he was evidently in direct touch with his SIS controlling section.

Charaudeau left Spain in May 1942 to devote himself to the organisation in France, leaving Georges Rotvan to look after the Spanish end of the network.

'Alibi' suffered heavy losses in some of its subsections: 'Klan', which had operated under Colonel de la Rocque, the Croix de Feu leader, was decimated in March 1943. 'Phill' had suffered greatly as early as October 1941 at the hands of the notorious French Bony-Lafont gang, which was working for the Germans. This subsection of 'Alibi' was led by a lady named Shoof and included among its subagents a well-known Billancourt coach-builder named Kellner. 'Alibi' is said at one stage to have used SOE communications and to have been in touch by this means with Langley of MI9. SOE seems even to have provided W/T operators for it on occasions.

From 23 February 1944, the date of the first GLOVER operation to Ile-à-Canton, 'Alibi-Maurice' formed a subsection working in the Lannion area under the immediate leadership of Lt Pierre Allart, who recruited a number of local people, including M Anastase Briand, a seaweed merchant at Ile-Grande in Pleumeur-Bodou. An agent named Guy Lemoine was sent to join them in April 1944. Lemoine's mission was to set up a group to collect intelligence relevant to the impending Allied landings in Normandy and to follow any eventual withdrawal of German forces into the Breton peninsula. Briand and his two brothers-in-law, Messieurs Le Goff and Lampalaer, formed the actual reception committee for the MGB operations. They managed, at a pinpoint no more than 500 metres from a German watch-post, to receive deliveries of material from Dartmouth and to dispatch clandestine mail collected from all over France. Material was hidden at, and W/T contacts were maintained from, Briand's seaweed depots.

Before these operations by sea had been organised as the result of an initiative by Charaudeau, the 'Alibi' network's mail had been sent to England in the course of Lysander and Hudson pick-up operations. Charaudeau went to London in October 1943 by one of these operations and there met 'Major Whytlaw' (Neil Whitelaw), the case officer dealing with 'Alibi', who had taken part in some of the pick-up operations.

In an address delivered on 28 May 1987 at Ile-Grande to a

reunion of those who had worked in 'Alibi-Maurice', Charaudeau said that it was he who suggested to 'Whytlaw' that operations should be organised by sea to collect the mail from the north coast of Brittany. He also said he had himself taken part on an experimental basis in three cross-Channel operations from Dartmouth to the Cap-Fréhel/Saint-Cast area between October and Christmas 1943. He returned to France by a Lysander operation shortly before Christmas 1943.

There were, as described in Chapter XVII, three cross-Channel operations from Dartmouth to the Baie-de-la-Fresnaie, which lies between Cap-Fréhel and Saint-Cast, in November and early December 1943 for Commander Cohen's Section of SIS – INDIFFERENT and INDIFFERENT II (two attempts). Two agents were to have been landed in the course of these, but the expected reception committee did not materialise; one of the agents chose to land 'blind' in the second sortie, but the other declined. These were probably the three operations on which Charaudeau was a passenger. December 1943 was a disastrous month for the Lysander Flight of 161 Squadron: three pilots were lost, and the aircraft returning Charaudeau to France must have been one of two that crashed on 16/17 December when attempting to land back at Tangmere in a fog severe enough to have closed all the airfields in southern England.

On his return to the field Charaudeau asked Allart to find a suitable pinpoint for putting his maritime project into effect. Allart chose a site at Ile-à-Canton, just south of Ile-Grande; this was accepted by DDOD(I). Charaudeau told his audience in 1987 that the first operation was fixed for the night of 9/10 February 1944, but Slocum's records show that the GLOVER I operation to Ile-à-Canton took place on 23 February. Charaudeau said he took part in the reception committee for this operation himself, with Allart and a W/T operator named Jonquet, transmitting on a set code-named 'Arsenic'. They were received and lodged by the Briand/Le Goff family for three days.

More than 50 agents are said to have worked for the 'Alibi-Maurice' organisation along the coast between Cherbourg and Brest. Two W/T transmitter/receivers, 'Tosti' and 'Nicotine', were attached to this subsection and were operated by two first-class naval radio-telegraphists, Yves Daniel and Isidore Duval.

'Alibi' acted as a collecting and dispatching agency for the intelligence from four other SIS networks that lacked rapid means of transmission. This material was placed by them in safe 'letter-boxes'.

David Birkin was involved in, and has left the official reports on, the naval side of six of the nine GLOVER operations.

Even by Breton standards, the Ile-Grande–Ile-Losquet area is a particularly broken piece of coast, fringed with numerous off-lying rocks and islets of pink granite that had to be skirted in boat-work, a process complicated by tidal streams of great strength. It says much for the efficiency of the surf-boat crews by this time that they succeeded in carrying out landings at such formidable pinpoints and in such difficult conditions. This was the area of which Davis had observed, 'Of all the festering collections of rocks on this rotten coast, the Ile-Losquet area wins the hamburger.'

The first GLOVER operation was carried out by MGB 503 on 23/24 February 1944. Mike Marshall was in command; David Birkin was navigating; Whitelaw of SIS and Lt Commander Guest, USN, were on board as conducting officer and observer respectively. Guest's presence at Dartmouth was followed a few weeks later by the arrival of two US Navy PT boats to train alongside the 15th MGB Flotilla for clandestine sea-transport work.

When 503 took her departure from Start Point the weather was moderate, with wind ENE 4–5 and sea 3, but the north-easterly swell was enough to make steering on the southerly course difficult. Earlier forecasts had suggested that conditions would improve, but unhappily they did not. The wind increased and the sea became rough, so that at 2154 hrs it was found necessary to reduce speed from the initial 20 knots. The gunboat overriding the sea and swell repeatedly seemed, in Marshall's words to be 'standing on her stern'. Although the conditions were far below the operational standard for boatwork, Marshall decided to ascertain if a windward shore might be found at the planned anchorage off Ile-Losquet.

The engines were silenced and speed further reduced at 2248. At 2310 the Triagoz light was sighted; it passed abeam to starboard at a distance of 3 km. (2 miles) seven minutes later. At 2350 they stopped for a fix and sighted land, altering course towards it when they got under way using only one engine. The weather seemed to improve, but only very slightly, and they anchored in 10 fathoms, with Losquet plainly visible 1,500 metres away; these were about the maximum conditions for boatwork that could be expected. The dinghy was lowered and loaded. Sub Lt Smith, who was to be in charge, was told that, if the weather proved too strong, they were to return forthwith. Smith reached Losquet quite quickly and found that it provided a good weather shore. On turning the south-west corner of the island, the dinghy soon reached the beach, as it was low water of a spring tide and the beach between Losquet and Ile-à-Canton had dried out to a considerable distance. The sea was calm and very little surf was experienced in this position.

The agents were about 200 metres apart on the beach where the boat landed. They had not been using light signals, as these would have been dangerous owing to the proximity of the enemy convoy route and the Triagoz lighthouse, but as the boat touched down they challenged in loud voices. Business was quickly transacted and a walkie-talkie was handed over to them for use on subsequent operations in view of the risks attendant on the use of normal light signals. It was to prove a very useful piece of equipment. The dinghy returned with the mail at 0120.

They weighed anchor and spent a few minutes in securing both anchor and surf-boats while 503 still had the benefit of a weather shore. After passing Triagoz, courses and speeds were dictated by the weather. At 0455 it was found necessary to alter course to the eastward as the very rough beam sea was becoming dangerous. A great deal of water was shipped and carried away the lashings of the forward towing bridle, allowing it to move freely, which only damaged paintwork; but the water also broke the perspex screen on the bridge, carried away the oar lashings and washed four oars overboard, as well as washing down below decks. Water also leaked into the W/T cabin, putting the W/T transmitter out of action, which made it impossible to pass a signal at 0640 giving position, course and speed. Oilskins and raincoats thrown over the W/T sets proved inadequate to protect them and it was not until 0900 that they were sufficiently dried for a signal to be sent. Dartmouth was entered at 0940. Marshall reported to DDOD(I) that, although most of the crew had been seasick all night, their behaviour was splendid and no engine trouble was experienced.

MGB 503 sailed again on 21 March to carry out GLOVER II. Once more David Birkin was navigating and Whitelaw accompanied the expedition on behalf of Commander Cohen's Section of SIS. MGB 503 proceeded in company with her sister ship 502, which was on her way to Beg-an-Fry for SEPTIMUS II. The weather was good, with a light north-westerly wind, slight sea and no swell. There was, however, a slight haze, which made it difficult to judge distances accurately. The lights at the Sept-Iles and Ile-de-Batz were flashing as they approached the French coast, but the Triagoz light was extinguished, though both the lighthouse and the rocks could be seen quite clearly.

At 2346 vessels were sighted on the port bow and course was altered to starboard while the matter was investigated. It was not immediately apparent in which direction they were heading and course was again altered to starboard and the wing engines stopped. There were at least four, possibly five, vessels, travelling at no great speed, identifiable as enemy E-boats about 100 feet long, with no, or very short, masts and low in the water. Their course proved to be easterly and 503 therefore proceeded on a course to the south-west until they were out of sight. At 0018, 503 attempted very slowly and with great caution to approach the Ile-Losquet anchorage. Visibility was now extremely poor and no points ashore could be recognised except for the general outlines of Losquet itself. Soundings caused concern as they shoaled to 6 fathoms, which was entirely unexpected. At 0047 the south-western side of Losquet was recognised, together with the bombing target the Germans had built on the island to simulate a ship. MGB 503 decided to anchor, but the strong northerly tide had set the gunboat well to the north of her intended position and, although 55 fathoms of grass line were used, the anchor would not hold. By this time the small rocks off the island were under water and manoeuvring promised to be dangerous, so the anchor had to be weighed and course set to the south-west before reanchoring in 13 fathoms. The tide was estimated to be running at 3 knots and Sub Lt Smith, in charge of the boat party, was instructed to return if it proved too strong. MGB 503's position turned out to be closer to the shore than at first estimated, though the visibility made it difficult to get good bearings.

The boat left the parent ship at 0125. The very strong tide turned her compass course of due south into an actual track of 151°. The crew could clearly hear and see the surf on Losquet as they approached. They rounded the southern tip of Losquet and explored among the many jagged rocks and attendant surf for a suitable landing-place on Ile-à-Canton. The boat grounded on a beach at 0155, but as there was no sign of a reception committee Sub Lt Smith and Whitelaw climbed to the nearest high point to see if they could see anyone. Whitelaw was convinced no-one was there and, after a fruitless attempt to make contact with the R/T set, Smith decided it was inexpedient to delay return to the mother ship any longer. The return journey was gruelling, but the boat was alongside at 0225.

The very strong northerly tidal set, which was running at 3–3.5 knots, made it extremely difficult to weigh anchor and eventually the wing engines had to be used to keep the ship's head in the right direction. The anchor was finally aweigh and course was set to the north-west. In the light of what happened on the third and final attempt to pick up mail from the Ile-à-Canton pinpoint, it seems possible that the starting and use of two engines so close to the shore alerted the Germans and led to increased vigilance in that area.

As 503 approached the German convoy route slowly, a vessel was sighted right ahead c. 1.6 km. (1 mile) away. The gunboat's engines were stopped immediately and the ship's head steadied in order to ascertain the enemy's course. A further four E-boats of the type sighted earlier were observed in line ahead, proceeding west at very slow speed. It was assumed this might be a patrol or the outer screen of a convoy, but nothing could be seen to the eastward and course was therefore set in that direction. Courses and speeds had to be altered in order to clear their convoy route as quickly as possible. A sharp look-out revealed nothing further. Courses and speeds were now set to the northward, allowance having been made for the instructions received as to the dispositions of other British forces. It was an uneventful passage and the Dartmouth boom gate was reached at 0808.

MGB 503 went back on 22 April to carry out GLOVER III. Weather was good and visibility fair when they took their departure from Start Point, but when they had gone no more than 5 km. (3 miles) on their southerly course they ran into a bank of fog and visibility quickly closed down to 50 metres, and then to less than 25. A QH fix an hour later showed that they were making 20.5 knots but speed was temporarily reduced by a broken water pump on the port engine. The pump proved to be beyond repair, so the cooling system was coupled up to the auxiliary engine pump and with this the engine could be run at 1,100 r.p.m. With the other two engines at 1,400 r.p.m. she was able to maintain a cruising speed of 18 knots.

As they neared Triagoz, clearer patches were encountered, but visibility remained poor. Marshall therefore decided to reduce speed 5 km. (3 miles) further to the north than originally intended as, from the intelligence received and their own experience on GLOVER II, there was a possibility that the Germans were maintaining an outer patrol.

Visibility improved as they closed in on Ile-Losquet and land was sighted on the port hand. At 0145 during the final approach, the fog lifted completely and the land and off-lying rocks were clearly defined. They anchored at 0158 and Whitelaw (who appears in the report as 'Lieutenant', though Charaudeau called him 'Major') quickly established contact on the R/T with the reception committee and code words were exchanged. Whitelaw was confident that they would be at the pinpoint used in GLOVER I. The surf-boat left at 0207 with Sub Lt Smith again in charge.

The boat reached the southernmost point of Ile-Losquet without incident and, shortly after this, R/T contact was again made with the reception committee, who confirmed that they would be at the GLOVER I pinpoint. The boat proceeded in that direction but the reception committee passed a message that the boat could not be seen. Smith therefore had the boat rowed back 100 metres to seaward to give them a better chance of sighting it, but without luck. They closed in on the beach on a northerly course. When they were a mere 20 metres from the shore, the reception committee informed Whitelaw, who was conducting the exchange in French, that there were Germans at the pinpoint and that they must leave immediately.

Since the SN1 surf-boats were double-ended, it was not even necessary to turn the boat round. Smith hastily transferred his steering oar to the opposite end of the boat and Leading Seaman Hibbert and Stoker Andrews swivelled round on their thwarts and shifted their oars, and the boat was off back to the southern end of Losquet, where it was found that a bank of fog had reduced visibility to approximately 50 metres. Course was set for the parent ship and R/T contact was established on the MAB equipment, requesting a homing signal. Thanks to this, the gunboat was sighted ahead at 40 metres. As soon as the dinghy was alongside, all possible haste was made to hoist it inboard, to weigh anchor and set course to the northward. The Triagoz light was seen quite clearly, but half an hour later 503 ran into a dense bank of fog. She reached Dartmouth at 0830 without further incident.

An alternative pinpoint was agreed in signals exchanged between London and the agent: it was on the north side of the Ile-Grande and six further operations were carried out to it. A first attempt at GLOVER IV was made on 19 May by two US PT boats, 71 and 72. No detailed report of it has come into the author's hands, but it is known to have been unsuccessful since, as emerged later, the reception committee were not there, having been delayed by travelling difficulties.

A second, attempt, this time successful, was made by the same two PT boats on 24 May. In addition to their normal complement of officers and men, Peter Williams, commanding officer of MGB 502 and senior officer of the 15th MGB Flotilla, was on board PT72 as commanding officer of the expedition, David Birkin accompanied him as navigating officer and Sub Lt Andrew Smith and two ratings from MGB 503 formed the leading boat's crew. The telegraphist of MGB 502 was also carried, together with Lt Whitelaw as conducting officer. Some difficulty was experienced from the outset as the flux-gate gyromagnetic compass was out of order and the ship had to be steered by a magnetic compass for which there was no deviation card. The flux-gate eventually functioned but not satisfactorily, as it swung continually and at times appeared to stick. However, Birkin obtained occasional fixes by QH and the ship maintained a fairly accurate course on the passage as far as Triagoz. At 2325, only an hour and 20 minutes after slipping from Dartmouth, the Sept-Iles light was sighted fine on the port bow. At 0027 hrs on 25 May all three engines suddenly cut out and it was found that the fuel filters were blocked. The ship had to be stopped for about 10 minutes while they were cleaned. At 0040 engines were restarted and course and speed were resumed.

At 0104 a large object was sighted on the port bow and the ship was stopped for two minutes to investigate. It turned out to be one of the larger of the Sept-Iles, clearly visible at a distance of 11 km. (7 miles). Although the Sept-Iles, Triagoz and Ile-de-Batz lights were showing during the approach, there was no standard compass available for taking bearings and estimated bearings relative to the ship's head only could be passed to the navigator, so that the ship found itself too far to the west and had to alter course radically to reach the anchorage, steering 097° for the last 20 minutes of the silent approach. At this distance, the land offered no immediate clues that might assist a landing. Just to help matters, the steering gear broke down at 0159 and for about five minutes the boat had to be steered on her engines. At 0222, when the characteristics of the land left no doubt that the correct position had been reached, both boats were lowered and preparations were made to anchor. The anchor was dropped at 0225 but did not hold and dragged back until a small rock called Ouerser-Sant-Duzec, showing about 60 cm. above the water, was discovered only about 3 metres away to port. Anchor was weighed with much haste and the ship was anchored again in 9 fathoms, closer to Le-Corbeau rock. The anchor never did hold properly and until 0309 the boat dragged gradually down towards Ouerser.

In the meantime the two surf-boats had left, walkie-talkie contact having been made at about 0225 with the party on the beach. Because of the low tide, Smith had some difficulty in identifying the pinpoint, but Lt Whitelaw requested the reception committee by walkie-talkie to show a light, which enabled contact to be made. Two bags of mail were brought back but no personnel were embarked. At 0257 the boats were sighted returning and at 0307 they were alongside. At 0309 boats were inboard, centre engine was started and anchor was weighed.

It was found at once that the steering gear had failed completely and PT72 started circling on centre engine only, dangerously near the Ouerser rock. It was decided to start wing engines but the port engine refused to start and until 0329 the boat circled helplessly round the rocks. However, the first lieutenant managed to rig the emergency hand-tiller steering and by 0332 it was possible to turn the ship slowly to starboard and steer clear of the rocks. Soon afterwards the port engine was started and course was set for home. The steering could not be repaired and the ship simply zigzagged her way back from Ile-Grande to Dartmouth, the commanding officer conning the ship by telephone to the men on the tiller aft.

Williams's report ended by saying that, apart from the commanding officer of PT72, who behaved with commendable calm and efficiency, and possibly some of the engine-room personnel, the other officers and crew appeared to be inexperienced and were far too complacent about the various breakdowns. Only stern encouragement from Sub Lt Smith and himself, when auxiliary steering had to be rigged or the anchor weighed in a hurry, obviated even greater difficulties.

Sub Lt Smith handled his part of the operation with admirable efficiency and speed and was certainly one of the best officers in the

15th Flotilla at this kind of work. Williams considered that much credit was due also to Lt Birkin for the way in which he handled and solved the difficulty with compasses. With very few minor alterations, Williams added, a PT boat could be made most suitable for this type of work.

Five further operations in the GLOVER series were carried out during the summer of 1944 to this new pinpoint on the north side of Ile-Grande, all by MGB 318 (Lt Jan McQuoid Mason, SANF(V)), the original 'C'-Class gunboat allocated to Slocum two years previously. MGB 318 had seen much hard service and her sustained cruising speed on passage was now sometimes no better than 15 or 16 knots (on the FELICITATE operation six months earlier she had actually averaged only 14). Indeed, Lt Cdr Bevil Warington Smyth, SOE's representative at the Helford base, wrote at the end of the war that many officers and men had been astonished that DDOD(I) should be compelled to use such a slow and antiquated gunboat (presumably through Admiralty inability or reluctance to provide him with a better vessel) in an operation of such admitted high priority as FELICITATE in the fourth winter of the war. 'Even allowing,' he continued, 'for German superiority in high-speed diesel marine engineering, the cynical observer was inclined to feel that the disparity in speed between the 35-knot E-boats (which were roaming the Channel as far west as the Scillies) and the 15-knot MGB 318 (employed for close approach to enemy territory on operations of high priority) was unduly great.'

Warington Smyth had suffered both injury and frustration during the war. He had lost a foot while flying with the Fleet Air Arm and he had seen SOE's Helford base relegated to the status of a training establishment. To be fair to the Admiralty, MGBs 502 and 503 had joined the 15th MGB Flotilla and become operational during the winter of 1943/44 and the 'D'-Class MGB 718, whose speed was similar to that of the German E-boats, had been sent straight from her builder's yard to work up and serve DDOD(I)'s needs in the spring of 1944. Conditions in the Channel had, moreover, changed significantly as 1944 wore on: the Luftwaffe no longer regularly flew the offensive sweeps that a year before had made it necessary to provide fighter escorts for DDOD(I)'s gunboats setting out to the north coast of Brittany in daylight and returning thence next morning. In 1943, MGB 318's slow speed had led to a suspension of cross-Channel operations from March until September, when the longer nights provided greater cover. In 1944, it was no longer considered foolhardy to send her south to carry out the GLOVER mail-run even during the short nights in June, July and August, sometimes without air cover, though the records show that this was still being provided, in some cases, as late as August.

GLOVER V was successfully completed by her on 17/18 June:

Slocum's 1946 report shows that she embarked mail, but no detailed account has survived. GLOVER VI, to land stores and pick up mail, failed on 16 July for lack of a reception committee.

GLOVER VII, whose objects were similar, took place only a week later (23/24 July) in fine weather – wind westerly, Force 2, slight WSW swell, sea slight – and these favourable conditions prevailed throughout the operation. Coastal Command aircraft were maintaining a good watch and persisted in flying across them as they headed south. One embarrassing incident occurred when a Wellington illuminated them with its submarine hunting Leigh light; 318 replied with a two-star recognition, one of which failed to ignite. However, the aircraft switched on its navigation lights in a friendly gesture and continued on its way. Navigation was left to the skill of David Birkin, who, with the use of QH, was able to give them the correct look-out bearings and place the ship within sight of Le-Corbeau rock.

Contact with the shore party was established at 0137 and they anchored eight minutes later a few yards east of their planned position. The SN1 surf-boat left ten minutes later. Gordon and Markham, two able-bodied seamen who had rowed in every one of 318's operations since the beginning of the previous winter, were again the boat's crew, and Sub Lt Bell was in charge. The SN1 surf-boat was back alongside at 0249 after a successful contact with the reception committee, though a fault in the ship's R/T set had prevented communication while the boat was away. The return passage to Dartmouth was uneventful.

MGB 318 had proved capable of 19 knots cruising speed, though admittedly conditions were ideal.

GLOVER VIII took place only six nights later (29/30 July). The object on this occasion was to embark Guy Lemoine as well as his mail. At the briefing on the afternoon of the operation, it was decided to sail 318 about 30 minutes earlier than originally planned, owing to the unfavourable weather report, which made it likely that speed would have to be reduced through engine trouble or sea. The timetable was otherwise too exacting under adverse conditions.

They left Dartmouth at 2114 and took their departure from a position off Start Point. The sea there was moderate, yet uncomfortable enough to make them wish they had done so from the Dart buoy, well clear of the disturbed waters south of Start. The wind was WSW Force 4–5 with a moderate south-westerly swell. There were not many white horses about and Mason thought that the spell of Force 5 was from the depression travelling eastward, as forecast by RAF Coastal Command, St Eval.

At 2213 trouble was reported from the engine-room and the first lieutenant was sent down to investigate. Speed was reduced to 15 knots and Bell reported that the port engine had a cracked manifold exhaust leaking badly over the distributor and likely to cause a fire: the centre engine oil temperature was also far too high. He added that the motor mechanic was being violently seasick, which made Mason think that the defects had perhaps been exaggerated. He sent Bell down again to see if the leak could be prevented from running over the distributor: this was done and he also placed a hand ready with a Pyrene fire extinguisher to in case a conflagration should occur. With reduction in speed, the centre engine returned to normal, indicating that there had been a temporary obstruction in the oil coolers. Until then, there had been a grave danger that the operation would have to be abandoned because of engine trouble; and the unseasonable weather almost tilted the scales in that direction. They proceeded at 17.5 knots to ease the engines and Mason instructed the engine room to report any immediate change in that department, while Birkin took a QH check on speed made good. Everything held well and they continued to log 17.5 knots, which would give them ten minutes in hand when the Triagoz came abeam.

Once again, Coastal Command aircraft were much in evidence and again one illuminated them with a beam from its Leigh light. Flak was seen in the Lézardrieux direction.

At 0115, they reduced speed, as they were actually running ahead of schedule, and the moon, still high and very bright, showed no signs of being obscured by cloud, although it was in fact hidden by haze ten minutes before it set at 0210. Engines were silenced. The Sept-Iles light (lit) was sighted at 0130 and Triagoz at 0222. At 0229 they further reduced speed to 10 knots when Triagoz was bearing N 78° W: the coastline was dimly visible through glasses. Seven minutes later a QH fix confirmed they were too far to the eastward, so course was altered to cross the Sausage Bank. At 0245 the Corbeau rock was identified and the ship conned in to the anchorage. While they were preparing to anchor, the conducting officer reported that he had made contact with the shore party by R/T and that everything was in order.

They anchored in 12 fathoms, a little closer inshore than usual, and also closer to Le-Corbeau to take advantage of the shelter these rocks afforded the boat's crew. The wind was WSW4, moderate westerly swell, haze on horizon, visibility about 1.6 km. (1 mile). The swell was high and Ouerser rock, which had 3 metres of water over it, was a swirling mass of foam.

Bell left at 0303, again with Gordon and Markham as oarsmen. They embarked Lemoine and the mail and returned to the ship at 0345. They made extensive use of the lee of the rocks and, when returning, rowed well beyond the ship before coming down with wind and swell as they crossed the open patch. Bell reported that the pinpoint beach was dead calm and it was like entering a lagoon. Considering the swell running, Mason felt the boat's crew did exceedingly well.

They weighed anchor and proceeded clear of the area at 0357, three minutes before their allotted time limit. Most of the lighthouses were operating, but no enemy traffic was sighted.

Coastal Command aircraft were as much in evidence on the return as they had been on the outward passage and at 0528 a Wellington again illuminated them with its Leigh light. Two Spitfires appeared at the agreed rendezvous at 0625 and gave the gunboat excellent air cover until it was well in sight of Start Point.

At 0645 the wind was NW4, moderate WNW swell, moderate sea, visibility good, but from then on weather improved and Start Bay was calm and sunny.

Further engine trouble was reported at 0655 – fuel starvation on the port engine – and the rest of the passage was completed by hand-pumping the fuel.

In view of the fact that all other Coastal Forces patrols in the Plymouth command had returned to harbour rather than continue their operation, Mason felt some statement on the weather was called for. For the first two hours it had been bad: many of the crew had been ill, including 318's well-hardened coxswain, but at no time had the ship laboured. Perhaps her trim was better than it had been, for she did not pound, though the bridge was as wet as on any previous occasion. After careful study of the Beaufort Scale, he did not think the wind force had ever been greater than 5. The boat's own speed often tended to increase the relative wind velocity and give a false impression: it was better to judge by the appearance of the sea. On the return passage the bridge was comparatively dry, spray coming over only occasionally.

Mason finished his report to DDOD(I) by expressing thanks to his navigator, Lt Birkin, and his first lieutenant, Sub Lt Bell, who carried out their duties with a high degree of efficiency. Most of the crew had been miserably ill and, knowing that other forces had returned to harbour, were cursing him for 'a mad so-and-so'.

Lemoine, the agent embarked on GLOVER VIII, was landed back on Ile-Grande by MGB 318 on the night of 5/6 August in the course of Operation GLOVER IX. No details of this mission are available, as David Birkin was not navigating. Lemoine made his way with his team ahead of the advancing American troops to Brest, where he remained throughout the siege, sending W/T messages daily reporting on the state of the German defences.

The Germans hunkered down in a series of such enclaves on the French Atlantic coast and remained in most of them until VE-Day, nine months later, though Brest itself fell into Allied hands within a few weeks: the rest of the Breton shore was free. DDOD(I)'s ships made expeditions from their Dartmouth and Helford bases to photograph the coast of France; to land stores, medical supplies and ammunition on SOE's behalf for the French Forces of the Interior (FFI), who were besieging the German redoubts; to embark returning agents; to visit pinpoints familiar only by night; and to make contact with the men and women who had formed the reception committees for this long series of nocturnal visitations to German-occupied Brittany. Nevertheless, the era of clandestine operations was at an end: the sea lines had served their purpose.

There had been some 120 genuinely clandestine operations from United Kingdom bases to the north and west coasts of France since the armistice of June 1940. Many required more than one sortie: one involved no fewer than ten. They are listed chronologically and summarised in Appendix A. Documentary evidence for operations by fishing vessels between July 1940 and May 1941 is fragmentary and the oral testimony in respect of the events in September 1940 somewhat confused. The list also includes 13 non-clandestine missions to liberated territory for SIS and SOE.

Slocum's recommendations for awards to the officers and ratings who took part in these operations are to be found in Appendix C.

CHAPTER XXI

Escapes by Sea from Brittany: 1940–44

T o complete this account of the clandestine sea lines to Brittany, mention must be made of escapes from Britanny, organised from within occupied France, on vessels lying in French ports.

It is not easy to assemble the full facts on this subject. There was no central control and there is no comprehensive record, though a considerable number of monuments on the Breton coast bear witness to exploits that were an epic of the Resistance. The list in Appendix B should perhaps be regarded as illustrative rather than exhaustive.[1]

Setting aside the many departures that took place before the armistice on vessels of every kind, there were escapes from Breton ports on at least 26 vessels before the end of 1940. Some, like Guéguen's *Pourquoi-Pas?* and Louis Tanguy's *Primel* made more than one voyage: others made a single crossing, left passengers in British ports or transferred them at sea to vessels fishing off the Cornish coast and then returned to their home ports. Some of these voyages were directly relevant to the development of Allied intelligence networks in the early days: Moreau, Mansion, Lomenech and Barlier all reached England initially or returned to England from missions to France, or both, on fishing vessels based in French ports.

The arrest of the *Monique* on 3 January 1941 at Douarnenez when she was preparing a large-scale escape provoked severe retribution and marked the end of the halcyon days in which fishing boats came and went fairly freely between the two countries across the line of war. German suspension of all fishing, though only temporary, enhanced the risk of denunciation by those who felt their livelihood to be at stake, and German controls became more systematic and difficult to evade. There was no further escape from Douarnenez until April 1943 (*Dalc'h-Mad*), but there were successful crossings from Paimpol and Loguivy on the north coast in January 1941, as well as one failure from Saint-Cast soon afterwards. Larger vessels reached England from Concarneau in September and November that same year.

Although escapes from the north coast had become difficult, a motor launch named *La-Korrigane* got away successfully from Bréhat in January 1942. Her passengers were picked up by an Royal Navy minesweeper and taken into Portsmouth: they included a future naval ADC to General de Gaulle[2] and the future captain of a Fighting French submarine.[3]

Ernest Sibiril was a boatbuilder with a yard on the Penzé River between Pont-de-la-Corde and Carentec, and at the end of June 1940 had repaired the engine of Jacques Guéguen's *Pourquoi-Pas?*, thus enabling him to continue to ferry clandestine passengers to England. In February 1942, Sibiril organised Guéguen's own escape on a small boat named *André* with his son and two other people. Guéguen, then aged 72, had been twice imprisoned by the Germans. He had been released temporarily on medical grounds and decided that another Channel crossing, even in winter, was preferable to serving the rest of his sentence in gaol at Rennes. Sibiril repeated the operation in July to enable five volunteers for the Fighting French forces to get to England with a consignment of intelligence mail. In the interval between these two departures, two boys aged 15 and 16 had escaped from Térénez-en-Plouézoc'h on the other side of Morlaix Bay on a small cutter-rigged open boat named *Yolande*.[4]

There were two attempted escapes from Camaret that year: *Sirène* got to England, but *Foederis Arca* did not.

Ernest Sibiril was only just getting into his stride: his yard was frequented by numbers of almost identical, small, sloop-rigged local vessels, all painted black with a white line along their sheer strake. These were used to collect sand and seaweed – much used in Brittany as a fertiliser – or for fishing. Sibiril set out to make it as difficult as possible for the local representatives of the GAST, the German military customs service, to keep track of movements of this flock of small boats, and succeeded brilliantly. When they came to enquire what had happened to a boat that had disappeared, he would show them pieces of wreckage and persuade them that the boat in question was no longer seaworthy and had been broken up. Between February and the end of June 1943 he managed to dispatch to England a further nine small vessels carrying no fewer than 105 passengers. His audacity and success, though greatly admired in London, raised fears for his safety and on 23 June a message broadcast on the BBC's French Service called on him to come to England himself.

The operation in July 1943, on which Sibiril, was not a passenger, was the only failure in the series: the *Armorick* sailed on the 17th with 18 passengers, in daylight since it was no longer possible to do so by night. After eight days, during which she had sailed round Guernsey and called at Trébeurden in Lannion Bay, she arrived back at the Ile-Callot, which lies off Carentec, having presumably been defeated by the weather. Her crew and passengers were not caught, but the Germans must have had wind of the event, since they ordered the Ile-Callot to be evacuated by its inhabitants. The five Le Ven brothers, who lived there and had contributed

much to previous escapes, decided it was time for them to leave, which they did, with two other people, on a boat called the *Pirate*.

At this point Ernest Sibiril went into hiding and asked his father, Alain, then 70 years old, to build him a boat on which he could himself cross the Channel to safety. Sibiril Senior, helped by two trusted shipwrights, complied. The new boat was built behind a partition closing off a narrow space at the inner end of the yard's covered building-shed. Her keel was arranged on stocks at right angles to the main axis of the shed. With these precautions the building operation was concealed from casual inspection. It was not until the night of 31 October that this boat, which they named *Requin*, was launched, had her mast stepped, her rigging set up, her sails bent, and escaped, carrying Ernest, his brother Léon, a son of Commandant Guizien who had been a passenger on the unfortunate *Armorick*, two other Morlaix inhabitants, a secret agent from Marseilles named Paul Daniel and an RAF pilot.

In the three months that had elapsed between the Sibirils' 13th and 14th operations, there had been an astonishing recrudescence of escapes from west-coast Breton ports. On 12 August, *La-Rose-Éffeuillée*, an old sardine *pinasse* converted into a cutter-rigged crabber, sailed from Morgat in daylight and picked up 19 passengers at a secluded and carefully chosen site on the east side of the Crozon peninsula, before setting course to England. On the following day, the *Rullanec*, a small, 5-m. cutter-rigged open boat, also sailed from Morgat in daylight with six on board. They landed at Penzance.

Ten days later a 19-m. sardine *pinasse* named *Moise* put to sea from Douarnenez with a seven-day fishing permit. She returned clandestinely on 23 August and picked up passengers from Porz-Lanvers. With 22 on board, including crew, they landed at Newlyn. This operation was organised by Victor Salez, Syndic des Gens de Mer at Douarnenez, at the request of a French naval lieutenant, Yves Le Henaff of the Aéronavale. It was jointly financed by MI9 and Paillole's Direction de la Surveillance du Territoire (DST), the Algiers-based French counter-espionage service.

There were escapes via, or from, Concarneau on 29 August and 9 September: two of the three boats concerned carried 12 and 7 passengers respectively. Then on 19 September a 17-m.-long liner named *Ar-Voulac'h* carried out a second escape organised by Yves Le Hénaff with the assistance of Victor Salez. On this occasion 25 passengers were smuggled on board at night in Rosmeur harbour at Douarnenez from a nearby sardine factory. They landed at Newlyn. Salez was forced to go into hiding in a garden shed: it was given out that he had gone to Le-Grau-du-Roi on the Mediterranean coast.

There were apparently two further escapes from Concarneau in September, on the *Anas* and the *Marpha*, though the list in the museum on the Ile-de-Sein does not show how many people they carried. On 2 October an 11-m.-long cutter named *La-Pérouse* sailed from Douarnenez with 22 on board, including Victor Salez, two French naval lieutenants and two US airmen – a third escape operation organised by Le Hénaff.

In October 1943 there was an escape from the Ile-de-Sein with four passengers; another from Camaret or Morgat organised by a BCRA/MI9 agent named J.C. Camors on the *Suzanne-Renée* carrying 19 shot-down airmen; and a further escape from Camaret of a 7-m., half-decked, sloop-rigged crabber. This vessel, *L'Yvonne*, was to have carried airmen left behind by the *Suzanne-Renée* but German surveillance was by then so tight that this proved impossible and she crossed to Newlyn under sail carrying only her crew of four. Sadly, just before these two successful escapes, Camors had been killed in Rennes by the German agent code-named Roger Le Légionnaire, who had inflicted much damage on earlier escape organisations operating in Brittany.

Le Hénaff met a young man named Yvon Jézéquel (*see* Chapter XX) of Lézardrieux whose ambition was to join the French navy. Together they worked out a plan to use an official French light-house-tender named *La-Horaine* on one of her regular visits to the Roches-Douvres lighthouse. They overcame the German armed guard placed on board the vessel on these expeditions but, owing to poor visibility, they failed to pick up a group of 20 would-be escapers who were waiting for them and had to cross to Dartmouth without them on 22/23 November 1943.

On 22 January 1944 a last large-scale escape took place on the *Breiz-Izel* from Tréboul, whose natural harbour lies immediately to the west of modern Douarnenez. It was financed with help from Georges Broussine, organiser of a BCRA escape line named 'Bourgogne'. There were 31 passengers on board – 12 Allied airmen evaders and 19 volunteers for the Fighting French forces, including Yves Vourc'h, the youngest of four sons of the doctor at Plomodiern. His three elder brothers had each escaped in turn to join the Fighting French forces, while Dr Vourc'h, their father, had escaped to French North Africa to seek safety when his involvement in the 'Johnny' intelligence network and other local Resistance activities had made flight necessary.

On 3 February 1944, Le Hénaff arranged for a small cargo coasting vessel named the *Jouet-des-Flots* to pick up 31 escapers from Ile-Tudy. They were a distinguished company and included Pierre Brossolette, Emile Bollaert, Emile Laffon and Jacques Maillet, who had been trying to get to London by an air pick-up operation for three months, but had been defeated by bad weather. The ship suffered damage by striking the bottom when entering Port-Tudy to pick up the passengers. The resulting leak got worse as they headed north for the Pointe-du-Raz in bad weather, and the engine was flooded. The skipper, Le Bris, managed to run the ship ashore in the Feunten-Aod creek near Plogoff. Brossolette, Bollaert and Le Hénaff were arrested, but Maillet and Laffon escaped to Paris.

Ernest Sibiril's own escape on the *Requin* on 31 October 1943 did not bring his family's epic series of operations to an end. The 15th and last escape by sea from Pont-de-la-Corde took place on 22 February 1944, when a second boat, built clandestinely by Ernest's father, Alain, and his two trusted shipwrights, in the record time of ten days, was launched at night and left with 22 local fishermen and seaweed-gatherers on board. They called the boat *Amity*. Between them, the two master shipwrights, Ernest and Alain, had made possible the flight to England of at least 146 people, including 12 Allied airmen on the run. To this remarkable total should be added the stragglers and volunteers whom Jacques Guéguen carried to England after Ernest repaired the engine of *Pourquoi-Pas?* at the end of June 1940, thus enabling Guéguen to resume his evacuations. No port in France can boast a prouder record in those sombre years of defeat and humiliation than the villages of Carentec and Pont-de-la-Corde, which lies above it on the Penzé River.

Footnotes

Chapter I

1 This chapter is based upon Sir Winston Churchill's *The Second World War*, Vol. II, Charles de Gaulle's *Mémoires de Guerre*, Vol. I, Sir Edward Spears's *Assignment to Catastrophe* and Jean Lacouture's fine *De Gaulle: The Rebel, 1890–1944*.

2 J. Lacouture: *De Gaulle: The Rebel, 1890–1944*, p. 147.

3 Guderian was Germany's leading proponent of mobile armoured warfare.

4 C. de Gaulle: *Mémoires de Guerre*, Vol. I, *L'Appel 1940–1942*, quoted by Lacouture.

5 Unpublished record by Admiral Odend'hal of de Gaulle's first meeting with Churchill (French naval archives via C. de V. Claude Huan).

6 *Mémoires de Guerre*, Vol. I, p. 44.

7 *De Gaulle: The Rebel, 1890–1944*, pp. 200–01.

8 Ibid., p. 189.

9 Ibid., p. 201, recording interview with G. Chaudron de Courcel.

10 Ibid., pp. 158–9 and 201.

11 N. Barber: *The Week that France Fell: June 1940*.

12 Laurent subsequently made his way to Tangier and Rabat. Charles Luizet, Military Attaché at the French Consulate-General at Tangier, offered his services to de Gaulle on 28 June and reported to him on 4 July via the British Consulate-General that Laurent's attitude had been so very reserved that he and those who shared Luizet's pro-de Gaulle views had been extremely careful in their dealings with de Gaulle's ex-Principal Private Secretary (unnumbered telegram of 4 July 1940 from Consul-General, Tangier, to Foreign Office).

13 Mandel was one of the ex-ministers and parliamentarians who took passage for Morocco on 20 June on board the *Massilia*. On arrival at Casablanca he (though his name was wrongly transcribed 'Moorl' in the relevant Consulate telegram) and Campinchi contacted Bond, the British Consul, on 25 June to say that they, Daladier and Yvon Delbos were awaiting the Italian armistice terms before deciding whether they would stay in North Africa to assist in prosecuting the war. If not, they would wish to leave immediately for England together with about 30 parliamentarians, wives and French *savants* for whom they vouched. They requested an urgent reply regarding the possibility of transport. Bond thought that senior French officers in North Africa anxious to prosecute the war would take it amiss if these politicians were given assisted passage. The Foreign Office, thereto persuaded by Jean Monnet, took the same view. But on 26 June, when Duff Cooper and Lord Gort arrived at Rabat by flying boat, they were not allowed to meet any of the people on the *Massilia* they had come to see, though by this time all the latter wished to proceed to England if possible. Daladier's son has recorded that a British submarine was to be sent to collect his father but failed to arrive. This is a misunderstanding, for no British submarine was available anywhere in the area. On 1 July Churchill did ask the Admiralty to mount a rescue operation (op. cit., Vol. 2, p. 194),

but this would have been impossible, particularly after Operation CATA-
PULT on 2 July, as the *Massilia* lay under the shore batteries of Casablanca. By 4 July, Mandel was under house arrest ashore. He was
subsequently transferred to France and interned, before being deported
and later murdered.

14 *Mémoires de Guerre*, Vol. I, p. 212.

15 Section D War Diary in the SOE archives.

16 K.A. Merrick: *Flights of the Forgotten*, Chapter I.

17 Roger Huguen: *Par les Nuits les Plus Longues*, p. 61.

18 Letter to the author from Tom Long, who served at Helford with van Riel;
and personal knowledge of the author, who succeeded van Riel there in
August 1941.

19 *De Gaulle: The Rebel, 1890–1844*, p. 257, quoting H. Amouroux, *Paris-Match*,
15 November 1970.

20 H.B. Verity: *We Landed by Moonlight*; totals as counted by the author.

Chapter II

1 Christopher Andrew: *Secret Service*, p. 126.

2 Ibid.

3 Donald Maclachlan: *Room 40*; C. Andrew: *Secret Service*, pp. 168–9.

4 *Secret Service*, p. 373.

5 Ibid., pp. 386–8.

6 Ibid., p. 419.

7 Ibid., pp. 373–4.

8 Ibid., pp. 419–22.

9 Ibid., p. 407.

10 Ibid., pp. 469–70.

11 L. de Jong: *Het Koninkrijk der Nederlanden in de Twede Wereldoorlog*, Vol. 2, pp. 73–
105, *Secret Service*, pp. 533–4.

12 Ladislas Farago: *The Game of the Foxes*, p. 113.

13 F.H. Hinsley and others: *British Intelligence in the Second World War: Its Influence on
Strategy and Operations*, Vol. I, p. 57.

14 *Secret Service*, p. 576.

15 Ibid., p. 575.

16 Ibid., p. 575.

17 Ibid., pp. 591–2.

18 Ibid., p. 602.

19 Ibid., p. 612.

20 Ibid., p. 615.

21 M.R.D. Foot: *SOE in France*, p. 6.

22 Ibid., p. 7.

23 *British Intelligence in the Second World War*, Vol. I, p. 400.

Chapter III

1   P. Beesly: *Very Special Admiral*, pp. 123, 127, 132–6, 190–92.

2   The form of radio communications used was termed 'wireless telegraphy', hence W/T.

3   Letter from the late Wing-Commander Ron Hockey to the author.

4   Letters from Steven Mackenzie and Patrick Whinney to the author.

5   Westblatt, according to Whinney, ended up in prison, having been arrested while lunching with the Captain of HMS *Hornet*, the Coastal Forces base at Gosport.

6   Information given by Colonel Pierre Fourcaud to the author.

7   Information provided by Steven Mackenzie to the author.

8   *We Landed by Moonlight*, pp. 35–8.

Chapter IV

1   The records of Slocum's Section and those of the BCRA list this operation, but it is not referred to in Passy's *Souvenirs* or in any other published work known to the author.

2   Information provided to the author by David Brown, Head of Naval Historical Branch, MoD.

3   René Pichavant: *Clandestins de l'Iroise (1940–42)*, pp. 37–64.

4   Articles published in Nos 80, 81 & 82 of the *Revue de la France Libre* by Hubert Moreau in 1955 form the basis of the account of his escape and of his first mission in this chapter; and of the first part of his second mission in Chapter V.

Chapter V

1   Passy: *Souvenirs*, Vol. I, *2e Bureau, Londres*.

2 & 3. Jean Le Roux recorded (on tape) a conversation between Mansion, Daniel Lomenech and himself over lunch at Les-Sables-d'Olonne in 1982, not long before Mansion's death. In the course of this meeting Mansion mentioned Plougasnou and Pointe-de-Saint-Mathieu. BCRA records show Pointe-de-la-Chèvre as his landing-place.

4   A view advanced by Jean Le Roux in a letter to the author.

5   The author is indebted to Lt Col Moreau, Hubert Moreau's son, and to Capitaine de Vaisseau Claude Huan who contacted him, for the text of this unpublished article.

6   Letter from Patrick Whinney to the author.

7   Obituary published in *The Daily Telegraph*, 17 February 1991.

8   The author is indebted to Capitaine de Vaisseau Claude Huan for tracking down both this document — *Renseignements de Burgaud sur Douarnenez* — and Moreau's personal file.

9   Pichavant: *Clandestins de l'Iroise (1940–42)*, p. 87.

10 Huguen: *Par les Nuits les Plus Longues*, pp. 91 & 93.

11 Anonymous booklet entitled *Lieutenant de Vaisseau Hubert Moreau* communicated to the author by Capitaine de Vaisseau Claude Huan.

12 Letter from Patrick Whinney to the author.

13 This document was found by Capitaine de Vaisseau Claude Huan in the Free French naval archives.

14 Letter from Patrick Whinney to the author.

15 Doornik's first name is variously recorded as Jan, Jean and Ian.

16 Letter from Robert Barclay to the author.

17 *Clandestins de l'Iroise (1940–42)*, p. 172.

18 Document dated 6 September 1940, headed 'NOTE pour le Chef du 2ᵉ Bureau Marine' and marked 'SECRET PERSONNEL', bearing the references in pencil 77C/10 and A118, found by Capitaine de Vaisseau Claude Huan in the Free French naval archives.

19 Letter from Jean Le Roux to the author.

20 *Clandestins de l'Iroise (1940–42)*, p. 175.

21 Report in Free French naval archives found by Capitaine de Vaisseau Claude Huan.

22 *Clandestins de l'Iroise (1940–42)*, pp. 177–8.

23 I am indebted to Dr Keith Sword for this information. See also Josef Garlinski: *Poland in the Second World War* (Macmillan, 1985), pp. 53–6 & 78–82.

24 M.Z. Rygor-Slowikowski: *In the Secret Service: The Lighting of the Torch*, pp. 10 & 14.

25 Information provided to the author by Daniel Lomenech.

26 *Clandestins de l'Iroise (1940–42)*, Vol. 4, pp. 42–5.

27 *Par les Nuits les Plus Longues*, p. 72.

Chapter VI

1 Information supplied to the author by Daniel Lomenech.

2 *Par les Nuits les Plus Longues*, p. 174.

3 Abwehr document communicated to the author by Capitaine de Vaisseau Claude Huan (*Abwehrleitstelle Frankreich* Br. Nr 9419/3.41 g III M dated 15.4.1941).

4 Ibid.

5 *Clandestins de l'Iroise (1940–42)*, p. 181.

6 Ibid., p. 181.

7 & 8. *Souvenirs*, p. 88.

9 *Par les Nuits les Plus Longues*, p. 21.

10 *La Vie Exemplaire du Commandant d'Estiennes d'Orves*, by his children.

11 *Par les Nuits les Plus Longues*, p. 21.

12 *Clandestins de l'Iroise (1940–42)*, p. 131.

13 Ibid., p. 195.

14 Information received from Capitaine de Vaisseau Claude Huan.

15 *Par les Nuits les Plus Longues*, p. 20.

16 Ibid., p. 113.

17 J. Lacouture: *De Gaulle: The Rebel, 1890–1944*, p. 227.

18 Information communicated by Col P. Fourcaud.

19 Ibid.

20 *Clandestins de l'Iroise (1940–42)*, Vol. 2, pp. 37–51.

21 *Par les Nuits les Plus Longues*, p. 56.

22 The escapes of fishing vessels from Breton ports between June 1940 and the Liberation are listed in the museum on the Ile-de-Sein. The author is indebted to his brother and sister-in-law, Mr and Mrs O.R. Richards, for photographs and transcripts of the lists there exhibited.

23 *Par les Nuits les Plus Longues*, with supplementary information communicated to the author by Jean Le Roux and Daniel Lomenech.

24 Information from the relevant British archives. This unidentified man would seem to have been, by two months, the first emissary of SOE's Independent French (F) Section. His mission is not recorded by M.R.D. Foot in his *SOE in France*.

25 *Par les Nuits les Plus Longues*, p. 91 and footnote.

26 Ibid., p. 92 and footnote.

27 Ibid., p. 175.

28 A. Crawley: *De Gaulle*, pp. 140–41, quoting Kenneth Younger.

29 *Par les Nuits les Plus Longues*, p. 176.

30 Having had first-hand experience of this indiscipline, Lomenech decided to use British naval crews when Steven Mackenzie and he began fishing-boat operations to the west coast of Brittany for Slocum.

Chapter VII

1 The whole of this chapter is based upon information provided by Jean Le Roux in correspondence with the author.

2 Their names were Cywinski and Slonininski.

3 *British Intelligence in the Second World War*, Vol. IV, p. 93–9.

4 Ibid., pp. 99n & 237.

Chapter VIII

1 The author researched the life of Leslie Humphreys from all the available sources when he contributed an article on him to the *Dictionary of National Biography*.

2 There is a detailed account of this abortive operation in the SOE archives.

3 H.B. Verity: *We Landed by Moonlight*; K.A. Merrick: *Flights of the Forgotten*.

4 M.R.D. Foot: *SOE in France*, p. 62.

5 Ibid., pp. 153–4, 157–8, 166, 521.

6 Article by J. Le Tac in *Les Réseaux Action de la France Combattante 1940–1944*, a collective work published in 1986 by the Amicale des Anciens Chefs de Mission Action et de leurs Collaborateurs recrutés en France, pp. 105–12.

7 *SOE in France*, p. 66.

8 Minshall in his *G(u)ilt Edged* made no reference to the existence of this supporting team. The present account of Operation SHAMROCK is based

largely on an account communicated to the author by Capitaine de Vaisseau Jean Pillet. Pillet was a member of the team of agents lent by SOE. It is confirmed by ADM 234/52 (i).

9 P. Wilkinson and J. Astley: *Gubbins and SOE*.

10 *SOE in France*; M. Langley: *Anders Lassen, VC, MC: The Story of Anders Lassen and the Men who Fought with Him*; documents in the SOE archives; author's own knowledge.

11 *Par les Nuits les Plus Longues*; *Les Clandestins de l'Iroise (1940–42)*; and information obtained from Lomenech by the author.

Chapter IX

1 This chapter is based on the author's own knowledge, amplified by documents in the SOE archives in respect of the period 1939–41.

Chapter X

1 The sections of this chapter dealing with Luard and the Operation POLISH are based on the author's own knowledge.

2 In 1981 the author learned by chance from Professor Guy Vourc'h the identity of the men met at sea by RAF 360 during Operation POLISH. Vourc'h sent him a copy of *Par les Nuits les Plus Longues*.

3 This total is the sum of the numbers of passengers shown in the museum on the Ile-de-Sein for each of the escapes organised by the Sibiril family. The monument erected at Carentec shows a total of 193. This higher figure is perhaps due to the inclusion of the boats' crews.

Chapter XI

1 This account of the Aber-Benoît operations from October 1941 to February 1942 is based on the author's own recollections and on an article by Joël Le Tac in *Les Réseaux Action de la France Combattante, 1940–1944*.

2 Guennoc has an alternative name Guénioc.

3 Marie-Claire Scamaroni (Fred's sister): *Fred Scamaroni 1914–43*.

4 *Par les Nuits les Plus Longues*, pp. 49, 369, 382, deals with the break-up of the OVERCLOUD organisation.

5 The woman's name was Anna Uspenskaya. She was arrested in July 1942 and shot.

6 *SOE in France*, pp. 190–94.

7 The author is indebted to Steven Mackenzie for the information in this paragraph.

8 Able-bodied Seaman William Alfred Savage, gun-layer of MGB 314's forward pom-pom, was wounded by shrapnel while waiting to re-embark Brigadier Newman. Savage continued to fire his gun and died on the way out. Awarded the VC posthumously.

9 Information from Steven Mackenzie.

Chapter XII

1 Apart from the official records made available by Gervase Cowell, SOE Adviser to the Foreign and Commonwealth Office, the author received much help from Steven Mackenzie and Daniel Lomenech in writing this chapter.

2   Steven Mackenzie: 'Operation MARIE LOUISE', *Blackwood's Magazine*, May 1946.

3   *We Landed by Moonlight*, p. 199 (Operations BACCARAT and BACCARAT II).

4   M.L. = a 112-foot Fairmile 'B'-Class Motor Launch.

5   For a fuller account of the problem of recognition, see Mackenzie's report in Appendix D.

6   MGB 501, according to Daniel Lomenech.

7   There is a full account of the French side of this operation in *Clandestins de l'Iroise (1940–42)*, Vol. 2, pp. 81–95.

8   Rémy: 'La Dernière Carte', *Le Parisien Libéré*, 18 November 1963, p. 2.

Chapter XIII

1   Bevil Warington Smyth's account of the SOE Base in the Helford River is in the SOE archives.

2   Newton had delivered coal to the lighthouse before the war.

3   David Birkin (see Chapter XIV) retained copies of Davis's reports on these LARDERING operations: they are chronologically the earliest operational sorties recorded in his collection of more than 30 reports of expeditions in which he was personally involved. Copies are now in the Imperial War Museum.

4   Letter from Tom Long to the author.

5   Long, a pre-war merchant seaman with considerable knowledge of the Narrow Seas, had served in destroyers until a percipient Divisional Officer recommended him for Special Service.

6   Slocum's Section records wrongly attribute this operation to MGB 324.

7   Lieut Cdr Sir Graham Esplen, Bt, RN.

8   Sub-Lieut R.O. Richards, RNVR.

9   *SOE in France*, p. 69.

Chapter XIV

1   Cecil Hampshire: *The Secret Navies*, p. 25.

2   Lomenech had retained the manuscript rough drafts of these documents, copies of which he made available to the author.

3   Lomenech's departure from NID(C) after three years of clandestine operations was marked by an episode revealing of an aspect of his character that was never far below the surface. His last assignment for Slocum was to take 2023 up from Helford to Cowes, where she was due for a refit at the hands of her builders. She sailed as part of the escort of a 6-knot convoy, whose senior officer was captain of a Hunt-class destroyer. Lomenech, being second in seniority among the commanding officers of the escort, was assigned to bring up the convoy's rear. Although she looked like a fishing boat, 2023 found it difficult to keep her speed down to 6 knots, so Lomenech tried to maintain station by proceeding by a series of starts and stops, alternately falling behind the convoy and catching it up. By the time they were off Fowey, the captain of the destroyer felt bound to investigate this unorthodox behaviour: he drew up alongside 2023 and asked Lomenech what was his maximum speed. Replying, 'You would be surprised,' Daniel raised his speed by several

knots. The destroyer did likewise. Daniel increased speed again until eventually they were both making their maximum (22 knots by his account). This race between a hare and what had looked like a tortoise was run blatantly in front of the whole convoy. Lomenech's seniors in NID(C) were more than a little displeased that the secret capabilities of their prized dispatch boat should thus be gratuitously compromised and 'Daniel le Téméraire' risked severe trouble, from which his outstanding services rescued him. Richard Townsend, his first lieutenant on six operations, questioned whether 2023 ever achieved 22 knots. He also recalled one occasion when fog came down as they were hanging about waiting for dark to make the passage past Ushant. Rather than wait longer, Daniel decided to take advantage of the fog to pass within a few miles of the lighthouse, but as they came abeam of it the fog cleared and left them in a flat, calm sea, bathed in bright evening sunshine. Immediately the lighthouse began to call them with a signal lamp. There was nothing they could do but carry on and hope that an E-boat would not be sent out to investigate. Nightfall came as a very great relief.

4   John Garnett has recorded that these presumed later operations by MFV 2023 were carried out direct from the Helford River, rather than from the Scillies. She went up to Frenchman's Creek to be repainted in French colours and then, after dark, motored very slowly out of the river. Only when she was beyond the range of the British coastal radar network did she open up her 500-h.p. Hall-Scott motors and begin to travel south at full speed.

Chapter XV

1   This chapter is based on notes and drafts of unpublished articles written by David Birkin after the war. They were made available to the author by the actress Judy Campbell, his widow.

2   Birkin recorded that sabotage did occur at Dartmouth on one occasion. At the final check of 318's petrol tanks, sugar was found at the bottom of one. This would have become apparent only when the fuel level was getting low and sugar was sucked into the carburettors, probably when restarting them for the return journey.

Chapter XVI

1   This account of the five operations carried out by MGB 318 in November and December 1943 to the Aber-Benoît estuary is based on five main sources:
   (a) The operational reports submitted to Captain Slocum by the officer in charge of each expedition, copies of which were retained by Birkin, who had acted as navigator of all five expeditions.
   (b) An unpublished account entitled *The Aber-Wrac'h Saga*, written by Birkin, which differs in some particulars from the official reports by Commander Davis and Lieutenant McQuoid Mason. It should be noted that, notwithstanding Birkin's choice of title, all these operations were in fact to pinpoints in the Aber-Benoît estuary rather than to the neighbouring Aber-Wrac'h estuary, which by this period was too well defended to be used by DDOD(I)'s MGBs.
   (c) A detailed account of the landward side of these events published by Roger Huguen in *Par les Nuits les Plus Longues*, who was in touch with Birkin when he wrote it. The map illustrating this chapter has been redrawn from one prepared by Huguen on the basis of the relevant Admiralty chart and is reproduced here by his kind permission.
   (d) An unpublished article by Steven Mackenzie, who took part in the fourth expedition and was standing by at Falmouth and Helford when the final, successful sortie was made.

(e) A report by Michael Pollard on what happened to the crews of the two surf-boats left behind by MGBs 318 & 329 on Operation ENVIOUS II communicated by the author by Mr Derek Caster of the Manaccan History Study Group.

2   Huguen spells the name Mao, but Alya Aglan, who interviewed Hentic when writing her *Mémoires Résistantes* book on the 'Jade-Fitzroy' network, uses 'Máho'.

3   This account of the disappointments and delays experienced in connection with the delivery of the ex-Turkish MGB to Slocum is based on letters to the author by Steven Mackenzie.

4   Slocum's section seems eventually to have received at least five MGBs of this class, two of which were delivered too late for operations to France. One (2209) was wrecked on arrival at Aberdeen, which was being used as a base for operations to Norway: the other was still being fitted out for operations in the Far East when the war ended.

5   Elizabeth Furse, who worked on the 'Pat' escape line, observed that the sudden transition of environment induced a state of shock in many shot-down airmen. Escaped POWs, particularly those with an Army background, were easier to handle.

6   'Philipson' was the pseudonym adopted by Pilot-Officer Philip Schneidau, the first agent parachuted into France (for SIS) and the first picked up by Lysander (see pp. 29 & 89). By 1944 he was a Squadron Leader and had been awarded the DSO.

Chapter XVII

1   H.B. Verity: *We Landed by Moonlight*, p. 211 (Operation DYER).

2   M.R.D. Foot: *SOE in France*, pp. 70–73. This account of the 'Var' line draws also extensively on R. Huguen's *Par les Nuits les Plus Longues* and on the MGBs' operational reports to DDOD(I) from the Birkin collection.

3   The author is indebted to Michel Guillou for information strongly suggesting that the agent who refused to land 'blind' on Operations INDIFFERENT and INDIFFERENT II must have been Georges Charaudeau, of the 'Alibi' network (see Chapter XX below).

4   Organised by Vic Gerson, MBE.

Chapter XVIII

1   *Par les Nuits les Plus Longues* contains well-researched chapters on MI9's 'Pat' organisation in Brittany, on OAKTREE and on SHELBURNE. Rémy devoted a book, *La Maison d'Alphonse*, to the local escape organisation at Plouha. Dominique le Trividic's *Une Femme du Réseau Shelburn* (sics) sets down Marie-Thérèse Le Calvez's recollections. Leon Dumais's *The Man Who Went Back* contains his own account of his escape from France via the 'Pat' escape line and a Polish felucca (see Chapter XXXI below) and of his SHELBURNE mission (which he consistently misspells 'SHELBURN'). Slocum's records of the operations of the 15th MGB Flotilla show, however, that Dumais's chronology is at fault in certain respects – in one case by as much as three months. These overlapping accounts differ in detail. The present chapter represents an attempt to draw the French, Canadian and British accounts into a single narrative.

2   There are, however, valuable references in a report by DDOD (I)'s staff.

3   See p. 122.

4   See Helen Long's *Safe Houses are Dangerous*, Abson Books, Abson, Wick, Bristol (1989), first published by William Kimber & Co. Ltd, 1985.

5   These passengers were not listed by name in the first English edition of *We Landed by Moonlight*. Operation MAGDALEN on 6/7 November 1943 is the only one shown to have succeeded at that time, at a third attempt.

6   The map illustrating this chapter is redrawn from one made by a former pupil of Roger Huguen's and published in his *Par les Nuits les Plus Longues*. The author is much indebted to M Huguen for his help in this matter.

7   See Note 1 above.

8   This must have been one of the contacts arranged via the W/T link of the ALLAH mission, manned by Jean Le Roux.

9   This account of Hamilton's enforced sojourn in Brittany is based on his own recollections, as set out in letters to the author.

10 The Vlasov Russians were followers of Andrey Vlasov (1900–46), an anti-Stalinist military commander who, after capture by the Germans in 1942, became a turncoat and fought with the Germans against the Soviet Union. His Russian Liberation Army, composed of former Russian soldiers captured by the Germans, numbered 50,000 near the end of the war.

Chapter XIX

1   This chapter is based on the operational reports in the Birkin collection.

Chapter XX

1   See *Par les Nuits les Plus Longues*, pp. 125–8.

2   The author is indebted to Michel Guillou for a booklet about Jézéquel which, incidentally, claims that his BLAVET mission provided the operational intelligence that led to the interception of a heavily escorted German convoy, an encounter known to naval historians as the Battle of the Ile-de-Batz. This seems an overstatement, as credit for the success of the venture was due primarily to signals intelligence.

3   John Watkins: 'Action off the Ile-de-Batz, 9 June 1944: A View from HMS *Ashanti*', *The Mariner's Mirror* (August 1992) p. 307–25.

4   The author is indebted to Michel Guillou for an account of an address given by Charaudeau to a gathering of veterans of his 'Alibi-Maurice' network at the Ile-Grande on 28 May 1987.

Chapter XXI

1   The list in Appendix B is based on that in the museum at the Ile-de-Sein, but incorporates amendments of dates and detail from the Abwehr report referred to in Chapter VI Note 3 above. The author is indebted to his brother and sister-in-law for a transcription of the Sein record, which is exhibited in the form of wall panels. The account in this chapter is also based on information in *Par les Nuits les Plus Longues* and *Les Clandestins de l'Iroise* (see Bibliography).

2   [Capitaine de Vaisseau] René Besnault.

3   [Capitaine de Vaisseau] Blondel.

Appendix A

CLANDESTINE SEA TRANSPORT OPERATIONS TO NORTH AND WEST COASTS OF FRANCE, 1940–44

Operation Code name	Department	Pinpoint	Ship	Object	Results and remarks
			Period: June – August 1940		
	SIS (Section D)	Carantec	MTB 29	To rescue Mme de Gaulle and family.	19–20/6 – Unsuccessful; family had left via Brest on a merchant ship.
AFB/SLO1	SIS (Cohen)	nr Brest	French MTB	(1) To land 1 agent 20/6. (2) To re-embark agent 1/7.	20/6 – Landing successful. 1/7 – Agent re-embarked.
AFB/SLO2	SIS (Cohen)	Cherbourg	French MTB	To land 2 agents.	2/7 – Attempt to land agents failed through faulty compass. No further attempt made.
ANGER	SIS (Cohen)	Guernsey (Icart Bay)	HM S/m H43	(1) To land 1 agent. (2) To bring him out to report.	7–8/7 – Agent (Lt Hubert Nicolle) successfully landed. 10/11 July–Agent successfully re-embarked.
	SIS (Dunderdale)	Le-Guilvinec	ex-French Navy F/V Le-Petit-Marcel	To land 1 agent (Hubert Moreau) for an intelligence reconnaissance and bring him back to the UK.	26/7 – Sailed from Falmouth. 27–28/7 – Landing successful. 30/7 – Returned to Falmouth.
A5/SLO1	SIS (Cohen for Free French)	nr St-Pabu (see Results and remarks)	MTB	To land 1 agent and later re-embark him.	30/7 – Agent taken to pinpoint but refused to land. Later landed and returned by fishing boat. This must have been Jacques Mansion, de Gaulle's first emissary. Mansion subsequently placed pinpoint at Plougasnou, near Morlaix.

NORTH AND WEST COASTS Continued

Operation Code name	Department	Pinpoint	Ship	Object	Results and remarks
			Period: August – October 1940		
	Free French 2e Bureau	Pointe-de-la-Chèvre	French F/V *Jiji*	To land Jacques Mansion.	Early August – Landing successful.
SO2/SLO1	Section D (SIS) (SO2/ SOE)	(1) Primel, near Morlaix (2) Anse-de-Bréhec	1/8 Belgian Motor Yacht; MTB for subsequent attempts	To land 4 agents.	1/8 Attempt by Section D failed, owing to expedition's encountering German convoy. 10 subsequent attempts organised by Section G3 (Slocum) failed, mostly owing to weather or enemy action. Agents machine-gunned 11/10 while attempting to land at Anse-de-Bréhec. Operation abandoned.
A5/SLO2	SIS (Cohen and Free French)	Hourtin lighthouse, nr Bordeaux	HM S/m *Talisman*	To land 3 agents (Bohec and 2 British agents, according to BCRA archives).	2/8 – Unidentified agents landed successfully.
DCO/SLO1	Directorate of Combined Operations	Guernsey	MA/SB 40	(1) To land 1 British Sergeant to contact 5 DCO personnel left behind in a raid on Guernsey. (2) To re-embark whole party of 6.	2/8 – Sergeant Ferbrache landed. 5/8 – Ferbrache re-embarked. Remainder of party had given themselves up to the Germans.
A5/SLO3	SIS (Cohen and Free French 2e Bureau)	Mouth of R. Orne (Lagrune)	MDV1 and MA/SB 40	(1) To land 2 agents 4/8. (2) To re-embark agents 7/8.	4/8 – Agents *St Jacques* and *Corvisart* successfully landed. 7/8 – No agents seen at pinpoint. Subsequently returned via Spain.
	SIS (Dunderdale)	Douarnenez	F/V *Rouanez-ar-Peoc'h*	(1) To land 2 agents (Hubert Moreau and another). (2) To re-embark them 12 days later.	4/8 – *Rouanez-ar-Peoc'h* sailed from Falmouth. 5/8 – Agents successfully landed. 17/8 – Hubert Moreau successfully re-embarked.
			Period: September – October 1940		
A5/SLO4	SIS (Cohen)	Guernsey	MTB	(1) To land 2 agents 3/9. (2) To pick up one or more agents 6/9.	3/9 – Landing successful. 6/9 – Operation failed owing to faulty compass. Weather prevented further attempts. One of the agents concerned was Lt Hubert Nicolle of the Guernsey Militia, who spent the rest of the war as a POW.

NORTH AND WEST COASTS Continued

Operation Code name	Department	Pinpoint	Ship	Object	Results and remarks
				Period: September – October 1940 continued	
	SIS (Dunderdale)	Douarnenez	Rouanez-ar-Peoc'h	(1) To land Hubert Moreau 6/9. (2) To re-embark Moreau and mail at subsequent date. (3) To land Roger Lefèvre, W/T operator, and collect mail 27/9.	5/9(?) – Sailed from Falmouth. Landing successful. Rouanez-ar-Peoc'h returned to base. Moreau, feeling himself compromised, took passage from Douarnenez before the agreed date on an Etel tunnyman, which returned him to England, where Burgaud, who accompanied him, was interrogated on 19/9. Rouanez-ar-Peoc'h returned to Douarnenez 27/9 with Lefèvre, after making a stop at Sein to land Prosper Couillandre.
A5/SLO5	SIS (Cohen)	Jersey	MTB	To land 1 agent.	5/9 –Strong tidal stream forced MTB to use main engines near coast. Noise alerted defences. Landing abandoned.
G3/SLO1	SIS (Slocum) (combined with operation for Free French 2e Bureau)	Ile-de-Sein	Rouanez-ar-Mor	(1) To land 2 British agents (Barclay and Arthur). (2) To land 1 Free French agent (Jan Doornik).	6/9 – Doornik successfully landed and transferred to mainland by local fishing boat (Porz-Loubous-en-Plogoff). It proved impossible to obtain papers for Barclay and Arthur in Ile-se-Sein, so they re-embarked on Rouanez-ar-Mor on 7/9 and returned to England.
	Free French naval forces (EM 2)	Bay of Biscay	Dom-Michel-de Nobletz	To collect intelligence from fishing vessels encountered.	24/9 – Sailed from Newlyn. 24/9. Contacted and spoke to two tunnymen before returning to port.
	Free French 2e Bureau	Pointe-du-Raz (Porz-Loubous)	Marie-Louise	To study possibility of reception at Le Normant house at Penneac'h-en-Plogoff	10/10 – E. de V. Georges Lequien landed and picked up after reconnaissance. Marie-Louise, under command of François Follic, sailed from and returned to Newlyn.
				Period: November – December 1940	
	SIS (Dunderdale)	Rospico (nr Pont-Aven)	Le-Grec	(1) To land 2 agents (Daniel Lomenech and Jean Milon) and return to base. (2) To pick up same 2 agents from same pinpoint and bring them back to base.	(1) Early November – Agents successfully landed: Le-Grec, using the name Rouanez-ar-Peoc'h, returned to base. (2) Early December – Le-Grec, on its way to pick up Lomenech and Milon, put into Port-Haliguen on Quiberon peninsula to repair engine defect. Boat went adrift while crew were ashore. Boat taken into custody by Inscription Maritime and Germans realised she had come from UK. Lomenech had to collect stranded crew and arrange their escape via Camaret on F/V Émigrant.

NORTH AND WEST COASTS Continued

Operation Code name	Department	Pinpoint	Ship	Object	Results and remarks
				Period: November – December 1940 continued	
SHAMROCK	NID/SO2 (SOE)	Ile-de-Groix area (not Gironde as claimed by Minshall)	HM S/m *Talisman* and F/V *Le-Clipper*	To reconnoitre procedures followed by U-boats entering and leaving French Atlantic ports.	Late November – Lt Merlin Minshall, RNVR, of NID, and 5 agents borrowed from SO2 took passage on s/m to Ile-de-Groix area, where they seized a French-sailing tunnyman trawler with no engine. Impressed half the crew and placed remainder on the s/m. After successful interrogation of F/V's crew, they sailed her back to Falmouth.
A5/SLO6	Free French 2e Bureau/ SIS	Pointe-du-Raz	F/V *Marie-Louise*	To land 2 agents (Maurice Barlier and Jacques Mansion) to prepare way for d'Estiennes d'Orves.	2/12 – Agents successfully landed at Porz-Bezellec. *Marie-Louise* fetched up in Weymouth.
	Free French 2e Bureau	Pointe-du-Raz (Porz-Loubous)	F/V *Marie-Louise*	To land d'Estiennes d'Orves and W/T operator Gaessler.	21–22/12 – Agents successfully landed: d'Estiennes d'Orves was sent to set up 'Nemrod' intelligence organisation, but was betrayed by Gaessler and arrested exactly a month after his arrival.
				Period: February – April 1941	
	Free French 2e Bureau	Pointe-du-Raz (Porz-Loubous)	F/V *Marie-Louise* (F. Follic)	To land a second W/T operator (J.-J. Le Prince) for d'Estiennes d'Orves.	5/2 – Vessel returned to base at Newlyn owing to compass trouble. Abwehr arrested Jan Doornik at Porz-Loubous: he had hoped to return to UK by this operation.
	Free French 2e Bureau	Pointe-du-Raz (Porz-Loubous)	F/V *Marie-Louise* (F. Follic)	As above.	14/2 – Vessel lured into trap by Abwehr (Col Dernbach) *Funkspiel* and arrested 27 miles west of Pointe-du-Raz. Towed into Brest.
G3/SR1 & SR2	SIS (Slocum)	Normandy coast	MTB	To carry out reconnaissance sweeps of the Normandy coast to ascertain the possibility of landing agents for SIS Belgian Section.	5 & 6/3 – Sea reconnaissance nos 1 & 2 successfully carried out. No subsequent attempts were made to carry out landings in this area.
SO2/SLO3	SOE (SO2)	nr Ile-Vierge	(1) MTB (2) *Korrigan*	To land 1 agent.	19/3 – Attempt by MTB failed owing to breakdown. 28/3 – Agent (unidentified) landed from F/V. Dinghy failed to return to *Korrigan*.

NORTH AND WEST COASTS Continued

Operation Code name	Department	Pinpoint	Ship	Object	Results and remarks
Period: February – April 1941 continued
A4/SLO1	SIS (Dunderdale)	Lampaul/ Ploudal-mezeau	F/V L'Émigrant	To land 4 agents, including 1 W/T operator: Alaterre, Jean Le Roux (W/T), Daniel Lomenech and Jean Milon.	20/3 – 4 agents successfully landed. This was the ALLAH mission, to set up 'Johnny' intelligence network. Should have been landed on west coast at Rospico.
SAVANNAH	SOE/BCRA	St-Gilles-Croix-de-Vie	HM S/m Tigris	To embark the 4-man SAVANNAH team.	4–5/4 – Lt Bergé and Sgt Forman successfully picked up by Major G. Appleyard. Sgt Le Tac left behind. Fourth member of team did not turn up at R/V.
	SIS (Dunderdale)	Plouha	F/V L'Émigrant	To pick up 3 agents (J. Milon, J. Mansion and 'Chemine').	19/4 – Vessel arrested 6 miles off Plouha by 2 Kriegsmarine launches when on way to pick up agents. Taken in to Cherbourg.
G3/SR3	SIS (Slocum)	W of Ushant	F/V Denise-Louise	Reconnaissance of fishing grounds W of Ushant.	24–27/4 – Cut short by engine trouble. No results obtained.
Period: May – September 1941
G3/SR4	SIS (Slocum)	W of Ushant	ML 107	Night reconnaissance of fishing grounds W of Ushant	May – Carried out in conjunction with air reconnaissance. No results obtained.
AUTOGYRO	SOE (SO2)	Anse-de-Bréhec	MTB	To land 3 agents.	May–June – Five unsuccessful attempts made. Two defeated by weather, three owing to agents' refusal to land.
A4/SLO2	SIS (Dunderdale)	Anse-de-Bréhec & W coast of France (20 miles off Pointe-de-Penmarc'h)	MTB & S/m Sealion (Lt-Cdr Ben Bryant, RN)	To embark 1 agent (Daniel Lomenech).	May–June – Four attempts made by MTB, three being combined with AUTOGYRO (at Anse-de-Bréhec). 2/7 – Agent embarked at sea rendezvous between F/V & s/m with a group of others (Michel de Kerdrel, Jacques Mansion and Gaston Kertan) who had left Pont-Aven on a small boat and transferred off Glénans to the larger Vincent-Michelle of Saint-Guénolé, with Henri Peron on board. Scuiller, skipper of V-M, landed mail, W/T set and money for 'Johnny' organisation.

NORTH AND WEST COASTS Continued

Operation Code name	Department	Pinpoint	Ship	Object	Results and remarks
			Period: May – September 1941 continued		
VALISE and VALISE II	SIS (Dunderdale)	Sea R/V off Pointe-de-Penmarc'h (52 miles S 22° W from the La-Jument buoy)	S/ms	To contact agents' vessel at sea and collect reports.	July – 2 attempts failed owing to agents' difficulties. 16/9 – Successfully completed by *Sealion*. D. Lomenech on board S/m. Boat was the 5-m.-long *Voltaire* (GV 3921) from Loctudy, manned by Pierre Dréau and Jean Bonoure, instead of *Malgré-Tout*, whose particulars had been given to the S/m. Rendezvous 12/9 according to Le Roux.
POLISH	SIS (Dunderdale)	Sea R/V off Ile-de-Batz	RAF 360 and ML 107	To contact agent's vessel and collect reports from 'Interallié' organisation.	11/9 – Successfully completed by Holdsworth in 360, escorted by ML107. R/V was with Jacques Guéguen, in his *Pourquoi-Pas?*, and his son François.
POLISH II	SIS (Dunderdale)	As above	MTB	As above.	29/9 – MTB waited 1 hour at R/V but agent's vessel (*Pourquoi-Pas?*) did not appear.
			Period: October – December 1941		
POLISH III	SIS (Dunderdale)	Sea R/V off Ile-de-Batz	MGB 325 (Lt P. Williams, RNVR)	To embark 1 agent and mail.	13/10 – Attempt failed owing to enemy action. 15/10 – Second failure, this time because of weather. MGB sailed from Portland with Lt-Cdr E. A. G. Davis, RNR, and Lt A. Letty, RNR, as commanding officer of expedition and as navigator.
LATAK (called OVER-CLOUD by SOE)	SOE & Free French BCRA	Aber-Benoît	RAF 360	To land 2 agents, Joël Le Tac and Alain de Kergorlay (W/T).	14/10 – Successful, using two Folboats lashed together catamaran-fashion.
POLISH IV	SIS (Dunderdale)	Pointe-de-Bihit	MGB 325 (P. Williams, RNVR)	As for POLISH III.	28/10 – MGB 325 reached pinpoint but, although signals were seen, sea was too rough for landing.
PILLAR	SIS (Dunderdale)	Ile-Rohein	MGB 319	To land a postbox on Ile-Rohein for use by A4 agents.	9/11 – Completed successfully.
CELERY	SIS (Cohen for BCRA)	Morlaix Bay	MA/SB 36	To land 1 agent.	20/11 – Completed successfully.
POLISH V	SIS (Dunderdale)	Pointe-de-Bihit	MGB 319	As for POLISH IV.	23/11 – Pinpoint reached: no agent present. It was later learned he had been arrested.

NORTH AND WEST COASTS Continued

Operation Code name	Department	Pinpoint	Ship	Object	Results and remarks
				Period: October – December 1941 continued	
VALISE III	SIS (Dunderdale)	Sea R/V off Penmarc'h	HM S/m P37 (*Sealion*)	To embark 4 agents – Alaterre, Hascoët (W/T), Lavalou, Paul Vourc'h – and mail.	17–18/11 – Successful at first attempt. D. Lomenech was on board to identify agents' F/V. Organised by Alaterre and Le Roux. Boat used was *Veac'h-Vad* (Sébastien Briec).
PILLAR	SIS (Dunderdale)	Ile-Rohein	MA/SB 36	To collect mail from postbox deposited on PILLAR I.	Prepared to sail on 1/12, 27/12 and 5/1/42. Finally cancelled as agent could not find box.
ANZAC	SIS (Slocum)	Ile-de-Bréhat to Ile-de-Batz	MGB 319 MA/SB 36	Sea reconnaissance from Ile-de-Batz to test defences and approaches.	9/12 – Successfully carried out from Falmouth.
HATCHET	SIS (Dunderdale)	Iles-Glénan	F/V *La-Brise*	To land food and stores for RAF evaders and escapers.	15/12 – Sailed from Falmouth with British crew and Daniel Lomenech. Returned unsuccessful, after accidental death of British skipper.
OVER-CLOUD (called OVER-CLOUD II by SOE)	SOE (RF Section for Free French)	Ile-Guénnoc	MGB 314 (Lt D. Curtis, RNVR)	(1) To land 1 agent (Moureau). (2) To embark up to 4 agents.	31/12 – Completed successfully at second attempt. 1 agent only embarked (F. Scamaroni).
				Period: January – February 1942	
OVER-CLOUD II (III for SOE)	SOE (RF Section for Free French)	Ile-Guénnoc	MGB 314 (Curtis)	To embark 4 agents.	6/1 – Completed successfully from Falmouth. 7 agents embarked (Forman, Labit, Chenal (Lt de l'Armée de l'Air), Peulevé, Paul Simon, Joël Le Tac, Yves Le Tac).
PICKAXE	SOE	Lannion Bay	MGB 314	To land 1 female Soviet agent.	10/1 – Completed successfully from Dartmouth.
VALISE IV	SIS (Dunderdale)	Sea R/V off Pointe-de-Penmarc'h	HM S/m *Tuna*	To embark 1 agent and mail from 'Johnny' organisation.	14/1 – *Tuna* sailed with D. Lomenech on board and reached R/V position 18/1. Agent cancelled operation at last moment. S/m interrogated other trawlers.
OVER-CLOUD III (IV for SOE)	SOE (RF Section for Free French)	Ile-Guénnoc	MGB 314 (Curtis)	To land 2 agents (Joël and Yves Le Tac).	1–2/2 – Completed successfully from Falmouth. Slocum listed this as OVERCLOUD Repeat II.

NORTH AND WEST COASTS Continued

Operation Code name	Department	Pinpoint	Ship	Object	Results and remarks
				Period: January – February 1942 continued	
TURQUOISE	SIS (? Cohen & Free French)	Ile-Guénnoc	MGB 314 (Curtis)	To land 1 agent (Peulevé, alias 'Le Neveu').	1–2/2 – Completed successfully. Combined with OVERCLOUD of same date.
WATER-WORKS	SOE (Buckmaster)	Moulin-de-la-Rive (Lannion Bay)	MGB 314 (Curtis)	(1) To land 2 agents (G.W. Abbott and G.C.B. Redding (W/T operator). (2) To pick up Pierre de Vomécourt, Mathilde Carré, Ben Cowburn.	12/2 – Agents landed. Surf prevented embarkation of 4 agents. Lt Ian Black, RNVR, became POW. 13/3 – Further attempts made but failed owing to surf. This operation and ROWAN were watched by the Germans and took place with their agreement.
ROWAN	SOE (Buckmaster)	Pointe-de-Bihit	MGB 314 (Curtis)	To embark 2 agents (Pierre de Vomécourt and Mathilde Carré).	19–20/2 & 21–22/2 – No agents at R/V. 26–27/2 – Agents embarked successfully. Nearly full moonlight conditions.
				Period: April – September 1942	
PILLAR WEST	SIS (Slocum)	Ile-Verte	F/V N51 (Le-Dinan)	To lay postbox.	20/4 – Successful. Lt S. Mackenzie in command, D. Lomenech first lieutenant.
MAC	SIS (Slocum)	W of Ushant	F/V Denise-Louise	Reconnaissance of fishing grounds.	23/5 – Attacked by German aircraft off Scillies and returned. 1 rating killed. Holdsworth in command.
MARIE-LOUISE I & II	SIS (Cohen for BCRA)	R/V off Iles-Glénan	F/V N51 (Le-Dinan) (Mackenzie & Lomenech)	(1) To embark agent (Rémy) and family. (2) To collect and lay postboxes.	20/5 Agent (Rémy) unable to keep R/V but postboxes laid round Iles-Glénan. 17/6 – 2 agents (Rémy and A. de Beaufort) + 5 members of Rémy's family collected from Les-Deux-Anges (Louis Yéquel).
GUILLOTINE (GILBERTE)	SOE/SIS (Cohen for BCRA)	Sea R/V off Ile-d'Yeu	F/V P11 (Ar-Morscoul) (Lomenech in command)	(1) To transfer SOE stores. (2) To embark 2 P1 agents from Rémy's CND.	4/8 – R/V with F/V Audacieux (Michel Bolloré) of Léchiagat successful and stores transferred. No agents present.
NEPTUNE	SIS (Slocum)	Western Approaches	MGBs 318 & 323	To contact and speak to French tunnymen to warn them of itensified RAF attacks by night in U-Boat hunting areas.	28/8 – Two tunnymen contacted. Were persuaded to come to England.

NORTH AND WEST COASTS Continued

Operation Code name	Department	Pinpoint	Ship	Object	Results and remarks
			Period: April – September 1942 continued		
GRENVILLE	SIS (Cohen for BCRA)	Sea R/V off Iles-Glénan with agent's boat Les-Deux-Anges	F/V P11 (Ar-Morscoul) (D. Lomenech in command)	(1) To land 2 agents (Rémy and M. Pichard). (2) To embark mail.	19/9 – R/V successful. Mail embarked. Agents could not land as strict control in force. (Author on board as observer.)
			Period: October – November 1942		
GRENVILLE II	SIS (Cohen for BCRA)	Sea R/V off Iles-Glénan with Les-Deux-Anges	F/V N51 (Le-Dinan) (Lomenech)	(1) To land 1 agent and gear. (2) To embark mail. (3) To embark 2 agents.	13/10 – R/V successful. Agent (Rémy) landed. Mail embarked. No agents present for embarkation.
CARPENTER	SOE	Near Ile-de-Batz	MGB 318 (Lt C. Martin, RNVR); MGB 323 as escort on first two occasions	To land and bury ½ thereon arms.	4 attempts in October failed because of weather. 2 attempts in November: first failed in bad weather, second succeeded on 10/11.
GRENVILLE III	SIS (Cohen for BCRA)	As for GRENVILLE I & II	F/V N51 (Lomenech in command)	(1) To land 1 agent and gear. (2) To embark mail from Rémy's 'Confrérie de Notre Dame' (CND).	12/11 – Successful in both objects.
			Period: January – March 1943		
HAWKINS	SIS (Cohen for BCRA)	Sea R/V 7 miles SW of La-Jument buoy, Iles-Glénan with LES-DEUX ANGES	MFV 2022 (Président-Herriot) (Sub Lt R. Townsend, RNVR)	(1) To land 2 agents and gear to CND. (2) To embark 2 agents and mail.	1st attempt – No date recorded. Failed owing to bad weather. 2nd attempt, 6/1, according to BCRA archives – Successful. Embarked Rémy and Fernand Grenier, Député for Saint-Denis and member of Central Committee of French Communist Party.
TENDERLY	SIS (Slocum)	(1) Triagoz (2) Ile-Losquet	MGB 318	To lay 2 special sonar buoys as navigational aids in connection with CARPENTER II.	24/1 – Completed successfully in spite of shocking weather conditions. Records incorrectly show MGB 326 as the ship involved.

NORTH AND WEST COASTS Continued

Operation Code name	Department	Pinpoint	Ship	Object	Results and remarks

Period: January – March 1943 continued

Operation Code name	Department	Pinpoint	Ship	Object	Results and remarks
CARPENTER II	SOE	7 miles SW of Ile-de-Batz	MGB 318 and MGB 324	To land and bury ½ ton of SOE stores.	25/1–13/2 – Bad weather. 28/2–11/3 – One attempt in MGB 324 failed because of fog. 28/3–1/4 – Attempt cancelled.
TENTATIVE	SIS (Slocum)	(1) Off Ile-de-Batz (2) Off Méan-Névez	MGB 318 (Lt E. Honer, RNVR, in command)	To lay 2 special sonar buoys in connection with CARPENTER II.	25/1–13/2 – As for CARPENTER II. 9/3 – Half-completed.
RODNEY	SIS (Cohen for BCRA)	Sea R/V 7 miles SW of La-Jument buoy	MFV 2022 (see Operation HAWKINS above)	(1) To land equipment. (2) To embark 4 agents and mail.	Postponed before sailing: agents' craft bombed. 14/2 – Successful. 2 agents (? Marty and Sermoy) and mail embarked.
CARPENTER III	SOE	Ile-Stagadon	MGB 318	To land and bury ½ ton SOE stores.	27/2 – Failed: no sand (see DRAPER below).
MIRFIELD	SOE (Section DF) (L. Humphreys)	Clogourouan	MGB 324	To embark 2 evaders (Sqn Ldr Gordon Carter, RAF, and Napoleon Barry, RCAF).	9/3 – Failed: no evaders on beach (?); but surf-boat went to wrong beach. Operation arranged through BCRA agent in Morbihan and Breton arm of 'Pat' escape line. Carter escaped soon after in Dalc'h-Mad (see Appendix B). As consequence of MIRFIELD, MI9 sent OAKTREE mission to Brittany.

Period: March – September 1943

Operation Code name	Department	Pinpoint	Ship	Object	Results and remarks
DRAPER	SOE	Ile-Stagadon (Aber-Wrac'h)	MGB 318 (Honer in command)	To land party to interview islander and establish dump.	10/3 – Party landed but islander not contacted. No further attempts to be made.
COOK	SOE	Ile-Guénnoc (Aber-Benoît)	MGB 318 (Honer in command)	To land and bury ½ ton SOE stores.	1st attempt, 28/3 – From Falmouth. Failed owing to fog. 2nd attempt, 3/4 – From Falmouth. Successful. Enemy activity seen on Stagadon.
MANGO	SOE (Section DF) (Humphreys)	Clogourouan	MGB 326	To land 1 agent and stores.	29/4 – Attempted but abandoned because of bad weather. Postponed indefinitely owing to short nights and slow speed of 'C'-Class MGBs.
EFFINGHAM	SIS (Cohen for BCRA)	Sea R/V with agent's vessel 5 miles S of La-Jument buoy (Iles-Glénan)	MFV 2023 (L'Angèle-Rouge) (D. Lomenech in command)	To embark 1 agent and mail of Rémy's CND organisation.	5/5–7/5 – Successful (6/5). Agent (Lechat) and mail embarked. The first expedition by this specially built fast vessel.

NORTH AND WEST COASTS Continued

Operation Code name	Department	Pinpoint	Ship	Object	Results and remarks

Period: March – September 1943 continued

Operation Code name	Department	Pinpoint	Ship	Object	Results and remarks
JERVIS	SIS (Cohen for BCRA)	Sea R/V with agent's vessel 5 miles S of La-Jument buoy (Iles-Glénan)	MFV 2023 (*L'Angèle-Rouge*) (D. Lomenech in command)	(1) To embark 3 agents and mail from Rémy's CND organisation. (2) To inspect *Narval* for refit.	6/6 – Attacked by enemy aircraft 30 miles S of Scillies and returned. 1 Mustang shot down. 7/6 – Postponed by agent. *Narval* bought by CND to replace *Les-Deux-Anges*.
ANSON	SIS (Cohen for BCRA)	Sea R/V 5 miles S 30° W of La-Jument buoy	MFV 2023 (Lomenech)	(1) To land 1 agent. (2) To embark 2 agents and mail.	18/8 – Successful. One agent embarked. Ship standing by in Scillies since 1/6. 24 changes of date.
REMEDY	As above	As above	As above (Sub Lt J.J. Allen, RN, in charge)	To embark 2 agents & mail.	7/9–9/9 – Successful.
HAPPEN	SOE (DF) (Humphreys)	nr Clogourouan	MGB 318 (Lt J. McQuoid Mason, SANF(V))	To reconnoitre beach.	27/9 – Sortie made but abandoned owing to bad weather. Squall Force 7. Very difficult return. MGB nearly capsized.

Period: September – November 1943

Operation Code name	Department	Pinpoint	Ship	Object	Results and remarks
INBRED I	SIS (Cohen for BCRA)	R/V 6 miles NW of Iles-Glénan	MFV 2023 (Sub Lt Allen)	(1) To trans-ship stores to R/V craft. (2) To embark agents and mail.	1st attempt, 27–29/9 – R/V vessel not at position.
INBRED II	As above	As above	MFV 2022 (ex-AO4) (*Président-Herriot*) Lt R. Townsend, RNVR	As above.	1st attempt, 4/10 – Ship returned owing to gale. 2nd attempt, 18/10 – Ship returned owing to gale, with damage to propeller.
INBRED III	As above	As above	MFV 2022 (ex-AO4) (*Président-Herriot*)	As above	27/10 – Ship unable to make sufficient speed and operation abandoned. Field then experienced such difficulties that sealine was never re-established.
JEALOUS (MANGO 4 for SOE)	SOE (Humphreys)	Pointe-de-Saint-Cast	MTB 697 (?)	To land 2 SOE agents (Erwin Deman and Raymond Langard) with stores and W/T gear.	1st attempt, 25/10 – Abandoned owing to late arrival at pinpoint in deteriorating weather. 2nd attempt, 28/10 – Successful. Agents landed.
INDIFFER-ENT	SIS (Cohen)	Baie-de-la-Fresnaie	MTB 697 (?)	To land 2 SIS agents.	3/11 – Abandoned owing to late arrival at pinpoint area. (German convoy delayed MTB.)

NORTH AND WEST COASTS Continued

Operation Code name	Department	Pinpoint	Ship	Object	Results and remarks
				Period: March – September 1943 continued	
ENVIOUS	SIS (Dunderdale)	Ile-Rosservor (Aber-Benoît)	MGB 318 (McQuoid Mason)	To reconnoitre island and evacuate 15 escapers and evaders under arrangements made by 'Jade-Fitzroy'.	3/11 – Island reconnoitred but no evaders found. Evaders later discovered to have gone to the neighbouring Ile-Guennoc. Signal informing SIS of the change of plan was not received in time.
ENVIOUS II (a)	SIS (Dunderdale)	Ile-Guénnoc	MGB 318	(1) To land 1 agent (Maho). (2) To embark up to 6 evaders.	26/11 – No reception committee and no evaders found on Ile-Guennoc. Maho decided to land on Rosservor and this was successfully accomplished. MGB 20 hours at sea.
				Period: November – December 1943	
JEALOUS II	SOE (DF) (Humphreys)	Pointe-de-Saint-Cast	MGB 502 (Lt P. Williams, RNVR)	(1) To land 4 SOE agents. (2) To embark 4–6 SOE agents.	1st attempt, 26/11 – Carried out in conjunction with INDIFFERENT II (see below). Unsuccessful because MGB arrived late, by which time Deman, the organiser, had stood the reception committee down. 2nd attempt, 1/12 – Also in conjunction with INDIFFERENT II. Successful. 4 agents landed; 5 evacuated. Inward passengers included Emile Minerault (OSS).
INDIFFER-ENT II	SIS (Cohen)	Baie-de-la-Fresnaie	MGB 673(?)	To land 2 SIS agents.	1st attempt, 26/11 – Carried out in conjunction with JEALOUS II. No reception committee. 1 agent landed; the other (Charaudeau) opted to return to UK. 2nd attempt, 1/12 – Unsuccessful. No reception committee present. Search lasted 1½ hours.
ENVIOUS IIb	SIS (Dunderdale)	Ile-Guennoc/ Ile-Tariec (Aber-Benoît)	MGB 318 (McQuoid Mason) and MGB 329	(1) To land stores. (2) To embark evaders and escapers.	1–2/12 – Reception committee found on Ile-Tariec. Stores landed. Weather then deteriorated rapidly and only 1 of 3 surf-boats regained MGB with 7 evaders. MGB left area at 0450 and regained Falmouth 1720 hrs 2/12 – S/Lt Pollard and 5 naval personnel left ashore.
JEALOUS III	SOE (DF) (Humphreys)	Pointe-de-Saint-Cast	MGB 502 (Williams)	(1) To land 6 SOE agents. (2) To embark up to 9 agents.	23/12 – Agent (Deman) contacted by S-phone but, visibility being good, MGB was sighted and fired on from shore. Operation abandoned. MGB withdrew behind smoke-screen.

NORTH AND WEST COASTS Continued

Operation Code name	Department	Pinpoint	Ship	Object	Results and remarks
		Period: November – December 1943 continued			
FELICITATE	SIS (Slocum)	Ile-Tariec (Aber-Benoît)	MGB 318 (McQuoid Mason)	(1) To embark 6 Section O personnel left behind on ENVIOUS IIb. (2) To embark evaders and escapers.	1st attempt, 23/12 – Unsuccessful owing to impossible weather conditions at pinpoint. 2nd attempt, 25/12 – Successful. 28 people embarked, including 6 Section O personnel, 2 women and remaining evaders and escapers. A 25-ft surf-boat was towed over and used successfully.
		Period: January – February 1944			
EASEMENT	SOE (DF) (Humphreys)	Beg-an-Fry	MGB 502	(1) To land 1 SOE agent. (2) To embark 10 agents.	28–29/1 – Unsuccessful. Reception committee had gone to a beach 300 metres further south, which Sicot, the organiser, thought better than that chosen and agreed by DDOD (I) and on which surf-boats landed.
BONAPARTE	SIS/MI9	Saint-Brieuc bay (Anse-Cochat/ Sous-Kéruzeau)	MGB 503 (Lt. R. M. Marshall, RNVR)	To embark up to 20 evaders and escapers.	28/1 – Successful. 19 embarked. First evacuation by 'Shelburne' organisation (Lucien Dumais).
FLANNEL-FOOT	SIS (Cohen for BCRA)	Ile-d'Er	MGB 318 Lt. J. McQuoid Mason, SANF(V)	To land 3 BCRA agents.	29/1 – Successful: Yvon Jézéquel, R. Weybel (or Neybel) and Etienne July (or Josse) (latter two W/T operators) landed (mission BLAVET).
GLOVER	SIS (Cohen)	Ile-à-Canton	MGB 503 (R. Marshall)	To land stores and embark mail.	23/2 – Successful. 'Alibi-Maurice' network.
EASEMENT II	SOE (DF) (VAR line)	Beg-an-Fry (pinpoint chosen by DDOD (I) but not what Deman and Sicot wanted)	MGB 502 (Lt P. Williams, RNVR)	(1) To land 3 SOE agents. (2) To embark up to 10 agents.	26/2 – Successful. 2 agents landed including François Mitterrand. Those embarked included Deman, Langard (W/T operator), Wally Mullet (Rhodesian airman) and 'Roy' evacuated on SOE orders. Capt Peter Harratt, conducting officer, Sub Lt Lloyd Bott in charge of surf-boats.
BONAPARTE II	SIS/MI9	Saint-Brieuc bay (Sous-Kéruzeau)	MGB 503 (R. Marshall)	(1) To land stores. (2) To embark evaders.	26/2 – Successful. Stores landed. 16 airmen–evaders and 2 volunteers for Fighting French forces evacuated.
EASEMENT III	SOE (DF) ('Var' line)	Beg-an-Fry	MGB 502 (Lt P. Williams, RNVR)	To land 2 SOE agents.	29/2 – Successful. 3 agents seem to have been landed: Defendini, Swatschko and Frager (for F Section).

NORTH AND WEST COASTS Continued

Operation Code name	Department	Pinpoint	Ship	Object	Results and remarks
			Period: March – April 1944		
BONAPARTE III	SIS/MI9	Saint-Brieuc bay (Sous-Kéruzeau beach)	MGB 502 (Lt P. Williams, RNVR)	(1) To land material. (2) To embark up to 25.	16/3 – Successful. MGB fired on by battery near Paimpol, withdrew and came back later. S-phone allowed Dumais to talk to ship. Tide very low and passengers had to cross 200–300 metres of bare beach. Material landed and 25 embarked in 4 surf-boats.
SEPTIMUS	SOE (DF) ('Var' line)	Beg-an-Fry	MGB 503 (Lt R. M. Marshall, RNVR)	(1) To land 6 SOE agents. (2) To embark up to 10 SOE agents.	17/3 – Successful. Inward passengers were Gilbert Védy alias Méderic, ('Arsinoë'), Courson de Villeneuve ('Pyramide'), Jollinon ('Excellence') and Ch. Entier ('Lateral'). 1 airman (Gérald Racine, RFCAF) embarked.
BONAPARTE IV	SIS/MI9	Saint-Brieuc bay (Sous-Kéruzeau)	MGB 503 (Lt. R. M. Marshall, RNVR)	(1) To land stores. (2) To embark evaders and escapers.	19/3 – Successful. Stores and (according to Huguen) 2 French agents landed. Those evacuated included 25 airmen and 1 French agent.
GLOVER II	SIS (Cohen)	Ile-à-Canton	MGB 503 (Lt R. M. Marshall, RNVR)	(1) To land stores. (2) To embark 1 agent and stores.	21/3 – Unsuccessful. No reception committee present.
SEPTIMUS II	SOE (DF) ('Var' line)	Beg-an-Fry	MGB 502 (Williams)	(1) To land 3 SOE-sponsored agents and material. (2) To embark up to 5 agents.	21/3 – Successful. Agents landed were 'Nubien', 'Oronte' and 'Pacha' (according to BCRA); perhaps also Mme Fontaine, courier to Mulsant ('Minister') of SOE's F Section.
BONAPARTE V	SIS/MI9	Saint-Brieuc bay (Sous-Kéruzeau)	MGB 503 (Marshall)	(1) To land stores. (2) To embark evaders and escapers.	23/3 – Successful. Stores landed and 30 evaders embarked (but, according to Huguen, 19 airmen and 2 young Frenchmen – Le Bourhis and Tréhiou, active members of Plouha Group, embarked).
FLANNEL-FOOT II (URVOIS) (PERRIN)	SIS (Cohen for BCRA)	Ile-d'Er	MGB 318 (McQuoid Mason)	To land 3 SIS agents.	1st attempt, 23/3 – Unsuccessful. R/T contact established with agents but, owing to low tide, landing party could not reach them. Operation abandoned. 2nd attempt, 25/3 – Successful. Party landed on W of island: Huguen suggests Pierre Serandour (alias 'Prax' of PRAXITELES mission), Louis Marec (W/T operator, COULINEC mission) and Théodore Le Doaré.
SEPTIMUS III	SOE (DF) ('Var' line)	Beg-an-Fry	MGB 503 (Marshall)	To land 4 SOE agents and material.	26/3 – Successful. Agents landed may have included Mme Fontaine, courier to Mulsant ('Minister').

NORTH AND WEST COASTS Continued

Operation Code name	Department	Pinpoint	Ship	Object	Results and remarks
colspan full			Period: March – April 1944 continued		
SCARF	SOE (DF) ('Var' line)	Beg-an-Fry	MGB 502 and MGB 718	(1) To land 6 SOE agents. (2) To embark up to 20 SOE and Allied personnel.	15/4 – Successful. Agents landed were M. H. Rouneau (Belgian), Capt. Martin Rendier ('Adolphe'), Félix Duffour ('Amédée'), Lt.-Col Ely, S/Lt Lazare, Racheline (ex-'Vic' line); to advise Parodi, and SOE F Section W/T operator A. Watt. Those embarked included Deman, Suzanne Warrenghem ('Charise'), Blanche Charlet and a number of airmen. German vessels met on the way out fired on MGBs. Latter did not return fire and the Germans then stopped shooting. 1 rating killed. No other damage sustained.
			Period: April – July 1944		
GLOVER III	SIS (Cohen)	Ile-à-Canton	MGB 503 (Marshall)	To land stores and embark mail.	22/4 – Unsuccessful. Agents contacted on R/T. They warned surf-boat that Germans were at pinpoint and told boat to go back. 'Alibi' network.
SPLINT	SIS (Cohen for BCRA)	Tréguier River	MGB 502 (Williams)	To embark 2 SIS agents and mail.	25/4 – Unsuccessful. Reception committee not present. It was ascertained later that they were arrested on 24/5 in Paris. Canadian destroyer engaged in sinking German destroyer fired on MGB but ceased at recognition signal.
GLOVER IV	SIS (Cohen)	Ile-Grande	PT 71 and PT 72 (Lt Cdr P. Williams in charge of expedition)	To embark 1 agent and mail from 'Alibi' network.	1st attempt, 19/5 – Unsuccessful. Reception committee not present, having been delayed by travel difficulties in France. 2nd attempt, 24/5 – Successful. Only mail embarked. Organised by 'Alibi-Maurice' group: Vallée and Briand based at Ile-Grande.
REFLEXION	SIS/MI9	Saint-Brieuc bay (Sous-Kéruzeau)	MGB 718 (Lt R. Seddon, RHVR)	To land 3 agents – Jean Tréhiou, Raoul Parent and Jean Hamon (W/T) – and equipment.	15/6 – Successful. Unfortunately dinghy could not find parent ship after landing. 1 officer and 2 ratings left behind and recovered 12/7.
GLOVER V	SIS (Cohen)	Ile-Grande	MGB 318 (McQuoid Mason)	To embark mail.	17/6 – Successful.

NORTH AND WEST COASTS Continued

Operation Code name	Department	Pinpoint	Ship	Object	Results and remarks
				Period: April – July 1944 continued	
GIRAFFE	OSS	Beg-an-Fry	PT 79 and PT 199	To land 4 OSS agents.	24/6 – Successful.
NOMINA-TION	SIS	Allied beach-head	MA/SB 36, MFV 2022 and MFV 2028	To land 1 Jeep and 6 officers for reconnaissance.	22/6 – Successful. Return delayed by bad weather.
CROZIER	SIS/MI9	Saint-Brieuc Bay (Sous-Kéruzeau)	MGB 503 (Marshall)	(1) To land stores. (2) To embark up to 15 evaders.	12/7 – Successful. Stores landed. 18 personnel embarked, including 3 left behind on Operation REFLEXION.
				Period: July – August 1944	
ROBES-PIERRE	SIS/MI9	SW of Ile-de-Batz	MGB 502 (Williams)	(1) To land stores. (2) To embark up to 15 evaders.	14/7 – Successful. Stores landed. Field had no evaders to evacuate.
GLOVER VI	SIS (Cohen)	Ile-Grande	MGB 318 (McQuoid Mason)	(1) To land stores. (2) To embark mail.	16/7 – Unsuccessful. No reception committee.
GLOVER VII	As above	As above	As above	As above.	23/7 – Successful.
CROZIER II	SIS/MI9	Saint-Brieuc Bay (Anse-Cochat)	MGB 502 (Williams)	To embark 4 escaped SAS personnel and any other evaders.	23/7 – Successful. 6 embarked: Major Cary-Elwes and his batman, Mills, survivors from Operation LOST; Major Smith, also SAS; F/Sgt Philip Farger, RAF; Major William A. Jones, USAF, and F. Gicquel.
GLOVER VIII	SIS (Cohen)	Ile-Grande	MGB 318 (McQuoid Mason)	To embark 1 agent (Lemoine) and mail.	29/7 – Successful.
GLOVER IX	As above	As above	As above	To land back agent embarked on GLOVER VIII.	5/8 – Successful.
CROZIER III	SIS/MI9	Saint-Brieuc Bay (Anse-Cochat)	MGB 718 (Seddon)	To embark 3 agents and any available escapers and evaders.	9/8 – Successful. 1 SAS and 2 French agents embarked. Operation took place in daylight after the Germans at the block-house on Pointe-de-la-Tour had surrendered. At least 138 persons were evacuated from the Saint-Brieuc pinpoint in the 8 BONAPARTE/CROZIER operations.

NORTH AND WEST COASTS Continued

Operation Code name	Department	Pinpoint	Ship	Object	Results and remarks
Period: July – August 1944 continued					
ROBES-PIERRE III (ROBES-PIERRE II was cancelled)	As above	SW of Ile-de-Batz (Clogourouan)	MGB 318 (McQuoid Mason)	To embark any escapers and evaders.	12/8 – No reception committee or evaders present (although, according to Huguen, Raoul Parent was present).
HAVEN	SOE	Lannion Bay	Minna MGB 718	(1) To embark 27 SOE agents and 3,200 lb. stores. (2) To land 1 cwt. of medical supplies.	23/8 – Successfully carried out in daylight to a liberated part of the coast. Embarked members of ALOES international mission (Col Eon), parachuted in at Kérien in early August.
Period: August – October 1944					
ROBES-PIERRE IV	SIS/MI9	SW of Ile-de-Batz (Clogourouan)	MGB 318 (McQuoid Mason)	To embark agents.	25/8 – Successful. Post-Liberation daylight landing. Met by Raoul Parent and Dr Le Duc. ADOLPHE-AMÉDÉE and LA-GIRAFFE missions embarked.
KORDA I & II	SIS (Slocum)	Aber-Wrac'h area	MGB 318 and MTB 718	To photograph coast of France.	1st sortie, 1/9–6/9 – Incomplete owing to bad weather. 2nd sortie, 12/9–17/9 – Successful.
IGNOBLE	SOE	Bénodet	Minna	(1) To land ammunition for French Forces of the Interior (FFI). (2) To embark 17 agents.	7/9–9/9 – Successful. 6 agents embarked.
HOUSING	SOE	Les-Sables-d'Olonne	HMS Ashanti HMS Kelvin	To land 48 tons of ammunition and 30 French officers.	9/9 -Successful.
KNOCKOUT	SOE	Ushant & Benodet	MGB 718, MFV 2021 and MFV 2022	To land 11 tons of stores for local population and for FFI.	16/9–19/9 – Expedition called at Aber-Wrac'h and proceeded independently to pinpoints. MFVs to Ushant; MTB 718 to Bénodet where photos were taken.
SCRUBBY	SOE	Lézardrieux	Jacques-Morgand	To land 7 tons of stores for FFI at Lorient.	22/9 – Successful. Expedition returned 25/9 after being delayed by weather. Contact was established with 'Shelburne'/'Bonaparte' agents and pinpoint visited in daylight.
HOUSING II	SOE	Les-Sables-d'Olonne	HM destroyer (name not recorded)	To land 40 tons of ammunition for FFI and disembark 16 men.	28/9 – Successful.

NORTH AND WEST COASTS Continued

Operation Code name	Department	Pinpoint	Ship	Object	Results and remarks
			Period: August – October 1944 continued		
SCRUBBY II	SOE	Lézardrieux	MGB 503 and PT 199	To photograph French coast.	4/10–9/10 – Unsuccessful owing to bad weather.
SOOTY	SOE	Ile-Guennoc, Ile-Stagadon	*Jacques-Morgand* and MFV 2025	To reconnoitre islands and see if arms buried in 1943 were still there.	27/10–1/11 – No arms found.
			Period: November 1944		
TELESCOPE	SIS (Cohen for BCRA)	Les-Sables-d'Olonne	MGB 321	To land stores for agents in Bordeaux.	22/11 – Arrangements for sending stores by destroyer failed; instead shipped to Dieppe for onward transport overland.
PICKWICK	SOE	Les-Sables-d'Olonne	Polish destroyer *Blyskawica*	To land 1 British and 1 French officer and 1,500 lb. of material for SOE parties.	11/11 – Successful.

Appendix B

CLANDESTINE ESCAPES AND CONTACTS AT SEA BY VESSELS FROM BRETON PORTS: 1940–44

Date	Name and Type of Vessel	Skipper	Remarks
		1940	
21 June	Dom-Michel-de-Nobletz (motor tunnyman)	Joseph Le Gloaguen	Escaped via Ushant to UK with crew composed of Louis Bernard, Hervé Habasq, François Bohut and Jean Chédhotel.
22 June	Ar-Zenith (Mail boat)		From Ile-de-Sein via Ushant.
22 June	Korrigan (pinasse)	Marcel Guénolé/ Raymond Le Corre	First clandestine escape from Le-Guilvinec. Arrived Mevagissey, sent to Falmouth.
24 June	Notre-Dame-de-Bon-Conseil		From Kérity (Penmarc'h).
24 June	L'Albatros (4.5-m. open boat)	Hubert Moreau	Escaped from Beg-Meil to Polperro with 1 passenger.
24 June	Ar-Morscoul (pinasse)		From Le-Guilvinec. Boat became P11 and was used by D. Lomenech for operations.
24 June	Velléda (lighthouse-tender)		24 soldiers and 25 civilians; also earlier voyage (19/6) with 20 passengers.
25 June	Primel (11-m. cutter)	Tanguy	From Plougasnou, at least twice to Guernsey (20/6 and 25/6), and ? once to British mainland (29/6).
25 June	La-Mouette (Roscoff/Ile-de-Batz ferry		
24–26 June	Maris-Stella	Martin Guilcher	From Ile-de-Sein. Estimates of passengers carried vary from 35 on each to 64 on the three boats. Rouanez-ar-Peoc'h used by SIS for operations in August and September.
	Rouanez-ar-Peoc'h (crabber/ long-liners)	François Fouquet	
	Rouanez-ar-Mor (crabber)	Prosper Couillandre	
26 June	Corbeau-des-Mers (crabber)	Pierre Couillandre	Corbeau-des-Mers returned to Sein in mid-August.
End June	Sainte-Marie (open boat)		Escaped from Camaret with 1 person.
June–July	Pourquoi-Pas? (8.4-m. half-decked sloop)	Jacques Guéguen	At least 4 voyages from Pont-de-la-Corde (Morlaix Bay), first to Jersey, then direct to UK. Subsequently used to carry mail for the 'Interallié' network to R/V with RAF 360 from England.
Early July	Petit-Emmanuel		Escaped from Le-Guilvinec.

BRETON PORTS Continued

Date	Name and Type of Vessel	Skipper	Remarks
		1940 continued	
5 Sept.	Marie-Louise (crabber)	Arsène Celton	Brought Jacques Mansion, de Gaulle's first agent, and Roger Lefèvre to England. Subsequently used by Free French for operations. Captured February 1941.
9 Sept.	Muse-des-Mers		Escaped from Concarneau with 7 passengers.
16 Sept.	Lusitania (sailing-tunnyman)		Sailed from Concarneau with 4 passengers incl. Daniel Lomenech and Joseph Burel. Trans-shipped to British trawler 20 miles off Penzance.
Mid-Sept.	Coeur-Sacré-de-Jésus (Etel tunnyman)		Took Hubert Moreau, SIS's first agent in France, back to UK when he was on the run during his 3rd mission. Boat returned to France.
9 Oct.	Étourdi (sailing crabber)	Raymond Morvan	Crossed from Camaret to Newlyn with 11 passengers (4, according to Huguen). Returned to Camaret 23/10. Crew denounced at end Jan. 1941 but denied guilt and freed for lack of evidence.
20 Oct.	Petite-Anna (pinasse)		Escaped from Douarnenez with Jean Vourc'h, Guy Vourc'h, Robert Alaterre, Charles de la Patellière (Nantes), Joseph Fréchaud and Bernard Scheidauer.
15 Dec.	La-Véga		Failed escape from Dourdoff: 16 on board all arrested.
16 Dec.	L'Émigrant (sailing crabber)		Jacques Andrieux and Daniel Lomenech organised successful escape from Camaret for themselves, René Grosnier, Paul L'Abbé, Fred Ashley (RAF), Albert Craight (RAF), Auguste le Monzé, Yann Le Roux, Jean Le Roux, Jean Milon, Jean-Marie Porsmouguer, Henri Le Goff, Raymond Le Corre, Marcel Guénolé (last 4 being marooned crew of Le-Grec) and 2 Poles.
		1941	
3 Jan.	Monique (motor crabber with auxiliary sail)	François Salaun (Camaret)	Failed escape from Douarnenez with 23 passengers, 16 of whom were arrested.
5 Feb.	Saint-Guillaume (seaweed-cutter)		Escaped from Loguivy-de-la-Mer (Lézardrieux) with 10 persons, including Yves Le Guen, François Gonidec, Jean Bonniot and a young French airman. Landed at Dartmouth.
8 Feb.	Aviso (7-m. launch)	Chaudron	Escaped from Loguivy with 9 persons including Comte de Mauduit, Jean Le Boédec and 5 students of Hydrographic School. Picked up by HMS Kelly.

BRETON PORTS Continued

Date	Name and Type of Vessel	Skipper	Remarks
		1941 continued	
9 Feb.	Gustave (sand barge)		Escaped from Paimpol with 30 on board.
12 Feb.	Buhara		Failed escape from Saint-Cast with 15 passengers, mostly French air force. Engine failed. Arrested west of Guernsey.
18 Feb.	Le-Misère		Sailed from Kérity (Penmarc'h). Lost at sea with all hands.
19 Feb.	Goyen (launch)		Failed escape from Audierne with 5 passengers.
2 July	Vincent-Michelle		From Saint-Guénolé (Penmarc'h). R/V with HM S/m Sealion: Daniel Lomenech and Jacques Mansion + 4 others transferred to s/m.
20 Sept.	Saint-Guénolé		Escaped from Concarneau with 8 passengers.
Sept.	Alsace-Lorraine		Escaped from Morgat with 3 on board.
27/28 Nov.	Veach-Vad	Sébastien Briec	Rendezvous with HM S/m P37 off Penmarc'h. 4 passengers (Alaterre, J. Lavalou, R. Hascoët, P. Vourc'h) transferred to s/m.
		1942	
15 Jan.	La-Korrigane (5–6-m. motor launch)		Although escapes from N coast of Brittany had become difficult, the following got away from Bréhat: Pierre Guélorget of Saint-Brieuc (wanted by Germans for sabotage); René Besnault of Hydrographic School at Paimpol, later promoted to Captain and ADC to Gen de Gaulle; Blondel, his fellow student, who also became Captain and commanding officer of Free French S/m Rubis; Claude Robinet, pharmacy student; and François Menguy. They were picked up by RN minesweeper and taken to Portsmouth.
10 Feb.	André	Jacques Guéguen	Escaped from Pont-de-la-Corde (Carentec). Guéguen's son François, Van Hacker, a Belgian intelligence officer and Mme Bruley de Vourane, a senior nursing sister, on board. Reached Fowey. First escape organised by Ernest Sibiril.
23 Feb.	?	Roger Bonnec	Failed escape from Ploujean. 14 arrests.
5 June	Yolande (small cutter-rigged open boat)		15-year-old Jean-Amaury Saladin and 16-year-old Victor Tudal escaped from Térénex-en-Flouézoc'h (E side of Morlaix Bay).

	BRETON PORTS Continued		
Date	Name and Type of Vessel	Skipper	Remarks

	1942 continued		
16 June	Les-Deux-Anges (small lug-sailed F/V)		Working from Pont-Aven, carried Rémy, his family and 1 other member of CND to R/V off Glénan Is with N51. Carried out 8 further R/Vs with NID(C) F/Vs in 1942–3.
20 July	Monique (small cutter)		Escaped from Pont-de-la-Corde with 5 volunteers for Free French forces and intelligence mail. Sibiril's 2nd operation.
4 Aug.	L'Audacieux (cutter-rigged crabber)		Successful R/V with D. Lomenech in P11. Arms transferred were landed in Glénan Is and at Léchigiat, a small port near Le-Guilvinec.
Aug.	Sirène (crabber)		Escaped from Audierne. Added to NID(C) flotilla at Helford but not used operationally.
Nov.	Foedris-Arca		Failed escape from Camaret.

	1943		
5 Feb.	Yvonne (small cutter)		Escaped from Pont-de-la-Corde (Carantec) with 10 passengers, including, for first time, 2 US airmen shot down in raid on Lorient, 1 RAF airman and mail for 'Alliance'. Ernest Sibiril's 3rd operation.
6 Mar.	S'ils-Te-Mordent (small cutter)		Escaped from Pont-de-la-Corde (Carantec) with 9 passengers including Gwenaël Bolloré, who had bought the old (1914) sailing boat rotting on mud and got Ernest Sibiril to repair it. A hard crossing. Ernest Sibiril's 4th operation and 2nd with 'Alliance'.
29 Mar.	Jean (6-m. seaweed-cutter)		Escaped from Pont-de-la-Corde (Carantec) with 18 passengers, including Yvonne Pétrement and 1 US airman. Carried mail from 'Alliance'. Ernest Sibiril's 5th operation.
4 Apr.	Jeanne (5-m. cutter-rigged boat)		Escaped from Pont-de-la-Corde (Carantec) with 5 passengers (Jourdain family from Carantec and Locanolé, including 1 woman, all volunteers for Free French forces. Picked up by RN 35 miles off English coast. Ernest Sibiril's 6th operation.
5 Apr.	Viking (yacht belonging to Comtesse de Ronseray)		Failed escape from Saint-Quay/Portrieux by a group of réfractaires (evaders from forced labour), none of whom knew how to handle a boat. Ended up in Guernsey in German hands.
6 Apr.	Dalc'h-Mad (sardine pinasse)	Louis Marec	Escaped from Tréboul (Douarnenez) with 19 on board, including Sqn Ldr Gordon Carter. Arrived at Coverack.

BRETON PORTS Continued

Date	Name and Type of Vessel	Skipper	Remarks
	1943 continued		
28 Apr.	Red-Atao		Escaped from Pont-de-la-Corde (Carantec) with 5 passengers and mail on board. Ernest Sibiril's 7th operation.
11 May	Tor-Eben		Escaped from Pont-de-la-Corde (Carantec) with 12 passengers including 1 Belgian and 3 French airmen, plus mail. Ernest Sibiril's 8th operation.
21–23 May	Sainte-Anne (4-m. open boat)	Henri Stéphane	Stéphane, an escaped French POW, sailed her from Ploumanac'h to Salcombe single-handed after a false start in a canoe.
29 May	Kermor (7-m. cutter)		Escaped from Pont-de-la-Corde (Carantec) with ? 13 passengers. Ernest Sibiril's 9th operation.
29 May	Météore (8-m. cutter)		Escaped from Pont-de-la-Corde (Carantec) with ? 10 passengers plus crew. Ernest Sibiril's 10th operation. According to Huguen, Kermor and Météore together carried 28 passengers. Alain Sibiril specified 1 US airman, 4 French officers and mail carried on the two boats.
7 June	Saint-Yves		Escaped from Pont-de-la-Corde (Carantec) with 24 passengers and mail. Ernest Sibiril's 11th operation. BBC message on 23/6 urged him to come to England himself.
10 June	Pierrot		Escaped from Landéda with 10 on board.
18 July	Armorick		Failed to escape from Pont-de-la-Corde with 18 passengers. Sailed in daylight as it was no longer possible to do so by night. Sailed round Guernsey to Trébeurden and back to Ile-Callot in Morlaix Bay, 8 days after leaving. Ernest Sibiril's 12th, and only unsuccessful, operation.
23 July	Pirate		Escaped from Pont-de-la-Corde with 7 passengers, including 5 brothers Le Ven from Ile-Callot. Germans had ordered evacuation of Ile-Callot, so Le Ven brothers, who had contributed so much to previous operations, decided to leave with 2 friends. Ernest Sibiril's 13th operation. Sibiril then went into hiding, having asked his father to build him a boat in which to escape. Boat completed in 10 days.
5 Aug.	Yvonne-Georges	Nicolas Foughet	Escaped from Ile-de-Sein to Newlyn with 5 on board.

BRETON PORTS Continued

Date	Name and Type of Vessel	Skipper	Remarks
		1943 Continued	
12 Aug.	La-Rose Éffeuillée (10-m. old sardine pinasse converted into crabber with cutter rig)	Joseph Ménesguen	Sailed from Morgat and picked up 19 passengers on E side of Crozon peninsula. (See Pichavant, Clandestins de l'Iroise, iii, pp. 317–36 for details and names.) Landed at Newlyn.
13 Aug	Rulianec (5-m. cutter, undecked yacht with 6-h.p. motor)		Escaped from Morgat in daylight with 6 on board. Landed at Penzance.
22 Aug.	Courlis II (open boat)		Escaped from Lilia with 1 on board.
23 Aug.	Moise (13-m. sardine pinasse with 24-h.p. motor)		Sailed on 19 Aug. from Douarnenez with 7-day permit. Returned clandestinely on 23 Aug. and picked up passengers from Proz-Lanvers. 22 on board including crew. Organised by Victor Salez. Landed at Newlyn. Salez acted in response to request from Lt Yves Le Hénaff, organiser of Lysander operations, to get a number of senior French officers to UK.
29 Aug.	Joie-des-Anges		Escaped from Ile-de-Groix via Concarneau.
29 Aug.	Marie-Joseph		Escaped from Concarneau with 12 passengers.
1 Sept.	Paul-André		Escaped from Locquenolé.
9 Sept.	Muse-des-Mers		Escaped from Concarneau with 8 passengers.
19 Sept.	Ar-Voulac'h (17-m. long-liner with 24-h.p. Bolinders motor)		The second escape organised by Le Hénaff with assistance of Victor Salex and Québriac. Former supposed to have gone to Le Grau-du-Roi, therefore had to hide in garden shed at Douarnenez. Passengers (25) smuggled aboard in Rosmeur harbour (Douarnenez) at night from a nearby sardine factory. Landed at Newlyn.
21 Sept.	Anas		Escaped from Concarneau, according to Ile-de-Sein list.
After 21 Sept	Marpha		Escaped from Concarneau, according to Ile-de-Sein list. No date or passenger details.
2 Oct.	La Pérouse (11-m. cutter)		Escaped from Douarnenez with 22 on board, including Victor Salez, 2 French naval commanders, 2 naval officers and 2 US airman. Organised by Le Hénaff. Port of Douarnenez closed in consequence and series of operations thus ended.
Oct.	Yvonne-Georges	Nicolas Fouquet	Escaped from Ile-de-Sein to Newlyn with 4 passengers, one of whom was in trouble with Germans for having smacked a girl who consorted with one of them.

BRETON PORTS Continued

Date	Name and Type of Vessel	Skipper	Remarks
		1943 continued	
23 Oct.	Suzanne-Renée	Joseph Morvan (ex-L'Étourdi) and M. Belcon, his brother-in-law	Escape organised by J.-C. Camors, a BCRA/ MI9 agent from Camaret or Morgat, with 19 airmen on board (13 US, 4 RAF, 1 RCAF and 1 Norwegian), after a passage of 133 hours (delay caused by storm). Camors had just previously been shot and killed in Rennes by the German agent Roger le Légionnaire.
30 Oct.	L'Yvonne (7-m. half-decked sloop-rigged crabber)		Escaped from Camaret. She was to have carried the airmen left behind by the Suzanne-Renée, but as German surveillance was now so tight she carried only her crew of 4. Crossed to Newlyn under sail.
31 Oct.	Requin	Ernest Sibiril	Boat built for Ernest Sibiril by his father Alain. Launched at night, carried 7 passengers including Ernest Sibiril, his brother Léon, a son of Commandant Guizien (a passenger on the unfortunate Armorick), 2 other Morlaix inhabitants, a secret agent from Marseilles named Paul Daniel and an RAF pilot (George Wood). Sibiril's 14th escape operation.
22–23 Nov.	La-Horaine (Ponts et Chaussées lighthouse-tender)		Le Hénaff met Yvon Jézéquel of Lézardrieux who wanted to join Free French forces. Decided to use La-Horaine on her regular visit to Roches-Douvres lighthouse. Overcame German armed guard but owing to poor visibility failed to pick up 20 planned passengers and crossed to Dartmouth without them.
		1944	
22 Jan.	Breiz-Izel		Escaped from Tréboul (Douarnenez) with 31 passengers on board – 12 airmen and 19 volunteers for Fighting French forces. Organised with financial help from Georges Broussine's 'Bourgogne' escape organisation. Landed at Falmouth.
3 Feb.	Jouet-des-Flots (small cargo coasting vessel)	Le Bris	Sailed from Ile-Tudy with 31 on board, including Pierre Brossolette, Emile Bollaert, Emile Laffon and Jacques Maillet, who had been trying to get to London by air pick-up operation for 3 months but were defeated by bad weather. Operation organised by Le Hénaff. The ship suffered damage by striking the bottom when entering Port-Tudy to pick up the passengers. This leak got steadily worse as they headed north for the Pointe-du-Raz in bad weather and the engine was flooded. Le Bris managed to run the ship ashore in the Feunten-Aod creek near Plogoff. Brossolette, Bollaert and Le Hénaff arrested: Maillet and Laffon escaped to Paris.

BRETON PORTS Continued

Date	Name and Type of Vessel	Skipper	Remarks
		1944 continued	
22 Feb.	*Amity*		15th and last escape operation organised from Carantec. Boat built clandestinely by Alain Sibiril (aged 70) and 2 trusted shipwrights in 10 days. Launched at night. Sailed with 22 local fishermen and seaweed-gatherers. A total of 146 passengers landed successfully by the efforts of Sibiril family.

Appendix C

FROM PUBLIC RECORD OFFICE, LONDON Ref ADM I/18977 (010501) DDOD
(1) *Ref C.D.C.3199/44.*

It is desired to bring to your notice the conduct of the following officers and ratings with a view to the award of some recognition:

Acting Commander E.A.G. Davis, DSO, RNR

Lieutenant D.L. Birkin, RNVR

Lieutenant M.P. Salmond, RNVR

Lieutenant J.T. McQuoid Mason, SANF (V).

Lieut Commander P.A. Williams, RNVR

Sub Lieutenant D.N. Miller, SANF (V)

Lieutenant K.M. Uhr-Henry, RANVR

Petty Officer H.E. Mould, DSM Off. No. P/JX 107084

Petty Officer F.S. Smith, Off. No. C/JX 143074

Leading Seaman A. Hibbert, Off. No. C/JX 259060

A.B. Roger Bartley, Off. No. C/JX 260016

A.B. Harold Pickles, Off. No. D/JX 272386

A.B. Paul Lumsley, Off. No. P/JX 254361

A.B. James J. Gordon, Off. No. P/JX 262137

A.B. John Markham, Off. No. P/JX 327761

A.B. John Hayden, Off. No. P/SSX 29812

Telegraphist Henry Banks, Off. No. C/JX 215426

Telegraphist C. Gadd; Off. No. D/JX 184213

Stoker Kenneth Peel, Off. No. P/KX 135977

Stoker Ronald Bracey, Off. No. D/KX 151590

Stoker Alfred A. Andrews, Off. No. C/KX 121798

Petty Officer W.H. Webb, Off. No. DM/DX 2399

2. Since 1941 the 15th MGB Flotilla has been engaged in maintaining a line of sea communication between United Kingdom and enemy occupied territory, notably France and Holland, and to-day the force consists of 5 Coastal Forces craft and some 125 seagoing officers and men.

3. The flotilla has benefitted from much scientific development and progress since its early days, and whilst its personnel have reached a high standard of efficiency in the special technique required of these clandestine operations into enemy waters the above named officers and men have been brought into prominence by their outstanding ability and conduct, some details of which are set forth below.

4. *Acting Commander E.A.G. Davis, DSO, RNR.*

(a) Commander Davis joined DDOD(I) (then NID(C)) early in 1941 and in September of that year he was appointed Senior Officer of the then 15th MGB Flotilla; Principal Operations Officer; and in charge of DDOD(I)'s main training and operational base at Dartmouth.

(b) By February 1942 Commander Davis had commanded 12 successful operations to the enemy controlled coasts of Holland and north Brittany in conditions of exceptional difficulty due partly to the unreliable and unsuitable type of Coastal Forces craft then available. For these services he was awarded the DSO in March 1942 (a copy of the citation which resulted in this award is attached).

(c) Since March 1942 Commander Davis has executed 22 further operations, the majority to the peculiarly difficult pilotage waters of the north coast of France west of the Cherbourg Peninsula.

(d) In December 1942 the Fighting French authorities desired to convey concrete expression of their appreciation of the services rendered by the 15th MGB

Flotilla to their cause; and Commander Davis was one of the four officers selected by DDOD(I) for recognition which resulted in the award of the Croix de Guerre in May of the following year.

(e) With the passage of time the improvement in the ships placed at DDOD(I)'s disposal, coupled with the introduction of QH gear and other aids to navigation and detection of enemy forces, have enabled faster passages to be made, and operations have continued well into the short summer nights of the year, but these advantages have been offset by increasing enemy vigilance both onshore and at sea along the convoy routes and coastal waters.

(f) A number of the limited pinpoints available have been compromised by disaster overtaking the intelligence and other organisations served by the flotilla, whilst others have been rendered useless by beach mining and enemy defences in the vicinity, leaving only those localities most difficult of access.

(g) As the launching of the allied invasion draws nearer the enemy convoys are more strongly escorted and his coastal patrols strengthened, with the result that the ships of the flotilla sailing singly and unsupported invariably have to run the gauntlet of numerous enemy forces at sea. Moreover, constant sweeps into enemy waters by ships of the Royal Navy necessitate the most careful planning to avoid untoward incidents and restrict the freedom of movement of our ships accordingly.

(h) Notwithstanding these mounting difficulties the volume of operations has steadily increased, and Commander Davis has trained a band of young officers second in skill and enthusiasm only to himself.

(i) The flotilla under this officer's leadership has been responsible for feeding the field organisations providing the intelligence vital to OVERLORD; has brought home the intelligence enabling the CROSSBOW targets to be attacked; has kept open the lines of communication with the SOE underground movements on the Continent, and in the three months ending 31 March last has evacuated upwards of 100 allied army and air force personnel which were proving an embarrassment to the intelligence organisations in France.

(j) The American OSS are now embarking on a programme of operations to the Continent, and a division of American Coastal Forces craft has joined the 15th MGB Flotilla to cater for the OSS's needs; to enable operations to continue well on into the summer (for which purpose the British craft are too slow) and to cope with the still increasing volume of operations. Commander Davis is now devoting his attention to the training of the American contingent, and in view of the increased importance and scope of his work he has recently been granted the acting rank of Commander whilst holding his present appointment.

(k) The brilliant leadership displayed by this officer; the enthusiasm and discipline he has engendered in the officers and men of the flotilla; his courage and skill in operations; the initiative and imagination with which he has interpreted DDOD(I)'s directives both in the operations and training spheres; and his physical and mental endurance throughout three years' hard work and continuous endeavour, and his unfailing cheerfulness and loyalty in the face of exasperating delays and disappointments, due to inadequate equipment and disasters in the field, are thought to be worthy of the highest praise and some further recognition.

5. *Lieutenant D.L. Birkin, RNVR.*

(a) Next to his Commanding Officer, Lieutenant Birkin is perhaps the most outstanding officer in the flotilla. He joined DDOD(I) in January 1942 on being commissioned from the rating of Telegraphist and after a course in navigation and pilotage was appointed to the 15th MGB Flotilla.

(b) From an enthusiastic amateur he has developed into an able navigator and pilot far in excess of his two years' experience, has 28 operations into enemy waters as Navigating Officer of the Expedition to his credit, and has on nine occasions been specifically mentioned by the Commanding Officer of the Expedition.

(c) Since precise navigation and pilotage are essential features of these clandestine operations, and Lieutenant Birkin is handicapped by a tendency to seasickness and a chronic sinus disability which frequently gives him considerable pain, his performance is the more noteworthy.

(d) He has experienced in full measure the dangers and discomforts already described in this history, which in the worst weather conditions under which the flotilla operates approach the limit of endurance of the physically fit, as DDOD(I) can testify from personal experience.

(e) He has in addition been in charge of surf-boats between the mother ship and the enemy shore, and on one occasion in the month of January he with another officer stood for 1½ hours in surf holding the boat in position since it could not be beached or withdrawn to seaward, whilst the negotiations were proceeding on shore practically under the noses of the enemy coast patrols.

6. *Lieutenant M.P. Salmond, RNR.*

(a) This officer's contribution to the work of the flotilla since his appointment in March 1942 includes 24 operations to France and Holland principally as Navigating Officer of the Expedition. He has also been in charge of surf-boat work.

(b) Lieut Salmond has also experienced in full measure the extreme discomfort of operations in the winter months when the ships of the 15th MGB Flotilla put to sea in weather which keeps normal operational Coastal Forces craft in harbour. Although a martyr to seasickness, this disability in no way detracts from Lieutenant Salmond's enthusiasm, determination and efficiency.

(c) He has on several occasions been in action with enemy forces during operations to the coast of Holland.

7. *Lieutenant J.T. McQuoid Mason, SANF (V).*

(a) Lieut McQuoid Mason is another particularly outstanding officer of the flotilla, whose experience since his appointment in May 1942 has covered a wide range of duties including, during the course of 19 operations, First Lieutenant and Commanding Officer of individual craft and latterly as Commanding Officer of the Expedition.

(b) This officer's qualities as a seaman and a leader early came into prominence, and on one occasion when the ship in which he was serving as First Lieutenant (MGB 501) was destroyed at sea by an internal explosion, DDOD(I) who was onboard at the time was impressed with his cool ability. He accompanied the latter below decks in search of survivors and subsequently tended the injured and made preparations for abandoning ship.

(c) After a short detachment in command of a specially constructed fast fishing vessel attached to DDOD(I)'s Bay of Biscay flotilla, Lieut Mason played a leading role in a series of trials to determine the best of several types of small surf boats constructed by DDOD(I) for carriage onboard MGBs. Here his natural gift for seamanship was evident.

(d) Subsequently he returned to the 15th MGB Flotilla where his judgment, ability and reliability in command of operations have brought him into special prominence.

8. *Lieutenant Commander P.A. Williams, RNVR.*

(a) This officer was first brought to DDOD(I)'s notice in October 1941 when in command of MGB 325 on temporary loan to DDOD(I) his outstanding qualities and natural aptitude for the type of work contributed largely to the success of six operations to the French and Dutch coasts.

(b) When a vacancy arose in the 15th MGB Flotilla in April 1943 Lieut Comdr Williams was given a command since when he has executed ten further operations, eight of them as Commanding Officer of the Expedition.

(c) On a recent occasion he was in command of a force consisting of two MGBs engaged on evacuating some 31 escaped prisoners of war and agents from a difficult pinpoint on the north coast of France. Having completed the embarkation he was standing out to sea along a narrow channel fringed by rocks and shoals whose only outlet was to the northward, when he found his way barred by three enemy patrol vessels waiting at the seaward entrance. By a judicious combination of speed and use of the special challenge and reply procedure provided by DDOD(I) for such emergencies, the enemy remained in doubt regarding his identity until they were abaft his beam. They then opened fire, but being still uncertain ceased firing 15 seconds later, with the result that the force escaped with the loss of one rating killed and superficial damage to both ships.

(d) On two other occasions when returning from an operation loaded with passengers he has sighted superior enemy forces and by a quick and correct appreciation of the situation followed by cool and skilful handling of his ship has escaped detection and compromise of the operation.

(e) Whilst engaged on an operation during the course of the recent action off the Ile de Bas in which HMS *Black Prince* and Tribal destroyers were engaged with Elbing-class destroyers, Lieut Comdr Williams spent a strenuous time avoiding the melee, but was eventually illuminated and fired on by heavy calibre guns, fortunately without result.

(f) By his constant study of the problem and intelligent grasp of the principles of clandestine operations in difficult pilotage waters flanked by enemy patrol vessels Lieut Comdr Williams has executed brilliantly a number of operations which have been models of how it should be done.

9. *Sub Lieutenant D.N. Miller, SANF (V).*

(a) This officer joined DDOD(I) in July 1943 and in addition to his duties as Executive Officer of Coastal Forces craft has specialised in surf-boat work in which he has become expert in the course of 14 operations to the French coast.

(b) He has three times been specially commended by the Commanding Officer of the Expedition for the skill and endurance he has displayed in this difficult aspect of clandestine operations.

(c) The normal task confronting the officer in charge of a convoy of surf-boats or a single craft is a journey of anything between six cables and two miles between the mother ship and the shore in complete darkness invariably athwart strong tidal streams for which the Brittany coast is notorious, and more often than not on to a lee shore. If the tide is low the surf-boats have to thread their way through a maze of rocks, and if the actual landing is on rocks great care and skill is needed if the boats are to avoid being swamped and smashed. It will be appreciated that all the more accessible and obvious landing beaches are mined or overlooked by strongposts, so that DDOD(I) is forced to use those landing-places least likely to be under enemy observation, and the more difficult the landing-place the more likely is the expedition to complete its business unmolested.

(d) The problem of the return passage to the mother ship includes pulling into a head sea with a heavily loaded boat if the operation is an evacuation, and finding the mother ship in the darkness. Recent trials with short-wave directional R/T enabling the expedition to communicate with the reception committee onshore and to assist the surf-boat in homing to the mother ship will remove some of the present difficulties, but the equipment cannot yet be relied upon since it must be highly selective and minutely tuned for security reasons, conditions unfavourable to the rough treatment inevitable in small craft and surf-boats. The use of a 'guide line' between the ship and the surf-boat is normally impracticable owing to the distance and the tortuous approach to the landing-place.

10. *Lieutenant K.M. Uhr-Henry, RANVR.*

(a) This officer joined DDOD(I) in May 1943 and like Sub Lieut Miller has distinguished himself as a specialist in surf-boat work in the course of 12 operations to France.

(b) The above remarks regarding Sub Lieut Miller apply equally to Lieut Uhr-Henry.

(c) In addition to his work as a surf-boat specialist he has acted as relief First Lieutenant of Coastal Forces craft.

(d) He was the second of the two officers referred to in the citation regarding Lieut Birkin in para. 5 (e) above.

(e) Lieut Uhr-Henry has been specially mentioned on five occasions by the Commanding Officer of the Expedition.

11. *Petty Officers Mould, Smith and Webb.*
    Leading Seaman Hibbert.
    A.B.s Bartley, Pickles, Lumsley, Gordon, Markham and Hayden.
    Telegraphists Banks and Gadd.
    Stokers Peel, Bracey and Andrews.

(a) From a seagoing company of over 100 the above named ratings have been selected for prominent conduct or individual acts of initiative and courage.

(b) The majority of these men have taken part in 27 operations to the coasts of France and Holland since mid-1942.

(c) Petty Officer Smith, Leading Seaman Hibbert, A.B.s Bartley, Gordon and Markham and Stoker Andrews have all been continuously employed as surf-boat crews.

(d) Petty Officer Mould, DSM, who joined the 15th MGB Flotilla in September 1943, has proved most outstanding in his duties as coxswain, and like Petty Officer Smith has spent long hours continuously at the wheel both while the ship has been conned into her anchorage through the dangerous rocky approaches to the north coast of France, and again when weather conditions have reached dangerous proportions necessitating expert steering to luff into seas or to avoid broaching to.

(e) Regarding the stokers, DDOD(I) has so often described in forceful detail the anxiety always attending these operations owing to the unreliability of the engines (particularly the diesels) of the 15th Flotilla, that the devotion to duty of these men in helping to effect running repairs at sea, resorting all night to hand pumping when mechanical pumps fail, working long hours in harbour to get defective ships ready for sea in time, all carried out with the utmost cheerfulness and zeal, needs no further emphasis.

(f) Regarding the telegraphists, who have the responsibility of certain special equipment in addition to the standard communications in the ship, it is felt that their duties below decks, for the most part carried out in conditions of extreme discomfort due to the invariably violent motion of the ship, coupled with their efforts to bring their sets into action again after being swamped by sea water, and their universally high example in the general work of the ship on operations when all hands irrespective of their special duties are employed in assisting to launch, store and subsequently re-embark surf-boats swiftly and silently, is worthy of some recognition.

(g) With regard to A.B.s Pickles, Lumsley and Hayden: they have been prominent by their example and enthusiasm in the general work of the ship and have shown outstanding attention to duty in the maintenance of the armament, and their initiative and skill when the ship's armament has been in action.

(h) Finally, Petty Officer Webb has distinguished himself by his work as coxswain during 16 operations, firstly in MGB 325 under Lieut Comdr Williams and secondly when, in view of his previously outstanding conduct, he was selected for draft to a vessel of the 15th MGB Flotilla in September 1943.

(signed) F. SLOCUM
DDOD(I)
2.5.44.

FROM PUBLIC RECORD OFFICE, LONDON Ref ADM I/16951 (010501) DDOD (1) Ewf O.D. 03325/44.

With the reduction of irregular operations in Home Waters and the paying off of the principal flotillas engaged on this work for the past five years, it is desired to bring to your notice the conduct of the undermentioned officers and ratings with a view to the award of some operational or periodical recognition as may be thought fit:

Operational

Act. Lt. Cdr. R.M. Marshall, DSC, RNVR
Lt. Andrew Smith, RNVR
Lt. L.F. Bott, RANVR
Lt. R.U.D. Townsend, RNVR
C.F. Hearn, Act. Ch. M.M.
Petty Officer G.C. Chambers, Off. No. D/SSX 30107
A.B. G.I. Hill, Off. No. C/JX 355797
A.B. O. Bleasdale, Off. No. D/SSX 20104
A.B. J. Daglish, Off. No. P/JX 295297
A.B. C.W. Wren, Off. No. C/JX 314255

A.B. A.L.G. Turner, Off. No. C/JX 374936
A.B. N.T.J. Hine, Off. No. P/JX 352292
A.B. J.G.S. Pringle, Off. No. D/JX 340460
Ldg. Sea. R.E.J. Rive, Off. No. LT/JX 199024

Periodical or Operational
Act. Lt. Cdr. S.M. Mackenzie, RNVR
Lt. Cdr. P.F. Whinney, RNVR (Sp.)
Lt. Cdr. W.B. Luard, RN (Retd.)
Lt. Cdr. N. Warington Smyth, RNVR

2. The 15th MGB Flotilla, from which the majority of the above named operations officers and ratings have been selected, has been the principal means of maintaining communications with enemy occupied France, particularly during the six months preceding D-Day. The Flotilla continued to work to parts of the coast behind the enemy lines until Brittany was liberated in August 1944. Seven officers and 15 men of this flotilla have been decorated for their work in earlier years. The officers and men now mentioned, who joined the 15th MGB Flotilla more recently, have been brought into prominence by their rapid mastery of the special technique required for work of this nature and by the high standard they achieved, some details of which follow.

3. Lt. Townsend and Ldg. Sea. Rive have been selected from the officers and men of the Inshore Patrol Flotilla, which maintained communications with western France throughout the summer of 1943 when Coastal Forces operations were not possible, and through whose hands a quantity of most valuable intelligence reports and political figures of importance reached this country.

4. The majority of the officers and men of these two flotillas are volunteers for similar work in the Eastern Theatre and are now undergoing courses in preparation for their new duties under tropical conditions.

15th MGB FLOTILLA

5. *Act. Lt. Cdr. R.M. Marshall,* DSC, RNVR.

(a) Lt. Cdr. (then Lt.) Marshall was appointed to the command of MGB 503 in November 1943, after a distinguished career in a regular operational flotilla, culminating in the award of the DSC.

(b) His first task was to get this ship into reliable running order. Being the first of her class she had suffered a series of serious mechanical breakdowns, which had undermined the morale of her crew and their faith in their craft. Under Lt. Marshall's direction the ship rapidly became operational.

(c) After accompanying two operations as an observer in another ship of the flotilla, Lt. Marshall embarked on a series of 12 faultlessly executed expeditions.

(d) Four of these operations were to parts of the North French coast not previously visited; Lt. Marshall displayed outstanding skill in locating accurately these new pinpoints, entering narrow, rock-strewn channels without hesitation. On one occasion he pressed on and completed an operation of great importance in a north-easterly gale gusting to force 8, under conditions which would have made a less determined officer give up long before reaching the French coast.

(e) MGB 503 embarked 100 Allied airmen from a beach in enemy occupied France between January and March 1944. The procedure involved lying at anchor within a mile of enemy watchposts for between two and four hours at a time. The standard of efficiency to which Lt. Marshall had trained his surf-boats' crews needs no emphasis in view of these figures.

(f) By skilful tactics and cool and correct judgment, Lt. Marshall avoided detection by enemy sea patrols and convoys indicated by Radar and visually on a number of occasions. His high qualities of leadership and seamanship are worthy of recognition.

6. *Lt. Andrew Smith,* RNVR.

(a) Lt. Smith joined the 15th MGB Flotilla in June 1942, as a Sub Lieutenant and Executive Officer of MA/SB 36, transferring to MGB 503 when she was commissioned in 1943. Apart from fulfilling his duties as First Lieutenant with outstanding efficiency, he specialised in surf-boat work in which he became expert in the course of 14 operations to the French coast.

(b) The orderly embarkation of the 100 evaders and escaped prisoners of war by MGB 503, referred to in para. 5 (e) above, was the work of Lt. Smith, whose personality and power of command in controlling a crowd of excited individuals on the verge of rescue was a notable achievement in so young an officer.

(c) The unhurried efficiency and calm demeanour of his surf-boats' crews, in circumstances where excitement and confusion are not uncommon, are a tribute to his skill and leadership.

(d) On two occasions he found his way to and from the pinpoint in thick fog. A number of the landings included pulling distances of $1\frac{1}{2}$ miles and over, mostly between rocks and through tortuous channels, with the time factor always present.

(e) On occasions of large landings or embarkations he has been in charge of convoys of surf-boats, which he has led into the pinpoint, supervised the unloading of stores and the embarkation of passengers, and led them back to the parent craft with the minimum delay. Such work has included launching the boats through surf and working in water waist high for considerable periods in mid-winter.

(f) He has on six occasions been specially mentioned in the report of the Commanding Officer of the expedition and his own Commanding Officer has remarked: 'He invariably uses his initiative under conditions of unexpected difficulty and, above all, inspires his boats' crews with confidence.'

(g) Lt. Smith received accelerated promotion to Lieutenant in August 1944.

(h) Add to the above facts the conditions of no moon and complete darkness save for the white loom of surf, and the conduct of this officer needs no further emphasis.

7. *Lt. L.F. Bott, RANVR.*

(a) Lt. Bott joined the 15th MGB Flotilla in February 1944 as Executive Officer of MGB 502 and has taken part in 12 operations, on four of which he has acted as Officer in charge of the surf boats and landing party.

(b) This officer has been brought to notice by his ability and industry as Executive Officer of the Senior Officer's ship, in which he was required to set a standard and example to the rest of the flotilla in smartness and efficiency.

(c) When a division of American Coastal Forces craft was attached to the 15th MGB Flotilla, Lt. Bott played a leading part in the practices and exercises designed for the benefit of the newcomers, and accompanied them on operations as surf-boat officer whilst they were gaining experience.

(d) On two occasions when MGB 502 was in action, Lt. Bott ably assisted his Commanding Officer to extricate the ship from a precarious situation with shoal water on three sides and enemy forces blocking the only way of escape to seaward.

(e) Whilst chance has not brought this officer into special prominence on any specific operations, it is considered that the high example he has set by his general conduct is worthy of some recognition.

8. *C.F. Hearn (Act. Ch. M.M.)*

(a) Act. Ch. M.M. Hearn joined MGB 502 early in 1944 as Senior Engine Room Rating.

(b) Since these Camper & Nicholson diesel Coastal Forces craft are fitted with experimental engines, they have for long been a notoriously difficult maintenance problem, and yet, due to the zeal and efficiency of Hearn, only on one occasion in ten expeditions was an operation postponed for reasons of mechanical break-down. On the occasion in question, which was no fault of Hearn's, he worked throughout the night and the following day to effect the necessary repairs which enabled the ship to sail that night.

(c) On leaving MGB 502 as a C.W. candidate his Commanding Officer reported: 'In a long experience of Coastal Forces craft I have never met such an enthusiastic, zealous and inspiring man as Hearn.'

9. *Petty Officer Chambers*

A.B. Hill		*A.B. Wren*	
A.B. Bleasdale	MGB 502	*A.B. Turner*	MGB 503
A.B. Daglish		*A.B. Hine*	
		A.B. Pringle	

(a) The above named ratings have all served as surf-boats' crews in addition to the general work of the ship and each has 12 to 15 operations to his credit.

(b) They have been brought into prominence by exceptional qualities of cheerfulness, physical endurance, skill as surf-boat crews, and cool and calm conduct in emergency under the conditions described in this narrative. In the general work of the ship they have been outstanding examples in zeal, efficiency and general bearing.

INSHORE PATROL FLOTILLA

10. *Lt. R.U.D. Townsend, RNVR.*

(a) This officer was transferred from the Army Intelligence Corps to the RNVR in March 1942. He was appointed as First Lieutenant of an ex-French trawler of the Inshore Patrol Flotilla, under the command of Lt. D. Lomenech, RNVR, who was awarded a DSC and Bar for his work in this and similar craft.

(b) Ships of this flotilla were used to maintain contact with western France, sailing under French colours and spending up to four days off the French Biscay coast under the pretence of fishing. Such work, carried out in face of close inspection by enemy surface vessels and aircraft, demanded cool deliberate courage. No defensive weapons could be carried other than light arms, and those concerned knew that they were liable to be shot for espionage if caught.

(c) Lt. Townsend took part in six operations under the leadership of Lt. Lomenech, carrying out his duties with outstanding efficiency. On two occasions he landed on the French coast in daylight dressed as a French fisherman in order to collect secret mail from a 'postbox' onshore. In July 1943, Lt. Townsend was appointed to command MFV 2022, an ex-French vessel of the same type, in which he carried out four further operations in command, displaying initiative and leadership of a high order including efficient seamanship in exceptionally bad weather. His calm and courageous conduct was an example to his crew.

(d) By the end of 1943 the mental and physical strain of these operations showed signs of affecting his health and he was transferred to the command of a training tender, in which capacity he has since rendered less spectacular but arduous and successful service.

11. *Ldg. Sea. Rive*

This rating joined the Inshore Patrol Flotilla in May 1942, and took part in eight operations to the west coast of France. He showed outstanding ability as a seaman, and his keenness, cheerfulness and disregard for the personal discomforts and unusual hazards of life in these small cramped ships was an example to the men with whom he sailed.

DDOD(I) H.Q. STAFF

12. *Act. Lt. Cdr. S.M. Mackenzie, RNVR.*

(a) Lt. Cdr. Mackenzie was one of DDOD(I)'s original staff officers, having joined the division as a Sub Lieutenant in June 1940 after a period on the staff of the British Naval Attaché, Paris, in which he took part in the retreat and evacuation from Bordeaux.

(b) His first task was as Executive Officer of the first Coastal Forces craft allocated to DDOD(I), an ex-French MTB in which he took part in two operations to the north coast of France before his ship was sunk during an air attack on Portsmouth Harbour.

(c) He then transferred to her sister ship and spent several months overcoming her various defects, including the manufacture of spare parts unobtainable from stocks in the United Kingdom. On the day that this craft was finally ready for sea she too was destroyed in an air raid.

(d) Lt. Cdr. Mackenzie then transferred to DDOD(I)'s H.Q. Staff and throughout the rest of 1941 was responsible for the planning and dispatch of numerous irregular operations to Norway by Norwegian fishing vessel.

(e) In 1942 he laid the foundation of the Inshore Patrol Flotilla, personally commanded the first three operations by French fishing vessel to the French Biscay coast, and trained and developed the officers and men of the rapidly expanding flotilla. It is a tribute to the care and attention to detail exercised by

Lt. Cdr. Mackenzie that this flotilla, manned by volunteer officers and ratings, disguised as French fishermen, achieved a long, unbroken series of successful operations, unarmed and unescorted to the enemy's doorstep in daylight, whilst the first Commanding Officer trained by Lt. Cdr. Mackenzie received a DSC and Bar for his work. The capture of one vessel of the flotilla would have wrecked the whole enterprise, since, although outwardly identical to a French vessel, the interiors of the ships of the IPF were fitted out with navigational aids, living quarters and armouries of hand weapons.

(f) So successful were the operations executed by this flotilla that in 1942 it was decided to construct a replica of a small French auxiliary trawler, but fitted with high-speed Coastal Forces engines in an attempt to reach a speed of 20 knots so as to shorten the time spent in the danger area of no man's land between British and enemy controlled waters at night. Lt. Cdr. Mackenzie played a leading part in the fitting out of this vessel which, when nearing completion, was obliterated in an enemy air attack on Cowes. A second vessel was laid down and eventually entered into service and proved highly successful.

(g) When the Inshore Patrol Flotilla was well launched, Lt. Cdr. Mackenzie returned to DDOD(I)'s H.Q. and became senior Staff Officer, under the direction of DDOD(I) in charge of home operations. He has made a notable contribution in the development and improvement of methods of conducting irregular operations, including investigation into improved navigational aids, design of surf-boats, and homing equipment between these boats and their parent craft. On occasions of exceptional importance he has accompanied expeditions to sea and landed in enemy territory to confer with agents and others onshore.

(h) In April 1943, he was, on the recommendation of DDOD(I), awarded the Croix de Guerre for his work in the F.F. cause.

(i) Now, after five years' hard work and outstanding service, during which he has planned some 200 irregular operations, he is leaving DDOD(I) to seek fresh experience, and it is fitting that this exceptionally able young officer should close this chapter of his career with the award of some recognition.

13. *Lt. Cdr. P.F. Whinney, RNVR (Sp).*

(a)   This officer joined DDOD(I) with Lt. Cdr. Mackenzie in June 1940, having also previously served on the staff of the British Naval Attaché, Paris.

(b) His early training as a Midshipman and Sub Lieutenant, RN, were of great assistance in the first months of DDOD(I)'s work when no adequate staff was available or trained.

(c) He commanded the first Coastal Forces craft allocated to DDOD(I), referred to in para. 12 (b) above, and took part in two expeditions to the north coast of France.

(d) During the early months of 1941 he acted as liaison officer onboard HMS *Fidelity* fitting out at Barry for service with DDOD(I). *Fidelity* was manned by Fighting French personnel with little or no knowledge of the British language, naval custom or procedure, so that Lt. Cdr. Whinney's task was arduous in the extreme.

(e) Thereafter, he was loaned for duty with SOE until the beginning of 1942 when he was detached to Gibraltar to organise a flotilla for the prosecution of irregular operations in the Western Mediterranean.

(f) After a brief return to H.Q. staff and a visit to Spain to arrange for the clandestine purchase of Spanish feluccas for augmenting the Mediterranean flotilla, he was detached to North Africa in the wake of Operation TORCH to reconnoitre suitable advanced bases and requisition Italian-type local craft for operations to the Italian mainland and islands.

(g) Throughout 1943 he was at H.Q. controlling Mediterranean operations, most of which at that time were inspired from this country.

(h) He was awarded the Croix de Guerre with Lt. Cdr. Mackenzie in April 1943.

(i) In January 1944 he was again detached to the Mediterranean to set up an advanced operational base at Bastia, where his reliability, imagination and independent initiative were evidenced to the full. The operations executed from this base were of the relatively short-range type to the Italian west coast and intervening islands, the Gulf of Genoa and as far west as Toulon. The only Coastal Forces craft available were loaned from the mixed force of British American and Italian craft based on Bastia. The crews were untrained in irregular operations, seldom could the same craft be loaned consecutively, and Lt. Cdr. Whinney, in addition to his duties in charge of the base and as coordinator and planner, personally assumed charge of the first 18 operations, assisted by trained surf-boat crews from the original Mediterranean irregular flotillas. So much has been said in previous citations on this type of work that further emphasis on the skill and determination exercised by Lt. Cdr. Whinney, in avoiding enemy forces and pressing on with operations in the face of winter weather conditions, is unnecessary. By March 1944 a sufficient number of trained officers was available to relieve Lt. Cdr. Whinney from the necessity of personally conducting operations. Shortly afterwards a temporary illness forced him to relinquish his command and return to the United Kingdom where, after sick leave, he recovered and was appointed for important liaison duties with the French section of ISLD.

(j) It is submitted that the record of Lt. Cdr. Whinney's service with DDOD(I) merits recognition.

14. *Lt. Cdr. W.B. Luard, RN (Retd.).*

(a) Lt. Cdr. Luard first joined DDOD(I) as an unpaid volunteer in the autumn of 1940, and played a leading part in the early investigations into fishing vessel operations to the north coast, as opposed to the Biscay coast, of France.

(b) In January 1942, when the enemy had prohibited all offshore fishing activities from ports on the north coast, Lt. Cdr. Luard was appointed to the RAF Station St Eval, as DDOD(I)'s naval operations liaison officer.

(c) Thereafter, for over 2½ years, he rendered outstanding service in arranging for the provision of intelligence, including special sorties to obtain information on French fishing vessel movements in the Bay of Biscay: air escort on the outward and homeward daylight passages of the Inshore Patrol Flotilla through no man's land, and for the 15th MGB Flotilla: search and patrol for overdue ships, etc. These duties included many hours spent in operational flying combat areas and, in the early days, Lt. Cdr. Luard himself conducted the navigation of the search and patrol aircraft.

(d) In 1943, the Admiralty entrusted him with the organisation of two large-scale combined air/surface sweeps for rounding up French tunny vessels in the western approaches to the Bay of Biscay, whose presence was a hindrance to the RAF anti-submarine campaign.

(e) Side by side with these activities, Lt. Cdr. Luard, who is an expert in small craft design and performance, rendered valuable service in the design and production of the following equipment and handbooks:

K-dinghy sailing gear. Aircraft catamaran dinghy. RAF dinghy drift tables.	Air/sea rescue
Submarine target for training crews in anti-submarine work. Handbook of fishing industries.	Coastal Command RAF

Design of catamaran power-driven
canoes for irregular operations
by submarine and unorthodox
offensive warfare in the Eastern
Theatre.
}
DDOD(I) and CCO

(f) Having in 1943 been awarded the Croix de Guerre with Lt. Cdr. Mackenzie and Lt. Cdr. Whinney, for his contribution to irregular operations on behalf of France, he was in 1944 officially thanked by the Air Council for the work described in para. (e) above.

(g) Lt. Cdr. Luard was originally invalided from the submarine service with a tubercular hip towards the end of the last war, and the resulting illness has left him badly lame. In spite of this disability he has served in a fully operational appointment with DDOD(I) for over four years and is more active than many people not so handicapped.

(h) With the reduction of irregular operations in Home Waters, his duties have come to an end, he is shortly leaving DDOD(I) for other spheres of activity, and it is desired to mark the close of his appointment with DDOD(I) by the award of some recognition.

15. *Lt. Cdr. N. Warington Smyth, RNVR.*

(a) This officer joined DDOD(I)'s H.Q. staff from sea service in the summer of 1942. His knowledge of small ship design and construction was of special value to DDOD(I) at a time when operations were increasing rapidly; no suitable Coastal Forces craft could be spared from normal offensive operations and the problem of penetrating surf in the small dinghies, which could be carried in Coastal Forces, remained unsolved.

(b) Four ex-Turkish diesel Coastal Forces craft were eventually allocated to DDOD(I) and Lt. Cdr. Warington Smyth was mainly responsible for the modifications which rendered them fit for irregular operations. Meanwhile, he carried out deep researches into surf-boat design and produced drawings of several types of boat.

(c) Prototypes were built and tried out by this officer in comprehensive tests under full surf conditions.

(d) Three types were developed as the result of these tests, and rendered invaluable service in clandestine operations to the coasts of Holland and France in the winters of 1942/3 and 1943/4, and the record of the experience gained on the above described and subsequent tests is now being printed as an Admiralty publication.

(e) Since June 1943 he has been in command of the Inshore Patrol Flotilla, consisting of a parent ship and nine MFVs and has been responsible for the preparation and despatch of all expeditions to the Bay of Biscay since that date.

(f) At one period during his command, the wholesale arrest of members of the field organisation along the Biscay coast left the flotilla for several months without any operational tasks. Such is the nature of the type of officer and rating who volunteers for this type of unorthodox work that, while quite magnificent when actively engaged on dangerous operations, he becomes depressed and temperamental when not so employed. By his leadership and imagination Lt. Cdr. Warington Smyth maintained the morale of his force, engaged them on constant practices and experiments, and brought them to the highest pitch of efficiency.

(g) With the paying off of the Inshore Patrol Flotilla he is proceeding to an appointment with DMWD, where his scientific knowledge will be of great value.

Signed. F. SLOCUM
DDOD(I)
31.12.44.

The work of these irregular flotillas having been in the main undertaken on behalf of that organisation in which I represent Admiralty interests, I can confirm the high value of the results achieved and would, from personal knowledge of the individuals concerned, endorse the specific recommendations made.

Signed.
ADMI (F)
4.1.45.

I fully concur with DDOD(I)'s recommendations. These officers and men are outstanding representatives of an irregular naval flotilla which has performed hazardous duties for all three services since the fall of France. The value of these services is fully confirmed.

Signed.
DNI
9.1.45.

Appendix D

Les-Deux-Anges was sighted from approximately four miles distant owing to her large white lugsail which was at first thought to be the white sail of the agent's yacht, of which a photograph had been provided. When the craft made for the correct rendezvous position and hove to N51 was some two miles off, at which distance it was impossible to see the flapping foresail but between one mile and half a mile this could be seen through glasses and at 1900 exactly one of the vessel's crew could be seen standing by the mast as if to climb it.

2. Considering that the vessel conformed exactly to the description given it was decided to close and pass the vessel to starboard so that her name could be read, but as N51 approached within 100 yards or so the rendezvous craft put fenders out and this was considered proof enough of her identity.

3. N51 therefore went alongside the starboard side of Les-Deux-Anges and made fast, the crew donning naval caps to give confidence to the agent. In the swell that was running the two craft bumped a good deal but no damage was done and the Frenchman handled his boat well. The agent and party were embarked in under ten minutes and no contact was made with the fishermen crew who were fully employed keeping Les-Deux-Anges out of danger.

4. A disturbing feature of the operation was that the agent states that the fishermen crew of Les-Deux-Anges sighted N51 from four miles off at approximately the same time that they were themselves sighted by us and decided at once that N51 must be the right craft as she was a strange vessel to them. No criticism of N51's appearance as a French fishing vessel was made but the fishermen who knew every boat on the coast could recognise her as a stranger.

5. The agent however stated that the Breton fishermen in this area are so anti-German that on no account would they inform the German authorities of strange vessels sighted, and the danger from careless talk by drunken fishermen is practically non-existent owing to the Germans having requisitioned the entire stock of drink in north-western France.

6. The agent considered that the rendezvous position two miles south of La-Jument was too close to the coast as it was in sight of Penfret lighthouse on the Iles-de-Glénan at which he thought there might be a German watch-post. In our opinion however there is no watch-post in this lighthouse, and since it was seven miles from the rendezvous position it is unlikely that two small fishing craft would attract attention.

7. The agent also considered that the fishing smocks and caps worn by N51's crew were noticeably new and would not pass muster at close quarters. It is hoped to rectify this, however, by importing ancient and patched smocks from France on the next operation.

8. Les-Deux-Anges has a small petrol engine and a permit to fish from any port on the west coast of Brittany. For this operation she had sailed from Port-Manech where the German control is notoriously slack. The agent states that the vessel could continue to keep regular rendezvous with craft from UK varying the position as much as possible and the port of departure in France from time to time. It is hoped that this line of communication will be developed accordingly.

9. It is of interest to note here that the attempt to rendezvous with Les-Deux-Anges on 20th May failed for the following reason: Les-Deux-Anges was due to sail from

Lorient a.m. 20th May but was suffering from magneto trouble and her departure was postponed one day, the agent's intention being to keep the second rendezvous on 21st May. On the night of 20th/21st May, however, the RAF bombed Lorient and laid mines in the harbour with the result that no vessels were allowed to leave Lorient on the 21st. It is also of interest to note that N51 was lying off the coast during this raid, observing it with great pleasure but without realising its serious effect.

Unsigned minute from DDOD(I)'s records. The author of these comments must have been Lt Steven Mackenzie, writing as Slocum's Staff Officer in charge of operations in Home Waters, or Captain Slocum himself, recording Mackenzie's observations on this important question.

PART TWO

*Operations from
Gibraltar and other bases
in the Western Mediterranean*

CHAPTER XXII

The Polish Predicament

U nder the terms of the armistice concluded in June 1940 between the Axis powers and the French Government formed by Pétain at Bordeaux, the Germans completed their occupation of France's Atlantic seaboard, but left her Mediterranean coast in French hands.

Vichy was hampered by severely restricted numbers of armed forces and shortages of fuel. The controls it exercised over this residual coastline and that of the unoccupied French North African territories were therefore less effective than the defences that the Germans proceeded to develop from the Hook of Holland to Hendaye. Gibraltar, the nearest base in British hands, was 1,100 km. (700 miles) or more from the beaches of Languedoc and the *calanques* – the long deep creeks on the coast of Provence. It was thus some time before the British clandestine services sought to exploit what was for them a rather roundabout route to and from occupied France.

For the Poles, who faced genocide at the hands of the Nazis, and, on a lesser scale, the Czechs, the problem of organising escape routes from unoccupied France was more urgent. In the eight months between Hitler's conquest of their homeland and the fall of France, the Poles had set up a Government in-exile in Paris and proceeded to regroup and re-form Polish forces on Allied territory. A number of their naval vessels and the bulk of their merchant fleet had found refuge and a new operational base in Great Britain. It was in Britain, too, and with the support of the RAF, that senior Polish air force officers would have preferred to concentrate the effort to rebuild an air force. But General Sikorski, who was both Prime Minister and Commander-in-Chief, believed profoundly in France as he remembered it from 1918 and wished this to be done in France. Under the terms of a compromise reached at the end of October 1939, Polish air force personnel who had made their way to the West were divided equally between the two countries. The new Polish army was wholly raised and equipped in France, however, though one brigade had been reconstituted in Syria, then French mandated territory.

To extricate Polish troops from the neutral countries where they had taken refuge and been interned at the end of the campaign in Poland was no easy task. They had first to escape from internment and then find civilian clothes, identity documents and transport.

There were about 40,000, including most of an armoured brigade, in Hungary and 30,000 troops and 20,000 civilian refugees in Romania: many of the latter had had military training and were of an age to be called up. 13,800 had sought refuge in Lithuania. By June 1940 22,000 had been extricated from Romania and 21,000 from Hungary. From these two countries the escape line to France ran through Yugoslavia and Italy, which, despite Mussolini's alliance with Hitler, showed sympathy with the Poles and respected their Embassy. The French authorities also allowed Sikorski to mobilise suitable age groups from the Polish community in France, which was almost half a million strong, many still Polish citizens. Though this process of re-forming and training the new Polish armed forces was still far from complete at the time of the German breakthrough north of the Maginot Line, those under arms in France or serving with the Podhalańska Brigade at Narvik numbered about 82,000.

It had been agreed between Sikorski and Gamelin, the French Commander-in-Chief, that Polish units, when ready for action, would form their own corps and operate as a single unit, but this had still not been done when the battle of France began and such Polish units as were ready for action were widely dispersed. The 1st Grenadier Division formed part of the French 20th Corps and was deployed south-west of Nancy in defence of the Maginot Line. The 2nd Infantry Fusiliers was in the Belfort area, not far from the Swiss border, and became part of the French 15th Corps. The 10th Armoured Cavalry Brigade was partly available and there were eight Polish infantry companies and two anti-tank batteries serving in French regimental formations. The still untrained 3rd Division and two equally untrained battalions at Coëtquidan in Brittany were drawn into the battle eventually, but none of these units, whose strength totalled approximately 40,000, was in action before 14 June, the day Paris was occupied. They were all determined to fight, and the 1st and 2nd Divisions both did so with distinction, but the battle was already lost and organised French military resistance crumbled around them in growing confusion.

The Polish government had by this time moved to Angers, but General Sikorski, wishing to be as near as possible to the two Polish divisions then in action, went forward to his field headquarters near Nancy but then only added to the confusion by moving from place to place and becoming difficult to find. His faith in France was such that he had never considered the possibility of her defeat or made any plans for the withdrawal of Polish forces – which their disper-sion and integration in French formations made impracticable in the prevailing chaos.

By 17 June, the Polish government and President had retreated to Libourne and their French counterparts to Bordeaux, where

Pétain succeeded Reynaud as Prime Minister and asked the Spanish Government to ascertain Hitler's terms for an armistice. Sikorski met Pétain next day and subsequently issued a declaration of Polish determination to fight on at the side of Great Britain. He flew to London in an aircraft provided by Churchill, who, at a conference on 19 June, confirmed that Great Britain would continue the war, receive the Polish President and Government and do what was possible to evacuate Polish troops from France. In a radio bulletin broadcast that same day by the BBC, General Sikorski ordered his men to break through to ports in southern France or cross into Switzerland.

The evacuation of Polish troops began forthwith from ports on the west coast of France. Some 3,000 left Brest before it fell into German hands on 19 June. Others embarked at Saint-Malo and La-Rochelle. Two days later the process continued from Bordeaux, Bayonne and Saint-Jean-de-Luz, where the Polish liners *Batory* and *Sobieski* took off 4,000 troops and 500 civilians. The evacuation continued until 25 June from south-western French ports while British naval vessels kept the Luftwaffe at bay. Polish airmen embarked meanwhile at Port-Vendres and Sète in the Mediterranean. Estimates of the numbers rescued vary between 16,000 and 23,000: the official figure quoted in London at a meeting of the Polish National Council some weeks later was 19,457.

As Garliński, historian of Poland in the Second World War, has pointed out, this was not a bad result given the chaos of the time, the lack of transport and the dispersion of Polish units. Moreover, a significant number of men mobilised in France were *émigrés* living there who would have preferred to stay. There remained however many thousands who had no roots in France and who were extremely bitter at finding themselves abandoned by their senior officers and civilian authorities in a foreign country, without money, papers or advice.

One of those who had failed to get away from Saint-Jean-de-Luz was a professional Polish intelligence officer named M.Z. Slowikowski, who had been serving at Kiev under consular cover when war broke out and had then, with his wife and 13-year-old son, quickly made his way to France via Finland, Sweden, Norway, Great Britain, Holland and Belgium.[2] Slowikowski, who held the rank of major and was already 53 years old, was given the job of second in command of one of the new Polish divisions being formed in France. Four months later, in February 1940, with the Russians in occupation of eastern Poland and the Russo–Finnish War in full swing, he was brought back to Paris to serve in the intelligence section of the Polish General Staff, where his knowledge of the Soviet Union could be put to use.

Early on, Slowikowski foresaw the outcome of the battle in

France and sent his wife and son for safety to Salies-du-Salat, a small town south of Toulouse. On the day before the Germans entered Paris he was put in charge of a group of officers from the General Staff and told to evacuate them by train to Saintes in the Charente-Maritime, not far north of Bordeaux, which he did with considerable difficulty. Together with another professional intelligence officer named Captain Jankowski, who had served in Germany before the war, he found lodgings and took stock of the situation, in which everyone seemed panic-stricken and obsessed with a desire to get out of France as quickly as possible. Slowikowski and Jankowski found it hard to decide whether to attempt to join in the evacuation or to stay on in France, where they felt there would be great opportunities for successful intelligence collection while the Germans digested the spoils. In any case, they drove to Toulouse next morning, having obtained permission to collect their families from their refuge. The Polish Consulate at Toulouse was packed up, expecting to be evacuated to Spain, but they persuaded the Consul to issue them passports, collected their families and somehow all reached Saint-Jean-de-Luz. There, the question whether to leave or stay was taken out of their hands because the Polish General acting as port commandant had decided to embark soldiers and airmen in priority and to relegate officers of their age with families to the back of the queue. The weather was most unpleasant, with heavy showers and strong winds, and they had to sleep in the open.

While awaiting embarkation Slowikowski and Jankowski went down to Hendaye to have a look at the Spanish frontier. There they ran into a French Deuxième Bureau officer whom they knew. He told them that, under the terms of the armistice, the Germans would occupy the whole of the French Atlantic coast, but that there would be a 'free zone' under French Government control and he advised them to make their way into it if they had to remain in France. Realising that the possibility of their being evacuated from Saint-Jean-de-Luz had vanished, the two families returned to Salies-du-Salat, where they found their previous accommodation still available. Moreover, the town and nearby Toulouse lay in what was to be the unoccupied zone.

Slowikowski was soon in contact with another Polish secret service officer named Zarembski, who had also worked in the Soviet Union under consular cover and had subsequently been briefly in charge of the Polish counter-intelligence post in Paris, this time with commercial diplomatic cover. They went together to Toulouse which they found packed with refugees: Polish could be heard spoken everywhere and Polish uniforms were much in evidence. The Consulate was overwhelmed by soldiers seeking documents and advice: the other ranks were bitterly hostile to officers, particularly those of senior rank. Slowikowski, who had been born near Warsaw in what was then part of Czarist Russia, was unpleasantly reminded of the behaviour of Russian troops during the 1917 Revolution. Fortunately the appointment of a diplomat named Bitner to take charge of the Consulate defused this explosive situation: his concern for the troops' welfare was unmistakable.

Bitner accepted in principle Slowikowski's suggestion that he and Zarembski should organise the evacuation to Great Britain of as many of the stranded Polish servicemen as possible, but he was less happy to cooperate in practice when he learned of Slowikowski's and Zarembski's secret service backgrounds. The arrival of Colonel Kobylecki, pushing a bicycle that had borne him south from the Breton battlefield, resolved the question. Kobylecki had been Slowikowski's chief on the latter's arrival in France and he had gone on to command the Podhalańska Brigade at Narvik. After the evacuation of the Allied Expeditionary Force from Norway, the Brigade had been disembarked at Brest and thrust immediately into the battle, notwithstanding the loss of all its heavy equipment. The active support of so senior an officer settled Bitner's qualms and the procedure began. Zarembski assumed responsibility for security vetting of candidates for evacuation.

During the first two months – as Szumlakowski, the Polish Ambassador at Madrid, subsequently told General Sikorski – anybody, irrespective of age, could and did travel through Spain – even those who bore arms and wore uniforms.[3] The Spanish authorities allowed Poles in without the Portuguese visas for which would-be evacuees later had to wait for weeks on end. The Ambassador considered that, because the evacuation from France had been inadequately organised, this period was not used to full advantage. After this there were two possible ways to get the evacuees across Spain to Portugal, whence passages to the United Kingdom were available. The evacuee could be equipped with a Polish passport and granted a visa to some exotic country such as China. This gave him the right to a Portuguese transit visa and a Spanish conditional visa. To obtain the Portuguese visa, he needed to produce a receipt from Cook's travel agency showing that he had paid part of the cost of the passage by sea to China. Provided the Polish passport proved the bearer to be less than 20 or more than 45 years of age, he could then travel to Perpignan and obtain, through the Polish Consulate there, a French exit permit from the local Prefecture. Anyone who had surmounted this series of bureaucratic obstacles could then travel to Lisbon legally.

The alternative was to introduce the evacuees illegally into Spain and hope to get them through to Portugal without their being arrested by the Spanish police. This became increasingly difficult. Szumlakowski had argued strongly against methods such as the use of false documents and visas, which he considered compromised his mission and damaged Polish interests in Spain. Police controls had been very much tightened up following a change of Spanish Foreign Minister and of pressure from the Gestapo. He complained that, in spite of this, Poles were still being sent over the border from France without adequate preparation and that of every 16 crossing the 'green frontier', not more than four succeeded in reaching Madrid.

There was, indeed, a great deal of mutual recrimination amongst the Polish authorities involved in the evacuation scheme. One of the officers concerned, Major Adam Szydlowski, who had been imprisoned in Spain, wrote subsequently to his former commanding officer that, thanks to the complete incompetence of the authorities in France responsible for organisating the evacuation and to the lack of coordination between the Polish authorities in France and in Spain, many wasted months passed; moreover, there was no prospect that the situation would improve in future.[4]

A more comprehensive appraisal, and one markedly more appreciative of Slowikowski's and Bitner's efforts at Toulouse, is contained in a report by a former staff officer of the Polish 2nd Infantry Division who managed to leave France at the end of July. His name appears at the head of the report as Lt Cdr Czeslaw Chieconski but he signed it Chiconski. In the report, written in London two months later, he recorded his own experiences and made his own recommendations to General Sikorski's Chief of Staff on ways of evacuating Polish troops left behind in southern France.[5]

Those who had not managed to leave France in June were, he reported, grouped in a few centres, which should be regarded as reservoirs of potential military manpower. The most important centres were Toulouse and Marseilles but there were smaller concentrations at Lyons, Nice and a camp near Port-Vendres. He estimated the number of Poles at Toulouse in July at 5,000: after dispersal of the soldiers who were inhabitants of France, there might possibly be 3–4,000 still left there.

The attitudes and quality of the men at Toulouse varied. They had been subjected to Gestapo and Soviet propaganda, to which some of the weaker characters – both officers and other ranks – had succumbed. Some were prepared to return to Poland; others shrank from active service and preferred to await the outcome of the war. Still others, however, of more robust outlook, were constantly looking for opportunities to leave for England to continue the fight against the Germans. The soldiers at Toulouse were very short of money and, if left there long, might be lost to the cause.

Chiconski predicted that relations between the French authorities and the Poles, which in most cases were at present quite good, would probably deteriorate. Quartering and food were bad. The

Polish Consulate at Toulouse was working efficiently and with tremendous dedication, but under very difficult circumstances.

At Marseilles the military element was prepared to take any risks to find ways of getting to England. Morale here was very high. The total number of officers and men in the Marseilles area was estimated at 600–700. The material circumstances of the officers were good because they had received their pay for June and some for July as well. For the other ranks, by contrast, living conditions were abysmal: they had been left to find their own quarters, as best they could, in hospices and places of refuge. Food was unsatisfactory and the French authorities was passive and unfriendly. The Polish Consulate at Marseilles was performing poorly and unproductively by comparison with the one at Toulouse.

Lyons was no more than a staging post for men on the way to Toulouse, Marseilles or other centres where Poles had congregated.

Nice was an assembly point for officers hoping to leave for Italy and thence travel to Poland. Some hoped to pursue their journey from Italy to Yugoslavia, Greece and Turkey with a view to joining the Polish Forces in Palestine, but this was a very unrealistic plan. Chiconski did not know how many soldiers were in the camp at Port-Vendres. Quarters and food there were not bad and the soldiers there were prepared to continue the fight against the Germans.

After describing the formalities for evacuation through Spain by the legal route, Chiconski set out in detail how to avoid trouble with the authorities while on Spanish soil. These ranged from tips about the currency regulations at the Spanish and Portuguese frontier posts to advice to the evacuee not to carry weapons or any part of his uniform, not to carry any documents about his real reason for travelling through Spain, not to stay in Spain even for the most plausible reasons, to avoid restaurants, coffee-houses and brothels; and to avoid any form of conflict with members of the public and particularly with the authorities. Any breach of Spanish law or currency regulations would lead to immediate arrest and incarceration. On arrival in Barcelona, the British Consulate would issue a third-class ticket to Madrid and the Polish Consulate would provide a small allowance and all necessary information. Evacuees should not overstay in Madrid without a valid reason. The Polish Consulate there would issue third-class tickets to the Portuguese border, but their advice that travel was allowed without payment in Portugal was incorrect: permission for free travel had to be obtained from the Polish Consulate in Lisbon. The Consulate in Madrid did not work well and tended to dismiss enquiries in a perfunctory and slapdash manner. Cooperation between the Consulates in the two capitals was very unsatisfactory, but the Consulate at Lisbon was very active and all matters concerning the evacuation of Polish military personnel were handled by Col Mally, the Military Attaché, or by Dubicza, the Minister, who was the most approachable official Chiconski had ever encountered.

Holders of Chinese, Portuguese and Spanish visas who lacked French exit permits might cross the French frontier illegally near Andorra or near a small town named Saint-Laurent, where the French authorities were usually cooperative. Soldiers crossing in such circumstances should report to the Spanish customs. The Spanish authorities would respect all visas even when the French exit visa was missing.

In Chiconski's opinion, group travel with the permission of the French authorities would not be practicable because of pressures exerted by the Gestapo, but it might be feasible, with the cooperation of the British Navy, to evacuate large groups of Poles assembled on the Mediterranean coastline, as already at the camp near Port-Vendres.

How far this report influenced official thinking at General Sikorski's headquarters in London is unclear: probably not very much, since an annotation in longhand, dated 1 October 1940, at the bottom of the document records the Chief of Staff's opinion that the above person was not trustworthy and was the subject of a pending criminal case.

The Polish Government-in-exile managed to establish, rather precariously, an Embassy at Vichy when the Pétain Government moved there from Bordeaux. Within it, General Kleeberg, the Military Attaché, assumed overall control of evacuation arrangements in July. But, by the autumn of 1940, under increasing German pressure, the French authorities had virtually ceased to cooperate over the issue of exit permits. At the beginning of October, moreover, Kleeberg had to order the route through Spain to be closed, owing to the complete lack of cooperation by the Polish agencies on the Spanish side of the border. As he subsequently reported to General Sikorski, anyone who attempted to escape by that route and whom luck did not favour generally found his way into Spanish internment camps or, if not, might be thrown back to the French side of the border, sometimes from as far away as Madrid or even the Portuguese frontier.[6]

Internment in Spanish camps such as that at Miranda-del-Ebro was a serious matter for Poles. The British Embassy was able to secure the release of British evaders and escapers within a few weeks, since the Spanish Government badly needed British cooperation over the contraband control of essential commodities such as flour and petrol. The Poles had no such leverage, however, and many of the 700 or so Polish escapers from France who were interned in Miranda languished there for two years or more.

Little wonder, then, that those concerned began seriously to consider the alternative of evacuation by sea from southern France. Even before the end of July 1940 Kleeberg had elaborated a scheme for removing several hundreds of soldiers by sea in one fell swoop. Having bought a cargo ship lying in Marseilles, he asked Slowikowski to transfer 250 men from the Toulouse area, for which he was responsible, to Marseilles for embarkation.[7] The men duly travelled by train in groups of ten, under the noses of the French gendarmerie, and once in Marseilles, were escorted to the English Seamen's Hospital to await embarkation. Kleeberg had, however, based his plan on the mistaken assumption that it would receive official approval by the Vichy authorities. Instead of granting Kleeberg permission, General Dentz, who, after surrendering Paris to the Germans, had become the general officer commanding the south-east military region, threatened to arrest him and anyone else using the ship for such a purpose. This turn of events, which ought to have been foreseen but was not, left the organisers with the acute administrative problem of dealing with the men assembled in the English Hospital, which also served as a reception centre for Polish troops arriving to be demobilised.

After this disaster, Kleeberg offered Slowikowski command of Polish evacuation from the whole of France – an offer which the latter felt unable to refuse. Having taken stock of the situation, Slowikowski, who adopted the alias Dr Skowronski, decided that Marseilles was the obvious centre for organising departures by sea. When he got there he found that nearly 300,000 Francs had been spent locally on 'research' but that not one man had as yet actually been evacuated. One officer was planning to ferry evacuees out to Gibraltar by motor boat. Slowikowski wanted him first to report to him on the cost and likely results but this advice was disregarded and a small party of officers set off anyhow, though Slowikowski noted that the organiser himself preferred to travel by the land line into Spain. Before leaving Marseilles he claimed to have been robbed at gunpoint by the Frenchmen who had helped him purchase the boat; for obvious reasons, he had been unable to report the matter to the police. Reproaching Slowikowski for forbidding evacuation by sea, the officer also maintained that by dispatching the boat to Gibraltar, he had proved this method to be possible. Slowikowski subsequently discovered that the boat had in fact been intercepted by the French maritime gendarmerie and its passengers sent to a special penal camp in the Pyrenees.

This was not the only unsuccessful attempt by Poles to escape by sea in small vessels. A fishing boat named *Marie-Thérèse*, of a type known locally as a *bateau boeuf* (because two worked together towing a single trawl, like yoked oxen with a plough), lay at the Quai-Aspirant-Herbert at Sète in November 1940.[8] 200 Polish soldiers were to be involved in this operation, which was headed by a Polish sapper Captain. He was assisted by a Lieutenant and a naval Sub-Lieutenant, who had left hospital clandestinely with the help of two Bretons who hoped to use this Polish venture to leave the country themselves. They were denounced by local fishermen and the two Bretons were arrested on board the *Marie-Thérèse* by two police inspectors from the crime squad, who came all the way from Vichy. René Poujade and Raymond Cauvel, the Bretons, admitted that they planned to escape to Gibraltar but they said nothing about the Poles involved in the enterprise, all of whom got away to Nîmes in a hurry.

The cargo ship bought by General Kleeberg for the abortive mass evacuation still lay in Marseilles port and, in due course, Slowikowski decided that, since the French police seemed to have lost interest in her, it was worth trying again to use her for an escape operation, this time without informing the French authorities.[9] Her holds were filled with bunks, which were supposed to be racks for oranges. The plan was that the ship would sail from Marseilles in ballast and would embark the evacuees by night from a nearby point on the coast. After dropping them at Gibraltar, she would put into a Spanish port and pick up a genuine cargo of crates of oranges before returning to land these at Marseilles. A French crew and captain were signed on and preparations were far advanced when news leaked out to the port authorities, who sealed the ship and denied access to her by anyone other than the crew. Since there was no longer any hope of reviving the project, the ship was sold, which realised a small profit.

On 1 October 1940 the Germans compelled Vichy to close down the Polish Embassy and all the Polish Consulates. With the Ambassador's departure, General Kleeberg lost his diplomatic status and was able to stay on in France as unofficial head of the Polish forces only by invoking his friendships with a number of high-ranking French officers. He moved to Marseilles and from then on all plans and arrangements for evacuation had to be pursued on a wholly clandestine basis.

The Germans tried several times to infiltrate agents into the Polish evacuation network; the network at least twice foiled the attempt by executing the individuals concerned. Fortunately Slowikowski had links with a pro-Allied French inspector of police at Marseilles who was prepared to lend them support and protection. Soon afterwards, warned by the Poles that his name was on a black-list at Vichy, this officer was able to get himself transferred to Morocco, where he eventually became one of Slowikowski's most valuable contacts in organising an intelligence network.

Direct evacuation by sea to Gibraltar proved extremely difficult. Permission to buy a boat had to be obtained from the port police and no ship could sail from a French port without the approval of the German Armistice Commission. There was, moreover, an acute shortage of fuel even on the black market. Nevertheless, Slowikowski felt that it was well worth evacuating men to French North Africa, from which escape might well prove easier. As early as October 1940 he had predicted that there would be an Allied landing in North Africa because of its strategic value. Poles who could get there would thus find themselves among friends sooner than would be the case if they remained in metropolitan France. Kleeberg agreed that in French North Africa they would be safer from the risk of falling into German hands. Lieutenant Kiersnowski, commander of the Polish naval outpost at Marseilles, was therefore ordered to establish friendly contacts with French merchant seamen on the Marseilles–North Africa run and to find out whether they would help stowaways. Kiersnowski knew his way around the waterfront bars of the Vieux-Port and spoke their argot; he soon gained their confidence and reported that evacuation by this route and method would be possible at a price of between 100 and 300 Francs per transportee, depending on the number to be carried.

The next step was to organise a network of evacuation outposts in French North Africa to receive men on arrival and direct them to safe houses pending their transfer to Casablanca, which Slowikowski judged would prove the best and safest port of refuge. Given the distances involved and the administrative division of French North Africa into three separate territories, each with guarded borders and the requirement for a permit to travel between them, there were substantial problems to be overcome. Five officers were selected to set up these outposts at Tunis, Algiers and Casablanca. They left for North Africa in November 1940 to make the necessary contacts and reported that conditions were rather better, and the officials more helpful, than in metropolitan France. Kleeberg therefore authorised Kiersnowski to begin shipments.

Batches of up to 40 evacuees would be assembled at the English Hospital reception centre when a suitable ship was due to sail and the necessary payments had been made. Late at night they were collected and moved to waiting boats, which, with all due precautions, rowed them round to the side of the ship remote from the quay. They climbed on board via a rope ladder hanging down the ship's side and were immediately ushered to their hide-outs in parts of the ship rarely visited by officers, such as the shaft tunnel and coal-bunkers. Conditions were often extremely uncomfortable and made great demands on the physical stamina of the stowaways, who needed to remain hidden for several days before being disembarked at a North African port with similar speed and secrecy. Any man who broke bounds and ventured forth from his cramped quarters to stretch his legs or snatch a breath of fresh air might ruin the whole venture. This is doubtless what happened in December 1940 when an early RAF evader, the future Air Chief Marshal Sir Lewis Hodges, whose Hampden bomber had made a forced landing in Brittany, arranged to be smuggled on board the *Ville-de-Verdun* to Casablanca.[10] On their first day at sea, the ship's Captain was alerted to the presence of other stowaways. The subsequent search brought to light altogether 40 illicit travellers. He turned the ship round and handed them all over to the Vichy police at Marseilles, who interned them, with the result that Hodges ended up with other British officers in what had been the French Foreign Legion transit depot in the Fort-Saint-Jean, instead of in Casablanca as he had hoped.

*   *   *

The Czechs had also had troops in France, though far fewer than the Poles, and these were equally subject to internment at the hands of the Vichy authorities. Among the places used for this purpose were camps on the coast between Sète and Perpignan, which had been built to accommodate interned Spanish Republican refugees. Gradually, groups of both Czech and Polish demobilised internees were transferred under armed guard into the Alps and Massif Central to do forestry work.

*   *   *

When the Polish Embassy had to be closed in November 1940, Kleeberg sought an audience with General Huntzinger, Pétain's Secretary of State for War, to discuss with him the status and future of the Polish soldiers in France. On 16 January 1941, when Huntzinger refused to see him, Kleeberg wrote to him instead.[11]

The situation imposed on the Poles, he wrote, seemed incompatible with the real feelings of the French population for his compatriots and with the mutual engagements, both moral and material, contracted between Poland and France. Polish soldiers had been called up, trained and engaged in combat in accordance with agreements concluded between the two Governments. On the orders of the French High Command, Polish units had been thrust into battle: the First and Second Infantry Divisions and even the Third, which was in process of being formed, the Northern Brigade, and the scarcely trained and formed Maczec Motorised Group. These units had all, without exception, done their duty. On the Polish side, all engagements had been fulfilled. Despite this, these soldiers, who had contributed unflinchingly to the vital task of holding back the enemy and saving honour, were now considered superfluous foreigners and treated on the same basis as the Spanish Reds (law of 27 September 1940). Not surprisingly therefore, Polish officers and soldiers, rejected by their erstwhile brothers in arms, sought to leave France.

Senior officers and soldiers with long service stripes, who had committed no other crime than to wish to fight on and to fulfil their duty as soldiers, found themselves in chains and treated as common criminals. Although the tribunal at Aix-en-Provence had recently set them free, the police were now about to send them to the camp at Le-Vernet with Communists, thieves and crooks. One of them, a senior officer of the greatest merit, had gone out of his mind. These soldiers asked for no favours. They wished only to be treated as ex-servicemen, with dignity.

Lastly, Kleeberg argued, it ought to be possible to avoid exposing these men to the risk of falling into enemy hands once more. It was clear, from reports of officers and other ranks who had escaped, that Polish soldiers captured in France by the Germans were particularly ill-treated. He concluded:

> I know that I am only doing my duty, General, in begging you to take the necessary steps to ensure that Polish soldiers, who have merely carried out the orders of their commanding officers, are not once more surprised by the enemy, as were, among others, the troops of the Narvik Brigade in Brittany.
>
> I ask you to facilitate their transfer to North Africa where they will know how to make themselves useful, whatever the circumstances.
>
> I beg you to believe, General, that I am not acting in a spirit of recrimination but from a sense of my responsibility as a chief, from a love of my soldiers and from my attachment to France, which long residence entitles me to consider my second homeland. We are at a moment of history where our actions are of more than passing consequence, for they will determine the future.

This plea seems to have elicited no response.

*   *   *

Slowikowski reckoned that almost 3,000 more Poles had been evacuated from France to the United Kingdom by one means or another before the beginning of May 1941. Several hundreds more had been smuggled to French North Africa. By Christmas 1940, Kleeberg thought he should send a more senior officer there to take charge and recommended Major Wysoczanski. Slowikowski did not know Wysoczanski, but he briefed him, explained his duties and told him he was expected to report on the local situation and on progress in carrying out his mission. He gave him funds and a list of the officers already actively engaged on the problem, but made it clear that Wysoczanski was free to make such changes as he thought necessary.[12]

Wysoczanski arrived at his post in North Africa at the end of 1940 with a team of his own associates and proceeded to replace most of the existing outpost commanders. Flouting orders, he sent no reports either to Slowikowski or to Kleeberg but instead sent telegrams demanding money. Slowikowski noted dourly that he and Kleeberg both thought it would be unwise to send money for unknown purposes.

Evacuation from the south of France to North Africa continued with reasonable success until mid-March 1941. It had been Slowikowski's policy to regroup the evacuees in North Africa according to their service of origin; the airmen had been concentrated in Tunisia, where good accommodation was available and Admiral Esteva, the French Resident-General, was particularly well-disposed.

Unfortunately the Polish commandant of this camp overreached himself by staging military parades on festive occasions. Alerted to this, the Italo–German armistice commission took the matter up officially with Esteva and a full-scale enquiry was launched, which brought to light not only the illegal camps in Tunisia but the clandestine sea traffic from France that had led to this concentration of Polish airmen in the Protectorate. A number of French officials who had been helpful to the Poles lost their jobs, while the airmen were transferred back to France and interned under penal conditions. The French sailors who had been involved in smuggling Poles into North Africa on merchant ships were arrested. Slowikowski had no choice but to suspend evacuation by this method.

Shortly afterwards, Slowikowski was himself appointed to North Africa to organise an intelligence network to cover the whole range of French territories from the Tripolitanian border to Dakar. He handed over the evacuation work in metropolitan France to his deputy, Major Mizgier-Chojnacki.

CHAPTER XXIII

Mass Evacuations from the Marseilles Area and the FIDELITY Tragedy

A quite separate scheme for a large-scale evacuation by sea of Polish ex-servicemen immobilised in southern France had been under discussion in London since December 1940 between the Polish General Staff and the British Admiralty.[1]

Sikorski's staff reckoned that there were still at least 3,000 officers and other ranks to be brought out. The original plan aimed to evacuate in a single operation all the internees in two main camps in the Marseilles area by means of a cargo steamer, the *Czardasz*. Slocum was in close touch with the Directorate of Naval Intelligence and it seems inherently likely that he was involved in these discussions as he was at the same time fitting out another small cargo steamer for an expedition to the south coast of France on behalf of the British clandestine services. He was quite prepared to meet Polish and Czech operational needs in the course of this projected voyage as well.

As a result of the *Czardasz* scheme, a Polish naval Lieutenant named Marian Kadulski was sent out to Gibraltar in March 1941.

Kadulski, who is one of the real heros of this book, was born in December 1909 in Nowy Sacz, south of Kraków, in the foothills of the Tatras. His father soon thereafter obtained a job in the Austro–Hungarian Imperial dockyard at Pola (now Pula) on the Adriatic coast of what subsequently became Yugoslavia. At the end of the First World War, in the resurrected Poland, Kadulski Senior joined the army, pieced together from ex-Austrian–German – and Russian – trained personnel. For the three Kadulski children, of whom Marian was the eldest, their father's changing assignments meant changing schools, which had also quite recently begun to merge satisfactorily. His mother often recalled in later years how surprisingly Marian caught up each time in the new surroundings and was always top of the class or very near it. When he was 13, his secondary schooling at Lwów (now L'viv in the Ukraine) was on the lines of a German *Realgymnasium* with a curriculum which stressed mathematics, physics and natural history. Again he was at the top. Languages came to him easily. He matriculated at 18, second out of about 30. He could well have been first, but he had a handicap, which also plagued him at naval college: he looked much younger than his age and, while not short of stature, did not look 100 per cent 'The Good Soldier Schweik'.

At the naval college (in Torun), where the three-year course was interspersed with summer cruises in warships, he was top in English and French, with quite good German as well.

Having read Jules Verne's *The Fifteen-Year-Old Ship's Captain*, he longed to learn astronomical navigation. Indeed, thanks to the manuals available at the school, he mastered the subject before the first lectures on it began, taking observations of Jupiter and Saturn in the morning watch on the training ship in order to identify them by the reversed mathematical process. It was a skill that, as will become apparent, stood him in good stead during his Gibraltar appointment in 1941 and 1942.

At the time of his arrival on the Rock, Kadulski was 31 years old and had been in the Polish navy since 1928. He had done an extra year's training on the French navy's *Jeanne-d'Arc*, where the cadets were required to take observations at noon each day and work out a fix, served in submarines and received some training in intelligence work during the summer of 1939. After postings to the Polish Naval Missions in Copenhagen and Amsterdam during the early months of the war, possibly on intelligence duties, he had become temporary first lieutenant of the destroyer *Blyskawica*, a post in which he was subsequently confirmed. He remained in this ship until November 1940 and saw active service in the Norwegian campaign. His appointment to Gibraltar on 3 March 1941 was nominally as head of a new Polish Naval Mission there, but this was no more than cover: he had in fact been detached from the navy to the branch of the Polish clandestine services dealing with evacuation operations. In this new capacity he was responsible to Colonel Frederyk Mally, whose cover post was Military Attaché in Lisbon, rather than to the Polish naval authorities. He adopted the name Krajewski for this new job and will be so described hereafter.[2]

Within a very few weeks of Krajewski's arrival at Gibraltar it became evident that the *Czardasz* plan was no longer practicable: mass escapes from the camps would be impossible in view of the enhanced French security measures adopted after Slowikowski's escape line to French North Africa was exposed. However, Commander Slocum's planned operation went ahead and it included a small-scale attempt to pick up Polish or Czech escapers from the coast of Languedoc. It also landed Bitner, previously Polish Consul at Toulouse, who was being sent back to investigate, in conjunction with SOE, whether the large Polish population in the Nord and Pas-de-Calais Departments could be drawn into active resistance.

The vessel to be used for this, Slocum's first operation in the Mediterranean, was an unusual ship which has passed into history as HMS *Fidelity*. For better security, *Fidelity* was to be sailed on this voyage direct from the United Kingdom, where she had been fitted out and commissioned, rather than from Gibraltar. She was built in 1920 at Hartlepool as a cargo vessel with an overall length of 270 feet, a beam of 41 feet and a gross registered tonnage of 2,450. Her triple-expansion Mackie and Baxter engine, yielding 1,100 h.p. from two boilers, had originally given her a top speed of 9.5 knots; 21 years later, in wartime service with poor coal, this was reduced to nearer 6 knots. Fitted to carry 20 passengers in seven cabins, she was put into service as *Le-Rhin* by the French firm of Devéry et Chaumet, who in 1923 sold her to the Compagnie Paquet of Marseilles. She was then used to transport vegetable oils from Senegal and general cargo to Morocco, the eastern Mediterranean and Black Sea ports.[3]

In June 1940, as organised French military resistance to the German onslaught was collapsing, *Le-Rhin* lay at Marseilles unloading a cargo from North Africa, when a French naval officer of Corsican origin, Claude André Péri, engaged on special service for the French Admiralty and the Cinquième Bureau, arrived there armed with an *ordre de mission* and looking for a ship to take him to Gibraltar to join the British.

Péri had a previous connection with *Le-Rhin*: indeed he had used her only six weeks earlier as a mobile base from which to mount an attack on a German merchant ship, the SS *Corrientes*, lying in Las Palmas harbour in the Canaries. This operation was carried out on 10 May, the day on which Hitler launched his western offensive into the Low Countries. Péri used limpet mines and plastic explosive, a novelty of Czech origin, in this attack. As *Le-Rhin* sailed from the neutral Spanish port, Péri had slipped back in her launch and placed the mines. He then rejoined the ship and was well offshore before they detonated. How much damage was caused is not clear: some accounts say Péri sank her, but an SIS report casts doubt on this.

Finding that almost all the evacuees had already gone, Péri took charge of the *Le-Rhin*, although he was a mere Sub Lieutenant, while her regular captain held the rank of Corvette Captain in the naval reserve. Helped by a handful of junior officers, he reloaded *Le-Rhin* with whatever lay to hand on the quay and joined a belated convoy sailing to Morocco. As the convoy was passing through the Straits of Gibraltar, Péri altered *Le-Rhin*'s course and brought her into Gibraltar harbour, complete with her cargo of silks, wines, bicycles, blankets and refrigerators. There she was kept idle for some months. Meanwhile, Péri was joined by a Belgian army doctor named Albert Guérisse, who shared his determination to fight on. The ship was finally sailed to Barry Docks to be refitted. In Britain Péri, who had scorned an attempt by the French Consul at Gibraltar to enlist him to carry out a sabotage attack on HMS *Hood*, opted to join the Royal Navy, rather than the Gaullist forces; so did his officers and they were accordingly granted RN ranks equivalent to their French ones. The ship had been visited by Admiral Muselier while she lay at Gibraltar, however, and the decision to allow Péri and his crew to join the Royal Navy caused great resentment at de Gaulle's Carlton Gardens headquarters – so much so that SOE decided not to take over the ship. They reckoned they already had enough trouble on their hands in the form of opposition from Passy and de Gaulle to their Independent French Section, which, however, they were determined to maintain because they could not be certain that their view of the need for paramilitary action in France would always coincide with de Gaulle's.

For reasons of security, Péri and his crew joined the Royal Navy under assumed names. Péri became Lt Cdr Jack Langlais, RN, and remained in command, with Guérisse as first lieutenant under the name Lt Cdr Patrick O'Leary, RN.

Slocum had fewer inhibitions than SOE and was ready to take over responsibility for *Le-Rhin*, which Langlais had proposed should be refitted as what would have been called in the First World War a Q-ship – a disguised armed merchant cruiser. Slocum's idea from the outset was to use her for clandestine sea-transport operations in the western Mediterranean. The refit at Barry was carried out under the direction of Langlais and with the help of one of Slocum's staff officers, Lt Patrick Whinney, RNVR. Whinney, like his colleague Steven Mackenzie, had been a member of the British Naval Mission at Admiral Darlan's headquarters at the Château de Maintenon before the fall of France. When they reached London and reported for duty at the Admiralty, they were sent by Ian Fleming, special assistant to the Director of Naval Intelligence, to join Slocum's Section of SIS.

At the end of her refit, *Le-Rhin* was renamed *Fidelity* and, with her French crew, commissioned under the white ensign, de Gaulle's objections notwithstanding. The programme for her first operational voyage in April 1941 involved landing two parties of agents and embarking three groups of evaders and escapers on the south coast of France. She needed to put into Gibraltar briefly to refuel and disembark some officers of SOE's Spanish Section, but it was decided to do this under cover of darkness, since ship movements in and out of the port could be observed from adjacent Spanish territory and it had to be assumed that the daily influx of 4,000 Spanish workers included a quota of Axis spies. Thereafter she proceeded through the Straits before dawn and up the Spanish coast.

Fidelity had been equipped with several disguises of Spanish and Portuguese character and her crew had been trained in altering the ship's appearance overnight. She passed inspection by German aircraft more than once and arrived on 25 April at her first pinpoint, the Étang-du-Cannet, close to the eastern end of the Pyrenees, where Bitner and an elderly Maltese civil engineer named Rizzo were landed by night. Rizzo had worked in Paris as a science teacher: he hated the Germans and was being infiltrated for Leslie Humphreys's Section of SOE, to establish a two-way link across the Pyrenees in conjunction with the professional Spanish smugglers working in the area. These were, for the most part, Republican exiles who made a living by carrying contraband tobacco into Spain. Rizzo accomplished his mission with great success and his trans-Pyrenean Spanish 'passers' formed an essential part of the land lines run by Humphreys into and out of France.

The next day *Fidelity* arrived off the small French port of Cerbère, which lies close to the Spanish frontier. She was due to collect a party of Polish evaders. The arrangement was that a boat would put into the harbour in daylight, embark passengers from the jetty in quick time and leave again before too many questions were asked. A small fishing boat of local type was carried for this purpose in the *Fidelity*.

On 26 April 1941 this boat entered Cerbère under command of Pat O'Leary (alias Albert Guérisse). A Polish agent met them and went off to collect his party, which was waiting nearby. But while he was doing this, two French gendarmes arrived and asked awkward questions, which forced O'Leary to leave hurriedly. His boat was pursued by a French *chasseur* and captured. O'Leary and his crew, with the exception of one man who got away by swimming into Spanish territorial waters, were taken prisoner by the Vichy authorities – but not for long: within three months every member of the boat's crew had escaped back to England except for O'Leary himself, who had also escaped, but remained in France to become one of the most successful SIS/MI9 agents aiding Allied evaders and escapers. Indeed, he was Belgium's greatest hero of the Second World War. Not long before Guérisse's death in 1989, the King of the Belgians broke with precedent and conferred on him the title of Count, in recognition of his outstanding services to the Resistance.

Fidelity's first voyage is not well documented. She had been due to pick up a group of British evaders and escapers from a pinpoint in the Gulf of Lyons but was prevented from doing so by the appearance of a French seaplane. Slocum's 1946 report on his Section's wartime activities says of *Fidelity*'s voyage only than that 'she completed her programmes satisfactorily and returned to the United Kingdom with a long list of defects and complaints.' The fact that he did not list any of the five operations that had been planned does not suggest that they were notably successful, apart from the landing of Bitner and Rizzo.

A major refit proved necessary and there were constant political squabbles over the crew, owing to continued Free French objections to the employment of Frenchmen in the Royal Navy. In September 1941 *Fidelity* was again ready for sea and this time her programme included operations on the Algerian coast. Again she sailed direct from the United Kingdom. The SOE records show that she once more made a stop, presumably nocturnal, at Gibraltar.

She had lost time on the outward passage owing to bad weather and poor coal. The first pinpoint in the Gulf of Lyons was reached 24 hours late on 14 September and the British evaders and escapers who should have been there could not be found. She then sailed for the Algerian coast where she was due to embark a second party of escaped British prisoners of war and evaders for MI9 on 16 September, but she again found no-one at the pinpoint. However, two other operations were, according to Slocum's 1946 report, carried out before *Fidelity* returned to the first pinpoint for a further attempt to embark the British evaders and escapers. She tried twice – on 20 and 21 September – but again failed.

The SOE files provide confirmation that four of their agents were successfully landed in the course of this voyage. This seems to have taken place at Barcaire, near Perpignan, on 19 September: the agents were F. Basin ('Olive'), R. Leary ('Alain'), R.B. Roche and A.J.R. Dubourdin – all of whom were destined to join the de Vomécourt brothers' 'Autogyro' circuit, the first such group that SOE's independent F Section had got going. They appear to have been landed as a single party. No details of a second disembarkation, as suggested by Slocum, have emerged.

Fidelity's September sortie to the western Mediterranean was thus not entirely fruitless, but Slocum apparently decided at this point that enough was enough and that she could not be further employed for his purposes. Apart from her slowness, she was too large and conspicuous for repeated clandestine ventures in the confined waters of the western Mediterranean. She was refitted once more towards the end of 1941, this time by Messrs Harland and Wolff at Southampton under the guidance of the Admiralty's Plans Division for work in the Far East, the 'spirit and personality' of her commanding officer having attracted the attention of the new C-in-C Eastern Fleet, Admiral Somerville.[4] Langlais, now promoted Acting Commander, knew the area well, having worked there before the war for the French Colonial Intelligence Service. The plan was that *Fidelity* should operate in this theatre as a proper Q-ship, carrying, for offensive purposes, Royal Marine Commando personnel, two small amphibious aircraft and a 45-foot motor torpedo boat of a type based on a First World War Coastal Motor Boat (CMB) design, capable of giving a top speed of 52 knots when fully loaded or 58 knots without armament, under the impulsion of a Rolls Royce Merlin main engine of the type used in Spitfire and Lancaster aircraft. This thorough refit was followed by intensive working-up with the Royal Marine Unit, which had been training at Chale on the south coast of the Isle of Wight.

In December 1942 *Fidelity* sailed for Panama as part of convoy ONS 154 on what proved to be her last voyage. Despite her apparent offensive capability, she was not considered a member of the escort. In fact, an Admiralty directive of November 1941 had said that, even if she were refitted (as she now had been), she was considered 'a most unsuitable ship to work on regular convoy escort as long as she is manned as she is at present.' Eight days later the two groups of German U-boats that had been shadowing ONS 154 since it emerged from St George's Channel pressed in and the biggest wolf-pack attack yet experienced began: it was to reduce the convoy of 45 ships to 30.

At the most critical moment of this running battle, at dusk on 29 December, Langlais was asked by the senior officer of the escort, Lt Cdr Windeyer, RCN, in HMCS *St-Laurent*, to fly off one of his two Kingfisher seaplanes to cover an alteration of course against submarine attack. Langlais, only too delighted to take part in the fight, complied and *Fidelity* hove to while the aircraft was hoisted out over the starboard quarter and deposited in the water. The pilot, Lt Cdr (A) Ben Schröder, RNVR – a distinguished Paris dentist in peacetime – and his observer/gunner, Sub Lt J.-J. Allen, RN, clambered into the tandem cockpits. Schröder realised that his chance of making a safe take-off in the prevailing conditions was poor. He shouted to Langlais to request the cooperation of the *St-Laurent*. The destroyer duly obliged and set off to steam at full speed into the wind, thus creating by her wake a broad strip of smooth water to provide a runway for the seaplane, but to no avail; the sea was altogether too rough and the Kingfisher became unstable. One wing-tip float dug into the water and broke off. The aircraft slewed round almost 90° and came to a standstill pointing back towards *Fidelity*. Very quickly the seaplane settled into the water. Schröder and Allen extricated themselves from their harness and clung on as long as they could to the waterlogged fuselage. Allen's attempt to inflate the dinghy was unsuccessful and he was swept away, sustained only by his Mae West. It was two hours before first Schröder and then he were picked up by the *St-Laurent*.

The Kingfisher had been equipped with six aircraft-type depth charges, three slung beneath each wing. They were set to go off at 50-foot depth and, as the aircraft sank, there was a series of explosions, which were felt with great force in *Fidelity*'s engine-room. The condenser was extensively damaged and the engines had to be shut down in some haste, leaving the ship disabled and dead in the water. The convoy pressed on with a Canadian corvette, HMCS *Shediac*, detached to stand by *Fidelity*, though she was forced to leave in the early hours of 29 December as she was short of fuel.

The U-boat pack had followed the main convoy, which continued to lose merchant ships. *Fidelity*, in improving weather, launched her MTB at about noon on 29 December and an hour later the second Kingfisher seaplane was able to take off for a brief reconnaissance, which revealed an apparently disabled U-boat on the surface some 16 miles to the south-west and two heavily laden lifeboats in the same area. The aircraft was hoisted back aboard and the MTB was sent to investigate the sightings, though only her auxiliary engine was working. Langlais subsequently ordered her to resume her anti-submarine patrolling and sent the two landing craft carried by *Fidelity* to search for the lifeboats.

In mid-afternoon, the fractured condenser pipes had been temporarily patched up and *Fidelity* got underway again at a speed that eventually rose to 5 knots. In due course the landing craft returned with some 40 survivors including the commander of the convoy.

That same evening *Fidelity* was twice attacked. U225 fired one torpedo, which missed. Langlais dropped a pattern of depth charges. The MTB sighted the U-boat on the surface and tried to close in on her, but at $7\frac{1}{2}$ knots this proved impossible. The U-boat dived and broke off the action. Less than an hour later U 615, which was making a sweep behind the convoy, sighted *Fidelity* and fired three more torpedoes, to no apparent effect. Once again Langlais dropped depth charges and the submarine withdrew. However, *Fidelity*'s engines broke down and, when she was able to get underway again, it was at no more than 2 knots. The MTB was in equally great mechanical trouble by this stage and lost sight of her mother ship during the night. With failing batteries, she lost R/T contact as well. Langlais had failed to make his position clear to the Admiralty when he left the convoy route, heading for the Azores; and in the forenoon of 30 December the Admiralty lost radio contact with *Fidelity*, which fell victim to two of three torpedoes fired by U 435 that afternoon. Langlais, belligerent to the last, fired two last depth charges as the ship sank.

Strelow, the U-boat commander, came up to periscope depth to view the destruction he had wrought. He estimated, with some accuracy, that there were between 300 and 400 survivors in the sea or on rafts in the gathering gloom, although he did not specify a figure in the signal he sent three hours later to his base at Saint-Nazaire, reporting the sinking. The reply told him in rather chilling tones to report if survivors were on board or whether 'their destruction in the weather prevailing can be counted on.'

Not one of the 406 souls on board *Fidelity* when she sank lived to tell the tale. Among those who died were Lt Cdr J.W.F. Milner-Gibson, her first lieutenant, who had played an important part in clandestine sea transport as one of only two navigators used by

Slocum on all cross-Channel operations of this type before September 1941. One of the ten members of the ship's company who survived because they were either on board the first Kingfisher aircraft or on MTB 105 was Schröder's observer, J.-J. Allen, later known as J.-J. Tremayne, real name Gilbert. Eight months later he assumed command of MFV 2023, Slocum's high-speed version of a French west-coast sardine *pinasse*, when Daniel Lomenech brought his three-year career as a clandestine operator to an end and transferred to submarines.

Fidelity and her commanding officer hold a unique, if controversial, place in the annals of the Royal Navy. Even three years after her demise, Slocum was predicting that many a supply officer would blench, many a civil servant tear his hair for years to come at the mere mention of her name. Seldom, he continued, could a single ship have caused such diverse opinions in high circles. The Flag Officer Commanding North Atlantic in Gibraltar referred to her as HMS *Futility*, but the ship and Langlais were highly thought of by the Commanders-in-Chief of Western Approaches and of the Far Eastern Fleet. Reviled by many and loved by few, she was the first British warship to sail in wartime with a female officer (First Officer Madeleine Barclay, WRNS, was her cipher officer). Under the name Bayard, this woman is said to have worked as an agent for Péri in the Far East and to have followed him home. At one time she had certainly been his mistress.

Péri was the only Frenchman in modern times to become an Acting Commander, RN. His methods of maintaining discipline included kicking a defaulter down the ladder leading to the ship's bridge. Slocum, who knew him well, described him as having the appearance and mentality of an 18th-century buccaneer, but he considered Péri a great man and his death a real loss to Britain. Peter Kingswell, in his carefully researched monograph *Fidelity Will Haunt Me till I Die*, written for the Royal Marine Historical Society, took a less charitable view: he deemed Péri a supreme opportunist who, in pursuit of his dream of personal glory and his insatiable lust for contest, caused vast sums of money to be squandered on converting an entirely unsuitable vessel into an armed merchant cruiser. He considered *Fidelity*'s very presence on convoy ONS 154 futile and her enormous armament pointless. For the loss of 406 lives and the waste of the invaluable assault troops in T Company of 40 Royal Marine Commando, Péri's megalomania and ability to bend people of influence and authority to his will qualify him, in Kingswell's view, for a heavy share of the blame.

CHAPTER XXIV

Operations from Gibraltar to Morocco:
July–October 1941

On 29 April 1941, after the plan to use the cargo steamer *Czardasz* to evacuate Poles from the Marseilles area was abandoned (see previous chapter), Krajewski, who had been sent to Gibraltar to organise that operation, received from Colonel Mally, his chief in Lisbon, details of a quite different plan, which the Polish General Staff had put to the Admiralty in London.[1]

The Poles suggested the British naval authorities should help them acquire a motor vessel that could be used to collect Polish internees from the Casablanca area. If a suitable craft could not be made available for their exclusive use from the existing stock of vessels at Gibraltar, a ship should be bought in Portugal or possibly Spain and sailed to Gibraltar. It would obviously attract undesirable attention if the Poles were seen to be the buyers. They would need help, too, in finding a crew for the vessel and a suitable place for it to be berthed at Gibraltar.

Once these conditions were fulfilled and they had been able to locate a suitable embarkation point at the Casablanca end, Mally would send a courier to Wysoczanski, their representative in Morocco, to discuss with him in secrecy how to put the plan into effect. The courier would take a letter from General Bohusz for Wysoczanski to give to Commandant de Mohl, Chief of Staff to the general commanding the French division in the area, asking de Mohl to give them all possible help. On the courier's return to Lisbon, Mally would inform the British authorities of the proposed arrangements so that they could issue the operation orders.

The evacuees would not be told how they were to be evacuated: they would, indeed, be given the misleading impression that it would be organised via Gambia or Tangiers. They would be required, as a condition of embarkation, to sign an undertaking to join the Polish Army in England. No families or other dependants would be taken off. Evacuation would be carried out in secret and at night. All immigration and security vetting procedures would be applied on arrival in the United Kingdom and evacuees would be held incommunicado while in transit through Gibraltar. The Poles asked that the costs of fitting out and maintaining the vessel, cost of fuel, pay for the crew and subsistence for the evacuees should be met locally from British sources and recovered from the Polish treasury in London.

The Admiralty was prepared to back the venture and written confirmation of this would be forthcoming. They suggested that Krajewski liaise in Gibraltar with Flag Officer Commanding North Atlantic (FOCNA) who would probably be able to provide a suitable craft from local resources but, if not, would be able to help Krajewski buy one in Spain or Portugal.

The Admiralty thought it would be better for the crew to be Polish, in case the boat were stopped by French patrols, when the presence of British sailors might endanger the whole operation. The British Ministry of Shipping would, if necessary, send a crew of Poles out from the United Kingdom, but it might be possible instead to recruit crew from the Polish motor ship *Oksywia*, which had been seized by the French authorities in Morocco but whose crew were expected to be released. Krajewski could choose volunteers and one officer to take command of the vessel. This crew should be retained in Gibraltar even if the required vessel had not been handed over when they arrived there.

FOCNA would give Krajewski advice and instructions about the operational aspects of the scheme – choice of a suitable time to approach the French Moroccan coast, embarkation point and possible support by British naval forces.

The Polish proposals presented the Admiralty with a means not only of rescuing their troops interned in the Casablanca area but also of meeting longer-term needs. A vessel based at Gibraltar and its Polish crew might be used to mount similar operations to other points on the French coast.

Mally was instructed by General Sikorski's Chief of Staff to put the plan into effect, in close cooperation with the British authorities and with Krajewski. Mally cabled Krajewski and followed this up with a letter telling him to begin the search for a vessel and asking whether it would be possible to draw from the crew of the *Oksywia*. Krajewski was to establish and maintain contact with FOCNA.

This was not the first clandestine sea contact with Morocco. In September 1940, a British destroyer from Gibraltar had landed three Gaullist emissaries between Mogador and Agadir, but their mission had been short-lived: all had been arrested soon after their arrival.[2]

As well as the Poles, a number of Allied ships and their crews were detained by the Vichy French authorities in Morocco. The Belgians had made one abortive attempt, through their Consulate in Lisbon, to smuggle out a group of about 40 people from Port Lyautey on a 200-ton Portuguese merchant ship, but the executants fell into the hands of a double agent working for the Vichy administration. The Portuguese captain, who was not privy to the plan, was arrested and sent to France.[3] Local initiatives by the interned ship's crews had been rather more successful. Six Danes and a Belgian had escaped from Port Lyautey in January 1941 in a ship's lifeboat, followed on 11 March by four more Danes and a Norwegian, by ten Danes a week later, and by three Norwegians at the beginning of April.[4] On the other hand, two Norwegians, who left Casablanca on 15 January in a ship's boat, were cast ashore near Fedhala, and five Danes, who had stolen a yacht to get away from Safi, were arrested off Mazagan by a French naval vessel. The project that emerged from the Poles' discussions with the Admiralty, however, was different in kind from any of these previous enterprises, and more ambitious, in that it envisaged an ongoing series of clandestine sea-transport operations from the Gibraltar base.

Krajewski reported on 9 May that he had found a boat that he could use without charge.[5] It was a seagoing motor fishing vessel, which could be used without arousing suspicion. She would require a maximum of four crew – possibly fewer – apart from the captain, a role he would take on himself. He would like to have a W/T operator who could double as a deck-hand, so as to maintain communications with Gibraltar when at sea.

The crew of the *Oksywia* were not at Gibraltar, nor could he find any trace of their having been there in transit. Foreigners arriving at Gibraltar were sent on to the United Kingdom as quickly as possible. There were no communications between Gibraltar and French Morocco. Since crew might therefore have to be chosen in Lisbon, Krajewski spelt out for Mally the qualities he was looking for. An ability to keep one's mouth shut was the first prerequisite. He stressed the need for stability of character because of prevailing conditions in the fortress of Gibraltar, where a lengthy stay must be anticipated, for his operations would take place over some months. On the positive side, a pay supplement would be available.

There was no regular means of smuggling letters to Morocco, Krajewski reported, but he had promises of help and hoped to know more within a few days. He assumed Mally would send detailed information and instructions by letter to Wysoczanski and asked permission to append details of his seagoing technical needs. Obviously rapid communications apart from these letters would be needed, W/T communications in particular, and these would need to be direct to avoid loss of time in decoding and recoding in Lisbon. But he confessed he was ignorant about conditions in Casablanca, and how much freedom their people enjoyed.

Krajewski knew that the British in Gibraltar had tried to evacuate a group of their own people by sending some form of naval vessel. The French authorities were terrified that, if they helped the Poles, the news would get back to Germany. While making these preparations for operations to Morocco, Krajewski had not lost sight of the far more important problem of evacuation from France. In a letter to Mally dated 17 May 1941, forwarding a report on communications to Morocco, he suggested that for urgent operational matters it would be better to use coded cable. Were there, he went on, direct communications between Lisbon and Marseilles? Was it General Kleeberg himself or his deputy who would be involved at the other end? He asked also if there had been any important change of status regarding the camps and what Kleeberg had replied to his earlier question about the delivery of people to certain places.

Mally replied on 21 May to both these letters.[6] He sent Krajewski Wysoczanski's address in Casablanca and an alternative means of contacting him through a bar. He had renewed a request to London headquarters for a code for use in direct communications between Mally and Casablanca which was indispensable for evacuation work. The Czechs, Mally continued, had recently been planning an evacuation of about 30 people from just north of Rabat, using a fishing boat. If this operation succeeded, they would be able to make use of the experience gained through it. Mally knew that there were at least 80 Poles to be evacuated from the Casablanca area, but this figure was some months out of date and he was convinced the total would turn out to be about 100. They were grouped in camps 150–200 km. (95–125 miles) from the coast and their freedom of movement was restricted. There was considerable difficulty about getting hold of passes to Casablanca; and it would not be easy to get these people down to the coast.

Wysoczanski had reported to Mally the names of the officers in charge of the camps in French North Africa. He was pessimistic about the chances of organising even the smallest evacuation without French complicity and thought that any attempt to take people out would cause a worsening of conditions in the camps. Mally said he was insisting that Wysoczanski should persist, as this was the only hope of getting these valuable people out of Africa. Wysoczanski had made proposals for evacuation by legal means, all of which, however, would require interminable efforts to get visas.

On 2 June Mally wrote to say that the French military and civilian authorities in Morocco were, for the time being, well disposed to the evacuation of the Poles from Africa.[7] This opportunity must be seized, for it was conceivable that the French would be obliged by the Armistice Commission to send the Poles who had reached Algeria and Morocco back to German-occupied France. Mally instructed Krajewski to get the British naval authorities to agree that, in that event, the ship carrying them would be intercepted and the Polish internees rescued: what had happened in Tunisia might equally well occur in Algeria and Morocco.

In a postscript, Mally wrote that a cable from London, just arrived, informed him that the British Admiralty had now issued the instruction for his own operations to France to begin. GHQ wanted Krajewski to report on progress. It was fairly typical that Mally's letter took three and a half weeks to reach Krajewski from Lisbon.

On 14 June Mally wrote again to Krajewski to say that he was still awaiting formal British Admiralty approval for operations to begin.[8] Wysoczanski meanwhile was urging the soonest possible evacuation because of the conditions prevailing in French North Africa.

Mally repeated that they must abandon the idea of using crew from the *Oksywia*, as the French were refusing to release them; Krajewski must find an alternative crew in Gibraltar.

Mally had sent Wysoczanski technical details, such as recognition signals, and he told Krajewski he must be ready to carry out an operation to Algeria at seven days' notice and to Morocco at five.

This letter must have crossed with one that Krajewski wrote on 15 June to Mally about the radio and courier problems he was experiencing in his communications with both Lisbon and Casablanca.[9] Friendly British Officers had just told him that a fishing vessel had arrived at Gibraltar from Morocco with Czechs on board. He attached a separate report on this subject, and sent another ten days later.

Particular circumstances accounted for the high cost of the Czech operation – 10,000 Francs per person. In fact, the price – a lump sum of 115,000 Francs – was to have covered the evacuation of 30 persons (i.e. 4,000 Francs per capita). This cost per head rose *de facto* when the police prevented 21 members of the expedition from making their way to the boat.

Krajewski's informants had been detained by the police with the other 21 Czechs. There was, however, no evidence against them since they were not carrying any bundles of possessions. (Evacuees, against organisers' orders, sometimes carried packages of belongings or suitcases with papers in them; one man had too many layers of clothing on.) The informants simply told the police that they had 'come to the beach' and were released with orders to return to camp before 10 o'clock.

Krajewski thought these events of obvious significance for the Poles; Wysoczanski must be informed of them. The Czechs, with their experience of evacuations, had proved a useful source of information. They advised that the best time of day for concentration at the evacuation point was the afternoon; evacuees should be divided into groups of two to four and should travel to the beach by various means. The police were in the habit of checking the papers of everyone who got off a bus. Nevertheless, the Czechs believed

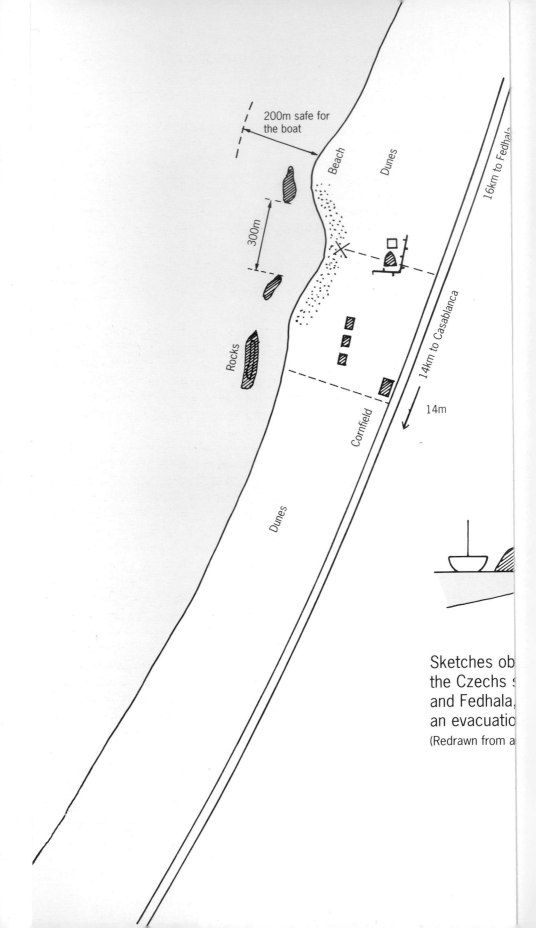

200m safe for
the boat

Beach

Dunes

300m

16km to Fedhala

Rocks

14km to Casablanca

14m

Dunes

Cornfield

Sketches ob
the Czechs :
and Fedhala,
an evacuatio
(Redrawn from a

that escape was easy so long as it was well organised. They gave Krajewski excellent sketches of the area. A person who knew the place well was a Czech Lieutenant named Riedel, who, had organised matters competently at the Casablanca end. Krajewski suggested it might be worth using him in cooperation with their own local representative. He gave Riedel's address in Casablanca.

Krajewski wrote that he could evacuate as many as 110 people if he used a passenger vessel that was available to him in Gibraltar. For any number over 50, he could ask for a British naval escort. If it proved impossible to get as many as 50 to the embarkation point, he would use an unescorted felucca. As regards crew, he wanted to have three, or at least two, Poles, rather than foreigners he could not trust. An engineer was indispensable, but he could do without a W/T operator.

Krajewski replied on 26 June to Mally's letter dated 14 June, which had taken ten days to reach him. They ought possibly to use Quennell's [SOE] bag.[10] He still had to find, requisition and fit out a vessel . He needed to hear from Casablanca about the place for the evacuation and the number of people, so as to decide on the most suitable type of boat. Then he would have to get Admiralty approval for the expenditure. All this would take time. He had suggested to Wysoczanski one possible pinpoint 14 km. south of Casablanca, but this was subject to Wysoczanski's report back on any buildings or guard posts in the area. An alternative, which he preferred, was 14 km. from Casablanca towards Fedhala. The Czechs had used it and been able to find a hide-out on the coast while waiting for evacuation. The spot was so isolated that they did not even consider a silenced engine in the boat necessary.

Krajewski pointed out that Casablanca was 190 nautical miles from Gibraltar. He estimated (not entirely accurately) that, allowing 12 hours in hand for contingencies, the round trip would take 70 hours at 7 knots or 52 hours at 10 knots. Oran was 250 nautical miles and a round trip would require 85 hours at 7 knots or 62 hours at 10 knots. Algiers was 450 nautical miles and a round trip would take 132 hours at 7 knots or 85 hours at 10 knots. He would need two months' notice and a no-moon period would be necessary.

Krajewski asked whether it would be possible to recruit a couple of Poles in Lisbon as crew. If not, he would attempt to find Spaniards, with discreet help from the British. Anticipating this, he had been learning Spanish for some time. He had proposed to Wysoczanski that priority be given to evacuating the crew of the *Oksywia*, including an engineer, but only if they agreed to serve in evacuation operations. In that case, the Spaniards would be needed for the first mission only.

On 13 June, Hugh Quennell, SOE's senior representative at Gibraltar, had informed Krajewski, to whom he was helpful in a number of ways, of a plan he had elaborated, which would involve leaving Polish military personnel in French North Africa for eventual use in special operations rather than evacuating them.[11] He told Krajewski he had been in Lisbon a week previously and had discussed this idea with Mally: he showed Krajewski a document in English, which purported to summarise Mally's reaction. The Polish military personnel left *in situ* would be organised in case the Germans invaded French North Africa or France entered into the Axis camp. The Poles would then disperse and place themselves at the head of Arab groups to create diversions. He undertook to provide money in sufficient quantity and would that week be sending 100,000 Francs to a named contact in Casablanca. Quennell claimed that Mally had more or less accepted his plan. Asked his own position, Krajewski replied that he could not adopt any policy but that of his own headquarters in London, which, to date, had given him instructions to evacuate. He was not prepared to hazard a personal view, not being familiar with the terrain in French North Africa. He suggested that Quennell might wire SOE Baker Street to discuss the matter with Polish headquarters in London.

Quennell set out his requirements in a memorandum to Krajewski dated 2 July 1941.[12] If Polish headquarters were to give permission for Polish military personnel other than air and armoured troops to be used for fifth-column activities, he would need answers to the following questions:

(a) How many Poles would be at SOE's disposal?

(b) In what districts could they become active?

(c) What were the numbers in particular districts?

(d) Who might become leaders of the proposed bands?

(e) Could the bands organise themselves as an effective fifth column for tasks such as cutting communications, sinking ships, distributing propaganda leaflets and other acts of sabotage?

(f) How much money would be necessary for such a scheme?

(g) What kind of material would need to be supplied?

(h) Could targets for sabotage be suggested?

In exchange, SOE could offer the following:

(i) To convey to French North Africa the radio station that was indispensable.

(j) Signals from the radio station could be transmitted to Gibraltar.

(k) Letters could be sent from Tangiers to the French North African territories.

(l) Money could also be forwarded by the same route.

Quennell asked if these questions and proposals could also be conveyed to the Czechs in French North Africa.

Mally replied on 8 July enclosing a record of a meeting he had had with Quennell and Jack Beevor, SOE's representative in Lisbon, on 12 June.[13] This, he said, would prove to Krajewski that Quennell had misled him. Agreement had been reached with Mr Quennell to stop evacuation of Polish military personnel from French North Africa and to leave them there for special operations, but only in the circumstances of a German invasion of French North Africa or of an attempt by the French to transfer Polish troops back to the French mainland. He asked Krajewski to remind Quennell of the basic assumptions on which their collaboration had been agreed.

The minutes of the meeting of 12 June recorded that Wyso-czanski had a certain freedom of movement and was able to travel all over French North Africa to visit the Polish camps. Mally had described the distribution of the camps and the numbers involved: Casablanca and Oran served as transit points. He had enumerated a range of possible means of arranging evacuation:

(a) United States visas, as had been obtained for individual British detainees.

(b) Evacuation by means of motor vessels under the command of Krajewski, working from Gibraltar. This project was in process of being firmed up in discussions between Polish GHQ and the British Admiralty.

(c) Evacuation with the help of British warships patrolling along the African coast. This would require that notice be given by Krajewski to Wysoczanski and would be possible only for small parties.

(d) Visas for neutral states via Lisbon: the British authorities had promised to evacuate most of the Poles from Portugal and, when this had been done, the Portuguese would be more likely to grant transit visas.

(e) The chartering of a Portuguese ship in Casablanca. In this case Portuguese visas would not be necessary: the ship would officially be sailing for Tangiers but would in fact go to Gibraltar.

(f) The remaining question was what should be done with their people should the Germans move into North Africa before evacuation was complete. Col Mally thought it would not be possible to disperse the Polish internees without the support of the Arab population because of the latter's pro-German sympathies. In the light of Mr Quennell's statement that there were Caids, tribal chieftains, of friendly disposition, matters presented themselves rather differently: dispersal would thus be an excellent solution if there were a German invasion or an order by the French authorities for the Poles to be returned to France. Proper preparations for their welfare and money for their subsistence would be necessary and should be arranged as for those held in the British camp at Carnot.

Mally had described the siting of the camps in French Morocco and the provenance of those held there; the Polish evacuation outposts at Algiers and Oran, whose personnel had a certain freedom of movement and access to the ports; and the 'Poloffices', which were the former Consulates at Algiers and Casablanca. Some further form of representation was contemplated in Tangiers.

The British wanted sabotage groups of six in Tangiers and Casablanca, and cooperation with preparations for an uprising of the local population.

The Polish side was uncertain whether it would be possible to establish Poles secretly in Tangiers, but could find people in French Morocco, including the crew of the *Oksywia* at Safi, where they were in contact with the interned Norwegians. With financial help they could achieve quite a lot. Lt Goguel, second mate of the OKSYWIA, would be a suitable leader. In Safi there were a number of large Norwegian ships whose crews were dreaming of escape. It would be worth helping them.

Mally noted that the possibility of an insurrection would depend on contact with the Arab chiefs and on the availability of money for them. It would be necessary to assign a liaison officer to the Caids. He had asked for 100,000 Moroccan Francs to be sent to an address he had given. Further financial needs would depend on progress with evacuation. Mally had said that French control of the port at Casablanca was stringent, but at Safi it was comparatively mild.

The Poles had excellent opportunities for monitoring movements of troops and merchant shipping at Oran and Safi and possibly also at Casablanca. This intelligence could be relayed to Krajewski in Gibraltar.

Code words had been agreed for the British emissary to Wysoczanski. He should bring greetings from Mally, who had worked with him in the registration office in Paris. Wysoczanski could be found via someone named Komar or the Poloffice.

Before receiving this information from Mally, Krajewski had reported (on 22 June) the arrival at Gibraltar of three boats carrying 15 Norwegians and Danes from Morocco: two were from Port Lyautey, one from Rabat.[14] The boats had simply been stolen during the night. The most important of their preparations was to provide a few boxes of biscuits and some fresh water. In the case of Port Lyautey, as the port lies some way up a river, they took advantage of the current and the ebb tide. The determination of the escapers could be judged from the fact that the boat from Rabat did not even have a compass. The voyage to Gibraltar had been accomplished in 3–4 days without incident. There were almost no controls on the coast and, if there were any look-out posts, they must have been asleep.

Krajewski felt that, if only the Poles had set about the task with energy, they would already have evacuated some dozens of their people.

On 3 July Krajewski wrote to Wysoczanski and copied the letter to Mally. He reported that Major Brzozowski had arrived from Africa.[15] To avoid further delay, he had begun preparations. The boat he had acquired had a diesel engine and auxiliary sails: it could carry up to 30 passengers and was said to be very reliable. Work on this vessel would take up to 12 July. The first evacuation operation would begin on 19 July at 0300. He was frustrated by the delay in their communications and had decided to take the initiative. He would use the embarkation point between Casablanca and Fedhala recommended by the Czechs and he attached to his letter a copy of their sketch of it. This stretch of coast was featureless and monotonous. He proposed to signal to the shore unless there was some other vessel in the vicinity. His crew on this first mission would consist of foreigners but he asked Wysoczanski to include some Polish sailors among the evacuees: he needed two reliable mechanics, only one of whom need be fully qualified, and one deck-hand. It would be desirable to get some undertaking from them of their readiness to serve. The second officer of the *Oksywia* (Goguel) would be useful. Each group of evacuees should include at least one person familiar with Morse code.

Krajewski said he was planning a second contact on Sunday 27 July and a third on Sunday 3 August, both at 0300. He repeated the Czech advice that the evacuees should avoid carrying bundles of their possessions and should be split into groups of not more than 2–4 persons, taking different routes to the pinpoint. He asked about the possibility of organising evacuation from the Oran area.

On 5 July Krajewski reported to Mally that he had taken on a Norwegian crew at a wage of £18, the rate paid on British ships.[16] They would also receive £20 by way of 'hard-lying' or danger money. He had not told them the whole story.

The conversion was progressing well: the additional fuel and freshwater tanks were being fitted by RN specialists, rather than by the civilian shipyard, in the interests of security. He expected to receive a second boat.

As regards communications, Quennell was being helpful at present, but in return he was asking Krajewski to help him over 'diversionary' activities.

He had received a reply from (Polish) GHQ to his telegram. After the evacuation of air force and armoured warfare personnel, they said that others could be used for 'diversionary activities'.

Krajewski had queried this: he wondered whether this ruling was not out of date in view of the decisive change in the political situation since the Germans had engaged themselves in the east. Perhaps a certain Father Misieuda might be landed at Casablanca for special operations of the type Quennell wanted.

In discussion with Krajewski, Admiral Collins (FOCNA) agreed that, if advised in time, and other commitments permitting, Royal Navy vessels might be used to intercept any French ship carrying Polish ex-service personnel back to metropolitan France.

Replying to earlier letters from Krajewski, Wysoczanski reported that on 7 July there had been a major change in the situation regarding the camps.[17] An order had been issued to transfer all the internees to the eastern frontier of Morocco, near the Algerian border, whence their chances of getting to the Atlantic coast would be impossible and to the Mediterranean coast nearly so. This forced Wysoczanski to make use of the fisherman Krajewski had recommended. The transfer was to begin on 11/12 July. A first group consisting of one officer and 16 other ranks must be ready for collection by this fisherman at midnight on 10 July and a second group, one officer and 24 other ranks, at midnight on 13 July. Mally would need to provide the funds.

Wysoczanski said he had reconnoitred the stretch of coast proposed by Krajewski and did not consider it suitable: the German Armistice Commission had an outpost at a village not many kilometres away and the whole district was closely patrolled. He had chosen an alternative approximately 7 km. south-west of Fedhala lighthouse and 14 km. north of the Roches-Noires lighthouse. The place would be easily recognisable. He had given it the code name HADDA.

There were, he said, more than 200 Polish internees in Algeria. As he could not bring them into Morocco, their evacuation from the Mediterranean coast should be considered. He had carried out a preliminary investigation and forwarded a report and map covering the area he thought of using for embarkation, code-named ZORRA.

Since he had started writing the letter, the first embarkation had had to be postponed for 24 hours as the fisherman had not turned up. Making use of a series of fishermen was an expensive and unsuitable method of evacuating large numbers. Events had shown that the fishermen were unreliable, which had meant that the intended evacuees were left in hiding near the beach.

The Czechs would be due to repay their share in the evacuation: The first combined Czech-Polish group had gone up from 1 + 16 to 1 + 24 and the bill would be 100,000 Francs in all: 20,000 of which should be reclaimed from the Czechs in respect of their 8 passengers.

*   *   *

After an abortive sortie on 19 July in the felucca he had been fitting out, Krajewski got back to Gibraltar on 25 July. On 3 August, just before he set off again on a further attempt, he wrote again to Mally. [18]

Communications with Casablanca continued to be unsatisfactory. Wysoczanski had not received via Quennell either the money or the radio. Quennell said he had a receipt from Tangiers signed by Komar, so they must face the possibility that someone in the line was either stealing or betraying. He would check with Wysoczanski as soon as possible to see whether he had after all now received the parcels.

If Krajewski's letter of 3 July had fallen into the wrong hands, it would be highly compromising, since it contained complete instructions for the evacuation operation and, what was worse, some intelligence and sabotage instructions sent by Major Brzozowski. The consequences would be catastrophic, so he asked Mally to try to find out through his own channels what had happened. Krajewski, for his part, had drawn the necessary conclusions and was using other means of contact with Casablanca.

Since Wysoczanski had not received his instructions by 20 July, Krajewski continued, it was entirely understandable that the first voyage should have been such a fiasco and that they had not found a single soul at the intended point of embarkation. Krajewski said he had tried to postpone the operation by telegram in code, but in the absence of the explanatory letter this would have meant nothing to Wysoczanski.

The boat's engine needed a thorough overhaul. There was no alternative vessel available at Gibraltar and looking for one in Spanish ports posed considerable security problems.

Krajewski was reticent about what was wrong with the engine but, three months later, when he had achieved a run of successes, he noted that the dockyard engineer had stopped reminding him of his felucca's 'spoiled engine'. This rather suggests that his improvised initial crew of two Norwegian seamen – survivors from a torpedoed ship – neither of whom was a mechanic, had been guilty of some sin of omission, such as failing to top up the oil in the crank-case, so that it had run dry and the big-end bearings had melted. Krajewski left no report of this abortive sortie and conferred the title of 'first evacuation mission' on what was actually his second voyage to Morocco, though he somewhat inconsistently called the immediately following operation his third and numbered the series consecutively thereafter.

The salient features of his first surviving report to Mally can be rendered thus in translation:

REPORT OF THE FIRST EVACUATION MISSION
(follows my cable of 8 viii '41)[19]

1) *AN UNEXPECTED OPPORTUNITY.* As I reported on 3 August, despite having a crew and being aware that people might still be waiting for me, my felucca was still undergoing basic repairs. In these circumstances . . . I received your telegram containing the information that dispersed all our doubts about possibly letting Major Wysoczanski down. The situation on that day made it glaringly obvious to us how exhausted our people must have been both physically and mentally, waiting since 10 July, and, in the majority of cases at least, sleeping on the beach.

When I informed Mr Quennell about my frustration he said, completely unexpectedly, 'Why don't you take my boat.' It turned out that he was prepared to give us his 'special operations' vessel for this task – an offer which, considering the situation here, I have to take as an expression of the utmost confidence.

I managed to prepare the ship for the voyage within 24 hours of being informed that we could use it (Sunday afternoon). On Monday 4 August I weighed anchor. I should add that I did not have my own crew (which would have been too small for this ship) but the ship's normal complement of personnel, together with its captain. Happily the latter was well disposed towards the operation, and also accepted certain suggestions from me regarding camouflage and the conduct of the ship, the route, etc. On board, apart from myself and the normal crew, there was Major Brzozowski, who was to be put ashore should we not find the people at the rendezvous, in order to make contact with them . . . There was in addition a young English officer, whom I took along at the request of Mr Quennell ostensibly to 'keep his hand in', although in reality perhaps as an apprentice for similar operations or as a discreet observer of our proceedings on behalf of the local representatives of British security intelligence. As it happened, it also served my purpose when we returned after a successful mission: his enthusiastic accounts of the operation helped our cause greatly and strengthened both the 'propaganda' success and its practical consequences at local level – the scale of support.

As for the first voyage, neutral identification signs were painted on the ship's side during the night. The journey to Casa was without incident. The number of ships and fishing vessels was even less than during my first trip. On 6 August at 0200 hrs we began to approach the coast, an operation of which I had already some considerable experience from my previous foray. Generally speaking, everything favoured an operation of our kind, since visibility had been reduced by a sea mist down to around 4,000 metres and the moon, which had been very bright (it was two days before the full moon) just before our arrival, became shrouded by a light layer of cloud. Having purposely arrived at our destination with time in hand. . . we began to patrol along the shore at a distance of 800 metres, giving our previously agreed identification signals as we went . . . The shoreline was generally rocky with some beaches and the hinterland was uninhabited for a distance of some kilometres. After half an hour of agitated suspense, when we had sighted what was beyond doubt the rock described by the Czechs and by Major Wysoczanski – and we had almost lost hope of receiving a reply from the shore – we made out the agreed signal. We approached the shoreline as far as the depth would allow, given the fairly large draught of our ship . . . and we dropped anchor. A small dinghy was launched and, having taken a volunteer in the shape of the English observer, I rowed the two of us towards the beach, towing behind me a light line, in accordance with the plan which I had drawn up to enable us to cross the breakers.

At a distance of 100 metres from the shore – as I soon realised – began the place where the waves broke into surf. Although we exercised the greatest care, we could not cross that line without a wetting, as we were thrown from the boat, which rapidly became filled with water. Since we had to swim across this none-too-pleasant stretch of water, we experienced this phenomenon for some 15 minutes.

Meanwhile, when thrown out of the boat, I had luckily managed to grab the line from it and, after I had swum to the shore, our people there helped me pull it out. Captain Roehr, the head of the local evacuation operation, was waiting for me on the beach together with 27 people, three of whom were Czechs. After an initial 'conference' with Captain R., which, because it was held in such difficult conditions, did not explore in full all the matters we had to discuss, I took a first group of nine people who knew how to swim. Since we were uncertain whether we could pass through the line of breakers with our wet clothes weighing down the boat, I ordered them to be left on the beach, allowing the men to take only their money, documents and items of value. I disposed the people around the boat, ordering them also to keep hold of the line. At an arranged signal the crew of the ship began to draw the line in, and we helped by walking alongside it until we were out of our depth. That line proved to be invaluable: the evacuees did not exhaust themselves, since their only efforts were expended in keeping afloat. The boat unfortunately filled with water once again, so that its contents were soaked. Apart from two people who at a certain point betrayed signs of panic and clawed their way on to the boat already filled with water, the whole group swam out most efficiently to the ship, where, with the help of the crew, they clambered up on to the deck. Each received a blanket and the crew made over its living quarters to them until the end of the voyage.

I returned to the shore; once again it proved impossible to cross the line of breakers without being tipped from the 'saddle' . . . After a final conversation with Captain Roehr, who made a favourable impression on me, and having received from him a letter for you [Mally] and me, I got together the second and final group. After the first attempt, I decided to risk the crossing with the whole remaining party at once (16 people). The procedure would be just the same – that is, we would cross the breakers to reach the ship. However, I must say that the second group conducted itself even more calmly than the first, even though its members did not know how to swim. The Englishman also returned from the shore with this second group. He – as it later turned out – was impressed by the courage and determination of our people in making their way from Africa to join the Polish army.

So, at 0530, after $2\frac{1}{2}$ hours, we completed the embarkation, after the disagreeable experience of touching the bottom a few times. The night was unsuitable for the operation insofar as the tides were concerned; high water being at 0200 hours, so we were compelled to work on a falling tide . . .

The only anxious moment of the voyage was the passage of a French aircraft some 1,000 metres away from us. Luckily it was a transport aircraft destined – to judge by its course – for Dakar. Also, as we approached the Straits of Gibraltar, where . . . we had a gale blowing against us, on the edge of Spanish territorial waters we met a Spanish patrol boat, which . . . suddenly, having passed us, turned about and followed us for a few minutes.

2) *ECHOES OF A SUCCESSFUL EXPEDITION.* Our mission acquired a relatively large, although discreet, fame amongst the senior people here. This is possibly because the attempts mounted so far, if my information is correct, have in general produced results such as the seizure of trawlers by the French or the failure of the evacuees to materialise, etc. The Governor himself [Lord Gort] took an interest in the mission and I have been informed that he will be summoning me within the next few days. Congratulations are coming in from all sides and, something that is most important in this situation, help for my

people in the form of uniforms, equipment, and many lesser items . . .

3) *NEWS FROM CAPTAIN ROEHR.* During the period when they were awaiting our arrival, 13 people were caught in a series of searches. One of them managed to escape for a second time. After the first escape on 25 July, Major Wysoczanski was called to the French military command and told that they did not believe that the escape had taken place without his knowledge, and that he had 'lost their confidence'. At present, as Captain R. says, they will await the reaction of the authorities for around two weeks, after which they were even going to inform the French that these people were 'already in Tangiers'.

They are not going to use the radio, although it is ready, as they are still exercising extreme care since the arrests. They have not given up the idea of using it, though, as long as it does not worsen the situation.

Apparently the French are going to clear the Casablanca region of foreigners, and house searches are being forecast (in the newspapers) under the pretext of requisitioning accommodation.

When the observation period has elapsed they will give us dates for further expeditions.

Wysoczanski will attempt to gain permission to travel to Algeria, where he will organise evacuations.

The Birgemayer affair, so strikingly coinciding with the Czechs' account, demands an immediate reaction. I am trying to establish the date on which the courier handed Mr Quennell the letter (there are difficulties and delays). If it is proved that the letter was deliberately delayed – this amounts to nothing other than treason. If they had received the letter on 19 July, I would have brought out 12 more people and there would have been less bad feeling from the French brought down on Wysoczanski's head, since the people would have disappeared without trace. . .'

(signed) M. Krajewski

*   *   *

The letter from Wysoczanski to Krajewski bears a note written by the latter to the effect that Roehr handed it over on the beach at Fedhala at 0400 on 6 August. It was written from Casablanca on 5 August and has survived time as well as immersion.[20] Wysoczanski wrote that he was assuming that the boat would come that night. He would need another operation to Morocco and, if he could obtain a permit, he would then go to Algeria. He would arrange for telegrams to be sent in code from Casablanca, Oran or Algiers about the next operation in the series. A telegram from Casablanca would mean that the boat should go to the HADDA pinpoint; sent from Oran or Algiers, to the ZORRA pinpoint. A reference in the telegram to 'transit visas' would indicate the number of evacuees, while one to 'resident's visas' would indicate the date on which the operation should take place. ZORRA was the beach from Les-Andalouses village to Cap-Falcon; because of its length, he had divided it into three sections: a reference in the telegram to 'IMMEDIATE' meant that the westernmost section, marked '1' on the plan (which he enclosed), would be the embarkation point; 'TRÈS URGENT' would denote the middle part of the beach; 'URGENT' the easternmost.

Wysoczanski said he would try to send the telegram about a week before the embarkation. If he had to cancel, he would telegraph at least 48 hours before the date on which the boat would need to sail from Gibraltar. He also indicated how Krajewski could warn him if the operation had to be cancelled from his side.

In a postscript, Wysoczanski said he had received Krajewski's letter dated 3 July only at 1800 hours that day: the courier had not distinguished himself and some other arrangement would be necessary in future. The arrest of his people on 25 July had led, as he saw it, to a vote of no confidence in him personally from the French authorities. The lack of premises made the installation of his W/T set more difficult. Household searches seemed likely and would affect foreigners first of all. The radio specialist mentioned by Krajewski did not reach Casablanca until the end of June and, owing to carelessness on the part of Marseilles, was picked up immediately after landing in Africa. The two sailors asked for by Krajewski should have been in the operation on 10 July but were arrested on 25 July. Arrangements for getting the crew of the *Oksywia* out were proving difficult, but he would include them in the next batch. Wysoczanski said he was in touch with Captain Nierojewski of the *Oksywia*, but, apart from a few officers and men of her crew, they had no-one who spoke English.

Mally too had written to Krajewski on 5 August, forwarding details of the number of people awaiting evacuation in Morocco and of the camps where they were held.[21] The arrests had been only partial: about 10 had been taken into custody, but approximately 30 were still awaiting Krajewski's arrival, in very difficult and arduous circumstances.

Mally asked Krajewski to pass on an order from himself as soon as effective contact with Wysoczanski was established: Wysoczanski's letters, cards and cables, all on the same subject, had attracted the attention of the censorship at Madrid; this kind of nonsense must cease forthwith.

Krajewski set sail once more for Morocco on 17 August and, when he returned eight days later, he reported as follows:

REPORT OF THE THIRD EVACUATION MISSION
(follows my cable of 26 August)[22]

1) As I reported in my evacuation report of 10 August, following the first evacuation, Major Wysoczanski intended to wait for some two weeks, in order to ascertain how the French authorities would react; after this waiting period, as long as their attitude did not worsen, he was to indicate by telegram his readiness to continue with further missions.

The first news from Wysoczanski in this regard was the cable you yourself received on 12th inst. with the information that Casablanca 'was asking why no-one has arrived to pick up the next group'.

As I reported by cable, replying to the above-mentioned enquiry, I had prepared a third evacuation mission irrespective of whether or not we received a signal from Casablanca. This was because I was aware of the unsatisfactory state of communications with Africa, especially regarding the speedy transmission of information *from Wysoczanski to me*, since the only route at the moment is via Lisbon.

2) My own evacuation vessel was still not ready (the workshops have promised to have it ready a week from now) so that, once again, certain technical difficulties arise. A trawler was not suitable on this mission, since I intended to wait close to the shore for up to a few days under the new plan I had devised for the mission.

Finally, I obtained, or rather borrowed, thanks to Mr Quennell's help, a fishing smack with room for cargo/passengers, although small. It had a 30 h.p. engine and sails. The motor, though, was 30 years old, and the condition of the sails left much to be desired. I include these details in order to convey to you some idea of the limited technical facilities here – despite the full-hearted support of the Gibraltar authorities and private help from a whole range of the officers here.

3) *PLAN OF THE MISSION.* This, by contrast with the evacuation of 4–8 August, was based on changing the evacuation point

a) because I regard the HADDA location as too severely compromised following the month-long vigil of some 40 of our people on this stretch of the coast;

b) because of the recruiting of a certain number of Arabs and one Frenchman into the organisation by our people (feeding them during the period of their vigil?); we had to count on the fact then that our activities might be revealed by idle chatter;

c) because the gendarmes seized 13 of our people on this precise stretch of coastline; this apart, during the night of 5/6 August, when the evacuation was underway, the gendarmerie was alerted by an Arab informer; they attempted to arrest one of our people, but were put to flight by superior numbers;

d) because, given the particular circumstances surrounding our embarkation and departure, our people had also left behind on the beach a number of items (clothing), and we had to assume that it might have come to the notice of the authorities (through markings left in the sand) even though Roehr had promised to send a friendly Frenchman to pick them up; we left though at a fairly late hour (0550 hrs).

After considering the above points, and sounding out the opinions of people who had been evacuated from that spot, I decided to change the point of evacuation. By a coincidence it seemed that one place definitely identified as suitable for evacuations already existed. A certain Officer Cadet Staggart, a Czech staying at Gibraltar, who himself wanted to use it for such purposes, knew the Moroccan terrain perfectly, having served for ten years in the Foreign Legion. He speaks Arabic, has fluent French, and he has to his credit a rather important achievement: he managed successfully to evacuate Czechs from Fedhala on 8–10 June *without any outside help.*

Staggart suggested a spot 3 km. to the north of the wall of the town of Sali (near Rabat). He claimed to have reconnoitred this place as an embarkation point during the spring, in connection with a certain evacuation plan devised with the aid of the Czech Consul in Lisbon (the plan though was never put into operation since the Consul was apparently transferred).

Nevertheless, Staggart undertook to accompany us, which ruled out any worries that by myself I might not recognise the correct location, etc. Staggart moreover was putting himself in some danger, since, if he were caught, he risked being put in front of a court martial and shot as a deserter from the Legion. This argued in his favour, but in any case, you only needed to look at him to have confidence in him. (The British authorities trusted him completely until . . . our return.)

My mission plan was based on putting Staggart ashore. He would then make contact with Major Wysoczanski and his own compatriots (only three of them were intending to leave), and he was to bring them to the agreed embarkation point within 24 hours. If this could not be accomplished in time, then within 2 days, during which I was to wait offshore (so as to conserve fuel).

An important advantage of the cooperation with Staggart was that he had a very good Czech friend in Rabat, the director of some business, who, as he said, would be sure to help by hiding our people for a few days.

4) We weighed anchor on 17 August after a week of the customary problems with technical preparations (by some dreadful quirk, circumstances forced me to prepare *three* different ships for these *three* missions . . .). The crew consisted of: Siembieda, in the role of engine-man; two Norwegians; and Staggart. At about 0300 hrs on the 19th we were already close to the port of Rabat, from where I began the passage along the coast to try to locate the agreed spot. However, in spite of the Czech's assurances that the spot could be discerned even at night 'thanks to the *marabout*' [Moslem shrine], we had to wait until dawn; then it became clear that, at the agreed point, *there was no beach*(!), simply a rock wall. (Staggart's comment: 'It looked different from above . . .') Because of this I moved further along the shore in a northerly direction, looking for some other suitable site. Only when I had travelled to a point almost halfway between Sali and Mehedia (Port Lyautey) did I come to a beach which was very long and suited our purpose completely – provided, of course, that the hinterland beyond the hills did not hide any surprises. Apart from numerous Arabs, there were no special patrols visible on the shore, nor a dense network of observation posts. The only thing, as it turned out later, was the spotter aircraft constantly flying along the coastline at a height of some 100 metres: they paid no attention to us at all because of our obvious 'fishing' appearance, complete with nets hung out to dry. Since I could not begin by putting Staggart ashore by day under the eyes of the Arabs, I dropped anchor some 500 metres from the shore to await dusk.

After sunset I advised the Czech to get into the water with a container tied to a line, inside which were his clothes, money, etc. I changed our anchorage specially in order to shorten the distance to the shore (to some 50 m.). The plan had of course been agreed with Staggart completely. I did not give him the rubber dinghy on purpose, since he said he was a good swimmer and it made the manoeuvre considerably easier. The line was to serve both for safety and to draw the container back to the ship (it was supposed to serve as a means of loading items without getting them wet – a need based on experience of the first trip). Twenty minutes after his descent into the water, as a result of calls from the water, we drew the line back in. It seemed that Staggart had not reached the shore; he explained that the line got in his way, etc. Since I still had complete confidence in him, I believed him, assuming that after all he probably lost his sense of direction in the dark.

We spent the night anchored further from the beach, since there is a powerful surf near the shore, and the presence of even a fishing boat would be suspect. On the morning of 20 August I once again approached to within 50 m., risking the loss of my anchor and the destruction of the felucca on the shore owing to the dangerous oceanic surf (for people swimming, or on a dinghy or life-raft, it presents a danger, as we learned during the embarkation on 6 August, when the state of the sea was the same. A clear beach without rocks is essential since the force of such waves falling on to rocks can kill . . .). I did in fact lose one anchor as the line broke, unable to withstand the tension. We were saved by the second anchor which was being held ready, the engine, which was also standing by, and – perhaps most important – the specially placed sailor, whose task was to observe the soundings taken to discover immediately the slightest dragging of the anchor.

Now, in such a perilous position, Staggart, having been called on deck, said that he was absolutely exhausted and in no state even to attempt making for the shore. After having tried vainly to persuade and entreat him, I again drew out from land to some 500 m., hoping that an additional day-long rest would restore his morale. At midday he was himself once more and, seeing that it was such a beautiful day and that the beach was completely safe (fine sand), he promised to set off the following night. At dusk on 20 August, I anchored once again, this time even closer (calmer spot) and – I must emphasise – I offered him a rubber boat with oars (from a German ship), together with a sailor to help him. In addition, he would be on the safety line. (I had already tried to send him by this inflatable boat in the morning.)

Staggart refused in spite of the fact that the whole crew volunteered to travel with him in the boat. (The conduct of the crew, including the Norwegians, deserves the highest praise. They displayed unflagging enthusiasm and energy as well as discipline. In spite of unbelievably difficult conditions and the fact that the voyage was eventually extended to eight days, two of them taken up by a fierce storm, there was not a word of complaint about the conditions, which were imaginable only by someone who has himself experienced life on a small fishing vessel.)

My further efforts to appeal to his sense of pride and to remind him that, because of him, some 40 people were going to have to wait, threatened by danger of arrest, etc, were in vain.

Given the situation, I began to weigh up the possibility of perhaps entering the port of Rabat or Mehedia at dawn, and dropping him off in the dock area, counting on the fact that the port police would not pay any attention since they would assume that it was one of their own boats returning with a catch. Staggart again promised that he would land, but when, at dawn on the 21st, I approached the entrance to Mehedia, he again began to display his symptomatic 'doubts'.

Since the risk of entering the port was too great to allow the Czech to proffer one more refusal – as usual at the last moment – I decided to return.

5) The return journey was not without adventure. Just before we entered the Straits of Gibraltar on the morning of 22 August (Friday), a strong gale blew up. With my weak engine I had no chance of making progress against the storm (which was from the east). After a few hours the storm blew itself out and I had to set a course for the north. In this way I tacked between Cadiz and Spanish Morocco for two days, driven by the ocean. After a lull on Sunday 24th, a wind from the south-west enabled me to return to Gibraltar at 2230 on the 25th.

6) As I discovered on reaching port, after a period of searching and waiting, the people here had almost given up hope of my return, which, in spite of the negative outcome, was a pleasant surprise. . . all the more so since they had been aware of the weather conditions at sea. Those who had been searching for us had not recognised us.

As regards Staggart, certain conclusions were drawn from the episode and he was sent to England.

7) Thinking over the case, I am now convinced that during his first attempt to swim, having arrived at the line of breakers, he was terrified by the waves, turned back and – not being able to find the boat in the darkness – experienced an overwhelming moment of fear, which broke him psychologically, so that even mentally he could not believe he could cross the breakers – a feat which 27 of our people had achieved previously.

8) Since people are waiting for me somewhere near Rabat, my intention is to repeat the mission, despite the risk, using HADDA, which after a few weeks will surely be a little safer. I intend to put to sea on Saturday 30 August and carry out the operation on the night of 31 August/1 September. As a precaution I am taking along Midshipman Kleybor, who has distinguished himself already by his courage and is a good swimmer. The object is

to establish communication, if no telegrams have arrived by then.

(signed) M. Krajewski

Krajewski followed up this report on 28 August with a long letter to Mally.[23] Simbieda, who had been used for the first time on the 17–25 August operation, had been a disappointment. The weather had been bad and he had felt seasick. The magneto had got wet and had had to be stripped down in particularly trying conditions. Simbieda had tried to do the job but had proved such a poor mechanic that Krajewski, though he had no particular mechanical aptitude, had had to spend a great deal of time working on the engine himself. This episode made it easier to understand why the *Sobieski* had been prepared to relinquish Simbieda to the army at a time when there was such an acute shortage of specialists. The man had positive qualities – he was a hard worker – but Krajewski was now looking to exchange him against someone better qualified from the crew of the *Oksywia*.

Krajewski was left with the two packets of Moroccan Francs and could not say how he would forward them. Also, he had not been able to land the new W/T set. He thought Casablanca were perhaps being unduly cautious in not using the set they already had.

He observed that all transients in Gibraltar, not just the Poles but also, for example, French and Belgians from Miranda, were accommodated in difficult conditions in the Spanish Pavilion, which was a kind of barracks. In spite of being disinfected every few weeks, even days, Polish soldiers still complained about fleas. They also had to sleep on the floor with a couple of blankets. A considerable part of the British garrison was similarly affected: London had met a request for beds with the rejoinder that there was a war on! It was really not possible for him to combine the functions of seagoing operations officer and liaison officer although he had achieved some progress in matters of this kind. It was only through his efforts that those arriving would be issued with tropical uniforms rather than battledress. Their soldiers were completely satisfied with the supply of equipment. The officers were separately quartered in hotels – admittedly cheap ones.

Father Misieuda had done his best on his first mission: he had even gone ashore in the rubber boat.

Reporting was a problem, as there was so little time between missions, and he had to deal with quartering of the evacuees and with their medical needs (malaria was on the increase). He could not delay missions to attend to the welfare of those already evacuated. After each operation, he had to report in detail to the

Admiral, his Chief of Staff, to naval intelligence, army intelligence, the Governor's Chief of Staff, the head of counter-intelligence, to the dockyard concerning technical matters and to a number of lesser figures. His courtesy visits elicited great interest and friendly offers of help. From him, for example, the Governor learned of the fleas and as a result the barracks were disinfected the next day. He also had to take care of his own crew. He cited the many tasks assigned to him not by way of complaint but because he had now been reproached a second time for being behind with his reports.

In the light of increased Polish business, the British authorities had suggested he ought to have an assistant, and Krajewski now concurred. The French, Belgians and Czechs all had or were forming missions. The other missions also had responsibility for evacuating their nationals from French North African territory, though only the French had actually got to the executive stage: he knew they had had boats arrested in the Casablanca area. The name of Kasimir Badeni, an officer cadet who spoke good English, was put forward as assistant to Krajewski, who suggested he be given the rank of second lieutenant.

Father Misieuda was taking the Belgian ship *René-Paul* to Lisbon. Quennell told him that Birgemayer had been arrested at Casablanca: the news had reached him via Madrid. It was not clear whether this was linked with their evacuation operations or not, but his arrest might affect future missions, as he might reveal too much under interrogation.

*   *   *

From: Marian KRAJEWSKI, Gibraltar, 8 September 1941.

To: Colonel Fryderyk MALLY (Lisbon)

REPORT OF THE FOURTH EVACUATION MISSION TO FRENCH AFRICA
(follows my cable of 6 September '41)[24]

1) Following the unsuccessful mission of 17-25 August I weighed anchor again, after the indispensable minimum period of time needed to

   a) inform Major Wysoczanski by telegram, giving him at the same time a few days to prepare things at his end;
   b) repair the felucca's engine, which had taken in water;
   c) add to our reserves, etc.

2) I informed Major Wysoczanski that, as he had concentrated his people in the vicinity of Rabat in line with my previous plan, I would not ask him to transfer them 70 km. to the south. I told

him that he alone should establish contact with me at the HADDA point, and show me the place at which he wanted them to embark (near Rabat).

3) We weighed anchor on 30 August, or just under five days from the time of our return from the third mission. On the felucca, apart from the crew, 2 Norwegians and Siembieda, were: Kleybor, taken in case the telegram had not reached Wysoczanski, and Lt Killick, an officer of the British army, whom I took along as a volunteer, in return for the great deal of help he had given me with technical preparations of the boat, which is formally under his care. This officer showed himself to be very brave and efficient, completely dedicated to the undertaking. He travelled with me already on the second mission (27 people brought back), when his official role was that of an observer.

For the first time, too, I carried some weapons, in case of a meeting with a motor patrol boat or, on land while we were embarking, an armed patrol: these consisted of a machine-pistol (tommy-gun), a carbine and two pistols.

4) The voyage to Casablanca passed without incident. I arrived at the spot several hours ahead of schedule (1750 hrs on 31 August). Until 2200 hrs I lay hove-to at a distance of 6 km. offshore. Then I began to make an approach to the correct location. Conditions at first were foul (v. thick fog) but luckily they improved at the last moment and we proceeded along the shore from the Fedhala lighthouse in order to find the rocks with which I was familiar. The moon was almost full, but a slight fog reduced visibility to around 5,000 metres. At 0030 hrs on 1 September I found myself near the rock. Immediately after giving the signal, we received the agreed response. I approached the shore as near as possible, to just a little more than the vessel's draft, as it seemed, and to the edge of the breakers (around 250 m.), which are dangerous on open oceanic beaches. Having dropped two anchors and taken soundings to establish whether the heavy swell might not cast the felucca on to the breakers, I launched the rubber boat which was already prepared and secured to a line, which was later paid out from the felucca. A second coil of rope was in the boat: this was later paid out from the beach, when the felucca drew the boat back in.

At a distance of around 20 m. from the rubber boat a watertight tin can was fastened to the line, in which I conveyed to the shore post for Casablanca, pistols for the look-outs covering the landing, and money. Additionally it had to serve to bring on board the documents, money, watches, etc. of those being evacuated. A distance of 20 m. was maintained so as not to injure those swimming in the surf.

5) I made my way to the beach with Kleybor. During the first trip to the shore in the rubber boat we had of course to row: on the next the 'ferry' system began to function, with the line being drawn in by turns from the boat and from the shore. We were dressed only in our swimming gear and lifebelts.

On the beach Major Wysoczanski was waiting with Capt Roehr and Lt Jozefkiewicz. After putting the embarkation procedure in motion, I left Midshipman Kleybor by the rubber boat in charge of the technical side of the operation, while I had a conference with the leaders of the evacuation.

As it turned out, the number of people brought together was 48, of whom four were Belgians.

The boarding operation passed off without incident: one Arab was chased away by a look-out.

6) At 0300 hrs I had already made my way back to the ship and, having weighed anchor, started on the return journey: first parallel with the shore and then direct to the Straits of Gibraltar.

As might have been foreseen, the conditions under which such a large group of people were accommodated on a small fishing boat were unspeakably difficult (it is 9 tons; my own felucca, which is bigger, will be ready in a few days). This was especially the case during the first night when these people were wet through (they received a ration of rum to warm them and a blanket each) and during the later nights of the voyage – of which more below. Half of the evacuees had to sleep on the deck, and the nights even in these regions are damp and cold at sea. Mind you, the crew had to put up with identical conditions.

In spite of these difficulties, the general mood was very good and one could see that these people were happy to have got out of Morocco. The meals were varied and, during the first days, until we were seriously delayed, of sufficient quantity.

Among the evacuees was the entire crew of the *Oksywia* with its Captain (Lipkowski).

7) After a day's sailing, we were at the entrance to the Straits (morning of 2 September), having travelled 140 nautical miles. But it was here that our difficulties began. A strong easterly wind began to blow, coming from the very direction in which I wanted to enter the Straits. After a few hours' unsuccessful attempts to make my way against the current and the storm-force wind, in conditions of dangerously heavy swell, and relentless soaking of half the evacuees and the crew, I turned

back and sought shelter behind Cape Spartel, the northernmost promontory of Africa (in the Straits of Gibraltar). There I prepared to ride out the storm, or at least wait for it to blow in a more favourable direction in relation to my course.

In these conditions we waited out the 2nd and 3rd of September. The wind neither weakened nor turned. The conditions under which we slept at night were worse than uncomfortable, and the food supplies were almost exhausted: the crew of OKSYWIA and the presence of other sailors among the evacuees – in other words, the absence of people suffering from seasickness – meant that food reserves ran low, they being limited because of the lack of space. So when, on the morning of 4 September, the wind seemed to abate, I made an attempt to break through to Gibraltar. I managed only to get to the Spanish coast and came under the lee of Tarifa, the southernmost promontory of Spain. The wind developed almost into a hurricane. I dropped anchor initially in the vicinity of Tarifa, off a beach where there happened to be a fort. Either in order to have a practice shoot or else to frighten away the intruding 'unknown fishermen', a Spanish army platoon came directly level with us (distance 500 m.) and began firing along the beach towards their target. Owing to the fact that bullets were falling in the water at a distance half-way between me and the shore – and not finding any pleasure in conjecturing whether it was being done accidentally or on purpose – I weighed anchor after a stay of two hours and, having made one further abortive attempt to make my way against the current, I put into the small fishing port of Tarifa. (Tarifa is called, because of its fortifications, the 'Spanish Gibraltar'.) According to the laws and customs of the sea, I always had the right to do this because of bad weather, and, in the event of questions from the Spanish authorities about the crowding on my felucca, I had a cover story prepared. For a few hours, nobody even turned up. Only when I requested supplies from a few 'fellow fishermen', who paid me a neighbourly visit and wanted to help me – did they go off to the authorities, in order to obtain not only fruit, which I had asked for, but also items distributed only on ration cards. They recounted to the authorities the story they had heard from me about having picked up the survivors from a torpedoed ship.

8) Eventually a Sub Lieutenant in the Spanish navy turned up (a sort of commissary-paymaster, or expert in maritime law) together with a couple of customs officials. After looking at the one document from Gibraltar that I had, on which it was noted that I had gone to sea to catch fish, and after listening to my story – that I was a fisherman from Gibraltar who at the

beginning of my voyage had come across a group of survivors from the SS *Kirken* – he invited me along to his office. There, in my presence, he telephoned through to the naval authorities in Algeciras, repeating my story faithfully, and asking whether he could give me supplies for the survivors. While awaiting the reply ($2\frac{1}{2}$ hours, since it was quite a late hour), I met the commander of the fortress, a Lt Colonel, who informed me very kindly that, given the difficult situation created by the presence of these survivors, they would certainly 'not let us starve to death'. They added that, once they had received a positive reply from Algeciras, for as long as I judged the weather too severe to put to sea, they would provide me with food on a daily basis. That night, despite the lateness of the hour, after 10 o'clock, the above-mentioned naval officer came with me around the shops and supply offices, in order to help me with provisions.

9) I had an unexpected visit after returning to the ship. Another naval officer appeared, a Lieutenant Commander, who spoke unexpectedly good English, although not well enough to realise that I am not English myself – which I had stated at the outset. After giving us tea and sugar (for the 'survivors'), he began some discreet questioning: which ship had it been (he asked for the exact name), where was it torpedoed, had it been travelling alone or in a convoy before being torpedoed, had any of the crew died? For most of the details of the ship, I called upon the officers of the *Oksywia* as the crew of the *Kirken*. Having listened to the story and asked searching questions, the Spanish officer left, promising to inform the British authorities.

We had a curious visit next day when the same officer approached again. He asked if he could see 'the Captain of the torpedoed ship'. Luckily, Captain Lipkowski (*Oksywia*) had been briefed on my fairy-tale, so there were no inconsistencies. To the question, 'Has the name of your ship been changed, since there seems to be no trace of it on Lloyd's List ?', Captain Lipkowski answered that it had, but he had only sailed in her under the new name and did not know the old one.

But this time too he was left with no doubts for even if there had been any inconsistencies, it would hardly have been surprising, since in wartime losses, names and other details are concealed. The only weak point in my story, which happily no-one pressed, was the professional aspect of my 'fishing knowledge'. But it was the regular navy with whom we were dealing, so they were not familiar with such things either.

10) Around 1500 hrs. on 5 September two British naval motor launches [110-foot 'B'-Class Fairmile MLs] from Gibraltar

arrived at the port of Tarifa. After being welcomed by the Spanish officer (mentioned above) they began preparations for loading the passengers. Since the wind was still at storm level and so too strong for my engine, I took a tow-line from them. During the towing, though, I helped by using my own engine, thanks to which we managed to reach Gibraltar at the 'exceptional' speed of 10 knots. I entered the port of Gibraltar and approached the pier under my own power (the weather, ironically, had improved markedly – after four days of storm – half-way to Gibraltar).

11) In Gibraltar quite a number of officers were awaiting my arrival – both in an official and in a private capacity. Also waiting was Major Brzozowski, whom the authorities had still not found a means of sending to England. Our return had something of a triumphal entry about it. In spite of my unusual dress (fisherman's) and the need to maintain a low profile, the congratulations began. People were immediately taken to cars and driven off to quarters prepared for them. In the meantime a number of things were put right: for example, each soldier received a mattress; they were divided among the regiments, because of overcrowding, which gave certain benefits, since the regiments, of their own initiative, are giving them many 'perks', and show a great deal of friendship and warmth towards them.

It turned out that the information from the Spanish authorities [about their arrival at Tarifa] was understood correctly [by the authorities in Gibraltar], in spite of lack of details, and only the number of 'survivors' was considered to be impossible for that sort and size of boat.

After settling in the new arrivals and the crew, there began the usual round of reporting on the mission: to the Admiral commanding the base, the naval Chief of Staff and other functionaries of the navy and army. In addition, Admiral Somerville, Commander of the Mediterranean Squadron, famous for the battle with the Italians, asked the base commander if he could put me up for a British decoration. They all expressed their sincere admiration for the morale and attitude of the Polish army, that, in the most difficult conditions, despite all adversities, the men manage to rejoin their forces. As for the undertaking itself, they themselves underlined the poverty of the resources with which such results were achieved.

12) As I anticipated, after two successes. the second larger than the first, thus ruling out any suspicion that it was all due to luck, all the officials here are asking in what way they can give more help. I am of course making the most of the situation with a view to evacuating the next region.

I should add that, up until, and including, the last evacuation, I was still forced to use a boat that was not my own, but borrowed, since mine is in the last stages of refitting.

13) *NEWS FROM WYSOCZANSKI.* 'With this last mission the evacuation from Morocco is completed' – Wysoczanski told me on the beach. The remaining element consists of people not suitable for evacuation (mainly from the Foreign Legion). He himself, together with his two helpers, will now attempt to secure an official transfer to Algeria: if the French authorities refuse this request, he will wire me via Lisbon, to come and pick them up, and put them ashore in Oran. There, being familiar already with the technique of evacuation and having now experience of the kind of embarkation point needed for such an operation (what was very important were places to hide large groups of people, in case of a delay in the date of departure and other obstacles), they will examine embarkation points suggested by me and also a plan of their own.

Birgemayer was arrested as a result of his own carelessness. When one hears assessments of his character from all sides, it is quite difficult to believe that he could be used for special duties. He talked too much and boasted of his 'special' missions: they found a radio code in his apartment.

As regards my letter of 3 July, which arrived in Major Wysoczanski's hands on 4 August, Wysoczanski discovered that Birgemayer received it on 21 July. In other words he allowed an unpardonable delay of two weeks to pass before handing it on – and this was in spite of the fact that the letter was opened and B. knew that the dates of my arrival mentioned therein would in the meantime have passed. Thus the fiasco of my first voyage.

As for Komar, the matter is not serious: he was arrested because a Morse key was found in his apartment, of the type that radio-telegraph operators use for training. They think that he will soon be released.

As for the money, I gave them only 75,000 *French* Francs, since these were the only kind in the package I received, despite the reference in the letter to 'Moroccan Francs'. I tore open the package en route, in order to load the contents into watertight containers. Major Wysoczanski was astonished by the French currency. He took the amount allocated, however, and asked for the rest to be sent on to him via the United States Consulate, which I will do. In case he leaves, 'Poloffice' will send it after him.

Incidentally I repeated to Major Wysoczanski the recommendation that correspondence using plain-language code should be kept to a minimum.

As for the radio, the matter is completely dead and buried,

according to Major Wysoczanski, following the arrest of the radio-telegraphist. They must be very careful. Files, for example, have been burned for the same reason.

14) As regards our successful mission, I consider it my duty to tell you that the expedition succeeded thanks to the good organisational work involved in concentrating the people on shore; credit for this must go to Major Wysoczanski and his helpers, Capt Roehr and Lt Jozefkiewicz, who ran considerable risks in making direct contacts.

After talking to a number of the people evacuated, I was able to appreciate the excellent organisation of the evacuation on the spot. After receiving a telegram from me, Major Wysoczanski managed, through skilful planning, to gather together people from such places as Berguent (500 km.), a whole crew from Safi who had come on a pass to Casablanca in order to have a 'medical examination'; and people from hospital; he managed to maintain the morale of people who had arrived too late for the first evacuation and who had to wait in the undergrowth or in a small hut for several weeks.

In addition I would like to inform you that the following distinguished themselves during this mission: Midshipman Kleybor, who ventured ashore with me, and Midshipman Pelipeyko. Kleybor was in fact a member of the crew and, in the course of the return journey lasting several days, his help in cooking and feeding the numerous passengers went unappreciated. He nevertheless carried out his normal watches day and night. Pelipeyko also kept watch (I know him from the navy) and when we were leaving Tarifa and other evacuees found themselves in more comfortable conditions on the MLs, he applied to make up the numbers of my small crew which – as might have been expected – meant a complete soaking for several hours and very hard work.

(signed) M. Krajewski

*   *   *

Although Wysoczanski had told Krajewski on 1 September at Fedhala that, with this last mission, evacuation from Morocco was complete, he did in fact require one more operation. On 27 September Mally wrote to Gibraltar asking what had happened with preparations for this further expedition: as he had already informed Krajewski by cable, Wysoczanski was pressing for news about the next date for embarking his people.[25] The letter reached

Krajewski only on 6 October, the day before he sailed once more in *Dogfish*, the ship lent to him by Quennell.

Mally asked for a repetition of a cable regarding a man named Sumliez, of which they had only been able to decode the beginning. He had orders from London that this man should on no account be admitted to England, even if they had to throw him back over the Portuguese border. He had been delivered to Mally by the Portuguese under armed guard straight from prison. The Madrid Embassy believed he was working for the Gestapo. London were furious that he had been embarked on a British warship without a British visa and Krajewski was enjoined to find some way of stopping him. It was not the first case in which Madrid had sent on someone working for foreign intelligence: not long before they had helped Ejsymont, who was working for the Germans and had given away all their evacuation arrangements. The evacuation organisation was still suffering from the effects. The file copy is annotated, 'Too late, he left on 2/x'.

Krajewski was asked to find out from the British whether they would be prepared to provide 700 blankets and how these could be forwarded to the Miranda-del-Ebro camp. He was also to investigate the possibility of sending food and reading matter via the British to the inmates of the camp. Gibraltar was also to send Lisbon a list of names of the soldiers they had collected from Casablanca, together with particulars of their experience in the military field. Krajewski was to report such information automatically in future.

Mally wrote that they had prepared in Lisbon a motor vessel, which could carry up to 20 people. They hoped this would spare them the task of keeping transients illegally in Portugal and avoid mass arrests such as had taken place a month previously.

Krajewski by this time had acquired an assistant and was probably glad to be able to leave him to wrestle with these problems and himself escape to sea, but it was to be a trying experience, as his report shows:

From: Marian KRAJEWSKI, Gibraltar, 13 October 1941

To: Colonel Fryderyk MALLY (Lisbon)

REPORT OF THE FIFTH EVACUATION MISSION
(Follows my cable 1938/10/10)[26]

1) Having learned from you that Major Wysoczanski was awaiting my news concerning the *date* of the evacuation, I once again found myself in a difficult situation because . . . the evacuation boat was still not ready. It is two months now and the workshops here have still not completed the refit of a 50 h.p. engine. (It appears that this is a fairly common occurrence in these parts:

all the workers in the dockyard are Spanish and they work at a slow pace.)

However, relying on the solemn promise of the engineer, and above all being myself aware that the engine had already been *assembled* and required only a few workshop tests, then to be fitted and tested on the boat itself, I sent a cable to Wysoczanski naming Sunday 5 October for the evacuation. Meanwhile the workshop, in spite of the intervention of the Chief of Staff, whom I kept *au courant* with the date of my departure, did not manage to have the engine working even by the time of the next deadline I gave to Major Wysoczanski, that is, Wednesday 8 October.

Not wanting to postpone the evacuation date yet again, I once more borrowed the *Dogfish*, familiar from my two previous missions. I had tried to avoid this since it is a coastal vessel rather than an ocean-going one and in any case is too small. Luckily the weather in general improved, exceptionally for the time of year, and as a result I was ready to weigh anchor on the morning of 7 October.

2) Composition of the crew, apart from myself, as captain: Siembieda, first mechanic; Filipkowski (for the first time) as second mechanic; and Jensen and Eggum (Norwegians) as deck-hands, the first in addition serving as cook.

I made efforts to take with me the radio-telegraphist, Lt Riedel (a Czech), in case of an accident, or the need to give our position to a ship sent to rendezvous with us, but I was not provided in time with suitable radio equipment for the difficult operating conditions on a small fishing boat.

An important improvement in the present plan was the promise that a British naval trawler would be sent to meet me, and an aircraft to relay my position. Because of this, the whole mission took on the character of a regular operation, in which the prerequisites for success were: my finding the people on the beach; my picking them up at any price, in spite even of adverse conditions which were always a possibility; and finally – something which caused a number of people to have doubts about the feasibility of the operation – to pick up the people *on time* and then *navigate precisely* after leaving the shore immediately after the pick-up, so that the rendezvous could take place. They knew that on the felucca there was no log and the compass was wildly inaccurate, so that the course of the operation was followed by the staff here with a certain interest, giving us an even greater incentive to succeed.

3) On 7 October at 0950 hrs we weighed anchor. The passage through the Straits and almost all the 190-mile journey down

was without incident. The weather was in our favour and at this point I was even expecting that the breakers – that most important factor on which both the timing and the success of the landing depends – would be less, since the swell was relatively small. Only at the end of the trip, after the whole of the second day of the journey out of sight of land, as I approached the shore of French Morocco near Fedhala to make a landfall, a thick fog descended, so I took a course parallel with the shore. (A foretaste of what would have awaited us had we travelled further came during a momentary thinning of the fog, when for a minute we saw huge surf breaking on to rocks at a distance of 2–3 thousand metres.) The fog continued, so that at around 1230 hrs on 8 October – having estimated our position to be in the vicinity of Fedhala (the lighthouse from which I start my usual 'march' along the shoreline to the rocks) – I stopped the engine so as not to 'overrun' the spot. In any case, ten minutes later the fog lifted and we saw Fedhala on course at a distance of 4,000 metres. Since I was too close to the shore, I pushed out to a distance of a few nautical miles to sit out the rest of the day until dusk, hove-to.

4) At 2115 hrs I started up the engine and moved to the pinpoint. The night was bright – a full moon – and visibility, depending upon the direction, was from 6,000 metres towards the moon to 4,000 away from it. At 2315 hrs we were already near the 'rock' and we began to send out the agreed signals. The answer came back after some 15 minutes – 'Everything in order'.

However the surf was unusually unfavourable. It turned out that there was a considerable swell, imperceptible from the open sea and, for the first time since I had started my evacuation missions, the breakers *began almost twice as far from the shore as usual*, at a distance of some 400–500 m. In the light of this I made an attempt to reach the shore in the rubber boat once again from outside the surf, not wanting to risk lying at anchor, given the exceptional size of the swell and, what was worse, the breakers, whose 'manes' represented a considerable danger because of the ease with which they can overturn small boats or break their anchor cables. At 2340 hrs I got into the dinghy, together with Filipkowski. As usual, one line was taken ashore in a coil and the other paid out from the boat. As early as the first minute on the line of the breaking surf, we were both thrown from the rubber boat by waves of huge size and it turned over. This story was repeated several times before we reached the neutral zone between two stretches of breakers (450 and 200 metres). There, however, in spite of strenuous rowing, we made no progress: the weight of the line's slack – in spite of being supported by several containers and a package of inflated life-belts (for the 'passengers') – turned out to be too great. We gave the signal for them to draw us back in. Filipkowski, after this half-hour spent in the water, had a feverish attack, so for the next two attempts I had to take the Norwegian, Eggum, with me in the rubber dinghy. Because of the difficult conditions, I decided to cross the line where the breakers began and anchor inside the surf line in the 'calm' zone. We crossed the critical line safely, in spite of a few dangerous moments, by proceeding in reverse. To reduce the distance to a minimum I dropped anchor for the second time just by the edge of the second line of breakers. After waiting to be sure that the anchor was hold-ing, I entered the water for the second time. We had hardly struck away from the ship's side when the crew began signalling to draw us back again. Owing to the pitching of the boat on the anchor chain, and because of the quite extraordinary difference of level caused by the ocean swell, the boat had struck the bottom once or twice, in spite of the fact that our soundings had shown there to be 4.5 metres' clearance. (The boat's draught was about 1.2 m.) Once again we were compelled to raise the anchor (especially difficult because of the surf) and move out a further 50 metres. Our distance from the shore at that point must have been about 300 m.

After half an hour's rowing – with, of course, inevitable falls from the rubber boat in spite of shouting a warning to each other before each major wave and then lying flat – we reached the shore and drew the boat up on to the beach. Only then did we appreciate how much heat we had lost through a soaking lasting by then a number of hours.

5) On the beach I found 13 Poles, three Belgians and Mr Wysocki, known to me already as the owner of one of the hide-outs. One of the Belgians told me what had happened. The day before my arrival Major Wysoczanski had been sent by the French authorities to Algeria. This was of course in accor-dance with his intentions, but he had wanted to see me before his departure in order to discuss embarkation sites and other details of evacuation from Oran. Wysoczanski, Roehr, Jozefkie-wicz and Komar, released from prison, also left. In addition I was informed that the whole Kasbah Tadla camp had been sent to Algiers some considerable time ago (that is, those who still remained after the last evacuation of 1 September). The Bel-gian, Durieux, known commonly as 'Maurice', was sent by Major Wysoczanski to the embarkation site, to show the others the way and also to receive the mail from me. Luckily, having

anticipated the absence of Major Wysoczanski or his helper, I had ready a letter, or rather a note, with my observations and the latest information about possible landing sites in Algeria. This apart, I handed over all the letters received from Lisbon for Wysoczanski and other addressees in Casablanca.

In addition, because of guarantees given by Mr Wysocki about the trustworthiness of the Belgian Officer, I handed him 100,000 French Francs for Major Wysoczanski.

The whole of the mail was to have reached its intended recipients, according to Durieux, 'the day after tomorrow'. He himself already had a visa and reckoned he would be at Gibraltar, via Lisbon, in two weeks.

Because of the trying cold, I kept the conversation down to the minimum and, having instructed the group how to use the life belts and tied two bags of clothes to the rubber dinghy, I gave the signal for those on the boat to draw in the line. Pushing the dinghy in front of us we moved out to the spot where the ground began to disappear beneath our feet, and then began to swim holding on to the line round the rubber dinghy.

Only then did we realise, as never before in any of the previous four expeditions, how horribly dangerous a strong surf can be. The extreme force of the waves – which on the way *to* the shore had acted to push us – was now opposing the efforts of the three-man crew, as they pulled the 15 of us hanging on the dinghy – a number which hitherto had been feasible. After some 20 minutes we felt that the pulling almost stopped, at precisely the moment when we were at the critical line where the surf broke. Even when the people involved are exceptionally brave, such a situation, when so protracted, can lead to panic. I had reason also to be very worried about the strength of the line, subjected to abnormal stress when the waves broke underneath the dinghy, which shot upwards at the impact of the wave. At last however we crossed the critical line and after another half an hour we reached the boat, where we found that the crew were at the limits of their endurance and had injured their hands.

It was 0300 hrs, $3\frac{1}{2}$ hrs since we had first put the boat into the water and we had brought only one group. During the fourth mission four trips took around $2\frac{1}{2}$ hours.

All those who came out of the water received a tot of rum and two blankets, after which we accommodated them, because they were so few in number, in the fo'c's'le. Our return through the outer line of breakers took place without difficulty. After two hours following the coast, we made a course straight for Cape Spartel, which was also the course for our rendezvous.

7) In the morning most of our passengers were 'as normal', that is, those who were suffering from seasickness felt worse, but morale was high, for the weather too was calm and generally sunny. It was then that I discovered to my astonishment that among the passengers I had *three Spaniards* – a very unpleasant surprise for reasons I detail below.

As I had calculated from a noon sight, I was as far north as Mehedia (Port Lyautey) at a distance of around 22 miles from the shore; in other words, in the area where our meeting was to take place. Indeed, at 1220 hrs an aircraft appeared (a Swordfish, as I later discovered) directly in front of us, flying very low. After the first 'look out, hide yourselves' – since I had encountered French aircraft too in the course of my missions – I ordered the passengers to come on deck and wave their hands to let the pilot know that the landing operations had succeeded, and so that he could send a message to that effect.

In the afternoon fog descended again and it had already begun to seem that the rendezvous with the trawler would not take place. When the fog lifted however, at 1430 hrs, I saw the outline of a ship. After changing course it became evident that it was the trawler, which also immediately picked up speed and moved in our direction. After we had recognised its colours and exchanged signals by means of the Aldis lamp, he came alongside and, without difficulty, since the sea was fairly calm, I transferred my passengers to him. Afterwards he got underway for Gibraltar. According to his calculations I was less than 5 miles off course.

In the end the trawler arrived at Gibraltar at 0330 hrs on 10 October; however the *Dogfish*, to the astonishment of all and sundry, came in exceptionally early, at 1215 that day; but, more important than the time saved, our passengers were spared an uncomfortable night and morning fighting against the usual east wind near Cape Spartel and in the Straits of Gibraltar.

8) Thanks to the presence, during my mission, of my new assistant in Gibraltar, the matter of organising the newcomers' stay, i.e. making lists, kitting them out, making payments on account, etc, does not have to wait for me but swings into operation immediately. Upon my return, as events have shown, I am still involved for a certain time with the maintenance and equipping of the ship since, because of my boat's lying in the [naval] dockyard, I have nowhere to keep stock for her. All these administrative and housekeeping matters now are dealt with quite smoothly, since we are working in tandem; and of course the paymaster now has a precedent, so there is no need to waste time in the tussle over some trivial items, as was

the case at the beginning. In any case, by contrast with the first two groups, this group of Poles is due to leave very shortly, around Wednesday 15 October.

9) Unfortunately, as I had feared from the beginning, bringing the three Spaniards to Gibraltar without the agreement of the British was nothing other than a 'blunder'; the British authorities were shocked since
a) the evacuation operation had been assumed to be for Allies only;
b) the Spanish are not trusted here;
c) the British were afraid that General Franco's people might demand they be handed over, if they heard of their arrival in Gibraltar (a similar case occurred a month ago when a runaway Spaniard attempted to swim across from La Linea but left his clothes on the beach).
I was given to understand quite clearly that such 'mistakes' were not desirable in the future.

I cannot explain why Wysoczanski added not only two Belgians but these Spaniards to the group as well. He should have understood that if we took Czechs or Belgians it was because they are Allies.

I hope, however, that this sorry incident will shortly be cleared up and forgotten, since the head of the Free French mission is due tomorrow, and it seems he is to recruit them to the Foreign Legion. . .

10) I must add in this report of the mission that during the boarding operation one of the containers holding a pistol broke away. Also, at the time the raft with evacuees was crossing the line of breakers, both bundles broke away, despite the fact that they had been secured with rope. This was an event that even perhaps tilted the scale to our advantage, owing to the considerably reduced area on which the waves broke. . .

11) Among those evacuated is – apart from the Polish soldiers without specialist qualifications – Mr Tadeusz Wysocki, born on 26 June 1899 in Dabrów, district of Nowy Sacz, a representative of the Bank of Poland. Although I cannot attempt to assess his professional banking qualifications, he creates a very favourable impression. He is however a special case, as a 42-year-old civilian who has never served in the army.

The decision to evacuate Wysocki should, in my opinion, be beyond discussion; Major Brzozowski agrees with this; Wysocki, as the official owner or subtenant of the hide-out, put himself in considerable danger helping the evacuations and without this safe house it is possible we would not have so many Poles evacuated from Morocco already. . .

(signed) M. Krajewski

On 10 October 1941, Mally wrote to Krajewski forwarding, with his heartiest congratulations, the following commendation bestowed on him by General Sikorski on 13 September:[27]

'On behalf of the Service I commend him for having evacuated from hostile territory in difficult circumstances, without any concern for his personal safety and in spite of two unsuccessful missions, 68 of our soldiers, as well as 3 Czechs and 4 Belgians.'

A covering letter addressed to Mally by General Klimecki, Sikorski's Chief of Staff, asked him for a list of the crew members of the boat, adding that he trusted that the Commander-in-Chief's commendation would not be the last that Major [sic] Kadulski [Krajewski] and the crew of his boat would receive, and that he would again have the opportunity to convey to him messages of similar content or, indeed, other means of bestowing distinctions in respect of Captain [sic] Kadulski and his crew.

By the time these accolades reached Gibraltar, the score of those evacuated by Krajewski had risen by a further 10 Poles, two Belgians and, of course, three controversial Spaniards.

...h maps of two beaches in Algeria
... by Lt. Krajewski in Polish evacuation
...ations during winter 1941-42.

...awn from originals in the Sikorski Institute archives)

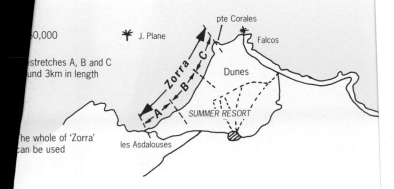

...0,000

...stretches A, B and C
...und 3km in length

✳ J. Plane

pte Corales

Falcos

Dunes

SUMMER RESORT

...he whole of 'Zorra'
...an be used

les Asdalouses

Received on 'Halda' beach
from major Wysoczanski
on 1-9-1941

1:250,000

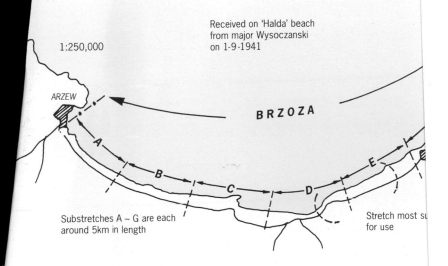

ARZEW

BRZOZA

Substretches A – G are each
around 5km in length

Stretch most su...
for use

Sket
used
oper
(Redr

1:2

Su
ard

CHAPTER XXV

Krajewski's Operations to Western Algeria: October 1941–January 1942

'Not until hair grows on the palms of my hands will the Poles in this camp join the Allies.'[1] This had been the habitual boast of the French camp commandant in Morocco where Krajewski's first Polish evacuees had been interned.

By the time he had completed his five missions to Morocco, Krajewski had begun to make his mark not only at Polish GHQ in London but also at senior levels on the Rock. When HRH the Duke of Gloucester paid a visit, Krajewski was not only invited to a garden party but presented to His Royal Highness by the Admiral. Krajewski elicited a laugh from the Duke with the story of the French camp commandant's boast and with his observation that the Frenchman must now be sporting some unwelcome hair. The fact that he had been singled out for presentation and had amused the royal visitor seemed to help Krajewski quite significantly. People who had previously belittled the importance of things he wanted done and had put difficulties in his way now invited him to their messes; and the dockyard engineer stopped reminding him of his felucca's spoiled engine. At a time when nothing much was happening in the western Mediterranean, his Scarlet Pimpernel role, enhanced by the hush-hush character of the business and the success of his embarkations, caught people's imaginations in the small official community on the Rock. He could not otherwise explain how he came to be awarded a DSO before he had begun his even more successful run of operations to the south of France.

He was first told he had been awarded a DSC. Soon afterwards he was officially notified that the award was a DSO and heard that the King had had to sign the relevant documents twice, probably because the Admiral and the Governor had put up separate, and uncoordinated, recommendations. He clearly thought the whole matter rather a joke, though he did claim credit for having swum ashore in the course of each successful operation in order to gain first-hand knowledge of the conditions and to establish effective liaison on shore in person.

The escapes by foreigners from the Protectorate came to the attention of the German Armistice Commission, which lodged protests both at Vichy and in Morocco.[2] On 18 October Admiral Darlan, Secretary of State for the French navy, called for a report from Admiral d'Harcourt, whose head of Deuxième Bureau replied on 23 October saying that no British fishing vessel had ever been reported off the coast of French Morocco nor did he think that clandestine escapers could have reached Gibraltar in that way.[3] He forwarded a list of 14 known escapes since 1 January 1941, which involved 77 foreign seamen from Danish, Norwegian and Greek ships interned in French Moroccan ports, but all these escapes had been made at night in ships' lifeboats or other small boats from the ships in question or which had been stolen locally. If these people had succeeded in reaching Gibraltar he thought they must have done so in the boats on which they had left, unless they had been picked up by Spanish feluccas, which fished in great numbers off the coast. The list also gave particulars of five further attempted escapes that had failed or been foiled. The 13 members of the crew from the *Oksywia*, who had been under enforced residence at Safi, had left there for Casablanca by bus on 31 August after obtaining the proper authorisation, but they had disappeared in the course of the journey and police enquiries had thus far failed to trace them.

D'Harcourt's staff had made a similar statement direct to Herr Laube, the armistice commission's local representative, giving figures of approximately 50 known escapes since 1 January and 10 since 1 August. He had appeared satisfied with this reply.

The number of escapes had, in fact, been twice as great as d'Harcourt reported. Apart from the 13 missing members of the *Oksywia*'s crew, Krajewski had successfully evacuated 65 other Poles, six Belgians and three Czechs. A French submarine-chaser was temporarily based at Port Lyautey to carry out patrols in an area extending 32 km. offshore, with the object of intercepting and seizing any possible British fishing vessels, but the horse had already bolted: Krajewski's objective was now Oran.

The first two operations to Algeria took place from 23 to 29 October and from 1 to 6 November in such quick succession that Krajewski had time to report to Mally between them only by telegraph. It was not until 8 and 9 November that his full accounts were completed and dispatched.

REPORT OF THE SIXTH EVACUATION MISSION
(follows my cables of 23 and 31 October)[4]

1) After the last evacuations from Morocco (my report of 13 October), I was waiting for the first signal from Major Wysoczanski following his transfer to Algeria, so that I could set out to pick up people from this – for me – new evacuation region.

The first word I received was Major Wysoczanski's cable of 10 October, sent on by letter. . . which I did not receive until 17 October. Major Wysoczanski's wire required me to arrive as early as 19 October, but since the message was conveyed to me by letter rather than by telegraph, clearly I was not informed in time to make the necessary preparations, which I could only do once I had definite knowledge of the *date* of evacuation. Indeed, the journey itself to the agreed spot (280 nautical miles to the Bay of Mostaganem) would take three days, given the speed of which the felucca is capable.

2) Faced with this situation, I sent you cable no. 1840/17/10 in which I drew attention to two possible evacuation sites: DOR-ULA and BRZOZA; also I requested that the necessary cable be sent 'en clair' to Oran. Not having received a reply before my departure, I sent cable no. 1620/23/10 on the day we weighed anchor, repeating the mission plan (place of embarkation).

3) We weighed anchor on 23 October at 0930 hrs. Once again, my own evacuation felucca had still not been finished by the workshops and once again I had to set out in the 'borrowed' DOGFISH, a small ship, not constructed for use on the open sea, but in fact perfectly suitable for our purposes. The crew was made up, apart from myself, of Siembieda and Filipkowski as mechanics, and Eggum (Norwegian) as a deck-hand and cook in place of Jensen (Norwegian) who had been dismissed for drunkenness. In addition, in the light of experience – 'just in case' – I took along Second Lt Lisek as a possible messenger who might be able to establish contact in the event of a 'jam', etc.

4) Our course led past the Tres-Forcas (Melilla) peninsula in order to fix our position and then from the Habibas Islands (about 25 nautical miles west of Oran) along the Algerian coast to the Bay of Mostaganem. The journey was very arduous, both because of the weather, which turned bad on the second day, and the fact that we were towing a sailing boat, which I was taking along for the first time in order to save people being drenched in sea-water, which by now was quite cold. It reached the stage that every few hours we had to let a sailor down into the small boat with a scoop to bail out the water. Worse was the fact that the extreme tension that built up in the tow-line tore away, one after the other, the cleats around which the line was fastened. Eventually, when the weather deteriorated even further, we were forced to attempt to haul the boat on to the felucca. This proved almost impossible, since we had to stop the engine and the boat itself was already full of water, but we succeeded, thanks to the efforts of the whole crew. This, I should underline, was one of many characteristic incidents that illustrated the exemplary attitude of the present crew.

5) On 25 October the stormy weather still continued, while the strong wind had turned about through 180° – a characteristic

occurrence for these regions – and taken the worst possible direction for us: from dead ahead. Under these conditions it took me six hours to travel 16 miles from the Habibas Islands to the Cap-Falcon lighthouse, while tons of water poured down on to the deck. My calculations showed that, travelling at such 'terrific' speed (around 3 knots), I would not reach the rendez-vous point on time, nor, more important, would we be in a position to carry out embarkation in a bay open to a wind from the north-east. I therefore decided on a complete change of plan. I changed to a diametrically opposite course, towards the embarkation point code-named DORULA, some 50 km. to the west of Oran. After turning about, we made a speed of 10 knots. Since the pilot-book warns that this bay 'is suitable only for small ships with knowledge of local conditions' and since our chart was too small-scale to show details of such a small bay – it did not give a precise idea of the location of the submerged rocks at the entrance – I ordered the crew to put on their life-jackets and gave instructions 'in case we founder'. The entry, though, passed off successfully. The little bay gave ideal shelter against storms from almost any direction, and it was situated in an almost unpopulated region, if you do not count Arabs tending their cattle, or one family group living in widely dis-persed huts.

6) After sunset I put into action the second stage of the plan – sending a messenger to Oran with the information that I was at another point and giving directions for reaching it. Second Lt Lisek was put ashore in the rubber dinghy, reckoning that he would be in Oran by the second day. All the following day I waited in the little bay, the one drawback of which was that it was visible from the high Habibas Islands, on which there is a lighthouse (distance about 10,000 metres). We waited through the whole of the next night for the agreed signal, enduring unusually cold temperatures.

On the morning of 27 October, when I had already started to fear that some accident had occurred, an individual appeared on the shore undressed and swam across to our boat, causing a near sensation among the Arabs. It turned out to be Second Lt Polanski, liaison officer to the division in Oran, who, having been shown the way by Second Lt Lisek, had at the last moment gone on ahead, fearing that we would weigh anchor and move off. A moment later Lisek also appeared and we fetched him in the rubber dinghy. After a few words of explanation, we weighed anchor and left the bay, just in time to make out a French patrol boat emerging from behind the headland and travelling slowly at a distance of some 4,000 metres from the shore. In order not to arouse suspicion, I continued on the same course, in other words towards him, and only at a distance of 2,000 metres did I change course towards Oran, which in the circumstances must have seemed normal behaviour. Fortunately it passed off without any questioning . . .

7) *A NEW SITUATION*. When sending Second Lt Lisek ashore I had asked him to recommend those in charge to organise a mass evacuation, that is, in groups of more than 25 people, like the one that Wysoczanski had arranged for me in Morocco. I even said that I was prepared to supply tinned food and fresh water to help keep people alive in empty desert regions. If we carried out the evacuation in small groups, we might alert the French authorities, who would probably step up their level of vigilance. Indeed, it emerged from Second Lt Lisek's account that, since their telegram to Lisbon on 10 October, the leaders of the Oran group were thinking along the same lines and had worked out a plan for total evacuation. As a result, on the night in question there were not 25 people at the embarkation point but only Major Wysoczanski and Capt Roehr. I was to take these two off because the French authorities in Algeria had issued an order for their arrest on the charge of arranging evacuations from Morocco. They had received prior warning in confidence and gone into hiding.

The DORULA site, the little bay in which I had sheltered for a day and a half, was unfortunately ruled out because of its distance from Oran (50 km.), as well as the necessity of travelling through desert regions and small settlements where the sight of any strange and white face immediately drew attention. The only possibility, they thought, was *Brzoza*; it was easy to reach (road and railway passed a few hundred metres away) without having to travel through Oran, and there was a hinterland covered in brush and bushes in which people could conceal themselves while awaiting the felucca.

On the way there I familiarised Second Lt Polanski with our sailing problems and at the same time I familiarised myself with the peculiarities of the new embarkation site and the plan for total evacuation.

8) *TOTAL EVACUATION FROM THE ORAN REGION*. The plan was based on the premise that for the two days of the forthcoming holiday – All Saints and Sunday – there would be no attempt to carry out a roll-call in the camps. So, starting on Friday evening, small groups of our people were to make their way in a trickle by bus, train and even by car (arrangements were being made) to the agreed spot, led by those who had been let into the secret – basically only a handful of officers. It was a

great risk but had considerable chance of success, and its success would have dramatically resolved the question of evacuation from all Africa.

My main difficulty was that I had very little time for technical preparations, because of the very large number of people involved. However, because of the high stakes I could not hesitate with my reply.

9) That evening (27 October), after passing the well-known Mers el-Kebir [naval base] at a distance of about 8 miles, we entered Mostaganem Bay. I was struck at first – and this was confirmed by my later observations as well as by those of others – by the lack of shipping movement of any kind, even of fishing boats, which are normally a very common sight on the coast of Morocco.

At 2140 hrs we altered course to travel parallel with the coast at a distance of 250 metres, in order to reconnoitre the shoreline. Second Lt Polanski helped me with my reconnaissance of the shore, he having been one of the first to check out this site. At 2200 hrs we received the agreed signal, which was followed by the usual preparations and the lowering of the raft. One fundamental difference struck me about this new location: the complete absence of breakers. Here it was connected with the fine weather and the direction of the wind (off shore). But on the Moroccan coast there are breakers *even in the finest weather.*

Major Wysoczanski, Capt Roehr, Lt Wyganowski and Lt Jozefkiewicz were already waiting on the beach and Polanski came ashore with me. While we were discussing the plan, it emerged that, after Polanski's departure, still further disturbing changes had taken place: an order was being prepared for the arrest of Polanski and Capt Szewalski, who played important roles in the local cell. Contacts had informed them of this confidentially. My proposal to off-load supplies was willingly accepted, as it would ease the logistical demands of maintaining a large group of people, for whom there was no question of purchasing food during the waiting period. In total I unloaded two boxes of biscuits, four boxes of tinned meat, 130 litres of fresh water and 400 litres of petrol for vehicles.

Those present accepted the plan for total evacuation and I promised to turn up at all costs on the night of Sunday/Monday 2/3 November. I warned that, in the event of an accident, very bad weather or other unexpected obstacles, I might turn up late – but *I would be coming.*

10) At 0145 hrs on 28 October we finished unloading the supplies and took on board Major Wysoczanski and Capt Roehr, after which we weighed anchor. The journey from

Oran to Gibraltar took place in excellent weather (an exception for these missions of ours . . .) and in phenomenal visibility: one could see the coastlines of Spain and of Spanish Morocco simultaneously from a distance of 50 nautical miles. This time I set a course to the small island of Alboran – the shortest route – so as to get used to the currents on this route (during the evacuations from Morocco, experience gained on frequent journeys allowed me to make use of currents, an important factor considering my speed of 6 knots).

That day at 2005 hrs we had a breakdown of the circulation pump (a pin had broken away), which happily the duty mechanic, Filipkowski, detected by ear immediately. He thus saved the engine: if it had continued working for a few minutes without being cooled, it would have been irreparably damaged and the return to Gibraltar would have had to be carried out under sail.

On 29 October at 2115 hrs I moored in Gibraltar, not without emotion, having been shot at by the trawler on guard off the port. The staff officer had not issued a warning in time and the trawler, seeing a 'mysterious' fishing boat approaching the entrance, fired a warning shot across our bow (as happened last with the Chief of Staff's launch).

11) During this trip Second Lt Lisek and the motor mechanic, Filipkowski, distinguished themselves.

Second Lt Lisek not only volunteered unhesitatingly for the dangerous mission of messenger but showed great strength of character and physical endurance. He travelled 50 km., partly at night, through hilly (400 m. above sea-level) terrain, the first section of it trackless. After only a few hours' rest, and having accomplished his mission entirely, he set out again on the return journey. In total he covered 100 km. and was on the move for 38 hrs with only a few hours' break. (How much more commendably this *one-armed* officer performed than the Czech Staggart during the third evacuation mission.)

Also deserving of commendation is Second Lt Polanski, for his brave and decisive action, demanding great physical effort, in informing the evacuation vessel of the change in situation, despite the fact that in doing so he jeopardised his very good official relations with the French authorities in Oran.

*   *   *

From: Marian KRAJEWSKI, Gibraltar, 9 November 1941.
To: Colonel Frederyk MALLY (Lisbon)

REPORT OF THE SEVENTH EVACUATION MISSION
(follows my cables of 31.x and 7.xi)[5]

1) After returning from the 6th evacuation mission, I had a little less than three days to prepare for the next mission. In the prevailing conditions, of which I will say more below, this was so little time that it was reminiscent, in the feverishness of the preparations and frequent disappointments, of the worst days of July, before the first expedition.

My plan was to use, for the first time, our own evacuation felucca; workshop tests were complete on the engine and it had only to be installed. The felucca could hold, not officially, but squeezed in together, 60 people, at a pinch. If it were merely to ferry them to another, larger ship, I estimated that I could take as many as 120 people – equivalent to the maximum the leaders of the local evacuation expected on the night of 2/3 November. On Monday 3 November a second group of some 30 people were to filter in, whom I planned to collect in a repeat performance on that night. A trawler-like vessel of around 70 tons, familiar to us from the second mission, would be standing by to take off any excess passengers. Using her presented a complication since in the first instance there was no engineer officer, no cook and no stoker. I made up the numbers from the crew of the *Oksywia*, not without trouble from one particular mechanic who at first allowed his anxiety not to miss the convoy to England to overshadow his patriotism. *Seawolf*, the evacuation felucca, might also have been ready, since the workshop had anticipated completing the job two days after our departure: following the intervention of the Chief of Staff at the base, they worked day and night, and it looked at long last as though she would be used for the first time.

2) On the day of our departure, Saturday, 1 November, we fitted the engine, which had supposedly been overhauled in the workshop, but it turned out that this was not the case and that once again the 'specialists' could not deliver the goods. I was forced to change the whole plan at the last moment and turn to a motor boat, the *Seagull*, of around 50 tons, which I had used in July. Luckily, thanks to the Chief of Staff, I was able to take charge of it immediately, although the owner (Customs and Excise) warned comfortingly that, ever since it had returned from the workshop, the engine was so undependable that they would be afraid to travel 20 miles with it. The mechanic and I looked over the engine and decided to take the motor boat and

demonstrate that it was not the engine but Spanish mechanics who are undependable.

It was characteristic of that morning that, almost simultaneously with the *Seawolf* fiasco, I was told that the *Quarto*, the civilian trawler that was to travel with me to carry back evacuees, had while raising steam burst some pipes in the boiler; as it turned out these pipes had corroded through repeated use of salt-water in the boiler. Happily the *Seagull* had enough room on board for all the people who might turn up.

Our departure was delayed, however, owing to various small difficulties such as requisitioning the motor boat, loading her up with an ample supply of stores (170 blankets, tinned food, biscuits and fresh water – enough for 150 people for four days). Thus we lost the extra reserve of time we had allowed in case of bad weather and unforeseen occurrences.

3) I cast off at 1525 hrs on 1 November. The crew was composed of: Siembieda and Filipkowski (mechanics), Eggum (deck-hand), and Skulimowski (cook and deck-hand taken on in place of Jensen . . .). In addition Capt Roehr, who knew local conditions, went with us, in order to contact the people on shore should any complications arise during the operation.

The outward passage took place without any incident worth mentioning, though a temporary breakdown of the engine occurred nine hours after our departure. It turned out that the cause was a blocked oil filter, which the Spanish mechanic had failed to clean. Once again our motor mechanic, Filipkowski, distinguished himself: he at once discovered the fault and sorted it out in 45 minutes. By Monday night (3/4 November) I had reached the latitude of Oran. Although the currents had been favourable to me on the first part of the journey, I had calculated that I would reach the agreed spot at 0400 hrs, the last possible moment to begin embarkation. However, at the last moment the weather and opposing currents dashed my hopes, so that it was not until 0300 hrs (after detour to avoid the Mers el-Kebir naval base that I reached the vicinity of Cap-Aiguille, in other words scarcely beyond Oran. I would not therefore arrive at the pinpoint until 0600 hrs. Accordingly, I had to make use of the remaining hours of darkness (very relative, as the night was bright and the moon full) to move away out of sight of the high shoreline (600 m.).

We spent the whole of the next day – in stormy weather particularly unsuitable for this motor boat, which was built for use in sheltered waters and was not sufficiently stable – riding out the storm some 35 miles north-east of Oran. In spite of our unfortunate outline and colours (typical of a motor torpedo boat), no-one paid any attention to us, as there was almost no traffic to speak of and all we saw was something like a trawler passing at a distance of around 10,000 m. Immediately the sun went down, I started the approach to Mostaganem Bay, in which I found the agreed embarkation point, familiar from the previous successful operation when we took aboard Major Wysoczanski and Capt Roehr.

4) The night fortunately was not as light as the previous one, since the full moon was obscured for most of the time by a layer of cloud. At 0015 hrs on 4 November we were already near Brzoza, or rather the stretch of shore where this pinpoint is situated, and we started on a course parallel to the shore. However, in spite of giving the agreed signals that had been used successfully several times before, no reply came back. After about half an hour of travelling along the coast, which at this point was a steep rock wall about 10 m. high, with a few small beaches below it (like BRZOZA), we noticed, to our amazement, several figures moving stealthily along the shoreline, trying with some difficulty to keep up with the boat, forcing their way through the bushes and the rocky terrain. We were able to see them because of our proximity to the shore (some 250 m.) and also because their silhouettes stood out against the background of the lighter sky. A few of them moved so incautiously that they were even more clearly discernible.

All of this was incomprehensible to us, so, in order to make absolutely sure that they were our people, . . . I changed course 180 degrees and gave out the agreed signals with a signalling lamp, although I knew that, if they were Frenchmen, our signals would be compromised. Figures on the shore began to run back in the other direction. These were certainly the same figures, since towards the end of the second tour a signal was given from the shore – an answer to my blue flashes – with a *white* light. The correct answer should have been a *blue* light, moreover not one flash but a series of short flashes. Whoever was faking the signals was confused by the fact that my signals were long, as had been agreed. Equally, it was obvious that they were not using an electric lamp but some improvised light. (The man in charge of the interception group, for such I took them to be, was caught by surprise by the blue lamp and improvised an answer – but it is not easy to improvise a blue lamp.)

Capt Roehr, who was on board with us, confirmed that our people invariably have a blue lamp at their disposal, since they carry several. I therefore set course for the open sea. Visibility was so good that we could see both sides of the bay and, if the trap had been better organised and they had called in the navy to cooperate, it would have been comparatively easy to have caught us. When the sun rose we could still see the shore.

5) On 4 November I set a course not directly to Gibraltar, but to the Spanish cape Cabo del Gata, so as to avoid any possible pursuit. In order to fix my position between the lighthouse and Mesa de Roldan, I took a course to the Isle of Alboran, which, because of a continuing heavy swell coming then from the east, slowed our progress tiresomely. The waves were at times dangerous for our shallow-draught motor boat, with no keel or ballast. We reached the level of Alboran at 1035 hrs on 5 November. On the same day at 1800 hrs a British Fulmar flew over and, as agreed before my departure, signalled in Morse, 'Please indicate number of passengers'. On this occasion I had to answer, 'No passengers'. On the next morning at 0800 hrs we were already moored at Gibraltar, where news of the trap set for us aroused a great deal of understandable interest and the comment, 'You were lucky' . . .

Krajewski went on to set out at some length the possible reasons for this failure. Perhaps when the first checks had been carried out in the camps at 10 a.m. on 3 November and most of the internees found to have disappeared (only 50 had not been included in the plan), the French authorities had immediately sounded the alarm and begun searching the coast, specifically, by deduction, the stretch of coast where the Brzoza pinpoint lay. Deploying an extended line of soldiers or police would have enabled them to capture, as in Morocco, if not all at least most of the escapers. The weak point in this hypothesis was that it assumed a very un-French organisational efficiency, since no more than 14 hours could have elapsed from the alarm to the time the vessel appeared off the coast.

A further possibility was that the escape had been accidentally discovered, perhaps though some indiscretion on the part of their people, a chance meeting with strangers in the forest or perhaps an encounter with some suspicious policeman who wanted to check their papers. But the most likely explanation, in his opinion, was that the plan had been given away by informers among the internees, whose existence had been suspected by their leaders in the camps for some time. It was too soon to lay the blame at anyone's door: they had known from the outset that any mass evacuation would be a risky venture. Still, if they had attempted to bring people out in small groups, the disappearance of the first 25 or so would have led to the present state of alert. The French authorities were undoubtedly very vexed by the successful 100 per cent evacuation from Morocco, as had been evident from their orders to arrest Wysoczanski, Roehr, Polanski and Szewalski, and were determined to apply preventive measures in Algeria. News from Algeria would soon show the real reason for the fiasco. Krajewski asked Mally to make sure that he was cabled any information arriving either from there or from Morocco, since it was quite possible that a certain number of the escapers might still be hiding near the coast or that the French might, even now, be unable to prevent the escape of smaller groups.

Krajewski then turned his attention to sea evacuation from France, which remained his main objective, since the number of Polish troops immobilised there was far larger than in Algeria.

Mally had written on 18 October instructing him to consult the British naval authorities about the possibility of carrying out two different types of evacuation operations from France and to report whether he would be able to put them into effect.[6]

The first of these plans, both of which emanated from General Kleeberg in France, would involve sending 100 evacuees to sea from Marseilles in a ship which would follow a predetermined course for a distance of 140 nautical miles from the French coast. There the ship would be met and her passengers taken off, and she would be given a return cargo of 10 tons of SOE stores.

To Mally the plan seemed wholly impracticable, though Klee-berg had had the benefit of naval advice in working it out. Sailors with whom Mally was in touch maintained that such transfers at sea would be impossible in the prevailing stormy season, but that they might be carried out later in the winter when seas would be calmer.

In Kleeberg's second plan, a British warship would take delivery at sea of groups of 50 evacuees travelling on foreign ships to Oran, Algiers or Tunis. He wanted to know if this would be possible, provided the Admiralty were informed a week before a ship's departure of her name and anticipated course.

Krajewski thought both proposals naive and said so in a letter to Mally.[7] He put forward his own ideas on tackling the problem in a paper for Mally, copies of which he sent to General Sikorski's Chief of Staff and to the Polish Naval Attaché in London.

He proposed that internees should be picked up from the coast of metropolitan France at night, using a small fishing vessel, which could transport them directly to Gibraltar. The distance from the Rock to Marseilles was 700 nautical miles – a passage of five days at 6 knots and a round trip of 12 days, allowing 48 hours for contingencies. At 10 knots, the round trip would take 8 days, with the same spare time in hand. At 12 knots, only 2½ days would be needed on passage to and from the pick-up area. From the technical and security points of view, groups of 50–100 could be managed. Operations would be easier than in North Africa, but a larger vessel would be needed. A minimum speed of 10–12 knots was desirable and the vessel's range must be sufficient for the double voyage of 700 miles, plus two additional days' steaming. The engine must be economical in its fuel consumption, simple to service and reliable: a diesel would probably best match these requirements.

The vessel should be able to carry 100, apart from the crew. She must be seaworthy and look like a fishing boat. She should not be too large – 70 gross registered tons would probably be about right. There should be no need to build a vessel for the job, since boats of that size were common on the coasts of Spain and Portugal. The British were looking for something similar.

Krajewski envisaged packing the evacuees into every corner of the ship, even if they had to sleep on deck. In wartime such conditions were acceptable.

He had views, too, about what would be needed at the Marseilles end. The English Hospital could accommodate only about 40 and there was the perennial problem of chatter in bars; he proposed to send Roehr to take charge.

Four days later, Krajewski wrote to Mally again.[8] He described their current communications problems, including the radio link they were trying to establish, and went on to say a new 50 h.p. engine was needed for the felucca (*Seawolf*) under repair. Four months had been wasted, during which he had had to struggle with various '*Dogfish*'es. A new engine was indispensable: a Kelvin A4 from Bergius of Glasgow could be made available in four weeks if the Admiralty backed the order and the factory were told.

In this winter period it was impossible to think of carrying out operations in the smaller vessel. The problem of a new engine was quite separate from his recommendation that a larger vessel be obtained for evacuations from France, advice based on six months' experience and a year's observation. Although his hitherto unavowed ambition had been to return to the fleet, he was putting forward this proposal because he saw the need to help their colleagues in France. Without capable and skilled assistance from outside, they were forced to take desperate steps, such as attempting to escape on yachts powered with car engines or, more frequently, to make their way over the 'green frontier', across the whole breadth of Spain and then over the Portuguese border. Unfortunately, most ended up in Miranda camp, from which there was no release until the end of the war. At the time of writing, there were 400 people in that notorious detention centre, compared with only 160 as recently as 26 June.

His plan was a counter to the proposals of Kleeberg, who lacked the necessary technical expertise. The serious drawbacks in Kleeberg's plan had become very evident when he had in vain asked the Admiralty to send a ship to intercept a French ship on which evacuees had been sent out. He knew that several dozen Poles were currently trying to escape from Sète on a motor fishing vessel.

The projected cooperation with the Belgians was not necessary. Objections to the smallness of the ship were ridiculous: small was best. They would manage without the Belgian ship and security and organisation would be better without their help.

As regards communications with Marseilles, Krajewski also found London HQ's objections to a direct link ridiculous.

Krajewski put to sea again on 18 November, still with no news of what had happened in the Orannais. His report to Mally on this mission was as follows:

From: Marian KRAJEWSKI, Gibraltar, 4 January 1942[9]
To: Col Fryderyk MALLY (Lisbon)

REPORT OF THE EIGHTH EVACUATION MISSION
(follows my wire of 27.xi.41)

1) The aim of the mission was chiefly to re-establish communications after the unsuccessful 7th mission. Major Wysoczanski had forecast that, even if the mission had failed through betrayal, communication would still be possible through certain intermediaries; in spite of this, we did not receive a single telegram, nor any other form of news. We considered beforehand that some of the officers and soldiers might possibly still be in hiding and that we would be able to direct them to the boarding-point.

This time we chose a different embarkation place, not BRZOZA, which had been revealed to the Vichy authorities after the previous mission, but Zorra to the west of Oran, near the Falcon lighthouse. Our felucca was the *Dogfish* (*circa* 10 tons) – the veteran of our missions.

2) Our departure from Gibraltar took place at 1100 hrs on 18 November. The first day of the voyage and almost the whole of the second passed in very difficult weather conditions; there was a strong wind (Force 4) and a heavy swell, and, to make things worse, the wind was from the east, which meant that in our small felucca we were continually taking water on deck, and everything became wet through, both on the deck and unfortunately in the living quarters. This gave us a foretaste of what to expect during the winter period, when even the local fishermen do not generally venture out to fish. Luckily, by the evening of the second day, the sea became almost completely calm, which gave us some hope that conditions would permit putting a runner ashore.

3) At 2110 hrs on 19 November we could already make out the lighthouse on the Habibas Islands; this came as a surprise since we had skirted Alboran Island (half-way to Oran) at such a

distance that it had been out of sight; I had estimated that we would have lost far more time as a result of the earlier bad weather. At 0230 hrs I passed around Plane Island, which is at the entrance to the bay – our destination. From this island we set a course to the landing point, which was a new one, but of which we would gain experience during this operation (from the land side it was to be reconnoitred by Capt Roehr).

At 0330 hrs I dropped anchor opposite a small beach; I was some 250 metres from it in water about 3–4 m. deep. Midshipman Buslowicz (the messenger) and Skulimowski (to help with the rowing) were put into the rubber dinghy and then we began the usual procedure of letting out the line to which the dinghy was attached, as those in it rowed their way towards the shore. Midshipman Buslowicz's effects were wrapped up in waterproof clothing, in case they fell into the water. The conditions here, by comparison with the Atlantic coast, were more favourable also in that the rowers got their legs wet to knee height only (and it was quite cold). At 0400 hours we weighed anchor, having of course pulled in Skulimowski once he had given the signal with his torch. Next, we set a course to the north, with the aim of distancing ourselves from the coast. At 1000 hrs we were hove-to some 25 miles from the coast, which was nevertheless still visible because of some high mountains.

We used this period of waiting until the evening to carry out some minor repairs such as changing the gaskets, changing the oil in the crank-case and trying out the sea anchor, which had been given us only recently. We also sighted an aircraft in the direction of the land, but it did not spot us. At 1700 hrs we set course again for the landing point.

4) The plan in putting the messenger ashore was as follows: the messenger had received from Major Wysoczanski a few addresses of people working with us; in the first place that of a Mr E., a Spaniard. He in turn was to find out what had happened to the Polish soldiers after the failed mission to La Macta; where and how they were being held; if they had freedom of movement, were able to communicate with us – and most important of all, he had to establish contact with Capt Szewalski and Lt Polanski (local leaders of the evacuation) if indeed they had not been arrested.

The messenger had received instructions to return in *24 hours*; if he did not appear, I was to return for him in 48 hours. However, if that too produced no answer to our signals as we moved along the coast, I would assume that the first had been arrested and would put a second messenger ashore. Since it was difficult to obtain an electric torch in Oran, I gave him a

ship's flashlight so as to ensure that he had something with
which to signal.

5) On reaching the narrow entrance to the bay, with Plane
Island in the centre and both shorelines plainly visible, we
slipped in successfully, at the last moment going 'at full speed'
(as fast as $7\frac{1}{2}$ knots) and moving out of the path of a patrol boat,
which was slowly following a course to the west, a mile from the
shore. In the bay we were comparatively safe. At 0015 hrs we
were level with the point on the shore where, proceeding slowly,
we sent out the agreed signal. There was, however, no answer. I
therefore withdrew further out into the middle of the bay, and,
after an hour had passed, I repeated the operation, again
without success. It seemed to us at one stage that we saw a
light but there was no answer to our repeated signalling. When,
after a further two hours (at 0200 hrs) we had had no further
success and the most probable period for our messenger to
arrive was drawing to a close, I set a course that would take
us out of the bay.

6) Meanwhile, out at sea, there was an unusual amount of
traffic for the time of year. The patrol boat that we had avoided
with difficulty three hours earlier was now returning from the
Habibas Islands. In addition, not very far from us, a small ship
with bright lights was moving from Oran to Plane Island, and,
having quite obviously noticed us (without lights), changed
course 90° and began to travel along with us. After a time he
did turn off his lights completely but at the same time he ceased
to tread on our heels. I took a course to the west in order to
shelter in Mersa Ben Nuar Bay, since the sea was becoming
heavier, and waiting all day in a small felucca in the open sea is
not one of life's more pleasurable experiences.

   This course however lay between a large ship, which, as we
guessed from the navigation lights, lay hove-to, but with its
engine still turning over (another unusual phenomenon in this
spot and at this hour) and the patrol boat mentioned earlier.
The patrol boat in the end passed us quite close by without
seeing us, perhaps because of our lowish profile.

7) At 0600 hrs, after passing the Habibas Islands, we
approached the shore with the intention of locating the small
bay of Mersa Ali, familiar to us from previous missions, and, of
putting Lt Lisek and Lt Polanski ashore there in broad daylight,
in spite of the presence of the Arabs. Even at a distance of 2,000
m. it was difficult to recognize the entrance to this crack in the
steep, high, rocky shoreline, since the night seemed somehow to
have become even darker. Eventually we managed to slip in past

the underwater rock at the entrance and at 0630 hrs we were already anchored and preparing to hang out the fishing nets in order to give ourselves an innocent look. The whole day passed quietly, except that we watched an Arab family group on the shore with some suspicion, worried that they might despatch a messenger to the nearest guard-post with the information that the people 'who once took on board a group of people on a raft' had come back. One Arab did pay us a visit, but he only asked about the fishing, to which we answered that the catch was poor.

This period of waiting was very much to our advantage, since we had been frozen and wet through during the night because of the swell and the cold. In addition, the crew had not had much sleep because of our night-time manoeuvres along the coast.

8) At 2130 hrs we weighed anchor. The weather had improved a great deal. At 0130 hrs we were again close to the shoreline, and we recognised the spot where the first messenger had been put ashore; it turned out too that the spot was at the edge of a village (Les Andalouses) of which we had not known beforehand (the stretch on which the landing had to be made was relatively short, only a few kilometres long, and was bounded at one end by underwater rocks and at the other by this village).

However on this occasion, too, there was no answer to our signals. So I at once withdrew from the vicinity and anchored, using two anchors (one anchor further from the shore, in order that we could haul ourselves off from the shallows if we touched bottom while our stern was close to the minimum depth; the position achieved by this method is parallel to the line of the coast and it permits lying closer to the shore, because the anchor further out provides added security).

According to the agreed plan, I put a second messenger ashore (Skulimowski), who had already spent some time in this area, so that at 0320 hrs we were able to weigh anchor. At 0430 hrs we had a breakdown of the cooling-pump, which was potentially very unpleasant, since we might have to remain after sunrise at a distance of less than 5,000 m. from the shore. Luckily at 0700 hrs we managed to repair the breakdown and precisely at that moment the familiar lights of the approaching patrol boat from the previous night appeared shining on the horizon.

9) At 1100 hrs we were waiting hove-to in the open sea in fine weather. The mechanics used this wait to improve the working of the pump, in which they displayed some ingenuity: they cut off two large brass pins and drilled holes and threaded them, then used them to bring together the broken bolts of the pump.

This incident boosted the morale of the crew, who were also cheered by the appearance of a shark right alongside the ship, together with the pilot fish, although we tried in vain to catch the shark to turn it into fishmeat.

10) At 2045 hrs on 23 November we started up the engine in order to move along the shore for the third time, now perhaps just a little concerned about the fate of the colleagues we had put ashore. At 0200 hrs, having approached the shore and given our 'call signal' for the first time, WE RECEIVED A REPLY. After anchoring at the nearest point we could (depth 2½ m.), we sent the raft to the shore. By 0245 hrs we had on board both messengers (Midshipman Buslowicz, Skulimowski), Second Lt Gromnicki and Branco Nekic (officer of the Yugoslav merchant navy). We had hardly made away from the beach, however, and were merely 1,000 metres from the shore when our engine broke down again. This time our situation was even more critical, since the spot was only a few kilometres distant from the Cap-Falcon lighthouse, which we knew to be also a look-out point. This time the problem was only damp in the magneto and at 0430 hrs the engine was working again.

11) Now everything seemed to turn against us as we were hurrying to return to base. The weather became stormy and, just when we could have done with an easterly wind such as there had been for several days, the storm came from the WEST. At 0830 hrs, when we were still at the latitude of the Habibas Islands and the wind had grown to Force 4–5, we began to worry about the stability of this shallow-draught boat during a journey of at least a day, and that against both waves and wind; so I decided to seek shelter, albeit perhaps not complete, in the Ali Bay again.

At 0930 hrs we entered the bay only to discover that it did not give real shelter and that the waves, because of the shallow depth, were transformed into SURF – the most dangerous kind of wave. We tried to shelter in one of the corners of the bay, behind a ridge, but the anchor we dropped would not hold and the felucca started to drag to the beach some 100 m. away. In these critical conditions I decided to seek alternative shelter where normally I would never have gone: the Habibas Islands, with their lighthouse-keeper's accommodation and – most probably – a telephone.

12) An hour later we entered the tiny bay of the main island of Habibas, where however, to our astonishment, we found a whole armada of our 'fellow fishermen' beckoning to us with friendly gestures to approach as near to them as possible, where

it was best to shelter from the wind. We did not of course show any enthusiasm for this idea, fearing their professional eye. Eventually I dropped anchor at the entrance to the bay, at a discreet distance from our 'colleagues', but not without great difficulty since the anchor – dropped several times – dragged along the rocky bottom.

The local fishermen looked on curiously and again, for a time, tried to encourage us to change our position; the lighthouse-keeper too came down from his lighthouse high aloft to satisfy his curiosity. Next, two fishermen made their way out in a small boat to meet us and they too encouraged us to move. Although they were very friendly, their conversation was sprinkled with intriguing remarks such as, 'We are all only fishermen' . . . 'There was once a ship of Spanish smugglers here' . . . 'There are no soldiers here, nor any navy; there is no telephone either'. It all pointed to the conclusion that they had recognised something unusual about the newcomers and this was confirmed when one of them said, 'We here read the newspapers from both sides' . . . I was not sure how far these two fishermen had gone in their speculation. They made good-natured but pointed complaints about the lack of food and lack of petrol for their engines (5 litres a month, which is nothing for a fisherman, enough for only half an hour under power . . .).

Eventually I established more intimate contact with them while we waited until the next morning. They were Algerians of Spanish origin, and did not harbour any particularly friendly sentiments towards the current French regime. A few litres of fuel, tinned meat or biscuits did a lot, of course, to loosen up our conversations. They answered in kind by supplying us with fresh bread. I gained a great deal of valuable information from them about the appearance of the motor patrol boat and the location of look-out posts, and was much reassured by their offers to 'help with anything at all'. After this I took their addresses, in case we needed to organise additional safe houses (I checked these addresses to confirm that the men were trustworthy, and that this was not merely a ploy, or a double-cross).

13) On 24 November I weighed anchor, since the weather had improved, and arrived at Gibraltar without further incident during the night of 25 November. The epilogue to this journey took place the following day when I moved the *Dogfish* to another mooring-place: the clutch broke. If this had happened at sea a day earlier, it would certainly have meant a return journey . . . under sail. This breakdown was of course a warning that the 30-year-old engine was already 'tired' and not completely reliable.

14) The following is a summary of the news brought by Lt Gromnicki from Algeria:

In the course of a few days, from Friday 30 October to Sunday 2 November, very nearly 200 people gathered on the coast at the secret concentration point called BRZOZA, near La Macta. This was possible mainly because of forged passes, breaking the number up into small groups and favourable conditions over the holiday period. This luck turned out to be only partial since, by real misfortune, the Prefect of Oran arranged a charity hunt (and, as though Fate intended to make fun of us, the proceeds were intended for the benefit of French POWs in German captivity) in exactly the same area of La Macta on Sunday 2 November. The result, completely unforeseen by the organisers of the escape, was that, during the hunt (with dogs) the hunting guests found under almost every bush of this fairly small forest not game but Poles. So THE ESCAPE WAS DISCOVERED A DAY EARLIER THAN HAD BEEN ANTICIPATED. In fact there was no immediate reaction on the spot.

However that same night the police and army were mobilised (a whole division of troops, since it was feared that a British landing was in the offing) and the navy was alerted too. The search was limited to one small area, with shooting in the air and calls to 'Give yourselves up!'; the results were, for the time being, poor (around 30–40 were caught). Next morning, however, several companies of soldiers and the police, walking abreast through the forest in daylight, caught almost all the rest; all those who were not caught then gave themselves up during the next few nights. At sea meanwhile warships and aircraft patrolled.

The French authorities were apparently aghast at this mass flight of two whole camps; for our troops and officers, however, it was to have regrettable results, since the other ranks were transferred immediately from Saida deep into the Sahara (Béchar) and the officers for the time being are held under guard with fixed bayonets. In due course they too are to be moved much further inland; their situation will be very unpleasant. The one person who remained at liberty was Capt Szewalski, saved by unusual quick-wittedness: he told the French that he had opposed the whole plan. They put him under guard nevertheless. And it was only with some difficulty that he managed to see my messenger and convey the above information to him.

15) The conclusions I draw from this information are as follows:

A mass evacuation had a chance of succeeding and we would have managed to take off at least half the people if

1) we had possessed on the day in question our own LARGE evacuation felucca, and not the *Dogfish*, which is good for around 40 people only, and that in awful conditions;

2) there had been an earlier decision from the organisers of the operation from the land side about the plan for the mass evacuation, and this had been communicated sufficiently early to the organisers of the seagoing part of the operation. Evacuation of 200 people required different preparations from those for groups of 40 people. The organisers of the naval side were not informed until the morning of Wednesday 29 October so that, after returning to Gibraltar on Wednesday night, we would have had to be ready on Saturday morning equipped with two new feluccas or ships, whereas only one was ready. This was why, at the organisational briefing on the beach at La Macta on the morning of 29 October, I had guaranteed only Monday 3 November as a deadline. The discovery of our people by the hunt took place on the Sunday;

3) the people on shore had been dispersed to several embarkation points, with the aim of not placing all our eggs in one basket, in case the operation were uncovered. At the very least, instructions should have been issued to the evacuees that, if one site were compromised, they should make their own way to another. Some of them would always have managed to get through.

Regarding the possession of a felucca – I reported on this earlier. The only one lying at Gibraltar was being prepared for our use, but, in spite of the intervention of HQ at my request and the assurances that there would be a positive and early conclusion to the refit, the dockyard spent four months repairing the engine in the workshop and then fitted it into the felucca (still expressing optimism), only to declare that . . . this engine was not suitable for the vessel in question.

16) The ship's complement during the voyage apart from myself consisted of: Siembieda and Filipkowski (mechanics), Skulimowski (cook and deck-hand), Eggum (Norwegian, deck-hand) and Midshipman Buslowicz as courier, to carry out the mission in Oran.

(signed) M. Krajewski

Further details of the failed mass evacuation from La Macta (Brzoza) reached Krajewski in a letter from Casablanca dated 20 November.[10] It confirmed that on 2 and 3 November French patrols had arrested 148 Polish soldiers and officers assembled at the agreed embarkation point near Oran. Evacuation from the camps at Saida and Mascara had gone off unusually well. After the departure from Saida of all those earmarked for embarkation, only 39 of the normal complement of 206 remained: at Mascara, only 6 of the previous total of 67 were left. Apart from the 148 arrested on the beach, the balance were rounded up on their way to the pinpoint. All of those arrested were transferred to Saida, where the other ranks were placed behind barbed wire and carefully guarded. Officers were confined to a barracks at Mascara. Those officers who had not left Mascara at all were not allowed to leave the hotel where they were accommodated: they were cut off from communication with the outside world. An enquiry was taking place.

According to information from Algeria, it was forestry guards and members of a shooting party who had on Sunday 2 November appeared in the district near the shore and chanced upon the tracks of groups of people in abnormal numbers. They alerted the gendarmes immediately and French naval patrols were carried out in the forest.

Szewalski was immediately directed by the French authorities to Mascara: there were hopes that he would be able to return to Oran. Lt Polanski had been arrested and imprisoned at Oran.

*   *   *

Though he did not send his full written report to Mally until 29 January 1942, Krajewski went back to Algeria in the *Dogfish* between 12 and 19 December. His account was as follows:

REPORT OF THE NINTH EVACUATION MISSION
(follows my wire of 30 Dec. 1941)[11]

1) As I have already reported, Capt Szewalski most insistently asked Midshipman Buslowicz, who was put ashore in Algeria between 22 and 25 Nov., to arrange for a felucca to be sent around 15 December in order to take off those people whom he had managed to collect and hide, and – he stressed the need most forcefully – that a sum of at least 500,000 Fr. Francs be sent to him by the same route.

However, prospects of finding available seagoing resources were gloomy then, and still are. I reported on this in my wire no. 1748 of 29 November, sent via the British Naval Attaché. Namely,
a) The *Seawolf*, our own felucca, was to have received a new engine after four months' overhaul of the old engine by this incompetent dockyard; discussions about this were beginning at the time we left for the 9th mission;

b) The *Dogfish*, a very small felucca with a very antique engine, was being repaired after a serious breakdown of the clutch mechanism. The breakdown indicated that many unpleasant surprises are hidden behind the general wear and tear on this 30-year-old engine;

c) There was no other felucca or smaller vessel at our disposal, and I knew only that the local agencies were looking on the Lisbon market for a 'special purposes' ship with the characteristics needed for our evacuations.

2) In these circumstances, and in view of the urgency of Capt Szewalski's requests and the dire situation of our people in Africa after the discovery of the escape at La Macta, I decided to embark on one more voyage with the *Dogfish*, the engine of which had had only its most basic faults repaired (the clutch – and that only partly). The weather posed another risk. According to the pilot-book and accounts of fishermen, the period of continuous bad weather should already have begun. I counted on another couple of days' delay.

As events showed, we succeeded almost completely, but we had to pay for our boldness during the next mission.

3) We weighed anchor at 1405 hrs on 13 December and, as if it wanted to indicate that to demand another 500 nautical miles from it was too much, the *Dogfish*'s engine took half an hour to start, seized up at the exit from the port – which was guarded very closely following the most recent sinkings and sabotages – and would not start again until an hour later.

Apart from myself, the crew was composed of: Siembicda and Filipkowski (mechanics), Skulimowski (cook), Eggum (deckhand) and Second Lt Gromnicki, brought back recently from Oran, as a courier to put ashore.

4) The voyage to Oran lasted almost two days and passed off without incident. At 2130 hrs on 14 December we sighted the now very familiar lighthouse on the Habibas Islands. The weather for almost all of the outward journey was tolerable and only at the end did the wind betray signs of growing to almost storm strength. At 0330 hrs I dropped anchor at a depth of $2\frac{1}{2}$ m. off the shore, at a point equidistant from the Falcon lighthouse and the village of Les Andalouses (about $1\frac{1}{2}$ km. from each), the Zorra pinpoint. After we had put Second Lt Gromnicki ashore with the money, I weighed anchor at 0400 hrs. Then, because of the increasingly heavy swell, happily then coming from ENE, which left Zorra sheltered, I withdrew about 15 miles to the west to the little bay of Ali Ben Nuar, which we had already used a couple of times, and which my crew had

christened 'Rio de Janeiro'. It is a small bay surrounded by mountains and has underwater rocks at the bar but, as we were familiar with this stretch of coastline, we had no trouble in locating it. We entered the bay at 0710 hrs 15 December.

5) Just before noon that day, a young Arab with only one arm paid us a visit. He came from a very poor family, who had recently settled in this desolate little bay . . . He did appear greatly suspicious. In the end we bought two chickens from him to vary our monotonous menu.

At 1430 hrs we had a far less welcome visit, which may yet have serious repercussions. A man in a boat borrowed from an Arab family approached our felucca. His dress contrasted strongly with the rags of the ordinary Arabs, although he may have had the same Semitic roots. He treated us to some very good cigarettes, certainly not an Arab custom. He asked some searching questions: 'Where have you come from?' 'Do you have any fish?' 'Do you know the Falcon family at Nemours?' (from which we had supposedly come). He also put some silly questions, such as, 'What do you catch using a net with such large holes?' (here he pointed to the net that we habitually hung out to improve our 'fishing appearance', although closer examination would reveal that it could be used in trawling for particular types of fish only). To which we answered, 'Anything we can'. After a time he gave up and returned to the shore, then walked rapidly uphill.

The identity of this person was of course clear to me: he was an agent of the secret police, or simply a police informer, of which in the French colonies – where a police regime prevails – there are a great many. So I ordered the anchor to be weighed, although we did not need to hurry especially, since the agent had to travel 25 km. to the nearest guard-post and the sun would set in three hours.

Whether we wanted to or not, we had to set out against a strong swell and wind and spend the night on the sea anchor. That night the man on watch at 0230 hrs saw lamp lights in the region of our bay, which of course did not come as a surprise to us.

6) Since I had arranged with Second Lt Gromnicki that I would pick him up *two* days later, in order to give him more time to sort things out, we continued to wait at sea the whole of the next day at a distance of about 30 nautical miles to the north-west of Oran – until 1900 hrs. At 0140 I entered the Andalouses Bay and, an hour later, having received the agreed signal from the shore, I anchored and sent the life-raft to the shore.

I took Second Lt Gromnicki on board again, along with five officers whom he had brought to the spot . . .

7) The return journey was initially propitious: there was almost no swell during the first day. However it grew heavier during the afternoon of 17 December, so that my speed dropped to 4 knots.

Worse came when the engine seized up that night about 20 miles from Gibraltar, almost in the Straits, in regularly patrolled waters. However, from that distance I was able to send an agreed recognition signal with the Aldis lamp to the look-out post at Gibraltar. As we had not returned to port at the expected time, they sent out a motor launch to help. We were towed for 10 minutes, after which the engine recovered and we were able to return to Gibraltar under our own steam at 0230 hrs on 18 December.

8) The news brought to me by Second Lt Gromnicki and the evacuated officers was communicated to you earlier. In short, the situation has not changed. Apparently there was a chance that former camp conditions might be restored (as at Saida and Mascara), but because of the treachery of two of our officers (Second Lt Schonfeld and Capt Jakubowski, according to Capt Szewalski), the French authorities moved the officers and the camps deeper inland . . .

9) This voyage showed once again that the *Dogfish* is not at all suitable for this time of the year. Its inadequate accommodation places excessive demands on the crew, who therefore have to spend the whole journey on deck, as do any passengers. This is to say nothing of its faults associated with age – leaks and the ancient engine.

(signed) M. Krajewski

On 20 December, the day after Krajewski returned from his ninth mission, Mally wrote to him agreeing that Roehr should leave for France to prepare evacuations by sea from there on the lines proposed by Krajewski.[12] He then raised the entirely new idea that some of those evacuated from France to Spain might possibly be directed into the Malaga area, where they would be hidden by priests. If so, the question would arise of exfiltrating these people by sea from somewhere in that vicinity. He asked Krajewski to look into this possibility on the basis of existing resources.

Mally had acquired a fishing vessel in Portugal but its delivery to Krajewski in Gibraltar had been delayed because the Belgian who was to act as skipper took fright when the Portuguese 'official' owner of the boat started to explain the navigational difficulties and the danger from submarines, and at the last minute refused to make the voyage. Mally was pressing the shipping office and would send her on as soon as a crew was available.

Meanwhile, he had been authorised by his London headquarters to buy a larger fishing vessel with the characteristics specified by Krajewski for operations to the south coast of France. His source of advice on seafaring matters in Lisbon thought, however, that it would be difficult to find a vessel which reconciled the required fuel capacity and range with the desired speed, carrying capacity and overall need to look like a fishing vessel. Furthermore London imagined the cost of a suitable ship would be of the order of £2,000. Mally doubted whether this price would buy anything suitable in Portugal. Mally asked Krajewski to confirm whether a new ship was still needed now that a new engine that had been promised for the existing felucca. To put Krajewski in the picture, Mally advised that the felucca they would be sending to Gibraltar for him would be able to carry 15 people in addition to the crew.

Krajewski was instructed to retain a radio operator who was in Gibraltar, rather than send him on to the United Kingdom. He was also to ask Captain Kaminski, who had been evacuated by the British from Madrid, whether Chojnacki would be suitable as organiser of the landward side of the planned sea evacuations from metropolitan France.

On 24 December Mally followed this letter up with a two-page plan for evacuations by sea from Spain, on very similar lines to those previously arranged from Africa, although he acknowledged that this scheme would not be necessary if direct evacuation from France proved possible. The landward side of any such operations would be organised by Madrid, the maritime side by Gibraltar. The object would be to extract groups of up to 50 people at a time on innocent-looking vessels.

On a day indicated by Gibraltar, the boat would turn up at the appointed place. Agreed identification signals would be needed. Embarkation might have to be carried out in rubber dinghies because of the surf. Mail might be handed over and there might be an opportunity for land and sea operational personnel to confer. The embarkation point might be between 100 and 200 km. from Gibraltar. He proposed Malaga as a suitable collecting point for evacuees. Naval charts indicated that the shore 10–18 km. outside the town might be suitable: there were beaches and no off-lying rocks. Embarkation points should be hidden and suitable for people to be picked up at night (2400–0200 hrs) without the need to wait for particularly dark conditions. Areas where there were underwater rocks should be avoided, to allow the ship to approach as near as possible and anchor in 4–5 m. of water. A little bay that would provide shelter from any breakers would be ideal, but an open beach might do.

There would have to be a recognisable navigational landmark on which the vessel could make its landfall: the boat would then follow the coast at distance of 500 m. Suitable landmarks might be a rock, a building or patches of undergrowth. At least three pinpoints should be chosen and, in order to facilitate recognition, each should be given a code name for telegraphic purposes, e.g. DORA.

The paper ended with notes about recognition signals and laid down coding arrangements to be used between Madrid and Gibraltar.

Krajewski's hopes of avoiding any further mid-winter operations in the 9-ton felucca *Dogfish* had been further raised by a visit paid to Gibraltar by Commander Slocum in December 1941. Slocum still held no Admiralty appointment: he was at that time no more than the SIS officer responsible for meeting that organisation's requirements for physical communications with occupied western Europe. He was, however, well on the way to establishing control of all Allied clandestine sea transport to the north and west coasts of France and his visit to Gibraltar proved a first step towards his acquiring at least theoretical control in the western Mediterranean as well.

In the event, his presence did not spare Krajewski from one further, unusually trying, sortie in *Dogfish*. This was the report submitted on it to Mally as follows:

REPORT OF THE TENTH EVACUATION MISSION[13]

1) In the course of a meeting between Second Lt Gromnicki and Captain Szewalski during the 9th mission (13–19.xiii. 1941), Captain Szewalski asked for a felucca to be sent on 10 January, by which date he expected to have gathered around 15 people in a newly organised safe house.

During that 9th mission, we expected to receive a new felucca more suited to the task, by the beginning of January. After Commander Slocum's visit, the matter of vessels for use in special operations moved forward much more energetically. It was possible we might be able to use either *Seawolf*, after the arrival of a new engine ordered by cable from London on 13.xi; or the *Ville-De-Fedala*, a very good fishing vessel freshly acquired by the authorities here. We did not take the *Dogfish* into consideration, because of her complete unsuitability for that kind of mission during bad weather. Moreover, according to Commander Slocum, two special ships for this kind of operation were due to arrive at Gibraltar from England.

By the time the operation was due to start, however, the feluccas I then had at my disposal were in just the same state as on so many previous occasions. Consequently, I was compelled to fall back on the 10-ton *Dogfish* with its old engine. This meant taking considerable risks, if only navigational, since she would be required to undertake a journey of some 600 miles, lasting at least six days, during the winter period. Having no other choice, I could only hope that, as on the last two missions, we would have the good fortune to encounter a period of mild weather and avoid any serious breakdown of the engine.

The sometimes turbulent 16-day voyage did not bear out our initial hopes . . .

2) We put to sea on the morning of 8 January. The crew, apart from myself, was composed of Siembieda and Filipkowski (mechanics), Skulimowski (cook), Eggum (deck-hand, Norwegian), Second Lt Gromnicki (liaison courier to be put ashore) and for the first time an English sergeant, Guilder. This man was seconded to me almost at the last moment in order to test some special radio apparatus for the authorities here. I was more than ready to do this favour for our hosts (and the owners of the *Dogfish*) since it provided a chance to use radio communications in the event of difficulties during the voyage. I do not use my own apparatus on the *Dogfish* because of the likelihood of damage from the damp, etc.

For the first two days of the voyage the wind was from the west – i.e. to our advantage – even though its strength (4–5) was rather dangerous for our little felucca. Far from easing, it strengthened, so that on the evening of 9 January, as we approached the Cap-Falcon lighthouse, near our usual landing and pick-up point, I had to decide whether to put Second Lt Gromnicki ashore on the *eastern* side of the peninsula, since the western shores were completely exposed to the north-west swell. Around 2200 hrs on the 9th we were only a few miles from the lighthouse and being driven in the direction of that rocky shoreline by the storm-force wind from aft. Passing us at a distance of a few thousand metres was a convoy of three French merchant vessels which, advancing slowly along the coast, exchanged recognition signals with the lighthouse. No-one could have noticed us in the complete darkness though.

3) At this point we suffered a mechanical breakdown. The clutch mechanism gave out a characteristic rattle and the propeller ceased to rotate, which was a sure indication of serious damage to the cog-wheels, something that just could not be repaired on a felucca. This was a very critical moment for a breakdown: we were drifting on to a rocky shore, now only a few thousand metres distant, in a very large swell. We raised the sails almost immediately, from the outset strongly reefed. After entering the Bay of Oran I realised that, unfortunately, I had not found the expected shelter from the north-westerly

storm; the swell was even more dangerous for us in the shallower waters, since it broke into surf. We had a foretaste of what awaited us as we approached the shore near the Falcon lighthouse, when the swell nearly covered us completely. I ordered the crew to put on their lifebelts. Taking shelter in the port of Oran or in Mers el-Kebir was out of the question, even if we did look like a fishing boat, because of the possibility that the entrance was closed by a boom.

In the light of this, I set a course as close to the wind as possible, about N 30° E, counting on being able to shelter in the little port of Arzew, east of Oran, and there dismantle the clutch.

4) In the midst of this severe storm, which demanded the full concentration of the crew in exceptionally difficult conditions, we were driven by the wind all night. In the end I was unable to manoeuvre in such a way as to enter the Bay of Arzew, which, with hindsight – after the experience of the shooting on 13 January – would have presumably ended in imprisonment, since our 'fishing appearance' had already been compromised. The storm remained at full force throughout 10 January and the following night. The only safe course I could hold was that of 30°, so that by the morning of the 11th, when it had calmed somewhat, we found ourselves drifting almost 100 miles from the Falcon light.

The dismantled clutch was immediately revealed to be seriously damaged and looked quite beyond repair. However, in view of the gravity of our situation (some 350 miles from Gibraltar, the proximity of the shore, the stormy season of the year), Siembieda undertook to attempt to repair the clutch, so that we could at least use the engine to go ahead. The experiment was entirely successful and, after two days of strenuous work, on the evening of 12 January, we were ready to set off in the direction of Oran. Siembieda again demonstrated the talent and experience of a fine specialist technician, since the repair required such things as drilling some 20 holes in iron or steel, threading them, cutting the bolts, etc, and all this while subjected to a continuous rolling motion, in conditions as remote from an engine repair-shop as could be imagined.

5) Nevertheless we had no guarantee that we could rely on the clutch, and we still lacked a reverse gear. With these considerations in mind, I decided to set a return course for Gibraltar. In spite of everything, though, I thought we could hazard careful use of the engine in order to approach the shore and put our runner ashore. The weather that night was considerably improved and, having travelled 300 miles, I did not want to

return without having picked up the people who were no doubt waiting impatiently in hiding. And lest that be thought something of a risk, then I must state that I considered any voyage in the *Dogfish* was one continuous risk.

On the morning of the 13th we were in the vicinity of Oran again, intending to wait 24 hours in order to carry out our assignment. Once more – although not for the last time on this trip – the weather forced us to change our plans. The wind rose again and became very strong, forcing us to search for a suitable sheltered anchorage. I moved off therefore in the direction of the Habibas Islands, which I knew from the 8th mission. The waves mounted and the wind grew ever stronger (Force 5), however, so that, after a day-long attempt to cross that scarcely 25-mile stretch, I was forced to seek shelter at all costs. The larger waves threatened to overturn the felucca, which has no keel or inside ballast.

The only place I could reach and seek shelter, given the direction of the wind, was in Oran Bay, specifically near Cap Falcon; this had the advantage of not being a port with the various customary authorities . . . also, it was the point indicated by the pilot-books. In other words, it was a natural place for a fisherman to seek shelter from the storm.

6) At around 1700 hrs, shortly before sunset, we dropped anchor. We intended to move closer to the shore during the night, hoping stlll to be able to put a courier ashore in the same place. Soon afterwards we noticed more than a dozen Arab soldiers, who appeared to be drawing in a net on the narrow beach. They must have seen us drop anchor (we were the only ship visible). A few of the soldiers then gathered opposite our anchorage (at some 250–300 m. from the shore) and called to us. Since we could not understand what they wanted, and there was not a great deal of choice of possible anchorages, we did not pay a great deal of attention to their shouting; sunset was near, and we hoped they would quickly tire of it. When, however, the watch informed me that an officer had joined them and was carefully studying us through a telescope, before evidently giving the order to launch their small boat, I understood that the game was starting to become more serious. Before they had travelled very far, I managed to turn the felucca around and set a course for the open sea, cutting the anchor cable without recovering the anchor to save time. We thus began a race. We were extremely lucky in all this since the engine started up at once: even a few minutes' delay would have delivered us into the hands of the French.

Not only did they give chase but they had hardly seen the movement on our deck indicating that we were getting under-way before they began firing with rifles – both from the boat and from the shore. Their shooting was reasonably accurate: no-one was hit but we found four bullet holes in the hull and on the mast. Two were on the stern, very close to me and to the fuel tank. Obviously they judged me, as helmsman, a more worth-while target than the others . . . Needless to add, we took cover, insofar as cutting the anchor cable and steering permitted. So once again we were on the open sea, in a storm that rated at least point 6 on the Beaufort scale.

7) This was decidedly the worst night we spent at sea during the evacuation missions, perhaps even during our whole careers at sea. We struggled continuously with the endless waves that poured over us. The trick was to avoid all the largest break-ers, which represented not just danger but possible disaster for our felucca. Worse, in spite of clothing that was generally excellent and waterproof, we were soaked through and suffered from the cold.

This lasted until the morning of 14 January. On that day as the sun rose, we made out the Spanish coast, viz. Mesa de Roldan. The Gata peninsula, known for its navigational features, was not much further. We had travelled all night under sail and with our engine running so as to get as far as possible out of range of the French air force, which might have been searching for us.

The weather gradually improved during the day, which was fortunate since the clutch was again refusing to respond to the controls. The pins that had been drilled into the cog-wheel and the propeller shaft to fasten them together had held for barely a single stormy night, although this was quite an achievement in itself. Luckily, this time the repair was easier. During the night, more pins were put in and we were able to move again.

8) There was only one direction we could choose: Gibraltar. Our supplies of fuel were exhausted and also the alarm had been raised among the French authorities on the coast after the last bout of shooting.

Our return journey seemed at first to be progressing well: the wind at Capo de Gata was in our favour and 15 January passed calmly. Indeed, we had enough fuel for the return only if the weather remained reasonably calm, but not if the winds against us were strong, reducing our speed from between 6 and 4 knots to 3 or even less – moreover, at the cost of severely straining the felucca's hull.

On the evening of the 15th, a stubborn westerly wind returned, which, forced me either to wait for a favourable wind or to change course. I ordered the engine to be switched off and we hoisted the sails.

9) The last phase of our protracted Odyssey began with our wait for an easterly wind. Lack of space prevents me from reporting on it more fully.

On the 16th, just before sunset, we were close to the African coast when a further storm compelled us to spend the night anchored in the shelter of the Tres Forcas peninsula, about 2 miles north of Melilla. On two occasions during the night an MTB passed close to us at a distance of a few score metres, but luckily either failed to see us or was not suspicious.

Since Spanish Morocco seemed to be so closely guarded and patrolled, I weighed anchor at first light on the 17th and until the 18th meandered about in the region of Alboran Island, in the centre of the western basin of the Mediterranean.

On 18 January, we established our first contact with a Hudson aircraft sent out to look for us as a result of radio messages I had been sending to Gibraltar . . . until the British radio operator discovered that the batteries had not been completely charged at the time when we sailed from Gibraltar.

We spent the night of the 18th/19th anchored close to Alboran, so as not to move too far from the position the aircraft must have reported to base. We remained there the next day, under sail in the vicinity of the island, in the expectation that someone from Gibraltar would turn up.

Because of a further storm on the night of the 19th, we anchored again near Alboran Island and stayed there at anchor during the 20th and 21st. On the second day a lighthouseman with one of the soldiers from the little island (600 m. long) paid us a visit, begging us for some tobacco, since the inclement weather had prevented any ship from visiting since the end of December. Asked about our nationality, I said that we were Norwegians, not wanting them to report to Melilla by telephone the presence of a possibly suspicious English fisherman.

10) On 21 January we had what was to be our final adventure, which we expected would lead to our being interrogated in Melilla.

Just before sunset I sighted a patrol boat heading for the island from the direction of Melilla. From the faintness of its navigational lights, I guessed that it was some 6,000 m. off and that it was Spanish – not the most desirable encounter in my position. I ordered the anchor raised but it was caught on some rock and this time we were not able to cut through the cable, which was chain not a grass warp. I therefore decided to re-enact the scene that had worked so well at Tarifa during the 4th mission.

In the meantime the patrol boat had reached the island, anchored and, having discovered us in its searchlight, let down a boat. Shortly the commander of the boat called to me that, as 'el capitano', I should come over 'con papel' [with the ship's papers] to his vessel.

I must add that, before he reached our side, I had ordered the men to throw overboard anything in the least compromising or that might indicate where we had been: grenades, revolvers, maps of the Oran region, notes and unfortunately French money, which, in the amounts we possessed (135,200 Francs), we would never have been able to explain away.

11) The captain of the patrol boat, a naval lieutenant aged around 35 years, received me on deck – to my astonishment, in quite friendly spirit. Having asked about my nationality ('British,' I replied) he then asked to see my papers. He copied precisely my clearance paper, in which were recorded both my 'British' nationality and the direction and purpose of my voyage, namely east, to trawl for fish. Clearly convinced of my identity as a fisherman, the Spanish captain then very kindly invited me to have a glass of cognac with him. In the course of conversation he asked how we came to be anchored there, and I explained that it was because of a breakdown right at the beginning of our fishing run. I gave him many true details, leaving aside, of course, our sojourn on the French African coast. He himself confirmed that the weather was exceptionally bad there that year and said that he had come to bring supplies to the group on the island and a change of both lighthouseman and soldiers. He added, 'I should bring supplies to the island every ten days, but I have not been able to do so since 27 December because of the weather.'

Eventually, while the supplies and men were being put ashore and the existing garrison was embarking (25 soldiers guard the island's neutrality . . .), I had the honour (rather awkward, to tell the truth, because of the technical questions with which he punctuated the conversation) of eating supper on the ship's bridge with the captain. He evidently had a soft spot for the British, having at one time sailed in the waters around Ireland, fishing, and visited British ports. (For a foreigner he spoke English well.)

Asked if we needed anything, I told him that in recent days we had greatly felt the lack of sugar. He agreed to provide me with some in return for butter, since he apparently was very fond of English butter (he smiled as he said this). Eventually, we worked out an exchange whereby he received English tobacco, corned beef and biscuits, while we received two pounds of sugar and some oranges.

12) Early on the following day the wind at long last veered around (after three weeks . . . !) and by the 23rd we had made our way under sail or engine power to within 20 miles of Gibraltar, where again we were almost completely becalmed and we had only enough fuel for port manoeuvring. But we were continually 'visited' by aircraft, which signalled to us that 'Everything is alright . . . help is coming'. That evening two Fairmile 'B'-Class MLs approached us, returning, as it turned out, from a second mission to locate us, which they had been unable to do as we had been forced in the meantime to change position.

Eventually, at 1900 hours on the 23rd, we entered harbour under our own steam using the remains of our fuel, and having thrown off the tow-line from the ML that had brought us to the port of Gibraltar. It was not before time, since for several days we had eaten only biscuits and dishes made from corned beef and for the whole 16 days of the voyage we had not managed to change our soaking clothing.

13) Analysing why the French shot at us, we may guess that the possible reasons were a) the usual suspicion of someone who attempts to run away; b) suspicion that we were smuggling, since we had no signs on the ship's side to indicate nationality; c) that the French in Africa were in possession of real information about us, through betrayal or idle talk, or perhaps the visit by that agent during the 9th mission. This last theory was supported by the most recent news received indirectly from Oran, recommending that I should not send a boat there at the beginning of February, as a trap was being prepared.

14) In addition, this journey proved indisputably that we can no longer use the *Dogfish* during the winter and spring transitional periods – in other words not until the beginning of April.

Luckily, the *Seawolf*, a much larger felucca with a new engine, will be ready in the meantime – although not until the end of this month (February).

15) In para. 4 I reported on Siembieda's contribution. In conclusion, I should like to report how Second Lt Gromnicki distinguished himself. In spite of the fact that he was at sea for the first time and has no previous knowledge of sailing, he set to the task with such enthusiasm and energy, in very difficult conditions, that he proved a great asset and in all senses a full member of the crew, which, given the reduced number of crew available (for sailing), was extremely valuable. I must emphasize

that this officer, unlike the other members of the crew, volunteered for the voyage knowing that it would not bring him any material reward at all.

(signed) M. Krajewski

Krajewski cannot have been best pleased to receive on 13 February, three weeks after his return from this ordeal, what amounted to a letter of reprimand from Mally.[14] The evacuation outpost in Africa had accused Krajewski of not having arrived at the rendezvous on the African coast where he had been expected about 11 January. From Krajewski's last report, Mally could not make out whether he had been on his way to North Africa or to France. Equally, Mally had asked, and now asked again, what was the situation about Roehr? Had Roehr yet made his way to French territory? As Mally had already pointed out several times, he was well aware of the great technical difficulties Krajewski had to surmount as a result of having to depend on other people's repair workshops to keep his felucca in operational order. Mally nevertheless drew Krajewski's attention to the equally difficult conditions under which their people had to work in North Africa. They required him to overcome all technical difficulties and make every possible effort to arrive at the meeting-points at the agreed time. Krajewski should choose the day and hour for meeting, but thereafter would he please do everything possible to ensure the arrangements for the meeting were adhered to? A bit tough!

CHAPTER XXVI

Krajewski's Further Plans for Operations to North Africa and Southern France, December 1941–March 1942

S locum had cogent reasons for visiting Gibraltar early in December 1941.[1]

Demands for clandestine transport were growing; German defences and controls were increasingly formidable, particularly on the north coast of France and in the Low Countries; attempts to carry out operations by sea from bases in the United Kingdom to these key areas had, in recent months, failed more often than they had succeeded.

The increased demand emanated mainly from SOE, whose Independent French Section had substantial numbers of agents under training, and from MI9, who were confronted with the task of rescuing from France growing numbers of shot-down aircrew.

By the end of April 1941, increased German vigilance had halted operations in and out of Brittany by fishing vessels, with the loss of two of the boats involved; and in the 13 months to September 1941 there had not been one successful cross-Channel operation to France by high-speed craft. Slocum expected shortly to be able to borrow a 'C'-Class MGB from Combined Operations and hoped that she would be allocated permanently to his Section in spring 1942. However, as the Germans tightened their hold on the occupied zone of France, it seemed all too likely that the increased vigilance and scale of their coastal, air and sea patrols, the building of their coastal defence system and the imposition of administrative controls on access to beaches and on the movements of fishing craft would make clandestine contacts with France by sea from the United Kingdom increasingly difficult. As the purveyor of physical communications to SIS and the guardian of their priority over those of other agencies, Slocum urgently needed landing areas that offered access to France but were less heavily guarded than those directly accessible from the United Kingdom. The south coast of France, still not occupied by the Germans, seemed in every way suitable for his purpose, notwithstanding *Fidelity*'s limited success, and it was in pursuit of this line of inquiry that he went to Gibraltar.

He found that the Poles, the Czechs and SOE were using what he termed 'their private means of transport' to mount forays into the western Mediterranean and down the Atlantic coast of Morocco. Although they had had a certain amount of success, he felt that this method of working left much to be desired. The craft employed were inadequate and the problem of maintaining them was insuperable. The dockyard would undertake no refits without the sanction of a recognised naval authority. This was almost unobtainable as the Navy, hard pressed for men and materials, viewed clandestine operations with suspicion and dislike, judging them a waste of ships and time. The Navy's indifference may perhaps be excused by the fact that requests for approval for such activities were inadequately explained although they came sandwiched between claims of importance.

In Slocum's view, there was insufficient liaison with, and control by, the naval and air authorities in the operational sphere. The inadequate craft employed had, as a consequence, to counter the dangers of attack by Allied, as well as enemy, submarines, ships and aircraft. He recorded, though on what evidence is unclear, that in many instances they were hindered by the attentions of friendly patrols to such an extent that their operations had to be abandoned, or at least postponed to the next no-moon period. This in turn disorganised the plans of the shore parties, often in desperate straits, awaiting embarkation from enemy coasts. Finally, there was always the danger that two craft, each working for its own organisation, would arrive at the same pinpoint without previous knowledge of the other's existence and thus that either or both operations would be jeopardised. If a vessel became overdue, air reconnaissance and assistance could not be organised with the necessary speed. As 1941 drew to a close, Slocum claimed that there was mounting misunderstanding between the naval authorities at Gibraltar and what he termed 'the purely military ones', operating their own craft, as a result of which the latter had 'reached a peak of their unpopularity'. The Navy was irritated at the way in which 'private navy' ships were sailed without reference to the situation at sea and without warning to the local naval port commands. The secret organisations themselves were becoming conscious of the difficulty of laying plans for operations when they were compelled to use unreliable craft, which were constantly breaking down through faulty maintenance, and with the knowledge that, when at sea, they could expect scant assistance from a Navy and Air Force whose sympathies had been 'so unfortunately alienated'.

By contrast with this untidy, unsatisfactory and even dangerous state of affairs in the Gibraltar Command, irregular operations in home waters had, as Slocum claimed, been a 'going concern' since 1940. The maritime interests of the clandestine departments were in the hands of a naval officer from the active list of the Royal Navy.

This officer [Slocum himself] had built up a good liaison between the clandestine services, the Admiralty and local naval authorities.

SOE would, of course, have regarded this description of the satisfactory state of affairs in home waters as quite unwarranted.

Krajewski's reports certainly bore out all Slocum's observations about inadequate craft and faulty maintenance, but Krajewski would hardly have been recommended for a DSO if his relations with the local naval authorities were as Slocum claimed. Perhaps Slocum's remark about the 'purely military ones' was meant to single Krajewski out from Quennell of SOE and the rest of the field. What is certain is that in December 1941 the Royal Navy at Gibraltar had its hands full: the Battle of the Atlantic was at its height and the difficulties of getting convoys through to beleaguered Malta were such that Gibraltar-based submarines of the Eighth Flotilla were being used to ferry aviation fuel through to keep the island's exiguous Spitfire fighter force flying. In such circumstances, it is hardly surprising that clandestine operations were merely tolerated rather than liked, and that Slocum's offer to take charge and reorganise them on a more satisfactory and coordinated basis should have been welcomed.

A series of consultations with Vice-Admiral Commanding North Atlantic (VACNA) and other interested parties culminated in a meeting at Government House at which a universally acceptable course of action was agreed. Slocum, who presented himself as the delegate of the Admiralty, announced that a Special Flotilla would be formed and that, as a temporary measure, the existing feluccas would be placed under the administrative and operational control of the Captain Commanding the Eighth Submarine Flotilla (S/m 8). Arrangements would be made for maintenance to be provided by HMS *Maidstone*, the submarine depot ship, and the dockyard. As soon as possible, a suitable officer and staff would be sent out by NID(C) to direct, under VCNA, all clandestine operations from the Rock. Slocum undertook to provide extra vessels, including a 200-ton diesel trawler and a fast escort vessel.

As has been seen, Krajewski felt that Slocum's visit had at last got things moving: *Seawolf* would receive her new engine, which was to be an 88 h.p. Kelvin, rather than the 50 h.p. model for which he had originally asked, unless it were decided to install it in another felucca, the *Vega* (original name *Ville-de-Fedala*), which had arrived in Gibraltar unexpectedly on 3 December from Casablanca, when stowaways forced her crew to proceed there.

Krajewski learned of this vessel's presence in the harbour only by chance.[2] She was an excellent open-sea type and very suitable for operations to the south coast of France. He hoped to be able to use her to begin his French evacuation scheme without needing to wait for the completion of *Seawolf*'s refit. The Contraband Control

Office had recommended to the Admiralty that the ship be released but, as de Bellaigue, the Free French liaison officer, independently needed a similar craft, he and Krajewski persuaded the CCO to rescind their advice and retain her for their clandestine operational purposes. They also wrote jointly to VCNA asking him to intervene in favour of their being allowed to have the boat.

Krajewski discussed his plans for using this vessel with Quennell, SOE's local representative, and it was agreed that she would be incorporated into the new Special Flotilla, initiated by Slocum. But SOE had a special task to carry out, for which Quennell received priority to use the new ship: Krajewski was promised that he could have her afterwards for his first expedition to the south coast of France, projected for the end of December 1941. But, as so often before in connection with *Seawolf*, his hopes were frustrated.

Quennell needed a vessel for an expedition to Casablanca. He had recently received from England a complete Polish crew, consisting of a naval Lieutenant, Jan Buchowski, three Leading Seamen and three Ordinary Seamen, all of whom had been seconded to SOE by Admiral Swirski, the Polish naval Commander-in-Chief, at the request of Brigadier Colin Gubbins, SOE's Chief of Training and Operations. Buchowski, who had been awarded the Polish Cross of Gallantry for courage in Norwegian waters while serving in the destroyer *Blyskawica* and a Bar to this decoration for courage during the Dunkirk evacuation, had been acting gunnery officer of the ship prior to his secondment. He had been put through a course of intensive and specialised training by SOE before being sent out to Gibraltar.

This operation to Casablanca in the *Vega* was scuppered by bad weather, which made landing impossible. While they were off Tangiers, on the return passage to Gibraltar, they were summoned by a Spanish warship to heave to. When they failed to comply, the warship opened fire, and *Vega* was placed under arrest. As they were being escorted into Tangiers, they managed to throw their explosive materials and arms overboard. The crew were interned for three weeks, when they were released after the intervention of the British Consulate-General, but the boat remained impounded. Krajewski was therefore obliged to use the *Dogfish* for his very trying 16-day sortie to Algeria in January 1942; and also to postpone his first expedition to the south coast of France until the following April, when *Seawolf* had been fitted with her new engine and was at last ready for sea.

Early in 1942, Patrick Whinney, Slocum's Staff Officer for Mediterranean operations, now a Lt Cmdr, RNVR, arrived at Gibraltar to lay the foundations of the new organisation and prepare for the advent of Captain C.B. Osborne, RNR, who was to take up the post of senior officer. Osborne assumed control in the spring of 1942. The trawler *Tarana* and escort vessel *Minna* followed in quick succession. These two vessels and the operational felucca were, for purposes of cover, styled the Coast Watching Flotilla (CWF). Slocum felt, in retrospect, that the cover designation had proved a satisfactory choice.

Buchowski's unit, having been formed for SOE's needs, was initially distinct from Krajewski's evacuation mission and was known as the Diversionary Group, but the two were old shipmates from the *Blyskawica* and when Krajewski went to sea in *Dogfish* for a final sortie to Oran in March, Buchowski must have gone with him as second in command.

SOE held substantial stocks of arms, ammunition and explosives at Gibraltar in connection with contingency plans to destroy communications should the Germans move into Spain and invade North Africa. They no doubt wished to be able to transport these stores wherever they were needed, including southern France. But the fact that Buchowski had been given training by SOE suggests they may also have planned to use him to carry out raids or sabotage or to instruct others to do so. The exact nature of the operation he was sent to carry out at Casablanca in December, when *Vega* was lost, is not clear; nor is the nature of a second operation for which he was subsequently sent to Tangiers, probably in *Dogfish*, when they were shot at by coastal guards. It is, however, certain that SOE Gibraltar made up and smuggled into Tangiers a 34-lb. explosive charge, which was used on 11 January 1942 to destroy a cliff-top villa containing a German infra-red monitoring device. Used in conjunction with a similar installation on the Spanish side of the 16-km.-wide Straits, this would have enabled the Abwehr to detect the movement of Allied shipping in and out of the western Mediterranean under cover of darkness. The threat was discovered by none other than Kim Philby, who consulted R.V. Jones, scientific adviser to SIS. In Abwehr signals they noted references to an operation code-named BODDEN, which was also the name of an enclosed stretch of water near Peenemünde on the Baltic coast of Germany, a known centre of scientific research and development for operational purposes. From this and collateral intelligence, they correctly deduced what was being built by the Abwehr on the two sides of the Straits. The Abwehr scored a savage tit-for-tat by blowing up a British diplomatic bag and killing 29 people on the Tangiers–Gibraltar ferry some weeks later, but the Germans were never able to replace what they had lost and thus the Allied invasion fleets destined for Oran and Algiers were able, in the first week of November 1942, to slip undetected through the Straits for the TORCH landings, an operation which, with El Alamein and Stalingrad, turned the tide of the Second World War.

On 8 March 1942, the new 88 h.p. engine for *Seawolf* arrived.

While it was being installed, Krajewski, cheered by the prospect that the vessel would at long last become available for operations, wrote formally to Captain Holland, Chief of Staff to the Governor and chairman of the local Joint Intelligence Committee, the body delegated to lay down priorities for clandestine operations from the Rock, outlining the tasks that the Polish mission wished *Seawolf* and her Polish crew to undertake.[3] Their object was to evacuate by sea the ex-Polish fighting forces immobilised in southern France, roughly estimated to number 3,000, though it was impossible to state how many could effectively be rescued. Krajewski noted that the plan to evacuate men went back to December 1940, when it had been discussed in outline between the Polish general staff and the Admiralty. In March 1941 he had been sent to Gibraltar, which he was to use as the base in carrying out the plan.

When the plan to organise a mass evacuation of the two main camps in the Marseilles area by means of the cargo steamer *Czardasz* was abandoned in April 1941 (see Chapter XXIV above), he was given the additional task of organising the rescue of Poles from Morocco and Algeria. At the same time he was to look for means to carry out the main scheme, evacuation from France.

The North African scheme had finally been put into effect from July 1941 onwards. In the course of ten expeditions, over 100 officers and men had been taken off, and he and his crew had gathered considerable experience in these rather unusual operations. On each journey at least 650 km. were covered in all weathers; there had been seven effective evacuations, five of which had been in heavy Atlantic surf; and three landings of officer–messengers.

The North African scheme, Krajewski continued, was based originally on the availability of the *Seawolf*, which he had taken over with the approval of VACNA and his Chief of Staff, Captain Duke, at the beginning of July 1941. Her engine having proved faulty, the boat was handed over to the dockyard about 20 July for an overhaul expected to last only two or three weeks. The African plan had been carried out mainly in the 10-ton *Dogfish*, which Mr Quennell had kindly lent him. At the beginning of November, after a $3\frac{1}{2}$-month refit, *Seawolf*'s engine had been declared unusable, so he had asked the Polish Government to buy a suitable replacement. This was done, but delivery from the United Kingdom had entailed considerable further delay in commissioning *Seawolf* and in the meantime other alterations were made, for instance to increase her radius of action.

At the beginning of December, when this refit was still in progress, Captain Slocum had informed a meeting of authorities and missions of the proposed new organisation of the Special

Flotilla. From this point on, Krajewski had received effective and substantial help from the officer specialists of HMS *Maidstone*.

The Polish mission intended to land an officer in southern France to take charge of the landward side of the evacuation scheme. They would then carry out a succession of expeditions to take off the maximum number of men, whom the officer would assemble at the appointed place. The designated officer had already been very successful in organising the landward side of the North African scheme and was, moreover, well acquainted with the area in which he would be operating. Exact numbers to be embarked on each occasion and consequently the duration of the scheme could not yet be specified. Besides, the situation might change at any moment if the boat or the land-based organisation were compromised. A figure of about 80 at a time seemed likely. Security was of the utmost importance, since the plan was based on the premise that it would be possible to repeat the operations. More information would be available when the officer concerned had reached France and seen things at first hand. It might, for example, be possible to assemble men at several different points on the same night or to carry out embarkation on several consecutive nights: 'passengers' would then have to be transferred to another ship and the boat would have to wait during the day at a safe distance from the coast.

Extrapolating from the operation in August–September, when the much smaller *Dogfish* had embarked and brought back 48 'passengers' in addition to her crew of six, Krajewski estimated that *Seawolf* would be able to take off and bring to Gibraltar a group of 80 men or, if necessary, 100. He proposed to carry out a first and exploratory operation as soon as *Seawolf* had passed her speed trials and was ready for sea. A favourable date for the embarkation would be Saturday/Sunday, 18/19 April. This would mean sailing about the 14th.

A few days after the land-based officer was put ashore, when he had had time to make the arrangements, the boat would pick up the first batch of men and the captain of the *Seawolf* would confer on the beach with the officer to plan further moves.

Communications were the subject of separate planning but, in general terms, the W/T link between Polish military HQ in London and the south of France was supposed to be at their disposal. They would also use plain-language code, which had proved both simple and successful in the case of North Africa.

In submitting this plan, Krajewski thought it his duty to make clear that it would not be possible for the Polish mission to put their long-planned French scheme into operation unless they were assured beforehand of priority for the use of *Seawolf*. He added that they had taken charge of this vessel in July 1941 and that the

Polish Government had incurred expenses on her, including £1,000 on buying the new engine.

This request for priority might appear superfluous, but the case of the *Vega* showed that no serious and far-reaching plan such as he outlined could be established unless the means to carry it out *in toto* were secured.

Krajewski then described how the *Vega* had arrived unexpectedly from Casablanca on 3 December and said that she was a very suitable boat in which to start operations to the south coast of France while *Seawolf* was being got ready. He recounted how he had told SOE about her qualities and his plans for using her. As a result, the boat had been added to the Special Flotilla. SOE had then laid claim to her for an operation and Krajewski had been told he could have use of her only after their own priority operation.

Krajewski passed lightly over the unfortunate end of *Vega*, which caused a delay not of weeks but of months in starting his French scheme. But he said that if he and his 'correspondents' in France had prepared an evacuation on a set date, the failure of *Vega* to arrive would have ruined the plan and exposed them to danger. He would in any case have had to postpone his arrival in France because of the delay caused by *Vega*'s use in the SOE operation.

In point of fact Krajewski had not been given even an approximate date for *Vega*'s availability and had therefore been unable to make any plans based upon her.

Krajewski said he would be very grateful if the Polish mission could have a written statement confirming that *Seawolf* would be available to them for the evacuation of Poles from southern France. He conceded that it was natural that *Seawolf* be used for other operations whenever she was not employed by the Polish mission for any length of time. He would be only too glad to help in any way by combining his operations off southern France with any similar operations planned by the authorities in Gibraltar. However, past experience told him that some sort of priority must be given to the use of the boat for *one* particular purpose if such a large scheme were to be put into effect. In support of his request for priority, Krajewski drew Captain Holland's attention to the potential contribution of the evacuated Polish personnel to the war effort, once they had been rescued from camps in southern France and incorporated in the Polish forces.

What reply Krajewski received to this cogently argued plea is not clear, but it must have been sufficiently emollient for him to continue with his proposed programme of operations to southern France. But by this time both SOE's Independent French Section and MI9 had emerged as potential users of any sea line of communications between Gibraltar and southern France and Captain

Osborne's job as the staff officer responsible for allocating priorities fairly was clearly not going to be a sinecure.

SOE's interest in the unoccupied zone was growing. In September 1941, the month Dubourdin and Basin of their Independent French Section had been landed from *Fidelity*, Squadron Leader Ron Hockey of 138 Special Duties Squadron had parachuted to a reception party at Fonsorbes, near Toulouse, the first of many consignments of arms and explosives that were to be delivered to south-western France over the next three years.[4] Gibraltar became involved at the end of 1941, when SOE's Independent F Section urgently needed to infiltrate Captain Peter Morland Churchill into southern France with new instructions for Dubourdin and Basin. They also wanted him to find out more about an organisation named 'Carte' and its eponymous chief, who claimed to have good contacts with the Vichy general staff. Quennell had some difficulty in arranging for Churchill to be landed – or rather, to land himself by means of a Folboat canoe – from *P36*, one of the Gibraltar-based submarines, at Miramar-de-l'Esterel on 9 January 1942, when the submarine was on its way to Malta with supplies.[5] Churchill returned from the mission via Spain and set about arranging to carry out two further landings of agents for F Section from HM S/m P42 (later renamed *Unbroken*), as is described in Chapter XXVII below.

Krajewski seems himself to have undertaken yet another expedition to Oran on 22 March, presumably in *Dogfish*. It was evidently unsuccessful and, since afterwards he was preoccupied with mounting his first operation to France in the re-engined *Seawolf*, it was Buchowski who, on 25 April, carried out Operation ORKAN in *Dogfish*, embarking from the Oran area four Poles for the Polish mission and for Dunderdale. This mission, the first to North Africa recorded by Slocum's representatives on the Rock, shows that the new Coast Watching Flotilla dispensation had begun to work. Although Buchowski had been sent to Gibraltar to work for SOE, he was in this case operating for Krajewski's evacuation mission and either for the intelligence network that Slowikowski was very successfully running from Algiers, with an outpost at Oran, or for some other group linked with Dunderdale's Section of SIS. Slowikowski himself was still unaware that his 'Agence Afrique' was really working for SIS: Dunderdale had asked Colonel Gano, head of the *émigré* Polish Deuxième Bureau, to establish such an organisation for North Africa.[6] This area was of little interest to the Poles as an intelligence target, but had considerable strategic importance for the British, though by no means easy for SIS to work in after Mers el-Kebir. French North Africa increasingly attracted the interest of Winston Churchill and of President Roosevelt: operations to it continued throughout the summer and autumn of 1942.

CHAPTER XXVII

Operations from Gibraltar to Southern France: April to June 1942

I n the no-moon period of April 1942, operations from Gibraltar to the Côte d'Azur began with a bang. In the five nights between 18/19 April and 22/23 April, *Seawolf* landed Roehr at Port-Miou to organise a first evacuation, put three SOE agents ashore at La Napoule and embarked 41 Poles from Port-Vau;[1] HM S/m *P42* landed two SOE W/T operators at Antibes and embarked de Gaulle's future Commissaire à l'Interieur before proceeding to land two other SOE agents at Miramar-de-l'Esterel on the following night;[2] and Slocum's newly arrived 200-ton diesel trawler *Tarana* put Pat O'Leary and a W/T operator ashore in the Port-Vendres area.[3] So concentrated was this activity that the felucca and the submarine actually sighted each other when *P42* was under-way on the surface without lights. *Seawolf* mistook her for a French naval patrol ship.

Of *Tarana*'s first operation, little is recorded. O'Leary, having escaped from Vichy police custody, had crossed the Pyrenees and made his way to Gibraltar for a meeting with Donald Darling, MI9's representative on the Rock, and Jimmy Langley from their London headquarters. They discussed plans for mass evacuations of Allied evaders and escapers by sea from southern France. O'Leary and a W/T operator then took passage back to France in *Tarana*, which was commanded by Lt E.B. Clarke, RNR, whom Krajewski found 'a very pleasant and cheery fellow'.

Peter Churchill, having also returned from his first mission, embarked with four SOE agents on *P42*, under command of Lt Alastair Mars, RN.[4] He landed the two W/T operators, who were to work for 'Carte', by folboat at the Pointe-de-l'Ilet, just outside the ancient walls of the city of Antibes, and walked with them into the town to show them the way to their safe house, the home of a Dr Levy. Emmanuel d'Astier de la Vigerie, founder and head of 'Libération-Sud', was staying there and, when Churchill arrived, decided on the spur of the moment to take advantage of the opportunity to leave France and return with him to the waiting submarine.

On the following night, Churchill landed the other two agents at Miramar-de-l'Esterel, which had been his own disembarkation point in January. They were Vic Gerson, the organiser of Leslie

Humphreys's remarkably efficient 'Vic' landline, who on an earlier mission to France had recruited as his deputy in the Paris area Jacques Mitterrand, a future General of the French air force and brother of François. His second passenger that night was Marcel Clech, the erstwhile Breton sailor and taxi-driver, who had survived 17 unsuccessful attempts to land him by sea in Brittany, 16 of them organised by Slocum. He had meanwhile trained as a W/T operator.[5]

The story of Operation JASMINE, Krajewski's first voyage to France in *Seawolf* is best told in his own words:

REPORT OF THE TWELFTH EVACUATION MISSION (14-27 April 1942)[6]

1) *READINESS OF THE FELUCCA 'SEAWOLF'*. Once the new engine for the evacuation felucca had arrived and in particular been unloaded from the ship that brought it (but not until 1 April, in spite of many appeals from various quarters), the firm hurried to finish off the fitting and adjustment, although this did not prevent them from failing to keep their word over the deadline.

Eventually however the *Seawolf* was handed over to 'the company' on 10 April, despite a whole number of outstanding small jobs that I did not want the firm to do, since this would have involved further delay, or that needed by their nature to be carried out by specialists from HMS *Maidstone*.

We had very little time to get the felucca into seaworthy condition, since we were constrained both by the date agreed with Midshipman Chciuk at Cassis – 18 April (we would have to raise anchor at least five days earlier) – and also by the approaching period of the new moon. Any slippage of the programme would mean postponing the long-awaited pioneering operation for almost a month.

As a result, the crew I and had barely three days to take charge of a completely bare felucca, equip it, test it and prepare it for a long voyage.

2) *PLAN OF OPERATION*. Lt Roehr[7] had arranged by letter with Midshipman Chciuk that he would meet him 'on a very important matter' in Cassis on 19 April. He was to brief him on current conditions in France and also smooth contacts with the local leaders.

My intention was to put Lt Roehr ashore at the same time so as to have someone permanently in France who is familiar with the techniques employed when evacuating by sea in our situation and with our resources, and to act as a personal link with the local leaders in France.

In order not to return empty-handed after a journey of 1,500 sea miles, Lt Roehr was to spend a few days collecting together a group of people for evacuation.

The authorities here asked me to put ashore three agents in the region of Antibes (near Cannes) – which readily fitted in with my operation, since I foresaw several days' wait in any case – so I agreed. I calculated that, as long as it did not clash with our evacuations, it would be to our advantage in that it would give me stronger grounds to put forward our requirements if the need for technical help arose.

3) *THE RAISING OF THE ANCHOR* took place on 14 April at 0500 hrs. Apart from the crew, the three above-mentioned 'passengers' were also taken on board. The composition of the crew apart from myself was: Mate Gorzelok, Leading Seaman Stanislawski (radio and deck-hand), Leading Seaman (Reserve) Chwastek (deck-hand), Petty Officer Siembieda (1st mechanic) and Seaman Kurzawa (greaser). Gorzelok had joined the crew on a permanent basis in place of Buchowski, which meant that none of my lads was familiar with the work of a deck-hand to anywhere near a satisfactory degree. I exchanged Seaman Schlauberg from my crew (cook) for Mate Gorzelok (deck-hand and also, of necessity, cook) in order to have someone who could help in case the engine broke down or if, at any other critical moment, it proved necessary to use the sails.

The journey began in a very strong wind (Force 4–5) but luckily it was a fair wind for us, which meant that I could exercise the crew in sail manoeuvres. In addition it meant a large saving in fuel and gave me experience in the art – totally new, and unknown to us – of lateen sailing. The results achieved were very interesting: under sails alone, our speed by the Walker log and in the prevailing wind conditions was 7.1 knots. Our speed when powered by our 88 h.p. diesel engine under the same conditions was not much greater – 8.5 knots. Linking both forms of traction (engine + sails) produced little more than 8.9 knots, which is the maximum speed attainable on average by a hull of this length, and thus to be expected. By using the sails and half power, we could reduce our consumption of fuel while at the same time maintaining a speed of around 7–8 knots in the strong wind.

14 and 15 April were spent in making finishing touches and modifications to the vessel, since new needs arise with new experience. On 15 April we had one of those typical incidents that attests to the manner in which tasks at Gibraltar are carried out by Spanish workmen. We discovered a fire in the galley – luckily still at an early stage – the cause being an absence of

asbestos between the coal stove and the wooden bulkhead. As a result, one of the spars had been charred and in none too favourable conditions we had to reinstall the stove provisionally with the means at our disposal.

From the very outset curious happenings began to occur with respect to the felucca's position. My instinct was to keep out of sight of land, since we had information that the Spaniards were observing every movement at sea by means of their coast-guard network and reporting to the Germans. The only means I had of checking my dead reckoning (Walker log) were a sextant (which had come from a German ship) and a chronometer (brought from Oran, where a ship's officer, in gratitude for our having evacuated him to Gibraltar, had removed it from a requisitioned Yugoslav ship without the knowledge of the French). Our position according to the stars repeatedly showed large discrepancies from our dead reckoning, unexplained by any currents that we were aware of. After a few days, when I was sure that I had recovered my old skills and that the discrepancies were not attributable to my faulty calculations, I realised that the real deviation of the compass was very different from what I had been told by the flotilla navigator – by more than 10° (!). The difference on 15 April amounted to 35 miles, as was confirmed by the appearance of the African coast to starboard. The situation was very worrying since we were only at the beginning of our journey and it was going to be very difficult, without a reliable means of reckoning our position, to take on such delicate operations as approaching unfamiliar coastlines, keeping rendez-vous, etc. I decided therefore to make a deviation table myself from the azimuth of the setting sun; however, for this I needed very good weather and a cloudless sunset.

At noon on the 16th I passed between the islands of Ibiza and Majorca. That evening a storm blew up, one of the heaviest of that season; worse to tell, this time it was against us. Because of the opposing swell, our speed was much reduced and a further reduction seemed inevitable to avoid damage to the hull (our average speed throughout the night was only 3.5 knots). A number of the crew were sick, which, together with the discovery of various defects in the new installations (e.g. a fault in the bilge pump, which sucked water into the boat rather than out of it), made it a rather unpleasant period for us.

On the 17th, the weather improved somewhat (speed 6.1 knots) and on the last day of our outward journey, arriving at the French coast, we encountered sunny weather. Behind us we had the best possible test of the excellent strength and endurance of our felucca, a successful sailing trial and a perfect idea of what still needed to be repaired on our vessel.

Astronomical observations continued to show a deviation of 18° (!) from our course. Fortunately I managed to catch sight of the sun or stars each day and in that way check the faults in our reckoning.

On 18 April we painted the French colours on our hull, as well as a registration number, and we carried out normal preparations for anchoring and putting someone ashore: lines, anchors, life-raft, etc. In the process the new crew had their first opportunity to familiarise themselves with the special techniques needed in these particular operations.

4) *PUTTING LT ROEHR ASHORE.* That same evening we saw the high coastline of the Marseilles region. Having waited until it grew dark, I moved in the direction of the Planier lighthouse, and then towards the little bay at Cassis. After midnight I entered the Port-Miou inlet, one of those known for their picturesque qualities as *calanques*, and dropped anchor. Lt Roehr was put ashore, having agreed to return in two hours' time with Chciuk. At 0200 hrs we did in fact make out the agreed signals, and then brought both of them off to the felucca, where we discussed the situation and our immediate plans.

The result was to fix a rendezvous for the night of 22/23 April – in four days' time – in En-Vau, the neighbouring *calanque*. Port-Miou had appeared busy of late; among other things, in a shack near the place where we had disembarked Lt Roehr a lamp was still burning, even at that late hour. In any case, while we were anchoring at a distance of around 300 m. from it, some man came to the door who appeared to have noticed the felucca. The number of people I asked for was 60.

At 0400 hrs I was already clear of the *calanque*, having landed both Lt Roehr and Midshipman Chciuk. I set a course for the east with the aim of putting the agents ashore. The distance to be covered was about 120 nautical miles.

5) *THE MEETING WITH THE 'MTB'.* The course I set for Antibes, where I was to drop the agents, was an average of 20 miles from the shore. On the evening of the 19th, being already to the south of the headland, I set a course for land, for the La-Garoupe lighthouse, a powerful light which we ought to have seen from a distance of 15 miles in spite of the poor visibility.

Here I made out a row of lights which seemed to me to be half-way between me and my objective, i.e. some five miles from the shore. Suspecting that it was a convoy, I began to man-oeuvre in order to discover the direction in which they were travelling, when suddenly I saw, no more than about 1,500–2,000 metres in front of me, the outline of a small warship, the shape of the French *chasseurs de sousmarins* – but UNLIT. (French military vessels and merchant ships always carry lights.) I immediately turned about and took an opposite course, increasing speed to our maximum (8.7 knots in a calm sea), since he might equally have detected me under these conditions. I decided to give up for that night, assuming that the convoy would pass and that, since I had a few days in hand during which I had to wait for *my* operation to come to fruition, there was no hurry to put the agents ashore.

After waiting hove-to in a position some 50 miles south-east of Antibes from 0700 hrs until 1530 hrs (on 20 April), I once again set a course for Antibes.

At around 2100 hrs that day, I was some 20 miles S-E of Cap d'Antibes, or at the edge of territorial waters according to current French claims. *Once again* I had seen the line of lights and, mindful of this and of the previous night's encounter with the unlit patrol boat, I called the agents to a conference. In the end they thought that it would be better to take them back to Gibraltar rather than risk trying to penetrate the line of patrols, which – as I emphasized – was a wholly unusual phenomenon in French waters and was particularly dangerous because of the presence of unlit vessels, which might be noticed too late. I postponed a decision until the following day and withdrew to our former position offshore.

6) *PUTTING THE AGENTS ASHORE.* On the morning of the 21st I worked out a completely different plan for putting the agents ashore: namely, slipping along as close as possible to the shore, on the assumption that the line of patrols was stationed far out at sea (as our experience seemed to bear out), and that there was no way of saturating the coastal stretch with patrols too. Being still uncertain of my degree of deviation, I based the whole plan of our route on the known position of the Camarat lighthouse to the east of Toulon, at which I had to arrive as early as possible (there was little time to make my way from it to Antibes), but security considerations permitted this only at dusk.

On the way – making use of a calm and clear sunset – I determined the degree of error for all the basic courses we needed – and this completely confirmed my guesses as to the degree of deviation. Our deviation amounted to a maximum not of 5° but of 10°. This was further confirmed by our landfall that evening, when the masts of the French naval radio station on Porquerolles in the Hyères Islands near Toulon appeared on our course, instead of the Camarat lighthouse.

The journey to the La-Napoule bay passed off without any incident: a solitary ship was all we saw. At 0115 hrs I entered the bay, where, because there was so little time left before dawn, the agents had agreed to disembark.

The rubber boat was put into the water and, after we had identified a suitable point on the generally very steep shoreline, the passengers were dropped off with their luggage. The landing-place turned out to be none too favourable, being not far from some huts in which, despite the lateness of the hour, we discerned some movement, no doubt because of the fierce barking of a dog. This sound, combined with the song of a nightingale in a nearby wood, created a strange and indescribable impression. What is more, our dinghy missed a passing fishing craft under oars by no more than a whisker. The craft must have been returning from a fishing trip and passed us at a distance of 50 metres, having, without doubt, seen the felucca.

At 0300 hrs I weighed anchor and set a course away from the shore. Then at a distance of some 20 miles from the coast, we set out for Marseilles, where a party of people was to be picked up the next night at a spot that was now familiar to me.

7) *EMBARKATION OF THE FIRST GROUP OF POLES FROM FRANCE.* On 22 April at 2330 hrs – as we had agreed with Lt Roehr – I was at the entrance to the Port-Vau *calanque* and gave the agreed signal. We immediately received a reply coming from the end of that rocky cleft in the shoreline, which was some 900 m. long and on average some 40 m. wide. The water, in these clefts is commonly deep in that region, which meant that I could go in almost to the very end. Accompanied by an oarsman (Gorzelok) I went ashore, where Lt Roehr was already waiting for me with three representatives of the Marseilles evacuation post and 41 other people. It was explained that the party numbered fewer that the 60 expected because of local difficulties. Given the short time available to organise collection, this did not surprise me at all. After discussing the local situation we went on to talk about plans for our next embarkation operation, which, as I emphasised, ought to involve a larger group of people – 60, if the felucca *Seawolf* alone was at our disposal, and this figure could be increased by 100 if it proved possible to secure the 'special operations' vessel I was counting on from our flotilla. Marseilles was to send a signal when they were ready to dispatch the next party (I asked for a date around 9 May) and I had to confirm whether there would be the extra vessel or not. Lt Roehr was to remain in France.

The embarkation process continued during our conference. At 0100 I was already back on the felucca and, after turning about in that narrow *calanque* so that I had my bow facing seawards, I made my exit. Immediately after leaving, we encountered a ship which, to judge by its course, could only have been a patrol boat. Owing to the local conditions it was difficult to give him the slip, but eventually we managed to escape undetected.

8) The return journey passed without any noteworthy events. At noon on the first day, we sighted an aircraft flying from Marseilles. A second followed a few hours later. Also two seaplanes flew low over us on the 22nd when we were passing Toulon at a distance of 30 miles, but at no time did they seem to pay any particular attention to us: indeed this was the very reason I relied on a fishing vessel (felucca) for the evacuations.

The weather in general was not too good and, since most of the people had to remain on deck because of the lack of space below (others because of seasickness), conditions for them were very arduous. Nevertheless they were all in good spirits and after a few days it was evident they were also in good appetite, since, leaving aside other considerations, all of them had eaten very little meat or fat lately in France.

On 27 April at 0830 hrs, 13 days after we had originally weighed anchor at the start of our mission, we entered the port of Gibraltar.

9) *RADIO CONTACT* turned out to be very unsatisfactory. On the day before our departure I was given a radio set (pack set) which did not work because it was lacking a valve. This became evident during tests before we put to sea. I was promised that they would drop a valve to me by aircraft en route but the aircraft could not find us owing to the bad weather and in any case the set was faulty in other respects. Because of this, I transmitted signals during the operation (after having completed particular tasks and after encountering the convoy) on a Polish-type set received from Commander Stoklas, but these, as it later transpired, were too weak and failed to be heard at all from that distance.

I was promised a set in better condition and better radio communications for future operations. Indeed, the receiver on my Polish set had broken down a long time before, but no-one here at Gibraltar was capable of repairing it, therefore we did not even attempt to receive signals.

10) *THE 'MTB' TURNED OUT TO BE . . . A SUBMARINE ON A SPECIAL OPERATION.* This was perhaps the most sensational aspect of this whole operation. When I gave the flotilla commander a report on the operation, the incident with the 'MTB' and the patrols, he informed me that at the time in question a submarine from our local flotilla was carrying out an operation,

and they were due to return in a few days. When the submarine's commander did get back and we exchanged information, it turned out that, on the same day and more or less at the same time, he had sighted a mysterious fishing boat, and what had struck him was that it was NOT BEARING LIGHTS, and that suddenly, as if having sighted him, it had turned about and apparently taken flight . . .

'Perhaps I should have given chase and attempted to disable her, in order to prevent her betraying my presence,' said the operational commander, 'but I was in a hurry myself, since I too had the task of putting agents ashore in that area.'

As it turned out, I had not been informed that one of our submarines was operating there, because it was supposed to have carried out its task *two days before* my operation, and the prospect of delay had not occurred to anyone. As it happened, the storm I encountered near Barcelona on the way to Marseilles had delayed the submarine by a whole 48 hours.

What was also interesting about this episode was that both our positions were imprecise: his was too close to the shore (3 miles) and, in addition, too far north, while mine was too far out (15 miles and, on the second day, 20 miles) because of the deviation error. I had thus assumed that the lights spotted 'not far off' belonged to ships, when in fact they were lights positioned on the high slopes of the shore, as is common in this region. I was all the more certain that they were not shore lights because the La-Garoupe lighthouse was not visible, and normally it would have been unmissable: on each occasion visibility was 25 miles. THE LIGHTS HOWEVER HAD APPARENTLY BEEN EXTINGUISHED NEAR THE ITALIAN FRONTIER and the last working lighthouse in this direction is the Camarat lighthouse near the Hyères Islands.

I requested my flotilla commander to inform me in future if any such operations were planned for the region in which I was engaged, and he agreed unreservedly, adding that he had not allowed for the possibility of such a delay on the part of the submarine.

(signed)
M. Krajewski (Captain)
Gibraltar, 25 May 1942

This episode – in which P42 and *Seawolf* sighted each other proceeding without navigation lights in suspicious circumstances near their respective operational objectives, and, thinking the other to be hostile, took evading action – delayed the landings Krajewski was due to carry out, but Mars, the submarine captain, made his way inshore and Churchill landed his two passengers at Antibes in the early hours of 20 April, as described above. It is the only recorded case of its kind in four years of clandestine operations on French coasts during the Second World War. Ironically enough, this was the very danger that Slocum had invoked as part of his case for letting NID(C) take over the running of such operations in the western Mediterranean, yet it happened just after the new coordinating arrangements he had devised were in place, rather than under the previous free-for-all that he had deplored.

This was the beginning of one of the most intensive and successful phases of clandestine sea-transport operations to wartime France. Marian Krajewski and his colleague Jan Buchowski, backed by the resources of Slocum's 'private navy', were to be its star performers, but it must be remembered that the coast to which they worked was in Vichy France, rather than in German hands. Nevertheless, the distances covered, the overcrowding of the feluccas and the endurance demanded far exceeded anything experienced in operations from the United Kingdom base to the west and north coasts of France.

In the May no-moon period, Krajewski went back to the Côte d'Azur in *Seawolf*, this time accompanied by *Tarana* – an arrangement Krajewski had contemplated using during his operations to Morocco, but which had proved possible only once because of the unreliable physical condition of the back-up ship. His account of Operation MIMOSA was as follows:

REPORT FROM THE THIRTEENTH EVACUATION MISSION (to France, from 5 to 21 May, 1942)[7]

1) *BACKGROUND AND PLAN OF THE OPERATION.* As I informed you in my report of the 12th mission, I came to an agreement with Lt Roehr, during our meeting at Calanque-en-Vau (near Cassis), that a second mission would take place at the beginning of May. They were to supply either 60 people if I was able to secure *Seawolf* alone or at least twice that number if I managed to obtain the use of one of the back-up ships. Our means of communication was to be radio via London, and Marseilles was to indicate if the situation permitted an operation; by way of reply, I was to let them know whether I had a back-up ship at my disposal.

Meanwhile I had made clear during our conference that I anticipated spending a week in port on minor modifications, which our first expedition in the new *Seawolf* had shown to be necessary.

France, however, did not keep to the letter of our Cassis agreement, since on the evening of 4 May I received an urgent telegram from London requiring my presence at the old meeting point to pick up 60 people during the night of 10/11 May.

In other words I HAD LESS THAN A DAY IN WHICH TO GET READY AND SET OUT. Of course, I was presented with a *fait accompli* in terms of the number of people. I aimed, and still aim, to take as many people as possible during such missions, which are long – at least 2,000 miles – and exhausting because of the poor standard of accommodation. Indeed, I had been promised the additional ship and, if the Marseilles outpost had been true to their word and had had the courage to organise a larger group of people, we would have been able to take at least twice as many passengers.

As luck would have it, the authorities here gave me the promised vessel anyway, because they asked me to put a further three agents ashore in southern France and they did not want them to be put at risk during the embarkation. Consequently they agreed to my plan to embark our people, take them to the Spanish–French frontier (one day's sailing) and there transfer them to the stand-by vessel (waiting 30 miles out at sea), collecting the agents at the same time. Indeed, I was going to suggest to the local leaders in France that within a few days they provide me with an additional party of people, for whom I would wait at sea after putting the agents ashore: I would then return with them direct to Gibraltar. The plan was not particularly convenient since it prolonged an already lengthy voyage and exhausted a crew who, after the last two-week mission, had not had the rest in port they deserved, since there was so much work to be done in altering and modifying the boat. I was forced into it however by the action of the Marseilles leadership.

2) *CABLE FROM MAJOR A. CHOJNACKI.* Just as we were making our way back to port after the previous (12th) evacuation mission, I received a cable from the Marseilles post, which altered the background to the mission and made our decision more difficult. The last sentence of this cable stated that the 'French police know about the evacuations and may be hunting him [Krajewski]', in the light of which the author 'requested help'.

What kind of help Major Chojnacki envisaged I have no way of knowing: indeed, I was already in the open sea after taking people on board and was due any moment to leave the danger region. What is more, this is a distance that requires a few days' sailing even for a destroyer. Even if they had sent a warship it would only have met me somewhere near the Balearic Islands. The result was just what I had been trying my best to avoid – to cause the naval authorities here problems by continual requests for help in the form of MLs, aircraft, etc (which in any case had happened enough times in cases of real emergency, such as for example on the little *Dogfish* with its museum-piece engine). The illogicality or irrationality of the telegram was pointed out by the Admiral himself when he called me for a report of the operation ('We didn't really know in what way we could help you,' our great friend declared).

The arrival of this telegram had a direct influence on the operation, because everybody here began to fear that the whole evacuation movement from France was, if not completely buried, at least rendered impossible for a period. We could not understand why a telegram suddenly requested us to come and pick up 60 people 'at the former place'. (Afterwards I understood the situation when one of the men evacuated during the previous mission, asked confidentially how he would explain the means by which the police could have discoved the operation, said, 'It is possible that Major Chojnacki sent that telegram just in case, because he is . . . very careful . . .')

3) We put to sea almost exactly 24 hrs after we received the telegram, which is never advisable because it imposes such haste on the last-minute preparations required for these special operations – things that one can do only when one knows the relevant conditions and the number of people (e.g. for supplies, since the space on a 20-ton felucca is limited and housekeeping must be very economical).

Crew: apart from myself – Petty Officer Siembieda (1st mechanic), Mate Tarnawski (2nd mechanic, newly sent), Seaman Kurzawa (greaser), Mate Zimny (helmsman, newly sent), Leading Seaman (of the Reserve) Chwastek (deck-hand, helmsman), Leading Seaman Stanislawski (radio operator, helm) and Mate Gorzelok as cook and 'handyman'.

So we weighed anchor on 5 May at 2220 hrs – unfortunately in a strong storm, from the east. The first two days were a nightmare, since the majority of the crew (not difficult to reach a majority among seven people!) fell sick. The worst affected however was the mate, Zimny, who, ironically, had been sent to me as chief and mainstay of the deck crew and my next in command. He became so terribly sick that he developed a temperature. Not only was he unable to steer – which others did despite being ill themselves – but I began to be concerned about him. He did not return to health and thus at the first opportunity I transferred him to the other ship, so that he did not continue to occupy a bunk (see below).

This weather lasted until 9 May when we were north of the Balearics. Unfortunately, the compass deviation had apparently again been wrongly plotted by the flotilla navigator, an error that had already convinced me of his incompetence. Luckily the conditions permitted astronomical observations almost every day, and usually I took three, sometimes more. We have an excellent chronometer and sextant too.

A new item on this voyage was the powerful radio receiver (of the British army officers' mess type), so that we had the opportunity not only to check our watches daily but also to hear the news bulletins and thus learn about current political events.

On 9 May, we painted the French colours and a registration number on the ship's side as usual (they had been painted over on our way back to Gibraltar after the previous mission). Then a Spanish aircraft flew over us, which, to judge by its course, was the communication flight between Valencia and Italy.

4) *EMBARKATION OF THE FIRST GROUP (31).* On the night of 10 May we were, in changeable weather conditions, at the entrance to Cassis Bay, where I began to look around for the familiar *calanque* (En-Vau). When we had found it and when the agreed light answered our signals, I entered and steered the felucca to the end of the *calanque*, before going ashore with the mate Gorzelok (0000 hrs on 11 May).

Once ashore we found Lt Roehr already waiting with 31 people. The embarkation began, while I had talks with Roehr and Cavalry Captain Iwaszkiewicz.

It turned out that 30 people had not turned up, as a result of local difficulties, I was told. Whatever the reason, this throws doubt on whether an operation to embark so few people is worthwhile, and not only from the strictly 'commercial' point of view: the risk to the 11 people involved in the operation and the enormous efforts of the crew must also be taken into account. Nor was the outlook in France much happier for clandestine evacuation by sea, according to a report by Lt Roehr. As a result, he anticipated being forced to leave with that same party. My plan, which depended on having someone in France who had experience of sea evacuations, lay in ruins.

All the more determined, in the light of the small party prepared for me, not to return to Gibraltar after putting the agents ashore, I asked Captain Iwaszkiewicz to have the next party ready for me in a few days' time. We decided to make it the night of 16/17 May and to choose a completely new location, namely by the Faraman lighthouse (at the mouth of the Rhône).

At 0115 we weighed anchor and set a course for the rendezvous with the ship.

5) *TRANSFER OF THE PASSENGERS.* The meeting with my colleague from the special flotilla had a particular significance. Since it was taking place at a considerable distance from the shore, it was a delicate operation not only from the point of view of the means of carrying out the transfer (which depended on the weather) but also in that it was to be something of a test of navigation. If we failed to meet, it would of course have been said that the *Seawolf* was in the wrong position. I had the feeling during our briefing that this test greatly intrigued everybody who was there; whether or not we succeeded in this mission might have a greater impact on our chances of obtaining this ship in future than at first appeared. So it was with the greatest care and effort that I took astronomical sights (luckily the sun, which that day had shown great reluctance to appear, came out from behind the clouds). The compass deviation, even after it had been defined, required repeated checking on a westerly course, because of the difficult conditions off Toulon under which I had swung the ship's compass.

It turned out that these astronomical observations rescued the situation for us, or at least saved us several hours' time and our reputation. After obtaining one position line and a noon latitude sight I discovered that I was 14 miles to the south-east of our meeting point (1255 hrs). I still had two hours before our rendezvous, so our honour was saved when, at 1425 precisely, we caught sight of the ship also steaming from the south. (In fact, rather more than saved, because in the Flotilla they talk about the *Seawolf* being accurate to the nearest mile, which makes pleasant hearing to Polish ears: our [British] hosts regard themselves as mariners without peer.)

The transfer took place without incident, other than an aircraft alert, during which the ship's captain asked me if I would hold away from his side while it lasted. It turned out – and the agents we took on board confirm this – that the ship's captain was a little edgy, after having apparently been tracked by aircraft earlier. Truth to tell, however, we could not make out the aircraft and after a further five minutes we came alongside again and completed the operation. Together with the 31 passengers I transferred the mate, Zimny, not only because he had requested it, but because I had come to the conclusion that he was no use at all to me at sea and was only taking up a bunk. We also transferred Lt Roehr but I kept behind Lt Biczysko in case the embarkation of the next party in a week's time became complicated and it was necessary to put someone ashore, which in fact proved to be the case.

All in all therefore the trans-shipment did not take more than ten minutes (the weather helped), after which the ship set course back to Gibraltar, where it arrived three days later; I however, turned to the east again, towards the Antibes region, where I had to put the agents ashore.

6) *PUTTING THE AGENTS ASHORE ... AND OTHER ADVENTURES.* En route to the pinpoint there were no note-worthy events. We met only two steamers, which I always try to avoid in such a way as not to draw attention and not to let them get a close look at us. At present one does not see any fishermen along the French coast – mainly through lack of fuel – except for those in rowing boats and these are no more than a kilometre from the shore, and usually close to some centre of settlement; this sad inactivity holds sway as a symptom of the war in these doubtless once busy waters.

At sunset (2005 hrs) Camarat – the last lighthouse lit to the east of Toulon – was visible. From there I started to move along level with the shore, at a distance, to start with, of about 5 km. Visibility however grew worse. After a few hours I was not even sure of my own position since even the bearings I had taken from the lighthouse, some 20 miles distant from the disembarkation point, were out because of the degree of compass error, which again amounted to 10°. At 2320 hrs on 12 May I arrived, or thought I did, at the spot and ordered the log line to be hauled aboard, since we would shortly have to undertake manoeuvres in a small bay.

However, I soon began to have doubts about whether it was the right bay. I had never been in it myself before and there were certain indications that the next bay might be the one; we could see it, apparently not far off.

Unfortunately, after moving in that direction for an hour, I realised that I still had a long journey before me, and that I had probably passed the right spot. In order to recognise the place, however, I had to travel further on.

At 0130 hrs (on 13 May) we entered a bay, which I was already almost certain was not the right one. Before putting the agents ashore in the dinghy, I therefore told them frankly that the location was uncertain and asked whether it made any difference to them if it was e.g. Villefranche. Seeing their hesitation, I added that we had enough time to put the operation off until the following day, since we no longer had enough time to continue that night and dawn comes at about 0430 hrs. As a result, we exited the bay, becoming aware for the first time of the critical nature of our situation, since at the narrow entrance of the bay a number of fishermen were attempting to catch fish by dazzling them, which meant illuminating everything around them and creating almost an enclosure of spotlights.

At 0700 hrs we were again, as during the previous voyage, hove-to some 40 miles to the south-west of the Cannes region, half-way between Corsica and France.

Having thoroughly considered the events of the previous night, I had no doubts at all that the spot in which I had eventually ended up was the Anse-de-Canton Bay, in other words . . . MONACO, and I had anchored just alongside the marine observatory. The fact that I had been a significant distance from the frontier (around 6 miles, or an hour's sailing even for me) and 15 miles from the spot I was aiming for was evidence that the Italian armistice commission's request for the French authorities to switch off the lighthouses in the frontier region had not been a wasted gesture.

After fixing my position during the day and working out a course, I moved off again (1230 hrs) in the direction of the Camarat lighthouse.

At 2320 hrs we were already in the right bay (i.e. Antibes), where we again had to pass by the line of fishermen. Under normal conditions they must have seen me, but I assume that with this kind of fishing (using lights to dazzle the fish) they themselves must be dazzled to a certain degree.

At 2350 hrs the disembarkation was completed, we then hoisted the dinghy back on board and set a course that would distance us from the shore.

After waiting a further 24 hours, during which I established the degree of compass error (again very large and, on westerly courses, 12° not 0°, as the flotilla navigator had entered on the deviation table), I set a course to the west, towards the Marseilles region.

7) *THE CHASE.* The new embarkation point was some 30 miles west of Marseilles at the mouth of the River Rhône, near the Faraman lighthouse. My intention was to approach the shore in daylight and reconnoitre, since the shoreline in that area is flat and very monotonous.

At around 1530 hrs, when we were some 18 miles south of the mouth of the Rhône and 25 miles to the south-west of Marseilles, I made out a small steamer on the horizon, on our port side. I was following a course of 300°. In order not to approach too close and fearing that it might be a patrol boat, I changed course to starboard to 320° (I could not turn too far since I was in any case heading in the direction of land). The closer the boat approached, the more it resembled a patrol boat or a small boat of the trawler type converted into a small trading vessel, displacement around 200 tons.

He did not seem to be paying any attention to me for the

moment but I watched him closely through my binoculars so as not to be caught out. When, however, he was level with me ('abeam') he suddenly altered *course towards me* and raised steam, as I concluded from the increased volume of smoke (coal-fired boiler) that he emitted, a characteristic effect of throwing more coal into the furnace. Just before this happened, a second patrol boat appeared, similar to the first, and began to behave in a similar manner. Having no longer any doubts as to their identity, I increased our speed to 'maximum', which produced (with the dinghy on the tow-line) 8.7 knots, as measured with my stop-watch. After a short while the patrol boats changed to a course that was parallel with mine (having reversed through 180° from their previous course), evidently realising that their route would be lengthened if they went *courbe de chien*, i.e. bow pointed towards me, instead of in front of me.

The situation was not at all pleasant, since it was only reasonable to expect that they had a speed advantage over me, and, furthermore, there were still more than five hours (!) to go until darkness, or rather until sunset. Worse, because of the proximity of the shore, the *Seawolf* would meanwhile have to change course *in their direction*. Accordingly I ordered that all our arms be prepared (pistols, machine-pistol, grenades) as well as radio codes, etc and the detailed maps of the French coast – everything to be loaded into one bag to be sunk on my order. I checked too that the crew remembered my instructions on how to conduct themselves if we were taken prisoner.

In the midst of this predicament, yet another patrol boat appeared, this time off the starboard bow, and sailed as though intending to cut me off. Certain that they would get us this time ('He who is to hang will not drown,' one of the crew called out jokingly at this point), I gradually changed course to 250° (at 1635 hrs). I now had pursuers abeam on both sides, the first group having fallen back a little, and the race continued. The course this time was more favourable since it led to the open sea and almost to the French–Spanish border.

After an hour I realised to my considerable surprise, and indeed contentment, that they were evidently dropping behind us. In fact, at 1800 hrs, in order not to move too far away and make myself late for the rendezvous – since leaving people until daylight would have been a catastrophe – I stopped the engine. Half an hour later, I set a course of 340°, with the aim of closing in to the coast. When I saw a patrol boat again (1915 hrs), I again took a course of 250°: I already felt more certain of the situation, since from the point of view of speed I had now tested them, and the sun would set in a little more than an hour.

At 2000 hrs we set a course for the Beauduc lighthouse, not far from Faraman.

8) *THE ACCIDENTAL DISCOVERY OF PEOPLE FOR EMBAR-KATION*. The new pinpoint appeared unsuitable from the very moment we approached it; it was certainly a beach, but with a very shallow level of descent, so that even the *Seawolf* (draught 1.8 m.), had to be anchored some 600 m. away. Indeed, if it had not been for the very calm sea that night, there could have been no thought of bringing people on board by the dinghy, nor – because of the distance – by the technique used during the African evacuations in the 'Atlantic breakers', i.e. with the life-raft on a line.

What was worse, however, was that *no-one* replied to our pre-arranged signals (2330 hrs). Because of this I sent Lt Biczysko ashore in the rubber dinghy, since he knew this region well, and I even requested him, if need be, to make his way to the Polish 'work brigade' based some 7 km. away, from which our evacuation party was, at least partly, to be recruited. Also – most important – Capt Iwaszkiewicz, with whom I had arranged a meeting, came from this detail.

We received the agreed signal unexpectedly early: the dinghy was sent out and brought back (0115 hrs) ten people. Lt Biczysko explained the mystery: it seemed that the people had been waiting two kilometres away and on seeing our signal had thought it was a lighthouse . . . (This is why I made efforts to have someone in France who is familiar with our procedures.)

Happily everything ended well and at 0205 hrs we weighed anchor and set a course for the Balearic Islands.

Our return did not pass off without one more encounter with the patrol boats. At dawn, directly ahead of us, and at the exact edge of the 20-mile territorial waters, I saw the lights of a ship. I went past him by making a turn to starboard of 50° (0440 hrs) but he barely remained on the port beam and I had returned to our old course when a second boat appeared, again to starboard (0515 hrs). Since it was already light, I had no doubts whatsoever that this was a patrol boat similar to the one we had seen the day before, if not the very same one. On this occasion, however, they showed no inclination to intervene, possibly because at that time almost everybody on board was asleep (they were moving very slowly). Thus at 0655 hrs, having a clear horizon in every direction, we were able to return to our old course.

At 1030 hrs excellent visibility allowed us to sight the high cliffs of the Spanish–French frontier region. The weather was very good for almost the entire voyage, which was especially useful in view of our 36 passengers, most of whom had to spend the journey on deck in any case.

On 19 May a favourable wind even enabled us to use our sails in order to spare the engine, and of course to economise on fuel.

On 21 May at 0100 hrs we entered the port of Gibraltar, having covered our route in the record time of four days, instead of the usual five.

9) *RADIO COMMUNICATIONS* were not at all satisfactory on this occasion either. None of our signals was received when we transmitted from the French coast (the transmitter was of the British 'Pack-set' type, strength 40 watts).

Our signals were first picked up when we had reached Barcelona and then with a strength level of only '1' (one), in other words very faintly. We too heard them at the same strength, since, as it turns out, that organisation has no transmitter on shore that is any stronger than ours (40 watts).

Indeed, proper communication was not established until we were south of the Balearic Islands. Near Barcelona we could hear only intermittently.

The reasons most probably lie both on the technical and the personnel side. My radio operator maintains that the people on land 'do not apply themselves' to getting hold of signals that are sent on the short wave by weak transmitters; if so, they will certainly miss ours, which are always in that category. This is an unacceptable state of affairs.

Indeed, the transmitter on land ought to be more powerful. I know that a stronger one is to be installed soon.

It is very likely too that the direction is very difficult because of geography, specifically because of the line of very high mountains on the track (through Spain). I know that from the Iberian peninsula there are greater difficulties in making contact on short wave with southern France than with London.

In the light of all this, it seems to me desirable in future operations of this type (southern France) to employ a stronger radio receiver of at least 50 watts, if not 100 watts. Even short-wave amateurs used this strength before the war . . .

10) *DISTINCTIONS.* Lt Biczysko distinguished himself during the operation, not only by volunteering to go ashore when the situation became complicated (which he settled most effectively) but also by acting almost as a member of the crew, as a result of which it was possible to use the crew for more specialised tasks.

Also worthy of note for his courageous and efficient execution of all landing tasks, associated as they are with the risk of arrest – Ernest Gorzelok.

Leading Seaman Chwastek demonstrated that he is currently the mainstay of my reduced deck crew.

M. Krajewski
(Naval) Captain
Gibraltar, 27 May 1942

On 17 May Lt Jankanty Roehr submitted a written report to Krajewski on his mission to France.[8] It throws interesting light on the prevailing conditions and the problems with which he had had to contend.

In preparation for his mission, he had written on 2 March to Commander Stoklas in London via British naval channels, forwarding samples of the identity documents that he would need. Stoklas replied by telegram, received on 25 March, that the matter was in hand but it would take between one and three weeks to produce them.

On 17 March Roehr had written to Midshipman Chciuk in France indicating, in terms that only Chciuk would understand, the place and date of a meeting between them. The date proposed was 18 April or one of the immediately following days. Roehr was working on the assumption that his identity documents would arrive in Gibraltar by 14 April, the date on which the felucca would have to sail. Allowing time for sending messages and mail to and from London, this left four full weeks for preparing the documents.

Chciuk confirmed by telegram on 4 April that he had received the letter designating their place and time of meeting.

On 11 April a telegram arrived from London stating, 'Impossible to send documents for Roehr earlier. Would draw your attention to the fact that Roehr must be supplied with French ration cards and also coupons.' This telegram made clear neither when he could count on receipt of the documents (they had still not turned up at the time he wrote more than a month later) nor who was supposed to provide him with ration cards. Perhaps they expected Gibraltar to do this?

Roehr decided to give up counting on any concrete help from London and to land without any documents, so as not to postpone indefinitely the beginning of evacuation from France.

He landed in France at 0100 hrs on 18 April at the agreed place, where he met Chciuk, with whom he made his way into Marseilles. Establishing contact with Major Chojnacki took the whole of the following day since the code name 'Hugo', given by London, was not known by anybody in the Marseilles area (Major Chojnacki seemed proud of this). Moreover, no-one at the British Hospital, which was being used by the Poles, knew an address for Chojnacki (who seemed proud of this too).

The search through various intermediaries for Chojnacki alerted a considerable number of people to Roehr's arrival. Moreover, London had apparently given Marseilles his real name as early as January in anticipation of his arrival. This equally did not help to keep the whole operation secret. It would have been possible to avoid this situation by simply giving Roehr Chojnacki's private address.

Having finally located Chojnacki on 20 April, he made his way to Lt Col Ejsymont, to whom he explained that the first group of around 60 had to be embarked on the night of 22/23 April and of whom he requested that some people be allocated to help with the arrangements.

Roehr repeated the instructions from the Commander-in-Chief's headquarters that priority be given to the evacuation of NCOs and other ranks; that not more than 5% should be officers; and that these officers should be of junior rank and not more than 30 years old. Priority was to be given to armoured-warfare specialists, R/T operators and airmen. Ejsymont and Chojnacki confirmed that they were familiar with this order, but that they were not observing it completely. In the light of this, Roehr made it clear that, since he had no say in the selection of evacuees, he would not assume any responsibility if any did not fit these criteria.

In a car rented from some friendly Frenchmen, Roehr took some helpers to show them the routes by which the evacuees were to be taken to the embarkation point and how they were to be moved. Along the journey into Marseilles and from Marseilles to the rendezvous, no-one had his documents checked. All of them had legal safe conducts in any case. Subsequently 41 people had been embarked efficiently at the pre-arranged place and time: it had not been observed from the landward side.

Roehr himself still had no documents at this point, but on the morning after the evacuation (23 April), he received from the French authorities, on the basis of a declaration by the Polish military office in Marseilles, a document directing him to be demobilised at Auch as a refugee from German captivity, which he had indeed been in September 1939.

At noon the same day Major Chojnacki informed Roehr that he had sent London a telegram reporting that 41 people had been evacuated at Cassis (which was not in fact the pinpoint). The operation had come to the attention of the police, who might look for them. He demanded immediate help for the ship from the British. Roehr asked what proof he had for this and Chojnacki replied that the police had been at the English Hospital asking for Major Szydlowski (who had left) and at the Villa La Ravelle, where they had asked for Captain Szulc (who had also left). He further alleged that the whole of the Polish community in Marseilles and especially those at the British Hospital, were abuzz and talking of leaving. There were French informers and the whole evacuation operation had been compromised. Roehr should disappear for a time because everybody knew he was organising sea evacuation operations.

Roehr replied that his information convinced him that he should keep out of sight for the next few days only, which fitted in with his plans to be demobilised at Auch. For his return from Auch in 3–4 days, he asked Chojnacki to prepare answers to two questions:

(i) Could Chojnacki organise the escape of people from the work details in such a way as to concentrate at various points on the coast, which he would indicate, parties of around 60 people every 48 hours?

(ii) Could Chojnacki prepare a first group of around 60 people for 10 May to be embarked at the previous place (Marseilles would serve as departure point)?

Decisions would be needed on these two points about 1 May. If plan (i) came off, Roehr would need to inform Krajewski at a reasonably early stage of the numbers and the dates of embarkation so that he could organise the transfer of people at sea to a British vessel.

Roehr went to Auch, where, with the help of Captain Oscar Ejsymont, he was demobilised under a false name as an escaped prisoner of war of 1939 vintage. The documents he received enabled him to remain legally in the Marseilles area. Travel beyond the Marseilles area was still legally prohibited but if one were caught in a document check the consequences would not be too severe. He returned to Marseilles on 28 April but found Chojnacki was away. Eventually on 2 May, he had a meeting with Chojnacki, at which Lt Col Ejsymont and Captain Ejsymont were present. Roehr was told that there had been no confirmation that the French authorities had discovered the evacuation plan and people had been needlessly alarmed that it may have been compromised. At present it was not possible to bring parties of 60 to the coast every 48 hours, but a group of about that size could be made available for 10 May at Marseilles.

Roehr then asked for new helpers and for a telegram to be sent to Krajewski calling on him to come and take off these people on the night of 10/11 May. It was agreed that on this occasion nobody from the Marseilles area should be included in the evacuation, the better to maintain security; it was also agreed that Roehr and Iwaszkiewiez should go down to the Salins-de-Girod on 5 May to see whether it would be possible to carry out an evacuation from that area (the place was found suitable from the landward side and an embarkation took place from it on 16/17 May).

On the next day, 3 May, Major Chojnacki came to see Roehr at noon and told him that, after considering new elements, he had sent the telegram but had added his own suggestion that, because of a renewed risk of discovery of the whole operation (the French authorities were on their tracks and had already arrested the brother of Midshipman Chciuk), sea evacuation be suspended until further notice. On 4 May, Major Chojnacki nevertheless declared that everything was in order and demanded confirmation that Krajewski would arrive on the night of 10/11 May!

With Captain Ejsymont, who had been allocated to help him, Roehr checked out the new approach routes. Of the 60 people promised only 29 materialised, although there had been more than enough time to organise the operation. They argued that one of the work-detail companies had been broken up and they had decided to reduce the number and so lower the risk of discovery.

The journey from Marseilles and visit to the embarkation point took place without any difficulty. As on the previous occasion, there was no check of identity documents on the way over: the routes and the pinpoint were not 'blown'. Patrolling of the shore from the landward side and of coastal waters from seaward simply did not exist, as Roehr's observations showed and Captain Krajewski confirmed. Nevertheless, Lt Roehr acceded to Major Chojnacki's demand that he leave because his activities were too widely known, and embarked on 11 May himself. Before he left he agreed with Chojnacki and Iwaszkiewicz details of how pinpoints should be chosen from both land and sea points of view, recognition signals, techniques of embarkation, telegraphic codes, etc. The embarkation on 16/17 May was to be carried out by Captain Iwaszkiewicz near the Salins-de-Girod: about 20 people were to be involved.

On 11 May, Krajewski transferred 29 evacuees, Roehr himself and Zimny (Mate) from the felucca to a British ship at sea. On arrival at Gibraltar, the following signal was sent to Stoklas: 'Roehr with 29 men arrived safely. K. should be back next week with approximately 20 men . . . Officers in France too talkative so Roehr suggests London orders France cease evacuation of officers only for two months. Evacuation should be carried out for other ranks only. K. sends back Zimny unfit for job . . . '.

On 28 May Krajewski forwarded Roehr's report to Mally, with a copy to Stoklas, Naval Attaché at the Polish Embassy in London. At the same time he said that, in spite of the positive results achieved, for which they should thank Roehr, he would assess the effectiveness of the April to May operations at about 50%: twice as many people should have been evacuated.[9] The organisation in France was weak and officers were talking too much. The French knew what was going on: the most up-to-date information on this subject was a report handed to them by Iwaszkiewicz at Faraman on 17 May. A French officer, in confidence, had shown the Polish officers of a work company at the Salins-de-Girod a warning from the authorities at Marseilles that in the Toulon district a group of Poles and their officers had made off to sea. The dates quoted coincided quite closely, if not exactly, with the first embarkation.

Indeed, Krajewski continued, evacuation by sea could not be continued with parties of 30–40 people as Marseilles seemed to contemplate, since it was highly uneconomic, not only from the viewpoint of expense but also taking into account the risks faced by the whole crew of the felucca in such difficult conditions. On each occasion they had to undertake a voyage of not less than 2,000 miles, or almost the distance to America. Also, they might well have difficulties sooner or later from the British side, who periodically cast envious eyes on the Poles' successes and who might argue, adducing the small numbers the Poles were bringing back, that their own operations were more important and that they needed the felucca.

Krajewski, indeed, had had enough. Having worked through the load of correspondence that faced him on return from his 13th evacuation mission, he wrote to Mally as follows on 25 May:[10]

8) *MY TRANSFER FROM GIBRALTAR.* Enclosed, amidst a whole pile of correspondence (it is a lot to send at once, but when do I have time to write except in port? – and there are so many matters to be seen to), there is one that may come as a surprise to you: my request to the Chief of Staff to transfer me from Gibraltar and to appoint another naval officer to my post.

The request I have submitted to the C-in-C's Chief of Staff is of course dry and formal, it cannot be anything else. You will be aware however of other, more understandable reasons – or rather, not only reasons, though the reasons are real – and . . . of my decision.

I am already exhausted both mentally and even physically with this treadmill and this drudgery for well over a year. Not only do I have too few people to help me, on the one hand, but on the other there are many who are willing to put spokes in one's wheel. I have quite simply exhausted the fervour that allowed me to achieve things last year that I would perhaps not be capable of today. It is perhaps not completely irrelevant that I have not had a holiday for a very long time, although I must emphasise, Commander, that I am not here asking for a holiday, because after all at Gibraltar there can be no thought of a holiday. I HAVE ALREADY REACHED THE STAGE WHERE I NEED A CHANGE.

I wanted very much to begin the evacuations from France, and I had placed a good deal of hope in them; they are progressing, perhaps even well, although not as I had wanted and had the right to expect. The leaders over there were not up to the task of organisation and the operation had even been penetrated to a certain extent. This was what struck me when – after a nightmare of a journey, during which I observed the efforts, dedication and COURAGE of the crew – I discovered that they had prepared 30 people for me. And then, when I had to return and expose myself to the comments of our various envious competitors at the base, I realised that . . . it was not worth it. Luckily, Capt Iwaszkiewicz agreed to have a second party ready in a week's time.

Or that telegram of Major Chojnacki's 'just in case'.

So – passing over my desire to return to the fleet, which I regard as a kind of self-indulgence at a time when I cannot withdraw without interrupting the evacuation programme – I most earnestly request you to intercede with the naval commander (Adm. Swirski) for him to pull me out, and to do it *now*, since I have delayed this decision for a long time (if I may recall my conversation with you last October). I understand that HQ may not agree, since they would always prefer to avoid the risks inherent in change. But in all honesty, *I can continue no longer.* The situation here is complicated even from angles that you would never imagine; certain British institutions place obstacles in each other's way and . . . one of them becomes irritated when I associate with another in my complicated role as both head of the Polish mission and at the same time head of the evacuation post. I do not want to give any examples, because of the Censor, but there will be opportunities later. As it turns out, I have managed so far to remain on good terms with everyone, even though on occasion I have had to defend our interests in a forthright manner and intervene most forcefully – but it is all very tiring.

[The letter finishes with a recommendation that Sub Lt Gromnicki be promoted; also a written note thanking Stoklas for sorting out so many matters for him.]

(signed)
M. Krajewski

Krajewski also enclosed a formal request for a transfer:

Lt Comm Marian KADULSKI (Krajewski) Evacuation Outpost Gibraltar

> To: The C-in-C's Chief of Staff
> *in London*

28 May 1942

Request for release from present post[11]

1. Since it will soon be 18 months since I was transferred from
shipboard duties to evacuation work – I request that you release
me from my post as head of the Polish Naval Mission at
Gibraltar.

2. My hope is to return to service on Polish warships, with
which I have completely lost contact since the time I was put
at the disposal of the C-in-C's headquarters (that is, since
December 1940).

3. I submit my request in the firm knowledge that today the
situation of the mission here is on such a firm footing that
changes in its command can take place without adversely
affecting its work. Furthermore I submit this request in the
knowledge that I have spent at this difficult outpost a period
of such length that even British officers would in similar circumstances receive a transfer.

4. The main task of this outpost is currently the evacuation
from southern France, the project which, while still experimental (sending a felucca a distance of 800 nautical miles), I
proposed in my letter of 10 November 1941. This plan has
now been successfully put into effect, as is proved by the first
two missions in April and May this year, during which 106
people in total were evacuated and some 4,220 nautical miles
were covered. The carrying capacity on this route could have
been even greater, were it not for an excessive caution on the
part of our evacuation leaders in France, who have observed
already so many attempts at evacuation by sea, of which literally
all in the course of the preceeding two years were unsuccessful.

5. This plan is now in a further stage of realisation, since a third
mission to France is now being prepared (departure set for some
time during the first ten days of June). I must however emphasise
that in any case this is a plan intended to continue for at least
one year; in other words, if I received orders to see it through to
the end, this would mean that I would be cut off completely
from the ranks of Polish navy officers and I would become a
specialist in an area which does not have a great deal in
common with the career of a naval officer.

6. The reasons that have led me to choose this moment to submit this request are, in addition, the gradual changes that have occurred at Gibraltar and the establishment of settled conditions, such that today any suitably chosen officer of the Polish navy could carry out the evacuation plan, since:

(a) we currently have a felucca whose thorough overhaul and fitting with a new engine lasted, thanks to local difficulties, more than nine months, but which has shown itself to be splendid for these duties and for which the expenses are now bearing fruit, since this felucca is capable of undertaking missions almost without a break;

(b) on technical–nautical grounds (repairs, supplies and equipment, etc), we are now dependent upon the local submarine base, and our felucca is released for an operation in almost the same way as their own regular warships. During the first phase, certainly, too many things depended upon the personal relationships established by the head of the mission, which would have meant, in the event of his replacement, that a newly dispatched officer would have to begin the evacuation work by . . . establishing good relationships and achieving a sound reputation among the (unfortunately numerous) authoritative agencies here;

(c) we have a crew from the navy which has been trained in the specific techniques of these difficult operations;

(d) we have an established operational practice for using feluccas; equipping them; embarking passengers in difficult conditions, etc), which has been worked on and is effective to such an extent that on a number of occasions the authorities here seek to benefit from our experience;

(e) it is not without significance that we, as Poles at this base, enjoy considerable moral credit and an excellent reputation, which is expressed from time to time in confidences that are overheard: 'Only the Poles are doing something . . . ' or 'The Poles are achieving things that we have not yet managed . . . '. Such prestige will strengthen the situation of the new head of the mission and will facilitate his adjustment at this base from the outset.

7. As my replacement in the position of head of the naval evacuation mission, I would suggest some young officer, a lieutenant commander or lieutenant.

8. I would also like to report that it is essential in the future (now even to a greater extent than heretofore) that the commander of the evacuation outpost here should be a post independent from that of head of the mission. I am concerned to ensure that the commander of the evacuation outpost here

(who is also captain of the felucca, and as such has his hands full) should be relieved of such matters as contacts with military authorities with regard to the payment of our people, their quartering, disciplinary problems, etc. There is also to be considered the question of the welfare of what is sometimes a large number of Polish troops at Gibraltar, looking after them during their long stay here, discipline, etc. During the evacuation campaign, the number of our troops easily reaches 100 people.

(signed)
M. Krajewski

(copied to: Senior Commander of the Polish Navy)

Having fired these salvos Krajewski set about organising his 14th evacuation mission – the June no-moon-period voyage to the Côte d'Azur. It required a good deal of planning since, in addition to his own monthly evacuation, he had undertaken to do four further operations for SOE and MI9 and those for MI9 had to take place at a fixed date.

On the day before he was due to sail in *Seawolf*, a cable arrived from Stoklas announcing that he was arriving soon, presumably prompted by Krajewski's application for a transfer.[12] It was then far too late to change his plans, so he had to leave others to deal with the visitor from London.

Krajewski's report on this mission was as follows:

SECRET

REPORT OF THE FOURTEENTH EVACUATION MISSION
(to Southern France; from 4 to 19 June 1942)[13]

1) *BASIS OF THE MISSION.* This was to have been one of the normal, periodic missions to France. The situation in France, although not altogether satisfactory, did not give us any reason to suspect that the *details* of the evacuation action, such as embarkation point, dates, type of vessel, etc, had been discovered. Unfortunately general information about the evacuation was already in the hands of the French authorities . . .

We waited for a favourable period of the moon and also to complete certain small repairs and improvements on the felucca before setting out.

The first date suggested by the Marseilles outpost in a cable handed me by the Polish Naval Attaché in London was 8 June at 0000 hrs.

I could not accept this date however because of a previously arranged pick-up of agents and war materials for the local British authorities (for 15 June, 0000 hrs). This did not allow me to move earlier, since it would have meant that the felucca had to wait unnecessarily for several days longer (according to the plan worked out, it already had to wait five days between picking up the first group and the second).

So on this basis I had the following cable sent by the Admiralty here on the evening of 30 May:

URGENT. TOP SECRET. FROM VACNA to ADMIRALTY

From Polish Mission to Polish Naval Attaché

Your ref: 1712 B/38/5

1) For HUGO
   a) intention is to take 80 (repeat 80) people from EN-VAU (repeat EN-VAU) during the night of 9/10 June.
   b) please prepare discreetly the next party of 60 (repeat 60) people on the night of 14/15 June.
   c) in the event of unforeseen difficulties on either side, all of these dates will be moved back automatically by 24 hours. (END HUGO)

2. Please emphasise to HUGO the necessity of making sure that the required numbers are available.

3. Regarding point a) – I propose that it be recommended to him that the party be split into two groups. The groups should arrive at the embarkation point each on a different night, with the proviso that they should be ready to be taken off on the night of 9/10 June. I suggest that a similar plan be adopted for the evacuation party due to leave on 14/15 June.

4. I intend to weigh anchor on the evening of 4 June.

2) It is true that the above cable shifted the pick-up date by two days, but on the other hand it gave ten days for a) the information to reach our authorities in London; b) to reach the Marseilles outpost; c) preparations in France to be set in motion.

Additional tasks that had to be carried out – during this mission – similar to those accomplished during both the previous missions for the British authorities – were:

a) to put ashore three agents in two separate places to the east of Toulon (the Cannes–Antibes region).
b) to pick up around three agents and bring them to Gibraltar or else to transfer them to a back-up ship together with some war material.

It was up to me to determine the pick-up point for the agents: since it had to be in the Marseilles region (luckily), I chose Port-

Miou, which was familiar to me from the first mission to France. I did not wish to designate En-Vau on principle (so as not to deliver the Polish embarkation points into unknown hands). In fact, Port-Miou was not really suitable for taking aboard whole groups of people because of the number of buildings in the area, but for three people it seemed safe enough.

3) On the day before our departure (3 June) I received a cable from London announcing the imminent arrival of Commander Stoklas as Gibraltar. I realised that unfortunately I would be weighing anchor before he arrived, since there was no way of postponing our departure, owing to the meeting times already agreed.

4) *THE WEIGHING OF ANCHOR* took place on 4 June at 2230 hrs. To the last minute the coupler was being finished off, which isolated the dynamo while the radio was being used, since a sparking of the brushes, unavoidable in such a small dynamo, would have rendered even the most basic reception virtually impossible.

In fact, half an hour after weighing anchor the coupler began to burn and we were forced to return to our . . . earlier situation, that is . . . turning off the engine completely whenever we made attempts to contact Gibraltar. Of course I had to limit these to less than the necessary minimum since each attempt took at least half an hour.

Composition of the crew: Krajewski – captain; Siembieda – 1st mechanic; Mate Tarnawski – 2nd mechanic; Mate Gorzelok – cook and in charge of the dinghy in 'alarm manoeuvres'; Leading Seaman Stanislawski – radio operator and watch helmsman; Leading Seaman (Reserve) Chwastek – watch helmsman and deck-hand. Seaman Kurzawa remained behind at base. He had fallen ill with some stomach complaint the day before we left and had been taken to the infirmary (he has made a full recovery).

Unfortunately, as has recently become almost a tradition, the weather on the day of our departure was stormy and the wind coming from the east made the first few days of our voyage very difficult. Once again the majority of the crew suffered from seasickness to a greater or lesser degree; water was leaking in everywhere; cooking was impossible; nor did these conditions prove favourable to astronomical observations. Our speed was noticeably reduced (5 knots).

The weather did not improve until 7 June and this lasted through the next day; however, this short period of settled weather had to suffice until the end of the voyage. I must say that in this regard the voyage was exceptionally difficult, more so even than that in April, in spite of the better time of year.

After midday on 7 June we passed between Ibiza and Majorca (Balearics).

The only vessels we encountered – there were no aircraft sighted - were two small schooners near Majorca and, on the 8th at the level of Cape St Sebastian, a steamer of some 10,000 tons moving on a southerly course.

In spite of the bad weather, we arrived at the French coast very early, so that, on 9 June at 0730 hrs, I stopped the engine and waited hove-to at a distance of some 40 km. to the south of La Ciotat.

5) *ARRESTS.* At 1700 hrs I moved in the direction of Cassis, adjusting my speed so as not to be nearer than ten miles to those high shores at dusk. The short night at this time of year meant that we could not afford to wait until it had grown completely dark.

At 23.10 hrs I was situated at the entrance to the En-Vau *calanque.* In reply to our recognition signals – sent out as usual at the *entrance* to this narrow (around 40 m.) rocky gorge, with cliffs some 50 m. high and altogether about a kilometre in length – there came a reply – BUT NOT THE CORRECT ONE (a white light instead of blue). I decided nevertheless to enter, since circumstances indicated that the wrong signal may have been given because of technical difficulties rather than because the authorities had discovered the plan.

It took us a whole hour to turn around so that our bow was pointing towards the entrance and then to anchor, the conditions were so unfavourable (rocky bottom, and the anchor would not hold; strong wind and a swell *along* the *calanque,* which in that narrow space made the manoeuvres very risky indeed).

At 0045 hrs the raft we had sent out returned with Gorzelok and Stanislawski, bringing however only three people and the news of the arrests – or dispersal – of our group in the area of the embarkation point – that afternoon. In the light of this I immediately weighed anchor and left the *calanque,* leaving more exhaustive enquiries until later.

At 0100 hrs our course was for the agreed meeting spot with the back-up ship, which was to have taken off the expected party of 80 people.

The situation ashore was, in spite of everything, unclear, since it turned out that a group of 82 people had waited three days, having expected my arrival from the first day (in other words from 7/8 June). Not surprisingly, such a concentration of people eventually led to their being discovered by a forester, and they dispersed because: a) people were not aware that I had announced I would arrive on the night of 9/10; after being shot at, they lacked the determination and will to remain in the area until the evening, as had happened with three previous embarkations; b) the manner in which the people were concealed left, it seems, much to be desired, since they had no instructions as to what they should do in particular cases where complications might arise; c) discipline too was not at the level it should have been, since people went to Cassis (small village) for water, etc.

Knowing Major Chojnacki ('Hugo') from the accounts of others, I assumed that after these arrests he would immediately suspend all evacuation moves and certainly the embarkation arranged for 14/15 June.

6) *THE PLAN TO PUT ASHORE A COURIER.* Knowing the French as I do, I did not assume that their level of watchfulness would be increased too greatly, and wanting at all costs to prevent such a long and tiring voyage from 'misfiring' completely because of some exaggerated danger, I decided to put ashore an officer–courier, who would clarify the situation on shore (i.e. at the Marseilles post) and whose arrival would give added motivation and prove that it was possible to slip through. I ordered him also to request Major Chojnacki most vigorously to send a party of people for the night of 14/15 June.

This is not to say that I prejudged the way the situation would develop; indeed, I ordered Lt Biczysko (courier) to have a good look around himself and form his own opinion about the situation and, if necessary to get someone else to prepare a party of people if the official leader was unduly fearful of the risks. I felt I could safely base such a plan on Lt Biczysko's assessment of the situation in the light of his character, as revealed to me by his exemplary conduct during the previous voyage.

The rendezvous with the ship taking off my passengers was to take place as previously – at a point 30 miles east of Cap Creus (in other words the Spanish-French frontier). In spite of the fog which reduced visibility at the last moment to 4,000 m., we managed to meet successfully, having fixed our position by observation during the morning. The meeting took place even earlier than had been anticipated in the programme, at 1240 rather than 1400 hrs. The transfer of passengers was effected successfully in spite of a swell, while at the same time we took on board the three agents who were to be put ashore, plus a number of packages, which were to be deposited together with the agents or at the time we took the people on board at Port-Miou.

We also picked up a series of signals, which unfortunately caused no small disturbance to the previous plan of my operation. I was warned that in the Antibes region, while putting ashore *two* of the agents, there MIGHT be an agent to pick up. I was not given the exact spot nor light signals or codes. I was further ordered to take on board at Port-Miou not three people but as many as ten, which made the whole Port-Miou operation very risky, since I had previously suggested it as a good embarkation point for three people but not for ten. It is too built-up.

All this showed up organisational shortcomings on the British side of my operation.

Not being able to influence or change any of the details, I decided to carry out the tasks insofar as possible.

7) *PUTTING ASHORE A COURIER AND THE AGENTS.* That evening (10 June) I was again in the Marseilles region, where, after avoiding a large steamer making its way from Marseilles to the south – and having avoided after sunset the lights of an extremely slow-moving ship not far from the coast in the Cassis–Toulon region (a patrol boat?) – we made the entrance to En-Vau. At 0135 hrs I dropped anchor. While manoeuvring in this very narrow *calanque* on such a dark night, however, I damaged the side of the ship's bow (bulwarks), having touched the almost vertical rock wall.

At 0210 hrs, after putting Lt Biczysko ashore, we were already heading south-east, in order to put the agents ashore.

In the morning, examination revealed that the collision had caused only a certain leakage of the deck and that the damage itself could be completely repaired, at least on a temporary basis. I had to wait for better weather, since the bow at that time was covered with water.

On 11 June at 2310 hrs we saw the coastal lights of the Cannes–Antibes region.

In the process of looking for the landing point – though I had been there once already – there were some anxious moments as regards navigation. These give an idea of the particular difficulties of pilotage in wartime conditions, when one is putting people ashore at an agreed point on an enemy coast. As I have already pointed out in previous reports, lighthouses east of Toulon (in fact the Camarat light) have been extinguished.

For considerations of safety, I could not approach the shore before the sun went down, but I needed to fix my position by daylight – from the afternoon's observed position. Indeed, since the coastline in this area is extremely varied, with peninsulas and little islands, it is not easy to draw close to the shore and recognise a place even when one has been there before. At midnight I was certain that I had identified points that seemed to tally more or less with the log's indications (although the current of 1–2 knots demanded that it be treated with caution).

Having passed a familiar headland, I entered the familiar bay and went to an anchorage point about 200 m. from the shore.

In spite of the presence of many features that resembled those of the little bay of Antibes, however, something was different about the look of this place.

After we had consulted the chart and the contours of the shoreline, it turned out that we had not gone far enough and that this was not the Antibes bay but a small bay between Juan-les-Pins and the island of Saint-Marguerite, where I had all but put the agents ashore. Indeed, within ten minutes our course would have run us aground in two metres of water.

Eventually, at 0105, we were in the right place. The dinghy was launched and Gorzelok and Stanislawski took the two agents and their 'freight' ashore. There was no agent waiting to be brought on board ship. Consequently, at 0145 hrs we were already on our way to the second pick-up point (third agent) – Cap-d'Ail, near Monaco.

8) This agent was to be dropped – according to the instructions that the back-up vessel had brought me – in La-Napoule bay, where I had already put ashore three people during the first mission to France. As I discovered from talking with him, however, this disembarkation point was of no value at all to the agent, and had only been chosen because I was familiar with it. The agent, who was very shy and clearly did not want to cause me any trouble, did admit that if he were put down somewhere near Cap-d'Ail he would be far better off. The distance from Napoule to Cap-d'Ail was not insignificant (25 miles as the crow flies), which could have presented considerable difficulties to someone who was new to the area; to me, however, it did not make any difference to add this much to our journey, so I decided to put him ashore there – to the agent's undisguised satisfaction. The spot at La-Napoule was in any case not too favourable, but Cap-d'Ail I knew from having accidentally arrived there in the course of the 13th mission: it lies just below Monaco. The greatest potential difficulty – recognising the spot – did not arise, because the coastline there is very distinctive.

I aimed to carry out the landing on that same night, since the agent was reacting badly to his stay on the felucca, especially in view of the poor weather. The difficulty was that the night was going to be very short.

At 0430 hrs we had already reached Cap-d'Ail, a very steep, rocky slope. Having hove-to, I put the agent on to the dinghy under the command of Gorzelok and recommended that he put him ashore at any point he could find where it looked possible for him to climb up: it did not look too pleasant a pastime from the felucca.

After the dinghy had left us, there followed a period of waiting amid growing tension, since the dinghy had not returned and the dawn had begun to lighten the area; earlier we had already made out the lights of residential buildings on the rocky wall. I had already begun to fear that Gorzelok had mixed up the courses I had given him, when the dinghy reappeared. We hoisted it on board and then sailed away from the shore as fast as we could. Half an hour later a thick fog descended. At dawn, although we were still close to the shore, it was impossible for anyone to see us.

Gorzelok informed me that after searching around for a long time he had managed to find a sufficiently quiet spot between Cap-d'Ail and the small village of Eze, at the foot of some château.

9) *HOVE-TO.* We had a further three days' wait before the next party was due to be picked up, and we spent these lying hove-to almost exactly where we had been in previous missions to France, around 40 miles south-east of Antibes. We made use of one exceptional day's weather (12 June) to carry out temporary repairs to the ship's side. And we relaxed a little.

Unfortunately the very next day we experienced a storm, coming from the west. Anticipating that it might make me late, at 1420 hrs I had to move towards Marseilles.

The storm was one of the most violent experienced in those regions. I had to reduce our speed to $3\frac{1}{2}$ knots in order to prevent our hull from being smashed. All the repairs we had carried out on the bow, although quite strong, were washed away. Our spare sail also was carried away during the night, in spite of the fact that it was securely fastened to the bow.

During the whole journey – that is until the evening of 14 June – we did not meet anyone except a three-masted schooner under French colours, running down full before the wind in the direction of Corsica.

A certain improvement in the weather (as it later turned out, only for a change of wind direction) occurred on the evening of the 14th, which we spent making good the damage to the sides with the remains of spare timber, which we always carry with us.

At 2315 hrs on the same day we were once again at the entrance to En-Vau. In response to my call signal we received the reply: 'DANGER'.

10) *WE TAKE ON BOARD A VERY MIXED PARTY.* Because of the recent penetration of our activities and arrests, as a result of which the police might have discovered our recognition signals, I had agreed with Lt Biczysko that the meaning of particular signal colours would be REVERSED: red would be 'All clear'; blue, 'Danger'. My call signal however would remain as it had been before (blue).

Having received the danger signal, therefore, I hesitated. As long as they were there, however, one had to assume that it could not be that dangerous, especially as from our position we could see nothing suspicious at all.

In addition, it occurred to me that Lt Biczysko might not have been able to remember that *our* call signal, i.e. that of the felucca, remained blue, and for some reason have assumed that the felucca was signalling danger.

In the light of the above I sent our call sign with a red light. The reply came back immediately: red. Everything was in order.

At 2345 hrs I was ashore where Captain Iwaszkiewicz was waiting with some people; others were still arriving in small groups led by guides. Also present was Lt Biczysko, who had acquitted himself extremely well, as the presence of so many people proved.

I was told that the signals had been understood perfectly but that Capt Iwaszkiewicz had quite simply used a different-coloured light by mistake.

As regards the situation on shore, it emerged that they had not received my cable – even by 14 June – although some 16 days had passed since I had sent it. What is more, as many as 82 people (among them two Free French) had been ready to leave earlier. However, 20 of them had been arrested in the end. The level of alertness of the authorities had been raised, although it was still possible to slip through, as we knew from the present embarkation.

According to Lt Biczysko's report, the leader of the Marseilles post was astonished when he arrived there, since, to his knowledge, the coast was – following the last penetration of the evacuation operations – cut off. He even declared that he would not allow him to return since 'it was only by a miracle that he had managed to get through'. On the first day he turned the idea down but on the second he agreed to provide a group of 20 people for 14 June. Luckily Capt Iwaszkiewicz persuaded Major Chojnacki to increase this figure to 40. (In the end I took 62 people on board that night.)

We agreed however that the boarding point we had used up until then (En-Vau) was now more or less compromised. I was not inclined to return to the Faraman site, though, owing to its

Sketch map showing pinpoints used by the Polish Feluccas for operations in 1942

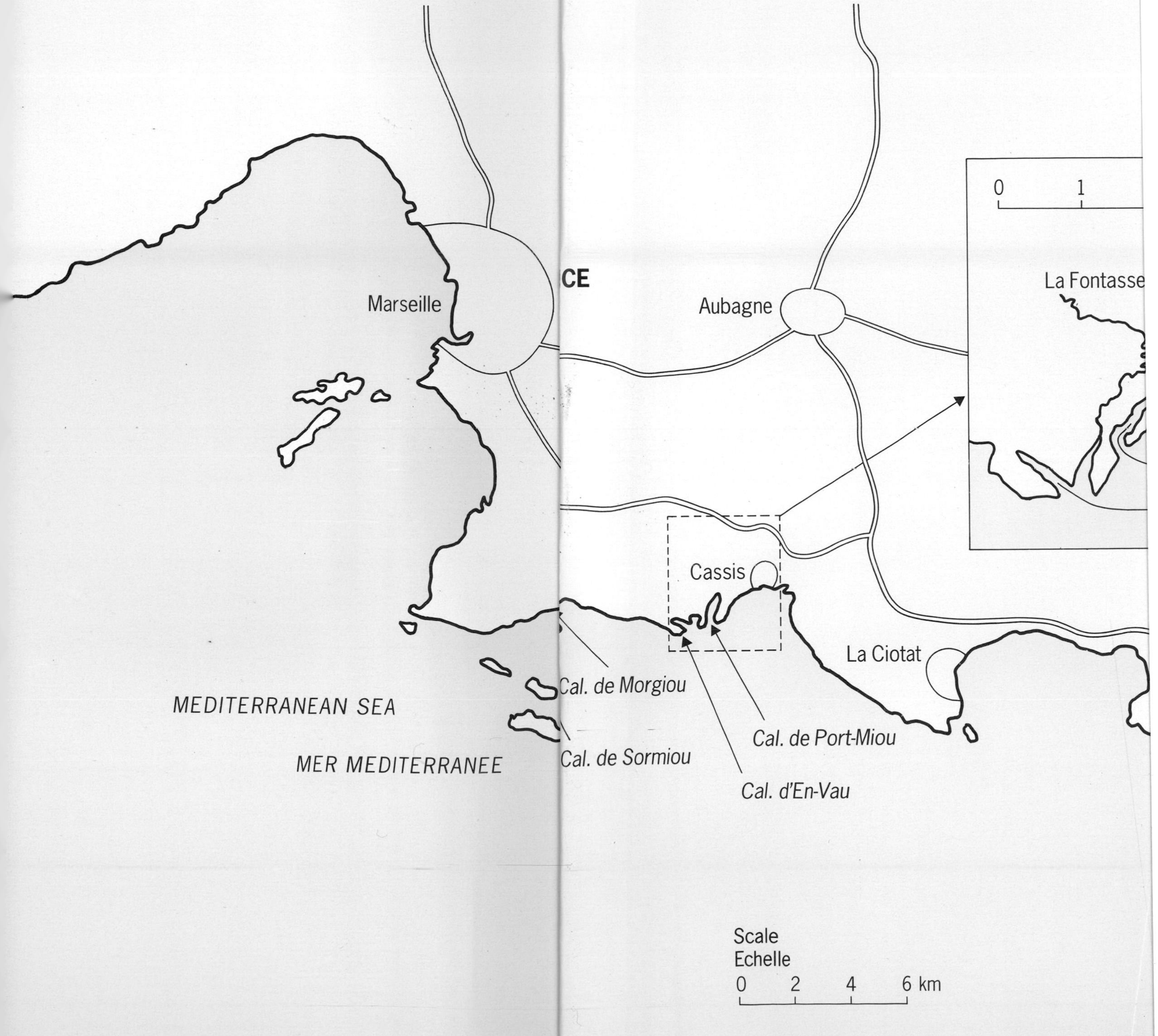

Marseille

CE

Aubagne

La Fontasse

0   1

Cassis

La Ciotat

Cal. de Morgiou

MEDITERRANEAN SEA

Cal. de Port-Miou

MER MEDITERRANEE

Cal. de Sormiou

Cal. d'En-Vau

Scale
Echelle

0   2   4   6 km

openness to bad weather from almost every direction, and its very shallow waters, which rendered it impossible to sail close in. Furthermore, it was not a suitable site in that it was difficult to reach from the land side (small workers' settlements along the way, which foreigners seldom visited).

In the light of this, Capt Iwaszkiewicz proposed a completely new place very close to Marseilles, not far from La-Madrague tram stop. Its advantages: beaches frequented by crowds of people during the day, so that, the presence of large numbers of people would not arouse much attention; the tramline ran close by, so if the ship did not turn up it would be easy to disperse people again; there were apparently no inhabited buildings in the vicinity, although an anti-aircraft battery was situated near by on the headland, about two kilometres away.

Upon my return to Gibraltar I was to confirm the suitability of this place from the point of view of sea operations.

The next embarkation date we decided should be 12 July at 0000 hrs.

In response to my proposal that we try to evacuate 100 people, Capt Iwaszkiewicz replied that it was not impossible. We agreed that I would, at a fairly early stage, indicate from Gibraltar whether I had the back-up ship at my disposal, since our ability to take off a large number of people depended on her availability.

I also gave him technical details of our operations, of our telegraphic communications and, above all, how many days our journeys lasted, since he seemed not to realise how slow communications were.

I also handed over a number of items I had been requested to get for him and for Major Chojnacki, and which it was impossible to obtain in France via normal trading channels.

Capt Iwaszkiewicz also passed on Major Chojnacki's wish that one of those who had been taken off (Dr Tomaszewski) should be sent back to them again(?!). 'What on earth for?' I asked. 'Intelligence duties?' 'I don't know myself what this is all about,' answered Capt Iwaszkiewicz.

I said that in general I did not believe that bringing people back served any useful purpose, and I was against it. The process was too arduous both for the passengers and for the crew (given that passengers occupy the sleeping berths) and too irregular for these matters to be decided so lightly. (A similar incident took place in the first party: Major Chojnacki wanted us to bring Mr Alvast back. According to Lt Roehr's information, however, this fellow had been under police observation for some time and was far too well known in Marseilles by the (unfortunately gossipy) Polish colony, for his disappearance by secret means and his equally mysterious reappearance to have been prudent.)

'If it is essential,' I replied, 'then I will always do it. But I would prefer Major Chojnacki to decide whether it is really necessary.'

11) At 0045 hrs the embarkation was complete, and we then moved to Port-Miou, which lies very close to En-Vau. At 0115 hrs I sent the raft commanded by Gorzelok into the *calanque* (we did not enter with the felucca itself since the *calanque* is inhabited, as we discovered during our first voyage to France). I gave him the password, so that he could collect people who would know the response.

To my amazement, after half an hour he brought back the first party, which included three women. He said that everything was in order, so I could not refuse to take them, in spite of the fact that our felucca can be used for almost anything except transporting women, especially since, for the whole of the journey lasting several days, it was to be crammed full of soldiers (there is, for example, no toilet on board).

At 0230 hrs we loaded the second group of people, after which I set course for home.

An hour later we passed a large passenger ship some 500 metres away. It was moving very slowly in the direction of Marseilles, apparently not wanting to arrive there by night.

12) *THE CURIOUS MYSTERY OF THE ST-CHRISTINE.* The first night was particularly difficult for the passengers, since we were taking a great deal of water on deck and almost all of them suffered from seasickness. Only after some time could we persuade our female passengers to go below to the cabin, which had been put at their disposal, since – as always in these cases – everyone was afraid that the suffering would be worse down below. The weather, which had been none too favourable for a considerable time, again turned into a heavy storm.

At 1105 hrs, being at the level of Cape Creus, in other words the Spanish frontier (at a distance of 65 kilometres), I made out on the starboard bow a steamer travelling most probably towards Marseilles. Anxious to pass her at a decent distance, which I habitually do during the day to prevent other seafarers getting too close a look at me, I changed course, doing my best to make the change imperceptible. However, when this ship saw us, it changed course . . . straight towards us. I made a further change of direction. Then, as though realising that it would pass too far away from us, the ship again changed its course towards us. There could no longer be any doubt: IT WAS HEADING FOR US ON PURPOSE. I therefore changed course gradually towards south-east. I ordered the passengers to hide themselves completely, an unimaginably difficult thing to do since there was no way that they could all be accommodated below. Some of them had to remain under the spare sails on deck.

The ship continued to approach, correcting its course regularly in order to intercept us. It was a ship of around 3,000 tons, with a single funnel, apparently quite modern and evidently with a speed of 12 knots, since my change of course put it on my starboard side and it still managed to catch up with us easily.

The name and colours were clearly visible: *St-Christine*, a French vessel.

And so it travelled behind us at a distance of around 500 m. for some 15 minutes. Anticipating trouble, I had prepared everything I could when our persecutor turned about and headed in a northerly direction. This mystery gave me no peace for the whole of the rest of the voyage. A merchant ship, however curious he might have been, however intrigued by a felucca seeking fish in the middle of the ocean where the water was 300 metres deep, would not have added so much distance to his journey simply to satisfy his private curiosity. The mystery was to be cleared up before long, however.

The storm continued to grow. Since it was coming from the north-west, it was hitting us abeam and causing our 20-ton felucca to pitch and roll, which was very unpleasant, especially with at least 50 people on deck. In addition we took a great deal of water on board.

Because of this I set a course for Cape Mahon (Minorca), with a view to leaving the Balearic Islands on my starboard side. All the time since we took our passengers on board I had been sending out a radio message in the hope of having them send me a transfer vessel, but we were unable to establish contact. I sent the message out 'into the ether' hoping that somewhere nearer I would be able to establish contact and would then find that the vessel was waiting for me along my course (I was giving out my position and course).

13) On the following day (16 June), from the morning on, we were sailing past the Balearic Islands. The weather improved for a time.

At midnight on the 17th we had a very odd meeting with a ship, which came towards us and then reduced its speed but did not approach us (the darkness was almost complete). Thinking that this might be the transfer vessel, I too reduced speed and gave out a call sign by switching off our navigation lights three times.

In response, an incomprehensible flashing came, after a time, from the other ship, whereupon I increased speed and moved off, leaving it still flashing.

14) *TRANSFER OF PASSENGERS*. At the level of Capo de Gata, in excellent weather, we encountered a squadron of the British fleet returning from convoy battles in the eastern Mediterranean, of which we had heard (on the radio). British patrol aircraft were in the air continually.

Taking advantage of the presence of a flying boat that dipped slightly and started to circle over us, I signalled by lamp, 'Please report my position. Here *Seawolf*', several times. He apparently had some difficulty reading it, but eventually answered, 'I will report your position'.

Because of my failure to make radio contact, I wanted to make sure that in Gibraltar they knew I was near, and would be prepared to receive this considerable number of passengers, something of a problem in that fortress. To prevent them from sending a ship out *now*, I signalled 'Need no help'.

The aircraft moved away. After a while we noticed a destroyer moving towards us at top speed. It ordered us to come alongside – and this was how in the end I transferred our passengers. I also took the astonished captain aside to give him some confidential information (1420 hrs).

Unfortunately our already-damaged felucca was further battered in the course of our transfer operation. A deck beam in the engine-room was shattered and the bowsprit, which would normally have projected a metre and a half beyond the bow, was broken off; it was dangerous to lie side by side in a strong swell, which was all that remained of the many days of inclement weather.

The next day at 0830 hrs we reached Gibraltar. I discovered that the passengers had arrived there – at 2100 hrs on the day we had transferred them.

15) *THE SOLVING OF THE ST-CHRISTINE MYSTERY.* After our arrival in port I was told, while giving my report to Commander Osborne, that the following signal had been sent to Gibraltar from London on 13 June:
'Sources in Marseilles report that on 6 June, "All captains of merchant ships have received orders to be on the look-out for, and to report, a small, brown-coloured vessel of some 10 metres in length, 4 metres in width, with *a four-seater dinghy*. This ship carried out an *operation on 10 April*."'
Needless to add, I recognised my own *Seawolf* in the descrip-

tion of the ship and indeed the incident with the *St-Christine* also became clear.

But how did they get hold of so many details in Marseilles?

My theory is as follows: THE REAL SOURCE LIES IN GIBRALTAR. After all, absolutely *nobody* along the French coast saw me from close quarters. And only someone very close could have noticed that the dinghy is a four-seater. None of the Poles engaged in helping with the loading could see either; it was night and the ship was several hundred metres from the shore.

Equally, the date of 10 April – although one must not lay too much emphasis upon this detail – seems to confirm my thesis, because that was the day we received the *Seawolf* from the civilian shipyard. The Blanda shipyard lies alongside the Spanish border and is even easier to observe than the dockyard. And of course we had to tell the firm, which was always late finishing work, that they must complete the felucca on time because we needed it. On 10 April the felucca came round to the dockyard area; in other words, it disappeared from the view of whoever was watching it in the Blanda shipyard, which does work both for the army and the navy.

16) *VARIOUS.* Radio communication is, to date, ineffective. After raising anchor I am completely deprived of any contact with base. It is essential to get hold of a powerful transmitter/ receiver (my previous report).

The following distinguished themselves in the course of this mission:

1) Lt Biczysko, Jozef – by taking on and executing the task of re-establishing contact with the Marseilles outpost; moreover, he faced the danger of landing in an area which, after all that had happened, must have been guarded and which we expected to be surrounded by the gendarmerie as soon as we landed.

In addition, during the whole voyage he distinguished himself by his willingness to help with deck work, at the same time learning such a lot that I used him as a helmsman and deck-hand, in spite of the fact that he had had no contact with the sea before.

2) Mate Gorzelok, Ernest – by courageously executing tasks associated with being in charge of the dinghy when we put agents ashore and when we brought people on board from difficult and sometimes dangerous spots. The fact that we carried agents considerably increased the risks if he were arrested, for then the charge would be not merely smuggling people (Poles) out but spying or indeed sabotage. The chances of being arrested were greater for him than for the rest of the crew

on the felucca, which was at anchor a few hundred metres from the shore.

Gibraltar, 28 June 1942

The destroyer to which Krajewski transferred his passengers off Capo de la Gata was HMS *Middleton*, which belonged to the 'Hunt' Class. As she steamed away from *Seawolf* at full speed to rejoin the anti-aircraft cruiser *Cairo*, Kinloch, her captain, told the ship's company that no-one should talk about the incident in case the Germans picked up a future 'run'. The refugees, who numbered over 60, included Pierre Fourcaud,[14] one of de Gaulle's first emissaries to return to France in the autumn of 1940, now returning from his third mission, and Henri Frenay, founder of the 'Combat' Resistance movement.[15] They were all placed in the tiller flat, under guard, and none of the crew allowed to speak to them. It was a most uncomfortable compartment, right in the stern and above the propellers. Fortunately they only had to endure the discomfort for seven hours before the ship berthed at Gibraltar. But Danny Jones, one of the ship's company, remembered half a century later that they seemed so happy to have been picked up that they sang all the time.[16] The *Middleton*'s first lieutenant, Edward Ashmore, was a future First Sea Lord.

CHAPTER XXVIII

The Coast Watching Flotilla and the Polish Special Operations Group

B y the time Krajewski got back from his 14th evacuation mission on 19 June, Stoklas had returned to London and reported to Admiral Swirski, commander of the Polish navy, copying the report to General Klimecki, Sikorski's Chief of Staff.[1]

The object of his visit to Gibraltar had been to familiarise himself with the new Special Flotilla and to ensure that the principles on which it was organised conformed with Polish needs; to clarify the present situation of the groups commanded respectively by Krajewski and Buchowski in relation to the local British authorities; and to look into a variety of administrative problems such as manning, uniforms, leave and promotions.

Unfortunately, Stoklas continued, he arrived at Gibraltar just at the moment when the recently created organisation had been replaced with a new one. Although this was partly working, at this early stage it was impossible for him to sort out the problems that arose, since decisions were required from higher authorities in London and, above all, direct negotiation was needed with the British Admiralty.

After a series of meetings with the British authorities concerned, he put to Captain Osborne, senior officer of the so-called Coast Watching Flotilla (CWF), proposals regarding Krajewski's and Buchowski's groups, stipulating that these arrangements would still require the approval of his superiors in London. Osborne was in complete agreement with what Stoklas had in mind but said that once Stoklas had obtained the agreement of the Polish authorities, matters would have to be settled directly with Captain Slocum at the Admiralty, who was Osborne's immediate superior. Stoklas's proposals were as follows:

(1) Buchowski's unit, the so-called Diversionary Group, would cease to exist and that Buchowski together with his crew should be transferred to the Coast Watching Flotilla under the same conditions as were applied to Krajewski's group.

(2) Both groups would be transferred to the Polish navy and would form a Special Operations Group (SOG) seconded to the CWF at Gibraltar.

(3) The aim of the SOG would be to evacuate by sea from North Africa and southern France Polish citizens conducted to embarkation points by the relevant Polish evacuation missions.

(4) The SOG would comprise two complete crews under the command of officers of the Polish navy, who would take charge of feluccas provided by the British authorities in Gibraltar.

(5) For administrative and disciplinary purposes, the SOG would be subordinated to the head of the Polish mission in Gibraltar, who would be a staff officer appointed by the senior Polish naval commander (i.e. Admiral Swirski).

(6) Pay would be at the rates prevailing in the Polish navy and the necessary arrangements would be made to enable it to be issued by the Polish mission.

(7) The head of the Polish mission would cooperate with the senior officer of the CWF on all operational matters affecting the SOG.

(8) On all other matters such as accommodation, payments and the transfer of Polish personnel arriving at Gibraltar by sea or other routes, the head of the Polish mission would deal directly with the relevant British agencies in Gibraltar.

(9) Both crews of the SOG could be entrusted with any tasks resulting from their operational secondment to the CWF: that is, in addition to strictly Polish evacuation tasks, they might take on special tasks to benefit British intelligence. However, additional duties had to be subordinate to the basic aim of the group, which was to evacuate Polish citizens.

(10) Any proposals concerning duties not connected with the evacuation of Polish citizens would be received by the head of mission only from the Flotilla commander, with whom he would allocate priorities to tasks and operations. (A handwritten addition specified that the head of the Polish mission would be directly subordinate to the [Polish] senior naval commander.)

(11) For the organisation of evacuations, the head of the Polish mission would follow the recommendation of the relevant department of Sikorski's headquarters. He would be a link between Sikorski's HQ and the relevant evacuation outposts. Operations concerning the evacuation of Polish citizens would be prepared by the head of the Polish mission, who would submit proposals to the Flotilla commander (i.e. Osborne), with proposed dates and places for embarking the evacuees.

(12) Operational orders would be issued by the Flotilla commander, whose responsibility it would be to ensure operational support

from the British naval authorities at Gibraltar in the event that the operation undertaken by the SOG was threatened by enemy action.

As regards (1) above, the main problem connected with the creation of the CWF at Gibraltar had been the status of Buchowski's group.

Buchowski, and his crew had been given four months' training in sabotage operations before they arrived in Gibraltar, where, Stoklas reported, Buchowski's group had been subordinated to a 'special organisation (non-military), headed, most probably, by the Ministry of Economic Warfare'. The head of this very conspiratorial organisation had representatives throughout the Empire and, under diplomatic cover, in neutral countries, they carried out sabotage and propaganda with the help of special agents and groups of specially trained people. The representative in Gibraltar of this organisation was Mr Hugh Quennell, whose second in command was Mr H. Morris.

Initially, Mr Quennell had had at his disposal a British sabotage group, whose operations had been unsuccessful. Then Buchowski's group had been sent to Gibraltar and placed under Quennell's orders.

Stoklas reported that Quennell's organisation [SOE] was not very popular at Gibraltar, especially in the military circles on the Rock. There seemed, moreover, to be a certain quiet rivalry between British military intelligence and Quennell's organisation. The head of intelligence on the Rock had made a whole series of attempts to have Buchowski's group removed from Quennell's authority. However, it seemed that the representative of British naval intelligence (affiliated to the Joint Intelligence Centre), Commander Clark, was fairly close to Quennell's organisation and had for a time played almost the role of naval Chief of Staff alongside Mr Quennell.

Buchowski's group had been seven months at Gibraltar and, up to the time that Krajewski began to use individual members of it for his own evacuation operations, the activities of the group as a 'sabotage organ' for Quennell had been limited to a series of unsuccessful operations – or operations that were prepared on a grand scale and then called off. These culminated in an unsuccessful mission to Casablanca, at the end of which Buchowski and his whole crew were arrested at Tangier and his borrowed felucca was confiscated by the Spaniards.

General Klimecki agreed to Stoklas's proposals but suggested that, if Admiral Swirski approved Krajewski's request for a transfer, his replacement should be sent out to Gibraltar as soon as possible so that he might familiarise himself with the technical aspects of the job by making a few voyages with Krajewski.[2] Swirski must also have agreed, since by 17 July a draft directive had emerged from discussions with Slocum to give practical effect to the proposed reorganisation.[3] The Polish contingent would normally man the feluccas *Seawolf* and *Seadog* but might be transferred to other feluccas of the CWF by agreement between CWF and the head of the Polish mission in Gibraltar.

The directive recognised that the main purpose of the Polish contingent of the CWF was the evacuation by sea from France and North Africa of Polish nationals, who would be delivered to the various points of embarkation by Polish evacuation missions established in those territories; but it went on to say that the primary task of the CWF was to provide sea lines of communication for intelligence organisations operating on behalf of the Allies. This latter objective, therefore, took precedence over all other operations of the CWF, including the evacuation of British, Polish and other Allied personnel. Thus the Polish contingent might be called on to execute any operation on behalf of the Allied cause, provided that any approved Polish evacuation plan would not be jeopardised by diversion of the Polish contingent to other tasks, except in cases of critical emergency.

With this significant emendation, Stoklas's proposals were agreed and adopted. The directive stipulated that the W/T channel of communication on all operational matters between the head of the Polish mission in Gibraltar and his headquarters in London would be via the CWF's office.

Though Buchowski had not carried out any operation to the south coast of France before the end of June, on 25 April he had used *Dogfish* to pick up four agents from near Cap Falcon in Algeria.[4] Though he undertook the operation (ORKAN) for Krajewski, it is clear from the record that at least one of those embarked must either have belonged to Rygor-Slowikowski's 'Agence Afrique' intelligence network, which was working for Dunderdale of SIS, though Slowikowski was still ignorant of the fact, or was an agent of Dunderdale's on a separate mission.

Buchowski's next operation was also undertaken for Krajewski: he set off in *Dogfish* for Casablanca in May with Lt Roehr, but the operation failed because of bad weather and they were recalled to Gibraltar, having encountered French warships on two occasions.

Dogfish went back to Casablanca to complete what was probably same evacuation mission (CASABLANCA) on 21 May, when she embarked 30 Allied evaders and escapers. It was the last large-scale venture of this kind to French North Africa by the Polish mission at Gibraltar. Who was in command is something of a mystery as neither Krajewski nor Buchowski recorded it among his achievements.

At this point *Seadog*, a second 20-ton felucca, was ready for sea and Buchowski took her up to the Oran area in an attempt to put

Gromnicki ashore. This operation (TANGERINE) failed on 9 June as they ran into a patrol on the Algerian coast and then encountered bad weather. After this there were no further felucca operations to North Africa: *Minna*, the fast escort vessel Slocum had sent out to join the CWF, took over this part of the Flotilla's work, leaving Buchowski and *Seadog* to join Krajewski and *Seawolf* on the run to the south coast of France.

Seadog's first appearance on the Côte d'Azur was at Cap-d'Antibes at the end of June.[5] Working without *Tarana*, which had just carried out a complex series of operations with *Seawolf*, she embarked one unidentified SOE agent and landed a consignment of SOE stores (Operation NETTLETREE). She returned a month later to the same area without *Tarana* to carry out Operation SASSAFRAS, in the course of which Buchowski landed Major Nicholas Boddington of SOE's F Section; Henri Frager, staff officer to Girard, head of the 'Carte' organisation, who had been in London discussing Girard's requests for propaganda broadcasts with the Political Warfare Executive (PWE); H.M.R Despaigne, an additional W/T operator for Peter Churchill; and Yvonne Rudellat, who was on her way to Tours to work as a courier for F.A. Suttill ('Prosper').[6]

CHAPTER XXIX

Problems and Methods of Operating from Gibraltar to the South of France

K rajewski's three first voyages to France had lasted 13, 16 and 15 days respectively and had served to evacuate 171 Poles and three others. The distances involved – 1,500–1,600 sea miles on passage, perhaps 2,000 miles in all, allowing for the extra distances steamed between operational pinpoints and waiting positions – greatly exceeded any previously tackled: it was by any standards a remarkable achievement.

Seawolf and the new *Seadog* were 47'6" long and, at 20 tons, twice the size of *Dogfish* (10 tons), but they were small, slow and extremely uncomfortable. There was no room below deck for the large numbers of passengers embarked, who had to be packed on deck like sardines, lying cheek by jowl along the felucca's gunwales. If it became necessary to conceal them from view or protect them from bad weather, they were covered by tarpaulins or sails.

All the feluccas employed were in a poor state of repair. Even *Seawolf*'s new Kelvin engine gave trouble, while *Seadog*'s Swedish semi-diesel was particularly temperamental and could be got going at all only with the aid of a blowlamp. Because of the shortcomings of her 30-year-old motor, which had required prodigies on the part of Siembieda, the mechanic who kept it going, *Dogfish* had been withdrawn from service after a year of voyages to the African coast. *Seawolf* was considered a better sea-boat than *Seadog*: she was of French Moroccan provenance, while *Seadog* was Spanish in origin. They used Spanish and French camouflage.

Things would have been a good deal worse if Krajewski had not found in Commander John Illingworth,[1] *Maidstone*'s senior engineer officer, a firm friend and ally. Illingworth, a future Commodore of the Royal Ocean Racing Club, was already well known in that context and had on the bulkhead of his cabin a blown-up photograph of his very successful Laurent Giles-designed cutter *Maid of Malham*. Writing 50 years later from Oslo, Krajewski, who had of course long since resumed his true patronymic Kadulski, said he owed the success of his last operations in *Seawolf*, and the markedly better conditions on board compared with *Dogfish*, to Illingworth's keenness to help, to his first-class technical engineering skills and to his knowledge of the requirements of very small boats. Illingworth even arranged for electric light to be installed in the *Seawolf*, which helped Krajewski to do his navigation properly and read charts at night!

Tarana's, which Slocum had sent out to operate in conjunction with the feluccas as well as on her own, was a Dutch-built, 200-ton deep-sea trawler. Under the command of Lt E. B. Clark, RNR, whom Krajewski describes as her 'jolly' captain, her mixed Anglo-Polish crew came to hold the record – six hours – for painting the ship overall during darkness, an operation that had to be undertaken at the beginning and end of each voyage. By transferring passengers to her from the feluccas at sea and thus saving a return trip of 750 miles to Gibraltar, it was possible for *Seawolf* and *Seadog* to embark twice – and, later, even three times – as many people in a fortnight as would otherwise have been possible. These rendezvous at sea also enabled the feluccas to embark agents for landing, without their having to make the whole uncomfortable trip from Gibraltar to the French coast in the smaller vessel; further, the agents avoided the risks inherent in being on board the felucca during preliminary operations that did not concern them – a distinct advantage from a security point of view. Of course weather conditions had to allow the wooden felucca to come alongside the steel trawler without sustaining damage, since the difference in their respective sizes made the felucca very vulnerable.

In the summer of 1942 the Poles estimated that there were still roughly 3,000 of their officers and men immobilised in southern France. Krajewski and Mally were prepared to run considerable risks to get them out, even after it became clear that the French authorities knew quite a lot about the felucca traffic from Gibraltar – as a result, they thought, of indiscretions by other people's agents, but no doubt also of the propensity of the Poles in France to gossip.

The hazards of operating under fishing-boat cover were aggravated by the fact that the French fuel ration for fishing vessels was very meagre and that the waters off the south coast of France were, even in normal times, not considered good fishing grounds. The triangle formed by Marseilles, Port-Vendres and Sète was something of an exception since it was an area where the nature of the bottom and depths were suitable for trawling. There was very little sea traffic of any kind east of Marseilles and the few ships that did sail these waters kept close inshore. Practically no vessels were to be found near Corsica and there was no fishing east of Marseilles except that close inshore. Fishermen at such places as Antibes and the Anse-de-Canton in Monaco fished by night, employing acetylene arc lights. Not only were the long-lines and ring-nets of these boats a hazard on the feluccas' approach to the shore to land agents but their brilliant lights would produce a good silhouette of another boat at a distance of 300–400 m. A felucca had therefore to be careful never to place herself between such lights and the shore.[2]

With a regular monthly service to the south coast of France, to a complex schedule involving combinations of three operating ships, and with *Minna* working to North Africa, an enormous amount of preparatory work was needed to achieve maximum results for each sailing.[3] The requirements of each organisation calling on the CWF for transport had to be coordinated. Great distances were involved and the short no-moon period of each month restricted operating time. For these reasons it was necessary to combine missions so that a felucca could carry them all out during her round voyage of about a fortnight.

The lion's share of this planning fell on Osborne himself. Apart from maintaining the Flotilla, he was responsible for the conduct of operations while the ships were at sea. Before provisional plans could be drafted for VACNA's approval, the customer organisations had to say how many operations they would require during the period under review, while the field sections had to supply details of their proposed pinpoints. When the number of individual missions had been settled, the craft made their final preparations for sailing. The suggested pinpoints needed to be checked from the naval angle, adjusted where necessary to suit naval requirements and sent back to the field for final approval. Then the customer organisations were asked which of their missions could, with due regard for security, be combined and the final sailing orders were completed. These included full details of pinpoints, any alterations, times of rendezvous, ship-to-shore and shore-to-ship signals and passwords. The navigational notes consisted of times of moonrise and moonset, courses to and from the pinpoints and the most suitable areas for lying to during daytime. To these were attached silhouettes of the pinpoint areas. Although wireless silence was enforced, a list of crack signals was always carried in case of last-minute alterations in the sequence of landings and embarkations. VACNA's final permission to sail was then sought and relevant details were passed to Operations for onward routing to the RAF liaison officer (who informed any aircraft in the vicinity) and to Captain S/m 8, who warned submarines.

Routes to and from France had to be chosen bearing in mind that the Spaniards, though neutrals, maintained a strict coast-watching service with look-out posts located at vantage points all along the coast and in the Balearics. A report by the watch-post at Carnero opposite Gibraltar of the sailing of a 'special' felucca from Gibraltar might be followed, two days later, by a similar report by the watch-post at Dragonera light in the Balearics. These two reports would give the Spaniards a valuable insight into the movements of the vessel and there was no telling whether it would not be passed on to Axis agents or to the French.

Once the vessel disappeared out of sight of land, the enemy had no means of tracking her unless one of his or a neutral reconnaissance aircraft spotted her day by day, which was not likely. The conclusion that the felucca should therefore keep constantly out of sight of land on passage to or from France had one potentially serious disadvantage: a fishing vessel sighted many kilometres away from any fishing ground must immediately appear suspicious. Trawling is impossible beyond a depth limit of about 250 metres and where the bottom is rocky. Long-lining, on the other hand, is seldom carried out in depths of over 50 fathoms (90 m.) and never in depths of over 100 (180 m.). A felucca might pass muster if spotted in an unlikely area by air or sea reconnaissance, but not if seen by a genuine fisherman.

Ships at sea had to be avoided as far as possible, but without making an excessive change of course, which itself might attract attention. When Krajewski had passengers on board he used them to make up look-out watches during daylight hours, but at other times he had to do without, as he could not spare his few crew for this duty. The feluccas, being small, normally sighted ships before they were themselves sighted. Even when they sighted another vessel close to, it was sometimes possible to alter course gradually by as much as 40°, enabling *Seawolf* to pass the other ship at sufficient distance to avoid close inspection.

Plans had to be made in advance if it was thought likely that the felucca would meet patrol vessels. The external appearance of the boat had to be prepared, as did a cover story in case they were boarded or examined and arrangements on board that were consistent with this. The feluccas on operations to the south of France were never in fact subjected to an examination such as *Dogfish* underwent at the hands of the Spanish authorities at Tarifa and in Alboran Island roads, though Krajewski had one narrow escape.

When it came to making a landfall, some moon was desirable, particularly where the pinpoint was inconspicuous or navigationally difficult to approach. The south coast of France offered a far better choice of places suitable for landing and embarkation in all states of weather than the Atlantic coast of Morocco. Port-Miou, near Cassis, was ideal in that it was sheltered against all winds. The *calanques* at Port-d'En-Vau and Sormiou were sheltered against all winds except from one direction.

CHAPTER XXX

Operations by *Seawolf, Seadog* and *Tarana*: July–September 1942

A t the beginning of July Krajewski still had no news of the appointment of a relief to take over command of *Seawolf* from him or of the appointment of a staff officer to replace him as head of the Polish mission in Gibraltar. Exhausted as he was, he had no choice but to prepare his felucca for what was to prove the longest, most complex, most successful, but also one of the most trying, of all his operations:

SECRET

REPORT OF THE FIFTEENTH EVACUATION VOYAGE
(to southern France, 7–26 July 1942)[1]

1) *TELEGRAMS PRIOR TO THE VOYAGE.* In the course of one of the embarkation operations during the 14th mission, Capt Iwaszkiewicz and I agreed that I was to let him know the *spot* where we would take on passengers, that is, I had to decide whether La-Madrague was suitable for that type of operation from the seagoing point of view. From the land side it had many advantages, such as its proximity to the tram stop, short journey time, etc. At the same time, its close proximity to Marseilles and to a fort was a disadvantage.

I was also to inform him by cable if I had a transfer vessel at my disposal; if so, Capt Iwaszkiewicz and I agreed, it would be better to aim to embark a larger group of around 100 people. He considered this to be quite feasible – and he was, after all, the one person (other than Major Chojnacki) entitled to give an opinion on what was clearly a local matter. I suggested this larger number to the local leaders of the evacuation, emphasising that we could mount only one voyage a month, encompassing at the most two pick-ups, because as a rule we spent a week at sea in the vicinity of the French coast. The period of bad weather due to start in October was another inducement to make the operation more productive by increasing the number of people taken off at each embarkation. The exact figures had to be decided by the people on the spot, i.e. in Marseilles, who had acknowledged that it would be possible to organise a *hundred* people at a time.

I emphasise the matter of numbers because of certain information received during the meeting with Major Chojnacki in France, about certain agencies in London intervening incomprehensibly with orders to reduce the number by *half*(!); I am submitting a separate report on this matter.

Against this background, I sent a cable on 22 June to Major Chojnacki. . . via London stating that from the seagoing point of view La-Madrague was a possibility and suggesting two embarkations; the first, of 100 people, the second, of 70 people. Further, I suggested a meeting with Major Chojnacki since there were many matters that required that I speak to him directly.

2) *MORGIOU AS A PROPOSED SITE.* Having sent my cable on 22 June I heard quite fortuitously, from one of the officers evacuated from Marseilles and from Major Chojnacki's immediate circle, that there was a spot for embarkation that was better, particularly from the seagoing point of view – at Morgiou. Accordingly, I sent a cable on 27 June suggesting this new site and – in case this caused the Marseilles outpost to change dates for technical reasons – an alternative date of 14 July. On 6 July I received a wire via London informing me that Major Chojnacki regarded Morgiou as inconvenient, and also that he could not change the dates. What struck me particularly about this wire was that the figures had been reduced by 50 per cent from those I had suggested (and had agreed with Marseilles). I thought however that conditions must have altered and that Major Chojnacki, and he alone, had set these new figures, which would have been natural in those circumstances.

In the light of this telegram, I brought forward our departure by 24 hours and before leaving sent a further cable (6 July) informing Major Chojnacki that I would arrive at La-Madrague on the required date.

3) We sailed at 2210 hrs on 7 July. The crew comprised: Capt Krajewski, Mate Tarnawski (1st mechanic), Leading Seaman Schlauberg (cook). Seaman Kurzawa (junior mechanic) remained behind in hospital in Gibraltar. For the first time Siembieda (mechanic from the merchant navy) did not take part, as he had been sent to England to have an essential operation on an advanced rupture and also he became increasingly demoralised with the conditions at Gibraltar, a problem on which I reported when the civilian crew were changed. He was kept on only because Bosun Buczek, sent out to Gibraltar as 1st mechanic, went to hospital before the first voyage and was judged unsuitable for service on seagoing units.

As the crew were considerably depleted, I received in addition merchant seaman Kreeman (Estonian) and Garcia (Spanish), both as mechanics. Futhermore, Sergeant Potter (British), who was familiar with the newer type of radio set which we were to use, travelled with us to establish proper radio communication.

As a passenger we took Mr Alvast – as requested by Major Chojnacki in his telegrams several times – with the aim of putting him ashore during one of our embarkation operations.

The first few days of the operation passed without incident. Our course led, as previously, far from land and was thus totally dependent on astronomical observations, except when it passed between the islands of Ibiza and Majorca (Balearics).

On 10 July, as we were having to regulate some valves, which during the short overhaul in port had been adjusted to completely wrong margins (too much tolerance), we took the opportunity to repaint the entire felucca, which I decided was advisable since our description had been passed out and was by now no doubt familiar to the captains of French merchant ships. The whole ship did not take longer than three hours.

On 12 July began the period of the severe mistral, which, I still imagined, should not have lasted longer than two to four days during this period.

Of our encounters with ships, the most interesting on the passage to Marseilles was our meeting with the ST CHRISTINE, known to us from the 14th mission (15 June), when she had changed course completely in order to examine our felucca from close quarters and then followed us for 15 minutes. This time, however, she did not undertake any suspicious man-oeuvres whatsoever (this was 40 miles to the south of Mar-seilles) and, without changing course, disappeared in the direction of the above-mentioned port. In spite of everything, it did not seem to augur well, although it was possible that she had not recognised us because of the complete repaint.

4) *THE STORM RUINS OUR ORIGINAL PLANS.* Just after midnight on 13 July I was already close to the shore where Capt Iwaszkiewicz and I had fixed our rendezvous, not far from the La-Madrague tram station. It is a place lying some 5 km. to the south of the port of Marseilles; the well-known little island of Château d'If lies even closer. The whole port can be seen from there like the palm of your hand. The shoreline is hardly less illuminated than it would presumably be in peace-time.

I received no reply to my signals at first and so, thinking that I had the wrong place, moved closer to the port of Marseilles, where I again began the parade along the coast, sending out signals aimed as far as possible at the level of the water. Only at 0100 hrs, when I reached what I assumed was the meeting-place for the second time, did I receive a reply. Our people on the shore had probably been obscured from the sea in an oblique direction to the line of the shore and therefore had not seen our signals.

The storm however grew to an ever more threatening level. The anchor did not hold and a very strong wind was driving us on to rocks. Anchoring manoeuvres, or rather the attempt to locate a sufficiently shallow spot and suitable ground, lasted until 0300 hrs, after which, in the end, I decided to heave to offshore and send a boat only *once* in order to tell the reception committee to change the embarkation point to the familiar En-Vau. Mainly by luck, Leading Seaman Stanislawski managed to reach the narrow strip (some 20 m.) of beach and tell Capt Iwaszkiewicz of the postponement of the operation because of the weather, and of the new location.

5) *TAKING ON BOARD THREE 'AGENTS'*. The next day (13 July) I waited as the mistral intensified to the south of the Ciotat–Cassis region, having moved away to a distance of some 40 miles from the shore. Until shortly after sunset I did not want to be within 12 miles of the coast, the limit of visibility from the shore in these regions.

At midnight we were already entering Port-d'En-Vau. Our signals received the correct replies and so I sent the rubber boat ashore; out of the ten 'agents' expected it came back with two men and one woman (the wife of one of the men). The others 'had not made it'. After leaving Port-d'En-Vau we passed (0145 hrs) a patrol boat heading slowly in the direction of Toulon (under lights).

During our short stay in Port-d'En-Vau I put Mr Alvast ashore.

Meanwhile the storm, far from relenting, seemed to intensify further. The felucca showed more and more leaks, to the extent that the mechanics had to pump bilge-water for more than half a watch. The putty seals and caulking carried out by the Blanda shipyard in March were proving inadequate somewhere in the submerged portion of the hull. Heating up materials on such a small vessel in such bad weather was of course out of the question. The sea water was coming in everywhere, and we had no dry blankets in the cabin quarters (I underline this since, only yesterday, I had to resist Captain Osborne's requests that – in order to keep to some dates set arbitrarily by the Admiralty for its operations – the *Seawolf* set out on its next operation as early as 5 August.)

The original plan was to transfer the passengers in two

batches: on 13 July, after the anticipated embarkation at La-Madrague, which of course had been cancelled because we had changed the pick-up of the Poles; and 14 July after taking on board the party of agents. Because of the storm I did not even move to the meeting-place but waited one more day riding out the storm beyond the extent of shoreline visibility, after which I moved once again towards d'En-Vau.

From the very beginning of the voyage I was in radio contact with Gibraltar, informing them of the changes in the situation. They sent on the information to the transfer vessel.

6) *RIDING THE STORM WITH 55 PASSENGERS.* At 2315 hrs I was again at the entrance to Port-d'En-Vau where I exchanged the normal signals with the shore. I made my way ashore on the dinghy, where it turned out that Major Chojnacki was waiting for me, as I had suggested in my previous cable, to confer with me on the current situation and plans for the future.

At 0030 hrs I returned to the felucca with the last group of evacuees, after which we weighed anchor and set a course to meet the transfer vessel. That night we took off 52 Poles.

Unfortunately, on that day too the weather was very stormy (waves 7–8 on the scale of sea conditions), so that when I eventually met the ship, transfers could not be contemplated. I did, though, let them know that I was forced to ride the storm with the swell (so as not to subject the passengers, most of whom were on the deck, to an irritating dousing from the waves, in testingly low temperatures); I also gave them a possible rendez-vous in case we lost contact with the ship.

The ship moved against the swell to the north, but the *Seawolf* turned in a south-westerly direction, trying to travel at minimum speed – indispensable requirement for steering in such a heavy swell – and also not to distance ourselves too far from the area of operations (I still had to return to Cassis).

That day we sighted the first and only aircraft of that voyage – a two-engined plane travelling at altitude towards the south-east, not in any case showing any interest in our felucca. In the Marseilles region I normally encounter several merchant vessels daily; sometimes also in the Cannes–Antibes area, where, how-ever, their course leads either to or from Italy; near Marseilles the course is to the south-west, or to Marseilles itself. To date I have never encountered any real warships (I do not count trawler-type patrol boats).

On the 15th conditions were very stormy.

When on 16 July the weather did not improve, the situation became ever more critical. Our whole strategic reserve was being used up; the dates of the operation were passing by;

and the agreed date – which lay particularly near to my heart – was approaching ever closer – the night of 19/20 July, fixed for our second embarkation of Poles from Port-d'En-Vau. Apart from all this, we were drawing worryingly close to Sardinia (at 1710 hrs our observed position was lat. 40° 52′ north, long. 6° 40′ east, barely 75 miles from the north-west point of Sardinia), and along this coastline we could expect regular patrols by the Italian air force and later by patrol boats too. I therefore had to force a passage against the swell in order not to take too great a risk.

7) *THE TRANSFER OF OUR PASSENGERS.* Luckily, as evening approached, there were indications that the storm was weakening and the swell eased somewhat. At 1840 hrs I changed course, bringing her about and moving in the direction of Cassis, at the same time suggesting by W/T signal, after much consideration, the only means of saving the whole plan, namely: instead of the agreed rendezvous with the ship, we should meet as close as possible to my point of operation (Cassis region), I would approach the shore that night, after the anticipated transfer (17 July), and, having landed several agents on the shore, still have time to get to the Antibes region – and, above all, to make it in time to pick up the second group of Poles afterwards.

That day, in exceptionally beautiful weather (the last for a long time), there was an emotion-filled race to the changed meeting points, since, what with the difficulties and limitations of radio communications, the explanations took up a great deal of precious time, and there was a point at which it seemed that the whole plan had already fallen apart.

Luckily, Gibraltar understood what I had in mind and eventually fixed a rendezvous so that the transfer could take place in the evening some 10 miles south of Cassis. The fact that I arrived at the meeting point barely ten minutes before the ship itself shows how close the game was to being lost. To have arrived a couple of hours late would have meant the loss of a whole day, because of the huge distance (140 miles) to the next point of our operation (Antibes). The agents we had agreed to pick up had in any case already been waiting for two days.

The transfer took place without any difficulties. Indeed I took a further six people to put ashore, and a certain amount of military stores. I also replenished our reserves of water and food and our fuel, just in case (it turned out not to be necessary; as before, we had enough of everything for the place and the purpose).

At 2210 hrs, or 40 minutes later, I moved away from the side of the ship setting a course for the Bay of Cassis.

A few minutes after midnight four of the new passengers had already been put down at the spot discussed with them earlier in my cabin.

At 0500 hrs I set a course for the south in order to distance myself from the shore, after which we turned east.

8) *THE STORM RETURNS.* During the operation to put the agents ashore we again saw (at the same time of day as before) the lights of a patrol boat moving slowly along the coast, but he could not see us against a background of high cliffs.

The mistral in fact returned after a day's break and again reached the unusual strength of Force 7. It came at us from the west. It delayed my arrival at the embarkation and landing spot until 0300 hrs, whereas the operational order had anticipated 0100 hrs. Indeed, as I received no answer to my signals, I could not be sure whether anyone was still waiting on the shore, or whether they had left after a couple of hours. Since the need to pick up the next group of Poles the following evening did not permit me to postpone the operation for a further 24 hours, I made my way to a place with which I was now familiar near Antibes (400 m. away) and I sent off the dinghy with the agents and material (0430 hrs).

Good fortune was not on our side at that point: the dinghy returned without having put anyone shore, since a few passers-by had taken an interest in her and one cyclist (it was already growing light) had even stopped to take a closer look.

I therefore left the bay at 0500 hrs, setting a course for Marseilles.

The storm however returned at its former strength. With the direction of the swell and the wind against me, I realised by 1305 hrs on 19 July that I would not make it by the agreed time to pick up the Poles. Consequently I decided to turn about and make one more attempt to put the agents ashore and to take on board some of the people who would be waiting, or so we had been notified by signal. After midnight, that is, on 20 July at 0020 hrs, I received a reply to my signals from the shore, indicating that the reception committee was waiting, this time in the agreed place. The dinghy was sent out, taking the agents to the shore, at the risk of capsizing with its passengers and heavy load, and in a location that was less than ideal for this type of operation. The British authorities do not employ *our* system of choosing embarkation points: first, the land-side organisers suggest a location, having familiarised themselves with the hinterland, and only then do the seagoing people put forward their point of view.

That spot had been chosen only from a nautical chart, which never gives a true picture of the coast.

The agents we were to have taken on board had not turned up and so at 0050 hrs I moved again in the direction of Marseilles, having successfully completed all the British tasks.

Our speed amounted to not much more than 4 knots because of the storm driving into us. . . In fact, it was obvious that we had been extremely unlucky in encountering this exceptional mistral, which lasted more than a fortnight.

9) *A FOREST FIRE NEAR CASSIS.* At 0130 hrs when I was approaching Cassis, but still a considerable distance away, I made out a phenomenon that we could not at first explain: the area projected for the pick-up seemed to be illuminated strangely for this area and this time of year. Drawing nearer, we discovered that it was a forest fire extending over a large area and fanned by the strong wind, which also made it extremely difficult to extinguish (as those we took on board confirmed later). I was afraid that no-one would be waiting at d'En-Vau because the security agencies were bound to be present. However, the *calanque* itself was not affected by fire: in fact the couriers from the Marseilles outpost were waiting. They told us that the operation had been postponed for 24 hours precisely because of the presence of police, linked to the blaze. We took on board a woman and two children (the agent's family) who had not turned up for embarkation on 14 July and had now been brought along by a delegate of the British organisation in Marseilles, kept 'au courant' with my visits to Port-d'En-Vau by the British Admiralty.

10) *THE EMBARKATION OF 53 NEW PASSENGERS.* The next night at 0225 hrs (22 July), the second party of Poles were embarked at Port-d'En-Vau. While this was under way I had yet another onshore conversation with Capt Iwaszkiewicz about the situation in France with regard to evacuations.

The boarding had to be speeded up even further at the last moment because the lights of some ship became visible at the mouth of the *calanque.*

At 0350 hrs we left the Port-d'En-Vau *calanque*, cutting across the course of the above-mentioned ship (which was heading towards La-Ciotat) without incident.

I took a return course this time to Minorca so as to leave it on my starboard side, thus avoiding any encounters with merchant ships and any repetition of the incident with the *St-Christine* during the previous voyage.

This course was not too unpleasant, as the storm was coming at us from the north-west.

We had a further meeting as arranged with the transfer ship near the island of Formentera (Balearic Islands) on the morning of 24 July. After that, in changeable weather, I set a course onwards to Gibraltar, arriving there on 26 July at 1245 hrs, after a voyage of 19 days (the longest to date) and some 2,520 nautical miles (the longest distance also).

It was a particularly arduous voyage because of the weather, which was tolerable for only a small proportion of the time.

In all, we evacuated 105 Poles and there would have been 50 more if it had not been for the interference of certain agencies in London (see below).

11) *INFORMATION FROM MAJOR CHOJNACKI AND CAPT IWASZKIEWICZ.* Something that came as a complete surprise to me, and astonished Major Chojnacki equally, was the fact that the reduction in the number of Poles – earlier agreed orally between the Gibraltar post and the Marseilles post – had come in orders from London and without any attempt to sound out the opinions of the two interested parties.

Another thing that struck both of us as very puzzling was the vehement tone of the telegram, which insisted that under no circumstances were the numbers given by London to be exceeded.

Major Chojnacki said that perhaps the Gibraltar post was not able to keep its word for some reason or could not guarantee to accommodate the promised number of evacuees on the felucca and on the transfer vessel. At the last moment (he emphasised the considerable delay in sending this telegram to him) he had been forced to change completely the instructions he and I had agreed, based on taking off 100 people.

We came to the conclusion that one of the newly arrived Polish officers in London had probably taken it upon himself to convince the evacuation department of the Commander-in-Chief's headquarters that it was impossible to take off more than 50 people, and that he had prompted the staff there to issue a categorical order to THE ONLY PEOPLE COMPETENT TO TAKE SUCH A DECISION in this respect – the Marseilles outpost. It looked as though someone was bent on undermining the success of the evacuation operations being carried out by the Gibraltar and Marseilles missions.

Here I must reiterate that it would be quite uneconomical and irrational to organise such very arduous voyages on a small fishing boat – in conditions that are not comparable with any other and are unimaginable even to people who have seen action on a surface ship or a submarine – just to take off a few dozen people. What we should be aiming for is to increase the efficiency of such evacuations. Moreover only four more evacuation voyages can be mounted before the approaching winter season (the last of them in the first half of October), after which the weather conditions will be too bad for a small felucca to travel about 2,000 nautical miles and remain at sea for at least two weeks.

Major Chojnacki brought me up to date about the evacuation situation in France and told me that the French authorities are moving all Poles from the coastal region to the north (near the demarcation line). Amongst others, they are winding up the work detail at the Salins-de-Giraud (mouth of the Rhône) and the (Polish) section of the Red Cross at Marseilles. He expected further moves and thought that this was being done to hamper the Polish evacuations. He also considered it quite possible that they might move him and other Polish officers from Marseilles but added that he would continue to carry out the evacuation operations as before.

He requested me also to report to the central authorities in London that Capt Iwaszkiewicz deserves special distinction for his unstinting efforts in the organisational work of evacuation. Naturally I warmly support this assessment, having had the opportunity to observe the results of his work at first hand: it is Capt Iwaszkiewicz whom I always see on the shore leading the embarkation operation. There is a good deal of personal risk involved in this and the French prisons and treatment of prisoners have already achieved a sad notoriety. (I know of documented cases of arrested officers being beaten about the face, being manacled, being locked in cells together with common criminals, of appalling sanitary conditions, of being held in prison for several months despite orders from Vichy to free them, and so on.)

I passed on the news and agreed the dates of our next embarkation on the nights of 13/14 August and 16/17 August. The location: if we have suitable weather, La-Madrague; if not, then Sormiou.

Major Chojnacki and Captain Iwaskiewicz were equally surprised to have received the order from London to evacuate 50 per cent British personnel; they say that there are not that many of them in the unoccupied zone of France, adding that the British are also carrying out evacuation missions independently (by the sea route), begun after the successes of the Polish seagoing evacuations. The numbers involved though are considerably smaller.

In addition, I received a letter to be forwarded to the C-in-C's Chief of Staff. The envelope has been spoiled from being in Capt Iwaszkiewicz's pocket when he had to undertake a long walk in hilly countryside. I enclose the letter in the same state I received it.

(signed) M. Krajewski
Gibraltar, 31 July 1942

On his return to Gibraltar on 27 July from this very trying 19-day expedition to southern France, Krajewski was confronted with a crisis over his plans to resume evacuation from French North Africa.

After the unsuccessful operation to this area in June, he had managed, with the help of the Americans, to re-establish contact with Captain Szewalski in Oran with a view to fixing a date for a renewed attempt, using a felucca.[2] Since it must be assumed that the places used on previous occasions were guarded by the French, he proposed that they try a new stretch of coastline, one that had been recommended in April to Gromnicki in Oran by a trusted Spaniard who had been extremely helpful to the Poles. Not only was this man familiar with the topography of this part of the coast and with the Spanish fishermen who lived there but he also offered to lend a hand with arrangements for the landward side of an operation. Particulars of the new venue were forwarded in a letter to Szewalski by the Polish mission in Gibraltar on 16 June. In his interim reply on 22 June, Szewalski promised to send within a couple of days a suggested date and time for the felucca's arrival and detailed information about the stretch of coast proposed.

It was not until 19 July that Gromnicki in Gibraltar received this promised letter from Szewalski, who had by then visited the area with the Americans. He reported that, as in the previous year, guards were deployed lightly throughout the region but that there were none at the proposed landing point. A man referred to as 'Papa' would be waiting there on 30 July with a bicycle, identity card and a pass stamped by the police, which would enable Gromnicki to travel to Oran and to Algiers. A main purpose of the proposed operation was to land Gromnicki in Algeria, where, having established contact with Szewalski in Oran and Czapski in Algiers, he was to work out with them plans for an early resumption of evacuation of the Poles interned in French camps and specifically for a first operational project that took account of the new conditions. Gromnicki would also carry letters of introduction to very influential Frenchmen and to one in particular who actively supported the Polish cause. Both Gromnicki himself and Krajewski were counting on this mission to relaunch the evacuation programme.

On the very day on which Szewalski's letter reached Gibraltar, the mission had applied to Captain Osborne, commander of the Coast Watching Flotilla, for the operation to be carried out on 29/30 July: they asked CWF to make available either one of its new feluccas or some suitable British ship, since their own two feluccas with Polish crews were absent on operations to France.[3] Osborne assured them that the operation to land Gromnicki would be carried out and that the ship (*Minna*) would sail on 29 July in the morning. On 28 July, when all the preparations for Gromnicki's departure were complete, the British Admiralty (i.e. Slocum) cancelled the operation. Krajewski, now back in Gibraltar after his 15th evacuation mission, sent a signal on 29 July asking the reasons for this decision. The Polish Naval Attaché in London replied laconically that the cancellation of the operation was 'confirmed repeat confirmed'; the reason was that no details of the operation had been communicated to London, and the authorities there saw no possibility of carrying out evacuation operations from North Africa at that time.

Furious, Krajewski expostulated that decision-making had been taken out of his hands and that, without consultation with him, there had been a change of policy with regard to evacuation from North Africa. He wrote at length on 31 July to Klimecki, Chief of Staff to General Sikorski, quoting a directive he had received from him in April, after the failure of the attempt to carry out a mass evacuation of Polish internees from the Oran area. Klimecki had urged Krajewski to give priority to the task of evacuating even a few people each month from Algeria, as it was the only possible way of bolstering the morale of the other internees. Krajewski was at that point uncertain whether responsibility for the cancellation of Gromnicki's mission was Polish or British, but he feared that the intervention of officers who had been evacuated from North Africa might have been to blame. This suspicion was none the less galling for being unjustified.

The problem was, of course, that nobody had told the Poles anything about the decision taken by Roosevelt and Churchill to carry out a major landing of Allied forces in French North Africa, which made attempts to evacuate penny-packets of interned Polish troops clandestinely from the African coast quite pointless, since they would soon all be free.

Krajewski's frustration was compounded by uncertainty as to how long he would have to continue to bear, after more than a year of unceasing activity, the intolerable burden of being both head of the Polish mission at Gibraltar and captain, navigator, mate and factotum of exiguous and unreliable operational vessels. On his return to Gibraltar on 27 July he had heard that his successor as head of the mission would be Commander K.E. Durski-Trzasko, but on 1 August there was still no news that anyone had been appointed to take over his command of *Seawolf* and he wrote to Stoklas, the Naval Attaché in London, in a mood of considerable bitterness:

Dear Commander,[4]

This letter, by contrast with earlier ones, is of a private nature since it concerns exclusively my personal affairs, namely the matter of my transfer.

Since your departure I have received in all two telegrams (from you). I am drawing attention to these at the outset, because they are the *only* – fairly modest – evidence I have of our authorities' intentions with regard to me.

I must point out to begin with that I was cheered when I read the phrase in your telegram of 9 July that my 'early relief (was) under consideration'. At the same time I must admit to a certain sense of bitterness that, although both matters were set in motion at the same time, my successor as head of the mission, Commander Durski, is virtually on his way here, whereas my replacement as captain of the felucca is still only 'under consideration'. For more than a year now I have been roaming around in conditions with which no-one, literally *no-one*, in our navy can be even remotely familiar. Moreover, my plight is considerably worse than that of my crew (I have had two crews already), because they can at least partly relax in port – indeed, I try to ensure that they do, for the good of the evacuation. By contrast, almost the minute I return to port I have to set to work on correspondence, repairs to the feluccas, and many other matters – including those associated with being Polish mission representative here. After the last, long (20 days) and exhausting mission, I did go to the beach – only once, and then with a guilty conscience – and I would have liked to go there today in order to unwind a little (it is Saturday, 1800 hrs as I write), but I cannot as I want to send this important and urgent *courrier* tomorrow.

It has been like this continuously, after every mission, for more than a year.

As a result I am physically tired to the point of exhaustion. If I have come this far, it is only because I have been supported by strong reserves of health and, above all, by an eagerness to do a necessary job, supplemented lately by the hope that very soon my well-deserved 'change of guard' will come about . . . I was counting on handing over the August voyage to my successor but I see in fact that, when I complete my outstanding correspondence, I will have to begin preparations for my next voyage myself. And I really cannot keep going so long, and as a resuslt the main thing that will suffer will be our very worthy cause.

So then [. . .] I strongly and respectfully request you to make the necessary approaches to the competent authorities, so that before the end of August I may also be able to hand over completely my functions as captain of the felucca.

I can see that the evacuation department might, in the interests of blissful inertia, want to believe that this next evacuation, which will be important in terms of numbers, will go just like the previous ones, and to delay my departure by various means, of which they have many (e.g. 'There is no room on the plane', etc). But these gentlemen, apparently acting on information from people who do not always have disinterested aims, are precisely the ones who are beginning to put obstacles in my way (see my report by this same post on the limitations being placed on numbers to be evacuated). They must know that, by putting off the change, they will bring the evacuation to a halt, by September at the latest. Because I now need a thorough rest before I will be fit for such demanding service at sea.

I declare today categorically that if my successor as captain of the felucca is not here before 5 September when we are due to weigh anchor, then there will be no evacuation mission that month. Indeed, I consider it my duty to myself and to the service to go to a doctor and request a check-up and a written certificate saying that I must have rest. I have no doubt at all that he will give me one.

A year of constant work and strain obviously takes its toll: I have been captain of the felucca, a junior officer (i.e. crew member), bosun (sic), because I never had a good junior deck officer in the crew), a writer, a liaison officer and sometimes commander of the unit of evacuees, since in certain groups there were no good officers like Capt Ejsymont. On top of all this, I spent generally at least half my time at sea and the other half in port sorting out outstanding matters, which none of my helpers is competent to do.

Do I have to add that a warship officer's duties (and I speak from experience, having served on warships in 1940, during the height of battle) never involve a major effort such as has been exacted from me – an amalgam of ship/sea/land functions and administration?

I reiterate in the strongest terms that I will not be able to sail in September. Moreover, since Captain Osborne is giving *Seawolf* more and more tasks, and the Admiralty is basing more and more plans on her – setting dates, incidentally, completely arbitrarily – there could be no felucca available and the operation could well be called into question, in which case *there may be a great stir.*

I am writing to you frankly and in this detail because it is important to me that you, with your known positive attitude to our needs, understand the background to my request, which is all the more urgent and importunate for having been put off for so long.

While I am writing, a question: is it possible to find out who at HQ is queering the pitch? Why, inexplicably, from month to month HQ arbitrarily limits the number of people being evacuated without sounding out my opinion or that of the people in Marseilles? Or why Second Lt Gromnicki's operation was cancelled (the background to this he probably explained to you in detail) with the assertion that evacuation from North Africa is already impossible? Is it not Roehr, who is known to share this view (at some time I will be able to explain a great deal about his game to you)? I ask for my own information only, so as to have some insight into the Chief of Staff's decision.

Yours sincerely,
M. Krajewski

Having fired this salvo at Stoklas about his own affairs, Krajewski wrote to the head of the evacuation section at Sikorski's GHQ in London about the mysterious limitations that had been imposed on the numbers of Poles to be evacuated by his mission from the south coast of France.[5]

He explained how he had discovered from Chojnacki when they met at Cassis on 15 July that the latter had been instructed at the last minute by London to scale down by 50 per cent the numbers agreed with Iwaskiewicz in June. On that occasion he had asked for 100 people to be available for the first July embarkation and 50 for the second. Chojnacki had been ordered to embark no more than 50 and 25. Though astonished by this peremptory change of plan, Chojnacki had concluded that Krajewski must have struck difficulty in obtaining a suitable back-up vessel and had therefore been compelled to make adjustments. He was as dumbfounded as Krajewski to discover that the restriction emanated from London.

Krajewski admitted that he knew nothing about the background to this decision but, if it were not the result of intervention by the British authorities or some other external factor, he wondered whether it was not based on false information brought back by an officer, whom he did not name but who was clearly Roehr. If so, it was an intolerable interference with responsibilities that belonged to the Marseilles and Gibraltar evacuation outposts and a stab in the backs of those who had to confront so many difficulties and dangers for the cause. He actually used the word 'crucified'.

On 8 August, a week after writing this letter, Krajewski was off to sea again, still without news of his relief. It proved to be another frustrating experience, for maintenance of the CWF feluccas had been handed back to the dockyard and was no longer carried out under the benevolent and rigorous scrutiny of Commander (E) John Illingworth of HMS *Maidstone.*

REPORT OF THE SIXTEENTH EVACUATION VOYAGE
(aborted)
(8–13 August 1942)[6]

1) *OVERHAUL OF THE ENGINE AND FELUCCA BEFORE THE MISSION.* The felucca was last caulked during its major refit in March. The material employed in this work was *putty* which however quite quickly began to dry out and even fall out, which gave us some concern on the last few voyages, for in the bad weather the amount of water that collected in the bilge could certainly not be explained by a leak of the stern gland or anything of that kind.

During the very strong storm at the beginning of July (15th mission), with normal petty breakdowns of the (hand-operated) bilge-pump, the amount of water threatened the stability of the felucca and meant that the watch mechanic had to pump for 45 minutes every hour. I therefore sent a signal to tell Gibraltar that the felucca must at all costs be recaulked when it was hauled out on the slip. On our return to port, the dockyard accordingly set to work giving her a thorough caulking and also took the opportunity to carry out other tasks such as repairing the freshwater tank, etc.

A second very important request we made was for the overhaul of the engine, which had run already for some 1,350 hours without being thoroughly serviced. The engine was taken to pieces (also by the dockyard) and reconditioned under a certain degree of 'supervision' by our senior mechanic Tarnawski.

2) *ENGINE TRIALS.* After the overhaul, with customary caution, I asked for a six-hour engine trial at sea in the presence of a representative from the mechanical workshop of the dockyard. Although this request was put forward by Commander Osborne, head of CWF, the dockyard commodore would not agree to put one of his mechanics at our disposal, arguing that they had an enormous amount of work in the workshop.

In the light of this I undertook tests with just my own crew; aboard as a guest I had Commander Osborne, who wished to take this opportunity to familiarise himself with sailing conditions on our felucca.

During the trial Tarnawski did not notice anything particularly worrying, although the temperature of the engine (crankcase, clutch) was certainly not normal. Since however this raised temperature had existed *from the beginning*, Tarnawski pronounced the engine in working order.

3) *THE RAISING OF THE ANCHOR* took place on 8 August just at sunset, in very good weather.

On board: Lt Cdr Krajewski – commanding officer; Chief Petty Officer Tarnawski – first mechanic; Leading Seaman Chwastek – helmsman; Leading Seaman Stanislawski – radio and helmsman; Seaman Schlauberg - cook and one turn at the helm daily; apart from this there were the foreigners, Garcia – second engine-room watch-keeper; Kreeman (Estonian) – third engine-room watch-keeper. Because of the shortage of crew, I myself had to take six-hour spells at the helm throughout the voyage, as well as my normal functions as captain. Not present: Seaman Kurzawa – in hospital once again.

4) *THE VOYAGE.* Only a few hours after weighing anchor (at 1020 hrs on 9 August) we again had cause to complain of the poor quality of work carried out by the Spanish workmen in the dockyard: there was a very serious leak, which was most strange in view of the very recent recaulking of the hull. After tearing away the ceiling in the commander's cabin aft we found that the leak had occurred through a seam puttied carelessly. In port, where the stern is not immersed so deeply as a result of the speed of the vessel, the unputtied spot was above the water-line and was, of course, painted with great care. To stem this leak of water took us three hours and all our reserves of cement, which luckily we always carry in case the felucca is damaged while manoeuvring.

At 1700 hrs warships overtook us: they were two corvettes escorting two tankers heading in the direction of Malta.

At 2010 hrs when the convoy was passing us, one of the escorts (K140) became interested in us: it approached quite near on a couple of occasions, apparently to get a better look at us. When after a while we heard orders to man the boats, we knew what it meant.

Our papers were checked by a Naval Lieutenant (RNVR), without any special incident, although he seemed to realise that there was something curious about this felucca covered by British papers, which I did not want him to examine too precisely, since I feared they might discover a case of explosive material the British authorities had asked me to take to a certain point in France.

5) *THE ENGINE BREAKS DOWN.* During my watch at the helm and the Spaniard's watch over the engine, at 0730 hrs on 10 August, I noticed from the sound of the engine that something was wrong. I went down to the engine-room, which was filled with smoke; Garcia was evidently not unduly worried by this but I was familiar with the phenomenon from our first voyage with an engine of this type. We woke Tarnawski, who opened up the crank-case and then we discovered . . . that

TWO BIG-END BEARINGS of the connecting-rods had melted, despite having been thoroughly oiled, at least in the part to which the watch technician had access. Further oiling did not help, neither did removing both forward pistons; the fuel pressure in this engine is too low for it to start under these conditions.

6) *UNDER SAIL.* Having a very favourable and fairly strong easterly wind, at least we did not worry about how to get home since our large area of sail gives us a sailing speed, in good conditions, of up to 7 knots. Here again, however, luck was not with us: at 1412 hrs, barely a few hours after we had started out under sail, the BOOM BROKE. Examination of a cross-section indicated that the wood had rotted. Our speed fell at once from 4 to $1\frac{1}{2}$ knots.

At 1755 hrs our observed position indicated a latitude of 36° 47′ north, longitude 1° 18′ west – still more than 150 miles from Gibraltar. (The breakdown had occurred a little less than 40 hours after starting up the engine after its overhaul in the dock-yard; in other words, this engine, which had worked for 1,350 hours WITHOUT BEING SERVICED, had not been able to withstand being overhauled by the. . . Spanish mechanics.)

We did not manage to establish radio contact with Gibraltar until 2330 hrs on the same day (10 August), when I reported that we had a breakdown that could not be repaired, gave our position, speed and course and asked for Marseilles to be informed that the operation had been called off.

On the next day our observed position at 1415 hrs was latitude 36° 18′ north, longitude 2° 29′ west. Our speed increased to 3 knots as a result of using both parts of the broken boom to stretch out the sail and employing the lateen rig (completely different from ours) – which made the felucca look very strange.

On the same day (11 August) at 2330 hrs we received a signal from Gibraltar reading, 'Inform Gibraltar when you pass the Isle of Alboran. I will try to send destroyer to tow you back.' We were in any case already at the position requested.

On the morning of the 12th the wind dropped completely. Sending out hourly communiqués of my position, I awaited the promised destroyer.

Around midday a heavily escorted British aircraft-carrier passed us, returning from the famous Malta convoy battle in which, among others, the aircraft-carrier *Eagle* was sunk.[7]

At 2015 hrs we sighted the destroyer. Half an hour later we were under tow.

We arrived at Gibraltar at 1100 hrs on 13 August.

7) *THE ENGINE REPAIR. CONCLUSIONS DRAWN FROM THE BREAKDOWN.* After my return I discovered at once from Commander Osborne that conclusions had been duly drawn from the breakdown. He had immediately requested the Admiralty to send an engineer officer to the Flotilla, saying that until then he had relied on the judgement of the dockyard regarding repairs, but that the dockyard was generally negatively disposed to such tasks, eager to see the back of them as quickly as possible and incapable of giving an assessment on which one could base the success of such important operations, not to mention the safety of the crew.

In addition, he reported that the mechanics tending the engine during the voyage – and making an excellent job of it – could not have had suitable training in regulating and adjusting an engine or in repairing the most serious breakdowns, since that demanded very good workshop specialists. We had such people on the *Maidstone* but they were no longer available to us, since the Flotilla had been made 'independent'.

Indeed, the first check of the engine by a 'borrowed' engineer officer showed that the filters were blocked up, the dockyard workers having cleaned the engine crank-case not with rags but with tow, leaving behind traces of fibre. Further, the senior mechanic recommended that the engine should most certainly have an oil-pressure manometer. But it was Tarnawski who pointed out that examination of the coupling showed a misalignment between the shaft and the clutch, which had caused the shaft to sag and the clutch consequently to run too hot, ever since it was installed.

As usual with this dockyard, the repair itself took longer than promised, here in spite of Commander Osborne's pleas.

Nevertheless it appeared that on 2 September everything would be ready. On that day, new white-metal bearings were installed, the alignment of the shaft was subjected to fresh examination and an already repaired universal coupling was fitted. We then set out on a six-hour test run. This time the dockyard did assign one of its mechanics to us as an observer. In addition there was an engineer officer on board, borrowed from one of the bigger ships in our Flotilla.

The test run already showed faults: the bearings were continuing to overheat. It was suggested that the oil could be cooled by installing piping to carry cooling water to the oil tank.

The issue of this cooling pipe (which requires very little work) is worth further mention as it is so characteristic of the technical difficulties we have to deal with.

The dockyard decided *not* to install it, their own engineer having concluded that it was not necessary. I told Commander

Osborne that it was indispensable: all engines designed for use on the open seas have an oil-cooling system, and our engine had always run too hot. The maker of the engine had probably not allowed for oil-cooling, since it was probably not designed for whole *weeks* in motion without a break but rather for intermittent work, perhaps in a port motor boat. We bought this engine because it was the only one of which we had full particulars and because there was a local mechanic representing the firm to carry out the installation. We also knew when that particular engine would be delivered to Gibraltar.

Commander Slocum, who is present here from the Admiralty, wrote a vigorous letter to the dockyard commodore, citing the above arguments and concluding that too much depended on this engine – from the viewpoint both of the operation and of the security of the crew and the felucca – for such simple tasks to be neglected, if there was just a chance that doing so might help the engine.

The results: none. The dockyard will not install an oil-cooling system and Commander Slocum's threats that the Admiralty will draw the appropriate conclusions if there is a further breakdown cut no ice.

As I write this report, we are preparing for a new sea trial of the engine (to take place on 9 September).

Gibraltar, 8 September 1942

While Krajewski was at sea on this abortive mission, Commander Durski-Trzasko arrived, to discover a poor state of morale among the Polish felucca crews, as he reported to Admiral Swirski:

Head of Polish Naval Mission,
Gibraltar[8]
Secret
25 August 1942

To: Commander of the Navy
(Adm. Swirski)

I wish to report that on the evening of 10 August I arrived at Gibraltar by flying boat, direct from Plymouth.

On the 11th I reported to Captain Osborne, head of the CWF (Coast Watching Flotilla). It took me a few days to pay all the necessary visits, first to the Governor and then to navy, army and intelligence organisations. I must point out that everywhere I went I heard the most sincere admiration expressed for the work of Captain Krajewski and Lt Buchowski.

At the time of my arrival, Captain Krajewski was engaged

on a mission from which, however, he was forced to return, because of a major engine failure.

I chose 15 August to arrange a review of the crews of the feluccas and the army. It was on this occasion that I announced the creation of the Polish Naval Mission.

On the same day Lt Michalkiewicz [subsequently known as Lukasz or Lucas] and Bosun Zawistowski arrived by flying boat from Plymouth.

On 19 August I carried out a detailed inspection of the crews of the feluccas and of the accommodation of the base ship, HMS *Araguana*. Earlier I had received information from Captain Krajewski and Lt Buchowski concerning the physical condition and state of morale of each member of the crews. I met each of them individually to discuss requests, complaints and regrets. Not surprisingly all of them wanted to return to England, adducing the most wide-ranging motives, and they all voiced various complaints about everyone and everything. Most of these grudges have been set out in detail by Captain Krajewski in his reports and are known to Commander Stoklas, but equally most of them have no foundation whatsoever, which suggests that they are the result of collusion. I can state with complete certainty that the men are nearly all exhausted and physically drained. Living on Gibraltar, with its very unpleasant climate, and in a completely isolated fortress, they spend their free time drinking, and their discontent manifests itself in a much more extreme form.

Lt Buchowski's crew in particular is suffering from low morale, one reason for which has been the failure to establish their relationship to the navy clearly and unequivocally. These people regarded themselves as civilians and were treated as such in most cases. The fact that on each occasion they were granted the best possible material conditions they demanded caused a loss of military identity and discipline.

My announcement that a new organisation was being created and my insistence that the crews of the feluccas are naval personnel and therefore soldiers in every respect caused dissatisfaction among Lt Buchowski's people, especially when I forbade them to walk about in civilian clothes and told them that they were subject to disciplinary regulations.

These symptoms of poor morale surfaced most clearly on 22 August, when Lt Buchowski reported to me that his crew members were asking for an immediate transfer and were refusing to put to sea.

I made my way to the warship *Araguana* and called Lt Buchowski's crew together. I explained to them that they are soldiers and work for the good of the homeland. I stressed that their refusal to carry out orders would inevitably harm their hitherto excellent reputation and might have far-reaching consequences, whereupon all of them announced their readiness to leave on the mission. Their commitment nevertheless was less than total, as evidenced by the fact that they tried to negotiate an increase in their wages before setting out. I immediately cut short any discussion on that point. Lt Buchowski left on his mission today.

In spite of everything, these people work conscientiously and with a great sense of duty; they are undoubtedly very good and worthwhile material and will return to equilibrium when their conditions change.

I consider it impossible that Lt Buchowski's crew can be used for further work here; especially as some members of the crew are absolutely exhausted physically. After their return from the mission, I shall send the whole crew to England by the next transport, irrespective of when the replacement crew is due in Gibraltar.

Captain Krajewski's crew is also displaying the first symptoms of loss of morale. I have sent a signal asking for a further replacement crew be sent as soon as possible. A replacement is unquestionably needed, so I repeat the request here. The success of the missions depends in large part on the hard work of the individuals involved; even the most severe disciplinary measures will not have the desired effect on the recalcitrant element.

The new organisation, CWF, which was agreed between yourself and the British Admiralty, does not yet seem to be familiar to the local authorities here. I assume that Captain Slocum, who is due to arrive any day, will bring the appropriate orders and instructions with him.

I will be able to send Captain Krajewski to England after he has carried out a joint mission with Lt Lukasz. I assume this will be during the second half of September.

Head of Polish Naval Mission
Cmdr Durski-Trzasko

While this was going on at Gibraltar, *Tarana* (none of whose operation reports has come to light) went up to the Agde area, where Clark landed six agents for SOE on the night of 15 August (Operation BULL) before going on to pick up seven men and one woman near Narbonne later the same night. This operation was for Cohen's Section of SIS and was therefore ultimately either for the Free French BCRA or for the 'Alliance' network, which Cohen also handled. CWF reports describe the evacuees as 'POWs', though this designation can scarcely have applied to the woman passenger, who was presumably a member of MI9's 'Pat' escape organisation. Food, stores and W/T sets were landed on the same occasion. This was the first time Cohen's Section had made use of the CWF service, perhaps because their needs were so largely catered for by the fishing-boat operations that were being conducted concurrently on the west coast of Brittany.

With the immediate morale problems of *Seadog's* crew reduced to operationally manageable proportions, Buchowski set off on 26 August for a further series of operations, on which he reported in due course as follows:

Lt Jan BUCHOWSKI
Report of voyage[9]

I beg to report, Commander,

that, in line with the orders I received, on 26 August 1942 at 0630 hrs I left port. At 0800 hrs I rounded Europa Point and set a course that would take me past Cabo de Gata at a distance of 15 miles bearing north.

During the first two days the weather was awful, the wind easterly with a strength of 4–5 and sea conditions 4. The passengers did not feel too well and betrayed no inclination to partake of the meals. There were no unusual events to report at this time.

On 29 August at 0320 hrs we suffered a breakdown of the oil pump, which was repaired in 20 minutes. At 2300 hrs I passed Ibiza and Majorca, sailing between them, and headed in the direction of our first operation.

On 30 August I received a signal from the captain of the CWF: 'Begin Operation WATCHMAN as soon as possible on Monday.' I replied: 'Impossible for me before 2400 hrs stop Request instructions', to which I received the answer: 'Continue with the operation'.

Operation No.1 (WATCHMAN)

On 31 August at 2300 hrs the shore became visible and I made out our location. On 1 September at 0300 hrs I entered the Rade-d'Agay and sent the first signal at the spot where the agents were supposed to have been waiting. Although I repeated the signal several times, I did not receive a reply. As a result I searched around the whole bay, giving signals at various points. I received a reply from beneath the railway bridge, but it was not given in the agreed colour, so I did not send out the dinghy. As I discovered later, it was most probably a police post. At 0145 hrs, I saw a signal correctly given from the right position. I sent the dinghy with one of the agents (female), whom I had to put ashore at this point. At 0205 hrs the dinghy returned in tow of a motorised fishing boat, and bringing with it seven passengers – five men and two women. I unloaded some 600 kilos of freight/cargo on to this motor boat. At 0220 hrs the loading and unloading was completed. After the fishing vessel had pulled away I moved to a position where I was to throw overboard (i.e. dispose of in the sea) the remainder of the freight. Unfortunately, one of the metal containers floated, but it was too late to do anything about it, since by this time a felucca was entering the bay, which is about 600 m. wide at this point. Owing to this, and not wanting to be noticed, I left the bay.

I discovered from the agents that they had been expecting me to arrive before 2400 hrs. It seems that they had sent a cable to London asking that the operation be completed by that time and, since I had not arrived by 2400 hrs, they went off to get some sleep, expecting me to turn up the next day. One of them happened to remain behind and, noticing my signal but not having a suitable lamp/torch, went to the nearest house and woke one of the others, who was able to give the signal. I feel, however, that we cannot blame the agents for the considerable delay in replying in this case, which is probably the result of a breakdown in communications between France, London and Gibraltar. Otherwise the organisation of the operation from the land side was excellent, proof of which was that the embarkation of people and off-loading of a considerable amount of material was done simultaneously and took barely 15 minutes. On the same day at 1100 hrs I was hove-to some 50 nautical miles from the coast. At 1700 hrs I started up the engine and made my way to the point where the second operation was to be carried out.

Operation No.2 (VAGRANT)

On 2 September at 0930 hrs I was at the place agreed and gave out the first signal. After five minutes I received a reply. I sent the boat to the shore. For the next hour the people on shore continued to signal to me but the boat did not return: I assumed that it had broken up on the rocks as the weather was none too good. At 0340 hrs I ordered the airman's rubber dinghy to be inflated and sent two people in it to render assistance.

Ten minutes after the dinghy had left, the boat returned bringing five passengers. I sent them back immediately for the rest of the passengers and ordered the dinghy to be hauled on board. After a further ten minutes both boats and the passengers were on the deck. I immediately weighed anchor. Asked the reason for the long delay on land, my crewman answered that when he reached the shore he could not find anybody. So he went off to search and after about half an hour he found one man at the top of a hillock intent on signalling out to sea. This fellow was startled by the appearance of my crewman and would have run off if it had not been for a well-aimed revolver under threat of which he led my crewman to the spot where the rest of the 'passengers' were hidden. Only here was he asked for the password. The passengers told me that they had been expecting a larger boat and had not come out of hiding when they saw the small boat, which they thought was only a fisherman. In my opinion, the land side of the operation failed in its duty here, since it is not desirable and is no part of our responsibility to force the passengers down at revolver point. Skilful use of the agreed signals should allow us to avoid that and the operation would take 30 minutes instead of two hours. Among the passengers was General Kleeberg.

Operation No.3 (KUMEL)

On 3 September at 0230 hrs I was situated at the predetermined location for operation No.3. Although I signalled several times I received no reply and consequently I sent out the boat with two people to search the rendezvous area, because it was possible that the passengers were again expecting something different. After an hour and a half the boat returned reporting that there was no-one there. On 4 September at the same time I returned to the rendezvous point, but the story repeated itself. When I returned to base I was told that there was indeed no-one there, as military manoeuvres were taking place in the area. It seems to me that one of the tasks of the organisers should be to find out about such occurrences at least a few days beforehand. Besides, the spot was one of the least secure on the whole of this coast (about 10 nautical miles from Toulon) and it would be desirable to avoid risking the two previous successful operations and the vessel by turning up there on two successive nights. Also, a signal that consists of two flashes on a white lamp for the party on shore seems rather ill-chosen, since I saw about 100 of these during my two-hour vigil there. If we were to put all these signals into service, we could, without much trouble, evacuate this entire stretch of shoreline, inhabitants, army units and all!

Operation No. 4 (LEDA)

On 5 September at 0115 hrs I was at the spot appointed for the operation. At 0130 hrs I sent the first signal. I received an answer immediately. I sent the boat out together with one agent. Approximately 20–30 minutes after the boat had left I noticed a suspicious white light on the beach, as though someone were shining a torch. Ten minutes later the boat returned carrying five passengers and immediately departed for the rest. At 0250 hrs it returned bringing only one passenger, who told me that, after the first party had embarked and the boat had left the shore, the police materialised. So the rest of the party had scattered in all directions and he himself had struck a policeman. As he was running away, he was lucky enough to chance on one of my sailors, and thus come to board our vessel. He appealed to me to send a machine-gun and a few people to the beach to liquidate the police. Unfortunately, I had to turn down this enticing proposition of opening up the second front, not having the permission of either parliament or government and being under quite contrary orders from my superiors. I decided, however, to wait for 20 minutes, in case one of those who were left on shore managed to escape the clutches of the police, in which case he would give me the signal and I would be able to pick him up. Unfortunately nothing happened.

At 0320 hrs I left the operation area. That night, expecting to be pursued eventually, I painted Spanish colours on our bow and raised the Spanish flag, meanwhile setting a course that would enable us to reach the Spanish frontier as quickly as possible. At 1225 hrs (position: lat. 42°15′ N, 03°50′ E) I noticed a flying boat about 3 nautical miles away to the east. I sent all our passengers below deck. A few moments later the plane noticed me, flew lower and approached. For 15 minutes it circled us, flying very low. On his tail and wings he had Spanish colours, in the centre of which were Italian colours. He moved off in the direction of Cape San Sebastian. When the aircraft had disappeared from sight, expecting that a warship would eventually be sent to examine my Spanish identity, I changed course 90 degrees to ENE. I travelled this course for 30 nautical miles and then changed it again, heading for the western headland of Majorca. During the following few days there were no special events to report. On 9 September at 1310 hrs I moored near the pier at base.

Having in mind the safety of future operations, the vessel and the crew, I must submit that I regard the presence of high-ranking officers in uniform and a line of cars and limousines as highly undesirable, and the security risk was heightened further by two tugboats just behind me, whose Spanish crew looked on with great interest at the ceremony of disembarking the passengers.

J. Buchowski (Lt)

Buchowski was not alone in his complaint about the public and very indiscreet manner in which *Seadog* was received at Ragged Staff

Steps. The Defence Security Officer wrote to Captain Osborne complaining that the entrance of a 'felucca'-type craft into the Admiralty Harbour was itself indicative of special operations.[10] A noteworthy number of important and well-known cars had arrived to pick up the passengers, who had disembarked in full view of many Spanish workmen, representatives of the Joint Intelligence Committee, the Assistant Chief of Staff and the Polish and French missions. The nature of the operation had been so evident that, as one report had pointed out, only the band, red carpet, press and news cameras had been lacking. The security officer recognised that there was perhaps no alternative to Admiralty Harbour but suggested that a more discreet hour be chosen, rather than midday, that the incoming vessel be met by representatives of the Security Service only and that passengers be taken off immediately to a pre-arranged rendezvous, perhaps to a nearby building for the necessary particulars to be taken.

Osborne replied, pointing out 'facts which might not be quite obvious to those unconnected with the sea.'[11] Use of Admiralty Harbour was indeed inevitable, but the feluccas frequently entered and left it for non-operational purposes such as trials. The problem of the arrival and disembarkation of passengers was far from being satisfactorily solved, but other berths in it had been tried, including both the north and south moles and none had been found more secure than Ragged Staff Steps. The Spanish workmen never failed to notice what went on. The number of important cars could, and must, be eliminated and passengers should be taken away in a covered lorry, though this was not his responsibility, any more than was preventing mission representatives from meeting the vessel. Timing was difficult to control: the felucca travelled comparatively slowly and had no reserve of speed, so an earlier arrival was impracticable. In this instance, too, *Seadog* had covered a great distance and was at the limit of her endurance; moreover it could not be desirable to keep the crew and passengers on such a small craft any longer than could be helped. In his view, security was jeopardised more by the length of time the passengers were talking and hanging about after landing than by where they came ashore.

Commander Durski-Trzasko pointed out that he had been present in response to Osborne's 'express proposal'.[12] To avoid attracting attention, he had come in plain clothes and on foot. He had watched *Seadog*'s arrival from a distance and had approached only when General Kleeberg came ashore, to accompany him to the car.

By the time *Seawolf*'s engine repairs were completed, to Krajewski's relief, Lt Marian Michalkiewicz, who called himself 'Lukasz' or 'Lucas' while serving with the CWF, had arrived and it was decided that he and Lt Tom Maxted, RNR, who had been sent out by NID(C) to understudy the Polish felucca captains, would sail with Krajewski on his final expedition in September to learn how the job was done.

Slocum arrived at Gibraltar when this, Krajewski's 17th evacuation voyage, was being planned and considerable friction surfaced at a briefing meeting held by Osborne. Slocum complained that the Poles in France had been indiscreet in their preparations for the abortive August evacuation and Krajewski protested that the British side, to fit into their requirements, were obliging him to operate much too far into the moon period for safety. Krajewski's account of this acrimonious exchange is contained in the report he wrote nearly a month later on his return from his last mission. Durski-Trzasko, however, wrote straight away to Stoklas, the Polish Naval Attaché in London, on 11 September, the day on which Krajewski put to sea, saying that, after a month in Gibraltar, he noted a tendency to limit evacuation operations and to accord them lower priority;[13] and, moreover, to make Polish evacuation objectives subject to what he described as 'imperial' (i.e. British) aims.

REPORT FROM THE SEVENTEENTH EVACUATION VOYAGE (to France, from 11–26 September)[14]

1) *FREQUENT CHANGES OF DATES.* When we had grounds to assume that the dockyard would have the engine and the felucca ready for operations by the promised date, we established the following dates and locations for Polish embarkations:

The nights of 15/16 and 16/17 September; the number of people, 25 (in one night); pick-up point, Sormiou *calanque*, close to Marseilles, or La-Madrague, 5 km. to the south of Marseilles – if the weather allows us to approach this coastline, which is open to winds from the west. Sormiou was suggested by Marseilles (Capt Iwaszkiewicz) during one of the earlier missions, but a personal inspection by Capt Iwaszkiewcz confirmed that En-Vau [or Calanque-d'En-Vau] was sufficiently safe too.

These first dates had already been imposed on me (indirectly) by the British side, which had settled the dates of *its* operations in advance, i.e. the tasks that *Seawolf* was to carry out under my command. As many as *six* of these operations had been anticipated initially.

When these first dates were being set, an incident occurred that was fairly trivial but nevertheless characteristic of a tendency by the British side (Capt Slocum, of NID, Admiralty) to contend that it is the Polish side of our combined Anglo–Polish operations that has to adapt its plans to suit British desiderata.

Thus Capt Slocum, who was present at my briefing with Capt Osborne, asked me to point out in my next cable to Marseilles (via London) proposing dates, that '. . . they should give an assurance that the preparations would be more discreet than during the preparations for the previous pick-up operation (which had failed because of our breakdown).' According to information received, apparently through the British authorities, Hugo's assistants were reportedly rounding up candidates and recommending that they make their getaway, giving the name both of the captain and of the felucca (*Seawolf*). Capt Slocum apparently received this information before he left London and was intending also to send it on to our central authorities . . .

2) As regards the embarkation dates thus established, the Polish side already had reservations of a fairly fundamental nature; they were too close to the full moon, which was to be on 24 September. Beyond the limit of 'dark' nights, one can count on a period of more than eight days clear of the 'full', because then the moon is still not large and also it rises and sets fairly early. Since the felucca was ready to depart on 7 September and that 'limit' fell on 16 September – even allowing for the five days we needed to make our way to the French coast – we were still left with quite a lot of time, even for the British operations (12–16 Sept), as long as we did not overwork *Seawolf* with too many of them.

3) These first operational dates were *at the limit* of the period of light nights – I should add that operation TITANIA was projected for the night after the Polish operation – this cannot be said of the dates established as the result of subsequent changes. On 3 September, after the dates for the British operations had been altered on cabled orders from the Admiralty, the British side proposed new dates: 16/17 September and, for a second embarkation, 18/19 September . . .

4) However, yet another change soon followed: on 5 September, after still more adjustments to the British operations, we were offered new dates: the night of 18/19 Sept. for the first pick-up; 19/20 Sept. for second pick-up. Reporting this in our signal no. 455 of 5 Sept., we added in paragraphs C and D that these people could not gather at the agreed location before 0130 hrs Greenwich time, since Operation ORLANDO (putting agents ashore and taking materials on board) was also due to take place at Sormiou, and the British side wanted to ensure that this operation remained clandestine.

All the same it is worth pointing out that Sormiou was 'borrowed' by the British from the Polish side (just as En-Vau and Miou had been earlier) although Capt Osborne had, with commendable loyalty and on instructions from the Admiralty, approached the Polish mission to ask if we had anything against their use of that spot.

Unfortunately, we had no alternative but to accept these dates, although reservations were at once expressed about the almost reckless proximity of the dates to the full moon. The last operation (TITANIA) was scheduled for 20/21 September, three days before the full moon.

In the light of all this, I formally advised Capt Osborne before our departure that if we were arrested the situation would be clear and the conclusions. . . easy to draw. En-Vau, where I was to carry out Operation MULLET (taking on board two agents), also caused me misgivings because it had been visited too often.

We ruled out La-Madrague as a possible embarkation site, even in good weather, because of the unusually bright nights expected during our operations.

6) *COMPOSITION OF THE CREW.* Lt Cmdr Krajewski, in command; Lt Lukasz (Michalkiewicz), taking over command at some future point; Sub Lt Maxted, RNR, future commander of a British felucca, also along 'for practice'; Coxswain Maszczynski, helm; Leading Seaman Chwastek, helm; Leading Seaman Stanislawski, helm and radio; Chief Petty Officer Tarnawski, 1st mechanic; Leading Seaman Latka, 2nd engine watch; Seaman Kurzawa, 3rd engine watch; Mate Kuston, cook. Two of the officers and three of the crew were taking part in an evacuation mission for the first time.

7) *THE WEIGHING OF ANCHOR* took place on 11 September at 2045 hrs, i.e. when it was already dark, so as to preserve the secrecy of the operation.

The weather was unfavourable, with a fairly strong wind (the 'Levanto' – Force 4–5) blowing from the east.

On the following day, the 12th, we released in succession, at distances of 50, 60 and 100 miles, three pairs of mail pigeons, which we had received in order to train them. In our report to base we gave the time and estimated location (in code) of their release. As a rule, the pigeons circled over the spot where they had been released for about ten minutes, after which we lost sight of them.

It turned out after our return to port that only one of the six pigeons had not returned to base.

8) *BREAKDOWN.* At 0120 hours on 13 September a breakdown of the engine cooling pump occurred, when the shaft broke in two. The fault was a serious one. Luckily the mechanic on duty (Leading Seaman Latka) immediately realised what was

happening and stopped the engine, thereby saving it from seizing up completely, which is what would have happened without any cooling. We were then about 5 miles away from Cabo de Gata.

Inspection of the cross-section of the shaft revealed that it had been split for a long time – most probably from the time it left the factory – and to such an extent that to the very last it could have been working only at $\frac{1}{5}$ of its strength.

We managed to get around the fault by shortening the shaft, which had broken at one end, and by screw-threading it (we always have sets of screw stock and dies with us after so many accidents of this kind). Working by the light of a lamp, Tarnawski was able to get the engine started again at 0400 hrs. At 08.40 hrs we had to stop it again in order to carry out certain improvements to the pump – but afterwards, to the end of the mission, it worked faultlessly.

The breakdown was further proof that on this kind of small ship, with a small crew and only one engine, and where there are urgent and important tasks to perform, it is absolutely essential there be *at least one experienced mechanic* on board. Indeed in many cases the safety of the felucca and the crew depend on it. Neither Leading Seaman Latka nor Seaman Kurzawa would have been able to repair this breakdown, so without a mechanic all five operations would have been frustrated.

It is perhaps unnecessary to add that a mechanic with enough experience for this kind of task will never be less than 28–30 years old.

From the time the engine was overhauled by the dockyard, it in fact never ran properly during the voyage, so that for the most part we travelled at half speed, or rather half power.

9) On 14 September at 2125 hrs we were already level with the Tagomago lighthouse (Island of Ibiza) travelling between Majorca and Ibiza and moving away from the Balearic archipelago.

On 15 Sept. we had our first encounter with an Italian aircraft during the whole period of our voyages. We had in fact just finished painting the felucca, in order to change its appearance, and I was in the process of checking the ship's side, when I received the warning that an aircraft was approaching. It was then at a distance of some 800 m. and was making a turn (very low, at around 100 m.) in order to get a better look at us. When it began to circle, it was possible to make out its Italian markings without any difficulty

We could not assume that nothing about us would arouse the suspicion of a critical observer; leaving aside the 'registration' letters, which we had only just painted on the bow, there was the very *position* of our felucca (very far from land and from waters usually frequented by fishermen) as well as its course. When the aircraft caught us unawares, we were heading straight for La-Ciotat, as we were already running out of time by then.

I ordered the helmsman to change course gradually to port by some 30°, which gave us a more 'natural' course, towards Cape St Sebastian. I also told the woman passenger and the second passenger (a man), who looked too refined to be a fisherman, to hide below deck. We carried out these man-oeuvres while the aircraft was circling further away from the felucca. In addition I ordered all those on deck to wave 'in a friendly fashion' in the direction of the aircraft.

After almost a quarter of an hour of circling, the aircraft, a two-engined Caproni (bomber and long-range reconnaissance) moved off towards the north but, as I could see through my binoculars, still continued to circle for a time on the horizon on west–east courses . . .

I reported this encounter to the base at Gibraltar, as we were now were already in contact.

The fact that Lt Buchowski had had a similar encounter just a few weeks previously at the level of the Spanish–French border indicated a recently increased level of sea patrols to the north of the Balearic Islands. I had to take this into account in the next phase of my voyage.

10) On 15 September the weather turned very much worse and in the evening a storm, typical of the Golfe-de-Lyon, came from the WNW. We then observed an electrical storm lasting several hours, a phenomenon that I had never before witnessed on such a scale: the lightning extended for a distance of several kilometres.

On 16 September we approached the French coast so as not to reach the area of visibility from the coast-watching posts too early, but nevertheless to enable us to begin the operation as early as possible. Unfortunately the storm grew in strength, creating, as usual, almost unbearable conditions – everything got soaked through, the charts and cabins were showered with water, in a word there was not a dry spot on the vessel and it seemed that the felucca was dripping from all sides.

11) *PUTTING THE AGENTS ASHORE AT LA-CIOTAT.* Luckily our first operation was to take place in the Bay of La-Ciotat which is sheltered from winds from the WNW.

At 0002 hrs on 17 September we entered the Bay. Half an hour later I hove to at a distance of some 400 m. from the shore at what I thought was the agreed spot (in fact very difficult to recognise) and ordered the dinghy lowered; into it we loaded luggage and two agents (one of them the woman). The spot, it turned out, was not suitable after all, not least because it lay 2 km. from the brightly lit town of La-Ciotat, which, because of its shipyard, must inevitably be well guarded. The dinghy, under the command of Leading Seaman Stanislawski, nevertheless put ashore both passengers safely and without incident, and reported to me that the agents recognised the agreed spot without any difficulty near the point where they had landed.

At 0150 hrs the dinghy was back on deck, after which we made away from the shore.

At 0845 hrs we lay hove-to, awaiting the next operation in an observed position at mid-afternoon (1530 hrs) of lat. 42° north; long. 5°13' east, around 40 miles to the south of the La-Ciotat area, a position to which I returned a few more times in breaks between operations. The weather had fortunately improved considerably.

This position, as my several earlier observations had indicated, was in something of a 'dead sector' as far as shipping movements were concerned.

12) *AN ERROR BY THE NEXT AGENT.* At 1605 hrs we set out once again. Since I found we were approaching the coast too early, at 2300 hrs (rendezvous was for 0100), and not wanting to spend that waiting period in the bay where we were due to meet (Sormiou) because it was populated, I hid behind the Isle of Riou, in whose shade (the moon, nearly full, was already shining very brightly) we passed the time by fishing. We repeated this manoeuvre several times, since it was the safest hiding-place, against the rocks, and not devoid of charm, because of the unusually picturesque scenery of that district. With each passing day (or rather, night) as we drew nearer to the full moon, it became increasingly lighter. In any case we had to spend our spare hours somewhere while waiting.

At 0030 hrs on 18 September I anchored in the *calanque* of Sormiou, to which, as with La-Ciotat, it was my first visit. My lamp signals, however, elicited no answer. When the situation did not change after 45 minutes, it became clear to me that the agent, who was to have met the other agent put ashore by me and collect some very heavy gear (radio station), was not there. Since my agent was not familiar with this region, I suggested putting him ashore in the Bay of Vau [Calanque-d'En-Vau], where I had to carry out the next operation that night, and where a reception committee was supposed to be waiting for us on shore.

At 0115 hrs I left the Bay of Sormiou, heading for En-Vau.

To our considerable surprise, as we passed the Morgiou *calanque*, which lies parallel with Sormiou, we perceived the AGREED SIGNALS. The agent had obviously made a mistake and taken up position in the adjoining bay. Finally, at 0230 hrs, our agent was put ashore and the delegate on land (the one who had made the mix-up) handed Leading Seaman Stanislawski, commander of the dinghy, around 50 kilos of material to take to Gibraltar (watches and stop-watches for the RAF).

13) *PICK-UP OF TWO AGENTS.* At 0310 hrs on the same night we were at the entrance of the En-Vau *calanque*. After an exchange of signals I entered it. Favourable weather conditions and our many past visits here saw to it that within minutes the dinghy had been put over the side, the two agents taken on board and we had left the *calanque* again, thereby establishing some sort of record for that kind of manoeuvre, which involves a certain amount of time taken to turn the felucca round in a *calanque* only 50 m. wide.

At 0815 hrs we were again lying hove-to at our former position.

Since the weather was exceptionally favourable, in the morning we had a bathing session with our passengers (Free French).

14) *TAKING ON BOARD THE FIRST 31 POLES.* At 0030 hrs on 19 September we were again at Sormiou (this time the Poles did not mistake the bay. . .). Signals were exchanged immediately: a moment later I was on the shore where, as usual, Capt Iwaszkiewicz was waiting for me.

While the group (31, of whom three were British) were being embarked, I held a conference with him. He said he thought Sormiou not completely convenient for our purposes, since passers-by were quite frequent. He therefore asked me if I would come to En-Vau the following night. Meanwhile he himself had to come aboard because his identity had been partially revealed.

At 0130 hrs we left the bay and moved to our usual position and hove to.

I now had enough people to organise, among other things, an anti-aircraft watch throughout the day, with changes of watch every two hours.

At 1400 hrs I ordered a general bathing session.

That day Tarnawski (1st mechanic) showed me a bearing newly made by the dockyard: white metal was falling off it, which threatened us with an unpleasant surprise at any moment. The engine too had been *heating up* more than usual ever since it left the dockyard.

At 1700 hrs we moved to the En-Vau *calanque.*

15) *TAKING A FURTHER 25 POLES ON BOARD.* That night at 2300 hrs we entered the En-Vau *calanque.* As we were still closer to the full moon the whole approach to the shore, which was fairly densely populated, was almost like a passage in full daylight. Almost every detail could be seen on the shore and also, we had to assume, on the felucca. I emphasise this because it gives an idea of the awkward situation in which the British Admiralty placed us by putting off the departure date, even though the felucca was ready; and how little in that institution they allow for rational security considerations and the secrecy of operations for the longer run (indeed 'the long run' was supposed to have been the reason for limiting the number of people evacuated in any one operation to 25 . . .).

Since Capt Iwaszkiewicz himself had to go ashore in the dinghy, this time I remained on the felucca during the embarkation operation, leaving arrangements on shore to Lt Lukasz, while I continually manoeuvred the vessel as we lay hove-to among so many rocks.

Capt Iwaszkiewicz came off again to the felucca to inform me that, despite everything, he would be *remaining* on land at the wish of Major Chojnacki, so we held our usual conference on the felucca (details below).

After taking 25 Polish evacuees on board, we left the *calanque* by 2350 hrs.

16) *THE INDISCREET BOARDING OF THE BRITISH PARTY.* The next operation (TITANIA), which involved picking up 15 POWs, was prepared by a British organisation [MI9] that apparently had an outpost at Gibraltar. The location: mouth of the River Tet below Perpignan. Having a considerable distance to cover, I set out to that point directly after leaving the En-Vau *calanque.*

Towards evening on that day we met a number of ships following the communication route from the Spanish border to Marseilles. Almost every night when we were in the vicinity of Marseilles we passed, at a decent distance, a few ships and perhaps even some patrol boats, but these were difficult to distinguish in the night, when we could see only their navigation lights.

The attempt to contact Gibraltar via the radio in order to arrange a new rendezvous with *Minna* (see para. 17) misfired. As the felucca was full to bursting – way above plan – I had suggested a meeting with the *Minna* to the *north* of the Balearic Islands, but received the answer 'Impossible'. *Minna* looks like a naval vessel and apparently they did not want to risk its being attacked by Italian aircraft.

Since all the lights are shining on that stretch of the French coast, I based our approach to the coast – which lacks any features by which to find one's bearings in the dark – on the red light of a fishing village and 'port' some 4 km. away to the north. At 0030 hrs, moving along the coast, which was lit up almost like daytime, we noticed the flashing of a light from a point that bore some resemblance to the agreed meeting point. THEY WERE HOWEVER IRREGULAR SIGNALS. After checking the position of a fort about ½ km. distant, I realised that it was one more case of unfortunate signalling from the land side. Our astonishment was all the greater when, after heaving to, WE HEARD CRIES AND SINGING AND SAW LAMPS BEING LIT among the party of people who were to be embarked. One even swam out towards us and in the water called out in our direction; in these conditions, as is well known, the sound carries a long way.

At 0130 hrs all of them had embarked. Again there were more in this party than anticipated: not 15 but 25 people, of whom the greater number were British from the RAF; there were also a few Frenchmen, one woman (Czech or, rather, 'Sudeten') and one Russian (the son of an emigrant).

All of them agreed that our vessel was visible 'as far as a mile out to sea', it was so clear.

17) *MEETING WITH THE MINNA.* Our journey back to base set a new record for our felucca in terms of numbers: in addition to the enlarged crew of ten for that voyage, we had *83 passengers* (54 Poles, 23 British, 4 French, 1 Russian, 1 Czech woman).

We therefore had 18 people altogether over the anticipated programme. Our drinking water being insufficient at the best of times, we had to ration this precious substance more than usual. Of course everybody had to be accommodated on deck, except the woman, a wounded Canadian (from the Dieppe raid), a wounded Pole and a wounded airman (who had been carrying out Special Operations flights and had had an accident on one of his missions).

The mood among the passengers was very good, irrespective of nationality, although I must state impartially that our people withstood the unspeakably awful conditions notably better than the others.

21 September was especially hard because of the return of the bad weather, and from a most unpropitious direction (south, Force 4–5). Being virtually certain that we would meet Italian aircraft in this region (Lt Buchowski's report), we set up a

specially rigorous anti-aircraft watch. In the end, we did not sight a single aircraft that day, possibly because of the poor weather . . .

We had to reduce our speed on a few occasions because of the heavy swell.

That day I had decided to change our usual return course (between Majorca and Ibiza) for a new one: between Majorca and Minorca, in spite of the narrowness of the straits. This enabled me to get to the south of the Balearic Islands during the night on the side that the Italian airmen 'did not like' to visit.

On 22 September, pouring rain, from which unfortunately not all our passengers were able to shelter. Between 0600 and 0800 hrs we passed between the islands, luckily in poor visibility.

Because of the shallow seas in this area we passed many offshore nets set out by fishermen. We tried to pull some in, to improve the menu of the passengers and crew, but there was too little time, the weather was not in our favour and in the end we succeeded only in tearing away a few of the buoys.

On the next day we passed a large French passenger vessel, the *O.G.Grévy* going – judging by its course – to Oran; this was the second time we had met it in the same place.

On 23 September we were to have met the *Minna* at a position 30 miles east of the south-easterly headland of the island of Formentera (Balearics). The rendezvous had been arranged for 1000 hrs. At 0930 hrs, however, lying hove-to, we sighted the mast of the ship to the south. The transfer of passengers was completed by 0940 hrs. We passed over materials we had brought on board at the Morgiou *calanque* and were given fresh supplies of food and water.

18) *THE RETURN.* That day, with a favourable wind, we raised the sails; however it lasted no longer than half a day, after which we had a head wind again.

On 24 September we sailed the stretch between Cape Nao and Cabo de Gata, through – unusually – countless shoals of fish, so that it seemed as if the whole sea was alive with them. . .

On 26 September at 1030 hrs we were back in the port of Gibraltar, having this time covered 'only' 1,800 miles and spent 14 days at sea.

19) *MY CONVERSATION WITH MAJOR IWASZKIEWICZ.* He asked me to hand on a list for the C-in-C's Chief of Staff (delivered by me personally to the C-in-C's HQ, 9 October) and requested that

a) we should not mention the names of the embarkation points, but use cryptonyms, namely: No.1 – La Madrague; No.2 – Sormiou; No.3 – Morgiou; No.4 – En-Vau;

b) we should add the figure 5 (five) to the date of the operation (which is to be understood as taking place at 0000 hrs), but at the same time give the *real* day of the week by way of confirmation;

c) the number of people being evacuated from France should be increased because of the great pressure of people;

d) we should support in London the suggestion of payment for the Marseilles evacuation 'outpost', because of the rising cost of living in France;

e) I should find out why orders had come from London reducing by ten the relatively modest number of 50 people to be evacuated, in order to take off ten Englishmen. The head of the British evacuation operation in Marseilles had shown him a signal from London notifying him that he 'might make use of the Polish organisation, but did not advise it.'

The 'coding' of dates of evacuations (point b) above), even though the signals go by a Polish intelligence W/T link, was advisable as a safety measure, he said: the number of arrests lately in those regions has been worryingly high and caused some loss of confidence.

Gibraltar, 6 October 1942
Capt M. Krajewski

Krajewski then returned to England, took three weeks' leave and, on 16 November 1942, rejoined *Blyskawica* as first lieutenant. He was awarded the Polish Cross of Gallantry and Bar 'for his courage, initiative and energy during special operations in the Mediterranean (1941–42) while evacuating Polish and Allied soldiers and citizens from occupied territories.' He served in the Battle of the Atlantic and in the North African invasion, but reckoned that his detachment to Gibraltar cost him his chances of a wartime command in the regular navy.

Buchowski sailed for France in *Seadog* again three days before Krajewski got back to Gibraltar from his epic 17th and last voyage. He took with him General Kleeberg[14] and Lt Cousens, RNR, who, like Maxted, had been sent out to Gibraltar by NID(C) to understudy the two Polish felucca captains and in due course relieve them in command. Buchowski's report on this expedition was as follows:

BUCHOWSKI, Jan, Lt

Report of voyage[15]

I beg to report, Commander, that, following my operational orders I left port on 23.ix.42 at 2030 hrs. After circling Europa Point I set a course that would take us around Cabo de Gata at a distance of 15 nautical miles bearing north. On the 23rd and 24th the weather was fairly good, the wind easterly, Force 3–4, and the sea conditions level 3. On 25.ix at 0905 hrs a French passenger ship (*Maréchal-Lyautey*) passed our stern at a distance of 3 miles, course N, speed 15 knots.

The weather worsened, the wind westerly Force 3–4 and visibility poor. On 26.ix at 0900 hrs an Italian seaplane flew over the ship. Two-engined monoplane, two large floats, markings; a white cross on the rudder and wings. Position: lat.38°42′ N, long. 01°58′ E. Course changeable, presumably on anti-submarine patrol.

On 27.ix from 0900 hrs to 1230 hrs we were passing through the straits between Majorca and Minorca. We noticed two French cargo vessels (coal-carrying), course S and N, speed around 7 knots. On 29.ix at 0800 hrs an Italian seaplane flew over the ship. The same type as that seen on the 26th. Changing course. The position at which we observed it: 42°57′ N, 07°21′ E. The plane remained visible to us until 1130 hrs. At 1330 hrs we were some 32 miles from the place of our first operation. I reduced our speed to 2½ knots. At 1500 hrs half speed. At 1600 full speed. At 1630 hrs the strong easterly wind suddenly dropped. At 1700 hrs there was an easterly wind Force 6–7, swell 4–5. We were in position at 2115. I began to give out the signals. By 2230 hrs I had received no reply, and as a result decided to move away. I could not travel to the second point, since it is impossible to land there in a strong easterly wind. On the 30th at 0420 hrs I was hove-to. We streamed the sea anchor. At 0630 hrs we had a breakdown of the engine, both bilge-pumps ceased operating. The ship started to take in a great deal of water. At 0900 hrs we had some 3 tons of water in the engine-room. We drew in the sea anchor in order to reduce the resistance and lifted the foresail, but within ten minutes the sail had been torn into shreds. The wind was blowing at Force 8–9, sea conditions 5–6. When we managed to repair the engine at 0930, we pumped out the water. On 1.x at 0930 hrs the weather was unchanged and we were unable to move to position. When the wind dropped at 1930 hrs to Force 4–5, the sea began to grow calmer. We set a course to the rendezvous spot. On 2.x at 1000 hrs the weather was fine. At 30 nautical miles from the meeting point we stopped the engine. We started the engine again at 1500 hrs, heading for the rendezvous. Entering La-Napoule Bay I passed at a distance of some 300 metres a French MTB making its way out into the open sea. In all probability, I was not observed. We were at the pinpoint by 2100 hrs and started to give out the requisite signals. There was no answer by 2100 hrs [sic], so I decided to put the two agents ashore, giving them the address and telling them how they could make contact with the individual who was organising everything on the land side. I suggested that they should ask him to organise a reception for me the following night in the Rade-d'Agay at 2200 hrs and that they should bring all the passengers to that spot. I decided also to put ashore General Kleeberg since a delay in his arrival, even by so little as a day, would be dangerous for him and I was not sure whether his party of people would be waiting for him at position no. 2 (as it later turned out there was nobody there).[16] I therefore landed General Kleeberg and two agents at the town of La-Napoule, 200 m. to the south of the railway station, half an hour before the departure of the train for Nice. At 2300 hrs I moved to the point fixed for our second operation. The place of the first operation was called Pointe-de-l'Aiguille, but two miles to the south there was a second point called Cap-de-l'Aiguillon [? l'Esquillon]: the similarity of the two names made me think that maybe they had made a mistake in London in giving out the position. I now had a lot of time in hand, since I did not need to be at the place of the second operation until 3.x at 0030 hrs, so I decided to move to 'Cap-de-l'Aiguillon'. At 2330 hrs I sent out the first signal and received an answer immediately. I sent out the boat again with the two agents whom I had to put ashore. I could not off-load the material since the promised motorboat had not materialised.

On 3.x at 0015 hrs I was at the position earmarked for the second operation. I remained there until 0130 hrs. I did not receive any reply to my signals. At 0136 hrs I moved out into the open sea. At 0900 hrs I stopped the engine some 35 miles from shore.

At 1500 hrs on 3.x I started up the engine and set a course for Rade-d'Agay. At 2200 hrs we were in position and I began to signal – but there was no answer. After about 20 minutes I saw a small boat moving in our direction. In the boat were two women – both French – who told me that I should make myself scarce since I had been observed by the gendarmes and police, and that I should go to the previous position. At 2230 hrs I left the Rade-d'Agay bay and had travelled half a mile from the shore when a flame about two metres long began to appear from the exhaust pipe. I covered the exhaust pipe in an old sail, but the sail caught fire, and so I organised three people with buckets to pour water on the sail.

On 4.x at 0000 hrs we were in position. I began to signal. By 0100 I had received no answer. The people pouring water on the sail were extremely tired, and so I decided to move out to sea. In the course of this short journey our engine stopped twice. At 1100 hrs I stopped the engine some 30 miles from the coast. The cause of our breakdown was coal-dust in the fuel. The filters were cleaned and the fuel tanks changed. At 1545 I started the engine and set a course for the site of the operation (Cap-de-l'Aiguillon). At 2130 hrs we were in position – gave out the signal – received a reply. I sent out the boat, which returned in ten minutes and the crew informed me that there was no motor boat. In the light of this I began to off-load the material using our own small boat. The unloading was completed on 5.x at 0030 hrs. The people on the shore conveyed the news to me from General Kleeberg and the agents that everyone was safe and sound and that there were no more passengers to be taken off. At 0035 hrs I moved away from the coast – set a course for Gibraltar. Close to the Balearic Islands we had a breakdown of the radio, and thus were able neither to receive nor to send messages. I reached Gibraltar on 10.x at 0730 hrs, having covered 2,300 miles. In the tanks there were 5 gallons of fuel left.

(signed)
Lt Jan BUCHOWSKI

CHAPTER XXXI

Last of the Polish Evacuation Missions

P atrick O'Leary, alias Albert Guérisse, having been landed near
Port-Vendres on 18 April 1942 from *Tarana* in one of the first
operations carried out under CWF auspices, set up one of the
largest and most effective of MI9's wartime organisations for
rescuing escaped prisoners of war and shot-down airmen who
had evaded capture. The so-called 'Pat' Line had built on foundations laid by Ian Garrow at Marseilles and, by the autumn of 1942,
its ramifications stretched up into the Pas-de-Calais and Belgium as
well as into Brittany, which of course harboured many evaders.[1]

Most of these evaders and escapers were passed over the
Pyrenees into Spain and, even if they fell into Spanish hands and
were interned in the camp at Miranda, it was unlikely they would
languish there for more than a few weeks since the Spanish
Government was dependent on imported oil products and flour
over which the British contraband control system had a strangle-
hold. However, O'Leary did organise a small-scale first evacuation
from Port-Miou in June, when, as recorded in Chapter XXX above,
a mixed party of nine agents, refugees and airmen were embarked
on *Seawolf* and subsequently transferred at sea to HMS *Middleton*
(Operation LUCALITE I).[2] In July, *Tarana*, working alone, picked
up 30–35 British escapers and evaders, mainly airmen, from the
Saint-Pierre-Plage near Narbonne, among them Whitney Straight,
a very distinguished American fighter pilot serving in the RAF, and
did a smaller operation to the same point in August.

Those embarked by O'Leary on *Seawolf* on Krajewski's final
expedition to France in September were mainly RAF aircrew who
had escaped from internment by Vichy at Fort-de-la-Révère in the
French hinterland behind Monaco. They included several well-
known pilots and the complete aircrew of a Halifax bomber from
138 Special Duties Squadron, which flew missions for the clandestine services from Tempsford in Bedfordshire. Krajewski put the
total number evacuated at 25, though other accounts speak of 38.[3]

The outward-bound passengers also included three French–
Canadian commandos, who had been taken prisoner during the
Dieppe raid a month previously but had escaped and fallen into
Vichy hands. A fourth – a Sergeant Major Lucien Dumais – had
already offered his services to O'Leary's escape line. He took part in
the operation at Saint-Pierre-Plage that night, but stayed behind
and was evacuated only a month later. He subsequently returned to

France as head of MI9's SHELBURNE Mission, where, based in Britanny, he applied the formula of an escape line linked to large-scale evacuation operations by sea, which O'Leary had copied from the Poles.[4]

As a result of the break-out from Fort-de-la-Révère, all the officers interned there were transferred to a camp in Italy. However, with the connivance of a Polish priest, the Abbé Mirda, and Caskie, the Missions to Seamen Scottish chaplain from Marseilles, who arranged for the internees to have access to a disused part of the fort once a week for recreation, 60 airmen and army other ranks made a second mass escape through the sewers in this area.

Thirty-four of these escapers were eventually collected by O'Leary at his safe house, a disused restaurant near Saint-Pierre-Plage. *Seawolf* should have picked them up on 5/6 October but made an error of some few hundred metres and thus failed to make contact with them. They had to cross and recross the River Tet four times, up to their necks in water, to get over to Saint-Pierre-Plage and back to the safe house before a new and more accurate rendezvous was arranged on the clandestine Gibraltar–Marseilles W/T link and they were all taken off by Lukasz on *Seawolf* on 11/12 October. Like those embarked by Krajewski at the same point on 20/21 September, the evacuees were so overwrought by fear, tension, boredom and frustration that their emotions erupted in a wave of reckless excitement when at last they saw the felucca's dinghy approaching the beach where they were assembled. Maxted, who was on board *Seawolf*, was appalled by the noise and feared that the French police or the dreaded *Milice* (Vichy auxiliary police units) would be alerted.[5]

Somehow, the whole party was ferried off safely and parked around the deck of the felucca. One man had escaped from hospital where he had been receiving treatment for a broken leg but had then broken an ankle jumping out of the hospital window: he was propped against the wheel-house.

Before long the weather deteriorated and seasickness was added to the passengers' other miseries. Food was running low too and there was a passage of another five or six days ahead. Lukasz, deeming it necessary to ask Gibraltar for assistance, broke radio silence and *Minna* was sent to the rescue. The evacuees were transferred to her off Majorca, while *Seawolf* received some much-needed bread, meat and other stores. This was one of the few CWF missions from Gibraltar that consisted of a single operation, but it had proved a trying experience for the ship as well as for the passengers. Here is Lukasz's account of this first operation under his command:

Lt M. Lukasz

Report of voyage[6]

(to) Head of Polish Naval Mission at GIBRALTAR

I report below, Commander, on the progress of the voyage of the *Seawolf* carried out between 30.9.1941 and 16.10.1942. The crew was composed of the following members: Lt Lukasz (commanding), Lt Long (RNR), Sub Lt Maxted (RNR), Mate Tarnawski (1st mechanic), Leading Seaman Latka, Seaman Kurzawa (mechanic), Mate Kuston (cook), Leading Seaman Stanislawski (radio operator), Leading Seamen Chwastek, Olesinski, Sieminski (deck-hands); PO Bates (British deck-hand).

AIM OF THE MISSION. Operation ROSALIND was intended to deliver a letter and two sacks of material to the British organisation in France as well as evacuate around 35 British POWs.

EXECUTION. In accordance with the orders of SOCWF I weighed anchor on 30 September at 2030 hrs and, at 2040, passed through the gate in the boom. After clearing Europa Point, I set a course that would take us along the Spanish coast so as to pass Cabo de Gata at a distance of 15 miles, continuing so as to stay 20 miles from the shore.

On 5 October at 1233 hrs, being some 42 miles from the embarkation point, I hove to, since we had around four hours to kill. At 1600 hrs I set out in the direction of the embarkation. I arrived at the location, i.e. on the southern bank of the River Tet estuary, at 0001 hrs on 6 October. A three-hour search of the coastline, continually signalling by lamp in the direction of the shore, produced no results (I covered a four-mile stretch of coast). At 0300 hrs I decided to withdraw and try my luck the following night. During the day I hove to at a distance of 36 miles from the coast.

On the next night I was at the agreed point at 0001 hrs (7 Oct.). On this occasion also, a two-hour search (covering some two miles of the coast) produced no results. At 0200 hrs I was forced to leave the area, as two vessels were heading in our direction, which I suspected were patrol boats. I decided to return to base, convinced that something must have happened ashore. I sent a radio report on the unsuccessful operation and of my decision to return to base. On 8 October at 1141 hrs I received a report giving the course followed by *Seadog* and requesting me to look out for her. Since my course was a little different from hers, I made a turn so as to arrive at her course as quickly as possible.

On 9 October at 1130 hrs I received a signal with the message: 'Return to embarkation point. The ROSALIND people have been waiting two nights and are still waiting . . .' I turned about immediately and went back. On 12 October at 0015 hrs I was at the embarkation point for the third time. This time when I signalled, I received the correct response immediately. At 0030 hrs I sent the dinghy to the beach and began to embark people. At 0200 hrs the operation was completed. I took on board 34 British former POWs, a Polish priest (a military chaplain called Mirda) and an officer of the French merchant navy. I left the letter and two sacks of material on shore. After hoisting the dinghy back on board, I set out on our return journey. On 16 October 1942 I passed through the gate in the boom at Gibraltar and at 0920 hrs handed over the passengers to the local authorities.

OBSERVATIONS. The journey passed off without any 'adventure'. I encountered over a dozen merchant ships and three transport aircraft, which did not pay us any attention. The weather, with the exception of the 2nd and 10th, was exceptionally fine. The wind did not go above Force 3. However on 11 October, the strong mistral (NW, Force 6–7) was in evidence. The swell did not ease until we were within three miles of the shore. At the embarkation point itself, conditions were calm and the use of the dinghy to embark the people did not present any problems.

RADIO COMMUNICATION. The radio operated effectively except on two days when we had no communication whatsoever with Gibraltar. It is difficult to find the reason for this. Probably on one day we were masked by high mountains, but on the second day the time assigned for communication with base was close to sunset (which on occasion causes problems).

The engine worked very satisfactorily. Small faults were caused by sloppy repair work in the workshops and perhaps too by ineffective servicing on the part of young, inexperienced mechanics.

GENERAL. I cannot explain how we were not seen on the nights of 5/6 and 6/7 October. I pulled along the shore at a distance of some 300 yards, certainly not more, and I touched the sandy bottom twice. Not only my light but the whole felucca must have been visible from the shore. According to eyewitnesses, during the first night even the fumes from the engine could be smelt . . . What is very curious is that, on my third approach to the embarkation point, I received a reply to my signal light immediately, although I was about a mile distant.

There can be no question of our having made an error as to the embarkation point, since I checked our position several times with bearings taken from lighthouses.

(signed)

M. Lukasz, Lt

Even before Lukasz returned from this job for MI9's 'Pat' escape line, Stoklas, the Polish Naval Attaché in London, had written to Slocum on 13 October, following up a conversation he had had with Lt Cdr Madden of NID(C) on 24 September.[7]

Making it clear that he was acting on the instructions of the Chief of the Polish General Staff, he pointed out that the evacuation of Polish nationals from France and North Africa, for which purpose the Polish mission in Gibraltar had been organised, had lately been very considerably restricted by the Admiralty's giving precedence to special operations by feluccas attached to the CWF and manned by Polish crews.

The Polish General Staff regarded this as a paticularly critical period. They wished to carry out as many evacuations from France as possible before the weather in the Golfe-de-Lyon broke and prevented any operations by these small boats. From experience of last year's campaign, they knew that September and October were the last favourable months.

On 1 September they had been unexpectedly informed by the Admiralty that all sea operations both for the south coast of France and for the north coast of Africa, from Gibraltar as base, were suspended from 1 October for an indefinite period, probably until 15 November.

According to this decision, which was communicated to Stoklas only on 13 September, the next evacuation from France, planned for the night of 4/5 and 5/6 October, had to be cancelled. This operation was considered especially important in view of the present serious deterioration of the situation of Poles in France.

Although the Poles were informed that all sea operations were to be stopped, both feluccas manned by Polish crews had been ordered to continue to carry out operations unconnected with the evacuation of Polish nationals from France. They were not informed whether any plans were being made for further such operations to be carried out during this period.

The Chief of the Polish General Staff instructed Stoklas to say that according to the *Proposals Concerning the Organisation of the Polish Mission in Gibraltar*, to which both sides had agreed, the Polish-manned feluccas might be used for such operations to a greater extent than originally anticipated, until special British crews were formed. As they had now heard that these crews had been put at the disposal of the senior officer CWF, Stoklas was further instructed to express the hope that from now on the Polish contingent would not be diverted from their main task – the evacuation of Polish nationals from southern France and north Africa; moreover that operations already proposed by the Polish mission in Gibraltar in cooperation with the Polish General Staff in London should, as far as possible, have first call on the Polish crews.

At any rate, the Chief asked for more detailed information, through the Polish Naval Attaché, about the way in which their crews were to be used in the immediate future, so that the Polish side might adapt their plans according to the circumstances in the countries from which evacuation was envisaged.

On the question of security and secrecy of the operations, which had already been raised, the Chief gave an assurance that he, for his part, had issued all the relevant instructions. He would be most grateful if the British authorities could note that very serious and dangerous indiscretions had allegedly been committed by non-Polish agents and possibly also by non-Polish civilians transported by their feluccas.

Such breaches of security, combined with the use of *Seawolf* and *Seadog* for British intelligence organisations had so increased the danger posed to operations purely for evacuation that the whole action to date might be compromised. Both sorts of operations had been carried out by the same boats, manned by Polish sailors, and their identity and the characteristics of the boats were now well known to the French authorities.

The Chief feared that all these factors might finally make the suspension of evacuation operations inevitable and consequently the existence of the Polish contingent in Gibraltar unnecessary. He had instructed Stoklas to say that he would be most grateful for an assurance that the task for which the Polish contingent had been attached to the CWF would not thenceforward be regarded as secondary, and that he would be informed, through the Polish Naval Attaché, of any important changes in the Admiralty's policy with respect to evacuation of Polish nationals from France to Gibraltar.

It was a good letter and it cannot, in the circumstances, have been an easy one to answer. Indeed, there is no evidence that it did receive an answer in written form.

That the Poles were compelled to cancel their own planned October evacuation from France and that *Seawolf* was then ordered by CWF to carry out an exactly similar operation on a smaller scale to rescue a group of British evaders and escapers was bound to engender resentment. It entirely bore out Durski-Trzasko's warnings, at the end of his first month at Gibraltar, that Polish needs were being subordinated to British requirements. The

Poles might have come round to accepting that, for reasons unkown to them, all forms of evacuation had temporarily to be relegated to lower priority than other forms of special operation; but that Slocum's organisation should then require a Polish crew to make a voyage to France to evacuate British nationals was a case of insult added to injury. Durski-Trzasko wrote to Admiral Swirski on 17 October, the day after Lukasz returned from his successful operation for MI9's 'Pat' escape line, to say he saw no hope of further evacuation of Poles from France.[8] Since this was the main purpose for which the Polish crews were attached to the CWF, confirmed in the orders he had been given, he proposed that they wind up the Polish mission. From what he heard in Gibraltar, he concluded that, although the situation had completely changed, the British had no intention of dispensing with the services of the Polish feluccas but wished to retain them for 'imperial' requirements. They made no secret of their view that, not only now but probably in the future too, the evacuation of large groups from the French coast must be entirely ruled out. The British understood perfectly well that they themselves were still not well enough prepared to take over the work carried out to date by Polish crews; nor did they have the experience and operational efficiency attained by the Poles through overcoming difficulties and set-backs. Durski-Trzasko imagined that the British would keep the Polish crews in place until they did have similar mastery of operational methods and means; but, equally, that the Poles would until then be employed serving British, not Polish aims. If all this were so, however, the role of the Polish evacuation mission would have ended and, with it, the financing from Polish sources of seagoing evacuation operations. If the feluccas were to go on being manned by Polish crews under the command of Polish officers, it seemed essential to give them a proper official status. In other words, the feluccas should become regular men-of-war under command of a Polish naval officer, sailing under the Polish naval ensign. On board the feluccas, the crews should wear or at least carry uniforms in case they fell into enemy hands, when they might otherwise be treated as saboteurs, spies or even pirates.

By the time Swirski replied to this letter on 2 December,[9] the strategic situation in the western Mediterranean had changed radically.

CHAPTER XXXII

The Changing Strategic Context in the Western Mediterranean

C hurchill claimed after the war that when the Japanese bombed the Pacific Fleet at its moorings in Pearl Harbour on 7 December 1941 and forced the United States into the Second World War, he knew that the war was won: Hitler and Mussolini would declare war on the United States and, in the prolonged coalition struggle that would follow, America's enormous resources, safeguarded by geography, would grind the Axis to defeat.[1] Great Britain, which had survived 17 months of lonely conflict under his leadership, would emerge, however mauled and mutilated, safe and victorious, as she had from eight earlier wars fought in the preceding two and a half centuries over the issue of hegemony in Europe. With America committed, all the rest was merely a question of what he called 'the proper application of overwhelming force'.

Churchill knew exactly where he most urgently needed the application of American force: in the Mediterranean, an area he feared the United States Joint Chiefs of Staff might 'too casually repudiate as not involving America's most vital interests.' Afraid that the whole fury of the United States would be turned on Japan, while Britain was left to fight Germany and Italy in Europe, Africa and the Middle East, the Prime Minister hastened to Washington. His object was to persuade Roosevelt and his service chiefs that the defeat of Japan would not spell the defeat of Hitler, but that, by contrast, if Hitler were defeated then finishing off Japan would be merely a matter of time and trouble.

Churchill, who was highly intuitive, suspected that Roosevelt might be sympathetic to some proposal for intervention in French North Africa.[2] The United States, unlike Great Britain, had maintained diplomatic relations with Vichy and the President had for some months had a personal representative in the Maghreb, Robert Murphy, entitled to report to the White House over the heads of the State Department. It was, in fact, an area of quite particular interest to the President. The policy pursued by Washington with regard to Vichy was very much Roosevelt's own and he had strong personal reasons for wishing to see it vindicated by positive benefits. North Africa was therefore the right card for Churchill to play and, as their first round of talks progressed in Washington over Christmas and the New Year of 1941–42, it was a subject to which the President returned with growing enthusiasm.

Before Churchill left in mid-January, the planners had been put to work on an Anglo-American project for landing in North Africa but the idea evoked little enthusiasm in the Washington military establishment: Admiral King wanted priority for the Pacific; General Marshall and General Eisenhower, his chief planner, thought the best way to beat Hitler was to build up large forces in Great Britain and launch them into Europe by the shortest sea route on a bee-line to Berlin. Despite the President's support for the North African plan, code-named SUPER-GYMNAST, Marshall and Eisenhower thought it a time-consuming diversion of resources, if not a devious Churchillian attempt to use American means to pluck British imperial chestnuts from the Middle Eastern fire. The case for the plan was further weakened by Auchinleck's resistance to Churchill's attempts to get him to mount an early offensive in the Western Desert. In the end it was laid aside by the US staff in favour of other projects.

However, the situation altered after Molotov's meetings in Washington in mid-May with the President, Hopkins, Marshall and King. He painted such a stark picture of what might happen on the Soviet front if no second front were opened in 1942 that Roosevelt, who faced mid-term elections in November, authorised him to tell Stalin that a second front could be expected before the end of the year. He did so without consulting Churchill and made the commitment public soon afterwards.[3]

During May, the British Chiefs of Staff had been conducting detailed surveys of available shipping resources, with particular attention to landing-craft availability, in order to assess their capacity for cross-Channel operations. They found that there were enough landing craft only to lift a force of 4,000 men to France: this finding demolished both General Marshall's SLEDGE-HAMMER plan to seize a limited beach-head in the Cotentin, and Churchill's idea for a landing in Norway. On 2 May 1942 the British Chiefs directed SOE to facilitate a still-hypothetical landing in French North Africa.[4]

Churchill flew to Washington in June 1942. While he was with Roosevelt at Hyde Park, the combined British and US Chiefs of Staff decided, with rare unanimity, not to proceed with SUPER-GYMNAST. Churchill held quite a different point of view, which he put to the President. If SLEDGEHAMMER was a non-starter, could they stand idle in the Atlantic theatre during the whole of 1942 ? Ought they not, while building up forces in the United Kingdom for a Continental invasion, to be preparing some other operation by which they might gain positions of advantage, and also directly or indirectly take some of the weight off Russia? That, the

Prime Minister suggested, was the light in which the French North African operation should be studied.[5]

Churchill had made a careful study of the President's thinking and reactions and he was sure that Roosevelt was powerfully attracted by the North African plan. Stimson, the Secretary for War, who shared General Marshall's views on the matter, believed that Churchill had taken up GYMNAST knowing full well that it was the President's 'great secret baby'.[6]

While Churchill was in Washington, news of the fall of Tobruk reached him and, as Rommel battered down the defences of Mersa Matruh and swept on to El Alamein, the Prime Minister faced a vote of censure in the House of Commons. He survived it by a massive majority, thanks partly to tactical errors by his critics. But from that point on, the needs of the 8th Army became a key factor in the ongoing strategic debate.

In July 1942 Roosevelt gave Marshall what was to prove a last chance to persuade the British Chiefs of the merits of SLEDGE-HAMMER, but by then he had firmly overruled Marshall's arguments in favour of concentrating United States resources on the Pacific war rather than on SUPER-GYMNAST. He also told Marshall he wanted a decision within a week.

Marshall found the British Staffs adamantly opposed to SLEDGEHAMMER: it would have tied up 250,000 tons of shipping and precluded the sending of supplies to the 8th Army or to besieged Malta, a crucial factor in the attack on Rommel's communications. On 22 July he had to concede defeat. Eisenhower's immediate reaction was that it 'might well go down as the blackest day in history.'[7]

Since the President was both publicly committed to, and privately determined on, action in the 'European' theatre in 1942, GYMNAST in some form was now the only runner. Marshall wanted to postpone a final decision until 15 September, but Hopkins advised the President to reject this proposal, which would have entailed delaying the landings until the meteorologically unpropitious month of December: he urged that 30 October be fixed as the latest date for the beginning of TORCH, as the operation was now renamed. The President, in his capacity as Commander-in-Chief, decided that TORCH should take place at the earliest possible date, which turned out to be 8 November.[8]

In 1947, when General George Marshall had become Secretary of State, a young Brazilian diplomat, who had accompanied his minister on an official visit to Washington, asked Marshall whether he had read the first volume of Churchill's *Second World War*. 'Yes, I have read it: it's a great book,' Marshall replied, 'but I am afraid of what he is going to say in the second volume.' Pressed to explain why, Marshall said that, in his wartime capacity as chairman of the

Joint Chiefs of Staff, he had opposed Churchill's concept of attacking the soft underbelly of Europe as opposed to the cross-Channel alternative, because he feared the consequent losses of life and of time. As Secretary of State, he realised just what a mistake he had made.[9]

Eisenhower, too, later revised his opinion about SLEDGE-HAMMER, when he came to realise how unseasoned the American troops were in 1942 and how inadequate the available air cover would have been.

From midsummer 1942, this high-level strategic debate began to influence the demands on the Allied clandestine services in the Western Mediterranean theatre and on the work of the CWF.

CHAPTER XXXIII

Renewed Priority for Operations to French North Africa

T he United States, having maintained diplomatic relations with the Vichy Government, still possessed consular posts at Casablanca, Oran, Algiers and Tunis. When President Roosevelt decided that United States strategic interests in French North and West Africa required him to appoint Robert Murphy as his quasi-diplomatic representative in the area, these served as a valuable infrastructure. The Americans were therefore far better placed to observe and influence events in the Maghreb during the run-up to TORCH than the British who, apart from their base at Gibraltar, had little more than their Consulate-General in Tangiers and were still suffering from the opprobrium of Mers el-Kebir. Murphy was, however, in no position to ask for the accreditation of attachés to represent the interests of the United States armed services, and the United States was still groping its way towards the creation of a clandestine service with functions similar to those of SIS and SOE. The need for such capabilities in French North Africa was felt quite quickly after Murphy's arrival. Agreements concluded between Murphy and Weygand, Vichy's Delegate-General, for the supply of US economic assistance, served to justify the appointment of 12 additional Vice-Consuls or 'observers', whose agreed role was to ensure that US aid shipments did not find their way into Axis hands, but whose covert function was to collect military intelligence. These so-called 'Twelve Apostles' reported to a new Washington agency, the Office of the Coordinator of War Information, predecessor of the Office of Strategic Services (OSS). Its director was Colonel William J. Donovan, a highly decorated World War I veteran turned New York attorney and a personal friend of Roosevelt's, though he was a Republican and known to harbour political ambitions.[1]

'Big Bill' Donovan had visited London in the course of 1941 and had, by Churchill's decision, been very fully briefed on British arrangements in the clandestine sphere. This had materially strengthened his hand in pressing for the establishment of the OSS.

During May and June 1942 Donovan was back in London for talks between OSS and SOE about combined working arrangements in the Western Mediterranean area in the event of Allied landings in North Africa.[2] It was agreed that an OSS headquarters

HMS *Fidelity* was used by Capt Slocum to land agents in the western Mediterranean in 1941.

Conditions on the Polish-manned feluccas can be judged from this photograph. Passengers had to be hidden under tarpaulins and sails when other ships or aircraft were in the vicinity, as there was no room for them below decks.

Lt Marian Kadulski ('Krajewski'), Polish Navy.

The felucca *Dogfish*, with which Krajewski carried out most of his operations to North Africa, was only half the size of *Seawolf*.

Seawolf, with which Krajewski carried out his remarkable series of operations from Gibraltar to the South of France, was a 17ft 6in Spanish Moroccan fishing felucca.

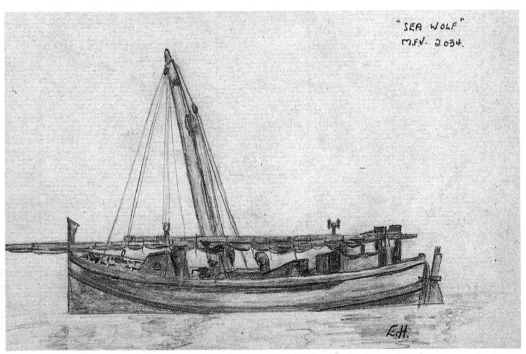

"SEA WOLF"
M.F.V. 2034.

Seawolf, drawn by Lt Cdr Eric Honer RNVR when serving in the Adriatic.

Seawolf meeting *Tarana* offshore to transfer passengers before going back to embark a second, or even third batch.

Minna as a Scottish fishery protection vessel after the end of her wartime employment with the so-called Coast Watching Flotilla in the Western Mediterranean.

Capitaine de Frégate Jean L'Herminier, here seen standing by *Casabianca's* periscope, was in his forties – substantially older than the Captains of British submarines doing similar operations.

French Submarine *Casabianca* in Algiers harbour, 1943.

The Officers of *Casabianca* in the submarine's wardroom: from left to right
L. V. Chailley, I. M. Kerneus (Chief Engineer), Cdt Jean L'Herminier, L. V. Bellet,
E.V. Lassure.

Admiral Darlan decorates Frigate Captain Jean L'Herminier on the quayside at Algiers after her return from her first operation to Corsica. This must have been one of Darlan's last official duties before his assassination.

Sir Winston Churchill meets captains of the Eighth Submarine Flotilla on board HMS *Maidstone.* Lt M. G. R. Lumby (*Saracen*) on left, Lt E. V. D. Turner (*Sybil*) shaking hands with the Prime Minister.

Major N. A. C. Croft, DSO (Essex Regiment), a pre-war Arctic explorer, was one of SOE's most versatile officers. His BALACLAVA team operated by sea from Bastia to SE France and NW Italy.

Commander Patrick Whinney, who joined Captain Slocum's section when it was created in July 1940, represented DDOD(I) in Corsica.

should be set up in Tangiers under Colonel William Eddy to work with the SOE mission in Gibraltar. Hugh Quennell had been withdrawn from Gibraltar at the behest of Lord Gort, the Governor, after a disastrous explosion on board the Tangiers–Gibraltar ferry, and replaced by Colonel Brien Clarke, a New Zealander in the Coldstream Guards. It was decided that a network of clandestine W/T posts should be established with SOE's help, to cover at least the main centres – Tunis, Algiers, Oran and Casablanca. Since OSS was responsible for collecting intelligence as well as for subversion, they wished these stations to be linked to Tangiers, but both parties recognised that, if there were to be landings in North Africa, the operational headquarters would undoubtedly have to be Gibraltar.[3]

The still-hypothetical North African invasion plans lent enhanced importance to Rygor-Slowikowski's 'Agence Afrique', which he had built up into an extensive network concentrating on military targets and which provided SIS's main insight into this field.

By great good fortune, the senior Vichy counter-espionage officer in Algeria, Achiary, was a secret sympathiser with the Allied cause. He became Slowikowski's friend and protector, but he came under suspicion and was replaced by an inspector from Vichy who did not share his pro-Allied views and came close to unmasking the *réseau*, in which Slowikowski used resident Poles as his subagents in Oran, Constantine, Casablanca and other centres.[4] Achiary himself was in touch with SIS, who arranged for a W/T receiver/transmitter to be delivered to him near Arzew in 1941 by a British submarine, which at the same time landed an agent of French nationality named Puech Sanson, who was on his way to Mostaganem, where his father had a factory producing Job cigarettes.[5]

Slowikowski's published account of his mission[6] is detailed and impressive: the coverage he achieved, which was passed straight to Dunderdale by Colonel Gano in London, must have been particularly welcome to SIS, since Dunderdale's Section had by then (mid-1942) lost a high proportion of its sources in metropolitan France as a result of German countermeasures.[7]

Slowikowski also made contact with the Americans in Algiers, but found, to his extreme annoyance, that they were dilatory in passing on to Washington the copies of the reports he gave them.

The growth and success of the 'Agence Afrique' network and the enhanced strategic importance of French North Africa in the months leading up to TORCH meant that, just when the Polish evacuation missions to Casablanca and Oran came to a halt, new requirements, viewed by SIS and NID(C) as of even higher priority, took their place. The ensuing run of operations was carried out for

CWF by *Minna*, Slocum's newly arrived fast escort vessel, which was by far the most suitable ship for the job.

Minna had been built in 1939 as a Scottish fishery protection vessel, but had never in fact served in that capacity, as she was sent straight from her builder's yard at Dumbarton to survey the west coast of Scotland for possible tanker anchorages, on behalf of the War Department.[8] After four months, in August 1939, she was taken over by the Admiralty and allocated to the Firth of Forth as an examination vessel on blockade-enforcement duties. In June 1940 she captured an Italian merchant vessel off May Island but in December she was seriously damaged by one of the then new German acoustic mines. This put her into a repair yard for six months. Back in service, she was attacked and damaged by a Heinkel bomber in November 1941. When she had been repaired again she was sent out to Gibraltar in April 1942 to join the CWF as the larger of the two ships Slocum had undertaken to provide as reinforcement for the Polish-manned feluccas.

Minna was 170 ft long, with a gross registered tonnage of 347. Designed to overhaul and arrest maritime poachers, she had been endowed with twin screws and the extra turn of speed necessary for that work. Ordinary deep-sea trawlers might well be capable of 9, or even 10, knots: *Minna*'s cruising speed of 14 meant that, if it came to a chase, poachers would not be able to show her a clean pair of heels. Her captain during this commission was Commander D.H.F. Armstrong, DSC, RNR, and her first lieutenant was another RNR officer, D.T. McCallum. She carried a 4-inch gun forward on her whale-back and sported the usual array of machine-guns on the wings of her bridge and aft for anti-aircraft protection.

Minna could even less afford to be seen close offshore on the Algerian or Moroccan coast than could *Tarana* on the south coast of France but, whereas *Tarana* under false Moroccan or Spanish colours might hope to pass muster as a genuine fisherman and thus avoid attack, *Minna* was unmistakably a minor warship and had to be prepared to fight her corner if sighted by a hostile patrolling aircraft. In mid-1942 there was always a chance of such an encounter in the Western Mediterranean, but it was not a routine occurrence, so she was able to exploit the fact that the Germans had as yet no air-bases in Southern France and that French coastal defences in Algeria were not sufficiently on the alert to include air-reconnaissance patrols. Nevertheless, her substantial silhouette and unsilenced engines meant that she needed to heave to at least a quarter of a mile offshore during a night operation; meanwhile, McCallum would conduct any necessary boatwork, for which she carried one of the 25-foot SN6 surf-boats that Nigel Warington Smyth had developed and Camper and Nicholson had built for NID(C)'s clandestine needs.

Minna's first mission from Gibraltar for the CWF was a rendez-vous in the Gibraltar Straits at the end of June 1942 with a felucca from Tangiers, to which she transferred a consignment of warlike stores for SOE – a method of shipment no doubt made necessary by the disaster in Tangiers harbour in March that had blighted Quennell's SOE career.

The fact that *Minna*'s next operation, GUYMAR, involved landing an agent near Oran for Kenneth Cohen's P1 Section of SIS is at first sight surprising. Cohen normally worked with de Gaulle's BCRA and the arrival of a Gaullist emissary in Algeria at that juncture would have been extremely unwelcome to President Roosevelt and Robert Murphy, his personal representative in the Maghreb. But, for historical rather than logical reasons, Cohen was also SIS's point of contact with an important intelligence network, 'Alliance', whose chiefs, Commandant Loustaunau-Lacau and Jacques Bridou, alias 'Navarre', had refused to work with de Gaulle. The links between 'Alliance' and North Africa and Navarre's ambition to provoke a revolt of the French Army there had led to the latter's arrest for the first time in May 1941. Commandant Léon Faye, chief of operations for 'Alliance', who was also arrested, had maintained close links with the small group of non-Gaullist conspirators in Algiers who were in touch with Murphy and planned to assist any Allied landings there.[9] The agent landed was a young officer of the Belgian merchant navy named Guy Verstraete, who had escaped from Dakar to Bathurst in a ship's lifeboat and on arrival in England had been recruited by SIS and trained as a W/T operator.[10] He was in touch with Ridgway Knight, one of Robert Murphy's OSS Vice-Consuls. His cover was that he was the son of a wealthy landowner. He and a considerably older local associate met the young and wealthy widow of a local colonist at an Oran hotel and were soon living with her in considerable style and comfort.

Minna's third operation, ORKAN II, successfully evacuated a subagent of Rygor-Slowikowski's from near Oran on 13 July, but the fourth, CASUAL, failed to land two, or possibly three, Polish agents in the same area on 19 July because the expected reception committee was not in place. This operation was successfully completed on 11 September, when it was combined with ZEBRA, an evacuation. The Oran subagent took the five men and one woman who were to be embarked on that night to the pick-up point as participants in an evening picnic party.[11] The agents landed on this occasion, Malinowski, Kowal and Piotrowski, had been on board *Minna* since May.

Another of *Minna*'s Algerian operations – ACCOST – an embarkation, failed at the beginning of October when a signal went astray leaving the agent too little time to arrive at the rendezvous. Last-minute intelligence was urgently required from Slowikowski's 'Agence Afrique' in the run-up to TORCH, but the successful landing of an agent from *Minna* on 1 October, the embarkation of six on 3 October (GIRAFFE II) and of a further individual on the same night (ULTRAMARINE) were recorded as for the 'Poles', rather than SIS (P5), the description applied to other 'Agence Afrique' operations.

Minna was attacked by an enemy aircraft on the return voyage after the abortive operation on 19 July, but drove off her assailant.

It is clear from the records that both she and *Tarana* were also used by CWF for a number of operations on the coast of Spain as well as in support of the Polish feluccas (see above).

CHAPTER XXXIV

SOE and OSS Prepare for TORCH

S OE's signals officer at Gibraltar, Squadron Leader Mallory
(real name Hugh Mallory-Falconer), and his staff had considerable difficulty in establishing the required W/T network to link all
the US consular posts in French North Africa to Tangiers, let alone
to Gibraltar. OSS brought various operators to Tangiers, where
Mallory had made arrangements for them to be instructed in
operating their sets, and sets were delivered to OSS in Tangiers
for distribution. But by the beginning of September a major
complication had arisen: the SOE signals station at the western
end of the tunnels in the Rock was able to send and receive signals
to and from Tangiers, Casablanca and Oran quite satisfactorily, but
contact with Algiers was very temperamental and Tunis permanently out of communication.[1]

Mallory put in a prodigious amount of work trying to discover
whether this difficulty was due to technical faults in the sets or to
errors by the operators: the sets were changed and the Tunis
operator brought back to Tangiers for further instruction. It eventually became clear that the trouble lay at the Gibraltar end: SOE
needed a branch W/T station at the eastern end of the Rock
directly connected with their main signals station.

Tunnelling in the Rock had been proceeding for a considerable
time and plans existed for the garrison and civil administration to
be dispersed in the tunnels in the event of siege, but the tunnelling
operation had still not caught up with the final requirements and all
the available space had been allocated with very high priorities.
Colonel Brien Clarke of SOE decided that, in view of the vital
importance of the SOE/OSS communications, he must approach
Mason Macfarlane, who had succeeded Field Marshal Lord Gort as
Governor in June 1942, to see whether the necessary further
accommodation could be allocated to SOE.

Brien Clarke was unaware that his call on the Governor fell at
an unfortunate juncture, because Mason Macfarlane had that very
morning held an urgent conference to decide requirements and
priorities for erecting further wireless installations on the Rock for
the Navy and the RAF in connection with the planned landings.
The Governor's first reaction to Clarke's request was distinctly
hostile but he relented when the problem was explained to him.
Not only did he agree to provide the accommodation but he went

so far as to allocate to SOE part of what would have been his own quarters, in case a crisis arose before tunnelling was complete.

Mallory and his staff worked day and night at the installation of this branch-signals equipment and, within a few days of the job's completion, Clarke was able to report that communications with Algiers had greatly improved and that a satisfactory link with Tunis had been established.

Clarke and Bill Eddy, his OSS opposite number, met quite frequently during this period, usually in Tangiers, as Eddy had no avowable reason for being seen frequently in Gibraltar. On these occasions they sent combined progress reports to London and Washington on the state of the clandestine W/T system and the assistance arrangements with the French groups with whom Murphy was working. In between these contacts, Major Wharton Tigar, SOE's man in Tangiers, who was working under cover as a clerk at the British Consulate-General, was in daily touch with his OSS counterparts.

Eddy, son of American missionary parents in the Middle East, was an Arabist and had taught at the American University in Beirut. After the war he became head of the US Mission in Saudi Arabia and in that capacity was reckoned by his British diplomatic colleagues as unfriendly to British interests. Clarke, on the other hand, considered that Eddy deserved the greatest credit for the cooperative spirit he showed and maintained throughout the planning and operational phases in the months leading up to TORCH.

The operational phase began for Brien Clarke at about tea-time on 19 October[2] when he was summoned to the drawing-room of Government House, where a conference of clearly distinguished visitors was in full swing. The Governor introduced him to Major-General Mark Clark, Colonel Lemnitzer, Colonel Hamblen and Colonel Julius Holmes, all of the US Army, though in civilian attire, and to Captain Gerald Wright, US Navy. It was evident to Brien Clarke that what he subsequently described as the long-expected, high-level staff talks with the French were about to begin.

At one point, VACNA, Sir Edward Collins, turned to Clarke and said, 'What do you know about all this? Do you realise that they are wanting to take one of my submarines to land on the North African coast? Isn't all this crazy?', or words to that effect. Clarke, who was evidently not fully informed about the state of negotiations between Murphy, General Mast and the self-appointed group of plotters under Lemaigre-Dubreuil, replied rather lamely that, in ancient days, before a tournament, the knights sometimes discussed whether lances, swords or clubs should be used and how the tournament should be conducted; perhaps pending events should be viewed in the same light. Collins, widely known as 'the Giant Panda', seemed far from comforted.

The Governor suggested that perhaps General Mark Clark would like to question Captain Barney Fawkes, who commanded the 8th Submarine Flotilla from HMS *Maidstone*, and Clarke himself about details of the impending submarine voyage and the W/T link between Gibraltar and Algiers. Mark Clark took the two officers concerned into a corner of the room to pursue these matters. One question he asked, among many others, was whether he and his party should land in North Africa in uniform or in plain clothes. Brien Clarke gave his opinion that they should land in uniform, as even a US Major General in plain clothes might have some difficulty in explaining to the Vichy authorities what he was doing there in civilian dress. Mark Clark said he received the same reply at Chequers from the Prime Minister a few evenings earlier.

Shortly afterwards the conference broke up and the American party adjourned to Captain Fawkes's quarters in *Maidstone*. Brien Clarke accompanied them. There the final details of the expedition were arranged. It was agreed that the party would leave Gibraltar in the submarine P219 (later named *Seraph*) under the command of Lt N.L.A. Jewell, RN, at about 2200 hours the same evening. For the first part of the voyage the submarine might maintain limited W/T communication with Gibraltar but when it reached the French North African coast W/T communication from the submarine would be prohibited.

P219 would be equipped with the necessary Folboats for landing and taking off the party. Brien Clarke suggested that they should take a small radio set to act as a link between ship and shore. Captain Fawkes undertook to provide this.

The landing pinpoint and recognition signals had already been agreed with Murphy, who would be in charge of the reception party, which would be headed on the French side by General Mast. Brien Clarke undertook to send a signal to Algiers forthwith to tell them that the party was on its way. In the event of trouble at the Algerian end, General Mark Clark said his party would try to make for the large salt-flats south-east of Oran and hoped that a signal would be sent from Algiers to the Gibraltar SOE post, in case he wanted the Flying Fortresses in which the party had flown out from the United Kingdom sent to take them off.

Mark Clark also asked that, on the return journey when the submarine was in mid-Mediterranean and no longer needed to observe wireless silence, a Catalina flying-boat should be sent to take him and his party off the submarine, weather permitting, thus saving several hours on the return journey.

At Gibraltar there was a small detachment of the Special Boat Section (SBS), which was trained in the use of Folboat canoes for clandestine landings and which had therefore the equipment and experience to land and pick up General Clark's party.[3] Three of their officers, Captain G.B. Courtney (known to his friends as 'Gruff'), Captain R.P. Livingstone and Lt J.P. Foot, were embarked on P219 with their equipment before she sailed at 2100.

The departure from England of the two B17 Flying Fortresses had been delayed: instead of taking off on the evening of Sunday 18 October, they left only at dawn on the 19th, which meant that the party's sailing from Gibraltar was delayed. Before leaving, Clark sent Murphy a message to say he would meet Mast on the night of 21/22 October. Murphy had in the meantime sent a signal to say he and the French group would expect Clark on the night of 20/21 October and, if that rendezvous was missed, they would hope to meet him 48 hours later.

Jewell took the risk of running *P219* on the surface in order to make the best possible speed, but further delay was caused by an indispensable exercise in the use of the Folboats in the dark and the submarine did not arrive at the agreed landing site of Messelmoun, some 12 km. west of Cherchell, until shortly before dawn on 21 October, by which time the reception party had left.

By then Murphy had received Clark's signal and the whole group was reassembled that evening, with some difficulty, at the villa on the unfrequented beach there. It had been chosen for the conference because it belonged to the father-in-law of an active member of the Cherchell Resistance. Shortly before midnight, the agreed light signal was shown to seaward and disembarkation began, using four Folboat canoes. This went very smoothly and Mark Clark and his colleagues were able to get some sleep while awaiting the arrival of General Mast and his team.

Historians have questioned whether General Clark's melo-dramatic mission accomplished anything useful. Tarbé de Saint Hardouin, one of the Group of Five with whom Murphy was negotiating the attempt to bring General Giraud into the affair, has argued that it actually did harm by creating an impression of too much confidence on the American side and too much distrust on the French.[4] The Allies were going to land in North Africa with or without French assistance, but A.L. Funk has pointed out that the planners of TORCH had grave reservations about the operation, at one time giving it no better than a fifty-fifty chance of success. They were very conscious of the lack of training, the shortage of equip-ment and, above all, the absolute novelty of an amphibious assault conducted from across the Atlantic. Any opportunity of securing an unopposed landing was therefore worth pursuing and far out-weighed the risks of General Clark's capture. But those involved, both French and American, greatly overestimated Giraud's influ-ence and relevance. Clark reported from Gibraltar that extremely valuable intelligence had been obtained and that the plan for the operation appeared sound.

The conference was brought to an abrupt and dramatic end at about 6 p.m. on 22 October, when two coastguards, who had assisted the landing, telephoned to say that the local police *commissaire* was on his way to inspect the villa. One of the Arab servants, who had twice before been evicted at short notice for security reasons by Tessier, the owner of the property, had told the police that something abnormal was afoot – probably smuggling.

The whole landing party took refuge in the empty wine cellar, while the French participants flew in all directions: the trap-door to the cellar was closed on Mark Clark and his companions, barrels were rolled on top of it and, as a finishing touch, someone scattered dust on the boards. Some of this percolated into the cellar, causing Gruff Courtney to have a coughing fit. As he struggled in the darkness to control it, choking and spluttering, he whispered to Clark, 'General, I'm afraid I'll choke,' to which Clark replied 'I'm afraid you won't.'[5] Clark slipped him a wad of chewing-gum, which he had already worked for a while, and this had the desired effect of silencing Courtney. They had to sit in pitch-darkness for two hours, getting more and more cramped, while Murphy, Ridgway Knight and Tessier explained that the American diplomats were his guests, that the occasion was a purely social one and included some imaginary ladies upstairs, and that the smuggling story was a ridiculous invention.

It was 8 p.m. before the police went and General Clark and his fellow sufferers were allowed to emerge from the cellar. To Courtney's remark that 'your American chewing-gum' had so little taste, Clark replied that he had chewed all the taste out of that particular piece.

All the French, except Tessier and a young man named Karsenty, had driven back to Algiers. Those who remained carried the Folboats down to a wood near the beach, where a considerable sea was running. Clark, who could see he was going to get soaked, took off his trousers and rolled them up around his heavy money-belt, which contained several hundred dollars in gold. Not wishing to be weighed down by it in the surf and heavy undertow, he put the roll into the Folboat. He and Livingstone tried to launch one of the canoes, wading out waist-deep and making a dash for it at what seemed a favourable moment. Just when they thought they were clear, an exceptionally large wave hit them: the boat reared up almost vertically and was rolled over, leaving them struggling in a boiling turmoil of foam. It had been impressed on everybody that on no account must the paddles be lost: accordingly, all that could be seen of Clark at one time was one arm holding a paddle firmly aloft above the swirling water. But the trousers and the money had disappeared (they were subsequently recovered and given to Murphy).

The disconsolate group stayed on the beach, cold and wet, not daring to return to the villa. They discussed the possibility of buying, chartering or stealing a fishing boat at Cherchell, driving to Spanish Morocco or making their way to Algiers, but all these courses involved unacceptable risks. They decided therefore to wait. About four o'clock in the morning the sea seemed to have abated slightly and they decided to make another attempt. Courtney knew that on the West African coast natives launched their canoes through surf by carrying them out beyond the breakers before climbing aboard. The shore party, consisting of Tessier, Karsenty and the two coastguards, stripped off their clothes and waded out into the cold surf with the canoes held above their heads. This tactic worked, although two of the canoes capsized at the beach and had to be righted. The last Folboat to come alongside the submarine was swamped and had to be abandoned, taking with it Julius Holmes's musette bag and its contents, which included letters written by Murphy and more gold coins.

The sky was already announcing the advent of the dawn and Jewell decided they must submerge without delay. Soaked and exhausted, the landing party made their way below. Mark Clark asked Jewell whether they had a rum ration on submarines. 'Yes, sir,' replied Jewell, 'but on submarines only in emergencies.' 'Well,' said General Clark, 'I think this is an emergency. What about a double rum ration?' 'OK, sir,' said the submarine's captain, 'if an officer of sufficient rank will sign the order.'

Clark actually did put his signature to the order.

The submarine ran submerged during the day of 23 October except for a brief surfacing to send a message reporting that conditions were ideal for transfer to a flying-boat. On the morning of 24 October Mark Clark and his party were picked up from *P219* by a Catalina and taken to Gibraltar, as planned. Before boarding the Flying Fortress for his return flight to London, General Clark dictated to Colonel Brien Clarke of SOE a signal reporting the main features of his talks with General Mast and outlining the more interesting episodes of his hazardous expedition. This was transmitted by SOE Gibraltar to SOE Baker Street with the prefix 'For Eisenhower's eyes only' and dated 24 October 1942.[6]

Mast had raised one matter with Clark that became SOE's direct concern: he said that if 2,000 Bren guns could be delivered to the young men under the orders of Henri d'Astier de la Vigerie and Colonel Van Hecke, the Belgian-born head of the local Chantiers de la Jeunesse youth training scheme, to replace the antique weapons on which they were relying, this group could become an underground force of political significance. Mark Clark foresaw no difficulty in meeting this request and agreed to make the arrangements.

During the previous few months SOE had accumulated a stock of some 600 tons of arms, explosives and other warlike stores at Gibraltar for various contingency plans on which they had been working; these included distribution to the French resistance elements in North Africa who were collaborating with Murphy and the fledgling OSS. The stores included special flares for airborne landings, automatic pistols, Sten guns, anti-tank 'Gammon' grenades, demolition materials, miniature tyre-bursters camouflaged to look like mule droppings, samples of which had been collected in Tangiers and flown home. There were some Bren guns and rifles, together with large stocks of ammunition of the relevant calibres. Brien Clarke was thus easily capable of meeting Mast's request, but the quantities asked for were unrealistically high. Indeed, a certain amount of such equipment – particularly flares and recognition signals – had already been dispatched in small consignments to the Americans in Tangiers. Brien Clarke reported to Baker Street that Colonel Lemnitzer (a future NATO Supreme Commander) had turned over to him 16,500 Algerian Francs 'to cover expenses', though this sounds more like an attempt to dispose of the contents of his money-belt than even a notional transaction.

Brien Clarke and Eddy worked out a plan which they agreed with Murphy. It called for the landing of some 10 tons of small arms, ammunition, grenades and small mines somewhere in the vicinity of Algiers. Osborne chose *Minna* for the operation, which was not very different in kind from others she had carried out since the beginning of July on the Algerian coast, though it required her to venture considerably further east than on her previous six expeditions, all of which had been to the Oran area.

SOE Baker Street had formed a small mission to take part in the TORCH landings and in any subsequent military operations. This included a naval officer who had already distinguished himself during the final stages of the East African campaign by sinking, or forcing ashore, off Djibouti a German merchant vessel of 8,000 tons, which was attempting to escape from Massawa through Vichy–French territorial waters. This officer, Anglo–Irish by descent, had left the Royal Navy after the First World War as a Sub Lieutenant and had spent the inter-war years as skipper of dhows in the Red Sea. His crews were Somali and he must have earned a living as a trader in pearls, arms and hashish. He had become a Muslim and, when recalled as a reserve officer at the outbreak of hostilities in 1939, he was widely known as Lt Cdr Abdullah Bey, RN.[7]

His feat in sinking the *Elbe* and capturing her crew of nearly 40, with a force of two engineless dhows whose armament consisted of a Bren gun and a 3-pounder Hotchkiss quick-firing gun, such as was mounted on naval steam packet-boats at the turn of the 19th century, earned him a recommendation for the DSO. However, while in command of a schooner supplying beseiged Tobruk (petrol in the bottom of the hold, bully beef on top, because they were so regularly shot up from the air), he incurred the severe displeasure of Admiral A.B. Cunningham, his Commander-in-Chief at Alexandria. Quite what led to this fall from grace is difficult to establish: people said at the time that he had 'swung on too many chandeliers'. Whatever the reason, he was sent home and Cunningham advised that he be no further employed. The recommendation for a DSO was rescinded.

SOE, however, impressed by his operational record, were about to send him off to join the impending landings in French North Africa when they realised that Cunningham was not only Eisenhower's deputy for the TORCH operation but would thereafter again become Commander-in-Chief of the whole Mediterranean: the last person he would wish to see there was Abdullah Bey. The fact that the Bey was also reported to have been talking to a group of strangers in a bar off Trafalgar Square about the forthcoming invasion sealed his fate: he was sent off to 'the cooler' – a particularly remote SOE establishment in the north of Scotland intended to keep such people out of harm's way. The author was summoned from Helford and flown to Gibraltar to take his place as the naval member of SOE's BRANDON mission. He landed there on 29 October with orders to act as conducting officer on the gun-running operation asked for by Mast. The matter was urgent: *Minna* would have to leave Algerian waters by dawn on 6 November at the latest, so as not to risk alerting the defences on the eve of the first major amphibious operation of the war.

CHAPTER XXXV

The Last Phase of the CWF's Operation: October–November 1942

A s winter approached, the weather broke and gale after gale made operations in the Western Mediterranean hazardous. Gibraltar became a main forward base and concentration point for the impending North African invasion. Orders from London banned the passage of agents to and from the Rock, bringing the Poles' highly successful felucca service to a halt. Then, on 29 October, *Seadog* was sent to France again and, on the night of 3/4 November, only four days before TORCH, Buchowski used her to carry out four successful landing operations at Port-Miou near Cassis, an ideal pinpoint, sheltered from all winds. His report was laconic in comparison with those of Krajewski:

> On 29 October I left port at 2030 hrs and, in compliance with my operational orders, after rounding Europa Point, set an easterly course so as to pass by the south of Cabo de Gata at a distance of 15 nautical miles. During the voyage there were no events worth reporting.[1]
>
> Arriving at the position on 3 November at 2130 hrs, I transferred command to [Capt] Pohorecki and made my way via the dinghy together with two other people to the Port-Miou *calanque*. After an hour's searching along the shoreline, I found the agents, who had not been waiting at the position agreed, and we exchanged the correct signals and code-signs. At 2330 hrs I returned to the ship. Nine (9) agents were put ashore and six (6) embarked. On 4 November at 0200 hrs the operation was completed. We moved away from the shore and set our course for the next operation point.
>
> On 5 November at 2200 hrs we were at the agreed position and we exchanged signals. The dinghy could not make its way to shore because of rough weather. At 2400 hrs we made away from the shore. During the day we rode out the storm 30 nautical miles distant from the coast. The weather worsened.
>
> On 6 November at 1500 hrs I set a course for the operation point. The wind was Force 8, the sea conditions Force 6, and the wind was continuing to increase in strength. At 2300 hrs, some five miles south of the point of the operation, the wind was Force 9–10 (from the NW). Working at full speed, the engine

produced a speed of 1 knot. At 2330 hrs I changed course. We left the shore. The wind force of 10 increased to 11. On 7 November at 0200 hrs a wave destroyed and tore away the wheel-house and galley. At 0900 hrs I sent a signal to Gibraltar, reporting our situation. At 2000 hrs the engine broke down and the vessel drifted in the direction of Sardinia.

On 8th at 0100 hrs the fault was repaired. We were then some 60 nautical miles from the Sardinian coast. Set a course for Gibraltar. Weather unchanged.

On the 10th at 19.00 hrs we were about 20 nautical miles east of the north-eastern promontory of Minorca. The weather improved.

On 13 November at 1000 hrs we entered the port of Gibraltar.

J. Buchowski, Lt

The following were landed at Port-Miou in the course of Operations WATCHMAN III, OVERGROW and DUBONNET on 3/4 November for SOE:[2] George Starr, Marcus Bloom, Mary Herbert, Mme M.T. Le Chêne and Odette Sanson. Embarked were: J.A.R. Starr, I. Newman, a W/T operator with Peter Churchill, a person with the field name 'Richard', his son and 'Quintet', recruited by 'Carte' for Radio Patrie, the clandestine broadcasting station operated by the British Political Warfare Executive, whose existence and tenor exacerbated relations with 4 Carlton Gardens. George Starr was bound for Gascony, where he became a Maquis organiser of such standing that the Germans believed him to be a British general: his homeward-bound brother John, whom he met briefly on the beach, was to return to France, where he was captured by the Sicherheitsdienst, taken to their Avenue Foch headquarters and manipulated to extract information from other SOE prisoners. Odette Sanson, courier to Peter Churchill, was subsequently captured with him, survived Ravensbrück and was awarded the George Cross.

One agent was landed for MI9 at Port-Miou that night, along with 1,000 lb. of stores for SOE.

The pinpoint chosen by Algiers for *Minna*'s gun-running expedition (Operation LEOPARD for CWF, PICNIC for SOE) was 12 km. west of Cherchell and 120 km. west of Algiers. Though nobody mentioned it at the time, this was near the Tessier villa, where General Mark Clark and his colleagues had landed ten days before. Presumably the complicity of the two local coastguards was thought to outweigh the risk of further trouble from the Arab servants and the police, though 10 tons of cargo could hardly have been removed without at least one heavy truck.

Since *Minna* could not afford to be seen anywhere near French territorial waters and must therefore approach the landing from well offshore, a passage of some 400 nautical miles was involved. By the time the weapons had been degreased, repacked in waterproof packages of a suitable size to be manhandled and loaded on to the ship, it was clear that the earliest time she could reach the rendez-vous was after nightfall on 2/3 November. Algiers was so advised by signal before *Minna* sailed.

Minna had no difficulty in maintaining the required timetable and she reached the area of the pinpoint on time. But she waited in vain for the agreed light signal and had to withdraw 20 miles offshore well before daybreak.

On the night of 3/4 November, she crept back to the coast, confident that she was at the agreed place, but again there was no light signal and she withdrew, expecting to have to return for a third night's vigil, as called for by her operation orders. But on the afternoon of 4 November a signal was received from SOE Gibral-tar saying that their friends would be prepared to receive the shipment that night but at an entirely different pinpoint, about 3 km. east of Alma Marine, which was 30 km. east of Algiers, and that they would, if necessary, repeat the reception arrangements on the following two nights.

The old and the new pinpoints were nearly 160 km. apart, as the seagull flies. *Minna* was lying 20 nautical miles offshore, and as she would have to skirt the coastal batteries on Cap Matifou just west of Alma Marine, she faced a passage of some 120 miles to reach the new venue. Obviously she could not arrive there in time to carry out the operation that night. *Minna* nevertheless steamed to the new operational area at top speed, determined to be in position on the second of the three appointed nights. The signal from the beach was to be a steady white light with a steady blue light beside it, starting at 2000 hrs local time: the landing was to begin at 2130.

José Aboulker and Bernard Karsenty were in charge of the reception arrangements. Aboulker says they expected the delivery would be made by submarine and that on the night of 2/3 November they were on the beach at Messelmoun, where Karsenty had helped General Clark and his party ashore 12 days before.[3] They decided next morning, in consultation with Murphy, that this was too dangerous a landing-place and switched to the Alma Marine alternative, which they had previously reconnoitred. There must therefore have been a delay of 24 hours or more in transmit-ting the new arrangements to *Minna* via SOE Gibraltar.

Brien Clarke's report to SOE says that *Minna* was in the vicinity of the new landing point from the night of 3 November and that 'in spite of the most careful and audacious search by the ship's commander [Armstrong] on the night of 4/5 November' no recognition signals could be picked up and the project eventually had to be abandoned, as the Admiralty had insisted that *Minna* be clear of the African coast by dawn on the 6th for fear that her presence would alert the defences and compromise the main landings.

Alma Marine beach was indeed used less than 48 hours later, for landings by troops that formed the easternmost flank of the invasion force. The author confirms that *Minna* was operating within the time limit to which Clarke refers, but the 'careful and audacious' search took place not on the night of 4/5 November but on the night immediately before *Minna*'s withdrawal, that is to say, on 5/6 November. Moreover, *Minna* arrived in the vicinity not on 3 November but on the 4th.

Brien Clarke's errors are understandable. No sooner had *Minna* returned to Gibraltar than she was ordered to join one of the invasion force convoys sailing eastwards. There was no time for a post-mortem at Gibraltar on what had gone wrong, nor did the participants have occasion to discuss the matter in Algiers, where the unforeseen presence of Admiral Darlan raised matters of more immediate moment. But the reasons for the failure of Operation LEOPARD are of some interest in the light of Murphy's conviction, shared with Eddy, that the British let them down because they had 'no confidence in our judgement or our French underground.' John Knox, one of Murphy's Vice-Consuls sent to London to help with the planning of TORCH, told A.L. Funk in November 1972 that Brigadier Mockler-Ferryman, the relevant regional director of SOE in 1943, had admitted as much. But Mockler-Ferryman had not even joined SOE at the time of TORCH. Funk was also told by Karsenty and Aboulker that they learned after the war that the shipment had been sent, but to the wrong rendezvous. This may well be the reason why *Minna* failed to make contact at Messelmoun on 2/3 November: as in other cases, a navigational error of even a few hundred yards on an unfamiliar coast can wipe out the chance of picking up light signals. Aboulker told the author in 1984 that he thought that the reception committee, which turned out at Alma Marine on 4/5 November and again on 6/7 November after *Minna*'s departure, may not have been there on the night in between, 5/6 November, which was the very night that *Minna* was cruising to and fro looking in vain for their lights, having been assured that the reception committee would be waiting on all three nights.

As for Murphy's suggestion that SOE had no confidence in 'our judgement and our underground', it should be recorded that, within a week of TORCH, most of the members of the Gaullist group who helped the Allies achieve an easy landing at Algiers had to be issued with British army battledress and pay books by SOE's BRANDON mission, to save them from retribution at the hands of Darlan and his administration, whom Murphy and Mark Clark, Roosevelt's plenipotentiaries, had maintained in power.

CHAPTER XXXVI

Final Preparations for TORCH

I n the minds both of Murphy and the of anti-Gaullist French group with whom he was negotiating in Algiers, General Giraud had a key role to play in TORCH and its immediate aftermath because he was a figure behind whom the French forces in North and West Africa might rally. The problem was that he was not only in the wrong place – still in France – but that communication with him was difficult; besides, he had still not been won over to the idea of Allied landings in North Africa and was instead strongly arguing the case for southern France.

On 27 October Brien Clarke received a signal from SOE Baker Street confirming and modifying a draft letter to Giraud from Murphy but no doubt emanating from Eisenhower, commander of the TORCH expeditionary force. It authorised Murphy to inform Giraud and Mast on 4 November of the date of the impending assault. The message also confirmed that, whether Giraud came to North Africa or not, Mast would be acceptable as his deputy.[1]

Another signal on 28 October indicated that Giraud's idea of a bridgehead in southern France to coincide with the launching of TORCH was out of the question. The final paragraph authorised Murphy to let Giraud know that the operation was now imminent and set for early November, so as to convince the General that his presence in North Africa was urgently needed. The message ended with the information that a British submarine under American command was moving in the direction of the Golfe-de-Lyon in order to expedite Giraud's removal from southern France.

At midnight on 31 October, by triple priority, a W/T message reached SOE Gibraltar. In it, Murphy stated that a messenger who had just returned from Giraud said that it was utterly impossible for him to leave France until about 20 November. Mast supported Giraud's plea for a delay, so Murphy suggested that TORCH be postponed until about that date.

Brien Clarke showed this remarkably silly signal to Admiral Sir Andrew Cunningham, Deputy Supreme Commander, who had just arrived in Gibraltar in HMS *Scylla*. The effect was dramatic. Cunningham pointed out that the assault forces were already well through the outer enemy submarine belt and that any change of plan would be quite disastrous. He told Brien Clarke that he would signal his view to the First Sea Lord through Admiralty channels and would be obliged if General Eisenhower could be notified that he had seen the telegram on its way through Gibraltar.

During the night of 1/2 November, a strongly worded reply from Eisenhower in London was received by SOE Gibraltar for onward transmission to Murphy. It was impossible to postpone the operation, he said: TORCH must proceed as planned.

On 4 November SOE Gibraltar received a signal from Murphy asking them to inform Eisenhower that Giraud had decided to come over immediately and requesting that the submarine should be at the pre-arranged point at 2300 French time on 4 November, and again on 5 November if the first attempt to embark him failed.

The submarine dispatched to fetch Giraud was *P219* (*Seraph*), the same vessel as had been used for Mark Clark's mission. It was normally commanded by Lt Cdr Jewell, but on this occasion it was deemed politically necessary that it should be at least nominally under command of an American officer. Thus Captain Jerauld Wright, USN – a future NATO Supreme Allied Commander Atlantic – to whom Gibraltar had wished Godspeed with Mark Clark's party on the night of 24 October, was back there on 28 October, ready for a second trip in the same submarine.[2]

A small ceremony took place in the captain's cabin of HMS *Maidstone* when Captain Barney Fawkes, Lt Cmdr Jewell, Captain Jerauld Wright and Colonel Brien Clarke were gathered together. Fawkes said that he had made considerable research into British naval history and believed the present to be a historic occasion, when for the first time a British submarine in war would be under command of an officer of another nation. He felt therefore that great responsibility rested on Captain Wright and himself to make a success of the operation and he had therefore drafted certain rules, regulations and instructions, which he hoped Captain Wright could master before he took command of his ship in about an hour's time. Captain Wright, who had not had active duty in submarines for some years, was by this time somewhat pale and obviously weighed down by his impending responsibilities. However, with a somewhat shaky hand, he took the scroll from Captain Fawkes and, on undoing the binding tape, found it to be a picture of an extraordinarily attractive pin-up girl from *La Vie Parisienne*.

Wright's orders were to proceed to 42° N latitude and 6° E longitude and stand by for further instructions. By 1 November *P219* was on station, about 50 miles south of Toulon.

At this time there were in fact two British submarines lying off the south coast of France. *P217* (*Sibyl*), under Lt E.J.D. Turner, RN, having sailed from Gibraltar 24 hours after *P219*, was also standing by in response to a request, through SIS, from Commandant Faye, operations officer of the 'Alliance' intelligence network, for a submarine to be stationed off Nice. But Faye and Cdt Beaufre, who was planning to leave France with Giraud, signalled SIS on the afternoon of 3 November recommending an embarkation point nearer Marseilles. Faye later confirmed a rendezvous at Le-Lavandou, about 75 miles east of Marseilles, for the following night.

Difficulties of transmission again prevented *P219* from receiving the order to proceed until 2100 on 4 November, when Giraud and his party were already waiting at Le-Lavandou. Giraud, his son Bernard and Cdt Beaufre were therefore picked up only on the next night, in rough sea conditions. *P219* headed back to Gibraltar as fast as possible, running submerged by day and on the surface at night. She was at the time unable to transmit because of a radio breakdown. Some historians have stated that, because of the breakdown of W/T communications, Gibraltar and Eisenhower were not informed that Giraud had been picked up until the submarine docked in Gibraltar's Admiralty Harbour alongside *Maidstone* on the afternoon of 7 November. This is incorrect: *P219* encountered a Catalina on pre-arranged patrol at 0850 on the morning of 7 November. After being contacted by signal, it landed and Giraud was paddled over by Lt Jimmy Foot of the SBS and transferred to the flying-boat. *Sibyl* picked up seven members of Giraud's entourage and Mme Beaufre from a small fishing boat that same night. The party had some problems with the French police just before embarking from Cros-de-Cagnes and three of the intended passengers were arrested.[3]

Though Cunningham had arrived in Gibraltar as scheduled on 30/31 October in *Scylla*, the weather had been extremely bad over a wide area during the previous ten days or so. Eisenhower and various members of his staff had been due to arrive there on 2 November and a second party the next night but impossible flying conditions – common enough during the Second World War in winter-time, since de-icing equipment was in its infancy – prevented any flights on Monday 2 November, Tuesday 3 November or Wednesday 4 November. In the meantime Admiral Cunningham, who had taken up his temporary headquarters at the Tower, held the fort. During that time, the few people in Gibraltar who were aware of the date of D-Day began to wonder whether the operation would have to begin without the Supreme Commander and most of his staff in place at their forward headquarters. However, flying became possible on Thursday 5 November, on which date Eisenhower, Mark Clark and Al Grunther, acting Chief of Staff, arrived, to be followed next day by the remainder of the chief staff officers, including General Doolittle, the Air Force commander. The B17 Fortress in which Doolittle and his party were travelling was attacked by two German fighters and the co-pilot was wounded.

The garrison commander's mess had decided as a form of light entertainment for the new arrivals to take tickets for a film showing publicly that week in Gibraltar, 'The First of the Few'. Doolittle watched himself (on the screen) being cheered and chaired some years earlier when he won the Schneider Trophy, but fortunately he was not recognised by the civilian audience.[4]

Eddy of OSS, after considerable urging on Brien Clarke's part, arrived in Gibraltar on 5 November, having previously sent over two of his officers from Tangiers, at the time of Mark Clark's secret mission to Cherchell, to acquaint the SOE signals staff with details of the OSS code and to assist generally with coding operations.

In the two or three weeks that followed, the US Army Signals Corps discovered that the Rock of Gibraltar was a lamentable place from which to transmit and receive radio communications without considerable previous experience and as a result the SOE/OSS network was to have heavy calls made upon it, particularly during the so-called Clark/Darlan negotiations, for which it had not been intended. Owing to the excellent and tireless work of the operational signals staff in North Africa and Gibraltar, this additional traffic was successfully carried and, before Allied Force Headquarters (AFHQ) moved on to Algiers, Brien Clarke received a letter from the Chief of Staff conveying the Supreme Commander's thanks.[5] It was just as well that SOE had made itself useful: before the year was out, it was to need, in the upper echelons of AFHQ, whatever goodwill it had accumulated over TORCH.

The SOE signals arrangements during the assault phase of the invasion were in fact quite ramified, since SOE technical communications staff had been provided by their Baker Street headquarters for each of the three task forces. Thus, in addition to the SOE/OSS network previously set up by Squadron Leader Mallory to link Robert Murphy's 'observers' in Tunis, Algiers and Casablanca to the OSS base at Tangiers and the SOE base at Gibraltar, and to interlink the OSS and SOE base stations, on D-Day there were SOE signals links between Gibraltar and the forces landing at Algiers, Oran and Casablanca. These elements with the task force did sterling work and in the case of Casablanca – where the Allies experienced the most sustained opposition from the forces under General Noguès's command – they were used by Admiral Hall for some days for all his operational priority communications with Admiral Cunningham at Gibraltar. SOE received a special telegram of thanks for this cooperation. SOE's signals, weaned from those of SIS, had won their spurs.

CHAPTER XXXVII

Unsuccessful Attempts to Revive Felucca Operations

A ttempts to restart the felucca operations from Gibraltar to the south of France after the Allied invasion of French North Africa were to prove fruitless. By the next moonless period at the end of November and beginning of December, the Germans were in control of the south coast of France and of airfields in its immediate vicinity. Ships as large as *Tarana* could no longer be used because they would be bound to attract the attention of Luftwaffe reconnaissance flights and, having attracted it, would be unable to get away before enemy strike aircraft or surface vessels arrived to investigate and attack.

The feluccas, reinforced by another named *Welcome*, made voyages in December and January but, in the few cases where they were able to struggle through the prevailing bad weather and get to the pinpoint, the Germans were waiting for them with machine-guns and ambushes.

Buchowski's original unit of three Leading Seamen and three Able-bodied Seamen had been returned to the Polish navy during the autumn, though they were relieved by a new group to operate under the Coast Watching Flotilla. Buchowski himself was recalled to the United Kingdom at the end of October, but stayed on long enough to carry out the final series of operations with *Seadog* at the beginning of November, just before TORCH. He was accompanied on this expedition by his replacement, an officer named Pohorecki. Gubbins of SOE asked Admiral Swirski to be allowed to retain Buchowski's services for another 12 months.[1] Swirski replied that, in recalling him from Gibraltar, he acted as much on Buchowski's own request as for other reasons, which he set out in a letter dated 23 October. He said he did not consider it advisable to employ a very young officer for longer than 12 months outside the regular service of the navy and he had therefore agreed that Buchowski should return to normal service on board Polish ships. Buchowski was, moreover, a very capable gunnery officer and, as this branch was extremely short of Polish crew to man new ships, it seemed imperative to release him for an appointment on board one of their destroyers as soon as possible. The Admiral understood the arguments but preferred to postpone his final answer to Gubbins until Buchowski reported to him in person and declared his preference.

Gubbins wrote again on 31 October and on 27 November to reiterate that Buchowski was urgently needed by SOE, particularly in view of developments in North Africa, but Swirski finally said that, on careful consideration, he was unable to spare him for work outside the Polish navy.

Buchowski's last contribution in the area of clandestine sea operations was the following report, apparently addressed to Colonel Mally:

Jan BUCHOWSKI, Lt
London, 18 December 1942
Top Secret

REPORT[2]

I wish to report to you, Colonel, my opinion that the occupation of France by the Germans has made evacuation by sea from the French coast impossible or in any event much more difficult. The French coastline is in all likelihood very strongly guarded by the Germans, so that the idea that a vessel might lie 30–40 miles offshore for the three days needed and remain unnoticed is unthinkable. The French patrolled a coastal strip of about 5 miles; it must be assumed that the current German patrols are covering more than 100 miles. The vessels used in clandestine work are fishing boats, which are very slow (7 knots). If there has been good observation from the air, a patrol ship can always be sent to check the identity of the vessel. Moreover, the Axis powers will be especially suspicious of a vessel travelling along a north–south route.

The only possible place for such operations at the moment on the southern French coast is the region of Perpignan, because it is close to the Spanish border (around 40 miles) and people can be taken on board and then . . . [typescript unclear] the vessel can be in Spanish territorial waters, with the Spanish flag raised, and can pretend to be a Spanish fisherman, heading for the Balearics.

There are two main obstacles:

1) As there are two German Panzer divisions stationed in the Perpignan district, that stretch of coast will presumably be strongly policed and it will be impossible either to gather groups of people together or to bring a vessel close in shore.

2) I know that this stretch of coast has been chosen by British intelligence (SOE) as the location of their operations. It is possible that they will not permit any other operations in this area. After all, they suspended the Polish evacuations from the Marseilles region three months ago when they began to increase their own activity in the area.

Thus it seems to me that evacuation by sea is feasible only if organised from the Spanish coast, north of Barcelona.

Organising an outpost in north-east Spain would spare the Poles who are continuing to trickle across into Spain the dangers of the overland journey towards Portugal. People currently in Spain would have to be chosen for the outpost, or suitable people sent there, who have an excellent knowledge of the country and could act on instructions from London. This outpost must have a hide-out, good communications with *centrala* [the 'centre' – presumably the Polish authorities in London] such that the ship would arrive within five days of the signal's being sent. The head of the outpost would have to be aware of the likely problems of the seaward side of the operation, as well as an expert in the land side.

The proposal to organise an outpost on Spanish territory would, in my opinion, meet with great opposition from the British, since the Foreign Office (especially Sir Samuel Hoare) are extremely scrupulous about observing Spanish neutrality (no British diversionary organisation has received Foreign Office permission to operate in Spain). I believe that the following is the only possible way of proceeding. First, Commander Durski, who has established very good relations with the British at Gibraltar, should try to gain the support of Mr Darling, head of the British evacuation operation, and of Col Codrington, head of SIS (Intelligence), in presenting this plan to the Governor of Gibraltar and the authorities in London, who will probably be won over by the fact that we will also be hiding and evacuating British airmen. Commander Durski should however immediately inform London (C-in-C's headquarters) of these overtures, so that the British authorities in London can be approached simultaneously with the notification of Gibraltar's consent.

If the plan receives official approval, it will be necessary to move the naval mission from Gibraltar to Algiers; since
1) it will shorten the voyage by some 600 miles;
2) it will allow the evacuation vessel to sail from Algiers to the Balearic Islands in 24 hours, to raise the Spanish flag there and to approach the coast as a fishing vessel. At present the only movement of neutral ships in the Mediterranean is between the Balearics and Spain, as Commander Durski is aware.

The transfer of our two vessels to Algiers should not present any problems since the CWF (Coast Watching Flotilla) is also going to transfer there shortly.

If the naval mission transfers to Algiers, I believe the consent of the American authorities should be sought, which I do not expect will present any difficulties, since they too are keen to see

American airmen evacuated. Both Lt Cdr Kadulski and I have already been approached on this matter by Col Holcomb, the American army liaison officer at Gibraltar, with whom Commander Durski is very friendly and who is extremely well disposed towards Poles.

It would further be desirable for the head of the mission to be accompanied by an officer who has excellent knowledge of North Africa and who enjoys good relations with both the American and the French authorities, since this would simplify administrative matters associated with the arrival and stay of Poles in Algiers and their speedy onward movement. It seems to me that Capt Szewalski admirably meets the above conditions.

An officer should be left at Gibraltar to look after Poles escaping from Spain overland.

(J. BUCHOWSKI, Lt)

On 14 and 15 April 1943 the *Polish Daily* published announcements that Jan Buchowski, naval lieutenant, decorated twice with the Polish Cross of Gallantry, the Golden Service Cross with Swords (Polish) and the Distinguished Service Order, had met 'a sudden death' (described also on 15 April as 'a tragic death').

On 2 June 1943 *The Times* reported that at the Central Criminal Court on 1 June a Polish officer, Lt Lubomir Chieński, 43, was found not guilty of the murder of Lt Jan Buchowski, attached to the Polish naval headquarters in London, and was discharged. He had pleaded 'not guilty'.

Lt Buchowski had been found shot dead at Lt Chieński's flat on 12 April. It was alleged that Lt Buchowski had 'formed an attachment for Lt Chieński's wife, to which the accused objected.'

CHAPTER XXXVIII

Operations by Sea for SIS and SOE in Tunisia

C hurchill now saw the task before the Allied armies in North Africa as twofold. They must conquer the African shore of the Mediterranean and set up the naval and air bases needed to open up an effective passage through it for military traffic. They should then use these facilities to strike at the 'underbelly of the Axis' in effective strength as rapidly as possible. Within ten days of the TORCH landings he was already directing the attention of the British Chiefs of Staff to the second of these objectives: North Africa, he said, was to be regarded as a springboard, not a sofa.

The United States Joint Chiefs of Staff, whom Roosevelt had had to overrule in ordering TORCH, continued to dislike very much the idea of committing US forces to operations east of the Straits of Gibraltar. For one thing, they viewed the whole North African enterprise and any ensuing operations in the Western Mediterranean as a diversion of naval resources from the Pacific war and of land forces from the build-up in the United Kingdom for the planned assault on mainland Europe across the short sea route. For another, they felt that their armies might be cut off on the shores of an inland sea by the severing of communications through the Straits of Gibraltar by the Axis. Churchill had been forced to argue that American occupation of Casablanca and its hinterland would not be enough: the thrust of the invasion must extend to Oran, Algiers and further east. If the Americans could not supply forces for all these operations, British troops, accompanied by small US contingents, might undertake the more easterly of them and supply the naval cover required.

Accordingly the Eastern Task Force that landed at Algiers consisted of the British First Army plus two US divisions. Eisenhower, having overcome his initial dismay at the decision to proceed with TORCH, now, as Supreme Allied Commander, shared the view that this task force should move as swiftly as possible up into Tunisia and that landings at Philippeville (now Skikda) and Bône (now 'Annaba) on D+3 should become an integral feature of the plan, though they could, of course, not be certain of reaching Tunis and Bizerta in time to forestall, or overcome, an enemy counter-landing.

Two SOE officers, Lt Col A.M. Anstruther and Major Hamish Watt Torrance, who, with Mr Knox of OSS, had been attached to the Eastern Task Force for the assault landings, were to accompany that force up into Tunisia and, with the help of some of the other

OSS officers deployed in the area under consular cover before TORCH, they were to organise any available resistance elements in support of whatever military campaign might develop.[1] This was a fairly tall order since SOE had been forbidden to work in Algeria and Tunisia before TORCH and, apart from the group of under 200 young men – largely Jewish – who had been organised by OSS to help the Allies land in Algiers, there was little in the way of organised and effective pro-Allied resistance movements in either Algeria or Tunisia. Most of the French population were fence-sitters (referred to colloquially as *attentistes*) or worse: the Arabs were anti-French and, to a lesser extent, anti-European.

What became known as SOE's BRANDON mission, or the Special Detachments, came into existence only on D-Day. It consisted initially of two officers and a small signals detachment, all without previous knowledge of the country and the conditions in which they had to operate. There were no trained recruits and the mission arrived without transport of its own. They were quite pleased to be joined by the naval member of the mission, with HMS *Minna* at his disposal, together with the cargo of 10 tons of arms and explosives that would have been landed before TORCH if ship and reception committee had been able to make contact.

The first three days after the ceasefire, which became effective at Algiers on the evening of D-Day, were spent acquiring vehicles, discussing plans and policy with the local OSS representatives, negotiating with the Chantiers de la Jeunesse youth organisation – from which the Algiers resistance group had derived many of its volunteers – and recruiting candidates from among these volunteers to be trained for guerilla and other paramilitary activities. A headquarters, base and training camp were set up on a farm at Aïn Taya near Cap Matifou and *Minna*'s cargo was offloaded in broad daylight into horse-drawn carts at a small jetty just behind a naval coastal battery that only 48 hours earlier had held up Allied troops advancing on Algiers from the east.

Although Colonel Van Hecke, head of the Chantiers de la Jeunesse, had failed at the last moment to take any active part in the coup on the night of the landings, his deputy, Henri d'Astier de la Vigerie, had been at the very centre of it and it seems inherently likely that some of BRANDON's recruits remained in contact with him as long as they were in the Algiers area. D'Astier de la Vigerie was a Royalist and a former member of the extreme right-wing Cagoule, which was active in metropolitan France in the 1930s. Rygor-Slowikowski rated him a brilliant and enigmatic *condottiere* and, reporting to SIS on 15 November, said that he and Lemaigre-Dubreuil were the most adroit of those involved in the Algiers resistance; but at the same time he noted that his friend and erstwhile protector Achiary, ex-head of the Algiers counter-espionage police, considered d'Astier a 'man without scruples'. It was presumably from this source, via SIS, that Admiral Cunningham knew as early as 19 November that a royalist plot was afoot to replace Darlan by the Comte de Paris, pretender to the throne of France. He commented to the Admiralty in a signal of that date: 'such a step regarded as catastrophic'.[2] The Comte, whose adherents always referred to him as 'the Prince', was in Churchill's bad books, not only for attempting to persuade Pétain to nominate him as his successor but also because the Prime Minister knew he had been attempting to enlist the Italians in support of his cause.

The political backgrounds of BRANDON's recruits were heterogeneous, but they were all Gaullist in sympathy, so the American decision to negotiate the ceasefire with Admiral Darlan, who was Pétain's deputy and was fortuitously in Algiers, provoked strong reactions among them. Seven of the group to which they belonged, under the command of Bernard Pauphilet, had actually placed the Admiral under house arrest on the night of the landings until Robert Murphy turned up at the villa where he was staying, as guest of his friend Admiral Fénard, and had Pauphilet's guard removed. The agreement with Darlan was no doubt justified in terms of military expediency, if only as a short-term measure, but it came as a bitter blow to a group united by their hatred of Vichy and all it stood for. In a barn at BRANDON's Aïn-Taya camp, four officer–cadets of the Special Detachments, on a proposal by Philippe Ragueneau, one of their number, drew straws for the 'honour' of executing the new occupant of the Palais-d'Eté. Nothing was said at the time to any of BRANDON's officers, but Bonnier de la Chapelle, who drew the short straw, found reasons for staying in Algiers when most of the volunteers took passage in *Minna* on 16 November, under arrangements made by the author. They disembarked on the following day at Bône, where 1 and 6 Commandos had landed unopposed and were being followed ashore by the British 78th Division.

Another BRANDON recruit who stayed behind in Algiers was a man named Sabatier, who had presented himself as a Captain and had been treated by BRANDON as its most senior recruit. He was in fact a Sergeant, a Cagoulard and a henchman of d'Astier de la Vigerie. It was Sabatier who arranged for Bonnier to be made an instructor under SOE's MASSINGHAM mission, which had begun to arrive in Algiers and had taken over the Aïn Taya camp; and to have a Colt Automatic pistol issued to him. It was Sabatier, too, who drove the car that fetched the Comte de Paris from the Moroccan border on 10 December. D'Astier had by then become deputy to Rigaud, Darlan's Commissaire à l'Intérieur, and was in fact chief of the police. Rigaud, also a former Cagoulard, was not a convinced Royalist and was seen by d'Astier as the main obstacle to his plan to restore the monarchy. In the end d'Astier failed to remove this obstacle, though there is first-hand evidence that he had talked of doing so by force if necessary.[3]

BRANDON knew nothing of the viper's nest it had left behind it in Algiers. By arrangement with the commander of 78th Division, then still at Bône, Anstruther established BRANDON's main base at Guelma, well away from the probable front, and set up a training camp at La Mahouna, a nearby mountain resort consisting of chalets among the native cedar trees. Here the Special Detachments could continue to be trained in comparative seclusion. On 20 November Ansthruther placed them at the disposal of 78th Division, the leading formation of General Anderson's First Army, which had crossed into Tunisia and had its headquarters at Souk el-Khemis (now El Khemis). When a formation called BLADE failed by a narrow margin to capture El Aouina, the airport of Tunis, one of BRANDON's first patrols led back to the Allied lines a parachute battalion that had been dropped south of Tunis and had lost all contact with the main Allied forces. There were other early patrols through the enemy lines, one of which attacked a German headquarters. Then the winter rains began, turning the RAF's improvised forward airstrips into quagmires, and First Army's thrust ground to a halt.

1 and 6 Commando had moved forward from Bône to Tabarka, a small port just over the Tunisian border, sending Captain Randolph Churchill ahead of them to requisition accommodation. The author turned up there shortly afterwards to see what use might be made by BRANDON of the landing craft that had brought the Commandos forward and that were lying there under the command of a thoroughly cooperative naval officer, Captain N.V. Dickinson. It emerged that, without waiting for his unit to arrive or asking anyone's permission, Captain Churchill had disappeared in the general direction of Tunis on the pillion of a motor cycle driven by an OSS agent who had crossed the lines and come westward seeking contact with the Allied vanguard. This had presented his Colonel with something of a dilemma: if the escapade went wrong, the Prime Minister's son might well land in Colditz as a prisoner of war, or worse. Colonel Glendinning decided to accept responsibility and said that he had authorised the reconnaissance.

The coastal area running east from Tabarka to Bizerta was mountainous and difficult for large-scale movement of troops: it formed a broad stretch of 'no man's land', which lay open to infiltration by both sides. BRANDON was to try to disembark a two-man patrol by landing craft as near to Bizerta as possible: the patrol was to establish what positions were occupied by the enemy and then make its way back on foot. This involved a jump forward by night of nearly 60 miles. Captain Dickinson approved the plan and placed two small infantry assault craft at the author's disposal. But when the target area was reached, there was too much sea running to make landing possible. The expedition started on its way back to Tabarka but found itself not more than half-way there when day began to break, so they decided to lie up in the lee of Cap Serrat, hoping that, by covering the two landing craft with camouflage nets, they might escape the attention of any prowling enemy aircraft till darkness returned. The headland was crowned with a lighthouse and French naval signal station but these stood back from the top of the cliff and the landing craft were screened from their field of vision. After posting look-outs and eating a breakfast of compo rations, those who were not on watch retired to the shade of a nearby Muslim shrine standing on a rock at the end of a long sandy beach and turned in as the sun rose.

The area was sparsely populated, but the scrub vegetation of arbutus and tall Mediterranean heaths that covered it was grazed by flocks of sheep and goats, followed by Arab herdsmen from villages of brushwood huts standing back from the coast. The expedition's presence did not long remain undetected. In the middle of the morning their look-outs reported a man approaching across the beach; his shirt, trousers and large straw hat proclaimed him to be a European. As he drew nearer they saw that, for all the gaping holes in the toes of his boots, there was a distinctly military air about their elderly visitor, a dismounted and unarmed North African Don Quixote. He presented himself to the author in an educated French with old-world courtesy: 'Chef d'Escadrons Perrin, artilleryman in retirement'. We were the first element of the Allied armies he had seen and he asked if there was anything he could do to help us. Well, as a matter of fact there was: if he could find us horses and guides, the reconnaissance begun by sea and defeated by weather might still be carried out by land. Had Monsieur le Commandant by any chance such resources? Yes, certainly he had.

The small BRANDON party – a Second Lt named Aynès, a Senegalese Sergeant named da Porto and the author, their conducting officer – walked back with the Commandant to his farm. He lived in a simple, single-storey building on the banks of a small river, the Oued Ziatine, spanned by a steel bridge. It was not like the substantial European colonists' farms of Algeria: the poorest peasants of the Cévennes or the Causses did not live more austerely than the Perrins, their son Jacques and their daughter-in-law, whose house stood nearby, though they belonged to a family whose factory at Grenoble produced the most famous gloves in France. But the Commandant had many hundreds of books in his living-room, in Arabic as well as French.

He had first come to the area in 1911 as a military surveyor and cartographer and he had liked the Ziatine valley well enough to retire from the army, obtain a concessionary grant of land and turn farmer. He was recalled to active service in 1914 and returned to Tunisia six years later to find that his house had been demolished, his cattle stolen and his fruit trees cut down by his Arab neighbours. He had started again from scratch and it was evident that he, the only European settler within 10 km., had come to enjoy some authority in the region, of which his knowledge was impressive. Arab villagers came from considerable distances to seek his advice, to ask him to write letters on their behalf or to seek first aid and medical advice from Mme Perrin.

Horses and guides were quickly forthcoming and soon the author made his way on horseback 5 km. up the hill to the lighthouse, which was manned by Tunisians, and the signal station, which had a crew of four French naval signals ratings, three of whom lived in married quarters with their families. What was termed the Semaphore was linked by telephone to the French naval headquarters in the Pêcherie at Bizerta; it seemed prudent to remove a substantial section of the telephone line before setting out on our mounted reconnaissance as dusk fell on the evening of 2 December. After we had been riding for five or six hours, the moon set and the guides lost their way, so we bivouacked until sunrise and, in due course, rode into a clearing where a German infantry platoon was drawn up for its morning inspection. We retreated over the brow of the hill before the bullets began to fly, but the object of the reconnaissance had been achieved: we knew how far west of Bizerta the Germans had deployed troops and that the Forestry Service track running west to Sedjenane and Cap Serrat was passable, even after rain, to light vehicles.

Our report, together with other reports indicating enemy penetration into the area, caused considerable anxiety to Fifth Corps, which had no Allied troops available to move into this sector. Further patrols by BRANDON personnel revealed that enemy penetration had not taken place on any large scale, but nevertheless the threat offered by this open flank continued to cause concern to the military authorities. It was therefore decided that BRANDON should establish two posts, one on the coast at Cap Serrat, the other further south at Sedjenane, from which observations could be made, unfriendly Arabs discouraged from cooperating with the enemy and sabotage and mining operations mounted against enemy communications, including the Bizerta–Tunis railway. These detachments were to operate under command of 36th Brigade. Torrance was given command of the post at Sedjenane and the author, having valuable access to the knowledge and wholehearted cooperation of the Perrin family, was to return by sea to set up the post at Cap Serrat.

With the establishment of a front line half-way between the Algerian–Tunisian border and the main centres of population in the eastern half of the Protectorate, the Arab population constituted a definite threat to Allied military security. Though initially apathetic in a struggle between two groups of foreign powers, both of which were invaders of their country, the Axis could take heart from the fact that the Tunisian Arabs' balance of sympathies soon tipped in favour of the Axis cause against the Allies when the latter were joined by French forces. They were easily persuaded that an Axis victory would mean the removal of their former colonial masters. This attitude represented a considerable menace to the Allied Forces during the period of military stalemate that prevailed until Spring 1943. A substantial Arab population, engaged almost exclusively in agricultural and pastoral pursuits, lived in small villages scattered over the hills and mountains that formed the battlefield. The paucity of motor roads, the hilly nature of the country and the comparatively small size of the opposing forces meant that in large areas there was no continuous front line and that considerable tracts of territory were neither occupied nor disputed by either side. This, coupled with the apparent unawareness of the Arabs of the dangers of attempting to follow their normal patterns of life near the fighting zones and in no man's land meant that they could, and did, pass freely in and out of territory controlled by the opposing forces. This would have been a danger even if the Arab population had been sympathetic to the Allied cause, which they were not. The people were poor and favourably impressed by the high wages paid by General von Arnim's forces. The Germans had distributed large stocks of French textiles to them: they admired the Germans' apparent strength and had so far seen little to convince them that the Axis ultimately faced defeat. The enemy was quick to take advantage of this state of affairs and organised members of the Arab population to provide intelligence, to reconnoitre and carry out sabotage behind the Allied lines, as well as to give them assistance in patrols and labour.

BRANDON, whose recruits included speakers of North African Arabic as well as French, Italian and Spanish, the other relevant languages, became substantially involved in dealing with this problem on behalf of First Army, and detachments were sent to other parts of the line, expanding until the mission's strength was ultimately 700. It would stray too far from the subject of this work to attempt to deal with BRANDON's operations and activities along the whole of the front. However, as No. 1 Special Detachment at Cap Serrat was landed by sea under cover of darkness, supplied initially in the same way and commanded by an officer of SOE's Naval Section, it may at least be worth summarising the relevant section of an official report on **BRANDON** written after the end of the campaign:

Cap-Serrat

No. 1 Special Detachment occupied the lighthouse at Cap-Serrat on December 16th and retained their position there until January 31st. Lieutenant Brooks Richards was in command with Sous-Lieutenant Ragueneau and 35–50 French troops, almost untrained and unfit owing to privations and, in some cases, imprisonment.

Provisioning was difficult owing to the weather, and communication by sea was possible on only two occasions. The landing place was 5 kilometres away with an unsatisfactory anchorage, and one assault landing craft was sunk there. Supply was finally brought by camel and horse 20 kilometres along the coast.

At first the local population was difficult partly because of enemy propaganda. The problem was dealt with in various ways, from taking hostages to supplying cloth and other stores to Arabs as a reward for assistance. This policy met with success and one of the villages formed an 'observer corps' to give notice of enemy activities and guard some of the French farms.

The detachment was attacked more than 50 times from the air; three enemy patrols penetrated to their defences and one attack by 200 Italians and armed Arabs was beaten off. A farm used by Italians was booby-trapped, agents were passed through the enemy's lines and reconnaissances made of Mateur, Ferryville, Tindja and Bizerta. There was a considerable amount of sickness and several men badly wounded. In the second half of January they were joined by Surgeon Lieutenant Chin, RNVR, who set up in addition a special clinic for the Arabs, which was much appreciated and useful in helping to extract information.

The detachment was faced by greatly superior numbers of enemy troops but, by tactical disposal of a very small number of men, the enemy was misled into believing that Cap Serrat was held by a much larger force than was the case, and the lines of communication were safeguarded on the whole northern flank of the front, this unit being the only one between Sedjenane and the coast.

Whatever No. 1 Special Detachment was able to achieve would have been inconceivable without the knowledge and wise counsel of Commandant Perrin. The Detachment was relieved by the RAF Regiment at the beginning of February.

The reason for the arrival of the RAF Regiment at Cap Serrat was that the RAF wanted to install there a ground-controlled interception (GCI) installation to monitor the take-off of German transport aircraft from airfields in Sardinia and in Sicily, so that when the Axis attempted to evacuate the 190,000 troops they had assembled in Tunisia, the twin-engined night fighters based at Souk el-Arba could shoot them down. One of the Atcherley brothers of Schneider Cup fame came to view the site and pronounced it perfect. But GCI had never been deployed in the front line and it took a decision by Roosevelt and Churchill at their Casablanca Conference to allow it to be done. They insisted that it be guarded by 4,000 troops. Ironically enough, only two weeks after No. 1 Special Detachment left the post, the unmetalled forest road leading eastwards to Mateur and Bizerta had dried out sufficiently to be used by motor vehicles and von Arnim launched an attack along it that dislodged the RAF Regiment from their Cap Serrat positions. The RAF were forced to run the GCI vehicles over the cliff and evacuate the vital radar tubes and the Perrin family by sea. The German thrust continued right through to Cap Negre, 25 km. further west.

BRANDON's outpost had been very lucky.

*   *   *

Submarines based on Malta had been used in February and April 1942 both to pick up and land agents on the east coast of Tunisia for SIS (see Appendix E).

BRANDON organised a number of long-range operations during the Tunisian campaign but these were bedevilled by the same unpropitious environment as their tactical activities: the soil for an effective resistance movement was just not there. In five of these cases infiltration was arranged by sea and only one by parachute.

The first two of these operations also involved landings from submarines based on Malta. Operation FELICITY (also known as FELICE I) was an attempt to destroy a vital bridge south of Hammamet on the east coast of Tunisia. The personnel taking part consisted of Captain Eyre, Lieutenant Thomas, four British and six French other ranks. The party, which was in uniform, was to land during the night, attack the bridge and re-embark the same night. The operation took place on the night of 28/29 January 1943 and, although the party was put ashore safely from HM S/m P42, the firing of Very lights shortly afterwards from near the point of landing made it obvious to those watching from seaward that the alarm had been given. The submarine waited as long as it safely could but was forced to withdraw without regaining contact with the party ashore. It was hoped that its members would be able to disperse and make their way overland back to the Allied lines, but they were all captured. Little or no damage was done to the bridge.

The second landing carried out that night, also in the Hamma-met area, but from *HM MTB* 307, involved Squadron-Leader Mallory, the SOE signals officer who had set up the North African signals system for OSS and SOE from Gibraltar before TORCH, and two French agents, Martinez and Bonjour. This party, code-named BLUE, was to organise resistance in the Tunis area.

After the end of the campaign, researches in Tunis showed that Mallory and his two associates must have been captured immedi-ately upon landing, but the enemy made such skilful use of Mal-lory's W/T set that they were able to convince BRANDON right up until the capture of Tunis that it was Mallory himself who was working it. This deception seems to have stemmed largely from the inadequate signals arrangements made by Mallory before his departure, which contained no reliable security check. The BRAN-DON signals personnel receiving BLUE's messages claimed to be confident that they were being sent by Mallory himself and a later opportunity to detect what was going on was lost by an error on the part of MASSINGHAM's signals section.

As a result of this successful *Funkspiel*, BRANDON made pre-parations to reinforce Mallory, including sending in a party of agents to a reception arranged through the BLUE W/T link. This operation was known as BEAR (or the BEARS).

The party consisted of ten Corsican agents and saboteurs in civilian clothes with a W/T link. They had been briefed to disrupt communications and destroy dumps and aircraft in eastern Tunisia. The original plan had been to parachute the team into the field but it was finally decided to infiltrate them by sea to a reception provided by BLUE. The pinpoint chosen was at Kelibia near the southern end of the Cap Bon peninsula, where the wreck of HMS *Havoc*, a British destroyer that had to be beached following damage sustained during a Malta convoy, provided an unmistakable land-mark. The operation was mounted from Malta, using two British Motor Torpedo Boats with the author as conducting officer. The landing took place on 6 April. Recognition signals and passwords were in order, and the author, who had gone ashore with the party, was allowed to re-embark safely and return to Malta under the illusion that all was well, unaware of the noose in which his head had reposed during the landing.

The BEARS were, of course, captured by the enemy as they left the beach. They tried unsuccessfully to escape and their leader Captain Brun was killed during the attempt. The enemy took possession of the W/T set and worked it back to BRANDON HQ as if things were perfectly normal, sending messages that reported considerable success by the BEARS and claiming the destruction of two ammunition dumps, an aircraft and three laden lorries, as well as the cutting of seven cables. At this point an opportunity arose to detect the deception that was being practised by the enemy. The first signal from CHAPTER, the new W/T set and signal plan that the BEARS had taken with them into the field, omitted the security check. MASSINGHAM signals, who were working this link, failed to notify the operations staff, but on their own authority pointed out the omission to CHAPTER and asked him to include the check in future. The facts of this incident were not brought to light until the campaign was finished.

As April progressed, it became obvious that the total defeat of the Axis forces in North Africa could not be long delayed. Allied Force Headquarters were extremely interested to know what plans were being made by the enemy for his evacuation from Tunisia. It seemed likely that von Arnim would use the sandy beaches of Cap Bon as an embarkation area and BLUE was accordingly asked to provide any available information. Meanwhile a representative of SIS had approached BRANDON on the same subject: they wished to land, blind, a W/T operator in Cap Bon who would observe and report back all movements.

SIS, however, had no operator available and therefore asked BRANDON's help in supplying one. BRANDON was not convinced of the soundness of the operation as proposed and agreed to supply an operator only after they had consulted with BLUE and he had agreed to provide a reception by him, which, not surprisingly, he did. He also asked that stores for himself should be sent in at the same time. An operation known as THIGH was consequently planned for the night of 6/7 May, to be mounted, in conjunction with SIS, from Sousse, which had just fallen to the advancing Eighth Army. The author travelled with two Jeeps from BRANDON's headquarters on the northern front all the way round the shrinking perimeter held by the Axis forces, to arrange this operation. It was to be carried out in two recently arrived and brand-new US Navy 72-foot Elco patrol torpedo (PT) boats. The party embarked according to plan but were forced back owing to engine trouble. Further delay was caused by bad weather on 8 May but the expedition sailed again before nightfall on 9 May and were halfway to the enemy-controlled reception in Cap Bon when they were recalled by a crack signal from the naval operating base at Sousse. Major Hamish Torrance had entered Tunis that day with the vanguard of the First Army and had attempted to contact Mallory at an address given by him, but found he was unknown there. Further enquiries in the prisons of Tunis revealed that a British officer answering approximately to Mallory's description had arrived in one of them at Le Bardo in February, soon after the BLUE landing operation, but had since been removed. Conclusive proof that this was Mallory was provided by a graffito on the wall of the relevant room; and prompt signalling by Torrance to BRANDON and by BRANDON to Sousse saved the THIGH expedition from falling into the trap that was no doubt awaiting them in Cap Bon peninsula. It seems unlikely that BRANDON's conducting officer (the author) would have been allowed to re-embark unmolested as had happened on BEAR a month previously. After the defeat of Germany, both Mallory and eight of the ten members of the BEARS party were recovered from prisoner of war and concentration camps in Germany. One of the BEARS had been killed in an Allied air raid while in Germany. The only positive feature of this sorry tale is that in both cases (BLUE and CHAPTER) the W/T sets had been worked by the enemy without the knowledge and assistance of Mallory or the BEAR party.

On the night of March 4/5 BRANDON carried out one other landing of agents by sea. This was ZODIAC, which involved the infiltration of an organiser (David) and a W/T operator (Dupont) in civilian clothes near Bizerta. Their mission was to organise a resistance movement in enemy-held territory to carry out sabotage.

The operation, in which both Holdsworth from MASSINGHAM and the author from BRANDON were involved, was carried out in conjunction with the African Coastal Flotilla organisation set up by Slocum (see next Chapter), from their forward base near Bône: it was the only BRANDON operation in which the ACF was involved.

The landing was successfully completed from an air/sea rescue launch in ideal conditions, using two of the dories built in Cornwall to the author's design and brought out from Helford on *Mutin*: Holdsworth and the author did the boatwork. But the ZODIAC party were forced to cache their W/T equipment and supplies when it was found that Arabs had raised the alarm.

When the two agents returned to the spot a few days later, they found that their equipment had been stolen, presumably by the same Arabs. Although several attempts were made, ZODIAC was unable to contact BRANDON headquarters until 27 March, when a message was passed on an SIS link explaining their predicament and asking that a new set be sent. An attempt was made to deliver this set by means of Operation THIGH, but this was, of course unsuccessful.

Meanwhile David and Dupont proceeded to find safe houses for the W/T station and set about forming a band of 150 men who might be used for reception work, street fighting; etc. As no reply came to their messages, they decided to cross the lines in person and report to BRANDON. They were, however, captured by the enemy during the attempt and were imprisoned until the liberation of Tunis, when they were set free and reported back to base.

BRANDON's most successful long-range operation, KIPLING, involved the dropping by parachute on March 25/26 of a party of eight in uniform, headed by Captain Evans, to cut the Tunis-Sfax railway. It was carried out at the request of 18 Army Group, recently formed under General Alexander to control the First and the Eighth Army, which had crossed from Libya into southern Tunisia. KIPLING was timed to interfere with the movement of enemy reinforcements to counter the Eighth Army offensive which was to outflank and break the Mareth Line.

The dropping operation was successful and aerial observation carried out on March 28 showed that railway communications in the area had been interrupted. Although the party had elaborate plans for making their way back to the Allied lines after the attack, none of them in fact arrived and it was later learned that Evans had broken a leg on landing and they had all been taken prisoner.

Considerable interest in this operation was shown by the Allied military authorities, although fighter aircraft attacks on any-pile up of traffic that resulted from the break failed to materialise. Interrogation of a railway official from the area revealed later that the line had been interrupted for 24 hours.

CHAPTER XXXIX

Clandestine Sea Transport Operations in the Western Mediterranean after TORCH

The advance guard of SOE's MASSINGHAM mission, which was to set up a base in Algeria to mount operations to Sardinia, Corsica, Italy and southern France, began to arrive at Algiers on 17 November 1942, as BRANDON and its recruits were moving up into Tunisia. Holdsworth and Laming, who were, with their crews, to provide MASSINGHAM with a naval component, sailed on 30 November from Helford for the Scillies in *Mutin* and *Serenini*. There they took on additional fuel and water before heading south under sail and power straight across the Bay of Biscay without escort. They reached Gibraltar in six and a half days – about the same time as was taken by convoys, which, of course, had to be routed far further out into the Atlantic because of the U-boat menace. After refuelling, they went straight on to Algiers, where they arrived, at the earliest, on 9 or 10 December. Neither of the ships was intended for operational use in the Mediterranean, but they provided accommodation for crews, transport for stores and personnel, as well as mobile base facilities from which operations could be organised, making use of such naval and local craft as might be available. SOE was concerned that SIS, in the shape of NID(C), should not be in a position to veto their use of clandestine sea transport in the new Western Mediterranean theatre, which is what it had recently done with regard to the west coast of France.

Slocum, too, had received a directive to prepare for operations by sea to Corsica, Sardinia, Sicily and southern Italy, as well as to southern France. CWF had, of course, been operating from Gibraltar to southern France in the seven months before TORCH, mainly by means of the Polish-manned feluccas. This directive must have emanated from within SIS, as Slocum did not at that time hold any Admiralty appointment. He sent Lt Cmdr Patrick Whinney, his staff officer for Mediterranean operations, to requisition local craft and investigate the possibility of setting up new bases.

A first such forward base had already been established near Bône as a result of *Minna*'s visit to that port in mid-November, when she had landed BRANDON's recruits on their way forward to Tunisia. During the approach to Bône, Armstrong, *Minna*'s captain, had been impressed by the look of a secluded villa, tucked away under the lee of Cap de Garde. On closer examination it seemed ideal as base for an advanced flotilla: the bay was sheltered from all directions except the south-east and was sufficiently far from the town to ensure security, yet near enough to allow full use of its maintenance facilities. The villa was requisitioned and, with the permission of the senior officer of the Inshore Squadron, Armstrong installed himself, one other officer and a number of ratings to form a nucleus for operating two craft. *Minna*, under the command of McCallum, his first lieutenant, then returned to Algiers. Slocum recorded that by the end of November two *balancelles*, the local form of felucca, were operating in support of the Allied armies in Tunisia, their duties being chiefly to run ammunition and supplies to isolated detachments marooned in the Cape Tabarka area. This rather overdramatises a useful but modest ration run to a ruined Genoese coral-fishing station at Sidi Mechrig, 20 kilometres to the rear of Cap Serrat, whence supplies were transported by camel or mule to BRANDON's No.1 Special Detachment.

The base Armstrong had established was in fact of limited operational use, though it was employed in March 1943 for ZODIAC, BRANDON's one and only operation with a high-speed vessel on the north coast of Tunisia. The Villa la Vie, or 'Hatter's Castle', served mainly as an agreeable staging post. Slocum described it as 'a centre of cloak-and-dagger activity for the area and a veritable haven for those of SIS, SOE and MI9 who were travelling forward to advanced sectors and who wished to break their journey or communicate back to headquarters.' No. 30 Commando, a unit formed under the command of Dunstan Curtis, erstwhile captain of MGBs 314 and 501, now a Commander, RNVR, was based there during the whole of its time in Africa, to accompany the assault phase of an advance and to collect any material of value to naval intelligence.

While relations between the naval representatives of SIS and SOE were excellent in forward areas, Slocum's 1946 report records an acrimonious and wholly unnecessary dispute at Algiers between the two organisations over future control of clandestine sea transport in the theatre. Slocum's NID(C) reckoned that Allied Force Headquarters would require an officer on their staff to coordinate all irregular sea operations. Both locally and in London they considered that Osborne, senior officer of NID(C)'s Coast Watching Flotilla at Gibraltar, would be the most suitable choice for the appointment but 'another nominee was put forward and during the month of December the whole question was under heated discussion.'

Slocum says an operation had been planned involving the use of a French submarine without the prior concurrence of Commander-in-Chief Mediterranean, and as a result the sailing had been peremptorily cancelled. What he describes as 'the inevitable repercussions' followed and, to avoid further recurrences of the kind, the 'only suitable officer' (i.e. Osborne) was applied for. Osborne arrived in Algiers at the beginning of 1943 and, from AFHQ, 'took control of clandestine operations under the title Senior Officer, African Coastal Flotilla (ACF).'

The surviving SOE archives throw no direct light on this episode, but the 'other nominee' can only be a coded reference to Holdsworth, with whom Slocum's relations had reached a nadir over NID(C)'s last-minute ban on SOE operations to the west coast of France. Holdsworth himself can hardly have reached Algiers when the dispute began, since the French submarine in question, the *Casabianca*, far from having its sailing cancelled, merely had it postponed by 24 hours while the RAF and naval units were informed. She put to sea on 11 December. The operation in any case had nothing to do with SOE, but was a first Franco-American intelligence mission to Corsica: there were now two new players – OSS and what had been Vichy's Deuxième Bureau, operating out of Algiers under the somewhat uncertain and controversial auspices of Giraud and Darlan. Coordination would certainly be required, but the situation was radically different from that in home waters, where, except in relation to Norway, NID(C) had established a monopoly of the relevant operational means of transport, such as they were. But it quite quickly emerged that feluccas could not establish contact with Sardinia, Corsica or with southern France under German occupation, either from Gibraltar or from North Africa, and that *Minna* and *Tarana* could no longer be employed operationally, though useful for non-clandestine sea transport. Operations to Corsica, Sardinia, the west coast of Italy and the south coast of France would in the next phase be carried out entirely by submarine.

By December 1942, the Royal Navy's submarine flotillas in the Mediterranean had long experience of carrying out special operations of the type required by the clandestine agencies: for nearly two years they had been working from Alexandria with the Folboat canoe specialists of the Special Boat Section of the Commandos. This unit was created in July 1940, when Roger Courtney (elder brother of 'Gruff', who had landed General Mark Clark) demonstrated to the first Chief of Combined Operations, Admiral Sir Roger Keyes – of Zeebrugge fame – his ability to use Folboats to approach, and even to board, anchored ships at night undetected.[1] Courtney's unit, which became No. 1 Special Boat Section early in 1941, was attached to the 1st Submarine Flotilla, whose depot ship, HMS MEDWAY, lay at Alexandria. After a pioneering beach reconnaissance on Rhodes, Courtney had gone on to use Folboats from submarines for a variety of small-scale raids and other operations, including the evacuation from the south coast of Crete of British,

Australian, New Zealand and Greek troops left behind when the island fell to German airborne forces in May 1941; and the landing and retrieval of agents for the clandestine services behind the enemy lines in Albania, Greece and Tunisia.

Courtney returned to the United Kingdom in December 1941 to form No.2 Special Boat Section on similar lines and a first contingent of this new unit was sent out to Gibraltar in September 1942 and attached to *Maidstone* to operate, as we have seen, with submarines of the 8th Flotilla in preparation for TORCH. Some over-cautious senior planner prevented No.2 SBS from carrying out the requisite beach reconnaissance for fear of compromising the assault landings, with results that were operationally serious at Oran,[2] but the new unit did land General Mark Clark and his companions for talks with General Mast and Robert Murphy at Messelmoun; and they had also collected Giraud and his entourage from Le-Lavandou. CWF seems not to have been involved in these operations, since they kept no record of them. Submarine operations from Algiers were in practice arranged directly by the agencies concerned with HMS *Maidstone*, depot ship of the 8th Submarine Flotilla, where the operations officer, Lt Cmdr Cowell, and Captain Barney Fawkes showed great interest in their work.

The French submarine, whose sailing on the first operation to Corsica touched off the dispute about coordination and control, was the *Casabianca*, one of five that on the night of 26/27 November had disobeyed Admiral de Laborde's order to ships of the French fleet at Toulon to scuttle themselves and had escaped from the port. Two of the five slunk away to Spain and were interned at Cartagena, but *Casabianca*, *Marsouin* and *Glorieux* turned up off Algiers and joined the Allies. They had been attacked by German aircraft using bombs and laying magnetic mines as they left Toulon and *Casabianca* had had to make a hurried crash-dive, leaving her captain's naval cap floating where she submerged.

Casabianca's displacement of 1,500 tons was more than twice that of the British 'S'-Class and larger than that of the 'T'-Class British submarines of the 8th Flotilla, so she offered great advantages in terms of carrying capacity for landing agents and supplies. This and the inspiring personality of her commanding officer, Capitaine de Frégate Jean L'Herminier, made her an obvious choice when a vessel was needed to carry a five-man mission, code-named PEARL HARBOR, to Corsica early in December.

L'Herminier came of a Breton family who had emigrated to the French West Indies at the time of the Revolution rather than live in France under a non-Royalist regime, but they had never considered that sending their sons to serve in the French navy ('la Royale') was inconsistent with their monarchist allegiance. He was in his early forties, while British submarine captains were mostly in their mid-twenties. The fact that *Casabianca* was not equipped with Asdic and that her torpedoes proved erratic meant that her offensive potential was not rated highly by the Royal Navy and Captain (S) 8 was the more ready for her to be used for 'cloak-and-dagger' missions.[3]

PEARL HARBOR was led by Commandant de Saule, a professional French intelligence officer of Belgian origin, whose experience in this field went back to the First World War.[4] He was accompanied by three Corsicans, all of whom had been on the fringes of the Algiers Resistance group. One, Pierre Griffi, was a W/T operator; a second, Regimental Sergeant Major Toussaint Griffi, was his first cousin: the third, a socialist and trade-union activist named Laurent Preziosi, born in Algeria of Corsican parents, was a friend of Albert Camus, whom he had met when they were both working as journalists on the *Alger Républicain*.[5] They were to be escorted on the maritime stage of their expedition by an OSS agent of indeterminate eastern European origin, who called himself Frederick Brown. Brown, who had worked for a variety of intelligence services, owned a radio shop in Algiers and had been one of the W/T operators manning the link between the US Consulate-General in Algiers, the OSS base in Tangiers and the SOE signals station at Gibraltar. He was presumably responsible for PEARL HARBOR's signals arrangements, but the mission seems in other respects to have been briefed by General Ronin, who had been head of air intelligence at Vichy and had been put in charge of General Giraud's Deuxième Bureau; and by staff of Colonel Rivet's Service de Renseignements working under him. Their task was to set up a military intelligence network covering the whole of the island, which had recently been occupied by 80,000 Italian troops.

Casabianca had been in Algiers no more than a fortnight when she put to sea on the evening of 11 December, carried out the usual diving trial and was escorted by a Royal Navy vessel to a position ten miles north of Cap Caxine. Both the voyage and its landward aftermath have been recorded by participants.[6]

As the submarine headed north on the surface under cover of night using her two diesels, L'Herminier took the head of the table in the submarine's diminutive wardroom for a first meal at sea and said to de Saule and his four companions, 'Gentlemen, I am fully confident in setting about the mission that lies before us. If you agree, I should like now to consider how best to carry out what is for a submarine a rather unusual operation – that of landing five men on a beach.'

Toussaint Griffi and Laurent Preziosi found it rather odd that this question should be raised only when they were already at sea. Where indeed on the Corsican coast could the landing be under-taken with a minimum of risk to the submarine and the members of the mission? Their ignorance about the deployment of the Italian occupation forces on the island was total, so it was difficult to say what the best choice of beach would be. For navigational and technical reasons, the submarine, too, could not go just anywhere. The problem was not easy to resolve. Options on both east and west coasts were discussed at length but there was still no decision when the party broke up and the five agents climbed into the hammocks allocated to them in the submarine's after-torpedo-flat.

There was further lengthy discussion next morning; eventually, one of *Casabianca*'s officers pointed out that the choice must not only be suitable from the submarine's point of view but should put the mission ashore as near as possible to a point where they could make contact with known patriots. Toussaint Griffi and Laurent Preziosi, who had been in Corsica most recently, said Bastia and Corte were the two towns where such contacts could be established most rapidly and de Saule had potential contacts in Corte. L'Herminier said that, in that case, a west coast landing would be best: it was nearer to the mountain chain that divided the island in two and better for the submarine as the deeper water would allow her to come closer inshore.

De Saule agreed: he had noted from their earlier discussion that there were several beaches between Ajaccio and Saint-Florent that provided access to roads and mule tracks leading over the mountains to Corte, which offered the best prospect of reaching the centre of the island in safety. L'Herminier and Bellet, his first lieutenant, had a closer look at beaches lying on both sides of a line from Porto to Corte. Bellet said that the beach at Chioni seemed to have everything in its favour from both their points of view. His remark met with general approbation. L'Herminier, calm and resolute as usual, added, 'Well then, we will put you ashore on that beach, which does seem to provide the best conditions – 300 metres length of sand and 40 metres depth of water within a mile of the coast – everything needed for a successful operation.'

The rest of 12 December gave the passengers leisure to see round the submarine and chat to the crew. Everyone seemed delighted to have escaped from the Germans and it was clear that their departure from Toulon had been carefully prepared. *Casabianca* had been due to be sent to a colonial station and L'Herminier and his officers, with the agreement of the German armistice commission, had carried out engine trials, tested equipment and done a series of diving trials to a depth of 80 m. over a period of months. They had gone to considerable lengths to train the younger members of the ship's company. L'Herminier raised a laugh when he said that of course the Germans had refused him permission to put what he described as 'the finishing touches' to these preparations. But the essential thing was that they had managed to retain a considerable quantity of diesel fuel on board.

Casabianca surfaced soon after nightfall on 13 December and members of the PEARL HARBOR team were able to go for a walk on deck as the submarine's powerful diesels drove her northwards at a spanking pace. But while they were having dinner in the wardroom mess, an aircraft was sighted astern, so a quick dive to 40 m. was necessary. After a time, L'Herminier brought her up to 16 metres and took a look through the periscope. Nothing could be seen, so they resurfaced and started up the diesels. Three quarters of an hour later, enemy aircraft were again sighted circling round the point where they had crash-dived. They had to dive again, but soon they were back on the surface and on course.

After dinner L'Herminier went up to smoke a cigarette and keep the officer of the watch company for a while. At about 2200 hrs the starboard look-out reported land in sight. This was a great surprise, as their course should have taken them well clear of Sardinia and southern Corsica, but there was no doubt about it and they had to alter course sharply to port to take them out of the coastal zone where they were likely to meet enemy patrols. The unexpected landfall gave rise to all sorts of conjectures, the most likely of which was that the gyro-compass was out of order, probably as a consequence of the shake-up it had received from the mine explosions as they were leaving Toulon. They decided that they must have sighted the island of Asinara off the north-west coast of Sardinia.

As they were unable to determine their position accurately, they set a course which they hoped would bring them to the point where L'Herminier planned to submerge – 15 miles west of Cap Rosso. At 0100 hrs on the morning of 14 December they judged they were in the right position and dived to about 40 m., proceeding eastward at two knots, through the enemy's assumed patrol zone. L'Herminier meanwhile snatched some sleep.

At about 0730, he was wakened by the officer of the watch and they came up to periscope depth and took a look around. They were unquestionably off Corsica, but they were still too far from land to fix their position, though they spent an hour in fruitless attempts to do so.

They submerged to a depth at which enemy planes would be unable to spot them and made their way slowly inshore. L'Herminier retired to his cabin, having left instructions that he was to be informed as soon as soundings indicated a depth of 100 metres. The 100-metre contour line ran along the coast about 2 miles offshore, following the shore fairly regularly except near the headlands, where it was closer: that would be the time for another cautious look around with the periscope.

Unfortunately the supersonic Langevin-Florisson sounding machine, a delicate and rather capricious instrument, let them down and began to show soundings only when they were some way inside the 100-metre isobath.

L'Herminier ordered the submarine to periscope depth and made his way to the conning-tower in a hurry.

The sounding machine was giving good readings now and showed that the sea-bed was rising rapidly. When the periscope broke surface, L'Herminier saw a reddish wall of rock straight ahead and quite close. He ordered 'hard aport'.

The rock face seemed so close that L'Herminier thought for a moment that he was using magnification 6 and turned the handle of the periscope to a different position. The texture of the cliff showed up in such detail that his head jerked back instinctively as though to avoid bumping against it. The periscope calibration had been set for magnification 1: they were very close inshore indeed!

Casabianca answered her helm in time and they slid past an island almost close enough to touch it.

A look around with the periscope showed that they were in Focolara Bay, with Cap-Gargalo towering above them and the semaphore station on Cap-Cavalo visible away to the north. They were 12 miles to the north of their chosen landfall at Cap-Rosso and 14 miles from their destination in Chioni Bay. They set course accordingly but had to increase speed to arrive there before nightfall, even though it meant greater discharge of their precious batteries. This presented a problem as they could not hope to finish the job in one night. The moon did not set before midnight and the remaining hours of darkness would be too short to complete the agreed plan, so they would have to remain close inshore for the next 48 hours, with no chance to use their diesels to recharge the batteries.

Before nightfall, which comes early in December, they had sighted Cargèse and Omignia. They took a last periscope sighting and altered course towards the shore before setting *Casabianca* very carefully down on a sandy bottom at a depth of about 45 m. Somebody made a joke about the lobsters they were probably crushing. Bellet, the first lieutenant, took in another 5 tons of water to anchor the submarine firmly to the bottom. It had been a calm day and they hoped it would remain so, but they had wasted time in finding their destination and everyone except the watch gladly turned in to snatch a few hours' sleep.

Towards midnight, L'Herminier gave orders to prepare for the landing. One group of seamen under command of an officer was equipped with small arms and stood ready to take up covering positions on deck as soon as the submarine surfaced. A second group was detailed to launch a boat carried on top of the pressure hull. Then L'Herminier ordered the submarine to be brought to the surface, a manoeuvre carried out in impressive silence. Bellet, with his eyes glued to the periscope, reported all clear. A few seconds later, the hatch leading from the control-room to the conning-tower was thrown open and the two groups of seamen climbed up through it and set about allotted tasks. Then the PEARL HARBOR team were invited up on to the bridge, where L'Herminier and a junior officer named Chaillet had already stationed themselves. It was a moment of high emotion: *Casabianca* seemed very close to the shore and the mountains loomed above them with their summits outlined against a grey sky, though they were in fact about 800 metres from the shore. The sea was flat calm and a light offshore breeze carried the aromatic scents of arbutus, myrtle, lentisk and the giant Mediterranean heath, which flowers in winter.

L'Herminier and Chaillet accompanied the landing party aft, where the boat, manned by two seamen, was waiting for them. As the party embarked, L'Herminier said that the submarine would tow the boat as close to the beach as possible. Then, when the time came to cast off, *Casabianca* would be stationed at right angles to their approach course, so that she could cover their withdrawal should they come under small-arms fire. If there was not time for them to get on board before she had to dive, the submarine would be forced to abandon them.

Everything went as planned: *Casabianca* moved gently ahead, towing the dinghy: its wake left a striking phosphorescent track on the surface. For all the apparent nearness of the mountains, the submarine was still quite a long way from the shore when it cast off the tow-line and left PEARL HARBOR and Frederick Brown to be rowed into the darkness. Everyone on the dinghy shook hands, their excitement tinged with apprehension: they were closing in on enemy-occupied territory with no idea of what might await them.

Luck was on their side. After a quarter of an hour, in which the silence of the night was scarcely broken by rhythmic oar-strokes into unruffled water, they found themselves close to a small sandy beach on which the boat grounded. Delighted as the three Corsicans were to step ashore on to their native soil, they were certainly not on a 300-metre-long beach. It was not the moment for questions: they took leave of the boat's crew, who disappeared back to the submarine, and set about looking for somewhere to hide Pierre Griffi, his W/T set and Mr Brown, who was to help Griffi establish radio contact with the base station at Algiers. The plan was that the two-man signals team would remain close to the beach until the following night, while the other three went in search of contact with local patriots who might help them carry inland the food, arms and second W/T set that were due to be landed from the submarine during the second night.

Once Pierre Griffi and Brown had been suitably installed, de Saule, Toussaint Griffi and Preziosi set off inland with the aid of a compass and a pocket torch in search of the Ajaccio–Porto road. They had gone no further than the top of the first small hill when, only 200 metres on their right, they caught sight of an Italian sentry who had betrayed his position by using an electric torch. The three infiltrators thought their footsteps must have been heard and took cover under some bushes. The sentry shone his torch in their direction and came some way towards them, as though aware of their presence. It was a moment of extreme tension for the agents. They were unarmed and in a place to which they had to return only a few hours later. Toussaint Griffi and Preziosi suggested they should move before the Italian came upon them. De Saule, an old practitioner of clandestinity, said no, the last thing they must do was to move: the sentry would not come as far as their position. No doubt he would be more frightened than they were. And indeed, after coming 40 or 50 metres in their direction, the Italian stopped, turned and went back to his guard-post. Soon they were able to resume their march through the thick *maquis* scrub vegetation towards the mountain.

It was hard going and at the end of an hour, when they had reached the top of a ridge, they thought they had lost their way and halted. Crouched at the foot of an old tree, surrounded by thick scrub and using their overcoats to screen the light of their torch, they consulted both map and compass. They concluded they were moving in the right direction to strike the road somewhere between Piana and Cargèse.

Day was beginning to break. Then, only a few minutes after they had resumed their march, de Saule suddenly collapsed: he was in his fifties, walked with a stick and had been given none of the rigorous physical training to which agents were subjected in the United Kingdom before being allowed to go into the field. The two young Corsicans were seized by momentary panic. But Toussaint Griffi had been in action on the Ailette in 1940 and had seen something of the sort before. He decided to try to bring the prostrate Commandant round by slapping his cheeks. There was no immediate response and for some seconds the two younger men feared their leader was dead. But Griffi set to once more and this time de Saule regained consciousness. 'What happened to you, mon Commandant?' 'Don't worry, it's nothing. I have just had a slight turn, because I am beginning to feel very tired.'

Preziosi had a bottle of wine in his knapsack and he persuaded de Saule to take a drink from it. He also gave him some dates he was carrying. This brought some colour back into the Commandant's cheeks. He smiled, got up, said he felt better and suggested they should move on. They followed a mule track leading down into a valley, which they could just make out in the growing light. It was easier going now as the zigzag path was used by shepherds and their flocks of goats and sheep. It led down to a little stream, swollen by winter rains.

From time to time they stopped to take stock of the lie of the land and to listen for any unaccustomed sound. It was quite cold: a light breeze had got up but the aromatic scents of the *maquis* on it raised their spirits. After three nights of very little sleep, the long-awaited moment when they would make contact with one or more Corsican patriots was at hand. They had been walking for several hours now and wondered where, when and with whom that first encounter would occur.

They were still coming down the mountainside when they heard the sound of a motor cycle. That meant they must be getting close to a road or some inhabited place. But under enemy occupation, a motor cycle must be Italian. It was 6 o'clock and becoming light. They took another look at their map. Yes, it must have been on the road from Ajaccio to Calvi and, if they had not strayed too far from their chosen route, they were about two kilometres from a bridge over a river. They walked on for another quarter of an hour and came down to a stream along which eucalyptus trees were growing. They crossed it and saw, 500 metres down a bank, a shepherd's house, with wisps of smoke rising slowly to the sky from the chimney. As they watched, a woman in a long woollen skirt and with a kerchief round her head came out of the house to fetch logs from a pile at the foot of a big tree. De Saule asked Preziosi to go and make contact with her. Preziosi wondered what sort of reception he might expect at 7 o'clock in the morning, his face lined by lack of sleep, a felt hat on his head and wearing an extremely crumpled overcoat. As he approached the door, she was standing in front of the hearth trying to put life into the fire, which she had just refuelled, by fanning it vigorously with a piece of cardboard. He addressed her in Corsican, 'Good day, Madame, I am on my way to Revinda. Could you please tell me the way?' 'It is not far from here', she replied, 'but if you wait a short while my son, who has gone to the sheepfold, will be back to drink his coffee; he'll show you the way.' And she added, 'But come in, Monsieur. Come and sit down.' Preziosi did so, with profound relief and pleasure: he had made a first contact and the woman's touching hospitality lent strength to his faith in the Corsican Resistance. Though she showed no signs of mistrust, she went on to ask questions that proved that she found his presence at that early hour distinctly unusual. Where had he come from at such a time to go to Revinda? Preziosi said he had come from Piana; he had set out very early and he had taken a short cut across country to save time. Was he alone? No; he was with two friends, who had stopped 200 metres back to relieve themselves. 'Well, tell them to come,' she replied. The lady's name was Santa di Notte and she wintered her sheep in the plain.

Preziosi fetched his companions and, by the time they reached the house, three cups had been set out on a small table by the fire. They had only just sat down when her son arrived; he was no doubt equally surprised to find visitors so early in the morning. As they sat sipping their coffee, the conversation turned to problems of everyday life under the Italian occupation. PEARL HARBOR learned that there were major Black Shirt units at Cargèse and some troops also at Piana: food supplies had become increasingly difficult as a result. However, troop movements on the nearby Route Nationale were infrequent.

This intelligence was most helpful, but they still had to decide where to go in search of the help that would be needed on the following night when the *Casabianca* would be landing further equipment and supplies. Revinda seemed as likely a place to look for such assistance as any, being well placed geographically in relation to their beach, so they decided to take advantage of their hostess's offer that her son guide them to that village. After breakfast he led them to the bridge they had noted on their map, where the Route Nationale crossed the nearby river. They followed the main road for some time in the direction of Piana and then took a track leading uphill to Revinda. The young shepherd told them they had only to follow this to reach their chosen destination. He then left them.

As they walked on alone they discussed whom they should approach for help in Revinda. The mayor or the village priest seemed obvious choices, provided they were not Pétainists. De Saule thought the priest the better choice. Griffi and Preziosi were surprised: admittedly a priest was used to safeguarding the secrets of the confessional, but might he not be a collaborator, an Italian by origin or the product of an Italian seminary? De Saule dismissed the idea: the two Corsicans should have known better than to suggest such a thing. They had to concede that the priest in such a place would probably be a Corsican, but they wondered whether indeed there would be one at Revinda.

They had reached the top of the hill from which they could catch a glimpse of the sea, with the Baie-de-Chioni and some of the roofs of Cargèse. It was a point where the *maquis* grew particularly high and thick. Then, as though de Saule had spoken with foreknowledge, from a mule path, which joined their track on the right, appeared a priest riding a donkey: it was the Abbé Mattei, the incumbent from Cargèse, known locally as Prête Santu, who was on his way to Revinda to say mass on the feast of Sainte-Lucie. Yes, he said, he was Corsican but, above all, a Frenchman. He came to Revinda to say mass only three or four times a year!

The priest was obviously no friend of the Italian occupation, which he said weighed heavily on the population at Cargèse: the

Corsicans had never accepted Genoese or other Italian tutelage. Clearly, PEARL HARBOR could have full confidence in him. He found them lodgings in Revinda and put them in contact with Dominique Antonini, a retired soldier, who had the mules they needed. Antonini was no fool and he subjected them to a searching cross-examination before he set out with them and his three mules at 5 o'clock that afternoon. Even then, he took care to bring up the rear of the procession and stay there.

It was completely dark when they got down to the beach. Their first calls to Pierre Griffi and Fred Brown produced no response. They tried several times more and were beginning to wonder what had gone wrong when the silhouettes of two men emerged from the night and came silently towards them. Dominique Antonini, still suspicious, had distanced himself from his companions and seemed ready to defend himself if need be. They called again and Pierre Griffi replied by switching on his torch. A few seconds later they were reunited. Antonini rejoined them, saying that he now knew that he was dealing with genuine members of the Resistance. He had been prepared for all eventualities: he showed them the automatic pistol that was stuffed into his belt.

The dinghy had got back to *Casabianca* at 0300 hrs on the previous night and, as it was hauled back on board, L'Herminier decided that it was really quite unsuitable for the work they were now engaged in: something far lighter was required and they must put in for it when they got back to Algiers. This had not been an ideal time for their operation, because the moon went down so late, but the urgency of establishing contact with the island had meant that they could not afford to wait for the next no-moon period.

On the night of 15/16 December the sea, unlike on the previous night, was very rough. A cold north-west wind – the mistral, which in Corsica is called the *libeccio* – was blowing directly on to their beach. The sea was getting worse and the reception party wondered whether landing stores would be possible. The understanding with L'Herminier was that they would stand by from about 0130 hrs, which was when the moon set. At the appointed time, Pierre Griffi flashed the agreed signal to seaward with his torch; after he had done so three or four times, the submarine broke surface at the same point as on the previous night. She was visible to them on the beach and had clearly seen and understood their signal: it remained only to wait for the boat to arrive. Some time went by and they could still not see any sign of its approach, so Toussaint Griffi and Preziosi climbed the hill that overlooked the beach. From this vantage point the boat could be made out at a distance of 300–400 metres. But at that very moment a big wave capsized the boat and it disappeared from sight. They rushed down the hill as fast as their legs would carry them. By the time they got to the beach, the boat's three occupants – Enseigne Lasserre, along with Lionnais and Vigot, the two seamen who had landed them the previous night – had swum ashore and were just emerging from the surf. Their sodden clothes were quickly replaced by three overcoats lent them by the reception party, so that everybody was left feeling frozen. But that was a small matter compared with the loss of the material the dinghy had been carrying.

For the three sailors to swim back to rejoin *Casabianca* at her present position was out of the question but L'Herminier needed to be told that they were safe. The waves were by now large enough to make it difficult to see the submarine and Pierre Griffi was not confident of being able to send a message using his torch as a signalling lamp. The only possible course of action was to ask Mr Brown, who was said to be an excellent swimmer, to swim out to the submarine and ask Commandant L'Herminier to bring the *Casabianca* in as close as possible to the rocky point north of the Anse-de-Topiti. Then it might be possible for the three members of crew to swim the shorter distance to the submarine. After some initial hesitation, Brown agreed to undertake this mission. With exemplary courage, he plunged into the tumultuous breakers and, with a few powerful strokes, he was away from the beach, vanquishing wave after wave till he disappeared into the night. A state of acute anxiety reigned on the beach. The waiting time seemed interminable and their scantily clothed bodies got colder and colder under the impact of the chill north wind from the sea. An hour later they heard, quite distinctly, the sound of the submarine's diesels. They hoped this meant she would be standing closer inshore. In fact, however, the submarine's batteries were running dangerously low and, after Brown had reached her at 0345 hrs and been hauled aboard with the news that all was well with PEARL HARBOR, L'Herminier had decided they must be left to fend for themselves in Corsica for the time being. *Casabianca* was heading north to reconnoitre the coast as far as Calvi. At 1945 hours that evening she turned and proceeded back to Algiers, the essential part of her mission successfully accomplished.

Though PEARL HARBOR had been sent into the field by professional French intelligence officers with OSS technical backing to collect military intelligence and de Saule had no wish to become involved in politics, political issues were inevitably raised: the Corsican Resistance being divided, which elements of it were to receive arms? Indeed, the politically unstable situation in Algiers in the aftermath of TORCH was itself a minefield, particularly for SOE's MASSINGHAM mission as it proceeded to set up its operational base.

As Admiral Cunningham reported to the Admiralty on 19 November, there was already a French Royalist plot afoot to replace

Admiral Darlan by the Comte de Paris, who was in Morocco. The Pretender was in Churchill's bad books and Cunningham quite rightly considered that his advent would be a disaster. Roosevelt was equally determined not to become the restorer of ousted European monarchies, but Bob Murphy's right-wing French connections, both social and professional, led the plotters to hope for support from that quarter. There was also a small, but potentially important, Gaullist group in Algiers, centred on Capitant's and Coste-Floret's local offshoot of the 'Combat' Resistance movement in metropolitan France. Between these two hotbeds of anti-Darlan sentiment stood the enigmatic figure of Henri d'Astier de la Vigerie, who regarded himself as the main organiser of the Algiers Resistance group that had risen to support the Allied landings on 8 November. Henri was a Royalist rather than a Gaullist,[7] but one of his brothers, Emmanuel, was head of the 'Libération-Sud' resistance organisation in metropolitan France and had visited London to meet de Gaulle earlier that year,[8] while a second brother, General François, had arrived in London by Lysander during the November moon and joined de Gaulle's staff.[9]

Since de Gaulle was in London and both SIS and SOE worked with his Bureau Central de Renseignements et d'Action as well as independently in the field, opponents of Darlan in Algiers looked to the British as their natural allies. In the absence of Foreign Office representation other than Harold Mack, who was the British political adviser to Eisenhower and whose contacts with the French were thereby inhibited, Lt Col David Keswick, MASSINGHAM's intelligence officer, and his deputy, Major Jacques de Guélis of SOE's Independent French Section, became important sources of information about this complex and precarious political situation. Keswick reported to Baker Street on 27 November that he was most anxious about the position as the British had not gained the adherence of their previous enemies and had forfeited the trust of their friends. Giraud had been side-tracked, Béthouard had been dismissed and Darlan and the Vichyists were completely in power.[10]

Churchill came under increasing domestic political pressure as a result of the situation in Algiers and on 10 December, a month after the landings, he was led to seek refuge in a secret session of the House of Commons. The speech he made was one of the most brilliant of his career but such was the delicacy of Anglo–American relations at that juncture that its text was not shown to General Eisenhower until nearly two months later.[11]

Both SIS and SOE became involved in establishing links between the Algiers Gaullists and General de Gaulle in London. What Churchill called 'the patchwork arrangement', whereby Darlan was at the head of civil affairs and Giraud was in command of the French armed forces in North Africa, came under increasing strain. Matters came to a head when de Gaulle's first emissary, General François d'Astier de la Vigerie, arrived in Algiers on 19 December. He had been flown from Tempsford to Gibraltar on an aircraft belonging to one of the RAF's Special Duties Squadrons, and carried from Gibraltar to Algiers on a British submarine.[12] He brought funds for the Algiers Gaullists under Professor René Capitant. Darlan's fate was sealed at meetings François had with his brother Henri and with the Comte de Paris in Algiers on 19 December, though the respective roles of the Gaullist and the Royalist brother, who was also chief of Darlan's police, have never been made clear.[13] On 20 December General François formally offered the military cooperation of the Fighting French forces to both Giraud and to Eisenhower. He was then put on a plane and summarily removed from North Africa by the Americans.

MASSINGHAM had, apparently on 18 December, received a very strong warning that if they offered any assistance to anti-Darlan or Gaullist elements, General Eisenhower would order the removal of the mission. MASSINGHAM, in the words of a report in the SOE archives, therefore 'trod warily'. But it was with MASSINGHAM's full, if undeclared, support that a second Gaullist emissary, who had arrived in Algiers unostentatiously with General François d'Astier, remained there after the latter's expulsion. This second Gaullist envoy was travelling under the name Grimaldi. For most of 1942 he had called himself Severi but he was in fact Fred Scamaroni, the young Sous-Préfet who had been one of de Gaulle's emissaries on the ill-fated Dakar expedition in October 1940 and, after his release from Vichy prisons, helped to found the 'Copernic' intelligence network in the non-occupied zone (see Chapter XI above).[14] He had visited his native Corsica in 1941, where he found the resistance divided and disorganised, and he longed to be sent back there to bring it into Gaullist allegiance. When he arrived back in England on New Year's Day 1942, he had adopted a new identity because he was well known to the Vichy authorities. Under the name Severi, he spent six months of 1942 working with Lagier on the Service Action side of the BCRA, which involved him in frequent liaison with SOE.[15] There seems to have been initial opposition in Baker Street to the idea of his returning to the field, on the grounds that he was compromised as an agent. However, Lt Col Jim Hutchison, head of SOE's RF Section, thought highly of the young man who in 1939 had torn up the paper that designated his post in the Préfecture at Caen a 'reserved occupation' in order to join the air force; who had joined de Gaulle in England on 27 June 1940; and who had made his way back from Dakar to rejoin de Gaulle in spite of immense difficulties. SOE eventually agreed to help him fulfil his ambition to return to Corsica as de Gaulle's representative.

Scamaroni's sister, who had access to relevant BCRA archives, stated that he was on the same SOE-organised training course as Jean Moulin, and that Operation SAMPIERO, which was to land him in Corsica from a British submarine, was originally to have taken place in November 1942 but had to be postponed because of the Allied landings in North Africa. The operation had been renamed SEA URCHIN by the time General de Gaulle signed his mission order on 9 December. In addition to Scamaroni, it included a French W/T operator named J.B. Hellier, provided by the BCRA, and a British arms instructor, James Anthony Jickell. It was the first time that BCRA agents and a member of SOE's Independent French Section, to whose existence de Gaulle objected strongly, had been sent into the field as members of a single team. Presumably that was itself a measure of the Gaullists' urgent concern to strengthen their foothold in Corsica and not leave the island's resistance movement to fall into the hands of the Darlan–Giraud Deuxième Bureau.

Four days after General François d'Astier de la Vigerie's expulsion and while the SEA URCHIN team were waiting, under MASSINGHAM's care, to be sent to Corsica by submarine, Admiral Darlan was assassinated. SOE's in-house history of MASSINGHAM recorded that, 'prior to the general publication of the news, MASSINGHAM told London that the assassin was an officer from the 10th Corps Franc camp at Matifou.' What this rather bland statement omits is that this unit was undergoing instruction by officers from MASSINGHAM and OSS; that Bonnier de la Chapelle, the assassin, who had been made one of the camp's French instructors at the request of Sabatier, Henri d'Astier's henchman, was accordingly issued by MASSINGHAM with a .38 Colt Automatic pistol; and that Sabatier had been accorded asylum *ex post facto* on Holdsworth's ship *Mutin*.[16] But the report of the autopsy on Darlan makes clear that the pistol used to kill him was not a Colt Automatic but a weapon of French naval origin. It had been removed from one of the sailors guarding Admiral Fénard's villa, where Darlan was staying, when a detachment of the Algiers Resistance arrived there, relieved the guard and placed Darlan temporarily under arrest on the night of the landings.[17]

Following the assassination, Darlan's immediate circle of friends persuaded General Bergeret that further violence was planned and he in turn persuaded General Giraud, who ordered Bonnier executed and a number of arrests to be made. These included everyone who had been in contact with General d'Astier during his visit and many who opposed the Darlan administration, notably the more prominent Gaullists, who were closely associated with many people recruited by BRANDON into the Special Detachments. The SOE report records that MASSINGHAM's intelligence officer Keswick attempted to find out who was the person responsible for the arrests. General Giraud began to regret his hasty action over the arrests and the execution of Bonnier amd appointed General Ronin to sift the evidence.[18]

Allied Force Headquarters quickly discovered that Bonnier had been issued with a pistol by MASSINGHAM and ordered an enquiry of their own. Eisenhower would probably have carried out his threat to remove MASSINGHAM, lock, stock and barrel, if General Jock Whitely, his British deputy Chief of Staff, had not told him this would be politically serious and, further, that he knew Dodds-Parker, MASSINGHAM's training officer, to be a reliable and efficient junior officer.[19] So the mission survived, minus Colonel Munn, its commanding officer, and 'Mouse' Glyn, his second in command. It acquired Douglas Dodds-Parker in Munn's place, and in mid-January 1943 moved to a new and better training camp and base at the Club des Pins, 20 km. to the west of Algiers.

How Scamaroni managed to avoid arrest in the aftermath of Darlan's assassination is not clear. No-one had been in closer touch with General d'Astier de la Vigerie than he, and he already knew Professor René Capitant, the acknowledged head of the Gaullists in Algiers and a friend of General de Gaulle since the time when de Gaulle and he both served at the headquarters of the French 5th Corps in 1939. Indeed Capitant confirmed to Scamaroni's sister and biographer before his death in 1971 that Fred had come to him as an accredited emissary of de Gaulle.[20] But he was also an SOE-sponsored agent on his way from London to the field: in that capacity he and his fellow members of the *Sea Urchin* team would have enjoyed MASSINGHAM's protection and support.

The BCRA archives consulted by Marie-Claire Scamaroni show that her brother wrote an eight-page report to the BCRA on 28 December, four days after Darlan's death. Its full contents were not disclosed to her but in the final paragraph he asked the BBC to broadcast the following message on 29, 30 and 31 December 1942: *'A nos amis de Corse, nous disons confiance: La Corse restera française, je répète, la Corse restera française. Gaston a mangé le saucisson, son ami ira manger la Coppa.'*[21]

Gaston Taviani, alias Collin, was a BCRA agent who had been sent from London to south-eastern France and to Corsica in 1942 at Scamaroni's request. He had been in the island no more than a fortnight, but the object of the BBC message was to inform the people with whom he had already been in touch of *Sea Urchin's* imminent arrival. Marie-Claire says that the mission should have been met by a reception committee on landing but apparently was not: indeed, in the absence of direct communications between Algiers and the island it is hard to see how the field could have been apprised of the intended time and place of landing.

The *Sea Urchin* mission left Algiers on 30 December 1942 in HM S/m *Tribune*, which was under the command of Lt S.A.Porter, RN.[22] *Tribune* proceeded directly to Corsica to land Scamaroni and his companions (Operation SIDELINE), arriving there on New Year's Day 1943, exactly one year after Scamaroni had been picked up from Yves Le Tac's Folboat canoe in the Aber-Benoît channel by MGB 314 and brought back to England. However, the weather was too bad for landing, so *Tribune* proceeded to the Cap-d'Antibes area to attack shipping until the weather looked more promising. On 3 January, while *Tribune* was patrolling on the surface at night off Cap-Ferrat, a searchlight was exposed in its direction several times, with a beam probably controlled by radar – a measure of the enhanced defences the Germans had established since their arrival on the coast in November.

By 4 January the weather had moderated, so *Tribune* headed back to Corsica. Lava Bay, the pre-arranged landing-place, which lies north of Ajaccio, was reached soon after daylight on 5 January and the beach was reconnoitred from periscope depth at one mile. It appeared quite deserted but there was a heavy ground swell. Porter decided to land the agents at 0030 on 6 January in the north-east corner of the bay, the only part sheltered from the swell. However, at 2038 they observed a small searchlight sweeping the beach in Lava Bay and an area half a mile to seaward: it was shown from an elevation of about 30 metres in the very corner of the bay where Porter had planned to put *Sea Urchin* ashore. The submarine's presence had apparently not been detected, as the light did not sweep anywhere in her vicinity. This light could not have been brought hurriedly into position as there were no roads to Lava Bay, only a rough track; it must therefore have been part of the fixed beach defences. Indeed, Porter and Scamaroni concluded that the whole Ajaccio peninsula must be a defended area. Cupabia Bay on the north shore of the Gulf of Valinco, 20 miles south of Ajaccio, was selected as an alternative. *Tribune* proceeded to seaward, to arrive off the new pinpoint at dawn. She dived at 0623 on 6 January, closed Cupabia Bay and carried out close reconnaissance from half a mile. The beach was quite deserted and a rock landingpoint was selected at U-Scogliu-Biancu. Shore marks were noted for the run in. There was no current or tidal set and the landing-place was better than Lava Bay, being sheltered from the wind and swell. The only disadvantage was its distance from Ajaccio. *Tribune* withdrew, submerged, went southwards into the middle of the Gulf and then turned west. After dark she surfaced and proceeded to seaward to charge batteries.

At 2140 Porter shaped course for the run in to the landing beach and proceeded on main motors. At 2345 the two rubber boats, baggage and a folding bicycle of SOE design were brought up on to the fore casing. The boats were inflated and the submarine trimmed down forward. At 0025, in position 41°44' N, 08°15' E and 600 yards from the landing-place, both rubber dinghies were launched and loaded: Porter noted in the log that the three agents embarked in high spirits. At 0035 the boats were slipped and proceeded shorewards on a steady course at a good speed. They were visible against the white rocks until they had nearly reached the shore. The night was bright with many stars and a haze to seawards. The boats' crews, presumably drawn from the men Holdsworth had brought with him from Helford, reported later that the submarine was invisible at a range of 140 metres, end on against the haze to seaward.

At 0125, the dinghymen reported on R/T that they had left the beach. *Tribune* was now beam-on to the shore at a distance of 550 metres, but they could not see her. R/T communication was maintained and the dinghymen eventually reported that they were 450 metres off the land. They flashed a torch to seaward at intervals but it was not sighted from the submarine. Porter was convinced that the rubber boats were now to seaward of him and had been blown to the westward by the offshore breeze. He instructed the boat to flash to the NE three times. The light was seen a mile south-west of the submarine's position and Porter closed in to the spot on the main electric motors. At 0230 he recovered the two boats and their crews. He then proceeded to seaward, still on the electric motors.

The dinghymen said the landing-place was excellent: the agents reached shore with all their baggage without getting wet and were delighted with the pinpoint. At 0315 *Tribune* was clear enough of the land to change over to main diesel engines and at 0632 she dived and shaped course to the NW with the intention of making a situation report later in the day. She resurfaced at 1848 hours and headed NW on main engines. At 1924 she received Captain (S) 8's signal ordering a situation report to be made 'as convenient before daylight on 9 January'. At 2047 *Tribune* reported completion of operation SIDELINE and shaped course for the Cassingdene Reef light, to arrive at dawn to intercept traffic between Marseilles and Toulon.

Scamaroni set off alone through the *maquis* for Ajaccio, 30 km. away, with the bicycle on his back. He left Hellier and Jickell near the beach to hide the W/T set, the team's baggage and a sealed suitcase of whose contents only Scamaroni was aware: it carried the greater part of his total funds, which amounted to a million Francs, intended to finance the mission's operations.

Scamaroni made his way across country until he reached the River Taravo, where he fell into a ditch and slept till dawn. He then proceeded by road on his bicycle to Ajaccio, arriving at nightfall, cold and hungry. Under cover as a commercial traveller, he knocked at the door of a man named Raimondi, a public works contractor and cinema-owner, who had been chosen by Achille Peretti, future President of the French Assemblée Nationale, to be Scamaroni's deputy head of mission. Scamaroni did not know Raimondi, but he identified himself by saying, '*Je viens de la part de Monsieur Tainturier.*' It was the name of a close family friend who had worked for many years with Fred's father in the Prefectural Corps and been sacked by the Vichy administration after many years of service at Toulouse. To Scamaroni's great relief, the man who had opened the door replied: '*Ah oui, Monsieur Tainturier de Toulouse.*' Peretti must have laid on these pre-arranged passwords before Fred left London. Raimondi was equally relieved, as he had received the BBC message but did not know what had become of his designated chief and had no means of making contact with him.

He gave Fred a meal and rapidly assembled some members of his Resistance team, which belonged to the 'Combat' movement: Colonel Ferrucci, who was to become deputy head of the military side of the organisation; Antoine Serafini, the departmental architect, a future mayor and parliamentary Deputy for Ajaccio; Fernand Poli, a journalist; whom he introduced to Scamaroni, their new chief and representative of the mythical General de Gaulle, who was known to them only as a voice on the BBC's French broadcasts. Fred immediately impressed them with his appraising gaze.

Jickell and Hellier, after hiding their baggage, seem also to have set off for Ajaccio. Poli and a man named Vignocchi went by car from Ajaccio to look for them and found them, ravenously hungry and having frequently lost their way. They were taken into Ajaccio and installed in a safe house.

Next day, 9 January, Hellier, with the help of Bianchi and three other members of the Ajaccio Resistance, set out in a taxi to collect the hidden baggage. They were disguised as fishermen and even greeted a passing Italian patrol. They pressed an errant donkey into service and readily found the spot where the material had been hidden but unfortunately one of the suitcases was missing. By four in the morning the rest of the luggage was by the roadside ready for departure when the group was challenged by an Italian patrol. They explained that they were taking the early morning postal bus to Ajaccio and were allowed to continue. The bus was searched by a gendarme who tapped the cases without opening them.

When they arrived in Ajaccio it was discovered that the missing suitcase belonged to Scamaroni and contained the greater part of the mission's war chest, 600,000 Francs and $500, as well as clothes, weapons and spare crystals for Hellier's W/T sets. Scamaroni dismissed speculation that the Italian OVRA must have discovered the cache: if they had, he said, they would have taken everything or nothing, and then lain in wait for whoever came to collect the kit.

Bianchi installed the W/T set in a safe house. Hellier's first signals were heard by MASSINGHAM in Algiers on 25 January but were unintelligible. This seems to have remained the case throughout the time the mission were in the field. SOE London received a first message from SEA URCHIN on 2 February 1943. It read, 'Team safely housed stop. Equipment Ajaccio stop. Congratulate submarine crew. POT A [Jickell] leaves tomorrow in search of landing grounds stop. Fishing days authorised and limited to certain gulfs.'[23]

Meanwhile, discreet enquiries were being made in the Gulf of Valinco area about the missing suitcase. A 17-year-old shepherd was spending wildly in the local bar with freshly minted banknotes. After a few traditional Corsican death threats and a vow of silence, the shepherd's parents finally handed over the suitcase and its contents, including three quarters of the money. The new notes the mission had brought contrasted with the ragged, soiled ones in circulation on the island, and Raimondi therefore arranged for all their cash to be exchanged for less conspicuous notes.

On 5 February MASSINGHAM were informed by SOE London that a reinforcement party, code-named MECHANIC/GURNET, had left London for Algiers and that MASSINGHAM were to arrange details of their infiltration direct with SEA URCHIN. MASSINGHAM explained that they had still not been able to establish radio contact with SEA URCHIN. They asked London to get SEA URCHIN to suggest a landing point on the west coast; but GURNET was never landed.[24]

Whether Scamaroni had deliberately arranged to communicate exclusively with London is not clear: he may have found MASSINGHAM's links with the Giraudist Service de Renseignements disturbing. He was finding that various Resistance groups in Corsica, particularly 'Franc Tireur', under General Mollard, who had been the military commander in the island in 1939 and 1940, and the 'Front National' under Benielli in Bastia and Giovoni in Ajaccio, both Communists, were reluctant to amalgamate behind de Gaulle. He discovered, too, that one of Benielli's men, Tavera, who had been offered to Scamaroni as liaison, was cultivating Hellier and plying him with drink to get information about the Free French. Scamaroni protested to Benielli about this, but the latter denied responsibility.

CHAPTER XL

Missions to Sardinia and Corsica: January–March 1943

O n the night of 8/9 January 1943, when *Tribune* had just resumed her offensive patrolling on the south-east coast of France, HM *S/m P228*, subsequently renamed *Splendid*, under command of Lt Ian McGeoch, RN, carried out a first infiltration of agents for the Italian Section of SOE's MASSINGHAM mission in Algiers.[1] The operation, code-named CONVERSE, involved landing two men, Adler and Pisani (alias 'Serra'), on the east coast of Sardinia and it was destined to have a direct effect on events in Corsica.[2] It had been planned in conjunction with Emilio Lussu, a brave and brilliant anti-Fascist leader from the days of Mussolini's 1922 march on Rome. Lussu, who combined left-wing politics with the cause of Sardinian separatism, had made a spectacular escape from the prison camp on the Lipari Islands in 1939. SOE had told Jack Beevor, their man in Lisbon, to arrange for Lussu to be brought out of France, where he was living under a false name, but Lussu and his wife turned up in Lisbon in 1941 without any action on Beevor's part. Beevor sent them on to London, but they were returned to France in June 1942 by felucca.[3]

The night of 8/9 January, which had been provisionally selected for CONVERSE, was perfectly suitable in terms of weather under the lee of Sardinia. The sea was calm; there was a light offshore breeze and an overcast sky, which made the night exceptionally dark. McGeoch closed the beach to within half a mile by 0230 on the 9th and then quickly sent the eight-man rubber dinghy away, manned by two men from Holdsworth's *Mutin*, Leading Seaman Taylor and Able Seaman Webb.[4]

Adler, who inspired great confidence in McGeoch and was certainly very intelligent, asked that the submarine return the next night, if she could do so without undue risk, to take him and Serra off, in case they thought their presence had been compromised and that they would soon be discovered. McGeoch felt that giving the agents some hope of retreat if events turned out against them would boost their morale and justified *P228*'s allotting another 24 hours of her patrol time to providing it. He therefore arranged a comprehensive set of light signals for use by Taylor and Webb. If Taylor were unable to find the submarine when coming away from the shore, McGeoch told him to proceed to seaward on a compass bearing due east from Mount Ferru, as far as possible, since it was not unlikely that P228 would be forced by patrol or other craft to dive or withdraw. Taylor had instructions from SOE to land with the agents and help them to carry their W/T gear a mile or so inland, where it would be buried. He was ordered to leave shore not later than 0430.

The rubber boat left *P228* at 0250 and was seen heading slowly but surely for the shore. At this time, some rather heavy gusts of wind were coming offshore, which must have slowed the boat down.

At 0445 one green flash was sighted to northward. McGeoch moved the submarine one cable in that direction but they did not see the light again. The flash was reported to be on the beach, some little way above the water; Taylor was intending to leave the shore shortly but, knowing it was after 0430, had flashed the signal before actually leaving. *P228* therefore returned to the exact waiting position.

At 0540 the boat had not returned and dawn was imminent. *P228* moved offshore, dived and then proceeded further to seaward on the line due east from Mount Ferru. During the forenoon one aircraft flying up the coast and one auxiliary schooner under sail and power, steering south, were seen.

Just after noon, they were proceeding very slowly towards the shore along the agreed line when Sub Lt Robert Balkwill, with his eyes glued to the search periscope, said, 'There they are, Sir!' The rubber boat was bearing 300°, 2,000 yards distant. They were four miles from land and it was a sunny day with a calm sea: McGeoch decided it would be better to surface and risk being seen than to leave Taylor and Webb drifting about in the Tyrrhenian Sea. As he subsequently reported:

'1223 Surfaced. Embarked boat and its occupants who were understandably relieved that we were not a U-boat, the periscope having looked at them, they said, in a hostile way.'

They dived again quickly, Balkwill having first leapt over the side to rescue the dinghy paddles, which were floating away and could have aroused suspicion. The dinghy was slashed with a knife so that it would deflate more quickly. A tot of rum restored Taylor and Webb's morale and they seemed thereafter entirely unmoved by their adventure. No enemy response followed *P228*'s brief stay on the surface. But it was not until a couple of nights later, when the submarine was well away from the scene of the operation, that McGeoch felt able to signal to Captain (S) 8 that CONVERSE had been completed.

Taylor reported that the landing had been successfully carried out and that no alarm had been raised. He and Webb had helped the agents carry the W/T gear some distance inland and bury it.

On the way inshore one of the agents (Pisani, alias Serra) had been absolutely useless and, as he would not paddle, the efforts of Adler, the other agent, were largely wasted because the boat turned round. The offshore breeze came in stronger gusts inshore and impeded the boat, so that the shoreward passage took an hour. He also reported that the agents had asked him not to flash any signals until 15 minutes after the boat had left the beach. In agreeing to this Taylor had not realised how much faster he would move downward away from the shore. In fact Webb saw the submarine and alerted Taylor, who thought they still had much further to go. They therefore paddled on and, not finding the submarine, continued to seaward as instructed.

McGeoch reported that both ratings had behaved admirably and cheerfully in trying circumstances, though not more so than was expected in view of their magnificent record in earlier operations.

*   *   *

In normal times Algiers was not a French submarine base, though Oran had the requisite facilities. From a maintenance point of view, it would have made good sense for *Casabianca*, which at the beginning of 1943 was the only French submarine in the Mediterranean in seagoing condition, to be transferred to Oran, but L'Herminier was determined to remain based on Algiers. The Allied intelligence services operated from Algiers and L'Herminier felt that his submarine, though less well equipped for offensive patrol duties than her smaller, but more modern, sisters of the Royal Navy's 8th Flotilla, was particularly qualified to serve their needs for clandestine sea transport. He persuaded the Deuxième Bureau without too much difficulty that *Casabianca* was big enough to carry out an operation to Provence as well as to Corsica in the course of a single patrol, but he stipulated that their next sortie should be delayed until the new moon so that they could take advantage of the long, dark nights for what promised to be protracted and heavy work when they began landing arms and explosives in Corsica.[5]

Casabianca's second mission was in fact threefold: she had, first of all, to land two secret agents in Corsica – Regimental Sergeant Major Bozzi and a W/T operator named Chopitel, together with two British B7-type suitcase sets, several accumulators and a transformer. ACF listed this operation, code-named AUBURN, as being for Cohen's Section of SIS and the mission was, therefore, supposed to work independently, but it was decided that the security advantages of doing so were outweighed by access to the experience gained by PEARL HARBOR and that they should therefore put themselves under the orders of Commandant de Saule.

The second part of the programme involved landing a cargo of

Sten guns and ammunition for PEARL HARBOR at the Anse-d'Arone. At the same time it was hoped that *Casabianca* would be able to re-embark the three members of her crew who had been left behind in December.

The third, and most important, part of the *Casabianca*'s mission in the February no-moon period was to land a three-man team on the coast of Provence, consisting of Captain Caillot, a cavalry officer who was to serve as W/T operator; Lieutenant Guillaume of the French counter-espionage service and Fred Brown of OSS.[6] Caillot was to operate an OSS signals plan code-named YANKEE. Brown had six SOE B-type suitcase sets with him: he thought in big terms, but his notions of security were, in the view of most wise men, quite unacceptable.[7]

A secondary task for *Casabianca* while on the coast of Provence was to embark a group of French officers who wanted to join the French Forces in North Africa.

The arms were supplied by SOE's MASSINGHAM packing station in watertight packages, none of which weighed more than 70 lb., but the boxes of ammunition were heavier and awkward to handle through the hatches and into their stowage places in the submarine. SOE could not immediately supply the secure R/T link that L'Herminier had requested or a lightweight replacement for *Casabianca*'s own heavy dinghy. Col Eddy of OSS, however, was able to produce a number of large, American, eight-man, inflatable aircraft dinghies, which MASSINGHAM modified by removing the inflatable centre thwarts and fitting removable, but rigid, bottom boards to distribute the weight of the cargo evenly over the bottoms of the boats, which consisted otherwise of no more than a reinforced rubber skin.[8]

Casabianca sailed on the evening of 31 January, after a last-minute change of plan when the 'field' in Provence signalled that they would be standing by on the night of 4/5 February. This was potentially awkward as PEARL HARBOR was expecting them at the Anse-d'Arone on the night of 6 February.[9]

The rendezvous in Provence was supposed to be at Cros-de-Cagnes and *Casabianca* crossed the Mediterranean without incident. Her navigator checked her position whenever possible with star sights, as they had rather lost confidence in their gyro-compass, which, having let them down on their first mission, could not be replaced or repaired at Algiers. They made a good landfall and, on the night of 3/4 February, observed searchlights in the vicinity of Toulon, on the Iles-d'Hyères and near La-Garoupe, the unlit light-house on the Cap-d'Antibes. The coast was obviously now well watched by the Germans and the British submarine *Tribune* had reported that the searchlights were apparently linked to a well-organised radar system. At 0150 *Casabianca* was just about to submerge: everybody was below and L'Herminier was ready to press the klaxon for the dive when the control-room reported on the voice-pipe that a W/T signal addressed to them was being received. L'Herminier instructed his British liaison crew to take the message and acknowledge receipt: it could be decoded at leisure after they had dived to 40 metres.

The signal was from the commander of the British 8th Submarine Flotilla. Referring by code name to the French agent who was due to meet them, it reported that reconnaissance of 'No. 1' was unfavourable. No. 1 was their chosen pinpoint at Cros-de-Cagnes. The warning had arrived just in the nick of time to save them from falling into a potential trap.

The message gave no clue as to what they were supposed to do about an alternative landing-place but L'Herminier decided to take the initiative. He went into conference with his three passengers. They decided against the Esterel, because the road and the railway followed the coast too closely and because there were a number of strategic key-points in that vicinity that were likely to be well guarded. The area south and west of Saint-Tropez was more promising: the coast there was broken and the main communications ran well inland. There was good cover for concealment of passengers and material. Cap-Camarat had a lighthouse and a semaphore station and Cap-Lardier was an obvious choice for an enemy observation post, but between the two lay Taillat Point, which might be less well guarded. They decided to feel their way along the coast either east or west of this feature, making themselves as inconspicuous as possible, and penetrate into one or other of the two bays, where, L'Herminier assumed, they would be completely safe both from the prowling searchlights on the Ile-du-Levant and from the enemy's radar network. Taillat itself, joined to the mainland by a narrow isthmus, would be silhouetted against sea and sky at night like an island and should be easy to identify.

They set course westwards, knowing they could not arrive before nightfall and that, when they got there, the submarine's batteries would be practically exhausted. During that day, the sea became rough and it was difficult to keep *Casabianca* at periscope depth, so that it was impossible to keep track of their exact position. Then, at nightfall, it became calmer and they had to dive deeper to avoid being spotted from the air. At 1800 hours they were proceeding at 2 knots when they touched bottom. That at least resolved doubts about their position, as there was only one shoal in the area: they knew that they must be 410 metres off the Tourelle-de-l'Esquillade. The current, reinforced by the east wind, had carried them further to the west than they had reckoned and they were now close to the Pointe-du-Titan, on which a searchlight was mounted. By 2000 hours they were far enough from it to risk surfacing and switching over to diesels, but remaining in deep trim so that as little as possible of their superstructure was clear of the surface.

They passed Lardier and could see Camarat on the horizon, but Taillat was lost against the background. Fortunately the sounding machine was working well enough to enable them to avoid shallow points in the sea-bed, many of which had never been properly charted.

At 2100 hours they headed into Bon-Porté Bay, which was quite shallow. The dinghymen and the three agents stood ready to leave and the submarine hove to about 275 metres short of the beach. The dinghy was launched and loaded and the shore party took their places on board. The indicator of the storage batteries read so low that the submarine would have been unable to submerge had anything gone wrong. At 2125 hours the dinghy left for the shore.

As their eyes became accustomed to the darkness, they became aware of the presence of what looked exactly like a blacked-out ship, less than 200 metres away to starboard. The gun crew, who were closed up and standing by, trained their weapon on to the target and were ready to fire: it was a moment of intense emotion for all on deck and for the shore party, who were still near enough to see what was happening. But the target did not move and gradually confidence returned. In reply to L'Herminier's whispered question down the voice-pipe from the bridge to the control-room, one of the officers confirmed that there was a large, detached rock jutting out of the water in the middle of the bay. It was called Escudelier rock and it became a well-known landmark to everyone who undertook subsequent operations to this pinpoint. There was in fact a German block-house only a short distance beyond it.

Within the record time of 17 minutes the dinghy was back alongside, having successfully completed the first landing from Algiers on the German-occupied south coast of metropolitan France. It was a good pinpoint, but suitable for use in only calm weather, as they were to learn on subsequent visits. Apart from the block-house, which lay 300 metres to one side of where the agents had landed, it subsequently transpired that there was a machine-gun nest only 200 metres in the other direction. A German-occupied farmhouse lay only a short distance above, north-east of the beach: it was badly blacked out and they had wrongly assumed that the light escaping from it was a star, although L'Herminier did think it strangely motionless among the myriad stars that twinkled through the pine trees.

Their success was cheering but this was countered by the ordeal they then had in engineering the submarine's withdrawal. The batteries, which had never been so low, had to provide power not only for the electric motors, to make a silent retreat , but thereafter to start the heavy diesels, which could not be brought into action by any other means. L'Herminier ran the motors dead slow so as to use a minimum of current.

At 2230, when they were still uncomfortably close to the coast, they saw a small white light behind them and to port. It went out, but they eventually made out the unmistakable silhouette of a small German patrol vessel, not very far away. L'Herminier decided that he had no alternative but to start up his diesels and rely on the submarine's surface speed of 17 knots to make their escape. While in Algiers there had been no time to arrange fitting of the exhaust-guards designed by Kerneur, their chief engineer, and, when the diesels started, there was a display of fireworks at water-level that must, L'Herminier thought, have greatly surprised the watch on the enemy patrol boat.

They still had two more operations to do in Corsica before they could head for home.

By this time Pierre Griffi's PEARL HARBOR W/T link had passed several dozen signals to base reporting progress in establish-ing the network and transmitting detailed intelligence of Italian military dispositions.[10] When Algiers told de Saule to stand by for a first consignment of arms to be landed from *Casabianca* on 6 February at the Anse-d'Arone, south of the Gulf of Porto – a region difficult of access because of its precipitous topography – Toussaint Griffi, Preziosi and four members of the Front National group from Ajaccio had piled into a large taxi and gone north along the coast through Sagone. They were particularly apprehensive about a permanently manned check-post at Cargèse, where there was a concentration of Italian troops, and were prepared to shoot if stopped, but, to their immense relief, they sailed past the road-block of sandbags without raising a movement from the Italian sentries behind it. As the taxi climbed from Cargèse to Piana and away from the sea, Preziosi and Griffi caught sight of the bay at Chioni and the spot where they had landed two months previously. It was a small creek close to the main beach and the beach was guarded by an Italian military unit; so they had had a very narrow escape. They drove past the little house with the eucalyptus trees where they had made their first contacts on their way to Revinda and shortly came to the point where they were to meet the two Nesa brothers, who had a sheep-fold not far from the road at U-Solognu. This was beginning to be a place of refuge for the local Resistance. The family were taking care of four of these patriots in addition to the three castaway members of *Casabianca*'s crew. Commandant de Saule joined them during the morning. It was the first meeting in the Maquis of a party of combatants from outside the island with a group of local patriots and everyone felt pleased to be involved in such an important step forward. *Casabianca*'s crew members were particularly happy at the prospect of being able to rejoin their submarine.

Soon they had to go down to the Baie-d'Arone, which lies just north of the Baie-de-Chioni on the way to the Gulf of Porto. Access to the beach was difficult as all the paths leading to it ran through the thick scrub that covered very steep hillsides. For reasons of prudence they went down in small groups and met at a small hut not far from the beach. A surprise awaited them when they reached the foreshore at about 1 o'clock in the morning and found four men there: the two agents, Sergeant Major Bozzi, Chopitel, the W/T operator, and two sailors named Asso and Cardot had been there since the previous night. *Casabianca* had arrived 24 hours earlier than expected and L'Herminier had decided to send them ashore without waiting for the reception party. But the submarine's heavy boat had run so hard aground that it had defied their efforts to refloat it, and once again, two sailors had been unable to return to their submarine. They told de Saule that the arms and ammunition would not be landed until the following night – 7 February – so the whole party went back to the hut. This information was misleading: *Casabianca* surfaced again on the night of 6 February and sent a flat-bottomed boat ashore, towing four of the rubber boats, which were loaded with a cargo of 450 Sten sub-machine-guns and 60,000 rounds of 9-mm ammunition. The landing party, who, on the previous night, had gone to check why the dinghy had not returned and had found it half-buried in the sand, unloaded their cargo and hid it under branches before returning to the submarine. The reception committee were unaware that they had come and gone, but fortunately they decided to return to the beach shortly before dawn to remove the stranded boat from sight, whereon they discovered the arms dump. They set to work and in less than an hour the arms and boxes of ammunition had been hidden provisionally in a more secure place half-way between the beach and the hut. They had finished before day broke. Toussaint Griffi and Preziosi noticed that quite a lot of the stranded boat remained visible, although it was supposed to have been broken up while the arms were being hidden, so they made a renewed attack on the wreckage with pick-axes and hid the pieces in the thick scrub that ran right down to the beach.

While this was being done, other members of the reception party had moved the material again. Some of it was stored in the shepherd's hut, some was loaded on to donkeys for early distribution to reliable local hands, starting with the Maquisards already gathered at the Nesa family's sheep-fold, who thus became the first armed Maquis group in the island; here PEARL HARBOR was soon to establish its base. It took a couple of hours for the first donkey convoys to scale the steep ascent from the shore and deliver their loads, but when they returned to the beach they brought back bread and good Corsican *charcuterie* for the 15 or so exhausted people at the hut with the remainder of the cargo.

The Sten guns and ammunition that had been landed represented less than half the total cargo *Casabianca* had on board, but the weather had deteriorated during the landing and L'Herminier had to use the electric motors all the time to prevent the submarine from drifting ashore.[11] He anchored to save his batteries and decided to wait another day in the hope of being able to land the rest of the arms cargo the following night. But the shore party, on leaving the beach, had to row off in the teeth of what had become a strong onshore wind. Seeing how difficult they found it to make headway towing the four rubber boats, L'Herminier weighed anchor and stood inshore to pick them up. As he did so, the rudder-guard bumped heavily on the bottom and the flat-bottomed boat was so damaged in coming alongside that it sank. They had now lost both their rigid boats and could only hope that the weather would improve substantially before the following night, as the rubber boats would be able to be used alone only in calm conditions. They waited on the bottom off the Anse-d'Arone all day but when they surfaced after dark that evening it was still blowing hard and they had to renounce the idea of further landings. They had seen lights on the beach before they submerged that morning and surmised that the reception party had at least turned up to collect what they had managed to put ashore.

Casabianca was back in Algiers on 10 February. On the same night the British submarine *Saracen*, under the command of Lt M.G.R. Lumby, RN, entered the Bay of Cupabia and landed three further agents there for SIS. The party's leader and W/T operator was Guy Verstraete, the Belgian merchant marine officer landed by *Minna* near Oran in July 1942, who had been in contact with Ridgway Knight. The mission, whose other two members were Corsicans named Antoine Colonna d'Istra and Simon Charles Andrei, recruited by SIS in Algiers, was known locally as FREDERICK.[12]

They used the same landing-place as Porter had used a month earlier to infiltrate Scamaroni and his *Sea Urchin* team. Lumby was not warned by S (8) that he would be using a 'hot bed' and subsequently complained of this omission.[13]

The Italians had indeed heard that a landing by submarine had been made in the Golfe-de-Valinco area. At 0210 on 11 February, when *Saracen* was less than 750 metres from the shore and on the surface preparing for the boatwork, a small searchlight on the beach one mile to the eastward started searching the sea. The submarine was illuminated six times but, though beam-on to the light, was apparently not detected. Lumby thought great credit was due to the three agents and two boat's crew, who carried on loading their boats as if they had not noticed the light. Verstraete and his companions were dispatched five minutes later in two rubber dinghies of American type. The landing was successfully accomplished and the boats were re-embarked only 40 minutes after they had left the submarine.

Lumby reported on his return to Algiers that the American-type rubber dinghy appeared to have every advantage for landing agents. It carried a very heavy load, as well as being seaworthy and robust. The latter point was very important. When the two dinghies were going inshore on 11 February they ran aground on a sharp reef and remained there until the swell managed to lift them right over. A Folboat would have sunk instantly and an ordinary rigid boat would have been holed; and as they were still over 25 metres from the beach, all the gear would have been lost. The only damage to the dinghies was a number of severe gashes in the canvas. The boats' crews had been supplied with binoculars and an R/T set, which were not used in this case as the dinghies had no trouble finding the submarine. However, they must be considered essential equipment for operations of this nature, where the burning of searchlights could compel the submarine to shift position violently.

Saracen's remarks on the American-type rubber dinghies confirmed Captain (S) 8's views based on his flotilla's previous experience. Their only disadvantage seemed to be that they could not navigate accurately over any great distance. (S) 8 thought therefore that the Folboat should be retained and, for certain operations where an unknown distance had to be traversed to and from shore, that the submarine should carry both types of boat.[14]

There was no reception committee on 11 February at Cupabia Bay and the FREDERICK team hid their luggage among the rocks. It consisted of a mountain rucksack, two suitcases of clothes, a suitcase W/T transmitter/receiver, another containing spare parts and a tin box containing an accumulator. They then made their way east to the small mountain village of Olmeto, some 18 km. away, where they arrived exhausted in the evening. Andrei had an old friend named Joseph Tramoni living there, who gave them food and a bed for the night. Andrei and Verstraete went back to the beach to collect their luggage on 15 February in company of a 16-year-old boy, Benoît Mondolni, and his donkey.[15]

*   *   *

All four submarine operations to Corsica so far had been to the west coast. At about this time, however, the Front National, under the leadership of Arthur Giovoni, the Communist chief at Ajaccio, conceived a plan to capture and abduct one of the four Italian divisional generals in the island, whose headquarters was at Petreto-Bicchisano, an operation whose effect would be all the more spectacular if he could be shipped out to Algiers as a prisoner of war. For this, an embarkation point on the east coast would be more suitable, as they wanted to take their prospective captive in that general direction via Aullène and Solenzara. Though far from convinced of the merits of the scheme, de Saule agreed to put it to his chiefs in Algiers and asked them to study the possibility of sending *Casabianca* to the east coast in the course of her next patrol. His feeling that the planned abduction involved disproportionately great risks was shared by the Palais d'Eté, so the plan was abandoned.[16]

De Saule worried that Toussaint Griffi and Preziosi were getting altogether too mixed up in the Front National, of which they had both become members, so he sent them off to join the Maquis group at U-Solognu, where the original castaways from *Casabianca*, Lasserre, Lionnais and Vigot, had now been joined by Cardot and Asso, left ashore after the second operation. The idea of a submarine operation on the east coast in March went ahead meanwhile and de Saule decided to send Toussaint Griffi and Preziosi back to Algiers by means of it. He felt that their close links with the Front National would make it difficult for them, in the coming paramilitary phase, to achieve effective coordination with all the other Resistance movements in the island.

The point for the operation, the Anse-de-Canelle, some way north of Porto-Vecchio, had originally been selected because a member of the Resistance had a farm near by capable of providing shelter for a substantial party, which made it particularly suitable in connection with the plan to kidnap the Italian general.

Casabianca sailed from Algiers on 2 March and on the night of 5/6 March made an unsuccessful attempt to land agents and pick up Captain Caillot and Lieutenant Guillaume (whom L'Herminier had landed a month before) and three other officers, including a general, from the Taillat pinpoint.[17] She then sailed to the Canelle rendezvous, where de Saule had assembled the whole PEARL HARBOR party and the five sailors. The coast in that area is featureless, with a sandy beach stretching away north and south for some 30 km. The party were in position on the night of 8/9 March, but Pierre Griffi flashed the recognition signal to seaward for two hours in vain and they got caught in a rainstorm as they were making their way back to their hotel at Solenzara, where they arrived drenched.[18] Preziosi and Toussaint Griffi had to go to bed naked, leaving their clothes to dry by the embers of the fire in their bedroom. They slept late and that night again made their way towards the Anse-de-Canelle, which lies 4–5 km. from the town. The area was malarial and the Italians had not deployed troops in it but, as they walked towards Favone, they saw the headlights of a car stopped on the road about 400–500 metres away. The lights were tinted blue, which suggested the vehicle was Italian, and, as they were shining in the direction of their rendezvous, which was only a kilometre away, they feared that an ambush was being prepared. Some of the party thought they should return to the hotel but in the end they agreed to split up into three groups and try to ensure that the submarine came to no harm. It fell to Preziosi and two of the local Resistance to act as the reconnaissance group. One of them, a man named Nicoli, went on alone to prospect. An hour later they saw a figure approaching, wearing a hat with its brim pulled down. They thought at first he must be an enemy and prepared to shoot. Preziosi called his name twice without response but the third time, just as they were on the point of firing, Nicoli identified himself. The vehicle did indeed belong to the enemy but it had broken down and was abandoned. Anyway, it seemed better to call off the operation for that night.

On 10 March they had better luck. During the day they made contact with a local fisherman who had a big boat moored in the creck at Favone and who was prepared to take everyone who was due to leave off to the submarine. They set off for the third time at about 1930 hours. It was less dark than on the two preceding nights and there was enough moonlight to enable them to find their way without difficulty. At 2000 one of the sailors, who was an engine-room rating, said he could hear the submarine's diesels. Everybody stopped and listened: other members of the submarine's crew thought they could perhaps also hear the sound. They had scarcely resumed their march when Lasserre said there was no doubt at all: the submarine was in the offing, expecting them, of course, at Canelle, whereas they were planning to embark at Favone. Unfortunately an east wind had arisen within the previous quarter of an hour which, as Lasserre observed, would not help the embarkation process. He set to work straight away with the signal torch to try to attract the submarine's attention and get L'Herminier to come closer to Favone. At 2300 hours they were on the little quay at Favone. Pierre Griffi was to board the fishing boat with the seven men who were due to leave, as he had messages from de Saule to deliver to L'Herminier. The motor started and less than quarter of an hour later they were in contact with the submarine, which was lying about 2 miles offshore. The fishing boat came alongside the submarine's bow and, although the fresh breeze complicated the manoeuvre, the sailors climbed on board, followed by Toussaint Griffi and Preziosi. L'Herminier was standing on the forward casing waiting for them. Pierre Griffi also came on board, had a few words with L'Herminier and then returned to the fishing boat, followed by two Corsicans from the Corps Franc French commando unit, who had been sent with six million Francs, arms and ammunition to prepare the insurrectional phase of the Resistance. The fishing boat was loaded and moved off slowly towards Favone, where de Saule and three members of the Resistance were awaiting them.

On board *Casabianca* L'Herminier still had the three intelligence agents he had been unable to land at Taillat. He was due to go back for a second attempt to do so and to pick up Captain Caillot and Lt Guillaume;[19] the revised rendezvous had been fixed for the night of 13/14 March. He decided to use the intervening time to fit in an offensive patrol off Bastia on his way north. He cross-examined Lasserre, who had spent part of his time ashore in Corsica at Bastia, where he and his companions had been taken care of by the local Resistance, about the timing of the shipping service organised by the Italians between Livorno, Elba and Bastia, which was the only port of any consequence in that part of the island. Lasserre told him that the small passenger ferry-boat *Francesco Crispi* and the cargo steamer *Tagliamento* maintained a weekly service, which would normally arrive on that very day. *Casabianca* therefore took up station off Bastia. At the beginning of the afternoon, the expected convoy appeared. L'Herminier fired four torpedoes but they missed their targets and hit the breakwaters of the Old Port. The submarine was then subjected to a prolonged depth-charge attack by the convoy's escorting destroyers. She dived to 80 m. and was pursued northwards almost to the Gulf of Genoa, or so it seemed to Preziosi. However, no sooner had the alert passed than L'Herminier, vexed by his failure, decided to return to Bastia next day with a view to shelling a large Italian military petrol dump close to the cemetery. Unfortunately the torpedo attack had alerted the whole of the enemy defence system in the area and, even before they surfaced, the submarine was detected and subjected to a renewed and intensive depth-charge attack. By an adroit manoeuvre, L'Herminier managed to escape from his pursuers again, but he was deeply disappointed by this second failure and made no attempt to hide it. Though they performed yeoman service in opening up and maintaining clandestine sea lines of communication with Corsica and south-eastern France, they all longed to strike at the enemy – a role for which their lack of Asdic and their unreliable torpedoes fitted them less well. On this occasion bad luck followed them back to the French coast: when they arrived in Bon-Porté Bay on 13 March, a combination of bad weather and the multiplicity of the German coastal batteries made it impossible to land the three-man team of intelligence agents they were carrying or to pick up the waiting party.

Submarine operations to Corsica
Embarquements de Corse par sous-marin

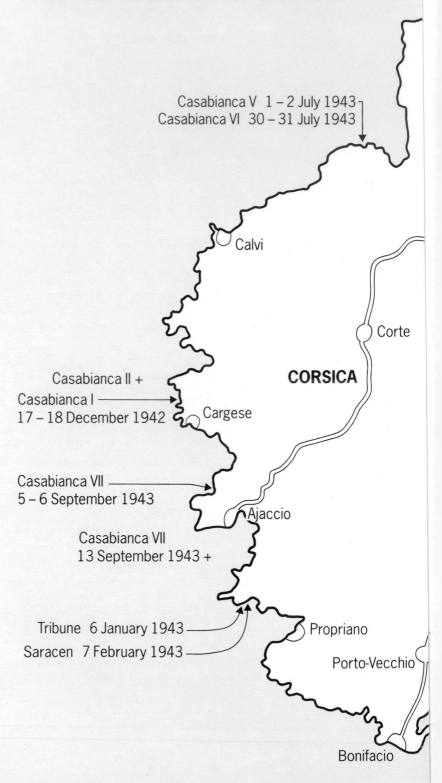

Casabianca V 1 – 2 July 1943
Casabianca VI 30 – 31 July 1943

Calvi

Corte

CORSICA

Casabianca II +
Casabianca I
17 – 18 December 1942

Cargese

Casabianca VII
5 – 6 September 1943

Ajaccio

Casabianca VII
13 September 1943 +

Tribune 6 January 1943

Saracen 7 February 1943

Propriano

Porto-Vecchio

Bonifacio

CHAPTER XLI

Last Missions to Corsica before the Italian Armistice and its Liberation

S OE's W/T contact with SEA URCHIN ceased abruptly on 15 March and reports trickled in from Deuxième Bureau sources that Scamaroni and Hellier were under arrest, which turned out to be true. Their undoing patently stemmed from the very prompt arrest of Adler and Serra, the SOE Italian Section agents landed in Sardinia in February, and their willingness to cooperate with the OVRA, Italian counterpart of the Gestapo. Serra had known Hellier in Algiers when they were waiting to be sent into the field by MASSINGHAM. The OVRA brought him over to Corsica, where he identified Hellier, doubtless without difficulty as he had taken to drinking heavily in the bars of Ajaccio. Hellier in turn betrayed his chief.[1]

Scamaroni, who had found it hard to unite the Corsican Resistance behind de Gaulle because the Front National's Communist leadership were suspicious of de Gaulle and thought they could get the arms they needed from PEARL HARBOUR, took his own life, having disclosed nothing under torture. Hellier told his captors enough to compromise not only his chief but a number of his local contacts as well. A fresh start was necessary. Verstraete and Andrei of FREDERICK had, incidentally, also been arrested by the Italians when they returned to Cupabia Bay, hoping for another submarine landing operation.[2]

It so happened that MASSINGHAM had already found and trained the man who stepped into the breach and became the leader of the Corsican Resistance. His name was Paul Colonna d'Istria, a cousin of Antoine Colonna d'Istria who had been landed in Corsica in February as a member of SIS's FREDERICK mission. He came of a family long established in the Sartenais and was a Commandant in the gendarmerie, serving on the staff of the general commanding that force at Algiers.[3]

MASSINGHAM discovered Colonna as a volunteer for a mission to Corsica in rather unusual circumstances.[4] Like many people from southern Corsica, where Arab cultural influence has left its mark, he was in the habit of having his horoscope cast each year. When this had last been done, some months before the Allied landings in North Africa, his astrologer had forecast that he would return to Corsica in dangerous circumstances within the year. At the time this prediction had not made much sense, as he could then travel to Ajaccio on the ferry from Algiers with no particular difficulty or danger. But after TORCH and the Italian occupation of the island, he realised that he was destined to return to his native island clandestinely, just as Sampiero Corso did in 1564, when he attempted, with the support of Catherine de Medici, to deliver it from Genoese domination. This historical precedent had appealed also to Fred Scamaroni, whose family background was not dissimilar: SAMPIERO was the name he chose for the original operation that was to have returned him to Corsica as an emissary of de Gaulle.[5]

Paul Colonna was prepared to work for SOE, as was his cousin for SIS. Although SOE had been willing to support Scamaroni as a BCRA agent, it had no doctrinal difficulty about sending a successor into the field who would be working directly for MASSINGHAM. Although de Gaulle much disliked the practice, Baker Street's Independent French Section under Maurice Buckmaster sent Frenchmen as well as British officers into France as agents all the time and Jacques de Guélis, head of MASSINGHAM's French Country Section, belonged by background to that side of SOE's French activities. Indeed, he had been back in London in February for a liaison visit, bringing with him two young Frenchmen whom he had found in Algiers as recruits for F Section.[6] Bob Maloubier and Alain Reynaud were both destined to win DSOs in France working for F Section. Paul Colonna was to earn one in Corsica.

Colonna, whom MASSINGHAM called 'Whiskers' or, more familiarly, 'Cesari', was not politically minded. MASSINGHAM hoped that his status as a British agent would allow him to hold himself aloof from the power struggle between de Gaulle and Giraud that was to be the principal preoccupation of the French in Algiers in the summer of 1943. They believed subsequently that his political independence had enabled him to weld together the disparate elements of the Corsican Resistance.[7] In retrospect, this was perhaps a somewhat naive view, but at the time it fitted in well enough with the need to work with the Americans, both in OSS and at AFHQ, who were still strongly anti-Gaullist. Indeed, Arthur Roseborough, head of OSS's Secret Intelligence (SI) operations at Algiers, lost his job because of his strong pro-de Gaulle views.[8]

By the end of March 1943 Scamaroni was dead and de Saule of PEARL HARBOR was on the run. It was decided to bring him out of Corsica during the operation (LEG) that would land Colonna d'Istria and his British W/T operator. The rendezvous fixed was on the east coast above the 42° parallel at the mouth of a river and the submarine chosen for the job was *Trident* (Lt P.E. Newstead, RN), which also carried an SOE prize crew to take over, if they could, an Italian schooner and bring it back to Algiers.[9]

Holdsworth had gone forward with *Mutin* to Bône for ZODIAC, but John Newton, skipper of *Serenini*, was embarked as captain of the prize crew and as conducting officer for SOE. The boatwork was to be carried out in conjunction with a Special Boat Section team consisting of Courtney and Lt E.J.A. Lunn.[10]

While *Trident* was 'dived' during the day before the operation, Newstead received a message altering the rendezvous to a point about 20 miles further south, at the mouth of the River Travo.

The operation itself, which took place on the night of 6 April at quarter moon, was comparatively straightforward: the SOE party paddled towards the shore in an inflatable rubber dinghy guided by Courtney and Lunn in a Folboat canoe, whose task was to keep the party on the right compass bearing for the river mouth. They approached the shore in silence, smelling the aromatic *maquis* stronger and heavier on the wind. Courtney noted that the whiteness of the sand at the river mouth first appeared as a long, grey, horizontal smudge, broken by the dark shapes of bushes.[11]

Once on shore, the men landing from the rubber boat threw restraint to the winds and clustered on the sand talking to the reception committee at the tops of their voices. De Saule told Colonna to get in touch with Pierre Griffi, who would brief him about the situation. Courtney and Lunn tried in vain to quieten them and the hubbub only grew when other members of the reception committee arrived and told them that a beautiful Maquisarde had been waiting to embrace the brave British commandos. She had, however, gone home about an hour before.

Courtney and Lunn were impatient to get away: de Saule and Jickell, who had avoided arrest when Hellier and Scamaroni were rounded up by the OVRA, were escorted into the rubber dinghy, which was taken in tow by their Folboat. Courtney recalled it making its unwieldy way, swaying across the crests of the rollers, until they reached the safety of the submarine.

Although de Saule had been picked up, other people connected with his PEARL HARBOR mission who were due to be evacuated had gone to the original rendezvous on the coast 20 miles further north, in case the message changing the venue had not got through to the submarine. Newstead therefore turned north, hoping the next night to collect these people, who must have included Pierre Griffi, de Saule's W/T operator.[12]

During the day he made an unsuccessful attack on a merchant vessel. This upset de Saule, who feared that it might prejudice the attempt to rescue the remaining members of his party.[13]

The attempt to make contact with them failed in any case, and Newstead, knowing that the unsuccessful attack would have stirred up the defences off Bastia, proceeded to the northernmost limit of his patrol area, on the coast west of Genoa. There *Trident* sighted what appeared to be a small coastal tanker of a few hundred tons close inshore. She was too small to justify using a torpedo so they surfaced and prepared to engage her with their guns. But appearances proved deceptive: she was in fact an Italian Q-ship, which proceeded to mount an intensive and accurate counter-attack on the submarine. *Trident* only just survived this. On 18 April she returned to Algiers.[14]

Trident sailed again from Algiers on 1 May, apparently under orders to attempt again to evacuate the remaining members of de Saule's party, as well as to land two Soviet agents on the Italian coast (Operation ETNA).[15] The Corsican operation on 10 May was again unsuccessful. Pierre Griffi, whose relationship with Colonna proved difficult, was arrested by the Italians on 16 June and executed in August.[16]

By the time *Trident* was free to attempt ETNA, moon conditions were no longer suitable and the operation was not carried out. She returned to Algiers on 18 May.

Colonna found that, despite Scamaroni's valiant efforts, the Resistance, though strongly anti-Fascist, was far from united. After carefully taking stock, he concluded that the Communist-led Front National provided the only nucleus around which a unified Resistance effort could be built.[17] De Gaulle, who was still in London at the time, was furious not to have been able to replace Scamaroni with one of his own men and chalked up yet another grievance against SOE's Independent French Section. Though Colonna had gone into Corsica under British auspices, the mission quite rapidly came under Giraud's aegis: Eisenhower involved Giraud, as Commander-in-Chief of French forces in North Africa, in the contingency planning for Corsica, which, if American strategy had prevailed in the Mediterranean theatre, would have had a more central role than the Quebec Conference decision to land in Sicily eventually awarded it.[18] When de Gaulle arrived in Algiers in June 1943, Colonna's mission was an accomplished fact.

Within two months Colonna had achieved some sort of co-ordination of the Resistance movement under his leadership, but it was an arrangement that conceded pride of place to the Front National. He claimed to have some good men at his command. He had also organised twelve dropping grounds for supplies. It was difficult for MASSINGHAM to keep pace with the demand for supplies created by this swift expansion. Colonna rightly insisted that arms must be sent without delay as a token of confidence, otherwise his men would lose heart and melt away.[19]

By June MASSINGHAM had four RAF Halifaxes from Tempsford temporarily based in Algeria for supply operations to Corsica, but the island proved difficult to supply by air.[20] Much of the eastern coastal plain was so heavily garrisoned by the Italians as to make clandestine reception impossible. The rest of the island was so mountainous that it was difficult to find dropping zones that were large enough and even approximately level: aircraft had to fly between mountain peaks and supplies that dropped wide of the mark fell down precipices. Supply by submarine therefore continued. In June HM S/m *Sibyl* (Lt E.J.D. Turner) was sent to southeastern Corsica with a consignment of arms. It carried, too, Lt R.J. Laming, RNVR, and PO Sam Smalley of SOE's Naval Section as conducting party. Laming was to meet Colonna by arrangement and discuss the situation with him. Colonna was at the pinpoint and came aboard the submarine for this discussion while the stores were being landed. As the boats pulled away from the beach after landing the last boatload, the Italians raised the alarm and began firing out to sea. The patriots on the beach fought their way out with the stores, but Colonna was marooned on the submarine. After failing next night to regain contact with his men on shore, he had to submit to returning on the submarine to Algiers.[21] This apparent mischance proved fortunate. The Allied Command, having decided on a major landing in Sicily (Operation HUSKY), ruled on 21 June that the liberation of Corsica should be a French military responsibility. SOE's – and hence Colonna's – activities in the island thus came under the operational control of the French general staff. In Algiers, Colonna was able to meet the French officers responsible and try to impress them with the potential represented by his organisation, of which they were, and remained, somewhat sceptical.[22]

The formation of the Bataillon de Choc under Commandant Fernand Gambiez was the limit of 'irregularity' the French officers concerned were capable of comprehending. For the training of this unit they gladly accepted the assistance of SOE instructors from MASSINGHAM, and they conceded that its function should be to stiffen Colonna's patriot units rather than to fight independently.

While he was in Algiers, Colonna was awarded the DSO. King George VI, who was on a visit to the British forces in North Africa and on more than one occasion came to MASSINGHAM's base at the Club des Pins for a swim and lunch, broke with precedent and bestowed it on Colonna personally, a rare honour for a non-British subject.[23]

Colonna also took advantage of his stay in Algiers to have a new horoscope cast. He was told that he would be surrounded by his enemies but that he would escape from them against all the odds.[24]

On the night of 1/2 July he was landed back in Corsica from the *Casabianca*. He had the satisfaction of knowing that his persistent demands for supplies were now being energetically met by MASSINGHAM, for on his return he brought with him an unprecedentedly large consignment of 11½ tons of arms. Many of these weapons had been salvaged by SOE after the surrender of the Axis forces in Tunisia, under an arrangement made by Dodds-Parker with AFHQ. They had been cleaned, greased and packed by SOE into manhandleable loads, using a variety of coverings, including Axis shell containers, to protect them from spray and damp while in transit.[25]

MASSINGHAM's Naval Staff and Training Section had been closely involved with *Casabianca*'s crew in devising and practising methods for landing these supplies, which were used operationally for the first time on this occasion. SOE had now been able to make available two of the lightweight plywood dories that the author designed and had built while at Helford in 1942. These had been adapted for submarine use by fitting in to their bottoms large, brass screw plugs or bungs – 'Kingstons' in submarine parlance – which, when removed, allowed the dories to flood and drain as the submarine dived or surfaced. With their thwarts removed, two of these dories could be nested one inside the other, like the heavier prototypes carried on the Grand Banks cod-fishermen which worked out of ports such as Saint-Malo under sail until the inter-war years. Two of these Helford dories were carried upside-down in a compartment on top of *Casabianca*'s pressure hull, under the forward deck casing. They had the directional stability that the aircraft rubber dinghies lacked, and the latter could, when loaded, be formed into a train of four or five boats, which would follow docilely in the dory's wake as a tow when the dory was rowed ashore. Ligthweight and secure radio-telephones had also been made available and were used for the first time to link the dories and the shore party back to the submarine.

Eight of *Casabianca*'s Seamen and Petty Officers had been put through a commando-type assault course by MASSINGHAM at the Club des Pins and were sent ashore first to reconnoitre, to 'stake out' the landing-point and find the best place to cache the landed material. While this was being done, the rubber dinghies provided by OSS were brought up on deck, fitted with their rigid wooden bottom boards and inflated by a lead from the ship's compressed-air system. They were then put into the water and aligned along one side of the surfaced submarine's deck casing; the submarine was in deep trim, with her bow resting on the sandy bottom, so that the boats could be more easily reached and loaded and there was no risk of her changing position while the landings were being carried out.

The beach chosen for the operation was the Plage-de-Saleccia, near Curza Point in the Désert-des-Agriates on the north coast – a region then so malarial that the Italians kept no permanent guard-posts there. It lies between the Genoese tower on Mortella Point –

the prototype of British Martello towers – and the cove where Nelson landed cannon from his squadron for the siege of Calvi.

It was a flat calm night and the scent of the *maquis* was pungent. As soon as the rubber boats were afloat and the dories had been lowered quietly into the water, *Casabianca*'s crew of 85 men were all put to work. A human chain was formed to convey the packages from the stowage-places that Bellet, the first lieutenant, had found for them in every part of the pressure hull – under the floor of the mess decks, in the shaft tunnels, in places where spare torpedoes would normally have been carried and even alongside the main diesel engines. The chain of dispatchers manhandled the packages, which weighed anything up to 70 lb., along slippery gangways and up through the hatches to a further chain of willing hands, which carried them forward and passed them down into the rubber boats.

The men worked rapidly and noiselessly, stripped to the waist and sweating like galley-slaves. They knew that a single slip, resulting in a metallic clang, might be picked up by enemy hydrophones and could lead to the loss of the submarine and all her crew.[26]

Each rubber boat could carry up to half a ton of material and, as soon as a 'train' of boats had been loaded, one of the dories would tow it ashore. The beach reconnaissance party, reinforced by men who had come ashore with the stores, then proceeded to unload the boats, passing the heavy packages from hand to hand to the place where they were to be concealed, pending collection by the Resistance. Though the whole ship's company toiled at the task all night, the job was not finished when imminent dawn brought proceedings to a halt not long after 0300 hours. All traces of the night's work were carefully effaced and everybody was brought back on board, except Colonna who decided to mount a discreet guard over the site until the following night and retained a radio-telephone for use when *Casabianca* surfaced after dark. The rubber boats were hauled on deck and deflated, the dories stowed away on top of the pressure hull, hatches closed and water was expelled from the ballast tanks so that *Casabianca*'s keel floated clear of the bottom. Then she slid silently astern into deep water to submerge and spend the daylight hours on the sea-bed a mile and a half offshore.

The author was on board as conducting officer for SOE, with Skipper Lt John Newton, LDG Seaman Frank Taylor and Able Seaman Don Miles, and went ashore at the outset. He had been involved for nearly two years in the problems of clandestine landings of material on enemy coasts. He found *Casabianca*'s achievement uniquely impressive. In one short summer's night L'Herminier and his crew had succeeded in landing and hiding 8 tons of arms and explosives in hostile territory without any outside help. No British submarine captain would have been allowed to take his submarine inshore to the point where she grounded, as a preliminary to sending the boats away. The way in which his large crew had worked together to make an operation of this size possible was in itself a remarkable tribute to L'Herminier's and Bellet's powers of leadership and to the efficiency and high morale of their crew.

It was much darker on the following night and one of the dories returning from the beach with a train of empty rubber boats missed *Casabianca*. Its departure from the beach had been reported by radio-telephone and, when it failed to appear alongside, L'Herminier decided to risk showing a few short flashes of light to seaward. It was not until 0230 hours that it came alongside, after an unnerving interlude in which it had pulled all round the bay looking for the submarine. But it was the only mishap in an otherwise flawless operation and by 0315 everyone was back on board except Colonna and his new W/T operator, Luc Le Fustec, who remained ashore, which was where their mission lay. Colonna was able to arrange for the entire cargo to be collected by the Resistance.

The author went down with malaria before the end of *Casabianca*'s 12-day patrol and, while he was away convalescing, L'Herminier was called upon to deliver a further large cargo of arms and ammunition to Corsica (Operation SCALP II). Colonna had told us that the next delivery would have to be made further south, because the material already landed would cater for the needs of the Resistance in the northern part of the island and it would be difficult for him to distribute to other areas because of Italian checks on movements by road. He asked MASSINGHAM by W/T to arrange that the next consignment be landed in the Gulf of Porto on the western coast of the island.[27]

Bellet again took careful stock of the available stowage space and this time all the rest of the ship's company joined in the hunt. With what L'Herminier later described as care and grim determination, they managed, by utilising every nook and cranny from one end of the submarine to the other, to stow away 20 tons of warlike stores, again carefully packaged by MASSINGHAM.

The Gulf of Porto is six miles deep and the dangers involved in mounting a large-scale landing of material in it on two successive nights were obvious, but L'Herminier felt that, if that was what Colonna needed, they must do their level best to respond. Four potential pinpoints were identified and Holdsworth arranged for high-level photographic reconnaissance to be carried out. L'Herminier's choice fell on the Anse-de-Gradella, though there were indications that there might be Italian coastal batteries not far from it.

MASSINGHAM's conducting party this time was led by Newton

and included Captain Michael Gubbins, son of SOE's chief executive, as well as PO Frank Taylor and Able Seaman Duff.

On the night of 29/30 July L'Herminier could not sleep and went up on to the bridge at 0100 hours. The smell of *maquis* was so strong that he could not help thinking they must be very much nearer land than they had reckoned, and he ordered the engines to be stopped. It was a warm, humid and very beautiful night, but he could see absolutely nothing through his night binoculars. He expected at that time to be 15 miles to the west of Cap Gargalo, where he planned to make his landfall at 0400 hours. The place had unpleasant memories for him, dating from their first mission to Corsica. He decided to stand north and south until the time came to submerge before dawn, when a quick periscope sighting would enable them to fix their position.

They proved to have been much closer to Gargalo than expected: indeed, they might have run straight on to it if L'Herminier's intuition had not told him to stop.

They proceeded into the middle of the gulf at a depth of 50 metres, travelling at 2 knots on the electric motors, and at 1430 hours settled down on the sea-bed within a short distance of their objective.

They surfaced at 2250 hours that night. Owing to the illusion that makes distances seem shorter at night, the southern shore of the gulf looked as if it was almost on top of them.

The coastal road passed above the Anse-de-Gradella but they hoped that they would be so close to the shore that they would be hidden from it by the dead angle of the cliffs. There was no signal from the reception committee they were expecting this time. L'Herminier set aside his misgivings and nosed in between the rocks until *Casabianca*'s stern touched bottom about 100 metres from the beach.

The rubber boats were brought up on deck. The dories entered the water soundlessly and the reconnaissance group took their places on board them, but they had gone no more than a few metres when heavy firing broke out from both sides and machine-gun bullets began to whistle around them. The dory crews clambered back on board and L'Herminier ordered full astern, instructing Bellet to put the submarine into deep trim by the stern as they disengaged themselves from the rocks and headed towards the open sea, six miles to the westward. L'Herminier did not dive because he was anxious to save the boats spread out on the foredeck, but the dories broke free and were lost in the darkness. Gradually the firing died away and it was possible to send men out on to the foredeck to collect the rubber boats. It had been a close shave.

But L'Herminier was *vir tenax propositi*. When he got to the open sea, he headed north at 17 knots under the diesels towards the

Curza pinpoint they had used successfully four weeks earlier. And, though bereft of their dories, they managed, with the help of their rubber dinghies and an ungainly steel boat they had had made in the dockyard at Oran, to land and conceal what must surely have been a world record of 20 tons of arms on the nights of 30/31 July and 31 July/1 August, again without the help of a reception committee.[28]

After this second success *Casabianca's* stock stood high with MASSINGHAM and Holdsworth attempted to get her permanently allocated to SOE for operations of this type. There had, however, been some friction between *Casabianca's* crew and the SOE conducting party in the course of SCALP II and consequently Holdsworth's proposal was turned down.

Casabianca did one further, though smaller, supply run to the Golfe-de-Lava on 5/6 September, when she landed Lt Giannesini, a Gaullist agent, together with a radio operator and 5 tons of stores, this time without any SOE conducting party. The reception party was organised by Henri Maillot, de Gaulle's cousin, who was prominent in the local Front National. This brought the total landed by this submarine to 61 tons. She also picked up Arthur Giovoni, the Communist leader of the Front National at Ajaccio. He was carrying a copy of the Italian defence plan for the island, which had been made available to the Resistance by a Lt Col Gagnoni, whose father had been a Republican senator and who had served three years in prison for his anti-Fascist views.

Weather had been bad for aircraft supply in July but in August and September the number of air drops was substantially increased to bring the total of supplies delivered by air to well in excess of 160 tons. A final delivery of 28 tons by *Serenini*, under temporary command of Lt C. Long, RNR, of the African Coastal Flotilla, and another by one of the ACF feluccas on 16 September, after the Italian armistice, brought the total of stores landed by sea and by air from MASSINGHAM to approximately 250 tons.[29]

After his return to Corsica at the beginning of July, Colonna had had a very narrow escape in circumstances that strikingly bore out the prediction of his astrologer. Circulating from one Maquis cell to another, frequently on bicycle and in the uniform of a gendarme, he was caught up one day in a major drive by Italian troops designed to flush Maquisards out of their protective scrub cover. He sought refuge by lying down on the ground in the middle of a flock of sheep and goats. If the flock had moved on, as they do when grazing, he would have been exposed and captured but they did not, perhaps because they were resting in shade from the heat of the day. He continued to arm his organisation and faced the problems of D-Day in Corsica with 12,000 armed men at his back.[30]

The nucleus of this force was the Communist-led Front National.

Colonna believed he had persuaded this organisation temporarily to lay politics aside and to accept in alliance any group that was genuinely patriotic and sought affiliation. Colonna saw to it that the supplies of arms, which he controlled, went only to those groups that were prepared to do so.

In the last days of August, the probability of an Italian capitulation – well known to MASSINGHAM, which was handling the signals traffic between the Badoglio Government and General Eisenhower, though not to General Giraud – began to have its effect on the Italian troops in Corsica. Colonna was in touch with Colonel Cagnoni at Bastia who controlled the defences of the port and the airfield. Shrewdly suspecting what was about to happen, Cagnoni promised to bring the troops under his command into action against the Germans and to persuade some of his colleagues to do the same. In the event, this was indeed the only area in which Italian troops played an active part in hampering the German withdrawal.[31]

The Germans already had 5,000 troops in southern Corsica and it was known in Algiers that they planned to withdraw their much larger force in Sardinia under command of General Ritter von Senger und Etterlin to Corsica. In view of this, proposals for a paramilitary insurrection of patriot forces in the island were rejected as too hazardous. Eisenhower knew from ULTRA that, though the Germans had originally intended to hold Corsica, they changed their minds on 13 September and proceeded to withdraw, via the ports and airfields of the island's eastern coastal plain, to the Italian mainland.[32]

When the armistice was made public on 8 September and the Corsicans saw the Germans executing an orderly and unhampered withdrawal, there was no holding them. It was their last chance to strike a blow at the enemy who had aroused their resentment in a way the easygoing Italians had never succeeded in doing. They brought their weapons out from their hiding-places and started an insurrection. Led by Colonna, who narrowly escaped being betrayed to the Germans (there was a price on his head), they joined with the Italians and seized Bastia. But the German-held area was limited to a narrow strip along the east coast, which was the only site of enemy movement. Elsewhere the Resistance had no enemy to attack, for the bulk of the 80,000 Italian troops followed their General into passive and ignominious neutrality. The bands were prepared to conduct guerilla warfare against second-rate troops in their own locality, but not to undertake a long march across country to fight far from their homes. Of two thoroughly practical prerequisites – boots and food – there was a lack that could not be made good. Consequently the brunt of the fighting was borne by the bands in the eastern coastal strip; the bulk of what SOE called at the time 'the patriot forces' were never engaged.[33]

Help was now on its way and on 11 September General Giraud sent Colonna an order to dispose his patriots in defence of Ajaccio in order to ensure a bridgehead for the landings of French troops.

Two days later the *Casabianca* arrived at Ajaccio, having made the passage from Algiers on the surface, carrying 109 men, almost all members of the Bataillon de Choc: L'Herminier had achieved his ambition to have *Casabianca* become the first French ship to enter a liberated port in metropolitan France. The French submarine *La-Perle* (under Lt Paumier) followed on 16 September in support. Paumier persuaded the captain of the Toulon–Ajaccio ferry to sail to Algiers and he also landed 3 tons of much-needed flour. The French submarine *Aréthuse* (Lt Goutier) arrived on 18 September carrying 5 tons of munitions, before going on to Cap-Camarat to land five officers and embark seven, together with the colours of the 2ième Dragon Regiment.[34]

Casabianca had also landed a joint SOE–Deuxième Bureau mission consisting of Major Jacques de Guélis, head of MASSING-HAM's French Country Section, and Commandant Clipet from General Ronin's office, for liaison with the patriot forces.[35] The task of the Bataillon de Choc was to consolidate and extend the bridgehead, which was held throughout the brief campaign. Colonna was by now a sick man, so Clipet assumed command of all patriot forces. He was handicapped in his task by the French professional soldier's characteristic dislike of the 'irregular'. Instead of using the patriot bands for sabotage and ambushes, to which they were suited, and supporting them with more highly trained and disciplined troops, he wanted to incorporate them as an integral part of the Bataillon de Choc and make them fight 'in the line'. One company of picked men, to whom he was able to give boots, rations and transport, fought with spirit and success; but other units, obliged reluctantly to leave their home areas and march on foot to the front, arrived there so hungry and exhausted as to be valueless as combatants.

On 13 September, the day the Bataillon de Choc landed at Ajaccio, the Germans, recovering from their surprise, drove the Italians out of Bastia and cleared their line of withdrawal up the coast road from Bonifacio and Porto-Vecchio. For a few days their retreat was hampered by demolitions and skirmishes with the local patriots and the Italians who had joined forces with them. But ammunition and explosives soon ran short and the penury of available transport in the island apart from Italian military vehicles meant that no reinforcements could be brought up. Thus, although many of the patriots had ammunition but no occasion to use it, others operating in vital areas were soon reduced, by lack of it, to guides and intelligence scouts. Certainly they did good service, but these were not the capacities for which they had been recruited and equipped by SOE.[36]

Meanwhile the Germans executed a leisurely withdrawal with the precision of a text-book manoeuvre. The French 'offensive', launched with African troops on 20 September, never caught up with them; indeed, it interfered with their movements far less than the Italians and the patriots had done in the first few critical days at Bastia, when the German commander on three occasions sent emissaries to Colonna endeavouring to persuade him, by a mixture of threats and promises, to call the patriots off. Two SOE parties established with their W/T sets in the forward areas could only report the day-to-day dispositions of the German units: they could not make good the French troops' lack of transport or clear the minefields that slowed their methodical advance. When the motorised 4th Spahis at last swept round Cap-Corse into Bastia on the morning of 4 October, they found that the last Germans had left the previous night.

SOE found it difficult to assess MASSINGHAM's contribution to the campaign: it was not clear whether the existence of a formidable patriot force in Corsica, of which the Germans were certainly aware, influenced the decision to withdraw their forces from Corsica as well as Sardinia. If it did, SOE's work in the island might be judged to have paid a handsome dividend in saving many French lives, which would certainly have been lost if a landing had encountered determined German opposition. If it did not, SOE itself conceded that the fruits of MASSINGHAM's labours were less easy to determine. Elaborate plans to isolate and hamper bodies of Italian troops scattered throughout the island could not abruptly be switched to provide a concentration of force against a narrow, though extended, area on one side of the island held by the Germans. The Corsican population had not been persecuted under Italian occupation to anything like the extent that the population of metropolitan France had been by the time the Allies landed there in 1944. Patriotic young Corsicans had not been driven into the mountains by the threat of forced labour in Germany, as befell their contemporaries in southern mainland France during 1943 and much of 1944. Nor had they experienced the savagery of reprisals against their relations and homes. When in September 1943 the Corsican patriot thought, in the peaceful security of his village, about the duty he had undertaken to perform, it was to wish he had a long-range rifle rather than a short-range Sten gun. If he failed to answer a blunt call to leave his home and undertake the unforeseen hazards of a campaign of movement, it was an understandable human failure.[37]

Colonna's insistence that SOE provide weapons for long-range fighting in mountainous country – rifles, anti-tank rifles and light machine-guns – was an important lesson, which certainly had an effect on SOE's future thinking.

In a memoir published 20 years after the end of the war, Senger und Etterlin described the reasons that led to the decision to evacuate Corsica rather than to defend it. The mission to evacuate Sardinia and defend Corsica, with which he was charged by Kesselring at the beginning of September, was political as well as military: he had to convince General Magli, the Italian corps commander in Corsica, to cooperate with him even in the event of a separate Italian armistice and, in the event of a refusal, to disarm the Italian troops.[38]

From the outset on 9 September the Germans were sufficiently mistrustful to take charge of strategic points on the east coast of Corsica. Magli had received Etterlin on the evening of 8 September and, Etterlin claims, had offered 'to support him in so far as was possible, to facilitate the transfer of German troops from Sardinia, to checkmate the rebellion of armed French bands and to have his coastal artillery reply to any bombardment from the sea.' Etterlin was pleased to have made these arrangements 'by the diplomatic channel' and considered them indispensable to allow him to act on his own initiative.

The agreement, if indeed it existed, fell to pieces immediately: the German garrison at Bastia, on an order given by the German naval authorities without Etterlin's knowledge, attempted to seize the port and the Italian vessels lying in it. The *coup de main* failed: Etterlin described it as foolish and contrary to Germany's own interests.

Magli, who asked for nothing better than to stay neutral, was informed by Colonna d'Istria on 9 September that an Allied expeditionary force was on its way. Called on to state immediately his position, 'With us, against us or neutral', Magli replied, 'With you'.

On 12 September the first elements of Senger und Etterlin's 90th Panzer–Grenadier Division landed at Bonifacio and on the mainland the Wehrmacht began to disarm the Italians. Magli realised that his two-faced posture was untenable: he was not going to be able to 'continue to collaborate with the Germans even as a neutral.' That evening there was a meeting between him and Etterlin, which the latter described as 'dramatic'. From that point on, the German commander realised that he, with one division and one brigade, 35,000 men in all, would be in no position to disarm four divisions of Italians. Still less would he be able to disarm the Corsican Resistance, whose numbers he did not know but who had given 'unmistakable proof of their fanaticism.' He decided to hold the eastern side only of the island's dorsal mountain chain. He was relieved next day, 13 September, to receive fresh orders not to defend Corsica but to transfer the German forces to the mainland. As he proceeded to put this plan into effect, he was disturbed by an astonishing order, brought to him on 16 September by General Westphal, Kesselring's Chief of Staff, to seize control of the road from Ajaccio to Bastia – an order he subsequently described as requiring him to reconquer the island before evacuating it. He managed to persuade his superior to renounce this stupid idea.

MASSINGHAM's achievement in arming virtually every mobilisable male member of the Corsican population had not been in vain.

On the political plane, the spectacle of the Front National taking over every Mairie in the island added fuel to the crisis in the relations between de Gaulle and Giraud. Giraud was forced out of his co-presidency of the Committee of National Liberation by de Gaulle even while the island was in the throes of liberation. De Gaulle put paid to Giraud's plans to install military government in the island and sent Charles Luizet there as Préfet. De Gaulle held SOE partly responsible for a situation he was determined to avoid in mainland France and de Guélis had to be replaced as head of MASSINGHAM's French Country Section. The author, instead of going to Corsica to conduct clandestine sea-transport operations for SOE to north-western Italy and south-eastern France, was asked to take over the Section.

Submarine operations had paid a unique part in the liberation of Corsica and it is no accident that when *Casabianca* came to be scrapped after the war, her bridge, conning-tower and gun-platform were preserved as a monument in the citadel at Bastia.

It is sad to have to record that Jean L'Herminier – far too old by the Royal Navy's standards for service in submarines – paid a terrible price for his determination to remain at his post until he had completed the job: a clot developed in one of his legs, and by the time his doctor had decided they must amputate, it had moved to the other leg, which had also to be sacrificed. His courage in affliction was as great as in war, but he died in 1947.

CHAPTER XLII

Operations from Bastia

I n April 1943, as a result of negotiations between SIS and the Admiralty and a suggestion that NID(C) should be merged into the Admiralty's Operations Division, Captain Slocum again visited North Africa. Admiral Cunningham, Commander-in-Chief Mediterranean, agreed to this proposal. He made it clear to Slocum that irregular operations did not interest him in the least but that he would suffer them provided that a clear-cut policy was laid down and that they came under one central control. Slocum became Deputy Director Operations Division (Irregular) – DDOD(I) – in June and his African Coastal Flotilla (ACF) was accepted by Allied Force Headquarters as the controlling authority for clandestine sea transport in the Western Mediterranean theatre of operations. In due course this arrangement was extended as far east as the Adriatic, but it was effectively rejected by Middle East Command, with the result that SIS, SOE and the Special Boat Squadron continued to operate separate flotillas of caiques and schooners in the Aegean, while sea transport to Yugoslavia and Albania involved a complex interface of command responsibilities.[1]

In the meantime, Captain Osborne had handed over command of the ACF to Captain R.E.T. Tunbridge, DSC, RNR. On the advice of the clandestine authorities in London, a Special Operations Committee was set up under the chairmanship of Brigadier Sugden of Allied Force Headquarters to decide transport priorities. Captain Tunbridge and Holdsworth, as naval representative of SOE, both attended as nautical advisers until Holdsworth was appointed head of SOE's MARYLAND mission to Italy, following the Italian armistice.[2]

Submarine transport, which played such a substantial part in operations to Corsica before the Liberation, in practice escaped the jurisdiction of ACF and DDOD(I). The feluccas, *balancennes* and a small, local motor trawler named *Cyrus-Joseph*, which were the only potentially operational craft under the direct control of ACF, made a peripheral contribution only to the liberation of Corsica. *Seawolf* was sent in April to attempt to land two agents in the north-west of the island, but failed owing to bad weather and active enemy shore patrols; the experiment was not repeated, as submarines were available and more effective. Indeed, with the eviction of the German and Italian forces from North Africa, enemy shipping targets had become scarce and the 8th Submarine Flotilla were glad to

carry out cloak-and-dagger operations; these, when successful, were added to the submarine's battle honours, in the form of a small dagger symbol on the piratical black flag with skull and cross-bones that British submarines had adopted and flew in celebration on their return from patrol.

United States PT boats – the equivalent of the Royal Navy's MTBs – were used in June and July to land agents for SIS in north-western and south-western Sicily before the Allied invasion of the island (HUSKY), but attempts by the ACF's feluccas *Welcome, Seawolf, Seadog* and the trawler *Cyrus-Joseph* to carry out operations to Sardinia and the Naples area failed in five cases out of seven; and on three occasions the vessels were attacked by friendly aircraft.

As the invasion of Sicily progressed, the demand for intelligence from Italy increased. Local fishing activities in Italian waters were so scarce that operations by vessels of fishing types were unlikely to provide a solution to the needs of the clandestine agencies. How-ever, once Sicily was in Allied hands, operations by fast craft out of Palermo seemed to be a good way of meeting their requirements. After preliminary arrangements with the American naval comman-der, DDOD(I)'s local organisation was given permission to use United States PT craft from that port, which was under complete American control. In July Slocum visited the area to obtain the approval of the British naval authorities for this arrangement. In spite of American willingness to cooperate, Admiral Cunningham categorically refused to release any craft possessing offensive poten-tialities for clandestine operations. Slocum returned to London and subsequent suggestions and requests from the Admiralty achieved nothing. Again all irregular operations had been brought to a standstill, as by now it was quite impossible to operate fishing vessels in the areas from which intelligence was so desperately required.[3]

However, Slocum sent Whinney out to the Mediterranean to carry out a reconnaissance of Bastia to assess the damage to the port. Geographically it offered important advantages for operations to the Italian mainland, as compared with Maddalena in Sardinia: whereas Maddalena and Anzio, which lie in the same latitude, are 320 km. apart, Bastia is a mere 40 km. from Elba.[4]

Maddalena had been in Allied hands since the German with-drawal in September 1943 and a British naval base had been established there under the redoubtable Captain N.V. Dickinson, who had been so helpful to SOE's BRANDON mission in the early days of the Tunisian campaign. Plans were already afoot to move the British, Canadian and American fast craft assembled at Mad-dalena forward to Bastia as soon as practicable and Whinney took passage northwards on a 'B'-Class ML to prospect.

SOE had already formed and sent forward from Algiers to

Corsica a mission code-named BALACLAVA, which was the first unit to arrive in the island with the intention of carrying out operations from there to the adjacent coasts of Italy and south-eastern France. Though an emanation of MASSINGHAM's Naval Section, it was under the command of Major N.A.C. Croft, well known before the war as an Arctic explorer, with Lt Fisher Howe, US Naval Reserve, an OSS officer, as his deputy. An advance party left Algiers on 28 September in *Serenini*, loaded down with 15 tons of boats, stores and equipment, which Croft had assembled with the care born of his experience in Greenland, North East Land and Spitzbergen. Skipper Lt John Newton, *Serenini* commanding officer, was in the United Kingdom on sick leave, so his place was taken by Lt Long of Slocum's African Coastal Flotilla. ACF volunteered the use of all their feluccas but only one of them proved able to carry a worthwhile amount of cargo. The expedition put in first to Ajaccio, where Croft made contact with de Guélis's mission, with Brigadier-General Peake, AFHQ's representative, and with General Martin, who commanded the French troops in the island. *Serenini* then proceeded to Calvi, where a base was established. A few days later, when the Germans had completed their leisurely evacuation of Corsica by air and sea, Croft moved to the port of Bastia, where he set up BALACLAVA's main headquarters.[5]

BALACLAVA's arrival at Bastia had preceded Whinney's and, on the morning after Whinney landed from Maddalena, he made contact with Croft with a view to sending a signal back to Maddalena. He found SOE's unit installed in a modern villa, with a tidy garden and a pleasant patio overlooking the sea, though the furniture consisted for the most part of ration boxes and army trestle tables. Over a bottle of gin, Croft offered Whinney all the help he might need. Cooperation between SIS and SOE seemed to have got off to a good start, but it was still quite unclear what vessels would be available to exploit the geographical advantages of Bastia as an operational base for the needs of the clandestine agencies.[6]

When Whinney reported back to Dickinson at Maddalena, a wonderful surprise awaited him. Maddalena had been an important base for the Italian navy's MAS boats – the equivalent of the Royal Navy's Coastal Forces craft or American PT boats – and, as a result of the armistice and the Badoglio Government's co-belligerency, these flotillas had passed under Allied command. The problem that faced Dickinson, however, was what operational use could be made of them. As he had pointed out when he took them over, it would be foolish in the extreme to expect the crews of these vessels to go out and engage their ex-Allies or, even worse, their own compatriots, at sea.[7]

While Whinney was making his report about the state of Bastia, Dickinson cut him short. After enquiring casually about Whinney's plans, which centred, perforce, on the ACF's unusable array of fishing vessels, he went on to explain his predicament over the MAS boats. He suggested that Whinney should consider using them as a better alternative to his fishing craft. It was a solution that would relieve him of the embarrassment of finding something for them to do and provide Whinney with fast craft suitable for clandestine sea-transport needs.

Whinney could hardly believe his luck, though he was by no means certain that DDOD(I) would approve the idea. He knew that for Slocum the safety of his passengers was always paramount and there were undeniable risks in employing what had so recently been enemy crews in a conflict in which Italian Fascists loyal to the ousted and discredited dictator were still fighting alongside the Germans.

There were three types of MAS boat: the largest, 120 feet long, was a copy of the German E-boats and fitted with diesel engines; there was a 60-foot variety with twin 500 h.p. Isotta-Fraschinis and a 47-foot version of rather similar Italian design. Whinney signalled all the relevant particulars to his master and, after a certain amount of humming and hawing arising out of his natural caution, Slocum accepted that there was really no alternative and sent his approval and good wishes.

Whinney concluded that the 60-foot boats were the most suitable for his purposes. By removing their torpedo tubes, which increased the deck space available for carrying dinghies, their top speed could be enhanced from 37 to 47 knots, speeds vastly superior to those of which even Slocum's 15th Motor Gunboat Flotilla working in the English Channel were capable. The MAS boats' auxiliaries gave them a cruising speed of 6 knots and they were supposed to be silent, though Whinney found that, with an onshore light air, they could be heard as a rather high-pitched whine when the boat was a mile or more from the beach.

Dickinson told the senior officer of the Italian naval base to arrange for his MAS boats to be sent up to Bastia as soon as he had finished what could be only a fairly perfunctory vetting of the crews. By this time several of the feluccas and other fishing vessels of the African Coastal Flotilla had joined *Seadog* at Maddalena and Whinney proceeded to select from their crews eight dinghymen to form four operational teams to accompany his conducting officers when work with the Italian MAS boats began. When he was ready to return to Bastia, Dickinson instructed him to find accommodation there for both himself and his staff, as he wished to move forward as soon as possible and begin the new operational phase in which he was to become Senior Officer Inshore Squadron.

Croft found it a great advantage during the critical settling-in period at Bastia to have an American, in the person of Fisher Howe, as his first lieutenant.[8] Before leaving Algiers, both officers had privately told the author, who was still handling SOE's Naval Section business while taking over MASSINGHAM's French Country Section, that they had doubts as to whether they could work well together, but their fears proved groundless: they rapidly came to appreciate each other's qualities and became firm friends. It was a very effective partnership. Liaison with the United States 63rd Fighter Wing and the OSS mission at Bastia under Lt Col Russell Livermore was excellent. Livermore had under his command two of the 15-man Operational Groups (OGs), created by 'Big Bill' Donovan as an integral part of OSS, on the lines of the British SAS. These particular OGs were composed of Italian-speaking officers and enlisted men. Donovan, who was up to his eyebrows in Washington politics and anxious for OSS to be seen to be where action lay, had rushed them to Corsica as soon as opportunity offered, and was in a hurry to see them operationally involved. Dickinson personified inter-Allied cooperation. The uniquely friendly atmosphere that emerged at Bastia in the closing months of 1943 was enhanced by the fact that the headquarters of Fighter Wing, Coastal Forces, ISLD (as SIS called itself for cover purposes), OSS and SOE's BALACLAVA mission were all situated within 150 metres of one another. Attached to BALACLAVA was an 'A' Force unit, which dealt with Allied escapers and evaders and operated usually under SIS auspices. In this case, for convenience, it joined up with Croft's mission. Also attached briefly to BALACLAVA was Commander Dunstan Curtis's intelligence procurement force, which also normally operated under the wing of SIS. This section was soon withdrawn to the United Kingdom for use in OVER-LORD, but Croft retained the services of its highly qualified intelligence officer, Lieutenant 'Paddy' Davies. At BALACLAVA's headquarters Davies helped Croft organise what proved to be a first-class intelligence 'pool', which was shared by members of the various special services and certain officers of Coastal Forces, the French general staff, Deuxième Bureau and Lt Col Fernand Gambiez's Bataillon de Choc. It was against this background of goodwill and efficiently coordinated planning that the local operational difficulties of the Allied Special Forces were tackled and resolved. The wise and firm guidance of Captain N.V. Dickinson was all-important. The author was present when Croft invited Dickinson to dinner at Bastia early in the New Year for a council of war. Something had to be done, Croft said, to keep SIS in general – and Lt Cmdr Pat Whinney in particular – from swallowing up SOE's BALACLAVA mission whole and removing all his freedom of action. Dickinson was firm: BALACLAVA could certainly help SIS when asked; they could also land agents for the Americans and the French, of course, since they had the expertise; but they were an independent group and must remain so.[9]

To Croft's regret, Howe, whose role in sorting out relations with the local American authorities had been so valuable, was ordered back to OSS headquarters in London two months after BALA-CLAVA's arrival in the island and before operations out of Bastia had begun. He was not replaced.

The crews of the Italian MAS boats, the first six of which were now at Whinney's disposal, remained an unknown quantity. Whinney, in his book *Corsican Command*, recalled how, on the day after their arrival from Maddalena, they were drawn up for his inspection, fallen in along the jetty with their backs to the water. Each crew was separated from its neighbour by a gap of two or three metres. Whinney felt that a formal inspection of this type was not really his form at all: he would have preferred to go round each boat while the hands were working but, as he discovered then and on a number of subsequent occasions, the Italians could be sticklers for formality. After a very grand salute from the Italian commanding officer, a formal handshake and a second, even grander salute, the commanding officer led off to introduce the first of the MAS boat captains, who were all somewhere between 25 and 30 years of age. The salute, which Whinney described as a sort of abrupt shading of the eyes, as if from a sudden blinding light, and the handshake were repeated and off they went to inspect the next crew, which was rigidly at attention, looking smart and clean.

They were half-way along this second crew when one of the ratings took a brisk pace forward, raised his arm palm downward in the Nazi salute and said quite loudly, 'Heil Hitler!' There followed a moment of acute embarrassment for everybody, not least for the man himself, who looked round sheepishly to see what his shipmates thought. They afforded him no comfort. Something had to be done. Whinney resisted an impulse to push the man into the water, which was only about two metres behind him. Turning to the commanding officer, whose face was locked in horror, he asked him to tell the man that he was now supposed to be fighting on the other side. The commanding officer favoured Whinney with an understanding shading of the eyes and then addressed himself to the offender. Under the ensuing avalanche of reprimand, the man dissolved into what Whinney described as a 'grease-spot'. The effect was not lost on his shipmates, although further down the long line there were one or two other 'Heil Hitler's. Each got the same impressive treatment, which Whinney felt would have done credit to a Whale Island instructor. It did provide some sort of rough yardstick of unreliability, but the changes made at that time did not, alas, eradicate all the culprits.

Over a glass of wine after the inspection, Whinney said that the episode should perhaps be regarded as a blessing in disguise – a means of separating goats from sheep. As he outlined what the

MAS boats might be expected to do, the formality of the proceedings gradually relaxed. There would be no offensive activity against
their compatriots fighting on the other side or against their erstwhile allies, the Germans. Of course, if the other side attacked, they
would have to reply in kind. But, as proof of their new peaceable
vocation, the Allies would be asking them to remove their torpedo
tubes, leaving them a couple of light machine-guns and a 20-mm.
cannon mounted on the stern to discourage pursuers. It was
impossible at that stage for him to go further, but the Italians
seemed relieved by what they had heard.

Next morning, the Italian commanding officer chose a young,
red-headed Lieutenant, who was captain of one of the boats, to be
Whinney's guide. He proved to a member of the well-known
Triestine ship-owning family of Cosulich. Because of his wiry red
hair, he quickly became known to his new British colleagues as
'Ginger'. Whinney found *MAS 541*, under Ginger's command,
all that he could have wished: a minimum of spit and polish, but
with everything neat, tidy and well maintained. Good morale
prevailed on board and Whinney was favourably impressed by
the personality and high professional competence of 541's engine-
room chief, Capo Pulchri. When invited into the diminutive wardroom for a first glass of wine, Whinney discovered that 541's battle
honours, inscribed on a bulkhead, included HMS *Fiji*, the British
cruiser sunk during the German airborne invasion of Crete in April
1941.

Notwithstanding Admiral Cunningham's ban, in the no-moon
period early in November, *ML 576*, a British 'B'-Class Fairmile
boat, was used to land two OSS agents in the Livorno area and,
three nights later, to put three officers and eight enlisted men of an
OSS Operational Group ashore on Capraia Island with stores and
a W/T set.[10]

By the end of November Whinney's ACF unit was ready to
operate with the Italian MAS boats. Careful observation had
convinced him that Ginger Cosulich was the most experienced
and reliable of the young Italian MAS boat captains; he was also
the one with whom he had worked first and got to know best.
Fortunately the Italian commander concurred in Whinney's choice
of Cosulich for this all-important first operation. In his book
Whinney described the operation that he and Andrew Croft undertook in *MAS 541* on the night of 2/3 December, in which two SOE
agents were landed at Deiva, between Sestri Levante and Moneglia
on the east side of the Gulf of Genoa. He called it the first such
expedition, but Slocum's records show a successful operation for
SOE to the Porto Potenza area on 27 November using an Italian
MAS boat to land an 'unspecified force'.[11]

Shortly after Christmas two operations to France became

necessary – one for OSS, the other for SIS. This posed a new problem because the pinpoints involved lay 150 miles from Bastia – a round trip of 300 miles, which was far longer than previous operations to the Italian mainland. This meant shipping extra fuel tanks in the form of mattress-like plastic bags and lightening the MAS boats by cutting down on crew numbers, though the sorties were certain to be protracted. Cosulich had often had to do this when fighting on the side of the Axis, but it was something no captain of a high-speed fighting vessel liked doing as it made the ship more vulnerable.

The first expedition involved landing two French agents for OSS, and was undertaken by Croft.[12] Tom Maxted of ACF was in overall charge of the expedition. In his report (to the author) dated 9 January 1943, Croft says that, owing to a misunderstanding, they sailed on 28 December later than had been planned but, after three and a half hours at 30 and then 35 knots, they switched over to the auxiliaries and, at about midnight, the loom of the Ile-du-Levant appeared ahead. Course was altered to the northward but, with a speed of only 6 knots, they did not reach the target area until 0425 hours. Five minutes later, some 825 metres ESE of the Cap-du-Pinet, the rubber dinghy, manned by himself and Able Seaman Don Miles, left with the two passengers.

The coast between the Cap-du-Pinet and the Pointe-du-Capon had been marked in a beach interpretation report as precipitous and studded with offshore rocks and shoals. The shallowness of the offshore water and the fact that the highest peak near the coast was only just over 120 metres had, however, been taken into account; and these factors, combined with a promising-looking stream valley, indicated that a suitable place for a 'blind' landing could be found, even though the hinterland appeared from intelligence to be well defended.

As it turned out, the landing-place was almost ideal, as the inshore rocks provided a natural camouflage for the rubber dinghy. Miles made a reconnaissance and discovered a track leading up through thick woods from the coast to the interior. The agents, who throughout had shown complete unconcern, now disembarked and went their way. Croft and Miles were back on board within 50 minutes of leaving the boat.

The operation had proved surprisingly easy, the only difficulty being to find the MAS boat, since she had shifted her position nearly a mile. In this one respect it was fortunate that the night was brightly starlit.

When dawn broke, 541 was only 30 miles from the French coast. Croft wrote that great credit was due to Maxted and Cosulich for their determination in proceeding with the operation in spite of their late arrival in the target area, and in carrying it out with decision and judgment.

The second operation, which was for SIS, involved handing over a parcel containing money to a member of Marie-Madeleine Fourcade's 'Alliance' network and collecting in return a parcel containing intelligence.[13]

On the morning of 29 December Whinney received a signal from London giving a pinpoint near Cavalaire, which, when plotted on to the chart, differed by about 900 metres from that previously indicated. He sent an urgent signal pointing out this discrepancy and asking for clarification, but the matter had not been resolved by the time they put to sea. It was a familiar problem, since agents in the field used map coordinates on Michelin maps, while sailors worked in latitude and longitude. Then there was a hold-up owing to late delivery of petrol, which was in very short supply in the island. They sailed an hour late but, by the time they reached Cap-Corse and turned west, they had used up enough fuel to increase speed from 30 to 35 knots. There was just enough swell to cause the plastic deck tanks to wallow awkwardly and make the boat lurch from time to time, but the problem resolved itself as the fuel was used up and finally the extra tanks were empty and could be rolled up and stowed amidships. Whinney found three and a half hours at 35 knots, with minimal protection on the bridge against wind and weather in mid-winter, a chilling experience and was glad when they reduced speed and switched over to the auxiliaries for the final approach, which lasted two full hours.

It was glassy calm as they closed in with the Iles-d'Hyeres to port and Cap-Camarat to starboard. The noise of the auxiliaries was worryingly loud to Whinney but they had made up for their late start and arrived punctually at the pinpoint. Whinney thought he had ordered the ship to stop 680 metres from the shore, but it turned out to be nearly double that distance. He and Petty Officer Bates reached the shore in their rubber dinghy at 0210 hours, ten minutes after schedule; but was it the right pinpoint? When nobody had turned up after 20 minutes, they decided to try the alternative position, about 900 metres to the east. There was nobody there either and, after another 20 minutes, they paddled round into the next bay before returning to their original position. While they were waiting beside the jetty that was supposed to be the meeting-place, a searchlight was switched on three times from somewhere just above their heads: it shone in the direction where the MAS boat had been when they left her but did not pick her up.

At 0400, half an hour before the agreed time limit would be up, they realised they must leave if they were to rejoin MAS 541 before she left for Bastia. Indeed, they had cut the time rather too fine, but fortunately Ranald Boyle, one of Whinney's officers, who was in charge of the MAS boat in Whinney's absence, realised that they were further from the shore than they had reckoned and stood inshore to collect them. Just when they were beginning to despair of finding 541 before the deadline ran out, there she was, bearing down on them. Five minutes later they were on the way back to base.

On two successive nights Cosulich and his crew had done two 300-mile expeditions, a feat achieved by none of the MGBs of Slocum's Dartmouth Flotilla. The operation was successfully completed at a third attempt on 28 January.

Between 6 December 1943 and 24 July 1944 there were 18 clandestine sea-transport operations to the coast of Provence by high-speed craft operating from Corsica. Five of the latter were undertaken by Italian MAS boats, the rest by United States PT craft. Details of these are listed in Appendix D. There were also ten operations to the Barcelona area on behalf of the French Deuxième Bureau, all by French submarines; this provided an alternative route to and from France after the Bon-Porté Bay pinpoint had to be abandoned.[14]

Since there were no Lysander or Dakota pick-up operations into southern France until June 1944, these contacts by sea were more important than their number might suggest and provided Rivet's Service de Renseignements and Paillole's Direction de Surveillance du Territoire with a large volume of intelligence. SOE's MAS-SINGHAM would have made greater use of operations by sea from Corsica if an agent named François Pelletier, whom they had trained and sent in to carry out the landward end, had not been betrayed, arrested and executed.[15]

The main importance of the Bastia base was, however, in relation to the campaign in Italy: Allied high-speed craft mounted more than 90 operations to the Ligurian coast and the off-lying islands between November 1943 and the end of July 1944 for the Allied clandestine services. These lie beyond the proper scope of this book but they were carried out by the same crews and the same boats as operated to Provence, and a number of them were for the French Deuxième Bureau, the Bataillon de Choc, the Service de Renseignements and the BCRA. When Cosulich's MAS 541 was blown up and sunk by a mine during an operation to the Italian coast with the loss of all hands, a French Frigate Captain was on board, as well as Lt Dow, RNR, one of Whinney's officers.[16]

Though the distances to many of these pinpoints were relatively short, conditions were by no means easy, as the craft had to cross continuous coastal traffic of well-armed and escorted convoys organised by the Germans to and from Genoa. Vessels due to carry out a landing quite often had to be escorted and the operation had to be staged in a bay, so as to be inside the enemy convoy traffic, which nevertheless hugged the coast with annoying affection. About a third of all these operations were carried out by MAS boats, though one Italian crew on passage from Bastia to Maddalena murdered their officers and defected.

The MAS and PT boats employed lacked the specialist navigational equipment and skills available in the 15th MGB Flotilla at Dartmouth and the success rate was correspondingly lower, but Croft's BALACLAVA team alone carried out a total of 24 successful operations using ACF fast craft, to the coasts of south-east France, north-west Italy and Elba. BALACLAVA infiltrated 85 agents and evacuated 24 agents together with important mail. Three operations were performed for MASSINGHAM, three for MARYLAND, SOE's mission in Italy, five for OSS, four for 'A' Force (MI9/19) and eight for the Deuxième Bureau. There was also one highly important joint operation, in the course of which Croft penetrated the harbour defences of Genoa to land ten SOE and SIS agents, together with six W/T sets, alongside a pier on which the Germans had a guard-post, at Voltri in the Genoa suburbs.[17]

The agents always 'came on the air' a few days after being infiltrated. On operations to Elba, the same three agents were infiltrated and evacuated for the French on four successive occasions and, while in the field, were in constant W/T communication with BALACLAVA headquarters. In an address to the French Forces just before the invasion of Elba, General de Lattre de Tassigny paid tribute to them, saying that no troops had ever been sent on an operation equipped with better intelligence.

It is also worth recording that two of Croft's Sergeants, Bourne-Newton and Jones, who were left behind after carrying out an operation to the Sestri-Levante area, escaped in a rubber boat to the island of Capraia, covering at least 90 miles in about 86 hours – a feat of presence of mind, initiative, skill, courage and endurance, which Croft, a qualified judge in such matters, considered of the highest order. They would not have succeeded but for the meticulous attention with which Croft equipped all his boats' crews for emergencies.[18]

When the invasion of southern France became imminent, BALACLAVA helped to organise operations by Lysander and Dakota aircraft. Meanwhile *Serenini* had left Corsica in order that the crew could man an Italian schooner, the *Marietta Madre*, and take part in the DRAGOON landings by ferrying SOE stores and personnel from Algiers to France. BALACLAVA's last sea operation was successfully completed on 29 July. On 5 August, the best all-rounders of BALACLAVA flew back to MASSINGHAM and a week later they parachuted into the Hérault Department, under the command of that most versatile of SOE's officers, Andrew Croft.[19]

Patrick Whinney, backed by Captain N.V. Dickinson and Andrew Croft, must be accorded the credit of organising, from a cold start, what was one of the most successful and intensive series of operations by high-speed craft for the Allied clandestine agencies in the whole of the Second World War. By March 1944 a sufficient number of trained officers was available to relieve Whinney from the necessity of personally conducting operations. Shortly afterwards, temporary illness forced him to relinquish his command and return to the United Kingdom. His place at Bastia was taken by Lt Cmdr McCallum, who had been first lieutenant, and subsequently captain, of *Minna*.

After the DRAGOON landings in Provence in August 1944, the Adriatic became the main centre for clandestine sea-transport operations. Apart from those in support of the Italian campaign, there were large numbers of operations from Italian ports in Allied hands, such as Bari and Monopoli, to the Dalmatian islands, carrying arms for Tito's Partisans. Slocum's local representatives recorded the astonishingly high total of 253 such missions. The last phase of clandestine sea-transport operations on the west coast of Italy was carried out from Livorno, rather than Bastia.

The French submarines based in North Africa carried more than 150 clandestine passengers to or from pinpoints in mainland France and Spain.

Epilogue

Immediately after the fall of France, the Admiralty's reluctance to appoint a serving officer to take charge of clandestine sea transport for the undercover agencies forced SIS and SOE to improvise in difficult circumstances. This worked well enough in the cases of Norway and Greece, where the sea lines required by both organisations could be started up with minimal demands on scarce British naval resources, but operations to the north coast of France and the Low Countries could not. Friction developed between SIS and SOE – the junior service, whose urgent needs could not be met.

The trouble was compounded by the Admiralty's initial refusal to allocate high-speed craft to the job on a permanent basis. This meant that operations had to be carried out by vessels borrowed from Coastal Forces, which could not be fitted with such specialist navigational equipment as was available and whose crews could not be trained to land boats on open beaches. The success rate was therefore low: there was in fact no successful operation by high-speed craft to the north coast of France between 2 August 1940 and September 1941. This was particularly serious for SOE, which was under political pressure to 'set Europe ablaze' and had fewer alternative means of transport than SIS.

The RAF, by creating the Special Duties Squadrons, avoided such a direct conflict of interest between SIS and SOE, but when Slocum, while remaining head of SIS's Operations Section, became the Admiralty's controller of all irregular operations to the north and west coast of France he was placed in a difficult position: he admitted at the end of the war that he never wholly gained SOE's confidence.

Though SOE maintained autonomous contact by sea with Norway, and on a larger scale than SIS, Slocum came by stages to control all clandestine operations by surface craft to the rest of German-held Western Europe as far east as the Adriatic. As we have seen, his attempt to bring the flotillas of local craft serving Greece under his authority as DDOD(I) foundered because of oppostion by GHQ Middle East. At the end of the war, he was preparing to send operational high-speed craft and a small depot ship to the Far East. He reckoned in 1946 that his Section under its various guises had landed 1,000 agents in enemy-occupied territory and extracted 3,500 agents and Allied evaders and escapers in the course of

1,150 operations involving 1,500 voyages, 75 per cent of which were successful. It was an impressive achievement, and attained in the face of enormous obstacles.

For all that, clandestine sea transport to France and French North Africa was never in practice controlled by any single authority. The present record has thus had to be compiled from a variety of sources.

In the period between the armistice of June 1940 and the spring of 1941, two Sections of SIS and also de Gaulle's Deuxième Bureau all operated more or less independently to the north and west coasts of France and SOE prepared to do likewise. Then, by the time Slocum's Section had emerged from the scrum as the controlling agency for all operations in the Narrow Seas, the Poles had begun to conduct felucca operations independently from Gibraltar to Morocco and western Algeria.

The creation of the Coast Watching Flotilla in spring 1942 extended Slocum's authority to clandestine operations by surface craft in the western Mediterranean and opened up a remarkable run of operations to the south coast of France, mainly by the Polish feluccas; but operations by submarines from Gibraltar, such as those that landed General Mark Clark in Algeria and picked up General Giraud from France, were not under the operational control of the CWF.

After the TORCH landings in North Africa the situation became more complex: both the American Office of Strategic Services and Giraud's Service de Renseignements began to operate from Algiers to Corsica and to France and a phase began in which submarine operations predominated. Slocum's African Coastal Flotilla had little, if any, involvement in missions for the Allied clandestine services by British or French submarines based on Algiers.

Between June 1940 and the Liberation of 1944 there were in all 77 successful or partly successful contacts with France by sea from bases in the United Kingdom. Details of these are set out in Appendix A. Though figures are in some cases approximate, it seems that 88 individuals were landed and 218 embarked.

The number of relevant operations in the Western Mediterranean was higher, though the tactical character of some of the sea transport during the Tunisian and Corsican campaigns makes precise reckoning difficult. There were certainly over 100 successful operations to French territory in this theatre, in the course of which 211 persons were landed and 665 evacuated.

Except in the case of Corsica, the quantities of warlike stores carried were insignificant by comparison with the 10,485 tons delivered to France by air. Though SOE exacerbated its relations with SIS by its insistence in 1941 and 1942 on planning for deliveries of arms and explosives by sea, it was driven to do so because Dr Dalton had oversold the immediately available potential of the French Resistance and because it was still not known whether aircraft would be available. By 1944 SOE's Country Sections had come to think exclusively in terms of parachute deliveries for the supply of stores and the ships at Helford that had been fitted out for the job were never used.

Notwithstanding the large number of Lysander pick-up operations, particularly in 1943, sea transport remained important throughout as a means of collecting qualitatively important intelligence, too bulky to be transmitted by W/T. Even in 1943, runs of bad weather over northern France frequently made pick-up operations impossible for weeks at a time. Rémy's 'Confrérie Notre Dame', the most productive and long-lasting of all the intelligence networks in France, remained more dependent on its monthly collection of mail by sea than on the Lysander pick-up operations that were supposed to alternate with it. The nine GLOVER operations carried out in 1944 by the 15th MGB Flotilla continued to deliver vitally important intelligence from all over the northern half of France to SIS right up to the liberation of Brittany.

For SOE, submarine operations to Corsica were of great importance and Buckmaster's F Section became very dependent on clandestine sea transport to Brittany at a critical period before D-Day OVERLORD: they had been obliged to close down Gilbert Déricourt's far too extensive Lysander operations because of well-founded suspicions that he was a double agent.

For the evacuation of groups of substantial size, sea transport had no competitor. Though by August 1944 Dakota aircraft were being landed clandestinely in southern France, this was exceptional: the Special Duties Squadrons would never have been able to tackle the Polish evacuation problem or the large numbers of evaders and escapers collected by MI9's 'Pat' and 'Shelburne' escape lines.

Just when Slocum seemed to have made good his case for permanently allocating suitable high-speed craft for operations to the north coast of Brittany, bad luck intervened. MGB 314, the first vessel to achieve a run of successful expeditions in this area, was lost at Saint-Nazaire; then MGB 501, first of the ex-Turkish gunboats allocated to NID(C), was sunk by misadventure only weeks after delivery. Finally, four of the ex-Turkish gunboat hulls that Slocum had expected to take over were reallocated to the Ministry of Economic Warfare and an inexplicable 12 months elapsed in bringing MGB 503, the first diesel-engined gunboat of this class, into operational service. In November 1943, while German diesel-engined E-boats capable of 35 knots ranged as far west as the Scillies, DDOD(I) was still dependent on that old and tired workhorse, MGB 318, capable of only half that speed.

In the Western Mediterranean Captain Fawkes was outstandingly helpful in making submarines available to the clandestine services in 1943. The chance availability of French submarines after the TORCH landings in North Africa allowed what Slocum considered the best of all forms of clandestine sea transport to be extensively used. However, after September 1943 the progress of the Italian campaign and the availability of Corsica as a base called for the use of high-speed craft. Admiral Cunningham's initial refusal to release a single British or American vessel of this type caused a deadlock, which was broken only when Italian MAS boats fortuitously became available after the Italian armistice. The cooperation of Captain Dickinson was invaluable in this and Cunningham's ban had by the end of January 1944 been relaxed.

Losses in the course of operations to France were surprisingly small: two fishing boats and their Breton crews early in 1941; two ratings killed by gunfire.[1] Boats' crews left ashore on five occasions were all safely rescued. But a number of ambushes were narrowly avoided. MGB 502 was lost by mine with only two survivors, but this happened after VE day and in Scandinavian waters. MAS 541 was also lost by mine with all hands including one of ACF's officers, though on an Italian operation. Because of Hitler's infamous secret instructions, no-one knew quite what fate might await them if they were captured in the course of special operations: two British captains of local craft taken prisoner in Greek waters were executed: one survivor of Gus March-Phillipps's raid on Saint-Vaast who escaped into Spain was extradited back into German hands and executed in France.

Though casualties were thus far smaller than in the RAF's Special Duties Squadrons, clandestine sea-transport operations involved very considerable feats of seamanship, navigation and endurance.

Krajewski's felucca operations from Gibraltar were outstanding: those to the south of France, which greatly benefited SOE and MI9, inexplicably received no official British recognition, his DSO having been awarded before the expeditions to France began. By the time this small Polish unit was disbanded in the Adriatic it had carried a total of over 600 people into or out of enemy-held territory and landed around 120 tons of war material. Their feluccas had spent 350 days at sea and travelled 35,000 nautical miles. Yet one has to search hard to find even an incidental reference in print to these feats.

The motor gunboat operations in the English Channel were equally impressive. The 'C'-Class MGB 318, too slow to operate safely in the short summer nights, was often at sea in weather that kept the regular Coastal Forces flotillas tied up in port. She and her larger sisters 502 and 503 worked, moreover, to a coast with notoriously strong tides and a daunting array of offshore dangers on moonless nights, without the normal navigational facilities, finding their way time and again to pinpoints inshore of these hazards.

*   *   *

This book will have succeeded in its *raison d'être* if it rescues from impending oblivion or from the realms of misleading myth the epic achievements of those, including the Poles, who opened up and maintained these clandestine sea lines of communication; and if it does justice to filling in a colourful and significant chapter of Anglo-French relations in the Second World War.

Footnotes

Chapter XXII

1 The account in this and the following seven paragraphs of the Polish Government-in-exile's attempts to reconstitute their armed forces, of the fate of those forces in the Battle of France and of the immediately ensuing evacuation to the United Kingdom is based on Garliński's *Poland in the Second World War*.

2 Rygor-Slowikowski: *The Lighting of the Torch*, Chapter II.

3 & 4 Tadeuz Wyrwa: 'The Polish Embassy in Madrid, 1940–44', *Zeszyty Historyczne* (Paris), No. 95 (1991).

5 The author's name is differently spelt at top and bottom of this document (A.XII.4/140), viz. Kpt. CIECHONSKI Czeslaw, former staff officer of 2nd Infantry Division, and Czeslaw CICHONSKI Kapitan.

6 *The Lighting of the Torch*, pp. 15–18.

7 Ibid.

8 R. Pichavant: *Clandestins de l'Iroise (1940–42)*, p. 151.

9 *The Lighting of the Torch*, pp. 15–18.

10 Personal communication to the author by Air Chief Marshal Sir Lewis Hodges.

11 A.XII. 4/140 (Sikorski Institute Archives).

12 *The Lighting of the Torch*, pp. 23–6.

Chapter XXIII

1 Documents from Sikorski Institute Archives.

2 Ibid., MAR A V 12/82.

3 M. Jullian: HMS *FIDELITY*, and information from British official archives.

4 Ibid. and P. Kingswell: *FIDELITY will Haunt Me till I Die*.

Chapter XXIV

1 Sikorski Institute Archives MAR A V 10/1 (HQ of the Commander-in-Chief); 1st Bureau; 1084 tjn/41/0.1/Ewak London, 8 April 1941, signed General Klimecki, Chief of Staff to the Commander-in-Chief.

2 Note de Renseignements No. 30 issued by Deuxième Bureau, EM Marine au Maroc on 20 Sept. 1940 and report dated 1 Oct. 1940, ref. 707 EM2. Affaire PECHERAL, Jacques: communicated to the author by Capitaine de Vaisseau Claude Huan, together with the document in footnote 4 below.

3 On 13 Nov. 1941, headed 'A/S de Manuel PEREIRA RAMAHEIRA'. Note de Renseignements dated 13 Nov. 1941 and issued from Casablanca.

4 Annex to a letter dated 23 October 1941 from Capitaine de Frégate Tariel to Amiral de la Flotte, Secrétaire d'Etat à la Marine [Darlan]. The author is grateful to Capitaine de Vaisseau Claude Huan for bringing this document, which is in the French naval archives, to his attention.

5–7 MAR A V 10/1.

8   L 614.

9–26 MAR A V 10/1.

Chapter XXV

1   Letter from Captain M. Kadulski [Krajewski] to author dated 12 Oct. 1992.

2   Letter from Amiral de la Flotte, Secrétaire d'Etat à la Marine, FM3–SECA dated 22 October, in French naval archives, tracked down and communicated to the author by C. de V. Claude Huan.

3   Reply to the above letter dated 23 October 1941 signed by Capitaine de Frégate Tariel.

4–9 MAR V A 10/1.

Chapter XXVI

1   The following two and a half pages are based on British official records made available to the author by Mr Gervase Cowell.

2 & 3 Sikorski Institute Archives MAR A V 10/2.

4   Information received from Group Captain H. B. Verity.

5   P.M. Churchill: *Duel of Wits*.

Chapter XXVII

1   Sikorski Institute Archives MAR A V 10/2.

2   *Duel of Wits*; M.R.D. Foot: *SOE in France*; and the relevant British official records.

3   Relevant British operational records made available to the author by Mr Gervase Cowell.

4   *Duel of Wits*, pp. 20–33.

5   *SOE in France*.

6–9 MAR A V 10/2.

10   MAR A V 10/5.

11–13 MAR A V 10/2.

14   Letters from Admiral Sir Edward Ashmore and from Danny Jones, the historian of HMS *Middleton*, to the author.

15   Personal communication to the author by Colonel Pierre Fourcaud, DSO.

16   As footnote 14.

Chapter XXVIII

1 & 2 Sikorski Institute Archives MAR A V 10/5; records of Polish Naval Attaché in London.

3   MAR A V 10/2.

4   Report by Buchowski, listing his operational achievements from Gibraltar, in MAR A V 10/5.

5   Relevant British official records.

6   *SOE in France*; personal communication to the author by C. M. Woods, CMG, then SOE Adviser to the Foreign and Commonwealth Office and custodian of the SOE Archives.

Chapter XXIX

1 Letter to the author from Captain M. Kadulski.

2 Memorandum in English language to NID(C) by Krajewski/Kadulski (copy in MAR A V 10/2).

3 Relevant British official records made available by Mr Gervase Cowell; and Krajewski's Memorandum referred to above.

Chapter XXX

1–6 MAR A V 10/2.

7 Operation PEDESTAL.

8 MAR A V 10/2.

9 MAR A V 10/1.

10–15 MAR A V 10/2.

16 General Kleeberg had been in London to report to General Sikorski.

Chapter XXXI

1 See pages 240–241.

2 See pages 480–494.

3 *Par les Nuits les Plus Longues*, page 221.

4 See Chapter XVIII, page 240.

5 C. Hampshire: *Undercover Sailors*, p. 155.

6–9 MAR A V 10/5.

Chapter XXXII

1 & 2 W.S. Churchill: *The Second World War*, Vol. III, p. 539, quoted in A.L. Funk: *The Politics of TORCH: The Allied Landings and the Algiers Putsch 1942*, p. 27.

3 A.L. Funk: *The Politics of TORCH*, p. 30.

4 SOE Archives.

5–8 *The Politics of TORCH*, Chapter 4.

9 Personal communication to the author by the Brazilian diplomat in question, Mario Gibson Barboso.

Chapter XXXIII

1 *The Politics of TORCH*, pp. 32–3.

2 & 3 Report by Col Brien Clarke to SOE Headquarters, communicated to the author by Sir Douglas Dodds-Parker.

4 *In the Secret Service: The Lighting of the Torch*, pp. 91, 95, 144–5, 166–70.

5 Information communicated by L'Hostis, W/T operator to Henri d'Astier de la Vigérie, to C de V Claude Huan.

6 *The Lighting of the Torch*.

7 Of 95 reports circulated by Dunderdale in June 1942, all but five came from his Polish liaison.

8 P.N. Thomas, 'Ships that Served: The Scottish Fishing Protection Vessel *Minna*', *Model Shipwright*, ii/3 (Spring 1973).

9 *The Politics of TORCH.*

10 The wartime career of Guy Verstraete was pieced together by Mr Terry Hodgkinson.

11 *The Lighting of the Torch.*

Chapter XXXIV

1 Report by Col Brien Clarke to SOE headquarters previously mentioned.

2 Col Clarke misdated his summons to Government House but it is clear from other sources that General Mark Clark and his party arrived at Gibraltar on 19 October and that the conference in question took place immediately thereafter.

3 R. Courtney: *The Special Boat Section.*

4 *The Politics of TORCH*, p. 164.

5 *The Special Boat Section.*

6 Report by Col Clarke referred to above.

7 This officer's unusual background was common knowledge among his colleagues in SOE's Naval Section.

Chapter XXXV

1 Sikorski Institute Archives MAR A V 10/5.

2 M.R.D. Foot: *SOE in France*; and a private communication to the author by C.M. Woods, when SOE Adviser to the Foreign and Commonwealth Office and custodian of the SOE archives.

3 Letter to the author from Professor José Aboulker.

Chapter XXXVI

1 & 2 Report by Col Brien Clarke referred to above (see Chapter XXXIV, footnote 1).

3 Letter from Captain N. L. A. Jewell to the author.

4 & 5 Report by Col Brien Clarke.

Chapter XXXVII

1 & 2 This correspondence is in the Sikorski Institute Archives MAR A V 10/5.

Chapter XXXVIII

1 These officers, the 'Twelve Apostles', had been deployed in North Africa before the creation of the Office of Strategic Services but Donovan's organisation had become OSS by the time of the TORCH landings. This chapter draws on a report on the BRANDON mission in the SOE Archives as well as on the author's knowledge.

2 Admiral Cunningham's signal is in Churchill's files in the Public Record Office, ref. PREM. 3/442.

3 Private communication to the author by Capitaine de Vaisseau Claude Huan.

Chapter **XXXIX**

1 G.B. Courtney: *S.B.S. in World War Two.*

2 The five 'marking' submarines from the 8th Submarine Flotilla sent to lead in the landing forces at Algiers and Oran received a last-minute instruction from Gibraltar based on considerations of secrecy that periscope reconnaissance only was to be made. The Combined Operations Pilotage Parties (COPP) carried on these submarines were, however, allowed to show the 'marking officers' the inner pilotage approaches to the landing beaches by means of canoe trips. This was carried out successfully in all cases but one. SHAKESPEARE's (P221) party was caught by a sudden storm on 4 November and the canoe was driven out to sea. The next day, waterlogged and suffering from cramp and exhaustion, the party was picked up by a trawler and taken into Algiers. Their cover story had been well rehearsed and was so well played that they were in danger of being shot as spies, but it was at least successful and nothing was given away to the French. (See Admiralty printed report BR 1736 (B1), Battle Summary No. 38 and *Role of Submarines in TORCH*, both in the Public Record Office.)

3 Author's personal knowledge.

4 De Saule's real name was Robert de Schrevel. He was a Belgian magistrate who had joined the French Foreign Legion at the outbreak of war. Also known as Dudule and René Tournier.

5 T. Griffi and L. Preziosi: *Première Mission en Corse Occupée, avec le Sousmarin Casabianca.*

6 Ibid. and Captain J. L'Herminier: *Casabianca*: The Secret Mission of a French Submarine. This chapter relies on L'Herminier's account of the maritime aspects of this operation and on Griffi's and Preziosi's record of PEARL HARBOUR once ashore.

7 This emerges from published and unpublished material communicated to the author by Capitaine de Vaisseau Claude Huan.

8 See Chapter **XXVII** above.

9 H.B. Verity: *We Landed by Moonlight.*

10 Letter in SOE Archives.

11 Copy in PREM. 3/442/14.

12 Author's personal knowledge.

13 Published and unpublished material communicated to the author by Capitaine de Vaisseau Claude Huan.

14 & 15 M.-C. Scamaroni: *Fred Scamaroni: 1914–1943.*

16 Author's personal knowledge.

17 A copy of the report on the autopsy was made available to the author by Capitaine de Vaisseau Claude Huan. The circumstances of Darlan's brief arrest on the night of the TORCH landings are recorded in *The Politics of TORCH*. That this was the origin of the naval pistol seems virtually certain.

18 SOE report on MASSINGHAM mission.

19 Private communications to the author by Sir Douglas Dodds-Parker.

20 *Fred Scamaroni: 1914–43.*

21 Capitaine de Vaisseau Claude Huan has searched the BCRA archives for this document in vain. The archives are in some disorder and it may have

migrated into a file where one would not expect to find it. But it may equally have been withdrawn because of its sensitivity.

22 Extracts from the operational report of HM S/m *Tribune* in the Public Record Office, made available to the author by Mr Terry Hodgkinson.

23 SOE Archives. Extracts from the relevant files were made available to Mr Terry Hodgkinson by Mr Gervase Cowell in a letter of which a copy was made available to the author by the latter.

24 Ibid.

Chapter XL

1 I. McGeoch: *An Affair of Chances: A Submariner's Odyssey 1939–42*.

2 It was Mr Terry Hodgkinson who drew the author's attention to the connection between the Adler/Serra case and the fate of Scamaroni, which had emerged from his correspondence with Mr Gervase Cowell.

3 J.G. Beevor: *SOE: Recollections and Reflections: 1940–1945*.

4 *An Affair of Chances*.

5 *Casabianca*: The Secret Mission of a French Submarine.

6 Ibid. The author is indebted to C. de V. Claude Huan for a list of many of those who travelled to or from France on the French Submarines based on Algiers. He derived his information on the subject from Capitaine P. Paillole. The results of his researches have been incorporated in Appendix D.

7 Lt Col F.C.A. Camimaerts, DSO ('Roger'), SOE's most successful agent in south-eastern France, formed a particularly adverse impression of Brown's blatant disregard of security when in occupied France. The author has a letter from him on the subject.

8 Author's personal knowledge.

9 *Casabianca*.

10 *Première Mission en Corse Occupée*.

11 *Casabianca*.

12 The author is indebted to Mr Terry Hodgkinson for information about FREDERICK, a subject he researched most thoroughly with a view to a possible television programme.

13 Private communication to the author by Captain M.G.R. Lumby.

14 Operational report by Lumby, made available to the author by Mr Terry Hodgkinson.

15 See footnote 12.

16 *Première Mission en Corse Occupée*.

17 *Casabianca*

18 *Première Mission en Corse Occupée*.

19 *Casabianca*; and Huan, see footnote 6.

Chapter XLI

1 See Chapter XL, footnote 2.

2 Unpublished memorandum by Mr Terry Hodkinson on FREDERICK referred to above.

3 & 4 Author's personal knowledge.

5 *Fred Scamaroni: 1914–43.*

6 G. Fleury and R. Maloubier: *Nageurs de Combat.*

7 Unpublished SOE report on operations in Corsica by MASSINGHAM.

8 Personal communication by A. L. Funk.

9 G.B. Courney: *S.B.S. in World War Two*; and letters from Captain P.E. Newstead, RN.

10 & 11 *S.B.S. in World War Two.*

12 Information from the Submarine Museum, Gosport, kindly made available by Mr Gus Britton.

13 *Première Mission en Corse Occupée.*

14 Official Admiralty report on submarines operating in the Western Mediterranean; also as footnote 12.

15 Records of Slocum's Section; report by Captain (S) 8 dated 17 July 1943 states that 'one of the agents had refused to land from *Trident.*'

16 P. Silvani: . . . *et la Corse fut Libérée.*

17 As footnote 7; and author's personal knowledge.

18 Personal communication by A.L. Funk to the author.

19 As footnote 7.

20 & 21 Author's personal knowledge.

22 As footnote 7.

23–25 Author's personal knowledge.

26–28 *Casabianca.*

29 & 30 As footnote 7.

31 . . . *et la Corse fut Libérée*; and author's personal knowledge.

32 Personal communication by A.L. Funk to the author.

33 As footnote 7.

34 *Casabianca.*

35 As footnote 7; also personal communication by A.L. Funk to the author.

36 & 37 As footnote 7.

38 General von Senger und Etterlin wrote in *Neither Fear nor Hope* (1988), p. 175: 'I believe that the inhabitants have become entirely apolitical due to their foreign rulers. This accounts for the fact that the numerous partisans, who were supplied with arms by air-drops, were not as active as might have been expected from their numerical strength and the contacts they had with the Allies along the open west coast. The ambush that I ran into after the Italian capitulation was laid by French gendarmes. The French were far more anti-German than the native Italians [sic].'

Chapter XLII

1 Author's personal knowledge.

2 MARYLAND, SOE's first mission established in ex-enemy territory, came, under the cover title No. 1 Special Force, to be the main source of supply and

strategic direction to the Italian partisans, with around 70–80,000 guerillas operating under its orders.

3   Report by F.A. Slocum; and P. Whinney: *Corsican Command.*

4   *Corsican Command.*

5   Report by N.A.C. Croft to the author in Algiers.

6   *Corsican Command*; and as footnote 5.

7   *Corsican Command.*

8   As footnote 5.

9   N.A.C. Croft: *A Talent for Adventure.*

10   As footnote 5.

11   *Corsican Command.*

12   As footnote 5.

13 & 14   *Corsican Command.*

15   A. Pelletier: 'Autrement qu'ansi', unpublished manuscript in the SOE archives.

16   *Corsican Command*; confirmatory evidence of the fate of MAS 541 and the position where she sank was communicated to the author by Capitaine de Vaisseau Claude Huan, from the French naval archives.

17   *A Talent for Adventure.*

18 & 19   As footnote 5.

Epilogue

1   Losses in Holland were more severe: six French 'fuseliers marins', forming part of 8 Commando, were killed or drowned conducting a reconnaissance at Wassenaar-Slag on 28 February 1944 to see whether it would be possible to resume sea landings of agents, notwithstanding the German coastal defences.

Appendix E

CLANDESTINE SEA OPERATIONS FROM GIBRALTAR TO FRENCH NORTH AFRICA AND THE SOUTH COASTS OF FRANCE AND SPAIN

Operation Code name	Department	Pinpoint	Ship	Object	Remarks and results
			Period: September 1940 – May 1941		
	Free French 2e Bureau	Agadir Bay	HM destroyer M . . . (from Gibraltar)	To land 3 agents: Guérin & Ter-Sarkissof – both officers – and Second Maître Jacques Pècheral.	21 Sept. 1940 – Agents successfully landed but arrested by French authorities in following month. They had taken passage to Gibraltar on 26 July from Scapa Flow in HMS Barham.
	Free French 2e Bureau	near Mostaganem	Small ship Johan, flying the Belgian flag, operating from Gibraltar	To land 3 agents: Lieutenants Puech-Samson and Bazaucourt, with W/T operator Papin.	26 Sept. 1940 – Agents successfully landed and remained in Algiers until mid-November. Taken prisoner in mid-November 1940, 30 miles west of Oran when they failed to embark for Gibraltar.
	SOE DF (Humphries) Section & EU/P (Polish Liaison) Section	Etang-du-C-annet	HMS Fidelity	To land 2 agents: E. H. Rizzo (DF) and Bitner (Polish).	25 April 1941 – Successful.
	Polish Evacuation Section	Cerbère	HMS Fidelity	To embark a party of Polish servicemen.	26 April 1941 – Unsuccessful. Attempt was made in broad daylight from within port of Cerbère. French gendarmerie intervened and Lt Cmdr P. O'Leary (Albert Guérisse) attempted to put to sea in the boat they were using but they were pursued by a French motor launch and arrested, except for one sailor who swam into Spanish waters.
	SIS/MI9	Gulf of Lyons	HMS Fidelity	To embark British POWs.	6 May 1941 – Attempt frustrated by appearance of French seaplane.
			Period: July – September 1941		
'KRA-JEWSKI'	Polish mission	Between Casablanca & Fedhala	Seawolf (felucca)	To evacuate Polish troops interned by Vichy authorities.	19–25 July 1941 – Krajewski's first attempt. Unsuccessful owing to poor communications with the organiser at Casablanca. Crew consisted of 3 Norwegians.

GIBRALTAR TO FRENCH NORTH AFRICA AND SOUTH COAST OF FRANCE Continued

Operation Code name	Department	Pinpoint	Ship	Object	Results and remarks
				Period: July – September 1941 continued	
'KRAJEWSKI I'; 'First Evacuation Mission'	Polish mission	As above	Seagull (lent by Quennell of SOE)	As above, and to land Major Brzozowski.	4–8 August – Successful. 6 August: 27 people evacuated, including 3 Czechs. 13 others arrested by Vichy police. Lt Killick (British, SOE) on board as observer.
'KRAJEWSKI III'	Polish mission	Between Sali & Mehedia (Port-Lyautey)	Dogfish (felucca)	To evacuate Polish escapers and to land Staggart (Czech volunteer).	17–25 August – Unsuccessful. Staggart lost his nerve and was unable to land. Krajewski called this his third evacuation mission, though he described its immediate predecessor as his first such operation. It was his third expedition to Morocco.
'KRAJEWSKI IV'	Polish mission	near Casablanca	Dogfish	To evacuate Polish evaders and escapers.	30 August–3 September – Successful. Embarked 48, including 4 Belgians, on night 1/2 September. Cadet Officer Kleybor and 2 Norwegians as crew. Lt Killick (British) on board.
IVz/SLO1	SIS/MI9)	Gulf of Lyons	HMS Fidelity	To embark party of escaped British POWs.	14 September – Unsuccessful. Fidelity arrived 24 hours late, having sailed from UK with brief call at Gibraltar during the night. Subsequent attempts on 20 and 21 September also failed.
ABRICOT	SIS/MI9)	Algeria (CapTénès)	Fidelity	To embark a party of escaped British POWs.	16 September – Unsuccessful. No-one at pinpoint.
KASBAH	BCRA	Algeria (nr Cherchell-Ti-paza)	Fidelity	To land 2 agents: Second Lt Jacquelin and Sgt Radio Carton; and 2 W/T sets.	17 September – Unsuccessful owing to presence of Italian submarine.
AUTOGYRO/ URCHIN	SOE	Barcarès, NE of Perpignan	Fidelity	To land 4 agents: F. Basin ('Olive'), R. Leroy ('Alain'), R.B. Roche and A.J.R. Doubourdin.	19/20 September – Successful.
'KRAJEWSKI V'	Polish mission	Fedhala	Dogfish	To pick up Polish evaders and escapers.	7–10 October – Successful. Embarked 13 Poles and two Belgians, and Mr Wysocki, owner of the safe house the Poles had been using.

GIBRALTAR TO FRENCH NORTH AFRICA AND SOUTH COAST OF FRANCE Continued

Operation Code name	Department	Pinpoint	Ship	Object	Results and remarks
			Period: July – September 1941 continued		
'KRAJEWSKI VI'	Polish mission	Mostaganem (DORULA)	*Dogfish*	To embark 2 agents: Major Wysoczanski and Lt Roehr.	23–29 October – Successful.
'KRAJEWSKI VII'	Polish mission	Mostaganem Bay	*Seagull*	To land supplies for 150 people for four days.	1–6 November – Unsuccessful. Saw people on shore at pinpoint, but they showed incorrect recognition signal (3/4 November). Trawler *Quarto*, which was to have been used as back-up, not available owing to boiler trouble.
'KRAJEWSKI VIII'	Polish mission	(1) Mostaganem Bay (BRZOZA) (2) Cap-Falcon nr Oran (Zorra)	*Dogfish*	(1) To pick up Polish escapers from R/V nr Mostaganem. (2) To land 1 agent nr Cap Falcon.	18–25 November – Planned evacuation of about 40 Polish soldiers, who had escaped from two interment camps, failed, as French authorities got wind of plan and frustrated it.
			Period: December 1941		
'BUCHOW-SKI I'	SOE	Casablanca	*Vega*, ex-*Ville-de-Fedhala* (Buchowski)	To land SOE stores.	December 1942 – Unsuccessful. Ship intercepted by Spaniards on return voyage and taken into Tangiers, where the crew were detained for several weeks and the ship was confiscated.
'KRAJEWSKI IX'	Polish mission	ZORRA, nr Cap Falcon (Andalousses Bay)	*Dogfish*	1) To land Lt Gromnicki carrying funds (600,000 Fr. Francs) for 'Szewalski' intelligence organisation. 2) To re-embark him.	13–18 December – Landing successful. Re-embarked Gromnicki two days later with 5 Polish officers. *Dogfish* not really fit for operations in winter: motor old and unreliable.
			Period: January – April 1942		
? DELAY	SOE	Miramar-de-l'Esterel	HM S/m P36 (Lt H.N. Edwards, RN)	To land Capt P.M. Churchill, using his own Folboat.	9 January 1942 – Successful. P36 left Gibraltar on 1 January and arrived back there on 15 January. The Naval Staff History omits this patrol completely but it was clearly offensive and took place in the Gulf of Lyons area as Naval Historical Branch have record of two Gibraltar signals telling her where merchant ships were to be.

GIBRALTAR TO FRENCH NORTH AFRICA AND SOUTH COAST OF FRANCE Continued

Operation Code name	Department	Pinpoint	Ship	Object	Results and remarks
				Period: January – April 1942 continued	
'KRAJEWSKI X'	Polish mission	Cap Falcon, nr Oran, Algeria	*Dogfish*	To land 1 agent (Lt Gromnicki) and to evacuate a party of Polish evaders and escapers.	8–23 January 1942 – Unsuccessful. Storm conditions made landing impossible at Cap Falcon. Motor broke down. Entered Oran Bay hoping to reach Arzew for shelter but could not. Blown 100 miles to the east. Continuous gales. Fired on in Oran Bay. Investigated by Spanish patrol boat at Alboran Island.
'KRAJEWSKI XI'	Polish mission	Oran area	*Dogfish*	? To evacuate Polish evaders and escapers.	22 March – Unsuccessful. There is no report on this operation in the Sikorski Institute archives. Buchowski accompanied Krajewski on it.
ABLOOM	SIS/MI9	Port-Vendres area	*Tarana* (Lt E.B. Clarke, RNR)	To land Pat O'Leary and W/T Operator.	18 April – Successful. This was the first operation to France under CWF auspices. *Tarana*, a Dutch-built trawler with secret armament, had a British and Polish crew. Operated sometimes under Moroccan, sometimes Portuguese flags.
				Period: April – June 1942	
JASMINE ('KRAJEW-SKI XII')	Polish mission, SOE and PWE	Cassis area, Antibes	*Seawolf* (Krajewski)	1) To land Lt Roehr at Port-Miou. 2) To land 3 agents at Antibes. 3) To evacuate Polish evaders and escapers from En-Vau.	18 April – Roehr successfully landed. 21/22 April – SOE and PWE agents successfully landed at Antibes. 22/23 April – 41 Poles evacuated. The SOE agents were Menesson ('Prunus') and Pertschuk ('Birch'). Le Chêne ('Plane') was for PWE.
DELAY II	SOE	Antibes & Miramar-de-l'Esterel	HM S/m P42 (UNBROKEN) (Lt A.G.C. Mars, RN)	1) To land 2 agents (Zeff and Newman) at Antibes. 2) To land 2 agents (Gerson and Clech) at Miramar, near Cannes.	1) 19/20 April – Successful. P. Churchill landed them using Folboat canoes and brought out Emmanuel d'Astier de la Vigerie ('Bernard'). 2) 20/21 April – Successful.
ORKAN	Polish Mission and SIS (P5)	Oran	*Dogfish* (Buchowski)	To evacuate 4 Poles.	25 April – Successful. Buchowski in command.

GIBRALTAR TO FRENCH NORTH AFRICA AND SOUTH COAST OF FRANCE Continued

Operation Code name	Department	Pinpoint	Ship	Object	Results and remarks
				Period: April – June 1942	
MIMOSA ('KRAJEW-SKI XIII')	Polish mission & SOE	Cassis area, Antibes & Rhône delta	Seawolf Tarana	To evacuate Polish evaders and escapers and land SOE agents (Denis Rake and Charles Hayes).	10/11 May – 31 Poles evacuated from En-Vau and transferred to Tarana at R/V on 11 May, when Seawolf embarked the agents from Tarana. 13/14 May – Agents successfully landed at Antibes. 15/16 May – 30 Poles embarked from nr Beauduc lighthouse in Rhône delta.
CASA-BLANCA	Polish mission	Casablanca area	Dogfish (Buchowski)	To evacuate 30 Allied evaders and escapers.	23 May – Successful.
* GOBLIN Ia ('KRAJEW-SKI XIV')	Polish mission	Cassis area (En-Vau)	Seawolf Tarana	To evacuate Polish evaders and escapers.	9 June – Picked up 3 Poles. Police had arrested others and group had dispersed. * Operation combined with GOBLIN II, SARDINE, LUCALITE I and LUCALITE II below; all one voyage.
	Polish mission	En-Vau	Seawolf	To land Polish courier (Lt Biczysko).	10/11 June – Courier landed.
* GOBLIN II	SOE	Antibes area	Seawolf Tarana	To land 2 SOE agents: Jickell and Boiteux; and stores.	11/12 June – Agents successfully landed. 1 embarked, according to Slocum (possibly Frager, staff officer to 'Carte').
* SARDINE	SOE	Cap-d'Ail, Monaco area	Seawolf Tarana	To land 1 SOE agent.	11/12 June – Agent (?Coppin) successfully landed.
* LUCALITE I	SIS (MI9), Polish mission	Port-Miou	Seawolf	1) To embark a non-Polish party. 2) To embark Polish evaders and escapers.	14/15 June – 9 mixed agents and refugees, including 3 women, successfully embarked.[1] 62 Poles successfully evacuated.
* LUCALITE II	SIS (VIb)	Port-Miou	Seawolf	To land 70lb. of war material.	14/15 June – Successful.
TANGERINE	Polish mission	Oran area	Seadog	To land 1 Polish courier (Gromnicki).	9 June – Failed. Bad weather.
NETTLE-TREE	SOE	Cap-d'Antib-es	Seadog Tarana	To embark 1 and land SOE stores.	30 June – Successful. Possibly Frager.
No name	SOE	Gibraltar Strait	Minna	To R/V at sea with felucca from Tangier and transfer stores.	26–30 June – Successful.

GIBRALTAR TO FRENCH NORTH AFRICA AND SOUTH COAST OF FRANCE Continued

Operation Code name	Department	Pinpoint	Ship	Object	Results and remarks
				Period: July 1942	
GUYMAR	SIS P1 Section (Cohen)	Oran area	*Minna*	To land 1 agent (J. Verstraete.)	7 July – Successful.
* LUCILE	SIS (P1) (BCRA *réseau* 'Ronsard')	Port-d'En-V-au	*Seawolf*	To embark up to 10.	13/14 July – Successful. Embarked 2 men and 1 woman (wife of one of the men). * Operation combined with MANDARIN I & II, 'KRAJEWSKI XV' and PEPPERTREE below; all one voyage.
* MAN-DARIN I & II; ('KRAJEW-SKI XV')	Polish	Port-d'En-V-au	*Seawolf Tarana*	To embark Polish evaders and escapers.	14/15 July – Successful. 52 embarked and transferred. 22 July – Successful. 53 embarked.
* PEPPER-TREE	SOE	1) Cassis Bay, Cap-Gros 2) Antibes	*Seawolf Tarana*	1) 15 July – to land 4 agents transferred from TARANA. 2) To land remaining 2 agents.	1) 15/16 July – Successful. 4 agents landed. 2) 19/20 July – Successful, after failed attempt on 19 July, because of too much traffic on the road. Passengers landed included R.H. Heslop ('Mahogany'), R. Leroy ('Buckthorn'), ? Lt Krumhorn ('Mangrove'), Capt Barnard.
† POST BOX	SOE Italian Section	'Marseilles area' (Port-Miou)	*Seawolf Tarana*	To land 2 (Emilio and Joyce Lussu)	18 July ? – Successful. † Operation combined with BLUEBOTTLE below; all one voyage. Krajewski's report does not in fact distinguish this operation from PEPPERTREE & LUCILE above.
† BLUE-BOTTLE	P15 (MI.9)	'Gulf of Lyons area' (Saint-Pierre-Plage, near Narbonne)	*Tarana*	To embark British escapers and evaders.	14/15 July ?[2] – Successful. Coast Watching Flotilla's first large-scale evacuation for the 'Pat' line; carried out directly by *Tarana*. 30–35 evacuated, including Whitney Straight, a very distinguished fighter pilot.
ORKAN II	SIS (P5) (Dunderdale)	Oran area	*Minna*	To evacuate 1 agent.	13 July – Successful. Group concerned was Rygor-Slowikowski's 'Agence Afrique'.
				Period: July – September 1942	
CASUAL	SIS (P5) (Dunderdale)	Oran area	*Minna*	To land 2 Polish agents to Rygor-Slowikowski's 'Agence Afrique'.	19 July – Failed. No reception committee present. *Minna* attacked by enemy aircraft on return voyage. Aircraft driven off.

GIBRALTAR TO FRENCH NORTH AFRICA AND SOUTH COAST OF FRANCE Continued

Operation Code name	Department	Pinpoint	Ship	Object	Results and remarks
				Period: July – September 1942 Continued	
SASSAFRAS	SOE	Cap-d'Antibes	*Seadog*	To land 4 agents: N. Boddington ('Professor'), Frager ('Architect'), Despaigne ('Magnolia') and Rudellat ('Soaptree').	30 July – Successful. Auguste Floiras left either on this operation or PEPPERTREE.
BULL	SOE	nr Agde	*Tarana*	To land 6 agents, including 1 woman, and stores.	15 August – Successful. Included Pilot Officer André Simon, Cdt Charles Clasen (Belgian) and 'Mercure' (BCRA).[3]
BLUE-BOTTLE (LEDA I for BCRA)	SIS (P1) (Cohen) (BCRA *réseau* 'Phalanx')	Saint-Pierre-Plage, near Narbonne	*Tarana*	To pick up evaders and escapers and to land stores.	15 August – Successful. 7 men and 1 woman embarked. Food, stores and W/T sets landed.
WATCHMAN	SOE	Agay	*Seadog*	To land agent and stores.	1 September – Successful. Landed 1 agent (Blanche Charlet) and 2,000 lb. stores. Brought off 5 men and 2 women: Boddington, André Gillois + wife and daughter; two Belgians.
VAGRANT	SIS (P5) (Dunderdale)	Agay area	*Seadog*	To evacuate mixed party.	2 September – Successful. Ten people evacuated, including General Kleeberg.
KUMMEL	SOE	nr Toulon	*Seadog*	To evacuate 5.	3 September – Failed. No-one at R/V. Military manoeuvres in area.
				Period: September 1942	
LEDA (LEDA II for BCRA)	SIS (P1) (Cohen for BCRA *réseau* 'Phalanx')	Narbonne	*Seadog*	To land 1 agent and evacuate others.	4 Sept. – Successful. 'Porthos' (W/T op.) landed. Brossolette, Charles Vallin, Denis Cochin, Dutrex, Sq Ldr Guy Lockhart (Lysander pilot), organiser 'Ronsard' (Quartier Maître Richard) evacuated. Christian Pineau, Jean Cavaillès and Saint Génies left behind owing to shore interference by customs patrol and arrested.

GIBRALTAR TO FRENCH NORTH AFRICA AND SOUTH COAST OF FRANCE Continued

Operation Code name	Department	Pinpoint	Ship	Object	Results and remarks
				Period: September 1942	
ZEBRA	SIS (P5) (Dunderdale)	Oran area	*Minna*	To land 3 agents to Slowikowski's 'Agence Afrique': Malinowski, Kowal, Piotrowski.	11 September – Successful. Agents had been on board since May. Also picked up Polish agents from Paris, refugees from treachery of 'La Chatte'. (see CASUAL below).
CASUAL	SIS (P5) (Dunderdale)	Oran area	*Minna*	To evacuate agents from 'Agence Afrique'.	11 September – Successful. 5 men and 1 woman embarked.
FALSTAFF (TRITON)	SIS (P1) (Cohen)	La-Ciotat	*Seawolf*	To land 2 agents (1 a woman)	17 September – Successful. (CND *réseau*).
ORLANDO	SIS (P5) (Dunderdale)	Sormiou, but Morgiou was point used	*Seawolf*	To land 1 agent and heavy W/T station.	18 September – Successful, but reception committee was at wrong pinpoint. Picked up 50 kilos of watches and stop-watches for the RAF.
MULLET	SOE	Port-d'En-V-au	*Seawolf*	To embark 2.	18 September – Successful.
NECTARINE I ('KRAJEW-SKI XVI')	Polish mission	Sormiou	*Seawolf*	To embark Polish evaders and escapers.	19 September – 31 embarked, including 3 British.
NECTARINE II	Polish mission	Port-d'En-V-au	*Seawolf*	As above.	20 September – Successful. 25 Poles embarked.
				Period: September – October 1942	
TITANIA	P15 (MI9)	Saint-Pierre-Plage, near Narbonne	*Seawolf*	To evacuate British evaders and escapers from the 'Pat' line.	21 September – Successful. Krajewski puts number of those embarked at 25; another account at 38. The party included a few Frenchmen, 1 Sudeten woman and a Russian, according to Krajewski.
SILKWORM	Poles & SIS (P5) (Dunderdale)	La-Napoule	*Seadog*	To land 1 and embark 6.	2 October – Buchowski landed 2 agents and General Kleeberg at La-Napoule. His record does not distinguish between the operations as listed in British records.
WATCHMAN II	SOE	Cap-de-l'Es-quillon	*Seadog*	To land stores, etc.	2/3 October – Promised motor boat did not appear. Material landed 4/5 October using own boat.

GIBRALTAR TO FRENCH NORTH AFRICA AND SOUTH COAST OF FRANCE Continued

Operation Code name	Department	Pinpoint	Ship	Object	Results and remarks
				Period: September – October 1942	
CHUB I	SOE (? and PWE)	La-Napoule, Cap-de-l'Es-quillon	*Seadog*	To land two parties of 2 agents at different pinpoints.	2/3 October – Buchowski landed all 4 agents including S.G. Jones, J. Goldsmith & Chalmers-Wright. He also decided to land General Kleeberg at the first pinpoint.
CHUB II	SOE	Rade-d'Agay	*Seadog*	To embark 6.	4 October – Failed. French police interfered.
ACCOST	SIS (P5)	Oran area	*Minna*	To embark 1.	Beginning October – Failed. A signal went astray and agent thus had too little time to arrive at R/V.
GIRAFFE I	'Poles'	Oran area	*Minna*	To land 1.	1 October – Successful.
GIRAFFE II	'Poles'	Oran area	*Minna*	To embark 6.	3 October – Successful.
ULTRA-MARINE	'Poles'	Oran area	*Minna*	To embark 1.	3 October – Successful.
				Period: October – November 1942	
ROSALIND	P15 (SIS for MI9)	St-Pierre-Plage, near Narbonne	*Seawolf* (Lukasz)	To embark British evaders and escapers from the 'Pat' line.	11/12 October – Successful. 34 embarked at a second attempt. No contact on 5/6 October.
SERAPH I	General Eisenhower	Messelmoun, near Cherchell, Algria	HM S/m P219 (later named *Seraph*) (Lt N.L.A. Jewell, RN)	To land Lt Gen Mark Clark and four staff officers for talks with General Mast, Col Jousse and Mr Robert Murphy.	21/22 October – Party successfully landed and re-embarked by No. 2 SBS.
* WATCH-MAN III * OVER-GROW * DUBON-NET	SOE (F Section & Italian Section)	Port-Miou	*Seadog* (Buchowski)	To land stores and personnel (Buchowski says 9 landed and 6 embarked).	3/4 November – Successful. 3 women, 5 men and 1,000 lb. stores landed; 4 men and 1 boy embarked. SOE records identify following landed: George Starr ('Wheelwright'); Marius Bloom ('Bishop'; W/T operator); Mary Herbert ('Jeweller'); Mme M.-T. Le Chêne ('Wisteria'); Odette Sanson ('Clothier'); plus Gracomino Galea for Italian Section. Embarked: J.A.R. Starr ('Walnut'); I. Newman ('Dividend'); 'Quintet' (Radio Patrie); 'Richard' and his son.
* PORTIA	P15 (SIS for MI9)	Port-Miou	*Seadog*	To land 1	3/4 November – Successful. * Part of WATCHMAN III.

GIBRALTAR TO FRENCH NORTH AFRICA AND SOUTH COAST OF FRANCE Continued

Operation Code name	Department	Pinpoint	Ship	Object	Results and remarks
	Period: November – December 1942				
LADYBIRD	SIS (P5) (Dunderdale)	Fréjus	Seadog	To land 1 and embark stores.	5 November – Failed owing to rough weather. 6 November – Further attempt failed for same reason.
SERAPH II		Le-Lavandou, 20 miles E of Toulon	HM S/m P219 (Lt N.L.A. Jewell, RN)	To embark General Giraud and 4 others, including his son and Viret, his bodyguard.	5 November – Successful. Party had been waiting since previous night. Party picked up by Catalina amphibious aircraft at 0900 7 November
LEOPARD (PICNIC for SOE)	SOE	1) Messelmoun 2) Alma-Marine (Algeria)	Minna	To land 10 tons of stores in preparation for TORCH landings at Algiers.	2/3 & 3/4 November – No reception found at Messelmoun. Ordered to new R/V east of Algiers. 5/6 November – No reception found at alternative R/V.
SIBYL		Cros-de-Cagnes	HM S/m Sibyl (Lt E.J.D. Turner, RN)	To embark 10 French staff officers and 1 woman.	8 November – 7 successfully embarked: Mme Beaufre, Cdt V. Boutron, 3 French officers and 2 men. Party had problems with French police just before embarking and 3 men were arrested.
WASP	SIS (P1) (Cohen)	Cros-de-Cagnes	Seawolf	To embark 2.	30 November & 4 December – Failed.
MELPO-MENE	SIS (P1) (réseau 'Denis')	La-Napoule	Seawolf	To embark 7.	1 & 5 December – Failed.
LADYBIRD	SIS (P1)	nr Fréjus	Seawolf	To embark stores for Ministry of Economic Warfare.	2 December – Failed.

On first attempts of above three operations, no contact with agents on shore. On second attempt at WASP and MELPOMENE, weather prevented embarkation.

Operation Code name	Department	Pinpoint	Ship	Object	Results and remarks
	Period: December 1942 – February 1943				
CRICKET	SIS (P5) (Dunderdale)	nr Agay (Cros-de-Cagnes)	Seawolf	To embark party of agents.	3 December – Cancelled by field after ship had sailed. Further attempts to be made.
LADYBIRD II	SIS (P1)	Fréjus	Welcome	To embark MEW stores.	2 January 1943 – Failed. Atmospheric conditions prevented ship from receiving W/T signal changing date after ship had sailed.
* WASP II	SIS (P1) (Cohen)	Cros-de-Cagnes	Seawolf	To embark 7.	January – Failed. Opposition from machine-guns at WASP/CRICKET pinpoint.

GIBRALTAR TO FRENCH NORTH AFRICA AND SOUTH COAST OF FRANCE Continued

Operation Code name	Department	Pinpoint	Ship	Object	Results and remarks
				Period: December 1942 – February 1943 continued	
* MELPO-MENE II	SIS (P1)	La-Napoule	*Seawolf*	To embark 7.	January – Failed. Weather very bad.
* CRICKET II	SIS (P5) Dunderdale)	Cros-de-Ca-gnes	*Seawolf*	To embark party.	January – Failed.
* LADYBIRD III	SIS (P1)	nr St-Aigulf	*Seawolf*	To embark MEW stores.	29 January – Failed. Ambush laid on beach. Felucca returned owing to illness of commanding officer. * Operation combined on same voyage with MELPOMENE III below.
* MELPO-MENE III	SIS (P1)	Cap-de-l'Aiguillon	*Seawolf*	To embark 7.	29 January – Failed.
MELPO-MENE IV & ROMEO	SIS (P1)	Cap-de-l'Aiguillon & Cavalaire	*Welcome*	To embark 7 at one pinpoint and up to 10 at another.	February – Failed. Agents cancelled arrangements after *Welcome* sailed. *Welcome* kept R/V but saw nothing and returned to Gibraltar 15 February.

Notes

1   Alya Aglan's *Mémoires Resistantes: Histoire du Réseau Jade-Fitzroy* 1940–44 identifies these passengers as Claude and Denise Lamirault and Emile Champion ('Parrain') with wife and son. Henri Frenay and Pierre Fourcaud were also evacuated on this occasion. All were transferred to HMS *Middleton*, met by chance at sea.

2   Some accounts quote 13 July as the date of this pick-up operation.

3   The BCRA archives show an agent code-named 'Mercure' as passenger on an operation near Narbonne on 10 August.

CLANDESTINE SEA OPERATIONS FROM VARIOUS BASES TO TUNISIA

Operation Code name	Department	Pinpoint	Ship	Object	Results and Remarks
Period: December 1942 – April 1943					
?	SIS (Malta)	Cap Kamart (E coast of Tunisia)	HM S/m Urge	To land agents.	16/17 February 1942 – Only 1 agent landed owing to foul weather.
?	SIS (Malta)	Off Sousse	HM S/m Utmost (Lt Cmdr R. Cayley, RN)	To pick up Cdt Breuillac and mail from Tunis at R/V with yacht belonging to Mounier.	15 April 1942 – Successful. Breuillac returned to Tunisia on 19 April by same means. (See Fleury and Maloubrier: Nageurs de Combat, P. 49–56, (La Table Ronde, Paris, 1989.)
FELICE I (called FELICITY by BRANDON)	SOE (BRANDON mission)	South of Hammamet	HM S/m P42 (Unbroken) (Lt A.G.V. Mars, RN), from Malta	To land party of 12 to demolish bridge.	28/29 January 1943 – Party successfully landed in uniform but captured during attack on bridge. Party consisted of Capt Eyre, Lt Thomas, 4 British and 6 French ORs.
FELICE II (BLUE)	SOE (BRANDON mission)	Gulf of Hammamet	HM MTB 307, from Malta	To land 3 agents: Sqn Ldr Mallory, Martinez and Bonjour (leader was W/T operator).	28/29 January 1943 – Agents successfully landed but captured almost immediately afterwards.
ZODIAC	SOE (BRANDON mission)	Bizerta	Air/sea rescue launch from Bône	To land 1 agent and 1 W/T operator: David and Dupont.	4/5 March 1943 – Agents safely landed.
BEAR	SOE (BRANDON mission)	Kelibia (E coast of Tunisia)	MTBs, from Malta (? MTB 307)	To land 10 agents to carry out sabotage in conjunction with BLUE.	6 April – Agents successfully landed, but to a reception party organised by the enemy. Conducting officer (Lt F.B. Richards) and boats' crews allowed by enemy to re-embark none the wiser.
BEAR II	SIS	Cap Bon area	2 US P/T boats from Sousse	To land W/T operator to reception committee provided by BLUE/BEAR organisation.	Early May 1943 – First attempt failed owing to mechanical breakdown. Expedition recalled from second attempt because the BLUE/BEAR organisation had been discovered to be under enemy control.

OPERATIONS FROM ALGIERS TO CORSICA, SOUTH COAST OF FRANCE AND SPAIN

Operation Code name	Department	Pinpoint	Ship	Object	Results and remarks
			Period: December 1942 – February 1943		
'CASA-BIANCA I'/ PEARL HARBOUR	OSS & Deuxième Bureau	Anse-de-To-piti (nr Chiuni, west coast of Corsica)	French S/m *Casabianca* (Captaine de Frégate L'Herminier)	1) To land 4-man intelligence mission and OSS W/T officer (F. Brown). 2) To land stores and arms; and re-embark OSS representative.	14/15 December – Successful landing of Cdt de Saule, Adjutant-Chief Toussaint Griffi, Sergeant Pierre Griffi, L. Preziosi and Fred Brown. 15/16 December – Attempt to land stores and arms failed. Dinghy lost and Lasserre, Lionnais and Vigot left ashore with PEARL HARBOUR mission. Brown swam off.
SEA URCHIN	SOE & BCRA	Cupabia Bay, Gulf of Valinco, Corsica	HM S/m *Tribune* (Lt S.A. Porter, RN)	To land BCRA/ SOE team of 3 agents: Scamaroni, Jickell and W/T operator.	6/7 January 1943 – Successful. Original choice of pinpoint in Lava Bay proved unsuitable.
'CASA-BIANCA II'/ AUBURN	OSS/Deuxiè-me Bureau/ SIS (P1)	1) Bon-Porté Bay nr Cap Lardier 2) Baie-d'Arone (Corsica)	French S/m *Casabianca*	1) To land 3 Deuxième Bureau and OSS agents. 2) To land 2 SIS agents on west coast of Corsica: Adj Bozzi and Sgt Chopitel ('Auburn'). 3) To land arms and ammunition to PEARL HARBOUR.	4/5 February – Operation 1) successfully completed without reception committee. Landed Capt Caillot, Lt Guillaume and Fred Brown (OSS). 5/6 February – Operation 2) successfully completed without reception committee. 2 crew stranded (Asso, Cardot). 6/7 February – Operation 3): 450 Sten guns and 60,000 rounds of ammunition successfully landed without reception committee.
FREDERICK	SIS (P1)	Cupabia Bay	HM S/m *Saracen* (Lt M.G.R. Lumby, RN)	To land 3 agents: Guy Verstraete, Antoine Colonna d'Istria, Andrei.	10/11 February – Successful.

ALGIERS TO CORSICA, SOUTH COAST OF FRANCE AND SPAIN

Operation Code name	Department	Pinpoint	Ship	Object	Results and remarks
			Period: March – May 1943		
'CASA-BIANCA III'/ PEARL HARBOUR	Deuxième Bureau	1) Pointe-de-Taillat, Bon-Porté Bay 2) Anse-de-Canelle (east coast of Corsica)	French S/m *Casabianca*	1) To land 3 agents: Capt de Peich, 'M Jean' and another. To pick up 2 of agents landed in Provence in February and Lt Col Bonneteau, General Arlebousse and Capt Raymond Bernard. 2) To pick up 2 members of PEARL HARBOUR Mission and 5 members of S/m's crew stranded in Corsica during two previous missions. Land 2 members of Corps Fanc d'Afrique.	5/6 March – Operation 1) unsuccessful. 10/11 March – Operation 2) successfully completed after two unsuccessful attempts. Motor fishing boat from Favone used to make contact with s/m. 13/14 March – Second unsuccessful attempt to carry out 1). A further attempt to take these people off on the following night also failed.
CATER-PILLAR I	SIS (P5) (Dunderdale)	NW Corsica	*Seawolf*	To land 2 agents.	10 April – Failed owing to bad weather and shore patrols.
ETNA	SOE	1) NW coast of Italy 2) East coast of Corsica	HM S/m *Trident*	1) To land 2 Soviet agents in Italy. 2) To make a further attempt to evacuate remainder of de Saule's mission from Corsica (? Pierre Griffi).	1) Not carried out. 2) 10 May – Unsuccessful.

ALGIERS TO CORSICA, SOUTH COAST OF FRANCE AND SPAIN

Operation Code name	Department	Pinpoint	Ship	Object	Results and remarks
			Period: March – May 1943 continued		
'MARSOUIN'	Deuxième Bureau (Giraud); OSS/SIS	Bon-Porté Bay	French S/m *Marsouin*	To land 5 agents: Jean Avallard, Christian Durrmeyer, E. Bolot (W/T operator) for OSS/SIS; Louis Gay for OSS, Gabriel Francart for SIS. To land 500 kg. arms for OSS. To pick up 2: Ingénieur Huet, Fred Brown (OSS).	8 May – Successful. Fabrizio Calvi lists Capitaine Jean Marie and Christophe Dunoyer (Service de Renseignements) among passengers. Submarine ran aground.
			Period: May – August 1943		
'CASA-BIANCA IV'	Deuxième Bureau	Barcelona	French S/m *Casabianca*	To land 4 agents (unidentified).	23 May 1943 – Successful. Patrol 20–24 May from Algiers.
LEG I/SKIN	SOE	SE Corsica (? mouth of River Travo)	HM S/m *Sibyl* (Lt E.J.D. Turner, RN)	1) To contact agent (Paul Colonna d'Istria) for consultations and then land him again. 2) To land stores (conducting party: Lt R.J. Laming, RNVR, and PO Sam Smalley).	Approx. 15 June – Only partly successful. Agent taken aboard s/m and stores successfully landed, but shooting broke out before agent could be disembarked. A further attempt was made on following night but there was no contact with shore party and it was decided it would be unwise for him to land 'blind'. He therefore returned to Algiers.
SCALP/'CA-SA- BIANCA V'	SOE	Curza Point, Désert-des-Agriates, N Corsica	French S/m *Casabianca*	1) To land Paul Colonna d'Istria and W/T operator (Luc Le Fustec). 2) To land 13 tons stores (conducting party: Lt F.B. Richards, Skipper Lt J.L. Newton, PO F. Taylor, Seaman D. Miles).	1/2 & 2/3 July – Successful.

ALGIERS TO CORSICA, SOUTH COAST OF FRANCE AND SPAIN

Operation Code name	Department	Pinpoint	Ship	Object	Results and remarks
				Period: May – August 1943 Continued	
'LA PERLE I'	Deuxième Bureau	Cap-Camarat area	French S/m *La-Perle*	1) To land 2 agents: Lt de Gasquet and Capitaine Vellaud alias Desforges. 2) To pick up a party.	2/3 July – Failed. Those due to be embarked were Estienne, Lt Col Bégue, Col. Agostini, Col. Serre and his son, Paul Schlochoff, Dautry.
'SIBYL I'	?	SE Corsica	HM S/m *Sybil*	To land 1 agent.	4/5 July – Successful, according to Naval Staff History of submarine operations.
SCALP II/ 'CASA-BIANCA VI'	SOE	Curza Point, N Corsica	French S/m *Casabianca*	To land 20 tons of stores (conducting party: Skipper Lt Newton, Capt. M. Gubbins, PO F. Taylor, Seaman J. Duff.)	30/31 July & 31July/1 August – Successful, after abortive attempt on W coast.
'SIBYL II'	?	E coast of Corsica	HM S/m *Sybil*	?	21/22 August – According to Naval Staff History (p. 172), carried out a special operation in Corsica and then patrolled east of the island.
'ARÉTHUSE'	Deuxième Bureau	Cap-Camarat	French S/m *Aréthuse* (Lieutenant de Vaisseau Goutier)	To land 6: Lt Chevée, Jean-Marie Sévère alias Bertino (W/T), E.V. Flichy, Claude Château, Jean-Paul Klotz ('Faure'), and an 'inspecteur de police'. To evacuate mail and personnel.	29 August – Successful. Also embarked: Ingénieur-Général Ziegler, 2 'inspecteurs de police' (Grino & another), Jacques Rivet, son of the General.
SCALP III/ 'CASA-BIANCA VII'	SOE	Golfe-de-La-va, due S of Piombata rock	French S/m *Casabianca*	1) To bring off 1 of leaders of Corsican Resistance (Giovoni). 2) To land 2: Lt Giannesini and W/T operator. 3) To land 5 tons of arms, ammunition and explosives.	5/6 September – Successful. Reception committee organised by Henri Maillot, de Gaulle's cousin.

ALGIERS TO CORSICA, SOUTH COAST OF FRANCE AND SPAIN

Operation Code name	Department	Pinpoint	Ship	Object	Results and remarks
			Period: May – August 1943 Continued		
'CASA-BIANCA VIII'	French general staff	Ajaccio, Corsica	French S/m *Casabianca*	To land 109 (members of Bataillon de Choc and SOE/Deuxième Bureau mission)	13 September – Successful. Passage carried out on the surface. Mission covered period 11–15 September.
			Period: September – October 1943		
'LA PERLE II'	French general staff	Ajaccio	French S/m *La-Perle* (L de V Paumier)	To land 3 tons of flour.	16 September – Successful. Mission undertaken in support of *Casabianca*. Paumier persuaded captain of Toulon-Ajaccio ferry to sail to Algiers.
STEELTON/EARDRUM	SOE	Gulf of Porto, Corsica.	*Serenini Seawolf Seadog Welcome*	To land 1 agent and material.	16 September – Successful.
'ARÉTHUSE II'	French general staff	Ajaccio	French S/m *Aréthuse* (L de V Goutier)	To land 5 tons of munitions.	18 September – Successful. Mission in support of *Casabianca* and Bataillon de Choc.
'ARÉTHUSE III'	Deuxième Bureau	Cap-Camarat	French S/m *Aréthuse*	To land 5: Capitaine Pauly (alias Pierson), 1 Lt, 3 *aspirants* (incl. Alfasser). To pick up mail and a party of French officers.	28 September – Successful. Picked up: Col Zeller, Col Chouteau, Col Granier, Cdt Etienne Rivet, Capitaine Vellaud, Capt de Neuchèze, Capitaine de Crovette Barthélemy and standard of 2e Dragons.
'LA PERLE III'	Deuxième Bureau	Barcelona	French S/m *La-Perle*	To land 1 agent (Capt d'Hoffelize) and stores.	16–17 October – Successful.
'LA PERLE IV'	Deuxième Bureau	Cap-Camarat	French S/m *La-Perle*	To land agents: Capt de Saint-Hilaire, Henri Bron (W/T), Paul-Marie Dubuc (W/T), Serge Deyres. Also to land stores.	26/27 October – Successful.

ALGIERS TO CORSICA, SOUTH COAST OF FRANCE AND SPAIN

Operation Code name	Department	Pinpoint	Ship	Object	Results and remarks
			Period: November 1943 – January 1944		
CREVASSE/ 'ORPHÉE I'	Deuxième Bureau	Barcelona	French S/m Orphée (L V Dupont)	To land 5 agents, including Capitaine E. Bertrand and Lt d'Hénin and a W/T set.	20 November – Successful.
'CASA-BIANCA IX'	Deuxième Bureau	Cap-Camarat	French S/m Casabianca (L de V Bellet)	Embarkation?	26 November – Operation interrupted by Germans. Alfasser shot and killed. Monique Giraud, daughter of General Giraud, managed to escape.
			Period: November 1943 – January 1944		
'PROTÉE'	Deuxième Bureau	Barcelona	French S/m Protée (L de V Millé)	To land 4 (?) agents: Capitaine Elie Rous ('Sera'), Capitaine Demettre ('Van der Brouck'), Georges Alain de Beauregard ('Gérard'), Georges Maignon ('Rivière').	6 December – Successful.
'ORPHÉE II'	Deuxième Bureau (DGSS)	Barcelona	French S/m Orphée (L de V Dupont)	To land 4 (?) agents: Marie-Andrée Bécu, wife of Capitaine de Corvette Mourman, C.C. Sanguinetti, Georges Espardeillat ('Christian'), Caubet ('Serge Patte'). To embark Auguste Larovier.	28 December – Successful.
'ORPHÉE III'	Deuxième Bureau (DGSS)	Barcelona	French S/m Orphée (L de V Dupont)	To land and embark agents and mail.	25 January 1944 – Successful. 9 agents picked up or landed (unidentified).

ALGIERS TO CORSICA, SOUTH COAST OF FRANCE AND SPAIN

Operation Code name	Department	Pinpoint	Ship	Object	Results and remarks
			Period: February – June 1944		
'ORPHÉE IV'	Deuxième Bureau (DGSS)	Barcelona	French S/m *Orphée*	To land and embark agents and mail.	22 February – Successful. Landed 7 agents. Picket up Lt Boffy, Lt Georges Riboullet ('Jojo').
DEPLETION 'ORPHÉE V'	Deuxième Bureau	Barcelona	French S/m *Orphée* (L de V Dupont)	As above.	1/2 March – Landed 12, including Paul Leduc ('Ledoux'; W/T operator), Lt Jeunot ('Tam'), André Marcel Pierrat ('Poiret'), Régis Witrand (W/T operator).
'SULTANE'	Deuxième Bureau (DGSS)	Barcelona	French S/m *Sultane* (L de V Javouhey)	As above.	28 March – Landed 4 agents including Mireille Molbert (W/T operator). Picked up Capitaine Demettre.
'ARCHI-MÈDE I'	Deuxième Bureau (DGSS)	Barcelona	French S/m *Archimède* (Capitaine de Corvette Bailleux)	As above.	20 April – Landed 5 or 6 agents, including a woman. Picked up Jean Diraison, his wife and child.
'CASA-BIANCA X'	Deuxième Bureau (DGSS)	Barcelona	French S/m *Casabianca* (L de V Bellet)	As above.	22 May – Landed Chartier, Perrier, Duchemin, Latour, Lt Riboullet, Abadie, Claire Dreyer ('Lenoir'). Picket up Marcel Picot, Jean-Marie Bresand.
'ARCHI-MÈDE II'	Deuxième Bureau (DGSS)	Barcelona	French S/m *Archimède*	As above.	2 June – Landed Lt Lucien Bardet (W/T operator), Charles Fareile (W/T operator), Isidore Fillion. Picked up a Lieutenant and Mireille Molbert.
'SULTANE II'	DGSS	Barcelona	French S/m *Sultane* (L de V Javouhey)	As above.	26 June – Picked up 3 or 4 agents, including a Colonel.

CLANDESTINE OPERATIONS FROM CORSICA TO SOUTH COAST OF FRANCE

Operation Code name	Department	Pinpoint	Ship	Object	Results and remarks
	Period: November 1943 – January 1944				
BOLIDE	Deuxième Bureau	Off Cap-de-l'Aiguillon	Jeaninou (French motor launch)	R/V at sea with Spanish ss REBECCA.	1 November 1943 – Failed owing to engine breakdown.
CLINTON (Known to OSS as CANAL II)	OSS	Cap-du-Pinet (Cap-Camar-at)	MAS 541 (Tenente di Vascello Cosulich) (ACF)	To land 2 agents.	28/29 December 1943 – Successful. Lt Maxted in command. Conducting party: Major Croft and OS Miles.
FURTIVE	SIS (P1/1.0)	Pointe-des-Issambres	MAS 541 (Tenente di Vascello Cosulich) (ACF)	To land 1 parcel and embark mail for 'Alliance'. 3 voyages.	29–30 December – Failed to find agents at pinpoint. Lt Cmdr Whinney in charge of expedition. 3 January 1944 – Failed. Again no agents at pinpoint. 28 January – Successful. 2 agents also embarked.
BROKER-AGE	SOE	Cap-de-l'Aiguillon	PT 200 PT 217	To land 2.	29 January – Failed. Enemy patrol encountered off pinpoint.
LADBROKE	SOE	Cap-Camarat	1) MAS 541 (Cosulich) 2) 2 PT boats	To land 2.	1) 27/28 January – Failed owing to poor navigation. Lt Cmdr Whinney in command. Party included Major Croft, Bourne-Newton, Ashton. 2) 30 January – Failed owing to hostile craft. Lt Maxted i/c. Party included Croft, Sgt Bourne-Newton, PO Smalley and OS Chalmers.
CROMER	SOE	Morgiou Bay	2 PT boats	To land 2 and embark mail.	19 March – Failed owing to bad weather. Maxted in command. 24 March – Failed (bad weather). 25 March – Failed (bad weather).
ABRAHAM	DGSS/BCRA	Cap-Camarat	PT 202 PT 216	To land 2.	18 April – Failed. Enemy destroyer encountered at pinpoint. Opened fire without challenging. No damage or casualties.

CORSICA TO SOUTH COAST OF FRANCE

Operation Code name	Department	Pinpoint	Ship	Object	Results and remarks
applies			Period: April – May 1944		
ABRAHAM (repeat)	DGSS/BCRA	Cap-Camarat	PT 209 PT 216	To land 2.	21 April – Successful.
CONISTON	SOE	Morgiou Bay	PT 207 PT 203	To land 2 and embark mail to Pelletier ('Reuben'). Meterological mission: Marcel Chaumien, operations officer and Jean Soupiron (W/T). Passed on to the Luberon.	28 April – Successful. Maxted in command. Conducting party: Capt Carson, PO Smalley, Sgt Bourne-Newton.
GORGE	SOE	Morgiou Bay (KARIKAL)	PT 556 + another	To land 4 and embark 5 including H. Rosencher ('Raoul').	19 May – Failed owing to fog and faulty navigation. Maxted in command. Conducting party: Major Croft, PO Smalley.
GORGE (repeat)	SOE	Morgiou Bay	PT 559	To land and embark agents.	20 May – Successful. Landed Henri Rosencher. Embarked Camille Rayon ('Archiduc'), Sobra ('Hercule') and W/T operator.
			Period: May – July 1944		
CHATHAM	OSS (AZUR mission)	Cap-Lardier	PT 217	To embark evaders and escapers.	24 May – Successful.
GRAPE-FRUIT	OSS (AZUR mission)	Cap-Lardier	PT 218	To embark 2: Marius Chavant ('Clement') and Lt Jean Veyrat.	24 May – Successful.
CORTE	DGSS/BCRA	Cap-Lardier	PT 558	To land 2.	26 May – Successful.
GORGE II	SOE	Morgiou Bay	PT 557 + another	To land 4 and embark 5.	23/24 June – Failed twice owing to bad navigation. Boyle in command. Conducting party: Croft and Smalley. 25 May – 3rd attempt called off as SPOC had learned of arrest of 'Octave' (W/T Operator) and Rayband family at La-Motte-d'Aigues on 21 May.
SWEET PEA	OSS	Cap-Lardier	PT 557	To land 2.	20 July – Successful.
SWEET PEA II	OSS	CAP-Lardier	PT 555	To embark 3.	24 July – Successful.

Bibliography

Unless otherwise stated, books in English were published in London, those in French in Paris.

AGLAN, Alya: *Mémoires Résistantes: Histoire du Réseau JADE-FITZ-ROY 1940–44* (Editions du Cerf, 1994).

ANDREW, Christopher: *Secret Service* (Heinemann, 1985).

BARBER, Noël: *The Week France Fell: June 1940* (Macmillan, 1976).

BEESLY, Patrick: *Very Special Admiral: The Life of Admiral J. H. Godfrey, C.B.*, with a Foreword by Stephen Roskill (Hamish Hamilton, 1980).

BEEVOR, J. G.: *SOE: Recollections and Reflections 1940–1945* (The Bodley Head, 1981).

BIRKIN, David: *The Aber-Wrac'h Saga*, unpublished typescript communicated by the author and by Judy Birkin.

BOTT, Lloyd: *Some Wartime Memoires of Lloyd Bott*, privately circulated in typescript by the author (Melbourne, 1991).

CALVI, Fabrizio, in collaboration with Olivier Schmidt: *OSS: La Guerre secrète en France, 1942–45: Les Services Spéciaux Américains, la Résistance et la Gestapo* (Hachette, 1990).

CAMPOS, Christophe, ed.: *Franco–British Studies* (Journal of the British Institute in Paris)

——— No. 2 (Autumn 1986), 'British Aid to Armed French Resistance':
I Maurice Hutt: The 1790s and the Myth of "Perfidious Albion"';
II M.R.D. Foot: '1940–44 and the Secret Services';

——— No. 7 (Spring 1989), 'Operation TORCH and its Political Aftermath: A Franco-Anglo-American Gordian Knot': papers by J. B. Duroselle, Anthony Verrier, Arthur Funk, Philippe Masson, Philip Bell, Jean-Pierre Azéma, Jean-Louis Crémieux-Brilhac, Charles-Robert Ageron. [Discussions of the roles of OSS and SOE in North Africa, Anglo–American policy towards Darlan and the Vichy administration, the death of Darlan.]

CHALOU, George C., ed.: *The Secrets War: The Office of Strategic Services in World War II* (National Archives and Records Administration, Washington, DC, 1992).

CHURCHILL, P. M.: *Of their Own Choice* (Hodder & Stoughton, 1952).

CHURCHILL, P. M.: *Duel of Wits* (Hodder & Stoughton, 1955).

CHURCHILL, Winston: *The Second World War*, Vols I–V (Cassell, 1948–52).

COLLIER, Richard: *D-Day: June 6, 1944: The Normandy Landings* (Cassell, 1992).

COON, Carleton S.: *A North African Story: The Anthropologist as OSS Agent 1941–43. With Historical Settings from the Editors of* Gambit (*Gambit*, Ipswich, MA, 1980).

COURTNEY, G. B.: *S.B.S. in World War Two* (Robert Hale, 1985).

COUTAU-BEGARIE, Hervé and HUAN, Claude: *Darlan* (Fayard, 1989).

CRAWLEY, Aidan: *De Gaulle: A Biography* (Collins, 1969).

CROFT, Andrew: *A Talent for Adventure* (SPA Ltd, Hanley Swan, Worcs., in conjunction with Andrew Croft, 1991).

DEACON, Richard: *A History of the British Secret Service* (Frederick Muller, 1969).

D'ESTIENNES D'ORVES, Family, eds: *La Vie Exemplaire du Commandant d'Estiennes d'Orves: Papiers, Carnets, Lettres* (Plon, 1950).

DILKS, David: *The Diaries of Sir Alexander Cadogan, 1938–45* (Cassell, 1971).

DODDS-PARKER, Douglas: *Setting Europe Ablaze: Some Account of Ungentlemanly Warfare* (Springwood Books, Windlesham, Surrey, 1984).

DUMAIS, Lucien A.: *The Man Who Went Back* (Leo Cooper, 1975).

FLEURY, Georges and MALOUBIER, Robert: *Nageurs de Combat* (La Table Ronde, 1989).

FOOT, M. R. D.: *SOE in France: An Account of the Work of the British Special Operations Executive in France 1940–1944* (HMSO, 1966).

FUNK, Arthur Layton: *The Politics of TORCH: The Allied Landings and the Algiers Putsch 1942* (The University Press of Kansas, Lawrence/ Manhattan/Wichita, 1974).

FUNK, Arthur Layton: *Hidden Ally: The French Resistance, Special Operations, and the Landings in Southern France, 1944*, Contributions in Military Studies, No. 122 (Greenwood Press, New York, Westpoint, CT, and London, 1992).

GAULLE, Charles de: *War Memoirs*, Vol. I: *The Call to Honour 1940–42* (Collins, 1955).

GILBERT, Martin: *Second World War* (Weidenfeld and Nicolson, 1989).

GILLOIS, André: *Histoire Secrète des Français à Londres de 1940 à 1944* (Hachette-Littérature, 1973).

GRIFFI, Toussaint and PREZIOSI, Laurent: *Première Mission en Corse Occupée, avec le Sousmarin CASABIANCA (Décembre 1942– Mai 1943)*, Preface by Henri Noguès (Editions L'Harmattan, 1988).

HAMPSHIRE, A. Cecil: *The Secret Navies* (William Kimber, 1978).

HAMPSHIRE, A. Cecil: *Undercover Sailors: Secret Operations in World War II* (William Kimber, 1981).

HINSLEY, F. H., with E. E. Thomas, C. F. G. Ransom and R. C. Knight: *British Intelligence in the Second World War: Its Influence on Strategy and Operations*, Vol. I (HMSO, 1979).

HUAN, Claude. *See* COUTAU-BEGARIE.

HUGUEN, Roger: *Par les Nuits les Plus Longues: Réseaux d'Evasion d'Aviateurs en Bretagne 1940–144* (Editions Breiz, La Baule, 4th edition, 1978).

JULLIAN, Marcel: *HMS FIDELITY* (Souvenir Press, 1957).

KINGSWELL, Peter: *FIDELITY Will Haunt Me till I Die*, privately published by the Royal Marines Historical Society (1991).

LACOUTURE, Jean: *De Gaulle: The Rebel, 1890–1944*; translated from the French by Patrick O'Brian (Collins Harvill, 1990).

LANGLEY, Mike: *Anders Lassen: VC, MC, of the SAS: The Story of Anders Lassen and the Men who Fought with Him* (New English Library, 1988).

LE GRAND, Alain and THOMAS, Georges-Michel: *39–45 Finistère* (Editions de la Cité, Brest–Paris, 1987).

LE TAC, Joël and others: *Les Réseaux Action de la France Combattante, 1940–1944* (Amicale des Réseaux de la France Combattante, 1986).

LE TRIVIDIC, Dominique-Martin: *Une Femme du Réseau Shelburn: L'Histoire de Marie-Thérèse Le Calvez de Plouha, en Bretagne recueillie par Dominique-Martin le Trividic*, Preface by Jacques Chaban-Delmas ('Témoignages', Editions le Cercle d'or, Les Sables d'Olonne, 1979).

L'HERMINIER, Captain J.: *CASABIANCA: The Secret Missions of a French Submarine*; translated from the French by Edward Fitzgerald (Frederick Muller, 1953).

McGEOCH, Ian: *An Affair of Chances: A Submariner's Odyssey 1939–42* (Imperial War Museum, 1991).

MACLACHLAN, Donald: *Room 39* (Weidenfeld and Nicolson, 1968).

MACMILLAN, Harold: *War Diaries: The Mediterranean, 1943–45* (Macmillan, 1985).

MERRICK, K. A.: *Flights of the Forgotten: Special Duties Operations in World War Two* (Arms and Armour Press, 1989).

MINSHULL, Merlin: *G(u)ilt Edged* (Bachman and Turner, 1975).

MOREAU, Hubert: 'Premières Missions', *Revue de la France Libre*, Nos 80, 81 and 82 (1955) [three articles].

MOREAU, Hubert and others: *Lieutenant de Vaisseau Hubert Moreau*, typescript booklet [communicated to the author by Capitaine de Vaisseau Claude Huan. Includes a separate and, in some respects, fuller account of Moreau's escape from France in June 1940 and his first two missions, a press release dated 25 August 1941 by the Free French information service entitled 'Le Léopard', and a biographical note headed 'MOREAU (Hubert Arnold Pierre), Lieutenant de Vaisseau, *Résistant–Premier Agent de Renseignements Français en France Occupée - 1920–1959*', compiled 13 October 1980 by le Maître Principal Dominique Lemaire from the Archives Centrales de la Marine, CC7 4ème Moderne 1331/4 and 3040/11].

'PASSY' (A. Dewavrin): *Souvenirs*, Vol. I: *2e Bureau, Londres* (Raoul Solar Editions, Monte Carlo, 1947).

PELLETIER, Antoine: *Autrement qu'ainsi*, unpublished manuscript.

PICHAVANT, René: *Clandestins de l'Iroise*, Vol. I: 1940–42 – Récits d'Histoire; Vol. II: 1942–3; Vol. III: 1943–4; Vol. IV: 1940–44 (Editions Morgane, Douarnenez, 1982, 1984, 1986, 1988).

'RÉMY' (Gilbert Renault, alias 'Roulier'): *Mémoires d'un Agent Secret de la France Libre* (Editions Robert Laffont, 1945).

'RÉMY': *Le Livre du Courage et de la Peur: Juin 1942–Novembre 1943*, 2 vols (Aux Trois Couleurs et Raoul Solar Editions, 1945).

'RÉMY': *La Maison d'Alphonse* (Librairie Académique Perrin, 1968).

RYGOR-SLOWIKOWSKI, Major General M. Z.: *In the Secret Service: The Lighting of the Torch*; translated by George Slowikowski; edited, English adaptation, Introduction and Afterword by John Herman (Windrush Press, 1988).

SCAMARONI, Marie-Claire: *Fred Scamaroni: 1914–43* (Editions France-Empire, 1986).

SENGER und ETTERLIN, Ritter von: *Neither Fear nor Hope* (Novara, CA, 1988).

SILVANI, Paul: . . . *et la Corse fut libérée* (La-Marge, Ajaccio, 1993).

SPEARS, Louis: *Assignment to Catastrophe*, 2 vols (Heinemann, 1947).

THOMAS, Georges-Michel. *See* LE GRAND, Alain.

VERITY, Hugh: *We Landed by Moonlight* (Ian Allan, 1973).

WHINNEY, Patrick: *Corsican Command* (Patrick Stephens Ltd, 1989).

WILKINSON, Peter and ASTLEY, Joan Bright: *Gubbins and SOE* (Leo Cooper, 1993).

Index

A

A4/SLO1 Operation 308
A4/SLO2 Operation 308
A5/SLO5 Operation 306
A5/SLO1 Operation 54, 304
A5/SLO2 Operation 30, 305
A5/SLO3 Operation 28, 305
A5/SLO4 Operation 305
A5/SLO6 Operation 307
'A' Force (MI9/19) 654
Abadie, – 687
Abbott, G.W. 122–3, 311
Aber-Benoît: COOK Operation
    158–61, 313; ENVIOUS Operation
    184–99, 301–2, 315; FELICITATE
    Operation 199–217; navigation 179;
    OVERCLOUD Operation 110,
    114–15, 116–17, 309; PICKAXE
    Operation 121
Aber-Wrac'h 158, 313, 320
ABLOOM Operation 453, 672
Aboulker, José 571, 572
ABRAHAM Operation 688, 689
ABRICOT Operation 670
Abwehr: double agents 122, 218;
    L'Émigrant 75, 83–6; Funkspiel 76,
    121, 307; infra-red monitoring 448;
    Le Grec 74; Marie-Louise 75;
    infiltration passport offices 18;
    Tangiers-Gibraltar ferry 448
ACCOST Operation 559–60, 677
ACF see African Coastal Flotilla
Achiary, – 557, 582–3
Acoustic mines 558
Adam, – 77
Adler, – 616, 618, 629
Admiralty: Air Ministry 24; CWF 549;
    Directorate of Combined
    Operations 21; HMS Fidelity 368;
    15th MGB FLOTILLA 284; Minna
    558; NID(C) 145; Operations
    Division 644–5; Polish evacuations
    361, 370–1, 421; Room 40 16–17;
    SIS/SOE control 656; Slocum 162;
    Special Flotilla 495; see also Naval
    Intelligence Division

'Adolphe' see Rendier, Captain Martin
ADOLPHE-AMÉDÉ mission 271,
    320
Adriatic 655
Aegean Sea 92
AFB/SLO1 Operation 304
AFB/SLO2 Operation 26, 304
AFHQ see Allied Forces Headquarters
African Coastal Flotilla (ACF):
    AUBURN operation 618;
    BALACLAVA 646–7; control 644;
    Corsica 638; creation 595–6; MAS
    boats 647; ZODIAC Operation 592
Agadir Bay 669
Agar, Lt Augustus xi
Agay 526, 543–4, 675, 677
Agde 525–6
'Agence Afrique' network 498, 557,
    560
Agostini, Colonel 684
Aïn Taya training camp 582, 583
Air operations: combined air/sea 24,
    165; de Gaulle family 12; records
    14; SOE 89; see also Royal Air Force
Ajaccio 613, 640, 646, 685
'Alain' see Leary, R.
Alaterre, Robert 78, 97, 308, 310, 323,
    324
Albania 597, 644
L'Albatros 38, 322
Alboran Island 415, 440
Alexander, General 593
Alfasser, – 685, 686
'Algèbre' see Ely, Colonel P.
Algeria: Arab hostility to Allies 587;
    arms supply 566–7; KASBAH
    Operation 670; Krajewski 409–43;
    Polish escapers 373, 374, 380, 399;
    Resistance 582; royalists 582–3; see
    also Algiers; Oran
Algiers: 'Agence Afrique' network 452;
    'Alliance' network 559; Casabianca
    base 618, 619, 624–5; Corsica
    missions 621–2, 626, 630, 633;
    French political situation 608–9,

630; MASSINGHAM mission 583, 616; Polish escapers 357, 378; 'Polofices' 378; resistance 582; SIS 164–5, 595–6; SOE 164–5, 567, 595–6; submarines 597; TORCH landings 581; W/T post 557, 561, 563

Ali Ben Nuar Bay 431

'Alibi-Maurice' network 275–7, 316

'Alibi' network 275, 318

ALLAH mission 78-9, 81, 83, 97, 308; see also Johnny's Group

Allard, General 222

Allart, Lt Pierre 276, 277

Allen, Sub Lt J.-J ('Tremayne') 171, 314, 367, 369

'Alliance' network 276, 325, 525–6, 559, 652–3, 688

Allied Command 633

Allied expeditionary force 642

Allied Forces Headquarters (AFHQ) 576, 630, 644

Alma Marine 571–2, 678

ALOES mission 320

Alsace-Lorraine 324

Altmeyer, General 6

Alvast, – 489–90, 506, 507

'Amédée' see Duffour, Félix

Amity 293, 329

Amphibious raids 21

Anas 291–2, 327

Les Andalouses 431

Andalouses Bay 432

Anderson, General 584

Anderson Manor, SSRF 147

André 113, 290, 324

'André, Dr' see Pfeiffer, Captain

Andrei, Simon Charles 624–5, 629, 681

Andrews, Stoker Alfred A. 281–2, 330, 334

Andrieux, Jacques 74, 83–4, 323

L'Angèle-Rouge see MFV 2023

ANGER Operation 304

Angers 348

Anglo-French Bureau 26

Anse-d'Arone 619, 622–4, 624

Anse-de-Bréhec 29, 96–7, 107, 305, 308

Anse-de-Canelle 626, 682

Anse-de-Canton Bay 468, 501

Anse-Cochat 246–7, 259, 263, 267

Anse-de-Gradella 636–7

Anse-de-Topiti 681

ANSON Operation 169, 314

Anstruther, Lt Col A.M. 581–2, 584

Antelme, J.F.A. 234

Antibes: DELAY II Operation 453, 672; fishing 501; GOBLIN II Operation 673; JASMINE Operation 455, 457–8, 672; Krajewski 485; MIMOSA Operation 673; PEPPERTREE Operation 674

Antonini, Dominique 606

ANZAC Operation 310

Anzio 645

AO4 see MFV 2022

Appleyard, Major Geoffrey 90–1, 114, 147–8, 308

Ar-Morscoul (MFV 2021, P11) 141–3, 165–6, 171, 311, 312, 320, 322

Ar-Voulac'h 291, 327

Ar-Zenith 322

HMS Araguana 524

Archimède 687

'ARCHIMEDE Operations 687

Aréthuse 640, 684, 685

'ARÉTHUSE' Operations 684, 685

d'Argenlieu, Commandant 31

'Aristide' 229

Arlebousse, General 682

Armistice Commission 356–7, 409–10; Morocco 380

Armorick 290, 291, 326

Arms supplies 657–8; Algeria 566–7; 'Shelburne' line 263–4; SOE 148–61; Tangiers 559; unoccupied zone 452

Armstrong, Commander D.H.F 558, 571, 594–5

Arrests: 'Alliance' network 559; CND 172; KRAJEWSKI XIV 483–4; Polish evacuations 541; SEA URCHIN Operation 629

'Arsenic' W/T set 277

'Arsinoë' see Védy, Gilbert

Arthur, Flight Sergeant René 64, 306

Arzew Bay 437

ASCENSION Operations 165

Asdic 155

HMS Ashanti 320

Ashley, Fred 323

Ashmore, Edward 494

Ashton, – 688

Asso, – 623, 626, 681

Astier de la Vigerie, Emmanuel d' ('Bernard') 231, 453, 608, 672

Astier de la Vigerie, General François d' 608, 609, 610–11
Astier de la Vigerie, Henri d' 566, 582–3, 608, 609
Astrape 149
Atcherley brothers 588–9
'L'Atelier' beach 228
HMCS *Athabascan* 261, 275
Atlantic, Battle of the 175
Attlee, Clement 21
AUBURN operation 618–24, 681
Auchinleck, General 553
L'Audacieux 142, 311, 325
'Autogyro' circuit 96, 122, 366
AUTOGYRO Operation 308, 670
Avallard, Jean 683
Aviso 323
Aynès, Lt 585

B

Badeni, Prince Kasimir 393
Badoglio, Marshal Pietro 639, 646
Baie-d'Arone 681
Baie-de-la-Fresnaie 218, 219–20, 314, 315
Bailleux, Capitaine de Corvette 687
Baker, OS Gordon 149, 150–1
BALACLAVA mission 646, 648–9, 654
Baldwin, Stanley 17
Balkwill, Sub Lt Robert 617
Baltas, – 35, 39
Banks, Telegrahist Henry 330, 334
Barbarin, Mlles 86
Barcaire 366
Barcarès 670
Barcelona 352, 653, 683, 685–7
Barclay, Lt Cdr Sir Colville 244
Barclay, First Officer Madeleine ('Bayard') 369
Barclay, Robert 64, 306
Bardet, Lt Lucien 687
Barker, P.O. 157
Barlier, Maurice 69, 75, 77, 289, 307
Barnard, Capt 674
HMS *Barham* 669
Barron, – 238
Barry, Napoleon 313
Bartélemy, Capitaine 685
Bartley, AB Roger 197, 214, 330, 334
Basin, F. ('Olive') 366, 452, 670
Bastia 599, 628, 631, 639, 640–1, 642, 644–55
Bataillon de Choc 633, 640, 648, 653, 685

Batalden Island 258
Bates, Petty Officer 547, 652
Batory 349
Battle of France 3–14
Baudet, – 255
Baudoin, Paul 5, 6, 7
'Bayard' *see* Barclay, First Officer Madeleine
Bayonne 349
Bazaucourt, Lt 669
BBC: de Gaulle 12; French Service 120, 205, 244, 290; messages 120, 188–9, 205, 225, 244, 248, 290
BCRA *see* Bureau Central de Renseignements et d'Action
BEAR I Operation 590, 592, 680
BEAR II Operation 680
Beatty, Captain Sam 123
Beauduc lighthouse 470
Beaufort, A. de 311
Beaufre, Cdt 574–5
Beaufre, Mme 575, 678
Beaumont-Nesbitt, Major-General 20
Beauregard, Georges Alain de ('Gérard') 686
Bécu, Marie-Andrée 686
Beevor, Jack 377, 616
Beg-an-Fry 224, 256; EASEMENT Operation 228, 230, 232–3, 316; GIRAFFE Operation 319; SCARF Operation 234–8, 318; SEPTIMUS Operations 231, 317
Beg-Meil 37, 38
Begué, Georges 96
Bégue, Lt Col 684
Belcon, Mons. 328
Belgium 3, 25, 29, 109, 545
Bell, Flight Lt J.N. 12
Bell, Sub Lt 270–1, 285, 286–7
Bellaigue, de 447
Bellet, Lt 599, 601–2, 635, 636, 686, 687
Benielli, – 615
Bénodet 320
Beresnikov, – (Corvisart) 28, 305
Bergé, Lt 90, 308
Bergeret, General 610
Bernard, – 87–8
Bernard, Louis 322
Bernard, Captain Raymond 682
Bertrand, Capitaine E. 686
Bertrand, Colonel Gustave 62
Besnault, Capt René 324
Best, Payne 19

Betrayals: *L'Émigrant* 83–6; *Étourdi* 323; fishing controls 289; 'Johnny' group 83; KRAJEWSKI XIV 480–94; Le Goff 79; *Marie-Thérèse* 356

Bey, Lt Cdr Abdullah 567–8

Bianchi, – 614–15

Bibundi 95

Bickford fuse 102

Biczysko, Lt Jozef 466, 470–1, 484, 485, 488, 493

Birgemayer, – 385, 393, 399

Birkin, Lt Cdr David 174–83; ENVIOUS Operations 186, 190–91, 194–5; FELICITATE Operation 204–5, 206, 212–13, 214–15, 217; GLOVER Operations 277–8, 279–81, 282, 283–4, 285, 286–7; operations format 180–3; recommendation for award 330, 331–2; ROBESPIERRE Operations 269, 270–1, 271–2; SEPTIMUS Operations 231–2, 232–3; SPLINT Operation 274; 'Var' line 227

Biscay, Bay of 30, 67, 106, 126, 306

Bitner, – 351, 352, 362, 365, 669

Bizerta 584–6, 680

Black, Lt Ian 122–3, 125, 311

HMS *Black Prince* 275, 333

Blackby, Petty Officer 166

BLADE Operation 584

Blanda shipyard 493

BLAVET mission 273, 303, 316

Bleasdale, AB O. 335, 337

Bleicher, Sergeant 122

Blondel, Captain 324

Bloom, Marcus ('Bishop') 570, 677

BLUE Operation 590–1, 592, 680

BLUEBOTTLE Operation 545, 674, 675

Blyskawica 321, 362, 447, 448, 541

Bocq, – 77

BODDEN Operation 448

Boddington, Major Nicholas ('Professor') 499, 675

Bodiger, Louis 190, 211, 217

Boédec, Jean Le 323

Boffy, Lt 687

Bohec, – 305

Bohusz, General 370

Bohut, François 322

Bois-de-la-Salle 263, 264, 268

Boislambert, Hettier de 118

Boiteux 673

BOLIDE Operation 688

Bollaert, Emile 235, 292–3, 328

Bolloré, Gwenaël 325

Bolloré, Michel 311

Bolot, E. 683

Bomelberg, – 218

Bon-Porté Bay 621, 628, 681, 683

BONAPARTE I Operation 240, 247–52, 316

BONAPARTE II Operation 230, 253–5, 316

BONAPARTE III Operation 255, 317

BONAPARTE IV Operation 255, 317

BONAPARTE V Operation 317

Bône 583, 592, 594

Bonifacio 640, 642

Bonjour, – 590, 680

Bonnec, Roger 324

Bonneteau, Lt Col 682

Bonnier de la Chapelle, – 583, 610–11

Bonniot, Jean 323

Bonoure, Jean 97, 309

Bony-Lafont gang 276

Bordeaux: operations to 305, 321; Pétain 347, 348–9; submarines base 30, 91, 114

Bott, Lt Lloyd 254, 316, 335, 337

'Bourgogne' escape line 241, 292, 328

Bourgoin, Commandant 264, 264–5

Bourne-Newton, Sergeant 654, 688, 689

Bouryschkine *see* Williams, Val

Boutron, Cdt V. 678

Boyle, PO Coxwain 157

Boyle, Lt Ranald 652–3, 689

Bozzi, Regimental Sergeant Major 618, 623, 681

Bracey, Stoker Ronald 330, 334

BRANDON mission 568, 582–93, 645; BLUE Operation 590; Darlan assassination 610–11; 'Hatter's Castle' 594–5; TORCH Operation 572, 582–4

Breeze 110, 172

Breiz-Izel 292, 328

Bresand, Jean-Marie 687

Brest 123; AFB/SLO1 26; ALLAH mission 79; bombing 67, 79, 123, 271; evaders 190; Moreau 55–7, 59; occupation 13; operations to 81–2, 109; Polish evacuees 349; Resistance 184; siege 287; submarine base 57, 93, 123, 126

Breuillac, Cdt 680

Briand, Anastase 276, 277, 318

Brickendonbury Hall 87, 92
'Bricklayer' circuit 234
Bridou, Jacques ('Navarre') 559
Briec, Sébastien 97, 310, 324
Brittany: Deuxième Bureau 27–8;
  fishing ban 78; fishing vessel escapes
  30, 289–93, 298, 322–9; Liberation
  271; navigation 174–6, 181–3;
  Prohibited Zone 148, 179;
  Resistance 82; SIS 26–7, 29, 31–45;
  SOE sea lines 29, 82, 99–104
Broc'h, Mme 188
Broc'h, Mons. 188
Brochu, General 87
BROKERAGE Operation 688
Bron, Henri 685
Brossolette, Pierre 198, 231, 235,
  292–3, 328, 675
Broussine, Georges 241, 292, 328
Brown, Frederick 598, 602–3, 606–7,
  619, 681, 683
Bruley de Vourane, Mme 113, 324
Brun, Captain 590
Brussels 184
Bryant, Lt-Cdr Ben 308
BRZOZA evacuation site 411, 413,
  418, 422
Brzozowski, Major 379, 381, 382, 398,
  407–8, 670
'BUCHOWSKI I' Operation 671
Buchowski, Lt Jan 535, 577–80;
  CASABLANCA Operation 498,
  673; CHUB I Operation 643–4,
  677; Coast Watching Flotilla 495–7;
  death 580; KUMEL Operation 528;
  LEDA Operation 528–9; morale
  524–5; ORKAN Operation 452,
  498, 672; SASSAFRAS Operation
  499; SILKWORM Operation
  542–3, 676; SOE 447, 462, 497;
  Special Flotilla 495; VAGRANT
  Operation 527–8; WATCHMAN
  Operations 526–7, 543–4, 569–70,
  677
'Buckmaster' circuit refugees 220–1
Buckmaster, Col Maurice 104, 232,
  234, 238, 630
Buczek, Bosun 505
Bugatti, Ettore 101
Buhara 324
BULL Operation 525–6, 675
Bureau Central de Renseignements et
  d'Action (BCRA): Algiers 164;
  'Bourgogne' 292; Darlan 608, 611;

Lefèvre 66; 'Mithridate' 241, 242;
  OVERCLOUD 114, 116, 119;
  Scamaroni 609, 610–11;
  SEPTIMUS Operation 231–2;
  Service Action 119–20; SIS
  operations 273
Burel, Joseph 323
Burgaud 62, 306
Buslowicz, Midshipman Josef 423,
  426, 429, 430
Buvette du Rosmeur safe house 62, 66

C

Cagnoni, Colonel 639
'Cagoule' organisation 275, 582–3
Caids 377–8
Caillot, Captain 619, 626, 628, 681
Cairo 494
Calcutta 26
Calvi 656, 683
Camarat lighthouse 458, 461, 467,
  468
Camaret 290
Camors, J.C. 292, 328
Campbell, Sir Ronald 8, 9
HMS *Campbelltown* 123–4
Campinchi, – 5, 7
Campinchi, Paul 243, 244, 245–6,
  253, 268, 294
Canaris, Admiral 18
Cap-de-l'Aiguillon 679, 688
Cap-d'Ail 486–7, 673
Cap-d'Antibes 619, 673, 675
Cap Bon 591–2, 680
Cap-Camarat 640; ABRAHAM
  Operation 688, 689; 'ARÉTHUSE'
  Operations 684, 685;
  'CASABIANCA IX' Operation 686;
  'LA PERLE' Operations 684, 685;
  LADBROKE Operation 688;
  lighthouse 620–1
Cap-Corse 652
Cap Creus 484, 490
Cap de Garde 594–5
Cap Falcon 498, 672
Cap-Fréhel radar station 219
Cap Gargalo 637
Cap-Gros, PEPPERTREE Operation
  674
Cap-Lardier 609, 620, 689
Cap-du-Pinet 651, 688
Cap Serrat, BRANDON 585–9
Capitant, Professor René 609, 611
Capo de Gata 439, 492

Capraia Island 650
Cap-de-l'Esquillon 676, 677
Cardot, – 623, 626, 681
Carentec 12, 113, 290, 293, 304
Cargèse check point 622
Cariou, Madame 50–1, 52, 60
CARPENTER I Operation 148–52,
    157, 162, 269, 312
CARPENTER II Operation 152–4,
    157, 312, 313
CARPENTER III Operation 157, 313
Carr, Frank 99
Carré, Mathilde ('La Chatte') 122–3,
    311
Carroll, Lt M. 269
Carson, Capt 689
'Carte' network 452, 453, 499, 570,
    673
Carter, Sqn Ldr Gordon 313, 325
Carton, Sgt Radio 670
Cary-Elwes, Major Oswald 264–5,
    266, 319
Casabianca 596, 597–607; AUBURN
    Operation 618–24, 681; Corsica
    640, 643; Operation I 681;
    Operation II 618–24, 681;
    Operation III 626–8, 682;
    Operation IV 683; Operation V
    683; Operation VI 684; Operation
    VII 684; Operation VIII 685;
    Operation X 687; Operation XI
    686; SCALP Operations 633–8,
    683, 684
Casablanca: 'BUCHOWSKI I'
    Operation 671; CASABLANCA
    mission 498, 673; Massilia 294–5;
    Norwegian escapers 372; Polish
    escapers 357, 370, 373; 'Polofices'
    378; sabotage 378; W/T post 557,
    561, 576; Wysoczanski 372–3
CASABLANCA mission 498, 673
Caskie, Chaplain 546
Casquets lighthouse 147
Cassis 457, 509–10, 511, 673, 674
CASUAL Operation 559, 674, 676
Catalina 678
CATAPULT Operation 73, 295
CATERPILLAR I Operation 682
Caubet ('Serge Patte') 686
Cauvel, Raymond 356
Cavaillès, Jean 675
Cavalaire 652, 679
Cayley, Lt Cdr R. 680
CELERY Operation 110–12, 309

Celton, Arsène 67, 323
Cerbère 365, 669
'Ceux de la Libération' movement 231
Chaillet, Lt 602
Chalmers, OS 688
Chalmers-Wright, – 677
Chamberlain, Austen 17
Chamberlain, Neville 13, 15
Chambers, Petty Officer G.C. 335
Champlain 11
Channel Islands 29, 96, 147; see also
    Guernsey; Sark
Chantiers de la Jeunesse 566, 582
CHAPTER radio link 591–2
Charaudeau, Georges 275–7, 302, 315
Charlet, Blanche 238, 318, 675
Chartier, – 687
Château d'If 506
Château, Claude 684
'Châteauvieux' see Estiennes d'Orves
CHATHAM Operation 689
'La Chatte' see Carré, Mathilde
Chaumien, Marcel 689
Chavant, Marius ('Clement') 689
Chciuk, Midshipman 454, 457, 472
Chédhotel, Jean 322
Chemine, – 80, 308
Chenal, Lt 120, 310
Cherbourg 26, 304
Cherchell 564
Chevée, Lt 684
Chiconski, Lt Cdr Czeslaw 352–4
Chieński, Lt Lubomir 580
Chin, Surgeon Lt 588
Chioni Bay 599–601, 622
Chojnacki, Major A. ('Hugo') 434,
    504–5, 518; KRAJEWSKI XIII
    463–4; KRAJEWSKI XIV 481,
    484, 488, 490; KRAJEWSKI XV
    505, 508, 512–13; MIMOSA
    Operation 472–3, 475, 477;
    TITANIA Operation 538
Chopitel, Sgt ('Auburn') 618, 623, 681
Choteau, Col 685
CHUB Operations 677
Churchill, Captain Peter Morland 452,
    453, 461–2, 570, 671, 672
Churchill, Captain Randolph 584
Churchill, Winston: Fall of France 3–4,
    6, 7; French political situation 608;
    Mediterranean importance 552–3;
    Muselier arrest 80; National
    Coalition Government 15; North

Africa 581; Security Executive 21; Sikorski 349
Chwastek, Leading Seaman: JASMINE Operation 455; KRAJEWSKI XIII 472; KRAJEWSKI XIV 482; KRAJEWSKI XVI 520, 533; MIMOSA Operation 464; ROSALIND Operation 547
Cinquième Bureau 87, 363
Clancey, OS 197
Clark, Commander 497, 525
Clark, Major-General Mark 596–7; Darlan negotiations 576; SERAPH I Operation 564–5, 657, 677; TORCH Operation 562–6, 575
Clarke, Colonel Brien 557; arms supply to Algeria 566–7; LEOPARD/PICNIC Operation 571; OSS 561–2; SERAPH II Operation 574; TORCH landings 562–3, 573–4; W/T network 561–2
Clarke, Lt E.B. 453, 501, 672
Clasen, Cadet Charles 675
Clech, Marcel 87–8, 92, 96, 454, 672
CLINTON Operation 650–2, 688
Clipet, Commandant 640
Clogourouan 162, 269, 313, 314, 320
Clubs des Pins 633, 634
CMB see Coastal Motor Boats
CND see Confrérie de Notre Dame
Coast Watching Flotilla (CWF) 495–9; Algiers 579; BULL Operation 525–6; creation 448, 657; detection 502–3; LEOPARD Operation 570–2; Minna 558–60; mission priorities 549–50; morale 524–5; ORKAN Operation 452; Polish escapers 495–9; replacements 577; Spain operations 560; submarine 8 flotilla 502; TORCH 557–8, 569–72
Coastal Forces: Bastia 648; flotillas 659; French MTBs 27; loans of craft 102, 106–7, 116, 124, 656; offensive sweeps 274–5
Coastal Motor Boats (CMBs) xi, xii, 366
Coat-Mallouen, Resistance 265
Cochin, Dennis 675
Code breaking: ENIGMA 22–3; history 16–17
Codrington, Colonel 579
Coëtquidan 348
Coeur-Sacré-de-Jésus 323

Cohen, Commander Kenneth: CELERY Operation 111; Dunderdale 81; INDIFFERENT Operation 277; 15th MGB Flotilla 273; North Africa 559; SIS section 24–5
'Cohors Asturies' network 257
College, Signalman George 222, 275
Collins, Vice-Admiral Sir Edward 275, 392, 398, 463, 562
Colonna d'Istria, Antoine 624–5, 629, 636, 681
Colonna d'Istria, Paul ('Whiskers' 'Cesari'): German withdrawal 638–42; LEG I/SKIN Operation 683; Resistance organisation 629, 630–4, 632–4; SCALP Operation 635, 683
'Combat' movement 494, 608, 614
'Comète' organisation 184, 242
Commandant-Dominé 48–9
Commandos: Corps Franc 627–8; Guernsey 27; Hitler's orders 147–8; MTBs 26; No. 1 584; No. 8 584; No. 30 595; No. 62 (SSRF) 96, 147–8
Committee of National Liberation 643
Concarneau 133, 142, 289, 291–2
Confrérie de Notre Dame (CND) 141, 179, 198, 312; air operations 165; arrests 166, 172; EFFINGHAM Operation 313; FALSTAFF Operation 676; German counter intelligence 164; GRENVILLE III Operation 312; HAWKINS Operation 312; JERVIS Operation 314; mail pick ups 142–3, 658; Rémy 129; W/T link 69
CONISTON Operation 689
Conseil National de la Résistance (CNR) 235
Contraband Control Office, Gibraltar 446–7
CONVERSE operation 616–18
Convoys: Gibraltar 594; Malta 521; ONS 154 367, 369
COOK Operation 158–60, 313
'Copernic' network 91, 119
Coppin, – 673
Corbeau-des-Mers 66, 82, 322
Corps Franc 627–8
SS Corrientes 363
Corsica: AUBURN Operation 618–24; BALACLAVA 646–9; CASABIANCA I 596; Colonna

629–43; FREDERICK Operation 624–5; German withdrawal 639, 641, 642–3; Italian capitulation 639; liberation 633; MASSINGHAM mission 594, 629–43; PEARL HARBOR 597–607, 618–24; Scamaroni 119; SEA URCHIN 609–10, 611–15; SIBYL Operations 684; submarines 596
Corte 599
CORTE Operation 689
'Corvisart' see Beresnikov
Cosulich, Tenente di Vascello 650, 651–3, 688
Côte d'Azur 453, 462–76, 499
Cotentin 147
Couillandre, Pierre 66, 82, 322
Couillandre, Prosper 63–4, 66, 82, 322
COULINEC mission 317
Coum family 198, 214
Courbet 32
Courcel, Lt Geoffrey Chaudron de 10, 31
Courlis II 327
Courtauld, Augustine 99
Courtney, Captain G.B 564, 565, 566
Courtney, Roger 596–7, 631
Cousens, Lt 541
Cowburn, Ben 122–3, 232, 311
Cowell, Lt Cmdr 597
Craight, Albert 323
Crete 596–7
CREVASSE Operation 686
CRICKET I Operation 678
CRICKET II Operation 679
Croft, Major N.A.C. 647–51, 654–5, 688, 689
'Croix de Feu' 275, 276
CROMER Operation 688
Cros-de-Cagnes 619–20, 678, 679
CROSSBOW Operation 331
CROZIER I Operation 263–4, 266, 319
CROZIER II Operation 267–8, 319
CROZIER III Operation 268, 319
Cumming, Sir Mansfield 17
Cunningham, Admiral Sir Andrew: Bey 568; clandestine ops 644–5, 650, 659; Darlan assassination 583, 607–8; TORCH landings 573, 575
Cupabia Bay 624–5, 629, 681
Curtis, Lt Cdr Dunstan 116, 122; BALACLAVA 648; MGB 501 124; No. 30 Commando 595;

OVERCLOUD Operations 310; ROWAN Operation 311; TURQUOISE Operation 311; WATERWORKS Operation 311
Curza Point 683, 684
CWF see Coast Watching Flotilla
CYGNUS Operation 258
Cyrus-Joseph 644, 645
Cywinski, – 298
Czapski, Count 514
Czardasz 361, 362, 370
Czechoslovakia 18, 20, 89
Czechoslovakian escapers 347, 358, 373, 374–5, 377, 380, 388, 393

D

Daglish, AB J. 335, 337
Dakar 118
Dakota aircraft 658
Daladier, Edouard 294
Dalc'h-Mad 289, 325
Dalton, Dr Hugh 21–2, 94, 658
Dalton, Major 18
Daniel, Paul 291, 328
Daniel, Yves 277
Danish escapers 372, 378
Dansey, Sir Claude 47, 81
Darlan, Admiral 26, 70–1; assassination 164, 583, 607–9, 610–11; Clark negotiations 576; Deuxième Bureau 596; French political situation 608–9; Krajewski 409–10; TORCH landings 572
Darling, Donald 453, 579
Dartmouth 109, 110, 301
Dautry 684
David, – 592, 680
Davies, Lt Paddy 648
Davis, Cdr E.A.G.: Birkin 176; CARPENTER Operations 149–54; CELERY Operation 110–12; COOK Operation 158–60; ENVIOUS Operations 186–7, 190–1, 193, 193–5; FELICITATE Operation 210; JEALOUS III Operation 199; MGB acquisitions 124; operations orders 180; OVERCLOUD Operation 116–17; POLISH III Operation 220, 309; recommendation for award 330–1; TENDERLY Operation 154–7, 177–8
DCO/SLO1 Operation 27, 305

DDOD(I) *see* Deputy Director Operations Division (Irregular)

De Gaulle, General Charles 657; Algeria 608–9; Commitee of National Liberation 164; Corsica 632, 643; Dunderdale 80–1; escape to England 9–11; fall of France 4–5, 6–7, 8, 9; Luizet 292–4; Mitterand 228; Moreau 31–2, 46; Péri 364; public opinion 53; radio appeal 12, 13; Roosevelt 164; SAVANNAH Operation 90; SOE 364, 630, 632; Védy 231; Weil-Curiel 77

De Gaulle, Mme 12, 13–14, 304

Defendini, – 230, 316

HMS *Defiance* 157

Deiva 650

DELAY I Operation 671

DELAY II Operation 453, 460–2, 672

Delbos, Yvon 294

Dellow, Leading Seaman Albert 260, 262

Deman, Erwin 162–3; EASEMENT II Operation 228–9, 316; JEALOUS Operations 218, 220, 314, 315; SCARF Operation 238, 318; SEPTIMUS Operation 231–2; 'Var' line 163, 221–7, 234, 269

Demettre, Capitaine ('Van der Brouck') 686, 687

Deniel, Abbé 62, 66

Denise-Louise 101, 105, 146, 308, 311

Denniston, – 22

Dentz, General 355

DEPLETION Operation 687

Deputy Director Operations Division (Irregular) 162; creation 644–5; evaders 184; Greece 656; Helford 172; mail pick ups 166; MAS boats 647; Normandy invasion 256; operations format 179–80; recommendations for awards 330–5, 338–42; 'Shelburne' line 244

Déricourt, Gilbert ('Farrier') 218, 234–5, 238, 658

Dernbach, Colonel 76–7, 86, 307

Derrien 188, 189–90, 198, 211

Désert-des-Agriates 634

Despaigne, H.M.R. ('Magnolia') 499, 675

Deuxième Bureau, Free French 306, 657; Estienne d'Orves 75, 79–80; Mansion 54; Passy 47; SAVANNAH Operation 90; SIS 24, 81; Slocum 27

Deuxième Bureau, Giraud: BALACLAVA 648; *Casabianca* 618; MAS/PT Operations 653; SEA URCHIN Operation 629

Deuxième Bureau, Polish: Interrallié network 107

Deuxième Dragon Regiment 640

Dewavrin, Col André ('Passy') 13, 25; Algiers 164; BCRA 114; Dunderdale 32, 80; Estiennes d'Orves 75; Mansion 65; Moreau 47–8, 53, 55; SAVANNAH Operation 90; Slocum 27; SOE Independent French Section 364

Deyres, Serge 685

DGER *see* Direction Général des Etudes et Recherches

Dhows 567–8

Dickinson, Captain N.V. 584–5, 645–8, 655, 659

Dimitri, Grand Duke 63

Dinghies 159, 160, 208, 213, 214–15, 625, 634, 635, *see also* Folboats; surf-boats

DINGSON base, Bourgoin 264

'Diplomat' circuit 235

Diraison, Jean 687

Direction de Surveillance du Territoire (DST) 83, 85–6, 164, 291, 653

Direction Général des Etudes et Recherches (DGER) 235

Directorate of Combined Operations 21; 62 Commando 96; loan of craft 116; SIS/SOE coordination 91

Diversionary Group 448, 495

Dobson, Cdr C.C. xii

Dodds-Parker, Douglas 164–5, 611

Dogfish 449, 450; Buchowski 448; CASABLANCA Operation 673; 'KRAJEWSKI III' Operation 670; 'KRAJEWSKI IV' Operation 670; 'KRAJEWSKI V' Operation 401–8, 670; 'KRAJEWSKI VI' Operation 410–15, 671; 'KRAJEWSKI VIII' Operation 422–9, 671; 'KRAJEWSKI IX' Operation 430–3, 671; 'KRAJEWSKI X' Operation 435–43, 672; 'KRAJEWSKI XI' Operation 672; operational problems 500; ORKAN Operation 452, 498, 672

Dolphin, Captain John 88

Dom-Michel-de-Nobletz 67, 306, 322
Donovan, General William J. 65, 556–7, 648
Doolittle, General 575–6
Doornik, Jan 63–4, 67–8, 75, 76–7, 297, 306, 307
Doornik, Yves 75
DORULA evacuation site 411, 412, 413
Douarnenez: *Monique* 77, 289; Moreau 49–52, 62, 305, 306
Double agents: 'Alliance' network 276; Carré 122; Déricourt 218, 658; *L'Émigrant* 85–6; Gaessler 76; Madrid 401; Musée de L'Homme group 77; OVERCLOUD Operation 121; Passport Control Office 18; Roger Le Légionnaire 242, 292; Vichy Government 371–2; Weil-Curiel 77
Doubourdin, A.J.R. 670
Dover 109
Dow, Lt 653
DRAGOON landings 654, 655
DRAPER Operation 157–8, 313
Dréau, Captain Pierre 97, 256, 309
Drévillion, – 83–5
Dreyer, Claire ('Lenoir') 687
DST *see* Direction de Surveillance du Territoire
Dubicza, – 354
DUBONNET Operation 569–70, 677
Dubourdin, A.J.R. 366, 452
Dubuc, Paul-Marie 685
Duchemin, Perrier 687
Duchessa d'Aosta 95–6
Duclos, Captain Maurice (Saint-Jacques) 27–8, 54, 305
Duff, Able Seaman 637
Duff Cooper, – 294
Duff, J. 684
Duffour, Félix ('Amédée') 234, 238, 318
Duke, Captain 449
Dukes, Sir Paul xi
Dumais, Sgt-Major Lucien: BONAPARTE Operations 247–52, 253–5, 316, 317; CROZIER II Operation 267–8; LOST Operation 265–6; MI9 244; OVERLORD Operation 256, 257; 'Pat'line 243, 545–6; REFLEXION Operation 266; Tunisia 243–4
Dunderdale, Cdr Wilfred 24–5, 61–2; *L'Émigrant* 86; fishing vessel

operations 29, 30; Free French 80–1; Jacolot 70; 'Johnny' Group 78–80; Moreau 46, 48; Mylor flotilla 81; Passy 32; SIS 498; Slowikowski 557
Dunoyer, Christope 683
Dupont, Lt 592, 680, 686, 687
Dupont, M.M.L. 235
Durieux (Maurice) 404–5
Durrmeyer, Christian 683
Durski-Trzasko, Cdr K.E. 515, 523–5, 530, 531, 550–1, 579–80
Dutrex, – 675
Duval, Isidore 277

E

E-boats 258, 279, 280–1, 284
Eagle 521
EARDRUM Operation 685
EASEMENT I Operation 227–8, 316
EASEMENT II Operation 228–30, 316
EASEMENT III Operation 230, 316
Eastern Task Force 581–2
Echo-sounders 187
Eddy, Colonel William 557, 561–2, 567, 576, 619
Eden, Anthony 5
Edwards, Lt H.N. 671
EFFINGHAM Operation 166–9, 313
Eggum, – 403, 404, 411, 417, 429, 431, 436
Eisenhower, General Dwight: Corsica 632; Darlan assassination 611; French political situation 608–9; Gen 216; Giraud 573; Italian capitulation 639; TORCH landings 553, 554, 555, 581
Ejsymont, – 401
Ejsymont, Captain Oscar 474, 475
Ejsymont, Lt Col 473
El Alamein 554
El Aouina 584
Elba 654
Elbe 567–8
Ely, Colonel P. (Algèbre) 235
Ely, Lt-Col 318
L'Émigrant 74–5, 78–80, 83–6, 97, 308, 323; see also *Marcel-Elénore*
ENIGMA 22–3
Entier, – ('Lateral') 317
ENVIOUS I Operation 185–98, 315
ENVIOUS II Operation 190–8, 315, 316
Eon, Colonel 320

Escapers and evaders 179, 184;
  BALACLAVA 648; Brittany 322–9;
  CWF evacuations 550;
  Czechoslovakian 347, 358, 373,
  374–5, 377, 380, 388, 393; Danish
  372, 378; discipline problems 302;
  L'Émigrant 74; HMS *Fidelity* 364,
  365, 366; fishing vessels 289–93;
  local support 242; MIRFIELD
  Operation 313; Morocco 370–408,
  410; Norwegian 372, 378; 'Pat' Line
  545; Poland 347–60; Port Lyautey
  371–2; POWs 546–9; 'Shelburne'
  line 240–68; 'Var' line 221; visa
  access 351–2
Escudier rock 621
Espardeillat, Georges ('Christian') 686
Esplen, Lt Cdr 158
Esterel 620
Esteva, Admiral 360
Estiennes d'Orves, Comte d' 68–9, 72,
  75–7, 307, 684
Etang-du-Cannet 365, 669
ETNA Operation 632, 682
L'Étourdi 71–2, 323
Evans, Captain 593
'Excellence' *see* Jolinon
Eyre, Captain 589, 680

F

F1 and F2 networks 107
Falmouth 116
FALSTAFF Operation 535–6, 676
Faraman lighthouse 465, 468
Farelle, Charles 687
Farger, Flight Sgt Philip 265, 319
Farley, Flight Lt W.R. 89
'Farrier' circuit 234–5
Favone 627
Fawkes, Captain Barney 563, 574,
  597, 658–9
Faye, Commandant Léon 559, 574–5
Fayolle, Engineer-General 56–7
Fedhala, evacuations 385, 388, 394,
  670
Fée-des-Eaux (MFV 2025) 127, 171, 321
FELICE I (FELICITY) Operation
  589–90, 680
FELICE II (BLUE) Operation 680
FELICITATE Operation 199–217,
  284, 316
FELICITY Operation 589–90, 680
Felixstowe 109
Felucca missions 164, 577–80; Algeria

410–15, 657; Gibraltar/Morocco
  381; JASMINE Operation 454–62;
  Krajewski 375, 659; MIMOSA
  Operation 462–71; North Africa
  499; O'Leary 243; operation format
  500–3
Fénard, Admiral 583
Ferbrache, Sergeant 27, 305
Fernando Po 95
Ferrucci, Colonel 614
FFI *see* French Forces of the Interior
HMS *Fidelity* 171, 339, 362–9, 669,
  670
Fighting French, escapers from
  Brittany 71, 290
HMS *Fiji* 650
Filipkowski, – 402, 403–4, 411, 415,
  417, 429, 431, 436
Fillion, Isidore 687
Fischer, Dr Franz 19
Fishing vessels: Breton ban 78;
  discipline problems 82; engine
  problems 128–9; escapes from
  Brittany 30, 289–93; Free French
  escapers 69, 77; fuel restrictions 256;
  German controls 289; Gibraltar to
  Morocco 372; 'Johnny' mail 98, 146;
  NID(C) 126–43, 146; Swedish iron
  ore routes 99–100; *see also* Inshore
  Patrol Flotilla; MFVs
Flag Officer Commanding North
  Atlantic (FOCNA) 371, 380
FLANNELFOOT Operations 273,
  273–4, 316, 317
Fleming, Ian 26, 93, 101–2, 364
Fleuriot, Lt 264–5
Flichy, E.V. 684
Floiras, Auguste 675
FOCNA *see* Flag Officer Commanding
  North Atlantic
Foederis Arca 290, 325
Folboat canoes: CELERY Operation
  111–12; rubber dinghy comparison
  625; OVERCLOUD Operation
  115–16, 117; SAVANNAH
  Operation 91; SBS 596; SERAPH I
  Operation 563, 564; SIS 110–12; *see
  also* dinghies; surf-boats
Follic, François 67, 68, 75, 76, 77, 306
Fontaine, Mme 233, 317
Foot, Lt J.P. 564, 575
Foot, Prof. M.R.D. 93, 235
Ford, Captain 269, 270–1
Foreign Office: amateurism 19;

intelligence assessment 18–19; propaganda 20–1; SIS relationship 17
Forman, – 91, 119–20, 310
Forman, Sgt 308
Fort-de-la-Révère 241, 546
HMS *Forte* IV 159, 160, 210
Fougères, – 226
Fouquet, François 322
Fouquet, Nicolas 326, 327
Fourcade, Marie-Madeleine 652
Fourcaud, Pierre 494
Frager, Henri 316, 499, 673, 675
'Franc Tireur' resistance group 615
Francart, Gabriel 683
Francesco Crispi 628
Franco, General 407
HMCS *Fraser* 26
Fraser, Sub Lt B.K. 234, 274
Fréchaud, Joseph 323
FREDERICK Operation 624–5, 629, 681
Free French: CND network 129; 'Copernic' intelligence network 91; Dunderdale relationship 80–1; HMS *Fidelity* 365–6; JOSEPHINE B Operation 91; Mansion 54; Mylor Creek 61; Naval Intelligence 67; Newlyn 61; 'Service Action' 114; SIS cooperation 24–5; volunteers 69, 77–8; W/T link 68–9
Frélhaud, Yves 35–7, 40–1, 60, 79, 678
Frenay, Henri 494
French forces: 2e Régiment de Chasseurs Parachutistes 264–5; Corps Franc 627–8; submarines 597, 659
French Forces of the Interior (FFI) 288
Frêne 55
Front National 632; Corsica 615, 622, 625, 626, 638, 638–9, 643; de Gaulle 629; Resistance links 246, 247
Funk, A.L. 564, 572
Funkspiel 76, 121, 307, 590
Furse, Elizabeth 302
FURTIVE Operation 650–1, 652, 688

G

G3/SLO1 Operation 63–4, 306
G3/SR1 & SR2 Operation 307
G3/SR3 Operation 308
G3/SR4 Operation 308
Gadd, Telegraphist C. 330, 334
Gaessler, Petty Officer 76, 307

Gagnoni, Lt Col 638
Galea, Gracomino 677
Galliou, Jean 188, 189–90
Gambiez, Commandant Fernand 633, 648
Gamelin, General 348
Gano, Colonel 452, 557
Garby-Czerniawski, Roman 107, 112, 122
Garcia, – 506, 520
Garliński, – 349
Garnett, Sub Lt John 143, 213, 215
Garrow, Major Ian 545
Gasquet, Lt de 684
GAST 74, 83–5, 290
Gauchard family 38, 39, 59
Gay, Louis 683
GC&CS *see* Government Code and Cipher School
Genoa 628, 654
George VI, King 633
Georges-Duhamel 79
'Georges France 31' network 120, 121
Georges, Mme 244–5
'Gérard' *see* Beauregard, Georges Alain de
German forces: eviction from North Africa 644; ill-discipline 263; Vlasov Russians 263, 265
Germany: counter intelligence 164; Polish evacuation network 356; South of France 577
Gerson, Vic 235, 453–4, 672
GESTAPO 352; escapers 354; 'Shelburne' line 252, 262, 263
GHQ Middle East 656
Giannesini, Lt 638, 684
Gibraltar: Coast Watching Flotilla 448; convoys 594; felucca operations 164, 577–80; HMS *Fidelity* 363; French sea lines 347, 453–94; Joint Intelligence Committee 449; Kadulski 362; Morocco 370–408; operational problems 479, 500–3; Polish escapers 355, 356–7; Polish Naval Mission 362; refugee camps 392; security problems 529–30; SIS 446; SOE 448, 452, 497, 567; Special Boat Section (SBS) 563, 597; Special Flotilla 446–7, 449–50; Special Operations Group 496; TORCH landings 569; tunnels 561–2; W/T station 561–2, 576
Gicquel, F. 319

Gicquel, Jean 248, 263, 265–6, 267
Gicquel, Mme 265, 266
GILBERTE Operation *see*
   GUILLOTINE
Giles, Laurent 165–6, 500
Gillois, André 675
Giovoni, Arthur 615, 625, 638, 684
GIRAFFE I Operation 319, 677
GIRAFFE II Operation 560, 677
Giraud, Bernard 575
Giraud, General: Corsica 632, 640,
   643; Darlan assassination 610–11;
   Deuxième Bureau 596; French
   political situation 608–9; North
   Africa 657; SERAPH II Operation
   574–6, 678; Service de
   Renseignements 164; TORCH
   landings 564, 573–4, 574
Giraud, Monique 686
Glénan Islands: EFFINGHAM
   Operation 166; evaders and escapers
   240; GRENVILLE Operation 142,
   312; HATCHET Operation 310;
   INBRED Operation 314; MARIE-
   LOUISE Operation 137–8, 311;
   SAVANNAH Operation 128
Glendinning, Colonel 584
Gloaguen, Joseph 63, 67
Glorieux 597
Gloucester, Duke of 409
GLOVER I Operation 275–9, 316,
   658
GLOVER II Operation 279–81, 317
GLOVER III Operation 281–2, 318
GLOVER IV Operation 282–4, 318
GLOVER V Operation 284–5, 318
GLOVER VI Operation 285, 319
GLOVER VII Operation 285, 319
GLOVER VIII Operation 285–7, 319
GLOVER IX Operation 287, 319
Glyn, 611
Gneisenau 79, 82, 97, 123, 126
GOBLIN Operation *see* KRAJEWSKI
   XIV
Godfrey, Rear-Admiral John 24, 102,
   116, 145
Goguel, Lt 378–9
Goldsmith, J. 677
Golfe-de-Lava 638, 684
Golfe-de-Valinco 624
Gonidec, François 323
Gordon, AB James J. 330, 334
Gordon, AS 285, 286
GORGE Operations 689

Gort, Field Marshal Lord 294, 384,
   557, 561
Gorzelok, Mate Ernest 459, 471;
   JASMINE Operation 455;
   KRAJEWSKI XIV 482, 483–4,
   486, 493; KRAJEWSKI XIV 487,
   490; MIMOSA Operation 464, 465
Goulding, Lt H.W. 25–6, 27, 28
Goutier, Lt de 640, 684, 685
Government Code and Cipher School
   (GC&CS) 17, 22–3, 24
Goyen 324
Grach-Dzu beach 269–71
Grande-Fourche rocks 190, 192
Granier, Col 685
GRAPEFRUIT Operation 689
Greece 353, 597, 656
Greene, Tom 32–3, 46, 48, 83
Grenier, Fernand 312
GRENVILLE I Operation 142, 312
GRENVILLE II Operation 312
GRENVILLE III Operation 165, 312
Grève-du-Mousselet 218, 220, 222
Griffi, Pierre 606–7; arrest 632; ETNA
   Operation 682; LEG Operation
   631; PEARL HARBOR Operations
   598, 602, 622, 626–7, 681
Griffi, RSM Toussaint 598–9, 602–6,
   622, 623, 626–7, 681
Grimaldi *see* Scamaroni, Fred
Grino, – 684
Groix Island 307
Gromnicki, Lt 477, 514–15;
   'KRAJEWSKI IX' 431–3, 671;
   'KRAJEWSKI X' 435, 436, 442,
   672; 'KRAJEWSKI XVIII' 426,
   428; Oran 514; TANGERINE
   Operation 499, 673
Grosnier, René 323
Gross, Alois 83–6
Ground-controlled interception (GCI)
   installation 588–9
Grunther, Al 575
Gubbins, Major General Colin 20, 90,
   94, 146, 447, 577
Gubbins, Captain Michael 637, 684
Guderian, General Heinz 3, 4
Guéguen, François 112–13, 309, 324
Guéguen, Jacques 71, 112–13,
   289–90, 293, 309, 322, 324
Guélis, Major Jacques de 630, 640,
   643
Guélis, Major Jacques de 608, 646
Guelma 584

Guélorget, Pierre 324
Guénolé, Marcel 35, 39, 42, 79, 322, 323
Guérin, – 669
Guérisse, Dr Albert 243, 363, 364, 365, 453, 545–6, 669, 672
Guernsey 27, 101–2, 304, 305
Guerrilla warfare 20–1, 582
Guers 234
Guest, Lt Cdr Raymond 202, 209, 210, 212; FELICITATE Operation 202, 204–5, 206, 212–14, 215; GLOVER Operation 278–9
Guilcher, Jos 66
Guilcher, Martin 322
Guilder, Sgt 436
Guillaume, Lieutenant , 626, 619, 628, 681
Guillerm, Abbé 65–6
Guillet, Pierre 108–9, 113, 115, 151–2
GUILLOTINE Operation 142, 311
Guimaëc 238
Guingamp 253–4, 263, 273
Guizien, Commandant 291
GURNET Operation 615
Gustave 78, 324
GUYMAR Operation 559, 674

H

HM S/m *H43* 304
Habasq, Hervé 322
Habibas Islands 412, 422–4, 426–7, 438
HADDA pinpoint 380, 386, 387–8, 391, 393–4
Halifax aircraft 165
Halifax, Lord 6, 15, 21
Hall, Virginia 232–3
Halsey *see* Kerdrel, Comte Michel de
Hamblen, Colonel 562
Hamilton, Lt Guy 173, 258–60, 259–61, 262, 270–1
Hammamet 589–90, 680
Hamon, Jean 258–9, 269, 271, 318
Hankey, Flt Lt Stephen 190
Hankey, Lord 15, 20, 21
HAPPEN Operation 314
Harcourt, Admiral d' 410
Harding, Sub Lt 166
Harratt, Captain Peter 229; Deman 218, 219; EASEMENT Operation 316; JEALOUS II Operation 220; SEPTIMUS III Operation 233; 'Var' line 162–3, 227, 269

Harris, Flight Sergeant C.W. 12
Harscoët, Mons 261
Hascoët, R. 310, 324
HATCHET Operation 128, 310
'Hatter's Castle' base 595
HAVEN Operation 320
HMS *Havoc* 590
Havoc aircraft 165
HAWKINS Operation 312
Hayden, AB John 330, 334
Hayes, Charles 673
Hearn, C.F. 335, 337
Hecke, Colonel Van 566, 582
Helford base 102, 108, 110, 284; FELICITATE Operation 201–2, 213–14, 215; IPF 172; NID(C) control 145; radio contact 171; reorganisation 171–2
Helford dories 634, 635
Hélie, – 88
Hellier, J.B. 610, 613, 614, 615, 629, 631
Hénin, Lt d' 686
Henriot family 228
Hentic, Pierre ('Maho'): arrest 216; ENVIOUS I Operation 184–5, 188, 189–90; ENVIOUS II Operation 192–8, 193, 195, 198, 199, 315; FELICITATE Operation 202–3, 205, 211, 214
Herbert, Mary ('Jeweller') 570, 677
Heslop, R.H. ('Mahogany') 674
Heydrich 19–20
Hibbert, Leading Seaman A. 281–2, 330, 334
Hill, AB G.I. 335, 337
Hine, AB N.T.J. 335, 337
Hitler, Adolf 147–8, 363, 659
Hoare, Sir Samuel 579
Hockey, Sqn Ldr Ron 452
Hodges, Air Chief Marshal Sir Lewis 218, 228, 358
Hodges, Bob 198
Hoffelize, Capt d' 685
Holbrook, Rear Admiral 145
Holcomb, Colonel 580
Holdsworth, Cdr G.A. 88–9, 91, 116, 631; ACF 596; *Casabianca* 638; Darlan assassination 610; Helford 146; LARDERING Operations 148; MAC Operation 311; MARYLAND Operation 644; MASSINGHAM mission 594; Newlyn 99, 100; North Africa 147;

OVERCLOUD 115, 116–17, 119, 120; POLISH Operation 109, 309; SCALP II Operation 636; SOE fishing vessel acquisitions 99–104; Swedish iron ore routes 99–100; ZODIAC Operation 592
Holland 3, 19, 25, 81, 91, 109–10
Holland, Captain 449, 451
Holmes, Colonel Julius 562, 566
Honer, Lt E. 313
HMS *Hood* 363
Hooper, Wing-Cdr Robin 198–9
Hope, Major Norman 12, 13, 26
HMS *Hornet* 296
HOUSING Operations 320
Howe, Lt Fisher 646, 649
Huan, Capitaine de Vaisseau Claude 296–7
Huet, Ingénieur 683
Huet, Pierre 257–8; BONAPARTE Operations 246–7, 250–1, 257–8; CROZIER II Operation 267; REFLEXION Operation 259, 260
'Hugo' *see* Chojnacki
Huguen, – 248, 317
Humphreys, Leslie 235, 453–4; communications 104; DF Section 162; Section D 87; SOE 87–8, 365; 'Var' line 221, 233
Hungary, Polish escapers 348
Hunter-Hue, – 264
Huntzinger, General 358
Hurd Deep 182
HUSKY 633, 645
Hutchison, Lt Col Jim 609
Hydrophone 260, 270

I

'Les Ibériques' Resistance group 121
IGNOBLE Operation 320
Ile-à-Canton 277, 278, 280, 316, 317, 318
Ile-de-Batz: ANZAC Operation 310, 312; CARPENTER Operations 148–54, 313; GLOVER Operations 282; POLISH Operations 309; ROBESPIERRE Operation 268, 270, 320
Ile-du-Bec 191
Ile-de-Bréhat 310
Ile-Callot 290–1
Ile-d'Er 316, 317
Ile-Grande 282, 283–4, 318, 319

Ile-de-Groix 67
Ile-de-Levant 620, 651
Ile-Guénnoc 114, 117, 120, 158–160, 311; COOK Operation 313; ENVIOUS Operations 188–9, 191, 192–6, 315; OVERCLOUD Operation 310; SOOTY Operation 321
Ile-Losquet 154–5, 278–80, 281, 312
Ile-Rohein 309–10
Ile-de-Sein 30, 64, 65–6, 306
Ile-de-Stagadon 157–8, 313, 321
Ile-de-Tariec 114, 188, 192–6, 211, 315, 316
Ile-Verte 311
Ile-Vierge lighthouse 187, 190
Ile-d'Yeu 311
Iles-d'Hyères 652
Illingworth, Commander John 500, 518
INBRED Operations 172, 314
Independent Companies 20, 94
INDIFFERENT I Operation 219–20, 314
INDIFFERENT II Operation 220–1, 315
Informers: Algeria 432, 442; KRAJEWSKI XIV 493; Polish mission 474; *see also* betrayals
Infra-red monitoring 448
Inscription Maritime 74, 93
Inshore Patrol Flotilla (IPF) 141–3, 171–2; FELICITATE Operation 213; fuel restrictions 256; recommendations for awards 335, 338–42; SOE 172
'Interallié' network 69, 107, 112, 122, 123, 220, 309, 322
IPF *see* Inshore Patrol Flotilla
Italy: Allied landings 645; capitulation 639; eviction from North Africa 644; MAS boats 649–55; MASSINGHAM mission 594; operations to 653; Polish escapers 348, 353
IVz/SLO1 Operation 670
Iwaszkiewicz, Captain 465, 470, 474–7; KRAJEWSKI XIV 488–9; KRAJEWSKI XV 504, 506–7, 511, 512–13, 607; KRAJEWSKI XVI 537–8, 540; KRAJEWSKI XVII 531

J

Jacob, Alice 227–8, 229–30, 237–8
Jacob, Raymonde 227–8, 229–30, 237–8
Jacob, Yvonne 226
Jacolet, – 70, 81
Jacquelin, Second Lt 670
Jacques-Morgand 172, 320, 321
'Jade-Fitzroy' network 184–98, 190, 203, 315
Jakubowski, Captain 433
Jankowski, Captain 350
JASMINE Operation 453, 454–62, 672
Javouhey, Lt 687
JEALOUS I Operation 219, 314
JEALOUS II Operation 220, 315
JEALOUS III Operation 199, 221–4, 227, 315
Jean 325
'Jeanette' *see* Sicot, Aristide
Jeaninou 688
Jeanne 325
Jeanne-d'Arc 362
'Jeannot' 184, 189, 192, 202–3, 205
Jeanson, Pierre ('Sarol') 184; arrest 216; ENVIOUS Operations 188, 189–90, 192, 198; FELICITATE Operation 202–3, 214, 216
Jensen, – 402, 411
Jersey 306
JERVIS Operation 169, 314
Jestin, Aline 218
Jestin, Mme 218
Jestin, Robert 211
Jestin sisters 226, 233
Jeunot, Lt ('Tam') 687
Jewell, Lt N.L.A. 563, 564, 566, 574, 677, 678
Jézéquel, Yvon 273–4, 292, 316, 328
Jickell, James Anthony 610, 613, 614, 631, 673, 681
Jiji 55, 305
Johan 669
'Johnny' organisation 69, 308; disbanded 83, 129; Lomenech family 71, 96–7; mail 78, 97–8, 126, 310; Vourc'h 292
Joie-des-Anges 327
Joint Intelligence Centre 497
Joint Intelligence Committee 19, 449
'Jojo' *see* Riboullet, Lt Georges
Jolinon ('Excellence') 317
Jones, Danny 494

Jones, Professor R.V. 448
Jones, Sergeant 654
Jones, S.G. 677
Jones, Major William A. 265, 266, 319
Jonquet, – 277
JOSEPHINE B Operation 91, 114, 119
Josse, Etienne 316
Jouan, Félix 221–4, 224, 225–6
Jouan, Mme 226
Jouet-des-Flots 235, 292, 328
Jourdain family 325
Jousse, Colonel 677
Joynson-Hicks 17
Jozefkiewicz, Lt 395, 400, 404; Algeria 414
July, Etienne 273, 316

K

Kadulski, Lt Cdr Marian *see* Krajewski
Kaminski, Captain 434
KARIKAL Operation 689
Karsenty, Bernard 565, 566, 571, 572
KASBAH Operation 670
Kasbah Tadla camp 404
Kelibia 590, 680
Kellner, Mons 276
HMS *Kelly* 323
HMS *Kelvin* 320
Kerdrel, Comte Michel de 97, 308
Kergorlay, Comte Alain de 115, 121, 309
Kerivel sisters 62
Kerloc'h, Jules 79
Kermor 326
Kérouartz, Château de 189–90
Kerquenn 197
Kertan, Gaston 308
Kesselring, General von 642–3
Keswick, Lt Col David 608, 611
Keyes, Admiral Sir Roger 596
Kiersnowski, Lt 357
Killick, Lt 394, 670
King, Admiral 553
King, Sub Lt R.G. 270–1
Kingfisher seaplane 367
Kingsmill, Peter 369
Kinloch, Captain 494
KIPLING Operation 593
SS *Kirken* 397
'Klan' network 276
Kleeberg, General 360, 373, 420; CHUB I Operation 677; escape plans 354, 355, 421; Huntzinger

358–9; sea evacuations 355, 356–7; SILKWORM Operation 541, 543, 676; VAGRANT Operation 528, 675; Wysoczanski 360, 373

Kleist, General 3, 4

Kleybor, Midshipman 391–2, 394, 395, 400, 670

Klimecki, General 408, 495, 497, 514–15

Klotz, John-Paul ('Faure') 684

Kluge, General von 13

Knight, Ridgway 559, 565, 624

KNOCKOUT Operation 320

Knox, John 572, 581

Kobylecki, Colonel 351

Koenig, Captain 13

Komar 378, 381, 399, 404

Komintern 17

KORDA Operations 320

Korrigan (MFV 2027) 32, 79, 171, 307, 322

Kowal 559; ZEBRA Operation 676

Krajewski (Kadulski) 361–2, 580; achievements 500, 659; Algeria evacuations 409–43; Coast Watching Flotilla 495; DSO award 409; plans for evacuation from France 373–4; French missions 420; GOBLIN Operation 673; Illingworth 500; JASMINE Operation 454–62, 672; MIMOSA Operation 462–76, 673; morale 524–5; Morocco/Gibraltar operations 370–2; NECTARINE I Operation 676; North Africa 514–15; Operation I 382–5, 669, 670; Operation III 387–92, 670; Operation IV 393–400, 670; Operation V 400–8, 670; Operation VI 410–15, 671; Operation VII 416–20, 671; Operation VIII 671; Operation IX 430–3, 671; Operation X 435–43, 672; Operation XI 672; Operation XII 672; Operation XIII 673; Operation XIV 480–94, 673; Operation XV 504–14, 674; Operation XVI 519–23, 537–8, 676; Operation XVII 531–41; Oran 452; plans for southern France 449–50; Quennell 375–9; SIS 446–7; Special Flotilla 495; *Tarana* 501; transfer 476–80, 497, 516–18; *Vega* 446–7; Wysoczanski 379

Kreeman, – 506, 520

Krumhorn, Lt ('Mangrove') 674

KUMEL Operation 528, 675

Kurzawa, Seaman 482, 520; JASMINE Operation 455; KRAJEWSKI Operations 505, 533, 534; MIMOSA Operation 464; ROSALIND Operation 547

Kuston, Mate 533, 547

L

La-Brise 90, 128, 240, 310

La-Ciotat 535–6, 676

La-Garoupe lighthouse 457, 461

LA GIRAFE mission 271

La-Horaine 273, 292, 328

La-Jeanine 77–8

La-Korrigane 289, 324

La Macta 423, 428

La-Madrague 504, 505, 508, 513, 531

La Mahouna 584

La Marnière, Dr de 214, 217

La Marnière, Mme de 190

La-Mouette 322

La-Napoule 458–9, 486, 543, 676, 677, 678, 679

La Patellière, Charles de 323

La-Perle 640, 684, 685

LA PERLE Operations 684, 685

La-Pérouse 292

La-Rochelle 349

La Rocque, Colonel de 276

La-Rose-Éffeuillée 291, 327

La-Véga 323

Labasque 63

L'Abbé, Paul 323

Labit, – 119–20, 310

Laborde, Admiral de 597

Labrosse, Raymond 241–5, 243; CROZIER Operation 263–4; OVERLORD Operation 257; REFLEXION Operation 266; 'Shelburne' 244–5, 247–8, 251; Williams escape 253

LADBROKE Operation 688

LADYBIRD I Operation 678

LADYBIRD II Operation 678

LADYBIRD III Operation 679

Laffon, Emile 292–3, 328

Laming, Lt R.J. 148–9, 151–2, 594, 633, 683

Lampalaer, – 276

Lampaul 308

Langard, Raymond 219, 226–7; arrest

238; EASEMENT II Operation 228–9, 316; JEALOUS Operation 314; SEPTIMUS Operation 231–2; 'Var' line 233
Langevin-Florisson sounding machine 600–1
Langlais, Lt Cdr Jack (Péri) 363–9
Langley, Major J. 243–4, 249–50, 276, 453
Lannion Bay 121–2, 276, 310, 311, 320
LARDERING Operations 148–61, 175, 179
Larovier, Auguste 686
Lassen, Major Anders 95–6, 147–8
Lasserre, Enseigne 607, 626, 627, 628, 681
LATAK Operation *see* OVERCLOUD
Latka, Leading Seaman 533, 534, 547
Latour, – 687
Lattre de Tassigny, General de 654
Laube, Herr 410
Laurent, Jean 9, 10, 294
Lava Bay 612
Lavalou, J. 310, 324
Lawn, PO Jasper 131, 137, 166
Lawrence, T.E. 103
Lazare, Sub Lt 318
Le Balch, Dr 246
Le Blais, Henri 246, 247, 252
Le Bourhis, – 317
Le Bris, – 293, 328
Le Calvez, Marie-Thérèse 249–50, 257, 261–2
Le Chêne, Mme M.-T ('Wisteria') 570, 672, 677
Le-Clipper 93, 171, 307
Le-Corbeau rock 283, 285, 286
Le Cornec, François 246–7; BONAPARTE Operations 250–1, 252, 253, 254–5, 256; LOST Operation 265–6; REFLEXION Operation 261–2
Le Corre, Raymond 32, 34–40, '45 53, 59–60, 79, 322–3
Le Corvaisier, – 229, 230, 237
Le-Dinan (MFV 2020, N51) 127–8, 131–41, 165, 171, 311, 312, 343–4
Le Doaré, Théodore 317
Le Duc, Anne 112, 271–2
Le Duc, Dr 112, 228, 230–1, 232, 271–2, 320
Le Fustec, Luc 636, 683
Le Gloaguen, Joseph 322

Le Goff, Henri 35, 39–42, 73–4, 79, 276, 277, 323
Le-Grec 73–4, 82, 306
Le Guen, Guillaume 203, 205, 211, 214, 216
Le Guen, Joseph 197–8, 211
Le Guen, Mme 189
Le Guen, Yves 323
Le-Guilvinec 34–8, 39–45, 53, 59–60, 304
Le Hénaff, Lt Yves 291, 292–3, 293, 327, 328
Le-Lavandou 575, 678
Le-Misère 324
Le Neveu, Roger 242–3
Le Normant 306
Le-Petit-Marcel 33, 40–1, 59, 304
Le-Petit-Marcel (L'Emigrant) 79
Le Prince, J.-J. 76, 77, 307
Le-Relec rock 187
Le-Rhin 363–4, *see also* HMS *Fidelity*
Le Roux, Jean 78–9, 81, 83, 85–6, 97, 308, 310, 323
Le Roux, Yann 323
'Le Studio' beach 228
Le Tac, Andrée 114–15, 121
Le Tac, Sgt Joël 90–1, 114–16, 118, 119, 120–1, 308, 309, 310
Le Tac, Mme 114–15, 120
Le Tac, Yves 116, 117–18, 120–1, 310
Le-Trépied rock 107–9
Le-Triomphant 76
Le Trocquer, Adolphe 246, 253
Le Ven brothers 290–1, 326
Leary, R. ('Alain') 366
Lebrun, President 7, 8
Lechat, – 313
LEDA Operation 528–9, 675
'Ledoux' *see* Leduc, Paul
Leduc, Paul ('Ledoux') 687
Lefèvre, Roger 65–6, 306, 323
Lefort, Cecily 218
LEG I/SKIN Operation 683
Lemaigre-Dubreuil, – 562, 582–3
Lemnitzer, Colonel 562, 567
Lemoine, Guy 276, 285, 287, 319
Léopard 63
LEOPARD Operation 570–2, 678
Lequien, Georges 61, 63, 67–8, 76, 82, 306
Leroy, R. (Alain) 670, 674
Les-Boeufs rocks 227, 232–3 236
Les-Deux-Anges 142, 325;

EFFINGHAM Operation 166–9;
GRENVILLE Operations 312;
JERVIS Operation 169;
MARIE-LOUISE Operation 134,
137–8, 311, 343–4
'Les Feux Follets' safe house 221, 223
Les-Sables-d'Olonne 320, 321
Letty, Lt Angus 110, 152, 158, 163,
220, 309
Levy, Dr 453
Lézardrieux 274–5, 320, 321
L'Herminier, Capitaine de Frégate
Jean: AUBURN Operation 618–24;
Corsican liberation 640; death 643;
PEARL HARBOR Operations
597–602, 626–8, 681; SCALP
operations 635–8
Libenter rocks 206
'Liberation-Sud' movement 453, 608
Likomba 95
Lionnais, – 607, 626, 681
Lipkowski, Captain 395, 397
Lisek, Second Lt 411–13, 415, 424
Livermore, Lt Col Russell 648
Livingstone, Captain R.P. 564
Lockhart, Sq Ldr Guy 675
Loiseau, – 144
Lomenech, Lt Daniel 308, 309, 369;
ALLAH mission 78–9; ANSON
Operation 169, 314; Ar-Morscoul
141–3, 322; L'Audacieux 325;
EFFINGHAM Operation 166–9,
313; L'Émigrant 74–5, 78–9, 86, 323;
fishing vessels 126–9, 289, 298; Le
Grec 73–4, 306; GRENVILLE
Operations 312; GUILLOTINE
Operation 311; HATCHET
Operation 310; JERVIS Operation
314; 'Johnny' organisation 96–7,
126; Lusitania 69–70; MARIE-
LOUISE Operation 131–41, 311;
NEPTUNE Operation 175–6;
PILLAR WEST Operation 311;
transfer to submarines 170, 300–1;
VALISE Operations 310;
Vincent-Michel 324
Lomenech, Mme 71
Lomenech, Mons 68, 71
Long, Lt C. 547, 638, 646
Long, PO Coxswain Tom 113, 151–2,
300
Lorient 60, 62, 93, 126, 142
Lorre, Louisette 252, 257, 268
LOST Operation 264, 319

Loustaunau-Lacau, – 276, 559
Luard, Lt Cdr W.B. 105–6, 127,
175–6, 335, 340–1
LUCALITE I Operation 480–94, 545,
673
LUCALITE II Operation 673
'Lucas' see Vomécourt, Pierre de
LUCILE Operation 674
Luftwaffe: Kampfgerschwader 100 90;
South of France 577
Luizet, Charles 294, 643
Lukasz, Lt (Michalkiewicz) 524, 525,
530–1, 533, 538, 546–9, 677
Lumby, Lt M.G.R. 624–5, 681
Lumsley, AB Paul 330, 334
Lunn, Lt E.J.A. 631
Lunna Voe, SOE missions 92
Lusitania 69, 323
Lussu, Emilio 616, 674
Lussu, Joyce 674
Lyons 352
Lyons, Gulf of 366, 669, 670
Lysander aircraft 165, 277, 658; early
problems 25; ENVIOUS II
Operation 198; 'Jade-Fitzroy'
network 190; mail pick-ups 184; pick
ups 89, 108, 276

M

'M Jean' 682
Ma-Gondole 62, 82
MA/SBs see Motor Anti-Submarine
Boats
MAB/DAV equipment 232, 233, 236,
282
MAC Operation 311
McCallum, Lt D.T. 558, 595, 655
Macfarlane, Mason 561
McGeoch, Lt Ian 616–18
Mack, Harold 608
Mackenzie, Lt Cdr Steven 364; A5/
SLO3 28; FELICITATE Operation
211–12, 213–14, 215; fishing vessel
acquisitions 98, 126–7; French
MTBs 26–7; JEALOUS III
Operation 199–217;
MARIE-LOUISE Operation
131–41, 311; MFV 2023 165–6;
MGB acquisitions 124; N51 129;
PILLAR WEST Operation 311;
recommendation for awards 335,
338–9; Rémy 129–31; 'Shelburne'
line 244
McQuoid Mason, Lt Jan 186, 314;

ENVIOUS Operations 315; FELICITATE Operation 199–209, 210–11, 212–13, 216; FLANNELFOOT Operations 316, 317; GLOVER Operations 284–7, 318, 319; recommendation for award 330, 332; ROBESPIERRE Operations 270–1, 320; SCARF Operation 234, 237
Maddalena, Sardinia 645, 646–7, 649
Madden, Lt Cdr 549
Madrid 352, 434
MAGDALEN Operation 303
Maginot Line 3, 348
Magli, General 642
'Maho' see Hentic, Pierre
Maid Honor Force (SSRF) 94–6, 147–8
HMS Maidstone 446, 450, 454, 500, 522, 563, 574, 597
Maignon, Georges ('Rivière') 686
Mail pick ups 275, 276, 658
Maillet, Jacques 292–3, 328
Maillot, Henri 638, 684
Mainguy, Job 257–8
Mainguy, Joseph 247, 250–1, 252, 261, 267
Maison d'Alphonse safe house 248–9, 251, 254, 257, 263, 265–6
Malaga 433, 434
Malgré-Tout 309
Malinowski, – 559, 676
Mallory, Sqd Ldr Hugh 561–2, 576, 590, 591–2, 680
Mally, Colonel Frederyk 354; arrests 386; Buchowski 578; craft acquisitions 433–4; Krajewski 362, 370, 420, 433, 443; MIMOSA Operation 475; Morocco/Gibraltar operations 371, 372–4; SOE 376–9
Maloubier, Bob 630
Malta 446, 589–90
MANDARIN Operations 674
Mandel, Georges 5, 7, 9, 10, 294–5
MANGO Operation 163, 313
MANGO 4 Operation see JEALOUS
Mankelow, Telegraphist 166
Mansion, Jacques 53–5, 296, 304–5; L'Émigrant 80, 308; Marie-Louise 64–5, 75, 289, 307; Moreau 56–7; Vincent-Michel 97, 324
Manuel, Commandant André 164
Maquis see Resistance
Marcel-Elénore (L'Émigrant) 78

March-Phillipps, Gustavus 94–6, 147, 659
Marec, Louis 317, 325
Maréchal-Lyautey 542
Mareth Line 593
Margiou Bay 689
Marie, Capitaine Jean 683
Marie-Joseph 327
Marie-Louise 64–5, 67–8, 75–7, 81, 84, 306, 307, 323
MARIE-LOUISE Operations 129–41, 311, 343–4
Marie-Thérèse 355–6
Marienne, Captain 265
Marietta Madre 654
Maris-Stella 322
Markham, AB John 285, 286, 330, 334
Marpha 291–2, 327
Marriott, H.R. 104
Mars, Lt Alastair 453, 461–2, 672, 680
Marseilles 352, 353; HMS Fidelity 363; fishing 501; JASMINE Operation 459; Krajewski 420–1, 506–7; MIMOSA Operation 462–71; North Africa sea lines 357–8; Polish escapers 355, 361, 504–5, 513
Marshall, General George 553–4
Marshall, Lt R.M.: BONAPARTE Operations 250–1, 316, 317; CROZIER Operation 319; GLOVER Operations 278–9, 281–2, 316, 317, 318; MGB 503 185; recommendations for awards 335, 336; SEPTIMUS Operation 231–2, 317
Marsouin 597, 683
MARSOUIN Operation 683
Martin, General 646
Martin, Lt Charles 124, 149, 156, 185, 312
Martin, Roger 121
Martinez, – 590, 680
Marty, Sergeant 264–5, 313
MARYLAND Operation 644, 654, 667–8
Marzin, M. 232
MAS boats 541, 646–7, 649–55, 659, 688
Mascara camp 430
Mason, Lt Jan McQuoid see McQuoid Mason
Massilia 294–5
MASSINGHAM 583, 594; Bataillon de Choc 633; BLUE 590, 591;

Casabianca 619, 634, 638; Colonna d'Istria 629–30; CONVERSE Operation 616; Corsica 632–4, 638–9, 641, 643; Darlan assassination 583, 607–11; French Country Section 640, 643, 648; MAS/PT boat missions 654; Naval Section 646; SCALP II Operation 636–7; SEA URCHIN 615

Mast, General 562, 563, 564, 566, 573, 597, 677

Masuy-Fallot gang 216

Maszczynski, Coxwain 533

Mattei, Abbé 605

Mauduit, Comte de 323

Maxted, Lt Tom 530–1, 533, 546, 547, 651–2, 688, 689

MDV 1 27, 28, 305

MDV 2 28–9

Méan-Névez 313

MECHANIC 615

'Médéric' *see* Védy, Gilbert

HMS *Medway* 596

Meffre, – 80

Mehedia 391

Melilla 440

MELPOMENE Operations 678, 679

Ménesguen, Joseph 327

Menesson ('Prunus') 672

Menguy, François 324

Menzies, Colonel Sir Stewart 15, 19, 22, 81, 99–100

Mercier, Louis 230

'Mercure' 675

Mers el-Kebir 26–7, 73, 414, 452, 556

Mersa Ali Bay 424

Messelmoun 564, 571, 677, 678

Météore 326

Meuçon airfield 90

Meynard, Dr 245–6

MFV 2020 (*Le-Dinan*, N51) 127–8, 131–41, 165, 171, 311, 312, 343–4

MFV 2021 (*Ar-Morscoul*) 141–3, 165–6, 171, 311, 312, 320, 322

MFV 2022 (*Président-Herriot*, AO4) 143, 171; HAWKINS Operation 312; INBRED Operations 172, 314; KNOCKOUT Operation 320; NOMINATION Operation 319; recommendations for awards 338; RODNEY Operation 313

MFV 2023 (*L'Angèle-Rouge*) 300–1, 369; ANSON Operation 169, 314; EFFINGHAM Operation 166–70,

313; INBRED Operations 172, 314; JERVIS Operation 314; REMEDY Operation 171, 314

MFV 2025 (*Fée des Eaux*) 127, 171, 321

MFV 2026 (*Sirène*) 171, 290, 325

MFV 2027 (*Korrigan*) 32, 79, 171, 307, 322

MFV 2028 (*L'Oeuvre*) 171

MGB *314* 116–24, 158, 310, 311, 658

MGB *318* 124–5, 658, 659; BONAPARTE Operations 248; CARPENTER Operations 148–52, 152–4, 312, 313; COOK Operation 158–60, 313; DRAPER Operation 313; EFFINGHAM Operation 168; ENVIOUS Operations 185–98, 190–91, 192–5, 315; FELICITATE Operation 199–217, 316; FLANNELFOOT Operations 273–4, 316, 317; GLOVER Operations 284–7, 318, 319; HAPPEN Operation 314; KORDA Operations 320; limitations 284; NEPTUNE Operation 174–5, 311; onboard conditions 176–7; ROBESPIERRE Operations 270–1, 271–2, 320; sabotage 301; TENDERLY Operation 154–7, 312; TENTATIVE Operation 313

MGB *319* 110, 309, 310

MGB *320* 109–10

MGB *321* 321

MGB *323* 149, 311, 312

MGB *324* 157, 313

MGB *325* 110, 220

MGB *326* 157, 163, 313

MGB *329* 192–5, 315

MGB *501* 124, 185, 658

MGB *502* 125, 185–6, 659–60; BONAPARTE Operations 254–5, 317; CROZIER II Operation 267, 319; EASEMENT Operations 228–30, 316; JEALOUS Operations 220–3, 315; recommendations for awards 337; ROBESPIERRE Operation 269–70, 319; SCARF Operation 234–8, 318; SEPTIMUS II Operation 232–3, 279, 317; SPLINT Operation 274–5, 318; 'Var' line 227

MGB *503* 185–6, 658, 659–60; BONAPARTE Operations 248, 250–1, 253, 255, 316, 317; CROZIER Operation 319;

GLOVER Operations 278–82, 316, 317, 318; recommendations for awards 336–7; SCRUBBY II Operation 321; SEPTIMUS Operations 231–2, 317
MGB *673* 219–21, 315
MGB *697* 219
MGB *718* 258–60, 268, 284, 318, 319, 320
15th MGB Flotilla 653; Aber-Benoît 184–217, 256–7; Cohen 273; craft acquisition 185–6; creation 161; operations format 179–82; recommendations for awards 330–5; 'Shelburne' line 240–68; surf boats 173; *Westward Ho!* 230
MI1c, creation 16
MI5 15, 21, 86
MI6 15
MI9: 'Alibi' network 276; evaders and escapers 179, 184, 216, 366; Gibraltar sea lines 451–2; *Moïse* escape 291; Normandy invasion 256; 'Pat' Line 365, 526, 545, 549, 658; ROBESPIERRE Operations 269–72; Saint-Brieuc Bay 258; 'Shelburne' line 240–68, 658; TITANIA Operation 538–9
Michalkiewicz, Lt Marian (Lucas) 524, 525, 530–1, 533, 538, 546–9, 671
Middle East Command 644
HMS *Middleton* 494, 545
Milan 6
Miles, Able-Bodied Seaman Don 635, 651
Miles, D. 683, 688
Milice 546
Millé, Lt 686
Miller, Sub Lt D.N. 234, 236–7, 269–70, 330, 333
Mills 33, 45, 46, 48
Mills, – (batman) 264–5, 266, 319
Milner-Gibson, Lt Cdr J.W.F. 25–6, 27, 28, 368–9
Milon, Jean 73, 78, 79, 80, 306, 308, 323
MIMOSA Operation 462–76, 673
Minefields, Plouha 257–8
Minerault, Emile 220–1, 238, 315
Mines, acoustic 105–6
Minesweeping 105–6
'Minister' circuit 233
Ministry of Economic Welfare 658
HMS *Minna* 655; ACCOST Operation

559–60, 677; BRANDON mission 582, 583, 594–5; CASUAL Operation 674, 676; CWF 448, 502, 558–60, 596; GIRAFFE Operations 560, 677; GUYMAR Operation 559, 674; HAVEN 320; Krajewsiki operations 514–15, 538, 540; LEOPARD Operation 568, 570–2; North Africa 499; ORKAN II Operation 559, 674; ROSALIND Operation 546; surfboats 211, 558; ULTRAMARINE Operation 677; ZEBRA Operation 676
Minshall, Lt Merlin 92–3, 307
MI(R) 20–1, 94
Miramar-de-l'Esterel 453, 671, 672
Miranda-del-Ebro camp 354, 401, 421, 545
Mirda, Abbé 546, 548
MIRFIELD Operation 162, 313
Misère 78
Misieuda, Father 380, 392, 393
'Mithridate' W/T link 241, 242
Mitterrand, François 228, 316
Mitterrand, Jacques 454
Mizgier-Chojnacki, Major 360
ML *107* 105, 106–9, 309
ML *576* 650
Mockler-Ferryman, Brigadier 572
Mohl, Commandant de 370
Moïse 291, 327
Molbert, Mireille 687
Mollard, General 615
Mollet, Wally 228
Molotov, – 553
Monaco 468
Mondolni, Benoît 625
Monique 77, 84, 289, 323, 325
Monnet, Jean 7, 294
Monzé, Auguste le 323
Moreau, Hubert 82, 88; Douarnenez operation 48–52, 55–60, 62–3, 305, 306; escape 289, 322, 323; Le-Guilvinec 31–45, 304; Passy 47–8
Moreau, Rear-Admiral Jacques 70–1
Moret *see* Moullec
Morgiou 505, 536–7, 676
Morlaix Resistance Group 228
Morlaix Bay 110–11, 309
Morocco: Allied ships 371–2; escapers 410; evacuation plans 377–8; French help in evacuations

373; operations from Gibraltar
370–408
Morvan, Joseph 328
Morvan, M. 84, 85
Morvan, Raymond 71–2, 323
Mostaganem Bay 411, 414, 418, 557, 671
Motor Anti-Submarine Boats 26; MA/
SB *36* 103, 110–12, 124, 174–5, 309, 310, 319; MA/SB *40* 305
Motor Gun Boats *see* MGB
Motor Torpedo Boats 306; MTB *29*
13, 304; MTB *105* 368–9; MTB *307*
590, 680; MTB *697* 314; MTB *718*
320; operations 25–6, 96–7, 308
Motor Yacht No. 77 88–9, 96
Mouden, ENVIOUS II Operation
192
Mouden, Joseph 188–9, 191–2, 217
Mould, Petty Officer H.E. 330, 334
Moulin de la Rive 122–3, 125, 311
Moulin, Jean 231, 610
Moullec, Commandant (Moret)
46–7
Moureau, – 116, 117, 118, 310
Mourman, Capitaine 686
MTBs *see* Motor Torpedo Boats
MULLET Operation 533, 537, 676
Mullet, Wally 316
Mulsant ('Minister') 233, 317
Munn, Colonel 611
Murphy, Robert 552, 597; 'Alliance'
network 559; appointment 556;
Darlan 583; Giraud 573, 574;
LEOPARD Operation 572; Royalist
plot 608; SERAPH I Operation
562–3, 564–5, 677
Muse-des-Mers 323, 327
'Musée de l'Homme' Resistance group
77
Muselier, Admiral 31, 46, 48, 63, 75,
80, 90, 364
Mutin 147, 149; fitting out 100–1, 108,
146, 151; MASSINGHAM mission
594; Sabatier 610; ZODIAC
Operation 592, 631
Mylor flotilla 60–1, 73, 74, 78, 79, 81,
82

N

N51 (MFV 2020, *Le-Dinan*) 127–8,
131–41, 165, 171, 311, 312, 343–4
Nantes, Resistance 77
Naples 645

Narbonne 675
Narval 314
Narvik 13, 348, 351, 359
Nash, 'Cookie' 131–2, 138–9
National Coalition Government 15
Naval Intelligence Division (NID):
history 16–17; operations 307;
Talisman mission 92–3
'Navarre' *see* Bridou, Jacques
Navigation: Brittany 174–9, 181–3;
Krajewski 464–5; North Africa coast
456–7; Poles 466
Nazarène 102
Neave, Major Airey 243, 244, 268
NECTARINE Operations 537–8, 676
Nekic, Branco 426
'Nemrod' organisation 75–6, 307
NEPTUNE Operation 175–6, 311
Nesa brothers, Corsica 622, 623
NETTLETREE Operation 499, 673
Neuchèze, Capt de 685
'Le Neveu' *see* Peulevé
New Grimsby Sound 132, 135, 140,
166, 169
Newlyn 61; discipline problems 82;
Free French operations 81;
Holdsworth 99, 100; *La-Brise* 90; No.
77 88; operations 306
Newman, I. ('Dividend') 570, 672,
677
Newstead, Lt P.E. 630–2
Newton, Lt John 101–2, 147, 631,
635–7, 646, 683, 684
Neybel, – 273
Neybel, R. 316
Nice 352
Nicoli, – 627
Nicolle, Lt Hubert 304, 305
'Nicotine' W/T set 277
NID(C): Bay of Biscay 126; CND 142;
fishing vessels 126–43, 146;
Gibraltar 446; Krajewski 530–1;
MGBs 124, 174; New Grimsby
Sound 169; Operations Division
644; Polish evacuations 531, 549;
Slocum 116, 145; SOE operations
ban 596; TORCH landings 557–8
NID *see* Naval Intelligence Division
NID(Q), Holbrook 145
Nierojewski, Captain 386
Noguès, General 576
NOMINATION Operation 319
NORDPOL Operation 110
Normant family 64, 67, 68, 76

North Africa: Allied landings 164;
anti-Gaullists 573; Belgian escapers
393; Czechoslovakian escapers 393;
felucca missions 499; French
escapers 393; Polish escapers 357,
359–60; SOE 147; W/T network
557, 561–2; *see also* Algeria;
Morocco; Tunisia
Norway 656; CYGNUS Operation
258; escapers and evaders 372, 378;
fishing vessel operations 338;
Independent Companies 20, 94;
invasion 3; iron ore routes 99–100;
SOE sea lines 91–2
Notre-Dame-de-Bon-Conseil 322
Notte, Santa di 604–5
Nouveau, Louis 241, 242
'Nubien' 317

O

'O' *see* Slocum
OAKTREE Operation 313
'Oaktree' organisation 241–5, 253,
268
'Octave', GORGE II Operation 689
Odend'hal, Admiral 5
L'Oeuvre (MFV 2028) 171
Office of the Coordinator of War
Information 556
Office of Strategic Services (OSS) 92,
164–5; Algiers 657; Bastia 648;
CANAL Operation 651; de Gaulle
630; establishment 556–7;
JEALOUS II Operation 220–1;
Mansion 65; MAS/PT boat missions
654; North Africa W/T network
561–2; PEARL HARBOR
Operation 598; radio networks 576;
SCARF Operation 238; Tangiers
557; TORCH landings 561–8;
Tunisia 581–2; W/T network 557;
YANKEE signals plan 619
O.G.Grévy 540
Oksywia 371–2, 374–5, 378, 386, 392,
395–7, 410, 416
O'Leary, Lt Cdr Patrick (Guérisse):
ABLOOM Operation 453, 672;
Dumais 243, 545–6; HMS *Fidelity*
364, 365, 669
Oleg xii
Olesinski, Leading Seaman 547
'Olive' *see* Basin, F.
Olmeto 625
Oran: ACCOST Operation 677; Bay

of 436–7; CASUAL Operation 674,
676; GIRAFFE Operations 677;
GUYMAR Operation 674;
Krajewski operations 410–11, 413,
414–15, 417–18, 422–30, 431, 452;
ORKAN Operations 559, 672, 674;
Polish evacuations 378, 399;
submarines 618; TANGERINE
Operation 498–9, 673; ULTRA-
MARINE Operation 677; W/T post
557, 561; ZEBRA Operation 676
ORKAN I Operation 452, 498, 672
ORKAN II Operation 559, 674
ORLANDO Operation 532, 536–7,
676
Ormesson, Vladimir d' 121
'Oronte' 317
Orphée 686, 687
Osborne, Captain C.B. 447–8, 451–2,
507, 519, 522, 644; ACF 595–6;
Durski-Trzasko 523; Gibraltar
security 530; Krajewski 492, 532–3,
519; planning 502; Polish mission
514–15; *Seawolf* repairs 522; Slocum
531; Special Operations Group 496;
Stoklas 495
OSS *see* Office of Strategic Services
Oued Ziatine 585
OVERCLOUD I Operation 114–21,
309, 310, 311
OVERCLOUD II Operation 310
OVERCLOUD III Operation 310
OVERCLOUD IV Operation 310
OVERGROW Operation 569–70, 677
OVERLORD Operation 235, 256–7,
276, 331
OVRA, Italy 629
Oxelösund 99–100
Oxley, – 61, 81

P

P11 (*Ar-Morscoul*) *see* MFV 2021
HM S/m *P36* 452, 671
HM S/m *P37* 97, 324
HM S/m *P42* (*Unbroken*) 452, 453,
460–2, 589, 672, 680
HM S/m *P217* (*Sibyl*) 574–5, 633, 678,
684
HM S/m *P219* (*Seraph*) 677, 678,
563–4, 566, 574–5
HM S/m *P221* (*Shakespeare*) 665
HM S/m *P228* (*Splendid*) 616–18
'Pacha' 317
Paillole, Captain Paul 62, 164, 291

Paimpol 317
Palermo 645
Palestine 353
Pallier, Mme 214
'Papa' 514
Papin 669
Parachute missions 89, 263
Parent, Raoul 258–9, 269, 271–2, 318, 320
Paris: 'Interallié' network 107; 'Phidias' organisation 273; 'Valmy' network 120
Paris, Comte de 583, 608, 609
Parodi, Alexandre 235
Passport Control Offices 18
'Passy' see Dewavrin, Colonel André
'Pat' line 184; betrayal 242–3; BLUEBOTTLE Operation 674; break-up 240–1; Campinchi 268; Krajewski 526; LUCALITE I Operation 545; MIRFIELD Operation 313; ROSALIND Operation 677; TITANIA Operation 676
Paul-André 327
Pauly, Capitaine (Pierson) 685
Paumier, Lt 640, 685
Pauphilet, Bernard 583
PCO see Passport Control Offices
Peake, Brigadier-General 646
PEARL HARBOR Operation 597–607, 618–19, 622–4, 626, 629, 631, 681, 682
Pècheral, Jacques 669
Peel, Stoker Kenneth 330, 334
Peich, Capt de 682
Pelipeyko, Midshipman 400
Pelletier, François ('Reuben') 653, 689
Pen, – 261
Penmarc'h 310
Penneac'h-en-Plogoff 67
PEPPERTREE Operation 674
Peretti, Achille 614
Péri, Claude André (Langlais) 363–9
Péron, Henri 97, 308
La Pérouse 327
Perpignan 358, 578
Perrin, Commandant 585–6, 588
Perrin, Jacques 585
PERRIN Operation see FLANNELFOOT II Operation
Pertschuk ('Birch') 672
Pétain, Marshall Philippe 3–4, 7–9, 13, 53, 347–9, 358, 583

Petit-Emmanuel 322
Petite-Anna 323
Petite-Fourche Buoy 191–2, 194
Pétrement, Yvonne 325
Petreto-Bicchisano, Corsica 626
Peulevé, – (Le Neveu) 120–1, 310, 311
Pfeiffer, Captain ('Dr André') 83, 84
'Phidias' organisation 273–4
Philby, Kim 448
Philipson see Schneidau
'Phill' network 276
Piana 622
Pichard, Michel 142, 198, 312
Pichavent, René 85
PICKAXE Operation 121–2, 310
Pickles, AB Harold 214, 330, 334
PICKWICK Operation 321
PICNIC Operation 570–2, 678
Picot, Marcel 687
Pierrat, André Marcel ('Poiret') 687
'Pierrot' 196–7, 198, 202–3
Pierrot 326
PILLAR Operation 309, 310
PILLAR WEST Operation 311
Pillet, Captain Jean 92, 299
Pillon, Charlotte 86
Pinckney, Roger 99
Pineau, Christian 675
Piotrowski, – 559, 676
Pirate 291, 326
Pisani, – ('Serra') 616, 618, 629
Plage-de-Saleccia 634
Plane Island 423, 424
Planier lighthouse 457
Pleven, René 7
Ploudal mezeau 308
Plougasnou 54
Plouha 240–68, 255–6, 257, 261–3, 268, 308
Plymouth 156–7
Pohorecki, Captain 569, 577
Point-du-Titan, France 620
Pointe-de-Bihit 123, 309, 311
Pointe-des-Issambres 688
Pointe-de-l'Ilet 453
Pointe-de-Penmarc'h 308, 309
Pointe-du-Raz 306, 307
Pointe-de-Saint-Cast 314, 315
Pointe-de-Taillat 682
'Poiret' see Pierrat, André Marcel
Poland: 2nd Infantry Division 352; 2nd Infantry Fusiliers 348; 10th Armoured Cavalry Brigade 348; Maczec Motorised Group 358;

Northern Brigade 358;
Podhalańska Brigade 348, 351; SOE
operations 89–90; W/T links 68
Polanski, Second Lt 412, 413–14, 415,
419–20, 423, 424, 430
Poli, Fernand 614
POLISH I Operation 107–9, 110,
112, 309
POLISH II Operation 309
POLISH III Operation 220, 309
POLISH IV Operation 220, 309
Polish evacuations and operations
577–80, 537–8; ban 549; Coast
Watching Flotilla 498; JASMINE
Operation 459; Marseilles-North
Africa line 357–8; North Africa 514;
numbers 501; priorities 473, 549–
50; routes 347–60; SOE 375–7;
Spain 434; Special Operations
Group 496; TORCH landings 515
Polish GHQ, Krajewski 409
POLISH V Operation 309
Polish Naval Attaché 550
Polish Naval Mission 524; Admiralty
interference 549; closure 551;
evacuation restrictions 518; feluccas
569; Gibraltar 362; morale 524–5;
organisational problems 476–7;
Special Operations Group 495–9,
496
Political Warfare Executive (PWE)
499, 570
Pollard, Sub Lt 193, 196–8, 200,
202–3, 207–8, 210, 214–16, 315
Ponte-de-la-Corde 293
Porquoi-Pas? 309
Porsmouguer, Jean-Marie 323
Port-d'En-Vau 453, 459, 503;
  KRAJEWSKI XII 457;
  KRAJEWSKI XIII 465;
  KRAJEWSKI XIV 483–5, 487–8;
  KRAJEWSKI XV 507, 508–9, 511;
  KRAJEWSKI XVII 531, 537;
  LUCILE Operation 674;
  MANDARIN I & II Operations 674;
  MULLET Operation 676;
  NECTARINE II Operation 538,
676
Port Lyautey 371–2, 378, 389, 410,
670
Port-Miou 457, 481–2, 484–5, 503;
  JASMINE Operation 453;
  KRAJEWSKI XIV 490;
  LUCALITE Operations 673;

PORTIA Operation 677; POST
  BOX Operation 674; WATCHMAN
  III Operation 569–70, 677
Port-Vau 453, 459
Port-Vendres 349, 352, 353, 501, 672
Portal, Marshall of the RAF C.F.A.,
  Chief of the Air Staff 90
Porte des Vaux, Jacquelin de la 48, 56
Porter, Lt S.A. 612–13, 624, 681
Portes, Comtesse Hélène de 6, 7
'Porthos', LEDA Operation 675
PORTIA Operation 677
Porto, Gulf of 636, 685
Porto Potenza 650
Portsmouth 109
Portugal 351, 352–3, 377–8, 401
Porz-Bezellec 307
Porz-Loubous-en-Plogoff 306–7
POST BOX Operation 674
POSTMASTER Operation 95
Potel, Marguerite 12
Potter, Sergeant 506
Poujade, René 356
Poulpiquet, Comtesse Geneviève de
241
Pourquoi-Pas? 71, 112–13, 289, 290,
293, 322
POWs *see* Prisoners of war
Praam dinghies 159, 160, 208, 213,
214–15
'Prax' *see* Serandour, Pierre
PRAXITELES mission 317
Président-Herriot see MFV 2022
President-Théodore-Tissier 33
Presqu'île Sainte-Marguerite 191, 196
Preziosi, Laurent 598–9, 602–6, 622,
623, 626–8, 681
'Priest' circuit 230
Primel 289, 322
Primel 305
Pringle, AB J.G.S. 335, 337
Prinz Eugen 97, 123
Prisoners of war: British, ROSALIND
  Operation 546–9
Prohibited Zone, Brittany 179
Propaganda: Foreign Office 20; SO1
22
'Prosper' *see* Suttill, F.A.
Protée 686
Provence 618, 619
PT boats 282, 282–4, 318, 319, 321,
645, 653–4, 688, 689
Puech-Samson, Lt 669
Pulchri, Capo 650

PWE *see* Political Warfare Executive
'Pyramide' 317
Pyrenees, SOE land line 365

Q

Q-ships 364, 366, 632
QH set 186–7, 190, 192
Quarto 417, 671
Quebec Conference 632
Québriac, – 35–7, 43–5, 46, 53,
    59–60, 327
Quennell, Hugh 375–7, 387, 559;
    Krajewski 379–80, 670; Ministry of
    Economic Warfare 497; supplies
    381; *Vega* 447; withdrawal 557
Quiberon Bay 146
Quimper 52–3, 55, 129, 228
'Quintet' 570, 677

R

Rabat 373, 378, 388–9, 389–91,
    393–4
Racheline, Lazare ('Socrate') 235, 318
Racine, Gérald 232, 317
Radar 174, 175, 176, 183, 219, 251,
    619, 620
Rade-d'Agay 526, 543–4, 677
Radio beacons 165
Radio communication *see* W/T
    communications
Radio Patrie 570
RAF 360 103–4, 145; COOK
    Operation 159; ENVIOUS II
    Operation 192; FELICITATE
    Operation 213; OVERCLOUD
    Operation 115–16; POLISH
    Operation 107–10, 309
RAF Regiment 588–9
RAF, *see* Royal Air Force
Ragueneau, Lt Philippe 583, 588
Raimondi, – 614, 615
Rake, Dennis 673
Rayband family 689
Rayon, Camille ('Archduc') 689
Raz-de-Sein 35
Rebecca, BOLIDE Operation 688
'Rebecca' radio beacons 165
Rechenmann, Charles 232
Reconnaissance: Bay of Biscay 67, 105,
    127; BRANDON 583–6, 588;
    reporting methods 25
Red-Atao 326

Red Cross (Polish section), Marseilles
    513
Red Sea, SOE operations 92
Redding, G.C.B. 122–3, 311
Redon 226
REFLEXION Operation 258–60,
    318, 319
Relec rock 191
REMEDY Operation 171, 314
Rémy *see* Renault, Colonel Gilbert
Renault, Colonel Gilbert ('Rémy')
    129–31, 325; German counter
    intelligence 164; GRENVILLE
    Operations 142, 312; intelligence
    importance 143–4; *Les-Deux-Anges*
    166; LYSANDER Operations 165;
    MARIE-LOUISE Operation
    132–41, 143–4, 311
Rendier, Captain Martin ('Adolphe')
    234, 238, 271–2, 318
Rendle, Howard 213, 215
René-Paul 393
Rennes 58, 120
Requin 291, 293, 328
Resistance: Bois-de-la-Salle 263, 264,
    268; Brest 184; Brittany 82, 289–93;
    Cherchell 564; CND network
    129–30; Coat-Mallouen 265;
    'Combat' movement 494, 608, 614;
    Corsica 629, 630, 632–3, 636;
    DINGSON base 264; ENVIOUS
    Operation 188–92, 197–8; evaders
    and escapers 184, 217; Front
    National 629, 638–9, 643;
    Guingamp 263; insurrectional phase
    628; 'Les Ibériques' 121; Liberation
    268; Morlaix Group 228; Musée de
    l'Homme 77; Nantes 77; North
    Africa 567, 582; Plouha 261–3;
    Royalist plot 607–8; SAMWEST
    base 264, 265; 'Shelburne' line 246;
    SOE arms drops 658; U-Solognu
    622, 626
Revinda 622
Reynaud, Alain 630
Reynaud, Paul 3–4, 5, 6, 7–8, 10
Rhodes 596
Riboullet, Lt Georges ('Jojo') 687
'Richard' 570, 677
Richards, Lt Cdr Brooks DSC*,
    RNVR 158; *Astrape* 149; BEAR
    Operation 680; BRANDON mission
    568, 583, 584–5; Cap Serrat 586,
    588; GRENVILLE Operation 142,

312; Helford 107; Luard 105–6; MASSINGHAM French Country Section 643, 648; OVERCLOUD Operation 116, 118, 119; POLISH Operation 107–9; *Pourquoi Pas* 113; SCALP Operation 635–6, 683; *Sevra* 105–6; surf-boat 125, 634; THIGH Operation 591–2; WATERWORKS Operation 122; ZODIAC Operation 592

Richards, R.O. 149, 300

Rickman, Alfred Frederick 99–100

Riedel, Lt 375, 402

Rigaud 583–4

Rive, Ldg Sea. R.E.J. 166, 335, 338

River Orne 27–8

Rivet, Cdt Etienne 685

Rivet, Colonel 61–2, 87, 164

Rivet, Jacques 684

'Rivière' *see* Maignon, Georges

Rizzo, E.H. 365, 669

ROBESPIERRE I Operation 269–70, 319

ROBESPIERRE II Operation 270–1

ROBESPIERRE III Operation 271–2, 320

ROBESPIERRE IV Operation 320

Robinet, Claude 324

Robinson, Motor Mechanic 166

Roche-Douvres lighthouse 219

Roche, R.B. 366, 670

Rockwood, Able Seaman 260, 262

RODNEY Operation 313

Rodocanachi, Georges 243

Roehr, Captain Jankanty 518; CASABLANCA mission 498; JASMINE Operation 453, 454–5, 457, 459, 672; KRAJEWSKI I 383–4, 385; KRAJEWSKI III 388, 489; KRAJEWSKI IV 395, 400; KRAJEWSKI VI 404, 413, 414, 671; KRAJEWSKI VII 419–20, 421; KRAJEWSKI VIII 423; MIMOSA Operation 462, 465, 466, 472–6

Roger Le Légionnaire 242–3, 292, 328

Rolland, Amédée 189, 192, 198, 211, 214

Romania, Polish escapers 348

ROMEO Operation 679

Rommel, Field Marshal 554

Rondelay, Colonel (Sapeur) 235

Ronin, General 164, 598, 611

'Ronsard', LEDA Operation 675

Ronseray, Comtesse de 325

Roosevelt, Franklin D.: Churchill 452, 515, 589; de Gaulle 164, 231, 608–9; North Africa 552–3, 556, 581

Ropers family 262, 263

ROSALIND Operation 546–9, 677

Roseborough, Arthur 630

Rosencher, Henri ('Raoul') 689

Rospico 306, 308

Rosservor Island 114, 186, 315

Rote Kappelle 122

Rotvan, Georges 276

Rouanez-ar-Mor 63–4, 66, 306, 322

Rouanez-ar-Peoc'h 32, 46, 48–52, 60, 62, 65–6, 73, 305, 306, 322

Rouneau, M.H. 234, 318

Rous, Capitaine Elie ('Sera') 686

ROWAN Operation 122, 123, 311

'Roy' 316

Royal Air Force (RAF): 54 Squadron 105–6; air escorts EFFINGHAM Operation 166–7; JARVIS Operation 169; LARDERING Operation 149, 159, 160; MARIE LOUISE Operation 136, 140; Brest bombing 79; Coastal Command 106, 175, 286–7; de Gaulle 90; evaders and escapers 157, 184–5, 240–68, 358, 539, 545; Flight 419 89; liaison 24, 145, 340–1; naval liaison 445, 502; parachute missions 89; Polish airman 347; reconnaissance 24; SAVANNAH Operation 90; SOE missions 161; Special Duties Squadrons 14, 138, 161, 163, 165, 190, 198–9, 277, 452, 545, 656, 658, 659;

Royal Australian Air Force, No.10 Squadron 12

Royal Cruising Club 99

Royal Marines 366-7, 369, *see also* Commandos

Royal Naval Patrol Service 101, 128

Royal Navy: 8th Submarine Flotilla 502, 618, 620, 625; cooperation 445; HMS *Fidelity* 369; Gibraltar 445–6; Péri 364; Polish escapers 380

Royal Patriotic School 70, 77, 113

Rubis 324

Rudellat, Yvonne ('Soaptree') 499, 675

Rullanec 291, 327

Russian Liberation Army 303

Russo-Finnish War 349
Rygor-Slowikowski, M.Z. 68, 498, 557, 582–3, 674

S

S-Phone 163, 193
Sabatier, Sgt 583, 610
Sabotage: BEAR Operation 590; Buchowski 497; Casablanca 378; Dartmouth 301; Guers 234; SOE 21–22; Tangiers 378, 448
Safi 372, 378
Saida camp 430
Saint-Brieuc 58, 273, 316, 317, 318, 319
St Christine 506, 511
Saint Génies 675
Saint-Géran 219–20
Saint-Guénolé 324
Saint-Guillaume 323
Saint Hardouin, Tarbé de 564
Saint-Hilaire, Capt de 685
'Saint-Jacques' see Duclos, Captain Maurice
Saint-Jean-de-Luz 349, 350
Saint-Malo 58–9, 349
Saint-Pabu 191
Saint-Pierre-Plage 545, 546, 674, 675, 676, 677
Saint-Tropez, France 620
Saint-Yves 326
Sainte-Anne 326
Sainte-Marie 322
Saladin, Jean-Amaury 324
Salaun, François
Salez, Victor 291–2, 292, 327
Sali 388
Salies-du-Salat 350
Salins-de-Girod 475–6, 513
Salmond, Lt M.P. 234, 330, 332
Salmond, Lt R. 220
SALVIA Operation 190
SAMPIERO operation 610, 630
Samuel, Hon. Tony 88
SAMWEST base 264, 265
Sanguinetti, C.C. 686
Sanson, Odette ('Clothier') 570, 677
Sanson, Puech 557
'Sapeur' see Rondelay, Col
HM S/m Saracen 624–5, 681
SARDINE Operation 480–94, 673
Sardinia 616–18, 645; evacuation 642; German withdrawal 639; KRAJEWSKI XV 509;

MASSINGHAM mission 594; submarines 596
Sark, SSRF raid 147–8
'Sarol' see Jeanson, Pierre
SASSAFRAS Operation 499, 675
Saule, Commandant de, – 598–9, 602–7, 618, 622, 626–8, 630–2, 681
Savage, AB William Alfred 299
SAVANNAH Operation 90–1, 114, 119, 308
SBS see Special Boat Squadron
SCALP Operations 633–8, 638, 683, 684
Scamaroni, Fred 231; Algeria 609; arrest 629, 631; Darlan assassination 611; OVERCLOUD Operations 117, 118–19, 310; SEA URCHIN 611–15, 624, 681
Scamaroni, Marie-Claire 611
SCARF Operation 234–8, 258, 318
Scharnhorst 79, 82, 97, 123, 126
Scheidauer, Bernard 323
Scheveningen Ferry 109–10, 149
Schlauberg, Leading Seaman 455, 505, 520
Schlochoff, Paul 684
Schneidau, Pilot-Officer Philip 89, 200–2, 210, 211–12, 213–14, 215–16, 302
Schofield, – 19
Schonfeld, Second Lt 433
Schrevel, Robert de see Saule, Commandant de
Schröder, Lt Cdr (A) Ben 367
Schwatschko, Lt 230
Scillies 124, 132, 133–4, 135, 140–1
Scott-Paine, Hubert 103
SCRUBBY I Operation 320
SCRUBBY II Operation 321
Scuiller, – 308
HMS Scylla 573, 575
SEA URCHIN 610, 611–15, 624, 629, 681
Seadog: Cap-d'Antibes 499; CHUB Operations 677; KUMMEL Operation 675; LADYBIRD Operation 678; LEDA Operation 675; NETTLETREE Operation 673; operational problems 500; PORTIA Operation 677; Sardinia 645; SASSAFRAS Operation 675; SILKWORM Operation 676; STEELTON/EARDRUM Operation 685; TANGERINE

Operation 498–9, 499, 673; *Tarana*
501; VAGRANT Operation 675;
WATCHMAN Operations 526–7,
569–70, 675, 676, 677
Seagull 416–17, 670, 671
Sealey, – 195
HM S/m *Sealion* 97, 126, 308, 309,
310, 324
Seawolf 503; CATERPILLAR I
Operation 682; Corsica 644;
CRICKET Operations 678, 679;
FALSTAFF Operation 676;
GOBLIN Operations 673;
JASMINE Operation 454–62, 672;
KRAJEWSKI I 669; KRAJEWSKI
XIII 462–71; KRAJEWSKI XV
504–14; KRAJEWSKI XVI
519–23; KRAJEWSKI XVII
531–41; LADYBIRD Operations
678, 679; LUCALITE I Operations
545, 673; LUCILE Operation 674;
MANDARIN I & II Operations 674;
MELPOMENE Operations 678,
679; MIMOSA Operation 462–71,
673; MULLET Operation 676;
NECTARINE Operations 676;
operational problems 500;
ORLANDO Operation 676;
PEPPERTREE Operation 674;
POST BOX Operation 674; repairs
416–17, 421, 430, 435, 442, 446,
448–9, 450–1; ROSALIND
Operation 546–9, 677; SARDINE
Operation 673; Sardinia 645;
STEELTON/EARDRUM
Operation 685; *Tarana* 501;
TITANIA Operation 676; WASP
Operations 678
Secret Intelligence Service (SIS):
Achiary 557; 'Agence Afrique' 557;
air operations 145; Algeria 452;
'Alibi' network 276; 'Alliance'
network 276, 652; AUBURN
Operation 618; BALACLAVA 648;
Bastia 646, 648; BLUE 591; Breton
North Coast 148; Brittany ban 148;
BULL Operation 525–6; CELERY
Operation 110–12; CND 142, 164;
corruption 18; Dartmouth base 110;
DDOD(I) 162; difficulties getting
craft 28–9; Dunderdale 61–2; early
confusion 18–19; ENIGMA 23;
HMS *Fidelity* 364; fishing-vessel mail
service 146; FLANNELFOOT

Operations 273–4; FREDERICK
mission 624, 629; Free French
relationship 80–1; French political
situation 608; FURTIVE Operation
651; German penetration 110;
Gibraltar control 446; Giraud 164;
GLOVER Operations 275–87;
GUYMAR Operation 559; Hankey
report 15, 20; history 15–19;
Holland networks 109–10;
INDIFFERENT Operations
219–21, 277; internal divisions 81;
MGBs 124; O'Leary 365;
Operations Section 25–9; ORKAN
Operation 498; OSS 164–5;
OVERCLOUD Operation 117; P1
559; parachute missions 89; passport
control 18; POLISH Operation 107;
Section D 20, 21, 22, 87–8, 99–100,
107, 128, 304, 305; Sicily 645; SOE
22, 82, 91, 94, 104, 594, 595, 656–7;
THIGH Operation 591; Tunisia
581–93; VALISE III Operation 310
Secret Service Bureau, creation 15
Section O 316
Security Executive 21
Seddon, Lt Ronald 234, 258, 260, 269,
318, 319
Sedjenane 586
Seine-et-Marne 233
Senger und Etterlin, General Ritter
von 639, 642
Sept-Iles 282, 286
SEPTIMUS I Operation 231–2, 317
SEPTIMUS II Operation 232–3, 279,
317
SEPTIMUS III Operation 233
Serafini, Antoine 614
Serandour, Pierre ('Prax') 317
SERAPH I Operation 562–6, 677
SERAPH II Operation 573–6, 678
Serenini 146, 147, 594, 638, 646, 654,
685
Sermoy 313
'Serra' *see* Pisani
Serre, Col 684
Service de Renseignements 24, 61–2,
87, 164, 598, 615, 653, 657
Sète 349, 355–6, 358, 421, 501
Sévère, Jean-Marie (Bertino) 684
Severi *see* Scamaroni, Fred
Sevra 105–6
Shackleton, Sqdn-Ldr Edward 106
Shad, – 217

SHAEF *see* Supreme Headquarters Allied Expeditionary Force
SHAMROCK Operation 92–3, 96, 171, 307
HMCS *Shediac* 367
'Shelburne' line 240–68, 316
SHELBURNE Mission 546
'Shipwright' circuit 230
Shoof, Mme 276
Sibiril, Alain 291, 293, 299, 326, 328, 329
Sibiril, Ernest 71, 113, 290–1, 293, 299, 324, 325–6, 328
Sibiril, Léon 291, 328
HM S/m *Sibyl (P217)* 574–5, 633, 678, 683, 684
Sicily 632, 633, 645
Sicot, Aristide 219, 220, 221–7, 228–30, 316
SIDELINE Operation 612–13
Sidi Mechrig 595
Sikorski, General 68, 347, 348–9, 354, 420, 495; evacuation plans 361; Krajewski 408; Morocco/Gibraltar operations 371
SILKWORM Operation 676
S'ils-Te-Mordent 325
Simbieda, Petty Officer 500; JASMINE Operation 455; KRAJEWSKI XIV 482; KRAJEWSKI III 389, 392; KRAJEWSKI IV 395; KRAJEWSKI V 402; KRAJEWSKI VI 411; KRAJEWSKI VII 417; KRAJEWSKI VIII 429; KRAJEWSKI IX 431; KRAJEWSKI X 436, 437, 442; KRAJEWSKI XV 505; MIMOSA Operation 464
Siminski, Leading Seaman 547
Simon, Paul 120, 310
Simon, Pilot Officer André 675
Simpson, Captain H.A 146
Sinclair, Admiral 16–17, 19
Sirène (MFV 2026) 171, 290, 325
SIS *see* Secret Intelligence Service
SKIN Operation 683
Skowronski, Dr *see* Slowikowski
Skulimowski, – 417, 423, 425, 426, 429, 431, 436
SLEDGEHAMMER plan 553–4, 555
Slocum, Cdr F.A.: Admiralty relationship 162; Adriatic operations 655; BONAPARTE Operations

255–6; CWF 499, 501; DDOD(I) 162, 644–5; HMS *Fidelity* 362–9; French MTBs 25, 26–7; Gibraltar 444–6, 531; gunboats 185; Inshore Patrol Flotilla 141–3; Krajewski 435; Lomenech 127, 170–1; Mansion 54; MAS boats 647; MTB operations 79; NID(C) 116, 145; Polish evacuations 361, 514–15, 531–2, 549, 550–1; Polish Special Operations Group 495; *RAF 360* 103; RAF liaison 105–6; resources 81–2; *Seawolf* repairs 523; Section D 87–8; 'Shelburne' 240; Sicily 645; SIS internal conflict 24–9, 81; conflict with SOE control 116, 595, 656–7; Special Flotilla 449–50; Special Operations Group 498
Slonininski, – 298
Slowikowski, M.Z. 349–52, 452; Achiary 557; Polish refugee troops 359–60; sea evacuations 355, 356–7; Wysoczanski 359–60
Small-Scale Raiding Force (SSRF) 96, 147–8
Smalley, PO Sam 633, 683, 688, 689
Smith, Lt Cdr A.H. 234
Smith, Sub Lt Andrew 232, 233, 254, 278–80, 283–4, 335, 336–7
Smith, Major 265, 319
Smith, Petty Officer F.S 330, 334
SO1, Vann 107
SO2/SLO1 Operation 305
SO2/SLO1 Operations 29
SO2/SLO3 Operation 307
Sobieski 349, 392
Sobra, – ('Hercule') 689
'Socrate' *see* Racheline, Lazare
SOE *see* Special Operations Executive
SOG *see* Special Operations Group
Somerville, Admiral 73, 366, 398
Sonar buoys 154–6, 177, 187, 312
SOOTY Operation 321
Sormiou 513, 531, 536–8, 676
Souk el-Khemis 584
Soupiron, Jean 689
Sous-Kéruzeau beach 247, 249, 255, 257, 262
Southgate, Maurice 230
Soviet Union, espionage 16, 17
Spain: 'Alibi' 275; CWF operations 560; evaders and escapers 407, 545; internment camps 354; look-out

posts 502; Polish evacuations 351–3, 352, 434, 578–9
Spears, Major-General Sir Edward 5, 8, 9, 10–11, 80–1
Special Air Service (SAS) 148, 264, 648
Special Boat Squadron (SBS) 147, 267, 575; control 644; Gibraltar 563; LEG Operation 631; No.1 596; No.2 597
Special Detachments 582, 584, 587–9, 595
Special Flotilla, Gibraltar 446–7
Special Operations Committee 644
Special Operations Executive (SOE): Aegean Sea 92; 'Alibi' network 276; 'Autogyro' circuit 122; BALACLAVA 646; Bey 568; BRANDON mission 568, 572, 582–93, 645; Brittany 79, 82, 99–104; Buchowski 497; 'Buckmaster' Section 218; BULL Operation 525–6; *Casabianca* 619, 638; Casablanca 447; Corsica 630, 641, 643; creation 21–2; Czechoslovakia 89, 377; Darlan assassination 608, 609, 610–11; DDOD(I) 162; de Gaulle 632; Dutch Section 95, 109–10; F Section 218, 366; FELICITY (FELICE I) Operation 589–90; HMS *Fidelity* 362–3; fishing vessel acquisitions 99–104; French Country Sections 161; German penetration 110; Gibraltar 375–6, 444, 448, 451–2, 497, 567; Giraud 164; Independent French Section 87, 96, 104, 146, 234, 264, 364; IPF 172; Italian section 616–17, 629; JASMINE Operation 454; JOSEPHINE B Operation 114; LARDERING Operation 148–61; *Le-Rhin* 364; LEG Operation 630–2, 630–4; Lussu 616; *Maid Honor* Force 94–6, 147; MANGO 4 Operation 219; MARYLAND mission 644, 654; MAS boats 646–7, 649–55; MASSINGHAM 594, 653; Mediterranean 164–5; Naval Section 146, 149, 158, 587–8, 633, 648; NETTLETREE Operation 499; NID(C) control 145; North Africa 147, 553, 561–2, 566, 570; Norwegian sea lines 91–2; OSS 556,

557; OVERCLOUD Operation 117, 309; OVERLORD Operation 257; PICKAXE Operation 121–2; PICNIC Operation 570–2; Poland 89–90; Polish escapers 375–7; Pyrenees land line 365; radio networks 576; RAF missions 161; Red Sea 92; Rizzo 365; SAVANNAH Operation 90–1; SCALP Operation 635; Scamaroni 609–10; SEA URCHIN 629; SEPTIMUS II Operation 232–3; SHAMROCK Operation 92–4; signals 576; SIS 22, 82, 87, 91, 94, 104, 594, 595, 656–8; Slocum 145, 656–7; Spanish Section 364; submarines ops 658; Tangiers sabotage 448; TORCH landings 553, 561–8, 573; Tunisia 581–93; unoccupied zone 452; 'Var' line 163, 220–1; *Vega* 446–7; WATCHMAN III Operation 569–70; weapons drops 148–61, 559, 566, 657–8; West Africa 95–6
Special Operations Group 495–9
HM S/m *Splendid* see HM S/m P228
SPLINT Operation 274–5, 318
SSRF *see* Small Scale Raiding Force
St-Aigulf 679
St-Christine 490–1, 492–3
St-Giles-Croix-de-Vie 308
HMCS *St-Laurent* 367
St-Nazaire 123–4
Staggart, Officer Cadet 388–9, 390–1, 670
Stallybrass, Cdr 27
Stanislawski, Leading Seaman: JASMINE Operation 455; KRAJEWSKI XIV 482, 483–4, 486; KRAJEWSKI XV 507; KRAJEWSKI XVI 520, 533, 536, 537; MIMOSA Operation 464; ROSALIND Operation 547
Starr, George ('Wheelwright') 570, 677
Starr, J.A.R. ('Walnut') 570, 677
'Stationer' circuit 230
Steele, Lt G.C. xii
STEELTON Operation 685
Stéphane, Henri 326
Stephenson, Sir William 99–100
Stevens, – 19
Stoklas, Commander 460; Gibraltar visit 482, 495; Krajewski transfer 515–16, 518; MIMOSA Operation

472; Polish evacuations 549; proposals for Coast Watching Flotilla 498
Stowaways, Marseilles-North Africa line 357–8
Straight, Whitney 545, 674
Strelow, Cdr 368
Submarines: Algiers 597; BRANDON 589; Corsica 616–28, 645–6; Gibraltar 461; 'Johnny' group 97, 126; mail pickups 310; Mediterranean 595–6; PEARL HARBOR Operation 597–607; Sardinia 616–28; SERAPH I Operation 562–3; SOE 658; TORCH landings 665; VALISE Operation 97–8
Sugden, Brigadier 644
Sultane 687
Sumliez, – 401
HM Yacht Sunbeam II 172, 215
SUPER-GYMNAST Operation 553–4
Supermarine Walrus amphibian L2312 12, 13
Supreme Headquarters Allied Expeditionary Force (SHAEF) 264–5
Surf-boats 173, 333; crews 337; dories 634; SN1 173, 213, 267, 271–2, 281–2, 285; SN2 173, 213, 215; SN6 211, 558, 214–15, 269–70, 558; training 172–3; see also dinghies
Suttill, F.A. ('Prosper') 499
Suzanne-Renée 292, 328
Swatschko, – 316
Sweden 99–100
SWEET PEA Operations 689
Swirski, Admiral 447, 495, 496, 497–8, 551, 577
Sykes-Wright, Miss 166
Szewalski, Captain 414, 419–20, 423, 428–31, 435, 514, 580
'Szewalski' organisation 671
Szulc, Captain 473
Szumlakowski, – 351–2
Szydlowdski, Major Adam 352, 473

T

Tabarka 584–5
Tagliamento 628
Taillat Point 620–1, 628
Talbot, Captain 26
HM S/m Talisman 30, 92, 305, 307

TANGERINE Operation 499, 673
Tangiers 378, 448, 557
Tangiers-Gibraltar ferry 557, 559
Tanguy, Claude 202–3, 211, 214, 322
Tanguy, Louis 289
Tarana 448, 596; ABLOOM Operation 453, 672; BLUEBOTTLE Operation 674, 675; BULL Operation 525–6, 675; fishing boat disguise 558; GOBLIN Operations 673; MANDARIN I & II Operations 674; MIMOSA Operation 673; NETTLETREE Operation 673; O'Leary 545; operational problems 501; PEPPERTREE Operation 674; POST BOX Operation 674; SARDINE Operation 673
Tarifa 396–8
Tarnawski, Mate 464, 482, 505, 519, 520–2, 533–4, 537, 547
Tavera 615
Taviani, Gaston ('Collin') 611
Taylor, Ldg Seaman Frank 635, 637, 683, 684
TELESCOPE Operation 321
Teller mines 257, 262
TENDERLY Operation 154–7, 177, 312
TENTATIVE Operation 313
Ter-Sarkissof 669
Tessier, – 565, 566
Théry, – 60
THIGH Operation 591–2
Thomas, Lt 589, 680
Thomson, Sir Basil 17
Tielan 197
Tigar, Major Wharton 562
HM S/m Tigris 90–1, 308
Tilly, – 87–8
TITANIA Operation 532–3, 538–9, 676
Tobruk, fall 554
'Todt' organisation 143, 253
Tomaszewski, Dr 489
Tor-Eben 326
TORCH landings 554, 573–6, 657; French involvment 564; intelligence 556; LEOPARD (PICNIC) Operation 678; OSS 164; Polish escapers 515; SBS 597; SERAPH I Operation 562–3; SOE 448; staff talks with French 563–6; submarines 665

Torrance, Major Hamish Watt 581–2, 586, 591–2
'Tosti' W/T set 277
Toulon 675
Toulouse 350–1, 352–3, 355
Tourelle-de-l'Esquillade 620
Tournier, Réné see Saule
Townsend, Lt R.U.D. 143, 301, 312, 314, 335, 338
Tramoni, Joseph 625
Tréguier River 318
Tréhiou, Jean 258–9, 269, 271, 317, 318
'Trellu' see Hentic, Pierre
'Tremayne', Lt J.-J. (Gilbert) 369, see also Allen
Triagoz 154–5, 232–3, 278–9, 282, 312
HM S/m Tribune 612–13, 616, 619, 632, 681
HM S/m Trident 630–2, 682
Tudal, Victor 324
HM S/m Tuna 98, 310
Tunbridge, Captain R.E.T. 644
Tunis 357, 557, 561, 590
Tunis-Sfax railway 593
Tunisia 360, 581–93, 587, 597
Turkey, Polish escapers 352
Turner, AB A.L.G. 335, 337
Turner, Lt E.J.D. 574–5, 633, 678, 683
'Turqoise' network 273
TURQOISE Operation 311
'Twelve Apostles' 556
Ty-Mad safe house 51, 53, 60
Tyrrhenian Sea 617

U

U-boats, convoys 367, 368, 594
U-Scogliu-Biancu 612
U-Solognu, Resistance 622, 626
Uhr-Henry, Lt K.M. 334;
    CARPENTER II Operation 153;
    ENVIOUS Operations 187, 190–1, 192, 193–6; FELICITATE
    Operation 200, 208–11, 214–15;
    MIRFIELD Operation 162; 'Var'
    line 227
ULTRA 639
ULTRAMARINE Operation 560, 677
HM S/m Unbroken (P42) 452, 453, 460–2, 589, 672, 680
United States of America: 63rd Fighter Wing 648; Army Signals corps 576;

Darlan 583; evaders and escapers 249; Joint Chiefs of Staff 581;
Mediterranean 552; North Africa 556; Polish evacuations from North
Africa 514; PT boats 278
URCHIN Operation 670
HM S/m Urge 680
URVOIS Operation see
    FLANNELFOOT II Operation
Ushant 105, 128, 132, 186, 308, 320
Uspenskaya, Anna 299
HM S/m Utmost 680

V

V1 and V2 rocket sites 216
VACNA see Vice-Admiral
    Commanding North Atlantic
VAGRANT Operation 527–8, 675
VALISE I Operation 97–8, 309
VALISE II Operation 309
VALISE III Operation 310
VALISE IV Operation 310
Vallée, François 318
Vallin, Charles 675
'Valmy' intelligence network 120
Van Hacker, – 113, 324
Van Riel 13–14, 26, 107
Vansittart, Sir Robert 7, 18, 64
'Var' line 163, 218–39, 256, 269, 316, 318
Veac'h-Vad 97–8, 310, 324
Védy, Gilbert (Médéric, 'Arsinoë') 231, 317
Védy, Maxime 231
Vega 446–7, 448, 451, 671
Vellaud, Capitaine (Desforges) 684, 685
Velléda 322
Verity, Sqn Ldr Hugh xiii–xiv, 190
Verney, Major John 267
HMS Vernon 27
Verstraete, Guy 559, 624–5, 629, 674, 681
Veyrat, Lt Jean 689
'Vic' line 219, 224, 235, 453–4
Vice-Admiral Commanding North Atlantic (VACNA) 446, 449, 481, 502, 562
Vichy Government 354, 355; Allied ship detentions 371;
    Czechoslovakian escapers 358;
    Dakar mission 118–19; de Gaulle 80; escapers 354; Krajewski 409–10;

Polish Consulates 356; treatment of prisoners 513; US links 556
'Victoire' *see* Carré, Mathilde
Vignocchi 614
Vigot, Timonier 607, 626, 681
Viking 325
Villa la Vie 595
Ville-de-Fedela 435, 446
Ville-de-Verdun 358
Villeneuve, Courson de ('Pyramide') 317
Vincent-Michelle 97, 308, 324
Viret, – 678
Visot, Rose 189–90
Vlasov Russians 263, 265, 303
Voltaire 97, 309
Vomécourt, Pierre de ('Lucas') 96, 122–3, 230, 311, 366
Von Arnim 591
Vourc'h, Dr 292
Vourc'h, Guy 323
Vourc'h, Jean 323
Vourc'h, Paul 310, 324
Vourc'h, Yves 292

W

W/T communications: Brittany 115; development 25, 68–9; *Funkspiel* 76; Gibraltar 576; infiltration by Germans 590; JASMINE Operation 459; North Africa 557, 561, 562, 563; S-Phone 163
Wagland, Sqn Ldr 198
'Walnut' *see* Starr, J.A.R.
Walsh, Fred 115–16
War Office, MI(R) 20–1
Warenghem, Suzanne 238, 318
Warington Smyth, Herbert 102
Warington Smyth, Lt Cdr Bevil 146, 147, 172, 284
Warington Smyth, Lt Cdr Nigel 172–3, 335, 341, 558
WASP Operations 678
WATCHMAN I Operation 526–7, 543, 675
WATCHMAN II Operation 676
WATCHMAN III Operation 569–70, 677
WATERWORKS Operation 122–3, 311
Watt, A.P.A. 234, 318
Watts, Captain O.M. 175, 177
Weapons drops *see* Arms supplies

Webb, Able Seaman 616–18
Webb, Petty Officer W.H. 330, 334
Weil-Curiel, Maître André 77
Welcome 577, 645, 678, 679, 685
West Africa, SOE 95–6
Westblatt, – 27, 296
Westphal, General 643
Westward Ho! 175, 181, 230
Weybel, – 273
Weybel, R. 316
Weygand, General Maxime 5, 6, 7, 8–9, 556
Whalley, Lt 155, 208, 556
'Wheelwright' *see* Starr, George
Whinney, Cdr Pat 335, 339–40, 652–3, 655; BALACLAVA 648; Bastia operations 645–50; HMS *Fidelity* 364; FURTIVE Operation 688; Gibraltar 447; LADBROKE Operation 688; MAS boat 649–55; MDV1 26, 27, 28; Mediterranean 594; *Rouanez-ar-Mor* 63
Whitelaw, Lt Neil (Major Whytelaw) 276–7, 278–81, 282, 283
Whitely, General Jock 611
Williams, Lt Cdr Peter 220–1, 236–8, 244; BONAPARTE III Operation 317; CROZIER II Operation 319; EASEMENT Operations 228, 316; GLOVER IV Operation 282, 283–4, 318; hydrophone 260; JEALOUS Operations 315; MGB 502 185–6; POLISH III Operation 309; recommendation for award 330, 332–3; ROBESPIERRE Operation 319; SCARF Operation 234; SEPTIMUS II Operation 317; SPLINT Operation 274–5, 318; 'Var' line 222–3
'Williams', Val 241–2, 252–3
Windeyer, Lt Cdr 367
Windham-Wright, Patrick 243, 244, 251, 254, 255, 256
Witrand, Régis 687
Wood, George 328
Wren, AB C.W. 335, 337
Wright, Captain Jerauld 562, 574
Wyganowski, Lt 414
Wysocki, Tadwusz 404–5, 407–8, 670
Wysoczanski, Major 359–60, 370, 418, 419–20; Algeria 410–11, 413, 414; evacuation plans 377–8; French military command 385; Krajewski

379–85, 386–7, 388, 399, 671;
Morocco/Gibraltar operations 372,
373, 374–5

Y

YANKEE signals plan 619
Yeo-Thomas, Wing-Cdr Forrest 121
Yéquel, Louis 311
Yolande 290, 324
Yugoslavia 348, 353, 644
L'Yvonne 292, 325, 328
Yvonne-Georges 326, 327

Z

Zarembski 350–1
Zawistowski, Bosun 524
ZEBRA Operation 559, 676
Zeff 672
Zeller, Colonel 685
Ziegler, Ingénieur-Général 684
Zimny, Mate 464, 466, 475
ZODIAC Operation 592, 595, 631,
680
ZORRA pinpoint 380, 386, 422, 431,
671

Y

YANKEE signal station, 113

Z

ZEBRA question for, 576
Zulu Council, 65
Zooper encampment, 83
Zunu No. 4, 361, 366, 376
Zulu, Lieutenant, 2, 350, 631
Zululand prisoner, 380, 380, 477, 451